THE BOOK OF VIDEO LISTS
THIRD EDITION

"This list format makes it useful as a viewer's adviser, and the price makes affordable for all collections . . . a welcome addition."
—*Booklist*

Thousands of video enthusiasts have already found *The Book of Video Lists* to be the easiest way to discover more movies to enjoy at home. Our exclusive list format provides thousands of suggestions for *every* movie lover . . . because it's organized the way most people shop for videos—by subject and star.

"Choose a category or star, run your eye down the list, and you may hit upon a title you would not have thought of otherwise."
—Peter Nichols, *The New York Times*

This new Third Edition is fully updated and expanded. It contains more than 600 lists of movies now available on video—a total of more than 5,350 movies— it includes all of the latest releases, the biggest stars, and the hottest directors.

"Provides very good film information in a concise format."
—*American Reference Books Annual*

This new edition also contains *six* new chapters: Stars, Directors, Writers, Historical/Fictional Characters, Essential Viewing, and Recommended Movies. Plus, there's a special list of the most requested movies not yet available on video . . . lists of Oscar-winning films . . . memorable movie debuts . . . and much, much more.

Skillfully organized and indexed . . ."
—*Library Journal*

Whether you're looking for a romantic comedy or a World War II drama . . . for a Judy Garland musical or a Clint Eastwood western . . . for a Sherlock Holmes mystery or a Walt Disney family film . . . for the latest releases starring Mel Gibson, Michelle Pfeiffer, or Michael Douglas . . . for movies directed by Ingmar Bergman, Sam Peckinpah, or John Waters, . . . *The Book of Video Lists* is the only video renter's guide that uncovers so many video treasures in such an organized, practical and fun-to-use format.

"A handy book . . . Wiener's sound judgment and thorough knowledge could save you time and money."
—Pat Dowell, *The Washingtonian*

THE BOOK
OF
VIDEO LISTS

THIRD EDITION

Tom Wiener

MADISON BOOKS
Lanham • New York • London

Published by Madison Books
4720 Boston Way
Lanham, Maryland 20706

3 Henrietta Street
London WC2E 8LU England

Distributed by National Book Network

ISBN 0-8191-7825-X (paperback)

British Cataloging in Publication Information Available

CONTENTS

3 Comedy (CO)   21

INTRODUCTION

You know the feeling:

You're in a video store, standing in front of a shelf full of tapes. Some of the films you've seen, a few titles sound familiar, and most you've never heard of. You know what *kind* of a movie you want to rent, but how do you find it? Your hands are sweating, the titles blur together, you're thinking about all the time you've been standing there looking for a movie when you could be home watching one. . . .

That's where *The Book of Video Lists* comes in. This book will make you a smarter video renter, because it provides you with hundreds of suggestions tailored to your tastes in movies, whether you're a fan of classic love stories, gangster dramas, or lavish musicals, whether your favorite actor is Cary Grant or Michelle Pfeiffer, whether you're looking for a film directed by Ingmar Bergman or John Waters.

Think of this book as a video matchmaker, designed to get you and the right movie together for an evening's entertainment. *The Book of Video Lists,* unlike any other video or movie guide, is organized by subjects and stars and directors, the way most people shop for movies on tape. It's a guide you can use every time you make a trip to the video store.

First, a few words on the contents of this book.

The only place in this Introduction where the word "complete" appears is in this paragraph. No video guide can be complete, because each month dozens of new releases arrive on the market. Nevertheless, the films listed here are as up-to-date as possible, accounting for many as many new releases on home video as I could confirm.

There are two types of lists in this book. The subject lists (for example, World War II, Romantic Comedies, Musical Films About Show Biz) are selective. To list every romantic comedy, every WW II drama, every backstage musical available on video would make this book longer than the Manhattan Yellow Pages and a lot less useful. The second type of lists, the Check Lists, attempt to be inclusive. More on those under How To Use This Book.

The lists are comprised almost entirely of theatrical films, the most popular form of home video entertainment. I have included a selection of comedy and music performance tapes, movies originally made for TV, and TV miniseries if they were of sufficient interest to merit a look on home video.

Every film in this book has been carefully checked for its availability on home video. However, some titles have been "discontinued" by their distributors. When a home video title is discontinued, rental copies may stay in circulation but cannot be replaced once they are defective. A discontinued movie cannot be purchased, unless a video retailer is willing to sell a used rental copy. I've made some judgment calls; if a title was only recently discontinued, there may still be enough rental copies in circulation to justify including the film here.

And finally, don't be disappointed if your video store doesn't carry all 5,300+ titles in this guide. In fact, if your video store *does* carry all the titles in this guide, write me. That's a store I'd like to see.

HOW TO USE THIS BOOK

The first portion of the book contains chapters on categories common to most video stores:

Action-Adventure (AC)	Foreign Films (FF)
Classics (CL)	Horror (HO)
Comedy (CO)	Musicals (MU)
Cult (CU)	Mystery/Suspense (MY)
Drama (DR)	Science Fiction (SF)
Family/Kids (FA)	Westerns (WE)

The two-letter codes after each category are used in the general index. More on that in a moment.

Each of these chapters contains lists of titles arranged by topic; the lists are numbered in sequence. For example, the first list in the ActionAdventure chapter lists a selection of World War II films (**AC1**). In the Comedy chapter, the seventh list is a collection of movie spoofs (**CO7**). Fans of British mysteries can begin their investigations with the 15th list under Mystery/Suspense (**MY15**).

For the Third Edition, I've added several chapters of lists:

Director Check Lists (DT)
Historical/Fictional Characters Check Lists (HF)
Star Check Lists (ST)
Writer Check Lists (WR)

Plus, I've expanded the Video Extra (**XT**) chapter, which contains miscellaneous collections of films not confined to one category.

Users of the first two editions of this book will note that many of these check lists were included in the Category chapters. For example, star Katharine Hepburn appeared in Classics, director David Lynch in Cult, fictional character Sherlock Holmes in Mystery, and writer Stephen King in Horror. To make it easier to locate Check Lists of films featuring your favorite star or a specific historical or fictional character, made by a certain director, or based on the work of a certain writer, I've created these separate chapters.

Turn to the Star Check Lists, for example, and you'll find everyone from Abbott & Costello to Bruce Willis, from Ingrid Bergman to Sigourney Weaver. The Director Check Lists include Woody Allen, Stanley Kubrick, and Billy Wilder. Under Historical/Fictional Characters, you'll find Charlie Chan, Adolf Hitler, and Tarzan. And, for films based on works by Charles Dickens, Edgar Allan Poe, or Tennessee Williams, turn to the Writer Check Lists.

The Check Lists are more inclusive than the subject lists. In a few cases, where the prodigious output of some stars (and the limited availability of some of their more obscure titles) warrants, I've been selective. But, with the Star Check Lists, I've included titles where the performer may have appeared only briefly. If you're unsure about a title featuring a star you're interested in, please check the film's entry in the Title Index before you rent. There, I've noted whether that actor is featured or plays a bit part. You may, for example, want to rent *Young Frankenstein* to see Gene Hackman's brief but hilarious cameo, but you may not necessarily want to sit all the way through *Dead Heat on a Merry-Go-Round* just to see Harrison Ford. (Then again, you might.)

As in the previous edition, the Video Extra Chapter contains a potpourri of lists, including all the major Academy Award winners available on videocassette, plus lists of Great Road Movies, Train Films, Film Debuts, Memorable Final Films, and more.

For this edition, I've also added two more chapters, Essential Viewing and Highly Recommended/Recommended. The nearly 400 films listed under Essential Viewing are intended as a guide to movies of enduring interest. If you want a capsule history of the movies from 1915 to 1980, this is a good place to start. If you want to consider yourself a well-informed movie person, start with this list. For convenience, I have divided this chapter into historical sections, in chronological order. And because I can't presume to know this soon which films of the 1980s are Essential Viewing, the list ends at 1980.

The Recommended Films are a matter of my personal taste, which is eclectic enough to include *The Fabulous Baker Boys*, *The Thin Blue Line*, *Pandora's Box*, and *The Band Wagon*. If none of those films is to your liking, you may still agree with some of my other recommendations. If you think in terms of a star rating system, a Highly Recommended title is ****, a Recommended title is ***. Again, if you're unsure of a title, read the description in the Title Index before you rent.

And finally, Chapter 20 is a long but by no means inclusive list of frequently requested movies still unavailable on videocassette. If you can't find a certain title in this book or in your favorite video store, check this list. Like all lists in this book, it is accurate as of our press time. Over two dozen titles from this list in the last edition have since been released on video. I've expanded the list to include many surprisingly popular films, as well as cult favorites that video stores get requests for regularly.

Every film in this book (except titles in Chapter 20) is listed alphabetically in the Title Index. Each index entry contains the year of release, color (C) or black & white (B&W), running time, and MPAA rating. Also included are a short description of the film and the code designation for the list or lists that film appears on. For example, *Always* is coded **CU18** (Remakes of Famous Movies), **CU19** (Letterboxed Movies), **DR1** (Romantic Dramas), **DT99** (Steven Spielberg Check List), **ST36** (Richard Dreyfuss Check List), **ST65** (Audrey Hepburn Check List), and **ST74** (Holly Hunter Check List). After the list codes, I've indicated if the title is Essential Viewing, and if I consider it Highly Recommended or Recommended.

The Title Index can be used in several ways. If you're browsing one of the lists in the first portion of the book and a title is unfamiliar, look it up in the Index. Or, you may want to start in the Index with a title you already know, to check out others on the same subject, or with the same star, by the same director, with the same fictional character, or based on the same author's work.

Some notes on dates, running times, and ratings.

On the lists, you'll notice that a title may be designated by a date. Where a date appears alone, it indicates that the same title has been used for more than one film. For instance, there are two movies named *Frantic,* a 1958 Jeanne Moreau drama and a 1988 thriller starring Harrison Ford. Where a date appears with the word "version," it's to show that the same story has been filmed more than once. *Henry V* was filmed in 1945 with Laurence Olivier and in 1989 with Kenneth Branagh. In some cases, I've indicated "version" even if a remake (or original) is not available on video, for the sake of clarity.

The dates reflect the film's original theatrical release (if it's a foreign film, release in its country of origin), its original TV air date, or its release to home video if it never showed in theaters or on TV.

Running times apply to the home video version of the film. Some films have been shortened or lengthened for release on home video, and I've tried to reflect that as faithfully as possible. (See List **CU10** in the Cult Chapter for a collection of movies which have added footage for home video release.)

MPAA ratings are to be used as guidelines, especially by parents. Any entry designated NR has not been rated by the MPAA. This includes most films released before 1968, movies made for broadcast or cable TV, and music performance videos. Some movies are available in two versions, one rated (usually "R"), another unrated. I've tried to indicate dual availability wherever possible.

This book may have one name below the title but, like a film, it was really a collaboration. Chuck Lean and Ron Castell were present at the creation; their love for good books and good movies nurtured the project. Mike Clark and Stephen Zito, two gentlemen whose writing and love of movies have inspired me, contributed enormously to this book. Pat Dowell, Patrick Sheehan, and Scott Simmon graciously lent advice on various lists.

I want to acknowledge several invaluable sources of published information: Leonard Maltin's *TV Movies and Video Guide* (still the best single volume movie reference at any price), *Variety's Complete Home Video Directory,* National Video Clearinghouse's *The Video Source Book, Video Movie Guide* by Mick Martin and Marsha Porter, *The Phantom's Ultimate Video Guide,* Michael Weldon's *Psychotronic Encyclopedia of Film* (the latter two especially helpful for off-the-beaten-track titles), and Roy Pickard's *Who Played Who on the Screen.*

I had support from these people as well: Lauren Malnati, Rich Swope and Liz Godin-Lee, who provided important research assistance; Bill Nuhn, who kept me abreast of new video releases (also thanks to Rich Swope, Michael James, Terri Nyman, and Michelle Lewis); Ray Heinrich of One to One Communications for unsurpassed expertise in all matters technical; Carlos Aguilar and Janet Egolf for brilliant design work; Bruce Eder for information on letterboxed titles; Al Hollin, Mark Miller, Rosemary Prillaman, and Tonda Hernandez for promoting the first edition; Pam Uhl, Roxanne Kavounis, and Jennifer Wyckoff for giving it a spectacular launch; Ty Burr for the kind words when they really counted; Joe Goluski for giving me lots of air time in Syracuse; Lori Shimabukuro and Joyce Woodward, who each give great lunch; Maureen Humphrys and Louise Millikan for ongoing culinary support; Bill Kenly and Jackie Sigmund for longtime moral support; Heidi Diamond (wherever you are) for fighting the good fight; and Mort Zedd, a man with superb taste in art and music.

Finally, to Barbara Humphrys, thanks for her insightful suggestions and painstaking proofreading; for her patience, her humor, her love, and Irish pancakes, I am always grateful.

I welcome comments and corrections from readers. Please address them to me at Madison Books, 4720 Boston Way, Lanham, MD 20706.

—Tom Wiener

Chapter One

ACTION/ADVENTURE
(AC)

See also: Historical/Fictional Character Check List HF2 James Bond; Star Check Lists ST12 Charles Bronson, ST21 Sean Connery, ST39 Clint Eastwood, ST43 Errol Flynn, ST88 Bruce Lee, ST97 Steve McQueen, ST114 Chuck Norris, ST128 Burt Reynolds, ST135 Arnold Schwarzenegger, ST140 Sylvester Stallone

WAR MOVIES: WORLD WAR II _____ **AC1**

Air Force
The Americanization of Emily
Anzio
Armored Command
Attack Force Z
Back to Bataan
Bataan
Battle Cry
Battle Force
Battle of Britain
The Battle of the Bulge
Battleground
The Big Red One
The Boat
Bombardier
Breakthrough
A Bridge Too Far
China Sky
Cross of Iron
D-Day the Sixth of June
Dangerous Moonlight
Days of Glory
The Desert Fox
Destination Tokyo
The Dirty Dozen
The Eagle Has Landed
The Enemy Below
Farewell to the King
Fires on the Plain
Flying Leathernecks
Flying Tigers
The 49th Parallel
Force 10 From Navarone
From Here to Eternity
Guadalcanal Diary
The Guns of Navarone
Halls of Montezuma

Hell in the Pacific
Home of the Brave
The Immortal Sergeant
In Harm's Way
In Which We Serve
Joan of Paris
The Longest Day
The Malta Story
Midway
The Naked and the Dead
Never So Few
North Star
One of Our Aircraft Is Missing
Patton
The Purple Heart
Pursuit of the Graf Spee
Run Silent, Run Deep
The Sands of Iwo Jima
The Sea Chase
The Sea Wolves
Sink the Bismarck!
Soldier of Orange
They Were Expendable
13 Rue Madeleine
Thirty Seconds Over Tokyo
This Is Korea/December 7th
To Hell and Back
To the Shores of Tripoli
Tobruk
Tora! Tora! Tora!
The Train
Twelve O'Clock High
A Walk in the Sun
The War Lover
Where Eagles Dare
The Young Lions

WAR MOVIES: WORLD WAR I _____ **AC2**

All Quiet on the Western Front
The Big Parade
The Blue Max

The Dawn Patrol (1938 version)
A Farewell to Arms (1932 version)
Forty Thousand Horsemen

Gallipoli
Hearts of the World
The Lighthorsemen
Paths of Glory

Sergeant York
What Price Glory
Wings

WAR MOVIES: KOREAN WAR _____ AC3

The Bridges at Toko-Ri
Field of Honor
M*A*S*H
Men in War
One Minute to Zero
Pork Chop Hill

Retreat, Hell!
Sergeant Ryker
The Steel Helmet
This Is Korea/December 7th
Torpedo Alley

WAR MOVIES: VIETNAM WAR (AND AFTERMATH) _____ AC4

Apocalypse Now
Bat 21
Born on the Fourth of July
The Boys in Company C
Braddock: Missing in Action 3
Casualties of War
China Gate
Dear America: Letters Home From
   Vietnam
The Deer Hunter
84 Charley Mopic
Fighting Mad (1977)
Full Metal Jacket

Go Tell the Spartans
Good Morning, Vietnam
The Green Berets
Hamburger Hill
The Iron Triangle
Missing in Action
Platoon
Purple Hearts
Rambo: First Blood II
The Siege of Firebase Gloria
Tornado
Uncommon Valor

WAR MOVIES: CIVIL WAR _____ AC5
See also: WE6 Civil War Westerns

The Birth of a Nation
Friendly Persuasion
Glory
Gone With the Wind

The Red Badge of Courage
She Wore a Yellow Ribbon
Shenandoah

WAR MOVIES: OTHER CONFLICTS _____ AC6

The Battle of Algiers
The Buccaneer
The Charge of the Light Brigade (1936
   version)
Damn the Defiant!
Drums Along the Mohawk
The Four Feathers

Heartbreak Ridge
Lost Command
Revolution
The Sand Pebbles
Soldiers of Fortune
Zulu
Zulu Dawn

WAR MOVIES: PRISONERS OF WAR _____ AC7

The Bridge on the River Kwai
Grand Illusion
The Great Escape
The Hanoi Hilton
King Rat

Merry Christmas, Mr. Lawrence
Missing in Action 2: The Beginning
POW: The Escape
Stalag 17
Von Ryan's Express

URBAN ACTION _____ AC8
See also: AC9 Cops and Robbers, AC22 Gangster Sagas

Above the Law
Action Jackson
Angel
Armed Response
Assault on Precinct 13
Avenging Angel
Band of the Hand
China Girl
Cold Sweat
Defiance
Detroit 9000
Die Hard
The Driver
8 Million Ways to Die
Enemy Territory
Fear City
Getting Even
Gloria

Gordon's War
Hard Times
The Hidden
The Hunter
The Killer Elite
Knights of the City
The Last of the Finest
The Mack
Point Blank
Savage Streets
Short Fuse
Streets of Fire
Sweet Sweetback's Badasssss Song
Switchblade Sisters
Thief
Tougher Than Leather
The Warriors (1979)

COPS AND ROBBERS _____ AC9
See also: AC8 Urban Action, AC22 Gangster Sagas

Across 110th Street
The Anderson Tapes
Badge 373
Black Rain
The Blue Knight
Bullitt
City in Fear
Cobra
Code of Silence
Colors
Coogan's Bluff
Dead-Bang
Dead Heat
The Dead Pool
The Detective (1968)
Dick Tracy
Dirty Harry
Downtown
Electra Glide in Blue
The Enforcer (1976)
Fatal Beauty
The First Deadly Sin
48HRS.
The French Connection
The French Connection 2
The Gauntlet
The Getaway
Hollywood Vice Squad
The Hot Rock
Hustle
Jackie Chan's Police Force

The January Man
The Laughing Policeman
Lethal Weapon
Lethal Weapon 2
Madigan
Magnum Force
Miami Blues
Nighthawks
Off Limits (1988)
The Presidio
Quiet Cool
Red Heat
Renegades
Robocop
Running Scared
The Seven-ups
Shakedown
Sharky's Machine
Stick
Sudden Impact
The Taking of Pelham One Two Three
Tango and Cash
They Call Me MISTER Tibbs!
Thunderbolt and Lightfoot
Tightrope
To Live and Die in L.A.
Under the Gun
Vice Squad
Walking Tall (series)
The Year of the Dragon

HOT WHEELS _____ AC10

Black Moon Rising
Cannonball
The Cannonball Run
Cannonball Run II
Convoy
Death Race 2000
Deathsport
Eat My Dust!
Electra Glide in Blue
Gone in 60 Seconds
Grand Prix
Grand Theft Auto
The Gumball Rally
The Last Chase

Mad Max
Mad Max Beyond Thunderdome
Race With the Devil
Rad
Return to Macon County
The Road Warrior
Rolling Vengeance
Safari 3000
Thunder Road
Vanishing Point
Wheels of Fire
The Wild Angels
The Wraith

THE WILD BLUE YONDER _____ AC11

The Aviator
Battle of Britain
The Blue Max
Blue Thunder
The Bridges at Toko-Ri
Choke Canyon
The Dawn Patrol (1938 version)
Firefox
Flying Tigers
The Great Waldo Pepper
High Road to China

Iron Eagle
Iron Eagle II
Only Angels Have Wings
The Right Stuff
The Spirit of St. Louis
Top Gun
Twelve O'Clock High
The War Lover
Wings
The Wings of Eagles

ADVENTURE IN THE GREAT OUTDOORS _____ AC12

The Abyss
The African Queen
Baby—Secret of the Lost Legend
Beneath the 12 Mile Reef
The Big Blue
The Bounty
A Breed Apart
The Call of the Wild
China Seas
Clan of the Cave Bear
Crusoe
Death Hunt
The Deep
The Eiger Sanction
The Emerald Forest
The Flight of the Eagle
Flight of the Phoenix
Greystoke: The Legend of Tarzan
Hatari!
King Solomon's Mines (1937, 1950 &
   1985 versions)
Leviathan

Lord of the Flies (1963 & 1990 versions)
The Man From Snowy River
The Man Who Would Be King
March or Die
Mogambo
Mountains of the Moon
Mutiny on the Bounty (1935 & 1962
   versions)
The Naked Jungle
The Naked Prey
Never Cry Wolf
Quest for Fire
Reap the Wild Wind
The Red Tent
Return to Snowy River, Part II
Shoot to Kill
Thunderball
The Treasure of the Sierra Madre
We of the Never Never
White Dawn
The Wind and the Lion

CLASSIC ADVENTURE _____ AC13
See also: AC14 Romantic Adventure, AC15 Costume Adventure, Historical/Fictional
Character Check List HF22 Tarzan

The Adventures of Robin Hood
Beau Geste (1939 version)
The Black Arrow
The Black Pirate
Captain Blood
Captains Courageous
The Charge of the Light Brigade (1936
    version)
The Corsican Brothers
The Crimson Pirate
Don Q: Son of Zorro
Drums
The Flame and the Arrow
The Four Feathers
Gunga Din
The Hurricane (1937 version)
Ivanhoe (1952 version)
Kim
King Solomon's Mines (1937 & 1950
    versions)
Knights of the Round Table
The Last of the Mohicans

The Lives of a Bengal Lancer
The Lost Patrol
The Lost World (1925 version)
Mutiny on the Bounty (1935 version)
Only Angels Have Wings
The Prisoner of Zenda (1937 & 1952
    versions)
Reap the Wild Wind
Red Dust
San Francisco
Scaramouche
The Scarlet Pimpernel (1934 version)
The Sea Hawk
The Seven Samurai
The Thief of Bagdad (1924 & 1940
    versions)
The Three Musketeers (1948 version)
Treasure Island (1934 version)
The Treasure of the Sierra Madre
The Vikings
The Wages of Fear
Yojimbo

ROMANTIC ADVENTURE _____ AC14
See also: AC13 Classic Adventure

The African Queen
American Dreamer
The Aviator
The Great Race
High Road to China
Into the Night
Jewel of the Nile
Ladyhawke
Lassiter

Mogambo
The Princess Bride
Raiders of the Lost Ark
Red Dust
Robin and Marian
Romancing the Stone
Time After Time
The Wind and the Lion

COSTUME ADVENTURE _____ AC15
See also: AC13 Classic Adventure

Blackbeard, the Pirate
The Four Musketeers
Nate and Hayes
The Pirate Warrior
Pirates

The Princess Bride
Robin and Marian
Sword of Sherwood Forest
The Three Musketeers (1974 version)

HISTORICAL ADVENTURE _____ AC16
See also: AC1-7 War Movies

Alexander the Great
The Bounty
The Buccaneer
The Charge of the Light Brigade (1936
    version)
The Conqueror
El Cid

The Flight of the Eagle
The Hindenburg
Lionheart
Mutiny on the Bounty (1935 & 1962
    versions)
The Sicilian
The Wind and the Lion

N

SUPER HEROES _____ AC17

The Adventures of Buckaroo Banzai
  Across the 8th Dimension
The Adventures of Hercules
Batman (1966)
Batman (1989)
Conan the Barbarian
Conan the Destroyer
Condorman

Doc Savage: The Man of Bronze
Greystoke: The Legend of Tarzan
Masters of the Universe
Sheena
Supergirl
Superman (series)
Teenage Mutant Ninja Turtles

SWORD & SORCERY FANTASIES _____ AC18

The Beastmaster
Blademaster
Conan the Barbarian
Conan the Destroyer
Deathstalker
Deathstalker 2
Dragonslayer
Excalibur
Fire and Ice
Flesh and Blood (1985)
Jason and the Argonauts
Krull
Ladyhawke

Legend
The Magic Sword
Metalstorm: The Destruction of Jared-
  Syn
Red Sonja
Robin Hood and the Sorcerer
The 7th Voyage of Sinbad
She (1985 version)
Ulysses (1955)
Warriors of the Wind
Willow
Wizards of the Lost Kingdom

TALES OF REVENGE _____ AC19

The Bounty Hunter
Death Wish (series)
The Exterminator
The Exterminator 2
Eye of the Tiger
F/X
Fighting Back
The Final Mission
Fleshburn
Hard to Kill
Instant Justice
The Killer Elite
The Ladies Club

The Mean Machine
Ms. 45
Next of Kin
No Mercy
Point Blank
Revenge (1990)
Rolling Thunder
Rolling Vengeance
Slaughter
Steele Justice
Underworld, U.S.A.
Vigilante
White Lightning

MERCENARIES AND OTHER COMBATANTS _____ AC20

American Commandos
Annihilators
Code Name: Wildgeese
Death Before Dishonor
The Delta Force
The Dogs of War
Gold Raiders
Gordon's War
Invasion U.S.A.
Let's Get Harry

Night Force
Opposing Force
Red Dawn
Red Scorpion
The Rescue
Terror Squad
Toy Soldiers
Uncommon Valor
The Wild Geese
Wild Geese II

SOLDIERS OF FORTUNE _____ AC21

Allan Quartermain and the Lost City of
  Gold
Big Trouble in Little China
Escape From New York
Firewalker
High Road to China
Indiana Jones and the Last Crusade
Indiana Jones and the Temple of Doom
Jake Speed
Jewel of the Nile

Jungle Raiders
King Solomon's Mines (1937, 1950 &
  1985 version)
The Mines of Kilimanjaro
Raiders of the Lost Ark
Romancing the Stone
Shanghai Surprise
Soldier of Fortune
Soldiers of Fortune
Treasure of the Four Crowns

GANGSTER SAGAS _____ AC22
See also: AC8 Urban Action, AC9 Cops and Robbers

Al Capone
Angels With Dirty Faces
The Big Heat
Black Caesar
Black Rain
Bloody Mama
The Cotton Club
Dick Tracy
Dillinger
The Godfather
The Godfather, Part II
Hell on Frisco Bay
Hell up in Harlem
High Sierra

Lepke
Little Caesar
The Long Good Friday
Lucky Luciano
Mean Frank and Crazy Tony
Once Upon a Time in America
Prime Cut
The Public Enemy
The Roaring Twenties
St. Valentine's Day Massacre
Scarface (1932 & 1983 versions)
The Untouchables
White Heat
The Yakuza

DISASTER STORIES _____ AC23

Airport (series)
Avalanche
Beyond the Poseidon Adventure
City on Fire
The Devil at 4 O'Clock
Earthquake
The Hindenburg
Hurricane

The Hurricane
Juggernaut (1974)
Meteor
A Night to Remember (1958)
The Poseidon Adventure
San Francisco
The Towering Inferno
When Time Ran Out

STORIES OF SURVIVAL _____ AC24

The Abyss
Avenging Force
Back From Eternity
The Blood of Heroes
Bridge to Nowhere
The Call of the Wild
Certain Fury
Crusoe
Cut and Run
Cyborg
Death Valley
Deliverance
Flight of the Phoenix

Grey Lady Down
Hunter's Blood
Lifeboat
Lord of the Flies (1963 & 1990 versions)
Mad Max Beyond Thunderdome
Man Friday
The Most Dangerous Game
The Naked Jungle
The Naked Prey
Never Cry Wolf
Opposing Force
Out of Control
Papillon

Predator
Quest for Fire
The Red Tent
The Road Warrior

Runaway Train
Southern Comfort
The Treasure of the Sierra Madre
White Dawn

ONE-MAN ARMIES _____ AC25

Above the Law
The Bounty Hunter
Bulletproof
Bullies
Commando
Die Hard
Equalizer 2000
First Blood
Ghost Warrior
Hard to Kill
Instant Justice
Mad Max
Mad Max Beyond Thunderdome
Nowhere to Hide
One Man Force
Point Blank

Predator
Rambo: First Blood II
Rambo III
Raw Deal
Red Scorpion
Road House
The Road Warrior
Robocop
The Soldier
Streets of Fire
The Terminator
Walking Tall
Walking Tall Part 2
Walking Tall: The Final Chapter
Wanted: Dead or Alive

MARTIAL ARTS ACTION _____ AC26
See also: Star Check Lists ST88 Bruce Lee, ST114 Chuck Norris

American Ninja
American Ninja 2: The Confrontation
American Ninja 3: Blood Hunt
The Big Brawl
Big Trouble in Little China
Billy Jack
Bloodfist
Bloodsport
Circle of Iron
Cleopatra Jones
Cleopatra Jones and the Casino of Gold

Cyborg
Hard to Kill
Jackie Chan's Police Force
Kickboxer
Kill and Kill Again
Kill or Be Killed
The Last Dragon
No Retreat, No Surrender
Pray for Death
The Protector
T.N.T. Jackson

Chapter Two

CLASSICS
(CL)

CLASSICS ILLUSTRATED: LITERARY ADAPTATIONS _____ **CL1**
See also: Writer Check Lists WR4 Charles Dickens, WR6 William Faulkner, WR7 F. Scott Fitzgerald, WR10 Ernest Hemingway, WR11 Henry James, WR14 D.H. Lawrence, WR17 Sinclair Lewis, WR20 Eugene O'Neill, WR22 William Shakespeare, WR25 John Steinbeck, WR27 Mark Twain

Anna Karenina
Barry Lyndon
Billy Budd
The Brothers Karamazov
Caesar and Cleopatra
Camille
Greed
Far From the Madding Crowd
The Heiress
The Hunchback of Notre Dame
The Importance of Being Earnest
Little Women (1933 & 1949 versions)

Madame Bovary
Moby Dick
The Picture of Dorian Gray
Pride and Prejudice
Pygmalion
The Red Badge of Courage
Tom Jones
Vanity Fair
War and Peace (1956 & 1968 versions)
Wuthering Heights (1939 & 1954 versions)

SCREEN BIOGRAPHIES _____ **CL2**

Abe Lincoln in Illinois
Abraham Lincoln
The Babe Ruth Story
Citizen Kane
Cleopatra (1934, 1963)
The Diary of Anne Frank
I'll Cry Tomorrow
Joan of Arc
Juarez
Knute Rockne—All American
Lawrence of Arabia
The Life of Emile Zola
Lust for Life

Marie Antoinette
Moulin Rouge
Napoleon (1927)
The Pride of St. Louis
Pride of the Yankees
The Private Life of Henry VIII
The Private Lives of Elizabeth and Essex
Sergeant York
Sister Kenny
The Spirit of St. Louis
To Hell and Back
Young Mr. Lincoln

HISTORICAL DRAMA _____ **CL3**

Beau Brummel (1924 version)
The Birth of a Nation
Caesar and Cleopatra
Cleopatra (1934, 1963)
Demetrius and the Gladiators
Desiree
Dr. Zhivago
The Egyptian
The Fall of the Roman Empire
Fire Over England
The Four Horsemen of the Apocalypse (1961 version)

Gone With the Wind
Jezebel
Mary of Scotland
Mutiny on the Bounty (1935 version)
A Night to Remember (1958)
Northwest Passage
The Private Lives of Elizabeth and Essex
Queen Christina
Raintree County

San Francisco
Scott of the Anarctic
Stanley and Livingstone
A Tale of Two Cities (1935 version)

That Hamilton Woman
The Virgin Queen
War and Peace (1956 & 1968 versions)

CLASSIC LOVE STORIES _____ CL4

The African Queen
Algiers
Anna Karenina
Back Street
Brief Encounter (1945 version)
Camille
Casablanca
The Clock
Dark Victory
Dr. Zhivago
The Enchanted Cottage
Flesh and the Devil
Gilda
Gone With the Wind
The Heiress
Intermezzo (1939 version)
Letter From an Unknown Woman

Love Is a Many Splendored Thing
Marty
Mayerling (1936 version)
Mr. Skeffington
Notorious
Now, Voyager
The Philadelphia Story
A Place in the Sun
Portrait of Jennie
Queen Christina
Random Harvest
Sabrina
The Shop Around the Corner
Summertime
Waterloo Bridge
Wuthering Heights (1939 version)

WOMEN'S PICTURES _____ CL5
See also: DR10 Today's Woman

Alice Adams
Autumn Leaves
By Love Possessed
Camille
Christopher Strong
Craig's Wife
Dance, Girl, Dance
I'll Cry Tomorrow
In This Our Life
Kitty Foyle
The Letter
Madame Bovary
Madame X (1966 version)

Mildred Pierce
Mr. Skeffington
Morning Glory
Now, Voyager
The Old Maid
Possessed
Since You Went Away
Stella Dallas
That Hamilton Woman
The Wind
A Woman Rebels
A Woman's Face
The Women

CLASSIC TEAR JERKERS _____ CL6
See also: DR2 For a Good Cry

Back Street (1961 version)
Blonde Venus
Casablanca
Dark Victory
Going My Way
The Heiress
Imitation of Life (1959 version)
In Name Only
It's a Wonderful Life
Johnny Belinda
King's Row
Kitty Foyle
Letter From an Unknown Woman

Limelight
Madame X (1966 version)
Made for Each Other (1939)
Magnificent Obsession (1954 version)
Mildred Pierce
Penny Serenade
A Place in the Sun
The Red Shoes
Since You Went Away
Stella Dallas
Summertime
Written on the Wind
Wuthering Heights (1939 version)

SHOW BUSINESS STORIES _____ CL7
See also: DR12 Backstage Dramas, MU4 Musical Films About Show Biz

All About Eve
The Bad and the Beautiful
The Country Girl (1954 version)
Dance, Girl, Dance
Dancing Lady
A Double Life
A Face in the Crowd
The Great Gabbo
The Greatest Show on Earth
The Last Command
Limelight
The Lost Squadron
The Red Shoes

The Seven Little Foys
Show People
Stage Door
A Star Is Born (1937 & 1954 versions)
Sunset Boulevard
Sweet Smell of Success
Sweethearts
Swing High, Swing Low
Trapeze
Twentieth Century
The Wings of Eagles
Young and Willing

SOCIAL PROBLEM DRAMAS _____ CL8

Bad Day at Black Rock
The Best Years of Our Lives
Black Fury
The Boy With Green Hair
Crossfire
The Crowd
Dead End
The Defiant Ones (1958 version)
The Grapes of Wrath
Home of the Brave
I Am a Fugitive From a Chain Gang
Inherit the Wind
Judgment at Nuremberg
Knock on Any Door
The Last Angry Man

The Lost Weekend
The Man With the Golden Arm
The Men
Mrs. Miniver
Mr. Deeds Goes to Town
On the Waterfront
Our Daily Bread
A Place in the Sun
The Prisoner
Rebel Without a Cause
Street Scene
They Drive by Night
Till the End of Time
Twelve Angry Men

GREAT COLOR FILMS _____ CL9

The Adventures of Robin Hood
The Barefoot Contessa
Black Narcissus
Black Orpheus
Cover Girl
DuBarry Was a Lady
Duel in the Sun
The Far Country
The Four Feathers
Funny Face
The Garden of Allah
The Golden Coach
Heller in Pink Tights
Henry V (1945 version)

Lust for Life
Moulin Rouge
Pal Joey
The Phantom of the Opera (1943
version)
The Pirate
The Quiet Man
The Red Shoes
The River (1951)
The Ten Commandments (1956 version)
The Thief of Bagdad (1940 version)
The Yearling
Yolanda and the Thief

CLASSIC SOUND COMEDIES _____ CL10

Adam's Rib
Arsenic and Old Lace
The Awful Truth
Ball of Fire

Born Yesterday
Bringing Up Baby
The Court Jester
Dinner at Eight

Duck Soup
The Front Page (1931 version)
Hail the Conquering Hero
The Great Dictator
Harvey
Heaven Can Wait (1943)
His Girl Friday
Holiday
It Happened One Night
It's a Gift
It's in the Bag
Kind Hearts and Coronets
The Lady Eve
The Ladykillers
Mr. Blandings Builds His Dream House
Mister Roberts
The More the Merrier
My Favorite Wife
My Little Chickadee

My Man Godfrey
Ninotchka
Nothing Sacred
One, Two, Three
The Palm Beach Story
Pat and Mike
The Philadelphia Story
The Senator Was Indiscreet
Some Like It Hot
Sons of the Desert
Sullivan's Travels
The Talk of the Town
The Thin Man
To Be or Not to Be (1942 version)
Twentieth Century
Unfaithfully Yours (1948 version)
Woman of the Year
You Can't Cheat an Honest Man
You Can't Take It With You

CLASSIC SILENT COMEDIES _____ CL11
See also: Director Check Lists DT18 Charlie Chaplin, DT54 Buster Keaton

The Circus
City Lights
College
The Freshman
The General
The Gold Rush
It
Modern Times

Our Hospitality
Running Wild
Safety Last
Show People
Steamboat Bill, Jr.
The Strong Man
The Three Ages

CLASSIC SILENT DRAMAS _____ CL12
See also: Director Check Lists DT42 D. W. Griffith, DT109 Erich Von Stroheim

Battleship Potemkin
Beau Brummel (1924 version)
Ben-Hur: A Tale of the Christ
The Big Parade
The Birth of a Nation
Blind Husbands
Broken Blossoms
The Covered Wagon
The Crowd
Diary of a Lost Girl
The Docks of New York
Earth
Flesh and the Devil
Foolish Wives
Greed
Intolerance
King of Kings (1927 version)
The Last Command

The Last Laugh
Metropolis (1925 edition)
Napoleon (1927)
Old Ironsides
Pandora's Box
Passion (1918)
The Passion of Joan of Arc
Queen Kelly
Sadie Thompson
Sparrows
The Ten Commandments (1923 version)
The Thief of Bagdad (1926 version)
Variety
Way Down East
The Wedding March
The Wind
Wings
A Woman of Paris

RELIGIOUS STORIES _____ CL13

Barabbas
Ben-Hur

Ben-Hur: A Tale of the Christ
The Bible

David and Bathsheba
The Greatest Story Ever Told
Jesus of Nazareth
King of Kings (1927 & 1961 versions)
Moses
The Robe
Salome
Samson and Delilah

The Silver Chalice
Sodom and Gomorrah
Solomon and Sheba
Song of Bernadette
The Story of Ruth
The Ten Commandments (1923 & 1956 versions)

DELAYED CLASSICS: MOVIES UNAPPRECIATED ————————— CL14
IN THEIR OWN TIME

Beat the Devil
Come and Get It
The Devil and Daniel Webster
The Golden Coach
Intolerance
Lola Montes
The Magnificent Ambersons
The Nutty Professor
Once Upon a Time in the West

Petulia
Rio Bravo
The Searchers
Sylvia Scarlett
To Be or Not to Be (1942 version)
Touch of Evil
The Trouble With Harry
Vertigo

MEMORABLE SCREEN TEAMS ————————————————— CL15
See also: Star Check List ST87 Laurel & Hardy

Katharine Hepburn & Spencer Tracy
Adam's Rib
Desk Set
Guess Who's Coming to Dinner
Pat and Mike
State of the Union
Woman of the Year

Humphrey Bogart & Lauren Bacall
The Big Sleep
Dark Passage
Key Largo
To Have and Have Not

Fred Astaire & Ginger Rogers
The Barkleys of Broadway
Carefree
Flying Down to Rio
Follow the Fleet
The Gay Divorcee
Roberta
Shall We Dance
The Story of Vernon and Irene Castle
Swing Time
Top Hat

William Powell & Myrna Loy
After the Thin Man
Another Thin Man
The Great Ziegfeld
The Shadow of the Thin Man
Song of the Thin Man
The Thin Man
The Thin Man Goes Home

Richard Burton & Elizabeth Taylor
Cleopatra (1963)
Divorce His, Divorce Hers
Doctor Faustus
Hammersmith Is Out
The Sandpiper
The Taming of the Shrew
Under Milk Wood
Who's Afraid of Virginia Woolf?

Nelson Eddy & Jeanette MacDonald
Bitter Sweet
The Girl of the Golden West
I Married an Angel
Maytime
Naughty Marietta
New Moon
Rose Marie (1936 version)
Sweethearts

Mickey Rooney & Judy Garland
Andy Hardy Meets Debutante
Babes in Arms
Babes on Broadway
Girl Crazy
Love Finds Andy Hardy
Strike up the Band
Words and Music

Bob Hope & Bing Crosby
The Road to Bali
The Road to Rio
Road to Utopia

Chapter Three

COMEDY
(CO)

See Also: Director Check Lists DT1 Woody Allen, DT13 Mel Brooks, DT18 Charlie Chaplin, DT54 Buster Keaton, DT103 Preston Sturges; Star Check Lists ST1 Abbott & Costello, ST18 Cheech & Chong, ST41 W. C. Fields, ST63 Goldie Hawn, ST69 Judy Holliday, ST70 Bob Hope, ST78 Danny Kaye, ST87 Laurel & Hardy, ST91 Jerry Lewis, ST99 Steve Martin, ST101 The Marx Brothers, ST109 Dudley Moore, ST125 Richard Pryor, ST137 Peter Sellers, ST158 Mae West; Writer Check List WR23 Neil Simon

ROMANTIC COMEDIES _____ CO1

All Night Long
Almost You
American Dreamer
Annie Hall
Arthur
Arthur 2 On the Rocks
Barefoot in the Park
Best Friends
Blind Date (1987)
Blume in Love
Broadcast News
Bull Durham
Cactus Flower
Chances Are
Continental Divide
"Crocodile" Dundee
"Crocodile" Dundee II
Cross My Heart
Crossing Delancey
The Electric Horseman
The Four Seasons
The Goodbye Girl
The Heartbreak Kid
Heartburn
House Calls
It Takes Two
It's My Turn
Joe Versus the Volcano
Living on Tokyo Time
Love at Large
Loverboy
Manhattan
Micki and Maude
A Midsummer Night's Sex Comedy
Modern Romance
Moonstruck
Murphy's Romance

Never on Sunday
A New Life
Night Shift
The Owl and the Pussycat
Pete 'n' Tillie
Pillow Talk
Play It Again, Sam
Pretty Woman
Quackser Fortune Has a Cousin in the
    Bronx
Reuben, Reuben
Roxanne
Say Anything
Shampoo
She's Gotta Have It
She's Having a Baby
Shirley Valentine
Skin Deep
Someone to Love
Splash
Starting Over
The Sure Thing
Surrender
Sweethearts Dance
Switching Channels
10
That Touch of Mink
A Touch of Class
True Love
Victor/Victoria
The War of the Roses
What's New, Pussycat?
When Harry Met Sally...
Who Am I This Time?
The Woman in Red
Working Girl
Worth Winning

COMEDIES FOR MODERN TIMES _____ CO2

After Hours
Annie Hall
Baby Boom
Being There
Between the Lines
Bob & Carol & Ted & Alice
Britannia Hospital
Broadcast News
Carbon Copy
Chan Is Missing
The Coca-Cola Kid
Cold Turkey
Crazy People
Creator
D.C. Cab
The Decline of the American Empire
Desk Set
Desperately Seeking Susan
Dr. Strangelove: or, How I Learned to
   Stop Worrying and Love the Bomb
Down and Out in Beverly Hills
Earth Girls Are Easy
The Experts
The First Monday in October
Gas-s-s-s
The Gods Must Be Crazy
The Graduate
Gung Ho (1986)
Heartburn
High Hopes
Honky Tonk Freeway
How to Get Ahead in Advertising
I Love You, Alice B. Toklas
In the Spirit
It's My Turn
King of Comedy
Little Murders
Living on Tokyo Time
Local Hero
The Lonely Guy
Lost in America
Making Mr. Right
Manhattan
Max Headroom
Melvin and Howard
The Milagro Beanfield War
Mr. Mom

Moon Over Parador
Mother, Jugs and Speed
Mystery Train
A New Life
New York Stories
Night Shift
One, Two, Three
Patti Rocks
Perfect!
Planes, Trains, and Automobiles
The President's Analyst
Private Benjamin
Putney Swope
Real Genius
Repo Man
Rosalie Goes Shopping
The Russians Are Coming! The
   Russians Are Coming!
School Daze
Scrooged
The Secret of My Success
Semi-Tough
Serial
Shampoo
She-Devil
She's Gotta Have It
Sidewalk Stories
Smile
Something Wild
Soul Man
Stars and Bars
Stay Hungry
Steel Magnolias
Steelyard Blues
Tanner '88
Three Men and a Baby
Tootsie
Valley Girl
Vibes
The War of the Roses
Where the Buffalo Roam
Where the Heart Is
Whoops Apocalypse
Wild in the Streets
Working Girl
Wrong Is Right

CONTEMPORARY COMEDY TEAMS _____ CO3

All of Me
Armed and Dangerous
Bedazzled
Bedtime Story
The Best of Times
Big Business
The Blues Brothers
Brewster's Millions

Buddy Buddy
City Heat
The Dream Team
Dirty, Rotten Scoundrels
Feds
A Fine Mess
The In-Laws
Ishtar

Macaroni
9 to 5
The Odd Couple
Outrageous Fortune
Planes, Trains, and Automobiles
Running Scared
See No Evil, Hear No Evil
Silver Streak
Stir Crazy
The Sunshine Boys

The Survivors
Three Amigos
Throw Momma From the Train
Tin Men
Tough Guys
Trading Places
Twins
Vibes
Volunteers
Wise Guys

GROWING UP _____ CO4

American Graffiti
Back to the Future
The Bad News Bears
Big
Big Shots
Breaking Away
Fandango
Fast Times at Ridgemont High
Ferris Bueller's Day Off
Footloose
For Keeps
The Graduate
Gregory's Girl
Heathers
Heaven Help Us
House Party
Johnny Be Good
The Joy of Sex
A Little Romance

My Bodyguard
My Life as a Dog
National Lampoon's Animal House
The Night Before
A Night in the Life of Jimmy Reardon
Porky's (series)
Real Genius
Revenge of the Nerds
Rich Kids
Risky Business
Rita, Sue and Bob Too
Say Anything
Sixteen Candles
Some Kind of Wonderful
Teen Wolf
Valley Girl
The World of Henry Orient
You're a Big Boy Now

FUNNY FAMILIES _____ CO5

Author! Author!
Back to the Future, Part II
Big Business
Brighton Beach Memoirs
A Christmas Story
Cookie
Coup de Ville
Crimes of the Heart
18 Again!
Family Business
First Family
Garbo Talks
The Great Outdoors
Hannah and Her Sisters
Honey, I Shrunk the Kids
Hope and Glory
The Hotel New Hampshire
I Ought to Be in Pictures
Irreconcilable Differences
Life With Father
Look Who's Talking
Lovers and Other Strangers
Max Dugan Returns
Mr. Mom

Morgan Stewart's Coming Home
National Lampoon's Christmas
   Vacation
National Lampoon's European Vacation
National Lampoon's Vacation
Overboard
Parenthood
Parents
The Plot Against Harry
The Prince of Pennsylvania
Radio Days
Raising Arizona
She's Out of Control
A Thousand Clowns
The Toy
True Love
Twins
Twister
Uncle Buck
Vice Versa
A Wedding
Where the Heart Is
Where's Poppa?
Yours, Mine and Ours

NUTTY NOSTALGIA —————————————————————————— CO6

American Graffiti
Back to the Future
Back to the Future, Part II
Biloxi Blues
Bloodhounds of Broadway
Brighton Beach Memoirs
A Christmas Story
Coup de Ville
Cry-Baby
Diner
Good Morning, Vietnam
The _____ _ce
Hairspray
Harlem Nights
Harry and Walter Go to New York
Heartbreak Hotel
Hearts of the West
History of the World—Part I
Hope and Glory
How I Won the War
I Wanna Hold Your Hand
In the Mood
The Lords of Flatbush

M*A*S*H
Mr. North
My Favorite Year
Nadine
The Night They Raided Minsky's
1941
Paper Moon
Parents
Peggy Sue Got Married
A Private Function
Privates on Parade
Radio Days
Shag
The Skin Game (1971)
Start the Revolution Without Me
The Sting
Sunset
The Twelve Chairs
Those Lips, Those Eyes
Those Magnificent Men in Their Flying
    Machines
Tin Men

MOVIE SPOOFS ———————————————————————————— CO7

Airplane!
Airplane II: The Sequel
Amazon Women on the Moon
The Big Bus
Blazing Saddles
Bullshot
Casino Royale
Cat Ballou
The Cheap Detective
City Heat
Cry-Baby
Dark Star
Dead Men Don't Wear Plaid
11 Harrowhouse
Erik the Viking
High Anxiety
I'm Gonna Git You Sucka
The Jet Benny Show
Johnny Dangerously
The Last Remake of Beau Geste
Loose Shoes

Love at First Bite
Lust in the Dust
The Man With Two Brains
Monty Python and the Holy Grail
Monty Python's Life of Brian
Movie Movie
Murder by Death
The Naked Gun
Rock 'n' Roll High School
The Rocky Horror Picture Show
Rustler's Rhapsody
Silent Movie
Sleeper
Spaceballs
Take the Money and Run
This Is Spinal Tap
Top Secret!
Transylvania 6-5000
What's Up, Tiger Lily?
Young Frankenstein
Zelig

THE LIGHTER SIDE OF SHOW BIZ —————————————————— CO8

After the Fox
The Big Picture
Broadway Danny Rose
Champagne for Caesar
Crimes and Misdemeanors
Enter Laughing

Gentlemen Prefer Blondes
Ginger and Fred
The Groove Tube
Hearts of the West
Hollywood Boulevard
Hollywood or Bust

Hollywood Shuffle
Home Movies
Hooper
The Loved One
Moon Over Parador
Movers and Shakers
My Favorite Year
The Producers
The Purple Rose of Cairo
Radio Days
Real Life
Rhinestone
Roadie
Romantic Comedy

S.O.B.
Smile
Songwriter
Stand-In
Stardust Memories
Sunset
The Sunshine Boys
Sweet Liberty
Tapeheads
Those Lips, Those Eyes
Tootsie
UHF
Under the Rainbow
Who Framed Roger Rabbit

ACTION COMEDIES _____ CO9
See also: CO10 Crime and Suspense Comedies

Any Which Way You Can
Beverly Hills Cop
Beverly Hills Cop II
Bird on a Wire
The Cannonball Run
Cannonball Run II
The Cheap Detective
Cold Feet
"Crocodile" Dundee
"Crocodile" Dundee II
Donovan's Reef
Every Which Way But Loose
Fuzz
Ghostbusters
Ghostbusters II
The Golden Child

The Gumball Rally
Howard the Duck
Innerspace
It's a Mad Mad Mad Mad World
Midnight Run
Raising Arizona
Running Scared
See No Evil, Hear No Evil
Short Time
Smokey and the Bandit (series)
Speed Zone
Think Big
Those Magnificent Men in Their Flying
     Machines
Weekend at Bernie's

CRIME AND SUSPENSE COMEDIES _____ CO10
See also: CO9 Action Comedies, MY17 Comic Mysteries, Star Check List ST137 Peter Sellers
(for Pink Panther titles)

The Black Marble
Breaking In
Burglar
The Choirboys
Clue
Compromising Positions
Cookie
Crazy Mama
Disorganized Crime
$ (Dollars)
Dragnet (1987)
11 Harrowhouse
Ernest Goes to Jail
Family Business
A Fish Called Wanda
Flashback
Fletch
Fletch Lives
Foul Play

Heart Condition
Hopscotch
The Hot Rock
How to Murder Your Wife
I Love You to Death
The In-Laws
Johnny Dangerously
Jumpin' Jack Flash
K-9
The Ladykillers
The Lavender Hill Mob
Loose Cannons
The Man With One Red Shoe
Married to the Mob
Moonlighting (1985)
Murder by Death
The Naked Gun
Opportunity Knocks
Pink Cadillac

The Plot Against Harry
Raising Arizona
Rough Cut
Ruthless People
Second Sight
See No Evil, Hear No Evil
Silver Streak
Some Like It Hot
Stakeout
Stir Crazy
Take the Money and Run

They All Laughed
The Thief Who Came to Dinner
Things Change
Three Fugitives
Throw Momma From the Train
Tough Guys
The Trouble With Harry
Turner and Hooch
Who Framed Roger Rabbit
Who's Harry Crumb?
Wise Guys

SPECIAL EFFECTS FOR LAUGHS ————————————————————— CO11

Back to the Future
Back to the Future, Part II
Beetlejuice
Big Top Pee-wee
Explorers
Ghostbusters
Ghostbusters II
The Golden Child
Gremlins
High Spirits
Honey, I Shrunk the Kids
Howard the Duck
The Incredible Shrinking Woman
Innerspace

Little Monsters
Max Headroom
Modern Problems
My Demon Lover
My Science Project
My Stepmother Is an Alien
Pee-wee's Big Adventure
Second Sight
Short Circuit
Short Circuit 2
Teen Wolf
Weird Science
Who Framed Roger Rabbit

OFFBEAT COMEDY ——————————————————————————————— CO12

The Adventures of Buckaroo Banzai
   Across the 8th Dimension
After Hours
Bagdad Cafe
Being There
Big Top Pee-wee
Bliss
Brewster McCloud
The Cars That Ate Paris
Catch-22
The Coca-Cola Kid
Cold Feet
Consuming Passions
A Day in the Death of Joe Egg
Dr. Strangelove: or, How I Learned to
   Stop Worrying and Love the Bomb
Down by Law
The End
Entertaining Mr. Sloane
Grace Quigley
Harold and Maude
Heathers
The Hospital
How I Won the War
I Love You to Death
In the Spirit
I've Heard the Mermaids Singing

King of Comedy
Little Murders
Lolita
Loot . . . Give Me Money, Honey
The Loved One
M*A*S*H
The Magic Christian
Malcolm
Me and Him
Miss Firecracker
My Dinner With Andre
Nasty Habits
Neighbors
A New Leaf
92 in the Shade
Outrageous
Parents
Pee-wee's Big Adventure
Pulp
Putney Swope
Repo Man
The Rocky Horror Picture Show
Salvation
A Shock to the System
Short Time
Silent Movie
Something Wild

Stranger Than Paradise
Swimming to Cambodia
The Trouble With Harry
UFOria

Used Cars
Where's Poppa?
Young Einstein
Zelig

STAR CHECK LISTS: THE ALUMNI OF *SATURDAY NIGHT LIVE* _____ CO13
see also: CO16 Performance Comics

Dan Aykroyd
The Best of Dan Aykroyd
The Blues Brothers
Caddyshack II
The Couch Trip
Doctor Detroit
Dragnet (1987)
Driving Miss Daisy
Ghostbusters
Ghostbusters II
The Great Outdoors
It Came From Hollywood
Loose Cannons
My Stepmother Is an Alien
Neighbors
1941
Spies Like Us
Trading Places
Twilight Zone: The Movie

Jim Belushi
About Last Night
Homer and Eddie
Jumpin' Jack Flash
K-9
Little Shop of Horrors
The Man With One Red Shoe
The Principal
Real Men
Red Heat
Salvador

John Belushi
The Best of John Belushi
The Blues Brothers
Continental Divide
Goin' South
National Lampoon's Animal House
Neighbors
1941
Old Boyfriends

Chevy Chase
The Best of Chevy Chase
Caddyshack
Caddyshack II
Deal of the Century
Fletch
Fletch Lives
Follow That Bird
Foul Play

Funny Farm
The Groove Tube
Modern Problems
National Lampoon's Christmas
    Vacation
National Lampoon's European Vacation
National Lampoon's Vacation
Oh! Heavenly Dog
Seems Like Old Times
Spies Like Us
Three Amigos
Under the Rainbow

Billy Crystal
Animalympics (character voice)
Memories of Me
The Princess Bride
Rabbit Test
Running Scared
This Is Spinal Tap
The Three Little Pigs
Throw Momma From the Train
When Harry Met Sally...

Jane Curtin
How to Beat the High Cost of Living
Suspicion (1987 version)

Garrett Morris
The Anderson Tapes
Critical Condition
The Stuff

Eddie Murphy
Best Defense
The Best of Eddie Murphy: Saturday
    Night Live
Beverly Hills Cop
Beverly Hills Cop II
Coming to America
48HRS.
The Golden Child
Harlem Nights
Trading Places

Bill Murray
Caddyshack
Ghostbusters
Ghostbusters II
Little Shop of Horrors
Loose Shoes

Meatballs
The Razor's Edge (1984 version)
Scrooged
Stripes
Tootsie
Where the Buffalo Roam

Laraine Newman
Invaders From Mars (1986 version)
Perfect!
Wholly Moses

Joe Piscopo
Dead Heat

Johnny Dangerously
Wise Guys

Gilda Radner
Animalympics (character voice)
The Best of Gilda
First Family
Gilda Live
Hanky Panky
Haunted Honeymoon
It Came From Hollywood
Movers and Shakers
The Woman in Red

CHECK LISTS: THE ALUMNI OF *SCTV* _____ **CO14**

John Candy
Armed and Dangerous
Brewster's Millions
Find the Lady
Going Berserk
The Great Outdoors
It Came From Hollywood
Little Shop of Horrors
National Lampoon's Vacation
1941
Planes, Trains, and Automobiles
Really Weird Tales
Spaceballs
Speed Zone
Splash
Stripes
Summer Rental
Uncle Buck
Volunteers
Who's Harry Crumb?

Joe Flaherty
Back to the Future, Part II
Going Berserk
One Crazy Summer
Speed Zone

Eugene Levy
Armed and Dangerous
Club Paradise
Going Berserk
National Lampoon's Vacation
Speed Zone
Splash

Andrea Martin
Black Christmas
Club Paradise
Worth Winning

*director only

Rick Moranis
Club Paradise
Ghostbusters
Ghostbusters II
Head Office
Honey, I Shrunk the Kids
Little Shop of Horrors (1986 version)
Parenthood
Spaceballs
Strange Brew
Streets of Fire
The Wild Life

Catherine O'Hara
After Hours
Beetlejuice
Really Weird Tales

Harold Ramis
Baby Boom
Caddyshack*
Club Paradise*
Ghostbusters
Ghostbusters II
National Lampoon's Vacation*
Stealing Home
Stripes

Martin Short
The Big Picture
Cross My Heart
Innerspace
Really Weird Tales
Three Amigos
Three Fugitives

Dave Thomas
The Experts*
Follow That Bird
Moving
Strange Brew

STARS CHECK LISTS: MONTY PYTHON'S FLYING CIRCUS ———————— CO15

The Troupe
And Now for Something Completely
  Different
Monty Python and the Holy Grail
Monty Python's Flying Circus, Volumes
  1-17
Monty Python's Life of Brian
Monty Python's The Meaning of Life

Individually (but sometimes together)
The Adventures of Baron Munchausen
  (Eric Idle; directed by Terry Gilliam)
All You Need Is Cash (Idle)
The Big Picture (John Cleese)
Brazil (Michael Palin; directed by
  Gilliam)
Clockwise (Cleese)
Erik the Viking (Cleese, Terry Jones;
  directed by Jones)
Fawlty Towers, Volumes 1-4 (Cleese)
A Fish Called Wanda (Cleese, Palin)
Jabberwocky (Palin; directed by
  Gilliam)

Labyrinth (Jones)
The Magic Christian (Graham
  Chapman, Cleese)
The Missionary (Palin)
National Lampoon's European Vacation
  (Idle)
Nuns on the Run (Idle)
Personal Services (directed by Jones)
The Pied Piper of Hamelin (Idle)
A Private Function (Palin)
Privates on Parade (Cleese)
Ripping Yarns (Jones, Palin)
The Secret Policeman's Other Ball
  (Chapman, Cleese, Jones, Palin)
The Secret Policeman's Private Parts
  (Chapman, Cleese, Gilliam, Jones,
  Palin)
Silverado (Cleese)
Spies Like Us (Gilliam)
Time Bandits (Cleese, Palin; directed by
  Gilliam)
Whoops Apocalypse (Cleese)
Yellowbeard (Chapman, Cleese, Idle)

PERFORMANCE COMICS ——————————————————————————— CO16
See also: CO29 Richard Pryor Check List

The Andy Kaufman Sound Stage
  Special
Bette Midler's Mondo Beyondo
The Best of Comic Relief
Bill Cosby: 49
Bill Cosby: Himself
Billy Crystal: A Comic's Line
Billy Crystal: Don't Get Me Started
Carlin at Carnegie
Comic Relief 2
Comic Relief III
Eddie Murphy: Delirious
Eddie Murphy Raw
An Evening With Bobcat Goldthwait:
  Share the Warmth
An Evening With Robin Williams
The First Howie Mandel Special
Gallagher: The Bookkeeper
Gallagher: The Maddest

Gallagher: Melon Crazy
Gallagher: Over Your Head
Gallagher: Stuck in the 60s
Gilda Live
HBO Comedy Club
Jackie Mason on Broadway
The Joe Piscopo Video
The Joe Piscopo New Jersey Special
Jonathan Winters: On the Ledge
Robert Klein: Child of the 60s, Man of
  the 80s
Robert Klein on Broadway
Robin Williams Live!
Steve Martin Live!
Steven Wright Live
Ten From Your Show of Shows
Whoopi Goldberg: Fontaine...Why Am I
  Straight?
Whoopi Goldberg Live

CLASSIC & CONTEMPORARY BRITISH COMEDY ——————————— CO17
See also: C015 Monty Python's Flying Circus Check Lists

Alfie
The Belles of St. Trinian's
Billy Liar
Britannia Hospital
Bullshot

Carry On Doctor
Comfort and Joy
Consuming Passions
A Day in the Death of Joe Egg
Doctor in the House

Eat the Peach
Educating Rita
Entertaining Mr. Sloane
A Fish Called Wanda
Georgy Girl
Getting It Right
The Goon Show Movie
The Gospel According to Vic
Gregory's Girl
Gumshoe
High Hopes
Hobson's Choice (1954 version)
Hope and Glory
The Horse's Mouth
How I Won the War
How to Get Ahead in Advertising
I'm All Right, Jack
Kind Hearts and Coronets
The Ladykillers
The Lavender Hill Mob
Letter to Brezhnev
Local Hero
Loot . . . Give Me Money, Honey!

The Magic Christian
Make Mine Mink
The Man in the White Suit
Morgan: A Suitable Case for Treatment
The Mouse That Roared
No Surrender
Nuns on the Run
Personal Services
A Private Function
Rita, Sue and Bob Too
The Ruling Class
Shirley Valentine
Stars and Bars
That Sinking Feeling
Tom Jones
Two Way Stretch
Waltz of the Toreadors
We Think the World of You
Whisky Galore
Whoops Apocalypse
Wish You Were Here
Withnail and I
The Wrong Box

CAMPUS COMEDY _____ CO18
See also: DR25 School Days

Bedtime for Bonzo
The Belles of St. Trinians
College
The Computer Wore Tennis Shoes
Fast Times at Ridgemont High
The Freshman
Getting Straight
The Gospel According to Vic
Gregory's Girl
Gross Anatomy
Heathers
Heaven Help Us
Horse Feathers
How I Got Into College
The Ladies' Man

My Bodyguard
My Science Project
National Lampoon's Animal House
National Lampoon's Class Reunion
The Nutty Professor
Porky's (series)
Real Genius
Revenge of the Nerds
Rock 'n' Roll High School
School Daze
Soul Man
Summer School
Teacher's Pet
The Trouble With Angels
Zero for Conduct

SPORTS FOR LAUGHS _____ CO19
See also: DR22 For Sports Fans

All the Marbles
The Bad News Bears
The Best of Times
The Bingo Long Traveling All-Stars and
    Motor Kings
Bull Durham
The Caddy
Fastbreak
Johnny Be Good
Let It Ride
The Longest Yard
Major League

Man's Favorite Sport?
Matilda
No Holds Barred
North Dallas Forty
Paper Lion
Pat and Mike
Semi-Tough
Ski Patrol
Slap Shot
Stroker Ace
Wildcats

FISH OUT OF WATER: FUNNY TALES OF MISPLACED PERSONS _____ CO20

Adventures in Babysitting
After Hours
All of Me
Back to the Future
Back to the Future, Part II
Bagdad Cafe
Beverly Hills Cop
Beverly Hills Cop II
Big
Bill and Ted's Excellent Adventure
Chances Are
Coming to America
Critical Condition
"Crocodile" Dundee
"Crocodile" Dundee II
Desperately Seeking Susan
Down and Out in Beverly Hills
Dream a Little Dream
The Dream Team
18 Again!
The Experts
Flashback
Freaky Friday
The Great McGinty
Hail the Conquering Hero

Heart Condition
Heaven Can Wait (1978)
Here Comes Mr. Jordan
Howard the Duck
Identity Crisis
Maxie
Mr. Mom
Moon Over Parador
Moscow on the Hudson
My Man Godfrey
Nuns on the Run
Peggy Sue Got Married
Pretty Woman
Rude Awakening
The Secret of My Success
Soul Man
Splash
Sullivan's Travels
Things Change
Tough Guys
Trading Places
Troop Beverly Hills
Vice Versa
We're No Angels (1989 version)
Yentl

UNIFORMLY FUNNY: SERVICE COMEDIES _____ CO21

At War With the Army
Biloxi Blues
Buck Privates
Catch-22
The Chaplin Revue (Shoulder Arms)
Good Morning, Vietnam
Great Guns
How I Won the War
Kelly's Heroes
The Last Detail
M*A*S*H
Off Limits (1953)

Operation Petticoat
Private Benjamin
Privates on Parade
The Secret War of Harry Frigg
She's in the Army Now
Soldier in the Rain
Stripes
Teahouse of the August Moon
Up in Arms
Up the Creek (1958)
The Wackiest Ship in the Army
Which Way to the Front?

Chapter Four

CULT FILMS
(CU)

See also: Director Check Lists DT2 Robert Altman, DT4 Allan Arkush, DT5 Paul Bartel, DT11 John Boorman, DT17 John Carpenter, DT19 Jean Cocteau, DT20 Larry Cohen, DT25 Joe Dante, DT28 Jonathan Demme, DT29 Brian DePalma, DT38 Bill Forsyth, DT40 Samuel Fuller, DT45 Walter Hill, DT52 Philip Kaufman, DT62 Richard Lester, DT66 David Lynch, DT67 Terrence Malick, DT72 Paul Morissey, DT73 Errol Morris, DT76 Max Ophuls, DT81 Michael Powell, DT83 Nicholas Ray, DT88 Nicolas Roeg, DT91 Alan Rudolph, DT92 Ken Russell, DT96 Ridley Scott, DT98 Douglas Sirk, DT110 John Waters, DT118 Ed Wood, Jr.

MIDNIGHT MOVIES _____ CU1

Angel Heart
Blue Velvet
A Clockwork Orange
Dawn of the Dead
Eraserhead
The Harder They Come
Harold and Maude
King of Hearts
Magical Mystery Tour
Myra Breckenridge
Night of the Living Dead
Outrageous!

Performance
Pink Flamingos
Reefer Madness
Rock 'n' Roll High School
The Rocky Horror Picture Show
Rude Boy
Sid and Nancy
Something Wild
Stranger Than Paradise
The Texas Chainsaw Massacre
200 Motels

CAMP CULT _____ CU2

Beyond the Valley of the Dolls
Bride of the Gorilla
The Conqueror
The Cool and the Crazy
Forbidden Zone
The Fountainhead
Heat (1972)
High School Confidential
Hush . . . Hush Sweet Charlotte
The Killers (1964 version)
The Lonely Lady

Mommie Dearest
Myra Breckenridge
The Private Files of J. Edgar Hoover
Sextette
Shack Out on 101
Sincerely Yours
Strait-Jacket
What Ever Happened to Baby Jane?
The Wicked Lady
The Wild One
The Women

"HEAD" MOVIES _____ CU3

Altered States
Cocaine Cowboys
Easy Rider
Head
Performance
The Trip

200 Motels
2001: A Space Odyssey
Up in Smoke
Yellow Submarine
Zabriskie Point

CULT HORROR & SCIENCE FICTION _____ CU4

The Abominable Dr. Phibes
Altered States
Android
Andy Warhol's Dracula
Andy Warhol's Frankenstein
Barbarella
Basket Case
Blood Couple
A Boy and His Dog
Brazil
The Bride of Frankenstein
The Brood
Carnival of Souls
A Clockwork Orange
Conqueror Worm
Dark Star
Daughters of Darkness
Dawn of the Dead
The Day the Earth Stood Still
Death Race 2000
Fahrenheit 451
Forbidden Planet
Freaks
Glen and Randa
Halloween
The Hills Have Eyes
I Walked With a Zombie

The Incredible Shrinking Man
The Incredibly Strange Creatures Who
   Stopped Living and Became Crazy
   Mixed-Up Zombies
Invasion of the Bee Girls
Invasion of the Body Snatchers (1956 &
   1978 versions)
King Kong (1933 version)
Liquid Sky
The Little Shop of Horrors (1960
   version)
The Man Who Fell to Earth
Martin
Night of the Living Dead
Night Tide
Piranha
Re-Animator
Scanners
Suspiria
The Texas Chainsaw Massacre
Theatre of Blood
Them
The Thing (From Another World)
2001: A Space Odyssey
The Wicker Man
Zardoz

CULT COMEDY _____ CU5

The Adventures of Buckaroo Banzai
   Across the 8th Dimension
After Hours
Angels Over Broadway
Beat the Devil
Bedazzled
Bedtime for Bonzo
Brewster McCloud
La Cage aux Folles
Eating Raoul
Get Crazy
Greetings
Harold and Maude
The Heartbreak Kid
Heathers
Hollywood Boulevard

It's a Gift
King of Comedy
King of Hearts
The Ladykillers
Little Murders
Morgan: A Suitable Case for Treatment
My Dinner With Andre
Pee-wee's Big Adventure
Repo Man
The Rocky Horror Picture Show
The Ruling Class
Something for Everyone
To Be or Not to Be (1942 version)
Used Cars
Where the Heart Is
Where's Poppa?

NOTORIOUSLY SEXY _____ CU6

Angel Heart
L'Annee des Meduses
Baby Doll
Barbarella
Betty Blue
Beyond the Valley of the Dolls
Big Bad Mama

Body Heat
Butterfly
Caligula
The Cook, The Thief, His Wife and Her
   Lover
Crimes of Passion
Daughters of Darkness

Devil in the Flesh
Ecstasy
The Fourth Man
The Girl in a Swing
Last Tango in Paris
Liquid Sky
The Night Porter
9½ Weeks
Pandora's Box
Rendez-vous

She's Gotta Have It
Something for Everyone
Summer Lovers
Sweet Movie
Tales of Ordinary Madness
Thief of Hearts
Two Moon Junction
The Unbearable Lightness of Being
Wild Orchid

FAMOUS FOR GORE AND VIOLENCE _____ CU7

Across 110th Street
Basket Case
The Brood
Caligula
The Cook, The Thief, His Wife and Her
    Lover
Dawn of the Dead
Enter the Dragon
The Evil Dead
Fingers
The Fly (1986 version)
From Beyond
Henry: Portrait of a Serial Killer
Mad Max

Maniac
Mother's Day
Ms. 45
Night of the Living Dead
Point Blank
Re-Animator
Scanners
Scarface (1983 version)
Shogun Assassin
Taxi Driver
The Texas Chainsaw Massacre
The Warriors
The Wild Bunch

CENSORED OR BANNED MOVIES _____ CU8

Baby Doll
Carnal Knowledge
The Commissar
Ecstasy
Freaks
Hail Mary

North Star
Oliver Twist (1948 version)
The Outlaw
Peeping Tom
Viridiana
Witchcraft Through the Ages

POLITICAL STATEMENTS _____ CU9
See also: DR21 Political Dramas

The Battle of Algiers
Billy Jack
Burn!
The Harder They Come
The Manchurian Candidate
The Parallax View
Potemkin

Salt of the Earth
Strike!
Sympathy for the Devil
Ten Days That Shook the World/
October
Winter Kills

FOOTAGE ADDED FOR VIDEO _____ CU10
*This list includes films with footage restored from early theatrical versions, as well as titles
with never-seen-before scenes. Check the Title Index for details on each film.*

And God Created Woman
Angel Heart
The Bad Sleep Well
Blade Runner

The Bullfighter and the Lady
Cheyenne Autumn
Colors
Crimes of Passion

Dr. Jekyll and Mr. Hyde (1932 version)
The Executioner's Song
The Fearless Vampire Killers
Frankenstein (1931 version)
Hawaii
Hellbound: Hellraiser II
The Hidden Fortress
Isadora
Johnny Be Good
Lawrence of Arabia
Lost Horizon
Mr. Skeffington
New York, New York
Oliver Twist (1948 version)
Pat Garrett and Billy the Kid
Red River
Richard III

Rocco and His Brothers
Salem's Lot
Scandal
The Sea Hawk
The Sicilian
Star Trek—The Motion Picture
Stealing Heaven
Stop Making Sense
Suspiria
Thief of Hearts
This Is Elvis
Touch of Evil
Two English Girls
The Wedding March
When Time Ran Out
Wild Rovers
The Wizard of Oz

"BAD" MOVIES _____ CU11

Attack of the Killer Tomatoes
Cocaine Fiends
The Creeping Terror
Frankenstein Island
Glen or Glenda?
Manos, the Hands of Fate
Night of the Bloody Apes

Plan 9 From Outer Space
Reefer Madness
Revenge of the Dead
Robot Monster
Tarzan, the Ape Man (1981 version)
Terror of Tiny Town
They Saved Hitler's Brain

BAD TASTE? YOU BE THE JUDGE _____ CU12

Andy Warhol's Bad
Blue Velvet
Desperate Living
Eraserhead
Female Trouble
Flesh
Heat (1972)
The Loved One

Mondo Trasho
Multiple Maniacs
Pink Flamingos
Polyester
Suburbia
Trash
Where's Poppa?

CULT MOVIES BY FAMOUS DIRECTORS _____ CU13

Beat the Devil (John Huston)
The Collector (William Wyler)
Fahrenheit 451 (François Truffaut)
Last Tango in Paris (Bernardo
  Bertolucci)

Rio Bravo (Howard Hawks)
The Searchers (John Ford)
Vertigo (Alfred Hitchcock)

DIRECTORS WHO GOT THEIR STARTS WITH ROGER CORMAN _____ CU14

Boxcar Bertha (Martin Scorsese)
Caged Heat (Jonathan Demme)
Dementia 13 (Francis Ford Coppola)
Grand Theft Auto (Ron Howard)

Hollywood Boulevard (Joe Dante and
  Allan Arkush)
Night Call Nurses (Jonathan Kaplan)
Targets (Peter Bogdanovich)

ONE-SHOT DIRECTORS _____ CU15

Carnival of Souls (Herk Harvey)
The Honeymoon Killers (Leonard
  Kastle)
The Night of the Hunter (Charles
  Laughton)

One-Eyed Jacks (Marlon Brando)
The Senator Was Indiscreet (George S.
  Kaufman)

DOCUMENTARIES _____ CU16
See also: MU10 Rock Concert Films, MU11 Rock Documentaries

Always for Pleasure
America at the Movies
Arruza
Athens, GA.
The Atomic Cafe
Best Boy
Burden of Dreams
Chicken Ranch
The Day After Trinity: J. Robert and the
  Atomic Bomb
Dear America: Letters Home From
  Vietnam
For All Mankind
Gates of Heaven
George Stevens: A Filmmaker's Journey
Gizmo!
Harlan County, U.S.A.
Hearts and Minds
Heaven
The Hellstrom Chronicle
Hotel Terminus
The James Dean Story
Jazz on a Summer's Day
Koyaanisqatsi
Land Without Bread
Lenny Bruce
Let There Be Light
Let's Get Lost
Lightning Over Water
Louisiana Story
Lulu in Berlin
Making of a Legend: Gone With the
  Wind

Marjoe
Marlene
Men of Bronze
Millhouse: A White Comedy
Nanook of the North
Night and Fog
Olympia
On Any Sunday
Pumping Iron
Pumping Iron II: The Women
Roger and Me
Roger Corman: Hollywood's Wild
  Angel
Salesman
Say Amen, Somebody
A Sense of Loss
Sherman's March
Shoah
The Sorrow and the Pity
Streetwise
Ten Days That Shook the World/
Tokyo Olympiad
Tokyo-Ga
October
Thelonius Monk: Straight, No Chaser
The Thin Blue Line
This Is Korea/December 7
The Times of Harvey Milk
Triumph of the Will
Vernon, Florida
Vietnam: In the Year of the Pig

CULT CASTING _____ CU17

Candy Mountain
Casino Royale
Catch-22
The Chase (1966)
Dancing Lady
Dinner at Eight
Grand Hotel
Harold and Maude
Into the Night

It's a Mad Mad Mad Mad World
Johnny Guitar
The Last Tycoon
The Loved One
The Magnificent Seven
The Outsiders
Spies Like Us
A Wedding
Winter Kills

REMAKES OF FAMOUS MOVIES _____ CU18
See also: FF8 Foreign Films and Their American Remakes
Note: Remake title is listed first; original title, if different, follows in parentheses.

Against All Odds (1984) (Out of the
    Past)
Always (A Guy Named Joe)
The Bride (The Bride of Frankenstein)
Body and Soul
Cat People
The Champ
D.O.A.
Diary of a Chambermaid
Farewell, My Lovely (Murder, My
    Sweet)
The Fly
Heaven Can Wait (Here Comes Mr.
    Jordan)
House of Wax (Mystery of the Wax
    Museum)
Invaders From Mars
Invasion of the Body Snatchers
The Jazz Singer
King Kong
The Lady Vanishes

Lord of the Flies
The Man Who Knew Too Much
Mogambo (Red Dust)
The Phantom of the Opera
The Postman Always Rings Twice
Scarface
Silk Stockings (Ninotchka)
Stage Struck (1958) (Morning Glory)
A Star Is Born
Stella (Stella Dallas)
Suspicion
Switching Channels (His Girl Friday)
The Thing (The Thing (From Another
    World))
The 39 Steps
To Be or Not to Be
Unfaithfully Yours
Walk, Don't Run (The More the
    Merrier)
We're No Angels

LETTERBOXED MOVIES _____ CU19
*Note: Many of these titles are reissues of films originally released on home video in standard
format. Always check the tape box or ask your video retailer before renting or buying, to
make sure you have the format you want.*

The Alamo
Always
L'Avventura
Ben Hur (chariot race only)
Can-Can (musical numbers only)
The Color Purple
The Cook, The Thief, His Wife and Her
    Lover
Glory
Guys and Dolls (final number only)
High and Low
Hit the Deck (final number only)
Indiana Jones and the Last Crusade
Indiana Jones and the Temple of Doom

Inner Space
King of Hearts
Lawrence of Arabia
Lola Montes
Manhattan
New York, New York
Picnic
Raiders of the Last Ark
Rendez-vous
Satyricon
Shoot the Piano Player
Tokyo Olympiad
Woodstock (some sequences)

Chapter Five

DRAMA
(DR)

ROMANTIC DRAMAS ———————————————————————— **DR1**

About Last Night
The Accidental Tourist
Always
The Americanization of Emily
Atlantic City
Baby, It's You
Breakfast at Tiffany's
Breathless (1983 version)
Children of a Lesser God
Chilly Scenes of Winter
Choose Me
Cocktail
The Cook, The Thief, His Wife and Her
  Lover
Dangerous Liaisons
Days of Heaven
Dirty Dancing
Elvira Madigan
Enemies, A Love Story
Everybody's All American
The Fabulous Baker Boys
Far From the Madding Crowd
The French Lieutenant's Woman
Fresh Horses
Goodbye, Columbus
A Handful of Dust
Hanover Street
Hard Choices
In a Shallow Grave
Independence Day
Last Tango in Paris
Love at Large
Love Story
Love With the Proper Stranger
Made in Heaven
Mrs. Soffel

An Officer and a Gentleman
Old Gringo
Pete 'n' Tillie
Petulia
The Rachel Papers
Racing With the Moon
The Rainbow
Robin and Marian
The Roman Spring of Mrs. Stone
The Romantic Englishwoman
sex, lies, and videotape
The Slugger's Wife
Somewhere in Time
Sophie's Choice
Splendor in the Grass
Stanley and Iris
Starman
The Sterile Cuckoo
Strangers When We Meet
A Summer Place
Tender Mercies
Tequila Sunrise
The Thorn Birds
Trouble in Mind
Turtle Diary
Two for the Road
The Unbearable Lightness of Being
Until September
Valmont
Violets Are Blue
The Virgin and the Gypsy
A Walk in the Spring Rain
The Way We Were
Winter People
Women in Love

FOR A GOOD CRY ———————————————————————— **DR2**
See also: CL6 Classic Tear Jerkers

Beaches
Careful, He Might Hear You
Clara's Heart
Dominick and Eugene
Duet for One
Field of Dreams
Gaby—A True Story

The Heart Is a Lonely Hunter
Imitation of Life (1959 version)
Love Story
Madame X (1966 version)
Mask
The Natural
Ordinary People

The Other Side of Midnight
Places in the Heart
Project X
Rage of Angels
Resurrection
Six Weeks

Sophie's Choice
Steel Magnolias
Stella
Sweet Dreams
Tender Mercies
Terms of Endearment

FORBIDDEN LOVE ───────────────────────────── DR3

American Gigolo
Betrayal
Betrayed
Body Heat
The Boys in the Band
Cal
The Collector
Coming Home
Crimes of Passion
Desert Hearts
Every Time We Say Goodbye
Falling in Love
Fatal Attraction
Five Days One Summer
Fool for Love
Georgy Girl
Hanna K.
Hard Choices
Jagged Edge
The Killing of Sister George
Lady Chatterly's Lover (1955 & 1981
   versions)
Last Tango in Paris
Lianna
Lilith
Looking for Mr. Goodbar

Making Love
Maurice
Mayerling (1936 version)
My Beautiful Laundrette
Nijinsky
9½ Weeks
A Patch of Blue
Personal Best
The Postman Always Rings Twice (1946
   & 1981 versions)
Pretty Baby
Prick Up Your Ears
Reflections in a Golden Eye
Romeo and Juliet (1936 & 1968 versions)
The Runner Stumbles
Ryan's Daughter
Shadows
Someone To Watch Over Me
Stealing Heaven
Sunday, Bloody Sunday
Swing Shift
Torch Song Trilogy
Two Moon Junction
Wild Orchid
Wonderland
X, Y, and Zee

THE FAMOUS AND NOTORIOUS ─────────────────── DR4
See also: MU5 Musical Life Stories

Amadeus
The Amazing Howard Hughes
The Birdman of Alcatraz
Blaze
Born on the Fourth of July
Bound for Glory
Cast a Giant Shadow
Coal Miner's Daughter
Cross Creek
84 Charing Cross Road
The Elephant Man
Fear Strikes Out
Frances
Gandhi
The Great White Hope
The Greatest
Heart Beat
Heart Like a Wheel
Hitler

The Incredible Sarah
Isadora
The Jackie Robinson Story
Julia
King
The Last Emperor
Lenny
MacArthur
A Man Called Peter
Mandela
The Miracle Worker
Mountains of the Moon
Mussolini and I
My Left Foot
The Naked Civil Servant
Nijinsky
Out of Africa
Patton
Pope John Paul II

Prick Up Your Ears
The Private Files of J. Edgar Hoover
Raging Bull
Reds
Romero
Saint Joan
Somebody Up There Likes Me
The Song of Bernadette

Stevie
Sunrise at Campobello
Sweet Dreams
Tucker: The Man and His Dream
Wired
A Woman Called Golda
Young Winston

HISTORICAL DRAMA ——————————————————————————— DR5

Anne of the Thousand Days
The Assassination of Trotsky
Barry Lyndon
Becket
Bonnie and Clyde
Burke and Wills
Burn!
Caligula
The Cotton Club
Cromwell
Dangerous Liaisons
Daniel
The Devils
Dreamchild
Eight Men Out
Empire of the Sun
Enemies, A Love Story
Exodus
Fat Man and Little Boy
Glory
Hannah's War
Haunted Summer
Hawaii
Henry V (1945 & 1989 versions)
Hester Street
Khartoum
The Kitchen Toto
Lady Jane
The Lion in Winter

A Man for all Seasons (1966 & 1988
   versions)
Marat/Sade
Matewan
The Mission
The Moderns
The Molly Maguires
Nicholas and Alexandra
A Night to Remember (1958)
1918
Old Gringo
On Valentine's Day
Places in the Heart
Playing for Time
Pretty Baby
Ragtime
The Return of the Soldier
Revolution
Ship of Fools
The Sicilian
Spartacus
Swing Shift
Tai-Pan
Three Sovereigns for Sarah
A Town Like Alice
Triumph of the Spirit
Valmont
Voyage of the Damned
White Mischief

TRUE-LIFE CONTEMPORARY DRAMA ——————————————————— DR6

Act of Vengeance
All the President's Men
At Close Range
Bill
Bill: On His Own
Buster
Castaway
Casualties of War
Chattahoochee
Conrack
Courage (1986)
Cry Freedom
A Cry in the Dark
Dance With a Stranger
The Desperate Hours

Dog Day Afternoon
84 Charing Cross Road
Eleni
The Executioner's Song
The Falcon and the Snowman
Fatal Vision
Gaby—A True Story
Gideon's Trumpet
Gorillas in the Mist
Helter Skelter
The Honeymoon Killers
In Cold Blood
The Killing Fields
Lean on Me
Marie

Mask
Midnight Express
Missing
Mississippi Burning
The Onion Field
Patty Hearst
Prince of the City
The Pursuit of D.B. Cooper
Raid on Entebbe
The Right Stuff
Sakharov
Scandal

Serpico
Sid and Nancy
Silkwood
Stand and Deliver
Star 80
The Sugarland Express
Sybil
Talk Radio
10 Rillington Place
The Terry Fox Story
Weeds

MODERN PROBLEMS ————————————————————————— DR7

About Last Night
Absence of Malice
Alamo Bay
Alice's Restaurant
Amazing Grace and Chuck
The Baby Maker
The Big Chill
Birdy
Blue Collar
The Boost
The Border
Born on the Fourth of July
Cal
Carnal Knowledge
The China Syndrome
Clean and Sober
Coming Home
The Conversation
Country
Cutter's Way
The Day After
The Deer Hunter
Distant Thunder (1988)
Do the Right Thing
Drugstore Cowboy
A Dry White Season
Dudes
Easy Rider
End of the Line
End of the Road
Executive Suite
F.I.S.T.
For Queen and Country
Four Friends
Gardens of Stone
Guess Who's Coming to Dinner
Hail, Hero!
The Handmaid's Tale
Hanna K.
Hardcore
Heart of Dixie
Iceman
In Country
Jacknife

Johnny Got His Gun
Katherine
King
Listen to Me
Looking for Mr. Goodbar
Mandela
Medium Cool
Miles From Home
Mississippi Burning
Music Box
My Beautiful Laundrette
Nightbreaker
El Norte
Over the Edge
Petulia
Powwow Highway
Project X
Promised Land
Return of the Secaucus 7
The River (1984)
Romero
Running on Empty
St. Elmo's Fire
Salvador
The Shadow Box
Shame (1961)
Special Bulletin
Streamers
Street Smart
Talk Radio
Testament
Twilight's Last Gleaming
The Ugly American
The Unbearable Lightness of Being
Under Fire
Wall Street
Wargames
Welcome Home
Who'll Stop the Rain?
Whose Life Is it, Anyway?
Windy City
A World Apart
Zabriskie Point

FAMILY TROUBLES _____ DR8

The Accidental Tourist
All My Sons
At Close Range
Autumn Sonata
The Baby Maker
Bloodbrothers
Bonjour Tristesse
Born on the Fourth of July
Clara's Heart
The Color Purple
Country
Crimes and Misdemeanors
Da
Dad
The Dead
Dead Ringers
Death of a Salesman (1985 version)
Desert Bloom
Distant Thunder (1988)
Distant Voices, Still Lives
Dominick and Eugene
The Dressmaker
Driving Miss Daisy
East of Eden (1955 & 1982 versions)
The Fabulous Baker Boys
Far North
Field of Dreams
First Born
Five Easy Pieces
The Good Father
The Good Mother
The Great Santini
Hail, Hero!
Harry and Son
High Tide
Home From the Hill
I Never Sang for My Father
Immediate Family
In Country
Interiors
Irreconcilable Differences
Islands in the Stream
Joshua Then and Now
King of the Gypsies

Kramer vs. Kramer
Light of Day
Long Day's Journey Into Night (1962 &
  1987 versions)
Mask
Memories of Me
Men Don't Leave
Misunderstood
The Mosquito Coast
Music Box
'night, Mother
Nothing in Common
Only When I Laugh
Ordinary People
Out of the Blue
Paris, Texas
Places in the Heart
The Prince of Pennsylvania
Providence
Rain Man
A Raisin in the Sun
The River Niger
Rocket Gibraltar
Running on Empty
See You in the Morning
September
Shoot the Moon
Shy People
Sometimes a Great Notion
Sons
Staying Together
The Stone Boy
Strangers: The Story of a Mother and
  Daughter
Tank
Terms of Endearment
Tribute
Twice in a Lifetime
A Voyage Round My Father
Wedding in White
The Whales of August
Who's Afraid of Virginia Woolf?
The World According to Garp
A World Apart

PROBLEM KIDS _____ DR9

All the Right Moves
Bad Boys
The Boy Who Could Fly
The Boys Next Door
The Breakfast Club
A Child Is Waiting
The Chocolate War
D.A.R.Y.L.
David and Lisa
Dead Poets Society

Empire of the Sun
The Escape Artist
Footloose
Foxes
Grandview, U.S.A.
The Heart Is a Lonely Hunter
Housekeeping
if . . .
The Karate Kid
The Karate Kid II

The Karate Kid III
The Kitchen Toto
Less Than Zero
Lord of the Flies (1963 & 1990 versions)
Lost Angels
Lucas
The Manhattan Project
Mask
The Member of the Wedding
My Little Girl
The New Kids
New York Stories
Ordinary People
The Outsiders
Over the Edge
Paperhouse
Permanent Record
Pretty in Pink
Rebel Without a Cause

Reckless
River's Edge
Rumblefish
A Separate Peace
Smooth Talk
Splendor in the Grass
Split Image
Square Dance
Stacking
Stand by Me
Suburbia
Taps
Tex
That Was Then, This Is Now
Ticket to Heaven
Vision Quest
Where the River Runs Black
The Wizard of Loneliness
Zelly and Me

TODAY'S WOMAN _____ DR10
See also: CL5 Women's Pictures

The Accused
Alice Doesn't Live Here Anymore
Anna
Another Woman
Beaches
The Bell Jar
Between Friends
The Burning Bed
Business as Usual
The Color Purple
Courage (1986)
Crimes of the Heart
Crossing Delancey
Darling
Desert Hearts
Diary of a Mad Housewife
The Dollmaker
Duet for One
Entre Nous
Extremities
First Monday in October
Gloria
The Good Mother
Gorillas in the Mist
The Group
The Handmaid's Tale
Hanna K.
Heart Like a Wheel
Heat and Dust
High Tide
Housekeeping
I'm Dancing as Fast as I Can
Independence Day

Just Between Friends
Marie
Men Don't Leave
Mystic Pizza
Norma Rae
The Nun's Story
Nuts
Old Boyfriends
Personal Best
Plenty
Rachel, Rachel
Rachel River
Raggedy Man
The Rain People
Rich and Famous
sex, lies, and videotape
She-Devil
Shirley Valentine
Shy People
Siesta
Steel Magnolias
Stella
Summer Wishes, Winter Dreams
Swing Shift
Testament
The Turning Point
An Unmarried Woman
Up the Sandbox
Vagabond
The Witches of Eastwick
Working Girl
Working Girls

GOLDEN OLDSTERS _____ DR11

Amos
Cocoon
Cocoon: The Return
Dad
Dreamchild
Driving Miss Daisy
Going in Style
Grace Quigley
The Grey Fox
Harry and Tonto

I Never Sang for My Father
Kotch
No Surrender
On Golden Pond
Right of Way
Summer Solstice
Tough Guys
The Trip to Bountiful
The Whales of August

BACKSTAGE DRAMAS _____ DR12
See also: CL7 Show Business Stories, MU4 Musical Films About Show Biz

Bird
Carny
The Competition
The Country Girl (1982 version)
Crossroads
Dancers
The Dresser
Eddie and the Cruisers
Eddie and the Cruisers II: Eddie Lives
The Fabulous Baker Boys
Fast Forward
Flashdance
The Front
The Gig
Great Balls of Fire!
Hearts of Fire
Honeysuckle Rose
Honky Tonk Man
I Could Go On Singing
The Idolmaker
The Incredible Sarah
Jo Jo Dancer: Your Life Is Calling

Nashville
Network
New York, New York
Nijinsky
One-Trick Pony
Payday
Pete Kelly's Blues
Punch Line
Purple Rain
The Rose
Round Midnight
Rude Boy
Sid & Nancy
Sing
Sparkle
Staying Alive
Sweet Dreams
Talk Radio
Tap
Tender Mercies
The Turning Point
Wired

INSIDE THE MOVIE BUSINESS _____ DR13

An Almost Perfect Affair
Anna
The Barefoot Contessa
Blow Out
The Comic
Day for Night
The Day of the Locust
8½
F/X
Frances
The French Lieutenant's Woman
The Goddess
Good Morning, Babylon
Inserts
The Last Movie

The Last Tycoon
Mommie Dearest
The Oscar
Star 80
A Star Is Born (1937 & 1954 versions)
The State of Things
Strangers Kiss
The Stunt Man
Stunts
Sunset Boulevard
Targets
The Way We Were
What Ever Happened to Baby Jane?
The Wild Party

BLACK LIFE _____ DR14

Aaron Loves Angela
The Autobiography of Miss Jane
    Pittman
Blue Collar
The Brother From Another Planet
Brother John
The Color Purple
Cornbread, Earl and Me
The Cotton Club
Cry Freedom
Do the Right Thing
A Dream for Christmas
A Dry White Season
The Emperor Jones
For Love of Ivy
For Queen and Country
Glory
The Great White Hope
The Greatest
Jo Jo Dancer: Your Life Is Calling
King
The Kitchen Toto
Lady Sings the Blues

The Learning Tree
The Liberation of L.B. Jones
Lost in the Stars
Mahogany
Mandela
The Mark of the Hawk
Marvin and Tige
Men of Bronze
Native Son
Purlie Victorious
The Quiet One
A Raisin in the Sun
The River Niger
School Daze
Shadows
She's Gotta Have It
The Sky Is Gray
A Soldier's Story
Something of Value
Sounder
Sparkle
Sweet Sweetback's Badasssss Song

LIFE IN THE BIG CITY _____ DR15

Aaron Loves Angela
Addict
Alphabet City
. . . And Justice for All
Barfly
Breakfast at Tiffany's
Bright Lights, Big City
The Brother From Another Planet
Chan Is Missing
The Chosen
Colors
Cornbread, Earl and Me
The Cotton Club
Crossing Delancey
Dim Sum: a little bit of heart
Do the Right Thing
Fear City
Five Corners
Flashdance
Fort Apache, The Bronx
Hester Street
House of Games
The Incident
The Last Angry Man
Last Exit to Brooklyn

Marvin and Tige
Mean Streets
Medium Cool
Midnight Cowboy
Moscow on the Hudson
New York Stories
On the Nickel
The Pawnbroker
Petulia
The Pope of Greenwich Village
Q & A
Saturday Night Fever
Signal 7
Slaves of New York
Smithereens
Someone to Watch Over Me
Stand and Deliver
Studs Lonigan
Taxi Driver
Times Square
Turk 182
Urban Cowboy
The Wanderers
The Warriors

LIVES OF CRIME _____ DR16
See also Action/Adventure, Mystery/Suspense Chapters

Against All Odds (1984)
At Close Range

Atlantic City
Badlands

Blood Simple
Bonnie and Clyde
The Brotherhood
Buster
Chiefs
Cop
Criminal Law
Cruising
Dance With a Stranger
Drugstore Cowboy
The Executioner's Song
The Falcon and the Snowman
Fatal Vision
Helter Skelter
The Honeymoon Killers
In Cold Blood
Internal Affairs
Johnny Handsdome
Kansas
Last Rites
Mean Streets

Mikey and Nicky
Miles From Home
Mona Lisa
Mrs. Soffel
The Onion Field
Patty Hearst
Performance
Point Blank
A Prayer for the Dying
Prince of the City
Prizzi's Honor
Q & A
Serpico
Star Chamber
Straight Time
Suddenly
10 Rillington Place
Thief
True Confessions
Wisdom
Witness

COURT'S IN SESSION _____ DR17

The Accused
Anatomy of a Murder
. . . And Justice for All
The Court-Martial of Billy Mitchell
Criminal Law
A Cry in the Dark
Inherit the Wind
Jagged Edge
Judgment at Nuremberg
Kramer vs. Kramer
Music Box

Nuts
The Paradine Case
Sergeant Ryker
Suspect
They Won't Believe Me
To Kill a Mockingbird
Twelve Angry Men
The Verdict
Witness for the Prosecution (1957
    version)

PRISON DRAMAS _____ DR18

Bad Boys
Birdman of Alcatraz
Brubaker
Chattahoochee
Cool Hand Luke
Crashout
The Criminal Code
Dead Man Out
Each Dawn I Die
Escape From Alcatraz
Fast-Walking
The Glass House
I Want to Live! (1958 version)

An Innocent Man
Kiss of the Spider Woman
Lock Up
The Longest Yard
Midnight Express
On the Yard
Papillon
Passage to Marseilles
Riot in Cell Block 11
Seven Miles From Alcatraz
Short Eyes
There Was a Crooked Man
Weeds

MODERN FICTION ON FILM _____ DR19
See also: Writer Check Lists WR6 William Faulkner, WR7 F. Scott Fitzgerald, WR10 Ernest Hemingway, WR11 Henry James, WR14 D.H. Lawrence, WR17 Sinclair Lewis, WR25 John Steinbeck

The Accidental Tourist
All the King's Men

Anthony Adverse
Arrowsmith

The Bell Jar
Bloodhounds of Broadway
The Bostonians
Bright Lights, Big City
Butterfield 8
Cannery Row
Catch-22
Charly
Chilly Scenes of Winter
A Clockwork Orange
The Color Purple
Daisy Miller
Daniel
The Day of the Locust
The Dead
Death in Venice
Deliverance
Dodsworth
East of Eden (1955 & 1982 versions)
Elmer Gantry
Encore
The End of the Road
Enemies, A Love Story
The Europeans
Fahrenheit 451
A Farewell to Arms (1932 version)
Fat City
From Here to Eternity
The Good Earth
Goodbye, Columbus
The Grapes of Wrath
The Great Gatsby
The Group
A Handful of Dust
The Handmaid's Tale
The Heart Is a Lonely Hunter
The Heiress
The Hotel New Hampshire
Housekeeping
The Human Comedy
In Country
Ironweed
Islands in the Stream
Johnny Got His Gun
Justine
The Killers (1964 version)
Last Exit to Brooklyn
The Last Picture Show
The Last Temptation of Christ
The Last Tycoon
Less Than Zero
Little Big Man
Lolita
The Lonely Passion of Judith Hearne
Lonelyhearts
Lord Jim
Lord of the Flies (1963 & 1990 versions)
The Loved One

The Man With the Golden Arm
The Manchurian Candidate
Maurice
The Milagro Beanfield War
The Mosquito Coast
Myra Breckenridge
The Name of the Rose
Native Son
The Natural
Neighbors
1984
92 in the Shade
Of Human Bondage
Of Mice and Men (1939 version)
Old Gringo
One Flew Over the Cuckoo's Nest
The Outsiders
A Passage to India
A Place in the Sun
Quartet (1949)
The Rainbow
The Razor's Edge (1946 & 1984
    versions)
The Red Pony (1949 & 1973 versions)
Reflections in a Golden Eye
The Reivers
Reuben, Reuben
A Room With a View
Rumblefish
Seize the Day
A Separate Peace
Ship of Fools
Slaughterhouse Five
Slaves of New York
Sometimes a Great Notion
Sophie's Choice
Steppenwolf
The Sterile Cuckoo
Studs Lonigan
Swann in Love
Tess
They Shoot Horses, Don't They?
The Tin Drum
To Have and Have Not
Tomorrow
The Trial
Trio
Turn of the Screw
Twister
The Unbearable Lightness of Being
Under the Volcano
The Virgin and the Gypsy
Who'll Stop the Rain?
Winter Kills
Wise Blood
The Witches of Eastwick
Women in Love
The World According to Garp

PLAYS ON FILM _____ DR20

See also: Writer Check Lists WR20 Eugene O'Neill, WR22 William Shakespeare, WR23 Neil Simon, WR30 Tennessee Williams

Agnes of God
All My Sons
Arsenic and Old Lace
Betrayal
The Boys in the Band
Bus Stop
Cat on a Hot Tin Roof
Children of a Lesser God
Come Back to the Five and Dime,
    Jimmy Dean, Jimmy Dean
Crimes of the Heart
Cyrano de Bergerac
Da
Dangerous Liaisons
A Day in the Death of Joe Egg
Dead End
Death of a Salesman (1985 version)
Deathtrap
Desire Under the Elms
A Doll's House (Bloom & Fonda
    versions)
Driving Miss Daisy
84 Charing Cross Road
The Emperor Jones
An Enemy of the People
Equus
Extremities
The Front Page (1931 version)
The Glass Menagerie
The Great White Hope
Harvey
I Am a Camera
I Never Sang for My Father
Inherit the Wind
Life With Father
The Little Foxes
Long Day's Journey Into Night (1962 &
    1987 versions)

Look Back in Anger
The Man Who Came to Dinner
Marat/Sade
The Member of the Wedding
The Miracle Worker
Miss Firecracker
'night, Mother
Nuts
Orphans
Our Town
The Petrified Forest
Picnic
Plenty
A Raisin in the Sun
The River Niger
Saint Joan
Separate Tables (1958 & 1983 versions)
The Shadow Box
Shirley Valentine
Sleuth
A Soldier's Story
Steel Magnolias
Strange Interlude (1988 version)
Streamers
A Streetcar Named Desire
Talk Radio
That Championship Season
These Three
Torch Song Trilogy
The Trojan Women
True West
Volpone
Watch on the Rhine
Who's Afraid of Virginia Woolf?
Whose Life Is It Anyway?
The Wild Duck
You Can't Take It With You
Young and Willing

POLITICAL DRAMAS _____ DR21

See also: CU9 Political Statements

Advise and Consent
All the King's Men
All the President's Men
Being There
The Best Man
Blaze
The Candidate
The Last Hurrah
The Manchurian Candidate
No Way Out

The Parallax View
Power
Scandal
The Seduction of Joe Tynan
Seven Days in May
Under Fire
White Nights
Winter Kills
The Year of Living Dangerously

FOR SPORTS FANS _____ DR22
See also: CO18 Sports for Laughs

Arm Wrestling
Over the Top

Baseball
The Babe Ruth Story
Bang the Drum Slowly
Eight Men Out
Fear Strikes Out
Field of Dreams
It's Good to be Alive
The Jackie Robinson Story
Long Gone
The Natural
The Pride of St. Louis
Pride of the Yankees
Tiger Town

Basketball
Hoosiers
Inside Moves
One on One
That Championship Season

Boxing
Body and Soul (1947 & 1981 versions)
The Champ (1931 & 1979 versions)
Champion
Fat City
Golden Boy
The Great White Hope
The Harder They Fall
Homeboy
Raging Bull
Rocky (series)
The Set-Up
Somebody Up There Likes Me
Split Decisions
Streets of Gold
Tough Enough

Cycling
American Flyers
Breaking Away
The Dirt Bike Kid
Rad

Football
All the Right Moves
Easy Living
Everybody's All American
Knute Rockne—All American

Gymnastics
American Anthem

Hockey
Youngblood

Horse Racing/Showing
Phar Lap
Sylvester

Martial Arts
Best of the Best
The Karate Kid
The Karate Kid II
The Karate Kid III

Motor Sports
Bobby Deerfield
Grand Prix
Greased Lightning
Heart Like a Wheel
The Last American Hero
Winning

Pool
The Color of Money
The Hustler

Rowing
The Boy in Blue
Oxford Blues

Rugby
This Sporting Life

Running
Chariots of Fire
On the Edge
Personal Best
Running Brave

Skateboarding
Thrashin'

Skiing
Downhill Racer

Soccer
Hot Shot
Victory

Surfing
Big Wednesday
North Shore

Swimming
Dawn!

Volleyball
Side Out

Wrestling
Vision Quest

CONTEMPORARY BRITISH DRAMA _____ DR23

Accident
Another Country
Betrayal
Billy Liar
Brimstone and Treacle
Business as Usual
Cal
Chariots of Fire
The Cook, The Thief, His Wife and Her
  Lover
Dance With a Stranger
Darling
Diamond Skulls
Distant Voices, Still Lives
The Dresser
The Dressmaker
For Queen and Country
Gandhi
The Good Father
A Handful of Dust
Heat and Dust
Henry V (1989 version)
A Kind of Loving
Knights and Emeralds
Lady Jane
Little Dorritt
The Lonely Passion of Judith Hearne
The Long Good Friday
Look Back in Anger
Marat/Sade
Mona Lisa

My Beautiful Laundrette
My Left Foot
No Surrender
O Lucky Man!
Paperhouse
Pascali's Island
The Ploughman's Lunch
A Prayer for the Dying
Prick Up Your Ears
The Rainbow
The Romantic Englishwoman
Sammy and Rosie Get Laid
Scandal
Seance on a Wet Afternoon
Separate Tables (1983 version)
The Servant
The Shooting Party
Steaming
Stevie
Stormy Monday
Sunday, Bloody Sunday
This Sporting Life
Turtle Diary
Victim
A Voyage Round My Father
Wetherby
When the Whales Came
White Mischief
Women in Love
Wonderland

THE WORLD OF BUSINESS _____ DR24

The Amazing Howard Hughes
The Arrangement
The Betsy
Citizen Kane
Executive Suite
F.I.S.T.
The Formula
Giant
The Godfather

The Godfather, Part II
Great Guy
The Man in the Grey Flannel Suit
Mr. Arkadin
Nothing in Common
Rollover
Save the Tiger
Tucker: The Man and His Dream
Wall Street

SCHOOL DAYS _____ DR25
See also: CO35 Campus Comedy

Absolution
An Annapolis Story
Au Revoir, les Enfants
The Breakfast Club
Carrie
The Chocolate War
The Class of Miss MacMichael
Class of 1984
Class of 1999

Conrack
The Corn Is Green (1945 version)
Dangerously Close
Dead Poets Society
The Devil's Playground
Fame
Goodbye, Mr. Chips
Heart of Dixie
High School Confidential

if . . .
Lean on Me
Listen to Me
The Paper Chase
The Prime of Miss Jean Brodie
The Principal
A Separate Peace

Sing
Taps
Teachers
To Sir, With Love
Vital Signs
Why Shoot the Teacher?

SMALL TOWN LIFE _____ DR26

All the Right Moves
Anatomy of a Murder
The Best Years of Our Lives
Blue City
Blue Velvet
Bus Stop
The Chase (1966)
Chiefs
Come Back to the Five and Dime,
  Jimmy Dean, Jimmy Dean
The Deer Hunter
East of Eden
Endangered Species
Footloose
Grandview, U.S.A.
The Heart Is a Lonely Hunter
Hoosiers
The Human Comedy
Independence Day
King's Row
The Last Picture Show
The Liberation of L.B. Jones
Maria's Lovers
The Milagro Beanfield War
Murphy's Romance

Mystic Pizza
The Naked Kiss
1918
Our Town
Picnic
Promised Land
Rachel River
Racing With the Moon
Raggedy Man
Shadow of a Doubt
Shame (1988)
Signs of Life
Some Came Running
Splendor in the Grass
Staying Together
Steel Magnolias
Testament
A Tiger Walks
To Kill a Mockingbird
Two Moon Junction
Vernon, Florida
Why Shoot the Teacher?
The Wild One
The Witches of Eastwick
The Wizard of Loneliness

Chapter Six

DIRECTOR CHECK LISTS
(DT)

FILMMAKER CHECK LIST: WOODY ALLEN ———————————————— DT1
All films writer-director-actor, unless noted.

Annie Hall
Bananas
Broadway Danny Rose
Crimes and Misdemeanors
Everything You Always Wanted to
   Know About Sex But Were Afraid to
   Ask
Hannah and Her Sisters
Love and Death
Manhattan
A Midsummer Night's Sex Comedy
New York Stories (co-director)
Sleeper
Stardust Memories
Take the Money and Run
What's Up, Tiger Lily?
Zelig

*also narrator

Writer-director only
Another Woman
Interiors
The Purple Rose of Cairo
Radio Days*
September

Writer-actor only
Play It Again, Sam
What's New, Pussycat?

Actor only
Casino Royale
The Front
King Lear (1987 version)

DIRECTOR CHECK LIST: ROBERT ALTMAN ———————————————— DT2

Aria (co-director)
Beyond Therapy
Brewster McCloud
Buffalo Bill & the Indians
Come Back to the Five and Dime,
   Jimmy Dean, Jimmy Dean
Countdown
Fool for Love
The James Dean Story (co-director)
M*A*S*H
McCabe and Mrs. Miller

Nashville
O.C. and Stiggs
Popeye
Quintet
The Room
Secret Honor
Streamers
Tanner '88
That Cold Day in the Park
A Wedding

DIRECTOR CHECK LIST: MICHELANGELO ANTONIONI ———————————————— DT3

L'Avventura
Blowup
The Eclipse
Love in the City (co-director)

The Passenger
Red Desert
Zabriskie Point

DIRECTOR CHECK LIST: ALLAN ARKUSH ———————————————— DT4

Caddyshack II
Deathsport
Get Crazy

Heartbeeps
Hollywood Boulevard (co-director)
Rock 'n' Roll High School

DIRECTOR CHECK LIST: PAUL BARTEL _____ DT5

Cannonball
Death Race 2000
Eating Raoul*
The Longshot
Lust in the Dust
Not for Publication
Scenes From the Class Struggle in
   Beverly Hills*

Actor only:
Amazon Women on the Moon
Caddyshack II
Chopping Mall
Hollywood Boulevard
Killer Party
Rock 'n' Roll High School

*also actor

DIRECTOR CHECK LIST: ROBERT BENTON _____ DT6

Bad Company
Kramer vs. Kramer
The Late Show

Nadine
Places in the Heart
Still of the Night

DIRECTOR CHECK LIST: INGMAR BERGMAN _____ DT7

After the Rehearsal
Autumn Sonata
Brink of Life
Cries and Whispers
The Devil's Eye
The Devil's Wanton
Dreams
Fanny and Alexander
From the Life of Marionettes
A Lesson in Love
The Magic Flute
The Magician
Night Is My Future
Persona

Port of Call
Sawdust and Tinsel (The Naked Night)
Scenes From a Marriage
Secrets of Women
The Serpent's Egg
The Seventh Seal
Smiles of a Summer Night
Summer Interlude
Three Strange Loves
Through a Glass Darkly
The Virgin Spring
Wild Strawberries
Winter Light

DIRECTOR/CHOREOGRAPHER CHECK LIST: BUSBY BERKELEY _____ DT8

Babes in Arms
Babes on Broadway
Dames*
Footlight Parade*
For Me and My Gal
42nd Street*
Girl Crazy*
Gold Diggers of 1933*
Gold Diggers of 1935
Jumbo*

Million Dollar Mermaid*
Roman Scandals*
Small Town Girl*
Stage Struck (1936)
Strike Up the Band
Take Me out to the Ball Game
Ziegfeld Girl*

NON-MUSIC
They Made Me a Criminal

*choreography only

DIRECTOR CHECK LIST: BERNARDO BERTOLUCCI _____ DT9

Before the Revolution
The Conformist
The Last Emperor

Last Tango in Paris
1900

DIRECTOR CHECK LIST: BUDD BOETTICHER ———————— DT10

Arruza
The Bullfighter and the Lady
The Human Gorilla
The Magnificent Matador
Tequila Sunrise*

WESTERNS
The Man From the Alamo
A Time for Dying

*actor only

DIRECTOR CHECK LIST: JOHN BOORMAN ———————— DT11

Deliverance
The Emerald Forest
Excalibur
Exorcist II: The Heretic
Hell in the Pacific

Hope and Glory
Point Blank
Where the Heart Is
Zardoz

DIRECTOR-ACTOR CHECK LIST: ALBERT BROOKS ———————— DT12

Lost in America
Modern Romance
Real Life

Actor only
Broadcast News
Private Benjamin
Taxi Driver
Twilight Zone: The Movie

FILMMAKER CHECK LIST: MEL BROOKS ———————— DT13
All films writer-director-actor, unless noted.

Blazing Saddles
High Anxiety
The History of the World: Part I
The Muppet Movie*
The Producers
Putney Swope*

Silent Movie
Spaceballs
To Be or Not to Be (1983 version)*
The Twelve Chairs
Young Frankenstein

*actor only

DIRECTOR CHECK LIST: TOD BROWNING ———————— DT14

The Devil Doll
Dracula (1931 version)
Freaks

Mark of the Vampire
Outside the Law

DIRECTOR CHECK LIST: LUIS BUÑUEL ———————— DT15

L'Age d'Or
The Brute
Un Chien Andalou (co-director)
The Criminal Life of Archibaldo de la
   Cruz
Diary of a Chambermaid (1964 version)
The Discreet Charm of the Bourgeosie
The Exterminating Angel
Land Without Bread
The Milky Way (1970)

Nazarin
Los Olvidados
The Phantom of Liberty
Simon of the Desert
Susana
That Obscure Object of Desire
Viridiana
A Woman Without Love
Wuthering Heights (1954 version)

DIRECTOR CHECK LIST: FRANK CAPRA _____ DT16

Arsenic and Old Lace
Here Comes the Groom
A Hole in the Head
It Happened One Night
It's a Wonderful Life
Lost Horizon
Meet John Doe

Mr. Deeds Goes to Town
Mr. Smith Goes to Washington
Pocketful of Miracles
State of the Union
The Strong Man
You Can't Take It With You

DIRECTOR CHECK LIST: JOHN CARPENTER _____ DT17

Assault on Precinct 13
Big Trouble in Little China
Christine
Dark Star
Escape From New York
The Fog

Halloween
Prince of Darkness
Starman
They Live
The Thing

FILMMAKER CHECK LIST: CHARLIE CHAPLIN _____ DT18

Short Films
The Chaplin Essanay Book I
The Chaplin Revue
Charlie Chaplin Carnival
Charlie Chaplin Cavalcade
Charlie Chaplin Festival
Charlie Chaplin—The Early Years,
  Vols. I–IV
Charlie Chaplin's Keystone Comedies
The Kid/The Idle Class
Kid's Auto Race/Mabel's Married Life
The Knockout/Dough and Dynamite
The Rink/The Immigrant
The Tramp/A Woman
Work/Police

Feature Films
The Circus
City Lights
The Gold Rush
The Great Dictator
A King in New York
Limelight
Modern Times
Monsieur Verdoux
Show People*
Tillie's Punctured Romance
A Woman of Paris

*actor only

DIRECTOR CHECK LIST: JEAN COCTEAU _____ DT19

Beauty and the Beast (1946 version)

Blood of a Poet

DIRECTOR CHECK LIST: LARRY COHEN _____ DT20

Black Caesar
Deadly Illusion (co-director)
God Told Me To
Hell Up in Harlem
It Lives Again
It's Alive!

The Private Files of J. Edgar Hoover
Q: The Winged Serpent
Special Effects
The Stuff
Wicked Stepmother

DIRECTOR CHECK LIST: FRANCIS FORD COPPOLA _____ DT21

Apocalypse Now
The Conversation

The Cotton Club
Dementia 13

Finian's Rainbow
Gardens of Stone
The Godfather
The Godfather, Part II
New York Stories (co-director)
One From the Heart
The Outsiders

Peggy Sue Got Married
The Rain People
Rip Van Winkle
Rumblefish
Tonight for Sure
Tucker: The Man and His Dream
You're a Big Boy Now

DIRECTOR CHECK LIST: ROGER CORMAN _____ DT22
Note: Corman has produced and "presented" scores of films too numerous to mention here.

Bloody Mama
Carnival Rock
Creature From the Haunted Sea
The Fall of the House of Usher
Gas-s-s-s
Last Woman on Earth
The Little Shop of Horrors (1960
   version)
The Masque of the Red Death (1964
   version)
The Pit and the Pendulum
Premature Burial
The Raven (1963)
The St. Valentine's Day Massacre
Shame (1961)
Swamp Diamonds

Tales of Terror
Tomb of Ligeia
Tower of London (1962 version)
The Trip
The Wild Angels
X: The Man With X-Ray Eyes

Actor only
Cannonball
The Godfather, Part II
The State of Things

Documentary subject
Roger Corman: Hollywood's Wild
   Angel

DIRECTOR CHECK LIST: DAVID CRONENBERG _____ DT23

The Brood
Dead Ringers
The Dead Zone
The Fly (1986 version)
Rabid
Scanners

They Came From Within
Videodrome

Actor only
Into the Night
Nightbreed

DIRECTOR CHECK LIST: GEORGE CUKOR _____ DT24

Adam's Rib
Born Yesterday
Camille
David Copperfield
Dinner at Eight
A Double Life
Gaslight
Heller in Pink Tights
Holiday
It Should Happen to You
Justine
Les Girls

Let's Make Love
Little Women (1933 version)
Love Among the Ruins
My Fair Lady
Pat and Mike
The Philadelphia Story
Rich and Famous
A Star Is Born (1954 version)
Sylvia Scarlett
Two-Faced Woman
A Woman's Face
The Women

DIRECTOR CHECK LIST: JOE DANTE _____ DT25

Amazon Women on the Moon (co-
   director)

The Burbs
Explorers

Gremlins
Hollywood Boulevard (co-director)
The Howling

Innerspace
Piranha
Twilight Zone: The Movie (co-director)

DIRECTOR-ACTOR CHECK LIST: VITTORIO DE SICA _____ DT26

After the Fox
The Bicycle Thief*
Bocaccio 70 (co-director)*
The Garden of the Finzi-Continis*
The Gold of Naples
Indiscretion of an American Wife*
The Roof*
Teresa Venerdi
Two Women*

Umberto D.*
Woman Times Seven*
Yesterday, Today & Tomorrow*

Actor only
Andy Warhol's Dracula
The Earrings of Madame de . . .
General Della Rovere
Shoes of the Fisherman

*director only

DIRECTOR CHECK LIST: CECIL B. DEMILLE _____ DT27

Cleopatra (1934)
The Greatest Show on Earth
The King of Kings (1927 version)
The Plainsman
Reap the Wild Wind
The Road to Yesterday

Samson and Delilah
The Ten Commandments (1923 & 1956
   versions)

Actor only
Sunset Boulevard

DIRECTOR CHECK LIST: JONATHAN DEMME _____ DT28

Caged Heat
Citizens Band
Crazy Mama
Last Embrace
Married to the Mob
Melvin and Howard
Something Wild

Stop Making Sense
Swimming to Cambodia
Swing Shift
Who Am I This Time?

Actor only
Into the Night

DIRECTOR CHECK LIST: BRIAN DEPALMA _____ DT29

Blow Out
Body Double
Carrie (1976)
Casualties of War
Dressed to Kill
The Fury
Greetings
Home Movies

Obsession
Phantom of the Paradise
Scarface (1983 version)
Sisters
The Untouchables
The Wedding Party (co-director)
Wise Guys

DIRECTOR CHECK LIST: STANLEY DONEN _____ DT30

Arabesque
Bedazzled
Blame It on Rio
Charade

The Grass Is Greener
Indiscreet
Saturn 3
Two for the Road

MUSICALS
Damn Yankees*
Deep in My Heart
Funny Face
It's Always Fair Weather**
The Little Prince

Movie, Movie
On the Town**
The Pajama Game*
Royal Wedding
Seven Brides for Seven Brothers
Singin' in the Rain**

*with George Abbott
**with Gene Kelly

DIRECTOR CHECK LIST: CARL DREYER ———————————— DT31

Day of Wrath
Master of the House
Ordet

The Passion of Joan of Arc
Vampyr

DIRECTOR CHECK LIST: BLAKE EDWARDS ———————————— DT32

Blind Date (1987)
Breakfast at Tiffany's
The Curse of the Pink Panther
The Days of Wine and Roses
Experiment in Terror
A Fine Mess
The Great Race
The Man Who Loved Women (1983
  version)
Micki and Maude
Operation Petticoat
The Party
The Perfect Furlough
The Pink Panther

The Pink Panther Strikes Again
The Return of the Pink Panther
The Revenge of the Pink Panther
S.O.B.
A Shot in the Dark
Skin Deep
Sunset
The Tamarind Seed
10
That's Life!
This Happy Feeling
The Trail of the Pink Panther
Victor/Victoria
Wild Rovers

DIRECTOR CHECK LIST: SERGEI EISENSTEIN ———————————— DT33

Alexander Nevsky
The General Line
Ivan the Terrible, Parts I and II
Potemkin

Que Viva Mexico!
Strike
Ten Days That Shook the World/
October

DIRECTOR CHECK LIST: RAINER WERNER FASSBINDER ——————— DT34

Ali—Fear Eats the Soul
Berlin Alexanderplatz
Despair
Fox and His Friends*
The Marriage of Maria Braun
Querelle

Subject only
A Man Like Eva

Actor only
Kamikaze '89

*also actor

DIRECTOR CHECK LIST: FEDERICO FELLINI ———————————— DT35

Amarcord
And the Ship Sails On

Il Bidone
Bocaccio '70 (co-director)

City of Women
The Clowns
La Dolce Vita
8½
Ginger and Fred
Juliet of the Spirits
Love in the City (co-director)
Nights of Cabiria

Satyricon
La Strada
Variety Lights (co-director)
I Vitelloni
The White Sheik

Actor only
We All Loved Each Other So Much

DIRECTOR CHECK LIST: JOHN FORD _____ DT36

Arrowsmith
Donovan's Reef
Drums Along the Mohawk
The Fugitive
The Grapes of Wrath
How the West Was Won
The Hurricane
The Informer
Judge Priest
The Last Hurrah
The Long Voyage Home
The Lost Patrol
Mary of Scotland
Mister Roberts (co-director)
Mogambo
The Quiet Man
They Were Expendable
This Is Korea/December 7th
Wee Willie Winkie

What Price Glory (1952 version)
The Wings of Eagles
Young Mr. Lincoln

WESTERNS
Cheyenne Autumn
Fort Apache
The Horse Soldiers
How the West Was Won (co-director)
The Man Who Shot Liberty Valance
My Darling Clementine
Rio Grande
The Searchers
She Wore a Yellow Ribbon
Stagecoach
Straight Shootin'
3 Godfathers
Two Rode Together
Wagonmaster

DIRECTOR CHECK LIST: MILOS FORMAN _____ DT37

Amadeus
The Firemen's Ball
Hair
Loves of a Blonde

One Flew Over the Cuckoo's Nest
Ragtime
Valmont

DIRECTOR CHECK LIST: BILL FORSYTH _____ DT38

Breaking In
Comfort and Joy
Gregory's Girl

Housekeeping
Local Hero
That Sinking Feeling

DIRECTOR/CHOREOGRAPHER CHECK LIST: BOB FOSSE _____ DT39

All That Jazz
Cabaret
Damn Yankees*
Kiss Me Kate**
The Little Prince*
The Pajama Game†
Sweet Charity

NON-MUSIC
Lenny
Star 80

  *actor, choreographer only
**actor only
†choreographer only

DIRECTOR CHECK LIST: SAMUEL FULLER _____ DT40

The Baron of Arizona
The Big Red One
China Gate
I Shot Jesse James
The Naked Kiss
Run of the Arrow
Shark!
The Steel Helmet
Underworld, U.S.A.

Actor only
The American Friend
Hammett
The Last Movie
Pierrot le Fou
Slapstick of Another Kind
Sons
The State of Things

DIRECTOR CHECK LIST: JEAN-LUC GODARD _____ DT41

Alphaville
Aria (co-director)
Band of Outsiders
Breathless (1959 version)
Contempt
First Name: Carmen*
Hail, Mary

King Lear (1987 version)
A Married Woman
Masculine-Feminine
My Life to Live
The Oldest Profession (co-director)
Pierrot le Fou
Sympathy for the Devil

*also actor

DIRECTOR CHECK LIST: D.W. GRIFFITH _____ DT42

Abraham Lincoln
The Avenging Conscience
The Birth of a Nation
Broken Blossoms
D.W. Griffith Triple Feature
Dream Street
Hearts of the World

Home Sweet Home
Intolerance
Orphans of the Storm
Sally of the Sawdust
The Short Films of D.W. Griffith, Vol. I
True Heart Susie
Way Down East

DIRECTOR CHECK LIST: HOWARD HAWKS _____ DT43

Air Force
Ball of Fire
The Barbary Coast
The Big Sleep (1946 version)
Bringing Up Baby
Come and Get It (co-director)
The Criminal Code
Gentlemen Prefer Blondes
Hatari!
His Girl Friday
Man's Favorite Sport?
Monkey Business (1952)
Only Angels Have Wings

Scarface (1932 version)
Sergeant York
To Have and Have Not
Twentieth Century

WESTERNS
The Big Sky
El Dorado
The Outlaw (co-director)
Red River
Rio Bravo
Rio Lobo

DIRECTOR CHECK LIST: WERNER HERZOG _____ DT44

Aguirre, The Wrath of God
Burden of Dreams*
Every Man for Himself and God Against
  All

Fitzcarraldo
Man of Flowers*
Werner Herzog Eats His Shoe*
Where the Green Ants Dream

*actor only

DIRECTOR CHECK LIST: WALTER HILL _____ DT45

Brewster's Millions
Crossroads
The Driver
Extreme Prejudice
48HRS.
Hard Times
Johnny Handsome

The Long Riders
Red Heat
Southern Comfort
Streets of Fire
Tales From the Crypt (1989; co-director)
The Warriors

DIRECTOR CHECK LIST: ALFRED HITCHCOCK _____ DT46

The Birds
Blackmail
Dial M for Murder
Easy Virtue
Family Plot
Foreign Correspondent
Frenzy
I Confess
Jamaica Inn (1939 version)
The Lady Vanishes (1938 version)
Lifeboat
The Lodger
The Man Who Knew Too Much (1934 &
    1956 versions)
The Manxman
Marnie
Mr. and Mrs. Smith
Murder
North by Northwest
Notorious
Number 17
The Paradine Case
Psycho

Rear Window
Rebecca
Rich and Strange
Rope
Sabotage
Saboteur
The Secret Agent
Shadow of a Doubt
The Skin Game (1931)
Spellbound
Stage Fright
Strangers on a Train
Suspicion
The 39 Steps (1935 version)
To Catch a Thief
Topaz
Torn Curtain
The Trouble With Harry
Under Capricorn
Vertigo
The Wrong Man
Young and Innocent

DIRECTOR CHECK LIST: TOBE HOOPER _____ DT47

Eaten Alive
The Funhouse
Invaders from Mars (1986 version)
Lifeforce
Poltergeist

Salem's Lot
Spontaneous Combustion
The Texas Chainsaw Massacre
The Texas Chainsaw Massacre II

DIRECTOR-ACTOR CHECK LIST: RON HOWARD _____ DT48

As Director
Cocoon
Grand Theft Auto*
Gung Ho (1986)
Night Shift
Parenthood
Splash
Willow

As Actor
American Graffiti
Bitter Harvest
Eat My Dust!
The Music Man
The Shootist
Village of the Giants
The Wild Country

*also actor

WRITER-DIRECTOR CHECK LIST: JOHN HUGHES _____ DT49

The Breakfast Club
Ferris Bueller's Day Off
The Great Outdoors*
Mr. Mom**
Nate and Hayes**
National Lampoon's Class Reunion**
National Lampoon's European
    Vacation**

National Lampoon's Vacation**
Planes, Trains and Automobiles
Pretty in Pink*
She's Having a Baby
Sixteen Candles
Some Kind of Wonderful*
Uncle Buck
Weird Science

*producer only
**writer only

DIRECTOR CHECK LIST: JOHN HUSTON _____ DT50

The African Queen
Annie
The Asphalt Jungle
The Barbarian and the Geisha
Beat the Devil
The Bible*
Casino Royale (co-director)
The Dead
Fat City
In This Our Life
Key Largo
Let There Be Light
The Life and Times of Judge Roy Bean*
The List of Adrian Messenger*
The Mackintosh Man
The Maltese Falcon
The Man Who Would Be King
The Misfits
Moby Dick
Moulin Rouge
The Night of the Iguana
Phobia

Prizzi's Honor
The Red Badge of Courage
Reflections in a Golden Eye
The Treasure of the Sierra Madre*
Under the Volcano
The Unforgiven
Victory
Wise Blood

Actor only
Angela
Battle for the Planet of the Apes
Battle Force
Breakout
Cannery Row (narrator)
The Cardinal
Chinatown
Lovesick
Myra Breckenridge
Tentacles
The Wind and the Lion
Winter Kills

*also actor

DIRECTOR CHECK LIST: NORMAN JEWISON _____ DT51

Agnes of God
. . . And Justice for All
Best Friends
The Cincinnati Kid
F.I.S.T.
Fiddler on the Roof
In the Heat of the Night
Jesus Christ Superstar

Moonstruck
Rollerball
The Russians Are Coming! The
    Russians Are Coming!
Send Me No Flowers
A Soldier's Story
The Thomas Crown Affair
The Thrill of It All

DIRECTOR CHECK LIST: PHILIP KAUFMAN _____ DT52

Invasion of the Body Snatchers (1979
    version)
The Right Stuff

The Unbearable Lightness of Being
The Wanderers
White Dawn

DIRECTOR CHECK LIST: ELIA KAZAN _____ DT53

The Arrangement
Baby Doll
East of Eden
A Face in the Crowd
The Last Tycoon

On the Waterfront
Splendor in the Grass
A Streetcar Named Desire
A Tree Grows in Brooklyn
Viva Zapata!

FILMMAKER CHECK LIST: BUSTER KEATON _____ DT54

Short Films
The Balloonatic/One Week
The Blacksmith/The Balloonatic
Buster Keaton Festival Vol. I
Buster Keaton Festival Vol. II
Buster Keaton Rides Again/The
   Railrodder

Feature Films
College
A Funny Thing Happened on the Way
   to the Forum*
The General
Limelight*
Our Hospitality
Steamboat Bill, Jr.
Sunset Boulevard*
The Three Ages

*actor only

DIRECTOR CHECK LIST: STANLEY KRAMER _____ DT55

Bless the Beasts and Children
The Defiant Ones
The Domino Principle
Guess Who's Coming to Dinner
Inherit the Wind
It's a Mad Mad Mad Mad World

Judgment at Nuremberg
On the Beach
The Pride and the Passion
R.P.M.
The Runner Stumbles
Ship of Fools

DIRECTOR CHECK LIST: STANLEY KUBRICK _____ DT56

Barry Lyndon
A Clockwork Orange
Dr. Strangelove: or, How I Learned to
   Stop Worrying and Love the Bomb
Full Metal Jacket
The Killing

Lolita
Paths of Glory
The Shining
Spartacus
2001: A Space Odyssey

DIRECTOR CHECK LIST: AKIRA KUROSAWA _____ DT57

The Bad Sleep Well
Dersu Uzala
Dodes'ka-den
Drunken Angel
The Hidden Fortress
High and Low
Ikiru
Kagemusha
The Lower Depths
The Men Who Tread on the Tiger's Tail

Ran
Rashomon
Red Beard
Sanjuro
Sanshiro Sugata
The Seven Samurai
Stray Dog
Throne of Blood
Yojimbo

DIRECTOR CHECK LIST: FRITZ LANG _____ DT58

Beyond a Reasonable Doubt
The Big Heat
Clash by Night
Cloak and Dagger (1946)
Contempt*
Destiny
The House by the River
Human Desire
Kriemhilde's Revenge
M
Metropolis
Rancho Notorious

The Return of Frank James
Scarlet Street
Secret Beyond the Door
Siegfried
Spiders
Spies
The Testament of Dr. Mabuse
Western Union
While the City Sleeps
The Woman in the Moon
You Only Live Once

*actor only

DIRECTOR CHECK LIST: DAVID LEAN _____ DT59

Blithe Spirit
The Bridge on the River Kwai
Brief Encounter (1945 version)
Dr. Zhivago
Great Expectations
Hobson's Choice

In Which We Serve (co-director)
Lawrence of Arabia
Oliver Twist (1948 version)
A Passage to India
Ryan's Daughter
Summertime

DIRECTOR-ACTOR CHECK LIST: SPIKE LEE _____ DT60

Do the Right Thing
School Daze

She's Gotta Have It

DIRECTOR CHECK LIST: SERGIO LEONE _____ DT61

A Fistful of Dollars
A Fistful of Dynamite
For a Few Dollars More
The Good, the Bad, and the Ugly
Once Upon a Time in the West

NON-WESTERN
Once Upon a Time in America

DIRECTOR CHECK LIST: RICHARD LESTER _____ DT62

Butch and Sundance: The Early Days
Cuba
Finders Keepers
The Four Musketeers
A Funny Thing Happened on the Way
    to the Forum
A Hard Day's Night
Help!

How I Won the War
Juggernaut (1974)
Petulia
The Ritz
Robin and Marian
Superman II
Superman III
The Three Musketeers (1974 version)

DIRECTOR CHECK LIST: ERNST LUBITSCH _____ DT63

Heaven Can Wait (1943)
Lady Windermere's Fan
The Merry Widow
Ninotchka

Passion (1918)
The Shop Around the Corner
That Uncertain Feeling
To Be or Not To Be (1942 version)

DIRECTOR CHECK LIST: GEORGE LUCAS _____ DT64

American Graffiti
Star Wars

THX-1138

DIRECTOR CHECK LIST: SIDNEY LUMET _____ DT65

The Anderson Tapes
Daniel
Deathtrap
Dog Day Afternoon
Equus
Fail-Safe
Family Business
The Fugitive Kind
Garbo Talks
The Group
Just Tell Me What You Want
Long Day's Journey Into Night (1962
    version)

The Morning After
Murder on the Orient Express
Network
The Pawnbroker
Power (1986)
Prince of the City
Q & A
Running on Empty
Serpico
Stage Struck
Twelve Angry Men
The Verdict
The Wiz

DIRECTOR CHECK LIST: DAVID LYNCH _____ DT66

Blue Velvet
Dune
The Elephant Man

Eraserhead
Zelly and Me*

*actor only

DIRECTOR CHECK LIST: TERRENCE MALICK _____ DT67

Badlands

Days of Heaven

DIRECTOR CHECK LIST: JOSEPH L. MANKIEWICZ _____ DT68

All About Eve
The Barefoot Contessa
Cleopatra (1963)
The Ghost and Mrs. Muir
Guys and Dolls

The Honey Pot
Julius Caesar (1953 version)
Sleuth
Suddenly, Last Summer
There Was a Crooked Man

DIRECTOR CHECK LIST: ANTHONY MANN _____ DT69

A Dandy in Aspic
Desperate
El Cid
The Fall of the Roman Empire
The Glenn Miller Story
God's Little Acre
He Walked by Night (co-director)
Men in War
Railroaded
Strategic Air Command

T-Men
Thunder Bay

WESTERNS
Bend of the River
The Far Country
The Man From Laramie
The Naked Spur
The Tin Star
Winchester '73

DIRECTOR-ACTRESS CHECK LIST: ELAINE MAY _____ DT70

As Director
The Heartbreak Kid
Ishtar
Mikey and Nicky
A New Leaf*

*also actress

As Actress
California Suite
Enter Laughing
In the Spirit
Luv

DIRECTOR CHECK LIST: VINCENTE MINNELLI _____ DT71

The Bad and the Beautiful
The Clock
Father of the Bride
Father's Little Dividend
The Four Horsemen of the Apocalypse
  (1961 version)
Home From the Hill
Lust for Life
Madame Bovary
A Matter of Time
The Sandpiper
Some Came Running

MUSICALS
An American in Paris
The Band Wagon
Bells Are Ringing
Brigadoon
Cabin in the Sky
Gigi
Kismet
Meet Me in St. Louis
On a Clear Day You Can See Forever
The Pirate
Yolanda and the Thief
Ziegfeld Follies

DIRECTOR CHECK LIST: PAUL MORISSEY _____ DT72

Andy Warhol's Dracula
Andy Warhol's Frankenstein
Flesh
Heat (1972)

The Hound of the Baskervilles (1977
  version)
Mixed Blood
Spike of Bensonhurst
Trash

DIRECTOR CHECK LIST: ERROL MORRIS _____ DT73

Gates of Heaven
The Thin Blue line

Vernon, Florida

DIRECTOR CHECK LIST: MIKE NICHOLS _____ DT74

Biloxi Blues
Carnal Knowledge
Catch-22
The Day of the Dolphin
Gilda Live

The Graduate
Heartburn
Silkwood
Who's Afraid of Virginia Woolf?
Working Girl

DIRECTOR CHECK LIST: MARCEL OPHULS _____ DT75

A Sense of Loss
The Sorrow and the Pity

Hotel Terminus

DIRECTOR CHECK LIST: MAX OPHULS _____ DT76

Caught
The Earrings of Madame De . . .
Letter From an Unknown Woman

Lola Montes
La Ronde

DIRECTOR CHECK LIST: SAM PECKINPAH _____ DT77

Bring Me the Head of Alfredo Garcia
Convoy
Cross of Iron
The Getaway
The Killer Elite
The Osterman Weekend
Straw Dogs

WESTERNS
The Ballad of Cable Hogue

*also actor

The Deadly Companions
Junior Bonner
Major Dundee
Pat Garrett and Billy the Kid*
Ride the High Country
The Wild Bunch

Actor only
Invasion of the Body Snatchers (1956
  version)

DIRECTOR CHECK LIST: ARTHUR PENN _____ DT78

Alice's Restaurant
Bonnie and Clyde
The Chase (1966)
Dead of Winter
Four Friends
The Left-Handed Gun

Little Big Man
The Miracle Worker
The Missouri Breaks
Night Moves
Penn and Teller Get Killed
Target

DIRECTOR CHECK LIST: ROMAN POLANSKI _____ DT79

Chinatown*
The Fearless Vampire Killers*
Frantic (1988)
Knife in the Water
Macbeth (1971 version)
Pirates
Repulsion

*also actor

Rosemary's Baby
The Tenant*
Tess

Actor only
The Magic Christian

DIRECTOR CHECK LIST: SYDNEY POLLACK _____ DT80

Absence of Malice
Bobby Deerfield
The Electric Horseman
Jeremiah Johnson
Out of Africa
The Scalphunters

*also actor

They Shoot Horses, Don't They?
This Property Is Condemned
Three Days of the Condor
Tootsie*
The Way We Were
The Yakuza

DIRECTOR CHECK LIST: MICHAEL POWELL _____ DT81
*All co-directed with Emeric Pressburger, except ***

Black Narcissus
The Forty-Ninth Parallel
Ill Met by Moonlight
The Life and Death of Colonel Blimp
One of Our Aircraft Is Missing

Peeping Tom*
Pursuit of the Graf Spee
The Red Shoes
The Spy in Black
Thief of Bagdad (1940 version)*

DIRECTOR CHECK LIST: OTTO PREMINGER _____ DT82

Advise and Consent
Anatomy of a Murder
Bonjour Tristesse
The Cardinal
The Court-Martial of Billy Mitchell
Exodus
In Harm's Way
Laura

The Man With the Golden Arm
The Moon Is Blue
River of No Return
Saint Joan

Actor only
Stalag 17
They Got Me Covered

DIRECTOR CHECK LIST: NICHOLAS RAY _____ DT83

The American Friend*
55 Days at Peking
Flying Leathernecks
In a Lonely Place
Johnny Guitar
King of Kings
Knock on Any Door

The Lusty Men
On Dangerous Ground
Rebel Without a Cause
They Live by Night

Documentary subject
Lightning Over Water

*actor only

DIRECTOR CHECK LIST: SATYAJIT RAY _____ DT84

Distant Thunder (1973)
The Home and the World

Two Daughters
The World of Apu

DIRECTOR CHECK LIST: ROB REINER _____ DT85

The Princess Bride
Stand by Me
The Sure Thing
This Is Spinal Tap*
When Harry Met Sally . . .

Actor only
Enter Laughing

*also actor

DIRECTOR CHECK LIST: JEAN RENOIR _____ DT86

La Bête Humaine*
Boudu Saved From Drowning
A Day in the Country*
Diary of a Chambermaid (1946 version)
Elena and Her Men

The Elusive Corporal
French Cancan
The Golden Coach
Grand Illusion
La Marseillaise

*also actor

The River (1951)
Rules of the Game*
The Southerner

This Land Is Mine
Toni

DIRECTOR CHECK LIST: MARTIN RITT ——————————— DT87

Back Roads
The Black Orchid
The Brotherhood
Casey's Shadow
Conrack
Cross Creek
The Front
The Great White Hope
Hombre
Hud
The Long Hot Summer (1958 version)

The Molly Maguires
Murphy's Romance
Norma Rae
Nuts
Paris Blues
Sounder
Stanley and Iris
The Spy Who Came in From the Cold

Actor only
The Slugger's Wife

DIRECTOR CHECK LIST: NICOLAS ROEG ——————————— DT88

Castaway
Don't Look Now
Eureka
Insignificance

The Man Who Fell to Earth
Performance (co-director)
Track 29
The Witches

DIRECTOR CHECK LIST: ERIC ROHMER ——————————— DT89

The Aviator's Wife
Le Beau Mariage
Boyfriends and Girlfriends
Chloe in the Afternoon
Claire's Knee

Full Moon in Paris
My Night at Maud's
Pauline at the Beach
Summer

DIRECTOR CHECK LIST: GEORGE ROMERO ——————————— DT90

The Crazies
Creepshow
Creepshow 2
Dawn of the Dead
Day of the Dead

Knightriders
Martin
Monkey Shines
Night of the Living Dead
Season of the Witch

DIRECTOR CHECK LIST: ALAN RUDOLPH ——————————— DT91

Choose Me
Endangered Species
Love at Large
Made in Heaven
The Moderns

Premonition
Roadie
Songwriter
Trouble in Mind
Welcome to L.A.

DIRECTOR CHECK LIST: KEN RUSSELL ——————————— DT92

Altered States
Aria (co-director)
Billion Dollar Brain

The Boy Friend
Crimes of Passion
The Devils

Gothic
Lair of the White Worm
Lisztomania
Mahler

The Rainbow
Salome's Last Dance
Tommy
Women in Love

WRITER-DIRECTOR-ACTOR CHECK LIST: JOHN SAYLES _____ DT93

Baby, It's You*
The Brother From Another Planet
Eight Men Out
Lianna
Matewan
The Return of the Secaucus 7

Writer only
Alligator
Breaking In
The Howling

Actor only
Hard Choices
Something Wild

*writer-director only

DIRECTOR CHECK LIST: JOHN SCHLESINGER _____ DT94

The Believers
Billy Liar
Darling
The Day of the Locust
The Falcon and the Snowman
Far From the Madding Crowd
Honky Tonk Freeway

A Kind of Loving
Madame Sousatzka
Marathon Man
Midnight Cowboy
Separate Tables (1983 version)
Sunday Bloody Sunday

DIRECTOR CHECK LIST: MARTIN SCORSESE _____ DT95

After Hours
Alice Doesn't Live Here Anymore
Boxcar Bertha
The Color of Money
King of Comedy
The Last Temptation of Christ
The Last Waltz
Mean Streets

New York, New York
New York Stories (co-director)
Raging Bull
Taxi Driver*

Actor only
Cannonball
Round Midnight

*also actor

DIRECTOR CHECK LIST: RIDLEY SCOTT _____ DT96

Alien
Black Rain
Blade Runner

The Duellists
Legend
Someone To Watch Over Me

DIRECTOR CHECK LIST: DON SIEGEL _____ DT97

An Annapolis Story
The Beguiled
The Black Windmill
Charley Varrick

Coogan's Bluff
Dirty Harry
Escape From Alcatraz
Flaming Star

Hell Is for Heroes
Invasion of the Body Snatchers (1956
    version)
Jinxed!
The Killers (1964 version)
Madigan
Private Hell 36
Riot in Cell Block 11

Rough Cut
The Shootist
Telefon
Two Mules for Sister Sara

Actor only
Into the Night
Play Misty for Me

DIRECTOR CHECK LIST: DOUGLAS SIRK ——————————————— DT98

The First Legion
Imitation of Life (1959 version)
Magnificent Obsession

A Time to Live and a Time to Die
Written on the Wind

DIRECTOR CHECK LIST: STEVEN SPIELBERG ——————————— DT99

Close Encounters of the Third Kind
The Color Purple
Duel
E.T. The Extra-Terrestrial
Empire of the Sun
Indiana Jones and the Last Crusade
Indiana Jones and the Temple of Doom

Jaws
Night Gallery (co-director)
1941
Raiders of the Lost Ark
The Sugarland Express
Twilight Zone: The Movie (co-director)

DIRECTOR CHECK LIST: JOSEF VON STERNBERG ——————— DT100

Blonde Venus
The Blue Angel
The Docks of New York
The Last Command

Macao
Morocco
The Shanghai Gesture

DIRECTOR CHECK LIST: GEORGE STEVENS ——————————— DT101

Alice Adams
Annie Oakley
A Damsel in Distress
The Diary of Anne Frank
Giant
The Greatest Story Ever Told
Gunga Din
I Remember Mama
The More the Merrier
Penny Serenade

A Place in the Sun
Quality Street
Shane
Swing Time
The Talk of the Town
Vivacious Lady
Woman of the Year

Documentary subject
George Stevens: A Filmmaker's Journey

DIRECTOR CHECK LIST: OLIVER STONE ——————————————— DT102

Born on the Fourth of July
The Hand
Platoon
Salvador

Seizure
Talk Radio
Wall Street

WRITER-DIRECTOR CHECK LIST: PRESTON STURGES ——————— DT103

The Beautiful Blonde From Bashful
    Bend

Christmas in July
The Great McGinty

The Great Moment
Hail the Conquering Hero
The Lady Eve
The Miracle of Morgan's Creek
The Palm Beach Story

Paris Holiday*
The Sin of Harold Diddlebock
Sullivan's Travels
Unfaithfully Yours (1948 version)

*actor only

DIRECTOR CHECK LIST: JACQUES TATI ———————————— DT104

Jour de Fête
Mr. Hulot's Holiday
My Uncle

Playtime
Sylvia and the Phantom*

*actor only

DIRECTOR CHECK LIST: JACQUES TOURNEUR ———————————— DT105

Appointment in Honduras
Berlin Express
Cat People (1942 version)
Curse of the Demon
Days of Glory
Easy Living
Experiment Perilous

The Flame and the Arrow
Great Day in the Morning
I Walked With a Zombie
The Leopard Man
Out of the Past
Volpone

DIRECTOR CHECK LIST: FRANÇOIS TRUFFAUT ———————————— DT106

Close Encounters of the Third Kind*
Confidentially Yours
Day for Night**
Farenheit 451
The 400 Blows
The Green Room**
Jules and Jim
The Last Metro
Love on the Run

The Man Who Loved Women (1977
  version)
Shoot the Piano Player
Small Change
The Soft Skin
Stolen Kisses
The Story of Adele H.
Two English Girls
The Woman Next Door

  *actor only
**also actor

DIRECTOR CHECK LIST: KING VIDOR ———————————— DT107

The Big Parade
Bird of Paradise
The Champ (1931 version)
The Citadel
The Crowd
Duel in the Sun
The Fountainhead
Man Without a Star
Our Daily Bread

Ruby Gentry
Show People
Solomon and Sheba
Stella Dallas
Street Scene
War and Peace (1956 version)

Actor only
Love and Money

DIRECTOR CHECK LIST: LUCHINO VISCONTI ———————————— DT108

Bellisima
Bocaccio 70 (co-director)

Conversation Piece
The Damned

Death in Venice   Senso
L'Innocente   La Terra Trema
Rocco and His Brothers

DIRECTOR-ACTOR CHECK LIST: ERICH VON STROHEIM _____ DT109

Blind Husbands   **Actor only**
Foolish Wives   Grand Illusion
Greed*   The Great Gabbo
Queen Kelly   Hearts of the World
The Wedding March   Intolerance
                                         Lost Squadron
                                         Napoleon (1955 version)
                                         North Star
                                         Sunset Boulevard

*director only

DIRECTOR CHECK LIST: JOHN WATERS _____ DT110

Cry-Baby   Pink Flamingos
Desperate Living   Polyester
Female Trouble
Hairspray*   **Actor only**
Mondo Trasho   Something Wild
Multiple Maniacs

*also actor

DIRECTOR CHECK LIST: PETER WEIR _____ DT111

The Cars That Ate Paris   Picnic at Hanging Rock
Dead Poets Society   The Plumber
Gallipoli   Witness
The Last Wave   The Year of Living Dangerously
The Mosquito Coast

DIRECTOR-ACTOR CHECK LIST: ORSON WELLES _____ DT112

Citizen Kane   Journey Into Fear
The Lady From Shanghai   The Long, Hot Summer (1958 version)
Macbeth (1948 version)   A Man for all Seasons (1966 version)
The Magnificent Ambersons*   Moby Dick
Mr. Arkadin   The Muppet Movie
The Stranger   Napoleon (1955 version)
Touch of Evil   Someone to Love
The Trial   Start the Revolution Without Me
                                           (narrator)
Actor only   The Third Man
Battle Force (narrator)   Transformers, The Movie (character
Butterfly   voice)
Casino Royale   The Vikings (narrator)
Catch-22   Voyage of the Damned

*narrator only

DIRECTOR CHECK LIST: WIM WENDERS ———————————— DT113

Alice in the Cities
The American Friend
The Goalie's Anxiety at the Penalty
  Kick
Hammett
Kings of the Road
Lightning Over Water

Paris, Texas
The Scarlet Letter (1980 version)
The State of Things
Tokyo-Ga
Wings of Desire
Wrong Move

DIRECTOR CHECK LIST: LINA WERTMÜLLER ———————————— DT114

All Screwed Up Blood Feud
Camorra
Joke of Destiny
Love and Anarchy
The Seduction of Mimi

Seven Beauties
Sotto . . . Sotto
Summer Night
Swept Away

DIRECTOR CHECK LIST: JAMES WHALE ———————————— DT115

The Bride of Frankenstein
Frankenstein (1931 version)
The Invisible Man

The Man in the Iron Mask (1939
  version)
Show Boat (1936 version)

DIRECTOR CHECK LIST: BILLY WILDER ———————————— DT116

The Apartment
Buddy Buddy
Double Indemnity
Irma La Douce
The Lost Weekend
Love in the Afternoon
One, Two, Three
The Private Life of Sherlock Holmes

Sabrina
The Seven Year Itch
Some Like It Hot
The Spirit of St. Louis
Stalag 17
Sunset Boulevard
Witness for the Prosecution (1957
  version)

DIRECTOR CHECK LIST: ROBERT WISE ———————————— DT117

The Andromeda Strain
Audrey Rose
Blood on the Moon
The Body Snatcher
Born to Kill
Criminal Court
Curse of the Cat People
The Day the Earth Stood Still
Executive Suite
The Haunting

The Hindenburg
I Want to Live!
Rooftops
Run Silent, Run Deep
The Sand Pebbles
The Set-Up
The Sound of Music
Star Trek—The Motion Picture
West Side Story (co-director)

DIRECTOR CHECKLIST: ED WOOD, JR. ———————————— DT118

Bride of the Monster
Glen or Glenda?
Jail Bait
Plan 9 from Outer Space

Revenge of the Dead
The Sinister Urge
The Violent Years

DIRECTOR CHECK LIST: WILLIAM WYLER _____ **DT119**

Ben-Hur
The Best Years of Our Lives
The Big Country
The Collector
Come and Get It (co-director)
Dead End
The Desperate Hours
Dodsworth
Friendly Persuasion
Funny Girl

The Heiress
Jezebel
The Letter
The Liberation of L.B. Jones
The Little Foxes
Mrs. Miniver
Roman Holiday
These Three
The Westerner
Wuthering Heights (1939 version)

DIRECTOR CHECK LIST: FRED ZINNEMANN _____ **DT120**

Behold a Pale Horse
The Day of the Jackal
Five Days One Summer
From Here to Eternity
High Noon
Julia

A Man for all Seasons (1966 version)
Member of the Wedding
The Men
The Nun's Story
Oklahoma!
The Sundowners

Chapter Seven

FAMILY/CHILDREN'S
(FA)

DISNEY LIVE ACTION FEATURES _____ **FA1**

Action/Adventure
Benji the Hunted
Black Arrow (1984 version)
Cheetah
Condorman
Davy Crockett
Davy Crockett and the River Pirates
The Fighting Prince of Donegal
The Great Locomotive Chase
In Search of the Castaways
The Incredible Journey
Island at the Top of the World
The Journey of Natty Gann
Kidnapped (1960 version)
King of the Grizzlies
The Last Flight of Noah's Ark
The Light in the Forest
Lightning: The White Stallion
Miracle of the White Stallions
Nikki, Wild Dog of the North
Swiss Family Robinson
The Sword and the Rose
Ten Who Dared
Third Man on the Mountain
Toby Tyler
Treasure Island (1950 version)
20,000 Leagues Under the Sea
The Wild Country

Comedy
The Absent-Minded Professor
The Barefoot Executive
The Billion Dollar Hobo
Blackbeard's Ghost
The Boatniks
Bon Voyage!
Candleshoe
The Cat From Outer Space
The Computer Wore Tennis Shoes
The Devil and Max Devlin
Freaky Friday
Gus
Herbie Goes Bananas
Herbie Goes to Monte Carlo
Herbie Rides Again
The Horse in the Gray Flannel Suit
Lt. Robin Crusoe, USN
Lots of Luck

The Love Bug
The Million Dollar Duck
The Misadventures of Merlin Jones
Monkeys Go Home!
The Monkey's Uncle
Moon Pilot
Never a Dull Moment
No Deposit, No Return
The North Avenue Irregulars
Now You See Him, Now You Don't
The One and Only Genuine Original
   Family Band
The Parent Trap
The Shaggy D. A.
The Shaggy Dog
Snowball Express
Son of Flubber
Superdad
That Darn Cat
The Trouble With Angels
The World's Greatest Athlete

Documentary
The Living Desert
Secrets of Life
The Vanishing Prairie
White Wilderness

Drama
Almost Angels
Amy
The Blue Yonder
Charley and the Angel
Child of Glass
Follow Me, Boys!
The Girl Who Spelled Freedom
Greyfriars Bobby
Johnny Tremain
The Littlest Horse Thieves
The Littlest Outlaw
Napoleon and Samantha
Night Crossing
Pollyanna
So Dear to My Heart
Summer Magic
Those Calloways
A Tiger Walks

Horror/Mystery/Suspense
Emil and the Detectives
Escape to Witch Mountain
The Moon-Spinners
Return to Witch Mountain
The Watcher in the Woods

Musical
Babes in Toyland
The Happiest Millionaire
Mary Poppins
Pete's Dragon

Science Fiction/Fantasy
Bedknobs and Broomsticks
The Black Hole

Darby O'Gill and the Little People
The Gnome-Mobile
The Three Lives of Thomasina
Tron
Unidentified Flying Oddball

Western
The Adventures of Bullwhip Griffin
The Apple Dumpling Gang
The Apple Dumpling Gang Rides Again
The Castaway Cowboy
Hot Lead and Cold Feet
Old Yeller
Savage Sam
Smith!

DISNEY ANIMATED FEATURES _____ FA2

Alice in Wonderland
Bambi
Cinderella
Dumbo
Lady and the Tramp
The Legend of Sleepy Hollow
The Little Mermaid (1989 version)
Oliver and Company

Peter Pan (1953 version)
Pinocchio (1940 version)
Robin Hood
Sleeping Beauty (1959 version)
The Sword in the Stone
The Three Caballeros
The Wind in the Willows

CLASSIC LITERATURE _____ FA3

The Adventures of Huckleberry Finn
   (1939 & 1985 versions)
The Adventures of Tom Sawyer (1938 &
   1973 versions)
Alice in Wonderland (1951 version)
Alice's Adventures in Wonderland
Anne of Green Gables
Captains Courageous
Casey at the Bat
A Connecticut Yankee in King Arthur's
   Court (1949 version)
David Copperfield
Great Expectations
Heidi (1937 version)

Huckleberry Finn
Little Lord Fauntleroy (1936 & 1980
   versions)
Mysterious Island
Oliver Twist (1922, 1933, & 1948
   versions)
The Prince and the Pauper (1937 & 1978
   versions)
Tom Brown's School Days (1940
   version)
Tom Sawyer
Treasure Island (1934 & 1950 versions)
20,000 Leagues Under the Sea

FAMILY ADVENTURE _____ FA4

Across the Great Divide
The Adventures of Robin Hood
The Adventures of the Wilderness
   Family
The Amazing Mr. Blunden
Any Friend of Nicholas Nickleby Is a
   Friend of Mine
Archer's Adventure
Around the World in 80 Days
Around the World Under the Sea

At the Earth's Core
The Black Pirate
Brighty of the Grand Canyon
Cold River
The Crimson Pirate
Five Weeks in a Balloon
Gunga Din
Island of the Blue Dolphins
Ivanhoe
Journey of Natty Gann

Journey to the Center of the Earth (1959
  & 1989 versions)
The Jungle Book (1942 version)
Kim
King Solomon's Mines (1950 version)
The Life and Times of Grizzly Adams
Lionheart
Lives of a Bengal Lancer
The Man in the Iron Mask
Mountain Family Robinson
My Pet Monster
My Side of the Mountain
Mysterious Island
Never Cry Wolf
The New Adventures of Pippi
  Longstocking
Pippi Longstocking (series)
The Prisoner of Zenda (1937 version)

The Quest
The Railway Children
Return to Oz
Scaramouche
The Scarlet Pimpernel
The Sea Gypsies
Superman (series)
Sword of the Valiant
Tarzan and the Trappers
Tarzan, the Ape Man (1932 version)
Tarzan, the Fearless
Tarzan's Revenge
Teenage Mutant Ninja Turtles
The Thief of Bagdad (1940 version)
Wee Willie Winkie
When the North Wind Blows
The Wilderness Family, Part 2
Young Sherlock Holmes

ANIMAL STORIES _____ FA5

All Creatures Great and Small
The Amazing Dobermans
The Bear
Benji
Benji Takes a Dive at Marineland
Benji, the Hunted
Big Red
Black Beauty (1946 & 1971 versions)
The Black Stallion
The Black Stallion Returns
Blue Fire Lady
Born Free
Brighty of the Grand Canyon
Casey's Shadow
Charlie, the Lonesome Cougar
Cheetah
Christian the Lion
The Day of the Dolphin
A Dog of Flanders
Flipper
For the Love of Benji
The Golden Seal

Goldy: The Last of the Golden Bears
Goodbye, My Lady
Hambone and Hillie
The Incredible Journey
International Velvet
Lassie Come Home
The Legend of Lobo
Lightning: The White Stallion
Living Free
The Magic of Lassie
Mighty Joe Young
The Miracle of the White Stallions
National Velvet
Nikki, Wild Dog of the North
Oh! Heavenly Dog
Old Yeller
Phar Lap
The Red Pony (1949 & 1973 versions)
Ring of Bright Water
Sylvester
Where the Red Fern Grows
The Yearling

COMEDY _____ FA6
See also: Director Check Lists DT18 Charlie Chaplin, DT54 Buster Keaton; Star Check Lists
ST78 Danny Kaye, ST87 Laurel and Hardy, ST101 The Marx Bros.

Big Top Pee-wee
C.H.O.M.P.S.
A Christmas Story
Cinderfella
Ernest Goes to Camp
Ernest Goes to Jail
Ernest Saves Christmas
The Great Race
Hawmps!
Hollywood or Bust

It's a Mad Mad Mad Mad World
Little Miss Marker (1980 version)
Matilda
Oh God!
Oh God! Book II
Oh God! You Devil
On the Right Track
The Peanut Butter Solution
Pee-wee's Big Adventure
The Prize Fighter

Short Circuit
Short Circuit 2
They Went That-a-Way and That-a-Way

The Young Magician
Yours, Mine and Ours
Who Framed Roger Rabbit

DRAMAS ABOUT CONTEMPORARY KIDS _____ FA7

Amazing Grace and Chuck
Big Shots
Birch Interval
Bless the Beasts and Children
Blue Fin
The Boy Who Could Fly
Casey's Shadow
The Champ (1979 version)
D.A.R.Y.L.
The Dirt Bike Kid
The Double McGuffin
The Earthling
The Escape Artist
Fast Talking
From the Mixed-Up Files of Mrs. Basil
    E. Frankenweiler
The Girl Who Spelled Freedom
Gregory's Girl

Hot Shot
I Am the Cheese
Jimmy the Kid
The Karate Kid
The Karate Kid II
The Karate Kid III
Lucas
My Side of the Mountain
The Peanut Butter Solution
Rad
Savannah Smiles
Somewhere Tomorrow
Tiger Bay
Tiger Town
Where the River Runs Black
Whistle Down the Wind
The Wizard

SCIENCE FICTION/FANTASY _____ FA8
See also: SF13 Family Fantasy/Sci-Fi

The Adventures of Baron Munchausen
Aladdin
*batteries not included
Battle for the Planet of the Apes
Beneath the Planet of the Apes
The Brothers Lionheart
Close Encounters of the Third Kind
Conquest of the Planet of the Apes
The Dark Crystal
The Day the Earth Stood Still
E. T. The Extra-Terrestrial
The Empire Strikes Back
The Enchanted Forest
Escape From the Planet of the Apes
Explorers
The 5,000 Fingers of Dr. T
Flight of the Navigator
From the Earth to the Moon
The Golden Voyage of Sinbad
Heartbeeps
The Hobbit
The Incredible Mr. Limpet
The Incredible Shrinking Man
Jason and the Argonauts
King Kong (1933 version)
Labyrinth
The Land of Faraway
Little Monsters

Lord of the Rings
Masters of the Universe
The NeverEnding Story
The Phantom Tollbooth
Planet of the Apes
Return of the Jedi
The 7 Faces of Dr. Lao
The 7th Voyage of Sinbad
Sinbad and the Eye of the Tiger
Something Wicked This Way Comes
Spaced Invaders
Star Trek (series)
Star Wars
Thief of Bagdad (1940 version)
Time Bandits
The Time Machine
tom thumb
Tuck Everlasting
The War of the Worlds
The Watcher in the Woods
The Water Babies
Willie Wonka and the Chocolate
    Factory
Willow
The Witches
The Wonderful World of the Brothers
    Grimm

MUSICALS _____ FA9

Annie
Bugsy Malone
Camelot
Carousel
Chitty Chitty Bang Bang
Cinderella (1964 version)
A Connecticut Yankee in King Arthur's
  Court (1949 version)
Doctor Dolittle
Fiddler on the Roof
Follow That Bird
Hans Christian Andersen
A Hard Day's Night
Help!
Jesus Christ Superstar
The King and I
Mary Poppins
Meet Me in St. Louis

The Music Man
My Fair Lady
Oklahoma!
Oliver!
The Pirates of Penzance
Popeye
1776
Singin' in the Rain
The Sound of Music
South Pacific
State Fair (1945 & 1962 versions)
West Side Story
Willie Wonka and the Chocolate
  Factory
The Wiz
The Wizard of Oz (1939 version)
Yankee Doodle Dandy

NON-DISNEY ANIMATED FEATURES _____ FA10

The Adventures of an American Rabbit
The Adventures of Mark Twain
Alakazam the Great
All Dogs Go to Heaven
An American Tail
Animalympics
Babar: The Movie
Bon Voyage, Charlie Brown
A Boy Named Charlie Brown
The Care Bears Movie
Charlotte's Web
The Chipmunk Adventure
Dorothy in the Land of Oz
The Dragon That Wasn't (Or Was He?)
Flight of the Dragons
Gnomes, Vol. 1
Gulliver's Travels (1939 version)
Here Come the Littles
Hey There, It's Yogi Bear
The Hobbit
It's an Adventure, Charlie Brown

Journey Back to Oz
Journey Through Fairyland
The Land Before Time
The Last Unicorn
The Lion, the Witch and the Wardrobe
Lord of the Rings
Mad Monster Party?
A Man Called Flintstone
My Little Pony: The Movie
Puff the Magic Dragon
Quackbusters
Scruffy
The Secret of NIMH
Shinbone Alley
Snoopy Come Home
Starchaser: The Legend of Orin
Teddy Ruxpin: Teddy Outsmarts
  M.A.V.O.
Transformers: The Movie
Watership Down
The Wizard of Oz (1982 version)

WARNER BROS. CARTOON COLLECTIONS _____ FA11

The Best of Bugs Bunny and Friends
Bugs and Daffy: The Wartime Cartoons
Bugs and Daffy's Carnival of the
  Animals
Bugs Bunny and Elmer Fudd Cartoon
  Festival
Bugs Bunny Cartoon Festival
Bugs Bunny Classics
Bugs Bunny in King Arthur's Court
Bugs Bunny/Road Runner Movie
Bugs Bunny Superstar

Bugs Bunny's 3d Movie: 1001 Rabbit
  Tales
Bugs Bunny's Wacky Adventures
Cartoon Moviestars: Bugs!
Cartoon Moviestars: Daffy!
Cartoon Moviestars: Elmer!
Cartoon Moviestars: Porky!
Daffy Duck Cartoon Festival
Daffy Duck: The Nuttiness
  Continues . . .
Daffy Duck's Movie: Fantastic Island

Elmer Fudd Cartoon Festival
Elmer Fudd's Comedy Capers
Foghorn Leghorn's Fractured Funnies
The Looney, Looney, Looney Bugs
   Bunny Movie
Pepe Le Pew's Skunk Tales

Porky Pig and Daffy Duck Cartoon
   Festival
Road Runner vs. Wile E. Coyote: The
   Classic Chase
A Salute to Chuck Jones
A Salute to Friz Freleng
A Salute to Mel Blanc

FAERIE TALE THEATRE CHECK LIST _____ FA12

Aladdin and His Wonderful Lamp
Beauty and the Beast (1984 version)
The Boy Who Left Home to Find Out
   About the Shivers
Cinderella (1984 version)
The Dancing Princesses
The Emperor's New Clothes
Goldilocks and the Three Bears
Hansel and Gretel
Jack and the Beanstalk (1983 version)
The Little Mermaid (1984 version)
Little Red Riding Hood
The Nightingale
The Pied Piper of Hamelin

Pinocchio (1984 version)
The Princess and the Pea
The Princess Who Never Laughed
Puss 'n' Boots
Rapunzel
Rip Van Winkle
Rumpelstiltskin
Sleeping Beauty (1985 version)
The Snow Queen
Snow White and the Seven Dwarfs (1983
   version)
The Tale of the Frog Prince
The Three Little Pigs
Thumbelina

CHRISTMAS STORIES _____ FA13

A Christmas Carol (1951 version)
Christmas in Connecticut
C' stmas Lilies of the Field
A Christmas Story
A Christmas to Remember
The Christmas Tree
A Dream for Christmas
Ernest Saves Christmas
It's a Wonderful Life

Miracle Down Under
Miracle on 34th Street
National Lampoon's Christmas
   Vacation
One Magic Christmas
Prancer
Santa Claus, The Movie
Scrooge (1970 version)
Scrooged

THE MUPPETS CHECK LIST _____ FA15

Children's Songs and Stories With the
   Muppets
Country Music with the Muppets
Fozzie's Muppet Scrapbook
The Great Muppet Caper
The Kermit and Piggy Story
Muppet Moments

The Muppet Movie
The Muppet Revue
Muppet Treasures
The Muppets Take Manhattan
Rock Music With the Muppets
Rowlf's Rhapsodies With the Muppets

Chapter Eight

FOREIGN FILMS
(FF)

FRANCE ———————————————————————————————————— **FF1**

See also: Director Check Lists DT41 Jean-Luc Godard, DT86 Jean Renoir, DT89 Eric Rohmer, DT104 Jacques Tati, DT106 François Truffaut

ACTION/ADVENTURE
L'Addition
La Balance
Bob le Flambeur
Quest for Fire

COMEDY
A Nous la Liberté
The Baker's Wife
Black and White in Color
Le Bourgeois Gentilhomme
Buffet Froid
La Cage aux Folles
La Cage aux Folles II
La Cage aux Folles 3: The Wedding
Cesar
La Chevre
Clean Slate (Coup de Torchon)
Les Comperes
Cousin, Cousine
The Crazy Ray
Fanny
Get Out Your Handkerchiefs
Happy New Year (1973 version)
Italian Straw Hat
Marius
Le Million
Mon Oncle d'Amerique
Murmur of the Heart
My New Partner
Next Year, If All Goes Well
A Pain in the A—
Pardon Mon Affaire
Princess Tam-Tam
Robert et Robert
Le Sex Shop
The Tall Blonde Man With One Black Shoe
Three Men and a Cradle
Under the Roofs of Paris
A Very Curious Girl
Zero for Conduct

DRAMA
A Nos Amours
And Now My Love

L'Annee des Meduses
L'Atalante
Au Revoir, Les Enfants
Bad Girls
Beatrice
Beau Pere
Betty Blue
La Boum
Camille Claudel
Cesar and Rosalie
Chocolat
Choice of Arms
Deathwatch
Diary of a Chambermaid (1964 version)
Diary of a Country Priest
Entre Nous
The Eternal Return
Forbbiden Games
The Game Is Over
Going Places
The Grand Highway
Heat of Desire
Hiroshima, Mon Amour
I Sent a Letter to My Love
Jean de Florette
Le Jour Se Leve
The Judge and the Assassin
Last Year at Marienbad
Les Liaisons Dangereuses
The Little Thief
Lola (1961)
Loulou
Love Songs
Lumiere
Madame Rosa
A Man and a Woman
A Man and a Woman: 20 Years Later
Manon of the Spring
Melo
Mr. Klein
The Moon in the Gutter
Mysteries
Napoleon (1927)
La Passante
The Passion of Joan of Arc
Providence

Ramparts of Clay
Rape of Love
Rendez-vous
The Return of Martin Guerre
La Ronde
A Simple Story
State of Siege
Sugar Cane Alley
A Sunday in the Country
Sundays and Cybelle
Swann in Love
Thérèse
La Truite
Vagabond
La Vie Continue
Vincent, Francois, Paul and the Others
Volpone
Wolf at the Door

HORROR
Eyes Without a Face

MUSICALS
Le Bal

The Umbrellas of Cherbourg
Zouzou

MYSTERY/THRILLER
Cat and Mouse
Dear Detective
Diabolically Yours
Diabolique
Diva
Investigation
Jupiter's Thigh
Melodie en Sous-Sol
Rider on the Rain
Rififi
Sincerely, Charlotte
This Man Must Die
The Wages of Fear
Wedding in Blood
Z

SCIENCE FICTION/FANTASY
Beauty and the Beast (1946 version)
Blood of a Poet
Le Dernier Combat
Fantastic Planet

ITALY _____ **FF2**

See also: Director Check Lists DT3 Michelangelo Antonioni, DT9 Bernardo Bertolucci,
DT26 Vittorio De Sica, DT53 Federico Fellini, DT108 Luchino Visconti, DT114 Lina
Wertmüller

ACTION/ADVENTURE
Hercules
Mean Frank and Crazy Tony

COMEDY
All the Way, Boys
Big Deal on Madonna Street
Down and Dirty
General della Rovere
The Immortal Bachelor
Lovers and Liars
Macaroni
Malicious
Seduced and Abandoned
Sex With a Smile
We All Loved Each Other So Much
Where's Picone?
Wifemistress

DRAMA
Allonsanfan
The Battle of Algiers
Brother Sun, Sister Moon
Burn!
China Is Near
Christ Stopped at Eboli
Cinema Paradiso
Dark Eyes
Devil in the Flesh

The Eyes, The Mouth
The Family (1987)
The Gospel According to St. Matthew
La Grande Bourgeoise
Henry IV
The Inheritance
Massacre in Rome
The Night of the Shooting Stars
1900
La Nuit de Varennes
Open City
Padre Padrone
Paisan
Passion of Love
Sacco and Vanzetti
A Special Day
Stromboli
Three Brothers
Time of Indifference

HORROR
Beyond the Door
Beyond the Door II

MYSTERY/THRILLER
The Bird with the Crystal Plumage

SCIENCE FICTION/FANTASY
The Tenth Victim

GERMANY _____ FF3
See also: Director Check Lists DT34 Rainer Werner Fassbinder, DT44 Werner Herzog, DT113 Wim Wenders

ACTION/ADVENTURE
The Boat

COMEDY
Men
Sugarbaby

DRAMA
The Blue Angel
Christiane F.
Coup de Grace
Diary of a Lost Girl
Faust
The Inheritors
Kameradschaft
Kamikaze '89
Kriemhilde's Revenge
The Last Laugh
The Lost Honor of Katharina Blum
M
Maedchen in Uniform (1931 version)
A Man Like Eva
Pandora's Box

Passion (1918)
Siegfried
Spies
The Tin Drum
Tonio Kroger
Variety
The Wannsee Conference
The White Rose
Westfront 1918
Woman in Flames

HORROR
The Cabinet of Dr. Caligari
The Golem

MUSICAL
The Threepenny Opera

SCIENCE FICTION/FANTASY
Destiny
Metropolis
The NeverEnding Story
The Testament of Dr. Mabuse

JAPAN _____ FF4
See also: Director Check List DT57 Akira Kurosawa, Star Check List ST106 Toshiro Mifune

ACTION/ADVENTURE
Kojiro
The One-Eyed Swordsman
Samurai Saga
The Samurai Trilogy
Shogun Assassin
Zatoichi Meets Yojimbo

COMEDY
The Family Game
Tampopo
A Taxing Woman

DRAMA
The Ballad of Narayama
Double Suicide
Early Summer
Fires on the Plain
Floating Weeds
The Forty-seven Ronin, Part One
The Forty-seven Ronin, Part Two
Gate of Hell
The Go Masters
The Golden Demon
Himatsuri
The Human Condition
Irezumi
The Island (1962)

The Life of Oharu
MacArthur's Children
The Makioka Sisters
Merry Christmas, Mr. Lawrence
Mishima
Mother
Odd Obsession
Sansho the Bailiff
Street of Shame
Tokyo Story
Ugetsu
Woman in the Dunes

HORROR
The Ghost of Yotsuya
Kwaidan

SCIENCE FICTION/FANTASY
Ghidrah, the Three-Headed Monster
Godzilla, King of the Monsters
Godzilla, 1985
Godzilla on Monster Island
Godzilla vs. Megalon
Godzilla vs. Monster Zero
Godzilla vs. Mothra
Gorath
The H-Man
The Human Vapor

The Last War
Mothra
The Mysterians

Rodan
Terror of Mechagodzilla

AUSTRALIA _____ FF5
See also: Director Check List DT111 Peter Weir

ACTION/ADVENTURE
Escape 2000
Fortress
Forty Thousand Horsemen
The Lighthorsemen
Mad Dog Morgan
Mad Max
Mad Max Beyond Thunderdome
The Man From Snowy River
The Odd Angry Shot
The Quest
Razorback
Return to Snowy River, Part II
The Road Warrior
Walk Into Hell
We of the Never Never

COMEDY
Bliss
The Cars That Ate Paris
"Crocodile" Dundee
"Crocodile" Dundee II
Don's Party
Malcolm
Norman Loves Rose
Rikky and Pete
Touch and Go (1980)
Young Einstein

DRAMA
Breaker Morant
Burke and Wills
Cactus
Caddie
Careful, He Might Hear You
Chain Reaction
A Cry in the Dark
Dawn!
The Devil's Playground

The Fringe Dwellers
The Getting of Wisdom
Ground Zero
Heatwave
High Tide
Kangaroo
The Killing of Angel Street
Kitty and the Bagman
The Last Wave
Lonely Hearts
Man of Flowers
The Mango Tree
Miracle Down Under
My Brilliant Career
My First Wife
Newsfront
Now and Forever
Puberty Blues
Rebel (1986)
Shame (1988)
Squizzy Taylor
Storm Boy
Summer City
Tim
A Town Like Alice
Traveling North
Warm Nights on a Slow-Moving Train
Weekend of Shadows
Who Killed Baby Azaria
The Wild Duck
Winter of Our Dreams

MUSICAL
Dogs in Space
Starstruck

MYSTERY/THRILLER
Dead Calm
Patrick

LATIN AMERICA _____ FF6
See also: Director Check List DT15 Luis Buñuel

ARGENTINA
Antonio das Mortes
Apartment Zero
Camila
Man Facing Southeast
Miss Mary
The Official Story
Subway to the Stars

BRAZIL
Black Orpheus
Bye Bye Brazil
Doña Flor and Her Two Husbands
Gabriela
Hour of the Star
I Love You
Kiss of the Spider Woman
Lady on the Bus
Pixote

CUBA
Memories of Underdevelopment

MEXICO
Erendira

NICARAGUA
Alsino and the Condor

OTHER COUNTRIES OF THE WORLD _____ FF7
See also: Director Check Lists DT7 Ingmar Bergman, DT15 Luis Buñuel, DT33 Sergei Eisenstein, DT84 Satyajit Ray

CZECHOSLOVAKIA
Closely Watched Trains
Ecstasy
The Firemen's Ball
Loves of a Blonde
The Shop on Main Street

DENMARK
Babette's Feast
Pelle the Conqueror

GREECE
Iphigenia

HOLLAND
The Assault
The Fourth Man
A Question of Silence
Spetters
Turkish Delight

HUNGARY
Colonel Redl
Father
Mephisto
The Revolt of Job
Time Stands Still

INDIA
Salaam Bombay!

POLAND
Ashes and Diamonds
Kanal
Knife in the Water
Man of Iron
Man of Marble
Moonlighting (1982)
A Year of the Quiet Sun

SOVIET UNION
Arsenal
The Commissar
Earth
The End of St. Petersburg
Little Vera
Moscow Does Not Believe in Tears
The Overcoat
Repentance
Shadows of Forgotten Ancestors
A Slave of Love
Storm Over Asia
War and Peace (1968 version)

SPAIN
El Amor Brujo
Carmen
Dark Habits
Half of Heaven
Holy Innocents
Law of Desire
The Spirit of the Beehive
What Have I Done to Deserve This!
Women on the Verge of a Nervous
    Breakdown

SWEDEN
Elvira Madigan
The Flight of the Eagle
June Night
My Life as a Dog
The Sacrifice
Swedenhielms
Witchcraft Through the Ages

SWITZERLAND
The Boat Is Full

YUGOSLAVIA
Hey Babu Riba
Montenegro
WR—Mysteries of the Organism

FOREIGN FILMS & THEIR AMERICAN REMAKES _____ FF8

La Bête Humaine/Human Desire
Boudou Saved From Drowning/Down
    and Out in Beverly Hills
Breathless (1959)/Breathless (1982)

Cousin, Cousine/Cousins
Diabolique/Reflections of Murder
Doña Flor and Her Two Husbands/Kiss
    Me Goodbye

Happy New Year (1973)/Happy New
   Year (1987)
Intermezzo (1937)/Intermezzo (1939)
The Man Who Loved Women (1977)/
   The Man Who Loved Women (1983)
A Pain in the A—/Buddy Buddy
Pardon Mon Affaire/The Woman in Red
The Seduction of Mimi/Which Way Is
   Up?

The Seven Samurai/The Magnificent
   Seven
The Tall Blonde Man With One Black
   Shoe/The Man With One Red Shoe
Three Men and a Cradle/Three Men and
   a Baby
La Vie Continue/Men Don't Leave
The Virgin Spring/Last House on the
   Left
Yojimbo/A Fistful of Dollars

Chapter Nine

HISTORICAL/FICTIONAL CHARACTER CHECK LISTS
(HF)

HISTORICAL CHARACTER CHECK LIST: BILLY THE KID _____ HF1

Billy the Kid Returns
Gore Vidal's Billy the Kid
The Left-Handed Gun
The Outlaw

Pat Garrett and Billy the Kid
Return of the Bad Men
Young Guns

FICTIONAL CHARACTER CHECK LIST: JAMES BOND _____ HF2

Casino Royale
Diamonds Are Forever
Dr. No
For Your Eyes Only
From Russia With Love
Goldfinger
Licence to Kill
Live and Let Die
The Living Daylights

The Man With the Golden Gun
Moonraker
Never Say Never Again
Octopussy
On Her Majesty's Secret Service
The Spy Who Loved Me
Thunderball
A View to a Kill
You Only Live Twice

HISTORICAL CHARACTER CHECK LIST: WILLIAM F. CODY (BUFFALO BILL) ___ HF3

Annie Oakley
Buffalo Bill and the Indians
The Plainsman (1936)

Pony Express
Young Buffalo Bill

FICTIONAL CHARACTER CHECK LIST: CHARLIE CHAN _____ HF4

Castle in the Desert
Charlie Chan at the Opera
Charlie Chan at the Wax Museum
Charlie Chan in Paris
Charlie Chan in Rio

Charlie Chan's Secret
Meeting at Midnight
Murder by Death
Murder Over New York

FICTIONAL CHARACTERS CHECK LIST: NICK & NORA CHARLES _____ HF5

After the Thin Man
Another Thin Man
Shadow of the Thin Man

Song of the Thin Man
The Thin Man
The Thin Man Goes Home

HISTORICAL CHARACTER CHECK LIST: GEORGE ARMSTRONG CUSTER _____ HF6

Little Big Man
The Plainsman (1936)

Santa Fe Trail
They Died With Their Boots On

FICTIONAL CHARACTER CHECK LIST: DRACULA _____ HF7

Abbott & Costello Meet Frankenstein
Andy Warhol's Dracula
Blacula
Count Dracula
Dr. Terror's Gallery of Horrors
Dracula (1931 & 1979 versions)
Dracula and Son
Dracula vs. Frankenstein

The Horror of Dracula
Love at First Bite
The Magic Christian
The Monster Club
Nosferatu
Scars of Dracula
Son of Dracula

FICTIONAL CHARACTER CHECK LIST: BULLDOG DRUMMOND _____ HF8

Bulldog Drummond
Bulldog Drummond at Bay
Bulldog Drummond Comes Back
Bulldog Drummond Escapes
Bulldog Drummond in Africa

Bulldog Drummond Strikes Back
Bulldog Drummond's Bride
Bulldog Drummond's Peril
Bulldog Drummond's Revenge
Bulldog Drummond's Secret Police

HISTORICAL CHARACTER CHECK LIST: WYATT EARP _____ HF9

Cheyenne Autumn
Gunfight at the O.K. Corral

My Darling Clementine
Winchester '73

FICTIONAL CHARACTER CHECK LIST: THE FRANKENSTEIN MONSTER _____ HF10

Abbott & Costello Meet Frankenstein
Andy Warhol's Frankenstein
The Bride
The Bride of Frankenstein
The Curse of Frankenstein
Dracula vs. Frankenstein
The Evil of Frankenstein
Frankenstein (1931 & 1973 versions)

Frankenstein—1970
Frankenstein Meets the Wolf Man
Horror of Frankenstein
The Monster Club
Son of Frankenstein
The Spirit of the Beehive
Transylvania 6-5000
Young Frankenstein

HISTORICAL CHARACTER CHECK LIST: WILD BILL HICKOK _____ HF11

Calamity Jane
Little Big Man
The Plainsman (1936)

Pony Express
The White Buffalo
Young Bill Hickok

HISTORICAL CHARACTER CHECK LIST: ADOLF HITLER _____ HF12

The Battle of Britain
The Desert Fox
The Great Dictator
Hitler
Hitler—Dead or Alive
Hitler: The Last Ten Days

The Miracle of Morgan's Creek
To Be or Not To Be (1942 & 1983
   versions)
Which Way to the Front?
Zelig

HISTORICAL CHARACTER CHECK LIST: DOC HOLLIDAY _____ HF13

Cheyenne Autumn
Gunfight at the O.K. Corral

My Darling Clementine
The Outlaw

FICTIONAL CHARACTER CHECK LIST: SHERLOCK HOLMES _____ HF14

The Adventures of Sherlock Holmes
Dressed to Kill (1946)
The Hound of the Baskervilles (1938,
   1959 & 1977 versions)
House of Fear
Masks of Death
Murder by Decree
Pearl of Death
The Private Life of Sherlock Holmes
Pursuit to Algiers
The Scarlet Claw
The Seven Percent Solution
Sherlock Holmes and the Secret
   Weapon

Sherlock Holmes and the Voice of
   Terror
Sherlock Holmes Faces Death
Sherlock Holmes in Washington
The Silver Blaze
The Speckled Band
Spider Woman
A Study in Scarlet
A Study in Terror
Terror by Night
The Triumph of Sherlock Holmes
Without a Clue
The Woman in Green
Young Sherlock Holmes

FICTIONAL CHARACTER CHECK LIST: ROBIN HOOD _____ HF15

The Adventures of Robin Hood
Ivanhoe
Robin and Marian
Robin Hood

Robin Hood and the Sorcerer
Sword of Sherwood Forest
Time Bandits

HISTORICAL CHARACTER CHECK LIST: JESSE JAMES _____ HF16

Days of Jesse James
The Great Northfield Minnesota Raid
I Shot Jesse James

Jesse James
Jesse James at Bay
The Long Riders

HISTORICAL CHARACTER CHECK LIST: JESUS CHRIST _____ HF17

Barabbas
Ben-Hur
Ben-Hur: A Tale of Christ
The Gospel According to St. Matthew
The Greatest Story Ever Told
The History of the World, Part I
Intolerance

Jesus Christ Superstar
Jesus of Nazareth
The King of Kings (1927 & 1961
   versions)
The Last Temptation of Christ
The Milky Way

HISTORICAL CHARACTER CHECK LIST: ABRAHAM LINCOLN _____ HF18

Abe Lincoln in Illinois
Abraham Lincoln
The Birth of a Nation
How the West Was Won
The Littlest Rebel

The Plainsman
Santa Fe Trail
They Died With Their Boots On
Young Mr. Lincoln

HISTORICAL CHARACTER CHECK LIST: NAPOLEON _____ HF19

Anthony Adverse
Desiree
Love and Death

Napoleon (1927 & 1955 versions)
Time Bandits
War and Peace (1956 & 1968 versions)

HISTORICAL CHARACTER CHECK LIST: ANNIE OAKLEY —————————— **HF20**

Annie Oakley   The Plainsman (1936)
Buffalo Bill and the Indians

FICTIONAL CHARACTER CHECK LIST: THE SAINT —————————— **HF21**

The Saint in London   The Saint Takes Over
The Saint in New York   The Saint's Vacation
The Saint Strikes Back

FICTIONAL CHARACTER CHECK LIST: TARZAN —————————— **HF22**

Greystoke: The Legend of Tarzan   Tarzan, the Ape Man (1932 & 1981
Tarzan and the Green Goddess   versions)
Tarzan and the Trappers   Tarzan the Fearless
Tarzan of the Apes   Tarzan's Revenge

Chapter Ten

HORROR
(HO)

See also: Writer Check Lists WR12 Stephen King, WR21 Edgar Allan Poe

CLASSIC HORROR ——————————————————————— HO1

The Black Cat
The Body Snatcher
The Bride of Frankenstein
The Cabinet of Dr. Caligari
Cat People (1942 version)
Curse of the Demon
Dead of Night (1945)
The Devil Doll
Dr. Jekyll and Mr. Hyde (1920, 1932 & 1941 versions)
Doctor X
Dracula (1931 version)
Eyes Without a Face
Frankentstein (1931 version)
Frankenstein Meets the Wolf Man
Freaks
The Golem
The Haunting
The Horror of Dracula
House of Wax

I Walked With a Zombie
The Invisible Man (1933 version)
— King Kong (1933 version)
M
The Masque of the Red Death (1964 version)
The Mummy (1932 version)
The Mystery of the Wax Museum
Nosferatu
The Phantom of the Opera (1925 version)
The Picture of Dorian Gray (1945 version)
Psycho
The Raven (1935)
Son of Dracula
Son of Frankenstein
White Zombie
The Wolf Man

GHOST STORIES ——————————————————————— HO2

The Changeling
The Curse of the Cat People
Dead of Night (1945)
The Fog
Ghost Story
The Haunting
The Haunting of Julia
Lady in White
Legend of Hell House

Poltergeist
Poltergeist II
Poltergeist III
The Shining
Sole Survivor
The Supernaturals
13 Ghosts
Turn of the Screw
The Watcher in the Woods

HAUNTED HOUSES ——————————————————————— HO3

The Amityville Horror
Amityville II: The Possession
Amityville 3D
Burnt Offerings
Castle of Blood
The Evil
The Haunting
The Haunting of Julia
House
House on Haunted Hill

House 2: The Second Story
The House Where Evil Dwells
Legend of Hell House
Poltergeist
Poltergeist II
The Shining
13 Ghosts
Twice Dead
The Watcher in the Woods
Witchtrap

WEREWOLVES _____ HO4

An American Werewolf in London
The Beast Must Die
The Beast Within
The Company of Wolves
The Curse of the Werewolf
The Howling
The Howling II
Howling III: The Marsupials

The Howling IV
Legend of the Werewolf
Silver Bullet
Teen Wolf
The Werewolf of Washington
The Wolf Man
Wolfen

VAMPIRES _____ HO5
See also: Fictional Character Check List HF7 Dracula

Andy Warhol's Dracula
Blacula
Blood Couple
The Bloodsuckers
Captain Kronos: Vampire Hunter
Count Dracula
Count Yorga, Vampire
Daughters of Darkness
Dracula (1931 & 1979 versions)
Dracula and Son
The Fearless Vampire Killers
Fright Night
Fright Night II
Graveyard Shift
The Horror of Dracula
The Hunger
Lair of the White Worm

Lifeforce
The Lost Boys
Love at First Bite
Lust for a Vampire
Mark of the Vampire
Martin
Near Dark
Nosferatu
The Return of the Vampire
Salem's Lot
Scars of Dracula
Son of Dracula
Vamp
The Vampire Lovers
Vampire's Kiss
Vampyr

ZOMBIES _____ HO6

Carnival of Souls
Children Shouldn't Play With Dead
   Things
Dawn of the Dead
Day of the Dead
Dead and Buried
Dead Heat
Deathdream
Hard Rock Zombies
I Walked With a Zombie

Isle of the Dead
Night of the Living Dead
Psychomania
The Return of the Living Dead
Revenge of the Zombies
The Serpent and the Rainbow
The White Zombie
Zombie
Zombie Island Massacre

PEOPLE WITH PSYCHIC POWERS _____ HO7

Cameron's Closet
Carrie (1976)
Creepers
Dark Forces
The Dead Zone
The Evil Mind
Eyes of Laura Mars
The Fury

The Initiation of Sarah
Jennifer
The Medusa Touch
Patrick
Scanners
The Shout
Sweet Sixteen

TALES OF POSSESSION ——————————————————————— HO8

The Awakening
Beyond the Door
Beyond the Door 2
The Boogeyman
Child's Play
Dark Places
The Evil Dead
The Evil Dead 2: Dead by Dawn

The Exorcist
Exorcist II: The Heretic
The Haunting of Morella
Horror Express
Magic
Mausoleum
Nightbreed

PSYCHO KILLERS ——————————————————————————— HO9

Alone in the Dark
The Bird With the Crystal Plumage
Blood and Black Lace
The Brute Man
Chamber of Horrors
Daughter of Horror
Deep Red: The Hatchet Murders
Don't Answer the Phone
Eyeball
Eyes of a Stranger
Fade to Black
The First Power
Halloween
Halloween II
Halloween IV: The Return of Michael
   Myers
Halloween 5
The Love Butcher

Myers
Happy Birthday to Me
He Knows You're Alone
The Hitcher
Honeymoon
The Human Monster
Jack the Ripper
The Night Visitor
The Phantom of the Opera (1925, 1943
   & 1989 versions)
Psycho
Psycho II
Psycho III
Schizoid
Shocker
Silent Night, Deadly Night
Slumber Party Massacre

DEAL WITH THE DEVIL ———————————————————————— HO10

Angel Heart
Angel on My Shoulder
Bedazzled
Black Sunday (1961)
Blood on Satan's Claw
Damien: Omen II
Damn Yankees
The Devil and Daniel Webster
The Devil and Max Devlin
The Devil's Nightmare
The Devil's Partner
The Devil's Rain

Faust
The Final Conflict
The First Power
The Gate
Heaven Can Wait (1943)
Leonor
The Mephisto Waltz
The Omen
Rosemary's Baby
To the Devil a Daughter
The Unholy

CULTS —————————————————— ——————————— HO11

Because of the Cats
The Believers
The Bloodsuckers
The Brotherhood of Satan
Curse of the Demon
The Dark Secret of Harvest Home
Deadly Blessing
The Devils
The Devil's Rain

The Legacy
Legend of the Minotaur
The Mephisto Waltz
Nomads
Race With the Devil
Rosemary's Baby
Season of the Witch
Videodrome
The Wicker Man

TEENS IN TROUBLE _____ HO12

April Fool's Day
Black Christmas
Brain Damage
Carrie (1976)
The Final Terror
Friday the 13th (series)
The Funhouse
Graduation Day
Hell Night
Killer Party

Last House on the Left
The Mutilator
A Nightmare on Elm Street (series)
Sleepaway Camp
Sorority House Massacre
Summer Camp Nightmare
Suspiria
Terror Train
The Texas Chainsaw Massacre
Zombie High

SCARY KIDS _____ HO13

Audrey Rose
The Baby
The Bad Seed
The Beast Within
The Brood
Cameron's Closet
Children of the Corn
Damien: Omen II
Evilspeak
The Exorcist
Exorcist II: The Heretic

Firestarter
The Godsend
It Lives Again
It's Alive
Jennifer
The Kindred
The Little Girl Who Lives Down the
   Lane
The Lost Boys
The Omen
Village of the Damned

BAD BLOOD: HORROR STORIES ABOUT FAMILIES _____ HO14
See also: HO15 Evil Twins

Arnold
The Beast in the Cellar
Crucible of Horror
The Curse
The Curse of the Cat People
Daughter of Dr. Jekyll
Dementia 13
Don't Look Now
Eraserhead
Flowers in the Attic

The Guardian
Hellbound: Hellraiser II
Hellraiser
The Hills Have Eyes
The Kiss
The Oblong Box
Psycho Sisters
Pumpkinhead
Seizure
Whatever Happened to Baby Jane?

EVIL TWINS _____ HO15

Basket Case
Basket Case 2
The Black Room
Blood Link
Dead Men Walk

Dead Ringers
The Man Who Haunted Himself
The Other
Sisters
Twins of Evil

ANIMALS AND OTHER CREEPY CREATURES _____ HO16

Alligator
Ants
Ben
The Birds
Bug

Child's Play
The Creature From Black Lake
Creepers
Critters
Critters 2: The Main Course

Cujo
Deep Star Six
Dogs of Hell
Dolls
Frogs
Ghoulies
— Gremlins
Humanoids From the Deep
In the Shadow of Kilimanjaro
Jaws (series)
King Kong (1933 & 1976 versions)
The Leopard Man
Link
Monkey Shines
The Nest
Nightwing
Of Unknown Origin

Orca
The Pack
Pet Sematary
Pin
Piranha
Puppet Master
Q
Razorback
Squirm
Swamp Thing
The Swarm
Tremors
Trolls
Venom
Willard
Wolfen

MEMORABLE TRANSFORMATIONS ⎯⎯⎯⎯⎯⎯⎯⎯⎯⎯ HO17

An American Werewolf in London
The Company of Wolves
Demons
Dr. Jekyll and Mr. Hyde (1932 version)

The Fly (1986 version)
The Howling
The Thing
The Wolf Man

GORY HORROR ⎯⎯⎯⎯⎯⎯⎯⎯⎯⎯⎯⎯⎯⎯⎯⎯ HO18

Basket Case
Basket Case 2
Blood Feast
Dawn of the Dead
Day of the Dead
Dr. Butcher, M.D.
The Evil Dead
The Evil Dead 2: Dead by Dawn
Friday the 13th (series)

Maniac (1980)
Mother's Day
Night of the Living Dead
Nightbreed
A Nightmare on Elm Street (series)
Rabid
Re-Animator
The Return of the Living Dead
Zombie

SCARY BUT NOT BLOODY ⎯⎯⎯⎯⎯⎯⎯⎯⎯⎯⎯ HO19
See also: HO1 Classic Horror

The Amityville Horror
The Body Snatcher
The Changeling
Coma
Curse of the Demon
The Dead Zone
Don't Look Now
Dracula (1979 version)
Freaks
Fright Night
Ghost Story
The Haunting
The Haunting of Julia

House
House of the Long Shadows
House of Wax
House on Haunted Hill
Lady in White
Link
Magic
Poltergeist
Rosemary's Baby
Something Wicked This Way Comes
Strait-Jacket
13 Ghosts
Turn of the Screw

SCIENCE RUNS AMOK _____ HO20
See also: Fictional Character Check List HF10 The Frankenstein Monster; SF5 Science Gone Wrong

The Abominable Dr. Phibes
Andy Warhol's Frankenstein
The Ape
Atom Age Vampire
The Brain That Wouldn't Die
The Bride
The Bride of Frankenstein
Circus of Horrors
The Curse of Frankenstein
Daughter of Dr. Jekyll
Deadly Friend
Dr. Jekyll and Mr. Hyde (1920, 1932 & 1941 versions)
Dr. Phibes Rises Again
Eyes Without a Face
Fiend Without a Face
The Fly (1958 & 1986 versions)

The Fly II
Frankenstein (1931 & 1973 versions)
From Beyond
Halloween III: Season of the Witch
The Invisible Man
The Island of Dr. Moreau
Link
The Man They Could Not Hang
The Mind Snatchers
Nightmare Weekend
Re-Animator
Return of the Fly
Scream and Scream Again
Screamers
Son of Frankenstein
Terminal Choice
Watchers

MUTANT MONSTERS _____ HO21

C.H.U.D.
City of the Walking Dead
Class of Nuke 'Em High
The Crazies
The Curse
Cyclops
The Invisible Ray

Mutant
Night of the Creeps
Slithis
Toxic Avenger
Transmutations
Tremors

MAD MACHINERY _____ HO22

Chopping Mall
Christine
Demon Seed

The Lift
Maximum Overdrive
Videodrome

HORROR ANTHOLOGIES _____ HO23

Asylum
Black Sabbath
Cat's Eye
Creepshow
Creepshow 2
Dead of Night (1945)
Dr. Terror's House of Horrors
From Beyond the Grave
The House That Dripped Blood
The Monster Club
Night Gallery

Nightmares
The Offspring
Tales From the Crypt (1972)
Tales From the Crypt (1989)
Tales From the Darkside: The Movie
Tales of Terror
Torture Garden
Trilogy of Terror
Twice-Told Tales
Twilight Zone - The Movie

HORROR FOR LAUGHS _____ HO24

An American Werewolf in London
Andy Warhol's Dracula
Andy Warhol's Frankenstein

Arnold
Basket Case 2
Critters

Critters 2: The Main Course
The Fearless Vampire Killers
Gremlins
— The Little Shop of Horrors (1960
    version)
Love at First Bite
Microwave Massacre
The Monster Squad
Motel Hell
Piranha
The Plumber

Psychos in Love
Return of the Living Dead
Slaughterhouse
The Stuff
Terror at Red Wolf Inn
Theatre of Blood
Toxic Avenger
Transylvania Twist
Tremors
Vamp
Witches' Brew

SEXY HORROR ———————————————————————— HO25

Because of the Cats
Cat People (1982 version)
Demon Seed
The Entity
From Beyond
Gothic

The Haunting of Morella
Humanoids From the Deep
Lair of the White Worm
Lust for a Vampire
The Vampire Lovers

HORROR WITH A BRITISH ACCENT ————————————————— HO26

The Abominable Dr. Phibes
And Now the Screaming Starts
Asylum
The Beast in the Cellar
Bloodbath at the House of Death
Captain Kronos: Vampire Hunter
Circus of Horrors
Conqueror Worm
The Creeping Flesh
The Curse of Frankenstein
The Curse of the Werewolf
Dead of Night (1945)
The Doctor and the Devils
Dr. Phibes Rises Again
Dr. Terror's House of Horrors
The Evil of Frankenstein
From Beyond the Grave
The Ghoul (1933)

The Ghoul (1975)
The Gorgon
The Haunting of Julia
Horror of Dracula
Horror of Frankenstein
Lust for a Vampire
The Mummy (1959 version)
The Picture of Dorian Gray (1945
    version)
Scars of Dracula
Scream and Scream Again
Tales From the Crypt
Terror in the Wax Museum
Theatre of Blood
To the Devil a Daughter
— Turn of the Screw
Village of the Damned
The Watcher in the Woods

PRODUCER CHECK LIST: VAL LEWTON ——————————————— HO36

Bedlam
The Body Snatcher ✔
Cat People (1942 version)
The Curse of the Cat People

I Walked With a Zombie
· Isle of the Dead
The Leopard Man

Chapter Eleven

MUSICALS
(MU)

MGM MUSICALS ——————————————————————————————— **MU1**

An American in Paris
Anchors Aweigh
Babes in Arms
Babes on Broadway
The Band Wagon
The Barkleys of Broadway
Bells Are Ringing
Born to Dance
Brigadoon
Broadway Melody of 1938
Broadway Melody of 1940
Cover Girl
Easter Parade
Gigi
Girl Crazy
Good News
The Great Caruso
The Harvey Girls
High Society
Hit the Deck
In the Good Old Summertime
Invitation to the Dance
It's Always Fair Weather
Kismet
Kiss Me Kate
Les Girls

Lili
Meet Me in St. Louis
Million Dollar Mermaid
Neptune's Daughter
On the Town
The Pirate
Rose Marie
Royal Wedding
Seven Brides for Seven Brothers
Show Boat (1951 version)
Silk Stockings
Singin' in the Rain
Small Town Girl
Strike Up the Band
Summer Stock
That's Entertainment
That's Entertainment, Part II
Three Little Words
Till the Clouds Roll By
Two Girls and a Sailor
The Unsinkable Molly Brown
The Wizard of Oz
Words and Music
Ziegfeld Follies
Ziegfeld Girl

THE BEST OF BROADWAY ——————————————————————————— **MU2**

Annie
The Best Little Whorehouse in Texas
Brigadoon
Bye Bye Birdie
Cabaret
Camelot
Can-Can
Carousel
A Chorus Line
Damn Yankees
Fiddler on the Roof
Finian's Rainbow
Flower Drum Song
42nd Street
Funny Girl
A Funny Thing Happened on the Way
   to the Forum
Grease

Guys and Dolls
Hair
Hello, Dolly!
How to Succeed in Business Without
   Really Trying
Jesus Christ, Superstar
The King and I
Kismet
Kiss Me Kate
A Little Night Music
Mame
Man of La Mancha
The Music Man
My Fair Lady
Oh! Calcutta!
Oklahoma!
Oliver!
The Pajama Game

Purlie Victorious
1776
Show Boat (1936 & 1951 versions)
The Sound of Music

South Pacific
Sweet Charity
West Side Story
The Wiz

GREAT DANCING MUSICALS _____ MU3
See also: Director Check List DT8 Busby Berkeley; Star Check Lists ST2 Fred Astaire, ST81
Gene Kelly

All That Jazz
Best Foot Forward
The Boy Friend
Carmen
A Chorus Line
Dirty Dancing
Flashdance
Footloose
Good News
Invitation to the Dance

Pennies From Heaven
The Red Shoes
Saturday Night Fever
Seven Brides for Seven Brothers
Stormy Weather
Sweet Charity
Tap
That's Dancing
West Side Story

MUSICAL FILMS ABOUT SHOW BIZ _____ MU4
See also: CL7 Show Business Stories, DR12 Backstage Dramas

All That Jazz
Babes in Arms
Babes on Broadway
The Band Wagon
The Barkleys of Broadway
The Boy Friend
Breaking Glass
Broadway Melody
Broadway Melody of 1938
Broadway Melody of 1940
Bye Bye Birdie
Carmen
A Chorus Line
Crossover Dreams
Dames
Eddie and the Cruisers
Eddie and the Cruisers II: Eddie Lives
   Fame
Footlight Parade
For Me and My Gal
42nd Street
Give My Regards to Broad Street
Gold Diggers of 1933
Gold Diggers of 1935
Holiday Inn
The Idolmaker

The Jazz Singer (1927 & 1980 versions)
Light of Day
New York, New York
Phantom of the Paradise
The Rose
Show Boat (1936 & 1951 versions)
Singin' in the Rain
Sparkle
Springtime in the Rockies
A Star Is Born (1954 & 1976 versions)
Starstruck
Staying Alive
Stormy Weather
The Story of Vernon and Irene Castle
Strike Up the Band
Summer Stock
Swing Time
That'll Be the Day
There's No Business Like Show
   Business
Tonight and Every Night
Wasn't That a Time!
White Christmas
Wonder Man
Young Man With a Horn
Ziegfeld Follies

MUSICAL LIFE STORIES _____ MU5

Amadeus (Mozart)
The Benny Goodman Story
Bird (Charlie Parker)
Bound for Glory (Woody Guthrie)
The Buddy Holly Story
Coal Miner's Daughter (Loretta Lynn)

Deep in My Heart (Sigmund Romberg)
The Fabulous Dorseys
Funny Girl (Fanny Brice)
Funny Lady (Fanny Brice)
The Glenn Miller Story
Great Balls of Fire! (Jerry Lee Lewis)

The Great Caruso
The Great Ziegfeld
Gypsy (Gypsy Rose Lee)
Jolson Sings Again
The Jolson Story
La Bamba (Ritchie Valens)
Lady Sings the Blues (Billie Holiday)
Lizstomania
Love Me or Leave Me (Ruth Etting)
Mahler
Night and Day (Cole Porter)
Seven Little Foys (Eddie Foy)
Song of Norway (Edvard Grieg)

A Song to Remember (Frédéric Chopin)
The Sound of Music (Maria von Trapp)
The Story of Vernon and Irene Castle
Sweet Dreams (Patsy Cline)
This Is Elvis
Three Little Words (Bert Kalmar &
    Harry Ruby)
Yankee Doodle Dandy (George M.
    Cohan)
Till the Clouds Roll By (Jerome Kern)
Wagner
Words and Music (Richard Rodgers &
    Lorenz Hart)

MUSICAL AMERICANA ———————————————————— MU6

Bye Bye Birdie
Calamity Jane (1953)
Carousel
Damn Yankees
Easter Parade
Flower Drum Song
Good News
Guys and Dolls
The Harvey Girls
Holiday Inn
Meet Me in St. Louis
The Music Man
Nashville

New York, New York
Oklahoma!
On the Town
Paint Your Wagon
Seven Brides for Seven Brothers
Show Boat (1936 & 1951 versions)
State Fair (1945 & 1962 versions)
Take Me out to the Ball Game
The Unsinkable Molly Brown
West Side Story
White Christmas
Yankee Doodle Dandy

MUSICALS WHICH WON MAJOR OSCARS ———————————— MU7

An American in Paris
Broadway Melody
Cabaret
Funny Girl
Gigi
The Great Ziegfeld
The King and I

Mary Poppins
My Fair Lady
Oliver!
The Sound of Music
West Side Story
Yankee Doodle Dandy

FANTASIES AND FAIRY TALES ———————————————— MU8

Brigadoon
Cabin in the Sky
Camelot
Cinderella (1964 version)
A Connecticut Yankee in King Arthur's
    Court
Doctor Dolittle
Finian's Rainbow
Kismet
Little Shop of Horrors (1986 version)

Mary Poppins
On a Clear Day You Can See Forever
Sergeant Pepper's Lonely Hearts Club
    Band
Tommy
The Wiz
The Wizard of Oz
Xanadu
Yellow Submarine
Yolanda and the Thief

ROCK MUSCIALS _____ MU9
See also: Star Check List ST123 Elvis Presley

Absolute Beginners
Beat Street
The Blues Brothers
Body Rock
Breakin'
Breakin' 2: Electric Boogaloo
Breaking Glass
Bye Bye Birdie
Can't Stop the Music
Dogs in Space
Fame
Get Crazy
The Girl Can't Help It
Give My Regards to Broad Street
Grease
Grease 2
Hair
A Hard Day's Night
The Harder They Come
Head
Help!
The Idolmaker
Jesus Christ, Superstar

Magical Mystery Tour
One-Trick Pony
Phantom of the Paradise
Pink Floyd: The Wall
Purple Rain
Quadrophenia
Roadie
Rock 'n' Roll High School
Rock, Pretty Baby
Rock, Rock, Rock
The Rocky Horror Picture Show
The Rose
Running Out of Luck
A Star Is Born (1976 version)
Starstruck
Tapeheads
That'll Be the Day
Times Square
Tommy
200 Motels
Wild Style
Yellow Submarine

ROCK CONCERT FILMS _____ MU10

The Concert for Bangladesh
Delicate Sound of Thunder
Divine Madness!
Elvis—The 1968 Comeback Special
Gimme Shelter
The Grateful Dead Movie
Heartland Reggae
Jimi Plays Berkeley
Joe Cocker: Mad Dogs and Englishmen
The Last Waltz
Let's Spend the Night Together
The MUSE Concert: No Nukes
Monterey Pop
Motown 25: Yesterday, Today, Forever

Nelson Mandela 70th Birthday Tribute
Rust Never Sleeps
Sign o' the Times
Simon & Garfunkel: The Concert in
   Central Park
Soul to Soul
Stop Making Sense
That Was Rock
U2 Live at Red Rocks "Under a Blood
   Red Sky"
Woodstock
Ziggy Stardust and the Spiders From
   Mars

ROCK DOCUMENTARIES _____ MU11

Bring on the Night
Chuck Berry: Hail! Hail! Rock 'n' Roll
The Compleat Beatles
The Decline of Western Civilization
The Decline of Western Civilization II:
   The Metal Years
Don't Look Back
Elvis '56
Elvis on Tour
Elvis—That's the Way It Is
Imagine: John Lennon

Janis
Jimi Hendrix
The Kids Are Alright
Let It Be
The Song Remains the Same
This Is Elvis
This Is Spinal Tap
25 X 5: The Continuing Adventures of
   the Rolling Stones
U2: Rattle and Hum
X, The Unheard Music

FILMS WITH POP STARS IN NON-MUSICAL ROLES _____ MU12

See also: Star Check Lists ST2 Fred Astaire, ST19 Cher, ST25 Bing Crosby, ST51 Judy Garland, ST81 Gene Kelly, ST105 Bette Midler, ST123 Elvis Presley, ST138 Frank Sinatra, ST146 Barbra Streisand

David Bowie
The Hunger
Into the Night
Just a Gigolo
Labyrinth
The Last Temptation of Christ
The Man Who Fell to Earth
Merry Christmas, Mr. Lawrence
Kris Kristofferson
Alice Doesn't Live Here Anymore
Big Top Pee-wee
Blume in Love
Bring Me the Head of Alfredo Garcia
Convoy
Flashpoint
Heaven's Gate
The Last Movie
Millennium
Pat Garrett and Billy the Kid
Rollover
Semi-Tough
Trouble in Mind
Welcome Home
Sting
The Bride
Brimstone and Treacle
Dune
Julia and Julia
Plenty
Stormy Monday
Others
The Alamo (Frankie Avalon)
Barbarosa (Willie Nelson)
Best Revenge (Levon Helm)
Bloodhounds of Broadway (Madonna)
Buster (Phil Collins)
Captain Newman, M.D. (Bobby Darin)
Carnal Knowledge (Art Garfunkel)
Carny (Robbie Robertson)
Catch-22 (Art Garfunkel)
Caveman (Ringo Starr)
Certain Fury (Irene Cara)
China Gate (Nat King Cole)
Clue (Lee Ving)
Coal Miner's Daughter (Levon Helm)
Cold Feet (Tom Waits)
Conan the Destroyer (Grace Jones)
Corrupt (John Lydon)
Critical Condition (Ruben Blades)
Cry-Baby (Iggy Pop)
Dead Man Out (Ruben Blades)
Desperately Seeking Susan (Madonna)
Disorganized Crime (Ruben Blades)

The Dollmaker (Levon Helm)
Down by Law (John Lurie, Tom Waits)
Dudes (Lee Ving)
The Electric Horseman (Willie Nelson)
End of the Line (Levon Helm)
Enemy Territory (Ray Parker, Jr.)
Escape From New York (Isaac Hayes)
Fatal Beauty (Ruben Blades)
Foxes (Cherie Curie)
Goldilocks and the Three Bears (Carole King)
Gunfight (Johnny Cash)
Hairspray (Ruth Brown, Debby Harry, Sony Bono)
Hamlet (1969 version) (Marianne Faithfull)
The Happy Ending (Robert (Bobby) Darin)
Harry Tracy (Gordon Lightfoot)
Homeboy (Ruben Blades)
How I Won the War (John Lennon)
Huckleberry Finn (Merle Haggard)
I'm Gonna Git You Sucka (Isaac Hayes)
Into the Night (Carl Perkins)
Ironweed (Tom Waits)
Jo Jo Dancer, Your Life Is Calling (Carmen McRae, Billy Eckstine)
Let It Ride (David Johansen)
Let's Get Harry (Glenn Frey)
Lost Angels (Adam Horovitz)
Love at Large (Neil Young)
Mad Max Beyond Thunderdome (Tina Turner)
McVicar (Roger Daltrey)
The Magic Christian (Ringo Starr)
The Milagro Beanfield War (Ruben Blades, Freddy Fender)
Mystery Train (Screamin' Jay Hawkins, Rufus Thomas, Joe Strummer, Tom Waits, Sy Richardson)
The Nightingale (Mick Jagger)
9 to 5 (Dolly Parton)
Nomads (Adam Ant)
North to Alaska (Fabian)
Oh, God! (John Denver)
Pat Garrett and Billy the Kid (Bob Dylan, Rita Coolidge)
The Red Headed Stranger (Willie Nelson)
The Right Stuff (Levon Helm)

Rio Bravo (Rick Nelson)
The Room (Annie Lennox)
Runaway (Gene Simmons)
Scrooged (David Johansen)
Shanghai Surprise (Madonna)
Short Fuse (Art Garfunkel)
Siesta (Grace Jones)
Smooth Talk (Levon Helm)
Staying Together (Levon Helm)
Steel Magnolias (Dolly Parton)
Straight to Hell (Elvis Costello, Dick
    Rude, Joe Strummer, Grace Jones)
Stranger Than Paradise (John Lurie)
Tales From the Darkside: The Movie
    (Deborah Harry, David Johansen)

Thief (Willie Nelson)
To Sir, With Love (Lulu, Michael Des
    Barres)
Tremors (Reba McIntire)
True Grit (Glen Campbell)
Union City (Debby Harry)
Vamp (Grace Jones)
Vibes (Cyndi Lauper)
Videodrome (Debbie Harry)
A View to a Kill (Grace Jones)
The Wackiest Ship in the Army (Rick
    Nelson)
Wanted: Dead or Alive (Gene
    Simmons)
Who's That Girl (Madonna)

ALL BLACK MUSICALS _____ **MU13**

Cabin in the Sky
The Duke Is Tops

Lost in the Stars
Stormy Weather

MUSICAL REMAKES OF NON-MUSICAL FILMS _____ **MU14**

Bundle of Joy
Cabaret High Society
In the Good Old Summertime
Kiss Me Kate
A Little Night Music
Little Shop of Horrors (1986 version)
Mame

Miss Sadie Thompson
My Fair Lady
Oliver!
Phantom of the Paradise Scrooge
Silk Stockings
A Star Is Born (1954 version)
Sweet Charity

MUSICAL REVUES _____ **MU15**

Glorifying the American Girl
The King of Jazz
Stage Door Canteen
Thank Your Lucky Stars

That's Dancing
That's Entertainment
That's Entertainment, Part II
Thousands Cheer

STRANGEST MUSICALS _____ **MU16**

Absolute Beginners
Aria
Le Bal
Bugsy Malone
The Fastest Guitar Alive
Forbidden Zone
The Last Dragon
The Little Prince
Little Shop of Horrors (1986 version)

Murder at the Vanities
One From the Heart
Pennies From Heaven
Pink Floyd: The Wall
The Rocky Horror Picture Show
Sergeant Pepper's Lonely Hearts Club
    Band
1776
The Umbrellas of Cherbourg

NON-SINGING ACTORS IN MUSICAL ROLES ——————————— MU17

The Best Little Whorehouse in Texas
  (Burt Reynolds)
Camelot (Richard Harris & Vanessa
  Redgrave)
Doctor Dolittle (Rex Harrison)
Guys and Dolls (Marlon Brando)
Idiot's Delight (Clark Gable)

A Little Night Music (Elizabeth Taylor)
Man of La Mancha (Peter O'Toole &
  Sophia Loren)
My Fair Lady (Rex Harrison)
Paint Your Wagon (Clint Eastwood &
  Lee Marvin)
Yankee Doodle Dandy (James Cagney)

Chapter Twelve

MYSTERY/SUSPENSE
(MY)

CLASSIC FILM NOIR _____ MY1

The Asphalt Jungle
The Big Combo
The Big Heat
The Big Sleep (1946 version)
Born to Kill
Cat People (1942 version)
Caught
The Chase (1946)
Cornered
Criss Cross
Crossfire
Cry Danger
D.O.A. (1949 version)
The Dark Mirror
Dark Passage
Dead Reckoning
Deadline at Dawn
Desperate
Detour
Double Indemnity
Follow Me Quietly
Force of Evil
Gilda
The Glass Key
He Walked by Night
High Sierra
His Kind of Woman
The Human Gorilla
I Wake Up Screaming
In a Lonely Place
Journey Into Fear (1943 version)
Key Largo
Killer Bait
The Killing
Knock on any Door

The Lady From Shanghai
Laura (1944)
The Maltese Falcon
Mildred Pierce
Moonrise
Murder My Sweet
The Narrow Margin
The Night of the Hunter
On Dangerous Ground
Out of the Past
The Postman Always Rings Twice (1946
    version)
Private Hell 36
The Racket
Scarlet Street
The Set-Up
Shack Out on 101
Slightly Scarlet
Sorry, Wrong Number
Split Second
The Strange Love of Martha Ivers
The Stranger (1946)
Suddenly
Sunset Boulevard
Sweet Smell of Success
T-Men
They Live by Night
They Won't Believe Me
This Gun for Hire
Touch of Evil
Try and Get Me
While the City Sleeps
White Heat
The Window
You Only Live Once

CONTEMPORARY FILM NOIR _____ MY2

Against All Odds (1984)
The American Friend
Angel Heart
The Big Easy
Blade Runner
Blood Simple
Blue Velvet
Body Heat
Bring Me the Head of Alfredo Garcia

Cape Fear
Chinatown
Cutter's Way
D.O.A. (1988 version)
Dance With a Stranger
The Driver
Experiment in Terror
Eyes of Laura Mars
52 Pick-up

Hustle
Kill Me Again
The Manchurian Candidate
Manhunter
Night Moves
No Way Out (1987)
Performance
Stormy Monday

Taxi Driver
Tequila Sunrise
To Live and Die in L.A.
True Believer
True Confessions
Union City
Who'll Stop the Rain

WOMEN IN DANGER _____ MY3

Apology
Berserk!
Beware, My Lovely
Blue Steel
Candles at Nine
Caught
Charade
The Collector
The Cradle Will Fall
Dead of Winter
Dial M for Murder
Experiment Perilous
Eyes of Laura Mars
Gaslight
Glitz
The House on Carroll Street
Impulse
Jack's Back
Jagged Edge
Jamaica Inn (1939 & 1985 versions)
Jane Doe
Klute
Lady in a Cage

Laura
Love From a Stranger
Masquerade
Midnight Lace
The Morning After
Ms. 45
Night Watch
No Way To Treat a Lady
Notorious
The Plumber
Positive I.D.
Rider on the Rain
Scream of Fear
Secret Beyond the Door
See No Evil
Sidney Sheldon's Bloodline
Someone to Watch Over Me
Sorry, Wrong Number
The Spiral Staircase
A Stranger Is Watching
Suspicion (1941 & 1987 versions)
The Very Edge
Wait Until Dark

TOUGH DAMES _____ MY4

Body Heat
The Dark Mirror
Dead Reckoning
Detour
Double Indemnity
Gilda
Kill Me Again

Killer Bait
Last Embrace
Niagara
Scarlet Street
Sea of Love
To Have and Have Not

SUSPENSE AND ROMANCE _____ MY5

Against All Odds (1984)
Betrayed
The Big Easy
Body Double
Body Heat
Cat Chaser
Double Indemnity
Dressed to Kill
Eyewitness
The Fourth Man

Jagged Edge
Klute
Laura
Marnie
Masquerade
The Morning After
No Mercy
No Way Out (1987)
Notorious
Obsession

Out of the Past
The Postman Always Rings Twice (1946
    & 1981 versions)
Sea of Love
Someone to Watch Over Me
Spellbound
Still of the Night

Suspicion (1941 & 1987 versions)
The Tamarind Seed
They're Playing With Fire
Thief of Hearts
The Thomas Crown Affair
To Catch a Thief
Vertigo

POLITICAL INTRIGUE _____ MY6

All the President's Men
The Amateur
Another Country
Arabesque
Billion Dollar Brain
Black Sunday (1977)
The Black Windmill
Blow Out
The Boys From Brazil
Cornered
A Dandy in Aspic
Dark Journey
The Day of the Jackal
Defense of the Realm
The Eagle Has Landed
The Eiger Sanction
Executive Action
Eye of the Needle
The Falcon and the Snowman
Foreign Correspondent
The Formula
The Fourth War
Funeral in Berlin
The General Died at Dawn
Gorky Park
Half Moon Street
The Holcroft Covenant
Hotel Reserve
The House on Carroll Street
The Hunt for Red October
Ice Station Zebra
The Ipcress File
The Jigsaw Man
Journey Into Fear
Keeping Track

The Killer Elite
Last Embrace
The Little Drummer Girl
The Looking Glass War
The Mackintosh Man
The Man Who Knew Too Much (1934 &
    1955 versions)
The Manchurian Candidate
Miracle Mile
No Way Out (1987)
Notorious
The Odessa File
The Osterman Weekend
The Package
The Parallax View
Philby, Burgess and Maclean: Spy
    Scandal of the Century
The President's Plane Is Missing
The Quiller Memorandum
Sabotage
Saboteur
The Salamander
The Secret Agent
Spy in Black
The Spy Who Came in From the Cold
The Stranger (1946)
The Tamarind Seed
Target
Telefon
The Third Man
The 39 Steps (1935 & 1978 versions)
Three Days of the Condor
Topaz
Torn Curtain
Winter Kills

WRONG MAN THRILLERS _____ MY7

The Bedroom Window
Criminal Court
Cry Danger
Frenzy
Hit and Run
I Confess
I Wake Up Screaming
An Innocent Man
Jack's Back
The Man Who Knew Too Much (1934 &
    1955 versions)

Marathon Man
Mirage
North by Northwest
Out of Bounds
The Paris Express
Pendulum
Physical Evidence
Saboteur
Slamdance
Star of Midnight
The Stranger on the Third Floor

10 Rillington Place
They Made Me a Criminal
They Won't Believe Me
The 39 Steps (1935 & 1978 versions)

Three Days of the Condor
The Wrong Man
Young and Innocent

TRUE-LIFE SUSPENSE _____ MY8
See also: DR6 True-Life Contemporary Drama

Adam
Agatha
Beyond Reasonable Doubt
The Boston Strangler
The Brink's Job
Buster
Dance With a Stranger
Fatal Vision

Hammett
Hide in Plain Sight
Philby, Burgess and Maclean: Spy
   Scandal of the Century
Robbery
10 Rillington Place
The Thin Blue Line
Without a Trace

CAT AND MOUSE GAMES _____ MY9

Apartment Zero
Bad Influence
Best Seller
Black Widow
Charley Varrick
Criminal Law
Deathtrap
Duel
F/X
The Formula
Highpoint

House of Games
Internal Affairs
Into the Fire
The Last of Sheila
Manhunter
Miami Blues
Rope
The Silent Partner
Sleuth
Strangers on a Train

PRIVATE EYES AND OTHER DETECTIVES _____ MY10
See also: Fictional Character Check Lists HF4 Charlie Chan, HF5 Nick & Nora Charles,
HF8 Bulldog Drummond, HF14 Sherlock Holmes, HF21 The Saint; Writer Check Lists WR2
Raymond Chandler, WR3 Agatha Christie, WR9 Dashiell Hammett, WR19 Ross MacDonald,
WR24 Micky Spillane

Angel Heart
The Big Fix
Chinatown
Columbo: Prescription Murder
Everybody Wins
From Hollywood to Deadwood
Gotham
In the Heat of the Night
The Kennel Murder Case
Kill Me Again

Klute
Lady in Cement
The Late Show
Love at Large
Moonlighting (1985)
Night Moves
Shamus
Sunburn
Tony Rome
An Unsuitable Job for a Woman

AMATEUR SLEUTHS _____ MY11

Blind Date (1984)
Blow Out
Blowup
Blue Velvet
Coma
Compromising Positions
The Conversation

Deadline at Dawn
The Detective (1954)
Dressed to Kill (1980)
Gumshoe
Her Alibi
Mike's Murder
The Naked Face

The Name of the Rose
A Night to Remember (1942)
The Parallax View
Rear Window

Rope
Stunts
True Believer
The Velvet Touch

WHODUNITS _____ MY12

And Then There Were None
Appointment With Death
The Body in the Library
Death on the Nile
Evil Under the Sun
Killjoy
The Last of Sheila
The List of Adrian Messenger

Murder at the Vanities
A Murder Is Announced
Murder on the Orient Express
A Pocketful of Rye
Rehearsal for Murder
Ten Little Indians (1975 version)
The Thirteenth Guest

CRAZY KILLERS _____ MY13

Blue Steel
The Boston Strangler
City in Fear
Criminal Law
Dressed to Kill (1980)
Fatal Attraction
Follow Me Quietly
Frenzy
Glitz
Henry: Portrait of a Serial Killer
The Housekeeper
Jack's Back
The Killer Inside Me

The Lodger
M (1931 version)
Manhunter
No Way To Treat a Lady
Play Misty for Me
Relentless
The Stepfather
Stepfather II
Strangers on a Train
Targets
Ten to Midnight
White of the Eye

SUSPENSE IN THE FAMILY WAY _____ MY14

The Bad Seed
The Cold Room
The Dark Mirror
Don't Look Now
Fatal Attraction
Murder by Natural Causes
Party Line
Reflections of Murder
Road to Salina
Scalpel

Secret Ceremony
Shadow of a Doubt
The Stepfather
Stepfather II
Torment
True Confessions
Where Are the Children?
White of the Eye
Winter Kills
Without a Trace

BRITISH MYSTERY/SUSPENSE _____ MY15
See also: Fictional Character Check List HF 14 Sherlock Holmes

And Then There Were None
Bellman and True
Candles at Nine
The Cat and the Canary (1977 version)
Dance With a Stranger
The Dark Corner
The Detective (1954)
Endless Night

The Evil Mind
Gumshoe
Hotel Reserve
Kind Hearts and Coronets
The Lady Vanishes (1938 version)
The Ladykillers
The Lavender Hill Mob
The Long Dark Hall

The Night Has Eyes
Number 17
Odd Man Out
Philby, Burgess and Maclean: Spy
  Scandal of the Century
Robbery
Sabotage
Scream of Fear
Seance on a Wet Afternoon
The Secret Agent

Sleuth
The Spy in Black
Stormy Monday
10 Rillington Place
The 39 Steps (1935 version)
Tiger Bay
An Unsuitable Job for a Woman
The Whistle Blower
Young and Innocent

SUSPENSE IN OTHER FOREIGN SETTINGS ───────────────── MY16

The American Friend
Cat Chaser
Clean Slate (Coup de Torchon)
Confidentially Yours
Dear Detective
Death Watch
Diabolique
Diva
The Fourth Man
Frantic (1958)
Frantic (1988)
Gorky Park
Heatwave

High and Low
The Hostage Tower
The Man on the Eiffel Tower
The Mighty Quinn
Off Limits (1988)
One Deadly Summer
The Plumber
Rififi
Road Games
Sincerely, Charlotte
The Wages of Fear
Wedding in Blood
Z

COMIC MYSTERIES ─────────────────────────────── MY17
See also: CO10 Crime and Suspense Comedies

Arsenic and Old Lace
Bullshot
Clue
Dead Men Don't Wear Plaid
Hanky Panky
Her Alibi
Kind Hearts and Coronets
Lady of Burlesque
The Ladykillers
The Lavender Hill Mob
Legal Eagles
The Mad Miss Manton

The Man With Bogart's Face
Mr. and Mrs. North
Murder by Death
A Night to Remember (1942)
Penn and Teller Get Killed
Scandalous
Star of Midnight
Sunset
The Thin Man (series)
The Trouble With Harry
Who Done It?
Without a Clue

HEISTS ────────────────────────────────────── MY18

The Anderson Tapes
The Asphalt Jungle
Bellman and True
Big Deal on Madonna Street
Bob le Flambeur
The Brink's Job
Buster
Charley Varrick
Dead Heat on a Merry-Go-Round
Diamonds

Disorganized Crime
$ (Dollars)
11 Harrowhouse
A Fish Called Wanda
Gambit
The Getaway
Going in Style
The Great Train Robbery
Happy New Year (1973 & 1987 versions)
The Hot Rock

How to Beat the High Cost of Living
The Killing
Lady Ice
The Lavender Hill Mob
Loophole
Malcolm

Ocean's Eleven
Rififi
Robbery
The Thomas Crown Affair
Thunderbolt and Lightfoot
Topkapi

Chapter Thirteen

SCIENCE FICTION/FANTASY
(SF)

CLASSIC 50S SCI-FI _____ **SF1**

The Blob
The Brain From Planet Arous
The Crawling Eye
The Creature From the Black Lagoon
The Day the Earth Stood Still
Destination Moon
Earth vs. the Flying Saucers
Fiend Without a Face
The Fly (1958 version)
Forbidden Planet
4D Man
I Married a Monster From Outer Space
The Incredible Shrinking Man

Invaders From Mars (1953 version)
Invasion of the Body Snatchers (1956 version)
It Came From Outer Space
Journey to the Center of the Earth
Kronos
On the Beach
Rocket Ship X-M
The Thing (From Another World)
This Island Earth
Them!
War of the Worlds
When Worlds Collide

CLASSIC PRE-50S SCI-FI/FANTASY _____ **SF2**

Angel on My Shoulder
Beauty and the Beast (1946 version)
The Bishop's Wife
Blood of a Poet
The Devil and Daniel Webster
Dr. Cyclops
Frankenstein (1931 version)
The Ghost and Mrs. Muir
The Ghost Goes West

Here Comes Mr. Jordan
I Married a Witch
King Kong (1933 version)
Lost Horizon
Metropolis (1926 edition)
The Testament of Dr. Mabuse
Things to Come
Topper

OUTER (AND INNER) SPACE TRAVEL _____ **SF3**

Alien
Aliens
The Angry Red Planet
At the Earth's Core
The Black Hole
Destination Moon
Explorers
Fantastic Voyage
First Men in the Moon
Flight to Mars
Innerspace
Journey to the Center of the Earth (1959 & 1989 versions)
Journey to the Far Side of the Sun

Marooned
Rocket Ship X-M
Saturn 3
Silent Running
SpaceCamp
Spacehunter: Adventures in the Forbbiden Zone
Star Trek (series)
This Island Earth
20,000 Leagues Under the Sea
2001: A Space Odyssey
2010: The Year We Make Contact
Voyage to the Bottom of the Sea

TIME TRAVEL _____ SF4

Back to the Future
Back to the Future, Part II
Biggles
Bill and Ted's Excellent Adventure
A Connecticut Yankee in King Arthur's
    Court
Daleks: Invasion Earth 2150 A.D.
Dinosaurus!
The Final Countdown
Highlander
The Land That Time Forgot
The Lost World (1925 version)

Millennium
The People That Time Forgot
The Philadelphia Experiment
Slaughterhouse Five
Sleeper
Somewhere in Time
Star Trek IV: The Voyage Home
Time After Time
Time Bandits
The Time Machine
Timerider
Where Time Began

SCIENCE GONE WRONG _____ SF5
See also: HO20 Science Runs Amok

Altered States
Android
The Andromeda Strain
The Asphyx
Brainstorm
Coma
Deathwatch
Dr. Cyclops
Dreamscape
Embryo

The Fly (1958 & 1986 versions)
The Fly II
4D Man
Looker
Metropolis
Spontaneous Combustion
The Terminal Man
Wargames
X: The Man With the X-Ray Eyes

MAD MACHINES _____ SF6

Colossus: The Forbin Project
Demon Seed
Futureworld
Runaway

Saturn 3
2001: A Space Odyssey
Westworld

SCI-FI DISASTER _____ SF7

The Andromeda Strain
The Day of the Triffids
The Day the Earth Caught Fire
Meteor

The Swarm
War of the Worlds
When Worlds Collide

SURVIVAL ADVENTURES _____ SF8

After the Fall of New York
The Andromeda Strain
Cherry 2000
Endgame
Enemy Mine
Escape From New York
Exterminators of the Year 3000
Firebird 2015 A.D.
Future-Kill

The Last Starfighter
Logan's Run
Planet of the Apes (series)
Quintet
Soylent Green
W
Warlords of the 21st Century
Warriors of the Wasteland
Zardoz

ALIEN VISITORS _____ SF9

The Blob
The Brain From Planet Arous
The Brother From Another Planet
Close Encounters of the Third Kind
Cocoon
Cocoon: The Return
Communion
The Crawling Eye
The Day the Earth Stood Still
The Day Time Ended
E.T. The Extra-Terrestrial
Earth Girls Are Easy
Earth vs. the Flying Saucers
I Married a Monster From Outer Space

Invaders From Mars (1953 & 1985
  versions)
Invasion of the Body Snatchers (1956 &
  1978 versions)
It Came From Outer Space
The Man Who Fell to Earth
Starman
Strange Invaders
They Live
The Thing
The Thing (From Another World)
This Island Earth
Village of the Damned
War of the Worlds
Wavelength

MUTANT MONSTERS _____ SF10

Creature From the Black Lagoon
Empire of the Ants
Food of the Gods
Godzilla (series)
Gorgo
The Hideous Sun Demon

It Came From Beneath the Sea
King Kong
Mysterious Island
Prophecy
Them!

FUTURE WARS AGAINST DICTATORS _____ SF11

Brazil
Dune
The Empire Strikes Back
Escape 2000
Fahrenheit 451
The Last Chase
1984

Return of the Jedi
Rollerball
Running Man
Star Wars
THX 1138
Tron

AFTER THE HOLOCAUST _____ SF12

After the Fall of New York
Aftermath
A Boy and His Dog
Creation of the Humanoids
Cyborg
Damnation Alley
The Day After
Glen and Randa
Last Woman on Earth

Lord of the Flies
Night of the Comet
On the Beach
Planet of the Apes (series)
The Quiet Earth
Testament
Things to Come
Threads
Virus

FAMILY SCI-FI/FANTASY _____ SF13
See also: FA8 Family Sci-Fi/Fantasy

The Adventures of Baron Munchausen
Aurora Encounter
Battle for the Planet of the Apes
Beneath the Planet of the Apes

The Black Hole
The Blue Bird (1940 version)
The Brothers Lionheart
Clash of the Titans

Conquest of the Planet of the Apes
The Dark Crystal
The Day the Earth Stood Still
E.T. The Extra-Terrestrial
The Empire Strikes Back
Escape From the Planet of the Apes
Explorers
From the Earth to the Moon
The Hobbit
Journey to the Center of the Earth (1959
   & 1989 versions)
King Kong (1933 version)
The Land of Faraway
Labyrinth
Laserblast
The Last Starfighter
Legend
Lord of the Rings
Making Contact
The Man Who Could Work Miracles
Masters of the Universe
The NeverEnding Story

Planet of the Apes
Return of the Jedi
Return to Oz
The 7 Faces of Dr. Lao
The 7th Voyage of Sinbad
Something Wicked This Way Comes
Space Raiders
Spaced Invaders
Spacehunter: Adventures in the
   Forbidden Zone
Star Trek (series)
Star Wars
Starchaser: The Legend of Orion
The Time Machine
Transformers
Tron
20,000 Leagues Under the Sea
The War of the Worlds
The Watcher in the Woods
Willow
The Wizard of Oz
Wizards

SPECTACULAR SETS _____ SF14

The Adventures of Baron Munchausen
Batman (1989)
The Black Hole
Blade Runner
Brazil

Legend
Metropolis
Things to Come
Transatlantic Tunnel

OSCAR-WINNING SPECIAL EFFECTS _____ SF15

Alien
Destination Moon
Dr. Cyclops
E.T. The Extra-Terrestrial
The Empire Strikes Back
Fantastic Voyage
Logan's Run
Marooned

Reap the Wild Wind
Star Wars
Superman
The Time Machine
tom thumb
20,000 Leagues Under the Sea
2001: A Space Odyssey
When Worlds Collide

SPECIAL EFFECTS MILESTONES _____ SF16

An American Werewolf in London
Close Encounters of the Third Kind
The Lost World (1925 version)
King Kong (1933 version)
Metropolis (1926 edition)

Star Wars
2001: A Space Odyssey
Them!
Tron

FUTURE COPS & ROBBERS _____ SF17

Alien Nation
Blade Runner
A Clockwork Orange
Crime Zone
The Hidden
The Killings at Outpost Zeta

Outland
Runaway
Slipstream
Space Rage
Trancers

JAPANESE SCI-FI _____ SF18

Dagora, the Space Monster
Ghidrah, the Three-Headed Monster
Godzilla, King of the Monsters
Godzilla, 1985
Godzilla on Monster Island
Godzilla vs. Megalon
Godzilla vs. Monster Zero
Godzilla vs. Mothra
Gorath

The H-Man
The Human Vapor
The Last War
Mothra
The Mysterians
Rodan
Terror of Mechagodzilla
Virus

SCIENCE FICTION WITH A FOREIGN ACCENT _____ SF19
See also: SF18 Japanese Sci-Fi

Alphaville
The Asphyx
Attack of the Robots
Barbarella
Biggles
Daleks: Invasion Earth 2150 A.D.
The Day of the Triffids
The Day the Earth Caught Fire
Deathwatch
Le Dernier Combat

Dr. Who and the Daleks
Fantastic Planet
Journey to the Far Side of the Sun
The Last Days of Man on Earth
Man Facing Southeast
The Quatermass Conclusion
Village of the Damned
Threads
Zardoz

SCI-FI HORROR _____ SF20

Alien
Alien Predators
Aliens
Altered States
Creature
The Fly (1986 version)
The Fly II
Galaxy of Terror

The Island of Dr. Moreau
Lifeforce
Phase IV
Star Crystal
Terrorvision
The Thing
Xtro

SCI-FI SPOOFS _____ SF21

The Adventures of Buckaroo Banzai
   Across the 8th Dimension
Dark Star
Death Race 2000
Earth Girls Are Easy
Flash Gordon
Galaxina
Heartbeeps
The Ice Pirates
The Incredible Shrinking Woman
Innerspace

The Jet Benny Show
The Last Days of Man on Earth
The Man With Two Brains
Monster in the Closet
Night of the Comet
Really Weird Tales
Simon
Sleeper
Spaceballs
Strange Invaders
The Tenth Victim

SEXY SCI-FI/FANTASY _____ SF22

Barbarella
A Boy and His Dog
Demon Seed

Galaxina
The Invasion of the Bee Girls
Liquid Sky

SCI-FI CHECK LIST: CLASSIC SERIES _____ SF23

Planet of the Apes
  Planet of the Apes
  Beneath the Planet of the Apes
  Escape From the Planet of the Apes
  Conquest of the Planet of the Apes
  Battle for the Planet of the Apes
Star Trek
  The Motion Picture

  II: The Wrath of Khan
  III: The Search for Spock
  IV: The Voyage Home
  V: The Final Frontier
Star Wars
  Star Wars
  The Empire Strikes Back
  Return of the Jedi

Chapter Fourteen

STAR CHECK LISTS (ST)

STARS CHECK LIST: ABBOTT & COSTELLO _____ ST1

Abbott and Costello in Hollywood
Abbott and Costello Meet Captain Kidd
Abbott and Costello Meet Dr. Jekyll and
  Mr. Hyde
Abbott and Costello Meet Frankenstein
Abbott and Costello Meet the Killer,
  Boris Karloff
Africa Screams

Buck Privates
Hit the Ice
Hold That Ghost
Jack and the Beanstalk (1952 version)
The Naughty Nineties
The Time of Their Lives
Who Done It?

Woody Allen _See:_ **Director Check List: DT1 Woody Allen**

STAR CHECK LIST: FRED ASTAIRE _____ ST2
See also: CL15 Memorable Screen Teams—Fred Astaire & Ginger Rogers

The Amazing Dobermans
Ghost Story
On the Beach
The Towering Inferno

MUSICALS
The Band Wagon
The Barkleys of Broadway
Belle of New York
Broadway Melody of 1940
Carefree
Damsel in Distress
Dancing Lady
Easter Parade
Finian's Rainbow
Flying Down to Rio
Follow the Fleet
Funny Face
The Gay Divorcee

Holiday Inn
Let's Dance
Roberta
Royal Wedding
Second Chorus
Shall We Dance
Silk Stockings
The Sky's the Limit
The Story of Vernon and Irene Castle
Swing Time
That's Dancing
That's Entertainment
That's Entertainment, Part II
Three Little Words
Top Hat
Yolanda and the Thief
You Were Never Lovelier
You'll Never Get Rich
Ziegfeld Follies (with Gene Kelly)

STAR CHECK LIST: GENE AUTRY _____ ST3

The Big Show
The Big Sombrero
Blue Canadian Rockies
Boots and Saddles
Call of the Canyon
Cow Town
Down Mexico Way
Git Along, Little Dogies
Heart of the Rio Grande
The Hills of Utah
In Old Santa Fe
Last of the Pony Riders
The Man From Music Mountain

Man of the Frontier
Melody Ranch
Night Stage to Galveston
The Old Barn Dance
The Old Corral
On Top of Old Smoky
Phantom Empire (serial)
Prairie Moon
Radio Ranch (condensed version of
  . Phantom Empire serial)
Ride, Ranger, Ride
Riders of the Whistling Pines
Ridin' on a Rainbow

Robin Hood of Texas
Rootin' Tootin' Rhythm
Round-Up Time in Texas
Saginaw Trail
Sioux City Sue
South of the Border

Valley of Fire
Winning of the West

NON-WESTERN
Manhattan Merry-Go-Round

Dan Aykroyd *See*: **CO13 The Alumni of Saturday Night Live**
Lauren Bacall *See*: **CL15 Memorable Screen Teams—Humphrey Bogart &**
   Lauren Bacall

STAR CHECK LIST: BRIGITTE BARDOT _____ ST4

A Coeur Joie
And God Created Woman (1957 version)
The Bride Is Much Too Beautiful
Contempt
Dear Brigitte
Doctor at Sea
The Legend of Frenchie King

Mademoiselle Striptease
Ms. Don Juan
Ravishing Idiot
Le Repos du Guerrier
Shalako
A Very Private Affair
Voulez-Vous Danser Avec Moi?

STAR CHECK LIST: WARREN BEATTY _____ ST5

Bonnie and Clyde
Dick Tracy*
$ (Dollars)
George Stevens: A Filmmaker's Journey
Heaven Can Wait**
Ishtar
Lilith

McCabe and Mrs. Miller
The Parallax View
Reds*
The Roman Spring of Mrs. Stone
Shampoo
Splendor in the Grass

*also director
**also co-director

STAR CHECK LIST: JEAN-PAUL BELMONDO _____ ST6

Breathless (1959 version)
Casino Royale
High Heels
Le Magnifique

Pierrot le Fou
Un Singe En Hiver
Two Women

Jim Belushi *See*: **CO13 The Alumni of Saturday Night Live**
John Belushi *See*: **CO13 The Alumni of Saturday Night Live**

STAR CHECK LIST: INGRID BERGMAN _____ ST7

Adam Had Four Sons
Arch of Triumph
Autumn Sonata
The Bells of St. Mary's
Cactus Flower
Casablanca
Doctor Jekyll and Mr. Hyde (1941
   version)

Elena and Her Men
Europa '51
Fear
From The Mixed-Up Files Of Mrs. Basil
   E. Frankenweiler
Gaslight
Goodbye Again
Indiscreet

The Inn of the Sixth Happiness
Intermezzo
Joan of Arc
June Night
A Matter of Time
Murder on the Orient Express
Notorious

Spellbound
Stromboli
Swedenhielms
Under Capricorn
Voyage to Italy
A Walk in the Spring Rain
A Woman Called Golda

STAR CHECK LIST: HUMPHREY BOGART ————————————————— ST8

The African Queen
Angels With Dirty Faces
The Barefoot Contessa
Beat the Devil
The Big Sleep
The Caine Mutiny
Call It Murder
Casablanca
Dark Passage
Dark Victory
Dead End
Dead Reckoning
The Desperate Hours
The Enforcer (1951)
The Harder They Fall
High Sierra
In a Lonely Place
Key Largo

Knock on Any Door
The Left Hand of God
The Maltese Falcon
Marked Woman
The Oklahoma Kid
Passage to Marseilles
The Petrified Forest
The Roaring Twenties
Sabrina
Sahara
Sirocco
Stand-In
Thank Your Lucky Stars
They Drive by Night
To Have and Have Not
Tokyo Joe
The Treasure of the Sierra Madre
We're No Angels (1955 version)

STAR CHECK LIST: SONIA BRAGA ———————————————————————— ST9

Doña Flor & Her Two Husbands
Gabriela
I Love You
Kiss of the Spider Woman

Lady on the Bus
The Milagro Beanfield War
Moon Over Parador

STAR CHECK LIST: MARLON BRANDO ———————————————————— ST10

Apocalypse Now
The Appaloosa
Bedtime Story
Burn!
The Chase (1966)
Desiree
A Dry White Season
The Formula
The Fugitive Kind
The Godfather
Guys and Dolls
Julius Caesar (1953 version)
Last Tango in Paris
The Men
The Missouri Breaks

Morituri
Mutiny on the Bounty (1962 version)
The Nightcomers
On the Waterfront
One-Eyed Jacks
Reflections in a Golden Eye
Sayonara
A Streetcar Named Desire
Superman
Teahouse of the August Moon
The Ugly American
Viva Zapata!
The Wild One
The Young Lions

STAR CHECK LIST: JEFF BRIDGES _____ **ST11**

Against All Odds (1984)
Bad Company
Cold Feet
Cutter's Way
Eight Million Ways to Die
The Fabulous Baker Boys
Fat City
Hearts of the West
Heaven's Gate
Jagged Edge
King Kong (1976 version)
Kiss Me Goodbye
The Last American Hero

The Last Picture Show
The Last Unicorn (character voice)
The Morning After
Nadine
Rapunzel
See You in the Morning
Starman
Stay Hungry
Thunderbolt and Lightfoot
Tron
Tucker: The Man and His Dream
Winter Kills
The Yin and Yang of Mr. Go

STAR CHECK LIST: CHARLES BRONSON _____ **ST12**

Assassination
Borderline
Breakheart Pass
Breakout
Caboblanco
Chato's Land
Chino
Cold Sweat
Death Hunt
Death Wish (series)
The Dirty Dozen
Drum Beat
The Evil That Men Do
The Family (1970)
The Great Escape
Hard Times
Honor Among Thieves
House of Wax
Jubal
Kid Galahad
Kinjite: Forbidden Subjects
Lola (1969)
Love and Bullets
The Magnificent Seven

Master of the World
The Mechanic
Messenger of Death
Mr. Majestyk
Murphy's Law
Never So Few
Once Upon a Time in the West
Pat and Mike
Raid on Entebbe
Red Sun
Rider on the Rain
Run of the Arrow
St. Ives
The Sandpiper
Showdown at Boot Hill
Soldiers of Fortune
Someone Behind the Door
The Stone Killer
Telefon
10 to Midnight
This Property Is Condemned
Villa Rides!
The White Buffalo

Mel Brooks *See*: **Director Check List: DT13 Mel Brooks**

STAR CHECK LIST: RICHARD BURTON _____ **ST13**
See also: CL15 Memorable Screen Teams: Richard Burton & Elizabeth Taylor

Absolution
Alexander the Great
Anne of the Thousand Days
The Assassination of Trotsky
Becket
Bluebeard
Breakthrough
Brief Encounter (1974 version)
Circle of Two
Cleopatra (1963)

Divorce His, Divorce Hers
Doctor Faustus
Equus
Exorcist II: The Heretic
Hammersmith Is Out
Ice Palace
The Longest Day
Look Back in Anger
Massacre in Rome
The Medusa Touch

The Night of the Iguana
1984
Raid on Rommel
The Robe
The Sandpiper
The Spy Who Came in From the Cold

The Taming of the Shrew
Under Milk Wood
Wagner
Where Eagles Dare
Who's Afraid of Virginia Woolf?
The Wild Geese

STAR CHECK LIST: JAMES CAGNEY _____ ST14

Angels With Dirty Faces
Blood on the Sun
Each Dawn I Die
Footlight Parade
Great Guy
Kiss Tomorrow Goodbye
Love Me or Leave Me
A Midsummer Night's Dream (1935
    version)
Mister Roberts
Never Steal Anything Small
The Oklahoma Kid

One, Two, Three
The Public Enemy
Ragtime
The Roaring Twenties
The Seven Little Foys
Something to Sing About
The Strawberry Blonde
13 Rue Madeleine
The Time of Your Life
What Price Glory (1952 version)
White Heat
Yankee Doodle Dandy

STAR CHECK LIST: MICHAEL CAINE _____ ST15

Alfie
Ashanti—Land of No Mercy
Battle of Britain
Beyond the Limit
Beyond the Poseidon Adventure
Billion Dollar Brain
The Black Windmill
Blame It on Rio
A Bridge Too Far
California Suite
Deathtrap
The Destructors
Dirty, Rotten Scoundrels
Dressed to Kill (1980)
The Eagles Has Landed
Educating Rita
The Fourth Protocol
Funeral in Berlin
Gambit
Half Moon Street
The Hand
Hannah and Her Sisters
Harry and Walter Go to New York
The Holcroft Covenant
The Ipcress File

The Island
Jaws: The Revenge
The Jigsaw Man
The Last Valley
The Man Who Would Be King
Mona Lisa
Pulp
The Romantic Englishwoman
A Shock to the System
Silver Bears
Sleuth
Surrender
The Swarm
Sweet Liberty
Too Late the Hero
Victory
Water
The Whistle Blower
The Wilby Conspiracy
Without a Clue
Woman Times Seven
The Wrong Box
X, Y and Zee
Zulu

John Candy *See*: **CO14 The Alumni of SCTV**

STAR CHECK LIST: LON CHANEY, SR. _____ ST16

Flesh & Blood (1922)
The Hunchback of Notre Dame (1923
    version)

Nomads of the North
Oliver Twist (1922 version)
Outside the Law

The Phantom of the Opera (1925 version)

Shadows
The Shock

STAR CHECK LIST: LON CHANEY, JR. _____ ST17

Abbott and Costello Meet Frankenstein
Behave Yourself!
The Black Sleep
Bird of Paradise (1932)
Bride of the Gorilla
Casanova's Big Night
Cyclops
The Defiant Ones (1958 version)
Dr. Terror's Gallery of Horrors
Dracula vs. Frankenstein
Frankenstein Meets the Wolf Man
High Noon
Hillbillys in a Haunted House

The Indestructible Man
My Favorite Brunette
Of Mice and Men
The Old Corral
One Million B.C.
Only the Valiant
Passion (1954)
Riders of Death Valley
Son of Dracula
Spider Baby
Undersea Kingdom
The Wolf Man

Charlie Chaplin *See*: **Director Check List: DT18 Charlie Chaplin**
Graham Chapman *See*: **CO15 Monty Python's Flying Circus**
Chevy Chase *See*: **CO13 The Alumni of Saturday Night Live**

STARS CHECK LIST: CHEECH & CHONG _____ ST18

After Hours
Born in East L.A.*
Cheech & Chong's Next Movie
Cheech & Chong's The Corsican Brothers
Get Out of My Room
Ghostbusters II*
It Came From Hollywood

Nice Dreams
Oliver and Company (character voice)*
Rude Awakening*
Still Smokin'
Things Are Tough All Over
Up in Smoke
Yellowbeard

*Cheech only

STAR CHECK LIST: CHER _____ ST19

Come Back to the Five and Dime, Jimmy Dean, Jimmy Dean
Mask
Moonstruck

Silkwood
Suspect
The Witches of Eastwick

John Cleese *See*: **CO15 Monty Python's Flying Circus**

STAR CHECK LIST: GLENN CLOSE _____ ST20

The Big Chill
Dangerous Liaisons
Fatal Attraction
Immediate Family
Jagged Edge

Maxie
The Natural
The Stone Boy
The World According to Garp

STAR CHECK LIST: SEAN CONNERY _____ ST21

The Anderson Tapes
Another Time, Another Place
A Bridge Too Far
Cuba
Darby O'Gill and the Little People
Diamonds Are Forever
Dr. No
Family Business
A Fine Madness
Five Days One Summer
From Russia With Love
Goldfinger
The Great Train Robbery
Highlander
The Hunt for Red October
Indiana Jones and the Last Crusade
The Longest Day
The Man Who Would Be King
Marnie

Meteor
The Molly Maguires
Murder on the Orient Express
The Name of the Rose
Never Say Never Again
Outland
The Presidio
The Red Tent
Robin and Marian
Shalako
Sword of the Valiant
The Terrorists
Thunderball
Time Bandits
The Untouchables
The Wind and the Lion
Wrong Is Right
You Only Live Twice
Zardoz

STAR CHECK LIST: GARY COOPER _____ ST22

Ball of Fire
Beau Geste (1939 version)
Blowing Wild
Cloak and Dagger (1946)
The Court-Martial of Billy Mitchell
A Farewell to Arms (1932 version)
The Fountainhead
Friendly Persuasion
The General Died at Dawn
Good Sam
It
Lives of a Bengal Lancer
Love in the Afternoon
Meet John Doe
Mr. Deeds Goes to Town

Morocco
Pride of the Yankees
Sergeant York
Wings

WESTERNS
Along Came Jones
Distant Drums
Fighting Caravans
High Noon
The Plainsman
They Came to Cordura
Vera Cruz
The Virginian
The Westerner

STAR CHECK LIST: KEVIN COSTNER _____ ST23

American Flyers
Bull Durham
Fandango
Field of Dreams
No Way Out

Revenge (1990)
Silverado
Stacy's Knights
Testament
The Untouchables

STAR CHECK LIST: JOAN CRAWFORD _____ ST24

Autumn Leaves
Berserk
Dancing Lady
Grand Hotel
Johnny Guitar
Mildred Pierce
Night Gallery
Possessed

Rain
Reunion in France
Strait-Jacket
Strange Cargo
Torch Song
What Ever Happened to Baby Jane?
A Woman's Face
The Women

STAR CHECK LIST: BING CROSBY _____ ST25
See Also: CL15 Memorable Screen Teams—Bob Hope & Bing Crosby

The Bells of St. Mary's
The Country Girl (1954 version)
Going My Way
The Legend of Sleepy Hollow (narration
  & songs)
Little Boy Lost

MUSICALS
A Connecticut Yankee in King Arthur's
  Court
Here Comes the Groom

High Society
Holiday Inn
The King of Jazz
Let's Make Love
Road to Bali
Road to Rio
Road to Utopia
Robin and the Seven Hoods
That's Entertainment
That's Entertainment, Part II
White Christmas

STAR CHECK LIST: TOM CRUISE _____ ST26

All the Right Moves
Born on the Fourth of July
Cocktail
The Color of Money
Legend
Losin' It

The Outsiders
Rain Man
Risky Business
Taps
Top Gun

Billy Crystal *See*: **CO13 The Alumni of Saturday Night Live**
Jane Curtin *See*: **CO13 The Alumni of Saturday Night Live**

STAR CHECK LIST: PETER CUSHING _____ ST27

Alexander the Great
And Now the Screaming Starts
Asylum
At the Earth's Core
The Beast Must Die
Biggles
Blood Beast Terror
Bloodsuckers
Call Him Mr. Shatter
A Choice of Weapons
The Creeping Flesh
The Curse of Frankenstein
Daleks—Invasion Earth 2150 A.D.
The Devil's Undead
Doctor Phibes Rises Again
Dr. Terror's House of Horrors
Dr. Who and the Daleks
Dynasty of Fear
The Evil of Frankenstein
Fear in the Night
From Beyond the Grave
The Ghoul (1975)
The Gorgon

Hamlet (1948 version)
Horror Express
Horror of Dracula
The Hound of the Baskervilles (1959
  version)
House of the Long Shadows
The House That Dripped Blood
Land of the Minotaur
Legend of the Werewolf
Masks of Death
The Mummy (1959 version)
Scream and Scream Again
Shock Waves
Silent Scream
Star Wars
Sword of Sherwood Forest
Sword of the Valiant
Tales from the Crypt
Top Secret!
Torture Garden
Twins of Evil
The Uncanny
The Vampire Lovers

STAR CHECK LIST: BETTE DAVIS _____ ST28

All About Eve
All This and Heaven, Too
Burnt Offerings

The Corn Is Green (1945 version)
Dangerous
The Dark Secret of Harvest Home

Dark Victory
Death on the Nile
Deception
The Disappearance of Aimee
The Empty Canvas
Fashions of 1934
The Great Lie
Hell's House
Hush . . . Hush, Sweet Charlotte
In This Our Life
Jezebel
Juarez
The Letter
The Little Foxes
Little Gloria . . . Happy at Last
Madame Sin
The Man Who Came to Dinner
Marked Woman
Mr. Skeffington
Now, Voyager

Of Human Bondage (1934 version)
The Old Maid
The Petrified Forest
Phone Call From a Stranger
Pocketful of Miracles
The Private Lives of Elizabeth and
   Essex
Return From Witch Mountain
Right of Way
A Stolen Life
Strangers: The Story of a Mother and
   Daughter
Thank Your Lucky Stars
The Virgin Queen
Watch on the Rhine
The Watcher in the Woods
The Whales of August
What Ever Happened to Baby Jane?
White Mama
Wicked Stepmother

STAR CHECK LIST: CATHERINE DENEUVE _____ ST29

The April Fools
Choice of Arms
Donkey Skin
La Grande Bourgeoise
The Hunger
Hustle
The Last Metro

Love Songs
March or Die
Repulsion
Scene of the Crime
A Slightly Pregnant Man
The Umbrellas of Cherbourg

STAR CHECK LIST: ROBERT DENIRO _____ ST30

Addict
Angel Heart
Bang the Drum Slowly
Bloody Mama
Brazil
The Deer Hunter
Falling in Love
The Godfather, Part II
Greetings
Jacknife
King of Comedy
The Last Tycoon
Mean Streets

Midnight Run
The Mission
New York, New York
1900
Once Upon a Time in America
Raging Bull
Stanley and Iris
The Swap
Taxi Driver
True Confessions
The Untouchables
The Wedding Party
We're No Angels (1989 version)

STAR CHECK LIST: GERARD DEPARDIEU _____ ST31

Buffet Froid
Camille Claudel
La Chêvre
Choice of Arms
Les Comperes
Danton
Get Out Your Handkerchiefs
Going Places
Jean de Florette

The Last Metro
Loulou
Mon Oncle d'Amerique
The Moon in the Gutter
1900
One Woman or Two
The Return of Martin Guerre
The Woman Next Door

STAR CHECK LIST: DANNY DEVITO ————————————————— ST32

Goin' South
Going Ape
Head Office
Jewel of the Nile
Joe Piscopo New Jersey Special
Johnny Dangeorusly
One Flew Over the Cuckoo's Nest
Romancing the Stone

Ruthless People
Terms of Endearment
Throw Momma From the Train*
Tin Men
Twins
The War of the Roses*
Wise Guys

*also director

STAR CHECK LIST: MARLENE DIETRICH ———————————————— ST33

Blonde Venus
The Blue Angel
Destry Rides Again
Judgment at Nuremberg
Garden of Allah
Just a Gigolo
Knight Without Armour
Morocco
Paris When It Sizzles
Rancho Notorious

Seven Sinners
The Spoilers (1942 version)
Stage Fright
Touch of Evil
Witness for the Prosecution (1957
version)

Documentary subject:
Marlene

STAR CHECK LIST: KIRK DOUGLAS ————————————————— ST34

Along the Great Divide
Amos
The Arrangement
The Bad and the Beautiful
The Big Sky
The Brotherhood
Cast a Giant Shadow
Champion
Draw!
Eddie Macon's Run
The Final Countdown
The Fury
A Gunfight
Gunfight at the O.K. Corral
Home Movies
In Harm's Way
The Light at the Edge of the World
The List of Adrian Messenger
Lonely Are the Brave
Lust for Life

The Man From Snowy River
Man Without a Star
My Dear Secretary
Once Is Not Enough
Out of the Past
Paths of Glory
Posse
Saturn 3
Seven Days in May
Spartacus
The Strange Love of Martha Ivers
Strangers When We Meet
There Was a Crooked Man
Tough Guys
20,000 Leagues Under the Sea
Ulysses
The Vikings
The War Wagon
The Way West
Young Man With a Horn

STAR CHECK LIST: MICHAEL DOUGLAS ———————————————— ST35

Adam at 6 A.M.
Black Rain
The China Syndrome
A Chorus Line
Coma
Fatal Attraction
Hail, Hero!

It's My Turn
Jewel of the Nile
Napoleon and Samantha
Romancing the Stone
The Star Chamber
Wall Street
The War of the Roses

STAR CHECK LIST: RICHARD DREYFUSS _____ ST36

Always
American Graffiti
The Apprenticeship of Duddy Kravitz
The Big Fix
Close Encounters of the Third Kind
The Competition
Dillinger
Down and Out in Beverly Hills
The Goodbye Girl

Inserts
Jaws
Let It Ride
Moon Over Parador
Nuts
Stakeout
Stand by Me (narrator)
Tin Men
Whose Life Is It, Anyway?

STAR CHECK LIST: FAYE DUNAWAY _____ ST37

The Arrangement
Barfly
Beverly Hills Madam
Bonnie and Clyde
Burning Secret
The Champ (1979 version)
Chinatown
The Country Girl (1982 version)
The Disappearance of Aimee
Eyes of Laura Mars
The First Deadly Sin
The Four Musketeers
The Handmaid's Tale

Little Big Man
Midnight Crossing
Mommie Dearest
Network
Ordeal by Innocence
Supergirl
The Thomas Crown Affair
Three Days of the Condor
The Three Musketeers (1974 version)
The Towering Inferno
Voyage of the Damned
The Wicked Lady

STAR CHECK LIST: ROBERT DUVALL _____ ST38

Apocalypse Now
Badge 373
The Betsy
Breakout
Bullitt
The Chase (1966)
Colors
The Conversation
Countdown
The Eagle Has Landed
The Godfather
The Godfather, Part II
The Great Northfield Minnesota Raid
The Great Santini
The Greatest
The Handmaid's Tale
Hotel Colonial
Joe Kidd

The Killer Elite
Lady Ice
Let's Get Harry
The Lightship
M*A*S*H
The Natural
Network
The Pursuit of D. B. Cooper
The Rain People
The Seven Percent Solution
The Stone Boy
THX 1138
Tender Mercies
The Terry Fox Story
To Kill a Mockingbird
Tomorrow
True Confessions
True Grit

STAR CHECK LIST: CLINT EASTWOOD _____ ST39

Any Which Way You Can
City Heat
Coogan's Bluff
The Dead Pool
Dirty Harry
The Eiger Sanction*

The Enforcer (1976)
Escape From Alcatraz
Every Which Way But Loose
Firefox*
The Gauntlet*
Heartbreak Ridge*

Honkytonk Man*
Kelly's Heroes
Magnum Force
Paint Your Wagon
Pink Cadillac
Play Misty for Me*
Sudden Impact*
Thunderbolt and Lightfoot
Tightrope
Where Eagles Dare

Bronco Billy*
A Fistful of Dollars
For a Few Dollars More
The Good, the Bad, and the Ugly
Hang 'Em High
High Plains Drifter*
Joe Kidd
The Outlaw Josey Wales*
Pale Rider*
Two Mules for Sister Sara

WESTERNS
The Beguiled

Director only
Bird

*also director

Nelson Eddy *See*: **CL15 Memorable Screen Teams—Nelson Eddy & Jeanette MacDonald**

STAR CHECK LIST: SALLY FIELD _____ ST40

Absence of Malice
Back Roads
Beyond the Poseidon Adventure
The End
Heroes
Home for the Holidays
Hooper
Kiss Me Goodbye
Murphy's Romance
Norma Rae

Places in the Heart
Punch Line
Smokey and the Bandit
Smokey and the Bandit II
Stay Hungry
Steel Magnolias
Surrender
Sybil
The Way West

STAR CHECK LIST: W. C. FIELDS _____ ST41

The Bank Dick
The Barber Shop
The Best of W. C. Fields
David Copperfield
The Dentist
The Fatal Glass of Beer/The Pool Shark
International House
It's a Gift

Mrs. Wiggs of the Cabbage Patch
My Little Chickadee
Never Give a Sucker an Even Break
Running Wild
Sally of the Sawdust
W. C. Fields Comedy Bag
W. C. Fields Festival
You Can't Cheat an Honest Man

STAR CHECK LIST: ALBERT FINNEY _____ ST42

Annie
The Dresser
The Duellists
Gumshoe
Looker
Loophole
Murder on the Orient Express
Orphans

Pope John Paul II
Scrooge
Shoot the Moon
Tom Jones
Two for the Road
Under the Volcano
Wolfen

Joe Flaherty *See*: **CO14 The Alumni of SCTV**

STAR CHECK LIST: ERROL FLYNN _____ ST43

The Adventures of Captain Fabian
The Adventures of Don Juan
The Adventures of Robin Hood
Against All Flags
Assault of the Rebel Girls (Cuban Rebel
    Girls)
Captain Blood
The Charge of the Light Brigade (1936
    version)
The Dawn Patrol (1938 version)
Dodge City
Gentleman Jim

Kim
Northern Pursuit
The Prince and the Pauper (1937
    version)
The Private Lives of Elizabeth and
    Essex
Santa Fe Trail
The Sea Hawk
Thank Your Lucky Stars
They Died With Their Boots On
The Warriors (1955)

STAR CHECK LIST: HENRY FONDA _____ ST44

Advise and Consent
Battle Force
The Battle of the Bulge
The Best Man
The Big Street
The Boston Strangler
The Cheyenne Social Club
City on Fire
Drums Along the Mohawk
Fail-Safe
Fort Apache
The Fugitive
Gideon's Trumpet
The Grapes of Wrath
The Great Smokey Roadblock
Home to Stay
How the West Was Won
I Dream Too Much
The Immortal Sergeant
In Harm's Way
Jesse James
Jezebel
The Lady Eve
The Last Four Days
The Longest Day
The Mad Miss Manton
Madigan
Meteor
Midway

Mister Roberts
The Moon's Our Home
My Darling Clementine
My Name Is Nobody
Night Flight From Moscow
The Oldest Living Graduate
On Golden Pond
Once Upon a Time in the West
The Ox-Bow Incident
The Red Pony (1973 version)
The Return of Frank James
Rollercoaster
Sometimes a Great Notion
Stage Struck
Summer Solstice
The Swarm
Tentacles
There Was a Crooked Man
The Tin Star
Too Late the Hero
Twelve Angry Men
War and Peace (1956 version)
Warlock
Wings of the Morning
The Wrong Man
You Only Live Once
Young Mr. Lincoln
Yours, Mine and Ours

STAR CHECK LIST: JANE FONDA _____ ST45

Agnes of God
Any Wednesday
Barbarella
Barefoot in the Park
California Suite
Cat Ballou
The Chase (1966)
The China Syndrome
Comes a Horseman

Coming Home
The Dollmaker
A Doll's House (Fonda version)
The Electric Horseman
Fun With Dick and Jane
The Game Is Over
Joy House
Julia
Klute

The Morning After
9 to 5
Old Gringo
On Golden Pond
Rollover

Stanley and Iris
Steelyard Blues
They Shoot Horses, Don't They?
A Walk on the Wild Side

STAR CHECK LIST: HARRISON FORD _____ ST46

American Graffiti
Apocalypse Now
Blade Runner
The Conversation
Dead Heat on a Merry-Go-Round
The Empire Strikes Back
Force 10 From Navarone
Frantic (1988)
The Frisco Kid
Getting Straight
Hanover Street

Heroes
Indiana Jones and the Last Crusade
Indiana Jones and the Temple of Doom
The Mosquito Coast
Raiders of the Lost Ark
Return of the Jedi
Star Wars
Witness
Working Girl
Zabriskie Point

OUSTAR CHECK LIST: JODIE FOSTER _____ ST47

The Accused
Alice Doesn't Live Here Anymore
Bugsy Malone
Candleshoe
Carny
Five Corners
Foxes
Freaky Friday
The Hotel New Hampshire

The Little Girl Who Lives Down the
  Lane
Napoleon and Samantha
Siesta
Stealing Home
Svengali
Taxi Driver
Tom Sawyer

STAR CHECK LIST: MORGAN FREEMAN _____ ST48

Brubaker
Clean and Sober
Driving Miss Daisy
Eyewitness
Glory
Harry and Son

Johnny Handsome
Lean on Me
Marie
Street Smart
That Was Then . . . This is Now

STAR CHECK LIST: CLARK GABLE _____ ST49

Boom Town
China Seas
Dancing Lady
Gone With the Wind
Idiot's Delight
It Happened One Night
The Misfits
Mogambo
Mutiny on the Bounty (1935 version)
No Man of Her Own
The Painted Desert

Possessed
Red Dust
Run Silent, Run Deep
San Francisco
Soldier of Fortune
Strange Cargo
The Tall Men
That's Entertainment
That's Entertainment, Part II
Teacher's Pet

STAR CHECK LIST: GRETA GARBO _____ ST50

Anna Christie
Anna Karenina
Camille
Flesh and the Devil
Gosta Berling's Saga

Grand Hotel
Ninotchka
Queen Christina
Two-Faced Woman
Wild Orchids

STAR CHECK LIST: JUDY GARLAND _____ ST51
See also: CL15 Memorable Screen Teams—Mickey Rooney & Judy Garland

A Child Is Waiting
The Clock
Judgment at Nuremberg

MUSICALS
Babes in Arms
Babes on Broadway
Broadway Melody of 1938
Easter Parade
For Me and My Gal
Girl Crazy
The Harvey Girls
I Could Go On Singing
In the Good Old Summertime

Meet Me in St. Louis
The Pirate
Presenting Lily Mars
A Star Is Born (1954 version)
Strike Up the Band
Summer Stock
That's Entertainment
That's Entertainment, Part II
Thousands Cheer
Till the Clouds Roll By
The Wizard of Oz
Words and Music
Ziegfeld Follies
Ziegfeld Girl

STAR CHECK LIST: RICHARD GERE _____ ST52

American Gigolo
Beyond the Limit
Bloodbrothers
Breathless (1983 version)
The Cotton Club
Days of Heaven
Internal Affairs

King David
Looking for Mr. Goodbar
Miles From Home
No Mercy
An Officer and a Gentleman
Power (1986)
Pretty Woman

STAR CHECK LIST: MEL GIBSON _____ ST53

Attack Force Z
Bird on a Wire
The Bounty
Gallipoli
Lethal Weapon
Lethal Weapon 2
Mad Max
Mad Max Beyond Thunderdome

Mrs. Soffel
The River (1984)
The Road Warrior
Summer City
Tequila Sunrise
Tim
The Year of Living Dangerously

Terry Gilliam *See*: CO15 Monty Python's Flying Circus

STAR CHECK LIST: LILLIAN GISH _____ ST54

The Adventures of Huckleberry Finn
   (1985 version)
The Birth of a Nation
Broken Blossoms
Commandos Strike at Dawn

D.W. Griffith Triple Feature
Duel in the Sun
Follow Me, Boys!
Hambone and Hillie
Hearts of the World

His Double Life
Hobson's Choice (1983 version)
Intolerance
The Night of the Hunter
Orphans of the Storm
Portrait of Jennie
Sweet Liberty

True Heart Susie
The Unforgiven
Way Down East
A Wedding
The Whales of August
The Wind

STAR CHECK LIST: DANNY GLOVER _____ ST55

Bat 21
The Color Purple
Dead Man Out
Lethal Weapon
Lethal Weapon 2

Mandela
Places in the Heart
Silverado
Witness

STAR CHECK LIST: JEFF GOLDBLUM _____ ST56

The Adventures of Buckroo Banzai
    Across the 8th Dimension
Between the Lines
Beyond Therapy
The Big Chill
Death Wish
Earth Girls Are Easy
Ernie Kovacs: Between the Laughter
The Fly (1986 version)
Into the Night

Invasion of the Body Snatchers (1979
    version)
Nashville
Rehearsal for Murder
The Right Stuff
Silverado
Thank God It's Friday
The Three Little Pigs
Threshold
Transylvania 6-5000
Vibes

STAR CHECK LIST: CARY GRANT _____ ST57

An Affair to Remember
Amazing Adventure
Arsenic and Old Lace
The Awful Truth
The Bachelor and the Bobby Soxer
The Bishop's Wife
Blonde Venus
Bringing Up Baby
Charade
Destination Tokyo
Every Girl Should Be Married
Father Goose
The Grass Is Greener
Gunga Din
His Girl Friday
Holiday
Houseboat
The Howards of Virginia
In Name Only
Indiscreet
Mr. Blandings Builds His Dream House
Mr. Lucky

Monkey Business (1952)
My Favorite Wife
Night and Day
None but the Lonely Heart
North by Northwest
Notorious
Once Upon a Honeymoon
Only Angels Have Wings
Operation Petticoat
Penny Serenade
The Philadelphia Story
The Pride and the Passion
She Done Him Wrong
Suspicion
Sylvia Scarlett
The Talk of the Town
That Touch of Mink
To Catch a Thief
The Toast of New York
Topper
Walk, Don't Run

STAR CHECK LIST: MELANIE GRIFFITH _____ ST58

Body Double
Cherry 2000
The Drowning Pool
Fear City
In the Spirit
Night Moves

She's in the Army Now
Smile
Something Wild
Stormy Monday
Working Girl

STAR CHECK LIST: CHARLES GRODIN _____ ST59

Catch-22
The Couch Trip
11 Harrowhouse
The Great Muppet Caper
The Heartbreak Kid
Heaven Can Wait (1978)
The Incredible Shrinking Woman
Ishtar
It's My Turn

King Kong (1976 version)
The Lonely Guy
Midnight Run
Movers and Shakers
Real Life
Rosemary's Baby
Seems Like Old Times
Sunburn
The Woman in Red

STAR CHECK LIST: ALEC GUINNESS _____ ST60

The Bridge on the River Kwai
Brother Sun, Sister Moon
The Captain's Paradise
Cromwell
Damn the Defiant!
The Detective (1954)
Dr. Zhivago
The Empire Strikes Back
The Fall of the Roman Empire
Great Expectations
A Handful of Dust
Hitler: The Last Ten Days
The Horse's Mouth
Kind Hearts and Coronets
The Ladykillers
The Lavender Hill Mob
Lawrence of Arabia

Little Dorritt
Little Lord Fauntleroy (1980 version)
Lovesick
The Malta Story
The Man in the White Suit
Murder by Death
Oliver Twist (1948 version)
A Passage to India
The Prisoner
The Promoter
The Quiller Memorandum
Raise the Titanic!
Scrooge (1970 version)
Star Wars
To Paris With Love
Tunes of Glory

STAR CHECK LIST: GENE HACKMAN _____ ST61

All Night Long
Another Woman
Bat 21
Bite the Bullet
Bonnie and Clyde
A Bridge Too Far
The Conversation
Doctors' Wives
The Domino Principle
Downhill Racer
Eureka
The French Connection
The French Connection 2
Full Moon in Blue Water

Hawaii
Hoosiers
I Never Sang for My Father
Lilith
Loose Cannons
March or Die
Marooned
Mississippi Burning
Misunderstood
Night Moves
No Way Out
The Package
The Poseidon Adventure
Power (1986)

Prime Cut
Reds
Scarecrow
Split Decisions
Superman
Superman II

Superman IV: The Quest for Peace
Target
Twice in a Lifetime
Uncommon Valor
Under Fire
Young Frankenstein

STAR CHECK LIST: TOM HANKS _____ ST62

Bachelor Party
Big
The Burbs
Dragnet (1987)
Every Time We Say Goodbye
He Knows You're Alone
Joe Versus the Volcano

The Man With One Red Shoe
The Money Pit
Nothing in Common
Punch Line
Splash
Turner and Hooch
Volunteers

STAR CHECK LIST: GOLDIE HAWN _____ ST63

Best Friends
Bird on a Wire
Butterflies Are Free
Cactus Flower
$ (Dollars)
The Duchess and the Dirtwater Fox
Foul Play
The Girl From Petrovka
Lovers and Liars
The One and Only, Genuine, Original
    Family Band

Overboard
Private Benjamin
Protocol
Seems Like Old Times
Shampoo
The Sugarland Express
Swing Shift
There's a Girl in My Soup
Wildcats

STAR CHECK LIST: RITA HAYWORTH _____ ST64

Affair in Trinidad
Angels Over Broadway
Blood and Sand (1941 version)
Circus World
Cover Girl
Fire Down Below
Gilda
The Lady From Shanghai
The Loves of Carmen
Miss Sadie Thompson
Only Angels Have Wings

Pal Joey
Renegade Ranger
Road to Salina
Salome
Separate Tables (1958 version)
The Strawberry Blonde
They Came to Cordura
Tonight and Every Night
You Were Never Lovelier
You'll Never Get Rich

STAR CHECK LIST: AUDREY HEPBURN _____ ST65

Always
Breakfast at Tiffany's
Charade
Funny Face
The Lavender Hill Mob
Love in the Afternoon
My Fair Lady
The Nun's Story
Paris When It Sizzles

Robin and Marian
Roman Holiday
Sabrina
Sidney Sheldon's Bloodline
They All Laughed
Two for the Road
The Unforgiven
Wait Until Dark
War and Peace (1956 version)

STAR CHECK LIST: KATHARINE HEPBURN _____ ST66
See also: CL15 Memorable Screen Teams—Katharine Hepburn & Spencer Tracy

Adam's Rib
The African Queen
Alice Adams
A Bill of Divorcement
Break of Hearts
Bringing Up Baby
Christopher Strong
Desk Set
Dragon Seed
George Stevens: A Filmmaker's Journey
Grace Quigley
Guess Who's Coming to Dinner
Holiday
The Lion in Winter
The Little Minister
Little Women (1933 version)
Long Day's Journey Into Night (1962 version)
Love Among the Ruins

Mary of Scotland
Morning Glory
On Golden Pond
Pat and Mike
The Philadelphia Story
Quality Street
The Rainmaker
Rooster Cogburn
Spitfire (1934)
Stage Door
Stage Door Canteen
State of the Union
Suddenly, Last Summer
Summertime
Sylvia Scarlett
That's Entertainment, Part II
The Trojan Women
Woman of the Year
A Woman Rebels

STAR CHECK LIST: DUSTIN HOFFMAN _____ ST67

Agatha
All the President's Men
Death of a Salesman (1985 version)
Dick Tracy
Family Business
The Graduate
Ishtar
Kramer vs. Kramer
Lenny

Little Big Man
Madigan's Millions
Marathon Man
Midnight Cowboy
Papillon
Rain Man
Straight Time
Straw Dogs
Tootsie

STAR CHECK LIST: WILLIAM HOLDEN _____ ST68

Alvarez Kelly
Ashanti, Land of No Mercy
The Blue Knight
Born Yesterday
The Bridge on the River Kwai
The Bridges at Toko-Ri
Casino Royale
The Christmas Tree
The Country Girl (1954 version)
Damien—Omen II
The Dark Past
Dear Wife
The Earthling
Executive Suite
Golden Boy
The Horse Soldiers
The Key
Love Is a Many Splendored Thing
The Man From Colorado

Miss Grant Takes Richmond
The Moon Is Blue
Network
Our Town
Paris When It Sizzles
Picnic
Rachel and the Stranger
S.O.B.
Sabrina
Stalag 17
Sunset Boulevard
Texas
The Towering Inferno
Union Station
When Time Ran Out
The Wild Bunch
Wild Rovers
The World of Suzie Wong
Young and Willing

STAR CHECK LIST: JUDY HOLLIDAY _____ ST69

Adam's Rib   It Should Happen to You
Bells Are Ringing   The Solid Gold Cadillac
Born Yesterday

STAR CHECK LIST: BOB HOPE _____ ST70
See also: CL15 Memorable Screen Teams—Bob Hope & Bing Crosby

Boy, Did I Get a Wrong Number!   The Princess and the Pirate
Cancel My Reservation   The Road to Bali
Casanova's Big Night   The Road to Rio
The Great Lover   Road to Utopia
The Lemon Drop Kid   The Seven Little Foys
My Favorite Brunette   Son of Paleface
Off Limits (1953)   Sorrowful Jones
The Paleface   Spies Like Us
Paris Holiday   They Got Me Covered

ACTOR CHECK LIST: DENNIS HOPPER _____ ST71

The American Friend   Night Tide
Apocalypse Now   O.C. and Stiggs
Black Widow   The Osterman Weekend
Blood Red   Out of the Blue*
Blue Velvet   The Pick-up Artist
Chattahoochee   Rebel Without a Cause
Cool Hand Luke   Riders of the Storm
Easy Rider*   Rumblefish
Flashback   Running Out of Luck
Giant   The Sons of Katie Elder
Gunfight at the O.K. Corral   Straight to Hell
Hang 'Em High   The Texas Chainsaw Massacre II
Hoosiers   Tracks
The Inside Man   The Trip
King of the Mountain   True Grit
The Last Movie*
Mad Dog Morgan   **Director only**
My Science Project   Colors

*also director

STAR CHECK LIST: BOB HOSKINS _____ ST72

Beyond the Limit   The Long Good Friday
Brazil   Mona Lisa
The Cotton Club   Mussolini and I
The Dunera Boys   Pink Floyd: The Wall
Heart Condition   A Prayer for the Dying
Inserts   The Raggedy Rawney*
Lassiter   Sweet Liberty
The Lonely Passion of Judith Hearne   Who Framed Roger Rabbit

*also director

STAR CHECK LIST: ROCK HUDSON ST73

The Ambassador
Avalance
Bend of the River
Embryo
Giant
Gun Fury
Ice Station Zebra
Lover Come Back
Magnificent Obsession
Man's Favorite Sport?

The Mirror Crack'd
Pillow Talk
Sea Devils
Send Me No Flowers
Something of Value
Tobruk
The Undefeated
Winchester 73
Written on the Wind

STAR CHECK LIST: HOLLY HUNTER ST74

Always
Animal Behavior
Broadcast News
End of the Line

Miss Firecracker
Raising Arizona
Roe vs. Wade
Urge to Kill

STAR CHECK LIST: WILLIAM HURT ST75

The Accidental Tourist
Altered States
The Big Chill
Body Heat
Broadcast News
Children of a Lesser God

Eyewitness
Gorky Park
I Love You to Death
Kiss of the Spider Woman
A Time of Destiny

Eric Idle *See*: **CO15 Monty Python's Flying Circus**

STAR CHECK LIST: JAMES EARL JONES ST76

Aladdin and His Wonderful Lamp
Allan Quartermain and the Lost City of
   Gold
Best of the Best
The Bingo Long Traveling All-Stars &
   Motor Kings
The Bushido Blade
Coming to America
Conan the Barbarian
Deadly Hero
Dr. Strangelove, or: How I Learned to
   Stop Worrying and Love the Bomb
The Empire Strikes Back (character
   voice)
End of the Road

Exorcist II: the Heretic
Field of Dreams
Gardens of Stone
The Great White Hope
The Greatest
The Hunt for Red October
The Last Remake of Beau Geste
Matewan
My Little Girl
A Piece of the Action
Return of the Jedi (character voice)
The River Niger
Soul Man
Star Wars (character voice)
Three Fugitives

Terry Jones *See*: **CO15 Monty Python's Flying Circus**

STAR CHECK LIST: BORIS KARLOFF ST77

Abbott and Costello Meet Dr. Jekyll and
   Mr. Hyde
Abbott and Costello Meet the Killer,
   Boris Karloff

The Ape
Bedlam
Before I Hang
The Bells

The Black Cat
The Black Room
The Black Sabbath
The Body Snatcher
The Bride of Frankenstein
Cauldron of Blood
Chamber of Fear
Charlie Chan at the Opera
Corridors of Blood
The Criminal Code
The Daydreamer (voice only)
Dick Tracy Meets Gruesome
Die, Monster, Die!
Doomed to Die
Frankenstein (1931 version)
Frankenstein 1970
The Ghoul (1933)
The Haunted Strangler
The Invisible Ray
Island Monster
Isle of the Dead

Juggernaut (1937)
The King of the Kongo
The Lost Patrol
Macabre Serenade
Mad Monster Party? (voice only)
The Man They Could Not Hang
Mr. Wong, Detective
Mr. Wong in Chinatown
The Mummy (1932 version)
Old Ironsides
The Raven (1935 & 1963)
Scarface (1932 version)
The Secret Life of Walter Mitty
Sinister Invasion
The Snake People
Son of Frankenstein
Targets
The Terror
Transylvania Twist
You'll Find Out

STAR CHECK LIST: DANNY KAYE _____ **ST78**

The Court Jester
Hans Christian Andersen
The Inspector General
The Kid From Brooklyn

The Secret Life of Walter Mitty
Up in Arms
White Christmas
Wonder Man

STAR CHECK LIST: DIANE KEATON _____ **ST79**

Annie Hall
Baby Boom
Crimes of the Heart
The Godfather
The Godfather, Part II
The Good Mother
Harry and Walter Go to New York
I Will, I Will . . . For Now
Interiors
The Little Drummer Girl
Looking for Mr. Goodbar
Love and Death

Lovers and Other Strangers
Manhattan
Mrs. Soffel
Play It Again, Sam
Radio Days
Reds
Shoot the Moon
Sleeper

Director only
Heaven

STAR CHECK LIST: MICHAEL KEATON _____ **ST80**

Batman (1989)
Beetlejuice
Clean and Sober
The Dream Team
Gung Ho (1986)

Johnny Dangerously
Mr. Mom
Night Shift
The Squeeze
Touch and Go (1986)

STAR CHECK LIST: GENE KELLY _____ **ST81**

The Black Hand
Forty Carats
Inherit the Wind

Marjorie Morningstar
The Three Musketeers (1948 version)

MUSICALS
An American in Paris
Anchors Aweigh
Brigadoon
Cover Girl
Deep in My Heart
DuBarry Was a Lady
For Me and My Gal
Invitation to the Dance
It's Always Fair Weather*
Les Girls
Let's Make Love
On the Town*
The Pirate
Singin' in the Rain*

Summer Stock
Take Me out to the Ball Game
That's Dancing
That's Entertainment
That's Entertainment, Part II
Thousands Cheer
Words and Music
Xanadu
Ziegfeld Follies (with Fred Astaire)

Director only
The Cheyenne Social Club
A Guide for the Married Man
Hello, Dolly!

*also co-director with Stanley Donen

STAR CHECK LIST: GRACE KELLY _____ ST82

The Bridges at Toko-Ri
The Country Girl (1954 version)
Dial M for Murder
High Noon

High Society
Mogambo
Rear Window
To Catch a Thief

STAR CHECK LIST: KLAUS KINSKI _____ ST83

Aguirre, The Wrath of God
Android
Beauty and the Beast (1984 version)
Buddy Buddy
A Bullet for the General
Burden of Dreams
Code Name: Wildgeese
Count Dracula
Crawlspace
Creature
Deadly Sanctuary
Fitzcarraldo

For a Few Dollars More
Jack the Ripper
The Little Drummer Girl
Operation Thunderbolt
The Ruthless Four
Schizoid
The Secret Diary of Sigmund Freud
Shoot the Living, Pray for the Dead
The Soldier
A Time to Love and a Time to Die
Venom

STAR CHECK LIST: KEVIN KLINE _____ ST84

The Big Chill
Cry Freedom
A Fish Called Wanda
I Love You to Death
The January Man

The Pirates of Penzance
Silverado
Sophie's Choice
Violets Are Blue

STAR CHECK LIST: BURT LANCASTER _____ ST85

Airport
Apache
Atlantic City
Birdman of Alcatraz
Buffalo Bill and the Indians

A Child Is Waiting
Control
Conversation Piece
The Crimson Pirate
Criss Cross

Elmer Gantry
Executive Action
Field of Dreams
The Flame and the Arrow
From Here to Eternity
Go Tell the Spartans
Gunfight at the O.K. Corral
The Island of Dr. Moreau
Judgment at Nuremberg
The Kentuckian*
The List of Adrian Messenger
Little Treasure
Local Hero
Moses
1900
The Osterman Weekend
The Professionals
The Rainmaker

Rocket Gibraltar
Run Silent, Run Deep
The Scalphunters
Separate Tables (1958 version)
Seven Days in May
Sorry, Wrong Number
Sweet Smell of Success
The Swimmer
Tough Guys
The Train
Trapeze
Twilight's Last Gleaming
Ulzana's Raid
The Unforgiven
Vengeance Valley
Vera Cruz
Zulu Dawn

*also director

STAR CHECK LIST: JESSICA LANGE _____ ST86

All That Jazz
Country
Crimes of the Heart
Everybody's All American
Far North
Frances
How to Beat the High Cost of Living

King Kong (1976 version)
Men Don't Leave
Music Box
The Postman Always Rings Twice (1981
   version)
Sweet Dreams
Tootsie

STARS CHECK LIST: LAUREL & HARDY _____ ST87

Atoll K
Block Heads
The Bohemian Girl
Bonnie Scotland
The Bullfighters
A Chump at Oxford
The Fighting Kentuckian*
The Flying Deuces
Great Guns
Laurel and Hardy Comedy Classics,
   Vols. I-IX

The Music Box/Helpmates
Our Relations
Pack Up Your Troubles
Pardon Us
Saps at Sea
Sons of the Desert
Swiss Miss
Way Out West
The Wizard of Oz (1925 version)*

*Hardy only

STAR CHECK LIST: BRUCE LEE _____ ST88

Bruce Lee: The Legend
Bruce Lee: The Man/The Myth
The Chinese Connection
Enter the Dragon
Fist of Fear, Touch of Death

Fists of Fury
Game of Death
The Real Bruce Lee
Return of the Dragon

STAR CHECK LIST: CHRISTOPHER LEE _____ ST89

Against All Odds (1969)
Airport '77
Albino
Bear Island
The Boy Who Left Home to Find Out
   About the Shivers
Caravans
Castle of Fu Manchu
Castle of the Living Dead
Circle of Iron
Corridors of Blood
Count Dracula
The Creeping Flesh
The Crimson Pirate
The Curse of Frankenstein
Dark Places
The Devil's Undead
Dr. Terror's House of Horrors
Dracula and Son
End of the World
An Eye for an Eye
The Four Musketeers
The Girl
The Gorgon
Horror Express
Horror Hotel
Horror of Dracula
The Hound of the Baskervilles (1959
   version)
House of the Long Shadows
The House That Dripped Blood

The Howling II
Jaguar Lives
Jocks
Julius Caesar (1970 version)
The Keeper
Killer Force
The Land of Faraway
The Magic Christian
The Man With the Golden Gun
Moulin Rouge
The Mummy (1959 version)
Murder Story
1941
The Oblong Box
The Private Life of Sherlock Holmes
Pursuit of the Graf Spee
Return from Witch Mountain
The Return of Captain Invincible
Safari 3000
The Salamander
Scars of Dracula
Scott of the Antarctic
Scream and Scream Again
Scream of Fear
Serial
Shaka Zulu
Theatre of Death
The Three Musketeers (1974 version)
To the Devil a Daughter
The Torture Chamber of Dr. Sadism
The Wicker Man

STAR CHECK LIST: JACK LEMMON _____ ST90

Airport '77
The Apartment
The April Fools
Bell, Book and Candle
Buddy Buddy
The China Syndrome
Dad
The Days of Wine and Roses
Fire Down Below
Good Neighbor Sam
The Great Race
How to Murder Your Wife
Irma La Douce
It Should Happen to You

Director only
Kotch

Long Day's Journey Into Night (1987
   version)
Luv
Macaroni
Mass Appeal
Missing
Mister Roberts
The Odd Couple
The Out-of-Towners
The Prisoner of Second Avenue
Save the Tiger
Some Like It Hot
That's Life!
Tribute
The Wackiest Ship in the Army

Eugene Levy *See*: **CO14 The Alumni of SCTV**

STAR CHECK LIST: JERRY LEWIS _____ ST91

At War With the Army*
The Bellboy**
The Best of Comic Relief
The Big Mouth**
The Caddy*
Cinderfella
Cookie
Cracking Up
The Delicate Delinquent
The Disorderly Orderly
Don't Raise the Bridge, Lower the River

The Errand Boy**
The Family Jewels
Hardly Working**
Hollywood or Bust*
Jerry Lewis Live
King of Comedy
The Ladies' Man
The Nutty Professor**
The Patsy**
Slapstick of Another Kind
Which Way to the Front?**

*with Dean Martin
**also director

STAR CHECK LIST: CAROLE LOMBARD _____ ST92

High Voltage
In Name Only
Made for Each Other (1939)
Mr. and Mrs. Smith
My Man Godfrey
No Man of Her Own
Nothing Sacred

Power (1928)
Racketeer
Swing High, Swing Low
They Knew What They Wanted
To Be or Not to Be (1942 version)
Twentieth Century

STAR CHECK LIST: SOPHIA LOREN _____ ST93

Aida
Angela
Arabesque
The Black Orchid
Blood Feud
Bocaccio '70
Brass Target
A Breath of Scandal
Brief Encounter (1974 version)
Courage (1986)
Desire Under the Elms
El Cid
The Fall of the Roman Empire
La Favorita

Firepower
The Gold of Naples
Heller in Pink Tights
Houseboat
The Key
Lady of the Evening
Legend of the Lost
Man of La Mancha
The Pride and the Passion
Sophia Loren: Her Own Story
A Special Day
Two Women
Yesterday, Today and Tomorrow

STAR CHECK LIST: MYRNA LOY _____ ST94
See also: CL15 Memorable Screen Teams—William Powell & Myrna Loy

After the Thin Man
Airport 1975
Another Thin Man
Ants
The April Fools
Arrowsmith
The Bachelor and the Bobby Soxer
The Best Years of Our Lives
Consolation Marriage

The End
From the Terrace
The Great Ziegfeld
Just Tell Me What You Want
Lonelyhearts
Midnight Lace
Mr. Blandings Builds His Dream House
The Red Pony (1949 version)
Shadow of the Thin Man

Song of the Thin Man
Summer Solstice
The Thin Man

The Thin Man Goes Home
Topaze
Vanity Fair

STAR CHECK LIST: BELA LUGOSI ——————————————— ST95

Abbott and Costello Meet Frankenstein
The Ape Man
Bela Lugosi Meets a Brooklyn Gorilla
  (The Boys From Brooklyn)
The Black Cat
Black Dragons
The Black Sleep
The Body Snatcher
Bowery at Midnight
Bride of the Monster
Chandu on the Magic Island
The Corpse Vanishes
The Death Kiss
Dracula (1931 version)
Frankenstein Meets the Wolf Man
Ghosts on the Loose
Glen or Glenda?
The Gorilla
The Human Monster
Invisible Ghost
The Invisible Ray

Killer Bats (The Devil Bat)
Mark of the Vampire
The Midnight Girl
Murder by Television
Mysterious Mr. Wong
The Mystery of the *Mary Celeste*: The
  Phantom Ship
Ninotchka
One Body Too Many
The Phantom Creeps
Plan 9 From Outer Space
The Raven (1935)
The Return of Chandu
Return of the Vampire
S.O.S. Coastguard
Scared to Death
Son of Frankenstein
Spooks Run Wild
White Zombie
The Wolf Man
You'll Find Out

Jeanette MacDonald *See*: **CL15 Memorable Screen Teams—Nelson Eddy &
  Jeanette MacDonald**

STAR CHECK LIST: SHIRLEY MACLAINE ——————————————— ST96

All in a Night's Work
The Apartment
Around the World in 80 Days
Being There
Can-Can
Cannonball Run II
A Change of Seasons
Gambit
Hot Spell
Irma La Douce

Loving Couples
Madame Sousatzka
Some Came Running
Steel Magnolias
Sweet Charity
Terms of Endearment
The Trouble With Harry
The Turning Point
Two Mules for Sister Sara
Woman Times Seven

STAR CHECK LIST: STEVE MCQUEEN ——————————————— ST97

Baby, the Rain Must Fall
The Blob
Bullitt
The Cincinnati Kid
An Enemy of the People
The Getaway
The Great Escape
The Hunter
Junior Bonner

Love With the Proper Stranger
The Magnificent Seven
Nevada Smith
Never Love a Stranger
Never So Few
On Any Sunday
Papillon
The Reivers
The Sand Pebbles

Soldier in the Rain
Somebody Up There Likes Me
The Thomas Crown Affair

Tom Horn
The Towering Inferno
The War Lover

STAR CHECK LIST: JOHN MALKOVICH _____ ST98

Dangerous Liaisons
Death of a Salesman (1985 version)
Eleni
Empire of the Sun

The Glass Menagerie (1987 version)
Making Mr. Right
Places in the Heart
True West

Andrea Martin *See*: CO14 The Alumni of SCTV

STAR CHECK LIST: STEVE MARTIN _____ ST99

All of Me
Dead Men Don't Wear Plaid
Dirty, Rotten Scoundrels
The Jerk
Little Shop of Horrors (1986 version)
The Lonely Guy
The Man With Two Brains
Movers and Shakers
The Muppet Movie

Parenthood
Pennies From Heaven
Planes, Trains, and Automobiles
Rowlf's Rhapsodies With the Muppets
Roxanne
Sergeant Pepper's Lonely Hearts Club
    Band
Steve Martin Live!
Three Amigos

STAR CHECK LIST: LEE MARVIN _____ ST100

Bad Day at Black Rock
The Big Heat
The Big Red One
The Caine Mutiny
Cat Ballou
The Comancheros
Death Hunt
The Delta Force
The Dirty Dozen
Dog Day
Donovan's Reef
Gorky Park
The Great Scout and Cathouse
    Thursday
Gun Fury

Hell in the Pacific
The Killers (1964 version)
The Man Who Shot Liberty Valance
Monte Walsh
Paint Your Wagon
Pete Kelly's Blues
Point Blank
Prime Cut
The Professionals
Raintree County
Sergeant Ryker
Shack Out on 101
Ship of Fools
Shout at the Devil
The Wild One

STARS CHECK LIST: THE MARX BROTHERS _____ ST101

Animal Crackers
At the Circus
The Big Store
The Cocoanuts
Copacabana*
A Day at the Races
Double Dynamite*
Duck Soup

A Girl in Every Port*
Go West
Horse Feathers
Love Happy
A Night at the Opera
A Night in Casablanca
Room Service
That's Entertainment, Part II

*Groucho only

STAR CHECK LIST: JAMES MASON ————————————————— ST102

Bad Man's River
The Blue Max
The Boys From Brazil
Caught
Cold Sweat
The Desert Fox
The Destructors
11 Harrowhouse
Evil Under the Sun
The Fall of the Roman Empire
ffolkes
Fire Over England
Georgy Girl
Heaven Can Wait (1978)
Hotel Reserve
Ivanhoe
Jesus of Nazareth
Journey to the Center of the Earth (1959
    version)
Julius Caesar (1953 version)
The Last of Sheila
Lolita

Lord Jim
The Mackintosh Man
Madame Bovary
Mandingo
Murder by Decree
The Night Has Eyes
North by Northwest
Odd Man Out
The Prisoner of Zenda (1952 version)
Salem's Lot: The Movie
The Seventh Veil
The Shooting Party
Sidney Sheldon's Bloodline
A Star Is Born (1954 version)
20,000 Leagues Under the Sea
The Verdict
Voyage of the Damned
Water Babies
The Wicked Lady
Yellowbeard
The Yin and the Yang of Mr. Go

STAR CHECK LIST: MARCELLO MASTROIANNI ————————————— ST103

Allonsanfan
Beyond Obsession
Big Deal on Madonna Street
Blood Feud
City of Women
Dark Eyes
The Divine Nymph
La Dolce Vita
8½
Gabriela
Ginger and Fred
Henry IV
Lady of the Evening
Lovers and Liars
Lunatics and Lovers

Macaroni
Massacre in Rome
La Nuit de Varennes
Shoot Loud, Louder, I Don't
    Understand
A Slightly Pregnant Man
A Special Day
Stay as You Are
The Tenth Victim
A Very Private Affair
We All Loved Each Other So Much
Where the Hot Wind Blows
Wifemistress
Yesterday, Today and Tomorrow

STAR CHECK LIST: WALTER MATTHAU ———————————————— ST104

The Bad News Bears
Buddy, Buddy
Cactus Flower
California Suite
Casey's Shadow
Charade
Charley Varrick
The Couch Trip
Earthquake
Ensign Pulver
A Face in the Crowd
Fail Safe
First Monday in October

A Guide for the Married Man
Hello Dolly!
Hopscotch
House Calls
I Ought To Be in Pictures
The Kentuckian
King Creole
Kotch
The Laughing Policeman
Little Miss Marker (1980 version)
Lonely Are the Brave
Mirage
Movers and Shakers

A New Leaf
The Odd Couple
Pirates
Plaza Suite
The Secret Life of an American Wife

Strangers When We Meet
The Sunshine Boys
The Survivors
The Taking of Pelham One Two Three

STAR CHECK LIST: BETTE MIDLER _____ ST105

Beaches
Bette Midler's Mondo Beyondo
Big Business
Divine Madness
Down and Out in Beverly Hills
Jinxed!

Oliver and Company (character voice)
Outrageous Fortune
The Rose
Ruthless People
Stella

STAR CHECK LIST: TOSHIRO MIFUNE _____ ST106

The Bad Sleep Well
Bushido Blade
The Challenge (1982)
Drunken Angel
The Gambling Samurai
Grand Prix
Hell in the Pacific
The Hidden Fortress
High and Low
The Life of Oharu
The Lower Depths
1941
Paper Tiger
Proof of the Man
Rashomon

Red Beard
Red Lion
Red Sun
Rikisha-Man
The Saga of the Vagabonds
Samurai Saga
The Samurai Trilogy
Sanjuro
The Seven Samurai
Stray Dog
Sword of Doom
Throne of Blood
Winter Kills
Yojimbo
Zatoichi Meets Yojimbo

STAR CHECK LIST: ROBERT MITCHUM _____ ST107

The Ambassador
Anzio
The Big Sleep (1978 version)
Blood on the Moon
Breakthrough
Border Patrol
Cape Fear
Crossfire
El Dorado
The Enemy Below
Farewell, My Lovely
Fire Down Below
Five Card Stud
The Grass Is Greener
Gung Ho! (1943)
His Kind of Woman
Home From the Hill
The Last Tycoon
The List of Adrian Messenger
The Longest Day
The Lusty Men
Macao
Maria's Lovers

Matilda
Midway
Mr. North
The Night of the Hunter
One Minute to Zero
Out of the Past
Pursued
Rachel and the Stranger
The Racket
The Red Pony (1949 version)
River of No Return
Ryan's Daughter
Scrooged
Secret Ceremony
The Sundowners
That Championship Season
Thirty Seconds Over Tokyo
Thunder Road
Till the End of Time
Villa Rides!
The Way West
The Yakuza

STAR CHECK LIST: MARILYN MONROE _____ ST108

All About Eve
The Asphalt Jungle
Bus Stop
Clash by Night
Gentlemen Prefer Blondes
How to Marry a Millionaire
Let's Make Love
Love Happy
The Misfits

Monkey Business (1952)
Niagara
The Prince and the Showgirl
River of No Return
The Seven Year Itch
Some Like It Hot
There's No Business Like Show
   Business

Monty Python's Flying Circus *See*: **CO15**

STAR CHECK LIST: DUDLEY MOORE _____ ST109

Alice's Adventures in Wonderland
Arthur
Arthur 2 On the Rocks
Bedazzled
Best Defense
Crazy People
Foul Play
The Hound of the Baskervilles (1977
   version)
Lovesick

Micki and Maude
Romantic Comedy
Santa Claus, The Movie
Six Weeks
10
30 Is a Dangerous Age, Cynthia
Unfaithfully Yours (1984 version)
Wholly Moses
The Wrong Box

Rick Moranis *See*: **CO14 The Alumni of SCTV**

STAR CHECK LIST: JEANNE MOREAU _____ ST110

Diary of a Chambermaid (1964 version)
Frantic (1958)
Going Places
Heat of Desire
Jules and Jim
The Last Tycoon
Les Liaisons Dangereuses
The Lovers

Lumiere*
Mr. Klein
Monte Walsh
The Oldest Profession
Querelle
The Train
The Trial
Your Ticket Is No Longer Valid

*also director

Garrett Morris *See*: **CO13 The Alumni of Saturday Night Live**
Eddie Murphy *See*: **CO13 The Alumni of Saturday Night Live**
Bill Murray *See*: **CO13 The Alumni of Saturday Night Live**
Laraine Newman *See*: **CO13 The Alumni of Saturday Night Live**

STAR CHECK LIST: PAUL NEWMAN _____ ST111

Absence of Malice
Blaze
Buffalo Bill and the Indians
Butch Cassidy and the Sundance Kid
Cat on a Hot Tin Roof
The Color of Money
Cool Hand Luke

The Drowning Pool
Exodus
Fat Man and Little Boy
Fort Apache, The Bronx
From the Terrace
Harper
Harry and Son*

Hombre
Hud
The Hustler
The Left-Handed Gun
The Life and Times of Judge Roy Bean
The Long Hot Summer (1958 version)
The Mackintosh Man
Paris Blues
Quintet
The Secret War of Harry Frigg
Silent Movie
The Silver Chalice
Slap Shot
Somebody Up There Likes Me

*also director

Sometimes a Great Notion*
The Sting
Sweet Bird of Youth
Torn Curtain
The Towering Inferno
The Verdict
When Time Ran Out
Winning
The Young Philadelphians

Director only
The Glass Menagerie
Rachel, Rachel
The Shadow Box

STAR CHECK LIST: JACK NICHOLSON _____ ST112

Batman (1989)
The Border
Broadcast News
Carnal Knowledge
Chinatown
Easy Rider
Ensign Pulver
Five Easy Pieces
Flight to Fury
Goin' South*
Heartburn
Hell's Angels on Wheels
Ironweed
The Last Detail
The Last Tycoon
The Little Shop of Horrors (1960
   version)
The Missouri Breaks
On a Clear Day You Can See Forever

*also director

One Flew Over the Cuckoo's Nest
The Passenger
The Postman Always Rings Twice (1981
   version)
Prizzi's Honor
Psych-Out
The Raven (1963)
Rebel Rousers
Reds
Ride in the Whirlwind
The Shining
The Shooting
Studs Lonigan
Terms of Endearment
The Terror
Tommy
The Wild Ride
The Witches of Eastwick

STAR CHECK LIST: NICK NOLTE _____ ST113

Cannery Row
Death Sentence
The Deep
Down and Out in Beverly Hills
Everybody Wins
Extreme Prejudice
Farewell to the King
48HRS.
Grace Quigley
Heart Beat

New York Stories
North Dallas Forty
Q & A
Return to Macon County
The Runaway Barge
Teachers
Three Fugitives
Under Fire
Weeds
Who'll Stop the Rain?

STAR CHECK LIST: CHUCK NORRIS _____ ST114

Braddock: Missing in Action 3
Breaker! Breaker!
Code of Silence
The Delta Force
An Eye for an Eye
Firewalker
A Force of One
Forced Vengeance
Game of Death
Good Guys Wear Black

Hero and the Terror
Invasion U.S.A.
Lone Wolf McQuade
Missing in Action
Missing in Action 2: The Beginning
The Octagon
Return of the Dragon
Silent Rage
Slaughter in San Francisco

ACTOR CHECK LIST: WARREN OATES _____ ST115

And Baby Makes Six
Badlands
Blue Thunder
The Border
Bring Me the Head of Alfredo Garcia
The Brink's Job
Cockfighter
Crooks and Coronets
Dillinger
Dixie Dynamite
Drum
East of Eden (1982 version)
The Hired Hand
In the Heat of the Night
Major Dundee
My Old Man

1941
92 in the Shade
Race With the Devil
Return of the Seven
Ride the High Country
The Shooting
Sleeping Dogs
Smith!
Stripes
There Was a Crooked Man
The Thief Who Came to Dinner
Tom Sawyer
Tough Enough
White Dawn
The Wild Bunch

Catherine O'Hara See: CO14 The Alumni of SCTV

STAR CHECK LIST: LAURENCE OLIVIER _____ ST116

As You Like It
Battle of Britain
The Betsy
The Bounty
The Boys From Brazil
A Bridge Too Far
Clash of the Titans
Clouds Over Europe
The Divorce of Lady X
Dracula (1979 version)
The Ebony Tower
Fire Over England
The 49th Parallel
Hamlet (1948 version)*
Henry V (1945 version)*
I Stand Condemned
The Jazz Singer (1980 version)
Jesus of Nazareth
The Jigsaw Man
Khartoum

Lady Caroline Lamb
A Little Romance
Love Among the Ruins
Marathon Man
Mr. Halpern and Mr. Johnson
Nicholas and Alexandra
Pride and Prejudice
The Prince and the Showgirl*
Rebecca
Richard III*
The Seven Percent Solution
The Shoes of the Fisherman
Sleuth
Spartacus
That Hamilton Woman
A Voyage Round My Father
Wagner
Wild Geese II
Wuthering Heights (1939 version)

*also director

STAR CHECK LIST: PETER O'TOOLE _____ **ST117**

Becket
The Bible
Caligula
Club Paradise
Creator
Foxtrot
High Spirits
Kidnapped
The Last Emperor
Lawrence of Arabia
The Lion in Winter
Lord Jim
Man Friday

Man of La Mancha
Murphy's War
My Favorite Year
The Night of the Generals
Power Play
The Ruling Class
The Stunt Man
Supergirl
Svengali
Under Milk Wood
What's New, Pussycat?
Zulu Dawn

STAR CHECK LIST: AL PACINO _____ **ST118**

. . . And Justice for All
Author! Author!
Bobby Deerfield
Cruising
Dick Tracy
Dog Day Afternoon
The Godfather

The Godfather, Part II
Revolution
Scarecrow
Scarface
Sea of Love
Serpico

Michael Palin *See*: **CO15 Monty Python's Flying Circus**

STAR CHECK LIST: GREGORY PECK _____ **ST119**

Amazing Grace and Chuck
Arabesque
Behold a Pale Horse
The Big Country
The Boys From Brazil
Cape Fear
Captain Newman, M.D.
David and Bathsheba
Days of Glory
Duel in the Sun
The Gunfighter
The Guns of Navarone
How the West Was Won
Keys of the Kingdom
MacArthur
Mackenna's Gold
The Man in the Grey Flannel Suit
Marooned

Mirage
Moby Dick
Old Gringo
The Omen
On the Beach
Only the Valiant
The Paradine Case
Pork Chop Hill
Roman Holiday
The Scarlet and the Black
The Sea Wolves
The Snows of Kilimanjaro
Spellbound
The Stalking Moon
To Kill a Mockingbird
Twelve O'Clock High
The Yearling

STAR CHECK LIST: MICHELLE PFEIFFER _____ **ST120**

Amazon Women on the Moon
Dangerous Liaisons
The Fabulous Baker Boys
Falling in Love Again
Grease 2
Into the Night

Ladyhawke
Married to the Mob
Scarface (1983 version)
Sweet Liberty
Tequila Sunrise
The Witches of Eastwick

Joe Piscopo *See*: **CO13 The Alumni of Saturday Night Live**

STAR CHECK LIST: SIDNEY POITIER ————————————— ST121

The Bedford Incident
Brother John
Buck and the Preacher*
The Defiant Ones (1958 version)
Duel at Diablo
For Love of Ivy
Goodbye, My Lady
Guess Who's Coming to Dinner
In the Heat of the Night
Let's Do It Again*
Lilies of the Field
Little Nikita
The Mark of the Hawk
The Organization
Paris Blues

A Patch of Blue
A Piece of the Action*
A Raisin in the Sun
Shoot to Kill
Something of Value
They Call Me MISTER Tibbs!
To Sir, With Love
Uptown Saturday Night*
The Wilby Conspiracy

Director only
Fast Forward
Hanky Panky
Stir Crazy

*also director

STAR CHECK LIST: WILLIAM POWELL ————————————— ST122
See also: CL15 Memorable Screen Teams—William Powell & Myrna Loy

After the Thin Man
Another Thin Man
Fashions of 1934
Feel My Pulse
The Great Ziegfeld
How to Marry a Millionaire
The Kennel Murder Case
The Last Command
Libeled Lady
Life With Father

Mr. Peabody and the Mermaid
Mister Roberts
My Man Godfrey
The Senator Was Indiscreet
Shdow of the Thin Man
Song of the Thin Man
Star of Midnight
The Thin Man
The Thin Man Goes Home
Ziegfeld Follies

STAR CHECK LIST: ELVIS PRESLEY ————————————— ST123
See also: MU10 Rock Concerts, MU11 Rock Documentaries

Blue Hawaii
Clambake
Double Trouble
Flaming Star
Follow That Dream
Frankie and Johnny
Fun in Acapulco
G.I. Blues
Girl Happy
Girls! Girls! Girls!
Harum Scarum
It Happened at the World's Fair
Jailhouse Rock
Kid Galahad
King Creole
Kissin' Cousins

Live a Little, Love a Little
Loving You
Paradise, Hawaiian Style
Roustabout
Speedway
Spinout
Stay Away, Joe
Tickle Me
The Trouble With Girls
Viva Las Vegas
Wild in the Country

NON-MUSIC
Change of Habit
Love Me Tender

STAR CHECK LIST: VINCENT PRICE _____ ST124

Abbott and Costello Meet Frankenstein
The Abominable Dr. Phibes
Adventures of Captain Fabian
The Baron of Arizona
Bloodbath at the House of Death
Casanova's Big Night
Champagne for Caesar
Conqueror Worm
Cry of the Banshee
Dangerous Mission
The Devil's Triangle (narrator)
Dr. Phibes Rises Again
The Fall of the House of Usher
The Fly (1958 version)
His Kind of Woman
House of the Long Shadows
House of Wax
House on Haunted Hill
Keys of the Kingdom
The Last Man on Earth
Laura
The Masque of the Red Death (1964 version)
Master of the World
The Monster Club

The Oblong Box
The Offspring
Pirate Warrior
The Pit and the Pendulum
The Private Lives of Elizabeth and Essex
The Raven (1963)
Return of the Fly
Scream and Scream Again
Shock
Snow White and the Seven Dwarfs (1983 version)
Son of Sinbad
Song of Bernadette
Tales of Terror
The Ten Commandments (1956 version)
Theatre of Blood
The Three Musketeers (1948 version)
The Tingler
Tomb of Ligeia
Tower of London (1962 version)
The Trouble With Girls
Twice Told Tales
The Whales of August
While the City Sleeps

STAR CHECK LIST: RICHARD PRYOR _____ ST125

Adios Amigo
The Bingo Long Traveling All-Stars & Motor Kings
Blue Collar
Brewster's Millions
Bustin' Loose
California Suite
Car Wash
Critical Condition
Greased Lightning
Harlem Nights
Jo Jo Dancer, Your Life Is Calling*
Lady Sings the Blues
The Mack
Moving
The Muppet Movie

Richard Pryor: Here and Now
Richard Pryor: Live and Smokin'
Richard Pryor: Live in Concert
Richard Pryor Live on the Sunset Strip
See No Evil, Hear No Evil
Silver Streak
Some Kind of Hero
Stir Crazy
Superman III
The Toy
Uptown Saturday Night
Which Way Is Up?
Wholly Moses
Wild in the Streets
The Wiz

*also director

Gilda Radner *See*: **CO13 The Alumni of Saturday Night Live**
Harold Ramis *See*: **CO14 The Alumni of SCTV**

STAR CHECK LIST: ROBERT REDFORD _____ ST126

All the President's Men
Barefoot in the Park
A Bridge Too Far

Brubaker
Butch Cassidy and the Sundance Kid
The Candidate

The Chase (1966)
Downhill Racer
The Electric Horseman
The Great Gatsby
The Great Waldo Pepper
The Hot Rock
Jeremiah Johnson
Legal Eagles
The Milagro Beanfield War*

*director only

The Natural
Ordinary People*
Out of Africa
The Sting
Tell Them Willie Boy Is Here
This Property Is Condemned
Three Days of the Condor
The Way We Were

STAR CHECK LIST: VANESSA REDGRAVE _____ ST127

Agatha
Bear Island
Blowup
The Bostonians
Camelot
Consuming Passions
The Devils
Isadora
Julia
A Man for all Seasons (1966 & 1988
   versions)
Morgan: A Suitable Case for Treatment

Murder on the Orient Express
Playing for Time
Prick Up Your Ears
The Seven Percent Solution
Snow White and the Seven Dwarfs (1983
   version)
Steaming
Three Sovereigns for Sarah
The Trojan Women
Wagner
Wetherby

STAR CHECK LIST: BURT REYNOLDS _____ ST128

All Dogs Go to Heaven (character
   voice)
Armored Command
Best Friends
The Best Little Whorehouse in Texas
Breaking In
The Cannonball Run
Cannnonball Run II
City Heat
Deliverance
The End*
Everything You Always Wanted To
   Know About Sex
Fuzz
Gator*
Heat
Hooper
Hustle
The Longest Yard
Malone
The Man Who Loved Cat Dancing

*also director

The Man Who Loved Women (1983
   version)
100 Rifles
Operation C.I.A.
Paternity
Physical Evidence
Rent-a-Cop
Rough Cut
Semi-Tough
Shamus
Shark!
Sharky's Machine*
Silent Movie
Smokey and the Bandit
Smokey and the Bandit II
Starting Over
Stick*
Stroker Ace
Switching Channels
White Lightning

STAR CHECK LIST: JASON ROBARDS _____ ST129

All the President's Men
Any Wednesday
The Ballad of Cable Hogue

A Boy and His Dog
Bright Lights, Big City
Burden of Dreams

By Love Possessed
Caboblanco
A Christmas to Remember
Comes a Horseman
The Day After
Dream a Little Dream
Fools
The Good Mother
Hurricane Isadora
Johnny Got His Gun
Julia
Julius Caesar (1970 version)
The Legend of the Lone Ranger
Long Day's Journey Into Night (1962 version)

The Long Hot Summer (1985 version)
Max Dugan Returns
Melvin and Howard
Murders in the Rue Morgue
The Night They Raided Minsky's
Once Upon a Time in the West
Parenthood
Pat Garrett and Billy the Kid
Raise the Titanic!
The St. Valentine's Day Massacre
Sakharov
Something Wicked This Way Comes
Square Dance
A Thousand Clowns
Tora! Tora! Tora!

STAR CHECK LIST: EDWARD G. ROBINSON _____ ST130

Barbary Coast
Cheyenne Autumn
The Cincinnati Kid
Double Indemnity
Good Neighbor Sam
Hell on Frisco Bay
A Hole in the Head
I Am the Law
Key Largo
Little Caesar
Mackenna's Gold

Mr. Winkle Goes to War
Never a Dull Moment
The Red House
Robin and the Seven Hoods
Scarlet Street
Song of Norway
Soylent Green
The Stranger
The Ten Commandments (1956 version)
Thunder in the City

STAR CHECK LIST: GINGER ROGERS _____ ST131
See also: CL15 Memorable Screen Teams—Fred Astaire & Ginger Rogers

Bachelor Mother
The Barkleys of Broadway
Carefree
Cinderella (1964 version)
Fifth Avenue Girl
Flying Down to Rio
Follow the Fleet
42nd Street
The Gay Divorcee
George Stevens: A Filmmaker's Journey
Gold Diggers of 1933
Having Wonderful Time
Kitty Foyle
Lucky Partners

Monkey Business (1952)
Once Upon a Honeymoon
Primrose Path
Roberta
Shall We Dance
A Shriek in the Night
Stage Door
The Story of Vernon and Irene Castle
Swing Time
The Thirteenth Guest
Tom, Dick & Harry
Top Hat
Vivacious Lady

STAR CHECK LIST: ROY ROGERS _____ ST132

Along the Navajo Trail
Apache Rose
The Arizona Kid
Bad Man of Deadwood
Bells of Coronado
Bells of Rosarita
Bells of San Angelo

The Big Show (with The Sons of the Pioneers)
Billy the Kid Returns
Carson City Kid
Colorado
Come on, Rangers
The Cowboy and the Señorita

Dark Command
Days of Jesse James
Don't Fence Me In
Down Dakota Way
Eyes of Texas
The Far Frontier
Frontier Pony Express
Gay Ranchero
The Golden Stallion
Grand Canyon Trail
Hands Across the Border
Heart of the Golden West
Heart of the Rockies
Helldorado
Home in Oklahoma
Idaho
In Old Amarillo
In Old Caliente
Jesse James at Bay
King of the Cowboys
Lights of Old Santa Fe
Man From Cheyenne
My Pal Trigger
Night Time in Nevada
North of the Great Divide
Old Barn Dance (billed as Dick Weston)
The Old Corral
The Ranger and the Lady

Ridin' Down the Canyon
Robinhood of the Pecos
Romance on the Range
Rough Riders Roundup
Saga of Death Valley
Shine on Harvest Moon
Silver Spurs
Son of Paleface
Song of Arizona
Song of Nevada
Song of Texas
South of Santa Fe
Southward Ho!
Springtime in the Sierras
Sunset in the West
Sunset on the Desert
Sunset Serenade
Susanna Pass
Texas Lightning
Trail of Robin Hood
Trigger, Jr.
Under California Stars
Under Nevada Skies
Under Western Stars
The Yellow Rose of Texas
Young Bill Hickok
Young Buffalo Bill

STAR CHECK LIST: MICKEY ROONEY _____ ST133
See also: CL15 Memorable Screen Teams—Mickey Rooney & Judy Garland

The Adventures of Huckleberry Finn
   (1939 version)
Andy Hardy Gets Spring Fever
Andy Hardy Meets Debutante
Andy Hardy's Private Secretary
The Atomic Kid
Babes in Arms
Babes on Broadway
The Big Wheel
Bill
Bill: On His Own
The Black Stallion
Boys Town
Breakfast at Tiffany's
The Bridges at Toko-Ri
Captains Courageous
The Comic
The Domino Principle

Erik the Viking
Find the Lady
Girl Crazy
The Human Comedy
It's a Mad Mad Mad Mad World
Journey Back to Oz (character voice)
Leave 'Em Laughing
Lightning: The White Stallion
Little Lord Fauntleroy (1936 version)
Love Laughs at Andy Hardy
The Magic of Lassie
A Midsummer Night's Dream
National Velvet
Off Limits (1953)
Pete's Dragon
Strike Up the Band
Thousands Cheer
Words and Music

STAR CHECK LIST: MICKEY ROURKE _____ ST134

Angel Heart
Barfly
Body Heat
City in Fear
Diner
Eureka
Johnny Handsome

9½ Weeks
The Pope of Greenwich Village
A Prayer for the Dying
Rape and Marriage: The Rideout Case
Rumblefish
Wild Orchid
The Year of the Dragon

STAR CHECK LIST: ARNOLD SCHWARZENEGGER _____ ST135

Commando
Conan the Barbarian
Conan the Destroyer
Predator
Pumping Iron
Raw Deal

Red Heat
Red Sonja
Running Man
Stay Hungry
The Terminator
Twins

STAR CHECK LIST: RANDOLPH SCOTT _____ ST136

Bombardier
Captain Kidd
China Sky
Follow the Fleet
Gung Ho! (1943)
My Favorite Wife
Rebecca of Sunnybrook Farm
Roberta
Susannah of the Mounties
To the Shores of Tripoli

WESTERNS
Abilene Town

Badman's Territory
Coroner Creek
Jesse James
The Last of the Mohicans (1936 version)
Man of the Forest
Rage at Dawn
Return of the Badmen
Ride the High Country
The Spoilers (1942 version)
Ten Wanted Men
To the Last Man
Western Union

STAR CHECK LIST: PETER SELLERS _____ ST137

After the Fox
Alice's Adventures in Wonderland
The Battle of the Sexes
Being There
The Blockhouse
The Bobo
Carlton Browne of the F.O.
Casino Royale
Dr. Strangelove: or, How I Learned to
   Stop Worrying and Love the Bomb
Down Among the Z-Men
The Fiendish Plot of Dr. Fu Manchu
Ghost in the Noonday Sun
The Goon Show Movie
The Great McGonagall
Heavens Above
I Love You, Alice B. Toklas
I'm All Right, Jack
The Ladykillers
Lolita
The Magic Christian
The Mouse That Roared
Muppet Treasures

Murder by Death
The Naked Truth
Never Let Go
The Party
The Pink Panther
The Pink Panther Strikes Again
The Prisoner of Zenda (1979 version)
The Return of the Pink Panther
The Revenge of the Pink Panther
Rowlf's Rhapsodies With the Muppets
A Shot in the Dark
There's a Girl in My Soup
tom thumb
Trail of the Pink Panther
Two Way Stretch
Up the Creek (1958)
Waltz of the Toreadors
What's New Pussycat?
Woman Times Seven
The World of Henry Orient
The Wrong Arm of the Law
The Wrong Box

Martin Short *See*: **CO14 The Alumni of SCTV**

STAR CHECK LIST: FRANK SINATRA _____ ST138

Cast a Giant Shadow
The Detective

The Devil at 4 O'Clock
Double Dynamite

The First Deadly Sin
From Here to Eternity
A Hole in the Head
Lady in Cement
The List of Adrian Messenger
The Man With the Golden Arm
The Manchurian Candidate
The Miracle of the Bells
Never So Few
Ocean's Eleven
The Pride and the Passion
Some Came Running
Suddenly
Tony Rome
Von Ryan's Express

MUSICALS
Anchors Aweigh
Can-Can
Guys and Dolls
High Society
Higher and Higher
On the Town
Robin and the Seven Hoods
Step Lively
Take Me out to the Ball Game
That's Entertainment
That's Entertainment, Part II
Till the Clouds Roll By
Young at Heart

STAR CHECK LIST: SISSY SPACEK _____ ST139

Badlands
Carrie (1976)
Coal Miner's Daughter
Crimes of the Heart
Ginger in the Morning
Heart Beat
Katherine
Marie

Missing
'night, Mother
Prime Cut
Raggedy Man
The River (1984)
Violets Are Blue
Welcome to L.A.

STAR CHECK LIST: SYLVESTER STALLONE _____ ST140

Bananas
Cannonball
Cobra
Death Race 2000
Farewell, My Lovely
F.I.S.T.
First Blood
Lock Up
The Lords of Flatbush
Nighthawks
Over the Top
Paradise Alley*
Rambo: First Blood II

Rambo III
Rebel (1973)
Rhinestone
Rocky
Rocky II*
Rocky III*
Rocky IV*
Tango and Cash
Victory

Director only
Staying Alive

*also director

ACTOR CHECK LIST: HARRY DEAN STANTON _____ ST141

Alien
The Black Marble
Christine
Cockfighter
Cool Hand Luke
Death Watch
Dillinger
Dream a Little Dream
Escape From New York

Farewell, My Lovely
Fool for Love
The Fourth War
The Godfather, Part II
Kelly's Heroes
The Last Temptation of Christ
The Missouri Breaks
Mr. North
One From the Heart

One Magic Christmas
Paris, Texas
Pat Garrett and Billy the Kid
Pretty in Pink
Private Benjamin
The Proud Rebel*
Rafferty and the Gold Dust Twins
Rebel Rousers*
Red Dawn
Repo Man

Ride in the Whirlwind
Rip Van Winkle
The Rose
Slamdance
Stars and Bars
Straight Time
Twister
UFOria
Wise Blood
Young Doctors in Love

*billed as Dean Stanton

STAR CHECK LIST: BARBARA STANWYCK _____ ST142

Annie Oakley
Ball of Fire
Blowing Wild
The Bride Walks Out
Cattle Queen of Montana
Christmas in Connecticut
Clash by Night
Double Indemnity
Escape to Burma
Executive Suite
Golden Boy

The Lady Eve
Lady of Burlesque
The Mad Miss Manton
The Maverick Queen
Meet John Doe
Roustabout
Sorry, Wrong Number
Stella Dallas
The Strange Love of Martha Ivers
The Thorn Birds
Walk on the Wild Side

STAR CHECK LIST: JAMES STEWART _____ STST143

After the Thin Man
Airport '77
Anatomy of a Murder
Bandolero
Bell, Book, and Candle
Bend of the River
The Big Sleep (1978 version)
Born To Dance
Broken Arrow
Cheyenne Autumn
The Cheyenne Social Club
Dear Brigitte
Destry Rides Again
The Far Country
Flight of the Phoenix
The Glenn Miller Story
The Greatest Show on Earth
Harvey
How the West Was Won
It's a Wonderful Life
Made for Each Other (1939)
The Magic of Lassie
The Man From Laramie
The Man Who Knew Too Much (1956
   version)

The Man Who Shot Liberty Valance
Mr. Hobbs Takes a Vacation
Mr. Smith Goes to Washington
The Naked Spur
The Philadelphia Story
Pot o' Gold
The Rare Breed
Rear Window
Right of Way
Rope
Rose Marie
Shenandoah
The Shootist
The Shop Around the Corner
The Spirit of St. Louis
Strategic Air Command
Thunder Bay
Two Rode Together
Vertigo
Vivacious Lady
Winchester '73
You Can't Take It With You
Ziegfeld Girl

ACTOR CHECK LIST: DEAN STOCKWELL _____ ST144

Alsino and the Condor
Anchors Aweigh
Blue Velvet
The Boy With Green Hair
Dune
The Dunwich Horror
Gardens of Stone
Kim
Long Day's Journey Into Night (1962
  version)

Married to the Mob
Paris, Texas
Psych-Out
Song of the Thin Man
To Live and Die in L.A.
Tracks
Tucker: The Man and His Dream
Werewolf of Washington
Wrong Is Right

STAR CHECK LIST: MERYL STREEP _____ ST145

A Cry in the Dark
The Deer Hunter
Falling in Love
The French Lieutenant's Woman
Heartburn
Holocaust
Ironweed
Julia
Kramer vs. Kramer

Manhattan
Out of Africa
Plenty
The Seduction of Joe Tynan
She-Devil
Silkwood
Sophie's Choice
Still of the Night

STAR CHECK LIST: BARBRA STREISAND _____ ST146

All Night Long
For Pete's Sake
The Main Event
Nuts
The Owl and the Pussycat
Up the Sandbox
The Way We Were
What's Up, Doc?

MUSICALS
Funny Girl
Funny Lady
Hello, Dolly!
On a Clear Day You Can See Forever
A Star Is Born (1976 version)
Yentl*

*also director

STAR CHECK LIST: ELIZABETH TAYLOR _____ ST147
See also: CL15 Memorable Screen Teams—Richard Burton & Elizabeth Taylor

Between Friends
Butterfield 8
Cat on a Hot Tin Roof (1958 version)
Cleopatra (1963)
A Date With Judy
Divorce His, Divorce Hers
Doctor Faustus
The Driver's Seat
Father of the Bride
Father's Little Dividend
Giant
Hammersmith Is Out
Ivanhoe
Lassie Come Home
The Last Time I Saw Paris
Life With Father
A Little Night Music
Little Women (1949 version)

Malice in Wonderland
The Mirror Crack'd
National Velvet
Night Watch
A Place in the Sun
Poker Alice
Raintree County
Reflections in a Golden Eye
Return Engagement
The Sandpiper
Secret Ceremony
Suddenly, Last Summer
The Taming of the Shrew
Under Milk Wood
Who's Afraid of Virginia Woolf?
Winter Kills
X, Y, and Zee

STAR CHECK LIST: SHIRLEY TEMPLE _____ **ST148**

Baby, Take a Bow
The Bachelor and the Bobby Soxer
The Blue Bird
Bright Eyes
Captain January
Curly Top
Dimples
Fort Apache
Heidi (1937 version)
Just Around the Corner
The Little Colonel
Little Miss Broadway

The Little Princess
The Littlest Rebel
Miss Annie Rooney
Our Little Girl
Poor Little Rich Girl
Rebecca of Sunnybrook Farm
Since You Went Away
Stand Up and Cheer
Stowaway
Susannah of the Mounties
To the Last Man
Wee Willie Winkie

Dave Thomas *See*: **CO14 The Alumni of SCTV**

STAR CHECK LIST: LILY TOMLIN _____ **ST149**

All of Me
Big Business
The Incredible Shrinking Woman

The Late Show
Nashville
9 to 5

ACTOR CHECK LIST: RIP TORN _____ **ST150**

Baby Doll
The Beastmaster
Beer
Birch Interval
The Cincinnati Kid
City Heat
Cold Feet
Coma
Cotter
Cross Creek
Extreme Prejudice
First Family
Flashpoint
Heartland
Hit List
Jinxed
The Man Who Fell to Earth

Misunderstood
Nadine
Nasty Habits
One-Trick Pony
Payday
Pork Chop Hill
The President's Plane Is Missing
The Private Files of J. Edgar Hoover
Rape and Marriage: The Rideout Case
The Seduction of Joe Tynan
Slaughter
Songwriter
A Stranger Is Watching
Summer Rental
Sweet Bird of Youth
You're a Big Boy Now

STAR CHECK LIST: SPENCER TRACY _____ **ST151**
See also: CL15 Memorable Screen Teams—Katharine Hepburn & Spencer Tracy

Adam's Rib
Bad Day at Black Rock
Boom Town
Boys Town
Captains Courageous
Desk Set
The Devil at 4 O'Clock
Dr. Jekyll and Mr. Hyde (1941 version)
Father of the Bride
Father's Little Dividend

Guess Who's Coming to Dinner
A Guy Named Joe
How the West Was Won*
Inherit the Wind
It's a Mad Mad Mad Mad World
Judgment at Nuremberg
The Last Hurrah
Northwest Passage
Pat and Mike
San Francisco

Stanley and Livingstone
State of the Union
That's Entertainment, Part II

Thirty Seconds Over Tokyo
Woman of the Year

*narrator only

STAR CHECK LIST: KATHLEEN TURNER ——————————— ST152

The Accidental Tourist
Body Heat
A Breed Apart
Crimes of Passion
Jewel of the Nile
Julia and Julia

The Man With Two Brains
Peggy Sue Got Married
Prizzi's Honor
Romancing the Stone
Switching Channels
The War of the Roses

STAR CHECK LIST: LANA TURNER ——————————— ST153

Another Time, Another Place
The Bad and the Beautiful
Bittersweet Love
By Love Possessed
Dr. Jekyll & Mr. Hyde (1941 version)
Green Dolphin Street
Imitation of Life

Love Finds Andy Hardy
Madame X (1966 version)
The Postman Always Rings Twice (1946 version)
The Sea Chase
The Three Musketeers (1948 version)
Ziegfeld Girl

STAR CHECK LIST: LIV ULLMANN ——————————— ST154

Autumn Sonata
The Bay Boy
A Bridge Too Far
Cold Sweat
Cries and Whispers
Dangerous Moves
Forty Carats
Gaby—A True Story

Leonor
The Night Visitor
Persona
Richard's Things
Scenes From a Marriage
The Serpent's Egg
The Wild Duck

ACTOR CHECK LIST: LEE VAN CLEEF ——————————— ST155

Armed Response
Bad Man's River
Beyond the Law
The Big Combo
Code Name: Wildgeese
The Conqueror
Death Rides a Horse
El Condor
Escape From New York
For a Few Dollars More
The Good, the Bad & the Ugly
Gunfight at the O.K. Corral

High Noon
Jungle Raiders
The Lonely Man
A Man Alone
The Man Who Shot Liberty Valance
Mean Frank and Crazy Tony
The Octagon
Speed Zone
The Stranger and the Gunfighter
Take a Hard Ride
The Tin Star
The Young Lions

STAR CHECK LIST: JOHN WAYNE ——————————— ST156

Back to Bataan
The Barbarian and the Geisha

Blood Alley
Brannigan

Cast a Giant Shadow
Circus World
The Conqueror
Donovan's Reef
The Fighting Seabees
Flying Leathernecks
Flying Tigers
The Green Berets*
Hatari!
The Hell Fighters
In Harm's Way
Lady for a Night
The Lady From Louisiana
Legend of the Lost
The Long Voyage Home
The Longest Day
McQ
The Quiet Man
Reap the Wild Wind
Reunion in France
The Sands of Iwo Jima
The Sea Chase
Seven Sinners
They Were Expendable
Tycoon
Wake of the Red Witch
Wheel of Fortune
The Wings of Eagles
Without Reservations

WESTERNS
The Alamo**
Allegheny Uprising
Angel and the Badman
Big Jake

The Big Trail
Cahill: United States Marshall
Chisum
The Comancheros
The Cowboys
Dakota
Dark Command
El Dorado
The Fighting Kentuckian
The Flame of the Barbary Coast
Fort Apache
The Horse Soldiers
How the West Was Won
In Old California
The Lady Takes a Chance
The Man Who Shot Liberty Valance
North to Alaska
Red River
Rio Bravo
Rio Grande
Rio Lobo
Rooster Cogburn
The Searchers
She Wore a Yellow Ribbon
The Shootist
The Sons of Katie Elder
The Spoilers (1942 version)
Stagecoach
Three Faces West
3 Godfathers
The Train Robbers
True Grit
The Undefeated
War of the Wildcats
The War Wagon

*also co-director
**also director

STAR CHECK LIST: SIGOURNEY WEAVER _____ **ST157**

Alien
Aliens
Deal of the Century
Eyewitness
Ghostbusters
Ghostbusters II
Gorillas in the Mist

Half Moon Street
Madman
One Man or Two
Working Girl
The Year of Living Dangerously
Orson Welles: See Director Check List
　　DT112 Orson Welles

STAR CHECK LIST: MAE WEST _____ **ST158**

My Little Chickadee
Myra Breckenridge

Sextette
She Done Him Wrong

STAR CHECK LIST: BILLY DEE WILLIAMS _____ **ST159**

The Bingo Long Traveling All-Stars &
　　Motor Kings

Brian's Song
Chiefs

Christmas Lilies of the Field
Courage (1986)
Deadly Illusion
The Empire Strikes Back
Fear City
The Glass House
Hostage Tower
Lady Sings the Blues

The Last Angry Man
Mahogany
Marvin and Tige
Nighthawks
Number One With a Bullet
Oceans of Fire
Return of the Jedi

STAR CHECK LIST: ROBIN WILLIAMS _____ ST160

The Adventures of Baron Munchausen
The Best of Comic Relief
The Best of Times
Club Paradise
Comic Relief 2
Comic Relief III
Dead Poets Society
An Evening With Robin Williams
Good Morning, Vietnam

HBO Comedy Club: Tenth Anniversary
    Young Comedians Special
Jonathan Winters: On the Ledge
Moscow on the Hudson
Popeye
Robin Williams Live!
Seize the Day
The Survivors
The Tale of the Frog Prince
The World According to Garp

STAR CHECK LIST: BRUCE WILLIS _____ ST161

Blind Date (1987)
Die Hard
In Country

Look Who's Talking (character voice)
Moonlighting (1985)
Sunset

STAR CHECK LIST: PAUL WINFIELD _____ ST162

Big Shots
Brother John
Blue City
Carbon Copy
Conrack
Damnation Alley
Death Before Dishonor
Gordon's War
Green Eyes

Hustle
It's Good To Be Alive
King
Mike's Murder
R.P.M.
The Serpent and the Rainbow
Sounder
The Terminator
Twilight's Last Gleaming

STAR CHECK LIST: DEBRA WINGER _____ ST163

Betrayed
Black Widow
Cannery Row
Everybody Wins
French Postcards
Legal Eagles
Made in Heaven

Mike's Murder
An Officer and a Gentleman
Slumber Party '57
Terms of Endearment
Thank God, It's Friday
Urban Cowboy

STAR CHECK LIST: SHELLEY WINTERS _____ ST164

Alfie
Bloody Mama
Blume in Love

City on Fire
Cleopatra Jones
The Delta Force

Diamonds
The Diary of Anne Frank
A Double Life
Enter Laughing
Executive Suite
Harper
I Am a Camera
King of the Gypsies
Knickerbocker Holiday
Lolita
The Night of the Hunter
A Patch of Blue
Pete's Dragon
Phone Call From a Stranger

A Place in the Sun
The Poseidon Adventure
Revenge (1971)
S.O.B.
The Scalphunters
The Tenant
Tentacles
Time of Indifference
Treasure of Pancho Villa
Who Slew Auntie Roo?
Wild in the Streets
Winchester 73
Wildfire

STAR CHECK LIST: JAMES WOODS _____ ST165

Against All Odds (1984)
Best Seller
The Boost
Cat's Eye
The Choirboys
Cop
The Disappearance of Aimee
Eyewitness
Fast-Walking
Immediate Family

Joshua Then and Now
Night Moves
Once Upon a Time in America
The Onion Field
Salvador
Split Image
True Believer
Videodrome
The Way We Were

STAR CHECK LIST: JOANNE WOODWARD _____ ST166

A Christmas to Remember
The Drowning Pool
The End
A Fine Madness
From the Terrace
The Fugitive Kind
Harry and Son
The Long Hot Summer (1958 version)

Paris Blues
Rachel, Rachel
The Shadow Box
The Stripper
Summer Wishes, Winter Dreams
Sybil
They Might Be Giants
Winning

Chapter Fifteen

WESTERNS
(WE)

See also: Historical/Fictional Character Check Lists HF1 Billy the Kid, HF3 Buffalo Bill (William F. Cody), HF6 George Armstrong Custer, HF9 Wyat Earp, HF11 Wild Bill Hickok, HF13 Doc Holliday, HF16 Jesse James, HF20 Annie Oakley

WESTERN EPICS _____ **WE1**

The Alamo
The Big Country
The Big Sky
The Big Trail
Cheyenne Autumn
Cimarron
The Covered Wagon
Duel in the Sun
The Good, the Bad, and the Ugly
Heaven's Gate

How the West Was Won
Little Big Man
Mackenna's Gold
The Magnificent Seven
Once Upon a Time in the West
The Plainsman
Red River
Silverado
The Unforgiven
The Way West

LONE GUNFIGHTERS _____ **WE2**

A Fistful of Dollars
For a Few Dollars More
The Gunfighter
High Noon
High Noon, Part Two: The Return of
   Will Kane
The Legend of the Lone Ranger
The Lonely Man
Man Without a Star
Pale Rider

The Red Headed Stranger
Rooster Cogburn
Shane
The Shootist
The Tin Star
True Grit
Warlock
The Westerner
The White Buffalo

SYMPATHETIC OUTLAWS _____ **WE3**

Bad Jim
Barbarosa
The Ballad of Gregorio Cortez
Butch Cassidy and the Sundance Kid
Butch and Sundance: The Early Days
The Good, the Bad, and the Ugly
Gore Vidal's Billy the Kid
The Grey Fox
Harry Tracy
Jesse James
The Left-Handed Gun
The Long Riders
Mad Dog Morgan

A Man Alone
The Missouri Breaks
Nevada Smith
The Outlaw
The Outlaw Josey Wales
Pat Garrett and Billy the Kid
Stagecoach
Tell Them Willie Boy Is Here
There Was a Crooked Man
3 Godfathers
Tom Horn
The Wild Bunch

CAVALRY STORIES ————————————————————————————— WE4

Fort Apache
The Horse Soldiers
Rio Grande
She Wore a Yellow Ribbon

Soldier Blue
They Died With Their Boots On
Ulzana's Raid

REVENGE IN THE OLD WEST ————————————————————— WE5

Cattle Queen of Montana
Coroner Creek
Death Rides a Horse
Django Shoots First
High Plains Drifter
Macho Callahan
The Man From Laramie
My Darling Clementine
Nevada Smith
Once Upon a Time in the West

One-Eyed Jacks
The Outlaw Josey Wales
The Ox-Bow Incident Pursued
Rancho Notorious
The Red Headed Stranger
The Return of Frank James
The Searchers
The Sons of Katie Elder
Young Guns

CIVIL WAR WESTERNS ————————————————————————— WE6
See also: AC5 War Movies—Civil War

Alvarez Kelly
Bad Company
The Beguiled
The Comancheros
Dark Command
The Fastest Guitar Alive
The Good, the Bad, and the Ugly
The Horse Soldiers
How the West Was Won (one segment)
Love Me Tender

Macho Callahan
Major Dundee
Massacre at Fort Holman
The Outlaw Josey Wales
Run of the Arrow
Santa Fe Trail
Shenandoah
The Skin Game (1971)
The Undefeated

INDIANS AS HEROES ————————————————————————— WE7

Apache
Broken Arrow
Chato's Land
Cheyenne Autumn
Eagle's Wing
Hombre
I Will Fight No More Forever
Little Big Man
A Man Called Horse
Mohawk
Naked in the Sun
100 Rifles
Return of a Man Called Horse

Run of the Arrow
The Searchers
Smith!
Soldier Blue
Tell Them Willie Boy Is Here
Triumphs of a Man Called Horse
Ulzana's Raid
The Unforgiven
The Vanishing American
War Party
When the Legends Die
Windwalker

WOMEN OF THE WEST ————————————————————————— WE8

Angel and the Badman
Annie Oakley
Bad Man's River
The Ballad of Cable Hogue

Barbary Coast
The Beautiful Blonde From Bashful
    Bend
Calamity Jane

Cat Ballou
Cattle Queen of Montana
Comes a Horseman
Destry Rides Again
Duel in the Sun
Girl of the Golden West
Heartland
Heller in Pink Tights
Johnny Guitar
Jubilee Trail
McCabe and Mrs. Miller
The Man Who Loved Cat Dancing
The Maverick Queen
The Misfits

My Darling Clementine
Once Upon a Time in the West
The Plainsman (1936)
Poker Alice
Rachel and the Stranger
Ramrod
Rancho Notorious
Renegade Ranger
River of No Return
The Stalking Moon
Texas Lady
Two Mules for Sister Sara
The Unforgiven

SOUTH OF THE BORDER _____ WE9

The Americano
The Appaloosa Bandolero!
Barbarosa
Bullet for Sandoval
Django El Condor
A Fistful of Dynamite
Goin' South
100 Rifles
Pancho Villa

The Professionals
Take a Hard Ride
They Came to Cordura
The Treasure of Pancho Villa
Vera Cruz
Villa Rides
Viva Zapata!
The Wild Bunch

NORTH OF THE BORDER _____ WE10

Blue Canadian Rockies
The Far Country
The Grey Fox
Harry Tracy

McCabe and Mrs. Miller
North of the Great Divide
North to Alaska
The Spoilers (1942 version)

LAST DAYS OF THE FRONTIER _____ WE11

The Ballad of Cable Hogue
Buffalo Bill and the Indians
Butch Cassidy and the Sundance Kid
The Grey Fox
McCabe and Mrs. Miller
The Man Who Shot Liberty Valance

Monte Walsh
Ride the High Country
The Shootist
Tell Them Willie Boy Is Here
Tom Horn
The Wild Bunch

THE CONTEMPORARY WEST _____ WE12

Bad Day at Black Rock
Bronco Billy
Comes a Horseman
Coogan's Bluff
Cotter
The Electric Horseman
Giant
Goldenrod
The Great American Cowboy
Hud

Junior Bonner
The Lady Takes a Chance
Last Night at the Alamo
Lonely Are the Brave
The Lusty Men
The Misfits
Three Faces West
Urban Cowboy
War Party
When the Legends Die

SPAGHETTI WESTERNS _____ WE13

Beyond the Law
Django
Django Shoots First
A Fistful of Dollars
A Fistful of Dynamite
For a Few Dollars More

The Good, the Bad, and the Ugly
Hang 'Em High
My Name Is Nobody
The Stranger and the Gunfighter
They Call Me Trinity
Trinity Is STILL My Name

WESTERN COMEDIES/SPOOFS _____ WE14

Adios Amigo
Along Came Jones
Bad Man's River
The Beautiful Blonde From Bashful
  Bend
Blazing Saddles
The Brothers O'Toole
Butch and Sundance: The Early Days
Butch Cassidy and the Sundance Kid
Cat Ballou
The Cheyenne Social Club
Destry Rides Again
Draw!
The Duchess and the Dirtwater Fox
The Frisco Kid
Go West (1940)
Goin' South

The Great Scout and Cathouse
  Thursday
The Lady Takes a Chance
The Last Ride of the Dalton Gang
Lust in the Dust
My Little Chickadee
The Paleface
Ruggles of Red Gap
Rustler's Rhapsody
The Scalphunters
Son of Paleface
Straight to Hell
Support Your Local Sheriff
There Was a Crooked Man
They Call Me Trinity
Trinity Is STILL My Name
The War Wagon Waterhole #3
Way Out West

CULT WESTERNS _____ WE15

Bad Company
The Culpepper Cattle Company
Duel in the Sun
The Great Northfield Minnesota Raid
The Hired Hand
Johnny Guitar
The Life and Times of Judge Roy Bean
McCabe and Mrs. Miller
The Missouri Breaks
The Oklahoma Kid
Once Upon a Time in the West
One-Eyed Jacks
The Outlaw

Pat Garrett and Billy the Kid
Rancho Notorious
Ride in the Whirlwind
Rio Bravo
The Searchers
The Shooting
The Skin Game (1971)
The Terror of Tiny Town
There Was a Crooked Man
3:10 to Yuma
Ulzana's Raid
Wild Rovers
Will Penny

Chapter Sixteen

WRITER CHECK LISTS
(WR)

WRITER CHECK LIST: JAMES M. CAIN ————————————————— **WR1**

Butterfly
Double Indemnity
Mildred Pierce

The Postman Always Rings Twice (1946
  & 1981 versions)
Slightly Scarlet

WRITER CHECK LIST: RAYMOND CHANDLER ————————————— **WR2**

The Big Sleep (1946 & 1978 versions)
The Brasher Doubloon
The Falcon Takes Over

Farewell, My Lovely
Murder My Sweet

WRITER CHECK LIST: AGATHA CHRISTIE ———————————————— **WR3**

And Then There Were None
Appointment With Death
The Body in the Library
Death on the Nile
Endless Night
Evil Under the Sun
Love From a Stranger
The Mirror Crack'd
A Murder Is Announced

Murder on the Orient Express
Ordeal by Innocence
A Pocketful of Rye
Ten Little Indians
Witness for the Prosecution (1957
  version)

Subject only
Agatha

WRITER CHECK LIST: CHARLES DICKENS ————————————————— **WR4**

A Christmas Carol (1951 version)
David Copperfield
Great Expectations (1946 version)
Little Dorritt
Miracle Down Under
Oliver!

Oliver and Company
Oliver Twist (1922, 1933 & 1948
  versions)
Scrooge
Scrooged
A Tale of Two Cities (1935 version)

WRITER CHECK LIST: DAPHNE DU MAURIER ————————————— **WR5**

The Birds
Don't Look Now

Jamaica Inn (1939 & 1985 versions)
Rebecca

WRITER CHECK LIST: WILLIAM FAULKNER ————————————————— **WR6**

Barn Burning
The Long Hot Summer (1958 & 1985
  versions)

The Reivers
Tomorrow

WRITER CHECK LIST: F. SCOTT FITZGERALD _____ WR7

The Great Gatsby   The Last Tycoon
The Last Time I Saw Paris

WRITER CHECK LIST: FREDERICK FORSYTH _____ WR8

The Day of the Jackal   The Fourth Protocol
The Dogs of War   The Odessa File

WRITER CHECK LIST: DASHIELL HAMMETT _____ WR9

After the Thin Man   The Thin Man
Another Thin Man   The Thin Man Goes Home
The Dain Curse   Watch on the Rhine
The Glass Key
The Maltese Falcon   **Subject only**
Shadow of the Thin Man   Hammett
Song of the Thin Man   Julia

WRITER CHECK LIST: ERNEST HEMINGWAY _____ WR10

A Farewell to Arms (1932 version)   The Snows of Kilimanjaro
Islands in the Stream   To Have and Have Not
The Killers (1964 version)
My Old Man   **Subject only**
                                        The Moderns

WRITER CHECK LIST: HENRY JAMES _____ WR11

The Bostonians   The Heiress
Daisy Miller   The Nightcomers
The Europeans   Turn of the Screw
The Green Room

WRITER CHECK LIST: STEPHEN KING _____ WR12

Based on Works by King   The Shining
Carrie (1976)   Silver Bullet
Children of the Corn   Stand by Me
Christine   Tales From the Darkside: The Movie
Cujo
The Dead Zone   **Original Screenplays**
Firestarter   Cat's Eye
Maximum Overdrive*   Creepshow**
Pet Sematary**   Creepshow 2
Salem's Lot

  *also director
**also actor

WRITER CHECK LIST: LOUIS L'AMOUR _____ WR13

Cancel My Reservation   The Quick and the Dead
Heller in Pink Tights   The Sacketts

WRITER CHECK LIST: D.H. LAWRENCE _____ WR14

Kangaroo
Lady Chatterly's Lover (1955 & 1981
   versions)

The Rainbow
The Virgin and the Gypsy
Women in Love

WRITER CHECK LIST: JOHN LECARRE _____ WR15

The Little Drummer Girl
The Looking Glass War

The Spy Who Came in From the Cold

WRITER CHECK LIST: ELMORE LEONARD _____ WR16

The Ambassador
Cat Chaser
52 Pick-up
Glitz
Hombre

Joe Kidd
Mr. Majestyk
Stick
3:10 to Yuma

WRITER CHECK LIST: SINCLAIR LEWIS _____ WR17

Ann Vickers
Arrowsmith

Dodsworth
Elmer Gantry

WRITER CHECK LIST: ROBERT LUDLUM _____ WR18

The Holcroft Covenant

The Osterman Weekend

WRITER CHECK LIST: ROSS MACDONALD _____ WR19

Blue City
The Drowning Pool

Harper

WRITER CHECK LIST: EUGENE O'NEILL _____ WR20

Anna Christie
Desire Under the Elms
The Emperor Jones

Long Day's Journey Into Night (1962 &
   1987 versions)
The Long Voyage Home
Strange Interlude (1988 version)

WRITER CHECK LIST: EDGAR ALLAN POE _____ WR21

The Avenging Conscience
Castle of Blood
The Fall of the House of Usher
The Haunting of Morella
The Masque of the Red Death (1964 &
   1989 versions)
Murders in the Rue Morgue (1971
   version)

The Oblong Box
The Pit and the Pendulum
The Premature Burial
The Raven (1963)
Tales of Terror
The Tomb of Ligeia
The Torture Chamber of Dr. Sadism

WRITER CHECK LIST: WILLIAM SHAKESPEARE _____ **WR22**

As You Like It (1936 version)
Forbidden Planet
Hamlet (1948 & 1969 versions)
Henry V (1945 & 1989 versions)
Julius Caesar (1953 & 1970 versions)
King Lear (1971 & 1987 versions)
Kiss Me Kate
Macbeth (1948 & 1971 versions)

A Midsummer Night's Dream (1935 version)
Ran
Richard III
Romeo and Juliet (1936 & 1968 versions)
The Taming of the Shrew
Throne of Blood

WRITER CHECK LIST: NEIL SIMON _____ **WR23**
(Based on Simon plays, or original screenplays by Simon, unless noted)

After the Fox
Barefoot in the Park
Biloxi Blues
Brighton Beach Memoirs
California Suite
Chapter Two
The Cheap Detective
The Goodbye Girl
The Heartbreak Kid*
I Ought to Be in Pictures
The Last of the Red Hot Lovers

Max Dugan Returns
Murder by Death
The Odd Couple
Only When I Laugh
The Out of Towners
Plaza Suite
The Prisoner of Second Avenue
Seems Like Old Times
The Slugger's Wife
The Sunshine Boys

*Simon screenplay, based on Bruce Jay Friedman story

WRITER CHECK LIST: MICKEY SPILLANE _____ **WR24**

The Girl Hunters

I, the Jury (1982 version)

WRITER CHECK LIST: JOHN STEINBECK _____ **WR25**

Cannery Row
East of Eden (1955 & 1982 versions)
The Grapes of Wrath

Of Mice and Men
The Red Pony (1949 & 1973 versions)

WRITER CHECK LIST: JIM THOMPSON _____ **WR26**

Clean Slate (Coup de Torchon)
The Getaway
The Killer Inside Me

The Killing
Paths of Glory

WRITER CHECK LIST: MARK TWAIN _____ **WR27**

The Adventures of Huckleberry Finn
(1939 & 1985 versions)
The Adventures of Mark Twain
The Adventures of Tom Sawyer (1938 &
1973 versions)
Bugs Bunny in King Arthur's Court

A Connecticut Yankee in King Arthur's
Court
Huckleberry Finn
The Prince and the Pauper (1937 & 1978
versions)
Pudd'nhead Wilson
Tom Sawyer

WRITER CHECK LIST: JULES VERNE _____ WR28

Around the World in 80 Days
Five Weeks in a Balloon
From the Earth to the Moon
In Search of the Castaways
Journey to the Center of the Earth (1959
   & 1989 versions)

The Light at the Edge of the World
Master of the World
Mysterious Island
20,000 Leagues Under the Sea
Where Time Began

WRITER CHECK LIST: H. G. WELLS _____ WR29

Empire of the Ants
First Men in the Moon
Food of the Gods
The Invisible Man
The Island of Dr. Moreau
The Man Who Could Work Miracles

Things to Come
Time After Time
The Time Machine
Village of the Giants
The War of the Worlds

WRITER CHECK LIST: TENNESSEE WILLIAMS _____ WR30

Baby Doll
Cat on a Hot Tin Roof
The Fugitive Kind
The Glass Menagerie (1987 version)
The Night of the Iguana

The Roman Spring of Mrs. Stone
A Streetcar Named Desire
Suddenly, Last Summer
Sweet Bird of Youth
This Property Is Condemned

Chapter Seventeen

VIDEO EXTRA
(XT)

ACADEMY AWARD CHECK LIST: BEST PICTURE _____ XT1

1927-28	Wings	1960	The Apartment
1928-29	Broadway Melody	1961	West Side Story
1929-30	All Quiet on the Western Front	1962	Lawrence of Arabia
		1964	My Fair Lady
1930-31	Cimarron	1965	The Sound of Music
1931-32	Grand Hotel	1966	A Man for all Seasons
1934	It Happened One Night	1967	In the Heat of the Night
1935	Mutiny on the Bounty	1968	Oliver!
1936	The Great Ziegfeld	1969	Midnight Cowboy
1937	The Life of Emile Zola	1970	Patton
1938	You Can't Take It With You	1971	The French Connection
1939	Gone With the Wind	1972	The Godfather
1940	Rebecca	1973	The Sting
1942	Mrs. Miniver	1974	The Godfather, Part II
1943	Casablanca	1975	One Flew Over the Cuckoo's Nest
1944	Going My Way		
1945	The Lost Weekend	1976	Rocky
1946	The Best Years of Our Lives	1977	Annie Hall
1948	Hamlet	1978	The Deer Hunter
1949	All the King's Men	1979	Kramer vs. Kramer
1950	All About Eve	1980	Ordinary People
1951	An American in Paris	1981	Chariots of Fire
1952	The Greatest Show on Earth	1982	Gandhi
1953	From Here to Eternity	1983	Terms of Endearment
1954	On the Waterfront	1984	Amadeus
1955	Marty	1985	Out of Africa
1956	Around the World in 80 Days	1986	Platoon
1957	The Bridge on the River Kwai	1987	The Last Emperor
1958	Gigi	1988	Rain Man
1959	Ben-Hur	1989	Driving Miss Daisy

Note: *Tom Jones*, the 1963 winner, has been discontinued; copies on videocassette are difficult to find.

ACADEMY AWARD CHECK LIST: BEST ACTOR _____ XT2

1927-28	The Last Command (Emil Jannings)	1937	Captains Courageous (Spencer Tracy)
1931-32	(tie) The Champ (Wallace Beery)	1938	Boys Town (Spencer Tracy)
	Dr. Jekyll and Mr. Hyde (Fredric March)	1939	Goodbye, Mr. Chips (Robert Donat)
1932-33	The Private Life of Henry VIII (Charles Laughton)	1940	The Philadelphia Story (James Stewart)
1934	It Happened One Night (Clark Gable)	1941	Sergeant York (Gary Cooper)
		1942	Yankee Doodle Dandy (James Cagney)
1935	The Informer (Victor McLaglen)		

1943	Watch on the Rhine (Paul Lukas)	1966	A Man for all Seasons (Paul Scofield)

1943 Watch on the Rhine (Paul Lukas)
1944 Going My Way (Bing Crosby)
1945 The Lost Weekend (Ray Milland)
1946 The Best Years of Our Lives (Fredric March)
1947 A Double Life (Ronald Colman)
1948 Hamlet (Laurence Olivier)
1949 All The King's Men (Broderick Crawford)
1950 Cyrano de Bergerac (Jose Ferrer)
1951 The African Queen (Humphrey Bogart)
1952 High Noon (Gary Cooper)
1953 Stalag 17 (William Holden)
1954 On the Waterfront (Marlon Brando)
1955 Marty (Ernest Borgnine)
1956 The King and I (Yul Brynner)
1957 The Bridge on the River Kwai (Alec Guinness)
1958 Separate Tables (David Niven)
1959 Ben-Hur (Charlton Heston)
1960 Elmer Gantry (Burt Lancaster)
1961 Judgment at Nuremberg (Maximilian Schell)
1962 To Kill a Mockingbird (Gregory Peck)
1963 Lilies of the Field (Sidney Poitier)
1964 My Fair Lady (Rex Harrison)
1965 Cat Ballou (Lee Marvin)

1966 A Man for all Seasons (Paul Scofield)
1967 In the Heat of the Night (Rod Steiger)
1968 Charly (Cliff Robertson)
1969 True Grit (John Wayne)
1970 Patton (George C. Scott)
1971 The French Connection (Gene Hackman)
1972 The Godfather (Marlon Brando)
1973 Save the Tiger (Jack Lemmon)
1974 Harry and Tonto (Art Carney)
1975 One Flew Over the Cuckoo's Nest (Jack Nicholson)
1976 Network (Peter Finch)
1977 The Goodbye Girl (Richard Dreyfuss)
1978 Coming Home (Jon Voight)
1979 Kramer vs. Kramer (Dustin Hoffman)
1980 Raging Bull (Robert DeNiro)
1981 On Golden Pond (Henry Fonda)
1982 Gandhi (Ben Kingsley)
1983 Tender Mercies (Robert Duvall)
1984 Amadeus (F. Murray Abraham)
1985 Kiss of the Spider Woman (William Hurt)
1986 The Color of Money (Paul Newman)
1987 Wall Street (Michael Douglas)
1988 Rain Man (Dustin Hoffman)
1989 My Left Foot (Daniel Day-Lewis)

ACADEMY AWARD CHECK LIST: BEST ACTRESS _____ XT3

1932-33 Morning Glory (Katharine Hepburn)
1934 It Happened One Night (Claudette Colbert)
1935 Dangerous (Bette Davis)
1936 The Great Ziegfeld (Luise Rainer)
1937 The Good Earth (Luise Rainer)
1938 Jezebel (Bette Davis)
1939 Gone With the Wind (Vivien Leigh)
1940 Kitty Foyle (Ginger Rogers)
1941 Suspicion (Joan Fontaine)
1942 Mrs. Miniver (Greer Garson)
1943 The Song of Bernadette (Jennifer Jones)
1944 Gaslight (Ingrid Bergman)
1945 Mildred Pierce (Joan Crawford)
1947 The Farmer's Daughter (Loretta Young)
1948 Johnny Belinda (Jane Wyman)
1949 The Heiress (Olivia de Havilland)
1950 Born Yesterday (Judy Holliday)

1951 A Streetcar Named Desire (Vivien Leigh)
1953 Roman Holiday (Audrey Hepburn)
1954 The Country Girl (Grace Kelly)
1958 I Want to Live! (Susan Hayward)
1960 Butterfield 8 (Elizabeth Taylor)
1961 Two Women (Sophia Loren)
1962 The Miracle Worker (Anne Bancroft)
1963 Hud (Patricia Neal)
1964 Mary Poppins (Julie Andrews)
1965 Darling (Julie Christie)
1966 Who's Afraid of Virginia Woolf? (Elizabeth Taylor)
1967 Guess Who's Coming to Dinner (Katharine Hepburn)
1968 (tie) The Lion in Winter (Katharine Hepburn)
       Funny Girl (Barbra Streisand)
1969 The Prime of Miss Jean Brodie (Maggie Smith)
1970 Women in Love (Glenda Jackson)

1971	Klute (Jane Fonda)	1981	On Golden Pond (Katharine Hepburn)
1972	Cabaret (Liza Minnelli)		
1973	A Touch of Class (Glenda Jackson)	1982	Sophie's Choice (Meryl Streep)
		1983	Terms of Endearment (Shirley MacLaine)
1974	Alice Doesn't Live Here Anymore (Ellen Burstyn)		
		1984	Places in the Heart (Sally Field)
1975	One Flew Over the Cuckoo's Nest (Louise Fletcher)	1985	The Trip to Bountiful (Geraldine Page)
1976	Network (Faye Dunaway)	1986	Children of a Lesser God (Marlee Matlin)
1977	Annie Hall (Diane Keaton)		
1978	Coming Home (Jane Fonda)	1987	Moonstruck (Cher)
1979	Norma Rae (Sally Field)	1988	The Accused (Jodie Foster)
1980	Coal Miner's Daughter (Sissy Spacek)	1989	Driving Miss Daisy (Jessica Tandy)

Note: *Room at the Top* (Simone Signoret), the 1959 winner, has been discontinued; copies on videocassette are difficult to find.

ACADEMY AWARD CHECK LIST: BEST SUPPORTING ACTOR ————————— XT4

1936	Come and Get It (Walter Brennan)	1963	Hud (Melvyn Douglas)
		1964	Topkapi (Peter Ustinov)
1937	The Life of Emile Zola (Joseph Schildkraut)	1965	A Thousand Clowns (Martin Balsam)
1939	Stagecoach (Thomas Mitchell)	1967	Cool Hand Luke (George Kennedy)
1940	The Westerner (Walter Brennan)		
1943	The More the Merrier (Charles Coburn)	1969	They Shoot Horses, Don't They? (Gig Young)
1944	Going My Way (Barry Fitzgerald)	1970	Ryan's Daughter (John Mills)
1945	A Tree Grows in Brooklyn (James Dunn)	1971	The Last Picture Show (Ben Johnson)
1946	The Best Years of Our Lives (Harold Russell)	1972	Cabaret (Joel Grey)
		1973	The Paper Chase (John Houseman)
1947	Miracle on 34th Street (Edmund Gwenn)		
		1974	The Godfather, Part II (Robert DeNiro)
1948	The Treasure of the Sierra Madre (Walter Huston)		
		1975	The Sunshine Boys (George Burns)
1949	Twelve O'Clock High (Dean Jagger)		
		1976	All the President's Men (Jason Robards)
1950	All About Eve (George Sanders)		
1951	A Streetcar Named Desire (Karl Malden)	1977	Julia (Jason Robards)
		1978	The Deer Hunter (Christopher Walken)
1952	Viva Zapata! (Anthony Quinn)		
1953	From Here to Eternity (Frank Sinatra)	1979	Being There (Melvyn Douglas)
		1980	Ordinary People (Timothy Hutton)
1954	The Barefoot Contessa (Edmond O'Brien)		
		1981	Arthur (John Gielgud)
1955	Mister Roberts (Jack Lemmon)	1982	An Officer and a Gentleman (Louis Gossett, Jr.)
1956	Lust for Life (Anthony Quinn)		
1957	Sayonara (Red Buttons)	1983	Terms of Endearment (Jack Nicholson)
1958	The Big Country (Burl Ives)		
1959	Ben-Hur (Hugh Griffith)	1984	The Killing Fields (Haing S. Ngor)
1960	Spartacus (Peter Ustinov)		
1961	West Side Story (George Chakiris)	1985	Cocoon (Don Ameche)
		1986	Hannah and Her Sisters (Michael Caine)
1962	Sweet Bird of Youth (Ed Begley)		

1987　The Untouchables (Sean Connery)

1988　A Fish Called Wanda (Kevin Kline)
1989　Glory (Denzel Washington)

Notes: Award debuted in 1936. The 1966 winner, *The Fortune Cookie* (Walter Matthau), has been discontinued; copies on videocassette are difficult to find.

ACADEMY AWARD CHECK LIST: BEST SUPPORTING ACTRESS _____ XT5

1936　Anthony Adverse (Gale Sondergaard)
1938　Jezebel (Fay Bainter)
1939　Gone With the Wind (Hattie McDaniel)
1940　The Grapes of Wrath (Jane Darwell)
1941　The Great Lie (Mary Astor)
1942　Mrs. Miniver (Teresa Wright)
1944　None but the Lonely Heart (Ethel Barrymore)
1945　National Velvet (Anne Revere)
1946　The Razor's Edge (Anne Baxter)
1948　Key Largo (Claire Trevor)
1949　All the King's Men (Mercedes McCambridge)
1950　Harvey (Josephine Hull)
1951　A Streetcar Named Desire (Kim Hunter)
1952　The Bad and the Beautiful (Gloria Grahame)
1953　From Here to Eternity (Donna Reed)
1954　On the Waterfront (Eva Marie Saint)
1955　East of Eden (Jo Van Fleet)
1956　Written on the Wind (Dorothy Malone)
1957　Sayonara (Miyoshi Umeki)
1958　Separate Tables (Deborah Kerr)
1959　The Diary of Anne Frank (Shelley Winters)
1960　Elmer Gantry (Shirley Jones)
1961　West Side Story (Rita Moreno)
1962　The Miracle Worker (Patty Duke)
1964　Zorba the Greek (Lila Kedrova)

1965　A Patch of Blue (Shelley Winters)
1966　Who's Afraid of Virginia Woolf? (Sandy Dennis)
1967　Bonnie and Clyde (Estelle Parsons)
1968　Rosemary's Baby (Ruth Gordon)
1969　Cactus Flower (Goldie Hawn)
1970　Airport (Helen Hayes)
1971　The Last Picture Show (Cloris Leachman)
1972　Butterflies Are Free (Eileen Heckart)
1973　Paper Moon (Tatum O'Neal)
1974　Murder on the Orient Express (Ingrid Bergman)
1975　Shampoo (Lee Grant)
1976　Network (Beatrice Straight)
1977　Julia (Vanessa Redgrave)
1978　California Suite (Maggie Smith)
1979　Kramer vs. Kramer (Meryl Streep)
1980　Melvin and Howard (Mary Steenburgen)
1981　Reds (Maureen Stapleton)
1982　Tootsie (Jessica Lange)
1983　The Year of Living Dangerously (Linda Hunt)
1984　A Passage to India (Peggy Ashcroft)
1985　Prizzi's Honor (Anjelica Huston)
1986　Hannah and Her Sisters (Dianne Wiest)
1987　Moonstruck (Olympia Dukakis)
1988　The Accidental Tourist (Geena Davis)
1989　My Left Foot (Brenda Fricker)

Note: Award debuted in 1936.

ACADEMY AWARD CHECK LIST: BEST DIRECTOR _____ XT6

1929-30　All Quiet on the Western Front (Lewis Milestone)
1934　It Happened One Night (Frank Capra)
1935　The Informer (John Ford)
1936　Mr. Deeds Goes to Town (Frank Capra)

1937　The Awful Truth (Leo McCarey)
1938　You Can't Take It With You (Frank Capra)
1939　Gone With the Wind (Victor Fleming)
1940　The Grapes of Wrath (John Ford)
1942　Mrs. Miniver (William Wyler)

1943 Casablanca (Michael Curtiz)	1969 Midnight Cowboy (John Schlesinger)
1944 Going My Way (Leo McCarey)	1970 Patton (Franklin J. Schaffner)
1945 The Lost Weekend (Billy Wilder)	1971 The French Connection (William Friedkin)
1946 The Best Years of Our Lives (William Wyler)	1972 Cabaret (Bob Fosse)
1948 The Treasure of the Sierra Madre (John Huston)	1973 The Sting (George Roy Hill)
1950 All About Eve (Joseph L. Mankiewicz)	1974 The Godfather, Part II (Francis Ford Coppola)
1951 A Place in the Sun (George Stevens)	1975 One Flew Over the Cuckoo's Nest (Milos Forman)
1952 The Quiet Man (John Ford)	1976 Rocky (John G. Avildsen)
1953 From Here to Eternity (Fred Zinnemann)	1977 Annie Hall (Woody Allen)
1954 On the Waterfront (Elia Kazan)	1978 The Deer Hunter (Michael Cimino)
1955 Marty (Delbert Mann)	1979 Kramer vs. Kramer (Robert Benton)
1956 Giant (Goerge Stevens)	
1957 The Bridge on the River Kwai (David Lean)	1980 Ordinary People (Robert Redford)
1958 Gigi (Vincente Minnelli)	1981 Reds (Warren Beatty)
1959 Ben-Hur (William Wyler)	1982 Gandhi (Richard Attenborough)
1960 The Apartment (Billy Wilder)	1983 Terms of Endearment (James L. Brooks)
1961 West Side Story (Robert Wise)*	
1962 Lawrence of Arabia (David Lean)	1984 Amadeus (Milos Forman)
1964 My Fair Lady (George Cukor)	1985 Out of Africa (Sydney Pollack)
1965 The Sound of Music (Robert Wise)	1986 Platoon (Oliver Stone)
1966 A Man for all Seasons (Fred Zinnemann)	1987 The Last Emperor (Bernardo Bertolucci)
1967 The Graduate (Mike Nichols)	1988 Rain Man (Barry Levinson)
1968 Oliver! (Carol Reed)	1989 Born on the Fourth of July (Oliver Stone)

*Wise and choreographer Jerome Robbins shared screen credit for directing; Robbins won a special Oscar for his contribution to the film.

Note: *Tom Jones* (Tony Richardson), the 1963 winner, has been discontinued; copies on videocassette are difficult to find.

ACADEMY AWARD CHECK LIST: BEST FOREIGN LANGUAGE FILM _____ XT7

1949 The Bicycle Thief (Italy)	1964 Yesterday, Today and Tomorrow (Italy)
1951 Rashomon (Japan)	
1952 Forbidden Games (France)	1965 The Shop on Main Street (Czechoslovakia)
1954 Gate of Hell (Japan)	
1955 Samurai (The Seven Samurai) (Japan)	1966 A Man and a Woman (France)
	1967 Closely Watched Trains (Czechoslovakia)
1956 La Strada (Italy)	
1957 Nights of Cabiria (Italy)	1968 War and Peace (Soviet Union)
1958 My Uncle (France)	1969 Z (France)
1959 Black Orpheus (Brazil)	1971 The Garden of the Finzi-Continis (Italy)
1960 The Virgin Spring (Sweden)	
1961 Through a Glass Darkly (Sweden)	1972 The Discreet Charm of the Bourgeoisie (France)
1962 Sundays and Cybele (France)	
1963 8½ (Italy)	1973 Day for Night (France)

1974   Amarcord (Italy)
1975   Dersu Uzala (Japan)
1976   Black and White in Color
          (France)
1977   Madame Rosa (France)
1978   Get Out Your Handkerchiefs
          (France)
1979   The Tin Drum (Germany)
1980   Moscow Does Not Believe in
          Tears (Soviet Union)

1981   Mephisto (Hungary)
1983   Fanny and Alexander (Sweden)
1984   Dangerous Moves (Switzerland)
1985   The Official Story (Argentina)
1986   The Assault (Holland)
1987   Babette's Feast (Denmark)
1988   Pelle the Conqueror (Denmark)
1989   Cinema Paradiso (Italy)

Note: Award debuted in 1947.

ALL IN THE FAMILY: MOVIES FEATURING MOTHERS, FATHERS, SONS, DAUGHTERS, SISTER, BROTHERS ——————————————————— XT8

At Close Range (Sean & Christopher
   Penn)
Big Jake (John & Patrick Wayne)
Big Wednesday (Barbara Hale &
   William Katt)
Boxcar Bertha (David & John
   Carradine)
The Chase (1966) (Marlon & Jocelyn
   Brando)
Cheech & Chong's The Corsican
   Brothers (Tommy, Rae Dawn &
   Robbi Chong; Cheech & Rikki Marin)
Do the Right Thing (Spike & Joie Lee)
The Fabulous Baker Boys (Beau & Jeff
   Bridges)
The Fog (Jamie Lee Curtis & Janet
   Leigh)
Hearts of the World (Lillian & Dorothy
   Gish)
Home Sweet Home (Lillian & Dorothy
   Gish)
Honkytonk Man (Clint & Kyle
   Eastwood)
In the Spirit (Elaine May & Jeannie
   Berlin)
The Long Riders (David, Keith &
   Robert Carradine; Christopher &

Nicholas Guest; Stacy & James
   Keach; Dennis & Randy Quaid)
Nightbreaker (Martin Sheen & Emilio
   Estevez)
On Golden Pond (Henry & Jane Fonda)
Orphans of the Storm (Lillian &
   Dorothy Gish)
Our Hospitality (Buster & Joseph
   Keaton, and Buster, Jr.)
The Proud Rebel (Alan & David Ladd)
Paper Moon (Ryan & Tatum O'Neal)
The Searchers (Natalie & Lana Wood)
That's Life! (Jack & Chris Lemmon;
   Julie Andrews & Emma Walton)
Think Big (Peter & David Paul)
Thunder Road (Robert & Jim Mitchum)
Tightrope (Clint & Alison Eastwood)
The Treasure of the Sierra Madre
   (Walter and John Huston)
Tucker: The Man and His Dream (Lloyd
   & Jeff Bridges)
Wall Street (Martin & Charlie Sheen)
The Wild Country (Ronny & Clint
   Howard)
Young Guns (Emilio Estevez & Charlie
   Sheen)

ON LOCATION: MOVIES THAT MAKE GOOD USE OF MAJOR CITIES

NEW YORK ————————————————————————————— XT9

Across 110th Street
Addict
After Hours
The Anderson Tapes
Annie Hall
Barefoot in the Park
The Believers
Breakfast at Tiffany's
Bright Lights, Big City

Broadway Danny Rose
China Girl
Coming to America
Coogan's Bluff
"Crocodile" Dundee
"Crocodile" Dundee II
Crossing Delancey
Death Wish
Desperately Seeking Susan

Do the Right Thing
Dog Day Afternoon
The Dream Team
Eyewitness
Falling in Love
Fame
Fort Apache, The Bronx
The French Connection
Funny Girl
Garbo Talks
Ghostbusters
Ghostbusters II
Greetings
Hair
Hannah and Her Sisters
Highlander
It Should Happen to You
It's My Turn
Just Tell Me What You Want
King Kong (1933 & 1976 versions)
King of Comedy
Legal Eagles
Liquid Sky
Love With the Proper Stranger
Madigan
Manhattan
Marathon Man
Married to the Mob
Mean Streets
Midnight Cowboy
Moscow on the Hudson
The Muppets Take Manhattan
New York Stories
Nighthawks
The Odd Couple
On the Town

The Out-of-Towners
The Pawnbroker
The Pick-up Artist
Prince of the City
Q & A
Q: The Winged Serpent
Radio Days
Raging Bull
Rooftops
Rosemary's Baby
Saboteur
Saturday Night Fever
Serpico
Slaves of New York
Smithereens
Someone to Watch Over Me
Sophie's Choice
Splash
A Stranger Is Watching
The Taking of Pelham One Two Three
Taxi Driver
They All Laughed
A Thousand Clowns
Times Square
Turk 182
An Unmarried Woman
Wall Street
The Warriors
West Side Story
When Harry Met Sally . . .
Where the Heart Is
Without a Trace
Wolfen
Working Girl
The World of Henry Orient
You're a Big Boy Now

LOS ANGELES _____ **XT10**

Against All Odds (1984)
Annie Hall
Beverly Hills Cop
Beverly Hills Cop II
Blue Thunder
California Suite
Chinatown
Colors
The Day of the Locust
Down and Out in Beverly Hills
Internal Affairs
The Loved One

Night of the Comet
Point Blank
Pretty Woman
Repo Man
Shampoo
Slamdance
To Live and Die in L.A.
True Confessions
Vice Squad
Welcome to L.A.
Zabriskie Point

CHICAGO _____ **XT11**

About Last Night
Adventures in Babysitting
Big Shots
The Blues Brothers

City That Never Sleeps
Code of Silence
Continental Divide
Ferris Bueller's Day off

Henry: Portrait of a Serial Killer
The Hunter
Medium Cool
Music Box
Nothing in Common

Red Heat
Risky Business
Running Scared
Windy City

WASHINGTON, D.C. _____ XT12

Advise and Consent
All the President's Men
Being There
Born Yesterday
Broadcast News
Chances Are
D.C. Cab
The Day the Earth Stood Still
Earth vs. the Flying Saucers
The Exorcist
Exorcist II: The Heretic
First Family
First Monday in October

Heartburn
Houseboat
In Country
Mr. Smith Goes to Washington
No Way Out
Power (1986)
The President's Analyst
Protocol
St. Elmo's Fire
The Seduction of Joe Tynan
Sherlock Holmes in Washington
Short Fuse
Suspect

SAN FRANCISCO _____ XT13

Bullitt
Chan Is Missing
The Conversation
The Dead Pool
Dim Sum: a little bit of heart
Dirty Harry
The Enforcer (1976)
Experiment in Terror
Fools
48HRS.
Foul Play
Invasion of the Body Snatchers (1979
    version)

The Killer Elite
The Laughing Policeman
Magnum Force
Petulia
Point Blank
The Presidio
Psych-Out
Signal 7
Vertigo
View to a Kill
What's Up, Doc?

NEW ORLEANS _____ XT14

Angel Heart
The Big Easy
The Cat People (1982 version)
Easy Rider
Hard Times

Johnny Handsome
Obsession
Pretty Baby
Tightrope

LONDON _____ XT15

Absolute Beginners
An American Werewolf in London
Blowup
Branningan
Darling
Frenzy
Georgy Girl
Gorgo

A Hard Day's Night
The Long Good Friday
Look Back in Anger
Midnight Lace
Mona Lisa
My Beautiful Laundrette
Sammy and Rosie Get Laid

PARIS _____ XT16

American Dreamer
La Balance
Bob le Flambeur
Breathless (1959 version)
Charade
The Day of the Jackal
The Destructors
Diva
The 400 Blows
Frantic (1988)

French Postcards
Funny Face
Last Tango in Paris
A Little Romance
The Man on the Eiffel Tower
Masculine-Feminine
Paris Blues
Round Midnight
Shoot the Piano Player

ROME _____ XT17

After the Fox
La Dolce Vita
Eclipse
Love in the City
Open City

Roman Holiday
The Roman Spring of Mrs. Stone
The Roof
The White Sheik

MOVIN' ON: ROAD MOVIES _____ XT18

Alice Doesn't Live Here Anymore
Around the World in 80 Days
Back Roads
Badlands
Bird on a Wire
Bonnie and Clyde
Bring Me the Head of Alfredo Garcia
Bustin' Loose
Cold Feet
Convoy
Coup de Ville
Crazy Mama
Duel
Easy Rider
Eddie Macon's Run
Fandango
Flashback
The Gauntlet
The Getaway
Going Places
The Great Race
The Great Smokey Roadblock
Harry and Tonto
Heroes
Hollywood or Bust
Homer and Eddie
It Happened One Night
It's a Mad Mad Mad Mad World
The Journey of Natty Gann

Kings of the Road
The Last Detail
Lost in America
Midnight Run
National Lampoon's European Vacation
National Lampoon's Vacation
Near Dark
North by Northwest
Outrageous Fortune
Paris, Texas
Pierrot le Fou
Planes, Trains, and Automobiles
Powwow Highway
Rafferty and the Gold Dust Twins
Rain Man
The Rain People
Saboteur
Scarecrow
Sherman's March
Something Wild
The Sugarland Express
Sullivan's Travels
The Sure Thing
They Live by Night
Think Big
The 39 Steps (1935 & 1978 versions)
Three Fugitives
Two for the Road
You Only Live Once

ALL ABOARD: TRAIN MOVIES _____ XT19

Breakheart Pass
Closely Watched Trains

Finders Keepers
Flashback

From Russia With Love
The General
Go West
The Great Locomotive Chase
The Great Train Robbery
The Grey Fox
Horror Express
How the West Was Won
The Incident
The Journey of Natty Gann
The Lady Vanishes (1939 & 1979
   versions)
Murder on the Orient Express

The Narrow Margin
The Palm Beach Story
Planes, Trains, and Automobiles
Runaway Train
Silver Streak
Strangers on a Train
The Taking of Pelham One Two Three
Terror Train
Tracks
The Train
Twentieth Century
Warm Nights on a Slow Moving Train

HERE COMES THE BRIDE: MEMORABLE WEDDING SCENES AND WEDDING MOVIES _____ XT20

Blind Date (1987)
La Cage aux Folles 3: The Wedding
Cousin Cousine
Cousins
The Deer Hunter
Father of the Bride
The Godfather
Goodbye, Columbus
The Graduate
Greed
The Heartbreak Kid
Here Comes the Groom

High Society
Lovers and Other Strangers
The Philadelphia Story
Prizzi's Honor
Seven Brides for Seven Brothers
Sixteen Candles
True Love
A Wedding
Wedding in White
The Wedding March
The Wedding Party

STUNNING DEBUTS: LEGENDARY FIRST STARRING ROLES _____ XT21

Adam's Rib (Judy Holliday)
Body Heat (Kathleen Turner)
Citizen Kane (Orson Welles)
East of Eden (James Dean)
48HRS. (Eddie Murphy)
Funny Girl (Barbra Streisand)
Golden Boy (William Holden)
Goodbye, Mr. Chips (Greer Garson)
Great Expectations (Alec Guinness)

The Invisible Man (Claude Rains)
Lawrence of Arabia (Peter O'Toole)
Mary Poppins (Julie Andrews)
The Men (Marlon Brando)
The Outlaw (Jane Russell)
Roman Holiday (Audrey Hepburn)
Splendor in the Grass (Warren Beatty)
The Trouble With Harry (Shirley
   MacLaine)

FOND FAREWELLS: MEMORABLE FINAL PERFORMANCES _____ XT22

Advise and Consent (Charles Laughton)
Bells Are Ringing (Judy Holliday)
Enter the Dragon (Bruce Lee)
Giant (James Dean)
Guess Who's Coming to Dinner
   (Spencer Tracy)
The Harder They Fall (Humphrey
   Bogart)
The Killers (1964 version) (Ronald
   Reagan)
The Misfits (Clark Gable, Marilyn
   Monroe)

Mister Roberts (William Powell)
Network (Peter Finch)
On Golden Pond (Henry Fonda)
Ride the High Country (Randolph Scott)
S.O.B. (William Holden)
Shane (Jean Arthur)
The Shootist (John Wayne)
To Be or Not to Be (1942 version)
   (Carole Lombard)
Walk, Don't Run (Cary Grant)

Chapter Eighteen

ESSENTIAL VIEWING LISTS

As explained in How to Use This Book, this is a check list of films which have made their mark on film history, usually for better, sometimes for worse. If you're looking to become a better educated person about the history of film, I suggest you start with this list.

The lists are broken down by half-decades, except for the silent film era and the first talkies. I feel this organization is especially useful for viewers looking for historical currents and trends as reflected in movies. It also gives a sense of the evolution (some would say devolution) of the art of film.

The numbers after each title indicate the date of its original release.

1915-1930
L'Age d'Or 30
All Quiet on the Western Front 30
The Big Parade 25
The Birth of a Nation 15
The Blue Angel 30
Broken Blossoms 19
The Cabinet of Dr. Caligari 19
The Chaplin Revue 18-22
Charlie Chaplin Cavalcade 16
Un Chien Andalou 28
The Circus 28
The Crowd 28
The Freshman 25
The General 27
The Gold Rush 25
Greed 25
Intolerance 16
It 27
The Jazz Singer 27
The Kid 21
The Last Command 28
The Last Laugh 24
Metropolis 26
Nanook of the North 22
Napoleon 27
Nosferatu 22
Pandora's Box 28
The Passion of Joan of Arc 28
Potemkin 25
Show People 28
Steamboat Bill, Jr. 28
The Ten Commandments 23
Ten Days That Shook the World/
   October 27
The Thief of Bagdad 24
Way Down East 20
The Wind 28
Wings 27

1931-35
A Nous la Liberté 31
L'Atalante 34

Blonde Venus 32
The Bride of Frankenstein 35
City Lights 31
Dr. Jekyll and Mr. Hyde 32
Dracula 31
Duck Soup 33
Footlight Parade 33
42nd Street 33
Frankenstein 31
Freaks 32
Grand Hotel 32
I Am a Fugitive From a Chain Gang 32
It Happened One Night 34
It's a Gift 34
King Kong 33
Little Caesar 31
M 31
Mutiny on the Bounty 35
A Night at the Opera 35
The Public Enemy 31
Queen Christina 33
Scarface 32
Sons of the Desert 33
Tarzan, the Ape Man 32
The Thin Man 35
The 39 Steps 35
Top Hat 35
Triumph of the Will 35
Twentieth Century 34
Zero for Conduct 33

1936-40
The Adventures of Robin Hood 38
Alexander Nevsky 38
Angels With Dirty Faces 38
The Awful Truth 37
Bringing Up Baby 38
Dark Victory 39
Dead End 37
Destry Rides Again 39
Dodsworth 36
Gone With the Wind 39
Grand Illusion 37

The Grapes of Wrath 40
The Great Dictator 40
The Great McGinty 40
Gunga Din 39
His Girl Friday 40
Holiday 37
The Lady Vanishes 38
Lost Horizon 37
Mr. Deeds Goes to Town 36
Mr. Smith Goes to Washington 39
Modern Times 36
My Man Godfrey 36
Ninotchka 39
Olympia 38
Only Angels Have Wings 39
The Philadelphia Story 40
Pinocchio 40
Rebecca 40
Rules of the Game 39
The Shop Around the Corner 40
Stagecoach 39
Stella Dallas 37
Swing Time 36
The Thief of Bagdad 40
The Wizard of Oz 39
The Women 39
Wuthering Heights 39
You Only Live Once 37
Young Mr. Lincoln 39

1941-45
Bambi 42
Brief Encounter 45
Casablanca 43
The Cat People 42
Citizen Kane 41
Double Indemnity 44
Going My Way 44
Henry V 45
High Sierra 41
Ivan the Terrible, Part One 43
King's Row 42
The Lady Eve 41
Laura 44
The Lost Weekend 45
The Magnificent Ambersons 42
The Maltese Falcon 41
Meet John Doe 41
Meet Me in St. Louis 44
Mildred Pierce 45
Mrs. Miniver 42
The Ox-Bow Incident 43
Shadow of a Doubt 43
Sullivan's Travels 41
To Be or Not To Be 42
A Tree Grows in Brooklyn 45
Woman of the Year 42
Yankee Doodle Dandy 42

1946-50
Adam's Rib 50
All About Eve 50
All the King's Men 49
The Asphalt Jungle 50
Beauty and the Beast 46
The Best Years of Our Lives 46
The Bicycle Thief 49
The Big Sleep 46
Born Yesterday 50
Diary of a Country Priest 50
Duel in the Sun 46
Father of the Bride 50
Force of Evil 48
Fort Apache 48
Great Expectations 46
Hamlet 48
Home of the Brave 49
It's a Wonderful Life 46
Ivan the Terrible, Part Two 46
Kind Hearts and Coronets 49
The Louisiana Story 48
My Darling Clementine 46
Notorious 46
Los Olvidados 50
On the Town 49
Open City 46
Out of the Past 47
The Postman Always Rings Twice 46
Red River 48
The Set-Up 49
She Wore a Yellow Ribbon 49
Sorry, Wrong Number 48
Sunset Boulevard 50
La Terra Trema 47
They Live by Night 49
The Third Man 49
The Treasure of the Sierra Madre 48
White Heat 49
Winchester '73 50

1951-55
The African Queen 51
An American in Paris 51
The Bad and the Beautiful 52
Bad Day at Black Rock 55
The Band Wagon 53
Beat the Devil 54
The Big Heat 53
The Crimson Pirate 52
The Day the Earth Stood Still 51
Diabolique 55
East of Eden 55
Forbidden Games 51
From Here to Eternity 53
High Noon 52
Ikiru 52
The Lavender Hill Mob 51

Limelight 52
The Man With the Golden Arm 55
Marty 55
Mr. Hulot's Holiday 53
Night and Fog 55
On the Waterfront 54
A Place in the Sun 51
The Quiet Man 52
Rashomon 51
Rear Window 54
Rebel Without a Cause 55
The Seven Samurai 54
Shane 53
Singin' in the Rain 52
Smiles of a Summer Night 55
Stalag 17 53
A Star Is Born 54
La Strada 54
Strangers on a Train 51
A Streetcar Named Desire 51
The Thing (From Another World) 51
Tokyo Story 53
Ugetsu 53
Umberto D 55
The Wages of Fear 52
The Wild One 54

1956-60
Anatomy of a Murder 59
The Apartment 60
Ashes and Diamonds 58
L'Avventura 60
Ben-Hur 59
Breathless 59
The Bridge on the River Kwai 57
La Dolce Vita 60
Forbidden Planet 56
The 400 Blows 59
Giant 56
Hiroshima, Mon Amour 60
The Incredible Shrinking Man 57
Invasion of the Body Snatchers 56
Look Back in Anger 58
North by Northwest 59
Paths of Glory 57
Pillow Talk 59
Psycho 60
Rio Bravo 59
The Searchers 56
The Seventh Seal 56
Some Like It Hot 59
Sweet Smell of Success 57
The Ten Commandments 56
Touch of Evil 58
Twelve Angry Men 57
Vertigo 58
Wild Strawberries 57
The World of Apu 59

1961-65
The Battle of Algiers 65
Cleopatra 63
Contempt 63
Darling 65
Dr. Strangelove or: How I Learned to
    Stop Worrying and Love the Bomb 64
8 1/2 63
The Exterminating Angel 62
Goldfinger 64
A Hard Day's Night 64
The Hustler 61
Jules and Jim 61
Knife in the Water 62
Last Year at Marienbad 62
Lawrence of Arabia 62
The Man Who Shot Liberty Valance 62
The Manchurian Candidate 62
Ride the High Country 62
The Servant 63
Shoot the Piano Player 62
A Shot in the Dark 64
The Sound of Music 65
This Sporting Life 63
Tom Jones 63
Viridiana 61
West Side Story 61
What Ever Happened to Baby Jane? 62
Yojimbo 61

1966-70
The Battle of Algiers 66
Blowup 66
Bonnie and Clyde 67
Butch Cassidy and the Sundance Kid 69
The Dirty Dozen 67
Don't Look Back 67
Easy Rider 69
Five Easy Pieces 70
Funny Girl 68
Gimme Shelter 70
The Good, the Bad & the Ugly 67
The Graduate 67
if . . . 69
In the Heat of the Night 67
Love Story 70
M*A*S*H 70
Medium Cool 69
Midnight Cowboy 69
My Night at Maud's 70
Night of the Living Dead 69
Once Upon a Time in the West 68
Patton 70
Persona 66
Petulia 68
Point Blank 67
The Producers 68
Rosemary's Baby 68

Salesman 69
The Sorrow and the Pity 70
Tokyo Olympiad 66
2001: A Space Odyssey 68
Who's Afraid of Virginia Woolf? 66
The Wild Bunch 69
Woodstock 70
Z 69
Zabriskie Point 70

1971-75
Aguirre, the Wrath of God 72
Amarcord 74
American Graffiti 73
Badlands 73
Cabaret 72
Chinatown 74
A Clockwork Orange 71
The Conformist 71
The Conversation 74
Cries and Whispers 72
Day for Night 73
Death Wish 74
Dirty Harry 71
The Discreet Charm of the Bourgeoisie
   72
Enter the Dragon 73
The Exorcist 73
The French Connection 71
The Godfather 72
The Godfather, Part II 74
Jaws 75
Last Tango in Paris 73
Mean Streets 73
Nashville 75
One Flew Over the Cuckoo's Nest 75
Shampoo 75
Straw Dogs 71
The Towering Inferno 74

The Way We Were 73
Young Frankenstein 74

1976-80
Alien 79
All the President's Men 76
Annie Hall 77
Apocalpyse Now 79
Carrie 76
The China Syndrome 79
Close Encounters of the Third Kind 77
Coming Home 78
Days of Heaven 78
The Deer Hunter 78
The Elephant Man 80
The Empire Strikes Back 80
Friday the 13th 80
Halloween 78
Heaven's Gate 80
Kramer vs. Kramer 79
The Last Waltz 78
Man of Iron 80
Man of Marble 77
Manhattan 78
The Marriage of Maria Braun 78
Network 76
Ordinary People 80
Raging Bull 80
Rocky 76
Saturday Night Fever 77
Seven Beauties 76
Star Wars 77
Superman 78
Taxi Driver 76
10 79
The Tin Drum 79
The Turning Point 77
The Warriors 79

Chapter Nineteen

HIGHLY RECOMMENDED & RECOMMENDED TITLES

As noted in How to Use This Book, these titles are my personal recommendations. My taste is pretty eclectic; however, discerning readers may note some trends toward certain genres or styles of filmmaking.

I will admit to one very broad prejudice. Because so many films are imitations, homages, ripoffs, sequels, and remakes, I prize originality above all other virtues. If a movie can't easily be compared to any other film, my interest is piqued. This doesn't mean I treasure only the weird and offbeat; there are plenty of *those* films which lack originality, too.

If a title on these lists is unfamiliar to you, check out the description in the Title Index before you rent. Your taste and mine are bound to intersect somewhere, but not at every point on the broad map of film history.

HIGHLY RECOMMENDED

Adam's Rib
The African Queen
All About Eve
All of Me
All Quiet on the Western Front (1930 version)
All the President's Men
Amarcord
Anatomy of a Murder
Annie Hall
Apocalypse Now
Babette's Feast
Bad Company
The Ballad of Cable Hogue
The Band Wagon
The Birth of a Nation
The Black Stallion
Bonnie and Clyde
Brazil
The Bride of Frankenstein
The Bridge on the River Kwai
Burden of Dreams
Chinatown
Chuck Berry: Hail! Hail! Rock 'n' Roll
Citizen Kane
City Lights
The Conversation
Cool Hand Luke
The Crimson Pirate
The Day the Earth Stood Still
Days of Heaven
Diner
The Discreet Charm of the Bourgeoisie
Do the Right Thing
Dr. Strangelove
Don't Look Back
Double Indemnity

Duck Soup
Dumbo
8 1/2
Eight Men Out
Elvis '56
Elvis—1968 Comeback Special
The Exterminating Angel
Fawlty Towers, Volumes 1-4
Five Easy Pieces
The 400 Blows
The Four Musketeers
From Here to Eternity
From Russia With love
The General
Ghostbusters
The Godfather
The Godfather, Part II
The Gold Rush
Goldfinger
Gone With the Wind
The Good, the Bad, and the Ugly
The Graduate
Grand Hotel
Grand Illusion
The Great Escape
Greed
Gunga Din
A Hard Day's Night
The Heartbreak Kid
Help!
His Girl Friday
Hope and Glory
The Hustler
Intolerance
Invasion of the Body Snatchers (1956 & 1978 versions)
It Happened One Night
It's a Gift

HIGHLY RECOMMENDED (cont.)
Ivan the Terrible, Part One
Ivan the Terrible, Part Two
Jaws
Juggernaut
Jules and Jim
The Kid/The Idle Class
King Kong (1933 version)
Lady and the Tramp
The Lady Eve
The Lady Vanishes (1938 version)
The Last Waltz
Lawrence of Arabia
Little Caesar
Local Hero
Long Day's Journey Into Night
The Long Good Friday
Lost in America
M
M*A*S*H
McCabe and Mrs. Miller
Mad Max
The Maltese Falcon
The Man Who Fell to Earth
The Manchurian Candidate
Mean Streets
Medium Cool
Melvin and Howard
Metropolis (1926 & 1984 editions)
Modern Times
Monterey Pop
Monty Python's Flying Circus, Volumes
   1-17
My Darling Clementine
Napoleon (1927)
Network
Night Moves
Night of the Living Dead
Ninotchka
North by Northwest
North Dallas Forty
Notorious
Los Olvidados
Olympia
On the Waterfront
Once Upon a Time in America
Once Upon a Time in the West
One-Eyed Jacks
One Flew Over the Cuckoo's Nest
One, Two, Three
Only Angels Have Wings
Out of the Past
The Palm Beach Story
Pandora's Box
Paths of Glory
Petulia
The Phantom of the Opera (1925
   version)
The Philadelphia Story
Pinocchio

Pixote
Point Blank
Potemkin
Psycho
The Public Enemy
Radio Days
Raging Bull
Ran
Rear Window
Rebel Without a Cause
Red Dust
Ride the High Country
Risky Business
The Road Warrior
Robin and Marian
Robin Williams Live!
Rosemary's Baby
S.O.B.
A Salute to Chuck Jones
Scarface (1932 version)
The Seven Samurai
The 7th Voyage of Sinbad
A Shot in the Dark
Singin' in the Rain
Some Like It Hot
Something Wild
Sons of the Desert
The Sorrow and the Pity
Southern Comfort
Stalag 17
A Star Is Born (1954 version)
Stop Making Sense
Strangers on a Train
A Streetcar Named Desire
Sullivan's Travels
Sunset Boulevard
Sweet Smell of Success
Swing Time
Sylvia Scarlett
Taxi Driver
The Ten Commandments (1956 version)
Ten From Your Show of Shows
Terms of Endearment
The Thin Blue Line
The Thin Man
The Third Man
The 39 Steps (1935 version)
The Three Musketeers (1974 version)
Throne of Blood
To Be or Not To Be (1943 version)
Tootsie
Top Hat
Touch of Evil
The Treasure of the Sierra Madre
Twentieth Century
Vertigo
Viridiana
The Wages of Fear
White Heat
Who Am I This Time?

HIGHLY RECOMMENDED (cont.)
Who Framed Roger Rabbit
Who'll Stop the Rain?
The Wild Bunch
The Wizard of Oz
Woman of the Year
The Women
Woodstock
Young Frankenstein
Zero for Conduct

RECOMMENDED
About Last Night
Absolute Beginners
Accident
The Adventures of Baron Munchausen
The Adventures of Buckaroo Banzai
The Adventures of Robin Hood
After Hours
L'Age d'Or
Aguirre, The Wrath of God
Airplane!
Alexander Nevsky
Alfie
Alice Doesn't Live Here Anymore
Alien
Aliens
All That Jazz
All the King's Men
All the Right Moves
All You Need Is Cash
Amadeus
American Graffiti
An American in Paris
An American Werewolf in London
And Now for Something Completely
   Different
Android
The Apartment
Arsenic and Old Lace
Arthur
Ashes and Diamonds
The Asphalt Jungle
Assault on Precinct 13
Atlantic City
The Atomic Cafe
The Bachelor and the Bobby-Soxer
Back to the Future
Bad Day at Black Rock
The Bad News Bears
Badlands
La Balance
Ball of Fire
Bambi
Bananas
Band of Outsiders
The Bank Dick
Barry Lyndon
Basket Case
Batman (1989 version)

Beauty and the Beast (1946 version)
Bedazzled
Beetlejuice
Being There
The Bellboy
Bellman and True
The Best of Comic Relief
The Best Years of Our Lives
Betrayal
Between the Lines
Big
The Big Combo
Big Deal on Madonna Street
The Big Red One
The Big Sleep (1946 version)
Billy Budd
Bird
Birdman of Alcatraz
The Black Cat
Black Orpheus
Blade Runner
Blaze
Blonde Venus
Blowup
The Blue Angel (1930 version)
Blue Velvet
Blume in Love
The Boat
Bob & Carol & Ted & Alice
Bob le Flambeur
Body Heat
Born Yesterday
Bound for Glory
Breakfast at Tiffany's
Breaking Away
Breaking In
Breathless (1959 version)
Brewster McCloud
Brief Encounter
Bringing Up Baby
Broadcast News
Broadway Danny Rose
The Brood
The Buddy Holly Story
Buffalo Bill and the Indians
Bugs and Daffy's Carnival of the
   Animals
Bull Durham
The Bullfighter and the Lady
Bullitt
Burn!
Buster Keaton Festival Vol. I
Buster Keaton Festival Vol. II
Buster Keaton Rides Again/The
   Railrodder
Cabaret
The Cabinet of Dr. Caligari
The Candidate
Cannery Row
Cape Fear

RECOMMENDED (cont.)

Carmen
Carnival of Souls
Carny
Carrie (1976)
Casablanca
Catch-22
Caught
Cesar and Rosalie
The Chaplin Essanay Book I
The Chaplin Revue
Charade
Charley Varrick
Charlie Chaplin Carnival
Charlie Chaplin Cavalcade
Charlie Chaplin Festival
Charlie Chaplin—The Early Years,
  Volumes I-IV
Charlie Chaplin's Keystone Comedies
The Chase
Un Chien Andalou
The China Syndrome
The Chocolate War
A Christmas Story
Cinderella
Cinema Paradiso
The Circus
Clean and Sober
Clean Slate
A Clockwork Orange
Close Encounters of the Third Kind
Coal Miner's Daughter
The Coca-Cola Kid
Cocoon
The Collector
The Color of Money
Come and Get It
Comes a Horseman
Comfort and Joy
The Concert for Bangladesh
The Conformist
Contempt
Coogan's Bluff
The Cook, The Thief, His Wife and Her
  Lover
Cousins
Cries and Whispers
Crossfire
Crossing Delancey
The Crowd
Crusoe
A Cry in the Dark
Cutter's Way
Damn Yankees
Dance With a Stranger
Dancing Lady
Dangerous Liaisons
Darling
David Copperfield
Dawn of the Dead

The Dawn Patrol (1938 version)
The Day After Trinity: J. Robert and the
  Atomic Bomb
Day for Night
A Day in the Country
The Day of the Jackal
The Day of the Locust
The Days of Wine and Roses
The Dead
Dead End
Dead Ringers
Dear America: Letters Home From
  Vietnam
Deliverance
Dersu Uzala
Desert Bloom
Desperately Seeking Susan
Destry Rides Again
Detour
The Devil's Playground
Diabolique
Diary of a Lost Girl
Die Hard
Dillinger
Dinner at Eight
The Dirty Dozen
Dirty Harry
Diva
Dr. Jekyll and Mr. Hyde (1932 version)
Dr. No
Dodes'ka-den
Dodsworth
Dog Day Afternoon
La Dolce Vita
Donovan's Reef
Don's Party
Don't Look Now
Down and Out in Beverly Hills
Dracula (1931 version)
Dreamchild
Driving Miss Daisy
A Dry, White Season
Duel
Duel in the Sun
The Duellists
Earth vs. the Flying Saucers
East of Eden (1955 version)
Easy Rider
Eat the Peach
84 Charing Cross Road
84 Charley Mopic
The Elephant Man
The Empire Strikes Back
Entre Nous
The Escape Artist
Escape From Alcatraz
Every Man for Himself and God Against
  All
Everything You Always Wanted to
  Know About Sex . . .

RECOMMENDED (cont.)

The Exorcist
The Fabulous Baker Boys
A Face in the Crowd
Fanny and Alexander
Far From the Madding Crowd
Fast Times at Ridgemont High
Fast-Walking
Fat City
Fatal Vision
Father of the Bride
Fiddler on the Roof
52 Pick-up
Finian's Rainbow
A Fish Called Wanda
Fitzcarraldo
The Fly (1986 version)
Footlight Parade
Forbidden Games
Forbidden Planet
Force of Evil
Fort Apache
42nd Street
The Fourth Man
Frances
Frantic (1988)
The French Connection
Frenzy
Full Metal Jacket
Gandhi
Gates of Heaven
George Stevens: A Filmmaker's Journey
Get Crazy
The Getaway
Gimme Shelter
The Girl Can't Help It
Glory
Going in Style
The Great Dictator
Great Expectations
Gung Ho (1986)
Hairspray
Halloween
Hamlet (1948 version)
Hammett
A Handful of Dust
Hannah and Her Sisters
Hardcore
The Harder They Come
Harold Lloyd
Harry and Tonto
Heart Like a Wheel
Heartland
Hearts and Minds
Hearts of the West
Heathers
Heaven Help Us
The Heiress
Hell in the Pacific
Hell Is for Heroes

Heller in Pink Tights
Helter Skelter
Henry V (1945 & 1989 versions)
Henry: Portrait of a Serial Killer
High and Low
High Sierra
High Society
High Tide
Holiday
The Honeymoon Killers
Hoosiers
Horse Feathers
House of Games
Housekeeping
How I Won the War
The Howling
Hud
Humanoids From the Deep
The Hunchback of Notre Dame (1939 version)
The Hunt for Red October
Hustle
I Married a Monster From Outer Space
I Walked With a Zombie
I Wanna Hold Your Hand
if . . .
Ikiru
I'm Gonna Git You Sucka
In Cold Blood
The Incredible Shrinking Man
The In-Laws
Internal Affairs
The Invivsble Man
Isadora
It Came From Outer Space
Jackie Mason on Broadway
Jack's Back
Jailhouse Rock
Jazz on a Summer's Day
Jean de Florette
Jimi Hendrix
Johnny Guitar
Julia
Julius Caesar (1953 version)
Junior Bonner
Kagemusha
Kanal
Key Largo
The Killing
The Killing Fields
Kind Hearts and Coronets
King of Comedy
King Rat
Klute
Knife in the Water
Kramer vs. Kramer
La Bamba
The Lady From Shanghai
The Ladykillers
The Last Command

RECOMMENDED (cont.)
The Last Detail
Last Embrace
The Last Emperor
The Last Laugh
The Last Picture Show
Last Tango in Paris
The Last Temptation of Christ
The Last Tycoon
The Late Show
Laura
Laurel and Hardy Comedy Classics
Lenny Bruce
Letter From an Unknown Woman
Libeled Lady
Lilith
Liquid Sky
The Little Drummer Girl
The Little Mermaid
The Lodger
Lolita
The Longest Day
Look Back in Anger
The Lost Patrol
Love Among the Ruins
Lulu in Berlin
Madigan
The Magnificent Ambersons
The Magnificent Seven
Making Mr. Right
The Makioka Sisters
The Man Who Shot Liberty Valance
The Man Who Would Be King
The Man With the Golden Arm
Manhattan
Manhunter
Manon of the Spring
Marat/Sade
Marlene
The Marriage of Maria Braun
Married to the Mob
Martin
Matewan
Max Headroom
Meet Me in St. Louis
The Men
Men of Bronze
Miami Blues
Midnight Cowboy
Mishima
Missing
Mrs. Soffel
Mr. Blandings Builds His Dream House
Mr. Hulot's Holiday
Mister Roberts
Mona Lisa
Moonlighting (1985)
Moonstruck
The More the Merrier

Motown 25: Yesterday, Today &
   Tomorrow
Mountains of the Moon
The Mummy (1932 version)
The Music Man
The Mutiny on the Bounty (1935
   version)
My Beautiful Laundrette
My Brilliant Career
My Favorite Year
My Left Foot
Nadine
The Naked Gun
The Naked Kiss
The Naked Prey
Nanook of the North
National Lampoon's Animal House
Near Dark
New York Stories
Newsfront
Night and Fog
A Night at the Opera
Night of the Comet
The Night of the Hunter
The Night of the Shooting Stars
Night Shift
1900
92 in the Shade
No Way Out
El Norte
Nothing in Common
O Lucky Man!
On the Town
The Onion Field
Ordinary People
Out of Africa
The Outlaw Josey Wales
Over the Edge
The Owl and the Pussycat
The Ox-Bow Incident
The Parallax View
The Passion of Joan of Arc
Pat and Mike
Pat Garrett and Billy the Kid
Patton
Pee-wee's Big Adventure
Pennies From Heaven
Performance
Persona
Peter Pan (1953 version)
Phase IV
Pierrot le Fou
A Place in the Sun
Platoon
Play Misty for Me
The Postman Always Rings Twice (1946
   version)
Prime Cut
Prince of the City
The Prisoner of Zenda (1937 version)

RECOMMENDED (cont.)

The Producers
The Professionals
Providence
Pulp
Q & A
Quadrophenia
Queen Christina
Queen of Hearts
The Quiet Man
Rain Man
Rashomon
Real Genius
Real Life
Red River
Reds
Repo Man
Repulsion
The Return of the Living Dead
The Return of the Secaucus 7
Reuben, Reuben
The Right Stuff
River's Edge
Road Runner vs. Wile E. Coyote: The
  Classic Chase
Roadie
The Roaring Twenties
Roger Corman: Hollywood's Wild
  Angel
Romancing the Stone
La Ronde
Round Midnight
Roxanne
Sabrina
Salesman
A Salute to Mel Blanc
Salvador
The Sand Pebbles
Say Amen, Somebody
Say Anything
Scandal
Scarlet Street
School Daze
The Searchers
The Secret Policeman's Other Ball
Seize the Day
The Seven Percent Solution
The Seventh Seal
sex, lies, and videotape
Shack Out on 101
The Shadow Box
Shadow of a Doubt
Shall We Dance
Shampoo
Shane
She Wore a Yellow Ribbon
Sherman's March
She's Gotta Have It
Shoah
Short Eyes

Show People
Sid and Nancy
The Silent Partner
Silkwood
Simon the Desert
Sisters
The Skin Game (1971)
Small Change
Smile
Smiles of a Summer Night
Song of the Thin Man
Songwriter
Sorry, Wrong Number
Special Bulletin
Splash
The Spy Who Came In From the Cold
The Spy Who Loved Me
Stagecoach (1939 version)
Star Wars
Stardust Memories
Start the Revolution Without Me
Starting Over
Stay Hungry
Steamboat Bill, Jr.
The Stepfather
The Stone Boy
Stormy Monday
Straight Time
The Stranger (1946)
Streetwise
The Stunt Man
Suburbia
The Sugarland Express
The Sure Thing
Swimming to Cambodia
The Taming of the Shrew
Tampopo
Tanner '88
Tapeheads
The Tenant
Tequila Sunrise
The Terminator
Them!
There Was a Crooked Man
They All Laughed
They Shoot Horses, Don't They?
They Won't Believe Me
The Thing (From Another World)
Things Change
This Is Elvis
This Is Spinal Tap
This Sporting Life
A Thousand Clowns
The Three Caballeros
Time After Time
Time Bandits
The Times of Harvey Milk
The Tin Drum
To Kill a Mockingbird
To Live and Die in L.A.

RECOMMENDED (cont.)

Tokyo Olympiad
Tom Jones
Topkapi
The Tramp/A Woman
Triumph of the Will
Trouble in Mind
True Confessions
True West
Tucker: The Man and His Dream
Turtle Diary
Twelve Angry Men
25 X 5: The Continuing Adventures of
   the Rolling Stones
20,000 Leagues Under the Sea
Two English Girls
Two for the Road
2001: A Space Odyssey
Ugetsu
Under Fire
Used Cars
Vagabond
Valley Girl
The Verdict
Vernon, Florida
Wait Until Dark
The Wanderers
The Wannsee Conference
The Warriors (1979)
Way Down East

A Wedding
West Side Story
What's Up, Tiger Lily?
Where the Heart Is
While the City Sleeps
White of the Eye
Who's Afraid of Virginia Woolf?
Wild Strawberries
Will Penny
The Wind
Wings of Desire
Wise Blood
Witness for the Prosecution
The Wolf Man
Wolfen
Women in Love
Women on the Verge of a Nervous
   Breakdown
Working Girl
Working Girls
The Wrong Box
Wuthering Heights (1939 version)
Yankee Doodle Dandy
Yellow Submarine
Yojimbo
Young Mr. Lincoln
Z
Zabriskie Point
Zelig

Chapter Twenty

UNAVAILABLE ON VIDEOCASSETTE

The following is a selected list of frequently requested titles that were still not on videocassette as of Fall 1990.

A few, such as *American Hot Wax*, are available on videodisc. Some are available in foreign-language versions. For example, a Japanese version of *Rocky Horror Picture Show* has been in circulation.

As with any popular titles, some are available in unauthorized, pirated cassettes whose quality is nearly always suspect.

Alexander's Ragtime Band
All Fall Down
All the Way Home
Alex in Wonderland
Alphaville
America, America
American Hot Wax
American Pop
The Americanization of Emily
Anastasia
Annie Get Your Gun
L'Atalante
Bad Timing: A Sensual Obsession
Beast of the City
The Big Carnival (Ace in the Hole)
The Big Clock
The Black Cauldron
Blithe Spirit (1945 version)
Bluebeard's Eighth Wife
The Boys in the Band
Bread and Chocolate
Breezy
Cabin in the Cotton
Carmen Jones
Carrie (1950)
Cattle Annie and Little Britches
Celine and Julie Go Boating
The Chant of Jimmie Blacksmith
Cheaper by the Dozen
Children of Paradise
Chimes at Midnight (Falstaff)
La Chinoise
Claudine
A Cold Wind in August
Comanche Station
Coming Apart
Cooley High
Cul-de-sac
The Dark at the Top of the Stairs
David Holtzman's Diary
Deadhead Miles
Death Takes a Holiday (1934 version)
Derby

Design for Living
Desperate Journey
Devil's Disciple
Drive, He Said
Dutchman
The Effect of Gamma Rays on Man-in-the-Moon Marigolds
El Topo
The Emigrants
F/M
Faces
Fantasia
A Farewell to Arms (1957 version)
Fellini's Casanova
Fellini's Roma
Five Million Years to Earth
For Whom the Bell Tolls
Forever Amber
The Fortune
Fury
The Gang's All Here
Gentleman's Agreement
The Glass Menagerie (1950 version)
Godspell
Gun Crazy
A Hatful of Rain
Having a Wild Weekend
Heaven Knows, Mr. Allison
Heavy Metal
Hell's Angels (1930)
Hi, Mom
The High and the Mighty
The Horn Blows at Midnight
Hot Tomorrows
How Green Was My Valley
The Hucksters
Humoresque
I Know Where I'm Going
I Walk the Line
I Was a Male War Bride
The Iceman Cometh
Images
The Innocents
Inside Daisy Clover

Jane Eyre (1944 version)
Jet Pilot
The Jungle Book (1967 version)
The Killers (1946 version)
The King of Marvin Gardens
Kiss Me, Stupid
Land of the Pharoahs
The Landlord
Leave Her to Heaven
Leo the Last
The Long Goodbye
The Long, Long Trailer
Loving
McClintock
Made for Each Other (1971)
Man of a Thousand Faces
Mickey One
Mississippi Mermaid
More American Graffiti
The Mother and the Whore
Mourning Becomes Electra
Muriel
My Cousin Rachel
The Nanny
The New Land
Night Nurse
Nightmare Alley
No Way Out (1950)
Nosferatu the Vampyre
Nothing but a Man
The Old Dark House
The Old Man and the Sea
101 Dalmatians
Out of It
Panic in Needle Park
Party Girl
The Passion of Anna
Peppermint Soda
Peyton Place
Pinky
Play It As It Lays
Point of Order
Porgy and Bess
The Power and the Glory
Pretty Poison
Rancho Deluxe
The Revolutionary
Ride Lonesome
The Road to Morocco

The Road to Singapore
The Road to Zanzibar
The Rose Tattoo
The Scarlet Empress
The Sea of Grass
Seconds
Sergeant Rutledge
Shame (1968)
Shanghai Express
Sherlock Jr.
Shock Corridor
The Snake Pit
Snow White and the Seven Dwarfs
The Song of the South
Sons and Lovers
Storm Warning
The Stranger (1967)
Summer and Smoke
The Sun Shines Bright
Sunrise
Susan Lennox: Her Rise and Fall
The Swan
Tales of Hoffmann
The Tall T
Tarzan and His Mate
Tea and Sympathy
Tempest
Thieves Like Us
Three Coins in the Fountain
The Three Faces of Eve
3 Women
Tobacco Road
Trouble in Paradise
Two-Lane Blacktop
Ulysses (1967)
Up the Down Staircase
The V.I.P.s
The Valley of Decision
Valley of the Dolls (1967 version)
Wanda
Weekend
White Dog
Who's That Knocking at My Door?
The Wild Child
Without Love
A Woman Under the Influence
Yanks
Young Girls of Rochefort

Discontinued Movies

These titles were made available on videocassette at one time but have been withdrawn from manufacture. Thus, copies are difficult to find. See "How To Use This Book" for further explanation.

The Fortune Cookie
Laura
A Letter to Three Wives (1949 version)
Love Is a Many-Splendored Thing

The Killing of Sister George
Room at the Top
They Shoot Horses, Don't They?
Tom Jones

TITLE INDEX

A Coeur Joie (1967, B&W, 100m, NR)
Brigitte Bardot plays a bored housewife who resumes her career, only to fall in love with another man. **ST4**

A Nos Amours (1984, C, 102m, R)
From France, a drama of a teenaged girl (Sandrine Bonnaire) with a string of lovers and family problems. Directed by Maurice Pialat. **FF1**

A Nous la Liberté (1931, B&W, 87m, NR)
French director René Clair's comic look at how machinery takes over people's lives. **FF1** *Essential*

Aaron Loves Angela (1975, C, 98m, R)
New York romance between a black Harlem youth (Kevin Hooks) and a Puerto Rican girl (Irene Cara). Moses Gunn costars. **DR14, DR15**

Abbott and Costello in Hollywood (1945, B&W, 83m, NR)
Bud and Lou invade the MGM lot and run into plenty of surprise guest stars. **ST1**

Abbott and Costello Meet Captain Kidd (1952, C, 70m, NR)
Charles Laughton hams it up as the notorious pirate in this A&C comedy. **ST1**

Abbott and Costello Meet Dr. Jekyll and Mr. Hyde (1953, B&W, 77m, NR)
Bud and Lou are in London where Lou is accidentally injected with the Mr. Hyde serum. Boris Karloff costars. **ST1, ST77**

Abbott and Costello Meet Frankenstein (1948, B&W, 83m, NR)
Dracula (Bela Lugosi) wants to use Lou's brain in the Frankenstein monster (Glenn Strange) and the Wolf Man (Lon Chaney Jr.) tries to warn him that he's in danger. Vincent Price has a bit at the end as the Invisible Man. **HF7, HF10, ST1, ST17, ST95, ST124**

Abbott and Costello Meet the Killer, Boris Karloff (1949, B&W, 84m, NR)
Karloff tries to do away with Lou in this A&C comic mystery. **ST1, ST77**

Abe Lincoln in Illinois (1939, B&W, 110m, NR)
Raymond Massey stars as the small-town lawyer who would eventually become our sixteenth President. **CL2, HF17**

Abilene Town (1946, B&W, 89m, NR)
Randolph Scott Western set in post-Civil War Kansas, where the townspeople are feuding over land rights. **ST136**

Abominable Dr. Phibes, The (1971, C, 94m, PG)
Vincent Price hams it up in this tongue-in-cheek horror film about a disfigured doctor seeking revenge. **CU4, HO20, HO26, ST124**

About Last Night (1986, C, 113m, R)
Comedy-drama about four young Chicago singles, two of whom think they've found love but aren't sure. Rob Lowe, Demi Moore, Jim Belushi, and Elizabeth Perkins star. Underrated film with some pointed observations about modern romance. **CO13, DR1, DR7, XT11** *Recommended*

Above the Law (1988, C, 99m, R)
Steven Seagall plays a super-agent (martial arts training, multi-lingual, weapons expert) with friends in the Mob. He's on the trail of a C.I.A.-sponsored drug ring. **AC8, AC25**

Abraham Lincoln (1930, B&W, 97m, NR)
Walter Huston stars in director D.W. Griffith's account of the sixteenth President's life. This is a restored version, with slavery sequences once thought lost. **CL2, DT42, HF17**

Absence of Malice (1981, C, 116m, PG)
Newspaper reporter tries for big scoop on Miami construction boss and his involvement with crime, only to find out her target is innocent. Sally Field and Paul Newman star. Sydney Pollack directed. **DR7, DT80, ST40, ST111**

Absent-Minded Professor, The (1960, B&W, 97m, G)
Fred MacMurray plays the forgetful inventor who discovers flubber—an amazing substance that raises his Model T and

basketball team to new heights in this classic Disney comedy. **FA1**

Absolute Beginners (1986, C, 107m, PG-13)
A stylized musical look at London in the late 1950s, when rock 'n' roll was about to break through and the teenager would become king. David Bowie, Ray Davies, and Sade perform musical numbers. Directed by Julien Temple. **MU9, MU16, XT15** *Recommended*

Absolution (1981, C, 105m, NR)
Richard Burton stars in this drama of a priest at a boys' school who's the victim of a cruel practical joke. Written by Anthony Shaffer. **DR25, ST13**

Abyss, The (1989, C, 140m, PG-13)
Undersea spectacular, with rescue mission trying to free a nuclear submarine from a precarious position. Ed Harris and Mary Elizabeth Mastrantonio star. Directed by James Cameron. **AC12, AC24**

Accident (1967, C, 105m, NR)
Drama set at a British univeristy, centering on a professor's affair with a lovely young student. Dirk Bogarde, Stanley Baker, Jacqueline Sassard, Delphine Seyrig, and Michael York star. Written by Harold Pinter; directed by Joseph Losey. **DR23** *Recommended*

Accidental Tourist, The (1988, C, 121m, PG)
A guidebook writer who hates to travel, his estranged wife, and a loopy dog trainer are the focus of this drama set in Baltimore. William Hurt, Kathleen Turner, and Oscar winner Geena Davis star, with Amy Wright, Ed Begley, Jr., David Ogden Stiers, and Bill Pullman. Lawrence Kasdan directed; based on Anne Tyler's novel. **DR1, DR8, DR19, ST75, ST152, XT5**

Accused, The (1988, C, 110m, R)
Oscar winner Jodie Foster stars as a woman who's been brutally assaulted in a bar. A determined prosecutor (Kelly McGillis) presses charges against the onlookers at the scene of the crime. **DR10, DR17, ST47, XT3**

Across 110th Street (1972, C, 102m, R)
Violent crime thriller, with New York police and the Mob in a race to catch freelance robbers who made off with $300,000 of Mob money. Anthony Quinn, Yaphet Kotto, and Anthony Franciosa star. **AC9, CU7, XT9**

Across the Great Divide (1977, C, 100m, G)
Family adventure about two orphaned children making the trek over dangerous Rocky Mountain terrain to earn their inherited land in frontier Oregon. **FA4**

Action Jackson (1988, C, 96m, R)
Carl Weathers plays Detroit's most determined police sergeant, Jericho "Action" Jackson. He keeps his cool as a ruthless auto tycoon, a scheming mistress, and his own police force cross his path in this thriller. Craig T. Nelson and Vanity co-star. **AC8**

Adam (1983, C, 100m, NR)
JoBeth Williams and Daniel J. Travanti play the real-life couple whose missing son case stirred controversy and congressional debate. Originally made for TV. **MY8**

Adam at 6 A.M. (1970, C, 100m, PG)
Michael Douglas plays a college professor who takes a laborer's job for the summer. With Lee Purcell, Joe Don Baker, and Meg Foster. **ST35**

Adam Had Four Sons (1941, B&W, 81m, NR)
Intense family drama starring Ingrid Bergman as a French governess for a widower (Warner Baxter) with four boys. With Susan Hayward, Fay Wray, Richard Denning, and June Lockhart. **ST7**

Adam's Rib (1949, B&W, 101m, NR)
Katharine Hepburn and Spencer Tracy are husband and wife lawyers who wind up on opposing sides of a marital dispute in court. Judy Holliday, in her film debut, is hilarious as the dizzy defendant. Written by Ruth Gordon and Garson Kanin; directed by George Cukor. **CL10, CL15, DT24, ST66, ST69, ST151, XT21** *Essential; Highly Recommended*

Addict (1971, C, 90m, R)
The life and very hard times of a New York City heroin addict, an ex-hairdresser, played by George Segal. Karen Black costars; Robert DeNiro has a small part. Directed by Ivan Passer. Original title: *Born To Win*. **DR15, ST30, XT9**

L'Addition (1985, C, 85m, R)
French prison drama, starring Richard Berry and Richard Bohringer. **FF1**

Adios Amigo (1975, C, 87m, PG)
In this western comedy, Fred Williamson (who also wrote and directed) costars with Richard Pryor as the hippest pair of gunslingers ever to ride the range. **ST125, WE14**

Adventures in Babysitting (1987, C, 99m, PG-13)
Shaggy dog tale of teen babysitter dragging her charges off to downtown Chicago to help a stranded friend. Elisabeth Shue stars. **CO20, XT11**

Adventures of an American Rabbit, The (1986, C, 85m, G)
Feature cartoon about Rob Rabbit, a normal bunny transformed into a superhero. **FA10**

Adventures of Baron Munchausen, The (1989, C, 125m, PG)
Spectacular adventure fantasy, based on real German nobleman with a penchant for spinning fabulous and less than credible tales. John Neville stars, with Sarah Polley as his young companion, and Eric Idle, Robin Williams (billed as "Ray Tutto"), Oliver Reed, and Uma Thurman. Directed with great flair by Terry Gilliam. **CO15, FA8, SF13, SF14, ST160** *Recommended*

Adventures of Buckaroo Banzai Across the 8th Dimension, The (1984, C, 103m, PG)
Adventure comedy about a super hero who's a brain surgeon, race car driver, and rock singer—among other talents. Peter Weller stars, with Ellen Barkin, Jeff Goldblum, and John Lithgow. **AC17, CO12, CU5, SF21, ST56** *Recommended*

Adventures of Bullwhip Griffin, The (1967, C, 110m, NR)
Disney western comedy, with a novice Bostonian who thinks he can make a bundle during the gold rush days. Roddy McDowall, Suzanne Pleshette, and Karl Malden star. **FA1**

Adventures of Captain Fabian (1951, B&W, 100m, NR)
Errol Flynn swashbuckler has the hero defending Micheline Presle from murder charge. Agnes Moorehead and Vincent Price costar. **ST43, ST124**

Adventures of Don Juan, The (1948, C, 110m, NR)
Costume adventure about history's roguish lover, starring Errol Flynn. Viveca Lindfors and Ann Rutherford costar as his conquests. **ST43**

Adventures of Hercules, The (1984, C, 89m, NR)
Lou Ferrigno plays the well-muscled hero of mythology in this adventure saga. **AC17**

Adventures of Huckleberry Finn, The (1939, B&W, 89m, NR)
Mark Twain's classic of a boy and a runaway slave in a thrilling raft trip down the Mississippi. Mickey Rooney stars. **FA3, WR27**

Adventures of Huckleberry Finn, The (1985, C, 121m, NR)
The most recent version of the Mark Twain classic about adventurous Huck (Patrick Day) rafting down the Mississippi with his runaway friend Jim (Samm-Art Williams). With Sada Thompson, Lillian Gish, Richard Kiley, and Butterfly McQueen. Originally made for public TV; shown at 240m. **FA3, ST54, WR27**

Adventures of Mark Twain, The (1985, C, 90m, G)
The art of claymation is used to capture the likeness of Mark Twain's literary characters (Tom Sawyer, Huck Finn, and Becky Thatcher) in this animated adventure story. **FA10, WR27**

Adventures of Milo in the Phantom Toll Booth, The *see* Phantom Tollbooth, The

Adventures of Robin Hood, The (1938, C, 102m, NR)
Errol Flynn plays the dashing Sherwood Forest outlaw. Olivia de Havilland, Basil Rathbone, and Claude Rains costar in this enchanting classic. **AC13, CL9, FA4, HF15, ST43** *Essential; Recommended*

Adventures of Sherlock Holmes, The (1939, B&W, 83m, NR)
Sherlock Holmes and Dr. Watson outsmart their arch-rival Professor Moriarity in the first Holmes movie to star Basil Rathbone and Nigel Bruce. **HF14**

Adventures of the Wilderness Family, The (1975, C, 100m, G)
A modern-day family trades in their big-city lifestyle for pioneer life in the West. **FA4**

Adventures of Tom Sawyer, The (1938, C, 77m, NR)
Mark Twain's classic about the Missouri boy whose endless curiosity gets him into all sorts of mischief. Tommy Kelly, Jackie Moran, Walter Brennan, and Victor Jory star. **FA3, WR27**

Adventures of Tom Sawyer, The (1973, C, 76m, NR)
Mark Twain's classic of a boyhood in Hannibal, Missouri, starring Josh Albee, with Jeff Tyler, Jane Wyatt, Buddy Ebsen, John McGiver, and, as Injun Joe, Vic Morrow. **FA3, WR27**

Advise and Consent (1962, B&W, 139m, NR)
From director Otto Preminger, a drama of Washington political wheeling and dealing over the controversial nomination of a left-wing Senator to become Secretary of State. Henry Fonda stars, with Don Murray, Charles Laughton (in his last film), Walter Pidgeon, Peter Lawford, and Gene Tierney. Based on a novel by Allen Drury. **DR21, DT82, ST44, XT12, XT22**

Affair in Trinidad (1952, B&W, 98m, NR)
Rita Hayworth and Glenn Ford star in this thriller of a cabaret singer and her brother-in-law tracking her husband's killer. **ST64**

Affair To Remember, An (1957, C, 115m, NR)
Shipboard romance between Cary Grant and Deborah Kerr. Directed by Leo McCarey; a remake of his 1939 film, *Love Affair*. **ST57**

Africa Screams (1949, B&W, 79m, NR)
Abbott and Costello go on safari with big game hunter Frank Buck. **ST1**

African Queen, The (1951, C, 105m, NR)
Romantic adventure teaming Humphrey Bogart (an Oscar winner) with Katharine Hepburn as the hard-drinking pilot and the uptight spinster who cruise treacherous waters to thwart the Germans in World War I. Directed by John Huston; written by James Agee. **AC12, AC14,**

CL4, DT50, ST8, ST66, XT2 *Essential; Highly Recommended*

After Hours (1985, C, 97m, R)
Ordinary guy finds himself stranded in the middle of the night in an unfriendly New York neighborhood. Offbeat comedy directed by Martin Scorsese. Griffin Dunne stars, with John Heard, Rosanna Arquette, Catherine O'Hara, Cheech & Chong, Teri Garr, Verna Bloom, and Linda Fiorentino. **CO2, CO12, CO14, CO20, CU5, DT95, ST18, XT9** *Recommended*

After the Fall of New York (1985, C, 95m, R)
Adventure saga set in post-holocaust America, where only the strong survive. Michael Sopikow stars. **SF8, SF12**

After the Fox (1966, C, 103m, NR)
Peter Sellers stars in a comedy about a frustrated film director on location in Rome. Victor Mature steals the show as a fading star. Directed by Vittorio De Sica; written by Neil Simon. **CO8, DT26, ST137, WR23, XT17**

After the Rehearsal (1984, C, 72m, R)
Swedish drama from director Ingmar Bergman about the intricate relationships of a theater director and his actresses. Erland Josephson, Ingrid Thulin, and Lena Olin star. **DT7**

After the Thin Man (1936, B&W, 113m, NR)
More parties, more hangovers, and more crime for the high-society detective couple Nick and Nora Charles (William Powell, Myrna Loy) in their second screen adventure. James Stewart costars as one of their suspects. **CL15, HF5, MY17, ST94, ST122, ST143, WR9**

Aftermath (1985, C, 96m, NR)
A trio of astronauts returns to Earth after a long journey to find a nuclear holocaust has ravaged the planet. **SF12**

Against All Flags (1952, C, 83m, NR)
Errol Flynn plays a British soldier who finds his way into a pirate stronghold—and into Maureen O'Hara's heart. Anthony Quinn costars. **ST43**

Against All Odds (1969, C, 93m, R)
The dastardly Fu Manchu plans to murder several world leaders by sending them

slave girls saturated in poison which will kill anyone who kisses them. Christopher Lee stars. Original title: *The Blood of Fu Manchu*. Also known as *Kiss and Kill*. **ST89**

Against All Odds (1984, C, 128m R)
An ex-jock (Jeff Bridges), hired to track down the runaway wife of a shady nightclub owner (James Woods), finds her and falls in love with her. Rachel Ward co-stars in this remake of the classic thriller, *Out of the Past*, set in contemporary Los Angeles. **CU18, DR16, MY2, MY5, ST11, ST165, XT10**

Agatha (1979, C, 98m, PG)
Vanessa Redgrave portrays mystery writer Agatha Christie in this dramatic account of her 11-day disappearance in 1926. Dustin Hoffman costars as an inquisitive reporter who tracks Christie down. **MY8, ST67, ST127, WR3**

L'Age d'Or (1930, B&W, 63m, NR)
Legendary surrealistic film directed by Luis Buñuel, co-written with Salvador Dali. A scandal in its time for its startling imagery. **DT15** *Essential; Recommended*

Agnes of God (1985, C, 97m, PG-13)
A young nun is the center of controversy over a murdered newborn infant. Jane Fonda, Anne Bancroft, and Meg Tilly star in this version of John Pielmeyer's play directed by Norman Jewison. **DR20, DT51, ST45**

Aguirre, The Wrath of God (1972, C, 90m, NR)
Adventure tale of mad conquistador driving his men to destruction in the jungles of South America. Klaus Kinski stars. Werner Herzog directed. **DT44, ST83** *Essential; Recommended*

Aida (1953, C, 96m, NR)
Screen version of the famed opera, starring Sophia Loren (with her singing voice dubbed). **ST93**

Air Force (1943, B&W, 124m, NR)
Howard Hawks' World War II drama about bomber crew action in Pearl Harbor, Manila, and the Coral Sea. John Garfield, John Ridgely, Gig Young, and Arthur Kennedy star. **AC1, DT43**

Airplane! (1980, C, 86m, PG)
Spoof of disaster movies (and the *Airport* series in particular), with a joke every 4 seconds, most of them quite funny. Robert Hays and Julie Hagerty star, with Lloyd Bridges, Peter Graves, Robert Stack, Leslie Nielsen, Kareem Abdul-Jabbar, and many guests. **CO7** *Recommended*

Airplane II: The Sequel (1982, C, 85m, PG)
Follow-up to *Airplane!* with same joke ratio, plus Robert Hays, Julie Hagerty, Lloyd Bridges, Peter Graves, and William Shatner. **CO7**

Airport (1970, C, 137m, G)
Original Disaster in the Sky adventure, with snowed-in runways, bomb-crippled planes, cute stowaways, and an all-star cast: Burt Lancaster, Dean Martin, George Kennedy, Helen Hayes (an Oscar winner), Van Heflin, Jacqueline Bisset, and Jean Seberg. **AC23, ST85, XT5**

Airport 1975 (1974, C, 106m, PG)
Second *Airport* film has Charlton Heston at the controls, Karen Black as a stewardess, and a passenger list including Helen Reddy (as a singing nun), Gloria Swanson (as herself), Myrna Loy, and Linda Blair. **AC23, ST94**

Airport '79 *see* The Concorde—Airport '79

Airport '77 (1977, C, 113m, PG)
The third edition of the Unfriendly Skies finds James Stewart's luxury jet-liner in the ocean with pilot Jack Lemmon attempting a rescue. Lee Grant, Brenda Vaccaro, George Kennedy, Joseph Cotten, Olivia de Havilland, Christopher Lee, and many more appear. **AC23, ST89, ST90, ST143**

Al Capone (1959, B&W, 105m, NR)
Rod Steiger plays Scarface in this bullet-riddled film biography. With Fay Spain, James Gregory, and Martin Balsam. **AC22**

Aladdin (1987, C, 95m, NR)
An updated version of the magic lamp tale, with Bud Spencer starring as the genie summoned by a boy who finds the lamp in a junk shop. **FA8**

Aladdin and His Wonderful Lamp (1984, C, 60m, NR)
Robert Carradine is the young man at odds with a wicked magician (Leonard Nimoy) until a powerful genie (James Earl Jones) and a beautiful princess appear before him. From the Faerie Tale Theatre series. Directed by Tim Burton. **FA12, ST76**

Alakazam the Great (1961, C, 84m, NR)
Animated adventure of a monkey who's made King of the Animals. Voices by Jonathan Winters, Frankie Avalon, Arnold Stang, and Sterling Holloway. **FA10**

Alamo, The (1960, C, 161m, NR)
The legendary battle of a small band of Texans against the Mexican army, directed by and starring John Wayne. With Richard Widmark, Laurence Harvey, Chill Wills, and Frankie Avalon. Now available in a letterboxed edition on two cassettes, with overture and entr'acte music by Dimitri Tiomkin. **CU19, MU12, ST156, WE1**

Alamo Bay (1985, C, 98m, R)
Texas fishermen clash with Vietnamese immigrants trying to make a living in the same waters. Amy Madigan and Ed Harris star in this topical drama directed by Louis Malle. **DR7**

Albino (1978, C, 85m, NR)
A murderous albino stalks beautiful women. Christopher Lee and Trevor Howard star. **ST89**

Alexander Nevsky (1938, B&W, 107m, NR)
Stirring historical drama about Russia's defense in the 13th century against invading German forces. Directed by Sergei Eisenstein; music by Sergei Prokofiev. **DT33** *Essential; Recommended*

Alexander the Great (1956, C, 141m, NR)
Richard Burton plays the great conqueror in this adventure drama. Fredric March, Claire Bloom, and Peter Cushing costar. Directed by Robert Rossen. **AC16, ST13, ST27**

Alfie (1966, C, 114m, NR)
Michael Caine is a roguish ladies' man in this British comedy with Jane Asher, Shelley Winters, and Millicent Martin. **CO17, ST15, ST164** *Recommended*

Algiers (1938, B&W, 95m, NR)
Classic romance stars Charles Boyer as Pepe Le Moko, who falls for a spoiled little rich girl (Hedy Lamarr) on her visit to the Casbah district of Algiers. **CL4**

Ali—Fear Eats the Soul (1974, C, 94m, NR)
A German widow in her sixties marries an Arab man thirty years younger. Werner Rainer Fassbinder directed this drama; he also plays a small role. **DT34**

Alice Adams (1935, B&W, 99m, NR)
Comedy with Katharine Hepburn as a social climber who finds true happiness with a modest young man (Fred MacMurray). Directed by George Stevens. **CL5, DT101, ST66**

Alice Doesn't Live Here Anymore (1975, C, 113m, PG)
A New Mexico housewife who is suddenly widowed decides to move with her adolescent son to California, where she can pursue her ambition to be a professional singer. Oscar winner Ellen Burstyn stars in this comedy-drama, with Kris Kristofferson, Dianne Ladd, Alfred Lutter III, and Jodie Foster. Written by Robert Getchell; directed by Martin Scorsese. **DR10, DT95, MU12, ST47, XT3, XT18** *Recommended*

Alice in the Cities (1974, B&W, 110m, NR)
Drama of the friendship between an American journalist and an abandoned 9-year-old German girl. Directed by Wim Wenders. **DT113**

Alice in Wonderland (1951, C, 75m, G)
Disney animation brings Lewis Carroll's enchanting classic to life as Alice ventures through the looking glass to discover a world of colorful and frightening characters. **FA2, FA3** *Recommended*

Alice's Adventures in Wonderland (1973, C, 97m, G)
Live action version of the Lewis Carroll story, filmed in England with a cast that features Peter Sellers, Dudley Moore, Ralph Richardson, and Spike Milligan. **FA3, ST109, ST137**

Alice's Restaurant (1969, C, 111m, PG)
Arlo Guthrie's famed song about a disastrous Thanksgiving Day and his problems with the draft is the basis for this amiable comedy-drama. Guthrie stars, with Pat

Quinn and James Broderick. Directed by Arthur Penn. **DR7, DT78**

Alien (1979, C, 116m, R)
Science fiction horror classic about life form invading space ship and destroying the crew one by one. Sigourney Weaver stars, with Yaphet Kotto, Ian Holm, Veronica Cartwright, Harry Dean Stanton, and John Hurt. Directed by Ridley Scott; Oscar winner for special effects. **DT96, SF3, SF15, SF20, ST141, ST157** *Essential; Recommended*

Alien Nation (1988, C, 89m, R)
In Los Angeles in the near future, a race of aliens resembling humans have become the new minority immigrant problem. An alien cop (Mandy Patinkin) and his human partner (James Caan) team up to uncover a criminal conspiracy within the alien community. **SF17**

Alien Predators (1987, C, 92m, R)
A trio of Americans visiting Spain help a scientist control an alien invasion which has taken over a small town. Martin Hewitt, Dennis Christopher, and Lynn-Holly Johnson star. **SF20**

Aliens (1986, C, 137m, R)
Smashing sequel to *Alien,* with survivor Sigourney Weaver returning to hunt down queen mother of creature from first film. Superb blend of action and suspense from director James Cameron. With Michael Biehn, Lance Henriksen, and Paul Reiser. **SF3, SF20, ST157** *Recommended*

All About Eve (1950, B&W, 138m, NR)
Witty, Oscar-winning look at life in the theater, with ambitious ingenue (Anne Baxter) trying to upstage aging but still formidable veteran (Bette Davis). With Oscar winner George Sanders, Gary Merrill, Celeste Holm, and Marilyn Monroe. Joseph L. Mankiewicz won Oscars for both his direction and original screenplay. **CL7, DT68, ST28, ST108, XT1, XT4, XT6** *Essential; Highly Recommended*

All Creatures Great and Small (1974, C, 92m, NR)
Drama adapted from James Herriot's autobiography, following the veterinarian's career from his apprenticeship to an established practice in England's lush countryside. Simon Ward and Anthony Hopkins star. Originally made for TV. **FA5**

All Dogs Go to Heaven (1989, C, 85m, G)
A junkyard dog gets a second chance at life with a new owner, a little girl who can predict the outcome of horse races. Among the character voices in this animated feature are Burt Reynolds, Dom DeLuise, and Judith Barsi. **FA10, ST128**

All in a Night's Work (1961, C, 94m, NR)
An office worker is victimized by a misunderstanding involving a respectable businessman. Comedy starring Shirley MacLaine and Dean Martin. **ST96**

All My Sons (1986, C, 122m, NR)
Adaptation of Arthur Miller's play about a family trying to deal with the loss of a son in World War II. James Whitmore, Aidan Quinn, Joan Allen, and Michael Learned star. Originally made for TV. **DR8, DR20**

All Night Long (1981, C, 88m, R)
A middle-aged manager of an all-night drug store falls in love with his neighbor's wife in this wacky romantic comedy starring Gene Hackman, Barbra Streisand, and Dennis Quaid. **CO1, ST61, ST146**

All of Me (1984, C, 93m, PG-13)
A swinging lawyer finds half his body possessed by a ditsy spinster in this frantic comedy. Steve Martin and Lily Tomlin star, with Victoria Tennant, Richard Libertini, Selma Diamond, and Jason Bernard. **CO3, CO20, ST99, ST149** *Highly Recommended*

All Quiet on the Western Front (1930, B&W, 130m, NR)
Harrowing, moving drama of German youth and his disillusionment during World War I combat. Lew Ayres stars. Oscar winner Lewis Milestone directed. An anti-war classic that won the Academy Award for Best Picture. **AC2, XT1, XT6** *Essential; Highly Recommended*

All Screwed Up (1976, C, 105m, PG)
Comedy-drama of two Italian farmers who move to the city and have problems adjusting to urban life. Directed by Lina Wertmuller. **DT114**

All That Jazz (1979, C, 123m, R)
Bob Fosse's autobiographical musical drama about a director-choreographer juggling too many balls in his professional and personal life. Roy Scheider stars, with Ann Reinking, Jessica Lange, Le-

land Palmer, Cliff Gorman, and Ben Vereen. Sensational dance numbers. **DT39, MU3, MU4, ST86** *Recommended*

All the King's Men (1949, B&W, 109m, NR)
Portrait of a Southern politician whose idealism is corrupted into demagoguery. Oscar winner for Best Picture, Actor (Broderick Crawford), Supporting Actress (Mercedes McCambridge, in her film debut), and Screenplay Adaptation (by director Robert Rossen). Based on Robert Penn Warren's novel, which mirrored the career of Louisiana's Huey Long. **DR19, DR21, XT1, XT2, XT5** *Essential; Recommended*

All the Marbles (1981, C, 113m, R)
Raucous comedy set in the world of ladies' professional wrestling, featuring a lovely tag team (Laurene Landon and Vicki Frederick) and their unscrupulous manager (Peter Falk). Robert Aldrich directed. **CO19**

All the President's Men (1976, C, 138m, PG)
Robert Redford and Dustin Hoffman play the real-life *Washington Post* reporters who uncovered the Watergate scandal. With Martin Balsam, Jack Warden, Jane Alexander, Hal Holbrook, and Oscar winner Jason Robards as Ben Bradlee. Directed by Alan J. Pakula. **DR6, DR21, MY6, ST67, ST126, ST129, XT4, XT12** *Essential; Highly Recommended*

All the Right Moves (1983, C, 90m, R)
In a small town in Pennsylvania, a high school football star breaks with his coach and finds that he's being shut out of a college scholarship—his only way out of the depressed town. Tom Cruise, Craig T. Nelson, and Lea Thompson star. **DR9, DR22, DR26, ST26** *Recommended*

All the Way, Boys (1973, C, 105m, PG)
Terence Hill and Bud Spencer star in this Italian comedy about two go-for-broke adventurers flying a decrepit airplane through the Andes. **FF2**

All This and Heaven Too (1940, B&W, 143m, NR)
Drama set in 19th-century France finds Bette Davis as a governess involved in a scandalous relationship with her aristocrat employer (Charles Boyer). **ST28**

All You Need Is Cash (1978, C, 70m, NR)
The Beatles are spoofed in this documentary about a popular British rock group called The Rutles. Eric Idle heads the cast of loonies. Also known as *The Rutles*; originally made for TV. **CO15** *Recommended*

Allan Quartermain and the Lost City of Gold (1986, C, 100m, PG)
Sequel to the latest version of *King Solomon's Mines* has title hero (Richard Chamberlain) on the trail of a legendary city, battling restless natives, hungry crocodiles, and other obstacles. With James Earl Jones. **AC21, ST76**

Allegheny Uprising (1939, B&W, 81m, NR)
This action saga of colonial America teams John Wayne with Claire Trevor against a British Army officer. **ST156**

Alligator (1980, C, 94m, R)
A pet alligator is flushed down the toilet; in the sewer system he grows into a monster and begins to terrorize the city. Tongue-in-cheek horror written by John Sayles, who also has a small role. Robert Forster stars, with Robin Riker, Michael Gazzo, Dean Jagger, and Jack Carter. **DT93, HO16**

Allonsanfan (1974, C, 117m, NR)
Comedy set in early 19th-century Italy about a group of idealists living in the not-so-distant past. Marcello Mastroianni stars; directed by Paolo and Vittorio Taviani. **FF2, ST103**

Almost Angels (1962, C, 93m, G)
Disney drama of young singer in the Vienna Boys' Choir whose voice is beginning to change. **FA1**

Almost Perfect Affair, An (1979, C, 93m, PG)
A young American filmmaker, on his first trip to the Cannes Film Festival, has a fling with the bored wife of an Italian producer. Keith Carradine and Monica Vitti star, with Raf Vallone. **DR13**

Almost You (1984, C, 96m, R)
Romantic comedy, with a New York woman questioning her marriage after she's injured in an auto accident. Brooke Adams and Griffin Dunne star. **CO1**

Alone in the Dark (1982, C, 92m, R)
Three psychopaths escape from an asylum and seek revenge on their psychiatrist. Jack Palance, Donald Pleasence, and Martin Landau star. **HO9**

Along Came Jones (1945, B&W, 90m, NR)
A western comedy with Gary Cooper as a cowboy who's the victim of mistaken identity. Loretta Young costars. **ST22, WE14**

Along the Great Divide (1951, B&W, 88m, NR)
Kirk Douglas is a western lawman trying to bring in a fugitive through a blinding sandstorm. **ST34**

Along the Navajo Trail (1945, B&W, 54m, NR)
Roy Rogers and Gabby Hayes ride to protect innocent ranchers. With Dale Evans. **ST132**

Alphabet City (1984, C, 98m, R)
Drama of life on New York's Lower East Side, where the mean streets are lettered—thus, the title. Vincent Spano stars. **DR15**

Alphaville (1965, B&W, 100m, NR)
French science fiction thriller, with Eddie Constantine as a detective trying to rescue a kidnapped scientist. Directed by Jean-Luc Godard. **DT41, SF19**

Alsino and the Condor (1982, C, 89m, R)
From Nicaragua, a drama of a young crippled boy who finds self-esteem fighting with a guerrilla band. Directed by Miguel Littin. Dean Stockwell stars. **FF6, ST144**

Altered States (1980, C, 102m, R)
Scientist lets his experiments in primal research overwhelm him. William Hurt stars, with Blair Brown, Charles Haid, and Bob Balaban. Science fiction film packed with dazzling imagery from director Ken Russell. **CU3, CU4, DT92, SF5, SF20, ST75**

Alvarez Kelly (1966, C, 116m, NR)
In this Civil War western, William Holden and Richard Widmark are on opposite sides of the conflict. **ST68, WE6**

Always (1989, C, 121m, PG)
Remake of *A Guy Named Joe*, updating that fantasy-drama's setting to contemporary Montana. A fire-fighting pilot (Richard Dreyfuss) returns after his death to encourage a young pilot (Brad Johnson) who begins romancing the dead man's girl (Holly Hunter). With John Goodman and Audrey Hepburn. Directed by Steven Spielberg. Available only in letterboxed format. **CU18, CU19, DR1, DT99, ST36, ST65, ST74**

Always for Pleasure (1979, C, 58m, NR)
Documentary portrait of New Orleans' Mardi Gras scene, with emphasis on the music; directed by Les Blank. **CU16**

Amadeus (1984, C, 158m, PG)
Oscar-winning film portrait of Wolfgang Amadeus Mozart, the brilliant and irritatingly immature composer, as told by his arch-rival Antonio Salieri. Thomas Hulce and F. Murray Abraham star under Milos Forman's direction. Abraham and Forman also won Oscars. Glorious use of Mozart music. **DR4, DT37, MU5, XT1, XT2, XT6** *Recommended*

Amarcord (1974, C, 127m, PG)
Federico Fellini's comic memoir of his youth in a seaside village is full of memorable characters and classic moments. Oscar winner for Best Foreign Film; arguably Fellini's best work. **DT53, XT7** *Essential; Highly Recommended*

Amateur, The (1979, C, 111m, R)
A computer operator (John Savage) swears revenge on the terrorists who murdered his girlfriend. **MY6**

Amazing Adventure (1936, B&W, 70m, NR)
On a bet, a wealthy man joins the working class to prove that his skills are worthy of a real job. Cary Grant stars in this British comedy. Original title: *The Amazing Quest of Ernest Bliss*. Released in the U.S. as *Romance and Riches*. **ST57**

Amazing Dobermans, The (1976, C, 94m, PG)
Fred Astaire plays a former con man whose trained dobermans help stop a gang of racketeers. **FA5, ST2**

Amazing Grace and Chuck (1987, C, 115m, PG)
A young boy gains international fame when he refuses to pitch in his Little League to protest the arms race. Joshua Zuehlke stars, with Gregory Peck, Jamie

Lee Curtis, and pro basketball player Alex English. **DR7, FA7, ST119**

Amazing Howard Hughes, The (1977, C, 119m, NR)
Dramatization of the life of the aviation pioneer/movie producer/casino owner/ legendary lover, starring Tommy Lee Jones, with Ed Flanders as Noah Dietrich and Tovah Feldshuh as Katharine Hepburn. Originally made for TV; shown at 215m. **DR4, DR24**

Amazing Mr. Blunden, The (1972, C, 100m, PG)
Two children travel in time with the help of a friendly ghost. Lynne Frederick and Gary Miller star in this family adventure with Laurence Naismith. **FA4**

Amazing Quest of Ernest Bliss, The
see Amazing Adventure

Amazon Women on the Moon (1987, C, 85m, R)
Catch-all parody of late-night TV movies and commercials, with series of skits featuring lots of stars (Rosanna Arquette, Michelle Pfeiffer, Griffin Dunne, Steve Allen, Henny Youngman, Arsenio Hall, Carrie Fisher, Paul Bartel). Joe Dante, Carl Gottlieb, Peter Horton, John Landis, and Robert K. Weiss directed. **CO7, DT5, DT25, ST120**

Ambassador, The (1984, C, 97m, R)
Robert Mitchum plays an American diplomat in Israel caught up in the Palestinean problem. With Rock Hudson, Ellen Burstyn, and Donald Pleasence. Loosely based on Elmore Leonard's crime novel, *52 Pick-up*. **ST73, ST107, WR16**

America at the Movies (1976, C/B&W, 116m, NR)
Compilation of scenes from over 80 movie classics, produced by the American Film Institute. **CU16**

American Anthem (1986, C, 100m, PG-13)
Gymnast Mitch Gaylord stars in this flashy drama about the triumphs and heartbreak of competitive gymnastics. **DR22**

American Commandos (1984, C, 89m, R)
An ex-Green Beret returns to Southeast Asia to carry on the war against deadly drug dealers. Christopher Mitchum stars. **AC20**

American Dreamer (1984, C, 105m, PG)
New Jersey housewife wins trip to Paris, finds herself involved in international intrigue and with a dashing Englishman. JoBeth Williams and Tom Conti star. **AC14, CO1, XT16**

American Flyers (1985, C, 114m, PG-13)
Two estranged brothers are reunited when they enter a grueling bicycle race, only to have one of them fall critically ill. Kevin Costner and David Grant star, with Alexandra Paul and Rae Dawn Chong. **DR22, ST23**

American Friend, The (1977, C, 127m, NR)
From director Wim Wenders comes this suspense story about an innocent German picture framer hired to kill a gangster. Bruno Ganz and Dennis Hopper star; film directors Nicholas Ray and Samuel Fuller have small roles. **DT40, DT83, DT113, MY2, MY16, ST71**

American Gigolo (1980, C, 117m, R)
Hollywood hustler is set up for murder, turns to the woman he really loves for help. Richard Gere and Lauren Hutton star. Paul Schrader directed. **DR3, ST52**

American Graffiti (1973, C, 110m, PG)
Cruising in a small California town, 1962; a nostalgic comedy with a cast full of future stars. Ron Howard, Richard Dreyfuss, Cindy Williams, Charles Martin Smith, Paul LeMat, and Candy Clark star, with Mackenzie Phillips, Harrison Ford, Bo Hopkins, Suzanne Sommers, and Wolfman Jack. George Lucas directed. Wall-to-wall rock soundtrack almost steals the show. **CO4, CO6, CU17, DT48, DT64, ST36, ST46** *Essential; Recommended*

American in Paris, An (1951, C, 113m, NR)
Artist Gene Kelly goes to the City of Light for inspiration and meets a young Parisian dancer (Leslie Caron). Winner of seven Academy Awards, including Best Picture, features an all-Gershwin score. Directed by Vincente Minnelli. **DT71, MU1, MU7, ST81, XT1** *Essential; Recommended*

American Ninja (1985, C, 90m, R)
Michael Dudikoff stars in this martial arts adventure about an American battling an

international arms dealer and his renegade army. Steve James costars. **AC26**

American Ninja 2: The Confrontation (1987, C, 90m, R)
More martial arts action with Michael Dudikoff and Steve James up against an army of warriors programmed by a madman. **AC26**

American Ninja 3: Blood Hunt (1989, C, 90m, R)
David Bradley takes over from Michael Dudikoff in this popular martial arts series. This chapter once again takes place at a tournament on a tropical island controlled by a madman (Marjoe Gortner). Steve James costars. **AC26**

American Tail, An (1986, C, 81m, G)
Fievel the mouse emigrates with his family from the Old World to a new life in America. He encounters many adventures along the way in this animated production. **FA10**

American Werewolf in London, An (1981, C, 97m, R)
Two Americans backpacking across the English moors are attacked by a werewolf; one is killed and one becomes a werewolf, in a series of elaborate transformation scenes. David Naughton, Griffin Dunne, and Jenny Agutter star. Directed by John Landis. Ground-breaking makeup effects by Rick Baker. **HO4, HO24, SF16, XT15** *Recommended*

Americanization of Emily, The (1964, B&W, 117m, NR)
Acidic comedy-drama of the U.S. Army's attempts to ensure that an American (James Garner) is the first man to hit the Normandy beaches on D-Day. Meanwhile, he's involved in an up-and-down affair with a British woman (Julie Andrews). With Melvyn Douglas and James Coburn. Written by Paddy Chayevsky. **AC1, DR1**

Americano, The (1955, C, 85m, NR)
A cowboy (Glenn Ford) travels to Europe with a herd of cattle, unaware that the rancher he's delivering them to has been murdered. **WE9**

Amityville Horror, The (1979, C, 117m, R)
A family moves into their dream house, which turns out to be haunted. Based on an allegedly true story. James Brolin, Margot Kidder, and Rod Steiger star. **HO3, HO19**

Amityville II: The Possession (1982, C, 110m, R)
A prequel to *The Amityville Horror* chronicles the events leading to the possession of the eldest son and his slaughter of the rest of the family. Burt Young and Rutanya Alda star. **HO3**

Amityville 3D (1983, C, 95m, PG)
Two journalists and a parapsychologist inhabit the Amityville house to find out once and for all if the house is haunted. Tony Roberts, Candy Clark, and Tess Harper star. **HO3**

Amor Brujo, El (1987, C, 100m, PG)
Romantic drama with dance from Spain, about two young lovers separated by a twist of fate. Choreographed by Antonio Gades. **FF7**

Amos (1985, C, 100m, NR)
A 70-year-old man in a nursing home and a nurse engage in a clash of wills. Kirk Douglas and Elizabeth Montgomery star in this drama originally shown on TV. **DR11, ST34**

Amy (1981, C, 100m, G)
In the early 1900s, a headstrong woman decides to leave her husband and embark on a career of teaching handicapped children. Jenny Agutter stars in this Disney drama, with Barry Newman, Kathleen Nolan, and Nanette Fabray. **FA1**

Anatomy of a Murder (1959, B&W, 161m, NR)
James Stewart is a small town lawyer who defends an Army officer (Ben Gazzara) on charges that he murdered the man who raped his wife (Lee Remick). Memorable courtroom drama, with George C. Scott, Eve Arden, Kathryn Grant, Arthur O'Connell, and Joseph Welch. **DR17, DR26, DT82, ST143** *Essential; Highly Recommended*

Anchors Aweigh (1945, C, 140m, NR)
Gene Kelly joins Frank Sinatra in a rousing musical about two sailor friends who fall for the same girl (Kathryn Grayson). With a very young Dean Stockwell. **MU1, ST81, ST138, ST144**

And Baby Makes Six (1979, C, 104m, NR)
A middle-aged couple (Warren Oates, Colleen Dewhurst) have mixed feelings when they learn they're about to have their fourth child. Originally made for TV. **ST115**

And God Created Woman (1957, C, 92m, NR)
Brigitte Bardot's signature role: the temptress of St. Tropez. Directed by Roger Vadim. Scandalous in its time, relatively tame now. **ST4**

And God Created Woman (1988, C, 100m, R)
Director Roger Vadim offers a remake (in name only) of his erotic drama, this time with Rebecca DeMornay as the free-spirited young woman. Also available in a re-edited, unrated version, with additional sexy footage added; running time: 98m. **CU10, CU18**

. . . And Justice for All (1979, C, 117m, R)
A Baltimore lawyer is asked to defend a corrupt judge on charges that he murdered a prostitute. Al Pacino and John Forsythe star, with Jack Warden and Christine Lahti. Directed by Norman Jewison; cowritten by Barry Levinson. **DR15, DR17, DT51, ST118**

And Now for Something Completely Different (1972, C, 89m, PG)
Collection of classic bits by the Monty Python troupe. **CO15** *Recommended*

And Now My Love (1975, C/B&W, 121m, PG)
French romantic drama about a wealthy woman (Marthe Keller) and rascal (Andre Dussolier) who manage to come together from widely different backgrounds. **FF1**

And Now the Screaming Starts (1973, C, 87m, R)
An aristocratic family is cursed by a disembodied hand which is avenging the rape of a virgin servant girl. Peter Cushing, Ian Ogilvy, and Stephanie Beacham star. **HO26, ST27**

And the Ship Sails On (1984, C, 138m, PG)
Federico Fellini parable set on a luxury liner cruise on the eve of World War I, with the usual assortment of Fellini grotesques and outrageous behavior. **DT53**

And Then There Were None (1945, B&W, 98m, NR)
Ten visitors to a lonely island begin to disappear one by one. Barry Fitzgerald and Walter Huston star in this version of the Agatha Christie tale. **MY15, WR3**

Anderson Tapes, The (1972, C, 98m, PG)
Thieves plan to rob apartments in a New York building over a summer holiday weekend. Sean Connery and Dyan Cannon star, with Martin Balsam, Christopher Walken, and Garrett Morris. Directed by Sidney Lumet. **AC9, CO13, DT65, MY18, ST21, XT9**

Android (1982, C, 80m, PG)
Low-budget, resourceful, amusing science fiction drama starring Klaus Kinski as a mad scientist and Don Opper as the title creation. Many references to classic film *Metropolis*; directed by Aaron Lipstadt. **CU4, SF5, ST83** *Recommended*

Andromeda Strain, The (1971, C, 130m, G)
Deadly virus threatens to trigger nuclear disaster in this science fiction adventure from director Robert Wise. Arthur Hill, David Wayne, James Olson, and Kate Reid star. **DT117, SF5, SF7, SF8**

Andy Hardy Gets Spring Fever (1939, B&W, 85m, NR)
Mickey Rooney plays that all-American boy who's up to his ears in trouble when he decides to produce his high school's annual play. **ST133**

Andy Hardy Meets Debutante (1940, B&W, 86m, NR)
Mickey Rooney and Judy Garland star in this romantic installment of the long-running series. **CL15, ST51, ST133**

Andy Hardy's Double Life (1942, B&W, 92m, NR)
More trouble for Andy (Mickey Rooney), as his romantic complications include Esther Williams. **ST133**

Andy Hardy's Private Secretary (1940, B&W, 101m, NR)
Mickey Rooney's affable lad mixes it up with Kathryn Grayson. **ST133**

Andy Kaufman Sound Stage Special, The (1983, C, 60m, NR)
An hour of offbeat humor with the very unpredictable comedian, assisted by comic Elayne Boosler. **CO16**

Andy Warhol's Bad (1971, C, 100m, R)
Suburban housewife runs a hit man squad out of her home—and that's just for starters in this movie that strives for outrageousness and bad taste at every turn. Caroll Baker, Perry King, Susan Tyrell star. **CU12**

Andy Warhol's Dracula (1974, C, 93m, R)
Campy horror film from producer Warhol and director Paul Morissey about vampire who needs virgins to survive. Udo Kier and Joe Dallessandro star, with Vittorio De Sica. **CU4, DT26, DT72, HF7, HO5, HO24**

Andy Warhol's Frankenstein (1974, C, 94m, R)
Gory update of the mad doctor story, produced by Warhol and directed by Paul Morissey, originally shown in 3-D to disbelieving audiences. Not for viewers with weak stomachs. **CU4, DT72, HF10, HO20, HO24**

Angel (1984, C, 92m, R)
Orphaned teenager goes to high school by day, but cruises Hollywood Boulevard as a prostitute at night, when she's befriended by a colorful collection of street characters. Donna Wilkes, Cliff Gorman, Susan Tyrell, Dick Shawn, and Rory Calhoun star. **AC8**

Angel and the Badman (1947, B&W, 100m, NR)
Western action and romance as a notorious gunslinger (John Wayne) mends his ways for the affections of a Quaker girl. **ST156**

Angel Heart (1987, C, 113m, R)
Detective thriller stars Mickey Rourke as a private eye hired to track down a missing singer, getting involved in a New Orleans voodoo cult. Robert DeNiro and Lisa Bonet costar. An unrated version is also available, containing a few seconds of footage that nearly got the film an "X" rating. **CU1, CU6, CU10, HO10, MY2, MY10, ST30, ST134, XT14**

Angel on My Shoulder (1946, B&W, 101m, NR)
Fantasy story of dead criminal sent to Earth as a judge and his battles with Satan. Paul Muni stars. **HO10, SF2**

Angela (1977, C, 100m, NR)
A middle-aged woman and younger man are attracted to one another, unaware that they're mother and son. Sophia Loren and Steve Railsback star, with John Huston. **DT50, ST93**

Angels Over Broadway (1940, B&W, 80m, NR)
Offbeat comedy from writer Ben Hecht and cinematographer Lee Garmes (they co-directed). Douglas Fairbanks, Jr. plays a hustler trying to redeem himself. With Rita Hayworth, Thomas Mitchell, and John Qualen. **CU5, ST64**

Angels With Dirty Faces (1938, B&W, 97m, NR)
Two childhood friends grow apart when one joins the clergy and the other becomes a gangster. James Cagney and Pat O'Brien star, with Humphrey Bogart, Ann Sheridan, and the Dead End Kids. **AC22, ST8, ST14** *Essential; Recommended*

Angry Red Planet, The (1959, C, 83m, NR)
Science fiction drama of trip to Mars, starring Gerald Mohr and Nora Hayden. **SF3**

Animal Behavior (1989, C, 90m, PG)
A researcher and composer find love in this romantic drama starring Karen Allen and Armand Assante, with Holly Hunter. **ST74**

Animal Crackers (1930, B&W, 98m, NR)
The Marx Bros. crash a party. Groucho sings "Hooray for Captain Spaulding." Margaret Dumont is appalled. **ST101**

Animal House *see* National Lampoon's Animal House

Animalympics (1979, C, 79m, NR)
Feature cartoon with various members of the animal kingdom competing in sporting events. Billy Crystal, Gilda Radner, and Harry Shearer are among the actors supplying the voices. **CO13, FA10**

Ann Vickers (1933, B&W, 72m, NR)
Drama based on the Sinclair Lewis novel of a woman who becomes pregnant by a cad and is redeemed by a judge. Irene Dunne, Walter Huston, and Bruce Cabot star. **WR14**

Anna (1987, C, 101m, PG-13)
Drama of the relationship (à la *All About Eve*) between an aging Czech film star and her young protegée, both living in New York. Oscar nominee Sally Kirkland and Paulina Porizkova star. **DR10, DR13**

Anna Christie (1930, B&W, 90m, NR)
Adaptation of Eugene O'Neill's classic play finds Greta Garbo as a former prostitute whose past begins to haunt her when she falls for a sailor (Charles Bickford). **ST50, WR20**

Anna Karenina (1935, B&W, 95m, NR)
Greta Garbo stars in Tolstoy's tragic love story of a forbidden affair. With Fredric March and Freddie Bartholomew. **CL1, CL4, ST50**

Annapolis Story, An (1955, C, 81m, NR)
John Derek and Kevin McCarthy play rival midshipmen, both in love with Diana Lynn. Directed by Don Siegel. **DR25, DT97**

Anne of Green Gables (1985, C, 195m, NR)
Adaptation of the children's classic about an orphan girl who brings joy to the older couple who adopt her. Megan Follows stars, with Colleen Dewhurst. Originally made for TV. **FA3**

Anne of the Thousand Days (1969, C, 145m, PG)
Historical drama of Henry VIII (Richard Burton) and his wife Anne Boleyn (Genevieve Bujold), who bore him an heir but was still executed. **DR5, ST13**

L'Annee des Meduses (1987, C, 100m, NR)
Sexy French drama of a battle between a nymphet (Valerie Kaprisky) and a gigolo (Bernard Giraudeau). Also known as *The Year of the Jellyfish*. **CU6, FF1**

Annie (1982, C, 128m, PG)
Lavish musical, based on the Broadway smash, about comic strip characters—a frizzy-haired orphan and her rich guardian, Daddy Warbucks. Aileen Quinn and

Albert Finney star, with support from Carol Burnett, Ann Reinking, Bernadette Peters, and Tim Curry. Directed by John Huston. **DT50, FA9, MU2, ST42**

Annie Hall (1977, C, 94m, PG)
Woody Allen's brilliant romantic comedy about an anxious New York comedian and a daffy singer from the Midwest finding—and losing—love. Oscar winner for Best Picture, Director, Actress (Diane Keaton), and Original Screenplay (Allen and Marshall Brickman). With Tony Roberts, Christopher Walken, Colleen Dewhurst, Carol Kane, and Shelley Duvall. Among other attributes, one of the best movies about life in both New York and Los Angeles. **CO1, CO2, DT1, ST79, XT1, XT3, XT6, XT9, XT10** *Essential; Highly Recommended*

Annie Oakley (1935, B&W, 88m, NR)
Barbara Stanwyck plays the legendary sharpshooter. Preston Foster costars, with Moroni Olsen as Buffalo Bill. Directed by George Stevens. **DT101, HF3, HF20, ST142, WE2, WE8**

Annihilators (1985, C, 87m, R)
A synchronized fighting unit just back from overseas gets some stateside action in a small Southern town overrun with sleazy criminals. Christopher Stone, Andy Wood, and Lawrence Hilton-Jacobs star. **AC20**

Another Country (1984, C, 90m, NR)
Drama set in 1930s Britain about two boarding school chums who eventually became spies for the Soviets. Based on the lives of Guy Burgess and Donald Maclean. Rupert Everett and Colin Firth star. **DR23, MY6**

Another Thin Man (1939, B&W, 105m, NR)
William Powell and Myrna Loy return as detectives Nick and Nora Charles in their third adventure, in which they not only solve another crime but start a family with the birth of Nick, Jr. **CL15, HF5, MY17, ST94, ST122, WR9**

Another Time, Another Place (1958, B&W, 98m, NR)
Lana Turner melodrama of wartime widow's nervous breakdown. Sean Connery has a small role. **ST21, ST153**

Another Woman (1988, C, 84m, PG)
Drama starring Gena Rowlands as a New York academic who becomes involved with the problems of a troubled younger woman (Mia Farrow). Woody Allen wrote and directed. Gene Hackman costars. **DR10, DT1, ST61**

Anthony Adverse (1936, B&W, 141m, NR)
Epic saga, based on bestselling novel, of young man's adventures in 19th-century America, including an encounter with Abraham Lincoln. Fredric March stars, with Olivia de Havilland, Claude Rains, and Oscar winner Gale Sondergaard. **DR19, HF18, XT5**

Antonio das Mortes (1969, C, 100m, NR)
True-life drama from Argentina about a bounty hunter, hired in 1939 to kill leftist rebels, who turns on his employers. Directed by Glauber Rocha. **FF6**

Ants (1977, C, 88m, NR)
An army of killer ants terrorizes a resort. Suzanne Sommers, Myrna Loy, and Lynda Day George star. **HO16, ST94**

Any Friend of Nicholas Nickleby Is a Friend of Mine (1981, C, 55m, NR)
Period family adventure set in small town, where a strange man (Fred Gwynne) takes a young boy into his confidence. Written by Ray Bradbury. **FA4**

Any Number Can Win *see* Melodie en Sous-Sol

Any Wednesday (1966, C, 109m, NR)
A New York executive tries to write off his mistress's apartment as a business expense in this comedy starring Jason Robards and Jane Fonda. **ST45, ST129**

Any Which Way You Can (1980, C, 116m, PG)
Sequel to *Every Which Way But Loose* has street brawler Clint Eastwood and his orangutan Clyde mixing it up with comic baddies. Sondra Locke, Geoffrey Lewis, and William Smith costar. **CO9, ST39**

Anzio (1968, C, 117m, PG)
Drama centering on the Allied invasion of a significant Italian beachhead in World War II. Robert Mitchum, Peter Falk, and Robert Ryan star. **AC1, ST107**

Apache (1954, C, 91m, NR)
Burt Lancaster stars in this historical account of the bitter battle between the Indians and the U. S. Cavalry. **ST85, WE8**

Apache Rose (1947, C, 75m, NR)
Roy Rogers western set on a gambling ship. Dale Evans pilots a tugboat, and Bob Nolan & the Sons of the Pioneers provide the harmonies. **ST132**

Apartment, The (1960, B&W, 125m, NR)
Writer-director Billy Wilder's Oscar-winning comedy about a schnook (Jack Lemmon) who lets his bosses borrow his pad for their little one-night stands. Shirley MacLaine and Fred MacMurray costar. **DT116, ST90, ST96, XT1, XT6** *Essential; Recommended*

Apartment Zero (1989, C, 114m, R)
Offbeat thriller from Argentina (shot in English) concerning a Buenos Aires film buff (Colin Firth) who takes in a strange boarder (Hart Bochner). Directed by Martin Donovan. **FF6, MY9**

Ape, The (1940, B&W, 62m, NR)
A kindly doctor becomes obsessed with his experiments after the death of his wife and child. He soon resorts to murder disguised as an ape. Boris Karloff stars. **HO20, ST77**

Ape Man, The (1943, B&W, 64m, NR)
Bela Lugosi experiments with a serum derived from ape blood to give humans the power of a gorilla. **ST95**

Apocalypse Now (1979, C, 153m, R)
Director Francis Ford Coppola's nightmarish vision of the Vietnam War, starring Martin Sheen, Marlon Brando, and Robert Duvall, with Harrison Ford, Dennis Hopper, Frederic Forrest, Timothy Bottoms, G.D. Spradlin, and Larry Fishburne. Effective use of rock music, brilliant imagery. **AC4, DT21, ST10, ST38, ST46, ST71** *Essential; Highly Recommended*

Apology (1986, C, 98m, NR)
Thriller about an artist (Lesley Ann Warren) who solicits confessions by phone, until a serial killer calls for her forgiveness. Peter Weller and John Glover costar. **MY3**

Appaloosa, The (1966, C, 98m, NR)
Western drama starring Marlon Brando as a cowboy who journeys to Mexico to retrieve his stolen horse. John Saxon and Anjanette Comer costar. **ST10, WE9**

Apple Dumpling Gang, The (1975, C, 100m, G)
Three frisky kids strike it rich and trigger a wild bank robbery in the gold-mad West. Bill Bixby, Susan Clark, Don Knotts, and Tim Conway star in this Disney western. **FA1**

Apple Dumpling Gang Rides Again, The (1979, C, 88m, G)
Two bumbling outlaws try to go straight, but they can't even seem to get that right. Disney western stars Tim Conway, Don Knotts, and Tim Matheson. **FA1**

Appointment in Honduras (1953, C, 79m, NR)
An American and his pals help out a Latin American country. Glenn Ford, Ann Sheridan, and Zachary Scott star. Directed by Jacques Tourneur. **DT105**

Appointment With Death (1988, C, 91m, PG)
Hercule Poirot (Peter Ustinov) solves a murder in 1937 Jerusalem. The suspects in this Agatha Christie whodunit include Lauren Bacall, Piper Laurie, and Carrie Fisher. **MY12, WR3**

Apprenticeship of Duddy Kravitz, The (1974, C, 121m, PG)
Richard Dreyfuss plays a Jewish hustler in this comedy-drama set in 1940s Montreal, based on Mordecai Richler's novel. With Micheline Lanctot, Jack Warden, Randy Quaid, Joseph Wiseman, and Denholm Elliott. **ST36**

April Fools, The (1969, C, 95m, PG)
A married man decides to start his life all over again by running off with a lovely French girl. Jack Lemmon and Catherine Deneuve star, with Charles Boyer and Myrna Loy. **ST29, ST90, ST94**

April Fool's Day (1986, C, 90m, R)
A rich college girl throws a party at her family's home on an island and her guests begin to disappear. Deborah Foreman stars. **HO12**

Arabesque (1966, C, 105m, NR)
Espionage thriller about a college professor (Gregory Peck) lured into political intrigue by a beautiful woman (Sophia Loren). Directed by Stanley Donen. **DT30, MY6, ST93, ST119**

Arch of Triumph (1948, B&W, 120m, NR)
Wartime drama stars Ingrid Bergman as a woman in love with an Austrian refugee (Charles Boyer). Charles Laughton costars. **ST7**

Archer's Adventure (1985, C, 120m, NR)
Family adventure, set in 19th century, about a young man and his horse crossing the trackless wastes of Australia. **FA4**

Aria (1988, C, 90m, R)
Ten directors concoct short films built around opera arias. Among the filmmakers: Jean-Luc Godard, Ken Russell, Robert Altman, Bruce Beresford, and Julien Temple. The stars include Theresa Russell, Bridget Fonda, Buck Henry, John Hurt, and Beverly D'Angelo. **DT2, DT41, DT92, MU16**

Arizona Kid, The (1940, B&W, 54m, NR)
Early Roy Rogers western has him singing and dispensing justice, with Gabby Hayes and Dale Evans along to help. **ST132**

Armed and Dangerous (1986, C, 88m, PG-13)
John Candy and Eugene Levy star in this comedy about pair of inept security guards. **CO3, CO14**

Armed Response (1986, C, 95m, R)
Chinatown gang war erupts in this drama starring David Carradine and Lee Van Cleef, with Mako and Dick Miller. **AC8, ST155**

Armored Attack *see* North Star

Armored Command (1961, B&W, 99m, NR)
World War II action, starring Howard Keel, with Tina Louise and Burt Reynolds. **AC1, ST128**

Arnold (1973, C, 100m, PG)
A rich old man dies but his fiancee goes through with the wedding so she and his family can spend his fortune. Then the members of the family begin to die in strange ways. Stella Stevens, Roddy

McDowall, and Elsa Lanchester star in this comic horror story. **HO14, HO24**

Around the World in 80 Days (1956, C, 178m, G)
Jules Verne tale of an outrageous wager—at least for the late 19th century. David Niven and Cantinflas play the champion travelers; Shirley MacLaine costars, with dozens of familiar faces in bit parts. Oscar winner for Best Picture and Musical Score. **FA4, ST96, WR28, XT1, XT18**

Around the World Under the Sea (1966, C, 117m, NR)
Family adventure of special submarine and its record-setting voyage. Lloyd Bridges stars, with Shirley Eaton, David McCallum, and Keenan Wynn. **FA4**

Arrangement, The (1969, C, 120m, R)
Business executive re-examines his life after a failed suicide attempt. Kirk Douglas stars, with Faye Dunaway, Deborah Kerr, and Richard Boone. Drama from director Elia Kazan, based on his novel. **DR24, DT53, ST34**

Arrowsmith (1931, B&W, 99m, NR)
From director John Ford comes the story of a country doctor who travels to the West Indies to study tropical ailments. Ronald Colman and Helen Hayes star, with Myrna Loy. Based on Sinclair Lewis' novel. **DR19, DT36, ST94, WR17**

Arruza (1972, C, 75m, NR)
A documentary portrait of Carlos Arruza, one of Mexico's great bullfighters. Directed by Budd Boetticher. **CU16, DT10** *Recommended*

Arsenal (1929, B&W, 70m, NR)
Classic silent anti-war drama from Soviet director Alexander Dovzhenko, set in the waning days of World War I and the early days of the Revolution. **FF7**

Arsenic and Old Lace (1944, B&W, 118m, NR)
Frantic mystery-comedy, based on the hit play about a couple of sweet, innocent-looking maiden aunts who poison their gentlemen callers. Cary Grant, Raymond Massey, and Peter Lorre star. Directed by Frank Capra. **CL10, DR20, DT16, MY17, ST57** *Recommended*

Arthur (1981, C, 97m, PG)
A tipsy millionaire playboy falls in love with a kooky shoplifter, although he's engaged to a socialite. Dudley Moore, Liza Minnelli, and Oscar winner John Gielgud star in this romantic comedy. **CO1, ST109, XT4** *Recommended*

Arthur 2 On the Rocks (1988, C, 113m, PG)
Sequel to *Arthur* finds the tipsy millionaire married to his true love, about to lose his fortune. Dudley Moore, Liza Minnelli, and John Gielgud (in ghostly form) reprise their roles from the first film. **CO1, ST109**

As You Like It (1936, B&W, 96m, NR)
William Shakespeare's comedy explores the many facets of love. Laurence Olivier and Elisabeth Bergner star. **ST116, WR22**

Ashanti: Land of No Mercy (1979, C, 117m, R)
The wife of a British doctor (Michael Caine) is kidnapped by a slave trader (Peter Ustinov). William Holden costars in this adventure set in the Middle East. **ST15, ST68**

Ashes and Diamonds (1958, B&W, 96m, NR)
Polish drama set in the immediate aftermath of World War II, when a Resistance youth assassinates the wrong man. Directed by Andrzej Wajda. Zbigniew Cybulski stars. **FF7** *Essential; Recommended*

Asphalt Jungle, The (1950, B&W, 112m, NR)
An aging criminal returns from prison to recruit his old gang for one final heist. Sterling Hayden and Sam Jaffe star, with Jean Hagen and Marilyn Monroe. Directed by John Huston. **DT50, MY1, MY18, ST108** *Essential; Recommended*

Asphyx, The (1972, C, 96m, PG)
British science fiction drama, set in the 1870s, with a scientist isolating the spirit of death and achieving immortality in the process. Robert Stephens, Robert Powell, and Jane Lapotaire star. **SF5, SF19**

Assassination (1987, C, 88m, PG-13)
A Secret Service agent (Charles Bronson) has reason to believe that the new First Lady (Jill Ireland) is in danger. **ST12**

Assassination of Trotsky, The (1972, C, 103m, R)
Brooding account of the final days of the Soviet leader, living in exile in Mexico. Richard Burton stars, with Alain Delon and Romy Schneider. Directed by Joseph Losey. **DR5, ST13**

Assault, The (1986, C, 149m, NR)
During the closing days of World War II, a young boy witnesses his family's betrayal to the Nazis and their deportation to the death camps. Oscar-winning drama from Holland. **FF7, XT7**

Assault of the Rebel Girls (1959, C, 68m, NR)
In Errol Flynn's last film, he plays himself in the fight to aid Fidel Castro's revolution. Also known as *Cuban Rebel Girls*. **ST43**

Assault on Precinct 13 (1976, C, 90m, R)
Isolated police station is besieged by vengeful street gangs in this low-budget thriller from director John Carpenter. Emphasis is on suspense rather than violence. **AC8, DT17** *Recommended*

Asylum (1972, C, 92m, PG)
Four scary stories by Robert Bloch are linked together by the conclusion of the fourth story. Peter Cushing stars, with Barbara Parkins, Britt Ekland, and Charlotte Rampling. **HO23, HO26, ST27**

At Close Range (1986, C, 115m, R)
A criminal tries to involve his young sons in his line of work, in this drama based on a true story. Sean and Christopher Penn star, with Christopher Walken and Mary Stuart Masterson. **DR6, DR8, DR16, XT8**

At the Circus (1939, B&W, 87m, NR)
The Marx Bros. take over the big top. Groucho sings "Lydia the Tattooed Lady." Margaret Dumont is not amused. **ST101**

At the Earth's Core (1976, C, 90m, PG)
Science fiction adventure, based on Edgar Rice Burroughs story, about scientists burrowing from England into subterranean kingdom of monsters. Peter Cushing, Doug McClure, and Caroline Munro star. **FA4, SF3, ST27**

At War With the Army (1950, B&W, 93m, NR)
Dean Martin and Jerry Lewis join the paratroopers in their first starring feature. **CO21, ST91**

L'Atalante (1934, B&W, 82m, NR)
Classic romance/fantasy about a French couple living on a barge on the Seine, directed by Jean Vigo. **FF1** *Essential*

Athens, GA (1987, C, 82m, NR)
Documentary of rock music scene in title town, focusing on R.E.M. and other local bands. **CU16**

Atlantic City (1980, C, 104m, R)
An aging gangster and an aspiring casino dealer are the improbable romantic couple in this offbeat drama set in Atlantic City. Burt Lancaster and Susan Sarandon star. Written by John Guare; directed by Louis Malle. **DR1, DR16, ST85** *Recommended*

Atoll K (1950, B&W, 80m, NR)
Laurel & Hardy inherit an island but don't realize they're sitting on top of an uranium mine. Their last film together. Also known as *Utopia*. **ST87**

Atom Age Vampire (1961, B&W, 87m, NR)
A mad doctor fixes a dancer's disfigured face, becomes obsessed with keeping her beautiful, and kills other women for their cells so he can preserve the dancer's looks. **HO20**

Atomic Cafe, The (1982, C/B&W, 88m, NR)
Collection of propaganda film clips from the 1950s about the dangers of nuclear war and how to survive one. Funny and chilling at the same time. **CU16** *Recommended*

Atomic Kid, The (1954, B&W, 86m, NR)
An innocent man wanders into an atomic test site and emerges alive but with extraordinary powers. Mickey Rooney stars in this comedy. **ST133**

Atonement of Gosta Berling, The *see* Gosta Berling's Saga

Attack Force Z (1981, C, 84m, NR)
Australian-produced World War II drama of commandos on a rescue mission. John

Phillip Law, Sam Neill, and Mel Gibson star. **AC1, ST53**

Attack of the Killer Tomatoes (1980, C, 87m, PG)
Cult "bad" movie that tries to spoof science fiction films about marauding giant vegetables and winds up being just plain awful. **CU11**

Attack of the Robots (1966, B&W, 88m, NR)
Combination of science fiction drama and spy thriller, with secret agent out to stop terrorists from programming robots for political assassinations. Shot in France; dubbed into English. Eddie Constantine stars. **SF19**

Au Revoir, les Enfants (1987, C, 103m, PG)
French director Louis Malle's autobiographical drama about a schoolboy befriending a Jewish classmate during the Occupation. **DR25, FF1** *Recommended*

Audrey Rose (1977, C, 113m, PG)
A twelve-year-old girl begins having nightmares about being in a fire and an investigation reveals that she is the reincarnation of Audrey Rose, a girl who died in a fiery car crash. Marsha Mason, Anthony Hopkins, and John Beck star. Robert Wise directed. **DT117, HO13**

Aurora Encounter (1986, C, 90m, PG)
A Texas town is the site for a friendly alien's visit in this humorous science fiction tale. Jack Elam stars. **SF13**

Author! Author! (1982, C, 110m, PG)
Domestic comedy starring Al Pacino as a playwright whose wife (Tuesday Weld) leaves him with a brood of children (most of them from her previous marriages). Dyan Cannon costars. **CO5, ST118**

Autobiography of Miss Jane Pittman, The (1974, C, 110m, NR)
Epic story of a black woman's journey from slavery to equality in the modern South, starring Cicely Tyson. Winner of 9 Emmys; originally made for TV. **DR14**

Autumn Leaves (1956, B&W, 108m, NR)
Joan Crawford is the middle-aged woman who finds romance with a man (Cliff Robertson) half her age. Their happiness turns sour when his secret past catches up with him. **CL5, ST24**

Autumn Sonata (1978, C, 97m, PG)
Ingrid Bergman and Liv Ullmann star in this drama of a mother and daughter reunited after seven years, with old wounds opened. Directed by Ingmar Bergman; dialogue in Swedish and English. **DR8, DT7, ST7, ST154**

Avalanche (1978, C, 91m, PG)
A new ski resort is about to get more powder than the weather forecasts predicted. Rock Hudson, Mia Farrow, Robert Forster, and Jeanette Nolan star in this disaster adventure. **AC23, ST73**

Avenging Angel (1985, C, 93m, R)
Sequel to *Angel,* with prostitute, now in college, gunning for killer of cop who befriended her. Betsy Russell stars, with Rory Calhoun and Susan Tyrell returning from first film. **AC8**

Avenging Conscience, The (1914, B&W, 78m, NR)
This early horror film from D.W. Griffith is based on Edgar Allan Poe's "The Tell-Tale Heart." **DT42, WR21**

Avenging Force (1986, C, 104m, R)
A terrorist group dumps a special agent in the midst of a swamp and forces him to fight for his life. Michael Dudikoff stars. **AC24**

Aviator, The (1985, C, 98m, PG)
Grounded pilot agrees to fly spunky young woman through treacherous territory, and romance develops. Christopher Reeve and Rosanna Arquette star. **AC11, AC14**

Aviator's Wife, The (1981, C, 104m, NR)
French comedy about a young man's disillusionment with his current lover and a chance encounter with a new possibility. Directed by Eric Rohmer. **DT89**

L'Avventura (1960, B&W, 145m, NR)
On a weekend boating trip to a remote island, a woman disappears, prompting the others in her party to examine their lives. Deliberately paced drama from Italian director Michelangelo Antonioni. Available in a letterboxed edition. **CU19, DT3** *Essential*

Awakening, The (1980, C, 102m, R)
An Egyptologist defies a curse and releases the spirit of an evil queen, who then possesses his daughter. Based on a

novel by Bram Stoker. Charlton Heston, Susannah York, and Stephanie Zimbalist star. **HO8**

Awful Truth, The (1937, B&W, 92m, NR)
Comedy classic pairs Irene Dunne and Cary Grant as a screwy divorced couple who interfere with one another's love life. Ralph Bellamy costars. Oscar-winning direction by Leo McCarey. **CL10, ST57, XT6** *Essential; Recommended*

Babar: The Movie (1989, C, 79m, G)
Animated feature starring the beloved children's storybook favorite, the gentle elephant, plus all his friends. **FA10**

Babe Ruth Story, The (1948, B&W, 106m, NR)
William Bendix plays the Sultan of Swat, as he bats and pitches his way out of a Baltimore orphanage to become the greatest New York Yankee of them all. **CL2, DR22**

Babes in Arms (1939, B&W, 96m, NR)
Judy Garland and Mickey Rooney put on a show to raise money for their vaudevillian parents. Directed by Busby Berkeley. **CL15, DT8, MU1, MU4, ST51, ST133**

Babes in Toyland (1961, C, 105m, NR)
Victor Herbert's music is featured in this Disney fantasy set in the make-believe world of Mother Goose. Annette Funicello, Ray Bolger, Ed Wynn, and Tommy Sands star. **FA1**

Babes on Broadway (1941, B&W, 118m, NR)
Mickey Rooney-Judy Garland musical extravaganza, in which the stars put on a show for poor kids. Busby Berkeley directed. **CL15, DT8, MU1, MU4, ST51, ST133**

Babette's Feast (1987, C, 102m, PG)
Remarkably subtle and rich drama, based on a story by Isak Dinesen. A pair of unmarried sisters in a Norwegian village take in a French woman as a cook and she unexpectedly enriches their lives. Oscar winner as Best Foreign Language Film. Gabriel Axel wrote and directed. **FF7, XT7** *Highly Recommended*

Baby, The (1973, C, 85m, R)
A retarded man is babied by his overprotective mother and sister. When a social worker gets involved with the case, mur-

der soon follows. Anjanette Comer and Ruth Roman star. **HO13**

Baby Boom (1987, C, 110m, PG)
A Manhattan business executive has her single life turned upside-down when she inherits an infant from a relative. Diane Keaton stars in this comedy, with Harold Ramis and Sam Shepard. **CO2, CO14, ST79**

Baby Doll (1956, B&W, 114m, NR)
Tennessee Williams' play about a poor Southern farmer who can't keep his teen-aged wife happy. Eli Wallach, Carroll Baker, and Karl Malden star, with Rip Torn. Directed by Elia Kazan. Condemned by the Catholic Church and banned in some cities on its original release. **CU6, CU8, DT53, ST150, WR30**

Baby, It's You (1983, C, 105m, R)
Romantic drama involving a Jewish girl and an Italian guy, starting in a New Jersey high school. Rosanna Arquette and Vincent Spano star. John Sayles wrote and directed. Four period rock 'n' roll songs from the film's original soundtrack were replaced for video version. **DR1, DT93**

Baby Maker, The (1970, C, 109m, R)
An infertile couple hire a free spirit (Barbara Hershey) as a surrogate mother, with predictably complicated results. Written and directed by James Bridges. **DR7, DR8**

Baby—Secret of the Lost Legend (1985, C, 92m, PG)
On an expedition in the jungles of Africa, a young couple stumble onto an infant dinosaur and wind up protecting it from a greedy scientist. William Katt and Sean Young star. **AC12**

Baby, Take a Bow (1934, B&W, 76m, NR)
Shirley Temple's first starring role has her helping her ex-con dad (James Dunn) to go straight. **ST148**

Baby, the Rain Must Fall (1965, B&W, 100m, NR)
Just out of prison, a drifter tries to settle down with his wife and child but soon becomes restless. Steve McQueen stars, with Lee Remick and Don Murray. **ST97**

Bachelor and the Bobby-Soxer, The (1947, B&W, 95m, NR)
A playboy (Cary Grant), hauled in for disturbing the peace, is sentenced by a judge (Myrna Loy) to court her younger sister (Shirley Temple). Written by Sidney Sheldon. **ST57, ST94, ST148** *Recommended*

Bachelor Mother (1939, B&W, 81m, NR)
Ginger Rogers comedy has her a single woman mothering an abandoned infant. With David Niven and Charles Coburn. **ST131**

Bachelor Party (1984, C, 106m, R)
Tom Hanks stars as a soon-to-be-married man whose buddies throw him the party of his life. **ST62**

Back From Eternity (1956, B&W, 97m, NR)
Adventure drama of survivors of jungle plane crash, starring Robert Ryan, Anita Ekberg, Rod Steiger, and Phyllis Kirk. **AC24**

Back Roads (1981, C, 94m, R)
Romantic comedy about a pair of drifters who fall in love while traveling the South together. Sally Field and Tommy Lee Jones star; directed by Martin Ritt. **DT87, ST40, XT18**

Back Street (1961, C, 107m, NR)
The classic Fannie Hurst soaper about a fashion designer (Susan Hayward) who is hopelessly in love with a married man (John Gavin). Vera Miles costars. **CL4, CL6**

Back to Bataan (1945, B&W, 95m, NR)
John Wayne leads American troops into the Philippines to battle the Japanese. Anthony Quinn costars. **AC1, ST156**

Back to the Future (1985, C, 116m, PG)
A teenager is transported back in time to the 1950s, where he plays matchmaker for his future parents. Michael J. Fox stars, with Christopher Lloyd, Lea Thompson and Crispin Glover. Robert Zemeckis directed. **CO4, CO6, CO11, CO20, SF4** *Recommended*

Back to the Future, Part II (1989, C, 107m, PG)
Followup to the time-travel comedy, with Michael J. Fox moving from the present to the future and back to the past. Emphasis is on saving his family—and town—from awful fate. Christopher Lloyd costars, with Lea Thompson, Thomas F. Wilson, and Joe Flaherty in a brief role. **CO5, CO6, CO11, CO14, CO20, SF4**

Bad *see* Andy Warhol's Bad

Bad and the Beautiful, The (1952, B&W, 118m, NR)
Hollywood tale of a tough producer (Kirk Douglas) and those who work under his thumb. With Lana Turner, Dick Powell, Gloria Grahame (an Oscar winner), and Barry Sullivan. Directed by Vincente Minnelli. **CL7, DT71, ST34, ST153, XT5** *Essential*

Bad Boys (1983, C, 123m, R)
Prison drama, set in facility for youth offenders, with the new loner taking on the established king of the cell block. Sean Penn and Esai Morales star, with Reni Santoni and Ally Sheedy. **DR9, DR18**

Bad Company (1972, C, 93m, PG)
Jeff Bridges and Barry Brown play a couple of drifters set loose on the frontier during the Civil War. With Jim Davis, David Huddleston, and Ed Lauter. Written by Robert Benton and David Newman; directed by Benton. **DT6, ST11, WE6, WE15** *Highly Recommended*

Bad Day at Black Rock (1955, C, 81m, NR)
Riveting drama of a one-armed stranger (Spencer Tracy) in a contemporary Western town to uncover a mystery. Great supporting cast includes Robert Ryan, Lee Marvin, Ernest Borgnine, Anne Francis, and Dean Jagger. **CL8, ST100, ST151, WE12** *Recommended*

Bad Girls (1968, C, 97m, R)
French romantic triangle involving an aging courtesan, a dissipated playboy, and a lovely street waif. Stephane Audran, Jean-Louis Trintignant, and Jacqueline Sassard star. Claude Chabrol directed. Originally released as *Les Biches* at 104m. **FF1**

Bad Influence (1990, C, 99m, R)
Cat-and-mouse thriller of a callow young man (James Spader) and his new, hedonistic, blackmailing pal (Rob Lowe). **MY9**

Bad Jim (1990, C, 90m, PG)
A trio of Western outlaws pull off a string of robberies, claiming to be the late Billy the Kid's gang. James Brolin, John Clark Gable, and Richard Roundtree star, with Harry Carey, Jr., Rory Calhoun, and Ty Hardin. **WE3**

Bad Man of Deadwood (1941, B&W, 54m, NR)
Roy Rogers western has him playing a man with a secret past who joins a circus as a sharpshooter. **ST132**

Bad Man's River (1972, C, 89m, PG)
Comic western starring Lee Van Cleef as an outlaw whose gang is harassed by a feisty woman (Gina Lollobrigida). With James Mason. **ST102, ST155, WE8, WE14**

Bad News Bears, The (1976, C, 102m, PG)
An inept Little League team and their beer-guzzling coach are saved from humiliation by a talented young pitcher, who just happens to be a girl. Walter Matthau and Tatum O'Neal star. Michael Ritchie directed. **CO4, CO19, ST104** *Recommended*

Bad Seed, The (1956, B&W, 129m, NR)
An innocent-looking little girl (Patty McCormack) holds the terrible secret to a rash of mysterious deaths. **HO13, MY14**

Bad Sleep Well, The (1960, B&W, 152m, NR)
Japanese drama of corporate corruption, directed by Akira Kurosawa, starring Toshiro Mifune. Based on a story by Ed McBain. New video version restores edited footage to the original theatrical running time. **CU10, DT57, ST106**

Badge 373 (1973, C, 116m, R)
Sequel of sorts to *The French Connection* starring Robert Duvall as a New York lawman fighting a lone battle against the Mob. **AC9, ST38**

Badlands (1973, C, 95m, PG)
Cult drama about a young couple's murder spree in the 1950s Midwest, loosely based on the Charles Starkweather-Caril Fugate case. Martin Sheen and Sissy Spacek star, with Warren Oates. Terrence Malick wrote and directed. **DR16, DT67, ST115, ST139, XT18** *Essential; Recommended*

Badman's Territory (1946, B&W, 97m, NR)
Randolph Scott is a sheriff clashing with outlaws who are out of his jurisdiction. **ST136**

Bagdad Cafe (1988, C, 91m, PG)
Off-center comedy about a German woman stranded in the California desert, and her relationship with a black woman who runs a greasy spoon. Marianne Sagebrecht and CCH Pounder star. **CO12, CO20**

Baker's Wife, The (1938, B&W, 124m, NR)
Classic French comedy, directed by Marcel Pagnol, of forlorn baker abandoned by his spouse. **FF1**

Bal, Le (1982, C, 112m, NR)
One-of-a-kind musical, set in Parisian dance hall, spanning fifty years, told with only music, no dialogue. French lyrics, with English subtitles. Ettore Scola directed. **FF1, MU16**

Balance, La (1982, C, 102m, R)
Cop drama from France about a Parisian prostitute and her boyfriend forced to inform on crime boss by a ruthless cop. Nathalie Baye, Philippe Leotard, and Richard Berry star. Bob Swaim directed. **FF1, XT16** *Recommended*

Ball of Fire (1941, B&W, 111m, NR)
To help his research, a language professor (Gary Cooper) and his seven colleagues consult a stripper (Barbara Stanwyck) for her interpretations of slang in this classic comedy. Directed by Howard Hawks; written by Billy Wilder and Charles Brackett. **CL10, DT43, ST22, ST142** *Recommended*

Ballad of Cable Hogue, The (1970, C, 121m, R)
From director Sam Peckinpah comes this gentle, comic tale of an old prospector (Jason Robards), his lady friend (Stella Stevens), and their misadventures in the desert. With David Warner, Strother Martin, L.Q. Jones, R.G. Armstrong, and Slim Pickens. **DT77, ST129, WE8, WE11** *Highly Recommended*

Ballad of Gregorio Cortez, The (1982, C, 99m, NR)
Drama based on the famous 1901 manhunt for a Mexican cowhand who, in self-

defense, killed a Texas sheriff and became a folk hero when he tried to escape. Edward James Olmos stars. Originally made for public TV. **WE3**

Balloonatic, The/One Week (1923/1920, B&W, 48m, NR)
A Buster Keaton double feature on one tape. In the first short, he's caught in a runaway hot-air balloon. In the second, Buster and his new bride buy a pre-fab home. **DT54**

Bambi (1942, C, 69m, G)
Classic Disney animated feature about a kind-hearted fawn and his forest friends. **FA2** *Essential; Recommended*

Bananas (1971, C, 82m, PG)
Wild Woody Allen comedy, basically a series of sketches starring Woody as Fielding Melish, product tester. Sight gags, puns, in-jokes, political humor—they're all here. Louise Lasser and Howard Cosell costar; Sylvester Stallone has a bit part. **DT1, ST140** *Recommended*

Band of Outsiders (1964, B&W, 97m, NR)
French director Jean-Luc Godard at his playful, provocative best, in a tale of theft that turns into a running political and cultural commentary. Anna Karina, Sami Frey, and Claude Brasseur star. **DT41** *Recommended*

Band of the Hand (1986, C, 109m, R)
Five buddies try to stay straight on the mean streets of Miami in this urban action thriller. James Remar and Stephen Lang star. **AC8**

Band Wagon, The (1953, C, 112m, NR)
Fred Astaire plays a fading movie star whose songwriting pals want him for their new Broadway show. Cyd Charisse, Jack Buchanan, Oscar Levant, and Nanette Fabray costar. Among the many highlights: the Girl Hunt Ballet. Directed by Vincente Minnelli; written by Betty Comden and Adolph Green. **DT71, MU1, MU4, ST2** *Essential; Highly Recommended*

Bandolero! (1968, C, 106m, PG)
James Stewart and Dean Martin are two fugitive brothers who take Raquel Welch hostage from Texas to Mexico. **ST143, WE9**

Bang the Drum Slowly (1973, C, 97m, PG)
A star pitcher tries to help his roommate, a third-string catcher, face up to a fatal illness. Michael Moriarty and Robert DeNiro star in this drama. **DR22, ST30**

Bank Dick, The (1940, B&W, 74m, NR)
W.C. Fields gets a job as a bank guard, and a robber decides to make his move. With Grady Sutton and Franklin Pangborn. **ST41** *Recommended*

Barabbas (1962, C, 134m, NR)
Anthony Quinn plays the robber whose freedom spelled doom for Jesus Christ in this biblical epic. With Silvano Mangano, Arthur Kennedy, Jack Palance, and Ernest Borgnine. **CL13, HF16**

Barbarella (1968, C, 98m, PG)
Science fiction spoof, with spacey heroine (Jane Fonda) experiencing all kinds of adventures. Considered sexy at the time of its release, but check the rating. **CU4, CU6, SF19, SF22, ST45**

Barbarian and the Geisha, The (1958, C, 105m, NR)
Historical drama starring John Wayne as a diplomat who helps open 19th-century Japan to the West. Directed by John Huston. **DT50, ST156**

Barbarosa (1982, C, 90m, PG)
Willie Nelson plays an aging outlaw who teaches a naive farm boy survival skills to carry on his legend along the Tex-Mex border. Gary Busey costars. Written by William Witliff; directed by Fred Schepisi. **MU12, WE3, WE9**

Barbary Coast (1935, B&W, 90m, NR)
Miriam Hopkins plays a saloon singer in the Gold Rush days of San Francisco, fending off the advances of her ruthless boss (Edward G. Robinson). Howard Hawks directed. **DT43, ST130, WE8**

Barber Shop, The (1933, B&W, 21m, NR)
Classic W.C. Fields short, with Bill playing a barber with a very sharp razor. **ST41**

Barefoot Contessa, The (1954, C, 128m, NR)
Humphrey Bogart stars as a manipulative director who promotes his protégée (Ava Gardner) into stardom, with the help of a cynical press agent (Oscar winner Edmond O'Brien). Striking color photogra-

phy; directed by Joseph L. Mankiewicz. **CL9, DR13, DT68, ST8, XT4**

Barefoot Executive, The (1971, C, 95m, G) Disney comedy finds Kurt Russell as a young employee at a struggling television network; with the help of a clever chimpanzee, he goes from the mailroom to executive row in no time. **FA1**

Barefoot in the Park (1967, C, 105m, NR) Neil Simon's romantic comedy about a young couple's struggles to make a life in New York, starring Jane Fonda and Robert Redford. Charles Boyer and Mildred Natwick offer fine support. **CO1, ST45, ST126, WR23, XT9**

Barfly (1987, C, 99m, R) Two skid-row alcoholics strike up a friendship of sorts, based on their mutual love of the bottle. Mickey Rourke and Faye Dunaway star in this comedy-drama based on the writings of Charles Bukowski. **DR15, ST37, ST134** *Recommended*

Barkleys of Broadway, The (1949, C, 109m, NR) Fred Astaire and Ginger Rogers play famous dancing partners who marry, separate, and then reunite. **CL15, MU1, MU4, ST2, ST131**

Barn Burning (1980, C, 40m, NR) Adaptation of William Faulkner short story about the infamous Snopes family, starring Tommy Lee Jones. Written by Horton Foote; originally made for public TV. **WR6**

Baron of Arizona, The (1950, B&W, 90m, NR) Vincent Price stars as a landgrabbing villain in 19th-century Arizona. Directed by Samuel Fuller. **DT40, ST124**

Barry Lyndon (1975, C, 183m, PG) Stanley Kubrick's epic about an 18th-century Irish scoundrel. Based on William Makepeace Thackeray's classic novel. Exquisitely photographed by John Alcott. Ryan O'Neal and Marisa Berenson star. **CL1, DR5, DT56** *Recommended*

Basket Case (1982, C, 89m, NR) Horror story of separated Siamese twins, one a deformed monster, both seeking revenge on the doctors who separated them. Has well-deserved cult reputation.

Frank Henenlotter wrote and directed; Kevin Van Hentenryck stars. **CU4, CU7, HO15, HO18** *Recommended*

Basket Case 2 (1990, C, 89m, R) Gruesome follow-up to the Siamese twins horror tale, with same star and writer-director. **HO15, HO18, HO24**

Bat 21 (1988, C, 88m, R) An American soldier, stranded behind enemy lines during the Vietnam War, has as his only hope a courageous chopper pilot. Gene Hackman and Danny Glover star. **AC4, ST55, ST61**

Bataan (1943, B&W, 114m, NR) Classic World War II drama of brave Americans holding out against impossible odds. Robert Taylor, George Murphy, and Thomas Mitchell star. **AC1**

Batman (1966, C, 105m, NR) Adventure starring the Caped Crusader from the comics, spun off from the popular TV series of the mid-1960s. Adam West and Burt Ward repeat their roles as Batman and Robin; comic villains are played by Burgess Meredith, Cesar Romero, and Lee Meriwether. **AC17**

Batman (1989, C, 126m, PG-13) Michael Keaton is the Caped Crusader, Jack Nicolson is the Joker in this extravagantly produced adventure of the comic book hero. With Kim Basinger, Robert Wuhl, Jack Palance, Billy Dee Williams, and Pat Hingle. Eye-popping sets; Tim Burton directed. **AC17, SF14, ST80, ST112, ST159** *Recommended*

*batteries not included (1987, C, 107m, PG) A group of tenants in a New York slum apartment house scheduled for demolition get some unusual help from an army of tiny aliens. Jessica Tandy and Hume Cronyn head the cast of this family fantasy drama. **FA8**

Battle Cry (1955, C, 149m, NR) World War II drama, taking Marine outfit through training and into combat. Based on Leon Uris's novel; directed by Raoul Walsh. Van Heflin, Tab Hunter, and Dorothy Malone star. **AC1**

Battle for the Planet of the Apes (1973, C, 92m, PG)
Fifth and final in the *Apes* series, featuring clips from earlier installments. Roddy McDowall, Paul Williams, and John Huston star. **DT50, FA8, SF8, SF13, SF23**

Battle Force (1978, C, 97m, NR)
Drama traces the lives of two families, one German and the other American, up to World War II. Helmut Berger and Samantha Eggar star, with John Huston, Henry Fonda, and Stacy Keach star. Newsreel footage narrated by Orson Welles. Also known as *The Great Battle.* **AC1, DT50, DT112, ST44**

Battle of Algiers, The (1965, B&W, 123m, NR)
Documentary-style drama of Algerian resistance to French colonialism during the 1950s. Powerful political film directed by Gillo Pontecorvo. **AC6, CU9, FF2** *Essential; Recommended*

Battle of Britain (1969, C, 132m, G)
All-star British cast enlivens this account of aerial combat over British soil during World War II. Michael Caine, Christopher Plummer, Laurence Olivier, Ralph Richardson, Harry Andrews, and Trevor Howard appear, with Rolf Stiefel as Hitler. **AC1, AC11, HF12, ST15, ST116**

Battle of the Bulge, The (1965, C, 141m, NR)
Henry Fonda, Robert Shaw, Robert Ryan, and Dana Andrews star in this account of the 1944 battle for Belgium against desperate German forces. Original running time: 163m. **AC1, ST44**

Battle of the Sexes, The (1960, B&W, 88m, NR)
Peter Sellers plays an auld Scot with murder in his heart in this British comedy. **ST137**

Battleground (1949, B&W, 118m, NR)
World War II drama centering on the Battle of the Bulge, starring Van Johnson, John Hodiak, Ricardo Montalban, and George Murphy. Directed by William Wellman. **AC1**

Battleship Potemkin *see* Potemkin

Bay Boy, The (1984, C, 107m, R)
Coming-of-age drama set in rural Canada during the Depression, starring Kiefer Sutherland, Liv Ullmann, and Peter Donat. **ST154**

Beaches (1988, C, 123m, PG-13)
The lifelong friendship of two women (Bette Midler, Barbara Hershey) is put to the test when one falls fatally ill. An unabashedly sentimental drama. Midler performs several songs. **DR2, DR10, ST105**

Bear, The (1988, C, 90m, PG)
French adventure tale of a bear cub's learning survival skills in the face of hunters and the vagaries of Mother Nature. **AC12, FA5**

Bear Island (1980, C, 118m, PG)
Adaptation of the Alistair MacLean novel about the race for a Nazi submarine loaded with gold, trapped under the Arctic ice. Donald Sutherland, Vanessa Redgrave, and Christopher Lee star. **ST89, ST127**

Beast in the Cellar, The (1970, C, 87m, R)
Two spinster sisters hide their maniacal brother in the basement in this British horror story. Beryl Reid and Flora Robson star. **HO14, HO26**

Beast Must Die, The (1974, C, 93m, PG)
A wealthy man believes one of his friends is a werewolf. He installs surveillance cameras throughout his home, then invites his friends for the weekend. Peter Cushing stars. **HO4, ST27**

Beast Within, The (1982, C, 98m, R)
A woman, raped on her wedding night by a deformed fiend, gives birth to a son who never misbehaves, until his 17th birthday. Ronny Cox, Bibi Besch, and Paul Clemens star. **HO4, HO13**

Beastmaster, The (1982, C, 118m, PG)
Sword and sorcery adventure, featuring a hero who communicates with animals, a lovely slave girl, and an evil priest. Marc Singer, Tanya Roberts, and Rip Torn star. **AC18, ST150**

Beat Street (1984, C, 106m, PG)
Inner city kids put on a show in this breakdancing musical, starring Rae Dawn Chong and Guy Davis. **MU9**

Beat the Devil (1954, B&W, 89m, NR)
Humphrey Bogart and Jennifer Jones head the cast of this unusual spoof of spy

films. Written by Truman Capote and John Huston (who also directed). Gina Lollobrigida, Robert Morley, and Peter Lorre costar. Misunderstood on its initial release, now a cult classic. **CL14, CU5, CU13, DT50, ST8** *Essential*

Beatrice (1988, C, 132m, R)
French drama, set during the Hundred Years War, of a warrior who comes home to bully his son and embark on an incestuous relationship with his daughter. Directed by Bertrand Tavernier. Also known as *The Passion of Beatrice.* **FF1**

Beau Brummel (1924, B&W, 92m, NR)
Silent historical drama of the famed ladies' man who led a life of dissolution after seeing his true love married off to a nobleman he despised. John Barrymore stars, with Mary Astor and Willard Louis. **CL3, CL12**

Beau Geste (1939, B&W, 114m, NR)
Classic Foreign Legion tale of three brothers surviving desert hardships, tribal warfare. Gary Cooper, Ray Milland, Robert Preston, and Brian Donlevy star. **AC13, ST22**

Beau Marriage, Le (1982, C, 97m, R)
From French director Eric Rohmer, a comedy about a determined young woman who decides it's time she got married—even though her intended has no idea of her plans. **DT89**

Beau Pere (1981, C, 120m, NR)
French comedy-drama about a man's relationship with his teenaged stepdaughter blossoming into romance after the death of her mother. Patrick Dewaere and Ariel Besse star. Bertrand Blier directed. **FF1**

Beautiful Blonde From Bashful Bend, The (1949, C, 77m, NR)
Comic western about a woman gunslinger who's mistaken for a proper lady. Betty Grable stars, with Cesar Romero, Rudy Vallee, and Sterling Holloway. Directed by Preston Sturges. **DT103, WE8, WE14**

Beauty and the Beast (1946, B&W, 92m, NR)
From French director Jean Cocteau, the classic fable of an impossible romance. Jean Marais and Josette Day star. **DT19, FF1, SF2** *Essential; Recommended*

Beauty and the Beast (1984, C, 60m, NR)
Love is in the eye of the beholder—as the beauty (Susan Sarandon) brings out the best in the beast (Klaus Kinski) in a romantic fantasy adventure from Faerie Tale Theatre. **FA12, ST83**

Because of the Cats (1973, C, 95m, R)
A gang of wealthy kids fall into a bizarre murder cult. Sylvia Kristel stars. **HO11, HO25**

Becket (1964, C, 148m, NR)
Historical drama of clash between England's King Henry II (Peter O'Toole) and the Archbishop of Canterbury, Thomas à Becket (Richard Burton). **DR5, ST13, ST117**

Bedazzled (1967, C, 107m, NR)
Comedy of nerdy man who makes several deals with the Devil to be near the woman he loves. Dudley Moore and Peter Cook star; Stanley Donen directed. **CO3, CU5, DT30, HO10, ST109** *Recommended*

Bedford Incident, The (1965, B&W, 102m, NR)
An aggressive U.S. naval captain tries to attack a Soviet submarine in international waters. Richard Widmark stars, with Sidney Poitier and Martin Balsam. **ST121**

Bedknobs and Broomsticks (1971, C, 117m, G)
An amateur witch (Angela Lansbury) helps the British win a few World War II battles in this Disney fantasy. **FA1**

Bedlam (1946, B&W, 79m, NR)
Val Lewton produced this horror story about a young lady (Anna Lee) who tries to reform conditions at an insane asylum and finds herself being committed. Boris Karloff stars. **HO27, ST77**

Bedroom Window, The (1987, C, 112m, R)
A wrong-man thriller in the Hitchcock mold. An innocent man (Steve Guttenberg) is accused of murder when he covers for the witness—his lover and his boss' wife. Isabelle Huppert and Elizabeth McGovern costar. **MY7**

Bedtime for Bonzo (1951, B&W, 83m, NR)
Comedy about a professor who takes a chimp into his house as an experiment. Ronald Reagan's name at the top of the

cast has made this a cult comedy. **CO18, CU5**

Bedtime Story (1963, C, 99m, NR)
Comedy of two rival seducers plying their trade on the French Riviera. Marlon Brando and David Niven star. Remade as *Dirty, Rotten Scoundrels*. **CO3, ST10**

Beer (1985, C, 82m, R)
A female ad executive comes up with a tasteless campaign to sell suds—and, of course, it works. Satire starring Sally Kellerman, with Rip Torn, Kenneth Mars, and Dick Shawn. **ST150**

Beetlejuice (1988, C, 92m, PG)
A pair of friendly ghosts can't scare away the obnoxious family that's moved into their house, so they call on a legendary "bio-exorcist" for help. Alec Baldwin, Geena Davis, and Michael Keaton star, with Catherine O'Hara, Winona Ryder, and Jeffrey Jones in this comedy packed with wild special effects. Directed by Tim Burton. **CO11, CO14, ST80** *Recommended*

Before I Hang (1940, B&W, 71m, NR)
A doctor working on a rejuvenation serum becomes a killer when he uses the blood of a murderer. Boris Karloff and Evelyn Keyes star. **ST77**

Before the Revolution (1964, C, 115m, NR)
Director Bernardo Bertolucci's second feature is an intense drama of a youth trying to decide between commitment to political activism and a marriage into a bourgeois family. **DT9**

Beguiled, The (1971, C, 109m, R)
Clint Eastwood plays a wounded Confederate soldier who seeks shelter in a girls' school, with disastrous results. With Geraldine Page and Elizabeth Hartman. Directed by Don Siegel. **DT97, ST39, WE6** *Recommended*

Behave Yourself! (1951, B&W, 81m, NR)
A couple is chased by a criminal gang after witnessing a crime. Farley Granger and Shelley Winters star, with Lon Chaney, Jr. in this thriller played for laughs. **ST17**

Behind Locked Doors *see* Human Gorilla, The

Behold a Pale Horse (1964, B&W, 118m, NR)
Drama of post-Civil War Spain, with exiled guerrilla Gregory Peck deciding to return to his homeland, in the face of certain death at the hands of an old enemy (Anthony Quinn). Fred Zinnemann directed. **DT120, ST119**

Being There (1980, C, 124m, PG)
A reclusive gardener is set loose on the world when his boss dies, and his cryptic remarks are mistaken for profound political observations. Peter Sellers stars in this satire, set in Washington, D.C., adapted from Jerzy Kosinski's novel. With Shirley MacLaine, Oscar winner Melvyn Douglas, Jack Warden, and Richard Dysart. **CO2, CO12, DR21, ST96, ST137, XT4, XT12** *Recommended*

Bela Lugosi Meets a Brooklyn Gorilla (1952, B&W, 74m, NR)
Duke Mitchell and Sammy Petrillo are shipwrecked on an island where a mad doctor (Bela Lugosi) is conducting bizarre experiments. Also known as *The Boys From Brooklyn*. **ST95**

Believers, The (1987, C, 114m, R)
A widowed police psychiatrist discovers his son has been chosen as the next sacrifice to a religious cult operating out of Harlem. Martin Sheen stars, with Helen Shaver, Robert Loggia, and Harley Cross. Directed by John Schlesinger. **DT94, HO11, XT9**

Bell, Book, and Candle (1958, C, 103m, NR)
Kim Novak plays a contemporary witch who casts a love spell on her next-door neighbor (James Stewart) in this comedy. With Jack Lemmon, Elsa Lanchester, Ernie Kovacs, and Hermione Gingold. **ST90, ST143**

Bell Jar, The (1979, C, 107m, R)
Drama set in the early 1950s about a sensitive college student's breakdown, based on the novel by Sylvia Plath. Marilyn Hasset stars, with Julie Harris, Anne Jackson, and Barbara Barrie. **DR10, DR19**

Bellboy, The (1960, B&W, 72m, NR)
Jerry Lewis stars in this series of comic sketches set in a plush Miami Beach hotel. Lewis's character never speaks; this

was his first film as a director. **ST91** *Recommended*

Belle of New York, The (1952, C, 82m, NR)
This musical set in the Gay 90s has Fred Astaire as a society playboy pursuing a missionary, played by Vera-Ellen. **ST2**

Belles of St. Trinians, The (1955, B&W, 90m, NR)
Classic British comedy set in a girls school run by a zany headmistress, whose bookie brother would like to use the students as part of his operation. Alastair Sim stars (in two roles), with Joyce Grenfell, George Cole, and Hermione Baddeley. **CO17, CO18**

Bellisima (1951, B&W, 112m, NR)
An overbearing mother pushes her daughter into a stage career in this Italian drama starring Anna Magnani. Luchino Visconti directed. **DT108**

Bellman and True (1988, C, 112m, R)
Bank robbers enlist the aid of a mildmannered computer expert, threatening his son if he doesn't cooperate. Bernard Hill stars in this British thriller. **MY15, MY18** *Recommended*

Bells, The (1926, B&W, 108m, NR)
Silent drama of an innkeeper who murders a traveler and is tormented by his conscience. Lionel Barrymore stars, with Boris Karloff. **ST77**

Bells Are Ringing (1960, C, 127m, NR)
Musical comedy about an answering service operator and a ladies' man. Judy Holliday (in her last film) stars with Dean Martin. Vincente Minnelli directed. Songs include "Just in Time" and "The Party's Over." **DT71, MU1, ST69, XT22**

Bells of Coronado (1950, B&W, 67m, NR)
Roy Rogers stars in this contemporary western about an insurance agent out to thwart a uranium deal with foreign agents. **ST132**

Bells of Rosarita (1945, B&W, 68m, NR)
Roy Rogers gallops to the rescue of a young girl. **ST132**

Bells of St. Mary's, The (1945, B&W, 126m, NR)
Sequel to *Going My Way*, with Father O'Malley (Bing Crosby) in a new parish with a wise Sister Superior (Ingrid Bergman). **ST7, ST25**

Bells of San Angelo (1947, B&W, 54m, NR)
Roy Rogers takes on evildoers who want to snatch a young girl's ranch. With Dale Evans. **ST132**

Ben (1972, C, 94m, PG)
A sequel to *Willard* has the lead rat, Ben, befriend a sick young boy. Lee Harcourt Montgomery and Joseph Campanella star. Michael Jackson sings the title song. **HO16**

Ben-Hur (1959, C, 217m, G)
Charlton Heston and Stephen Boyd star as former friends, now rivals in a spectacular chariot race. This religious epic won a record 11 Academy Awards; Heston, director William Wyler, and supporting actor Hugh Griffith won Oscars. New edition has chariot race presented in letterboxed format. **CL13, CU19, DT119, HF16, XT1, XT2, XT4, XT6**

Ben-Hur: A Tale of the Christ (1926, B&W/C, 148m, NR)
Silent classic, shot with then-record budget, about rival charioteers in the time of Christ. Ramon Novarro and Francis X. Bushman star. Video version includes original tinted and Technicolor sequences. **CL12, CL13, HF16**

Bend of the River (1952, C, 91m, G)
Wagon train saga set in 1840s Oregon, starring James Stewart, Arthur Kennedy, and Rock Hudson. Directed by Anthony Mann. **DT69, ST73, ST143**

Beneath the Planet of the Apes (1970, C, 95m, PG)
Second *Planet of the Apes* story features the simian heroes battling human mutants who somehow survived the holocaust. James Franciscus, Kim Hunter, and Charlton Heston star. **FA8, SF8, SF13, SF23**

Beneath the 12 Mile Reef (1953, C, 102m, NR)
The scenery's the star in this adventure of a Florida family of sponge divers. Robert Wagner and Terry Moore star. **AC12**

Benji (1980, C, 87m, G)
Benji, the Laurence Olivier of the dog world, stars in his first adventure story. **FA5**

Benji Takes a Dive at Marineland (1984, C, 60m, NR)
America's canine hero takes a tour of Marineland—and comes up swimming in this family adventure. **FA5**

Benji the Hunted (1987, C, 88m, G)
The lovable mutt uses his wits in the wilderness to protect some lion cubs in this adventure from the Disney studios. **FA1, FA5**

Benny Goodman Story, The (1955, C, 116m, G)
Film bio of America's premier jazz clarinetist, with Steve Allen as the King of Swing. Benny's great sidemen, Gene Krupa, Lionel Hampton, and Teddy Wilson, appear as themselves. **MU5**

Berlin Alexanderplatz (1980, C, 931m, NR)
Epic portrait of Berlin during the 1920s from director Rainer Werner Fassbinder, adapted from novel by Alfred Doblin. Originally produced for German TV in 13 episodes. Gunter Lamprecht, Hanna Schygulla, and Barbara Sukowa star. **DT34**

Berlin Express (1948, B&W, 86m, NR)
In Berlin after World War II, several Allied agents attempt to free a German government offical kidnapped by members of the Nazi underground. Merle Oberon, Robert Ryan, and Paul Lukas star. Directed by Jacques Tourneur. **DT105**

Berserk! (1967, C, 96m, NR)
A circus owner (Joan Crawford) becomes frantic when a series of murders occur under her big top. **MY3, ST24**

Best Boy (1979, C, 111m, NR)
Oscar-winning documentary about filmmaker Ira Wohl's retarded cousin, a 52-year-old man named Philly. **CU16**

Best Defense (1984, C, 94m, R)
Comedy about the arms race, featuring two related stories. In one, Dudley Moore bumbles through the development of a super tank, and in the other, Eddie Murphy plays a soldier stationed in the Middle East who has to employ the weapon. **CO13, ST109**

Best Foot Forward (1943, C, 95m, NR)
Big Broadway star decides to pay a visit to a small town in this musical comedy featuring outstanding dance numbers. Lucille Ball stars. **MU3**

Best Friends (1982, C, 108m, PG)
When a screenwriting team changes their status from Living Together to Married, their love life suffers. Burt Reynolds and Goldie Hawn star, with Ron Silver and Richard Libertini. Directed by Norman Jewison. **CO1, DT51, ST63, ST128**

Best Little Whorehouse In Texas, The (1982, C, 114m, R)
The hit Broadway musical about a sheriff (Burt Reynolds) who tries to close down the infamous Chicken Ranch, run by his girlfriend (Dolly Parton). **MU2, MU17, ST128**

Best Man, The (1964, B&W, 102m, NR)
Gore Vidal adapted his own play about dirty and double dealing at a poltical convention. Henry Fonda and Cliff Robertson star, with Edie Adams and Shelley Berman. **DR21, ST44**

Best of Bugs Bunny and Friends, The (1986, C, 53m, NR)
Collection of Warner Bros. classic cartoon stars features *Duck Soup to Nuts, A Feud There Was,* and *Tweetie Pie.* Bugs' costars include Daffy Duck, Tweetie Pie, and Porky Pig. **FA11**

Best of Chevy Chase, The (1987, C, 60m, NR)
Chevy's brief stint on *Saturday Night Live* yields this hour of comedy, featuring his Gerald Ford impression and his "Weekend Update" bits. **CO13**

Best of Comic Relief, The (1986, C, 120m, NR)
Highlights of a benefit show to help homeless people, hosted by Robin Williams, Billy Crystal, and Whoopi Goldberg. Among the comics featured are Jay Leno, Garry Shandling, Howie Mandel, Bobcat Goldthwait, and Jerry Lewis. **CO16, ST91, ST160** *Recommended*

Best of Dan Aykroyd, The (1986, C, 60m, NR)
Classic Aykroyd bits from *Saturday Night Live*, including the Bass-o-matic salesman, Richard Nixon, and the Cone-heads. **CO13**

Best of Eddie Murphy: Saturday Night Live, The (1989, C, 79m, NR)
Eddie's memorable bits from Saturdays gone by, including Mr. Robinson's Neighborhood, Little Richard Simmons, James Brown, Bill Cosby, and Buckwheat. **CO13** *Recommended*

Best of Gilda, The (1989, C, 59m, NR)
Highlights from Gilda Radner's skits on *Saturday Night Live*, featuring Roseanne Roseannadanna, Baba Wawa, Emily Litella, Lisa Loobner, and more. **CO13**

Best of John Belushi, The (1985, C, 60m, NR)
The Killer Bees, Samurai Everything, Joe Cocker—they're all here on this collection of Belushi highlights from *Saturday Night Live*. **CO13**

Best of the Best (1989, C, 95m, PG-13)
Drama set around a martial arts competition in Korea. Eric Roberts stars, with James Earl Jones, Sally Kirkland, and Phillip Rhee. **DR22, ST76**

Best of Times, The (1986, C, 105m, PG-13)
A pair of former high school football teammates get a chance to redeem themselves in a 20-year anniversary rematch of the Big Game they lost. Robin Williams and Kurt Russell star in this comedy, with Pamela Reed and Holly Palance. **CO3, CO19, ST160**

Best of W. C. Fields, The (1930, B&W, 58m, NR)
Three of Fields' early short comedies, produced by Mack Sennett. **ST41**

Best Revenge (1984, C, 92m, NR)
Two Americans in Spain try to pull off a major hashish deal, with the usual double crosses. John Heard and Levon Helm star. **MU12**

Best Seller (1987, C, 110m, R)
A former hit man for a corporation turns to a bestselling novelist (and former cop) to write his life story. James Woods and Brian Dennehy star in this cat-and-mouse thriller. **MY9, ST165**

Best Years of Our Lives, The (1946, B&W, 170m, NR)
Three World War II veterans (Dana Andrews, Oscar winners Fredric March and Harold Russell) adjust to life back home in this stirring drama. Oscar winner for Best Picture and Director (William Wyler). With Myrna Loy, Hoagy Carmichael, Teresa Wright, and Virginia Mayo. **CL8, DR26, DT24, ST94, XT1, XT2, XT4, XT6** *Essential; Recommended*

Bête Humaine, La (1938, B&W, 106m, NR)
French drama of a railway worker's obsession with a married woman, who tries to persuade him to kill her husband. Jean Renoir directed; Jean Gabin, Simone Simon, and the director star. U.S. remake: *Human Desire*. **DT86, FF8**

Betrayal (1983, C, 95m, R)
Harold Pinter's play about a romantic triangle begins at the very end of the affair, flashing back in stages to the beginning. Jeremy Irons, Ben Kingsley and Patricia Hodge star. **DR3, DR20, DR23** *Recommended*

Betrayed (1988, C, 127m, R)
An inexperienced F.B.I. agent (Debra Winger) is assigned to go undercover to investigate a white supremacist group. What she doesn't count on is falling in love with one of the group's leaders (Tom Berenger). With John Heard and John Mahoney; Costa-Gavras directed. **DR3, MY5, ST163**

Betsy, The (1978, C, 125m, R)
Laurence Olivier stars as the head of a family-owned auto manufacturing plant. Trashy drama from Harold Robbins' bestseller. Blockbuster cast includes Robert Duvall, Katharine Ross, Tommy Lee Jones, Jane Alexander, Kathleen Beller, Lesley-Anne Down, and Edward Herrmann. **DR24, ST38, ST116**

Bette Midler's Mondo Beyondo (1988, C, 60m, NR)
Bette stars in this comedy special (made for cable TV) as an Italian sexpot hosting a raunchy cable TV show. **CO16, ST105**

Betty Blue (1986, C, 121m, NR)
Erotic story of a writer's affair with a free-spirited young woman, whose mental instability begins to threaten their lives. Jean-Hughes Anglade and Beatrice Dalle star; Jean-Jacques Beneix directed. **CU6, FF1**

Between Friends (1983, C, 100m, NR)
Elizabeth Taylor and Carol Burnett play middle-aged women who offer each other moral support as they begin a new life in the singles world. Originally made for cable TV. **DR10, ST147**

Between the Lines (1977, C, 101m, R)
An alternative newspaper in Boston is the setting for this charming comedy about a group of idealistic friends. Outstanding cast of young performers: Lindsay Crouse, John Heard, Jeff Goldblum, Jill Eikenberry, Gwenn Welles, Bruno Kirby, and Stephen Collins. Directed by Joan Micklin Silver. **CO2, ST56** *Recommended*

Beverly Hills Cop (1985, C, 105m, R)
Eddie Murphy plays Axel Foley, a Detroit cop who travels to California to investigate the murder of a friend. Action comedy costarring Lisa Eichorn, Judge Reinhold, Ronny Cox, and John Ashton. **CO9, CO13, CO20, XT10**

Beverly Hills Cop II (1987, C, 103m, R)
The further adventures of Axel Foley; this time, he's on the trail of a gang of murderous thieves. Eddie Murphy stars, with Ronny Cox, John Ashton, Judge Reinhold, Brigitte Nielsen, Dean Stockwell, and Jürgen Prochnow. **CO9, CO13, CO20, ST144, XT10**

Beverly Hills Madam (1986, C, 100m, PG-13)
Faye Dunaway plays the title role in this drama of a woman with a very lucrative business. Among her associates: Robin Givens, Donna Dixon, and Melody Anderson. Originally made for TV. **ST37**

Beware, My Lovely (1952, B&W, 77m, NR)
A lonely woman (Ida Lupino) hires a handyman (Robert Ryan), only to discover that he's a psychopath. **MY3**

Beyond a Reasonable Doubt (1956, C, 80m, NR)
Mystery, based on true story, of a usually peaceful New Zealand town that turns violent when an innocent farmer is charged with double murder. Fritz Lang directed. **DT58, MY8**

Beyond Obsession (1984, C, 116m, NR)
Marcello Mastroianni and Tom Berenger star in this thriller, set in Marrakesh, about an Italian ex-diplomat and an American and their mutual interest in the same woman. **ST103**

Beyond the Door (1974, C, 94m, R)
Horror film from Italy about the possession of a young girl, with *Exorcist* overtones. Juliet Mills and Richard Johnson star. **FF2, HO8**

Beyond the Door 2 (1979, C, 92m, R)
A little boy is possessed by the soul of his dead father seeking revenge on his wife. Horror drama from Italy, directed by Mario Bava. **FF2, HO8**

Beyond the Law (1968, C, 91m, NR)
Lee Van Cleef plays an outlaw who decides to go straight when he learns that, as sheriff, he can claim a silver mine. **ST155, WE13**

Beyond the Limit (1983, C, 103m, R)
A British doctor in a South American country gets in over his head when he becomes involved with a diplomat's wife and with revolutionaries. Richard Gere, Michael Caine, and Bob Hoskins star in this adapatation of Graham Greene's *The Honorary Consul*. **ST15, ST52, ST72**

Beyond the Poseidon Adventure (1979, C, 122m, PG)
Sequel to *The Poseidon Adventure* about a race to recover treasure from the capsized ship before it sinks. Michael Caine, Sally Field, Telly Savalas, Slim Pickens, and Shirley Knight star. **AC23, ST15, ST40**

Beyond the Valley of the Dolls (1970, C, 109m, R)
Spoofy "sequel" to famous trash story of three casualties of wicked Hollywood, with all-girl rock band clawing and sleeping their way to the top. Directed by Russ Meyer; written by Roger Ebert. **CU2, CU6**

Beyond Therapy (1987, C, 93m, R)
Comedy of two souls trying for romance but thwarted by their respective therapists. Julie Hagerty and Jeff Goldblum

star, with Glenda Jackson, Tom Conti, and Christopher Guest. Robert Altman directed. **DT2, ST56**

Bible, The (1966, C, 174m, NR)
Religious epic detailing many familiar stories from the first book of Genesis. John Huston directed and stars as Noah; also in the cast: Michael Parks (as Adam), George C. Scott (as Abraham), plus Peter O'Toole, Ava Gardner, and Richard Harris. **CL13, DT50, ST117**

Biches, Les *see* Bad Girls

Bicycle Thief, The (1949, B&W, 90m, NR)
Classic Italian drama of a poor man and his son searching the streets of Rome for their stolen bicycle. Vittorio De Sica directed; winner of a special Oscar. **DT26, XT7** *Essential*

Bidone, Il (1955, B&W, 92m, NR)
Federico Fellini's comedy-drama of three crooks setting up operation in Rome. Broderick Crawford, Giulietta Masina, and Richard Basehart star. Also known as *The Swindle*. **DT35**

Big (1988, C, 102m, PG)
Tom Hanks stars in this comedy of a 12-year-old boy who wakes up one morning in the body of a 30-year-old man. With Elizabeth Perkins, Robert Loggia, and John Heard. **CO4, CO20, ST62** *Recommended*

Big Bad Mama (1974, C, 87m, R)
Depression-era action comedy with a shady lady, her male accomplices, and her two sexy daughters. Angie Dickinson stars, with Tom Skerritt, William Shatner, Susan Sennett, and Robbie Lee. Has a cult following for its numerous sex scenes. **CU6**

Big Blue, The (1988, C, 118m, PG)
Adventure story of a pair of rival French free divers (men who use no equipment in their underwater diving), one of whom falls in love with an American woman. Rosanna Arquette stars, with Jean-Marc Barr and Jean Reno. **AC12**

Big Brawl, The (1980, C, 95m, R)
Martial arts star Jackie Chan is featured in this action drama set in 1930s gangster-era Chicago. Lots of action and not a few laughs. **AC26**

Big Bus, The (1976, C, 88m, PG)
Spoof of disaster movies set on a mammoth bus making an accident-prone cross-country trip. Stockard Channing, Joseph Bologna, John Beck, Lynn Redgrave, and Ned Beatty head the cast. **CO7**

Big Business (1988, C, 97m, PG)
Comedy starring Bette Midler and Lily Tomlin as two sets of twins mismatched at birth. One set grows up to run a New York corporation; the other grows up poor in rural West Virginia. Trouble starts when the country sisters travel to New York and run into you-know-who. **CO3, CO5, ST105, ST149**

Big Chill, The (1983, C, 103m, R)
A group of college friends from the 1960s are reunited when one of their group commits suicide. Slick portrait of a generation, starring William Hurt, Glenn Close, Kevin Kline, JoBeth Williams, Mary Kay Place, Tom Berenger, and Jeff Goldblum, with Meg Tilly. **DR7, ST20, ST46, ST56, ST84**

Big Combo, The (1955, B&W, 89m, NR)
A cop (Cornel Wilde) takes on a mobster with the help of the crook's mistress. With Jean Wallace, Brian Donlevy, Richard Conte, and Lee Van Cleef. **MY1, ST155** *Recommended*

Big Country, The (1958, C, 166m, NR)
From director William Wyler comes an epic tale of the Old West, with a land battle erupting between settlers. Gregory Peck and Charlton Heston head the cast, which also includes Oscar winner Burl Ives, Jean Simmons, Carroll Baker, and Chuck Connors. **DT24, ST119, WE1, XT4**

Big Deal on Madonna Street (1956, B&W, 91m, NR)
Classic Italian comedy about an inept band of crooks and their bungling attempts to pull off a heist. Vittorio Gassman and Marcello Mastroianni star. **FF2, MY18, ST103** *Recommended*

Big Easy, The (1987, C, 101m, R)
A thriller set in New Orleans, with an easy-going police detective (Dennis Quaid) trying to solve a series of drug-related murders and a nosey district attorney (Ellen Barkin) getting in his way. **MY2, MY5, XT14**

Big Fix, The (1978, C, 108m, PG)
Richard Dreyfuss plays Moses Wine, a
hippie turned private eye. He's on the
trail of a fellow former activist. **MY10,
ST36**

Big Heat, The (1953, B&W, 90m, NR)
An ex-cop becomes obsessed with a case
when his wife is killed by a car bomb
meant for him. Glenn Ford, Gloria Grahame, and Lee Marvin star. Directed by
Fritz Lang. **AC22, DT58, MY1, ST100** *Essential; Recommended*

Big Jake (1971, C, 110m, PG)
John Wayne swings into action to save his
grandson's life. Richard Boone, Maureen
O'Hara, and Wayne's real-life son Patrick
costar in this western drama. **ST156, XT8**

Big Mouth, The (1967, C, 107m, NR)
Jerry Lewis comedy about a treasure
hunt and its unscrupulous participants.
ST91

Big Parade, The (1925, B&W, 141m, NR)
Silent classic set in World War I Europe,
starring John Gilbert and Renee Adoree.
Box-office smash was also one of the first
major films to deal with the war. Directed
by King Vidor. **AC2, CL12, DT107** *Essential*

Big Picture, The (1989, C, 99m, PG-13)
Satire of contemporary Hollywood, with
Kevin Bacon as an up-and-coming direc-
tor, Martin Short as an agent. The sup-
porting cast also includes Emily Long-
streth, J.T. Walsh, Jennifer Jason Leigh,
Michael McKean, and, in a cameo, John
Cleese. **CO8, CO14, CO15**

Big Red (1962, C, 89m, NR)
Disney drama of a young boy's adven-
tures with one very special Irish setter.
FA5

Big Red One, The (1980, C, 113m, PG)
World War II drama of tough sergeant
(Lee Marvin) pushing his young recruits
through several European campaigns.
Samuel Fuller directed. **AC1, DT40,
ST100** *Recommended*

Big Shots (1987, C, 91m, PG-13)
A pint-sized version of *The Sting*, with
streetwise Darius McCrary and his new-
found suburban pal Ricky Busker hustling
their way through the streets of Chicago.

With Paul Winfield. **CO4, FA7, ST162,
XT11**

Big Show, The (1936, B&W, 70m, NR)
Gene Autry plays two roles, a conceited
movie cowboy and his look-alike stunt
man, in this musical western. The Sons
of the Pioneers (with Roy Rogers, billed
as Leonard Slye) do some harmonizing.
ST3, ST132

Big Sky, The (1952, B&W, 122m, NR)
Kirk Douglas and a rowdy band of 1830s
furtrappers set out on a back-breaking
expedition up the Missouri River. Howard Hawks directed. **DT43, ST34, WE1**

Big Sleep, The (1946, B&W, 114m, NR)
Private eye Philip Marlowe (Humphrey
Bogart) falls for the lovely sister (Lauren
Bacall) of a girl he's hired to protect in
Raymond Chandler's classic thriller.
Howard Hawks directed. **CL15, DT43,
MY1, ST8, WR2** *Essential; Recom-
mended*

Big Sleep, The (1978, C, 100m, R)
Robert Mitchum plays Philip Marlowe in
an updated version of Raymond Chandler's novel, closer to the actual story
than the Bogart version, although the setting is London. With Sarah Miles, Candy
Clark, Oliver Reed, Richard Boone, and
James Stewart. **ST107, ST143, WR2**

Big Sombrero, The (1949, C, 77m, NR)
Gene Autry comes to the aid of a lovely
señorita whose fiance is in cahoots with a
swindler. **ST3**

Big Store, The (1941, B&W, 80m, NR)
The Marx Bros. go shopping at a department store. Margaret Dumont is not buying any of their nonsense. **ST101**

Big Street, The (1942, B&W, 88m, NR)
A Damon Runyon story about a shy bus-
boy (Henry Fonda) idolizing an embittered former show girl (Lucille Ball) who
is wheelchair-bound. **ST44**

Big Top Pee-wee (1988, C, 86m, PG)
Pee-wee Herman finds a circus in his farm
yard and he decides to join the action,
especially when he catches sight of a
lovely trapeze artist. With Kris Kristofferson and Valeria Golino. **CO11, CO12,
FA6, MU12**

Big Trail, The (1930, B&W, 110m, NR)
Epic western featuring John Wayne in one of his first starring roles, as a giant-sized, tender-hearted cowboy. Filmed in 70mm. **ST156, WE1**

Big Trouble in Little China (1986, C, 99m, PG-13)
A truck driver agrees to help his Chinese-American pal rescue the guy's fiancee from a cult operating beneath the streets of Chinatown. Kurt Russell stars in this action adventure from director John Carpenter. **AC21, AC26, DT17**

Big Wednesday (1978, C, 120m, PG)
Three surfing buddies from the 1960s find that the passing years aren't kind to them. Jan-Michael Vincent, Gary Busey, and William Katt star, with Barbara Hale (Katt's real-life mother). John Milius wrote and directed. **DR22, XT8**

Biggles (1986, C, 100m, PG)
Time travel drama, with British man (Alex Hyde-White) moving between 1986 New York and World War I Europe, where he assists an aviator. With Neil Dickson and Peter Cushing. **SF4, SF19, ST27**

Bill (1981, C, 100m, NR)
True story of a retarded man released to the world after 46 years in a mental hospital. Mickey Rooney won an Emmy for his starring performance. With Dennis Quaid; originally made for TV. **DR6, ST133**

Bill and Ted's Excellent Adventure (1989, C, 90m, PG)
Time-travel comedy featuring a pair of lame-brained high school buddies (Keanu Reeves and Alex Winter) who get a crash course in history, thanks to a hip dude of a wizard (George Carlin). **CO20, SF4**

Bill Cosby: 49 (1987, C, 67m, NR)
The comedian holds forth on his impending middle age, his family, and a host of other topics, all grist for his comic mill. **CO16**

Bill Cosby: Himself (1981, C, 104m, NR)
An extended Cosby concert, filmed in Canada, featuring his observations on fatherhood and other modern dilemmas. **CO16**

Bill of Divorcement, A (1932, B&W, 69m, NR)
Katharine Hepburn's first film, in which she's the daughter of a man (John Barrymore) just released from a mental hospital. **ST66**

Bill: On His Own (1983, C, 100m, NR)
Sequel to *Bill* has Mickey Rooney returning as the mentally retarded man trying to make his way in the world after years of confinement in a mental hospital. With Teresa Wright and Dennis Quaid; originally made for TV. **DR6, ST133**

Billion Dollar Brain (1967, C, 111m, NR)
Michael Caine plays international spy Harry Palmer in this drama of espionage set in Scandinavia. Based on a Len Deighton novel; directed by Ken Russell. **DT92, MY6, ST15**

Billion Dollar Hobo, The (1978, C, 96m, G)
Disney comedy featuring Tim Conway as a man who becomes a bum to gain an inheritance. **FA1**

Billy Budd (1962, B&W, 112m, NR)
Terence Stamp, Robert Ryan, and Peter Ustinov star in this version of Herman Melville's classic novel about a naive sailor's court martial. Directed by Ustinov. **CL1** *Recommended*

Billy Crystal: A Comic's Line (1984, C, 59m, NR)
The *Saturday Night Live* alumnus leaves no comic stone unturned in this concert tape. **CO16**

Billy Crystal: Don't Get Me Started (1986, C, 60m, NR)
Plenty of Billy's best bits, plus a "documentary" on his life and a spoof of a 1950s kiddie TV show. **CO16**

Billy Jack (1971, C, 114m, PG)
Pacifist schoolteacher is harassed by bullies at her school for Indians; karate expert shows up to help her out. Cult movie that preaches non-violence, starring Tom Laughlin and Delores Taylor. **AC26, CU9**

Billy Liar (1963, B&W, 96m, NR)
British comedy-drama about a young man who prefers fantasies of heroic action to his drab everyday life. Tom Courtenay and Julie Christie star. John Schlesinger directed. **CO17, DR23, DT94**

Billy Rose's Jumbo *see* Jumbo

Billy the Kid Returns (1938, B&W, 60m, NR)
Roy Rogers is mistaken for the legendary outlaw. **HF1, ST132**

Biloxi Blues (1988, C, 106m, PG-13)
Neil Simon comedy, a sequel to *Brighton Beach Memoirs*, with Eugene Jerome (Matthew Broderick) now in the U.S. Army. Christopher Walken costars. Mike Nichols directed. **CO6, CO21, DT74, WR23**

Bingo Long Traveling All-Stars & Motor Kings, The (1976, C, 110m, PG)
The comic adventures of a black baseball team barnstorming the countryside in the 1930s. Billy Dee Williams, James Earl Jones, and Richard Pryor star. **CO19, ST76, ST125, ST159**

Birch Interval (1977, C, 104m, PG)
Drama of an 11-year-old girl who is sent to live with relatives in Pennsylvania's Amish community. Eddie Albert, Rip Torn, Ann Wedgeworth, and Susan McClung star. **FA7, ST150**

Bird (1988, C, 161m, R)
The life of pioneering jazz musician Charlie Parker, marked by artistic triumphs and personal setbacks, leading to his death at age 34. Forest Whitaker stars, with Diane Venora as Parker's wife, Chan. Clint Eastwood directed. **DR12, MU5, ST39** *Recommended*

Bird of Paradise (1932, B&W, 80m, NR)
A soldier of fortune falls in love with a native woman. Joel McCrea and Dolores Del Rio star, with Lon Chaney, Jr. Directed by King Vidor. **DT107, ST17**

Bird on a Wire (1990, C, 110m, PG-13)
Action comedy starring Mel Gibson as a man hiding out with the Federal Witness Protection program, Goldie Hawn as his long-ago fiancée who runs into him just as the men he fingered are released from prison. With David Carradine and Bill Duke. **CO9, ST53, ST63, XT18**

Bird with the Crystal Plumage, The (1969, C, 98m, PG)
An American writer in Rome witnesses a Jack the Ripper style murder, tries to help the police, but finds himself involved with the case. Tony Musante and Suzy Kendall star. **FF2, HO9**

Birdman of Alcatraz (1962, B&W, 143m, NR)
True story of Charles Strouse, a convicted murderer confined to the famed maximum security prison and how he became an expert on birds. Burt Lancaster stars, with Karl Malden, Thelma Ritter, Neville Brand, and Edmond O'Brien. **DR4, DR18, ST85** *Recommended*

Birds, The (1963, C, 120m, NR)
Alfred Hitchcock's classic chiller finds a coastal California community terrorized by thousands of birds. Rod Taylor, Tippi Hedren, Jessica Tandy, and Suzanne Pleshette star. Based on a story by Daphne du Maurier. **DT46, HO16, WR5**

Birdy (1984, C, 120m, R)
Two boyhood friends go to Vietnam and come back shattered, one with his face disfigured, the other retreating into his boyhood fantasies of being a bird. Matthew Modine and Nicolas Cage star. Based on William Wharton's novel; Alan Parker directed. **DR7**

Birth of a Nation, The (1915, B&W, 159m, NR)
D.W. Griffith's controversial account of the Civil War and Reconstruction from the South's perspective. Lillian Gish, Henry B. Walthall, Mae Marsh, and Miriam Cooper star, with Joseph Henabery as Abrhaam Lincoln. A landmark in film history. **AC5, CL3, CL12, DT42, HF17, ST54** *Essential; Highly Recommended*

Bishop's Wife, The (1947, B&W, 108m, NR)
David Niven plays a bishop in need who's visited by a charming angel (Cary Grant). Loretta Young costars in this classic fantasy. **SF2, ST57**

Bite the Bullet (1975, C, 131m, PG)
Western drama of an epic horse race, starring Gene Hackman, James Coburn, Ben Johnson, Jan-Michael Vincent, and Candice Bergen. **ST61**

Bitter Harvest (1981, C, 104m, NR)
Ron Howard and Art Carney star in this topical drama about dairy farmers whose herd is dying from chemical poisoning. Originally made for TV. **DT48**

Bitter Sweet (1940, C, 94m, NR)
Nelson Eddy and Jeanette MacDonald teamed up for the sixth time in this musical drama set in turn-of-the-century Vienna, with songs by Noel Coward. **CL15**

Bittersweet Love (1976, C, 92m, PG)
Soap opera story of a young couple about to have their first child, discovering that they are half-brother and sister. Lana Turner stars, with Robert Lansing, Celeste Holm, Robert Alda, Scott Hylands, and Meredith Baxter-Birney. **ST153**

Black and White in Color (1976, C, 90m, NR)
Frenchmen living in Africa at the outbreak of World War I decide to attack a nearby German fort. This droll comedy won an Oscar for Best Foreign Language Film. **FF1, XT7**

Black Arrow, The (1948, B&W, 76m, NR)
Robert Louis Stevenson swashbuckling adventure set in England follows the exploits of a young soldier (Louis Hayward) out to solve his father's murder. George MacReady is the villain, Janet Blair the lady fair. **AC13**

Black Arrow (1984, 93m, C, NR)
Remake of the 1948 film of an exiled archer who returns to England and swears revenge on the villain (Oliver Reed) who drove him from his homeland. Disney swashbuckler made for cable TV. **FA1**

Black Beauty (1946, B&W, 74m, NR)
Mona Freeman stars as the young girl who develops a very special bond with a wild horse. Based on Anna Sewell's famed novel. **FA5**

Black Beauty (1971, C, 105m, G)
This version of Anna Sewell's classic tale takes a dramatic stand for animal rights. Mark Lester and Walter Slezak star. **FA5**

Black Caesar (1973, C, 96m, R)
Fred Williamson stars in this violent gangster melodrama directed by Larry Cohen. With Art Lund, Julius W. Harris, and Gloria Hendry. **AC22, DT20**

Black Cat, The (1934, B&W, 65m, NR)
The bizarre home of an architect who is also a devil worshipper is the setting for this tale about a man who seeks vengeance for the death of his wife. Boris Karloff and Bela Lugosi star in this horror classic that is genuinely scary without resorting to on-screen gore. Not based on Edgar Allan Poe's story; directed by Edgar G. Ulmer. **HO1, ST77, ST95** *Recommended*

Black Christmas (1974, C, 100m, R)
Sorority sisters prepare for their Christmas holiday while a madman stalks them. Margot Kidder, Olivia Hussey, and Keir Dullea star, with Andrea Martin. **CO14, HO12**

Black Dragons (1949, B&W, 62m, NR)
Japanese agents sabotage the American war effort. Bela Lugosi and Clayton Moore star. **ST95**

Black Fury (1935, B&W, 92m, NR)
Paul Muni plays a coal miner who attempts to improve conditions for his fellow laborers in this classic social drama. **CL8**

Black Hand, The (1950, B&W, 93m, NR)
In a rare dramatic role, Gene Kelly plays a young man in turn-of-the-century New York who avenges his father's murder by a secret society. **ST81**

Black Hole, The (1979, C, 97m, PG)
Disney science fiction adventure of distant space travelers encountering title phenomenon. Maximillian Schell and Anthony Perkins star. **FA1, SF3, SF13, SF14**

Black Magic (1944) *see* Meeting at Midnight

Black Marble, The (1980, C, 113m, PG)
Romance blossoms between cops Paula Prentiss and Robert Foxworth when they're assigned to the case of a dognapper. Harry Dean Stanton costars in this adaptation of Joseph Wambaugh's novel. **CO10, ST141**

Black Moon Rising (1985, C, 100m, R)
A high-tech car is the bone of contention between an organized car theft ring and a freelance thief. Tommy Lee Jones, Linda Hamilton, and Robert Vaughn star. **AC10**

Black Narcissus (1946, C, 99m, NR)
Drama set in the Himalayas finds three nuns (Deborah Kerr, Jean Simmons, Flora Robson) faced with overwhelming obstacles when they try to set up a hospital. Breathtaking color photography by

Jack Cardiff; directed by Michael Powell. **CL9, DT81**

Black Orchid, The (1959, B&W, 96m, NR)
A businessman and a widow fall in love, but she must persuade her children that the marriage will make them happy, too. Anthony Quinn and Sophia Loren star. Directed by Martin Ritt. **DT87, ST93**

Black Orpheus (1959, C, 98m, NR)
Oscar-winning drama from Brazil is based on Greek myth, transferred to Rio at Carnival time. Colorful imagery, with memorable music by Luis Bonfa and Antonio Carlos Jobim. **CL9, FF6, XT7** *Recommended*

Black Pirate, The (1926, B&W, 132m, NR)
Douglas Fairbanks' silent swashbuckler classic. Billie Dove and Donald Crisp co-star in this adventure for the entire family. **AC13, FA4**

Black Rain (1989, C, 126m, R)
A pair of American cops (Michael Douglas, Andy Garcia) invade Japan to bring an escaped gangster back to the States. With Ken Takakura, Kate Capshaw, and Yusaku Matsuda. Directed by Ridley Scott. **AC9, AC22, DT96, ST35**

Black Room, The (1935, B&W, 75m, NR)
Boris Karloff plays cursed twins, one of whom is literally a ladykiller. When he's suspected of the murders, he kills the good brother and impersonates him. **HO15, ST77**

Black Sabbath (1964, C, 99m, NR)
A compilation of three horror stories. *The Drop of Water* is about a nurse who steals a ring from a corpse, which comes back to haunt her through her tap. *The Telephone* is about a prostitute who receives mysterious phone calls. *The Wurdalak* features a Russian vampire who infects his whole family. Boris Karloff stars. Directed by Mario Bava. **HO23, ST77**

Black Sleep, The (1956, B&W, 81m, NR)
Standard horror tale of mad doctor and brain transplants, energized by excellent cast: Basil Rathbone, Akim Tamiroff, Lon Chaney, Jr., John Carradine, and Bela Lugosi. **ST17, ST95**

Black Stallion, The (1980, C, 118m, G)
Walter Farley's magical tale of the famed black horse and the boy who loved him.
Mickey Rooney, Kelly Reno, Teri Garr, and Hoyt Axton star. Directed by Carroll Ballard, lovingly photographed by Caleb Deschanel. **FA5, ST133** *Highly Recommended*

Black Stallion Returns, The (1983, C, 103m, PG)
The young hero of *The Black Stallion* is off to Morroco when his best friend is horsenapped. Kelly Reno, Vincent Spano, and Teri Garr star. **FA5**

Black Sunday (1961, B&W, 83m, NR)
Barbara Steele stars in an Italian-made horror opus about an emissary from Satan wreaking havoc on the descendants of her executioners. **HO10**

Black Sunday (1977, C, 143m, R)
Arab terrorists plot to kill the President at the Super Bowl. Bruce Dern stars, with Marthe Keller and Robert Shaw. **MY6**

Black Widow (1986, C, 103m, R)
An offbeat thriller about a woman who's been widowed by wealthy men so many times that she's aroused the suspicions of a government investigator. Theresa Russell and Debra Winger star in this cat-and-mouse thriller. With Sami Frey, Nicol Williamson, and Dennis Hopper. **MY9, ST71, ST163**

Black Windmill, The (1974, C, 106m, PG)
A secret agent (Michael Caine) investigates the kidnapping of his son. Directed by Don Siegel. **DT97, MY6, ST15**

Blackbeard, The Pirate (1952, C, 99m, NR)
Robert Newton plays the infamous buccaneer, the terror of the Seven Seas. With Linda Darnell, William Bendix, and Richard Egan. **AC15**

Blackbeard's Ghost (1980, C, 106m, G)
Dean Jones conjures up the spirit of the famed pirate (Peter Ustinov) to protect his descendants' home from racketeers. Suzanne Pleshette costars in this Disney comedy-adventure. **FA1**

Blackmail (1929, B&W, 85m, NR)
Alfred Hitchcock's first talking picture, about a woman who kills a man in self-defense and then has to prove her innocence when she's trapped between her detective boyfriend and a blackmailer. Originally shot as a silent film. **DT46**

Blacksmith, The/The Balloonatic (1922/ 1923, B&W, 57m, NR)
Two Buster Keaton comedy shorts on one tape. In the first, he's the apprentice to the village smithy. In the second, he's trapped on a runaway hot-air balloon. **DT54** *Recommended*

Blacula (1972, C, 92m, PG)
An African prince is transformed into a vampire, imprisoned in a coffin, then unleashed in modern Los Angeles. William Marshall and Vonetta McGee star. **HF7, HO5**

Blade Master, The (1984, C, 92m, PG)
Adventure saga featuring the title character, who leads the forces of good against the evil ones who would possess the Sword of Knowledge. Miles O'Keefe and Lisa Foster star. **AC18**

Blade Runner (1982, C, 123m, R)
Harrison Ford plays a cop hunting down criminal androids in Los Angeles of the next century. With Rutger Hauer, Sean Young, Joanna Cassidy, and Daryl Hannah. Ridley Scott directed; spectacular sets almost steal the show. Video contains some scenes of violence not shown in theaters. **CU10, DT96, MY2, SF14, SF17, ST46** *Recommended*

Blame It on Rio (1984, C, 90m, R)
Comedy about two married men on holiday in Rio with their daughters and the trouble that develops when one man begins an affair with his pal's daughter. Michael Caine, Joseph Bologna, Demi Moore, and Michelle Johnson star. Directed by Stanley Donen. **DT30, ST15**

Blaze (1989, C, 108m, R)
Raucous portrait of legendary Louisiana politican Earl K. Long and his well-publicized affair with exotic dancer Blaze Starr. Paul Newman stars, with Lolita Davidovich, Jerry Hardin, Gaillard Sartain, and Jeffrey DeMunn. Written and directed by Ron Shelton. **DR4, DR21, ST111** *Recommended*

Blazing Saddles (1974, C, 93m, R)
Mel Brooks takes a satirical look at westerns in this free-for-all, starring Gene Wilder and Cleavon Little, with Harvey Korman, Madeline Kahn, Slim Pickens, and David Huddleston. Brooks also plays two roles. **CO7, DT13, WE14** *Recommended*

Bless the Beasts and Children (1972, C, 109m, PG)
At a summer camp, six city youths plan to save a herd of buffalo from their demise. Directed by Stanley Kramer. **DT55, FA7**

Blind Date (1984, C, 100m, R)
A blind man (Joseph Bottoms), obsessed that a psychopathic killer be brought to justice, implants a sight-giving computer chip in his head. Kirstie Alley costars. **MY11**

Blind Date (1987, C, 95m, PG-13)
A young executive is fixed up with an unpredictable woman for an important business dinner, with wildly comic events leading to apocalyptic wedding scene. Bruce Willis and Kim Basinger star, with John Laroquette and William Daniels. Directed by Blake Edwards. **CO1, DT32, ST161, XT20**

Blind Husbands (1919, B&W, 98m, NR)
Erich von Stroheim stars in and directed this silent drama about a military man who falls for a doctor's wife. **CL12, DT109**

Blind Man's Bluff *see* Cauldron of Blood

Bliss (1985, C, 93m, R)
From Australia, a dark comedy about a successful businessman who suffers a nearly fatal heart attack and recovers with a new perspective on his greedy lifestyle and uncaring family. Barry Otto stars. **CO12, FF5**

Blithe Spirit (1945, C, 96m, NR)
Rex Harrison stars in this comic fantasy about a man haunted by the ghost of his first wife, who tries to ruin his second marriage. Margaret Rutherford costars. David Lean directed. **DT59**

Blob, The (1958, C, 86m, NR)
Jelly-like mass from outer space begins devouring everything—and everyone—in a small town, whose teens rush to the rescue. Classic 1950s science fiction, starring Steve McQueen. **SF1, SF9, ST97**

Block Heads (1938, B&W, 55m, NR)
Laurel and Hardy comedy, with Stanley still thinking World War I is on, Ollie having to bring him out of the trenches. **ST87**

Blockhouse, The (1973, C, 90m, NR)
Drama of men trapped in an underground bunker during the D-Day invasion. Peter Sellers stars, with Per Oscarsson and Charles Aznavour. **ST137**

Blonde Venus (1932, B&W, 97m, NR)
Marlene Dietrich becomes the sole provider when her husband becomes ill; she returns to her career as a nightclub singer until a suave playboy (Cary Grant) makes her an irresistible offer. With Herbert Marshall and Dickie Moore. Directed by Josef von Sternberg. **DT100, ST33, ST57** *Essential; Recommended*

Blood Alley (1955, C, 115m, NR)
Action drama starring John Wayne and Lauren Bacall as a couple fleeing the Chinese Communists for Hong Kong. **ST156**

Blood and Black Lace (1964, C, 90m, NR)
A man becomes a psychopathic killer when he can no longer hide his desire for beautiful women. Cameron Mitchell and Eva Bartok star. Directed by Mario Bava. **HO9**

Blood and Sand (1941, C, 123m, NR)
A bullfighter spurns his faithful love for an attractive temptress. Tyrone Power stars, with Linda Darnell and Rita Hayworth. Oscar-winning color cinematography. **ST64**

Blood Beast Terror (1969, C, 81m, NR)
An entomologist conducts experiments on his own daughter, turning her into a bloodthirsty insect. Peter Cushing stars. **ST27**

Blood Couple (1973, C, 83m, R)
Cult horror film involving a black vampire, African rituals, and a deadly romance. Duane Jones, Marlene Clark, and Bill Gunn star; Gunn directed. Also known as *Ganja and Hess*. **CU4, HO5**

Blood Feast (1963, C, 75m, PG)
An Egyptian preparing to bring a goddess to life needs body parts and organs from various women to complete the ritual. One of the first horror films to use explicit gore; directed by Herschell Gordon Lewis. **HO18**

Blood Feud (1979, C, 112m, NR)
Drama set in Sicily in the 1920s, with widow (Sophia Loren) romanced by two men (Marcello Mastroianni, Giancarlo Gi-

annini). Directed by Lina Wertmüller. **DT114, ST93, ST103**

Blood Link (1986, C, 98m, R)
A doctor begins to have a recurring dream that he is committing a murder. He discovers that he was once a Siamese twin and that his brother is still alive and deranged. Michael Moriarty stars. **HO15**

Blood of a Poet (1930, B&W, 55m, NR)
French director Jean Cocteau's meditation on an artist's inner world is a study in striking imagery, although not for every taste. **DT19, FF1, SF2**

Blood of Fu Manchu, The see Against All Odds (1969)

Blood of Heroes, The (1990, C, 102m, R)
Rutger Hauer stars in this action-adventure tale of a futuristic band of warriors known as "juggers." With Joan Chen. **AC24**

Blood on Satan's Claw (1970, C, 93m, R)
A farmer unearths the corpse of a half man/half beast and evil takes hold of the community, eventually possessing a young girl. Linda Hayden and Patrick Wymark star. **HO10**

Blood on the Moon (1948, B&W, 88m, NR)
Western drama starring Robert Mitchum and Robert Preston as rivals in a land fraud scheme. Robert Wise directed. **DT117, ST107**

Blood on the Sun (1945, B&W, 98m, NR)
James Cagney stars in this drama about an American living in Japan during the 1930s and foreseeing that country's war plans. **ST14**

Blood Red (1988, C, 91m, R)
Western drama, set in Northern California, focuses on immigrant grape growers and their struggle against a tyrannical industrialist. Eric Roberts stars, with Giancarlo Giannini, Dennis Hopper, Burt Young, and Susan Anspach. **ST71**

Blood Simple (1984, C, 97m, R)
A jealous husband hires a seedy private detective to murder his wife and her lover. Contemporary cult thriller, written by Joel and Ethan Coen, directed by Joel. John Getz, Frances MacDormand, M. Emmet Walsh, and Dan Hedaya star. **DR16, MY2**

Bloodbath at the House of Death (1983, C, 92m, NR)
British spoof of horror films, about a group of paranormal researchers setting up shop in a house which has been the scene of many murders. Kenny Everett, Pamela Stephenson, and Vincent Price star. **HO26, ST124**

Bloodbrothers (1978, C, 116m, R)
Young New Yorker is torn between following his father and uncle into construction work and following his own dream of becoming a teacher. Richard Gere stars, with Paul Sorvino and Tony LoBianco. Based on Richard Price's novel. **DR8, ST52**

Bloodfist (1989, C, 85m, R)
Martial arts action featuring Don (The Dragon) Wilson as a man off to Manila to investigate the murder of his brother after a kickboxing match. **AC26**

Bloodhounds of Broadway (1989, C, 101m, PG)
Four Damon Runyon stories set in 1928 New York are the basis for this nostalgic comedy of colorful horse players, showgirls, and mobsters. Among the stars: Julie Hagerty, Randy Quaid, Madonna, Matt Dillon, Jennifer Grey, and Rutger Hauer. **CO6, DR19, MU12**

Bloodline *see* Sidney Sheldon's Bloodline

Bloodsport (1987, C, 92m, R)
Martial arts drama of American who enters the Kumite, a secret fighting contest. Jean Claude Van Damme stars; based on a true story. **AC26**

Bloodsuckers, The (1970, C, 87m, R)
An Oxford don visiting Greece takes up with a mysterious woman who leads him into black magic and vampirism. Patrick Mower stars, with Peter Cushing. **HO5, HO11, ST27**

Bloody Mama (1970, C, 90m, R)
Shelley Winters plays the notorious Ma Barker, the gangster who included her sons in her criminal affairs. Robert DeNiro, Don Stroud, Pat Hingle, and Bruce Dern costar. Directed by Roger Corman. **AC22, DT22, ST30, ST164**

Blow Out (1981, C, 107m, R)
From director Brian DePalma comes a suspense thriller about a sound effects engineer (John Travolta) who becomes involved in a political conspiracy. With Nancy Allen, John Lithgow, and Dennis Franz. **DR13, DT29, MY6, MY11**

Blowing Wild (1953, B&W, 90m, NR)
Barbara Stanwyck romances two men: oil tycoon husband (Anthony Quinn) and a wildcatter (Gary Cooper). **ST22, ST142**

Blowup (1966, C, 100m, NR)
An innocent London photographer takes snapshots of a couple which later, when enlarged, expose what appears to be a murder. Michelangelo Antonioni directed. David Hemmings stars, with Vanessa Redgrave and Sarah Miles. **DT3, MY11, ST127, XT15** *Essential; Recommended*

Blue Angel, The (1930, B&W, 103m, NR)
German classic about an aging professor's pathetic infatuation with a heartless nightclub singer. Marlene Dietrich and Emil Jannings star. Josef von Sternberg directed; his first of seven films with Deitrich. **DT100, FF3, ST33** *Essential; Recommended*

Blue Bird, The (1940, C, 83m, NR)
Classic fantasy about the search for the special bird which will bring happiness. Shirley Temple stars. **SF13, ST148**

Blue Canadian Rockies (1952, B&W, 58m, NR)
Gene Autry's boss sends him to Canada on a personal expedition to discourage his daughter's marriage to a fortune hunter. **ST3, WE10**

Blue City (1986, C, 83m, R)
Thriller of a young man (Judd Nelson) trying to solve the murder of his father in a corrupt small town. With Ally Sheedy and Paul Winfield; based on a Ross MacDonald novel. **DR26, ST162, WR19**

Blue Collar (1978, C, 114m, R)
A trio of auto workers discover their union has been ripping off its workers, and they decide to get even. Hard-bitten drama from director Paul Schrader, starring Richard Pryor, Yaphet Kotto, and Harvey Keitel. **DR7, DR14, ST125** *Recommended*

Blue Fin (1977, C, 93m, NR)
Family adventure of a young boy on a fishing trip; he must take over the boat from his father in a storm. **FA7**

Blue Fire Lady (1983, C, 96m, NR)
Family drama of a girl's love for horses and her training of an obstinate mare, Blue Fire Lady, for racing. Cathryn Harrison stars. **FA5**

Blue Hawaii (1961, C, 101m, NR)
Elvis Presley musical has The King as a cashiered soldier working in a tourist agency in Honolulu. Angela Lansbury co-stars. **ST123**

Blue Knight, The (1973, C, 103m, NR)
Veteran cop, about to retire, wants to bring in one more criminal. William Holden stars in this adaptation of the Joseph Wambaugh novel. Originally made for TV. **AC9, ST68**

Blue Max, The (1966, C, 156m, NR)
Drama of aerial combat during World War I, starring George Peppard, James Mason, and Ursula Andress. **AC2, AC11, ST102**

Blue Steel (1990, C, 102m, R)
A female cop is stalked by a psycho in this urban thriller starring Jamie Lee Curtis and Ron Silver. **MY3, MY13**

Blue Thunder (1983, C, 110m, R)
Los Angeles police develop super-helicopter for crowd control, but political conspiracy has other ideas. Roy Scheider stars, with Daniel Stern, Malcolm McDowell, Warren Oates, and Candy Clark. **AC11, ST115, XT10**

Blue Velvet (1986, C, 120m, R)
Nightmarish, disturbing story from director David Lynch about a naive young man's discovery of the dark side of a small American town. Kyle MacLachlan, Dennis Hopper, and Isabella Rossellini star, with Laura Dern, Dean Stockwell, and Brad Dourif. **CU1, CU12, DR26, DT66, MY2, MY11, ST71, ST144** *Recommended*

Blue Yonder, The (1985, C, 89m, NR)
Disney drama of a young boy (Huckleberry Fox) who travels back in time to share flying adventures with his grandfather (Peter Coyote), an ace aviator. Originally made for cable TV. **FA1**

Bluebeard (1972, C, 125m, R)
Richard Burton plays the legendary ladykiller whose victims include Raquel Welch, Virna Lisi, and Joey Heatherton. **ST13**

Blues Brothers, The (1980, C, 113m, R)
John Belushi and Dan Aykroyd extend their *Saturday Night Live* routine into a gargantuan musical comedy, featuring a great array of black performers, including Aretha Franklin, James Brown, Ray Charles, Cab Calloway, and many more. The streets of Chicago take a pounding in this grand finale car chase. **CO3, CO13, MU9, XT11**

Blume in Love (1973, C, 117m, R)
A lawyer's brief indiscretion has his wife packing her bags and has him pleading to get her back. Sharp romantic comedy-drama from director Paul Mazursky, starring George Segal and Susan Anspach, with Kris Kristofferson, Marsha Mason, and Shelley Winters. **CO1, MU12, ST164** *Recommended*

Boat, The (1981, C, 145m, R)
Stunning World War II drama set aboard a German submarine, starring Jürgen Prochnow, directed by Wolfgang Petersen. This is the dubbed version of the original German-language film, *Das Boot*. **AC1, FF3** *Recommended*

Boat Is Full, The (1983, C, 104m, NR)
German refugees fleeing the Nazis are turned away by neutral Swiss officials in this drama produced in Switzerland. **FF7**

Boatniks, The (1970, C, 99m, G)
Disney comedy has an accident-prone Coast Guard ensign (Robert Morse) tangling with a band of jewel thieves. With Phil Silvers, Stephanie Powers, Norman Fell, Wally Cox, and Don Ameche. **FA1**

Bob & Carol & Ted & Alice (1969, C, 104m, R)
A California couple are happily married until they meet a "modern" husband and wife, who believe in getting in touch with one's real inner feelings. Hilarious satire directed by Paul Mazursky, starring Robert Culp & Natalie Wood & Elliott Gould & Dyan Cannon. **CO2** *Recommended*

Bob le Flambeur (1955, B&W, 102m, PG)
A middle-aged Parisian gambler decides to pull off a casino heist in this first-rate

crime story directed by Jean-Pierre Melville. Roger Duchesne and Isabel Corey star. **FF1, MY18, XT16** *Recommended*

Bobby Deerfield (1977, C, 124m, PG)
Drama of a race car driver and his love for a German woman who is afflicted with a terminal disease. Al Pacino and Marthe Keller star. Sydney Pollack directed. **DR22, DT80, ST118**

Bobo, The (1967, C, 105m, NR)
Peter Sellers plays an aspiring singing matador who tries to seduce a lovely but remote senorita (Britt Ekland). **ST137**

Bocaccio '70 (1962, C, 165m, NR)
Three-part Italian sex comedy: a timid man wins a night with a lovely woman in a raffle, the bored wife of a businessman takes a job as his mistress, and a voluptuous poster girl comes to life. Directed by Federico Fellini, Vittorio De Sica, and Luchino Visconti, featuring Anita Ekberg, Sophia Loren, and Romy Schneider. **DT26, DT35, DT108, ST93**

Body and Soul (1947, B&W, 104m, NR)
John Garfield stars in the classic boxing drama of man who cuts every corner on his way to the championship. Written and directed by Robert Rossen. **DR22**

Body and Soul (1981, C, 100m, R)
Remake of the John Garfield classic, with Leon Isaac Kennedy as the hard-driving fighter. **CU18, DR22**

Body Double (1984, C, 109m, R)
From director Brian DePalma comes the story of an unemployed actor whose spying on a voluptuous neighbor involves him in a twisted plot. Craig Wasson and Melanie Griffith star. **DT29, MY5, ST58**

Body Heat (1981, C, 113m, R)
A lawyer and a married woman plot to murder her wealthy husband. Steamy thriller stars William Hurt and Kathleen Turner (her film debut), with Richard Crenna, Ted Danson, and Mickey Rourke. Written and directed by Lawrence Kasdan. **CU6, DR3, MY2, MY4, MY5, ST75, ST134, ST152, XT21** *Recommended*

Body in the Library, The (1984, C, 153m, NR)
Miss Marple, Agatha Christie's elderly sleuth, investigates the murder of a young woman whose corpse is found in a stately mansion. Joan Hickson stars. Originally made for British TV. **MY12, WR3**

Body Rock (1984, C, 93m, PG-13)
Breakdancing musical about a group of "downtown" kids showing the folks at an "uptown" club what good music and dancing is all about. Lorenzo Lamas stars. **MU9**

Body Snatcher, The (1945, B&W, 77m, NR)
Val Lewton production about the macabre relationship between a doctor and the grave robber who steals bodies for the doctor's experiments. Boris Karloff stars, with Bela Lugosi. Directed by Robert Wise. **DT117, HO1, HO19, ST77, ST95**

Bohemian Girl, The (1936, B&W, 70m, NR)
Laurel and Hardy adopt an abandoned girl who turns out to be the heir to a throne. **ST87**

Bombardier (1943, B&W, 99m, NR)
Randolph Scott plays a fighter cadet being trained for battle during air raids over World War II Japan. **AC1, ST136**

Bon Voyage! (1962, C, 130m, NR)
Disney comedy of a family touring Europe, starring Fred MacMurray, Jane Wyman, Michael Callan, and Deborah Walley. **FA1**

Bon Voyage, Charlie Brown (1980, C, 76m, G)
The *Peanuts* comic strip gang go overseas as exchange students in this feature-length animated film. **FA10**

Bonjour Tristesse (1958, C/B&W, 94m, NR)
Drama of relationship between a young woman (Jean Seberg) and her unattached father (David Niven), who's romancing an old friend (Deborah Kerr). Set in Paris and the South of France; based on Francoise Sagan's bestseller. Directed by Otto Preminger. **DR8, DT82**

Bonnie and Clyde (1967, C, 111m, NR)
Brilliant, controversial portrait of Depression-era outlaws who became folk heroes. Warren Beatty and Faye Dunaway star, with Gene Hackman, Oscar winner Estelle Parsons, Michael J. Pollard, and Gene Wilder. Written by Robert Benton

and David Newman; directed by Arthur Penn. **DR5, DR16, DT78, ST5, ST37, ST61, XT5, XT18** *Essential; Highly Recommended*

Bonnie Scotland (1935, B&W, 80m, NR)
Laurel and Hardy are a pair of Scots assigned to a military outpost in the desert. **ST87**

Boogeyman, The (1980, C, 86m, R)
A boy kills his mother's lover but is witnessed by his sister. Years later the girl returns to the scene of the crime to confront her fears. **HO8**

Boom Town (1940, B&W, 116m, NR)
Oil drilling saga stars Clark Gable and Spencer Tracy as rival wildcatters, Claudette Colbert and Hedy Lamarr as their women. **ST49, ST151**

Boost, The (1989, C, 95m, R)
A young couple find that sudden success in business has exacted a heavy price—they've become cocaine addicts. James Woods and Sean Young star. **DR7, ST165**

Boot, Das, *see* Boat, The

Boots and Saddles (1937, B&W, 59m, NR)
A young Englishman becomes a real western rancher after Gene Autry shows him the ropes. **ST3**

Border, The (1982, C, 107m, R)
Jack Nicholson plays a Tex-Mex border cop who begins taking bribes to let illegals in and becomes involved with a desperate Mexican woman and her child. With Valerie Perrine, Warren Oates, and Harvey Keitel. Music by Ry Cooder. **DR7, ST112, ST115**

Borderline (1980, C, 105m, PG)
Charles Bronson is a Border Patrol officer tracking a dangerous killer. With Bruno Kirby, Bert Remsen, and Kenneth McMillan. **ST12**

Born Free (1966, C, 96m, NR)
Drama based on the true story of Joy Adamson, the wife of a British game warden living in Kenya who raised a lioness as a pet in the wilds of Africa. **FA5**

Born in East L.A. (1987, C, 84m, R)
Cheech Marin stars in a comedy about a legal resident of Los Angeles who's rounded up with a group of illegals and deported to Mexico. With Paul Rodriguez, Daniel Stern, and Jan-Michael Vincent. **ST18**

Born on the Fourth of July (1989, C, 144m, R)
The true story of Ron Kovic, decorated and crippled Vietnam veteran who became an antiwar activist. Tom Cruise stars, with Raymond J. Barry, Caroline Kawa, Kyra Sedgwick, Willem Dafoe, and Tom Berenger. Kovic and Oscar-winning director Oliver Stone adapted Kovic's memoir. **AC4, DR4, DR7, DR8, DT102, ST26, XT6**

Born To Dance (1936, B&W, 105m, NR)
MGM musical featuring Eleanor Powell and James Stewart dancing and singing to a Cole Porter score that includes "I've Got You Under My Skin." **MU1, ST143**

Born To Kill (1947, B&W, 92m, NR)
Classic film noir about a man who marries a woman for her money, but is really attracted to her divorced sister. Lawrence Tierney, Claire Trevor, Walter Slezak, and Audrey Long star. Directed by Robert Wise. **DT117, MY1**

Born To Kill (1974) *see* Cockfighter

Born To Rock *see* That Was Rock

Born To Win *see* Addict

Born Yesterday (1950, B&W, 103m, NR)
Garson Kanin's Broadway comedy about a wisecracking girl (Oscar winner Judy Holliday) in need of some polish. Her sugar daddy (Broderick Crawford) hires a tutor (William Holden) to smooth over her rough edges. George Cukor directed. Some scenes shot on location in Washington, D.C. **CL10, DT24, ST68, ST69, XT3, XT12** *Essential; Recommended*

Boston Strangler, The (1968, C, 120m, NR)
Intense, gripping drama based on the exploits of the crazed killer who terrorized Boston for over a year. Henry Fonda and Tony Curtis star, with George Kennedy. **MY8, MY13, ST44**

Bostonians, The (1984, C, 120m, NR)
In 19th-century New England, feminists have a new young spokeswoman. She's also the center of a tug-of-war between a Southern reporter and one of her col-

leagues in the movement. Vanessa Redgrave, Christopher Reeve, and Madeleine Potter star in this version of Henry James's novel. **DR19, ST127, WR11**

Boudu Saved From Drowning (1932, B&W, 87m, NR)
French comedy from director Jean Renoir about a tramp rescued by a book dealer and the havoc he wreaks on the man's household. Michel Simon stars. American remake: *Down and Out in Beverly Hills*. **DT86, FF8**

Boum, La (1981, C, 100m, PG)
A teenaged girl tries to stay out of the way of her quarreling parents in this comedy-drama from France. Claude Brasseur, Brigitte Fossey, and Sophie Marceau star. **FF1**

Bound for Glory (1976, C, 147m, PG)
Superb portrait of folk music composer and singer Woody Guthrie, concentrating on his life during the Great Depression. David Carradine stars and sings Guthrie's music; Ronny Cox, Melinda Dillon, and Randy Quaid costar. Directed by Hal Ashby; photographed by Haskell Wexler. **DR4, MU5** *Recommended*

Bounty, The (1984, C, 130m, PG)
Latest version of the *Mutiny on the Bounty* story, with Mel Gibson as Fletcher Christian and Anthony Hopkins as Captain Bligh. Laurence Olivier has a small role. **AC12, AC16, ST53, ST116**

Bounty Hunter, The (1989, C, 91m, R)
Robert Ginty stars as a one-man wrecking crew out to avenge a buddy's death. **AC19, AC25**

Bourgeois Gentilhomme, Le (1958, C, 97m, NR)
Performance of Moliere's classic stage comedy about a social climber, featuring Jean Meyer, Louis Seigner, Jacques Charon, and other members of the Comedie-Francaise. **FF1**

Bowery at Midnight (1942, B&W, 63m, NR)
A killer is stalking the inhabitants of the Bowery. Bela Lugosi stars. **ST95**

Boxcar Bertha (1972, C, 97m, R)
Trashy tale of Depression-era train robbers, starring David Carradine and Barbara Hershey, directed by Martin Scor-

sese. Produced by Roger Corman. John Carradine has a small role. **CU14, DT95, XT8**

Boy and His Dog, A (1975, C, 87m, R)
A post-nuclear wasteland is the setting for this cult science fiction tale of a young hustler and his "dog" robot. Don Johnson and Jason Robards, Jr. star. **CU4, SF12, SF22, ST129**

Boy, Did I Get a Wrong Number! (1966, C, 99m, NR)
Bob Hope comedy, costarring Phyllis Diller and Elke Sommer, with Ol' Ski Nose a fast-talking real estate man helping to conceal a fugitive movie star. **ST70**

Boy Friend, The (1971, C, 135m, G)
Lavish spoof of old-fashioned Hollywood musicals, starring Twiggy, with Christopher Gable (who choreographed), Moyra Fraser, and Tommy Tune. Directed by Ken Russell. **DT92, MU3, MU4**

Boy in Blue, The (1986, C, 98m, R)
True story of 19th-century rowing champion Ned Hanlon, starring Nicolas Cage, with Christopher Plummer and David Naughton. **DR22**

Boy Named Charlie Brown, A (1969, C, 85m, G)
Movie debut of the "Peanuts" gang, with Charlie Brown going for the grand prize in a national spelling bee. **FA10**

Boy Who Could Fly, The (1986, C, 108m, PG)
Story of a 14-year-old boy whose fantasy is to soar away from his unhappy home life. Jay Underwood, Lucy Deakins, and Bonnie Bedelia star. **DR9, FA7**

Boy Who Left Home to Find Out About the Shivers, The (1981, C, 60m, NR)
Brothers Grimm tale about a boy (Peter MacNichol) who's fearless until he's put to a test against the Evil Sorcerer. Christopher Lee and Dana Hill costar in this Faerie Tale Theatre production. **FA12, ST89**

Boy With Green Hair, The (1948, C, 82m, NR)
Dean Stockwell stars in this social parable about a war orphan who's an outcast because of his unusually colored locks. With Pat O'Brien, Robert Ryan, and Bar-

bara Hale. Directed by Joseph Losey. **CL8, ST144**

Boyfriends and Girlfriends (1988, C, 102m, PG)
The concluding chapter in French director Eric Rohmer's six-film "Comedies and Proverbs" series. It's about a quartet of young people in the throes of romantic angst in a Paris suburb. **DT89**

Boys From Brazil, The (1978, C, 123m, R)
Bizarre tale of an army of Hitler-cloned youth intended for use in a neo-Nazi takeover. Gregory Peck is the villain; Laurence Olivier costars as a Nazi hunter. With James Mason. **MY6, ST102, ST116, ST119**

Boys From Brooklyn see Bela Lugosi Meets a Brooklyn Gorilla

Boys in Company C, The (1977, C, 127m, R)
Tough Army sergeant trains young recruits for Vietnam combat. Stan Shaw, Andrew Stevens, and Craig Wasson star. **AC4**

Boys in the Band, The (1970, C, 119m, R)
Mart Crowley's play about a group of homosexual friends at a birthday party, starring Kenneth Nelson, Peter White, Leonard Frey, Cliff Gorman, and Laurence Luckinbill. **DR3, DR20**

Boys Next Door, The (1985, C, 90m, R)
Disturbing drama of two seemingly normal teenagers who go on a crime spree on the eve of their graduation. Charlie Sheen and Maxwell Caulfield star. Penelope Spheeris directed. **DR9**

Boys Town (1938, B&W, 96m, NR)
Oscar winner Spencer Tracy is kindly Father Flanagan and Mickey Rooney is Whitey, the kid he reforms, in this stirring drama of the real-life priest and his orphanage. **ST133, ST151, XT2**

Braddock: Missing in Action 3 (1988, C, 103m, R)
Chuck Norris returns once again to Vietnam as former POW Colonel Braddock, this time to rescue his long-lost Vietnamese wife and their son. **AC4, ST114**

Brain Damage (1988, C, 94m, R)
From Frank Henenlotter, the director of *Basket Case*, a horror story of a teenager

plagued by a monstrous parasite which acts like a narcotic. **HO12**

Brain From Planet Arous, The (1958, B&W, 70m, NR)
Title creature inhabits scientist John Agar's head, while the brain of a cop occupies Agar's dog in this low-budget science fiction drama. **SF1, SF9**

Brain That Wouldn't Die, The (1963, B&W, 81m, NR)
A doctor keeps alive the head of his decapitated fiancee while he searches for a body. **HO20**

Brainstorm (1983, C, 106m, PG)
Research scientists discover a telepathic device; the military can't wait to use it for a weapon. Christopher Walken, Louise Fletcher, Cliff Robertson, and Natalie Wood (in her last film) star. **SF5**

Brannigan (1975, C, 111m, PG)
A tough Chicago detective (John Wayne) is off to London to bring home a fugitive. Richard Attenborough costars. **ST156, XT15**

Brasher Doubloon, The (1947, B&W, 72m, NR)
Raymond Chandler's detective mystery stars George Montgomery as Philip Marlowe, who's after some rare coins linked to a series of murders. **WR2**

Brass Target (1978, C, 111m, PG)
World War II drama that imagines General Patton was murdered to cover up a gold theft by his men. John Cassavetes, Sophia Loren, and George Kennedy star. **ST93**

Brazil (1985, C, 131m, R)
Futuristic tale of a bureaucrat mistakenly targeted as a terrorist, brilliantly directed by Terry Gilliam. Jonathan Pryce stars, with Robert DeNiro, Kim Greist, Bob Hoskins, and Michael Palin. Eye-filling sets, special effects. **CU4, CO15, SF11, SF14, ST30, ST72** *Highly Recommended*

Break of Hearts (1935, B&W, 78m, NR)
Katharine Hepburn plays a young composer married to a famous conductor (Charles Boyer) in this drama. **ST66**

Breaker! Breaker! (1977, C, 86m, PG)
Trucker uses his CB to rescue son from a crooked judge. Chuck Norris stars. **ST114**

Breaker Morant (1979, C, 107m, PG)
Edward Woodward stars in this Australian drama set during the Boer War, about the court-martial of several soldiers on questionable charges. Directed by Bruce Beresford. **FF5**

Breakfast at Tiffany's (1961, C, 115m, NR)
Audrey Hepburn is Holly Golightly, a non-working girl living off a series of wealthy men in New York. With George Peppard, Patricia Neal, Buddy Ebsen, Mickey Rooney, and Martin Balsam. Based on Truman Capote's story; directed by Blake Edwards. **DR1, DR15, DT32, ST65, XT9** *Recommended*

Breakfast Club, The (1985, C, 92m, R)
Five high school students, confined to the school for a Saturday detention, become fast friends, despite their outward differences. Emilio Estevez, Molly Ringwald, Ally Sheedy, Anthony Michael Hall, and Judd Nelson star; written and directed by John Hughes. **DR9, DR25, DT49**

Breakheart Pass (1976, C, 95m, PG)
Western drama about secret agent (Charles Bronson) on the trail of gunrunners. Action takes place mostly on a train; good supporting cast includes Ben Johnson, Richard Crenna, Charles Durning, Ed Lauter, Archie Moore, and Jill Ireland. **ST12, XT19**

Breakin' (1984, C, 90m, PG)
A waitress hopes to crash the show business world as a break dancer. Lucinda Dickey stars in this musical drama. **MU9**

Breakin' 2: Electric Boogaloo (1984, C, 94m, PG)
Lucinda Dickey and her break dancing partners are back for more musical numbers in this sequel to *Breakin'*. **MU9**

Breaking Away (1979, C, 100m, PG)
A Midwestern teenager trains for a major bike race in this warm comedy-drama starring Dennis Christopher, Dennis Quaid, and Paul Dooley. Written by Steve Tesich. **CO4, DR22, DR26** *Recommended*

Breaking Glass (1980, C, 104m, PG)
British musical drama of a singer (Hazel O'Connor) determined to make it with her own style of punkish music. Phil Daniels, Jon Finch, and Jonathan Pryce co-

star in this look behind the scenes of the music business. **MU4, MU9**

Breaking In (1989, C, 91m, R)
Wry comedy-drama from director Bill Forsyth, starring Burt Reynolds as an aging burglar who takes on a young apprentice (Casey Siemaszko). Written by John Sayles. **CO10, DT38, DT93, ST128** *Recommended*

Breakout (1975, C, 96m, PG)
True-life action drama of an American held in Mexican prison and a helicopter pilot's attempts to spring him. Charles Bronson, Robert Duvall, Randy Quaid, and John Huston star. **DT50, ST12, ST38**

Breakthrough (1978, C, 115m, PG)
Sequel to World War II drama *Cross of Iron*, starring Richard Burton, Robert Mitchum, Rod Steiger, and Curt Jurgens. **AC1, ST13, ST107**

Breath of Scandal, A (1960, C, 98m, NR)
Costume drama starring Sophia Loren as a princess wooed by an American (John Gavin). Maurice Chevalier and Angela Lansbury costar. **ST93**

Breathless (1959, B&W, 89m, NR)
A petty thief and an American girl find romance and death on the streets of Paris. Director Jean-Luc Godard's highly influential feature debut. Jean-Paul Belmondo and Jean Seberg star. U.S. remake released in 1983. **DT41, FF8, ST6, XT16** *Essential; Recommended*

Breathless (1983, C, 100m, R)
American remake of the French classic; this time the drifter is an American who's enthralled with rock music and comic books and his lover is a French exchange student. Richard Gere and Valerie Kaprisky star. **DR1, FF8, ST52**

Breed Apart, A (1984, C, 95m, R)
Adventure drama of a couple living in the mountains of North Carolina, protecting a rare species of bird. Enter a mysterious stranger, with orders to capture the bird. Kathleen Turner, Rutger Hauer, and Powers Boothe star. **AC12, ST152**

Brewster McCloud (1970, C, 101m, R)
Offbeat comedy about a young man who believes he's a bird and tries to fly in the Houston Astrodome. Packed with absurd bits and throwaway gags, this comedy has

a cult following. Directed by Robert Altman. Bud Cort stars, with Sally Kellerman, Michael Murphy, Shelley Duvall, Stacy Keach, and Margaret Hamilton. **CO12, CU5, DT2** *Recommended*

Brewster's Millions (1985, C, 97m, PG)
Frequently filmed comic story about a man who must spend $30 million in 30 days in order to inherit $300 million (the amounts in this version have been adjusted for inflation). Richard Pryor and John Candy star. Walter Hill directed. **CO3, CO14, DT45, ST125**

Brian's Song (1970, C, 73m, NR)
Tearjerker about the friendship between Chicago Bears running back Gayle Sayers (Billy Dee Williams) and his terminally ill teammmate, Brian Piccolo (James Caan). Originally made for TV. **DR2, DR22, ST159**

Bride, The (1985, C, 113m, PG-13)
Remake of *The Bride of Frankenstein,* starring Sting as the mad doctor and Jennifer Beals as his creation. **CU18, HF10, HO20, MU12**

Bride Is Much Too Beautiful, The (1958, B&W, 90m, NR)
Brigitte Bardot plays a simple farm girl whose life is turned upside-down when she's recruited to become a fashion model. Louis Jourdan costars. **ST4**

Bride of Frankenstein, The (1935, B&W, 75m, NR)
Masterful follow-up to the first great Frankenstein film, with Boris Karloff "wed" to Elsa Lanchester. Colin Clive and Ernest Thesiger play the matchmakers. James Whale directed. **CU4, DT115, HF10, HO1, HO20, ST77** *Essential; Highly Recommended*

Bride of the Gorilla (1951, B&W, 76m, NR)
Camp classic about a newlywed who discovers that her husband is regularly transformed into a hairy beast. Raymond Burr, Barbara Payton, and Lon Chaney, Jr. star. **CU2, ST17**

Bride of the Monster (1955, B&W, 69m, NR)
Inept horror film from the king of inept movies, Ed Wood, Jr. Bela Lugosi stars as a mad scientist; Tor Johnson is his

immense assistant Lobo. Must be seen to be believed. **DT118, ST95**

Bride Walks Out, The (1936, B&W, 81m, NR)
Romantic comedy starring Barbara Stanwyck and Gene Raymond as a young couple trying to make ends meet. **ST142**

Bridge on the River Kwai, The (1957, C, 161m, NR)
British prisoners of war are forced to construct a bridge vital to the Japanese; meanwhile, commandos are sent to destroy it. Winner of seven Oscars, including Best Picture, Director (David Lean), and Actor (Alec Guinness). William Holden, Sessue Hayakawa, and Jack Hawkins costar. **AC7, DT59, ST60, ST68, XT1, XT2, XT6** *Essential; Highly Recommended*

Bridge to Nowhere (1986, C, 82m, NR)
Five city kids head into trouble on a hike in the country when they trespass on a madman's property. **AC24**

Bridge Too Far, A (1977, C, 175m, PG)
World War II epic about ill-fated Allied attempt to surround German forces in Holland. Among the many stars: Dirk Bogarde, James Caan, Michael Caine, Sean Connery, Edward Fox, Gene Hackman, Laurence Olivier, Robert Redford, and Liv Ullmann. Richard Attenborough directed; Joseph E. Levine produced. **AC1, ST15, ST21, ST61, ST108, ST116, ST154**

Bridges at Toko-Ri, The (1954, C, 103m, NR)
Korean war drama focusing on fighter pilot and his qualms about the U.S. involvement. William Holden, Grace Kelly, Fredric March, and Mickey Rooney star. **AC2, AC11, ST68, ST82, ST133**

Brief Encounter (1945, B&W, 85m, NR)
Classic romance finds Celia Johnson and Trevor Howard in World War II England as ordinary, middle-aged people who have a bittersweet affair. Directed by David Lean. **CL4, DT59** *Essential; Recommended*

Brief Encounter (1974, C, 103m, NR)
Richard Burton and Sophia Loren star in this made-for-TV remake of the classic romance. **ST13, ST93**

Brigadoon (1954, C, 108m, NR)
Lerner and Loewe Broadway hit, with
Gene Kelly and Van Johnson as two
Americans discovering a magical Scottish
village. Directed by Vincente Minnelli.
DT71, MU1, MU2, MU8, ST81

Bright Eyes (1934, B&W, 90m, NR)
Shirley Temple sings "On the Good Ship
Lollipop" in this sentimental story of a
custody battle. With Shirley's fellow
child star Jane Withers. **ST148**

Bright Lights, Big City (1988, C, 110m, R)
Portrait of young New Yorker coming
apart at the seams, as his partying and
drug habit take their toll on his marriage
and job at a prestigious magazine. Michael J. Fox stars, with Kiefer Sutherland, Phoebe Cates, Tracy Pollan, and
Jason Robards. Based on Jay Mc-
Inerney's novel. **DR15, DR19, ST129,
XT9**

Brighton Beach Memoirs (1986, C, 110m,
PG-13)
Nostalgic comedy about growing up in
Brooklyn in the 1940s, adapted by Neil
Simon from his Broadway hit. Jonathan
Silverman, Bob Dishy, Blythe Danner,
and Judith Ivey star. **CO5, CO6, WR23**

Brighty of the Grand Canyon (1967, C,
89m, NR)
The adventures of a lovable pack mule,
set in the splendor of northern Arizona,
starring Joseph Cotten and Dick Foran.
FA4, FA5

Brimstone and Treacle (1982, C, 85m, R)
Bizarre tale of strange young man who
moves in uninvited with a couple; their
teenaged daughter is in a coma from an
auto accident. Sting stars, with Denholm
Elliot, Joan Plowright, and Suzanna Hamilton. **DR23, MU12**

Bring Me the Head of Alfredo Garcia
(1974, C, 112m, R)
Director Sam Peckinpah's story of honor
and revenge, with Warren Oates as a
lowly piano player who tangles with a
greedy Mexican. With Isela Vega, Gig
Young, Robert Webber, Kris Kristofferson, and Emilio Fernandez. **DT77, MU12,
MY2, ST115, XT18**

Bring on the Night (1985, C, 97m, PG-13)
Documentary about rock star Sting and
his formation of a jazz-rock band. **MU11**

Bringing Up Baby (1938, B&W, 102m,
NR)
Classic screwball comedy featuring a so-
cially inept zoologist, a ditsy heiress, and
her Baby—a pet leopard. Katharine Hepburn and Cary Grant star; Howard Hawks
directed. **CL10, DT43, ST57, ST66** *Essential; Recommended*

Brink of Life (1958, B&W, 84m, NR)
Drama from director Ingmar Bergman
about the lives of three women in a mater-
nity ward. Eva Dahlbeck, Ingrid Thulin,
and Bibi Andersson star. **DT7**

Brink's Job, The (1978, C, 103m, PG)
Seriocomic version of the famed 1950
robbery of armored car offices in Boston
by a motley crew, played by Peter Falk,
Peter Boyle, Allen Goorwitz, and Warren
Oates. Directed by William Friedkin.
MY8, MY18, ST115

Britannia Hospital (1982, C, 115m, R)
British comedy, set in an ineptly run hospital, takes swipes at socialized medicine,
quack medical research, corrupt unions.
Malcolm McDowell stars. Lindsay Anderson directed. A loose continuation of
the McDowell/Anderson film, *O Lucky
Man*. **CO2, CO17**

Broadcast News (1987, C, 131m, R)
Romantic comedy set in a Washington,
D.C., TV newsroom, involving a dynamo
producer (Holly Hunter) and two reporters (William Hurt, Albert Brooks) who
both love her. With Joan Cusack, Robert
Prosky, and Peter Hackes; Jack Nicholson has a small role as a network anchorman. James L. Brooks wrote and directed. **CO1, CO2, DT12, ST74, ST75,
ST112, XT12** *Recommended*

Broadway Danny Rose (1983, C, 85m, PG)
A luckless New York talent agent gets
mixed up with a mobster's wife. Woody
Allen and Mia Farrow star in this gentle
comedy about the less glamorous side of
show business. **CO8, DT1, XT9** *Recommended*

Broadway Melody (1929, B&W, 104m,
NR)
A pair of sisters try to break into show
biz and fall for the same entertainer. The
first musical to win the Best Picture Oscar. Bessie Love and Anita Page star.
MU4, MU7, XT1

Broadway Melody of 1938 (1937, B&W, 110m, NR)
Eleanor Powell stars as a dancer torn between two men (Robert Taylor and George Murphy). Judy Garland and Sophie Tucker costar. **MU1, MU4, ST51**

Broadway Melody of 1940 (1940, B&W, 102m, NR)
Fred Astaire and George Murphy are dance partners and rivals for dancing star Eleanor Powell. Songs by Cole Porter. **MU1, MU4, ST2**

Broken Arrow (1950, C, 93m, NR)
Classic western drama of the Apache Indian chief Cochise and his struggle to make peace with white settlers. James Stewart and Jeff Chandler star. **ST143, WE7**

Broken Blossoms (1919, B&W, 95m, NR)
D.W. Griffith's silent tragedy, with Lillian Gish as an abused child who's befriended by a gentle Chinaman (Richard Barthelmess). **CL12, DT42, ST54** *Essential*

Bronco Billy (1980, C, 119m, PG)
A Wild West Show entrepreneur (Clint Eastwood) leads his ragged troupe from one improbable adventure to the next. With Sondra Locke and Scatman Crothers. **ST39, WE12**

Bronze Venus *see* The Duke Is Tops

Brood, The (1979, C, 90m, R)
David Cronenberg directed this gory story of a therapist experimenting with a treatment that allows patients to express their inner rage in physical ways. Art Hindle, Samantha Eggar, and Oliver Reed star. Like many Cronenberg films, this has a cult following, but the faint of heart should beware. **CU4, CU7, DT23, HO13** *Recommended*

Brother From Another Planet, The (1984, C, 109m, NR)
Dark-skinned alien fugitive lands in Harlem, where he's treated like just another strange dude. Science fiction with its tongue in its cheek; written and directed by John Sayles, who also plays a small role. Joe Morton stars. **DR14, DR15, DT93, SF9**

Brother John (1972, C, 94m, PG)
Sidney Poitier stars in this story of the return of the Messiah in the form of a black man, who can't get anyone to believe him. With Will Geer, Beverly Todd, and Paul Winfield. **DR14, ST121, ST162**

Brother Sun, Sister Moon (1973, C, 121m, PG)
Italian director Franco Zeffirelli's portrait of Francis of Assisi, starring Graham Faulkner and Judi Bowker, with Alec Guinness. Music by Donovan. **FF2, ST60**

Brotherhood, The (1968, C, 98m, NR)
Kirk Douglas and Alex Cord play clashing brothers in this drama of organized crime. Directed by Martin Ritt. **DR16, DT87, ST34**

Brotherhood of Satan (1971, C, 92m, PG)
A coven of witches takes over a small town and three outsiders fight for their lives. Strother Martin stars. **HO11**

Brothers Karamazov, The (1958, C, 146m, NR)
Dostoyevsky's classic tragedy, an exploration of good, evil, and faith involving a father and his three sons. Lee J. Cobb, Yul Brynner, Richard Basehart, and William Shatner star. Directed by Richard Brooks. **CL1**

Brothers Lionheart, The (1977, C, 108m, G)
Family fantasy of siblings brought together in death in a medieval world, where they fight dragons. **FA8, SF13**

Brothers O'Toole, The (1973, C, 94m, NR)
This western comedy follows the misadventures of two drifters who ride into a broken-down 1890s mining town. **WE14**

Brubaker (1980, C, 132m, R)
An idealistic warden at a Southern prison farm uncovers massive corruption. Robert Redford stars, with Yaphet Kotto, Jane Alexander, Brian Keith, Morgan Freeman, and Tim McIntire. **DR18, ST48, ST126**

Bruce Lee: The Legend (1984, C, 88m, NR)
Documentary about the great martial arts star, with rare footage and out-takes, plus interviews with Steve McQueen and other friends of Lee. **ST88**

Bruce Lee: The Man/The Myth (1984, C, 90m, PG)
Dramatized biography of the martial arts star, featuring real footage of Lee in action. **ST88**

Brute, The (1952, B&W, 81m, NR)
To break a tenants' strike, a slumlord hires an ignorant slaughterhouse worker, who falls into an affair with the slumlord's wife. Luis Buñuel directed this drama, filmed in Mexico. Katy Jurado and Pedro Armendariz star. **DT15**

Brute Man, The (1946, B&W, 60m, NR)
A college football hero is disfigured by a lab accident, which turns him into the Creeper, a psychopathic killer. Rondo Hatton stars. **HO9**

Buccaneer, The (1958, C, 121m, NR)
Drama set during the War of 1812, with Andrew Jackson (Charlton Heston) teaming up with pirate Lafitte (Yul Brynner) to fight the bloody British. Produced by Cecil B. DeMille; directed by Anthony Quinn. **AC6, AC16**

Buck and the Preacher (1972, C, 102m, PG)
Sidney Poitier stars in and directed this western about a couple of con men. Harry Belafonte and Ruby Dee costar. **ST121**

Buck Privates (1941, B&W, 84m, NR)
Abbott and Costello's first starring roles, in a wacky service comedy. The Andrews Sisters sing "Boogie Woogie Bugle Boy." **CO21, ST1**

Buddy Buddy (1981, C, 96m, R)
A suicidal man and a hit man wind up in the same hotel room in this comedy starring Jack Lemmon and Walter Matthau. Billy Wilder directed. Klaus Kinski costars. Remake of French comedy *A Pain in the A—*. **CO3, DT116, DT7, ST83, ST90, ST104**

Buddy Holly Story, The (1978, C, 113m, PG)
The short but brilliant life of rock music pioneer Buddy Holly, portrayed with gusto by Gary Busey, who also performs Holly's ground-breaking music. Don Stroud and Charlie Martin Smith costar. **MU5** *Recommended*

Buddy System, The (1984, C, 110m, PG)
Romantic comedy starring Richard Dreyfuss and Susan Sarandon as a couple trying to decide whether to get involved. **ST36**

Buffalo Bill and the Indians (1976, C, 120m, PG)
A moody portrait of the Hero of the Plains in his final days, when he ran a traveling Wild West Show. Paul Newman stars, with Burt Lancaster as Ned Buntline, Geraldine Chaplin as Annie Oakley, Frank Considine, Harvey Keitel, and Will Sampson. Directed by Robert Altman. **DT2, HF3, HF20, ST85, ST111, WE11** *Recommended*

Buffet Froid (1979, C, 95m, NR)
French comedy of a bumbling trio of killers (Gerard Depardieu, Bernard Blier, Jean Carmet). Directed by Bertrand Blier, son of actor Bernard. **FF1, ST31**

Bug (1975, C, 100m, PG)
An earthquake lets loose a swarm of insects capable of setting anything on fire. Bradford Dillman stars. **HO16**

Bugs and Daffy: The Wartime Cartoons (1943-5, C, 120m, NR)
Time-capsule look at World War II through the eyes of the Warner Bros. cartoon gang. **FA11**

Bugs and Daffy's Carnival of the Animals (1976, C, 26m, NR)
Bugs Bunny and Daffy Duck combine their talents with a live orchestra conducted by Michael Tilson Thomas in this fantasy based on Camille St. Saens' title composition. Directed by Chuck Jones; originally made for TV. **FA11** *Recommended*

Bugs Bunny and Elmer Fudd Cartoon Festival (1940-6, C, 54m, NR)
Seven classic Bugs and Elmer shorts, including *Wabbit Twouble*, *Stage Door Cartoon*, and *The Big Snooze*. **FA11**

Bugs Bunny Cartoon Festival (1942-6, C, 34m, NR)
Cartoon delights from directors Friz Freleng, Chuck Jones, and Bob Clampett. **FA11**

Bugs Bunny Classics (1941-8, C, 60m, NR)
Among the highlights of this collection are "Heckling Hare," directed by Tex

Avery, and "Haredevil Hare," directed by Chuck Jones. **FA11**

Bugs Bunny in King Arthur's Court (1977, C, 25m, NR)
That wascally wabbit and his pals retell Mark Twain's *Connecticut Yankee in King Arthur's Court*. Directed by Chuck Jones; originally made for TV. **FA11, WR27**

Bugs Bunny/Road Runner Movie, The (1979, C, 90m, G)
Warner Bros. classic cartoon compilation features Bugs, Daffy Duck, Elmer Fudd, The Road Runner, Wile E. Coyote, Porky Pig, and Pepe Le Pew. **FA11**

Bugs Bunny, Superstar (1975, C, 90m, G)
A nine-cartoon collection from the 1930s and 1940s, most of them directed by Bob Clampett. **FA11**

Bugs Bunny 3rd Movie: 1001 Rabbit Tales (1982, C, 74m, G)
A collection of old and new Warner Bros. favorites. Voices by Mel Blanc. **FA11**

Bugs Bunny's Wacky Adventures (1957, C, 59m, NR)
Eight prized tales featuring that wascally wabbit. **FA11**

Bugsy Malone (1976, C, 93m, G)
Jodie Foster heads the all-child cast in a musical which spoofs gangster films. Music by Paul Williams; directed by Alan Parker. **FA9, MU16, ST47**

Bull Durham (1988, C, 108m, R)
A veteran catcher, wrappping up his career in the minor leagues, befriends a goofy young pitcher with great talent but no brains for the game, while the team's most devoted female fan makes a play for both men. Kevin Costner, Tim Robbins, and Susan Sarandon star in this sensational comedy from writer-director Ron Shelton. **CO1, CO19, ST23** *Recommended*

Bulldog Drummond (series)
Bulldog Drummond (1929, B&W, 85m, NR)
Bulldog Drummond at Bay (1937, B&W, 62m, NR)
Bulldog Drummond Comes Back (1937, B&W, 64m, NR)
Bulldog Drummond Escapes (1937, B&W, 65m, NR)

Bulldog Drummond in Africa (1938, B&W, 60m, NR)
Bulldog Drummond Strikes Back (1947, B&W, 65m, NR)
Bulldog Drummond's Bride (1939, B&W, 55m, NR)
Bulldog Drummond's Peril (1938, B&W, 66m, NR)
Bulldog Drummond's Revenge (1937, B&W, 60m, NR)
Bulldog Drummond's Secret Police (1939, B&W, 56m, NR)
The exploits of Hugh "Bulldog" Drummond, a high-flying ex-British officer with dashing good looks who always got his man with the help of his constant companion Algy. Ronald Colman stars in the first film; John Howard appears in all others in the series. **HF8**

Bullet for Sandoval, A (1970, C, 96m, PG)
A Civil War veteran swears revenge on those who caused the death of his son. Western action starring Ernest Borgnine. **WE9**

Bullet for the General, A (1967, C, 115m, NR)
Italian-made western with American gunfighter joining marauding Mexicans for mayhem. Gian Maria Volonte, Lou Castel, and Klaus Kinski star. **ST83**

Bulletproof (1988, C, 95m, R)
Gary Busey plays a seemingly unstoppable ex-CIA agent who takes on a gang of terrorists. With Darlanne Fluegel and Henry Silva. **AC25**

Bullfighter and the Lady (1951, B&W, 125m, NR)
An American visiting Mexico finds a matador to teach him bullfighting. Robert Stack and Gilbert Roland star, with Joy Page and Katy Jurado. Budd Boetticher directed and was Stack's stand-in on many of the bullfighting scenes. New video version adds footage to restore film to original running time. **CU10, DT10** *Recommended*

Bullfighters, The (1945, B&W, 61m, NR)
Laurel and Hardy comedy, with Stanley mistaken for a famed matador and forced into the ring. **ST87**

Bullies (1986, C, 96m, R)
A clan of mountain rednecks terrorize a small community, with only a teenaged boy to stand up to them. **AC25**

Bullitt (1968, C, 113m, PG)
Modern classic cop drama, with Steve McQueen the cool San Francisco detective caught up in political machinations, trying to protect a criminal witness. With Robert Vaughn, Jacqueline Bisset, and (in a small part) Robert Duvall. Memorable car chase sequence. **AC9, ST38, ST97, XT13** *Recommended*

Bullshot (1983, C, 85m, PG)
Send-up of Bulldog Drummond detective series, adapted from a play by Alan Shearman, Diz White, and Ron House, who all star as well. **CO7, CO17, MY17**

Bundle of Joy (1956, C, 98m, NR)
Debbie Reynolds takes custody of an abandoned baby, creating problems with fiance Eddie Fisher, in this musical remake of *Bachelor Mother*. **MU14**

Burbs, The (1989, C, 103m, PG)
Tom Hanks plays a suburbanite who's suspicious of his new neighbors in this comedy from director Joe Dante. **DT25, ST62**

Burden of Dreams (1982, C, 94m, NR)
Documentary about the filming of *Fitzcarraldo,* a movie plagued by physical hardships, a feuding star (Klaus Kinski) and director (Werner Herzog), and remote locations. Jason Robards and Mick Jagger appear briefly in clips from an earlier version of Herzog's film. Directed by Les Blank. **CU16, DT44, ST83, ST129** *Highly Recommended*

Burglar (1987, C, 103m, R)
A bookshop owner who moonlights as a cat burglar witnesses a murder and can't go to the police with her story. Whoopi Goldberg stars in this comedy with Bobcat Goldthwait. **CO10**

Burke and Wills (1986, C, 140m, PG-13)
Historical drama, set in 1860 Australia, of the first two men to cross that continent. Jack Thompson, Nigel Havers, and Greta Scacchi star. **DR5, FF5**

Burn! (1969, C, 112m, PG)
Marlon Brando stars in this political drama of British meddling on an 18th-century Caribbean island. Superb political drama from Italian director Gillo Pontecorvo; dialogue in English. **CU9, DR5, FF2, ST10** *Recommended*

Burning Bed, The (1984, C, 100m, NR)
An abused wife reaches the breaking point and sets fire to the bed in which her husband is sleeping. Farrah Fawcett and Paul LeMat star in this harrowing true-life story. Originally made for TV. **DR10**

Burning Secret (1988, C, 107m, R)
Post-World War I Vienna is the setting for this romantic drama starring Faye Dunaway as an American woman seduced by a dashing nobleman (Klaus Maria Brandauer). **ST37**

Burnt Offerings (1976, C, 115m, PG)
There's something spooky about the summer house Karen Black and Oliver Reed have rented for their family. Bette Davis costars. **HO3, ST28**

Bus Stop (1956, C, 96m, NR)
Marilyn Monroe stars as a small-town singer bound for Hollywood; she has a boisterous rodeo cowboy (Don Murray) in love with her. Based on a play by William Inge. **DR20, DR26, ST108**

Bushido Blade, The (1979, C, 104m, R)
In 19th-century Japan, Commander William Peary attempts to recover a valuable stolen sword. Action adventure starring Richard Boone, James Earl Jones, and Toshiro Mifune. **ST76, ST106**

Business As Usual (1988, C, 89m, PG)
British drama of a sexual harassment suit, starring Glenda Jackson and Cathy Tyson. **DR10, DR23**

Buster (1988, C, 94m, R)
Pop star Phil Collins plays the mastermind behind Britain's 1962 Great Train Robbery. Julie Walters costars as Buster's wife. **DR6, DR16, MU12, MY18**

Buster Keaton Festival Vol. I (1923, B&W, 55m, NR)
Three classic comedy shorts: *The Boat, The Frozen North,* and *The Electric House.* **DT54** *Recommended*

Buster Keaton Festival Vol. II (1920/1923, B&W, 54m, NR)
Three more great silent comedy shorts: *Daydreams, The Balloonatic,* and *The Garage.* **DT54** *Recommended*

Buster Keaton Rides Again/The Railrodder
(1965, B&W, 81m, NR)
The Railrodder is one of Keaton's last films; shot in Canada, it tries to recreate his classic style, as Buster travels cross-country on a railroad handcar. *Rides Again* is a documentary on the making of *The Railrodder,* with revealing footage about Keaton's working methods. **DT54** *Recommended*

Bustin' Loose (1981, C, 94m, R)
Richard Pryor plays an ex-con who's hustled into driving a school bus full of ornery kids to a camp. Cicely Tyson costars in this comedy. **ST125, XT18**

Butch and Sundance: The Early Days
(1979, C, 110m, PG)
Prequel to *Butch Cassidy and the Sundance Kid* shows the formative years of the famous outlaw duo. Tom Berenger and William Katt star. Directed by Richard Lester. **DT62, WE3, WE14**

Butch Cassidy and the Sundance Kid
(1969, C, 112m, PG)
Paul Newman and Robert Redford play the legendary outlaws in this comic western. With Katharine Ross, Strother Martin, and Ted Cassidy. Written by William Goldman; directed by George Roy Hill. **ST111, ST126, WE3, WE11, WE14** *Essential*

Butterfield 8 (1960, C, 110m, NR)
Elizabeth Taylor won an Oscar as the call girl of John O'Hara's novel. She's attracted to a married client (Laurence Harvey) and counseled by her best friend (Eddie Fisher). **DR19, ST147, XT3**

Butterflies Are Free (1972, C, 109m, PG)
Romance blossoms between a young blind man (Edward Albert) and his goofy neighbor (Goldie Hawn), despite the interference of his mother (Oscar winner Eileen Heckart). **ST63, XT5**

Butterfly (1981, C, 107m, R)
Sexy young woman seduces a man who may be her father in this trashy version of the James M. Cain story. Pia Zadora, Stacy Keach, and Orson Welles star. **CU6, DT112, WR1**

By Love Possessed (1961, C, 115m, NR)
Romantic drama of relationship between lovelorn woman (Lana Turner) and a prominent attorney (Efrem Zimbalist,

Jr.). With Jason Robards and George Hamilton. **CL5, ST129, ST153**

Bye Bye Birdie (1963, C, 112m, NR)
Musical about rock star, loosely modeled on Elvis, coming to small town just before he's drafted. Janet Leigh, Dick Van Dyke, Ann-Margret, and Paul Lynde star. **MU2, MU6, MU9**

Bye Bye Brazil (1980, C, 110m, R)
A troupe of entertainers tour the Brazilian countryside in this comedy-drama. **FF6**

C.H.O.M.P.S. (1979, C, 89m, G)
The title means: Canine HOMe Protection System. A young inventor perfects a mechanical guard dog in this family comedy starring Wesley Eure and Valerie Bertinelli. **FA6**

C.H.U.D. (1984, C, 90m, R)
Derelicts who live in the New York sewer system are turned into flesh eating mutants, Cannabilistic Humanoid Underground Dwellers, by nuclear waste. John Heard, Daniel Stern, and Kim Greist star. **HO21**

Cabaret (1972, C, 128m, PG)
Hit Broadway musical, set in the early days of the Third Reich, about a decadent Berlin nightclub featuring an American singing star (Liza Minnelli) and nasty emcee (Joel Grey). Minnelli, Grey, and director Bob Fosse won three of the film's 8 Oscars. Musical remake of *I Am a Camera.* **DT39, MU2, MU7, MU14, XT3, XT4, XT6** *Essential; Recommended*

Cabin in the Sky (1943, B&W, 100m, NR)
Black musical fantasy about one man's struggle with the forces of good and evil. Eddie "Rochester" Anderson is the man, and the musical stars include Lena Horne, Ethel Waters, and Louis Armstrong. Directed by Vincente Minnelli. **DT71, MU8, MU13**

Cabinet of Dr. Caligari, The (1919, B&W, 69m, NR)
Silent German classic about an evil doctor and his zombie-like creation. Sensational sets and imagery. Werner Krauss stars; Robert Wiene directed. **FF3, HO1** *Essential; Recommended*

Caboblanco (1980, C, 87m, R)
Intrigue set in wartime South America, with bartender Charles Bronson keeping an eye on Nazi Jason Robards and other characters. Dominique Sanda and Fernando Rey costar. **ST12, ST129**

Cactus (1986, C, 95m, NR)
Love story involving a blind man (Robert Menzies) and a woman who is losing her sight (Isabelle Huppert). Australian Paul Cox directed. **FF5**

Cactus Flower (1969, C, 103m, PG)
Goldie Hawn won an Oscar for her role as the kookie girl friend of a swinging middle-aged dentist (Walter Matthau). Ingrid Bergman plays Matthau's nurse, who breaks out of her shell when she realizes she's in love with him. **CO1, ST7, ST63, ST104, XT5**

Caddie (1976, C, 107m, NR)
Helen Morse stars in this true story of an Australian woman trying to raise two children and manage a career during the 1920s. **FF5**

Caddy, The (1953, B&W, 95m, NR)
Martin and Lewis comedy set on the golf links, with Donna Reed and guest appearances by several golf pros. **CO19, ST91**

Caddyshack (1980, C, 90m, R)
Comic shenanigans at a snooty country club, starring Rodney Dangerfield, Ted Knight, Bill Murray, and Chevy Chase. Directed by Harold Ramis. **CO13, CO14**

Caddyshack II (1988, C, 98m, PG)
More hijinks at Bushwood Country Club, featuring Jackie Mason, Dyan Cannon, Robert Stack, Paul Bartel, and "guest appearances" by Chevy Chase and Dan Aykroyd. Directed by Allan Arkush. **CO13, DT4, DT5**

Cadillac Man (1990, C, 97m, R)
Robin Williams stars as a fast-talking car salesman whose talents are put to the test when a madman invades his dealership and holds everyone there hostage. With Tim Robbins, Pamela Reed, Fran Drescher, and Zack Norman. **ST160**

Caesar and Cleopatra (1946, C, 134m, NR)
Rendition of George Bernard Shaw's play with Claude Rains and Vivien Leigh as the mighty conqueror and his young Egyptian queen. **CL1, CL3**

Cage aux Folles, La (1978, C, 91m, R)
French comedy about a gay couple (Ugo Tognazzi, Michel Serrault), one with a son about to be married, both trying to keep their private lives secret from the future in-laws. **CU5, FF1**

Cage aux Folles II, La (1981, C, 100m, R)
More misadventures with the popular gay couple (Ugo Tognazzi, Michel Serrault), this time involving espionage and multiple mistaken identities. **FF1**

Cage aux Folles 3: The Wedding, La (1985, C, 88m, PG-13)
In the third chapter, the oddest couple are about to land an inheritance, but only if one of them is married. **FF1, XT20**

Caged Heat (1974, C, 84m, R)
Women-in-prison drama, directed by Jonathan Demme, produced by Roger Corman, has Barbara Steele as warden confined to a wheelchair, the usual shower scenes, etc. **CU14, DT28**

Cahill: United States Marshal (1973, C, 103m, PG)
John Wayne plays a lawman whose son is tempted by a life of crime. **ST156**

Caine Mutiny, The (1954, C, 125m, NR)
Humphrey Bogart stars in the Herman Wouk story of Navy officers who join forces to relieve their captain of his ship when they find him mentally unfit. With Jose Ferrer, Van Johnson, Fred MacMurray, E. G. Marshall and Lee Marvin. **ST8, ST100**

Cal (1984, C, 102m, R)
An Irish youth who was involved in the murder of a British policeman falls in love with his widow. John Lynch and Helen Mirren star. Produced by David Puttnam; music by Mark Knopfler. **DR3, DR7, DR23**

Calamity Jane (1953, C, 101m, NR)
Doris Day plays the Wild West sharpshooter. Howard Keel costars as Wild Bill Hickok. Features the Oscar winning song "Secret Love." **HF11, MU6, WE8**

California Suite (1978, C, 103m, PG)
A series of comic sketches, all set in the Beverly Hills Hotel. The cast features

Jane Fonda, Richard Pryor, Bill Cosby, Maggie Smith (an Oscar winner), Michael Caine, Elaine May, Walter Matthau, and Alan Alda. Written by Neil Simon. **DT70, ST15, ST45, ST104, ST125, WR23, XT5, XT10**

Caligula (1980, C, 156m, NR)
Lavish, violent, sexually explicit portrait of ancient Rome from *Penthouse* magazine publisher Bob Guccione, starring Malcolm McDowell, Peter O'Toole, and John Gielgud. Also available in a R-rated version with a running time of 105m. **CU6, CU7, DR5, ST117**

Call Him Mr. Shatter (1976, C, 90m, R)
Stuart Whitman plays a hit man in Hong Kong who's had enough. Peter Cushing costars. **ST27**

Call It Murder (1934, B&W, 80m, NR)
Humphrey Bogart stars in a mystery about a jury foreman's daughter who gets the death penalty when she's romantically linked to a gangster. Also known as *Midnight*. **ST8**

Call of the Canyon (1942, B&W, 71m, NR)
Gene Autry and his radio ranch are caught under hoof when a crooked meat packer starts a stampede. **ST3**

Call of the Wild, The (1972, C, 100m, PG)
The Jack London adventure tale of gold fever in the turn-of-the-century Klondike, starring Charlton Heston. **AC12, AC24**

Camelot (1967, C, 178m, NR)
Broadway musical of the Knights of the Round Table, featuring Vanessa Redgrave, Richard Harris, and Franco Nero as Guinevere, King Arthur, and Sir Lancelot. **FA9, MU2, MU8, MU17, ST127**

Cameron's Closet (1988, C, 86m, R)
Horror tale of a psychic child whose powers cause the deaths of those who would control him. Cotter Smith, Mel Harris, and Tab Hunter star. **HO7, HO13**

Camila (1984, C, 105m, NR)
Romantic drama, based on true events, of a young socialite's love for a priest. This Argentinean film was nominated for an Oscar for Best Foreign Language Film. **FF6**

Camille (1936, B&W, 108m, NR)
Greta Garbo, Robert Taylor, and Lionel Barrymore star in Alexandre Dumas' story of the tragic heroine who is thwarted in her desire for the man she truly loves. Directed by George Cukor. **CL1, CL4, CL5, DT24, ST50**

Camille Claudel (1988, C, 149m, R)
Isabelle Adjani plays the student-mistress of sculptor Auguste Rodin who eventually became an artist in her own right. Gerard Depardieu costars as Rodin. Original French running time: 173m. **FF1, ST31**

Camorra (1986, C, 115m, R)
Italian thriller of an ex-prostitute taking on the Mob in Naples. Angela Molina stars. Lina Wertmüller directed. **DT114**

Can-Can (1960, C, 131m, NR)
Gay Nineties setting for this lavish musical featuring Cole Porter music. Frank Sinatra, Shirley MacLaine, Maurice Chevalier, Louis Jourdan, and Juliet Prowse star. Muscal numbers are presented in letterboxed format. **CU19, MU2, ST96, ST138**

Cancel My Reservation (1972, C, 99m, G)
Bob Hope comedy of a New York talk show host, on vacation in Arizona, becoming implicated in murder. Based on a novel by Louis L'Amour. **ST70, WR13**

Candidate, The (1972, C, 109m, PG)
A novice office seeker suddenly finds himself the front-runner in a Senatorial race against a veteran incumbent. Sharp observations on the media-dominated political climate in contemporary America. Robert Redford stars, with Don Porter, Melvyn Douglas, and Peter Boyle. Oscar-winning screenplay by Jeremy Larner; directed by Michael Ritchie. **DR21, ST126**
Recommended

Candles at Nine (1944, B&W, 84m, NR)
In order to inherit her late uncle's estate, an innocent showgirl must first live a month in his home, which his other relatives have booby-trapped. Jessie Matthews stars in this British thriller. **MY3, MY15**

Candleshoe (1977, C, 101m, G)
Jodie Foster stars as an orphan pawn in a con man's swindle to steal heiress Helen Hayes's fortune. Disney comedy costars David Niven. **FA1, ST47**

Candy Mountain (1987, C, 91m, PG)
Unusual tale of musician's search for legendary guitar maker, with several prominent pop musical figures playing roles, including Dr. John, Tom Waits, Leon Redbone, Joe Strummer, and David Johansen (Buster Poindexter). Directed by photographer Robert Frank and writer Rudolph Wurlitzer. **CU17**

Cannery Row (1982, C, 120m, PG)
An adaptation of John Steinbeck's story about opposites who attract: a marine biologist (Nick Nolte) meets a goofy drifter (Debra Winger) in Monterey, California, in the 1930s. John Huston narrates this sweet tale of love. **DR19, DT50, ST113, ST163, WR25** *Recommended*

Cannonball (1976, C, 93m, R)
Low-budget road race movie starring David Carradine, Veronica Hamel, and Robert Carradine. Directed by Paul Bartel. Watch for Roger Corman, Sylvester Stallone, Martin Scorsese, and others in bit parts. **AC10, DT5, DT22, DT95, ST140**

Cannonball Run, The (1981, C, 95m, PG)
Burt Reynolds and pals race across country in vehicles of all makes and descriptions. Roger Moore, Farrah Fawcett, Dom DeLuise, Dean Martin, Sammy Davis, Jr., and many more guest drivers and pedestrians show up. **AC10, CO9, ST128**

Cannonball Run II (1984, C, 108m, PG)
More road racing action with Burt Reynolds and friends, this time including Dom DeLuise, Shirley MacLaine, and Marilu Henner. Look quickly for Frank Sinatra. **AC10, CO9, ST96, ST128**

Can't Stop the Music (1980, C, 118m, PG)
Rock musical featuring The Village People, with Valerie Perrine, Bruce Jenner, and Steve Guttenberg on hand for dramatic flourishes. **MU9**

Cape Fear (1962, B&W, 105m, NR)
An ex-convict, out for revenge, terrorizes the family of the attorney who convicted him. Robert Mitchum and Gregory Peck star. **MY2, ST107, ST119** *Recommended*

Captain Blood (1935, B&W, 99m, NR)
Doctor turns pirate but doesn't ignore a certain attractive damsel. Errol Flynn's first swashbuckler; Olivia de Havilland and Basil Rathbone costar. **AC13, ST43**

Captain January (1936, B&W, 76m, NR)
Shirley Temple drama of a kindly lighthouse keeper (Guy Kibbee) and his charge. Buddy Ebsen and Shirley trip the light fantastic. **ST148**

Captain Kidd (1945, B&W, 89m, NR)
Adventures on the high seas with the notorious pirate (Charles Laughton) in search of treasure. Randolph Scott co-stars. **ST136**

Captain Kronos: Vampire Hunter (1974, C, 91m, R)
From Britain's Hammer Studios, a spoof of horror and adventure serials, with a caped superhero and his two sidekicks who travel the world searching for vampires to kill. **HO5, HO26**

Captain Newman, M.D. (1963, C, 126m, NR)
Army psychiatrist (Gregory Peck) counsels patients, does battle with military brass in this comedy-drama. Angie Dickinson, Tony Curtis, and Bobby Darin co-star. **MU12, ST119**

Captains Courageous (1937, B&W, 116m, NR)
Classic family adventure about a spoiled little rich kid (Freddie Bartholomew) whose attitude improves when he falls from a cruise ship and into the custody of a very wise Portuguese fisherman (Oscar winner Spencer Tracy). Based on Rudyard Kipling's novel. **AC13, FA3, ST151, XT2**

Captain's Paradise, The (1953, B&W, 77m, NR)
Alec Guinness stars in this British comedy about a sea captain with wives in two ports. Yvonne de Carlo and Celia Johnson are his mates. **ST60**

Car Wash (1976, C, 97m, PG)
Multi-character comedy set at an inner-city car wash. Richard Pryor and Franklin Ajaye head the cast; fine rock soundtrack. **ST125**

Caravans (1978, C, 123m, PG)
Adventure tale of the search in the Middle East for a U.S. Senator's daughter. Anthony Quinn and Jennifer O'Neill star, with Michael Sarrazin, Christopher Lee, and Joseph Cotten. **ST89**

Carbon Copy (1981, C, 92m, PG)
Comedy of a successful executive confronted with a 17-year-old black youth who claims he's the man's son from a long-ago affair. George Segal, Susan Saint James, Denzel Washington, and Paul Winfield star. **CO2, ST162**

Cardinal, The (1963, C, 175m, NR)
From director Otto Preminger comes the epic story of a priest's rise to power in the Catholic Church. Tom Tryon stars, with Romy Schneider, Carol Lynley, Burgess Meredith, Raf Vallone, and John Huston. **DT50, DT82**

Care Bears Movie, The (1985, C, 75m, G)
Those roly-poly, lovable little bears are on a mission to help people share their feelings and to prevent evildoers like Professor Coldheart from taking over the world. **FA10**

Carefree (1938, B&W, 80m, NR)
Fred Astaire plays a psychiatrist, with Ginger Rogers as his patient, in this Irving Berlin musical. **CL15, ST2, ST131**

Careful, He Might Hear You (1983, C, 116m, PG)
Moving drama from Australia, based on Sumner Locke Elliott novel of a young boy caught in a bitter custody battle between two aunts. Wendy Hughes, Robyn Nevin, and Nicholas Gledhill star. **DR2, FF5** *Recommended*

Carlin at Carnegie (1983, C, 60m, NR)
Comedian George Carlin in concert at New York's venerable Carnegie Hall. **CO16**

Carlton Browne of the F.O. (1959, B&W, 88m, NR)
The British Foreign Office discovers a forgotten island that's still part of the Commonwealth and dispatches a bumbling diplomat to take charge. Terry-Thomas and Peter Sellers star. Also known as *Man in a Cocked Hat.* **ST137**

Carmen (1983, C, 102m, R)
Spanish troupe rehearses for dance interpretation of the famed opera, with the choreographer and his female star playing out the story backstage. Antonio Gades and Laura Del Sol star. Carlos Saura directed. Brilliant dance numbers. **FF7, MU3, MU4** *Recommended*

Carnal Knowledge (1971, C, 96m, R)
Drama of two college friends who treat women as objects and don't understand why they can't find love. Jack Nicholson, Art Garfunkel, Ann-Margret, and Candice Bergen star. Banned in at least one state and subject of a famous trial. Directed by Mike Nichols; written by Jules Feiffer. **CU8, DR7, DT74, MU12, ST112**

Carnival of Souls (1962, B&W, 80m, NR)
After surviving a car crash into a river, a woman is pursued by a zombie-like man. Low-budget horror film with cult following. Candace Hilligoss stars. Written and directed by Herk Harvey, his only feature film; he also plays the zombie man. **CU4, CU15, HO6** *Recommended*

Carnival Rock (1957, B&W, 75m, NR)
Early film from director Roger Corman, a romantic triangle drama set in the nightclub world, with appearances by The Platters and David Houston. Susan Cabot and Dick Miller star. **DT22**

Carny (1980, C, 107m, R)
Life behind the scenes at a traveling carnival, with young runaway (Jodie Foster) getting a liberal education from barker (Robbie Robertson) and his pal (Gary Busey). **DR12, MU12, ST47** *Recommended*

Carousel (1956, C, 128m, NR)
Colorful Broadway musical of a ne'er-do-well carnival barker and his love. Gordon MacRae and Shirley Jones star, with Cameron Mitchell and Barbara Ruick. Rodgers and Hammerstein songs include "If I Loved You" and "Soliloquy." **FA9, MU2, MU6**

Carrie (1976, C, 97m, R)
High school wallflower gets even with her tormentors and her strict mother by using her telekinetic powers. Horror shocker directed by Brian DePalma, based on a story by Stephen King. Sissy Spacek stars, with Piper Laurie, William Katt, Nancy Allen, Amy Irving, and John Travolta. **DR25, DT29, HO7, HO12, ST139, WR12** *Essential; Recommended*

Carry On Doctor (1968, C, 95m, NR)
British comedy in the long-running *Carry On . . .* series, with hospital setting and the usual bedpan humor. **CO17**

Cars That Ate Paris, The (1974, C, 91m, PG)
Black comedy from Australia, about a small town which creates traffic accidents to reap scrap metal and spare parts. Directed by Peter Weir. **CO12, DT111, FF5**

Carson City Kid (1940, B&W, 54m, NR)
Roy Rogers cleans up yet another Western town and gets in a few tunes as well. With Dale Evans and Gabby Hayes. **ST132**

Cartoon Moviestars: Bugs! (1942-8, C, 60m, NR)
Among the highlights of this collection of Warner Bros. cartoons are "Bugs Bunny & the 3 Bears" and "Bugs Bunny Gets the Boid." **FA11**

Cartoon Moviestars: Daffy! (1938-48, B&W/C, 60m, NR)
Eight cartoons featuring that crazy duck, including the debut of Elmer Fudd in "Daffy Duck and Egghead." **FA11**

Cartoon Movietstars: Elmer! (1940-8, B&W/C, 60m, NR)
First-wate cowection featuwing that bald butt of Bugs' and Daffy's jokes. **FA11**

Cartoon Moviestars: Porky! (1935-47, B&W/C, 60m, NR)
The stuttering porker is featured in this collection which includes his debut in "I Haven't Got a Hat." **FA11**

Casablanca (1943, B&W, 102m, NR)
The Oscar-winning romantic classic that just gets better and better. Humphrey Bogart and Ingrid Bergman make the perfect pair of war-torn lovers. Sydney Greenstreet, Dooley Wilson, Claude Rains, and Paul Henreid costar. Director Michael Curtiz also won an Academy Award. **CL4, CL6, ST7, ST8, XT1, XT6** *Essential; Recommended*

Casanova's Big Night (1954, C, 86m, NR)
Joan Fontaine mistakes Bob Hope for the infamous Casanova (Vincent Price) and havoc ensues throughout Venice. With Lon Chaney, Jr. **ST17, ST70, ST124**

Casey at the Bat (1986, C, 52m, NR)
The famous poem of the blustering baseball slugger, starring Elliott Gould, with narration by Howard Cosell. Entry in Shelley Duvall's Tall Tales & Legends series. **FA3**

Casey's Shadow (1978, C, 117m, PG)
A free-wheeling horse trainer has to raise three sons when his wife leaves him. Walter Matthau stars in this family drama. Directed by Martin Ritt. **DT87, FA5, FA7, ST104**

Casino Royale (1967, C, 130m, NR)
Anything-for-a-laugh spoof of James Bond movies with amazing cast (Peter Sellers, Woody Allen, David Niven, Ursula Andress, Orson Welles, William Holden, Deborah Kerr, Jean-Paul Belmondo) and plenty of sight gags, including explosive finale in Monte Carlo casino. Co-directed by John Huston. **CO7, CU17, DT1, DT50, DT112, HF2, ST6, ST68, ST127**

Cast a Giant Shadow (1966, C, 142m, NR)
True-life drama about Mickey Marcus, Israeli freedom fighter. Kirk Douglas stars, with Angie Dickinson and many guest stars in bit parts, including John Wayne and Frank Sinatra. **DR4, ST34, ST138, ST156**

Castaway (1987, C, 118m, R)
True story of middle-aged man and young woman who intentionally set themselves up on a desert island for a year. Oliver Reed and Amanda Donohoe star. Nicolas Roeg directed. **DR6, DT88**

Castaway Cowboy, The (1974, C, 91m, G)
Cowboy James Garner goes Hawaiian to help a farm widow (Vera Miles). Robert Culp costars as the bad guy in this tropical Disney western. **FA1**

Castle in the Desert (1942, B&W, 62m, NR)
It's the crafty detective Charlie Chan (Sidney Toler) up against a modern version of the Borgia clan in this mystery. **HF4**

Castle of Blood (1964, B&W, 85m, NR)
A poet decides to spend a night in a haunted castle in this adaptation of Edgar Allan Poe's poem, "Berenice." Barbara Steele stars. Also known as *Castle of Terror*. **HO3, WR21**

Castle of Fu Manchu (1968, B&W, 92m, PG)
Fu Manchu and his minions are out to create havoc in the world one more time. Christopher Lee stars. **ST89**

Castle of Terror *see* Castle of Blood

Castle of the Living Dead (1964, B&W, 90m, NR)
A mysterious nobleman turns his visitors into mummies. Christopher Lee stars, with Donald Sutherland. **ST89**

Casualties of War (1989, C, 113m, R)
True story of Vietnam War atrocity, starring Michael J. Fox and Sean Penn. Directed by Brian DePalma. **AC4, DR6, DT29**

Cat and Mouse (1975, C, 107m, PG)
Comic mystery from France about a murdered husband whose less-than-faithful ways leave a long list of suspects. Michele Morgan and Serge Reggiani star. Claude Lelouch directed. **FF1**

Cat and the Canary, The (1978, C, 96m, NR)
British remake of the classic tale finds a group of guests visiting a mansion on your basic dark and stormy night, becoming victims of a series of bizarre pranks. Michael Callan, Carol Lynley, and Olivia Hussey star. **MY15**

Cat Ballou (1965, C, 96m, NR)
Comic western featuring Jane Fonda as a cowgirl avenging her father's murder and Oscar winner Lee Marvin in two roles: a broken-down gunslinger and his evil twin brother. **CO7, ST45, ST100, WE8, WE14, XT2**

Cat Chaser (1989, C, 90m, R)
Thriller about a former Marine, who once fought in Santo Domingo, returning there, becoming involved with the wife of the former chief of secret police. Peter Weller and Kelly McGillis star, with Charles Durning, Frederic Forrest, and Tomas Milian. Based on a novel by Elmore Leonard. **MY16, WR16**

Cat From Outer Space, The (1978, C, 104m, G)
An extraterrestrial feline crashes on Earth, creating mayhem with the U.S. government. Disney comedy starring Ken Berry, Sandy Duncan, Harry Morgan, and McLean Stevenson. **FA1**

Cat on a Hot Tin Roof (1958, C, 108m, NR)
Elizabeth Taylor and Paul Newman star in this drama of a deceptive Southern family who cozy up to their dying patriarch (Burl Ives), hoping to get a piece of his inheritance. Based on Tennessee Williams's play. **DR20, ST111, ST147, WR30**

Cat People (1942, B&W, 73m, NR)
Producer Val Lewton's first horror film is about a mysterious bride obsessed with a curse that will transform her into a deadly panther. Directed by Jacques Tourneur. **DT105, HO27, MY1** *Essential*

Cat People (1982, C, 118m, R)
An erotic remake of the 1942 Val Lewton classic, set in New Orleans. Nastassja Kinski, Malcolm McDowell, John Heard, and Annette O'Toole star. Directed by Paul Schrader. **CU18, HO25, XT14**

Catch-22 (1970, C, 121m, R)
Joseph Heller's darkly comic view of World War II, with pilot Alan Arkin frustrated and near a breakdown. Incredible supporting cast includes Martin Balsam, Bob Newhart, Buck Henry, Jon Voight, Orson Welles, Art Garfunkel, Martin Sheen, Charles Grodin, Anthony Perkins, and Paula Prentiss. Directed by Mike Nichols. **CO12, CO21, CU17, DR19, DT74, DT112, MU12, ST59** *Recommended*

Cat's Eye (1985, C, 93m, PG13)
A trio of Stephen King short stories are linked by a cat involved in all three. James Woods, Drew Barrymore, and Robert Hays star. **HO23, ST165, WR12**

Cattle Queen of Montana (1954, C, 88m, NR)
Barbara Stanwyck stars in the title role; Ronald Reagan's an undercover federal agent investigating cattle thievery. **ST142, WE5, WE8**

Caught (1949, B&W, 88m, NR)
A young woman (Barbara Bel Geddes) trapped in a miserable marriage to a millionaire (Robert Ryan) finds happiness with a struggling doctor (James Mason). Directed by Max Ophuls. **DT76, MY1, MY3, ST102** *Recommended*

Cauldron of Blood (1967, C, 97m, PG)
A blind sculptor uses skeletons provided by his murderous wife. Boris Karloff, Viveca Lindfors, and Jean-Pierre Aumont star. **ST77**

Caveman (1981, C, 92m, PG)
Comedy of life in prehistoric times, featuring Ringo Starr as a lovable Neanderthal. Barbara Bach, John Matuszak, Shelley Long, and Dennis Quaid costar. **MU12**

Certain Fury (1985, C, 88m, R)
Two girls, accused of a crime they didn't commit, are on the run from both police and hoods. Tatum O'Neal and Irene Cara star. **AC24, MU12**

Cesar (1936, B&W, 170m, NR)
Third in classic trilogy of life in France's Provence region, with Fanny's son learning the true identity of his father. Preceded by *Marius* and *Fanny*. Raimu, Pierre Fresnay, and Orane Demazis star. Marcel Pagnol wrote and directed. **FF1**

Cesar and Rosalie (1972, C, 110m, R)
Yves Montand, Romy Schneider, and Sami Frey star in this French drama of a woman's longtime love for two men. **FF1** *Recommended*

Chain Reaction (1980, C, 87m, NR)
An accident at a nuclear power plant forces a worker to confront the dangers of nuclear power. Australian drama stars Steve Bisley. **FF5**

Challenge, The (1982, C, 112m, R)
An American boxer visiting Japan becomes embroiled in a feud between two brothers. Scott Glenn and Toshiro Mifune star. John Frankenheimer directed. **ST106**

Chamber of Fear (1968, C, 88m, NR)
A madman tortures all those who visit his castle. Boris Karloff and Isela Vega star. Also known as *The Fear Chamber*. **ST77**

Chamber of Horrors (1940, B&W, 80m, NR)
A charming man (Leslie Banks) is secretly a killer of beautiful women; he has already selected his next victim (Lili Palmer). **HO9**

Champ, The (1931, B&W, 87m, NR)
Wallace Beery won an Oscar for his portrayal of a broken-down boxer trying to keep custody of his son (Jackie Cooper). A classic three-hankie movie directed by King Vidor. Remake released in 1979. **CL6, DR22, DT107, XT2**

Champ, The (1979, C, 121m, PG)
An ex-fighter (Jon Voight) may lose custody of his son (Ricky Schroder) in this tear-jerker remake of the 1931 film. Faye Dunaway costars. **CU18, DR22, FA7, ST37**

Champagne for Caesar (1950, B&W, 99m, NR)
This comedy poking fun at television game shows features a contestant (Ronald Colman) winning big prizes and the show's worried sponsor (Vincent Price) trying to distract him. **CO8, ST124**

Champion (1949, B&W, 90m, NR)
Kirk Douglas plays the ultimate boxing machine in this drama of an overly ambitious fighter. Marilyn Maxwell and Arthur Kennedy costar. **DR22, ST34**

Chan Is Missing (1982, B&W, 80m, NR)
Two San Francisco cabdrivers hunt for the title character, a Chinese who has their $4,000. Comedy-drama directed by Wayne Wang. **CO2, DR15, XT13**

Chances Are (1989, C 108m, PG-13)
A Washington widow (Cybill Shepherd) has a new man in her life—a young man to whom her daughter is attracted. The real complication: he's her late husband reincarnated. Robert Downey, Jr., Mary Stuart Masterson, and Ryan O'Neal costar. **CO1, CO20, XT12**

Chandu on the Magic Island (1940, B&W, 67m, NR)
Chandu the magician travels to a lost island to battle an evil cult of devil worshippers. Bela Lugosi stars. **ST95**

Change of Habit (1969, C, 93m, G)
Elvis Presley stars in this drama with no musical numbers about an inner-city physician and his relationship with a nun (Mary Tyler Moore). **ST123**

Change of Seasons, A (1980, C, 102m, R)
A professor takes one of his students for a lover, and his wife retaliates by taking up with a younger man, too. Anthony Hopkins, Shirley MacLaine, Bo Derek, and Michael Brandon star in this comedy. **ST96**

Changeling, The (1979, C, 107m, R)
A composer who has lost his wife and child in an accident rents an old house, discovers it is haunted by the ghost of a

murdered child, then sets out to solve the murder. George C. Scott, Trish Van Devere, and Melvyn Douglas star. **HO2, HO19**

Chaplin Essanay Book I, The (1915, B&W, 51m, NR)
Collection of Charlie Chaplin's early short films, including *The Tramp* and *The Champion*. **DT18** *Recommended*

Chaplin Revue, The (1958, B&W, 121m, NR)
Charlie Chaplin personally assembled this collection in 1958 of his early silent shorts, including *Shoulder Arms* (1918) and *The Pilgrim* (1922). **CO21, DT18** *Essential; Recommended*

Chapter Two (1979, C, 124m, PG)
Neil Simon's autobiographical drama of a writer trying to get over the death of his wife and falling all too quickly in love with another woman. James Caan and Marsha Mason star. **WR23**

Charade (1963, C, 114m, NR)
A young widow finds that several men are interested in a secret that killed her husband. Audrey Hepburn and Cary Grant star in this romantic mystery set in Paris, with Walter Matthau, George Kennedy, and James Coburn. Directed by Stanley Donen. **DT30, MY3, ST57, ST65, ST104, XT16** *Recommended*

Charge of the Light Brigade, The (1936, B&W, 116m, NR)
Adventure tale of fateful British maneuver during the Crimean War, starring Errol Flynn and Olivia de Havilland. Directed by Michael Curtiz. **AC6, AC13, AC16, ST43**

Chariots of Fire (1981, C, 123m, PG)
Oscar-winning drama, based on a true story, of rival runners in the 1924 Olympics. Ben Cross, Ian Charleson, Ian Holm, and Alice Krige star, with guest appearances by John Gielgud and Lindsay Anderson. Directed by Hugh Hudson; produced by David Puttnam. **DR22, DR23, XT1**

Charley and the Angel (1973, C, 93m, G)
Fred MacMurray learns a heavenly lesson from a wise angel (Harry Morgan): shape up his strict ways with his family or he'll be shipped off to the hereafter. Drama from the Disney studios. **FA1**

Charley Varrick (1973, C, 111m, PG)
Robber of small town bank gets more than he bargained for when he learns the loot is laundered Mob money. Walter Matthau stars, with Joe Don Baker, Felicia Farr, John Vernon, and Andy Robinson. First-rate action drama directed by Don Siegel. **DT97, MY9, MY18, ST104** *Recommended*

Charlie Chan at the Opera (1936, B&W, 68m, NR)
An opera singer (Boris Karloff) seems the perfect suspect for the sleuthing of Chan (Warner Oland). William Demarest co-stars as a rival detective. **HF4, ST77**

Charlie Chan at the Wax Museum (1940, B&W, 64m, NR)
An escaped killer vows vengeance against the wily detective (Sidney Toler) who put him behind bars. **HF4**

Charlie Chan in Paris (1935, B&W, 72m, NR)
On the trail of forged bank bonds, Chan (Warner Oland) is soon caught up in a murder investigation in the City of Light. **HF4**

Charlie Chan in Rio (1941, B&W, 62m, NR)
A suspected murderess is herself found dead, and Chan (Sidney Toler) sets out to find the real killer. **HF4**

Charlie Chan's Secret (1936, B&W, 72m, NR)
A seance turns deadly, and Chan (Warner Oland) must divine the killer's identity. **HF4**

Charlie Chaplin Carnival (1916, B&W, 80m, NR)
This collection of silent comedy classics includes *The Vagabond, The Fireman, The Count,* and *One A.M.* **DT18** *Recommended*

Charlie Chaplin Cavalcade (1916, B&W, 81m, NR)
Includes these silent shorts: *One A.M., The Pawnshop, The Floorwalker,* and *The Rink*. **DT18** *Essential; Recommended*

Charlie Chaplin Festival (1917, B&W, 80m, NR)
More Chaplin classics: *The Cure, The Adventurer, The Immigrant,* and *Easy Street*. **DT18** *Recommended*

Charlie Chaplin—The Early Years, Volumes I-IV (1916-1917, B&W, approx. 60m each, NR)
Gems from Chaplin's first years in Hollywood. Volume I includes *The Immigrant* and *Easy Street*. Volume II features *The Pawnshop* and *One A.M.* Volume III has *The Cure* and *The Vagabond*. Volume IV: *The Rink* and *The Fireman*. **DT18** *Recommended*

Charlie Chaplin's Keystone Comedies (1914, B&W, 59m, NR)
Six one-reelers that helped to introduce Chaplin to the world: *Making a Living* (Chaplin as a villain), *Kid's Auto Races, A Busy Day, Mabel's Married Life, Laughing Gas,* and *The New Janitor.* **DT18** *Recommended*

Charlie, the Lonesome Cougar (1968, C, 75m, G)
Disney's animal adventure-comedy stars a likable cougar who befriends a rugged logger. **FA5**

Charlotte's Web (1972, C, 94m, G)
E.B. White's famous story of Wilbur the pig and his friendship with Charlotte the spider is transformed into an animated musical. **FA10**

Charly (1968, C, 103m, NR)
Through a scientific experiment, a retarded man is given powers of superintelligence. Oscar winner Cliff Robertson and Claire Bloom star. Based on Daniel Keyes' story, "Flowers for Algernon." **DR19, XT2**

Chase, The (1946, B&W, 86m, NR)
The chauffeur for a crooked Miami businessman decides to help his employer's unhappy wife escape to Cuba. Robert Cummings, Michele Morgan, and Steve Cochran star. **MY1**

Chase, The (1966, C, 135m, NR)
Delirious melodrama, with super cast, about a small Texas town awaiting the return of a notorious escaped convict. Marlon Brando, Robert Redford, Jane Fonda, Robert Duvall, Angie Dickinson, E.G. Marshall, James Fox, and Janice Rule star, with Jocelyn Brando, Paul Williams, and Martha Hyer. Written by Lillian Hellman; directed by Arthur Penn. **CU17, DR26, DT78, ST10, ST38, ST45, ST126, XT8** *Recommended*

Chato's Land (1972, C, 110m, R)
Charles Bronson plays an Indian accused of murdering a U.S. marshal. With Jack Palance, Richard Basehart, and Jill Ireland. **ST12, WE7**

Chattahoochee (1990, C, 103m, R)
True story of a Korean war veteran (Gary Oldman) confined, after a shooting spree, to a hellhole of a prison. With Dennis Hopper, Frances McDormand, Pamela Reed, M. Emmet Walsh, and Ned Beatty. **DR6, DR18, ST71**

Cheap Detective, The (1978, C, 92m, PG)
Peter Falk stars in this Neil Simon spoof of Humphrey Bogart's detective movies. With Ann-Margret, Eileen Brennan, Sid Caesar, Madeline Kahn, and Marsha Mason. **CO7, CO10, WR23**

Cheech & Chong's Next Movie (1980, 95m, R)
The second set of adventures featuring that stoned L.A. comedy team. **ST18**

Cheech & Chong's The Corsican Brothers (1984, C, 90m, R)
C&C play three roles each in this broad spoof of the swashbuckler adventures. Among the supporting cast: Rae Dawn and Robbi Chong (Tommy's kids) and Rikki Marin (Cheech's wife). **ST18, XT8**

Cheetah (1989, C, 84m, G)
American teens (Lucy Deakins, Keith Coogan) adopt an orphaned cheetah cub in Africa, then try to teach it to adapt to the wild. Disney drama shot on location. **FA1, FA5**

Cherry 2000 (1988, C, 93m, PG-13)
Futuristic adventure saga with Melanie Griffith as a kind of bounty hunter guiding a male companion (David Andrews) in search of a female robot. With Ben Johnson and Harry Carey, Jr. **SF8, ST58**

Chevre, La (1986, C, 91m, NR)
French comedy starring Pierre Richard and Gerard Depardieu as a pair of inept detectives on the trail of a kidnapped businessman's daughter. Also known as *The Goat*. **FF1, ST31**

Cheyenne Autumn (1964, C, 154m, NR)
Director John Ford's last western tells the epic story of the Cheyenne tribe's relocation by the U.S. government. Richard Widmark stars, with Carroll Baker, Ed-

ward G. Robinson, Karl Malden, and Dolores Del Rio. A Dodge City sequence featuring James Stewart as Wyatt Earp and Arthur Kennedy as Doc Holliday was restored to the home video edition. **CU10, DT36, HF9, HF13, ST109, ST143, WE1, WE7**

Cheyenne Social Club, The (1970, C, 103m, PG)
Comic western has James Stewart inheriting a house of ill repute, running it with the help of Henry Fonda. Directed by Gene Kelly. **ST44, ST81, ST143, WE14**

Chicken Ranch (1983, C, 84m, NR)
Documentary on Nevada's notorious—and legal—house of prostitution. Directed by Nicholas Broomfield and Sandl Sissel. **CU16**

Chiefs (1983, C, 200m, NR)
A murder in a small Southern town goes unsolved from 1924 to 1962, until the town's first black chief takes a personal interest in the case. Charlton Heston, Billy Dee Williams, Brad Davis, and Keith Carradine star in this epic drama. Originally made for TV. **DR16, DR26, ST159**

Chien Andalou, Un (1928, B&W, 20m, NR)
Surrealistic film, directed by Luis Buñuel and Salvador Dali, is a series of memorable images. A preview of things to come from both artists. **DT15** *Essential; Recommended*

Child Is Waiting, A (1963, B&W, 102m, NR)
Burt Lancaster and Judy Garland star in this drama of teachers trying to help retarded children. With Gena Rowlands; directed by John Cassavetes. **DR9, ST51, ST85**

Child of Glass (1978, C, 93m, NR)
Disney drama of a boy who discovers a ghost in his parents' New Orleans home; together they solve a mystery. Originally made for TV. **FA1**

Children of a Lesser God (1986, C, 119m, R)
A teacher at a school for the deaf and one of his most difficult pupils embark on a tempestuous affair. William Hurt and Oscar winner Marlee Matlin star, with Piper Laurie. Based on Mark Medoff's play. **DR1, DR20, ST75, XT3**

Children of the Corn (1984, C, 93m, R)
A Stephen King short story is the basis for this tale of a young couple passing through a small Midwestern town, discovering that the children are murderers. Linda Hamilton and Peter Horton star. **HO13, WR12**

Children Shouldn't Play With Dead Things (1973, C, 91m, PG)
An acting company goes to a burial island to shoot a movie. When the director tries to raise the dead to use in his film, he succeeds too well. **HO6**

Children's Songs and Stories With the Muppets (1985, C, 56m, NR)
The Muppets are joined by guest stars Julie Andrews, Judy Collins, John Denver, Brooke Shields, and Twiggy. **FA14**

Child's Play (1988, C, 87m, R)
An innocent-looking toy doll is possessed by the soul of a mass killer, who continues his crime spree. Chris Sarandon, Catherine Hicks, and Alex Vincent star. **HO8, HO16**

Chilly Scenes of Winter (1979, C, 96m, PG)
A determined young man tries to win back his former sweetheart in this adaptation of Ann Beattie's novel. John Heard and Mary Beth Hurt star, with Peter Riegert, Kenneth McMillan, and Gloria Grahame. Also known as *Head Over Heels*. **DR1, DR19**

China Gate (1957, B&W, 95m, NR)
In one of the first films to deal with the Vietnam War, French soldiers attack a communist outpost. Gene Barry, Angie Dickinson, and Nat King Cole star. Samuel Fuller directed. **AC4, DT40, MU12**

China Girl (1987, C, 90m, R)
Gang warfare breaks out between hot-headed youths in the adjoining New York neighborhoods of Chinatown and Little Italy. An interracial couple is caught in the crossfire. Directed by Abel Ferrara. **AC8, XT9**

China Is Near (1967, B&W, 110m, NR)
Italian drama from director Marco Bellochio, who depicts a man in political and

sexual turmoil. Glauco Mauri and Elda Tattoli star. **FF2**

China Seas (1935, B&W, 90m, NR)
Clark Gable takes to the high seas as the captain of a shipping vessel bound for the Orient, with pirates and a deadly typhoon to contend with. **AC12, ST49**

China Sky (1945, B&W, 78m, NR)
Randolph Scott plays a doctor who joins the Chinese to fight the Japanese in World War II. Based on a story by Pearl Buck. **AC1, ST136**

China Syndrome, The (1979, C, 123m, PG)
A TV news reporter and her cameraman learn that officials at a nuclear power plant are covering up certain details of an accident. Jane Fonda, Michael Douglas, and Jack Lemmon star. **DR7, ST35, ST45, ST90** *Essential; Recommended*

Chinatown (1974, C, 131m, R)
Director Roman Polanski's tale of love and mystery in Depression-era Los Angeles. A moody, hard-boiled detective, (Jack Nicholson) is hired to find the missing husband of a shady lady (Faye Dunaway). John Huston costars. Written by Robert Towne. **DT50, DT79, MY2, MY10, ST37, ST112, XT10** *Essential; Highly Recommended*

Chinese Connection, The (1980, C, 107m, R)
Bruce Lee martial arts saga of young man avenging the death of his instructor. **ST88**

Chino (1976, C, 98m, PG)
Western drama starring Charles Bronson as a half-breed whose ranch is under attack from prejudiced locals. **ST12**

Chipmunk Adventure, The (1987, C, 76m, G)
Alvin, Simon, and Theodore take to the skies in this full-length animated feature. **FA10**

Chisum (1970, C, 111m, G)
A cattle baron (John Wayne) wages war on local political corruption. **ST156**

Chitty Chitty Bang Bang (1968, C, 142m, G)
Dick Van Dyke portrays an eccentric inventor whose wild imagination takes him, his two children, and a beautiful woman

named Truly Scrumptious (Sally Ann Howes) into a mystical world—all in a magical car. Family musical fun. **FA9**

Chloe in the Afternoon (1972, C, 97m, NR)
Eric Rohmer directed this French comedy of a married man's obsession with a store clerk. Bernard Valery and Zouzou star. **DT89**

Chocolat (1989, C, 105m, PG-13)
A woman recalls his girlhood in French Cameroon in this drama set in the 1950s. Cecile Ducasse and Isaach de Bankole star; Claire Denis directed. **FF1**

Chocolate War, The (1988, C, 103m, R)
At a Catholic boys' school, a freshman defies both the stern principal and a secret student society known as The Vigils. Ilan Mitchell-Smith, John Glover, and Wally Ward star in this drama based on Robert Cormier's novel. **DR9, DR25** *Recommended*

Choice of Arms (1983, C, 114m, NR)
Yves Montand and Gerard Depardieu are the antagonists in this French drama of a retired mobster and a young punk who threatens him and his wife (Catherine Deneuve). **FF1, ST29, ST31**

Choice of Weapons, A (1976, C, 88m, NR)
A man's investigation into the death of his father leads him to a society of modern-day knights. David Birney, Barbara Hershey, Donald Pleasance and Peter Cushing star. Also known as *Dirty Knight's Work*. **ST27**

Choirboys, The (1977, C, 119m, R)
Joseph Wambaugh's comic novel of a profane and rowdy group of Los Angeles cops, adapted for the screen by director Robert Aldrich. Among the cast: Charles Durning, Louis Gossett, Jr., Perry King, Tim McIntire, Randy Quaid, and James Woods. **CO10, ST165**

Choke Canyon (1986, C, 95m, PG)
Scientist attempts to keep ruthless conglomerate out of protected wilderness area. Plenty of high-flying aerial action. Bo Svenson and Stephen Collins star. **AC11**

Choose Me (1984, C, 106m, R)
Romantic drama set largely in a big-city bar run by a loveless woman (Lesley Ann

Warren). She's is attracted to a smooth-talking newcomer (Keith Carradine); he's attracted to a radio talk show host (Genevieve Bujold). Alan Rudolph directed. **DR1, DT91**

Chopping Mall (1986, C, 76m, R)
Horror story of shopping mall's automated security robots going haywire, with quartet of shoppers trapped inside after hours. Russell Todd and Barbara Crampton star, with Paul Bartel. **DT5, HO22**

Chorus Line, A (1985, C, 118m, PG-13)
Film version of Broadway's long-running musical, the backstage tale of a group of dancers auditioning for a show that may give them their first break. Michael Douglas stars, with Alyson Reed, Audrey Landers, Janet Jones, and Nicole Fosse. Directed by Richard Attenborough. **MU2, MU3, MU4, ST35**

Chosen, The (1981, C, 108m, G)
In 1940s Brooklyn, two Jewish boys, one Hassidic, the other Americanized, strike up a wary friendship. Robby Benson and Barry Miller star, with Rod Steiger and Maximillian Schell. **DR15**

Christ Stopped at Eboli (1979, C, 120m, NR)
Italian drama of an anti-Fascist writer living in exile at a small village during the 1930s. Gian Maria Volonte stars. Francesco Rosi directed. **FF2**

Christian the Lion (1976, C, 89m, G)
Family drama of a lion raised in the London Zoo, then returned to the wild. Bill Travers and Virginia McKenna (the stars of *Born Free*) star, with George Adamson (whom Travers portrayed in *Born Free*). **FA5**

Christiane F. (1981, C, 124m, R)
A teenager enters Berlin's seamy underworld of prostitution and drug addiction in this disturbing German drama based on true events. Nadja Brunkhorst stars; David Bowie concert appearance is included. **FF3**

Christine (1983, C, 111m, R)
A 1958 Plymouth Fury turns into a killing machine in this adaptation of the Stephen King novel, directed by John Carpenter. Keith Gordon stars, with Alexandra Paul

and Harry Dean Stanton. **DT17, HO22, ST141, WR12**

Christmas Carol, A (1951, B&W, 86m, NR)
Charles Dickens' classic story of the nasty, stingy Scrooge; he learns a few of life's lessons through the help of the ghost of his late partner, Marley, and the ghosts of Christmas Past, Present, and Future. Alistair Sim stars. **FA13, WR4**

Christmas in Connecticut (1945, B&W, 101m, NR)
Barbara Stanwyck stars in this comedy about a recipe author who's really at a loss in the kitchen, and her attempts to host a lonely sailor with no place to go for the holidays. Dennis Morgan and Sydney Greenstreet costar. **FA13, ST142**

Christmas in July (1940, B&W, 67m, NR)
Preston Sturges wrote and directed this comedy of a man who mistakenly thinks he has won the grand prize in a contest. Dick Powell stars, with Ellen Drew, William Demarest, and Franklin Pangborn. **DT103**

Christmas Lilies of the Field (1984, C, 98m, NR)
Billy Dee Williams takes on the Sidney Poitier role in this holiday-themed follow-up to the story of a black handyman and a group of German nuns in the Arizona desert. With Maria Schell; originally made for TV. **FA13, ST159**

Christmas Story, A (1983, C, 98m, PG)
Nostalgic holiday story, set in the Midwest of the early 1950s, about a boy whose only wish is to have a Red Ryder BB gun for Christmas. Peter Billingsley stars, with Darren McGavin and Melinda Dillon. Written and narrated by Jean Shepherd. **CO6, FA6, FA13** *Recommended*

Christmas To Remember, A (1978, C, 100m, NR)
During the Depression, an elderly farm couple is visited by their grandson for the holidays. Jason Robards, Eva Marie Saint, and Joanne Woodward star. Originally made for TV. **FA13, ST129, ST166**

Christmas Tree, The (1969, C, 110m, G)
Sentimental tale of a wealthy man's reconciliation with his dying young son. Wil-

liam Holden stars. Also known as *When Wolves Cry*. **FA13, ST68**

Christopher Strong (1933, B&W, 77m, NR)
A female aviator (Katharine Hepburn) goes into a tailspin over a married man (Colin Clive). **CL5, ST66**

Chuck Berry: Hail! Hail! Rock 'n' Roll (1987, C, 120m, PG)
Documentary about one of rock's Founding Fathers intersperses interview material with footage from a historic concert in Berry's hometown, St. Louis. Performers include Keith Richards, Eric Clapton, Linda Ronstadt, Etta James, and Robert Cray; interviewees include Bruce Springsteen, Little Richard, Bo Diddley, the Everly Brothers, and Jerry Lee Lewis. **MU11** *Highly Recommended*

Chump at Oxford, A (1940, B&W, 63m, NR)
Laurel and Hardy matriculate at England's most prestigious university. **ST87**

Cimarron (1931, B&W, 124m, NR)
Oscar-winning western epic of a family settling the frontier, based on Edna Ferber's novel. Richard Dix stars, with Irene Dunne and Estelle Taylor. **WE1, XT1**

Cincinnati Kid, The (1965, C, 113m, NR)
Steve McQueen stars as a poker-playing ace who challenges rich Edward G. Robinson to a high-stakes game. With Ann-Margret, Tuesday Weld, Rip Torn, Karl Malden, and Joan Blondell. Directed by Norman Jewison. **DT51, ST97, ST130, ST150**

Cinderella (1950, C, 75m, G)
Disney's full-length animated fairy tale finds a beautiful maiden dominated by an evil stepmother and ugly stepsisters until her fairy godmother and Prince Charming come to her rescue. **FA2** *Recommended*

Cinderella (1964, C, 77m, NR)
Musical version of the famed fairy tale, with Lesley Ann Warren, Ginger Rogers, Celeste Holm, and Walter Pidgeon, plus a Rodgers and Hammerstein score. Originally made for TV. **FA9, MU8, ST131**

Cinderella (1984, C, 60m, NR)
Jennifer Beals is the over-worked, under-loved maiden, Matthew Broderick is the charming prince, Jean Stapleton plays her

fairy godmother, and Eve Arden is the wicked stepmother in this Faerie Tale Theatre presentation. **FA12**

Cinderfella (1960, C, 91m, NR)
Jerry Lewis spoofs the famed fairy tale as an orphaned boy who has to cook and clean for his evil step*brothers*. **FA6, ST91**

Cinema Paradiso (1988, C, 123m, NR)
Oscar-winning drama from Italy, set in a Sicilian village, where a young boy befriends the projectionist at the local theater. Filled with clips from classic Italian and American films of the 1930s and 1940s. Philippe Noiret stars, with Salvatore Cascio and Jacques Perris. Written and directed by Giuseppe Tornatore. **FF2, XT7** *Recommended*

Circle of Iron (1979, C, 102m, R)
Martial arts combines with fantasy in this tale of an American searching for perfect peace and Zen awareness. David Carradine, Jeff Cooper, Roddy McDowall, and Christopher Lee star. Based on an idea by James Coburn and Bruce Lee. **AC26, ST89**

Circle of Two (1980, C, 105m, PG)
Richard Burton plays an artist who develops a special friendship with a young model (Tatum O'Neal). **ST13**

Circus, The (1928, B&W, 72m, NR)
Charlie Chaplin classic silent comedy finds him charmed by the circus owner's stepdaughter. Also available on a tape which includes Chaplin's 33-minute short, *A Day's Pleasure*, about a family's mishaps during a day set aside for fun and games. **CL11, DT18** *Essential; Recommended*

Circus of Horrors (1960, C, 89m, NR)
A plastic surgeon and his nurse hide out in an unusual circus to escape a patient they once disfigured. Donald Pleasence stars. **HO20, HO26**

Circus World (1964, C, 135m, NR)
After a fifteen-year absence, a circus owner attempts to locate his ex-lover, who's also the mother of the child he's raised. John Wayne and Rita Hayworth star. **ST64, ST156**

Citadel, The (1938, B&W, 112m, NR)
Robert Donat plays a doctor who compromises his ideals for a life of luxury in

this version of the A.J. Cronin novel. With Rosalind Russell, Ralph Richardson, and Rex Harrison. Directed by King Vidor. **DT107**

Citizen Kane (1941, B&W, 120m, NR)
The story of publishing tycoon Charles Foster Kane marks the stunning Hollywood debut of Orson Welles, who stars and also co-wrote, directed, and produced. Joseph Cotten, Agnes Moorehead, Everett Sloane, Dorothy Commingore, and Ruth Warrick are among the supporting players. **CL2, DR24, DT112, XT21** *Essential; Highly Recommended*

Citizens Band (1977, C, 98m, PG)
Comedy focusing on activities of CB enthusiasts in a small town, full of rich characters. Paul LeMat stars, with Candy Clark, Ann Wedgeworth, Marcia Rodd, Charles Napier, and Bruce McGill. Directed by Jonathan Demme. Also known as *Handle With Care*. **CO2, DT28**

City Heat (1984, C, 94m, PG)
Spoof of 1930s gangster films starring Clint Eastwood as a cop and Burt Reynolds as his pal, a private eye. Rip Torn is the villain; Richard Roundtree, Madeline Kahn, Jane Alexander, and Irene Cara head the supporting cast. **CO3, CO7, ST39, ST128, ST150**

City in Fear (1980, C, 150m, NR)
David Janssen plays a reporter on the trail of a psycho killer who's terrorizing a city. Robert Vaughn, Perry King, and Mickey Rourke costar. Originally made for TV. **AC9, MY13, ST134**

City Lights (1931, B&W, 86m, NR)
Charlie Chaplin is the poor tramp whose sudden fortune brings sight to a blind girl in this delightful silent classic. **CL11, DT18** *Essential; Highly Recommended*

City of the Walking Dead (1983, C, 92m, R)
Zombies come to life in search of humans to feast on. Mel Ferrer stars. **HO21**

City of Women (1981, C, 139m, NR)
Federico Fellini fantasy of a man (Marcello Mastroianni) who dreams that he is a prisoner in a town run by females. **DT35, ST103**

City on Fire (1979, C, 101m, R)
Disaster story of a city endangered by a blaze set by an embittered refinery worker. Barry Newman, Henry Fonda, Ava Gardner, Shelley Winters, and Susan Clark star. **AC23, ST44, ST164**

City That Never Sleeps (1953, B&W, 90m, NR)
A Chicago cop (Gig Young) is involved in an affair with a nightclub singer, which leads to blackmail and murder. With Mala Powers, William Talman, and Edward Arnold. **MY1, XT11**

Claire's Knee (1971, C, 103m, PG)
A groom-to-be develops an obsession with the daughter of a friend, or more specifically, the knee of a daughter of a friend. Comedy from French director Eric Rohmer. **DT89**

Clambake (1967, C, 97m, NR)
Elvis Presley musical, with El as a rich boy who wants to be treated just like everyone else. Set in Miami; Shelley Fabares costars. **ST123**

Clan of the Cave Bear (1985, C, 100m, R)
Prehistoric adventure saga, based on Jean M. Auel novel, starring Daryl Hannah, Pamela Reed, and James Remar. Directed by Michael Chapman. **AC12**

Clara's Heart (1988, C, 108m, PG-13)
A Jamaican housekeeper brings a young boy out of his emotional shell in this sentimental drama starring Whoopi Goldberg. Neil Patrick Harris, Kathleen Quinlan, and Michael Ontkean costar. **DR2, DR8**

Clash by Night (1952, B&W, 105m, NR)
Barbara Stanwyck plays a restless woman who finally settles down with a fisherman (Paul Douglas), but she's hooked on her husband's best friend (Robert Ryan). Marilyn Monroe has a small part. Fritz Lang directed. **DT58, ST108, ST142**

Clash of the Titans (1981, C, 118m, PG)
Fantasy adventure retells ancient Greek mythology with the help of contemporary special effects by Ray Harryhausen. Laurence Olivier stars as Zeus, with Harry Hamlin, Maggie Smith, Claire Bloom, Ursula Andress, and Burgess Meredith. **SF13, ST116**

Class of Miss MacMichael, The (1978, C, 99m, R)
Glenda Jackson is the teacher of a class of disadvantaged rebels in this schoolroom drama. Oliver Reed costars. **DR25**

Class of 1984 (1982, C, 93m, R)
Violent melodrama of a lone teacher (Perry King) confronting a vicious gang of "students." Timothy Van Patten leads the truants; watch for Michael J. Fox. **DR25**

Class of 1999 (1990, C, 98m, R)
Futuristic look at high school life which Andy Hardy wouldn't recognize: gangs have taken over schools and a trio of androids are trying to whip (literally) the kids into shape. Bradley Gregg stars, with Traci Lind, Malcolm McDowell, and Stacy Keach. **DR25**

Class of Nuke 'Em High (1986, C, 81m, R)
A New Jersey high school becomes a nuclear waste dump and the students are transformed into obnoxious mutants. **HO21**

Clean and Sober (1988, C, 121m, R)
Abosorbing drama of an investment counselor (Michael Keaton) and his battle against alcohol abuse and drug addiction. With Morgan Freeman, Kathy Baker, and M. Emmet Walsh. **DR7, ST48, ST80** *Recommended*

Clean Slate (1981, C, 128m, NR)
French black comedy, set in colonial Africa, about a police chief who gains revenge on everyone who has mistreated him. Philippe Noiret, Stephane Audran, and Isabelle Huppert star. Bertrand Tavernier directed. Based on Jim Thompson's novel, *Pop. 1280.* French title: *Coup de Torchon.* **FF1, MY16, WR26** *Recommended*

Cleopatra (1934, B&W, 95m, NR)
Claudette Colbert plays the Queen of the Nile in this lavish historical drama directed by Cecil B. DeMille. With Warren William and Henry Wilcoxon. **CL2, DT27**

Cleopatra (1963, C, 243m, G)
The legendary film that made Elizabeth Taylor and Richard Burton the celebrity couple of our time and nearly bankrupted one movie studio. Rex Harrison costars, with Roddy MacDowall and Martin Landau. Joseph L. Mankiewicz directed.

Also available in a 194m. version. **CL2, CL3, CL15, DT68, ST13, ST147** *Essential*

Cleopatra Jones (1973, C, 89m, PG)
Tamara Dobson stars as a secret agent skilled in the martial arts in this adventure saga. Shelley Winters plays her nemesis. **AC26, ST164**

Cleopatra Jones and the Casino of Gold (1975, C, 96m, R)
Second chapter in Cleo saga, with Tamara Dobson squaring off against dragon lady Stella Stevens. **AC26**

Cloak and Dagger (1946, B&W, 106m, NR)
Gary Cooper plays a professor caught up in espionage on his way to Germany. Fritz Lang directed. **DT58, ST22**

Clock, The (1945, B&W, 90m, NR)
Classic romance between soldier on leave in New York and an office worker. Robert Walker and Judy Garland star, with James Gleason and Keenan Wynn. Directed by Vincente Minnelli. **CL4, DT71, ST51**

Clockwise (1986, C, 96m, PG)
A British schoolmaster who prides himself on his punctuality encounters a series of comic disasters on the most important day of his career. John Cleese stars. **CO15**

Clockwork Orange, A (1971, C, 137m, R)
In the ultra-violent future, Alex and his droogs (gang members) lead merry lives of crime until the authorities catch him and subject him to a gruesome form of rehabilitation. Malcolm McDowell stars in director Stanley Kubrick's version of Anthony Burgess's novel. **CU1, CU4, DR19, DT56, SF17** *Essential; Recommended*

Close Encounters of the Third Kind (1977, C, 135m, PG)
Steven Spielberg's science fiction drama of aliens landing in Wyoming, tipping off their arrival ahead of time to certain Earthlings. Richard Dreyfuss and Melinda Dillon star, with François Truffaut. This is the Special Edition, which contains footage added for the film's theatrical rerelease. **FA8, DT99, DT106, SF9, SF16, ST36** *Essential; Recommended*

Closely Watched Trains (1966, B&W, 89m, NR)
Oscar-winning comedy-drama from Czechoslovakia about a young railway worker's first brush with sex. Set during the Nazi occupation. Directed by Jiri Menzel. **FF7, XT7, XT19**

Clouds Over Europe (1939, B&W, 78m, NR)
Laurence Olivier stars with Ralph Richardson in a light-hearted mystery about a test pilot and British inspector assigned to unravel a case of missing bombers. Also known as *Q Planes*. **ST116**

Clowns, The (1971, C, 90m, NR)
Documentary from Federico Fellini about the merry men and women of the circus, with some serious commentary on the human condition as well. **DT53**

Club Paradise (1986, C, 104m, PG-13)
A Chicago fireman moves to a Caribbean island with hopes of opening a swank resort for swingin' singles. Robin Williams stars, with Twiggy, Jimmy Cliff, Peter O'Toole, Andrea Martin, Rick Moranis, and Eugene Levy. Directed by Harold Ramis. **CO14, ST117, ST160**

Clue (1985, C, 96m, PG)
Comic mystery, based on the popular board game, starring Tim Curry, Eileen Brennan, Madeline Kahn, Martin Mull, Michael McKean, Christopher Lloyd, Lesley Ann Warren, and Lee Ving among the suspects. Released theatrically with three different endings; all are featured on the video version. **CO10, MU12, MY17**

Coal Miner's Daughter (1980, C, 125m, PG)
Oscar winner Sissy Spacek stars as country music queen Loretta Lynn in this drama about her roller-coaster life and career. Tommy Lee Jones plays her husband, Beverly D'Angelo is Patsy Cline, Levon Helm is Lynn's father. Both actresses do their own singing. **DR4, MU5, MU12, ST139, XT3** *Recommended*

Cobra (1986, C, 88m, R)
Sylvester Stallone is a take-no-prisoners police detective who's after a gang of vicious killers. Brigitte Nielsen costars. **AC9, ST140**

Coca-Cola Kid, The (1985, C, 94m, R)
Charming, offbeat comedy about a brash American marketing expert sent to the Australian outback to push the title product. Eric Roberts and Greta Scacchi star. Directed by Dusan Makavejev. **CO2, CO12** *Recommended*

Cocaine Cowboys (1979, C, 87m, R)
Andy Warhol produced this comedy about a rock band that doubles as dope smugglers. Jack Palance, Tom Sullivan, and Warhol star. **CU3**

Cocaine Fiends (1937, B&W, 74m, NR)
Serious "message" film from the distant past warning audiences of the consequences of cocaine use (prostitution, suicide) is now regarded a camp "bad" movie. **CU11**

Cockfighter (1974, C, 83m, R)
Warren Oates plays a man who drifts through the rural South, training fighting birds, in this cult film adapted from Charles Willeford's novel. With Harry Dean Stanton, Troy Donahue, and Millie Perkins. Also known as *Born To Kill*. **ST115, ST141**

Cocktail (1988, C, 104m, R)
Tom Cruise stars in this light romantic drama about a young man whose claim to fame in New York is his considerable bartending skills. Bryan Brown plays his mentor, Elisabeth Shue his girlfriend. **DR1, ST26**

Cocoanuts, The (1929, B&W, 96m, NR)
The Marx Brothers' debut film, about phony land sales in Florida, adapted from their Broadway hit. **ST101**

Cocoon (1985, C, 117m, PG-13)
Senior citizens in Florida and aliens disguised as humans collide in this comedy-drama starring Hume Cronyn, Wilford Brimley, Jessica Tandy, Maureen Stapleton, Gwen Verdon, Steve Guttenberg, Brian Dennehy, and Oscar winner Don Ameche. Directed by Ron Howard. **DR11, DT48, SF9, XT4** *Recommended*

Cocoon: The Return (1988, C, 102m, PG)
This sequel to the story of alien visitors and oldsters in Florida reunites virtually the entire cast of the first film for more adventures. **DR11, SF9**

Code Name: Wildgeese (1984, C, 101m,R)
Action in the jungles of Southeast Asia,
as a hand-picked mercenary force lays
siege to a major opium smuggling operation. Lee Van Cleef, Klaus Kinski, and
Ernest Borgnine star. **AC20, ST83, ST155**

Code of Silence (1985, C, 100m, R)
Chicago police detective is shunned by
his colleagues when he turns in a crooked
cop, and is also caught between warring
gangs. Chuck Norris and Henry Silva
star. **AC9, ST114, XT11**

Cold Feet (1989, C, 91m, R)
Loopy, offbeat comedy, set in the contemporary West, of jewel smugglers using
a horse to carry their booty. Keith Carradine, Sally Kirkland, and Tom Waits star,
with Bill Pullman, Rip Torn, and in a
cameo role, Jeff Bridges. Written by Jim
Harrison and Thomas McGuane. **CO10,
CO12, ST11, ST150, XT18**

Cold River (1982, C, 94m, PG)
Family adventure of a brother and sister
stranded in the wilderness when their father suffers a fatal heart attack. Filmed
on location in the Adirondack Mountains;
set in 1932. **FA4**

Cold Room, The (1984, C, 95m, NR)
A German vacation for a father (George
Segal) and his college-age daughter
(Amanda Pays) turns into a series of bizarre incidents when a mysterious man is
found hiding out in her hotel room. Originally made for cable TV. **MY14**

Cold Sweat (1971, C, 94m, PG)
Charles Bronson plays an American expatriate in France who gets involved with
drug dealing. James Mason, Liv Ullmann,
and Jill Ireland costar. **AC8, ST12, ST102,
ST154**

Cold Turkey (1971, C, 99m, PG)
Comedy of small-town minister who tries
to get his entire community to give up
smoking for a huge cash reward. Dick Van
Dyke stars, with Pippa Scott, Tom Pos-
ton, Bob Newhart, and Bob Elliott & Ray
Goulding (Bob & Ray). Directed by Norman Lear; music by Randy Newman.
CO2

Collector, The (1965, C, 119m, NR)
A shy young man (Terence Stamp) wins a
fortune in a football pool and buys an
estate, where he keeps a beautiful girl

(Samantha Eggar) captive in hopes that
she'll fall in love with him. Cult film directed by William Wyler. **CU13, DR3,
DT119, MY3** *Recommended*

College (1927, B&W, 65m, NR)
Buster Keaton goes out for the football
team to impress a sweet coed. **CL11,
CO18, DT54**

Colonel Redl (1985, C, 144m, R)
Klaus Maria Brandauer stars in this Hungarian drama about an army officer's rise
to power in the days before World War I.
Istvan Szabo directed. **FF7**

Color of Money, The (1986, C, 117m, R)
Sequel to *The Hustler*, set 25 years later,
with Paul Newman's Eddie Felson training a hot new young prospect (Tom
Cruise). With Mary Elizabeth Mastrantonio and Helen Shaver. Newman won an
Oscar under Martin Scorsese's direction.
DR22, DT95, ST26, ST111, XT2 *Recommended*

Color Purple, The (1985, C, 152m, PG-13)
Drama of two black sisters and their pain-
ful separation and enduring love for one
another. Whoopi Goldberg stars, with
Danny Glover, Oprah Winfrey, Margaret
Avery, Rae Dawn Chong, and Adolph
Caesar. Steven Spielberg directed; based
on Alice Walker's novel. Available in let-
terboxed format. **CU19, DR8, DR10,
DR14, DR19, DT99, ST55**

Colorado (1940, B&W, 54m, NR)
Roy Rogers and partner Gabby Hayes
saddle up and head out for the wilds of
Colorado. **ST132**

Colors (1988, C, 120m, R)
On the streets of Los Angeles, two police
officers (Robert Duvall, Sean Penn) try to
keep the peace amid warring gangs. Directed by Dennis Hopper; some brief
footage added for video release. **AC9,
CU10, DR15, ST38, ST71, XT10**

Colossus: The Forbin Project (1970, C,
100m, PG)
Science fiction tale of a super-computer
that begins to develop a mind of its own,
overriding all attempts to thwart it. Eric
Braeden and Susan Clark star. Also
known as *The Forbin Project*. **SF6**

Columbo: Prescription Murder (1967, C, 99m, NR)
The disarming sleuth in the rumpled raincoat, Lt. Columbo (Peter Falk), is on the trail of a philandering psychiatrist. Originally made for TV; pilot for the successful series. **MY10**

Coma (1978, C, 113m, PG)
A doctor discovers a horrifying secret when her patients begin to suffer major brain damage after relatively minor surgery. Genevieve Bujold stars, with Michael Douglas and Rip Torn. **HO19, MY11, SF5, ST35, ST150**

Comancheros, The (1961, C, 107m, NR)
A Texas ranger (John Wayne) goes undercover in an attempt to halt the sale of guns and liquor to the Comanches. Lee Marvin costars. **ST100, ST156, WE6**

Come and Get It (1936, B&W, 99m, NR)
Frances Farmer plays dual roles in this drama set in Wisconsin timber country. Edward Arnold and Joel McCrea star as the men in her life; Oscar winner Walter Brennan costars. A cult favorite, mainly for Farmer's amazing performance. Co-directed by Howard Hawks and William Wyler. **CL14, DT43, DT119, XT4** *Recommended*

Come Back to the Five and Dime, Jimmy Dean, Jimmy Dean (1982, C, 110m, NR)
A reunion of women who hung around the set of Dean's last film (*Giant*) in a small Texas town is shaken up by the arrival of a stranger. Cher, Sandy Dennis, and Karen Black star. Robert Altman directed this drama based on Ed Graczyk's play. **DR20, DR26, DT2, ST19**

Come On, Rangers (1938, B&W, 54m, NR)
Roy Rogers and Gabby Hayes demonstrate the cowboy way in this musical western. **ST132**

Comes a Horseman (1978, C, 118m, PG)
A cattle baron plots to rustle up the land in his territory, but there's a feisty woman in his way. James Caan, Jane Fonda, Jason Robards star in this western set in the late 1940s. **ST45, ST129, WE8, WE12** *Recommended*

Comfort and Joy (1984, C, 93m, PG)
Disarmingly charming comedy about a Scottish disc jockey who looks for "meaning" in his life after his girlfriend leaves him; he gets involved in a feud between local ice cream truck companies. Bill Paterson stars. Bill Forsyth directed. **CO17, DT38** *Recommended*

Comic, The (1969, C, 94m, PG)
Drama of a self-destructive silent film clown, played by Dick Van Dyke. With Mickey Rooney and Michele Lee. **DR13, ST133**

Comic Relief 2 (1987, C, 120m, NR)
The second comedians' benefit concert to aid the homeless, hosted by Robin Williams, Billy Crystal, and Whoopi Goldberg. **CO16, ST160**

Comic Relief III (1989, C, 120m, NR)
More stand-up comedy from Billy Crystal, Whoopi Goldberg, Robin Williams, and friends in a benefit concert to aid the homeless. Among the guests: Bobcat Goldthwait, Arsenio Hall, Shelley Long, Garry Shandling, and Steven Wright. **CO16, ST160**

Coming Home (1978, C, 127m, R)
In the late 1960s, a crippled Vietnam vet, now opposed to the war, has an affair with the wife of a gung-ho Marine. Oscar winners Jon Voight and Jane Fonda star, with Bruce Dern, Penelope Milford, and Robert Carradine. **DR3, DR7, ST45, XT2, XT3** *Essential*

Coming to America (1988, C, 116m, R)
Eddie Murphy comedy about an African prince who decides to look for a bride in the land of the brave and the home of the free—namely, Queens, New York. Arsenio Hall heads the supporting cast; he and Murphy play several character parts in disguises. With James Earl Jones, Madge Sinclair, John Amos, and Shari Headley. **CO13, CO20, ST76, XT9**

Commando (1985, C, 90m, R)
Former fighting man (Arnold Schwarzenegger) swings into action when nasties kidnap his daughter. A one-man army movie if ever there was one. Rae Dawn Chong costars. **AC25, ST135**

Commandos Strike at Dawn (1942, B&W, 96m, NR)
A Norwegian comes to the aid of British soldiers when Nazis invade his homeland. Paul Muni stars, with Anna Lee and Lillian Gish. **ST54**

Commissar, The (1967, B&W, 105m, NR)
Soviet drama, long banned in its native land, about the oppression of Jewish villagers by a female bureaucrat. **CU8, FF7**

Communion (1989, C, 103m, R)
Novelist Whitley Striebler's nonfiction account of an encounter he had with alien visitors. Christopher Walken stars as the author; Lindsay Crouse plays his wife. **SF9**

Company of Wolves, The (1984, C, 95m, R)
Fantasy about a granny (Angela Lansbury) who tells various werewolf stories to her granddaughter (Sarah Patterson), which culminate in an erotic twist on the Little Red Riding Hood fairy tale. **HO4, HO17**

Comperes, Les (1985, C, 109m, PG)
A French comedy about two bachelors with an ex-lover in common whose missing child may be one of theirs. Gerard Depardieu and Pierre Richard star. **FF1, ST31**

Competition, The (1980, C, 129m, PG)
Richard Dreyfuss and Amy Irving play rival pianists at a classical contest who fall in love. **DR12, ST36**

Compleat Beatles, The (1982, C, 120m, NR)
Documentary portrait of the four lads from Liverpool, packed with familiar and rare footage of their performances and fans. Narrated by Malcolm McDowell. **MU11** *Recommended*

Compromising Positions (1985, C, 99m, R)
Long Island housewife turns sleuth when her lecherous dentist is murdered. A suspense comedy starring Susan Sarandon, with Raul Julia, Judith Ivey, and Mary Beth Hurt. **CO10, MY11**

Computer Wore Tennis Shoes, The (1970, C, 91m, G)
Disney comedy with Kurt Russell as a college student who accidentally gets zapped by a computer and then has gangsters, gamblers, and college deans fighting for his knowledge. **CO18, FA1**

Conan the Barbarian (1982, C, 115m, R)
Arnold Schwarzenegger plays Robert Howard's pulp hero in this tale of his origins and battle against Thulsa Doom

(James Earl Jones). With Max von Sydow and Sandahl Bergman. John Milius directed. **AC17, AC18, ST76, ST135**

Conan the Destroyer (1984, C, 101m, PG)
Arnold Schwarzenegger returns for more sword-wielding action. Grace Jones and Wilt Chamberlain costar. **AC17, AC18, MU12, ST135**

Concert for Bangladesh, The (1972, C, 90m, G)
Documentary of 1971 rock concert in Madison Square Garden to benefit victims of famine in Asia. George Harrison (who organized) performs, along with Bob Dylan, Leon Russell, and Ringo Starr. **MU10** *Recommended*

Concorde, The—Airport '79 (1979, C, 123m, PG)
Fourth *Airport* adventure has more midair disasters with an entirely new lineup of stars, featuring Robert Wagner, Alain Delon, Susan Blakely, Sylvia Kristel, John Davidson, and Martha Raye. **AC23**

Condorman (1981, C, 90m, PG)
A cartoonist is transformed into a super hero to help a lovely Russian spy to defect. Michael Crawford, Oliver Reed, and Barbara Carrera star. Produced by the Disney studios in Britain. **AC17, FA1**

Confidentally Yours (1983, B&W, 110m, PG)
A French comedy-mystery about a wrong man framed for murder, while his devoted secretary (Fanny Ardant) tries to prove his innocence. Director François Truffaut's last film. Based on Charles Williams' *The Long Saturday Night*. **DT106, MY16**

Conformist, The (1971, C, 115m, R)
In the 1930s, an Italian fascist is ordered to murder his former professor. Chilling, atmospheric drama from director Bernardo Bertolucci. Jean-Louis Trintignant, Dominique Sanda, and Stefania Sandrelli star. **DT9** *Essential; Recommended*

Connecticut Yankee in King Arthur's Court, A (1949, C, 107m, NR)
Bing Crosby plays Mark Twain's resourceful hero in this musical version of the time-travel tale. With Rhonda Fleming, William Bendix, and Cedric Hardwicke. **FA3, FA9, MU8, SF4, ST25, WR27**

Conqueror, The (1956, C, 111m, NR)
John Wayne portrays the mighty warlord Genghis Khan in this adventure drama which has acquired a cult following for its unintentionally hilarious moments. With Susan Hayward, Pedro Armendariz, Agnes Moorehead, and Lee Van Cleef. **AC16, CU2, ST155, ST156**

Conqueror Worm (1968, C, 98m, NR)
Horror tale set in Cromwell's England, about a lustful witchfinder (Vincent Price). Cult horror film directed by Michael Reeves. Edgar Allan Poe's title poem is quoted, but the story is unrelated. **CU4, HO26, ST124**

Conquest of the Planet of the Apes (1972, C, 87m, PG)
Fourth in the *Apes* series is a flashback story to the origin of the famed planet, and how the apes took control. Roddy McDowall stars. **FA8, SF8, SF13, SF23**

Conrack (1974, C, 107m, PG)
True story of Pat Conroy, an idealistic young Southerner who tries to give a good education to poor black children living in rural Georgia. Jon Voight stars, with Paul Winfield, Hume Cronyn, and Madge Sinclair. Directed by Martin Ritt. **DR6, DR25, DT87, ST162**

Consolation Marriage (1931, B&W, 82m, NR)
Drama of a couple who marry when their respective lovers desert them. Years later, they face a tough decision when their ex-lovers return. Pat O'Brien and Irene Dunne star, with John Halliday and Myrna Loy. **ST94**

Consuming Passions (1988, C, 98m, R)
Dark British comedy of a candy firm which discovers success with its new flavor—created when several workers accidentally fall into a vat of chocolate. Based on a play by Monty Python's Michael Palin and Terry Jones. Vanessa Redgrave and Jonathan Pryce star. **CO12, CO17, ST127**

Contempt (1963, C, 103m, NR)
Director Jean-Luc Godard's wry comedy about modern filmmaking, with respectable writer selling out to write a potboiler version of *The Odyssey*. Jack Palance stars, with Brigitte Bardot, Michel Piccoli, and Fritz Lang as himself. **DT41, DT58, ST4** *Essential; Recommended*

Continental Divide (1981, C, 103m, PG)
A Chicago reporter and a Colorado ornithologist manage to find love on a disastrous hiking expedition in the Rockies. John Belushi and Blair Brown star. **CO1, CO13, XT11**

Control (1987, C, 83m, NR)
Fifteen people volunteer to be confined to a fallout shelter in an experiment. They're trapped when a real nuclear emergency occurs. Burt Lancaster stars, with Kate Nelligan and Ben Gazzara. **ST85**

Conversation, The (1974, C, 113m, PG)
Gene Hackman plays a professional surveillance man who thinks he's heard a couple plotting a murder. With John Cazale, Robert Duvall, Harrison Ford, Cindy Williams and Frederic Forrest. Brilliantly directed by Francis Ford Coppola on location in San Francisco. **DR7, DT21, MY11, ST38, ST46, ST61, XT13** *Essential; Highly Recommended*

Conversation Piece (1976, C, 112m, R)
A middle-aged professor becomes involved with a woman, her wild children, and her young lover. Burt Lancaster, Silvana Mangano, and Helmut Berger star. Directed by Luchino Visconti. **DT108, ST85**

Convoy (1978, C, 110m, R)
A big rig driver (Kris Kristofferson), accompanied by his good buddies of the road, form the world's longest truck escort. Directed by Sam Peckinpah. **AC10, DT77, MU12, XT18**

Coogan's Bluff (1968, C, 100m, R)
A modern-day sheriff pursues his quarry from the West to the streets of New York. Clint Eastwood stars, with Don Stroud and Susan Clark. Directed by Don Siegel. **AC9, DT97, ST39, WE12, XT9** *Recommended*

Cook, the Thief, His Wife and Her Lover, The (1990, C, 126m, NR)
Controversial British drama from director Peter Greenaway, set in and around a swanky French restuarant. Exceptionally violent, sexually explicit; perhaps the ultimate Love It or Hate It film. The title roles are played by Richard Bohringer, Michael Gambon, Helen Mirren, and Alan Howard. Widescreen photography

can only be appreciated in letterboxed version. Also available in a "R"-rated version; r.t.: 98m. **CU6, CU7, CU19, DR1, DR23** *Recommended*

Cookie (1989, C, 93m, R)
Comedy of mobster released from prison, reuniting with his street-smart daughter. Peter Falk and Emily Lloyd star, with Dianne Wiest, Brenda Vacarro, Michael V. Gazzo, and Jerry Lewis. Directed by Susan Seidelman. **CO5, CO10, ST91**

Cool and the Crazy, The (1958, B&W, 78m, NR)
1950s version of *Reefer Madness*, with high school kids "turned on" to marijuana, suffering dire consequences. **CU2**

Cool Hand Luke (1967, C, 126m, NR)
A rebellious prisoner on a Southern chain gang becomes a folk hero to his fellow cons. Paul Newman stars, with Oscar winner George Kennedy, Strother Martin, Harry Dean Stanton, Wayne Rogers, Clifton James, Joe Don Baker, Ralph Waite, Dennis Hopper, J.D. Cannon, and Jo Van Fleet. **DR18, ST71, ST111, ST141** *Highly Recommended*

Cop (1987, C, 110m, R)
James Woods plays a policeman at the breaking point in this intense drama, costarring Lesley Ann Warren, Charles Durning, and Charles Haid. **DR16, ST165**

Copacabana (1947, B&W, 92m, NR)
Comedy about the mix-ups that occur at a famous New York nightclub when a girl applies for two different jobs. Groucho Marx and Carmen Miranda costar (their only film together), with Abel Green and Earl Wilson. **ST101**

Corn Is Green, The (1945, B&W, 114m, NR)
Bette Davis plays a middle-aged teacher who devotes much of her time and attention to one of her star pupils. **DR25, ST28**

Cornbread, Earl and Me (1975, C, 95m, R)
A black youth's idolization of a neighborhood basketball star is shattered when the older boy is accidentally shot by a policeman. Moses Gunn, Bernie Casey, Rosalind Cash, and Keith (Jamal) Wilkes star. **DR14, DR15**

Cornered (1945, B&W, 102m, NR)
Thriller staring Dick Powell, who's on a manhunt in Buenos Aires chasing his wife's killer. Directed by Edward Dmytryk. **MY1, MY6**

Coroner Creek (1948, C, 93m, NR)
Randolph Scott western has him seeking revenge for the murder of his fiancée. **ST136, WE5**

Corpse Vanishes, The (1942, B&W, 64m, NR)
A scientist kidnaps young women to use in his rejuvenation serum for his elderly wife. Bela Lugosi stars. **ST95**

Corridors of Blood (1958, B&W, 86m, NR)
A 19th-century doctor experiments with a way to anesthetize patients, becomes addicted to one of the drugs he tries, and resorts to robbing graves to maintain his experiments. Boris Karloff stars, with Christopher Lee. **ST77, ST89**

Corrupt (1983, C, 99m, PG)
A New York cop (Harvey Keitel) finds himself immersed in illegal activities in order to catch a killer. Rock singer John Lydon costars, with Nicole Garcia and Sylvia Sidney. **MU12**

Corsican Brothers, The (1941, B&W, 112m, NR)
Classic swashbuckler, based on the Dumas tale of separated twins. Douglas Fairbanks, Jr. stars. **CL13**

Cotter (1973, C, 94m, NR)
An Indian rodeo clown returns to his small town to pick the pieces of his life after a tragic accident. Don Murray stars, with Rip Torn, Carol Lynley, and Sherry Jackson. **ST150, WE12**

Cotton Club, The (1984, C, 124m, R)
Colorful tale of Harlem's famed night spot, where gangsters and movie stars mingled to watch the likes of Duke Ellington and Cab Calloway perform. Richard Gere, Diane Lane, Gregory Hines, Bob Hoskins, Fred Gwynne, and James Remar head the cast. Directed by Francis Ford Coppola. **AC22, DR5, DR14, DR15, DT21, ST52, ST72**

Couch Trip, The (1988, C, 98m, R)
Dan Aykroyd stars in this comedy about an escaped mental patient who takes over the radio call-in show of a vacationing

therapist. Charles Grodin, Walter Matthau, and Donna Dixon costar. **CO13, ST59, ST104**

Count Dracula (1970, C, 98m, R)
Christopher Lee plays the vampire with an eye for ladies' necks. Klaus Kinski costars. **HF7, HO5, ST83, ST89**

Count Yorga, Vampire (1970, 90m, PG)
A vampire in modern Los Angeles holds seances as a way of attracting women into his lair. Robert Quarry stars. **HO5**

Countdown (1968, C, 101m, NR)
Drama centering on the approaching launch of a manned satellite, starring Robert Duvall and James Caan. Directed by Robert Altman. **DT2, ST38**

Country (1984, C, 109m, PG)
An embattled farm couple struggle to hold on to their land against overwhelming economic pressures. Jessica Lange and Sam Shepard star. **DR7, DR8, ST86**

Country Girl, The (1954, B&W, 104m, NR)
Drama of aging alcoholic singer trying for a comeback. Bing Crosby and Oscar winner Grace Kelly star; William Holden plays a director with a professional interest in Crosby and personal one in Grace. **CL7, ST25, ST68, ST82, XT3**

Country Girl, The (1982, C, 137m, NR)
Remake of the 1954 drama of an aging alcoholic actor (Dick Van Dyke), his younger wife (Faye Dunaway), and their director friend (Ken Howard). Originally made for TV. **DR12, ST37**

Country Music with the Muppets (1985, C, 55m, NR)
Compilation of favorite country music highlights from *The Muppet Show* feature Johnny Cash, Roy Clark, Crystal Gayle, and Roger Miller. **FA14**

Coup de Grace (1976, C, 96m, NR)
German drama of a countess pining for the love of a no-good military officer. Margarethe von Trotta stars; her husband, Volker Schlöndorff, directed. **FF3**

Coup de Torchon *see* Clean Slate

Coup de Ville (1990, C, 99m, PG-13)
Road comedy set in the early 1960s, involving three brothers who drive a 1954 powder-blue Cadillac convertible from Detroit to their father's home in Florida. Patrick Dempsey, Arye Gross, and Daniel Stern star, with Annabeth Gish, Rita Taggart, and Alan Arkin. **CO5, CO6, XT18**

Courage (1986, C, 141m, NR)
In this true-life drama, Sophia Loren plays an American housewife who becomes a drug agent after she discovers that her own son is an addict. Billy Dee Williams costars. Originally made for TV. **DR6, DR10, ST93, ST159**

Court Jester, The (1956, C, 101m, NR)
Danny Kaye impersonates a clown; soon the joke's on him when a band of outlaws ask him to dethrone their nasty king. Glynis Johns, Basil Rathbone and Angela Lansbury costar in this comedy classic. **CL10, ST78**

Court-Martial of Billy Mitchell, The (1955, C, 100m, NR)
Gary Cooper stars as the Army officer whose obstreperous ways landed him in trouble with the brass in 1925. Charles Bickford, Ralph Bellamy, and Rod Steiger costar. Directed by Otto Preminger. **DR17, DT82, ST22**

Cousin, Cousine (1975, C, 95m, R)
French comedy about an affair between two people who have become cousins by marriage. Marie-Christine Barrault and Victor Lanoux star. American remake: *Cousins*. **FF1, FF8, XT20**

Cousins (1989, C, 110m, R)
American remake of French romantic comedy *Cousin, Cousine*, with married man and woman falling in love at a wedding which is about to make them cousins. Ted Danson and Isabella Rossellini star, with William Petersen, Sean Young, Lloyd Bridges, Keith Coogan, and Norma Aleandro. Directed by Joel Schumacher. **CO1, FF8, XT20** *Recommended*

Cover Girl (1944, C, 107m, NR)
Colorful musical starring Rita Hayworth as the title character, an overnight success, romanced by Gene Kelly. With Phil Silvers and Eve Arden. **CL9, ST64, ST81**

Covered Wagon, The (1923, B&W, 60m, NR)
Silent western epic, directed by James Cruze, with pioneers making their way

across the frontier. J. Warren Kerrigan stars, with Lois Wilson and Alan Hale, Sr. **CL12, WE1**

Cow Town (1950, B&W, 70m, NR)
Gene Autry's homesick on the range when ranchers take stake in their land with a fence war to protect it from cattle rustlers. **ST3**

Cowboy and the Señorita, The (1944, B&W, 56m, NR)
Roy Rogers finds a missing girl and wins the love of her cousin (Dale Evans). **ST132**

Cowboys, The (1972, C, 128m, PG)
A veteran cattleman is forced to employ a group of young boys on his 400-mile cattle drive. John Wayne stars, with Bruce Dern as a dastardly villain. **ST156**

Cracking Up (1983, C, 83m, PG)
Jerry Lewis comedy, a series of skits revolving around stories told by a suicidal patient to his shrink. With Herb Edelman, Dick Butkus, Sammy Davis, Jr., and Foster Brooks. Directed by Lewis; originally titled *Smorgasbord*. **ST91**

Cradle Will Fall, The (1983, C, 100m, NR)
Thriller about a desperate woman (Lauren Hutton) who can't convince her family and friends that she witnessed a murder. Ben Murphy and James Farentino costar. Originally made for TV. **MY3**

Craig's Wife (1936, B&W, 75m, NR)
Rosalind Russell plays a material girl who loves her possessions more than her man (John Boles). **CL5**

Crashout (1955, B&W, 90m, NR)
Prison drama of an escape attempt, starring William Bendix, Arthur Kennedy, Luther Adler, and William Talman. **DR18**

Crawling Eye, The (1958, B&W, 85m, NR)
A small town in the Swiss Alps is plagued by an immobile cloud and a series of gruesome murders. A psychic discovers that the cloud is an alien invader that resembles a large eye. **SF1, SF9**

Crawlspace (1986, C, 80m, R)
A landlord spies on his female tenants from an elaborate network in the ceilings of their apartments. Klaus Kinski stars in this horror drama. **ST83**

Crazies (1973, C, 103m, R)
A strange plague transforms and controls the inhabitants of a small town. Directed by George Romero. **HO21, DT90**

Crazy Mama (1975, C, 82m, R)
Comic crime saga, set in the 1950s, about a grandmother, mother, and daughter as they wend their way from California to Arkansas. Ann Sothern, Cloris Leachman, and Linda Purl star. Directed by Jonathan Demme. **CO10, DT28, XT18**

Crazy People (1990, C, 90m, R)
Comedy of an ad man (Dudley Moore) who suggests telling the truth to customers and winds up in an asylum. With Daryl Hannah, Paul Reiser, and Mercedes Ruehl. **CO2, ST109**

Crazy Ray, The (1924, B&W, 60m, NR)
Silent comedy from French director Rene Clair, about a scientist's experiment that paralyzes virtually all of Paris. Also available on this tape: *Entr'acte*, Clair's 1924 surrealistic short film. **FF1**

Creation of the Humanoids (1962, C, 78m, NR)
In a post-World War III world, robots which thrive on human blood perform menial tasks, and a security officer discovers that his sister has fallen in love with one. **SF12**

Creator (1985, C, 108m, R)
Peter O'Toole stars in this comedy-drama about a scientist who preserves some of his late wife's tissue in the hopes that he can recreate her in his laboratory. With Mariel Hemingway, Vincent Spano, and Virginia Madsen; Ivan Passer directed. **CO2, ST117**

Creature (1985, C, 97m, R)
Science fiction horror drama about an expedition to one of Saturn's moons making a gruesome and deadly discovery. Stan Ivar and Klaus Kinski star. **SF20, ST83**

Creature From Black Lake, The (1976, C, 97m, PG)
Two men come across Bigfoot in a Louisiana swamp. Jack Elam stars. **HO16**

Creature From the Black Lagoon (1954, B&W, 79m, NR)
Trip to Amazon results in find of Gill-Man who lives underwater. Classic 1950s sci-

ence fiction starring Richard Carlson, Julia Adams, Richard Denning, and Ricou Browning as the Creature. **SF1, SF10**

Creature From the Haunted Sea (1961, B&W, 72m, NR)
A gangster aboard a boat fakes a story about a sea monster killing off his companions—only to discover that he's unwittingly telling the truth. Anthony Carbone and Edward Wain (writer Robert Towne) star; Roger Corman directed. **DT22**

Creepers (1985, C, 82m, R)
A psychopath stalks a young girl who can communicate with insects via telepathy. Donald Pleasence and Jennifer Connelly star. Directed by Dario Argento. **HO7, HO16**

Creeping Flesh, The (1972, C, 91m, PG)
A scientist injects his daughter with an experimental serum which turns out to be the essence of evil. Peter Cushing and Christopher Lee star. **HO26, ST27, ST89**

Creeping Terror, The (1964, B&W, 75m, NR)
Legendarily awful monster movie, with no dialogue, about a creepy, carpet-like creature. Directed by Art J. Nelson, who also stars under the name Vic Savage. **CU11**

Creepshow (1982, C, 120m, R)
Five tales of revenge by Stephen King filmed in the style of the old E.C. comic books. Hal Holbrook, Adrienne Barbeau, Leslie Nielsen, Ted Danson, and King star. Directed by George Romero. **DT90, HO23, WR12**

Creepshow 2 (1987, C, 89m, R)
George Romero adapted three Stephen King short stories for this sequel to *Creepshow*. Lois Chiles and George Kennedy are among the stars. **DT90, HO23, WR12**

Cries and Whispers (1972, C, 106m, R)
Stunning drama from Ingmar Bergman about four women: three sisters (one of whom is dying) and their servant. Harriet Andersson, Liv Ullmann, Ingrid Thulin, and Kari Sylwan star. Oscar-winning photography by Sven Nykvist. **DT7, ST154** *Essential; Recommended*

Crime Zone (1989, C, 92m, R)
Futuristic crime saga of a fugitive couple from the wrong "caste" and their mentor, starring David Carradine, Peter Nelson, and Sherilynn Fenn. **SF17**

Crimes and Misdemeanors (1989, C, 104m, PG-13)
Woody Allen's two-fold story of a prominent physician (Martin Landau) becoming involved with murder-for-hire, and a documentary filmmaker (Allen) hired to record the life of his obnoxiously successful brother-in-law (Alan Alda). With Mia Farrow, Jerry Orbach, Anjelica Huston, and Sam Waterston. **CO8, DR8, DT1**

Crimes of Passion (1984, C, 101m, R)
Successful businesswoman moonlights as a prostitute, runs into trouble from a crazed preacher. Kathleen Turner and Anthony Perkins star. Ken Russell directed. An unrated version of the film is also available, containing more explicit sexual material; running time: 107m. **CU6, CU10, DR3, DT92, ST152**

Crimes of the Heart (1986, C, 105m, PG-13)
A trio of Southern sisters (Diane Keaton, Sissy Spacek, Jessice Lange) muddle through life in this adaptation of Beth Henley's play. Sam Shepard and Tess Harper costar. **CO5, DR10, DR20, ST79, ST86, ST139**

Criminal Code, The (1931, B&W, 98m, NR)
From director Howard Hawks comes the story of a young man convicted of manslaughter and sent off to prison. Walter Huston, Phillips Holmes, Boris Karloff, and Constance Cummings star. **DR18, DT43, ST77** *Recommended*

Criminal Court (1946, B&W, 63m, NR)
A lawyer involved in a murder trial knows the defendant is innocent—because he committed the crime. Robert Wise directed this thriller starring Tom Conway. NOTE: Packaged on videocassette with *The Saint Strikes Back*. **DT117, MY7**

Criminal Law (1989, C, 113m, R)
After a young attorney successfully defends his client on a murder charge, he begins to suspect that the man really is a killer. Gary Oldman and Kevin Bacon star. **DR16, DR17, MY9, MY13**

Criminal Life of Archibaldo de la Cruz, The (1955, B&W, 91m, NR)
Offbeat drama from director Luis Buñuel of a man fascinated by death as a result of a childhood trauma. Also known as *Ensayo de un Crimen (Rehearsal of a Murder)*. **DT15**

Crimson Pirate, The (1952, C, 104m, NR)
Exhilirating pirate classic, with Burt Lancaster and former fellow acrobat Nick Cravat swinging, climbing, and somersaulting their way across the Mediterranean. With Christopher Lee. **AC13, FA4, ST85, ST89** *Essential; Highly Recommended*

Criss Cross (1949, B&W, 87m, NR)
Moody thriller with Burt Lancaster as a loser whose fatal flaw is his devotion to his deceitful ex-wife (Yvonne de Carlo). Tony Curtis's film debut. **MY1, ST85**

Critical Condition (1987, C, 99m, R)
A convict in the hospital for treatment finds himself mistaken for a doctor during a power failure. Richard Pryor stars in this comedy, with Rachel Ticotin, Ruben Blades, and Garrett Morris. **CO13, CO20, MU12, ST125**

Critters (1986, C, 86m, PG-13)
Hairy little aliens crashland in Kansas and proceed to eat all the humans they can. A little boy and two intergalactic hunters try to save the day. Dee Wallace Stone and Scott Grimes star. **HO16, HO24**

Critters 2: The Main Course (1988, C, 87m, PG-13)
More chompin' by those furry little demons from outer space. Scott Grimes and Liane Curtis try to stay out of the sauce. **HO16, HO24**

"Crocodile" Dundee (1986, C, 102m, PG-13)
Romantic comedy with an international twist: an American journalist travels to Australia to interview a rough-and-tumble bush guide. He then comes to New York and learns how to "survive" in the urban jungle. Paul Hogan and Linda Kozlowski star. **CO1, CO9, CO20, FF5, XT9**

"Crocodile" Dundee II (1988, C, 110m, PG)
Sequel to the romantic comedy about an Australian bush guide (Paul Hogan) and his American sweetheart (Linda Kozlowski). This time, the couple's adventures begin in New York and continue Down Under. **CO1, CO9, CO20, FF5, XT9**

Cromwell (1970, C, 145m, G)
Richard Harris plays the British rebel soldier in this historical epic, with Alec Guinness, Robert Morley, Frank Finlay, and Timothy Dalton. **DR5, ST60**

Crooks and Coronets (1969, C, 106m, PG)
Telly Savalas and Warren Oates are con artists at work on an elderly English lady (Edith Evans) in this comedy. Also known as *Sophie's Place*. **ST115**

Cross Creek (1983, C, 122m, PG)
True story of author Marjorie Kinan Rawlings, who abandoned Long Island society in the 1920s to homestead in a Florida swamp and become a writer. Mary Steenburgen stars, with fine support from Rip Torn, Alfre Woodard, Dana Hill, and, as Maxwell Perkins, Malcolm McDowell. Directed by Martin Ritt. **DR4, DT87, ST150**

Cross My Heart (1987, C, 90m, R)
Comic chronicle of a modern couple's "crucial" third date, starring Martin Short and Annette O'Toole. **CO1, CO14**

Cross of Iron (1977, C, 119m, R)
Director Sam Peckinpah's drama follows the lives of German officers (James Coburn and Maximilian Schell) amidst World War II. With James Mason. **AC1, DT77, ST102**

Crossed Swords *see* The Prince and the Pauper (1978)

Crossfire (1947, B&W, 86m, NR)
One of the first postwar films to explore the issue of bigotry. A Jewish man is beaten to death, and three soldiers are held for questioning. Robert Young stars, with Robert Mitchum and Robert Ryan. Directed by Edward Dmytryk. **CL8, MY1, ST107** *Recommended*

Crossing Delancey (1988, C, 97m, PG)
A New York woman finds herself the object of an arranged courtship in this romantic comedy-drama starring Amy Irving and Peter Riegert, with Reizl Bozyk, Jeroen Krabbe and Sylvia Miles. **CO1, DR10, DR15, XT9** *Recommended*

Crossover Dreams (1985, C, 86m, NR)
Musical drama about a salsa singing star (Ruben Blades) who gets a swelled head over his forthcoming album. **MU4**

Crossroads (1986, C, 100m, R)
Young guitar player journeys the Mississippi back roads in search of someone to teach him authentic blues licks. Ralph Macchio and Joe Seneca star. Walter Hill directed; music by Ry Cooder. **DR12, DT45**

Crowd, The (1928, B&W, 104m, NR)
Classic silent drama from director King Vidor about the triumphs and tragedies of an "ordinary" couple living in New York. Eleanor Boardman and James Murray star. **CL8, CL12, DT107** *Essential; Recommended*

Crucible of Horror (1971, C, 91m, PG)
A man murdered by a member of his family comes back to haunt them. **HO14**

Cruising (1980, C, 106m, R)
A New York cop goes undercover to solve a series of murders in the gay community. Al Pacino stars. **DR16, ST118**

Crusoe (1989, C, 95m, PG-13)
The classic adventure tale of a marooned man, this time portrayed as an American slave trader (Aidan Quinn). Written by Walon Green; directed by Caleb Deschanel. **AC12, AC24** *Recommended*

Cry-Baby (1990, C, 85m, PG-13)
Early 1950s Baltimore is the setting for this affectionate send-up of teen movies, directed by John Waters. Johnny Depp and Amy Locane star, with Susan Tyrrell, Polly Bergen, Iggy Pop, Ricki Lake, Traci Lords, David Nelson, Joey Heatherton, and Mink Stole. **CO6, CO7, DT110, MU12**

Cry Danger (1951, B&W, 79m, NR)
Wrong-man thriller stars Dick Powell as Rocky, framed for murder and robbery, sent to prison, now trying to prove his innocence. With Rhonda Fleming and William Conrad. **MY1, MY7**

Cry Freedom (1987, C, 157m, PG)
True drama of South African activist Steven Biko and his friendship with white reporter Donald Woods, who smuggled the story of Biko's torture and death to the outside world. Denzel Washington and Kevin Kline star. Richard Attenborough directed. **DR6, DR14, ST84**

Cry in the Dark, A (1988, C, 122m, PG-13)
Australian fact-based drama about the sensational case of Lindy Chamberlain, a mother accused of murdering her infant baby (whom she claimed was carried off by a wild dog). Meryl Streep and Sam Neill star. Directed by Fred Schepisi. **DR6, DR17, FF5, ST145** *Recommended*

Cry of the Banshee (1970, C, 87m, PG)
A witch and a satanist seek revenge against a nobleman who is on a witch hunt. Vincent Price stars. **ST124**

Cuba (1979, C, 121m, PG)
Love story set against the downfall of dictator Batista and rise of Castro, starring Sean Connery and Brooke Adams. Directed by Richard Lester. **DT62, ST21** *Recommended*

Cuban Rebel Girls *see* Assault of the Rebel Girls

Cujo (1983, C, 91m, R)
Stephen King story about a woman and her son who are terrorized by a rabid dog. Dee Wallace stars. **HO16, WR12**

Culpepper Cattle Company, The (1972, C, 92m, PG)
A western cult favorite about a 16-year-old boy who quickly becomes a man when he joins a cattle drive through violent post-Civil War Texas. Gary Grimes stars, with Billy "Green" Bush, Luke Askew, and Bo Hopkins. **WE15**

Curly Top (1935, B&W, 75m, NR)
Shirley Temple classic finds the greatest child star of them all playing matchmaker and singing "Animal Crackers in My Soup." **ST148**

Curse, The (1987, C, 90m, PG-13)
A meteorite lands on a farm in Tennessee, and soon everyone in the family, except the young son, is acting strangely. Wil Wheaton and John Schneider star. **HO14, HO21**

Curse of Frankenstein, The (1957, C, 83m, NR)
The first horror film from Britain's Hammer Studios, about Mary Shelley's doctor who becomes obsessed by his experi-

ments and his creation. Peter Cushing, Christopher Lee, and Hazel Court star. **HF10, HO20, HO26, ST27, ST89**

Curse of the Cat People, The (1944, B&W, 70m, NR)
A lonely little girl is befriended by the ghost of her father's first wife in this sequel to *Cat People*. Produced by Val Lewton; directed by Robert Wise. **DT117, HO2, HO14, HO27**

Curse of the Demon (1957, B&W, 82m, NR)
An American professor (Dana Andrews) comes face to face with the dark side of the occult when he tries to solve the mysterious death of a colleague. Directed by Jacques Tourneur. **DT105, HO1, HO11, HO19**

Curse of the Living Dead *see* Kill, Baby, Kill

Curse of the Pink Panther (1983, C, 109m, PG)
The final Pink Panther film, made after Peter Sellers' death, with Ted Wass playing Inspector Clouseau. Cameo appearances by Panther alumni David Niven, Herbert Lom, Bert Kwouk, and Capucine. Directed by Blake Edwards. **DT32**

Curse of the Werewolf, The (1961, C, 91m, NR)
A servant girl is raped and eventually gives birth to a son who, when he reaches adulthood, discovers that strange things happen to him when the moon is full. Oliver Reed stars in this British horror film. **HO4, HO26**

Cut and Run (1985, C, 87m, R)
A pair of ambitious reporters stumble onto a big scoop when they travel to South America in search of an evil disciple of Jim Jones. Lisa Blount, Willie Aames, and Karen Black star. **AC24**

Cutter's Way (1981, C, 105m, R)
In Santa Barbara, California, a cynical, crippled Vietnam vet (John Heard), his alcoholic girl friend (Lisa Eichorn), and their beach bum pal (Jeff Bridges) set out to prove that a local pillar of society is involved in a sordid murder case. Directed by Ivan Passer; written by Jeffrey Alan Fiskin. **DR7, MY2, ST11** *Recommended*

Cyborg (1989, C, 85m, R)
Martial arts star Jean Claude Van Damme plays the title role in this post-apocalyptic tale of revenge. **AC24, AC26, SF12**

Cyclops (1957, B&W, 75m, NR)
An expedition discovers the man they are searching for has been transformed into a monster by a radiation blast. Gloria Talbott, Lon Chaney, Jr., and Tom Drake star. Directed by Bert I. Gordon. **HO21, ST17**

Cyrano de Bergerac (1950, B&W, 112m, NR)
Jose Ferrer won an Oscar for his portrayal of the long-nosed romantic of Edmond Rostand's play. **DR20, XT2**

D.A.R.Y.L. (1985, C, 99m, PG)
A young boy (Barrett Oliver) baffles his parents because he is too "perfect." He soon becomes the most popular kid around—wanted even by the government. Michael McKean and Mary Beth Hurt costar. **DR9, FA7**

D.C. Cab (1983, C, 99m, R)
Amiable comedy about a wacked-out collection of cabbies cruising the streets of Our Nation's Capital. Adam Baldwin stars, with Max Gail, Gary Busey, Mr. T, and Irene Cara. **CO2, XT12**

D-Day the Sixth of June (1956, C, 106m, NR)
Dramatic recreation of the Normandy invasion, starring Robert Taylor and Richard Todd as, respectively, American and British officers. **AC1**

D.O.A. (1949, B&W, 83m, NR)
A man is given poison—he has a few days to find his killer. Edmond O'Brien stars in this classic thriller. **MY1**

D.O.A. (1988, C, 96m, R)
Remake of the film noir classic, with Dennis Quaid as the poisoning victim trying to track down his killer. Meg Ryan costars. **CU18, MY2**

D.W. Griffith Triple Feature (1913, B&W, 50m, NR)
A trio of short films from the movies' first great director: *The Battle of Elderbush Gulch*, *Iola's Promise*, and *The Goddess of Sagebrush Gulch*. Lillian Gish, Mary Pickford, and Mae Marsh are among the stars. **DT42, ST54**

Da (1988, C, 102m, PG)
An Irish-American playwright returns to his homeland when his father dies. The old man's ghost confronts his son as they recall their good and bad times together. Martin Short and Barnard Hughes star; based on Hugh Leonard's play. **DR8, DR20**

Dad (1989, C, 117m, PG)
Heartfelt drama of the relationship between an ailing, elderly man (Jack Lemmon) and his grown son (Ted Danson). With Olympia Dukakis, Kathy Baker, Kevin Spacey, and Ethan Hawke. **DR8, DR11, ST90**

Daffy Duck Cartoon Festival (1942-8, C, 35m, NR)
Donald Duck's Number One cartoon rival stars in these frenetic adventures, featuring Bob Clampett's "The Wise Quacking Duck." **FA11**

Daffy Duck: The Nuttiness Continues . . . (1956, C, 59m, NR)
Daffy's very own collection of cartoon classics, including *Beanstalk Bunny, Deduce You Say, Dripalong Daffy,* and *The Scarlet Pumpernickel.* **FA11**

Daffy Duck's Movie: Fantastic Island (1983, C, 78m, G)
Collection of ten classic Warner Bros. cartoon features Speedy Gonzales, Bugs Bunny, Porky Pig, Sylvester, Tweety, Pepe Le Pew, Pirate Sam, Foghorn Leghorn, and, of course, Daffy Duck, who provides linking storyline that spoofs TV's *Fantasy Island.* **FA11**

Daffy Duck's Quackbusters *see* Quackbusters

Dagora, the Space Monster (1964, C, 80m, NR)
Japanese science fiction drama of a flying jellyfish, gangsters, and stolen diamonds. **SF18**

Dain Curse, The (1978, C, 118m, NR)
James Coburn and Jean Simmons star in this Dashiell Hammett thriller. A private eye assigned to a relatively easy case of theft uncovers a series of complex murders in the process. Originally made for TV. **WR9**

Daisy Miller (1974, C, 91m, G)
Cybill Shepherd stars as the heroine of Henry James's comic novel about a headstrong American girl touring the Continent. With Barry Brown, Cloris Leachman, Mildred Natwick, and Eileen Brennan. Directed by Peter Bogdanovich. **DR19, WR11**

Dakota (1945, B&W, 82m, NR)
John Wayne battles land grabbers in this western saga. Vera Miles costars. **ST156**

Daleks: Invasion Earth 2150 A.D. (1966, C, 81m, NR)
Dr. Who travels to London 2150 A.D. and helps out a small band of resistance fighters in their battle against the Daleks, robots who want to kill all humans. Peter Cushing and Bernard Cribbens star. **SF4, SF19, ST27**

Dames (1934, B&W, 90m, NR)
Busby Berkeley's film about a millionaire who tries to prevent the opening of a Broadway show. Dick Powell and Ruby Keeler costar. **DT8, MU4**

Damien: Omen II (1978, C, 110m, R)
Sequel to *The Omen* opens seven years later, with Damien a student at a military academy where he discovers his true identity as the anti-christ. William Holden and Lee Grant star as Damien's uncle and aunt, who are now his legal guardians. **HO10, HO13, ST68**

Damn the Defiant! (1962, C, 101m, NR)
Adventure of sea battles during Napoleonic wars, with Dirk Bogarde and Alec Guinness on opposing sides. **AC6, ST60**

Damn Yankees (1958, C, 110m, NR)
Musical fantasy of baseball fan who makes deal with the Devil to be a young star who will help his beloved Washington Senators beat the hated New York Yankees. Tab Hunter, Ray Walston, and Gwenn Verdon star. Directed by Stanley Donen and George Abbott; choreography by Bob Fosse, who appears in one dance number. **DT30, DT39, HO10, MU2, MU6**
Recommended

Damnation Alley (1977, C, 91m, PG)
Five survivors of a nuclear holocaust travel the wasteland in search of other human life. Jan-Michael Vincent, George Peppard, Dominique Sanda, Paul Win-

field, and Jackie Earle Haley star. **SF12, ST162**

Damned, The (1969, C, 146m, R)
A dark portrait from Italian director Luchino Visconti of a decadent family of German arms merchants and their ties to the Third Reich. Dirk Bogarde, Ingrid Thulin, Helmut Griem, Helmut Berger, and Charlotte Rampling star in this controversial drama, originally rated "X." **DT108**

Damsel in Distress, A (1937, B&W, 101m, NR)
George Gershwin musical comedy stars Fred Astaire as a London dancer who pursues Joan Fontaine. With George Burns and Gracie Allen. George Stevens directed. **DT101, ST2**

Dance, Girl, Dance (1940, B&W, 89m, NR)
Classic woman's picture with cult following: Maureen O'Hara stars as a dancer with serious ambitions who gets sidetracked into a career in burlesque. With Louis Hayward, Lucille Ball, and Ralph Bellamy. Directed by Dorothy Arzner. **CL5, CL7**

Dance With a Stranger (1985, C, 101m, R)
The true story of Ruth Ellis (Miranda Richardson), a divorced woman who killed her younger lover (Rupert Everett) and was hanged for her crime—the last woman in Britain to be executed. Ian Holm costars. **DR6, DR16, DR23, MY2, MY8, MY15** *Recommended*

Dancers (1987, C, 97m, PG)
Mikhail Baryshnikov stars in this drama set in the ballet world, where a pair of dancers imitate in real life the love story they're performing on stage. Directed by Herbert Ross. **DR12**

Dancing Lady (1933, B&W, 94m, NR)
Clark Gable romances dancer Joan Crawford in this backstage musical that also features Fred Astaire in his film debut and comic relief from the original Three Stooges. **CL7, CU17, ST2, ST24, ST49** *Recommended*

The Dancing Princesses (1984, C, 60m, NR)
A princess (Lesley Ann Warren) teaches her overly strict father a lesson when his daughters break out of their locked rooms

and into their dancing slippers with the help of a handsome prince (Peter Weller). From The Faerie Tale Theatre series. **FA12**

Dandy in Aspic, A (1968, C, 107m, NR)
A Russian double agent (Laurence Harvey) tires of his dangerous profession but can see no way out. With Tom Courtenay and Mia Farrow. Director Anthony Mann died during production; Harvey finished the film. **MY6, DT69**

Dangerous (1935, B&W, 72m, NR)
Oscar winner Bette Davis plays a star on the downside of her career who finds redemption in the arms of a handsome suitor (Franchot Tone). **ST28, XT3**

Dangerous Liaisons (1988, C, 120m, R)
Intrigue in 18th-century France, with villainous schemers John Malkovich and Glenn Close plotting to divest innocent married woman Michelle Pfeiffer of her virtue. With Uma Thurman, Keanu Reeves, and Swoosie Kurtz. Christopher Hampton adapted his play; Stephen Frears directed. Material previously filmed as *Les Liaisons Dangereuses* and subsequently as *Valmont*. **DR1, DR5, DR20, ST20, ST84, ST120** *Recommended*

Dangerous Mission (1954, C, 75m, NR)
A witness to a gangland killing flees across country with the killers in hot pursuit. Piper Laurie and Vincent Price star. **ST124**

Dangerous Moonlight (1941, B&W, 83m, NR)
British drama of classical musician turned bomber pilot, set during World War II. Anton Walbrook stars. **AC1**

Dangerous Moves (1984, C, 95m, PG)
Oscar-winning drama from Switzerland about an international chess match and the behind-the-scenes machinations that accompany it. Michel Piccoli, Leslie Caron, and Liv Ullmann star. **ST154, XT7**

Dangerously Close (1986, C, 95m, R)
Melodrama of a society of high school vigilantes bullying kids who don't fit their clean-cut standards. John Stockwell stars. **DR25**

Daniel (1983, C, 130m, R)
Drama about a brother and sister whose parents were executed as spies in the

1950s and how that event still haunts them years later. Timothy Hutton and Amanda Plummer star, with Lindsay Crouse, Mandy Patinkin, Ed Asner, and Ellen Barkin. Based on E.L. Doctorow's novel, *The Book of Daniel;* directed by Sidney Lumet. **DR5, DR19, DT65**

Danton (1982, C, 136m, PG)
French-language drama from Polish director Andrzej Wajda, about the stormy days of the French Revolution. Gerard Depardieu stars in the title role. **ST31**

Darby O'Gill and the Little People (1959, C, 90m, G)
Deep in the emerald forest of Ireland, a weaver of tall tales falls into the land of leprechauns in this Disney fantasy. An early role for Sean Connery. **FA1, ST21**

Dark Command (1940, B&W, 94m, NR)
In Civil War Kansas, John Wayne is the town marshal who clashes with local vigilante leader Walter Pidgeon. With Claire Trevor, Gabby Hayes, and Roy Rogers. **ST132, ST156, WE6**

Dark Corner, The (1946, B&W, 99m, NR)
Lucille Ball plays an amateur sleuth in this mystery about a secretary who clears her boss from a murder charge. With Mark Stevens, Clifton Webb, and William Bendix. **MY15**

Dark Crystal, The (1983, C, 93m, PG)
Fantasy adventure from director Jim Henson and producer George Lucas, about the quest to replace the missing shard in the all-powerful Dark Crystal. Family entertainment, packed with unique creatures. **FA8, SF13**

Dark Eyes (1987, C, 118m, NR)
Marcello Mastroianni stars in this comedy-drama about a faded Italian aristocrat who takes one last, mad fling at love. **FF2, ST103**

Dark Forces (1980, C, 96m, PG)
An updating of the Rasputin story, about a faith healer who gains access into a Senator's family by apparently curing the son, then developing a psychic power over the Senator. Robert Powell stars. **HO7**

Dark Habits (1984, C, 116m, NR)
Irreverent comedy by Spanish director Pedro Almodóvar: a singer on the lam hides out in convent. Christina Pascual, Julieta Serrano, and Carmen Maura star. **FF7**

Dark Journey (1937, B&W, 82m, NR)
Romantic suspense with Vivien Leigh as a World War I British spy who gets involved with a German intelligence officer (Conrad Veidt) while in Stockholm. **MY6**

Dark Mirror, The (1946, B&W, 85m, NR)
Twin sisters, one evil and the other good, are implicated in a murder case. Olivia de Havilland plays both sisters. **MY1, MY4, MY14**

Dark Passage (1947, B&W, 106m, NR)
An escaped convict (Humphrey Bogart) undergoes plastic surgery to cover up his identity while a beautiful girl (Lauren Bacall) tries to prove his innocence. **CL15, MY1, ST8**

Dark Past, The (1948, B&W, 75m, NR)
Hostage tale of a psycho killer and a psychologist. William Holden and Lee J. Cobb star. **ST68**

Dark Places (1973, C, 91m, PG)
Three people out to defraud a man of his inheritance are haunted by the ghost of a murderer. Christopher Lee and Joan Collins star. **ST89**

Dark Secret of Harvest Home, The (1978, C, 200m, NR)
A New York City family moves to a small town in New England. A mysterious old woman (Bette Davis) slowly draws the wife and daughter into her circle while the husband tries to solve some mysterious happenings. Originally made for TV. **HO11, ST28**

Dark Star (1974, C, 83m, PG)
Low-budget science fiction adventure from director John Carpenter that pokes fun at sci-fi epics such as *2001*. **CO7, CU4, DT17, SF21**

Dark Victory (1939, B&W, 106m, NR)
A young woman (Bette Davis) with a fatal disease decides to live her last few months to the fullest in this classic love story. With George Brent, Humphrey Bogart, Geraldine Fitzgerald, and Ronald Reagan. **CL4, CL6, ST8, ST28** *Essential*

Darling (1965, C, 122m, NR)
Drama of a successful London fashion model and her inability to find real love or meaning in her life. Oscar winner Julie Christie stars, with Dirk Bogarde and Laurence Harvey. Written by Frederic Raphael; directed by John Schlesinger. **DR10, DR23, DT94, XT3, XT15** *Essential; Recommended*

Date With Judy, A (1948, C, 113m, NR)
Comedy with music revolving around two mischievous teenagers and their families. Wallace Beery, Jane Powell, Elizabeth Taylor, and Carmen Miranda star. **ST147**

Daughter of Dr. Jekyll (1957, B&W, 67m, NR)
A young woman believes she is cursed by the experiments of a famous relative. Gloria Talbott and John Agar star. Directed by Edgar G. Ulmer. **HO14, HO20**

Daughter of Horror (1955, B&W, 60m, NR)
Offbeat horror film, with no dialogue, about a woman whose paranoia edges her into murder. Adrienne Barrett stars. Also known as *Dementia*. **HO9**

Daughters of Darkness (1971, C, 87m, R)
Horror film with a cult following about a pair of lesbian vampires who prey on honeymooning couples. Filmed in France; Delphine Seyrig stars. **CU4, CU6, HO5**

David and Bathsheba (1951, C, 116m, NR)
Gregory Peck and Susan Hayward play the title roles in this religious drama of the Biblical king and his consort. **CL13, ST119**

David and Lisa (1963, B&W, 94m, NR)
Two mentally disturbed young people meet in a therapy session and develop a friendship that slowly blossoms into romance. Keir Dullea and Janet Margolin star, with Howard Da Silva. Written by Eleanor Perry; directed by Frank Perry. **DR9**

David Copperfield (1935, B&W, 130m, NR)
An all-star production of the life and times of Charles Dickens' character in Victorian England. Directed by George Cukor. Freddie Bartholomew stars, with Frank Lawton, W.C. Fields (as Micawber), Lionel Barrymore, Roland Young,

Basil Rathbone, and Maureen O'Sullivan. **DT24, FA3, ST41, WR4** *Recommended*

Davy Crockett (1955, C, 88m, G)
Disney portrait of the King of the Wild Frontier (Fess Parker), as he takes on wild bears and nasty Indians before making his last stand at the Alamo. Buddy Ebsen costars. **FA1**

Davy Crockett and the River Pirates (1956, C, 81m, G)
Two episodes from the Disney TV series: Davy and riverboat king Mike Fink (Jeff York) square off in a boat race; Davy and his sidekick George Russell (Buddy Ebsen) take on some pesky Indians. **FA1**

Dawn! (1976, C, 114m, NR)
Australian film bio of Olympic swimming champ Dawn Fraser. Bronwyn Mackay-Payne stars. **DR22, FF5**

Dawn of the Dead (1979, C, 126m, NR)
Gruesome and darkly funny sequel to *Night of the Living Dead* finds a quartet of humans holed up in an abandoned shopping mall besieged by flesh-eating zombies. George Romero directed. **CU1, CU4, CU7, DT90, HO6, HO18** *Recommended*

Dawn Patrol, The (1938, B&W, 82m, NR)
World War I drama of brave pilots on the edge of collapse from exhaustion, starring David Niven and Errol Flynn. **AC2, AC11, ST43** *Recommended*

Day After, The (1983, C, 126m, NR)
Controversial portrait of America undergoing nuclear attack and the attendant devastation. Jason Robards, JoBeth Williams, Steve Guttenberg, and John Lithgow star. Nicholas Meyer directed; originally made for TV. **DR7, SF12, ST129**

Day After Trinity: J. Robert and the Atomic Bomb, The (1981, C/B&W, 88m, NR)
Superb documentary about the building of the first nuclear weapons and the devastating effect the experience had on scientist J. Robert Oppenheimer. **CU16** *Recommended*

Day at the Races, A (1937, B&W, 111m, NR)
The Marx Bros. invade a race track. Chico sells tutti-frutti ice cream and hot

tips on the ponies. Margaret Dumont tries to ignore him. **ST101**

Day for Night (1973, C, 120m, PG)
Loving look at filmmaking from director François Truffaut, who also plays the director of a romantic comedy in production, with the usual behind-the-scenes crises, affairs, hopes, and dreams. Jean-Pierre Léaud, Jacqueline Bisset, Jean-Pierre Aumont, and Valentina Cortese co-star. Oscar winner for Best Foreign Film. **DR13, DT106, XT7** *Essential; Recommended*

Day in the Country, A (1936, B&W, 36m, NR)
French director Jean Renoir's short film, about a family's outing, suggests some of the inspirations for Impressionist painters like his father. A mini-classic. **DT86** *Recommended*

Day in the Death of Joe Egg, A (1972, C, 106m, R)
Darkly comic story of a British couple trying to deal with their severely handicapped daughter. Alan Bates and Janet Suzman star in this adaptation of Peter Nichols' play. **CO12, CO17, DR20**

Day of the Dead (1985, C, 91m, NR)
The third of the . . . *Dead* trilogy that began with *Night of the Living* and continued with *Dawn of the* has the zombies in control of everything and the last of the humans in a bunker waiting for the final battle. Directed by George Romero. **DT90, HO6, HO18**

Day of the Dolphin, The (1973, C, 104m, PG)
A marine biologist uses his trained dolphins to thwart an assassination plot. George C. Scott stars. Mike Nichols directed. **DT74, FA5**

Day of the Jackal, The (1973, C, 141m, PG)
Thriller based on the Frederick Forsyth bestseller about a young British assassin's plot to kill DeGaulle in Paris and French officials' desperate race to catch him. Edward Fox stars. Directed by Fred Zinnemann. **DT120, MY6, WR8, XT16** *Recommended*

Day of the Locust, The (1975, C, 144m, R)
Drama about the dark underside of Hollywood in the 1930s, with an impression-able painter meeting a gallery of grotesque show-biz characters. Adapted from Nathanael West's classic novel. William Atherton stars, with Donald Sutherland, Karen Black, Burgess Meredith, and Geraldine Page. Directed by John Schlesinger. **DR13, DR19, DT94, XT10** *Recommended*

Day of the Triffids, The (1963, C, 95m, NR)
Science fiction drama about blinding meteor showers and invasion of mutant monsters. Howard Keel stars in this British production. **SF7, SF19**

Day of Wrath (1943, B&W, 110m, NR)
From Danish director Carl Dreyer, a tale of 16th-century superstition and revenge. An old woman, accused of witchcraft, places a curse on the clergyman who fingered her. **DT31**

Day the Earth Caught Fire, The (1962, B&W, 99m, NR)
Earth comes dangerously close to the sun in this British science fiction drama starring Edward Judd and Leo McKern. **SF7, SF19**

Day the Earth Stood Still, The (1951, B&W, 92m, NR)
Classic 1950s science fiction drama, with spaceship landing in Washington, D.C., alien trying to warn Earth of its disastrous nuclear arms race. Michael Rennie, Sam Jaffe, Patricia Neal, Billy Gray, and "Gort" star. Robert Wise directed. **CU4, DT117, FA8, SF1, SF9, SF13, XT12** *Essential; Highly Recommended*

Day Time Ended, The (1980, C, 79m, PG)
Family living in the desert experience a strange alien visitation. Jim Davis, Dorothy Malone, and Christopher Mitchum star. Also known as *Time Warp*. **SF9**

Daydreamer, The (1966, C, 98m, NR)
Live action mixes with animation in this tale of a young Hans Christian Andersen thinking of the fairy tale characters he will later write about. Jack Gilford and Margaret Hamilton star, with the voices of Boris Karloff and Tallulah Bankhead. **ST77**

Days of Glory (1944, B&W, 86m, NR)
World War II action between the Nazis and the Russians, with Gregory Peck in

his starring debut. Directed by Jacques Tourneur. **AC1, DT105, ST119**

Days of Heaven (1978, C, 95m, PG)
Romantic drama, set in Texas wheatfields at the turn of the century, about a farm owner who woos an itinerant worker, only to find that her "brother" is really her lover. Stunning photography by Nestor Almendros and Haskell Wexler won an Oscar. Richard Gere, Brooke Adams, Sam Shepard, and Linda Manz star. Directed by Terrence Malick; music by Ennio Morricone. **DR1, DT67, ST52** *Essential; Highly Recommended*

Days of Jesse James (1939, B&W, 63m, NR)
Roy Rogers plays the notorious outlaw in one of his early films. **HF16, ST132**

Days of Wine and Roses, The (1962, B&W, 117m, NR)
Drama of an alcoholic couple and how they ruin their lives before one of them makes a recovery. Jack Lemmon and Lee Remick star. Blake Edwards directed. **DR7, DT32, ST90** *Recommended*

Dead, The (1987, C, 82m, PG)
James Joyce's short story is the basis for this drama of family life in turn-of-the-century Dublin, centering around a holiday party and the memories it evokes. Anjelica Huston stars; her father, John, directed—his last film. **DR8, DR19, DT50** *Recommended*

Dead and Buried (1981, C, 92m, R)
A sheriff investigating a series of bizarre murders discovers that some of his neighbors are actually zombies. James Farentino, Melody Anderson, and Jack Albertson star. **HO6**

Dead-Bang (1989, C, 105m, R)
Don Johnson stars in a crime saga of a relentless police detective whose pursuit of a cop killer uncovers a nest of verminous white supremacists. **AC9**

Dead Calm (1989, C, 96m, R)
Australian suspense drama has a couple on a yacht encountering a stranger on another boat who, they belatedly discover, has murdered all on board. Sam Neill, Nicole Kidman, and Billy Zane star. Phillip Noyce directed. **FF5**

Dead End (1937, B&W, 93m, NR)
Drama set on New York's Lower East Side during the Depression. Sylvia Sidney, Joel McCrea, and Humphrey Bogart star, with the film debut of The Dead End Kids, later The Bowery Boys. Lillian Hellman adapted Sidney Kingsley's hit play; directed by William Wyler. **CL8, DR20, DT119, ST8** *Essential; Recommended*

Dead Heat (1988, C, 86m, R)
Buddy-cop/horror story, with a pair of detectives (Joe Piscopo, Treat Williams) on the trail of a mad doctor who's reviving criminals from the dead. **AC9, CO13, HO6**

Dead Heat on a Merry-Go-Round (1966, C, 107m, NR)
Heist drama centering on the robbery of an airport bank. Plenty of twists and double crosses. James Coburn stars, with Camilla Sparv, Aldo Ray, and Ross Martin. Harrison Ford makes a brief appearance, in his first film. **MY18, ST46**

Dead Man Out (1989, C, 87m, NR)
A state-appointed psychiatrist attempts to deal with a convict whose insanity has prevented the state from executing him. Danny Glover and Ruben Blades star. Originally made for cable TV. **DR18, MU12, ST55**

Dead Men Don't Wear Plaid (1982, B&W, 91m, PG)
A comedy thriller starring Steve Martin as a private detective with a very bizarre assortment of suspects. Includes scenes from many film noir classics of the 1940s skillfully woven into the story. Directed by Carl Reiner. **CO7, MY17, ST99**

Dead Men Walk (1943, B&W, 64m, NR)
An evil twin involved with the black arts resorts to vampirism to get back at his good brother. **HO15**

Dead of Night (1945, B&W, 102m, NR)
An architect discovers that the cottage he is to redesign and its occupants are exactly the same as in his recurring nightmare. His story prompts the other guests to tell of their own brushes with the supernatural. Highlight: the tale of the nervous ventriloquist and his independent dummy, featuring Michael Redgrave. **HO1, HO2, HO23, HO26**

Dead of Night (1973) *see* Deathdream

Dead of Winter (1987, C, 100m, R)
An aspiring actress (Mary Steenburgen) is lured to a remote farmhouse with the promise of a movie role. Once there, she finds herself trapped in a bizarre game of deception. Directed by Arthur Penn. **DT78, MY3**

Dead Poets Society (1989, C, 128m, PG)
Drama set in a private boys' school in 1959, with an unorthodox teacher (Robin Williams) inspiring devotion from his pupils, controversy among his colleagues and the boys' parents. Robert Sean Leonard and Ethan Hawke costar. Directed by Peter Weir. **DR9, DR25, DT111, ST160**

Dead Pool, The (1988, C 91m, R)
Clint Eastwood's fifth outing as Dirty Harry has him trailing a killer with a hit list of San Francisco celebrities—a list which includes Harry. **AC9, ST39, XT13**

Dead Reckoning (1947, B&W, 100m, NR)
A World War II veteran (Humphrey Bogart) attempts to solve the murder of a fellow officer. **MY1, MY4, ST8**

Dead Ringers (1988, C, 117m, R)
Disturbing psychological study of twin doctors who share an apartment, a gynecological practice—and more. Jeremy Irons stars as both twins, with Genevieve Bujold. Brilliantly directed by David Cronenberg; based loosely on a true story. **DR8, DT23, HO15** *Recommended*

Dead Zone, The (1983, C, 104m, R)
An accident victim comes out of a coma after five years and discovers he now has psychic powers. Christopher Walken, Martin Sheen, Brooke Adams, and Tom Skerritt star. Directed by David Cronenberg; based on a novel by Stephen King. **DT23, HO7, HO19, WR12**

Deadline at Dawn (1946, B&W, 83m, NR)
A mystery with Susan Hayward as an aspiring actress who tries to clear the name of a sailor accused of murder. Written by Clifford Odets. **MY1, MY11**

Deadly Blessing (1981, C, 102m, R)
A young couple move to a farm that borders the compound of a community called The Hittites. A series of strange murders begins. Maren Jenson and Lisa Hartman star. Directed by Wes Craven. **HO11**

Deadly Companions, The (1961, C, 90m, NR)
Brian Keith plays a tough gunfighter who accidentally kills the son of a dance hall girl (Maureen O'Hara). Director Sam Peckinpah's first film. **DT77**

Deadly Friend (1987, C, 91m, R)
A teenaged genius has two friends—the girl next door and his special robot. When the girl dies, he pushes his experiments into a deadly realm. Directed by Wes Craven. **HO20**

Deadly Hero (1975, C, 102m, PG)
Cop drama of a policeman who seems to be a hero when he kills a woman's attacker. Don Murray stars, with Diahn Williams, James Earl Jones, and Lilia Skala. **ST76**

Deadly Illusion (1987, C, 87m, R)
A detective is framed for murder in this thriller starring Billy Dee Williams, with Vanity, Morgan Fairchild, and John Beck. Written and co-directed by Larry Cohen. **DT20, ST159**

Deadly Sanctuary (1970, C, 93m, R)
Horror drama focusing on the writings of the Marquis De Sade (Klaus Kinski), starring Jack Palance, Sylvia Koscina, and Mercedes McCambridge. **ST83**

Deal of the Century (1983, C, 99m, PG)
Chevy Chase stars in this satire on the arms race; he plays a fast-talking salesman of high-tech military hardware. Gregory Hines and Sigourney Weaver costar. **CO13, ST157**

Dear America: Letters Home From Vietnam (1987, C/B&W, 87m, NR)
Moving documentary composed of TV news footage and home movies of the war in Vietnam, with a soundtrack of actual letters written by servicemen and nurses (read by such stars as Robin Williams, Robert DeNiro, Kathleen Turner), plus well-chosen pop and rock music of the period. Originally made for cable TV. **AC4, CU16** *Recommended*

Dear Brigitte (1965, C, 100m, NR)
James Stewart stars in a comedy about an 8-year-old boy's infatuation with French "sex kitten" Brigitte Bardot. Glynis Johns and Fabian costar; Bardot makes a guest appearance. **ST4, ST143**

Dear Detective (1977, C, 105m, NR)
A French thriller starring Annie Girardot as a detective who takes time out from several murder investigations for a little romance with a college professor. Also known as *Dear Inspector*. **FF1, MY16**

Dear Inspector *see* Dear Detective

Dear Wife (1949, B&W, 88m, NR)
William Holden stars in this comedy about an aspiring politician competing against a much older man (Edward Arnold) for state office. **ST68**

Death Before Dishonor (1986, C, 95m, R)
A Marine sergeant (Fred Dryer) and his elite unit track down a terrorist in the Middle East. With Paul Winfield. **AC20, ST162**

Death Hunt (1981, C, 97m, R)
A Mountie (Lee Marvin) pursues a trapper (Charles Bronson) accused of murder across the frozen Canadian landscape. **AC12, ST12, ST100**

Death in Venice (1971, C, 130m, PG)
Italian drama, based on Thomas Mann novel, of a composer's final days in Venice, as he struggles to come to terms with his homosexuality and art. Dirk Bogarde stars; Luchino Visconti directed. **DR19, DT108**

Death Kiss, The (1933, B&W, 75m, NR)
During the filming of a movie, an actor is murdered. Bela Lugosi and David Manners star. **ST95**

Death of a Salesman (1985, C, 150m, NR)
Dustin Hoffman plays Willy Loman in the latest adaptation of the classic Arthur Miller play. Kate Reid, John Malkovich, Stephen Lang, and Charles Durning costar. Directed by Volker Schlöndorff. Originally made for TV. **DR8, DR20, ST67, ST98**

Death on the Nile (1978, C, 140m, PG)
An all-star production of the Agatha Christie novel, in which Hercule Poirot (Peter Ustinov) must determine who killed an heiress aboard a ship. Bette Davis, Angela Lansbury, and David Niven are among the suspects. **MY12, ST28, WR3**

Death Race 2000 (1975, C, 78m, R)
Low-budget science fiction adventure about a road race that awards points for hitting pedestrians. David Carradine, Sylvester Stallone, and Mary Woronov star; Paul Bartel directed. Sequel: *Deathsport*. **AC10, CU4, DT5, SF21, ST140**

Death Rides a Horse (1969, C, 114m, PG)
Western tale of revenge, starring John Phillip Law as a man tracking a gang of killers, unaware that one of them is riding with him. With Lee Van Cleef. **ST155, WE5**

Death Sentence (1974, C, 78m, NR)
A juror discovers that the wrong man is on trial for murder when her husband is revealed as a killer. Cloris Leachman stars, with Nick Nolte. Originally made for TV. **ST113**

Death Valley (1982, C, 87m, R)
A young boy visiting Arizona is witness to a murder and flees for his life from a psychotic killer. Paul LeMat, Catherine Hicks, Peter Billingsley, and Stephen McHattie star. **AC24**

Death Wish (series)
Death Wish (1974, C, 93m, R)
Death Wish II (1982, C, 89m, R)
Death Wish III (1985, C, 100m, R)
Death Wish IV: The Crackdown (1987, C, 100m, R)
Charles Bronson plays Paul Kersey in these violent action melodramas. In the first film, his wife is killed and his daughter brutally assaulted by street thugs, and he goes on a vigilante-style killing spree. Subsequent chapters have him in both New York and Los Angeles, dealing out his brand of justice to criminals. Jeff Goldblum makes his film debut as a mugger in the first film. **AC19, ST12, ST56** (first film), **XT9** (first film) *Essential (first film)*

Deathdream (1973, C, 90m, PG)
A veteran is discovered to be responsible for a series of murders because he is a zombie in need of human blood. Directed by Bob Clark. Also known as *Dead of Night*. **HO6**

Deathsport (1978, C, 82m, R)
Sequel to *Death Race 2000*, with deadly road race featuring killer cycles. David

Carradine and Claudia Jennings star. Allan Arkush directed. **AC10, DT4**

Deathstalker (1984, C, 80m, R)
Sword and sorcery saga featuring a lovely princess (Barbi Benton), who's the prize for the bravest warrior of them all. **AC18**

Deathstalker 2 (1987, C, 85m, R)
Name-only sequel in this adventure tale of a brave fighting man. Monique Gabrielle and John Terlesky star. **AC18**

Deathtrap (1982, C, 118m, PG)
A complicated thriller about a burned-out playwright, his smothering wife, and an ambitious student who's written a very good play. Michael Caine, Dyan Cannon, and Christopher Reeve star. Based on Ira Levin's hit play; directed by Sidney Lumet. **DR20, DT65, MY9, ST15**

Deathwatch (1980, C, 128m, R)
A dying woman is followed by a TV reporter who has a camera imbedded in his head, transmitting her story on national TV. Romy Schneider, Harvey Keitel, and Harry Dean Stanton star in this science fiction drama from France, with English dialogue. Directed by Bertrand Tavernier. **FF1, MY16, SF5, SF19, ST141**

Deception (1946, C, 112m, NR)
Bette Davis melodrama of a pianist whose benefactor (Claude Rains) keeps a tight rein on her. **ST28**

Decline of the American Empire, The (1986, C, 102m, R)
Canadian drama, with French dialogue, about a group of Quebec University professors and their wives. The men prepare a dinner while the women work out at a gym; the groups engage in conversation at the dinner. Directed by Denys Arcand. **CO2**

Decline of Western Civilization, The (1981, C, 100m, NR)
Documentary of the Los Angeles punk music scene, directed by Penelope Spheeris, featuring such household names as Black Flag, Fear, X, and Catholic Discipline. **MU11**

Decline of Western Civilization Part II: The Metal Years, The (1988, C, 90m, R)
Director Penelope Spheeris follows up her documentary on the punk music scene with a look at the heavy metal artists who've made it (Ozzy Osbourne, Joe Perry, Steve Tyler, Gene Simmons) and the younger generation of musicians looking for the same kind of fame. **MU11**

Deep, The (1977, C, 123m, PG)
Couple on an innocent skindiving expedition in Caribbean wind up finding treasure and drugs. Nick Nolte, Jacqueline Bisset, and Robert Shaw star. **AC12, ST113**

Deep in My Heart (1954, C, 132m, NR)
Jose Ferrer plays Sigmund Romberg in this biographical musical which features guest stars Gene Kelly, Ann Miller, and Tony Martin. Directed by Stanley Donen. **DT30, MU5, ST81**

Deep Red: The Hatchet Murders (1975, C, 98m, R)
A man who witnessed an ax murder and a journalist set out to investigate a series of similar killings. David Hemmings and Daria Nicolodi star. Directed by Dario Argento. **HO9**

Deep Star Six (1988, C, 103m, R)
An underwater expedition encounters a sea monster in this high-tech horror story. Greg Evigian, Cindy Pickett, and Taurean Blacque star. **HO16**

Deer Hunter, The (1978, C, 183m, R)
Drama of small-town buddies whose experiences in Vietnam shatter their lives. Robert DeNiro, Christopher Walken, John Savage, John Cazale, and Meryl Streep star. Directed by Michael Cimino. Oscar winner for Best Picture, Director, and Supporting Actor (Walken). **AC4, DR7, DR26, ST30, ST145, XT1, XT4, XT6, XT20** *Essential*

Defense of the Realm (1985, C, 96m, PG)
A journalist's story forces a British officer to resign. When the writer learns of the result, he attempts to uncover the entire story. **MY6**

Defiance (1980, C, 102m, PG)
Urban loner (Jan-Michael Vincent) takes on New York street gangs. With Art Carney, Theresa Saldana, and Danny Aiello. **AC8**

Defiant Ones, The (1958, B&W, 97m, NR)
Tony Curtis and Sidney Poitier play two escaped cons who must look past the color of their skin to survive. With Lon

Chaney, Jr. and Cara Williams. Directed by Stanley Kramer. **CL8, DT55, ST17, ST121**

Delicate Delinquent, The (1957, B&W, 100m, NR)
Jerry Lewis stars in his films *sans* Dean Martin as a hoodlum reformed by a friendly cop. With Darren McGavin and Martha Hyer. **ST91**

Delicate Sound of Thunder (1989, C, 100m, NR)
Concert film of rock group Pink Floyd's Momentary Lapse of Reason tour, featuring four songs not on the album of the same name. **MU10**

Deliverance (1972, C, 109m, R)
Four men on a canoe trip down an isolated stretch of river encounter disaster. Burt Reynolds, Jon Voight, Ned Beatty, and Ronny Cox star. John Boorman directed this adaptation of James Dickey's novel; Dickey makes a brief appearance as a sheriff. **AC24, DR19, DT29, ST128** *Recommended*

Delta Force, The (1986, C, 125m, R)
When terrorists commandeer an airliner and its terrified passengers, a special squad of fighting men swing into action. Chuck Norris and Lee Marvin are the rescuers; Shelley Winters and Martin Balsam are among the hostages. **AC20, ST100, ST114, ST164**

Dementia *see* Daughter of Horror

Dementia 13 (1963, B&W, 81m, NR)
Low-budget thriller about murders in and around an Irish castle. Directed by Francis Ford Coppola; produced by Roger Corman. **CU14, DT21, HO14**

Demetrius and the Gladiators (1954, C, 101m, NR)
Saga of ancient Rome, with Victor Mature the stalwart hero, Susan Hayward his royal lover, and a flamboyant Jay Robinson as the emperor Caligula. **CL3**

Demon *see* God Told Me To

Demon Seed (1977, C, 94m, R)
Computer goes mad, attacks scientist's wife for purposes of reproduction in this science fiction thriller. Julie Christie and Fritz Weaver star; Donald Cammell directed. **HO22, HO25, SF6, SF22**

Demons (1986, C, 89m, R)
An audience watching a slasher film is terrorized by a demonic army and transformed into hideous creatures. Directed by Lamberto Bava. **HO17**

Dentist, The (1932, B&W, 22m, NR)
W.C. Fields stars in this comedy short about a man with a mission for removing molars. **ST41**

Dernier Combat, Le (1984, B&W, 90m, R)
After the apocalypse, a survivor wanders a bizarre landscape and encounters equally strange characters. French film with no dialogue, only music and sound effects. Directed by Luc Besson. **FF1, SF19**

Dersu Uzala (1975, C, 124m, G)
Oscar-winning drama from Japan's Akira Kurosawa about the friendship between a Japanese guide and a Russian explorer in turn-of-the-century Siberia. Slow-moving, but worthwhile. **DT57, XT7** *Recommended*

Desert Bloom (1986, C, 106m, PG)
Sensitive portrait of a teenager with family problems in 1950s Las Vegas, at the time of A-bomb testing. Annabeth Gish stars, with Jon Voight, JoBeth Williams, and Ellen Barkin. **DR8** *Recommended*

Desert Fox, The (1951, B&W, 88m, NR)
James Mason plays Field Marshall Rommel in this World War II drama. With Cedric Hardwicke, Jessica Tandy, and Luther Adler as Adolf Hitler. **AC1, HF12, ST102**

Desert Hearts (1986, C, 96m, R)
In the 1950s, a female professor in Reno to get a divorce falls in love with another woman. Helen Shaver and Patricia Charbonneau star. **DR3, DR10**

Desire Under the Elms (1958, B&W, 114m, NR)
Drama based on Eugene O'Neill play set in 19th-century New England. Mother loves stepson, family bickers over land. Sophia Loren, Anthony Perkins, and Burl Ives star. **DR20, ST93, WR20**

Desiree (1954, C, 110m, NR)
Marlon Brando plays Napoleon, Jean Simmons his love object, Merle Oberon Empress Josephine in this historical drama. **CL3, HF18, ST10**

Desk Set (1957, C, 103m, NR)
Spencer Tracy-Katharine Hepburn comedy of a computer expert and a TV network researcher matching wits. With Joan Blondell, Gig Young, and Dina Merrill. **CL15, CO2, ST66, ST151**

Despair (1979, C, 119m, R)
A Russian emigré starts a successful business in Germany, only to see the Nazis come to power and ruin his life. Dirk Bogarde stars in this version of Vladimir Nabokov's book. Written by Tom Stoppard; directed by Rainer Werner Fassbinder. **DT34**

Desperate (1947, B&W, 73m, NR)
Thriller of a truck driver who is victimized by gangsters and flees for his life with his wife. Steve Brodie and Audrey Long star, with Raymond Burr. Directed by Anthony Mann. **DT69, MY1**

Desperate Hours, The (1955, B&W, 112m, NR)
Humphrey Bogart stars in this drama of an escaped convict and his gang hiding out in the house of a middle-class family. Fredric March, Arthur Kennedy, and Martha Scott costar. Loosely based on a true incident. William Wyler directed. **DR6, DT119, ST8**

Desperate Living (1977, B&W, 87m, NR)
Baltimore's gift to movies, director John Waters, strikes again with this story of a murderous housewife (Mink Stole), her accomplice maid (Jean Hill), and other not-of-this-earth characters. Edith Massey and Liz Renay costar. Don't say you weren't warned. **CU12, DT110**

Desperately Seeking Susan (1985, C, 104m, PG-13)
New Jersey housewife and New York con artist get their identities switched in this madcap, modern comedy. Rosanna Arquette and Madonna star, with Aidan Quinn. **CO2, CO20, MU12, XT9** *Recommended*

Destination Moon (1950, C, 91m, NR)
Early example of postwar science fiction, with rocketship making perilous trip to the moon. Oscar-winning special effects; co-written by Robert Heinlein. **SF1, SF3, SF15**

Destination Tokyo (1943, B&W, 135m, NR)
World War II drama set aboard a submarine in Japanese waters. Cary Grant stars, with John Garfield, Alan Hale, and Dane Clark. **AC1, ST57**

Destiny (1921, B&W, 122m, NR)
Early film from German director Fritz Lang, a fantasy of a woman's desperate attempt to rescue her lover from the hands of death. **DT58, FF3**

Destructors, The (1974, C, 89m, R)
Paris is the setting for this crime drama, starring Michael Caine as an assassin, Anthony Quinn as a federal drug agent, and James Mason as a narcotics kingpin. **ST15, ST102, XT16**

Destry Rides Again (1939, B&W, 94m, NR)
One of the great western comedies, with sheriff James Stewart trying to clean up the town—without resorting to violence. Marlene Dietrich costars. **ST33, ST143, WE8, WE14** *Essential; Recommended*

Detective, The (1954, B&W, 91m, NR)
Alex Guinness stars as Father Brown, the cleric-turned-detective created by G.K. Chesterton. **MY11, MY11, ST60**

Detective, The (1968, C, 114m, NR)
Frank Sinatra plays a police detective who's overzealous in his search for a killer and sends the wrong man to the electric chair. Al Freeman, Jr. and Lee Remick costar. **AC9, ST138**

Detour (1945, B&W, 69m, NR)
A hitchhiker gets involved in a murder after he encounters a mysterious woman. A low-budget classic, starring Tom Neal and Ann Savage, directed by Edgar G. Ulmer. **MY1, MY4** *Recommended*

Detroit 9000 (1973, C, 106m, R)
Jewel thieves and cops shoot it out on the streets of Motown. Alex Rocco, Hari Rhodes, and Vonetta McGee star. **AC8**

Devil and Daniel Webster, The (1941, B&W, 85m, NR)
Fantasy about a young farmer who meets up with the Devil. A flop in its original release, now a cult favorite. Edward Arnold and Walter Huston star. **CL14, HO10, SF2**

Devil and Max Devlin, The (1981, C, 96m, PG)
Deceased Max Devlin (Elliott Gould) bargains with the Devil (Bill Cosby) for another chance at life—in exchange, he'll provide three souls. Comedy from the Disney studios. **FA1, HO10**

Devil at 4 O'Clock, The (1961, C, 120m, NR)
Spencer Tracy plays a priest sent to rescue sickly children from the shadow of an erupting volcano. Frank Sinatra costars. **AC23, ST138, ST151**

Devil Bat, The see Killer Bats

Devil Doll, The (1936, B&W, 80m, NR)
A madman shrinks humans to the size of small dolls and gets them to carry out various crimes. Lionel Barrymore and Maureen O'Sullivan star. Directed by Tod Browning. **HO1, DT14**

Devil in the Flesh (1986, C, 110m, R)
Sexually explicit drama of a young woman who's torn between her terrorist lover and a younger man. Maruschka Detmers, Federico Pitzalis, and Riccard de Torrebruna star. Italian filmmaker Marco Bellochio directed. Also available in an unrated version which contains footage that earned the film its original "X" rating. **CU6, FF2**

Devil Walks at Midnight, The see Devil's Nightmare, The

Devils, The (1971, C, 109m, R)
Religious hysteria grips a convent in 17th-century France, and a lecherous priest attempts to aid the delirious nuns. Ken Russell directed this controversial drama starring Oliver Reed and Vanessa Redgrave. **DR5, DT92, HO11, ST127**

Devil's Eye, The (1960, B&W, 90m, NR)
Director Ingmar Bergman's drama of the Devil's emissary sent to take a young woman's virginity. Jarl Kulle and Bibi Andersson star. **DT7**

Devil's Nightmare, The (1971, C, 90m, R)
A sexy succubus seduces and slays seven travelers at a remote villa, with each killing paralleling the Seven Deadly Sins. Erika Blane stars. Also known as *The Devil Walks at Midnight* and *Succubus*. **HO10**

Devil's Partner, The (1958, B&W, 75m, NR)
An old man possessed by the devil returns to life as his mysterious "nephew," to torment a small town in New Mexico. Ed Nelson stars. **HO10**

Devil's Playground, The (1976, C, 107m, NR)
Life at an Australian Catholic boys' school, whose students and teachers are wrestling with sexual problems. Fred Schepisi directed. **DR25, FF5** *Recommended*

Devil's Rain, The (1975, C, 86m, PG)
Ernest Borgnine is the reincarnation of a 17th-century witch who is to deliver souls to the Devil. He and his coven melt everyone who gets in his way. William Shatner costars. **HO10, HO11**

Devil's Triangle, The (1978, C, 59m, NR)
Vincent Price narrates this documentary about the strange occurrences in the Bermuda Triangle area. **ST124**

Devil's Undead, The (1972, C, 90m, PG)
A satanic cult who yearn for immortality try to project their souls into children. Christopher Lee, Peter Cushing, and Diana Dors star. **ST27, ST89**

Devil's Wanton, The (1949, B&W, 72m, NR)
Ingmar Bergman drama of an unhappy prostitute and her love affair with a writer. Doris Svenlund stars. Released in the U.S. in 1962. **DT7**

Diabolically Yours (1967, C, 94m, NR)
French thriller of a man who awakens after an accident with a wife and huge house he has no memory of. Alain Delon and Senta Berger star. Directed by Julien Duvivier. **FF1**

Diabolique (1955, B&W, 107m, NR)
Classic French thriller about a wife and mistress who murder a heartless schoolteacher—and the surprising aftermath. Simone Signoret and Vera Clouzot star; Henri-Georges Clouzot directed. **FF1, MY16** *Essential; Recommended*

Dial M for Murder (1954, C, 105m, NR)
A faithless husband (Ray Milland) plots the murder of his wealthy, adulterous wife (Grace Kelly). Robert Cummings co-

stars. Directed by Alfred Hitchcock. **DT46, MY3, ST82**

Diamond Skulls (1989, C, 87m, NR)
Drama of the decadent British aristocracy, involving a murder coverup and sexual infidelity. Gabriel Byrne, Amanda Donohoe, and Michael Horder star. **DR23**

Diamonds (1975, C, 101m, PG)
Heist drama, with Robert Shaw playing two roles: the lead crook and his twin brother, the designer of the target vault's security system. Richard Roundtree, Shelley Winters, and Barbara Seagull (Hershey) costar. Filmed in Israel. **MY18, ST164**

Diamonds Are Forever (1971, C, 119m, PG)
James Bond travels to Las Vegas, but it's not to catch any of the shows or play the slots. Sean Connery stars, with Jill St. John and Charles Gray in support. Car chases galore. **HF2, ST21**

Diary of a Chambermaid (1946, C, 81m, NR)
Jean Renoir directed this English-language drama about a disruptive servant (Paulette Goddard). Written by and costarring Burgess Meredith. Original running time: 98m. **DT86**

Diary of a Chambermaid (1964, B&W, 97m, NR)
A French maid (Jeanne Moreau) discovers a world of hypocrisy and corruption when she takes a job with a country family during the Nazi Occupation. Luis Buñuel directed this remake of Jean Renoir's film. **CU18, DT15, FF1, ST110**

Diary of a Country Priest (1950, B&W, 120m, NR)
French director Robert Bresson paints a moving portrait of a young idealist assigned to a rural parish. **FF1** *Essential*

Diary of a Lost Girl (1929, B&W, 104m, NR)
Silent classic from Germany starring Louise Brooks as a woman whose life is a virtual catalogue of tragedy, from rape to residence in a bordello. Directed by G.W. Pabst. **CL12, FF3** *Recommended*

Diary of a Mad Housewife (1970, C, 94m, R)
A Manhattan woman, fed up with her status-seeking husband, tries to find solace in an affair with an actor. Carrie Snodgress stars, with Richard Benjamin and Frank Langella. **DR10**

Diary of Anne Frank, The (1959, C, 150m, NR)
The true account of a Jewish family's hiding out from the Nazis, as told by a teenaged daughter in her diary. Millie Perkins stars, with Oscar winner Shelley Winters, Joseph Schildkraut, Richard Beymer, and Ed Wynn. George Stevens directed. **CL2, DT101, ST164, XT5**

Dick Tracy (1990, C, 103m, PG)
The square-jawed police detective of the comic strips battles a rogue's gallery of villains. Warren Beatty stars, with Al Pacino, Dustin Hoffman, Madonna, Glenne Headly, Mandy Patinkin, and Charlie Korsmo. Beatty directed; production design by Richard Sylbert; cinematography by Vittorio Storraro. **AC9, AC22, ST5, ST67, ST118**

Dick Tracy Meets Gruesome (1947, B&W, 65m, NR)
Dick Tracy is on the trail of master criminal Gruesome, who is using a gas to freeze people in the middle of his bank robberies. Ralph Byrd stars, with Boris Karloff. **ST77**

Die Hard (1988, C, 131m, R)
Riveting, breathlessly paced thriller set in a Los Angeles high-rise office building, with a terrorist gang holding hostages and battling a lone New York cop trapped inside. Bruce Willis stars, with Alan Rickman, Alexander Gudonov, and Bonnie Bedelia. **AC8, AC25, ST161** *Recommended*

Die, Monster, Die! (1965, C, 80m, NR)
Boris Karloff stars in this British horror story of a hermit who's given strange powers by a fallen meteor. Based on an H. P. Lovecraft story. **ST77**

Dillinger (1973, C, 96m, R)
Portrait of America's most notorious Depression-era gangster, played with roguish charm by Warren Oates. Costarring Ben Johnson (as Melvin Purvis), Cloris Leachman (as the Lady in Red), Richard Dreyfuss (as Baby Face Nelson), Michelle Phillips, and Harry Dean Stanton.

Directed by John Milius. **AC22, ST36, ST115, ST141** *Recommended*

Dim Sum: a little bit of heart (1984, C, 89m, PG)
Drama set in San Francisco's Chinatown, focusing on the relationship between a mother with her Old World ways, and her more modern, Americanized daughter. Directed by Wayne Wang. **DR15, XT13**

Dimples (1936, B&W, 78m, NR)
Shirley Temple classic finds the child star taking on the burden of her father's financial difficulties to help ease his mind. Songs include: "Oh Mister Man Up In the Moon," "What Did the Bluebird Say." **ST148**

Diner (1982, C, 110m, R)
Baltimore in the late 1950s is the setting for this nostalgic comedy about five young men reluctant to get on with their adult lives. Mickey Rourke, Daniel Stern, Kevin Bacon, Steve Guttenberg, Paul Reiser, and Timothy Daly star, with Ellen Barkin and Michael Tucker. Written and directed by Barry Levinson. **CO6, ST134** *Highly Recommended*

Dinner at Eight (1933, B&W, 113m, NR)
Comedy classic from George Cukor stars Lionel Barrymore and Billie Burke as a highfalutin' couple who throw swell parties, where guests open up to reveal deep-dark secrets. All-star MGM cast also includes Wallace Beery, Jean Harlow, Lee Tracy, John Barrymore, Jean Hersholt, Marie Dressler, and many more. **CL10, CU17, DT24** *Recommended*

Dinosaurus! (1960, C, 85m, NR)
Science fiction adventure about a pair of cavemen and a dinosaur discovered on a remote tropical island. **SF4**

Dirt Bike Kid, The (1986, C, 90m, PG)
Peter Billingsley plays a precocious teen with an unusual bike that rides him right into mischief. **DR22, FA7**

Dirty Dancing (1987, C, 100m, PG-13)
Romantic drama, set in the summer of 1963 at a mountain resort hotel, where a 16-year-old girl blossoms under the eye of a handsome dance instructor. Jennifer Grey and Patrick Swayze star. **DR1, MU3**

Dirty Dozen, The (1967, C, 150m, NR)
Allies recruit 12 convicts for nasty job behind Nazi lines. Lee Marvin trains the misfit gang, which includes Charles Bronson, Jim Brown, John Cassavetes, Telly Savalas, and Clint Walker; Robert Ryan and Ernest Borgnine also star. Directed by Robert Aldrich. **AC1, ST12, ST100** *Essential; Recommended*

Dirty Harry (1971, C, 102m, R)
The first film in the series about the San Francisco cop (Clint Eastwood) who makes his own rules—whatever it takes to keep the streets clean. A psychotic killer (Andy Robinson) is terrorizing the city, and Harry Callahan is ordered to bring him in. Directed by Don Siegel. **AC9, DT97, ST39, XT13** *Essential; Recommended*

Dirty Knight's Work *see* Choice of Weapons, A

Dirty, Rotten Scoundrels (1988, C, 110m, PG)
A pair of hustlers who romance wealthy women wager on a common target—the one who succeeds first has the French Riviera to himself. Steve Martin and Michael Caine are the title characters. Remake of *Bedtime Story*. **CO3, ST15, ST99**

Disappearance of Aimee, The (1976, C, 110m, NR)
Faye Dunaway and Bette Davis star in this drama, set in the 1920s, about the much-publicized disappearance and reappearance of the evangelist Aimee Semple McPherson. With James Woods. Originally made for TV. **ST28, ST37, ST165**

Discreet Charm of the Bourgeoisie, The (1972, C, 100m, R)
Straight-faced comedy about the inability of a group of well-to-do friends to conclude a dinner party. Director Luis Buñuel's film deservedly won the Oscar for Best Foreign Film. Dialogue in French. **DT15, XT7** *Essential; Highly Recommended*

Disorderly Orderly, The (1964, C, 90m, NR)
Jerry Lewis comedy set in a nursing home. Directed by Frank Tashlin. **ST91**

Disorganized Crime (1989, C, 101m, R)
A quartet of inept crooks, waiting for their leader to show up for a big heist,

manage to create plenty of havoc in the meantime. Fred Gwynne, William Russ, Ruben Blades, and Lou Diamond Phillips are the crooks; Corbin Bernsen is their leader. **CO10, MU12, MY18**

Distant Drums (1951, C, 101m, NR)
Gary Cooper is swamped by Seminole Indians in 19th-century Florida. **ST22**

Distant Thunder (1973, C, 100m, NR)
Indian director Satyajit Ray presents a devastating drama of the great 1942 famine in Bengal. Soumitra Chatterji stars. **DT84**

Distant Thunder (1988, C, 114m, R)
A Vietnam veteran, living in isolation in a woodsy retreat since the war, confronts his teenaged son, whom he abandoned 16 years before. John Lithgow and Ralph Macchio star. **DR7, DR8**

Distant Voices, Still Lives (1989, C, 85m, PG-13)
Drama set in 1940s Liverpool, England, centering on one family and important events: the death of the father and weddings of two of the children. Terence Davies directed. **DR8, DR23**

Diva (1982, C, 123m, R)
Contemporary French thriller, set in Paris, about a young courier's obsession with an opera singer and his accidental possession of a valuable tape recording. Stylish fun, directed by Jean-Jacques Beneix. **FF1, MY16, XT16** *Recommended*

Divine Madness (1980, C, 95m, R)
Concert film featuring Bette Midler, in all her campy glory. **MU10, ST105**

Divine Nymph, The (1979, C, 90m, R)
Costume drama starring Marcello Mastroianni, Laura Antonelli, and Terence Stamp as points of a love triangle. **ST103**

Divorce His—Divorce Hers (1972, C, 144m, NR)
Richard Burton and Elizabeth Taylor play a husband and wife who offer two sides to the story behind a marriage breakup. Originally made for TV. **CL15, ST13, ST147**

Divorce of Lady X, The (1938, C, 91m, NR)
A British debutante (Merle Oberon) pretends she's married to trick her lawyer (Laurence Olivier). **ST116**

Dixie Dynamite (1976, C, 89m, PG)
After their father is killed by a deputy sheriff, two lovely sisters arm for revenge. Jane Anne Johnstone and Kathy McHaley star, with Warren Oates and Christopher George. **ST115**

Django (1968, C, 90m, PG)
Spaghetti western finds a group of Americans feuding with Mexican bandits. **WE9, WE13**

Django Shoots First (1974, C, 96m, NR)
In this spaghetti western, a cowboy is out to avenge the murder of his father. Glenn Saxon stars. **WE5, WE13**

Do the Right Thing (1989, C, 120m, R)
Writer-director-actor Spike Lee's uncompromising look at contemporary race relations in New York City, in a one-day portrait of Brooklyn's Bedford Stuyvesant neighborhood. The action centers around a pizza parlor run by Italians. Danny Aiello costars, with Ossie Davis, Ruby Dee, John Turturro, Richard Edson, Giancarlo Esposito, Joie Lee, and John Savage. **DR7, DR14, DR15, DT60, XT8, XT9** *Highly Recommended*

Doc Savage: The Man of Bronze (1975, C, 100m, G)
Pulp hero created by author Kenneth Robeson makes his movie debut in this adventure about a super scientist/muscle man and his five colleagues. Ron Ely stars. **AC17**

Docks of New York, The (1928, B&W, 76m, NR)
Classic silent drama about a man who falls for the emotionally unstable woman he's just saved from drowning. Directed by Josef von Sternberg. **CL12, DT100**

Doctor and the Devils, The (1985, C, 93m, R)
Two grave robbers provide corpses to a dedicated surgeon who needs them for practice. Based on a screenplay written in the 1940s by Dylan Thomas. Timothy Dalton, Jonathan Pryce, and Twiggy star. **HO26**

Doctor at Sea (1955, C, 93m, NR)
British comedy-drama of young doctor
signing on to work a freighter. Dirk Bogarde and Brigitte Bardot star. **ST4**

Dr. Butcher, M.D. (1980, C, 88m, NR)
An investigation of mutilated corpses
leads a doctor and scientist to an island
where cannibalism is practiced. They find
a mad doctor experimenting with strange
transplants and creating a race of monstrous zombies. **HO18**

Dr. Cyclops (1940, C, 75m, NR)
A mad scientist in the Peruvian jungle
transforms a quartet of colleagues into
miniaturized humans. Oscar-winning special effects highlight this classic fantasy.
SF2, SF5, SF15

Doctor Detroit (1983, C, 89m, R)
A college professor finds himself involved
with pimps, prostitutes, and other low-
lifes in this comedy starring Dan Aykroyd
and Howard Hesseman. **CO13**

Doctor Dolittle (1967, C, 144m, NR)
Rex Harrison is the magical doctor who
can talk to the animals, in a musical based
on Hugh Lofting's children's stories. Samantha Eggar and Anthony Newley costar. **FA9, MU8, MU17**

Doctor Faustus (1968, C, 93m, NR)
Richard Burton stars in this drama based
on Christopher Marlowe's play of an embittered scholar in need of some soul
searching. Elizabeth Taylor appears
briefly as Helen of Troy. **CL15, ST13,
ST147**

Doctor in the House (1954, C, 92m, NR)
Classic British comedy about medical stu-
dents majoring in female anatomy. Dirk
Bogarde stars. **CO17**

Dr. Jekyll and Mr. Hyde (1920, B&W,
63m, NR)
A silent version of Robert Louis Stevenson's story about a doctor (John Barrymore) who is experimenting with a way
to separate the good half and the evil half
in humans. **HO1, HO20**

Dr. Jekyll and Mr. Hyde (1932, B&W,
98m, NR)
Superb version of the Robert Louis Stevenson tale, with an Oscar-winning performance by Fredric March, solid support
from Miriam Hopkins, excellent direction

by Rouben Mamoulian. The transformation scenes are especially effective. Video
version restores footage trimmed by cen-
sors after the film's initial release. **CU10,
HO1, HO17, HO20, XT2** *Essential; Recommended*

Dr. Jekyll and Mr. Hyde (1941, B&W,
114m, NR)
Spencer Tracy and Ingrid Bergman star in
this version of Robert Louis Stevenson's
classic tale. With Lana Turner and Donald Crisp. **HO1, HO20, ST7, ST151, ST153**

Dr. No (1963, C, 111m, PG)
The first film appearance of James Bond
(Sean Connery), as he battles a sinister
mastermind (Joseph Wiseman) in the Ca-
ribbean. Ursula Andress costars. **HF2,
ST21** *Recommended*

Dr. Phibes Rises Again (1972, C, 89m, PG)
Sequel to *The Abominable Dr. Phibes* has
the bad doctor in Egypt to perform a
ritual that will bring his late wife back to
life. Vincent Price, Robert Quarry, and
Peter Cushing star. **HO20, HO26, ST27,
ST124**

**Dr. Strangelove or: How I Learned to Stop
Worrying and Love the Bomb** (1964,
B&W, 93m, NR)
Landmark black comedy about a crazy
Air Force general who orders U.S. planes
to bomb the Soviet Union, triggering fran-
tic actions by the President to save the
world. Peter Sellers stars in three roles,
with Sterling Hayden, George C. Scott,
Keenan Wynn, Slim Pickens, Peter Bull,
and James Earl Jones in support. Di-
rected by Stanley Kubrick. **CO2, CO12,
DT56, ST76, ST137** *Essential; Highly
Recommended*

Dr. Terror's Gallery of Horrors (1967, C,
90m, NR)
Five-part horror anthology featuring John
Carradine as a warlock, Lon Chaney, Jr.,
as a mad doctor, Mitch Evans as Dracula,
and more. **HF7, ST17**

Doctor Terror's House of Horrors (1964,
C, 98m, NR)
Five tales are linked together by the mysterious Dr. Schreck, foretelling the futures of five people on a train. Peter Cushing, Christopher Lee, and Donald
Sutherland star. **HO23, HO26, ST27, ST89**

Dr. Who and the Daleks (1965, C, 85m, NR)
Science fiction adventure, inspired by popular British TV character, with Dr. Who and his friends on another planet with robot-like creatures. Peter Cushing and Jennie Linden star. **SF19, ST27**

Doctor X (1932, C, 77m, NR)
The path of a murderer is traced back to a mysterious doctor. Lionel Atwill and Fay Wray star. **HO1**

Dr. Zhivago (1965, C, 197m, NR)
An epic of the Russian Revolution and the people whose lives it changed. Omar Sharif and Julie Christie star, with Geraldine Chaplin, Rod Steiger, Alec Guinness, and Tom Courtenay. Based on Boris Pasternak's novel; directed by David Lean. **CL3, CL4, DT59, ST60**

Doctors' Wives (1971, C, 100m, R)
Trashy drama about the murder of a wife who had been cheating on her physician husband. Gene Hackman stars, with Richard Crenna and Rachel Roberts. **ST61**

Dodes'ka-den (1970, C, 140m, NR)
Japanese drama centering on the lives of shanty dwellers in a Tokyo slum is both funny and terribly moving. Directed by Akira Kurosawa. **DT57** *Recommended*

Dodge City (1939, C, 105m, NR)
Western saga starring Errol Flynn as a two-fisted marshal. With Olivia de Havilland, Ann Sheridan, Bruce Cabot, Alan Hale, and Ward Bond. **ST43**

Dodsworth (1936, B&W, 101m, NR)
A middle-aged American couple discover on a European holiday that their marriage is no longer solid. Walter Huston, Ruth Chatterton, and Mary Astor star in this excellent version of Sinclair Lewis's novel, directed by William Wyler. **DR19, DT119, WR17** *Essential; Recommended*

Dog Day (1983, C, 101m, NR)
French drama starring Lee Marvin as a U.S. traitor on the run who bargains with some farmers for refuge. **ST100**

Dog Day Afternoon (1975, C, 130m, R)
True-life drama of a bank robbery in summertime New York that goes awry, with the desperate thieves holding hostages. Taut suspense mixed with humor. Al Pacino and John Cazale star, with John Forsythe and Chris Sarandon. Directed by Sidney Lumet. **DR6, DT65, ST118, XT9** *Recommended*

Dog of Flanders, A (1959, C, 96m, NR)
A badly abused dog is cared for and loved back to good health by a Dutch boy and his grandpa in this animal story. **FA5**

Dogs in Space (1986, C, 105m, NR)
Australian musical drama set in the late 1970s, centering on that country's punk music scene. Michael Hutchence stars. **FF5, MU9**

Dogs of Hell (1983, C, 90m, R)
The U.S. Army trains a pack of Rottweilers to be the perfect killing machines. The dogs escape and terrorize a nearby town. Earl Owensby stars. **HO16**

Dogs of War, The (1981, C, 109m, R)
Frederick Forsyth's story of a band of ruthless mercenaries who try to overthrow a sadistic African dictator. Christopher Walken and Tom Berenger star, with JoBeth Williams. **AC20, WR8**

Dolce Vita, La (1960, B&W, 175m, NR)
Exuberant, sobering, one-of-a-kind look at contemporary Rome from director Federico Fellini. Marcello Mastroianni stars as a jaded journalist who thinks he's seen it all, but really hasn't. Anita Ekberg heads the supporting cast of this drama filmed on many well-known locations in Rome. **DT53, ST103, XT17** *Essential; Recommended*

$ (Dollars) (1972, C, 119m, R)
Comic tale of elaborate heist, with wild chase sequence. Warren Beatty and Goldie Hawn star in this caper film shot in Germany. **CO10, MY18, ST5, ST63**

Dollmaker, The (1984, C, 140m, NR)
Drama of one woman's struggle to keep her family together when they move from the rural South to Detroit in search of work. Jane Fonda won an Emmy for her performance; Levon Helm costars as her husband. Originally made for TV. **DR10, MU12, ST45**

Dolls (1987, C, 77m, R)
A family and a couple of hitchhikers are forced by a storm to take refuge in a mysterious house owned by an old couple

who make dolls that can kill. Directed by
Stuart Gordon. **HO16**

Doll's House, A (1973, C, 95m, G)
Claire Bloom and Anthony Hopkins star
in Henrik Ibsen's drama of one woman's
struggle for respect and independence.
With Ralph Richardson, Denholm Elliott,
Anna Massey, and Edith Evans. **DR20**

Doll's House, A (1973, C, 103m, G)
Jane Fonda stars in this adaptation of the
Ibsen play about a 19th-century house-
wife's fight for independence. With David
Warner, Trevor Howard, Delphine Seyrig,
and Edward Fox. **DR20, ST45**

Dominick and Eugene (1988, C, 111m, PG-
13)
Sentimental tale of two Pittsburgh brothers (Tom Hulce, Ray Liotta), one a slow-
witted, well-meaning child-man, the other
an aspiring doctor. Trouble arises when
the intern must continue his studies in
another city. With Jamie Lee Curtis.
DR2, DR8

Domino Principle, The (1977, C, 97m, R)
Thriller about a man recruited by a polit-
ical conspiracy to be an assassin. Gene
Hackman stars, with Candice Bergen,
Richard Widmark, and Mickey Rooney.
Directed by Stanley Kramer. **DT55, ST61,
ST133**

Don Q: Son of Zorro (1925, B&W, 148m,
NR)
Douglas Fairbanks stars in this silent classic about the Mexican swordsman and his
offspring, who is determined to follow in
his father's famous footsteps. **AC13**

Doña Flor and Her Two Husbands (1977,
C, 105m, R)
Brazilian comedy about a lovely young
widow who remarries, then has to satisfy
her sex-starved husband's ghost. Sonia
Braga stars. U.S. remake: *Kiss Me Goodbye*. **FF6, FF8, ST9** ·

Donkey Skin (1971, C, 90m, NR)
Comic fairy tale starring Catherine Deneuve as a princess whose mother's dying
request leads to a rather delicate situation
with her father. **ST29**

Donovan's Reef (1963, C, 109m, NR)
Classic action comedy stars John Wayne
as an ex-Navy man living the island high-
life in the South Pacific until a prudish

New England girl arrives in search of her
dad. With Elizabeth Allen, Lee Marvin,
Jack Warden, Cesar Romero, and Mike
Mazurki. John Ford directed. **CO9, DT36,
ST100, ST156** *Recommended*

Don's Party (1976, C, 91m, NR)
Australian comedy about an election-
night bash featuring heated political de-
bates and some sexual escapades as well.
Bruce Beresford directed. John Hargreaves heads the splendid cast. **FF5** *Recommended*

Don't Answer the Phone (1980, C, 94m, R)
A psychopath stalks and attacks the patients of a beautiful talk show psychologist. James Westmoreland and Flo Ger-
rish star. **HO9**

Don't Fence Me In (1945, B&W, 71m, NR)
Roy Rogers plays a singin' cowpoke who
can't be tied down. **ST132**

Don't Look Back (1967, B&W, 96m, NR)
Unsparing, often very funny documentary about singer Bob Dylan's 1965 tour
of England. Incisive portrait of a brilliant,
difficult subject. Directed by D. A. Pen-
nebaker. **MU11** *Essential; Highly Recommended*

Don't Look Now (1973, C, 110m, R)
Julie Christie and Donald Sutherland star
in a gripping thriller about a couple who
try to make contact with their dead child.
Directed by Nicolas Roeg; adapted from
a Daphne du Maurier story. **DT88, HO14,
HO19, MY14, WR5** *Recommended*

Don't Raise the Bridge, Lower the River
(1968, C, 99m, NR)
Jerry Lewis plays an American living in
England whose free-spending ways are
financed by his get-rich-quick schemes.
ST91

Doomed To Die (1940, B&W, 68m, NR)
Boris Karloff plays Mr. Wong, the wily
Chinese detective, in this mystery of a
fire aboard a luxury liner. **ST77**

Dorothy in the Land of Oz (1981, C, 60m,
NR)
Animated musical based on the popular
Wizard of Oz tales, with old friends and
some new members added to the Oz fam-
ily. **FA10**

Dorritt's Story *see* Little Dorritt

Double Dynamite (1951, B&W, 80m, NR)
Frank Sinatra stars in this comedy about a bank clerk mistakenly accused of embezzlement. With Jane Russell and Groucho Marx. **ST101, ST138**

Double Indemnity (1944, B&W, 106m, NR)
Classic film noir with Barbara Stanwyck the ultimate femme fatale, Fred MacMurray the ultimate sap in this murder for love story. Edward G. Robinson co-stars. Billy Wilder directed and wrote the screenplay with Raymond Chandler, based on the James M. Cain novel. **DT116, MY1, MY4, MY5, ST130, ST142, WR1** *Essential; Highly Recommended*

Double Life, A (1947, B&W, 104m, NR)
A serious actor (Oscar winner Ronald Colman) finds he can't separate his work from his personal life when he takes on the role of Othello. With Signe Hasso, Edmond O'Brien, and Shelley Winters. Directed by George Cukor. **CL7, DT24, ST164, XT2**

Double McGuffin, The (1979, C, 101m, PG)
A trio of inquisitive kids get mixed up in a plot to assassinate a Middle Eastern leader. The adult stars of this family adventure include Ernest Borgnine, George Kennedy, Elke Sommer, and Lyle Alzado. **FA7**

Double Suicide (1969, B&W, 105m, NR)
Japanese drama of ill-fated affair between a merchant and a prostitute. Directed by Masahiro Shinoda. **FF4**

Double Trouble (1967, C, 90m, NR)
Elvis Presley musical about a pop star (guess who) and one of his teen fans in Britain. With Annette Day and John Williams. **ST123**

Down Among the Z-Men (1952, B&W, 70m, NR)
Britain's Goon Show radio team stars in this comedy about an inept gang of crooks trying to steal a secret formula. Harry Secombe, Spike Milligan, and Peter Sellers head the cast. Also known as *Stand Easy*. **ST137**

Down and Dirty (1976, C, 115m, NR)
Italian comedy, directed by Ettore Scola, about a poverty-stricken family and their ribald adventures in a Rome slum. Nino Manfredi stars. **FF2**

Down and Out in Beverly Hills (1985, C, 103m, R)
Homeless man tries to commit suicide in Beverly Hills swimming pool, is rescued and moves in with nutsy family. Comic look at modern lifestyles starring Nick Nolte, Richard Dreyfuss, and Bette Midler, with Elizabeth Pena, Tracy Nelson, and Little Richard. Directed by Paul Mazursky, who plays a small role. Remake of French classic, *Boudu Saved From Drowning*. **CO2, CO20, FF8, ST36, ST105, ST113, XT10** *Recommended*

Down by Law (1986, B&W, 90m, R)
A trio of jailbirds escape from a Louisiana pokey for a series of comic adventures. John Lurie, Tom Waits, and Robert Benigni star. Jim Jarmusch directed this offbeat comedy. **CO12, MU12**

Down Dakota Way (1949, B&W, 67m, NR)
Roy Rogers is on the trail of the bad guys when he learns of his friend's death. Dale Evans costars. **ST132**

Down Mexico Way (1941, B&W, 78m, NR)
Gene Autry and sidekick Smiley Burnette wind up among a ring of thieves. **ST3**

Downhill Racer (1969, C, 102m, PG)
Cocky ski champ and his coach clash all the way to the Olympics. Robert Redford and Gene Hackman star. Michael Ritchie directed. **DR22, ST61, ST126**

Downtown (1990, C, 96m, R)
A white Philadelphia cop is transferred from a suburban beat to one of the city's worst neighborhoods, where he's teamed up with a young black cop. Anthony Edwards and Forest Whitaker star in this action film with moments of comedy. **AC9**

Dracula (1931, B&W, 85m, NR)
Bela Lugosi recreates his famous stage role as the mysterious nobleman who only comes out at night and lives to drink human blood. With Dwight Frye. Directed by Tod Browning. **HF7, HO1, HO5, DT14, ST95** *Essential; Recommended*

Dracula (1979, C, 109m, R)
Frank Langella plays the famous vampire in this version of Bram Stoker's novel, which gives the old count sexier appeal.

Laurence Olivier costars. **HF7, HO5, HO19, ST116**

Dracula and Son (1979, C, 90m, PG)
Dracula's boy just wants to play football and date girls; he won't bite anyone, even when his father punishes him. Christopher Lee stars. **HF7, HO5, ST89**

Dracula vs. Frankenstein (1971, C, 90m, PG)
Dracula (Lon Chaney, Jr.) goes to see Dr. Frankenstein (J. Carroll Naish) to arrange for a continuous blood supply. **HF7, HF10, ST17**

Dragnet (1987, C, 106m, PG-13)
Dan Aykroyd stars as the nephew of TV's Sgt. Joe Friday in this continuation of that show's tight-lipped traditions, with a few contemporary comic touches. Tom Hanks costars, with Dabney Coleman, Alexandra Paul, Christopher Plummer, and Harry Morgan. **CO10, CO13, ST62**

Dragon Seed (1944, B&W, 145m, NR)
A Chinese town bands together to ward off a Japanese invasion in this classic drama based on Pearl Buck's novel. Katharine Hepburn and Walter Huston star. **ST66**

Dragon That Wasn't (Or Was He?), The (1983, C, 96m, NR)
An animated feature about Ollie B. Bear, a jolly bruin who raises a baby dragon he finds on his doorstep. **FA10**

Dragonslayer (1981, C, 108m, PG)
Sorcerer's apprentice (Peter MacNicol, not Mickey Mouse) learns his craft well when he takes on an enormous dragon. Caitlin Clark and Ralph Richardson costar in this adventure tale with dazzling special effects. **AC18**

Draw! (1981, C, 98m, NR)
Kirk Douglas and James Coburn play a couple of has-been outlaws in this old-fashioned Western comedy. Originally made for cable TV. **ST34, WE14**

Dream a Little Dream (1989, C, 114m, PG-13)
A smitten teenager exchanges personalities with an old man in this comedy-drama starring Corey Feldman and Jason Robards. With Meredith Salenger, Piper Laurie, and Harry Dean Stanton. **CO20, ST129, ST141**

Dream for Christmas, A (1973, C, 100m, NR)
Family drama of a black pastor moving his brood to California to start a new congregation. George Spell, Hari Rhodes, and Beah Richards star. **DR14, FA13**

Dream Street (1921, B&W, 138m, NR)
D.W. Griffith's silent drama looks at London's seamy lower depths, where two brothers are both in love with the same girl. **DT42**

Dream Team, The (1989, C, 113m, PG-13)
A quartet of psychiatric patients are set adrift in New York City when their doctor is injured during a field trip. Comedy starring Michael Keaton, Christopher Lloyd, Peter Boyle, and Stephen Furst. **CO3, CO20, ST80, XT9**

Dreamchild (1985, C, 94m, PG)
Imaginative drama of elderly English woman who, as a little girl, was the inspiration for Lewis Carroll's *Alice in Wonderland,* now coming to New York to attend a program honoring the late author. Coral Browne stars, with Ian Holm (as Carroll in flashbacks), Peter Gallagher, and Nicola Cowper. Written by Dennis Potter. **DR5, DR11** *Recommended*

Dreams (1955, B&W, 86m, NR)
Drama from Ingmar Bergman about a model and the head of her photo agency, their problems with men and their careers. Eva Dahlbeck and Harriet Andersson star. **DT7**

Dreamscape (1984, C, 99m, PG-13)
A research project into dreams is secretly used for sinister political purposes in this science fiction thriller. Dennis Quaid, Kate Capshaw, and Max von Sydow star. **SF5**

Dressed To Kill (1946, B&W, 72m, NR)
Super sleuth Sherlock Holmes uncovers a music box with some valuable hints as to a theft at the Bank of England. Basil Rathbone and Nigel Bruce star. **HF14**

Dressed To Kill (1980, C, 105m, R)
Brian DePalma's thriller finds an adulterous wife (Angie Dickinson) brutally murdered. Her son launches his own investigation by seeking out a prime witness. Michael Caine, Keith Gordon, and Nancy Allen costar. **DT29, MY5, MY11, MY13, ST15**

Dresser, The (1983, C, 118m, PG)
In postwar Britain, the temperamental star of a traveling troupe is tended to by his loyal valet. Albert Finney and Tom Courtenay star, with Edward Fox. **DR12, DR23, ST42**

Dressmaker, The (1988, C, 92m, NR)
In 1944 Liverpool, England, a 17-year-old girl under the care of two aunts falls in love. Joan Plowright, Billie Whitelaw, and Jane Horrocks star. **DR8, DR23**

Driver, The (1978, C, 90m, R)
Stripped-down thriller (characters have no names) about a getaway man (Ryan O'Neal), a detective (Bruce Dern), and a lovely lady (Isabelle Adjani). Directed by Walter Hill. **AC8, DT45, MY2**

Driver's Seat, The (1973, C, 101m, R)
Thriller, made in Italy, stars Elizabeth Taylor as a psychotic on a rendezvous with death. **ST147**

Driving Miss Diasy (1989, C, 99m, PG)
The ongoing relationship between a Southern Jewish widow and her black chauffeur form the basis for this touching drama. Jessica Tandy and Morgan Freeman star, with Dan Aykroyd. Based on the play by Alfred Uhry; directed by Bruce Beresford. Six Oscars, including Best Picture and Actress. **CO13, DR8, DR11, DR20, ST48, XT1, XT3** *Recommended*

Drowning Pool, The (1976, C, 108m PG)
Paul Newman plays private eye Lew Harper in Ross MacDonald's mystery about the murder of a businessman. With Joanne Woodward, Anthony Franciosa, and Melanie Griffith. **ST58, ST111, ST166, WR19**

Drugstore Cowboy (1989, C, 100m, R)
Matt Dillon stars in a comedy-drama set in the early 1970s about a junkie who steals drugs or cash in a one-day-at-a-time lifestyle. With Kelly Lynch, James LeGros, Heather Graham, and William Burroughs. Directed and co-written by Gus Van Sant. **DR7, DR16**

Drum (1976, C, 110m, R)
Sequel to *Mandingo*, with further adventures of fighting slaves, lusting massas, and their women. Warren Oates, Ken Norton, and Pam Grier star. **ST115**

Drum Beat (1954, C, 111m, NR)
Alan Ladd western about Indian wars. Audrey Dalton costars; watch for Charles Bronson in a small role. **ST12**

Drums (1938, C, 99m, NR)
British troops in India are aided by a native lad in this classic adventure tale. Sabu, Raymond Massey, and Valerie Hobson star. **AC13**

Drums Along the Mohawk (1939, C, 103m, NR)
Henry Fonda and Claudette Colbert star in this drama of settlers living in upstate New York during the colonists' fight against the British. Directed by John Ford. **AC6, DT36, ST44**

Drunken Angel (1948, B&W, 108m, NR)
A young gangster (Toshiro Mifune) is treated by a kindly doctor (Takashi Shimura) for a bullet wound and learns that he has tuberculosis. Japanese drama from director Akira Kurosawa. **DT57, ST106**

Dry White Season, A (1989, C, 105m, R)
Intensely felt drama of racial divisions in contemporary South Africa, focusing on one white man's growing realization of the injustices of apartheid. Donald Sutherland stars, with Winston Ntshona, Zakes Mokae, Jürgen Prochnow, Susan Sarandon, Janet Suzman, and Marlon Brando. Directed by Euzhan Palcy. **DR7, DR14, ST10** *Recommended*

DuBarry Was a Lady (1943, C, 101m, NR)
Red Skelton plays a patsy who dreams he's in the court of Louis XIV. With Lucille Ball and Gene Kelly. Outstanding color photography and sets. **CL9, ST81**

Duchess and the Dirtwater Fox, The (1976, C, 103m, PG)
Western comedy teams George Segal and Goldie Hawn; he's a bumbling cardsharp and she's a kooky dance hall girl. **ST63, WE14**

Duck Soup (1933, B&W, 70m, NR)
The Marx Bros. take over a country called Freedonia. Zeppo's last appearance with Groucho, Chico, and Harpo. Margaret Dumont acts offended. A classic satire on politics, perhaps the best Marxist movie. **CL10, ST101** *Essential; Highly Recommended*

Duck, You Sucker *see* A Fistful of Dynamite

Dudes (1988, C, 90m, R)
On a cross-country trip, a trio of punk rockers from New York are harassed by a gang of rednecks. Jon Cryer, Daniel Roebuck, Catherine Mary Stewart, and Lee Ving star. Penelope Spheeris directed. **DR7, MU12**

Duel (1971, C, 90m, NR)
Steven Spielberg directed this terrifying tale of a businessman (Dennis Weaver) being stalked on the highway by an unseen truck driver. Originally made for TV. **DT99, MY9, XT18** *Recommended*

Duel at Diablo (1966, C, 103m, NR)
James Garner and Sidney Poitier star in an Indians vs. the cavalry western. **ST121, WE4**

Duel in the Sun (1946, C, 130m, NR)
Producer David O. Selznick's colorful western saga, with Jennifer Jones a hot-blooded half-breed caught between brothers Gregory Peck and Joseph Cotten. The supporting cast includes Lionel Barrymore, Walter Huston, Lillian Gish, and Butterfly McQueen. Directed by King Vidor. **CL9, DT107, ST54, ST119, WE1, WE8, WE15** *Essential; Recommended*

Duellists, The (1977, C, 101m, PG)
A pair of feuding soldiers carry their grudge through many years and campaigns in this drama set in the Napoleonic era. Harvey Keitel and Keith Carradine star, with Christina Raines and Albert Finney.Ridley Scott directed. **DT96, ST42** *Recommended*

Duet for One (1987, C, 110m, R)
A concert violinist is struck with a debilitating disease, throwing her shaky marriage onto the rocks, forcing her into therapy. Julie Andrews stars, with Alan Bates, Max von Sydow, and Rupert Everett. **DR2, DR10**

Duke Is Tops, The (1938, B&W, 80m, NR)
All-black musical about a girl trying for her first break in show business. Lena Horne stars, in one of her first screen appearances. Also known as *Bronze Venus*. **MU13**

Dumbo (1941, C, 63m, G)
Disney animation brings this poignant tale of the tiny elephant with oversized ears to life. **FA2** *Highly Recommended*

Dune (1984, C, 137m, PG-13)
Science fiction epic, based on Frank Herbert's classic novel, about intergalactic war and intrigue in the distant future. David Lynch directed. Kyle MacLachlan stars, with Jürgen Prochnow, Sting, Francesca Annis, Sean Young, Kenneth McMillan, Brad Dourif, Dean Stockwell, and Linda Hunt. **DT66, MU12, SF11, ST144**

Dunera Boys, The (1985, C, 150m, R)
Epic drama set during World War II, when a POW camp was set up in Australia to house Jewish outcasts from Britain who incredibly were suspected of being Nazi spies. Joseph Spano and Bob Hoskins star. **ST72**

Dunwich Horror, The (1970, C, 90m, PG)
An evil warlock (Dean Stockwell) menaces a lovely young woman (Sandra Dee). Based on a story by H.P. Lovecraft. **ST144**

Dynasty of Fear (1973, C, 93m, NR)
The wife and assistant of a headmaster at a boys school conspire to murder him. Peter Cushing, Joan Collins, and Ralph Bates star. **ST27**

E.T. The Extra-Terrestrial (1982, C, 115m, PG)
Box-office champion about friendly visitor and the kids who protect him from uncaring adults. Directed by Steven Spielberg, with Oscar-winning special effects. Henry Thomas, Drew Barrymore, Robert McNaughton, Peter Coyote, and Dee Wallace star. **FA8, DT99, SF9, SF13, SF15**

Each Dawn I Die (1939, B&W, 92m, NR)
James Cagney prison drama, with our hero a framed man trying to prove his innocence. George Raft and George Bancroft costar. **DR18, ST14**

Eagle Has Landed, The (1977, C, 133m, PG)
World War II espionage drama about an attempt to kidnap Winston Churchill. Michael Caine, Donald Sutherland, Robert Duvall, Jenny Agutter, and Donald Pleasence star. Based on the Jack Higgins novel. **AC1, MY6, ST15, ST38**

Eagle's Wing (1979, C, 100m, PG)
An Indian renegade and a white trapper come to blows over a white stallion in this British-made western. Martin Sheen, Sam Waterston, and Harvey Keitel star. **WE7**

Early Summer (1951, B&W, 135m, NR)
Japanese drama from director Yasujiro Ozu, with a young woman resisting an arranged marriage. **FF4**

Earrings of Madame de . . . , The (1954, B&W, 105m, NR)
Elegant costume drama of wealthy woman's gift passing from hand to hand and eventually ruining her marriage. Danielle Darrieux, Charles Boyer, and Vittorio De Sica star; Max Ophuls directed. **DT26, DT76**

Earth (1930, B&W, 63m, NR)
Russian silent classic dealing with the formation of a peasant farm in the Ukraine. **CL12, FF7**

Earth Girls Are Easy (1989, C, 99m, PG)
Comedy with musical numbers about a manicurist (Geena Davis) living in the San Fernando Valley and her close encounter with three handsome aliens (Jeff Goldblum, Jim Carrey, Damon Wayans). With Julie Brown and Michael McKean. Julien Temple directed. **CO2, SF9, SF21, ST56**

Earth vs. the Flying Saucers (1956, B&W, 82m, NR)
Unfriendly aliens come out of the skies in this 1950s science fiction classic starring Hugh Marlowe and Joan Taylor. Finale featuring the destruction of Washington, D.C. is not to be missed. **SF1, SF9, XT12** *Recommended*

Earthling, The (1980, C, 102m, PG)
Family drama of an orphaned boy (Ricky Schroder) and a terminally ill man (William Holden) learning the ways of the bush country. **FA7, ST68**

Earthquake (1974, C, 129m, PG)
Los Angeles is hit by a catastrophic quake in this all-star disaster drama. Charlton Heston, Ava Gardner, Lorne Greene, Genevieve Bujold, Marjoe Gortner, Richard Roundtree, George Kennedy, and (in a bit part) Walter Matthau try to keep their balance. **AC23, ST104**

East of Eden (1955, C, 115m, NR)
Two brothers become rivals for the love of their father in John Steinbeck's transplanting of the Cain and Abel story to early 1900s California. James Dean's starring debut won him an Oscar nomination. Raymond Massey, Julie Harris, and Oscar winner Jo Van Fleet costar. Elia Kazan directed. **DR8, DR19, DR26, DT53, WR25, XT5, XT21** *Essential; Recommended*

East of Eden (1982, C, 240m, NR)
TV miniseries based on the Steinbeck classic, starring Timothy Bottoms and Bruce Boxleitner as the rival brothers, with Jane Seymour and Warren Oates. **DR8, DR19, ST115, WR25**

East Side Kids Meet Bela Lugosi *see* Ghosts on the Loose

Easter Parade (1948, C, 103m, NR)
MGM musical, with tunes by Irving Berlin, about a dancer (Fred Astaire) caught between his current partner (Judy Garland) and his old one (Ann Miller). **MU1, MU6, ST2, ST51**

Easy Living (1949, B&W, 77m, NR)
An aging football star (Victor Mature) can't face his impending retirement or his nagging wife (Lizabeth Scott) until the team secretary (Lucille Ball) comes up with her own strategy. Directed by Jacques Tourneur. **DR22, DT105**

Easy Rider (1969, C, 94m, R)
Two California bikers hit the road for New Orleans with money from a drug deal. Legendary "head" movie starring Dennis Hopper (who directed), Peter Fonda, and Jack Nicholson. Superb rock soundtrack. **CU3, DR7, ST71, ST112, XT14, XT18** *Essential; Recommended*

Easy Virtue (1927, B&W, 79m, NR)
Early film from Alfred Hitchcock, a silent melodrama about a married woman whose husband is an alcoholic and whose lover commits suicide. Based on a play by Noel Coward. **DT46**

Eat My Dust! (1976, C, 90m, PG)
Ron Howard stars in this car-chase comedy, produced by Roger Corman. **AC10, DT48**

Eat the Peach (1987, C, 95m, NR)
Irish comedy about two friends who come up with a plan to put their village on the map with a daring motorcycle act borrowed from the Elvis Presley movie *Roustabout*. Stephen Brenna and Eammon Morrissey star, with Catherine Byrne. **CO17** *Recommended*

Eaten Alive (1976, C, 96m, NR)
A demented hotel owner keeps a live crocodile in his front yard and feeds it any troublesome guests. Neville Brand, Carolyn Jones, and Mel Ferrer star in this horror film from director Tobe Hooper. **DT47**

Eating Raoul (1982, C, 87m, R)
Strange comedy about a couple who murder swingers for their money to pay for a new restaurant. Paul Bartel and Mary Woronov star; Bartel directed. **CU5, DT5**

Ebony Tower, The (1983, C, 80m, NR)
An aging artist living in a country house with two young women hosts an art critic, who begins a romance with one of the women. Laurence Olivier, Roger Rees, and Greta Scacchi star. Based on a novel by John Fowles. Originally made for cable TV. **ST116**

Eclipse, The (1962, B&W, 123m, NR)
From Italian director Michelangelo Antonioni, a drama of doomed love between a young Roman translator and a handsome broker, starring Monica Vitti and Alain Delon. **DT3, XT17**

Ecstasy (1933, B&W, 88m, NR)
Notorious film, banned for many years in some states, mainly for brief nude swimming and suggestive love-making scenes. The story is of a bored young wife (Hedy Lamarr) and her affair with a workman. **CU6, CU8, FF7**

Eddie and the Cruisers (1983, C, 90m, PG)
A rock group's debut album is a smash hit, but their leader disappears with the tapes for their follow-up record. Years later, a journalist opens an investigation of the mystery. Tom Berenger, Michael Pare, and Ellen Barkin star. **DR12, MU4**

Eddie and the Cruisers II: Eddie Lives (1989, C, 103m, PG-13)
Second chapter in the Eddie saga, with Michael Pare returning as the mysterious rock 'n' roll singer. **DR12, MU4**

Eddie Macon's Run (1983, C, 95m, PG)
An escaped con (John Schneider) leads a determined lawman (Kirk Douglas) on a wild chase across the Southwest toward Mexico. **ST34, XT18**

Eddie Murphy: Delirious (1983, C, 60m, NR)
This live concert, taped at Washington, D.C.'s Constitution Hall, features some of Murphy's most outrageous routines, with no-holds-barred language and wit. **CO16**

Eddie Murphy Raw (1987, C, 91m, R)
More concert comedy featuring the outrageous humor of Eddie Murphy, filmed at New York's Madison Square Garden. Directed by Robert Townsend. **CO16**

Educating Rita (1983, C, 110m, PG)
A young wife (Julie Walters) who works as a hairdresser wants to improve her life, and she selects an alcoholic professor (Michael Caine) to do the job. **CO17, ST15**

Egyptian, The (1954, C, 140m, NR)
Elaborate historical drama set in ancient Egypt, centering on a physician to the Pharoah and his love affairs. Edmund Purdom stars, with Victor Mature, Michael Wilding, Jean Simmons, and Peter Ustinov. **CL3**

Eiger Sanction, The (1975, C, 128m, R)
Clint Eastwood directed and stars in this drama of a professor who moonlights as a CIA agent. He leads a mountain-climbing expedition designed to expose a traitorous agent. **AC12, MY6, ST39**

8 1/2 (1963, B&W, 135m, NR)
Oscar-winning film from Federico Fellini about a film director unsure what his next project is to be. This autobiographical film has had an enormous influence on many other movies. Marcello Mastroianni stars, with Claudia Cardinale and Anouk Aimee. **DR13, DT35, ST103, XT7** *Essential; Highly Recommended*

Eight Men Out (1988, C, 120m, PG-13)
Superbly detailed recreation of the major league scandal that forever changed the sport, when players on the 1919 Chicago White Sox conspired to "fix" the World Series. John Cusack, David Strathairn, D.B Sweeney, and Charlie Sheen star, with Christopher Lloyd, Clifton James,

Michael Rooker, and Studs Terkel. Written and directed by John Sayles, who plays sportswriter Ring Lardner. **DR5, DR22, DT93** *Highly Recommended*

8 Million Ways to Die (1986, C, 115m, R)
Urban action drama of an alcoholic ex-cop (Jeff Bridges) involved with a prostitute (Rosanna Arquette) and her vicious pimp (Andy Garcia). With Alexandra Paul. **AC8, ST11**

18 Again! (1988, C, 100m, PG)
A teenager (Charlie Schlatter) recovers from an accident to find that the mind of his lively grandfather (George Burns) has taken over his body. **CO5, CO20**

84 Charing Cross Road (1987, C, 100m, PG)
True-life drama of New York writer Helene Hanff and her twenty-year correspondence with a London bookseller. A small gem of a film starring Anne Bancroft and Anthony Hopkins. Based in part on a play adapted from Hanff's memoirs. **DR4, DR6, DR20** *Recommended*

84 Charley Mopic (1989, C, 95m, R)
Vietnam War drama, presenting events as seen through the eyes (and lens) of a documentary filmmaker. Written and directed by Patrick Duncan. **AC4** *Recommended*

El Cid (1961, C, 184m, R)
The story of the legendary eleventh-century Christian hero (Charlton Heston) who freed Spain from Moorish invaders. Directed by Anthony Mann. Sophia Loren costars. **AC16, DT69, ST93**

El Condor (1970, C, 102m, R)
Western tale set in Mexico, with two cowpokes searching for a cache of gold. Jim Brown and Lee Van Cleef star. **ST155, WE9**

El Dorado (1967, C, 126m, NR)
From director Howard Hawks comes this tale of an aging gunslinger (John Wayne) who stands up to a land-grabbing cattle baron. Robert Mitchum costars. **DT43, ST107, ST156**

Electra Glide in Blue (1973, C, 106m, R)
Robert Blake stars as a Arizona highway patrolman in this hot wheels action drama. **AC9, AC10**

Electric Horseman, The (1979, C, 120m, PG)
A reporter (Jane Fonda) rounds up a rodeo star (Robert Redford) for a scoop, but she winds up with more than she bargained for. Willie Nelson costars. Sydney Pollack directed this romantic comedy. **CO1, DT80, MU12, ST45, ST126, WE12**

Elena and Her Men (1956, C, 98m, NR)
Ingrid Bergman plays a Polish princess who's juggling affairs with the likes of Jean Marais and Mel Ferrer. Jean Renoir directed. Also known as *Paris Does Strange Things*. **DT86, ST7**

Eleni (1985, C, 116m, PG)
Drama based on New York reporter Nicholas Gage's search for the man who executed Gage's mother in war-torn Greece in the late 1940s. John Malkovich and Kate Nelligan star. **DR6, ST98**

Elephant Man, The (1980, B&W, 125m, PG)
The life of John Merrick, a Victorian-age Briton who suffered from a terrible, deforming disease. John Hurt and Anthony Hopkins star, with Anne Bancroft and Freddie Jones.Directed with enormous ingenuity by David Lynch. **DR4, DT66** *Essential; Recommended*

11 Harrowhouse (1974, C, 98m, PG)
Spoof of heist movies, written by and starring Charles Grodin as a diamond merchant who decides to pull off the ultimate jewel theft. Candice Bergen and James Mason costar. **CO7, CO10, MY18, ST59, ST102**

Elmer Fudd Cartoon Festival (1940-8, C, 33m, NR)
A quartet of cartoons starring that balding, wovable, wittle man. **FA11**

Elmer Fudd's Comedy Capers (1957, C, 57m, NR)
Cartoon comedy at its finest, including *The Rabbit of Seville, Hare Brush,* and *What's Opera, Doc?* **FA11** *Recommended*

Elmer Gantry (1960, C, 145m, NR)
Burt Lancaster won an Oscar as the smooth-talking tent preacher of Sinclair Lewis's novel. Jean Simmons and Oscar winner Shirley Jones costar as the women in Elmer's life—and his downfall. Richard Brooks directed. **DR19, ST85, WR17, XT2, XT5**

Elusive Corporal, The (1962, B&W, 108m, NR)
From French director Jean Renoir, the story of a World War II P.O.W. and his attempts to escape. **DT86**

Elvira Madigan (1967, C, 89m, NR)
Lushly filmed romance from Sweden, about two young people who run away to be together, only to meet tragedy. Pia Degermark and Thommy Berggren star. Directed by Bo Widerberg. **DR1, FF7**

Elvis '56 (1987, C, 61m, NR)
Documentary, narrated by Levon Helm, focuses on the year when Elvis rocked the nation with stunning performances in concert and on national television. Directed by Alan and Susan Raymond; originally made for cable TV. **MU11** *Highly Recommended*

Elvis—1968 Comeback Special (1968, C, 76m, NR)
This live television broadcast marked The King's long-awaited return to the concert stage. **MU10** *Highly Recommended*

Elvis on Tour (1972, C, 93m, NR)
Elvis Presley, on-stage and off, on one of his cross-country tours. **MU11**

Elvis: That's the Way It Is (1970, C, 97m, NR)
Behind the scenes with Elvis, as he prepares for his debut on the Las Vegas stage. **MU11**

Embryo (1976, C, 104m, PG)
Rock Hudson plays a scientist who develops a fetus into a full-grow woman right in his laboratory. **SF5, ST73**

Emerald Forest, The (1985, C, 113m, R)
Adventure tale, based on fact, of an American father looking in the Amazon jungles for his long-lost son, who was actually kidnapped and raised by natives. Powers Boothe and Charley Boorman star; John Boorman (Charley's father) directed. **AC12, DT11**

Emil and the Detectives (1964, C, 99m, NR)
Disney adventure about a young boy who is robbed and enlists the help of his detective friends to catch the thief. **FA1**

Emperor Jones, The (1933, B&W, 72m, NR)
Paul Robeson stars in this adaptation of the Eugene O'Neill play about a black fugitive who escapes a chain gang and becomes the king of a Caribbean island. **DR14, DR20, WR20**

Emperor's New Clothes, The (1984, C, 60m, NR)
This story from the Faerie Tale Theatre collection features Art Carney and Alan Arkin as two con men who pull the invisible wool over the eyes of a vain king (Dick Shawn). **FA12**

Empire of the Ants (1977, C, 90m, PG)
Vacationers on an island are attacked by monster ants in this loose adaptation of an H.G. Wells story. Joan Collins and Robert Lansing star. **SF10, WR29**

Empire of the Sun (1987, C, 152m, PG)
A British boy living in Shanghai when Japanese invade in the 1930s finds himself separated from his parents and on his own during the war. Based on J.G. Ballard's autobiographical novel; Steven Spielberg directed. Christian Bale and John Malkovich star. **DR5, DR9, DT99, ST98**

Empire Strikes Back, The (1980, C, 124m, PG)
The first sequel to *Star Wars* features a developing romance between Han Solo (Harrison Ford) and Princess Leia (Carrie Fisher), while Luke Skywalker (Mark Hamill) meets the kindly sage Yoda. With Billy Dee Williams, Alec Guinness, and James Earl Jones as the voice of Darth Vader. Special effects won an Oscar. **FA8, SF11, SF13, SF15, SF23, ST46, ST60, ST76, ST159** *Essential; Recommended*

Empty Canvas, The (1964, B&W, 118m, NR)
Bette Davis plays the mother of a model who is the obsession of a young French artist. Horst Bucholz and Catherine Spaak costar. **ST28**

Enchanted Cottage, The (1945, B&W, 91m, NR)
Dorothy McGuire and Robert Young portray two misfits who fall in love in a magical New England cottage. **CL4**

Enchanted Forest, The (1945, C, 78m, NR)
Fantasy of a young boy who learns about life from his visits to an old man who lives in the forest. Edmund Lowe stars. **FA8**

Encore (1952, B&W, 89m, NR)
Sequel to *Quartet* and *Trio* presents three more tales by W. Somerset Maugham, with Anthony Pelissier, Nigel Patrick, and Glynis Johns heading the cast. **DR19**

End, The (1978, C, 100m, R)
Burt Reynolds stars in this black comedy about a terminally ill man whose friends and relatives can't seem to deal with his imminent demise. Sally Field, Dom De-Luise, Joanne Woodward, Myrna Loy, Pat O'Brien, and Kristy McNichol costar. **CO12, ST40, ST94, ST128, ST166**

End of St. Petersburg, the (1927, B&W, 75m, NR)
Silent Soviet drama from director V.I. Pudovkin, about a worker becoming aware of the need to participate in the Revolution. **FF7**

End of the Line (1987, C, 105m, PG)
Drama of a railroad man and his buddy (Wilford Brimley, Levon Helm) from Arkansas who protest the closing of a depot. With Mary Steenburgen, Holly Hunter, and Kevin Bacon. **DR7, MU12, ST74**

End of the Road, The (1969, C, 110m, R)
Drama of romantic triangle in college community is a springboard for commentary on variety of late-1960s social issues. Bizarre film stars Stacy Keach, Harris Yulin, Dorothy Tristan, and James Earl Jones; based on John Barth's novel. **DR7, DR19, ST76**

End of the World (1977, C, 87m, PG)
Christopher Lee plays two roles: a priest and his grotesque, murderous double in this science fiction drama about alien invaders. **ST89**

Endangered Species (1982, C, 97m, R)
New York cop on vacation stumbles onto mystery in small Wyoming town involving cattle mutilations. Robert Urich, Jo-Beth Williams, Paul Dooley, and Hoyt Axton star. Alan Rudolph directed. **DR26, DT91**

Endgame (1985, C, 98m, PG-13)
Science fiction adventure set in a vaguely post-apocalyptic world, with survival the real name of the game. Al Cliver and Moira Chen star. **SF8**

Endless Night (1971, C, 99m, NR)
A chauffeur marries an heiress (Hayley Mills), and they move into a mysterious old house. Based on an Agatha Christie novel. **MY15, WR3**

Enemies, A Love Story (1989, C, 119m, R)
Seriocomic story of a man living in 1949 New York who is married, has a mistress—and then is stunned when his first wife, whom he thought had died in a World War II concentration camp, shows up. Ron Silver stars, with Margaret Sophie Stein, Lena Olin, and Anjelica Huston as his women. With Alan King and Paul Mazursky, who also directed. Based on an Isaac Bashevis Singer story. **DR1, DR5, DR19**

Enemy Below, The (1957, C, 98m, NR)
World War II submarine action, with Robert Mitchum, Curt Jurgens, and Theodore Bikel. **AC1, ST107**

Enemy Mine (1985, C, 108m, PG-13)
When an astronaut crashes on a remote planet, he is forced to join with an alien to survive various hardships. Dennis Quaid and Louis Gossett, Jr. star. **SF8**

Enemy of the People, An (1977, C, 103m, G)
Steve McQueen stars in this version of Henrik Ibsen's 19th-century drama about a doctor warning a small town of the dangers of water pollution. With Bibi Andersson and Charles Durning. **DR20, ST97**

Enemy Territory (1987, C, 89m, R)
A white insurance salesman is trapped inside a ghetto tenement by a vicious street gang. Only a local resident can help him escape. Gary Frank and Ray Parker, Jr. star. **AC8, MU12**

Enforcer, The (1951, B&W, 87m, NR)
Humphrey Bogart stars as a crusading district attorney determined to put a syndicate boss (Everett Sloane) behind bars. **ST8**

Enforcer, The (1976, C, 96m, R)
Third in the *Dirty Harry* series, with Clint Eastwood taking on a female partner (Tyne Daly), as they hunt down terrorists

who have kidnapped the mayor of San Francisco. **AC9, ST39, XT13**

Ensayo de un Crimen (Rehearsal of a Murder) *see* Criminal Life of Archibaldo de la Cruz, The

Ensign Pulver (1964, C, 104m, NR)
This sequel to *Mister Roberts* follows the shenanigans of Ensign Pulver (Robert Walker, Jr.) as he tries to save the captain (Burl Ives), who has been washed overboard. With Walter Matthau, Jack Nicholson, and Larry Hagman. **ST104, ST112**

Enter Laughing (1967, C, 112m, NR)
Carl Reiner wrote and directed this semi-autobiographical comedy about a struggling young actor. Reni Santoni stars, with Jose Ferrer, Shelley Winters, Elaine May, and Rob Reiner in a small role. **CO8, DT70, DT85, ST164**

Enter the Dragon (1973, C, 90m, R)
Martial arts classic, with cult following, starring Bruce Lee in his last finished film. He's invited to a fighting tournament on an island stronghold run by a criminal kingpin. Exciting action sequences. **CU7, ST88, XT22** *Essential; Highly Recommended*

Entertaining Mr. Sloane (1970, C, 94m, NR)
In this offbeat comedy based on the Joe Orton play, a handsome young criminal becomes sexually involved with both a widow and her brother. Beryl Reid, Harry Andrews, and Peter McEnery star. **CO12, CO17**

Entre Nous (1983, C, 110m, PG)
Drama of two women whose friendship for each other over a 20-year span proves stronger than what they feel for their husbands. Isabelle Huppert and Miou-Miou star. Diane Kurys directed. **DR10, FF1** *Recommended*

Equalizer 2000 (1986, C, 85m, R)
In a post-apocalypse world, only Slade, the one-man army, will take on the brutal dictatorship of The Ownership. Richard Norton and Corinne Wahl star. **AC25**

Equus (1977, C, 138m, R)
A psychiatrist (Richard Burton) tries to unravel the problems of a stable boy (Peter Firth) who intentionally blinds horses.

Based on the Peter Shaffer play; directed by Sidney Lumet. **DR20, DT65, ST13**

Eraserhead (1978, B&W, 90m, NR)
Director David Lynch's legendary cult film about a reclusive young man (John Nance), the deformed baby he fathers, and his bizarre imaginary life. A midnight-screening favorite. **CU1, CU12, DT66, HO14**

Erendira (1983, C, 103, NR)
Offbeat drama, based on a story by Gabriel Garcia Marquez, about a woman who travels the countryside with a carnival starring her young granddaughter as a sexual slave. Irene Papas stars; filmed in Mexico. **FF6**

Erik the Viking (1989, C, 103m, PG-13)
Spoof of Viking films stars Tim Robbins, with Gary Cady, Mickey Rooney, John Cleese, and Terry Jones, who also wrote and directed. **CO7, CO15, ST133**

Ernest Goes to Camp (1987, C, 93m, PG)
Ernest P. Worrell, world's most inept human, gets his wish when he envisions himself as a camp counselor. Jim Varney stars in this silly family comedy. **FA6**

Ernest Goes to Jail (1990, C, 81m, PG)
A bank janitor is wrongly fingered for a robbery and winds up in stir with hardened cons. Jim Varney plays the title character in this family comedy. **CO10, FA6**

Ernest Saves Christmas (1988, C, 89m, PG)
Jim Varney stars as Ernest P. Worrell, the good-natured hayseed who's out to fill in when Santa can't make his annual trip. **FA6, FA13**

Ernie Kovacs: Between the Laughter (1984, C, 100m, NR)
Jeff Goldblum stars as TV's pioneering comic genius; this drama focuses on his bitter battle for custody of his two daughter from his first marriage. With Melody Anderson as Edie Adams. **ST56**

Errand Boy, The (1961, B&W, 92m, NR)
Star Jerry Lewis directed this tale of a nutty young nerd set loose in a movie studio. **ST91**

Escape Artist, The (1982, C, 96m, PG)
Young magician tries to follow in his late father's footsteps in this offbeat drama starring Griffin O'Neal, with Teri Garr, Raul Julia, Joan Hackett, and Desi Arnaz. Directed by Caleb Deschanel; written by Stephen Zito and Melissa Mathison. **DR9, FA7** *Recommended*

Escape From Alcatraz (1979, C, 112m, PG)
Clint Eastwood stars as bank robber Frank Morris, who led the only escape from the famed maximum security prison in which no one was caught. Directed by Don Siegel. **DR18, DT97, ST39** *Recommended*

Escape From New York (1981, C, 99m, R)
In the near-future, Manhattan has become a maximum-security prison for the worst criminal elements. When the President's plane crashes there, the government hires a soldier of fortune to rescue him. John Carpenter directed; Kurt Russell stars, with Lee Van Cleef, Harry Dean Stanton, Isaac Hayes, and Adrienne Barbeau. **AC21, DT17, MU12, SF8, ST141, ST155**

Escape From the Planet of the Apes (1971, C, 98m, PG)
Third in the *Apes* series of science fiction adventures, with the ape characters in contemporary Los Angeles. Roddy McDowall, Kim Hunter, and Bradford Dillman star. **FA8, SF8, SF13, SF23**

Escape to Burma (1955, C, 87m, NR)
Barbara Stanwyck's the tough mistress of a tea plantation who's confronted by a desperate fugitive (Robert Ryan). **ST142**

Escape to Witch Mountain (1975, C, 97m, G)
Two children with mysterious powers are the object of a villain's plans in this Disney adventure. Ray Milland, Eddie Albert, and Donald Pleasence costar. **FA1**

Escape 2000 (1981, C, 92m, R)
Futuristic action drama about a society where criminals are hunted down like animals. Filmed in Australia; Steve Railsback and Olivia Hussey star. **FF5, SF11**

L'Ete Meurtrier *see* One Deadly Summer

Eternal Return, The (1943, B&W, 100m, NR)
French drama, based on the Tristan and Isolde legend, starring Jean Marais. Jean Cocteau contributed to the screenplay. **FF1**

Eureka (1981, C, 130m, R)
Offbeat drama, set on a Caribbean island, about a wealthy ex-prospector, his daughter and her shady lover, and a pair of hit men. Gene Hackman, Theresa Russell, Rutger Hauer, and Mickey Rourke star. Nicolas Roeg directed. **DT88, ST61,ST134**

Europa '51 (1951, B&W, 110m, NR)
Ingrid Bergman stars in a drama of a wealthy woman's search for peace after the death of her son. Roberto Rossellini, then Bergman's husband, directed. Also known as *The Greatest Love.* **ST7**

Europeans, The (1979, C, 90m, NR)
A staid American family living in 19th-century New England tries to cope with the arrival of two foreign cousins. Ismail Merchant produced and James Ivory directed this drama, based on the Henry James novel. Lee Remick stars. **DR19, WR11**

Even More Ripping Yarns *see* Ripping Yarns (series)

Evening With Bobcat Goldthwait, An: Share the Warmth (1987, C, 83m, NR)
The comedian whom one critic called "a cross between Joe Cocker and a serial killer" performs in concert. **CO16**

Evening With Robin Williams, An (1982, C, 92m, NR)
The fastest funny man in America goes wild in this energetic comedy special. **CO16, ST160**

Every Girl Should Be Married (1948, B&W, 85m, NR)
Comedy about a determined girl (Betsy Drake) who sets out to capture the affections of a bachelor (Cary Grant). **ST57**

Every Man for Himself and God Against All (1975, C, 110m, NR)
German drama, based on fact, about a strange, child-like man who appeared one day in 19th-century Nuremberg. Directed by Werner Herzog. Also known as *The Mystery of Kasper Hauser.* **DT44** *Recommended*

Every Time We Say Goodbye (1987, C, 97m, PG-13)
An American soldier recuperating in a Jerusalem hospital falls in love with a Jewish girl, whose family opposes the romance. Tom Hanks and Christine Marsillach star in this drama set during World War II. **DR3, ST62**

Every Which Way But Loose (1978, C, 114m, PG)
Clint Eastwood plays a two-fisted truck driver who travels the country with his pet orangutan Clyde in pursuit of a country and western singer (Sondra Locke). Beverly D'Angelo and Ruth Gordon co-star in this action comedy. **CO9, ST39**

Everybody Wins (1990, C, 97m, R)
Nick Nolte is an insurance investigator, Deborah Winger a small-town prostitute who hires him in this mystery written by Arthur Miller. With Will Patton and Judith Ivey. **MY10, ST113, ST163**

Everybody's All American (1988, C, 127m, R)
Dennis Quaid and Jessica Lange star in a romantic drama of a college football star and homecoming queen who marry and then have to deal with his post-sports career problems. With Timothy Hutton and John Goodman. **DR1, DR22, ST86**

Everything You Always Wanted to Know About Sex But Were Afraid to Ask (1972, C, 87m, R)
Writer-director Woody Allen serves up seven comic sketches, each answering a valid question about sexuality. With Gene Wilder, John Carradine, Louise Lasser, Lou Jacobi, Lynn Redgrave, Burt Reynolds, and Tony Randall. The last bit, "What Happens During Orgasm?", is particularly funny. **DT1, ST128** *Recommended*

Evil Dead, The (1982, C, 85m, NR)
Gruesome horror film about five college pals on a woodsy vacation in a remote cabin and how they're possessed by spirits of the dead. Directed by Sam Raimi. **CU7, HO8**

Evil Dead 2: Dead by Dawn (1987, C, 85m, X)
The remaining survivor from *The Evil Dead* returns to the sight of the murders, where supernatural demons once again take over. Directed by Sam Raimi. **HO8**

Evil Mind, The (1934, B&W, 80m, NR)
A phony clairvoyant begins to predict events which do happen. Claude Rains and Fay Wray star. **HO7, MY15**

Evil of Frankenstein (1964, C, 98m, NR)
The baron tries to manipulate his monster with the help of a hypnotist, but the monster runs amok. Peter Cushing stars in this British-made film. **HF10, HO26, ST27**

Evil That Men Do, The (1984, C, 89m, R)
Charles Bronson action thriller, with the hero tracking down a doctor who advises dictators on torture techniques. Joseph Maher plays the villain. **ST12**

Evil Under the Sun (1982, C, 102m, PG)
Hercule Poirot (Peter Ustinov) investigates a murder at a resort hotel. Based on the Agatha Christie novel. Jane Birkin, James Mason, Sylvia Miles, Diana Rigg, and Maggie Smith costar. **MY12, ST102, WR3**

Evilspeak (1982, C, 90m, R)
An orphan at a military academy uses black magic on the cadets who have tormented him. **HO13**

Excalibur (1981, C, 140m, R)
The King Arthur legend, starring Nigel Terry, Helen Mirren, Nicol Williamson, and Cherie Lunghi. Directed by John Boorman. **AC18, DT11**

Executioner's Song, The (1982, C, 157m, NR)
Dramatic account of murderer Gary Gilmore and his fight to be executed by the state of Utah. Emmy winner Tommy Lee Jones costars with Rosanna Arquette; Norman Mailer adapted his own book. Originally made for TV; video version contains footage not shown in original broadcast. **CU10, DR6, DR16**

Executive Action (1973, C, 91m, PG)
Burt Lancaster stars in this thriller claiming a conspiracy was behind President Kennedy's assassination. Robert Ryan costars in one of his last screen appearances. **MY6, ST85**

Executive Suite (1954, B&W, 104m, NR)
High-powered corporate soap opera, with all-star cast: William Holden, June Allyson, Barbara Stanwyck, Fredric March, Walter Pidgeon, and Shelley Winters. Di-

rected by Robert Wise. **DR7, DR24, DT117, ST68, ST142, ST164**

Exodus (1960, C, 213m, NR)
Paul Newman and Eva Marie Saint star in this epic drama of the birth of the modern state of Israel and the Palestinean war that resulted. With Ralph Richardson, Sal Mineo, John Derek, Peter Lawford, and Jill Haworth. Directed by Otto Preminger; based on Leon Uris's novel. **DR5, DT82, ST111**

Exorcist, The (1973, C, 122m, R)
A young girl is possessed by the devil and a special priest is called in to perform a horrifying ritual of exorcism. Linda Blair, Ellen Burstyn, Max von Sydow, and Jason Miller star in this modern horror classic. Based on the bestseller by William Peter Blatty, set in Washington, D.C.. **HO8, HO13, XT12** *Essential; Recommended*

Exorcist II: The Heretic (1977, C, 110m, R)
Delirious sequel to *The Exorcist,* with Linda Blair the subject of experiments by priest Richard Burton and researcher Louise Fletcher. With James Earl Jones. Directed by John Boorman; some scenes shot in Washington, DC. **DT11, HO13, ST13, ST76, XT12**

Experiment in Terror (1962, B&W, 123m, NR)
An F.B.I. agent (Glenn Ford) tracks a killer who has terrorized a bank teller (Lee Remick) into embezzlement by kidnapping her sister. Directed by Blake Edwards on location in San Francisco. **DT32, MY2, XT13**

Experiment Perilous (1944, B&W, 91m, NR)
An unsuspecting wife (Hedy Lamarr) is tormented by her overbearing husband (Paul Lukas), who is set on driving her mad. Directed by Jacques Tourneur. **MY3, DT105**

Experts, The (1989, C, 94m, PG-13)
Comedy adventures of a pair of hip (but not too bright) dudes who travel from New York to what they think is a Nebraska town to open a night club. In reality, they're in a mock American town inside the Soviet Union, unwittingly teaching pop culture to Russian agents masquerading as Americans. John Travolta and Arye Gross star, with Charlie Martin Smith and Kelly Preston. Directed by Dave Thomas. **CO2, CO14, CO20**

Explorers (1985, C, 109m, PG)
A young science fiction buff gets his wish for space travel in a scheme concocted by his friend. Joe Dante directed this special effects comedy. **CO11, DT25, FA8, SF3, SF13**

Exterminating Angel, The (1962, B&W, 95m, NR)
Surrealistic masterwork from director Luis Buñuel: a party of well-to-do friends suddenly find they cannot leave a room. Silvia Pinal stars. **DT15** *Essential; Highly Recommended*

Exterminator, The (1980, C, 101m, R)
Robert Ginty plays a Vietnam veteran with vengeance on his mind when his buddy is blown away by the Mob. This extremely violent action thriller was directed by James Glickenhaus. **AC19**

Exterminator 2, The (1984, C, 88m, R)
Star Robert Ginty and director James Glickenhaus return for more adventures of the man with the blowtorch. **AC19**

Exterminators of the Year 3000 (1983, C, 101m, R)
Science fiction adventure with the world gone dry from years without rain and warring factions fighting for every precious drop of water. **SF8**

Extreme Prejudice (1987, C, 104m, R)
Violent action drama about boyhood friends who grow up on opposite sides of the law and on opposite sides of the Tex-Mex border. Nick Nolte is the Texas Ranger, Powers Boothe the drug kingpin. With Maria Conchita Alonso and Rip Torn. Walter Hill directed. **DT45, ST113, ST150**

Extremities (1986, C, 89m, R)
A woman is nearly raped in her home but turns the tables on her attacker and holds him prisoner, trying to decide how to dispense justice. Farrah Fawcett stars, with James Russo, Alfre Woodard, and Diana Scarwid. Based on a play by William Mastrosimone. **DR10, DR20**

Eye for an Eye, An (1981, C, 106m, R)
Chuck Norris is a cop whose partner is killed by drug dealers. He swears ven-

geance and singlehandedly takes on the gang leader (Christopher Lee) and his men. **ST89, ST114**

Eye of the Needle (1981, C, 112m, R)
Donald Sutherland is a German spy stranded on a British island during World War II. He seduces a lonely woman (Kate Nelligan) in hopes of using her to effect his plans. **MY6**

Eye of the Tiger (1986, C, 88m, R)
A newcomer to a small town battles local corruption, goes on a rampage when his wife and child are murdered. Gary Busey and Yaphet Kotto star. **AC19**

Eyeball (1977, C, 87m, R)
Horror story of a psychopathic murderer and his particularly gruesome calling card. **HO9**

Eyes of a Stranger (1980, C, 85m, R)
A newswoman is on the trail of a psychopathic killer after she finds that her sister, a blind and deaf young girl, could be his next victim. **HO9**

Eyes of Laura Mars (1978, C, 103m, R)
A fashion photographer (Faye Dunaway) has premonitions of brutal murders, but she can't persuade anyone to believe her. Tommy Lee Jones costars in this stylish thriller. **HO7, MY2, MY3, ST37**

Eyes of Texas (1948, B&W, 54m, NR)
Roy Rogers turns his ranch into a camp for boys orphaned by World War II. With Andy Devine. **ST132**

Eyes, the Mouth, The (1982, C, 100m, R)
A young man tries to come to grips with his twin brother's suicide in this drama from Italian director Marco Bellochio. Lou Castel stars. **FF2**

Eyes Without a Face (1959, B&W, 88m, NR)
Classic French horror film about a scientist's experiemts on his disfigured daughter. Georges Franju directed; cinematography by Eugen Shuftan. Pierre Brasseur stars. Also known as *The Horror Chamber of Dr. Faustus.* **FF1, HO1, HO20**

Eyewitness (1981, C, 102m, R)
A New York janitor (William Hurt) pretends he has access to evidence in a baffling murder case, just to get acquainted with a TV news reporter (Sigourney Weaver) he admires. With Christopher Plummer, James Woods, Morgan Freeman, and Pamela Reed. **MY5, ST48, ST75, ST157, ST165, XT9**

F.I.S.T. (1978, C, 145m, PG)
Sylvester Stallone plays a union boss who unsuccessfuly attempts to resist corruption in this drama based loosely on the life of Jimmy Hoffa. With Rod Steiger, Peter Boyle, and Melinda Dillon. Directed by Norman Jewison. **DR7, DT51, ST140**

F/X (1986, C, 106m, R)
A movie special effects expert is hired to stage the phony killing of a government witness against the Mob. When the man actually dies, the effects man realizes he has been set up. Bryan Brown stars, with Jerry Orbach and Mason Adams. **AC19, DR13, MY9**

Fabulous Baker Boys, The (1989, C, 113m, R)
Real-life brothers Jeff and Beau Bridges star as a piano-playing act whose career is on the skids—until they hire a lovely singer (Michelle Pfeiffer). Written and directed by Steve Kloves. **DR1, DR8, DR12, ST11, ST120, XT8** *Recommended*

Fabulous Dorseys, The (1947, B&W, 88m, NR)
Biography of those great bandleaders and musicians, Tommy and Jimmy Dorsey, with the brothers playing themselves. Musicians Art Tatum and Charlie Barnet appear in one memorable jam session. **MU5**

Face in the Crowd, A (1957, B&W, 125m, NR)
Andy Griffith portrays a country bumpkin who rises to sudden fame as a television star and develops dangerous political ambitions. Patricia Neal and Walter Matthau costar, with Lee Remick making her film debut. Written by Budd Schulberg; directed by Elia Kazan. **CL7, DT53, ST104** *Recommended*

Fade to Black (1980, C, 100m, R)
A lonely young man who fantasizes about movies begins dressing up like famous film villains and eliminating his tormentors. Dennis Christopher stars. **HO9**

Fahrenheit 451 (1967, C, 111m, NR)
In a future society, firemen start fires, urged by a dictatorship to burn books and

keep the population ignorant. Oskar Werner and Julie Christie (playing two roles) star. Cult film was directed by François Truffaut and based on Ray Bradbury's novel. **CU4, CU13, DR19, DT106, SF11**

Fail-Safe (1964, B&W, 111m, NR)
A U.S. Air Force plane is accidentally ordered to bomb the Soviet Union, which could start a nuclear war. Henry Fonda stars, with Walter Matthau and Fritz Weaver. Sidney Lumet directed. **DT65, ST44, ST104**

Falcon and the Snowman, The (1985, C, 131m, R)
True story of two boyhood friends (Timothy Hutton, Sean Penn) who grow up to become spies and sell American secrets to the Russians. Directed by John Schlesinger. **DR6, DR16, DR26, DT94, MY6**

Falcon Takes Over, The (1942, B&W, 63m, NR)
George Sanders stars as the suave crime-solver in this entry of the popular mystery series. Based on Raymond Chandler's *Farewell, My Lovely.* **WR2**

Fall of the House of Usher, The (1960, C, 79m, NR)
A beautiful young girl is brought to her fiance's mysterious house, where the skeletons come out of the closets with hair-raising results. Vincent Price stars; Roger Corman directed this first of his eight films based on the works of Edgar Allan Poe. Also known as *House of Usher.* **DT22, ST124, WR21**

Fall of the Roman Empire, The (1964, C, 153m, NR)
An epic drama of Livius, the renegade general (Stephen Boyd) who's torn between his country and his lover (Sophia Loren). Anthony Mann directed; the cast also includes Alec Guinness, James Mason, Christopher Plummer, and Omar Sharif. **CL3, DT69, ST60, ST93, ST102**

Falling in Love (1984, C, 106m, PG-13)
Robert DeNiro and Meryl Streep star as two married Manhattan-bound commuters who strike up a friendship that develops into something more serious. **DR3, ST30, ST145, XT9**

Falling in Love Again (1980, C, 103m, R)
Middle-aged man is nostalgic for his youthful, romantic days. Elliott Gould

stars, with Susannah York and Michelle Pfeiffer. **ST120**

Fame (1983, C, 134m, R)
New York City's High School for the Performing Arts is the backdrop for this story of aspiring students who struggle to make it in show business. Directed by Alan Parker. **DR25, MU9, XT9**

Family, The (1970, C, 100m, R)
An ex-con seeks retribution against the man who framed him and stole his girl friend while he was in prison. Charles Bronson stars, with Jill Ireland and Telly Savalas. **ST12**

Family, The (1987, C, 127m, PG)
Drama of eighty years in the life of one family in Rome, directed by Ettore Scola. Vittorio Gassman stars, with Fanny Ardant, Philippe Noiret, and Stefania Sandrelli. **FF2**

Family Business (1989, C, 115m, R)
Crime comedy of three generations of a Mob clan: irrepressible grandfather (Sean Connery), reluctant son (Dustin Hoffman), and eager grandson (Matthew Broderick). Directed by Sidney Lumet. **CO5, CO10, DT65, ST21, ST67**

Family Game, The (1984, C, 107m, NR)
Comedy centering on Japanese family who hires a tutor for one its sons and winds up being totally dominated by the teacher. Directed by Yoshimitsu Morita. **FF4**

Family Jewels, The (1965, C, 100m, NR)
Jerry Lewis plays seven outrageously different roles, as potential guardians to a little heiress. **ST91**

Family Plot (1976, C, 120m, PG)
Alfred Hitchcock's final film is about a phony psychic who, along with her private-eye boyfriend, tries to find a missing heir. Barbara Harris, Bruce Dern, William Devane, and Karen Black star. **DT46**

Fandango (1985, C, 91m, PG)
Five college friends decide to go off for one last fling before they're drafted to fight in the Vietnam War. Judd Nelson and Kevin Costner star. **CO4, ST23, XT18**

Fanny (1932, B&W, 120m, NR)
Second part of famed trilogy by French writer-director Marcel Pagnol (*Marius* is

first, *Cesar* is last). Fanny (Orane Demazis) is abandoned by her true love Marius
(Pierre Fresnay). **FF1**

Fanny and Alexander (1983, C, 197m, R)
Oscar-winning family epic from director
Ingmar Bergman, a mixture of comedy
and drama set in turn-of-the-century Sweden. The point of view is that of a young
boy and his sister, as they witness their
beloved father's death and their mother's
remarriage to a stern minister. **DT7, XT7**
Recommended

Fantastic Planet (1973, C, 72m, NR)
From France, an animated science fiction
adventure about a planet where men are
slaves to gigantic mechanical creatures.
FF1, SF19

Fantastic Voyage (1966, C, 100m, NR)
Team of scientists is miniaturized and injected into the body of a patient in need
of advanced micro-surgery. Oscar-winning special effects highlight this science
fiction adventure. Donald Pleasence, Stephen Boyd, Raquel Welch, and Edmond
O'Brien star. **SF3, SF15**

Far Country, The (1955, C, 97m, NR)
Western tale about a cattleman (James
Stewart) in search of a boomtown on the
Alaskan tundra. Directed by Anthony
Mann; outstanding color photography.
CL9, DT69, ST143, WE10

Far From the Madding Crowd (1967, C,
169m, NR)
Thomas Hardy's story of one passionate
woman's effect on three very different
men, starring Julie Christie, Alan Bates,
Peter Finch, and Terence Stamp. Cinematography by Nicolas Roeg; adapted by
Frederic Raphael and directed by John
Schlesinger. **CL1, DR1, DT94** *Recommended*

Far Frontier, The (1948, B&W, 67m, NR)
Roy Rogers rides to the rescue of a kid-
napped Border Patrol agent. With Andy
Devine. **ST132**

Far North (1988, C, 88m, PG-13)
Sam Shepard wrote and directed this
drama of a woman's struggle to reconcile
herself with her father. Jessica Lange and
Charles Durning star, with Anne Wedgeworth. **DR8, ST86**

Farewell, Friend *see* Honor Among
Thieves

Farewell, My Lovely (1975, C, 97m, R)
Robert Mitchum plays Philip Marlowe,
Raymond Chandler's famous detective,
who is hired to find an ex-con's sweetheart. With Charlotte Rampling, John Ireland, Harry Dean Stanton, and in a small
role Sylvester Stallone. Filmed in 1944 as
Murder My Sweet. **CU18, ST107, ST140,
ST141, WR2**

Farewell to Arms, A (1932, B&W, 78m,
NR)
Tragic love story, based on the Ernest
Hemingway novel, about an affair be-
tween an army nurse (Helen Hayes) and
a young soldier (Gary Cooper) during
World War I. **AC2, DR19, ST22, WR10**

Farewell to the King (1989, C, 117m, PG-
13)
During World War II, a renegade American soldier successfully leads natives on
a South Pacific island against the Japanese. Nick Nolte stars in this action
drama from writer-director John Milius.
AC1, ST113

Farmer's Daughter (1947, B&W, 97m,
NR)
Loretta Young gave an Academy Award-
winning performance in this comedy of a
Swedish housemaid and her boss, a
Washington politician. With Joseph Cot-
ten, Ethel Barrymore, and Charles Bick-
ford. **XT3**

Fashions of 1934 (1934, B&W, 78m, NR)
Bette Davis plays a fashion designer who,
along with a con man (William Powell),
conquers the Paris fashion world. **ST28,
ST122**

Fast Break (1979, C, 107m, PG)
A New York City basketball coach accepts a position in the Midwest and brings
his street-wise players with him. Gabe
Kaplan stars in this comedy. **CO19**

Fast Forward (1985, C, 110m, PG)
Eight teenagers from a small town in Ohio
venture to New York City to enter a national dance contest. Directed by Sidney
Poitier. **DR12, ST121**

Fast Talking (1986, C, 93m, NR)
A bright 15-year-old from a broken home
uses his wits to wriggle out of sticky

situations. Family comedy-drama stars Steve Bisley. **FA7**

Fast Times at Ridgemont High (1982, C, 92m, R)
Sean Penn stars as Spicoli, the ultimate party animal, in this comedy about high school life. Jennifer Jason Leigh, Phoebe Cates, and Judge Reinhold are his less laid-back classmates. Directed by Amy Heckerling. **CO4, CO18** *Recommended*

Fast-Walking (1982, C, 116m, R)
James Woods is Fast-Walking Miniver, a cynical prison guard who is ordered to assassinate a new black con (Robert Hooks) but can't resist an offer of $50,000 to help the same man escape. With Tim McIntire and Kay Lenz. **DR18, ST165** *Recommended*

Fastest Guitar Alive, The (1968, C, 88m, NR)
Civil War western starring rock star Roy Orbison. He's the leader of a band of Confederate soldiers trying to return money they stole just before the end of the conflict. Title refers to Orbison's instrument, which converts to a gun; he does sing several songs. **MU16, WE6**

Fat City (1972, C, 100m, PG)
John Huston directed this story of a small time boxer trying to pass on some of his ring savvy to a young fighter. Stacy Keach and Jeff Bridges star, with Susan Tyrrell and Candy Clark. Written by Leonard Gardner; based on his novel. **DR19, DR22, DT50, ST11** *Recommended*

Fat Man and Little Boy (1989, C, 126m, PG-13)
True-life drama of the development of the atomic bomb at Los Alamos, New Mexico. Paul Newman stars as General Leslie Groves, Dwight Schultz as J. Robert Oppenheimer. With Bonnie Bedelia, John Cusack and Laura Dern. Directed by Roland Joffe. **DR5, ST111**

Fatal Attraction (1987, C, 102m, R)
A family man (Michael Douglas) has a weekend fling with a young woman (Glenn Close), who turns murderously possessive, threatening to ruin his entire life. With Anne Archer. Directed by Adrian Lyne. **DR3, DR6, MY13, MY14, ST20, ST35**

Fatal Beauty (1987, C, 105m, R)
Whoopi Goldberg goes undercover to track the dealers of a dangerous drug, Fatal Beauty. She gets help from a bodyguard (Sam Elliott) whom she suspects of knowing more about distribution of the drug than he admits. With Ruben Blades. **AC9, MU12**

Fatal Glass of Beer, The/Pool Shark, The (1933/1915, B&W, 29m, NR)
Two classic shorts starring W.C. Fields. In the first, Fields is in the frozen North battling the elements. In the second, one of his early silent films, Fields gets involved in a duel over a beautiful girl; no pistols or swords are brandished, only pool cues. **ST41**

Fatal Vision (1984, C, 200m, NR)
True story about an army doctor accused of killing his wife and two daughters. His father-in-law is sure of his guilt, and pursues the case in a bitter trial. Karl Malden, Gary Cole, and Andy Griffith star. Originally made for TV. Based on the book by Joe McGinniss. **DR16, MY8** *Recommended*

Father (1966, B&W, 96m, NR)
Hungarian drama of a young boy (András Bálint) who imagines a new father for himself after his real one dies in World War II. Written and directed by Istvan Szabo. **FF7**

Father Brown *see* The Detective (1954)

Father Goose (1964, C, 115m, NR)
Cary Grant plays a beach bum on a South Pacific island during World War II. He winds up protecting a teacher (Leslie Caron) and her girl students, who are fleeing the Japanese. **ST57**

Father of the Bride (1950, B&W, 93m, NR)
Spencer Tracy is the father, Elizabeth Taylor is the bride in this warm comedy about preparations for a wedding. Vincente Minnelli directed. **DT71, ST147, ST151, XT20** *Essential; Recommended*

Father's Little Dividend (1951, B&W, 82, NR)
Sequel to *Father of the Bride* has Spencer Tracy adjusting to the idea of becoming a grandfather. Elizabeth Taylor costars. Vincente Minnelli directed. **DT71, ST147, ST151**

Faust (1926, B&W, 100m, NR)
Silent German drama based on the famed
legend, with Gosta Ekerman in the title
role, Emil Jannings as The Devil. Directed by F.W. Murnau. **FF3, HO10**

Favorita, La (1952, B&W, 82m, NR)
Film version of the opera, with Sophia
Loren in an early supporting role. **ST93**

Fawlty Towers, Volumes 1-4 (1975, C, approx. 75m. each, NR)
Each of these four volumes contains three
episodes of the hilarious British TV series
starring John Cleese as the hyperbolic
owner of a slightly rundown seaside hotel.
Prunella Scales and Connie Booth costar;
Cleese and Booth wrote the scripts. **CO15**
Highly Recommended

Fear (1954, B&W, 84m, NR)
Ingrid Bergman stars as a woman who
begins to collapse from the everyday
pressures of life. Directed by Roberto
Rossellini, then her husband. **ST7**

Fear Chamber, The *see* Chamber of Fear

Fear City (1984, C, 96m, R)
Tom Berenger and Jack Scalia plays the
owners of a New York talent agency that
specializes in "exotic dancers." They're
looking for a killer who has been eliminating their clients. With Billy Dee Williams,
Melanie Griffith, and Rae Dawn Chong.
AC8, DR15, ST58, ST159

Fear in the Night (1972, C, 94m, NR)
Peter Cushing and Joan Collins star in
this tale of a tormented wife whose fear
drives her to the brink of insanity. **ST27**

Fear Strikes Out (1957, B&W, 100m, NR)
Tony Perkins stars as Red Sox outfielder
Jimmy Piersall, whose battle with mental
illness nearly cost him his ballplaying career. With Karl Malden. **DR4, DR22**

Fearless Vampire Killers, The (1967, C,
111m, NR)
Roman Polanski's comic vampire story
features footage added for home video
release. Jack MacGowran, Sharon Tate,
and the director star. **CU10, DT79, HO5,
HO24** *Recommended*

Feds (1988, C, 83m, PG-13)
A pair of female recruits (Rebecca De-
Mornay, Mary Gross) bungle their way

through training at the F.B.I. Academy.
CO3

Feel My Pulse (1928, B&W, 65m, NR)
Silent comedy about a girl who discovers
that a santiarium she has inherited is a
haven for rumrunners. Bebe Daniels
stars, with Richard Arlen and William
Powell. **ST122**

Fellini Satyricon *see* Satyricon

Female Trouble (1975, B&W, 95m, NR)
Director John Waters' follow-up to *Pink
Flamingos* stars Divine as a girl gone
wrong who finally suffers for her sins in
the electric chair. Camp or crude? It's up
to the viewer. **CU12, DT110**

Ferris Bueller's Day Off (1986, C, 103m,
PG-13)
A suburban high school senior (Matthew
Broderick) with a knack for ducking trou-
ble takes a day off from school with two
pals and heads for downtown Chicago.
Written and directed by John Hughes.
Mia Sara and Alan Ruck costar, with
Jeffrey Jones, Jennifer Grey, and Charlie
Sheen. **CO4, DT49, XT11**

ffolkes (1980, C, 99m, PG)
Tongue-in-cheek action film, with Roger
Moore as an unorthodox agent (loves
cats, hates women) hired to battle terror-
ists on two North Sea oil rigs. With James
Mason and Anthony Perkins. **ST102**

Fiddler on the Roof (1971, C, 184m, G)
Popular Broadway musical about a hum-
ble Ukrainian farmer at the turn of the
century who has no dowries for his five
unwed daughters. Great family viewing.
Directed by Norman Jewison. **DT51, FA9,
MU2** *Recommended*

Field of Dreams (1989, C, 106m, PG)
An Iowa farmer (Kevin Costner) builds a
baseball diamond in his corn field, where
the spirits of long-gone baseball stars like
Shoeless Joe Jackson (Ray Liotta) come
to play. Sentimental drama also features
Amy Madigan, James Earl Jones, and
Burt Lancaster. **DR2, DR8, DR22, ST23,
ST76, ST85**

Field of Honor (1986, C, 93m, R)
Drama of a Dutch soldier's horrifying experiences in the Korean War. Based on a
true story; Everett McGill stars. **AC3**

Fiend Without a Face (1958, B&W, 74m, NR)
Great special effects enhance this gruesome tale of a scientist whose thoughts materialize in the form of invisible creatures. These creatures then seek out victims to feed on their brains. **HO20, SF1**

Fiendish Plot of Dr. Fu Manchu (1980, C, 108m, PG)
Peter Sellers' last film casts him in two roles: Fu Manchu and his nemesis, Inspector Nayland Smith. As Fu Manchu tries to conquer the world, his bumbling foe tries to stop him. **ST137**

Fifth Avenue Girl (1939, B&W, 83m, NR)
Ginger Rogers comedy has her playing a homeless lass taken in by a friendly millionaire (Walter Connolly). **ST131**

55 Days at Peking (1963, C, 150m, NR)
Epic account of events in China surrounding the 1900 Boxer Rebellion, starring Charlton Heston, Ava Gardner, and David Niven. Directed by Nicholas Ray. **DT83**

52 Pick-up (1986, C, 114m, R)
A self-made businessman (Roy Scheider) is blackmailed by three creeps who know he has been cheating on his wife (Ann-Margret). With John Glover and Clarence Williams III. Based on Elmore Leonard's novel; directed by John Frankenheimer. **MY2, WR16** *Recommended*

Fighting Back (1982, C, 98m, R)
A deli owner in South Philadelphia organizes his neighbors into a vigilante group to fight local thugs, with unexpected results. Tom Skerritt stars, with Patty LuPone, Michael Sarrazin, and Yaphet Kotto. **AC19**

Fighting Caravans (1932, B&W, 80m, NR)
Gary Cooper takes to the great outdoors in this western based on a Zane Grey story. **ST22**

Fighting Kentuckian, The (1949, B&W, 100m, NR)
John Wayne comes to rescue of homesteaders in colonial Kentucky. Oliver Hardy costars in a rare dramatic role. **ST87, ST156**

Fighting Mad (1977, C, 96m, R)
A soldier in Vietnam is left to die by his company, only to be captured by Japa-

nese troops who think that World War II is still on. James Iglehart, Jayne Kennedy, and Leon Isaac Kennedy star. **AC4**

Fighting Prince of Donegal, The (1966, C, 112, NR)
Disney swashbuckler has the new head of an Irish family in the 16th century fighting for his people against British troops. **FA1**

Fighting Seabees, The (1944, B&W, 100m, NR)
John Wayne and Dennis O'Keefe are soldiers stationed in the South Pacific, both fighting for the same woman (Susan Hayward). **ST156**

Final Conflict, The (1981, C, 108m, R)
This third and final chapter of *The Omen* saga follows anti-christ Damien Thorn to adulthood, as he moves toward the Presidency. **HO10**

Final Countdown, The (1980, C, 104m, PG)
Modern aircraft carrier passes through a time warp to Pearl Harbor on the eve of the Japanese attack. Kirk Douglas and Martin Sheen star in this science fiction adventure. **SF4, ST34**

Final Mission, The (1984, C, 101m, NR)
A Vietnam veteran, now a policeman, gets a chance for revenge against a man who betrayed him in Southeast Asia. **AC19**

Final Terror, The (1983, C, 82m, R)
A psychopathic killer stalks teenagers in a forest. Daryl Hannah and Rachel Ward star. **HO12**

Find the Lady (1976, C, 79m, NR)
John Candy and Lawrence Dane play a pair of inept cops looking for a kidnapped socialite. With Mickey Rooney and Peter Cook. **CO14, ST133**

Finders Keepers (1984, C, 96m, PG)
Frantic comedy, set mostly on a train, involving con men, coffins, hired killers, and a fortune in stolen money. Michael O'Keefe, Beverly D'Angelo, and Louis Gossett, Jr. star. Richard Lester directed. **DT62, XT19**

Fine Madness, A (1966, C, 104m, NR)
Sean Connery plays an iconoclastic poet in this comedy-drama about society's attempts to tame a misfit. Joanne Wood-

ward and Jean Seberg costar. **ST21, ST166**

Fine Mess, A (1986, C, 88m, PG)
Comedy about a pair of bumblers (Ted Danson, Howie Mandel) who overhear plans to fix a horse race, and wind up with the Mob and the police on their trail. Directed by Blake Edwards. **CO3, DT32**

Fingers (1978, C, 91m, R)
Cult movie with exceptionally violent scenes about a young man torn between career as a concert pianist and loyalty to his father, a numbers runner. Harvey Keitel stars, with Michael V. Gazzo and Jim Brown. James Toback directed. **CU7**

Finian's Rainbow (1968, C, 145m, NR)
Musical fantasy, adapted from the Broadway hit, starring Fred Astaire as an Irishman who moves to the American South in search of his pot of gold. With Petula Clark, Tommy Steele, Keenan Wynn, Al Freeman, Jr. and Don Francks. Francis Ford Coppola directed; songs include "That Old Devil Moon" and "Look to the Rainbow." **DT21, MU2, MU8, ST2**
Recommended

Fire and Ice (1983, C, 81m, PG)
Animated adventure saga based on Frank Frazetta's dungeon & dragons characters, directed by Ralph Bakshi. **AC18**

Fire Down Below (1957, C, 116m, NR)
Shipboard romantic triangle, with Robert Mitchum and Jack Lemmon in conflict over Rita Hayworth on a tramp steamer. **ST64, ST90, ST107**

Fire Over England (1936, B&W, 89m, NR)
Vivien Leigh and Laurence Olivier portray young lovers in the court of Queen Elizabeth during the British-Spanish conflict. With James Mason. **CL3, ST102, ST116**

Firebird 2015 A.D. (1981, C, 97m, PG)
In this science fiction adventure, cars have been banned because of an oil shortage. Darren McGavin and Doug McClure star. **SF8**

Firefox (1982, C, 124m, PG)
An American undercover agent (Clint Eastwood) steals a super-secret plane from the Russians and heads for the border with Soviet aircraft in pursuit. Eastwood also directed. **AC11, ST39**

Firemen's Ball, The (1968, C, 73m, NR)
Comedy from Czechoslovakia about a volunteer firemen's dance that turns into a full-scale disaster. Directed by Milos Forman. **DT37, FF7**

Firepower (1979, C, 104m, R)
Action drama, set in the Caribbean, starring Sophia Loren as a woman seeking revenge for the murder of her husband. With James Coburn, O.J. Simpson, and Eli Wallach. **ST93**

Fires on the Plain (1959, B&W, 105m, NR)
Japanese war drama focuses on the suffering of several soldiers during the final days of World War II. Directed by Kon Ichikawa. **AC1, FF4**

Firestarter (1984, C, 115m, R)
Drew Barrymore plays a child who inherits the ability to start fires at a glance. Based on the Stephen King bestseller. With George C. Scott, Art Carney, and Martin Sheen. **HO13, WR12**

Firewalker (1986, C, 96m, R)
Tongue-in-cheek adventure story, with Chuck Norris and Louis Gossett, Jr. as two bumbling soldiers of fortune. **AC21, ST114**

First Blood (1982, C, 97m, R)
Sylvester Stallone's first appearance as John Rambo, the Vietnam vet with a chip on his shoulder. Here, he's harassed by a small town sheriff and he leads law enforcement officials and a National Guard company on a wild backwoods chase. With Richard Crenna and Brian Dennehy. **AC25, ST140**

First Born (1984, C, 100m, PG-13)
A teenager is suspicious of his divorced mother's new boyfriend, especially when he finds evidence that the man is dealing drugs. Christopher Collet, Teri Garr, and Peter Weller star in this underrated drama. **DR8** *Recommended*

First Deadly Sin, The (1980, C, 112m, R)
Frank Sinatra stars as a New York City cop who tracks a psycho. With Faye Dunaway, Brenda Vaccaro, and James Whitmore. **AC9, ST37, ST138**

First Family (1980, C, 104m, R)
This political satire casts Bob Newhart as a President trying to deal with his scatterbrained wife (Madeline Kahn) and sex-

crazed daughter (Gilda Radner). With Rip Torn, Richard Benjamin, and Harvey Korman. Written and directed by Buck Henry. **CO5, CO13, ST150, XT12**

First Howie Mandel Special (1983, C, 53m, NR)
The former star of T.V.'s *St. Elsewhere* gives an energetic standup comedy performance. **CO16**

First Legion, The (1951, B&W, 86m, NR)
A priest is skeptical of events surrounding a miracle in his town. Charles Boyer stars in this drama directed by Douglas Sirk. **DT98**

First Men in the Moon (1964, C, 85m, NR)
H.G. Wells tale of space explorers, with outstanding special effects by Ray Harryhausen. Edward Judd, Martha Hyer, and Lionel Jeffries star. **SF3, WR29**

First Monday in October (1981, C, 98m, R)
This light comedy concerns the first female member of the Supreme Court locking horns with a fellow justice. Jill Clayburgh and Walter Matthau star. **CO2, DR10, ST104, XT12**

First Name: Carmen (1983, C, 85m, NR)
French director Jean-Luc Godard's meditation on the Carmen story, with updating to make the heroine a terrorist/filmmaker. Maruschka Detmers stars; Godard plays her "Uncle Jean," a has-been director. **DT41**

First Power, The (1990, C, 98m, R)
The Devil grants a mad killer immortality, and he immediately seeks vengeance against a young cop. Lou Diamond Phillips stars as the cop, with Jeff Kober and Tracy Griffith. **HO9, HO10**

Fish Called Wanda, A (1988, C, 108m, R)
British caper comedy featuring a gang composed of one thick-headed macho American (Oscar winner Kevin Kline), his sexy girl friend (Jamie Lee Curtis), and a stuttering accomplice (Michael Palin)—all mixed up with a confused barrister (John Cleese). Co-written by Cleese. Small dog or tropical fish lovers, beware. **CO10, CO15, CO17, MY18, ST84, XT4** *Recommended*

Fist of Fear, Touch of Death (1980, C, 90m, R)
Drama set at a karate championship at Madison Square Garden, starring Fred Williamson and Ron Van Clief. Bruce Lee appears in a short segment. **ST88**

Fistful of Dollars, A (1964, C, 96m, NR)
A mysterious gunfighter (Clint Eastwood) is caught between two feuding families in this classic spaghetti western directed by Sergio Leone. Remake of Japanese samurai drama, *Yojimbo*. **FF8, DT61, ST39, WE2, WE13**

Fistful of Dynamite, A (1972, C, 138m, R)
A peasant thief (Rod Steiger) and an explosives mastermind (James Coburn) join forces during the Mexican Revolution. Directed by Sergio Leone. Also known as *Duck, You Sucker*. **DT61, WE9, WE13**

Fists of Fury (1972, C, 103m, R)
Bruce Lee's first feature film has him playing a martial arts student out to avenge his teacher's death. **ST88**

Fitzcarraldo (1982, C, 157m, NR)
Epic drama from German director Werner Herzog about an obsessed man's attempt to build an opera house in the midst of the Amazon jungles. Klaus Kinski stars in this bold, memorable drama. **DT44, ST83** *Recommended*

Five Card Stud (1968, C, 103m, NR)
Western action with Dean Martin as a gambler, Robert Mitchum as a psychotic preacher. With Inger Stevens and Roddy McDowall. **ST107**

Five Corners (1988, C, 92m, R)
In 1964, a Bronx neighborhood is shaken by the return of an ex-con looking for revenge. A young idealist (Tim Robbins) agrees to protect a girl (Jodie Foster) from the criminal. Written by John Patrick Shanley; directed by Tony Bill. **DR15, ST47**

Five Days One Summer (1983, C, 93m, PG)
A middle-aged man and his young female companion travel in 1930s Switzerland posing as man and wife—although their relationship is secretly quite different. Sean Connery and Betsy Brantley star. Fred Zinnemann directed. Original running time: 108m. **DR3, DT120, ST21**

Five Easy Pieces (1970, C, 96m, R)
Breakthrough role for Jack Nicholson in this tale of a drifter who chooses a blue-collar job rather than follow his family of classical musicians. Written by Carol Eastman (under the name Adrien Joyce) and directed by Bob Rafelson. Karen Black and Susan Anspach costar, with Billy "Green" Bush, Lois Smith, Toni Basil, and Helena Kallianotes. **DR8, ST112** *Essential; Highly Recommended*

5000 Fingers of Dr. T, The (1953, C, 88m, NR)
Classic children's fantasy of a little boy who suffers nightmares dominated by his strict piano teacher. Tommy Rettig and Hans Conried star; written by Dr. Seuss. **FA8**

Five Weeks in a Balloon (1962, C, 101m, NR)
Jules Verne adventure about a hot air balloon expedition to Africa. Red Buttons, Barbara Eden, and Fabian star. **FA4, WR28**

Flame and the Arrow, The (1950, C, 88m, NR)
Burt Lancaster stars as a swashbuckler in medieval Italy who leads his people to victory against the Hessians. Virginia Mayo and Nick Cravat costar. Jacques Tourneur directed. **AC13, DT105, ST85**

Flame of the Barbary Coast (1945, B&W, 91m, NR)
John Wayne western with the Duke competing for the hand of a saloon singer (Ann Dvorak). **ST156**

Flaming Star (1960, C, 92m, NR)
Elvis Presley plays a half-breed who must choose sides when an Indian uprising threatens his family. Directed by Don Siegel. **DT97, ST123**

Flash Gordon (1980, C, 110m, PG)
The hero of the old movie serials gets a big-budget, tongue-in-cheek treatment in this spoofy adventure. Sam J. Jones, Max von Sydow, Ornella Muti, Melody Anderson, Topol, and Timothy Dalton star. Music by Queen. **SF21**

Flashback (1990, C, 108m, R)
A legendary 1960s activist, a fugitive from the law, is captured and transported by a young FBI agent from San Francisco to Washington State to stand trial. Com-

edy stars Dennis Hopper and Kiefer Sutherland, with Carol Kane, Paul Dooley, Cliff DeYoung, Richard Masur, and Michael McKean. **CO10, CO20, ST71, XT18, XT19**

Flashdance (1983, C, 96m, R)
A young female welder moonlights as an exotic dancer, although she aspires to audition for a ballet company. Jennifer Beals and Michael Nouri star; music by Giorgio Moroder. **DR12, DR15, MU3**

Flashpoint (1984, C, 94m, R)
A pair of border cops stumble onto some evidence that will help solve an old mystery. Kris Kristofferson and Treat Williams star, with Rip Torn. **MU12, ST150**

Flesh (1968, B&W, 90m, NR)
Paul Morissey directed and Andy Warhol produced this cult comedy about a male hustler (Joe Dalessandro) and his many conquests. **CU12, DT72**

Flesh & Blood (1922, B&W, 74m, NR)
A lawyer goes to jail for 15 years for a crime he didn't commit. Lon Chaney, Sr. stars in this silent melodrama. **ST16**

Flesh & Blood (1985, C, 126m, R)
Adventure tale of lovely young princess captured by a band of roving thieves, with her intended in hot pursuit. Rutger Hauer, Jennifer Jason Leigh, and Tom Burlinson star. Paul Verhoeven directed. **AC18**

Flesh and the Devil (1927, B&W, 103m, NR)
Greta Garbo silent drama in which she plays the ultimate temptress, breaking up the friendship of John Gilbert and Lars Hanson. **CL4, CL12, ST50**

Fleshburn (1984, C, 91m, R)
Confined to an asylum for five years, a Vietnam veteran escapes and seeks revenge against the doctors who had him committed. **AC19**

Fletch (1985, C, 96m, PG)
Chevy Chase plays a wise-guy reporter who relies on disguises to get the scoop on a drug ring. **CO10, CO13**

Fletch Lives (1989, C, 95m, PG-13)
Chevy Chase returns as the investigative reporter and master of disguises. Here, he inherits a Southern mansion and a

mystery that goes with the house. **CO10, CO13**

Flight of Dragons, The (1982, C, 98m, NR)
Enter a world of dragons, dungeons and castles, and mysterious happenings in this full-length animated feature. **FA10**

Flight of the Eagle, The (1982, C, 139m, NR)
Swedish adventure story, based on historical events, about a daring hot-air balloon trip to the North Pole in 1897. Max von Sydow stars. **AC12, AC16, FF7**

Flight of the Navigator (1986, C, 90m, PG)
Fantasy about a 12-year-old boy who leaves earth on an alien spacecraft, but returns as a 12-year-old eight years later. Veronica Cartwright and Joey Cramer star. **FA8**

Flight of the Phoenix (1966, C, 147m, NR)
Tense tale of survival, starring James Stewart as the leader of a squadron whose plane crashes in the Arabian desert. With Richard Attenborough, Peter Finch, and Ernest Borgnine. Directed by Robert Aldrich. **AC12, ST143** *Recommended*

Flight to Fury (1966, B&W, 80m, NR)
Adventure saga set in the Philippines, about a search for missing diamonds. Dewey Martin, Fay Spain, and Jack Nicholson star. Directed by Monte Hellman. **ST112**

Flight to Mars (1951, C, 72m, NR)
Low-budget science fiction adventure about trip to the Red Planet and discovery of a lost civilization. **SF3**

Flipper (1963, C, 90m, NR)
Family adventure of a boy and his friendly dolphin, the basis for the TV series. Chuck Connors, Luke Halpin, and Kathleen McGuire star. **FA5**

Floating Weeds (1959, C, 119m, NR)
From Japan, a drama about an actor visiting his illegitimate son and ex-lover after many years' absence. Directed by Yasujiro Ozu. **FF4**

Flower Drum Song (1961, C, 133m, NR)
Rodgers and Hammerstein musical about life in San Francisco's Chinatown. Nancy Kwan, James Shigeta, and Miyoshi Umeki star. **MU2, MU6**

Flowers in the Attic (1987, C, 95m, PG-13)
A widowed mother of four is desperate to be reinstated in her father's good graces—and in his will. She and her kids move into his house, where she keeps the children confined to one room. Based on the novel by V. C. Andrews. **HO14**

Fly, The (1958, B&W, 94m, NR)
An experiment turns into a disaster as a scientist's machine mixes some of his molecules with those of a fly. Vincent Price, Herbert Marshall, and David Hedison star. **HO20, SF1, SF5, ST124**

Fly, The (1986, C, 96m, R)
Remake of the horror science fiction film about an experiment gone terribly wrong, with much more explicit and gruesome detail. Jeff Goldblum and Geena Davis star. David Cronenberg directed. **CU7, CU18, DT23, HO17, HO20, SF5, SF20, ST56** *Recommended*

Fly II, The (1989, C, 105m, R)
Follow-up to 1986 remake of the sci-fi horror classic has the son of the scientist/insect following in his father's fateful footsteps. Eric Stoltz and Daphne Zuniga star. **HO20, SF5, SF20**

Flying Deuces (1939, B&W, 65m, NR)
Laurel and Hardy join the foreign legion to forget Ollie's recent lost love. **ST87**

Flying Down to Rio (1933, B&W, 89m, NR)
Fred Astaire and Ginger Rogers dance "The Carioca" in their first screen teaming. Dolores Del Rio costars. **CL15, ST2, ST131**

Flying Leathernecks (1951, C, 102m, NR)
John Wayne and Robert Ryan play two Marine officers who argue over Wayne's treatment of his troops during World War II. Nicholas Ray directed. **AC1, DT83, ST156**

Flying Tigers (1942, B&W, 102m, NR)
World War II action over China, starring John Wayne. **AC1, AC11, ST156**

Fog, The (1980, C, 91m, R)
An old fisherman in a California coastal town creates havoc when he tells a ghost story to a group of young children. John Carpenter directed. Jamie Lee Curtis and John Houseman star, with Janet Leigh. **DT17, HO2**

Foghorn Leghorn's Fractured Funnies (1986, C, 58m, NR)
Collection of classic Warner Bros. cartoons featuring the best of Foghorn Leghorn's adventures. Included are *Lovelorn Leghorn, The Leghorn Blows at Midnight,* and *Leghorn Swaggled.* **FA11**

Follow Me, Boys! (1966, C, 131m, NR)
Disney drama set in 1930s Midwest, with Fred MacMurray starting a Boy Scout troop in a small town. With Vera Miles, Lillian Gish, and Kurt Russell. **FA1, ST54**

Follow Me Quietly (1949, B&W, 59m, NR)
Thriller about a vigilante killer who calls himself The Judge. William Lundigan, Dorothy Patrick, and Jeff Corey star. **MY1, MY13**

Follow That Bird (1985, C, 88m, G)
Big Bird, *Sesame Street*'s favorite giant, is placed in a foster home, and slowly makes his way back to his friends. Many guest stars include Dave Thomas, John Candy, and Chevy Chase. Also known as *Sesame Street Presents Follow That Bird.* **CO13, CO14, FA9**

Follow That Dream (1962, C, 110m, NR)
Elvis Presley musical about a young man whose family moves to Florida and is not accepted by the local townspeople. **ST123**

Follow the Fleet (1936, B&W, 110m, NR)
Fred Astaire dances his way through the Navy to Irving Berlin tunes. Ginger Rogers and Randolph Scott costar. **CL15, ST2, ST131, ST136**

Food of the Gods (1976, C, 88m, PG)
H.G. Wells tale of animals growing to gigantic proportions after eating an unusual substance. Marjoe Gortner, Pamela Franklin, and Ida Lupino star. **SF10, WR29**

Fool for Love (1985, C, 118m, R)
Two lovers meet at a desert motel and try to sort out their past in this drama written by and starring Sam Shepard, with Kim Basinger, Harry Dean Stanton, and Randy Quaid. Robert Altman directed. **DR3, DT2, ST141**

Foolish Wives (1922, B&W, 107m, NR)
Erich Von Stroheim directed and stars in this classic silent movie about a corrupt man who poses as a Russian count. **CL12, DT109**

Fools (1970, C, 97m, PG)
San Francisco is the setting for this May-December romance between a middle-aged actor (Jason Robards) and the bored wife (Katharine Ross) of an attorney. **ST129, XT13**

Footlight Parade (1933, B&W, 104m, NR)
Classic backstage musical about the difficulty of putting on a show. James Cagney, Ruby Keeler, and Dick Powell star, with choreography by Busby Berkeley. **DT8, MU4, ST14** *Essential; Recommended*

Footloose (1984, C, 106m, PG)
A young high school student (Kevin Bacon) shakes up a town where dancing has been outlawed by a powerful minister. With Lori Singer and John Lithgow. **CO4, DR9, DR26, MU3**

For a Few Dollars More (1965, C, 130m, PG)
In this sequel to *A Fistful of Dollars,* Clint Eastwood is a cigar-smoking bounty hunter out to track down a vicious bandit. Lee Van Cleef costars, with Klaus Kinski. Directed by Sergio Leone. **DT61, ST39, ST83, ST155, WE2, WE13**

For All Mankind (1989, C, 90m, NR)
NASA footage of the nine manned space flights to the moon between 1968 and 1972, compiled and edited by Al Reinert. **CU16**

For Keeps (1988, C, 98m, PG-13)
In this comedy, Molly Ringwald plays a high school senior whose unplanned pregnancy forces her to postpone college. **CO4**

For Love of Ivy (1968, C, 102m, NR)
A brother and sister fix up their family's black maid with a trucking company owner. Romantic comedy stars Sidney Poitier and Abbey Lincoln as the lovers; Beau Bridges and Lauri Peters are the matchmakers. **DR14, ST121**

For Me and My Gal (1942, B&W, 104m, NR)
Gene Kelly made his film debut opposite Judy Garland in this musical about a vaudeville couple's attempts to hit the big time. Busby Berkeley directed. **DT8, MU4, ST51, ST81**

For Pete's Sake (1974, C, 90m, PG)
Barbra Streisand stars as the well-intentioned wife of a cab driver (Michael Sarrazin); her schemes to help him make money immerse them in comic misadventures. **ST146**

For Queen and Country (1988, C, 105m, R)
Denzel Washington stars in a British drama of a veteran who finds his home country hostile to his aspirations. **DR7, DR14, DR23**

For the Love of Benji (1977, C, 84m, G)
The lovable canine stars in his second adventure; this time, he's running through the streets of Athens, dodging criminals who want a formula tattoed on his paw. **FA5**

For Your Eyes Only (1981, C, 127m, PG)
James Bond adventure, with the usual exotic locales and sinister villains, but less emphasis on gadgetry and gimmicks. Roger Moore stars, with Carole Bouquet, Chaim Topol, and Lynn-Holly Johnson. **HF2**

Forbidden Games (1951, B&W, 87m, NR)
Oscar-winning French film about an orphan girl and her stepbrother retreating into their own world. Brigitte Fossey stars; Rene Clement directed. **FF1, XT7** *Essential; Recommended*

Forbidden Planet (1956, C, 98m, NR)
Classic 1950s science fiction drama about astronauts discovering planet occupied by wicked scientist and his lovely daughter. A loose version of Shakespeare's *Tempest,* starring Walter Pidgeon, Anne Francis, and Leslie Nielsen. **CU4, SF1, WR22** *Essential; Recommended*

Forbidden Zone (1980, C, 76m, R)
This unusual, campy musical deals with an underground kingdom set in the sixth dimension. Herve Villechaize stars. **CU2, MU16**

Forbin Project, The *see* Colossus: The Forbin Project

Force of Evil (1948, B&W, 78m, NR)
A small-time attorney (John Garfield) gives up his ideals to find success working for a racketeer. Classic film noir, written and directed by Abraham Polonsky. **MY1** *Essential; Recommended*

Force of One, A (1979, C, 90m, PG)
Chuck Norris stars in this karate-kicking sequel to *Good Guys Wear Black,* about a small California town overrun by drug dealers and the man who would stop them. **ST114**

Force 10 From Navarone (1978, C, 118m, PG)
This sequel to *The Guns of Navarone* features Harrison Ford and Robert Shaw as members of a force out to blow up a bridge that is vital to the Nazis. **AC1, ST46**

Forced Vengeance (1982, C, 90m, R)
In Hong Kong, a Vietnam War veteran, now the head of security at a casino, tangles with some gangsters. Chuck Norris stars. **ST114**

Foreign Correspondent (1940, B&W, 119m, NR)
Joel McCrea is a journalist who falls for a British girl and uncovers a spy ring headed by her father. With Laraine Day, Herbert Marshall, and George Sanders. Directed by Alfred Hitchcock. **DT46, MY6**

Formula, The (1980, C, 117m, R)
A Los Angeles cop investigates the murder of his friend and discovers a conspiracy involving a formula for synthetic fuel. Marlon Brando and George C. Scott star. **DR24, MY6, MY9, ST10**

Fort Apache (1948, B&W, 127m, NR)
John Ford directed this classic western about cavalrymen (John Wayne and Henry Fonda) who protect the frontier from the Indians. Shirley Temple, Victor McLaglen, and Ward Bond costar. **DT36, ST44, ST148, ST156, WE4** *Essential; Recommended*

Fort Apache, The Bronx (1981, C, 125m, R)
Paul Newman plays a weary, streetwise cop trying to do his job against often impossible odds in a dangerous neighborhood. With Ed Asner, Ken Wahl, Pam Grier, and Danny Aiello. **DR15, ST111, XT9**

Fortress (1985, C, 89m, NR)
Australian action drama of kidnapping of a teacher and her students in the Australian outback. Rachel Ward stars. **FF5**

Forty Carats (1973, C, 110m, PG)
Liv Ullmann is a middle-aged divorced woman who falls in love with a man half her age. Gene Kelly and Edward Albert costar in this comedy. **ST81, ST154**

48HRS. (1982, C, 97m, R)
Eddie Murphy made his screen debut in this action/thriller about a weary San Francisco cop (Nick Nolte) who gets a con (Murphy) out of jail for two days to help track a deranged killer. With Annette O'Toole, James Remar, and Frank McRae. Directed by Walter Hill. **AC9, CO13, DT45, ST113, XT13, XT21**

49th Parallel, The (1941, B&W, 105m, NR)
When a Nazi U-boat is sunk in Canadian waters, its survivors struggle to reach neutral territory. Suspense from director Michael Powell, starring Anton Walbrook, Eric Portman, Leslie Howard, and Laurence Olivier. **AC1, DT81, ST116**

42nd Street (1933, B&W, 89m, NR)
The star of a Broadway show gets sick, and a naive girl (Ruby Keeler) is picked to go on in her place. Great songs, including "Shuffle Off to Buffalo," and superb choreography by Busby Berkeley. Watch quickly for Ginger Rogers. **DT8, MU4, ST131** *Essential; Recommended*

Forty-Seven Ronin, The
  Part One (1941, B&W, 113m, NR)
  Part Two (1942, B&W, 112m, NR)
Epic Japanese historical drama about a group of royal retainers out to avenge the honor of their lord. Directed by Kenji Mizoguchi. **FF4**

Forty Thousand Horsemen (1941, B&W, 84m, NR)
World War I adventure of the Australian Light Brigade's adventures in Palestine. Grant Taylor and Chips Rafferty star. **AC2, FF5**

Foul Play (1978, C, 116m, PG)
Suspense comedy, set in San Francisco, about a woman caught in a murder plot. No one will believe her, except a detective who happens to be falling in love with her. Goldie Hawn and Chevy Chase star, with Dudley Moore. **CO10, CO13, ST63, ST109, XT13**

Fountainhead, The (1949, B&W, 114m, NR)
Gary Cooper plays an idealistic architect who won't compromise his designs for the company he works for, or for the woman he loves (Patricia Neal). Cult camp based on the Ayn Rand novel. Directed by King Vidor. **CU2, DT107, ST22**

4D Man (1959, C, 85m, NR)
Science fiction drama of a scientist whose experiments give him the power to pass through solid matter. Robert Lansing and Lee Meriwether star. **SF1, SF5**

Four Feathers, The (1939, C, 115m, NR)
A cowardly British officer decides to prove his prowess when he helps fellow soldiers in the Sudan uprising. Ralph Richardson and C. Aubrey Smith star in this Technicolor saga. **AC6, AC13, CL9**

Four Friends (1981, C, 115m, R)
A young Yugoslavian immigrant to the U.S. grows up during the turbulent 1960s. Craig Wasson stars, with Jodi Thelen and Jim Metzler. Written by Steve Tesich; directed by Arthur Penn. **DR7, DT78**

Four Horsemen of the Apocalypse (1961, C, 153m, NR)
Vincente Minnelli directed this remake and updating of the silent classic about the break-up of a family whose members fight on opposite sides during World War II (World War I in the original). Glenn Ford and Charles Boyer star. **CL3, DT71**

400 Blows, The (1959, B&W, 99m, NR)
Stunning account of a young Parisian boy's desperate search for affection in a loveless household. Jean-Pierre Léaud stars in this first of several films about the same character, Antoine Doinel. Director François Truffaut's groundbreaking debut. **DT106, XT16** *Essential; Highly Recommended*

Four Musketeers, The (1975, C, 108m, PG)
Sequel to 1974 version of *The Three Musketeers* (filmed at the same time), with grand cast indulging in more swordplay and double-dealing. Oliver Reed, Faye Dunaway, Frank Finlay, Michael York, and Richard Chamberlain star, with Christopher Lee, Charlton Heston, Raquel Welch, and Roy Kinnear. Brilliantly directed by Richard Lester. **AC15, DT62, ST37, ST89** *Highly Recommended*

Four Seasons, The (1981, C, 107m, PG)
Three middle-aged couples vacation together during each of the seasons of the year. Alan Alda stars, with Carol Burnett, Rita Moreno, Jack Weston, Len Cariou, and Bess Armstrong. Alda wrote and directed. **CO1**

Fourth Man, The (1979, C, 104m, NR)
A bisexual writer begins an affair with a seductive young woman, but is more attracted to her current boyfriend. Then he learns that the woman's three husbands all died mysteriously. Dutch film with cult reputation for its sexy explicitness, directed by Paul Verhoeven. **CU6, FF7, MY5, MY16** *Recommended*

Fourth Protocol, The (1987, C, 119m, R)
A British spy (Michael Caine) tries to stop a Russian plot to sever ties between England and America. Pierce Brosnan and Joanna Cassidy costar as the Russian agents. Based on a Frederick Forsyth novel. **ST15, WR8**

Fourth War, The (1990, C, 91m, R)
Roy Scheider and Jürgen Prochnow play rival American and Soviet military officers poised on opposite sides of the Eastern Europe border in this pre-glasnost thriller. With Harry Dean Stanton and Tim Reid. **MY6, ST141**

Fox and His Friends (1975, C, 123m, NR)
German drama of a gay carnival worker who is exploited by his wealthy lover. Rainer Werner Fassbinder directed himself in the title role. **DT34**

Foxes (1980, C, 106m, R)
The trials and tribulations of four teen-aged girls growing up fast in the San Fernando Valley, starring Jodie Foster, Cherie Curie, Marilyn Kagan, and Kandice Stroh, with Scott Baio, Sally Kellerman, and Randy Quaid. **DR9, MU12, ST47**

Foxtrot (1976, C, 91m, R)
Peter O'Toole stars in this drama about a wealthy couple who flee Europe in the late 1930s to escape the approaching madness of World War II. They settle on an island off the coast of Mexico. With Charlotte Rampling and Max von Sydow. **ST117**

Fozzie's Muppet Scrapbook (1985, C, 58m, NR)
Milton Berle, Raquel Welch, and Beverly Sills join Sesame Street's lovable Fozzie Bear in some of his greatest adventures. **FA14**

Frances (1982, C, 140m, R)
Jessica Lange plays Frances Farmer, the Hollywood actress of the 1930s whose brushes with the law and conflicts with her domineering mother cut short her career. Kim Stanley and Sam Shepard costar. **DR4, DR13, ST86** *Recommended*

Frankenstein (1931, B&W, 71m, NR)
The definitive Man-Made Monster movie, with Boris Karloff the creation of mad scientist Colin Clive. Video version restores footage not seen since the original release. Directed by James Whale. **CU10, DT115, HF10, HO1, SF2, ST77** *Essential; Recommended*

Frankenstein (1973, C, 200m, NR)
Made-for-television version of the Mary Shelley story features Michael Sarrazin as the creation, more a dashing rogue than a monster. Robert Foxworth and James Mason costar. **HF10, HO20**

Frankenstein Island (1978, C, 88m, NR)
Four balloonists crash on an uncharted island and encounter zombies, mad doctors, scantily clad women, and . . . well, more we dare not tell. Deservedly obscure "bad" film. **CU11**

Frankenstein Meets the Wolf Man (1943, B&W, 72m, NR)
Summit meeting of film monsters, starring Bela Lugosi and Lon Chaney, Jr. **HF10, HO1, ST17, ST95**

Frankenstein—1970 (1958, B&W, 83m, NR)
This version of the classic horror story stars Boris Karloff as a mad scientist and takes more of a science fiction approach to the familiar material. **HF10, ST77**

Frankie and Johnny (1966, C, 87m, NR)
Elvis Presley plays a riverboat gambler caught in a love triangle. **ST123**

Frantic (1958, B&W, 90m, NR)
A man and woman plan to murder her husband, but the plan backfires, and the man gets accused of murders he didn't

commit. Jeanne Moreau stars. Louis Malle directed. **MY16, ST110**

Frantic (1988, C, 120m, R)
Thriller starring Harrison Ford as an American whose wife is kidnapped while they're vacationing in Paris. With Emmanuelle Seigner and Betty Buckley. Directed by Roman Polanski. **DT79, MY16, ST46, XT16** *Recommended*

Freaks (1932, B&W, 66m, NR)
Classic horror film, banned for many years in Britain, about circus troupe, starring real "human oddities." Directed by Tod Browning. **CU4, CU8, DT14, HO1, HO19** *Recommended*

Freaky Friday (1977, C, 95m, G)
This Disney comedy features Barbara Harris and Jodie Foster as a mother and daughter who switch personalities for a day. **CO20, FA1, ST47**

French Cancan (1955, C, 102m, NR)
Jean Renoir directed this colorful story of the early days of the Moulin Rouge. Jean Gabin plays a showman who invents the title dance. Also known as *Only the French Can*. **ST86**

French Connection, The (1971, C, 104m, R)
Oscar winner Gene Hackman plays Popeye Doyle, a hard-driving New York City detective on the trail of a heroin smuggling ring. Oscars for Best Picture and Director (William Friedkin). Roy Scheider and Fernando Rey costar. **AC9, ST61, XT1, XT2, XT6, XT9** *Essential; Recommended*

French Connection 2, The (1975, C, 119m, R)
Popeye Doyle travels to France in an attempt to locate the drug kingpin who eluded him in New York. Gene Hackman and Fernando Rey star. John Frankenheimer directed. **AC9, ST61**

French Lieutenant's Woman, The (1981, C, 123m, R)
Screen version of John Fowles' story of ill-fated Victorian love affair adds a parallel modern story about actor and actress shooting a film and becoming lovers. Meryl Streep and Jeremy Irons star. Written by Harold Pinter and directed by Karel Reisz. **DR1, DR13, ST145**

French Postcards (1979, C, 92m, PG)
A group of American teenagers studying in Paris get involved in many misadventures. Early screen appearances for Debra Winger, Mandy Patinkin, and Blanche Baker. **ST163, XT16**

Frenzy (1972, C, 116m, R)
Alfred Hitchcock directed this tale of a London strangler known as The Necktie Murderer, and the innocent man who is suspected of the killer's crimes. Jon Finch and Barry Foster star, with Barbara Leigh-Hunt, Anna Massey, Alec McCowen, and Vivien Merchant. **DT46, MY7, MY13, XT15** *Recommended*

Fresh Horses (1988, C, 104m, PG-13)
A soon-to-be-married young man has second thoughts when he meets a sensual young woman, although they're from very different backgrounds. Andrew McCarthy and Molly Ringwald star in this romantic drama. **DR1**

Freshman, The (1925, B&W, 70m, NR)
In this silent comedy classic, Harold Lloyd plays a college freshman who will do anything to be accepted by his fellow students. **CL11, CO18** *Essential*

Friday the 13th (series)
Part I (1980, C, 90m, R)
Part II (1981, C, 87m, R)
Part III (1982, C, 96m, R)
The Final Chapter (1984, C, 91m, R)
Part V: A New Beginning (1985, C, 102m, R)
Part VI: Jason Lives (1986, C, 87m, R)
Part VII: The New Blood (1988, C, 90m, R)
Part VIII: Jason Takes Manhattan (1989, C, 100m, R)
This horror series portrays a mad, seemingly indestructible killer named Jason, who masquerades behind a hockey mask, murdering innumerable teenagers at a summer camp. **HO12, HO18** *Essential (first film)*

Friendly Persuasion (1956, C, 140m, NR)
A family of Quakers hold fast to their faith during the Civil War. Gary Cooper and Dorothy McGuire star. William Wyler directed. **AC5, DT119, ST22**

Fright Night (1987, C, 105m, R)
A teenager hires a TV horror movie host to kill a new neighbor, whom he suspects of being a vampire. William Ragsdale,

Chris Sarandon, and Roddy McDowall star, with Amanda Bearse. **HO5, HO19**

Fright Night II (1989, C, 108m, R)
Sequel to first *Fright Night* has same teen and TV horror show host teaming to trap a seductive vampire (Julie Carmen). **HO5**

Fringe Dwellers, The (1986, C, 98m, PG)
Australian drama about an aborigine family moving into a white, middle-class neighborhood, with expected problems. Directed by Bruce Beresford. **FF5**

Frisco Kid, The (1979, C, 122m, PG)
A wild western about a Polish rabbi (Gene Wilder) who sets out on the 1850s frontier to meet his San Francisco congregation. Harrison Ford costars. **ST46, WE14**

Frogs (1972, C, 91m, PG)
Ray Milland stars as a man who destroys the natural wildlife near his home, only to have his family threatened by an onslaught of avenging reptiles. **HO16**

From Beyond (1986, C, 85m, R)
A scientist's insatiable search for a sixth sense eventually drives his staff to insanity. Based on a H.P. Lovecraft tale; exceptionally gory. **CU7, HO20, HO25**

From Beyond the Grave (1973, C, 97m, PG)
Four horror stories centering on a British antique shop, where the mysterious owner (Peter Cushing) helps his customers meet terrible fates. Margaret Leighton, Diana Dors, and David Warner costar. **HO23, HO26, ST27**

From Here to Eternity (1953, B&W, 118m, NR)
The James Jones story of army life in Pearl Harbor, just before the Japanese attack, starring Burt Lancaster, Deborah Kerr, Montogmery Clift, and Oscar winners Frank Sinatra and Donna Reed. Winner of six other Academy Awards, including Best Picture and Director (Fred Zinnemann). **AC1, DR19, DT120, ST85, ST138, XT1, XT4, XT5, XT6** *Essential; Highly Recommended*

From Hollywood the Deadwood (1989, C, 102m, R)
A pair of private eyes (Scott Paulin, Jim Haynie) go looking for a missing movie star. Written and directed by Rex Pickett. **MY10**

From Russia With Love (1963, C, 118m, NR)
The second James Bond adventure, and one of the very best, with Sean Connery sparring with lovely Soviet spy Daniela Bianchi. Robert Shaw and Lotte Lenya make an especially colorful pair of villains. Outstanding fight sequence aboard the Orient Express. **HF2, ST21, XT19** *Highly Recommended*

From the Earth to the Moon (1958, C, 100m, NR)
Jules Verne's fantasy adventure about man's first voyage to the moon, starring George Sanders, Debra Paget, and Cedric Hardwicke. **FA8, SF13, WR28**

From the Life of the Marionettes (1980, C/B&W, 104m, R)
Drama from director Ingmar Bergman about a respectable businessman involved in the murder of a prostitute. Robert Atzorn stars. **DT7**

From the Mixed-Up Files of Mrs. Basil E. Frankenweiler (1973, C, 105m, NR)
Two children hide out in New York City's Metropolitan Museum and befriend a reclusive woman (Ingrid Bergman). **FA7, ST7**

From the Terrace (1960, C, 144m, NR)
John O'Hara story of a war veteran rising to social prominence on the backs of everyone who gets in his way. Paul Newman stars, with Joanne Woodward and Myrna Loy. **ST94, ST111, ST166**

Front, The (1976, C, 94m, PG)
Woody Allen stars in a drama of a restaurant cashier who fronts for a group of blacklisted television writers in 1950s New York. He slowly becomes a celebrity as he accepts the praise and recognition for their work. Written by Walter Bernstein (himself a blacklisted writer); directed by Martin Ritt. **DR12, DT1, DT87**

Front Page, The (1931, B&W, 101m, NR)
First screen version of the Ben Hecht-Charles MacArthur stage comedy about the ruthless world of journalism. Pat O'Brien plays the star reporter, and Adolphe Menjou is his hard-driving editor. Remade in 1940 (as *His Girl Friday*), in 1974 (unavailable on video), and in 1988 (as *Switching Channels*). **CL10, DR20**

Frontier Pony Express (1939, B&W, 54m, NR)
Roy Rogers and Trigger ride into action to round up Pony Express bandits. **ST132**

Fugitive, The (1947, B&W, 104m, NR)
Drama of a priest (Henry Fonda) in Mexico involved with revolutionaries. Directed by John Ford. **DT36, ST44**

Fugitive Kind, The (1959, B&W, 122m, NR)
A drifter (Marlon Brando) arrives in a Southern town and begins romancing two women (Joanne Woodward and Anna Magnani). Tennessee Williams drama directed by Sidney Lumet. **DT65, ST10, ST166, WR30**

Full Metal Jacket (1987, C, 117m, R)
After a grueling basic training period, a cynical young army journalist (Matthew Modine) is plunged into combat in Vietnam. A gritty, violent tale from director Stanley Kubrick. With Vincent D'Onofrio, Lee Ermey, and Adam Baldwin. **AC4, DT56** *Recommended*

Full Moon in Blue Water (1988, C, 96m, R)
Gene Hackman plays the owner of a rundown seaside bar whose bad fortune is reversed by the arrival of a young woman (Teri Garr). **ST61**

Full Moon in Paris (1984, C, 102m, R)
French comedy about an independent young woman juggling three lovers. Pascale Ogier stars. Eric Rohmer directed. **DT89**

Fun in Acapulco (1963, C, 97m, NR)
Elvis Presley plays a lifeguard by day and nightclub entertainer at night in this musical set in Mexico. **ST123**

Fun With Dick and Jane (1977, C, 95m, PG)
Jane Fonda and George Segal star as an upwardly mobile couple who turn to robbery when he loses his job. Ed McMahon costars in this comedy about modern lifestyles. **ST45**

Funeral in Berlin (1966, C, 102m, NR)
Michael Caine's second film as British spy Harry Palmer; here he arranges for the defection of a Russian officer. **ST15, MY6**

Funhouse, The (1981, C, 96m, R)
Four teenagers decide to spend the night in a carnival funhouse, where they are terrorized by an unknown assailant. Directed by Tobe Hooper. **DT47, HO12**

Funny Face (1957, C, 103m, NR)
Fred Astaire is a fashion photographer who takes a plain Audrey Hepburn and turns her into a beautiful Paris model. Stanley Donen directed; songs by George Gershwin. **CL9, DT30, ST2, ST65, XT16**

Funny Farm (1988, C, 101m, PG)
Chevy Chase is a sportswriter looking for a rural retreat—and finding nothing but trouble. Madolyn Smith costars. **CO13**

Funny Girl (1968, C, 151m, G)
Barbra Streisand, in her debut film, won an Academy Award for recreating her Broadway success as Fanny Brice, the comedy legend who rose to stardom in the Ziegfeld Follies. With Omar Sharif and Kay Medford. Directed by William Wyler. **DT119, MU2, MU5, MU7, ST146, XT3, XT9, XT21** *Essential*

Funny Lady (1975, C, 137m, PG)
This sequel to *Funny Girl* portrays Fanny Brice (Barbra Streisand) at the peak of her career, married to showman Billy Rose (James Caan). **MU5, ST146**

Funny Thing Happened on the Way to the Forum, A (1966, C, 99m, NR)
Zero Mostel portrays a sly slave in ancient Rome with a yearning to be free. Based on the Broadway musical, with costars Buster Keaton, Jack Gilford, and Michael Crawford. Directed by Richard Lester. **DT54, DT62, MU2**

Fury, The (1978, C, 118m, R)
Young girl and boy with telekinetic powers are united against evil American agents. Brian DePalma directed; Kirk Douglas, Amy Irving, John Cassavetes, and Andrew Stevens star. **DT29, HO7, ST34**

Future-Kill (1985, C, 83m, R)
Science fiction action with a band of rowdy fraternity boys taking on anti-nuclear activists in a city wasteland. Edwin Neal and Marilyn Burns star. **SF8**

Futureworld (1976, C, 104m, PG)
Sequel to *Westworld,* with that film's robots hatching a Take Over the World

scheme. Science fiction drama starring Peter Fonda, Blythe Danner, and Yul Brynner. **SF6**

Fuzz (1972, C, 92m, PG)
Cop drama, with moments of dark humor, about Boston policemen and their attempts to stay sane amid the chaos of big city life. Burt Reynolds stars, with Raquel Welch, Yul Brynner, Jack Weston, Tom Skeritt, and Peter Bonerz. **CO10, ST128**

G.I. Blues (1960, C, 104m, NR)
Elvis Presley stars as a guitar-playing soldier in Germany who romances a leggy dancer (Juliet Prowse). **ST123**

Gabriela (1983, C, 102m, R)
Barkeeper takes on lovely young woman as a cook, and romance follows. Marcello Mastroianni and Sonia Braga costar in this Brazilian film. **FF6, ST9, ST103**

Gaby—A True Story (1987, C, 110m, R)
True-life drama of a young woman afflicted with cerebral palsy, struggling to overcome her handicap and her parents' overprotectiveness to become a bestselling writer. Rachel Levin stars, with Liv Ullmann, Robert Loggia, and Norma Aleandro. **DR2, DR6, ST154**

Galaxina (1980, C, 95m, R)
Science fiction spoof of both *Star Wars* and *Star Trek* movies, starring Avery Schreiber and sexy Dorothy Stratten. **SF21, SF22**

Galaxy of Terror (1981, C, 80m, R)
Astronauts confront monsters while on a rescue mission in this science fiction/horror tale. Edward Albert, Erin Moran, and Ray Walston star. **SF20**

Gallagher (series) (1984-85, C, approx. 60m ea., NR)
Stand-up comic Gallagher, appears in this series of five separate performances: *The Bookkeeper, The Maddest, Melon Crazy, Over Your Head,* and *Stuck in the 60s.* **CO16**

Gallipoli (1981, C, 110m, PG)
World War I drama, starring Mel Gibson and Mark Lee as two naive young Australian recruits thrown into fierce battle. Directed by Peter Weir. **AC2, DT111, ST53**

Gambit (1966, C, 109m, NR)
A crook (Michael Caine) wants to steal a valuable statue, and he hires a kooky young woman (Shirley MacLaine) to help him do the job. **MY18, ST15, ST96**

Gambling Samurai, The (1960, C, 93m, NR)
Toshiro Mifune stars in this tale of a wandering warrior. **ST106**

Game Is Over, The (1966, C, 96m, NR)
French drama of a woman's marriage to a wealthy man and her affair with his son. Jane Fonda stars; Roger Vadim directed. **FF1, ST45**

Game of Death (1979, C, 102m, R)
Bruce Lee finished twenty minutes of fighting scenes for this film before he died; a story was composed around those sequences to take advantage of his phenomenal popularity. With Chuck Norris, Kareem Abdul-Jabbar, Gig Young, and Hugh O'Brian. **ST88, ST114**

Gandhi (1982, C, 200m, PG)
Ben Kingsley won an Oscar for his portrayal of India's modern spiritual leader, whose courage inspired his countrymen to reject British colonial rule. With John Gielgud, Edward Fox, and Martin Sheen. The film and director Richard Attenborough also won Academy Awards. **DR4, DR23, XT1, XT2, XT6** *Recommended*

Ganja and Hess *see* Blood Couple

Garbo Talks (1984, C, 103m, PG-13)
A son works to grant his mother's dying wish—she wants to meet Greta Garbo, who is living in seclusion in New York City. Anne Bancroft and Ron Silver star, with Carrie Fisher, Catherine Hicks, Steven Hill, Howard da Silva, Dorothy Loudon, and Harvey Fierstein. Directed by Sidney Lumet. **CO5, DT65, XT9**

Garden of Allah (1936, C, 86m, NR)
Charles Boyer and Marlene Dietrich star in this romance set in the Algerian desert. Lovely color photography. **CL9, ST33**

Garden of the Finzi-Continis, The (1971, C, 95m, R)
Oscar-winning drama from Italy about an aristocratic Jewish family in wartime Italy oblivious to the Holocaust until it is too late to escape. Vittorio De Sica directed. Dominique Sanda stars. **DT26, XT7**

Gardens of Stone (1987, C, 112m, R)
Title refers to Arlington National Cemetery, scene of this drama set during the early days of the Vietnam War. An army company that buries the dead welcomes a young recruit yearning for combat experience. James Caan, James Earl Jones, and D.B. Sweeney star, with Mary Stuart Masterson, Anjelica Huston, Dean Stockwell, and Bill Graham. Francis Ford Coppola directed. **DR7, DT21, ST76, ST144**

Garry Shandling: Alone in Vegas (1984, C, 52m, NR)
The popular comedian is shown in a live performance in Las Vegas. **CO16**

Gaslight (1944, B&W, 114m, NR)
Ingrid Bergman won an Academy Award for playing a tormented woman whose husband (Charles Boyer) is slowly driving her insane. Directed by George Cukor. **DT24, MY3, ST7, XT3**

Gas-s-s-s (1970, C, 79m, PG)
Roger Corman directed this free-spirited comedy about a lethal gas destroying everyone in the United State over 30. Robert Corff and Elaine Giftos star, with Bud Cort, Cindy Williams, Ben Vereen, and Talia Coppola (Shire). Full title: *Gas-s-s-s . . . Or It May Become Necessary to Destroy the World in Order to Save It!* **CO2, DT22**

Gate, The (1987, C, 92m, PG-13)
A young boy is grounded, and he and a friend discover the gate to hell in his back yard. **HO10**

Gate of Hell (1954, C, 89m, NR)
Japanese drama of a 12th-century samurai who falls in love with a married woman, then discards her. Oscar winner for Best Foreign Language Film. **FF4, XT7**

Gates of Heaven (1978, C, 85m, NR)
Funny and surprisingly touching documentary about pet cemeteries, the people who use them, the people who run them. Directed by Errol Morris. **CU16, DT73** *Recommended*

Gator (1976, C, 116m, PG)
Good ol' boy Burt Reynolds teams up with the feds to get the goods on a crooked politican in this sequel to *White Lightning*. **ST128**

Gauntlet, The (1977, C, 109m, R)
A cop is assigned to escort a prostitute, set to testify against the Mob, from Las Vegas to Phoenix; both are unaware they've been set up for assassination. Clint Eastwood and Sondra Locke star. **AC9, ST39, XT18**

Gay Divorcee, The (1934, B&W, 107m, NR)
Fred Astaire and Ginger Rogers dance to Cole Porter music. Also includes the first Oscar-winning song, "The Continental." **CL15, ST2, ST131**

Gay Ranchero, The (1947, B&W, 53m, NR)
Roy Rogers and sidekick Andy Devine go searching for a downed airplane in this contemporary western. **ST132**

General, The (1927, B&W, 74m, NR)
Buster Keaton plays a man trying to steal a train during the Civil War, with riotous results. One of the truly great comedies. **CL11, DT54, XT19** *Essential; Highly Recommended*

General Della Rovere (1960, B&W, 129m, NR)
Vittorio De Sica stars in a drama of an Italian impersonating a general during World War II and beginning to believe his ruse. Roberto Rossellini directed. **DT26, FF2**

General Died at Dawn, The (1936, B&W, 97m, NR)
Gary Cooper stars in this tale of romance and intrigue in the mysterious East, with Madeleine Carroll as the agent he falls for, Akim Tamiroff his wily adversary. **MY6, ST22**

General Line, The (1929, B&W, 90m, NR)
Soviet director Sergei Eisenstein's silent drama of a rural woman's struggle to start a collective. **DT33**

Gentleman Jim (1942, B&W, 104m, NR)
Errol Flynn plays Jim Corbett, the famed heavyweight boxing champion of the early 20th century, in this colorful drama. With Alexis Smith, Jack Carson, and Alan Hale. **ST43**

Gentlemen Prefer Blondes (1953, C, 91m, NR)
Marilyn Monroe and Jane Russell are two showgirls who set out to find themselves

husbands in this vibrant adaptation of the Broadway musical. Monroe proves that "diamonds are a girl's best friend." Directed by Howard Hawks. **CO8, DT43, ST108**

George Stevens: A Filmmaker's Journey (1984, C, 110m, NR)
Katharine Hepburn, Ginger Rogers, and Warren Beatty are three of the performers who add insight to this documentary of director Stevens' films. Includes scenes from *Alice Adams, Giant,* and *A Place In the Sun.* Directed by George Stevens, Jr. **CU16, DT101, ST5, ST66, ST131** *Recommended*

Georgy Girl (1966, B&W, 100m, NR)
Lynn Redgrave is an ugly duckling London girl who's romanced by a wealthy older gentleman (James Mason). Alan Bates and Charlotte Rampling costar. **CO17, DR3, ST102, XT15**

Get Crazy (1983, C, 90m, NR)
A theater owner plans to stage the biggest rock concert ever on New Year's Eve, but everything goes wrong. Cult comedy with many characters resembling real-life rock stars, lots of in-jokes about the music business. Daniel Stern stars, with Malcolm McDowell, Ed Begley, Jr., Lou Reed, Bobby Sherman, and Fabian Forte. Directed by Allan Arkush. **CU5, DT4, MU9** *Recommended*

Get Out of My Room (1985, C, 53m, NR)
Cheech and Chong perform in this compilation of four crazy comedy and music videos, including *Love Is Strange* and *Born in East L.A.* **ST18**

Get Out Your Handkerchiefs (1978, C, 109m, R)
Dark comedy from France about a man so desperate to keep his wife happy that he urges her to take a lover. Gerard Depardieu, Patrick Dewaere, and Carole Laure star. Directed by Bertrand Blier. Oscar winner for Best Foreign Langauge Film. **FF1, ST31, XT7**

Getaway, The (1972, C, 122m, PG)
Sam Peckinpah's tale about a bank robber and his wife (Steve McQueen and Ali McGraw) who lead a corrupt politician and the police on a wild chase across Texas. With Ben Johnson, Al Letieri, Sally Struthers, Dub Taylor, John Bryson, and Slim Pickens. Based on a novel by Jim Thompson. **AC9, DT77, MY18, ST97, WR26, XT18** *Recommended*

Getting Even (1986, C, 90m, R)
A crazed businessman threatens to unleash poison gas on Dallas if he's not paid $50 million. Joe Don Baker stars, with Edward Albert and Audrey Landers. **AC8**

Getting It Right (1989, C, 101m, R)
British comedy of a 31-year-old virgin and his one-night initiation into the world of sex. Jesse Birdsall stars, with Helena Bonham Carter, Peter Cook, John Gielgud, Jane Horrocks, and Lynn Redgrave. **CO17**

Getting of Wisdom, The (1977, C, 100m, NR)
Australian drama of a girl from the outback holding her own at a stuffy boarding school. Directed by Bruce Beresford. **FF5**

Getting Straight (1970, C, 124m, R)
A graduate student (Elliott Gould) is caught between his loyalty to his studies and the student activist movement taking place on campus. Candice Bergen costars; watch for Harrison Ford in a small role. **CO18, ST46**

Ghidrah, the Three-Headed Monster (1965, C, 85m, NR)
Monster movie from Japan, with Godzilla, Mothra, and Rodan battling the title character. **FF4, SF18**

Ghost and Mrs. Muir, The (1947, B&W, 104m, NR)
Fantasy of lonely woman (Gene Tierney) romanced by a suave spirit (Rex Harison). Written by Philip Dunne and directed by Joseph L. Mankiewicz. Music by Bernard Herrmann. **DT68, SF2**

Ghost Goes West, The (1936, B&W, 82m, NR)
The new owner of a castle finds it's haunted by the ghost of a playboy. Eugene Pallette and Robert Donat star. Rene Clair directed. **SF2**

Ghost in the Noonday Sun (1973, C, 89m, NR)
Pirate comedy starring Peter Sellers, Tony Franciosa, Spike Milligan, and Peter Boyle. **ST137**

Ghost of Yotsuya, The (1950, C, 100m, NR)
Japanese horror film about a man tortured by an evil spirit. **FF4**

Ghost Story (1981, C, 104m, R)
Four elderly men are tormented by an event which took place 50 years before. Fred Astaire, Melvyn Douglas, Douglas Fairbanks, Jr., John Houseman, and Patricia Neal star in this horror tale. **HO2, HO19, ST2**

Ghost Warrior (1984, C, 86m, R)
A samurai warrior found frozen in modern-day Japan is brought to Los Angeles. When he thaws out and someone tries to steal his sword, all hell breaks loose on the streets. **AC25**

Ghostbusters (1984, C, 107m, PG)
A trio of nutty paranormal researchers (Bill Murray, Dan Aykroyd, Harold Ramis) decide to start their own business, flushing out ghosts in New York. Dazzling special effects and a brilliant comic performance by Murray. With Sigourney Weaver, Ernie Hudson, Rick Moranis, William Atherton, and Annie Potts. **CO9, CO11, CO13, CO14, ST157, XT9** *Highly Recommended*

Ghostbusters II (1989, C, 102m, PG)
Return of the spook-chasing trio and their associates, with stars from first installment reprising their roles. Watch for Cheech Marin in a cameo. **CO9, CO11, CO13, CO14, ST18, ST157, XT9**

Ghosts on the Loose (1943, B&W, 65m, NR)
A honeymooning couple has to spend the night in a haunted house, and the East Side Kids go there pretending to haunt the place. Bela Lugosi and Ava Gardner, in one of her first roles, star. Also known as *East Side Kids Meet Bela Lugosi*. **ST95**

Ghoul, The (1933, B&W, 73m, NR)
British horror tale, with Boris Karloff as a man buried with jewels from an Egyptian tomb, resurrected when they're stolen. With Cedric Hardwicke, Ernest Thesiger, and (in his film debut) Ralph Richardson. **HO26, ST77**

Ghoul, The (1975, C, 88m, NR)
Innocent people are accosted by the monster of a wealthy man (Peter Cushing). John Hurt costars. **HO26, ST27**

Ghoulies (1984, C, 81m, PG-13)
On his 18th birthday, a young man inherits a rambling mansion and an ability to conjure up evil spirits. **HO16**

Giant (1956, C, 201m, G)
Elizabeth Taylor, Rock Hudson, and James Dean (in his last film) star in Edna Ferber's sprawling story of Texas cattlemen who strike it rich with oil. With Mercedes McCambridge, Dennis Hopper, Carroll Baker, Chill Wills, Jane Withers, and Sal Mineo. Directed by Oscar winner George Stevens. **DR24, DT101, ST71, ST73, ST147, WE12, XT6, XT22***Essential*

Gideon's Trumpet (1980, C, 104m, NR)
Henry Fonda plays a convict whose battle for his basic rights became a landmark Supreme Court decision. Jose Ferrer costars; originally made for TV. **DR6, ST44**

Gig, The (1986, C, 95m, NR)
An amateur group of jazz musicians get their first big break—but aren't sure if they can handle the pressures. Wayne Rogers and Cleavon Little star. **DR12**

Gigi (1958, C, 119m, NR)
Winner of nine Academy Awards, including Best Picture, this is the story of a young Parisian girl (Leslie Caron) who chooses marriage over becoming a courtesan. Louis Jourdan, Maurice Chevalier, and Hermione Gingold costar. Directed by Oscar winner Vincente Minnelli. **DT71, MU1, MU7, XT1, XT6**

Gilda (1946, B&W, 110m, NR)
Rita Hayworth's most famous role, a woman married to a wealthy South American casino owner, whose right-hand man (Glenn Ford) is a love from her past. **CL4, MY1, MY4, ST64**

Gilda Live (1980, C, 90m, NR)
Former *Saturday Night Live* regular Gilda Radner recreates many of her characters in this filmed version of her Broadway show. Directed by Mike Nichols. **CO13, CO16, DT74**

Gimme Shelter (1970, C, 91m, NR)
This stunning documentary of The Rolling Stones' 1969 concert tour of America includes footage from their tragic appearance at Altamount, where an audience member was murdered. Directed by Albert and David Maysles, with Charlotte Zwerin. **MU10** *Essential; Recommended*

Ginger and Fred (1986, C, 126m, PG-13)
A couple of small-time Italian entertainers who once imitated Astaire and Rogers are reunited thirty years later for a television show. Giulietta Masina and Marcello Mastroianni star. Directed by Federico Fellini. **CO8, DT53, ST103**

Ginger in the Morning (1973, C, 89m, PG)
Love story between an unlikely pair: a lonely traveling salesman (Monte Markham) and a free-spirited hitchhiker (Sissy Spacek). **ST139**

Girl, The (1986, C, 104m, R)
A wealthy attorney's affair with a teenager soon leads to murder in this thriller starring Franco Nero and Christopher Lee. **ST89**

Girl Can't Help It, The (1956, C, 99m, NR)
A gangster hires an agent to promote his girlfriend, who wants to be a singer. Edmond O' Brien, Tom Ewell, and Jayne Mansfield are the leads, but the real stars are the rock performers (Little Richard, Eddie Cochran, Gene Vincent) who appear in concert segments. Directed by Frank Tashlin. **MU9** *Recommended*

Girl Crazy (1943, B&W, 99m, NR)
Mickey Rooney plays a hypochondriac who moves from New York to Arizona, where he falls for a local girl (Judy Garland). Directed by Busby Berkeley, with songs by George and Ira Gershwin. **DT8, MU1, ST51, ST133**

Girl From Petrovka (1974, C, 104m, PG)
A Russian ballerina (Goldie Hawn) falls in love with an American correspondent (Hal Holbrook). **ST63**

Girl Happy (1965, C, 96m, NR)
Elvis Presley chaperones a gangster's daughter (Shelley Fabares) to Ft. Lauderdale. **ST123**

Girl Hunters, The (1963, B&W, 103m, NR)
Author Mickey Spillane wrote and starred in this tale of detective Mike Hammer, who travels to Europe to find his missing secretary. **WR24**

Girl in a Swing, The (1989, C, 112m, NR)
Erotic drama starring Meg Tilly as a mysterious woman who marries a lonely ce-ramics dealer (Rupert Fraser). Based on a Richard Adams novel. **CU6**

Girl in Every Port, A (1952, B&W, 86m, NR)
Groucho Marx and William Bendix star in a comedy about two sailors who hide a racehorse aboard ship. **ST101**

Girl of the Golden West, The (1938, B&W, 121m, NR)
Jeanette MacDonald and Nelson Eddy star in a musical western about a desperado and the woman who loves him. Walter Pidgeon, Leo Carillo, and Buddy Ebsen head the supporting cast. **CL15, WE8**

Girl Who Spelled Freedom, The (1986, C, 90m, NR)
Disney drama, based on a true story of a Cambodian girl who comes to the United States and becomes a spelling bee champion. Wayne Rogers, Mary Kay Place, and Jade Chinn star; originally made for TV. **FA1, FA7**

Girls! Girls! Girls! (1962, C, 106m, NR)
Elvis Presley musical about a man with women on his mind. El sings "Return to Sender." Stella Stevens costars. **ST123**

Git Along, Little Dogies (1937, B&W, 60m, NR)
Gene Autry sings his heart out for a banker's daughter. **ST3**

Give My Regards to Broad Street (1984, C, 109m, PG)
A rock star (Paul McCartney) searches for his stolen master recordings. Paul plays some new tunes, as well as a few ditties he wrote when he was with a band called The Beatles. With Bryan Brown, Ringo Starr, Linda McCartney, Barbara Bach, Tracey Ullman, Ralph Richardson, and Dave Edmunds. **MU4, MU9**

Gizmo! (1977, C/B&W, 77m, G)
Documentary tribute to inventors and their wacky creations, directed by Howard Smith. **CU16**

Glass House, The (1972, C, 73m, NR)
Truman Capote story of life behind bars, starring Vic Morrow, Clu Gulager, and Billy Dee Williams. Originally made for TV. **DR18, ST159**

Glass Key, The (1942, B&W, 85m, NR)
An unscrupulous politician calls on his right-hand man to clear him of a murder frameup in this version of the Dashiell Hammett novel. Brian Donlevy, Alan Ladd, and Veronica Lake star. **MY1, WR9**

Glass Menagerie, The (1987, C, 135m, PG)
Paul Newman directed this adaptation of the Tennessee Williams play about a timid cripple (Karen Allen), her faded Southern belle mother (Joanne Woodward), her shiftless brother (John Malkovich), and the dream worlds they live in. **DR20, ST98, ST111, WR30**

Glen and Randa (1971, C, 94m, R)
Science fiction drama with cult following about the end of the world and a surviving couple (Steven Curry, Shelley Plimpton). Directed by Jim McBride. **CU4, SF12**

Glen or Glenda? (1953, B&W, 61m, NR)
Contender for title of Worst Movie Ever, with (naturally) a cult following. Serious attempt to document one man's struggle with sexuality winds up a hilarious comedy. Bela Lugosi "hosts." Directed by Ed Wood, Jr., who also stars. **CU11, DT118, ST95**

Glenn Miller Story, The (1954, C, 116m, G)
A sentimental musical biography that follows the life of the legendary big band leader. James Stewart stars, with June Allyson. Anthony Mann directed. **DT69, MU5, ST143**

Glitz (1988, C, 100m, NR)
Elmore Leonard story, set in Atlantic City, of a cop, a psycho killer devoted to his mother, and a lounge singer. Jimmy Smits, Markie Post, and John Diehl star. Originally made for TV. **MY3, MY13, WR16**

Gloria (1980, C, 121m, R)
A feisty New York woman takes a young Puerto Rican boy under her protection after his parents are rubbed out by mobsters. Gena Rowlands stars, with John Adames, Buck Henry, and Julie Carmen. John Cassavetes directed. **AC8, DR10**

Glorifying the American Girl (1929, B&W, 87m, NR)
Flo Ziegfeld produced this musical revue featuring the top talent of the day, including Helen Morgan, Rudy Vallee, and Eddie Cantor. **MU15**

Glory (1989, C, 122m, R)
Stirring, true story of the first black regiment to fight in the Civil War, commanded by a white New Englander. Matthew Broderick stars, with Morgan Freeman and Oscar winner Denzel Washington. Available in a letterboxed format. **AC5, CU19, DR5, DR14, ST48, XT4** *Recommended*

Gnome-Mobile, The (1967, C, 90m, NR)
Disney adventure starring Walter Brennan as an elderly businessman who, along with his grandchildren, discovers gnomes in a forest. The three try to protect them from being captured by freak show owners. **FA1**

Gnomes, Vol. 1 (1980, C, 52m, NR)
This animated feature introduces the Gnomes, tiny creatures who battle the Trolls, who are trying to ruin a Gnome wedding. **FA10**

Go Masters, The (1982, C, 123m, NR)
Japanese-Chinese production traces relationship of two families, one from each country, from the 1920s to the 1950s. Title refers to chess-like game played by various members of each clan. **FF4**

Go Tell the Spartans (1978, C, 114m, R)
Vietnam War drama starring Burt Lancaster as a commander during the early days of that conflict. With Craig Wasson and Marc Singer. **AC4, ST85**

Go West (1940, B&W, 81m, NR)
The Marx Brothers take a train ride through the Old West. **ST101, WE14, XT19**

Goalie's Anxiety at the Penalty Kick, The (1971, C, 110m, NR)
German drama about a soccer player's depression over a crucial misplay and his subsequent breakdown. Directed by Wim Wenders; adapted from a Peter Handke story. **DT113**

Goat, The *see* Chevre, La

God Told Me To (1977, C, 95m, R)
Horror film about normal New Yorkers driven to unexplained acts of madness. Larry Cohen directed. Also known as *Demon.* **DT20**

Goddess, The (1958, B&W, 105m, NR)
Drama, loosely based on Marilyn Monroe story, of Hollywood star at the breaking point. Kim Stanley and Lloyd Bridges star; screenplay by Paddy Chayevsky. **DR13**

Godfather, The (1972, C, 175m, R)
Sensational adaptation of Mario Puzo's look into the world of a Mafia chieftain (Marlon Brando) in 1930s New York City. The supporting cast includes James Caan, Diane Keaton, Robert Duvall, and Al Pacino. Winner of three Oscars, including Best Picture and Actor (Brando). Masterfully directed by Francis Ford Coppola. **AC22, DR24, DT21, ST10, ST38, ST79, ST118, XT1, XT2, XT20** *Essential; Highly Recommended*

Godfather, Part II, The (1974, C, 200m, R)
Sequel to *The Godfather* combines two stories: the rise to power of the Corleones' youngest son, Michael (Al Pacino), and the struggles of his young immigrant father (Robert DeNiro) in early 20th-century New York City. Winner of six Oscars, including Best Picture, Best Director (Francis Ford Coppola), and Best Supporting Actor (DeNiro). With Diane Keaton, John Cazale, Robert Duvall, Talia Shire, Lee Strasberg, Michael V. Gazzo, Harry Dean Stanton, Roger Corman (as a Congressman), and, in one flashback scene, James Caan. **AC22, DR24, DT21, DT22, ST30, ST38, ST79, ST118, ST141, XT1, XT4, XT6** *Essential; Highly Recommended*

God's Little Acre (1958, B&W, 110m, NR)
A Georgia farmer (Robert Ryan) destroys his land in search of sunken treasures. This version of the Erskine Caldwell novel was directed by Anthony Mann. **DT69**

Gods Must Be Crazy, The (1981, C, 108m, PG)
Comedy, set in South Africa, with two intertwining tales: a community of Bushmen encounter civilization in the form of a soft drink bottle, and a clumsy scientist romances a pretty schoolteacher. **CO2**

Godsend, The (1979, C, 93m, R)
Horror story of a couple who take in a little girl left with them by a strange woman, and the death and destruction she brings to their lives. **HO13**

Godzilla, King of the Monsters (1956, B&W, 80m, NR)
The film that started the cycle of Japanese monster movies, featuring that Tokyo-stomping behemoth. Raymond Burr costars. **FF4, SF10, SF18**

Godzilla, 1985 (1985, C, 91m, PG)
The big guy returns and is reunited—more or less—with Raymond Burr. **FF4, SF10, SF18**

Godzilla on Monster Island (1971, C, 90m, NR)
A children's amusement park is the site for this version of Monster Wrestlemania, starring Godzilla, Ghidrah, Gaigan, and Angorus. **FF4, SF10, SF18**

Godzilla vs. Megalon (1976, C, 80m, G)
Godzilla, now a good guy, joins forces with a robot monster to square off against Megalon and his buddy in a monster tag-team match. **FF4, SF10, SF18**

Godzilla vs. Monster Zero (1970, C, 98m, G)
Nick Adams and Rodan costar with the Big Guy, as he takes on yet another foe of Japanese civilization. **FF4, SF10, SF18**

Godzilla vs. Mothra (1964, C, 91m, G)
The Protector of Japan meets a flying monster that no moth ball could hope to stop. Also known as *Godzilla vs. The Thing*. **FF4, SF10, SF18**

Godzilla vs. The Thing *see* Godzilla vs. Mothra

Goin' South (1978, C, 109m, PG)
Jack Nicholson stars in this romantic western comedy about an outlaw who ties the knot to save his neck. With Mary Steenburgen, John Belushi, and Danny DeVito. Nicholson directed. **CO13, ST32, ST112, WE9, WE14**

Going Ape (1981, C, 87m, PG)
Tony Danza plays a man who must care for three primates to qualify for an inheritance. Comedy costars Danny DeVito and Jessica Walter. **ST32**

Going Berserk (1983, C, 85m, R)
John Candy plays a scatter-brained chauffeur who saves his future father-in-law from a religious cult. With Joe Flaherty and Eugene Levy. **CO14**

Going in Style (1979, C, 96m, PG)
Touching comedy-drama about a trio of
elderly men (George Burns, Art Carney,
Lee Strasberg) who decide to rob a bank
for the hell of it. Directed by Martin
Brest. **DR11, MY18** *Recommended*

Going My Way (1944, B&W, 126m, NR)
Bing Crosby and Barry Fitzgerald play
parish priests with different approaches
to their flock in this heartwarming classic.
Oscars went to both actors, writer-director Leo McCarey, and the film. **CL6,
ST25, XT1, XT2, XT4, XT6** *Essential*

Going Places (1974, C, 117m, R)
French drama, with darkly comic overtones, of two drifters (Gerard Depardieu,
Patrick Dewaere) and their determinedly
carefree lifestyle. With Brigitte Fossey
and Jeannne Moreau. Directed by Bertrand Blier. **FF1, ST31, ST110, XT18**

Gold Diggers of 1933 (1933, B&W, 96m,
NR)
Busby Berkeley choreographed this mu-
sical about a songwriter (Dick Powell)
who can't finance his extravaganza until
some spunky showgirls (Ginger Rogers,
Ruby Keeler) save the day. **DT8, MU4,
ST131**

Gold Diggers of 1935 (1935, B&W, 95m,
NR)
More singing and dancing from Busby
Berkeley and his talented collection of
performers, headed by Dick Powell. With
Adolphe Menjou and Gloria Stuart. Mu-
sical highlight: "Lullaby of Broadway."
DT8, MU4

Gold of Naples, The (1954, B&W, 107m,
NR)
Vittorio De Sica directed this quartet of
vignettes of Italian life, starring Sophia
Loren, Silvano Mangano, Toto, and the
director. **DT26, ST93**

Gold Raiders (1983, C, 106m, NR)
A plane carrying $200 million in gold is
shot down over Laos and a commando
squad tries to retrieve the precious cargo.
Robert Ginty stars. **AC20**

Gold Rush, The (1925, B&W, 72m, NR)
Charlie Chaplin classic set in the Yukon
gold rush days. With Georgia Hale and
Mack Swain. **CL11, DT18** *Essential;
Highly Recommended*

Golden Boy (1939, B&W, 99m, NR)
A would-be musician turns to boxing to
make a living. Clifford Odets drama has
William Holden making his screen debut
opposite Barbara Stanwyck. With Lee J.
Cobb and Adolphe Menjou. **DR22, ST68,
ST142, XT21**

Golden Child, The (1986, C, 96m, PG-13)
A youth with magical powers is kid-
napped by a cult, and it's up to Eddie
Murphy to rescue him in this adventure
comedy packed with special effects. **CO9,
CO11, CO13**

Golden Coach, The (1952, C, 105m, NR)
French director Jean Renoir's classic
drama of a theatrical troupe in 18th-cen-
tury Peru, starring Anna Magnani as a
lady of many affairs. Superb color photography. **CL9, CL14, DT86**

Golden Demon, The (1953, C, 95m, NR)
From Japan, a drama about a young man
in love with the daughter of his adopted
parents. His frustration grows when she
is given in an arranged marriage to a
wealthy businessman. **FF4**

Golden Seal, The (1983, C, 93m, PG)
Family drama about a young boy who
befriends a seal. Steve Railsback, Penelope Milford, and Michael Beck star. **FA5**

Golden Stallion, The (1949, B&W, 67m,
NR)
Trigger gets the spotlight in this Roy
Rogers western, as he tries to set a small
mare free from her nasty owners. **ST132**

Golden Voyage of Sinbad, The (1974, C,
104m, G)
John Phillip Law stars as the swashbuckling pirate in this adventure/fantasy which
features great special effects. **FA8**

Goldenrod (1977, C, 100m, NR)
A rodeo champion (Tony LoBianco)
reevaluates his life after a debilitating accident. Originally made for TV. **WE12**

Goldfinger (1964, C, 111m, NR)
Third James Bond adventure has 007 foiling plan to rob Fort Knox. Sean Connery
stars, but Gert Fröbe, Harold Sakata, and
Honor Blackman steal the show as Goldfinger, Odd Job, and Pussy Galore. **HF2,
ST21** *Essential; Highly Recommended*

Goldilocks and the Three Bears (1985, C, 60m, NR)
Tatum O'Neal stars as the little girl who invades the lives of three bears in this Faerie Tale Theatre adventure. John Lithgow, Alex Karras, and Carole King costar. **FA12, MU12**

Goldy: The Last of the Golden Bears (1984, C, 91m, NR)
An orphaned child adopted by a prospector goes on an incredible adventure to rescue a golden bear from the circus. **FA5**

Golem, The (1920, B&W, 118m, NR)
Classic silent horror film about a legendary robot-like creature created to save German Jewish peasants from persecution. **FF3, HO1**

Gone in 60 Seconds (1974, C, 103m, PG)
A professional car thief eludes police with his incredible driving skills. This action drama features a 40-minute car chase. Written and directed by H.B. Halicki. **AC10**

Gone With the Wind (1939, C, 222m, G)
Civil War epic of Scarlett O'Hara (Vivien Leigh) and her tempestuous romance with Rhett Butler (Clark Gable). Winner of 10 Oscars, including Best Picture, Best Actress, Best Supporting Actress (Hattie McDaniel), and Best Director (Victor Fleming). Olivia de Havilland and Leslie Howard costar. **AC5, CL3, ST49, XT1, XT3, XT5, XT6** *Essential; Highly Recommended*

Good Earth, The (1937, B&W, 138m, NR)
Oscar winner Luise Rainer costars with Paul Muni in Pearl Buck's story of Chinese peasants coming to ruin over greed. **DR19, XT3**

Good Father, The (1987, C, 90m, R)
An embittered man whose marriage has just broken up takes out his frustrations by interfering in the domestic problems of a friend. Anthony Hopkins stars in this British drama. **DR8, DR23**

Good Guys Wear Black (1979, C, 96m, PG)
Karate action drama with Chuck Norris, featuring his incredible stunt of leaping through the windshield of a moving car. Anne Archer costars. **ST114**

Good Morning, Babylon (1987, C, 115m, NR)
Two Italian stonemasons emigrate to American in search of work, wind up laboring on the sets of D.W. Griffith's silent film epic, *Intolerance*. Vincent Spano and Joaquim de Almeida star, with Greta Scacchi, Desiree Becker, and Charles Dance as Griffith. Dialogue in Italian and English. **DR5, DR13**

Good Morning, Vietnam (1987, C, 120m, R)
Robin Williams stars as a zany disc jockey who shakes up Armed Forces Radio during the Vietnam War. With Forest Whitaker, Bruno Kirby, and J.T. Walsh. Barry Levinson directed. **AC4, CO6, CO21, ST160** *Recommended*

Good Mother, The (1988, C, 104m, R)
Diane Keaton plays a divorced woman locked in a bitter battle for custody of her young daughter. With Liam Neeson, Jason Robards, Ralph Bellamy, and Teresa Wright. **DR8, DR10, ST79, ST129**

Good Neighbor Sam (1964, C, 130m, NR)
An advertising executive out to impress a new client gets caught up in a complicated masquerade involving a lovely neighbor who's mistaken for his wife. Jack Lemmon stars, with Edward G. Robinson, Romy Schneider, and Dorothy Provine. **CO20, ST90, ST130**

Good News (1943, C, 93m, NR)
A college football star (Peter Lawford) won't graduate unless he passes his French exam in this MGM musical set in the Roaring Twenties. June Allyson costars. **MU1, MU3, MU6**

Good Sam (1948, B&W, 128m, NR)
A good samaritan (Gary Cooper) creates tension in his home life when he overdoes his generosity. Ann Sheridan costars. **ST22**

Good, the Bad, and the Ugly, The (1967, C, 161m, NR)
Three unscrupulous men (Clint Eastwood, Lee Van Cleef, Eli Wallach) hunt for a treasure while the Civil War rages around them. Directed by Sergio Leone. **DT61, ST39, ST155, WE1, WE3, WE6, WE13** *Essential; Highly Recommended*

Good To Go *see* Short Fuse

Goodbye Again (1961, B&W, 120m, NR)
Ingrid Bergman stars in the melodrama of a lonely woman's affair with a younger man (Anthony Perkins). Yves Montand costars. **ST7**

Goodbye, Columbus (1969, C, 105m, R)
Romantic comedy-drama of a naive young Jewish man falling for snobbish girl, getting involved with her family. Richard Benjamin and Ali MacGraw star, with Jack Klugman, Nan Martin, and Michael Myers. Based on Philip Roth's short novel. **DR1, DR19, XT20**

Goodbye Girl, The (1977, C, 110m, PG)
An aspiring actor (Oscar winner Richard Dreyfuss) shares an apartment with a divorced woman (Marsha Mason) and her precocious daughter (Quinn Cummings) in this Neil Simon comedy. **CO1, ST36, WR23, XT2**

Goodbye, Mr. Chips (1939, B&W, 114m, NR)
Robert Donat won an Oscar for his portrayal of a devoted schoolmaster in this classic drama. Greer Garson costars in her film debut. **DR25, XT2, XT21**

Goodbye, My Lady (1956, B&W, 95m, NR)
Family drama, set in rural Mississippi, of a boy and his dog. Brandon de Wilde stars, with Walter Brennan, Phil Harris, and Sidney Poitier. **FA5, ST121**

Goon Show Movie, The (1953, B&W, 75m, NR)
The zany antics of Britain's Goon Show are presented in this collection of their sketches. Spike Milligan, Harry Secombe, and Peter Sellers star. Also known as *Stand Easy*. **CO17, ST137**

Gorath (1964, C, 77m, NR)
Japanese science fiction drama about a meteor forcing scientists to change Earth's orbit. **FF4, SF18**

Gordon's War (1973, C, 90m, R)
Paul Winfield plays a Vietnam veteran who returns to the States to find his wife hooked on drugs. He forms a fighting force to rid his neighborhood of drugs pushers. **AC8, AC20, ST162**

Gore Vidal's Billy the Kid (1989, C, 96m, NR)
Val Kilmer plays the legendary western outlaw in this new version of the Vidal TV play, previously filmed as *The Left-Handed Gun*. Originally made for cable TV. **HF1, WE3**

Gorgo (1961, C, 78m, NR)
A baby sea monster is captured and placed in a London zoo, and its giant parent comes to the rescue. Bill Travers stars. **SF10, XT15**

Gorgon, The (1964, C, 83m, NR)
After she is possessed by an evil spirit, a beautiful girl's gaze turns people to stone. Peter Cushing, Christopher Lee, and Barbara Shelley star. **HO26, ST27, ST89**

Gorilla, The (1939, B&W, 66m, NR)
The Ritz Brothers play detectives who investigate a series of murders that take place at the stroke of midnight. With Bela Lugosi. **ST95**

Gorillas in the Mist (1988, C, 129, PG-13)
Sigourney Weaver plays Dian Fossey, the anthropologist whose defense of mountain gorillas from hunters led to her murder. Bryan Brown costars. **DR6, DR10, ST157**

Gorky Park (1983, C, 128m, R)
Three corpses found in Moscow's Gorky Park set a Russian police captain (William Hurt) off on a twisted case. Based on the bestseller by Martin Cruz Smith. With Lee Marvin, Brian Dennehy, and Joanna Pacula. **MY6, MY16, ST75, ST100**

Gospel According to St. Matthew, The (1966, B&W, 135m, NR)
Low-key dramatization of the life of Christ, from Italian director Pier Paolo Pasolini. Enrique Irazoqui stars. **FF2, HF16**

Gospel According to Vic, The (1985, C, 92m, PG)
A teacher at a Catholic school embarks on a skeptical inquiry into miracles that have been occurring at his school. Tom Conti and Helen Mirren star in this offbeat British comedy. **CO17, CO18**

Gösta Berling's Saga (1924, B&W, 123m, NR)
Silent Swedish drama of a defrocked priest (Lars Hanson) and a married

woman (Greta Garbo). Directed by Maurice Stiller. Also known as *The Atonement of Gösta Berling*. **ST50**

Gotham (1988, C, 93m, NR)
A private eye (Tommy Lee Jones) is hired by a man who's certain that his dead wife (Virginia Madsen) is following him. Originally made for cable TV. **MY10**

Gothic (1987, C, 87m, R)
One dark and stormy night in the lives of writers Lord Byron, Percy Shelley, and Mary Shelley, as imagined by flamboyant director Ken Russell. Julian Sands, Gabriel Byrne, and Natasha Richardson star. **DT92, HO25**

Grace Quigley (1985, C, 87m, PG)
Katharine Hepburn plays an elderly woman who hires hit man Nick Nolte to kill her and other friends who would rather be dead. Also known as *The Ultimate Solution of Grace Quigley*. **CO12, DR11, ST66, ST113**

Graduate, The (1967, C, 105m, PG)
A naive college graduate (Dustin Hoffman) is seduced by a middle-aged woman (Anne Bancroft) but falls in love with her daughter (Katharine Ross). Director Mike Nichols won an Oscar for this brilliant comedy. **CO2, CO4, DT74, ST67, XT6, XT20** *Essential; Highly Recommended*

Graduation Day (1981, C, 96m, R)
Horror story about members of a high school track team who are brutally murdered a few days before graduation. **HO12**

Grand Canyon Trail (1948, B&W, 68m, NR)
Roy Rogers' mine may have him sitting pretty on pay dirt, or it could just be useless gravel. Only the town swindler knows for sure. **ST132**

Grand Highway, The (1988, C, 104m, NR)
French drama of a 9-year-old boy sent to live in a village in Brittany while mother has a baby. Directed by Jean-Loup Hubert, based on his own experiences. **FF1**

Grand Hotel (1932, B&W, 113m, NR)
Drama set in luxury hotel featuring a mind-boggling cast of MGM stars: Wallace Beery, Greta Garbo, John Barrymore, Joan Crawford, Lionel Barrymore, and Jean Hersholt, for starters. Grand, old-fashioned entertainment; winner of

Best Picture Oscar. **CU17, ST24, ST50, XT1** *Essential; Highly Recommended*

Grand Illusion (1937, B&W, 111m, NR)
Director Jean Renoir's masterful anti-war drama, set in a World War I prisoner of war camp. Jean Gabin, Erich Von Stroheim, and Pierre Fresnay star. **AC7, DT86, DT109** *Essential; Highly Recommended*

Grand Prix (1966, C, 176m, NR)
Big-budget, all-star drama about racing on the European circuit. James Garner, Eva Marie Saint, Yves Montand, and Toshiro Mifune head the cast. John Frankenheimer directed. **AC10, DR22, ST106**

Grand Theft Auto (1977, C, 89m, PG)
Ron Howard is the star, co-writer, and debuting director of this car-chase comedy. Produced by Roger Corman. **AC10, CU14, DT48**

Grande Bourgeoisie, La (1974, C, 115m, NR)
Italian drama, based on true story, of a man who murders his sister's no-good husband. Giancarlo Giannini and Catherine Deneuve star. **FF2, ST29**

Grandview U.S.A. (1984, C, 97m, R)
Smalltown drama of kids trying to stay out of trouble, with C. Thomas Howell, Patrick Swayze, and Jamie Lee Curtis. **DR9, DR26**

Grapes of Wrath, The (1940, B&W, 129m, NR)
John Steinbeck story of a poor family in the midst of the Depression and their hopes for a better life in California. Henry Fonda stars; Oscars went to actress Jane Darwell and director John Ford. **CL8, DT36, ST44, WR25, XT5, XT6** *Essential; Recommended*

Grass Is Greener, The (1960, C, 105m, NR)
Cary Grant and Deborah Kerr play a British couple whose marriage is threatened by a handsome tourist (Robert Mitchum) in this comedy. Directed by Stanley Donen. **DT30, ST57, ST107**

Grateful Dead Movie, The (1977, C, 131m, NR)
Rock concert film starring those tie-dyed wonders of laid-back rock 'n' roll. Out-

standing animated sequence opens the film. **MU10**

Graveyard Shift (1987, C, 89m, R)
Horror story about a New York cabbie with a deadly secret—he's a vampire who prefers a nip on the neck to a tip. **HO5**

Gray Lady Down (1978, C, 111m, PG)
A downed submarine is the object of a daring rescue mission in this adventure saga. Charlton Heston and David Carradine star, with Stacy Keach, Ned Beatty, and Ronny Cox. **AC24**

Grease (1978, C, 110m, PG)
Olivia Newton-John and John Travolta star in this screen version of the long-running Broadway musical about high school life in the 1950s. In the supporting cast: Stockard Channing, Eve Arden, Edd Byrnes, and Frankie Avalon. **MU2, MU9**

Grease 2 (1982, C, 114m, PG)
More musical adventures of the students at Rydell High in the 1950s. Maxwell Caulfield and Michelle Pfeiffer star. **MU9, ST120**

Greased Lightning (1977, C, 94m, PG)
In a dramatic change of pace, Richard Pryor portrays Wendell Scott, the first black racing car driver. **DR22, ST125**

Great American Cowboy, The (1974, C, 90m, NR)
An Oscar-winning documentary about modern day rodeo cowboys. Narrated by Joel McCrea. **WE12**

Great Balls of Fire! (1989, C, 108m, PG-13)
Dennis Quaid plays rock legend Jerry Lee Lewis in this flamboyantly told account of his early career, including his controversial marriage to a cousin (Winona Ryder). With Alec Baldwin as Jimmy Swaggart and Michael St. Gerard as Elvis Presley. **DR12, MU5**

The Great Battle *see* Battle Force

Great Caruso, The (1951, C, 113m, NR)
Ann Blyth and Mario Lanza star in this biographical film about the opera star's life. **MU1, MU5**

Great Day in the Morning (1956, C, 92m, NR)
In pre-Civil War Colorado, a separationist wants to finance the impending war with gold. Robert Stack and Ruth Roman star. Directed by Jacques Tourneur. **DT105**

Great Dictator, The (1940, B&W, 128m, NR)
Charlie Chaplin's classic spoof of Hitler, as he plays "Adenoid Hynkel," dictator of Tomania. Jack Oakie costars as "Benzino Napaloni." **CL10, DT18, HF12** *Essential; Recommended*

Great Escape, The (1963, C, 168m, NR)
Superb drama of World War II POWs and a massive breakout from a Nazi prison, based on a true story. James Garner, Steve McQueen, Charles Bronson, Richard Attenborough, James Coburn, and Donald Pleasence head the cast. **AC7, ST12, ST97** *Highly Recommended*

Great Expectations (1946, B&W, 118m, NR)
David Lean directed this adaptation of Charles Dickens' story of a poor orphan who becomes a wealthy young gentleman, thanks to an unknown benefactor. John Mills, Alec Guinness (in his film debut), and Jean Simmons star. **DT59, FA3, ST60, WR4, XT21** *Essential; Recommended*

Great Gabbo, The (1929, B&W, 95m, NR)
Erich Von Stroheim plays a boastful ventriloquist in this backstage drama with musical numbers. **CL7, DT109**

Great Gatsby, The (1974, C, 144m, PG)
Robert Redford portrays the mysterious Jay Gatsby in this lavish adaptation of F. Scott Fitzgerald's novel of the Jazz Age. With Mia Farrow, Sam Waterston, Bruce Dern, and Karen Black. **DR19, ST126, WR7**

Great Guns (1941, B&W, 74m, NR)
After their boss joins the army, a gardener and a chauffeur (Stan Laurel and Oliver Hardy) enlist, too. **CO21, ST87**

Great Guy (1936, B&W, 75m, NR)
James Cagney plays an inspector out to crack down on illegal dealings in the meat business. **DR24, ST14**

Great Lie, The (1941, B&W, 107m, NR)
Bette Davis soap opera of a woman who marries a man with a scheming ex-wife. With George Brent and Oscar winner Mary Astor. **ST28, XT5**

Great Locomotive Chase, The (1956, C, 85m, NR)
Disney adventure based on the true story of a Union spy who led a band of renegades in the theft of a train during the Civil War. Story previously filmed as *The General*. **FA1, XT19**

Great Lover, The (1949, B&W, 80m, NR)
Bob Hope plays a boy scout leader aborad a cruise ship with a lovely redhead (Rhonda Fleming) and a fugitive killer (Roland Young). **ST70**

Great McGinty, The (1940, B&W, 81m, NR)
Classic comedy of a bum maneuvered into the governor's mansion by a political machine, which finds to its dismay that their man is actually honest. Brian Donlevy and Akim Tamiroff star. Written and directed by Preston Sturges. **CO20, DT103** *Essential*

Great McGonagall, The (1975, C, 95m, NR)
British comedy of a Scot trying to become poet laureate of England. Spike Milligan stars, with Peter Sellers as Queen Victoria. **ST137**

Great Moment, The (1944, B&W, 83m, NR)
Joel McCrea plays the inventor of anasthesia in this comedy-drama from director Preston Sturges. **DT103**

Great Muppet Caper, The (1981, C, 90m, G)
Kermit, Fozzie, and Gonzo travel to London as newspaper reporters in search of jewel thieves. Miss Piggy is close on their heels to keep an eye on "Kermie." Featuring guest stars Diana Rigg and Charles Grodin. **FA14, ST59**

Great Northfield Minnesota Raid, The (1972, C, 91m, PG)
Western with cult following about Cole Younger (Cliff Robertson) and Jesse James (Robert Duvall) and their ill-fated attempt to rob a bank in the title town. Written and directed by Philip Kaufman. **HF16, ST38, WE15**

Great Outdoors, The (1988, C, 90m, PG)
Comic tale of a family's vacation ruined by the arrival of obnoxious relatives. John Candy and Dan Aykroyd star. Written by John Hughes. **CO5, CO13, CO14, DT49**

Great Race, The (1965, C, 150m, NR)
Blake Edwards directed this old-fashioned, big-budget comedy about an intercontinental road race. Jack Lemmon, Tony Curtis, and Natalie Wood star. **AC14, CO6, DT32, FA6, ST90, XT18**

Great Santini, The (1979, C, 116m, PG)
Portrait of a career Marine whose peacetime battles are mainly with his teenaged son. Robert Duvall, Michael O'Keefe, and Blythe Danner star. **DR8, ST38**

Great Scout and Cathouse Thursday (1976, C, 102m, PG)
Lee Marvin, Oliver Reed, and Robert Culp star as a crazy trio of gold prospectors who strike it rich in 1908 Colorado. **ST100, WE14**

Great Smokey Roadblock, The (1976, C, 84m, PG)
An aging truckdriver's rig is reposessed while he is in the hospital. He escapes, steals the truck, and decides to go across the country one last time. Henry Fonda stars, with Eileen Brennan and Susan Sarandon. **ST44, XT18**

Great Train Robbery, The (1979, C, 111m, PG)
Victorian England is the setting for this heist thriller, starring Sean Connery, Donald Sutherland, and Lesley-Anne Downe. **MY18, ST21, XT19**

Great Waldo Pepper, The (1975, C, 107m, PG)
Robert Redford stars as a barnstorming pilot of the 1920s in this affectionate comedy-drama about aerial daredevils. With Susan Sarandon. Directed by George Roy Hill. **AC11, ST126**

Great White Hope, The (1970, C, 101m, PG)
Howard Sackler's play, based on the life of Jack Johnson, the first black heavyweight boxing champion. James Earl Jones recreates his stage role, with Jane Alexander as his mistress. Directed by

Martin Ritt. **DR4, DR14, DR20, DR22, DT87, ST76**

Great Ziegfeld, The (1936, B&W, 176m, NR)
Musical bio of the legendary showman, played by William Powell. Oscar winner for Best Picture and Actress (Luise Rainer). Also in the cast: Myrna Loy, Fanny Brice, and Ray Bolger. **CL15, MU5, MU7, ST94, ST122, XT1, XT3**

Greatest, The (1977, C, 101m, PG)
This screen biography of Muhammad Ali traces his life from boyhood in Louisville to his incredible achievements as heavyweight champ. Ali stars as himself, with support from Ernest Borgnine, James Earl Jones, and Robert Duvall. **DR4, DR14, ST38, ST76**

Greatest Love, The see Europa '51

Greatest Show on Earth, The (1952, C, 153m, NR)
Oscar-winning drama about life in the circus, directed by Cecil B. DeMille, starring Charlton Heston, Betty Hutton, and James Stewart. **CL7, DT27, ST143, XT1**

Greatest Story Ever Told, The (1965, C, 196m, NR)
George Stevens directed this lavish epic detailing the life of Christ. Max von Sydow plays the lead, with guest appearances by many Hollywood stars. **CL13, DT101, HF16**

Greed (1925, B&W, 133m, NR)
Director Erich Von Stroheim's masterpiece, a searing version of the Frank Norris novel *McTeague*. A simple dentist (Gibson Gowland) and his wife (Zasu Pitts) become bitter enemies over money and her former suitor (Jean Hersholt). Video version contains new musical score by Carl Davis. **CL1, CL12, DT109, XT20** *Essential; Highly Recommended*

Green Berets, The (1968, C, 141m, NR)
John Wayne stars this Vietnam War drama that makes no apologies for American involvement in that conflict. Wayne and Ray Kellogg directed. **AC4, ST156**

Green Dolphin Street (1947, B&W, 141m, NR)
Romantic drama set in 17th-century New Zealand, starring Lana Turner, Donna Reed, and Van Heflin. **ST153**

Green Eyes (1976, C, 100m, NR)
Paul Winfield plays a Vietnam veteran returning to Southeast Asia to find the son he left behind. Originally made for TV. **ST162**

Green Room, The (1978, C, 95m, PG)
A writer obsessed with World War I casualties builds a memorial in their honor. Adaptation of Henry James story directed by François Truffaut, who also stars. **DT106, WR11**

Greetings (1968, C, 88m, R)
Comedy of a trio of New Yorkers (Jonathan Warden, Robert DeNiro, Gerrit Graham) and their obsessions: women, ducking the draft, and the Kennedy assassination. Directed by Brian DePalma. Originally rated "X." **CU5, DT29, ST30, XT9**

Gregory's Girl (1981, C, 91m, PG)
A young Scottish goalie develops a crush on the new girl on the soccer team. Comedy from director Bill Forsyth. **CO4, CO17, CO18, DT38, FA7**

Gremlins (1984, C, 111m, PG)
A teenager's unusual pet produces offspring which turn violent when not properly cared for. Frantic horror comedy directed by Joe Dante. **CO11, DT25, HO16, HO24**

Grey Fox, The (1982, C, 92m, PG)
After thirty-three years in prison, a gentleman bandit (Richard Farnsworth) just can't go straight, so he stages a train robbery. Western drama filmed in Canada. **DR11, WE3, WE10, WE11, XT19**

Greyfriars Bobby (1961, C, 91m, NR)
Disney drama about a terrier who became a "community pet" in Edinburgh in the 19th century. **FA1**

Greystoke: The Legend of Tarzan (1984, C, 130m, PG)
This version of the Tarzan story starts at the very beginning when, as a baby, Greystoke's parents are shipwrecked in Africa and die, leaving the jungle apes to raise him. Christopher Lambert stars, with Ralph Richardson, Ian Holm, and Andie McDowell. **AC12, AC17, HF22**

Groove Tube, The (1972, C, 75m, R)
Chevy Chase is among the stars in this wild collection of satirical skits about television. **CO8, CO13**

Gross Anatomy (1989, C, 107m, PG-13)
Comedy-drama of life in medical school, with Matthew Modine and Daphne Zuniga the students, Christine Lahti their hardnosed teacher. **CO18**

Ground Zero (1988, C, 99m, PG-13)
Australian drama, based on actual events, about a 1950s atomic test that turned disastrous, leading to a government coverup, which a cameraman discovers thirty years later. Colin Friels stars. **FF5**

Group, The (1966, C, 150m, NR)
Film version of Mary McCarthy novel about a clique of Vassar students and their lives after college. Candice Bergen, Joanna Pettet, Joan Hackett, Elizabeth Hartman, Shirley Knight, Jessica Walter, Kathleen Widdoes, and Mary-Robin Redd star. Directed by Sidney Lumet. **DR10, DR19, DT65**

Guadalcanal Diary (1943, B&W, 93m, NR)
World War II action in the South Pacific, with Preston Foster, Lloyd Nolan, William Bendix, Richard Conte, and Anthony Quinn. **AC1**

Guardian, The (1990, C, 98m, R)
A couple entrust their young daughter to a nanny (Jenny Seagrove) who is secretly a child-stealer who sacrifices infants to a monstrous tree. Directed by William Friedkin. **HO14**

Guess Who's Coming to Dinner (1967, C, 108m, NR)
Spencer Tracy (in his last film) and Katharine Hepburn (an Oscar winner) team in this drama about a couple whose daughter tells them she's marrying a black doctor (Sidney Poitier). Directed by Stanley Kramer. **CL15, DR7, DT55, ST66, ST121, ST151, XT3, XT22**

Guide for the Married Man, A (1967, C, 89m, NR)
Walter Matthau stars as a befuddled husband who is guided in the fine art of adultery by a lecherous pal (Robert Morse). Gene Kelly directed this comedy, essentially a series of skits with guest stars including Lucille Ball, Jack Benny, Sid Caesar, and Jayne Mansfield. With Inger Stevens as Matthau's wife. **ST81, ST104**

Gulliver's Travels (1939, C, 74m, NR)
Jonathan Swift's adventure comes to the screen in this full-length animated feature. **FA10**

Gumball Rally, The (1976, C, 107m, PG)
A variety of characters gather for a cross-country road race in this action-filled comedy. Michael Sarrazin, Tim McIntire, Raul Julia, and Gary Busey star. **AC10, CO9**

Gumshoe (1972, C, 88m, NR)
Albert Finney stars in this comic thriller about a man obsessed with Bogart who decides to solve a murder. Directed by Steven Frears. **CO17, MY11, MY15, ST42**

Gun Fury (1953, C, 83m, NR)
Rock Hudson plays a cowboy who tracks down the men who kidnapped his fiancée. Lee Marvin and Donna Reed costar. **ST73, ST100**

Gunfight, A (1971, C, 90m, PG)
Two aging gunslingers decide to sell tickets to a final shootout with themselves as the star attractions. Kirk Douglas, Raf Vallone, and Johnny Cash star. **MU12, ST34**

Gunfight at the O.K. Corral (1957, C, 122m, NR)
Burt Lancaster and Kirk Douglas join forces as Wyatt Earp and Doc Holliday in this western classic about the fabled Dodge City shootout. With Rhonda Fleming, Jo Van Fleet, John Ireland, Lee Van Cleef, and Dennis Hopper. **HF9, HF13, ST34, ST71, ST85, ST155**

Gunfighter, The (1950, B&W, 84m, NR)
Gregory Peck plays Johnny Ringo, a disillusioned gunslinger who feels it's time to hang up the holster. **ST119, WE2**

Gung Ho! (1943, B&W, 88m, NR)
Randolph Scott prepares Marine recruits for World War II action. With Robert Mitchum. **ST107, ST136**

Gung Ho (1986, C, 111m, PG-13)
The foreman of an auto plant about to go under persuades a Japanese car company to take over management of the factory. Michael Keaton stars in this comedy,

with Gedde Watanabe, George Wendt, and Mimi Rogers. Directed by Ron Howard. **CO2, DT48, ST80** *Recommended*

Gunga Din (1939, B&W, 117m, NR)
Rousing adventure classic, from Kipling's poem, about three British soldiers fighting the natives—and each other—in 19th-century India. Cary Grant, Douglas Fairbanks, Jr., and Victor McLaglen star, with Sam Jaffe in the title role. George Stevens directed. **AC13, DT101, FA4, ST57** *Essential; Highly Recommended*

Guns of Navarone, The (1961, C, 157m, NR)
Adventure yarn about a group of World War II commandoes out to destroy massive Nazi guns. Gregory Peck, David Niven, Anthony Quinn, and Stanley Baker star. **AC1, ST119**

Gus (1976, C, 96m, G)
This Disney comedy features a mule named Gus with a talent for kicking footballs. A group of evildoers plots to kidnap the talented animal for their own purposes. Edward Asner, Don Knotts, and Tim Conway star. **FA1**

Guy Named Joe, A (1943, B&W, 120m, NR)
Spencer Tracy plays an angel who comes to earth to help a World War II soldier in trouble. With Irene Dunne, Van Johnson, Ward Bond, Barry Nelson, and Lionel Barrymore. Remade as *Always*. **SF2, ST151**

Guys And Dolls (1955, C, 150m, NR)
Frank Sinatra, Marlon Brando, and Jean Simmons star in this classic Damon Runyon story about a gambler and a missionary, set to a Frank Loesser score. Joseph L. Mankiewicz directed. Final number is presented in letterboxed format. **CU19, DT68, MU2, MU6, MU17, ST10, ST138**

Gypsy (1962, C, 149m, NR)
Natalie Wood plays Gypsy Rose Lee in this musical account of the stripper's life, with Rosalind Russell as Mama Rose. **MU5**

HBO Comedy Club (1987, C, 60m each, NR)
This series of three tapes highlight the best of today's comedy. The first is *Howie From Maui*, featuring Howie Mandel in concert. The second, *Tenth Anni-*

versary Young Comedians Special is a reunion of comics featuring Robin Williams. The third, *Roseanne Barr,* stars the witty, sharp-tongued comedienne. **CO16, ST160**

H-Man, The (1958, C, 79m, NR)
Japanese science fiction story set in Tokyo with twin plots: radioactive substance causes havoc, while police and dope dealers battle it out. **FF4, SF18**

Hail! Hail! Rock 'n' Roll *see* Chuck Berry: Hail! Hail! Rock 'n' Roll

Hail, Hero! (1969, C, 100m, PG)
Michael Douglas' film debut, as he plays a son rebelling against his parents over the Vietnam War. With Arthur Kennedy and Teresa Wright. **DR7, DR8, ST35**

Hail Mary (1985, C, 107m, NR)
Director Jean-Luc Godard's controversial drama about a contemporary young woman's unexplained pregnancy. Any resemblances to the well-known Biblical story are purely intentional. **CU8, DT41**

Hail the Conquering Hero (1944, B&W, 101m, NR)
An Army reject is mistakenly taken for a war hero by his hometown. Preston Sturges wrote and directed this satire starring Eddie Bracken. **CL10, CO20, DT103**

Hair (1979, C, 121m, R)
The Broadway musical about a group of New York hippies opposed to the Vietnam War. Treat Williams, John Savage, and Beverly D'Angelo star. Milos Forman directed; choreography by Twyla Tharp. **DT37, MU2, MU9, XT9**

Hairspray (1988, C, 90m, PG)
Baltimore in the early 1960s: a TV teen dance show is disrupted when one of the "regulars" tries to bring her black friends to the show. A marvelously nostalgic comedy from director John Waters, starring Ricki Lake, Divine (in two roles), Jerry Stiller, Sonny Bono, Debby Harry, and Ruth Brown. **CO6, DT110, MU12** *Recommended*

Half Moon Street (1986, C, 90m, R)
Sigourney Weaver plays an American researcher in London who turns to prostitution to make ends meet, becomes involved in political intrigue. Michael Caine costars in this adaptation of Paul Theroux's novella. **MY6, ST15, ST157**

Half of Heaven (1987, C, 127m, NR)
Spanish drama, with elements of comedy and fantasy, starring Angela Molina as a woman who molds herself into a successful restaurant owner. Directed by Manuel Guttierez Aragon. **FF7**

Halloween (1978, C, 85m, R)
A young boy murders his teenaged sister, is locked up, and escapes years later, looking for more victims. Cult horror film was also a hit movie spawning dozens of imitators and several sequels. Jamie Lee Curtis and Donald Pleasence star. John Carpenter directed. **CU4, DT17, HO9** *Essential; Recommended*

Halloween II (1981, C, 92m, R)
Terror continues as the killer stalks his victims on Halloween night, taking up where *Halloween* left off. Jamie Lee Curtis and Donald Pleasence return, too. **HO9**

Halloween III: Season of the Witch (1983, C, 96m, R)
A mad scientist hatches a plot to slaughter millions of children on Halloween. Not a sequel to earlier *Halloween films*. **HO20**

Halloween IV: The Return of Michael Myers (1988, C, 88m, R)
As the title suggests, the monstrous killer from the first two *Halloween* horrorfests is back, with the same good doctor (Donald Pleasence) in pursuit. **HO9**

Halloween 5 (1989, C, 96m, NR)
Dr. Loomis (Donald Pleasence) continues to explore the psychic connection between madman Michael Myers and his young niece (Danielle Harris). **HO9**

Halls of Montezuma (1950, C, 113m, NR)
Marines hit the beach in this World War II saga, starring Richard Widmark, Walter (Jack) Palance, Robert Wagner, and Jack Webb. Directed by Lewis Milestone. **AC1**

Hambone and Hillie (1984, C, 89m, G)
Lillian Gish plays a woman who's separated from her beloved dog at an airport in this family drama. **FA5, ST54**

Hamburger Hill (1987, C, 104m, R)
War drama of American company caught up in bloody battle for a strategic position in Vietnam. Michael Dolan, Daniel O'Shea, and Dylan McDermott star. **AC4**

Hamlet (1948, B&W, 153m, NR)
Laurence Olivier directed and stars in this adaptation of the Shakespeare play about the tormented Danish prince. With Jean Simmons and Peter Cushing. Winner of four Academy Awards, including Best Picture and Actor. **ST27, ST116, WR22, XT1, XT2** *Essential; Recommended*

Hamlet (1969, C, 114m, G)
Nicol Williamson stars in this version of Shakespeare's tragedy, with Gordon Jackson, Anthony Hopkins, and Marianne Faithfull as Ophelia. Directed by Tony Richardson. **MU12, WR22**

Hammersmith Is Out (1972, C, 108m, R)
Elizabeth Taylor and Richard Burton team up in this story of a violent mental patient who is determined to escape from the hospital. **CL15, ST13, ST147**

Hammett (1983, C, 97m, PG)
Real-life author Dashiell Hammett gets involved in a real-life mystery. Based on Joe Gores' novel about Hammett's career as a Pinkerton detective. Frederic Forrest stars, with Peter Boyle, Marilu Henner, Elisha Cook, Samuel Fuller, and R.G. Armstrong. Wim Wenders directed. **DT40, DT113, MY8, WR9** *Recommended*

Hand, The (1981, C, 104m, R)
Michael Caine plays a cartoonist whose severed hand comes back to haunt him. Written and directed by Oliver Stone. **DT102, ST15**

Handful of Dust, A (1988, C, 118m, PG)
The Evelyn Waugh story of a failed marriage between a sensitive aristocrat (James Wilby) and his self-centered wife (Kristin Scott-Thomas). With Rupert Graves, Judi Dench, Anjelica Huston, and Alec Guinness. **DR1, DR19, DR23, ST60** *Recommended*

Handle With Care *see* Citizens Band

Handmaid's Tale, The (1990, C, 109m, R)
Futuristic tale of society where a class of women is subservient to men only for procreation. Natasha Richardson stars, with Robert Duvall, Faye Dunaway, Aidan Quinn, Elizabeth McGovern, and Victoria Tennant. Adapted by Harold Pinter from Margaret Atwood's novel; directed by Volker Schlöndorff. **DR7, DR10, DR19, ST37, ST38**

Hands Across the Border (1944, B&W, 54m, NR)
Roy Rogers does his bit to promote good relations between the U.S. and Mexico in this western adventure. **ST132**

Hang 'Em High (1968, C, 114m, NR)
A cowboy (Clint Eastwood) vows revenge on the men who tried to kill him in this American-made spaghetti western. With Inger Stevens, Ed Begley, Pat Hingle, Ben Johnson, and Dennis Hopper. **ST39, ST71, WE13**

Hanky Panky (1982, C, 105m, PG)
Comic thriller about a woman looking for the men who murdered her brother and involving an innocent bystander in her investigation. Gilda Radner and Gene Wilder star; directed by Sidney Poitier. **CO13, MY17, ST101**

Hanna K. (1983, C, 108m, R)
Jill Clayburgh plays a lawyer in Israel who is juggling a persistent ex-husband, an amorous district attorney, and a mysterious Arab defendant she is representing. Topical drama from director Costa-Gavras. **DR3, DR7, DR10**

Hannah and Her Sisters (1986, C, 106m, PG)
Woody Allen comedy-drama of a family of neurotic New Yorkers whose lives mingle over three Thanksgivings. Dianne Wiest and Michael Caine won Oscars, as did Allen's screenplay. With Mia Farrow and Barbara Hershey. **CO5, DT1, ST15, XT4, XT5, XT9** *Recommended*

Hannah's War (1988, C, 148m, PG-13)
True-life drama of a Hungarian woman who worked for the Allies in World War II on rescue missions. She was captured and tortured by the Nazis. Maruschka Dettmers stars, with Ellen Burstyn, Anthony Edwards, and Donald Pleasence. **DR5**

Hanoi Hilton, The (1987, C, 126m, R)
Drama of Vietnam War POWs; the title refers to their sarcastic name for their quarters. Michael Moriarty, Jeffrey Jones, and Paul LeMat star. **AC7**

Hanover Street (1979, C, 109m, PG)
World War II romance between British wife and American serviceman, starring Harrison Ford and Lesley-Anne Downe. **DR1, ST46**

Hans Christian Andersen (1954, C, 120m, NR)
Danny Kaye stars in this family musical about the famous storyteller. **FA9, ST78**

Hansel and Gretel (1984, C, 58m, NR)
Two hungry children (Ricky Schroder, Bridgette Andersen) stop to snack on a gingerbread house and almost become dinner for the witch (Joan Collins) who lives there. A Faerie Tale Theatre presentation. **FA12**

Happiest Millionaire, The (1967, C, 118, NR)
This Disney musical features Fred MacMurray and Greer Garson as an eccentric Philadelphia couple dealing with life in the early 1900s. With Geraldine Page and Lesley Ann Warren. **FA1**

Happy Birthday to Me (1981, C, 107m, R)
Horror story of a high school student who may be killing off her classmates in retribution for the accidental death of her mother. **HO9**

Happy Ending, The (1969, C, 112m, PG)
Contemporary drama of a middle-aged woman walking out on her marriage, starring Jean Simmons, with John Forsythe, Lloyd Bridges, Shirley Jones, and Robert (Bobby) Darin. **DR10, MU12**

Happy New Year (1973, C, 112m, PG)
A pair of jewel thieves plot a heist, only to have one fall in love with the proprietor of the store next to their target. French comedy stars Lino Ventura, Françoise Fabian, and Charles Gerard. U.S. remake released in 1987. **FF1, FF8, MY18**

Happy New Year (1987, C, 85m, PG)
Remake of French comedy about two jewel thieves and romantic complications, starring Peter Falk, Wendy Hughes, Charles Durning, and Tom Courtenay. **FF8, MY18**

Hard Choices (1984, C, 90m, NR)
Drama of social worker and her teenaged client, a juvenile offender, falling in love, with her helping him to escape custody. Gary McCleery and Margaret Klenck star, with John Sayles. **DR1, DR3, DT93**

Hard Day's Night, A (1964, B&W, 85m, NR)
Richard Lester directed this brilliant rock musical about a day in the life of The

Beatles, shot on location in London.
DT62, FA9, MU9, XT15 *Essential; Highly Recommended*

Hard Rock Zombies (1987, C, 90m, R)
Four heavy metal musicians are murdered but return from the grave for their scheduled concert as zombies. **HO6**

Hard Times (1975, C, 97m, R)
Drama about street fighter in Depression-era New Orleans, starring Charles Bronson, James Coburn, and Strother Martin. Directed by Walter Hill. **AC8, DT45, ST12, XT14**

Hard To Kill (1990, C, 95m, R)
Steven Seagal stars as Mason Storm, an agent left for dead by his enemies, back after seven years in a coma, looking for revenge. With Kelly LeBrock. **AC19, AC25, AC26**

Hardcore (1979, C, 108m, R)
Religious father from the Midwest tries to find runaway daughter in the midst of the porno film and prostitution worlds. George C. Scott stars, with Season Hubley. Paul Schrader wrote and directed. **DR7** *Recommended*

Harder They Come, The (1973, C, 98m, R)
A poor youth in Jamaica gains fame as both a singer and an outlaw in this midnight movie classic starring Jimmy Cliff. Great reggae music soundtrack. **CU1, CU9, MU9** *Recommended*

Harder They Fall, The (1956, B&W, 109m, NR)
Humphrey Bogart's last screen appearance has him playing a press agent who befriends an exploited prizefighter. Rod Steiger costars. **DR22, ST8, XT22**

Hardly Working (1981, C, 91m, PG)
An unemployed circus clown (Jerry Lewis) stumbles through a series of odd jobs, all with disastrous results. With Susan Oliver, Steve Franken, and Lewis J. Stone. Lewis directed. **ST91**

Harlan County, U.S.A. (1977, C, 103m, PG)
Oscar-winning documentary about a bitter and violent coal miner's strike in Kentucky. Directed by Barbara Kopple. **CU16**

Harlem Nights (1989, C, 118m, R)
Comedy set in 1930s New York, with Eddie Murphy and Richard Pryor as club owners fighting off a crime boss who wants a piece of their action—a *big* piece. With Redd Foxx, Della Reese, Danny Aiello, Michael Lerner, and, in a small role, Arsenio Hall. **CO6, CO13, ST125**

Harold and Maude (1972, C, 90m, PG)
Offbeat romantic comedy about a suicidal rich boy (Bud Cort) and a life-loving 80-year-old (Ruth Gordon) finding romance. A cult favorite at midnight screenings. **CO12, CU1, CU5, CU17**

Harold Lloyd (1962, B&W, 80m, NR)
Compilation of the classic silent comedian's short films from the early 1920s, including his masterpiece, *Safety Last*. **CL11** *Recommended*

Harper (1966, C, 121m, NR)
Paul Newman plays detective Lew Harper, hired by a frustrated wife (Lauren Bacall) to find her missing husband. With Janet Leigh, Arthur Hill, Robert Wagner, Shelley Winters, Julie Harris, Strother Martin, and Robert Webber. Based on the Ross MacDonald novel, *The Moving Target*. **ST111, ST164, WR19**

Harry and Son (1984, C, 117m, PG)
Paul Newman cowrote, coproduced, directed, and stars in this tale of a strained relationship between a widowed construction worker and his idealistic son. Robby Benson costars, with Joanne Woodward and Morgan Freeman. **DR8, ST48, ST111, ST166**

Harry and Tonto (1974, C, 115m, R)
Odyssey of a senior citizen and his pet cat on the road from New York to California, with Oscar winner Art Carney magnificent. With Ellen Burstyn and Larry Hagman. Directed by Paul Mazursky. **DR11, XT2, XT18** *Recommended*

Harry and Walter Go to New York (1976, C, 123m, PG)
Two unsuccessful vaudevillians (Elliott Gould, James Caan) resort to theft and land in jail in 1890s New York. Diane Keaton costars in this comedy. **CO6, ST15, ST79**

Harry Tracy (1982, C, 100m, PG)
A wanted criminal's exploits made him the envy of all and a folk hero to most.

Bruce Dern and singer Gordon Lightfoot star in this Canadian-produced western. **MU12, WE3, WE10**

Harum Scarum (1965, C, 86m, NR)
Elvis Presley musical about a movie star who gets involved in an attempted assassination in the Middle East. **ST123**

Harvey (1950, B&W, 104m, NR)
James Stewart stars in the screen version of Mary Chase's play about Elwood P. Dowd, a man who has a large, invisible rabbit for a companion. With Oscar winner Josephine Hull. **CL10, DR20, ST143, XT5**

Harvey Girls, The (1946, C, 101m, NR)
Judy Garland stars in this musical about a girl who travels west to work for Fred Harvey and his railroad-stop restaurants. Ray Bolger, Angela Lansbury, and Preston Foster costar. **MU1, MU6, ST51**

Hatari! (1962, C, 159m, NR)
John Wayne is the leader of a group of big-game stalkers who capture wild animals for zoos. Directed by Howard Hawks; music by Henry Mancini. **AC12, DT43, ST156**

Haunted Summer (1988, C, 106m, R)
Drama based on actual meeting of 19th-century English poets Lord Byron (Philip Anglim) and Percy Bysshe Shelley (Eric Stoltz). Laura Dern and Alice Krige costar. **DR5**

Haunted Honeymoon (1986, C, 82m, PG-13)
A recently married couple (Gene Wilder, Gilda Radner) spend their honeymoon in a haunted house. Dom DeLuise costars in this horror comedy. **CO13**

Haunted Strangler, The (1958, B&W, 81m, NR)
A mystery writer (Boris Karloff) investigates a series of murders which took place in London twenty years before, believing that an innocent man was hanged for the crimes. **ST77**

Haunting, The (1963, B&W, 113m, NR)
Two women who have had clairvoyant experiences are invited to a mysterious house where strange and terrifying events have occurred. Claire Bloom and Julie Harris star. Directed by Robert Wise. **DT117, HO1, HO2, HO3, HO19**

Haunting of Julia, The (1976, C, 96m, R)
Mia Farrow stars as a tormented woman who, after the death of her young daughter, moves to a house inhabited by a spirit. Keir Dullea and Tom Conti costar in this British horror film. **HO2, HO3, HO19, HO26**

Haunting of Morella, The (1990, C, 87m, R)
Sexy rendering of Edgar Allan Poe story of a witch executed, then coming back to life to possess her nubile niece. Produced by Roger Corman. **HO8, HO25, WR21**

Having Wonderful Time (1938, B&W, 71m, NR)
Ginger Rogers comedy set in the Catskills, where she finds romance on her vacation. With Douglas Fairbanks, Jr., Lucille Ball, Red Skelton, and Eve Arden. **ST131**

Hawaii (1966, C, 171m, NR)
Missionaries try to bring Christianity to Hawaiian Islands in the 19th century. Julie Andrews, and Max von Sydow star, with Gene Hackman. Directed by George Roy Hill, from the James Michener novel. Also available in a 192-minute "director's cut" version. **CU10, DR5, ST61**

Hawmps! (1976, C, 113m, G)
Camels are trained as army mounts for desert maneuvers in this family comedy based on a true story. **FA6**

Haxan *see* Witchcraft through the Ages

He Knows You're Alone (1981, C, 94m, R)
A mad killer is after women who are about to be married. Don Scardino and Caitlin O'Heaney star; watch for Tom Hanks in a small part. **ST62**

He Walked by Night (1948, B&W, 79m, NR)
Los Angeles homicide investigators are looking for a cop killer in this classic thriller. Anthony Mann co-directed, with Alfred Werker. **DT69, MY1**

Head (1968, C, 86m, G)
The Monkees made their film debut in this wild collection of skits, written by Jack Nicholson and directed by Bob Rafelson. **CU3, MU9**

Head Office (1986, C, 86m, PG-13)
A naive college graduate (Judge Reinhold) gets a job with a powerful conglomerate after his father pulls some strings. Comedy about big business also features Rick Moranis, Danny DeVito, Eddie Albert, and Jane Seymour. **CO14, ST32**

Head Over Heels *see* Chilly Scenes of Winter

Heart Beat (1980, C, 109m, R)
The life and times of Beat writer Jack Kerouac (John Heard) and his pal Neal Cassidy (Nick Nolte). Sissy Spacek plays Carolyn Cassidy and Ray Sharkey is very funny as Allen Ginsberg. **DR4, ST113, ST139**

Heart Condition (1990, C, 95m, R)
A racist cop suffers a heart attack, winds up with the transplanted heart of a murdered black lawyer. The lawyer's spirit appears to the cop, and they solve the mystery of the killing. Bob Hoskins and Denzel Washington star in this comedy, with Chloe Webb and Roger E. Mosley. **CO10, CO20, ST72**

Heart Is a Lonely Hunter, The (1968, C, 125m, G)
Touching version of Carson McCullers novel about a young girl's coming of age in a small Southern town. Sondra Locke and Alan Arkin star, with Stacy Keach, Chuck McCann, and Cicely Tyson. **DR2, DR9, DR19, DR26**

Heart Like a Wheel (1983, C, 113m, PG)
The true story of Shirley Muldowney, the first woman to dent the all-male barrier in modern drag racing. Bonnie Bedelia, Beau Bridges, and Hoyt Axton star. **DR4, DR10, DR22** *Recommended*

Heart of Dixie (1989, C, 95m, PG)
At a girls' college in 1957 Alabama, a young white student learns of the civil rights struggle firsthand. Ally Sheedy stars, with Virginia Madsen, Phoebe Cates, and Treat Williams. **DR7, DR25**

Heart of the Golden West (1942, B&W, 54m, NR)
Roy Rogers comes to the rescue of Cherokee City ranchers. **ST132**

Heart of the Rio Grande (1942, B&W, 70m, NR)
Gene Autry sings his way out of the middle of a family feud. **ST3**

Heart of the Rockies (1951, B&W, 54m, NR)
Roy Rogers plays a highway engineer battling a crooked rancher in this contemporary western. **ST132**

Heartbeeps (1981, C, 79m, PG)
The ultimate futuristic romance: two robots fall in love. Andy Kaufman and Bernadette Peters star. Allan Arkush directed. **DT4, FA8, SF21**

Heartbreak Hotel (1988, C, 101m, PG-13)
To cheer up his widowed mother who's an avid Elvis Presley fan, her teen son and his buddies kidnap The King from his hotel and take him to their small Ohio town. Comedy, set in the early 1970s, stars Charlie Schlatter and Tuesday Weld, with David Keith as Elvis. **CO6**

Heartbreak Kid, The (1972, C, 104m, PG)
A Jewish man (Charles Grodin) marries, but has a change of heart when he meets a beautiful WASP (Cybill Shepherd) on his honeymoon in Miami. Elaine May directed this dark comedy, adapted by Neil Simon from a Bruce J. Friedman story. With Jeannie Berlin and Eddie Albert. **CO1, CU5, DT70, ST59, WR23, XT20**
Highly Recommended

Heartbreak Ridge (1986, C, 130m, R)
A tough Marine sergeant (Clint Eastwood) shapes up his young recruits for action in the Grenada invasion. With Marsha Mason, Everett McGill, and Mario Van Peebles. Eastwood directed. **AC6, ST39**

Heartburn (1986, C, 108m, R)
Jack Nicholson and Meryl Streep are a seemingly happily married couple, until she learns during her pregnancy that he's having an affair. Directed by Mike Nichols from the novel by Nora Ephron. Filmed partly on location in Washington, D.C. **CO1, CO2, DT74, ST112, ST145, XT12**

Heartland (1979, C, 96m, PG)
A western woman's saga of life on the 1910 Wyoming frontier, based on a true story. Conchata Ferrell and Rip Torn star. **ST150, WE8** *Recommended*

Heartland Reggae (1980, C, 87m, NR)
Concert film shot in Jamaica in April 1978, featuring some of reggae's superstars, including Bob Marley and Peter Tosh. **MU10**

Hearts and Minds (1974, C, 110m, R)
Oscar-winning documentary explores America's involvment in the Vietnam War. Directed by Peter Davis. **CU16** *Recommended*

Hearts of Fire (1987, C, 95m, R)
Drama of a romantic triangle among pop singers, starring Bob Dylan, Fiona, and Rupert Everett. **DR12**

Hearts of the West (1975, C, 102m, PG)
Jeff Bridges plays an aspiring novelist in the 1930s who goes to Hollywood to work as a screenwriter, but winds up acting in low-budget westerns. Charming comedy also stars Blythe Danner, Alan Arkin, and Andy Griffith. **CO6, CO8, ST11** *Recommended*

Hearts of the World (1918, B&W, 152m, NR)
Sentimental silent drama from director D.W. Griffith, made to persuade America to enter World War I. Robert Harron is the young man who goes off to fight; Lillian and Dorothy Gish costar. Erich Von Stroheim has a small role as a German soldier. **AC2, DT42, DT109, ST54, XT8**

Heat (1972, C, 100m, NR)
Andy Warhol-produced takeoff on *Sunset Boulevard,* with Joe Dallessandro and Sylvia Miles as the writer and faded star. Directed by Paul Morissey. **CU2, CU12, DT72**

Heat (1987, C, 101m, R)
Burt Reynolds is a mystery man based in Vegas, protecting the innocent, teaching a neophyte gambler the ropes. Written by William Goldman from his novel. **ST128**

Heat and Dust (1983, C, 130m, NR)
Two-pronged story of a pair of English-women (Greta Scacchi, Julie Christie) who a century apart journey to India and fall in love with the country and one of its natives. From the filmmaking team of producer Ismail Merchant, director James Ivory, and writer Ruth Prawer Jhabvala. **DR10, DR23**

Heat of Desire (1980, C, 90m, R)
A respectable professor is seduced by a free-spirited woman, and both his marriage and career are ruined. Patrick Dewaere, Clio Goldsmith, and Jeanne Moreau star. **FF1, ST110**

Heathers (1989, C, 103m, R)
Dark comedy starring Winona Ryder as a high school girl vying to be accepted into a clique of snotty princesses, until she meets a rebel student (Christian Slater). Murders trumped up to look like suicides are his specialty. Written by Daniel Waters; directed by Michael Lehmann. **CO4, CO12, CO18, CU5** *Recommended*

Heatwave (1983, C, 99m, R)
A radical activist leads a fight against a multi-million dollar development which will destroy a neighborhood. Matters get complicated when she and the project architect fall in love. Australian drama starring Judy Davis. **FF5, MY16**

Heaven (1987, C, 80m, NR)
Diane Keaton directed this documentary about people's perceptions of heaven. Film alternates between clips of Hollywood movies on the subject and interviews. **CU16, ST79**

Heaven Can Wait (1943, C, 112m, NR)
Ernst Lubitsch directed this comedy classic of a man (Don Ameche) who recalls his wicked past as he awaits admission through the Pearly Gates. With Gene Tierney, Charles Coburn, Marjorie Main, and Laird Cregar as the Devil. **CL10, DT63, HO10** *Recommended*

Heaven Can Wait (1978, C, 100m, PG)
Remake (and updating) of *Here Comes Mr. Jordan,* with Warren Beatty as a football player taken to heaven before his time and allowed to return to Earth. With Julie Christie, James Mason, Dyan Cannon, and Charles Grodin. Co-directed by Beatty and screenwriter Buck Henry. **CO20, CU18, ST5, ST59, ST102**

Heaven Help Us (1985, C, 104m, R)
A New York Catholic boy's school in the early 1960s is the setting for this coming of age comedy. Andrew McCarthy and Kevin Dillon are the students; Donald Sutherland, John Heard, and Wallace Shawn are in charge. **CO4, CO18** *Recommended*

Heavens Above (1963, B&W, 113m, NR)
A deeply devoted reverend wreaks havoc
when he becomes a bishop on a nuclear
missile base in outer space. Peter Sellers
stars. **ST137**

Heaven's Gate (1980, C, 219m, R)
Western epic of a war between immigrant
settlers and cattle barons in Johnson
County, Wyoming. Kris Kristofferson,
Christopher Walken, Isabelle Huppert,
and Jeff Bridges star. Michael Cimino
directed; photographed by Vilmos Zsig-
mond, with music by David Mansfield.
(Also available in a 149m version.) **MU12,
ST11, WE1** *Essential*

Heidi (1937, B&W, 88m, NR)
Shirley Temple stars as the little girl living
in the Swiss Alps with her grandfather
whose life turns upside down when she
moves to the city to live with a wealthy
invalid girl. **FA2, ST148**

Heir to Genghis Kahn, The *see* Storm
Over Asia

Heiress, The (1949, B&W, 115m, NR)
The plain daughter of a wealthy doctor is
threatened with disinheritance when she
falls in love with a young social climber.
Oscar winner Olivia de Havilland stars,
with Ralph Richardson and Montgomery
Clift. Directed by William Wyler; based
on the Henry James novel, *Washington
Square*. **CL1, CL4, CL6, DR19, DT119,
WR11, XT3** *Recommended*

Hell Fighters, The (1969, C, 121m, NR)
John Wayne leads a team of brave men
who put out oil well fires. Jim Hutton and
Katharine Ross costar. **ST156**

Hell in the Pacific (1968, C, 103m, G)
A Pacific island during World War II is
the setting for this survival drama, as a
U.S. Marine (Lee Marvin) and Japanese
officer (Toshiro Mifune) match wits. Directed by John Boorman. **AC1, AC24,
DT11, ST100, ST106** *Recommended*

Hell Is for Heroes (1962, B&W, 90m, NR)
World War II action, with Steve McQueen
as a cynical loner whose outfit includes
Bobby Darin, Fess Parker, Harry Guar-
dino, Nick Adams, and Bob Newhart.
Directed by Don Siegel. **AC1, DT97,
MU12, ST97** *Recommended*

Hell Night (1981, C, 101m, R)
Four girls pledging a sorority must spend
the night in a haunted mansion supposedly occupied by the ghost of a killer. But
as the night wears on, they're not sure
he's really dead. **HO12**

Hell on Frisco Bay (1955, C, 98m, NR)
Gangster saga, set in contemporary San
Francisco, with good guy Alan Ladd
against baddie Edward G. Robinson.
With Joanne Dru, William Demarest, Fay
Wray, and Jayne Mansfield. **AC22, ST130**

Hell up in Harlem (1973, C, 96m, R)
Sequel to *Black Caesar* stars Fred Wil-
liamson as a vengeance-seeking gangster.
Directed by Larry Cohen. With Julius W.
Harris, Gloria Hendry, and Margaret Av-
ery. **AC22, DT20**

Hellbound: Hellraiser II (1988, C, 93m, R)
The demons who haunted the couple in
the first *Hellraiser* are back for more
sport, this time with the couple's daughter (Ashley Laurence). Available in an
unrated version with a 98m running time.
CU10, HO14

Helldorado (1946, B&W, 54m, NR)
Roy Rogers and Dale Evans travel to Las
Vegas for Nevada's Frontier Days.**ST132**

Heller in Pink Tights (1960, C, 100m, NR)
Sophia Loren travels the 1880s West with
a theatrical troupe, entertaining in the
face of Indian uprisings, bill collectors,
and thieves. With Anthony Quinn, Steve
Forrest, Eileen Heckart, Margaret
O'Brien, and Ramon Novarro. Directed
by George Cukor; based on a Louis L'A-
mour story. Outstanding use of color.
CL9, DT24, ST93, WE8, WR13 *Recommended*

Hello, Dolly! (1969, C, 146m, G)
In this screen version of the Broadway
smash, Barbra Streisand plays Dolly
Levi, a widowed matchmaker in old New
York who finds herself attracted to a
bachelor merchant (Walter Matthau). Di-
rected by Gene Kelly. **MU2, ST81, ST104,
ST146**

Hellraiser (1987, C, 94m, R)
Clive Barker wrote and directed this harrowing tale about a man whose dead
brother comes back to haunt him and his
family. **HO14**

Hell's Angels on Wheels (1967, C, 95m, NR)
Low-budget nonsense about the infamous motorcycle gang. Jack Nicholson stars as a gas station attendant named Poet. **ST112**

Hell's House (1932, B&W, 72m, NR)
A young boy is sent to a reformatory after he takes the blame for a crime to protect someone else. Bette Davis appears in one of her first film roles. **ST28**

Hellstrom Chronicle, The (1971, C, 90m, G)
Oscar-winning documentary which proposes that insects may take over the world from man by weight of sheer numbers. **CU16**

Help! (1965, C, 90m, NR)
In their second film, The Beatles dodge a crazy cult that's after a sacrificial ring that Ringo possesses. With Leo McKern, Eleanor Bron, Victor Spinetti, and Roy Kinnear. Richard Lester directed. **DT62, FA9, MU9** *Highly Recommended*

Helter Skelter (1976, C, 194m, NR)
Chilling dramatization of the Charles Manson murders and the subsequent trials, based on prosecutor Vincent Bugliosi's book. Steve Railsback is a very creepy Manson. Originally made for TV. **DR6, DR16** *Recommended*

Henry V (1945, C, 137m, NR)
Laurence Olivier produced, directed, and stars in this colorful adaptation of Shakespeare's classic. Olivier won a special Oscar for his achievement. **CL9, DR5, ST116,WR22** *Essential; Recommended*

Henry V (1989, C, 137m, NR)
Kenneth Branagh stars as Shakespeare's dashing warrior monarch. He also directed a cast that includes Derek Jacobi, Brian Blessed, Ian Holm, and Paul Scofield. **DR5, DR23, WR22** *Recommended*

Henry IV (1984, C, 95m, PG-13)
Marcello Mastroianni stars as a mad nobleman who believes he's Emperor Henry IV in this version of the Pirandello play, directed by Marco Bellochio. Claudia Cardinale costars. **FF2, ST103**

Henry: Portrait of a Serial Killer (1990, C, 83m, NR)
Violent, affecting crime drama stars Michael Rooker as a character whose exploits are loosely based on a real-life murderer. Directed by John McNaughton on locations in and around Chicago. **CU7, MY13, XT11** *Recommended*

Her Alibi (1989, C, 94m, PG)
Comic mystery of a novelist (Tom Selleck) who's not sure if the lovely new woman in his life (Paulina Porizkova) is really guilty of murder. With William Daniels. **MY11, MY17**

Herbie Goes Bananas (1980, C, 93m, G)
Herbie, the magical Volkswagen from *The Love Bug,* travels to South America to enter a car race. Fourth in the series from the Disney studios. **FA1**

Herbie Goes to Monte Carlo (1977, C, 104, G)
Herbie gets involved in a Monte Carlo race and his driver (Dean Jones) is unaware that a spy ring has a diamond hidden in the gas tank. Third in the Disney series. **FA1**

Herbie Rides Again (1974, C, 88m, G)
This sequel to *The Love Bug* casts Helen Hayes as a woman trying to thwart a villain who wants to get his hands on Herbie. **FA1**

Hercules (1959, C, 107m, NR)
Strongman Steve Reeves plays the mighty warrior in this adventure that set off a wave of sequels and imitators. **FF2**

Here Come the Littles (1985, C, 72m, G)
Based on the children's books, this animated feature follows the adventures of the Littles, tiny people who live in the walls of people's houses. In this story, they get involved with a 12-year-old boy. **FA10**

Here Comes Mr. Jordan (1941, B&W, 93m, NR)
Classic comic fantasy of boxer taken to heaven before his time and returned to Earth in another man's body. Robert Montgomery, Claude Rains, Evelyn Keyes, and Edward Everett Horton star. Remade in 1978 as *Heaven Can Wait.* **CO20, SF2**

Here Comes the Groom (1951, B&W, 113m, NR)
Bing Crosby musical has him playing odd man out at his old flame's wedding, trying to disrupt the proceedings. With Jane

Wyman and Franchot Tone; musical appearances by Louis Armstrong and Phil Harris. Directed by Frank Capra. Oscar-winning Johnny Mercer song: "In the Cool Cool Cool of the Evening." **DT16, ST25, XT20**

Hero and the Terror (1988, C, 97m, R)
Chuck Norris plays a cop who puts away a super-human killer, only to have the man escape, precipitating another manhunt led by you-know-who. **ST114**

Heroes (1977, C, 113m, PG)
A disturbed Vietnam vet (Henry Winkler) embarks on a cross-country trip and meets a confused young girl (Sally Field) along the way. Harrison Ford costars in this comedy-drama. **ST40, ST46, XT18**

Hester Street (1975, B&W, 92m, PG)
In turn-of-the-century New York, a young immigrant wife struggles to adapt to the ways of her new life. Carol Kane stars. Joan Micklin Silver directed. **DR5, DR15** *Recommended*

Hey Babu Riba (1986, C, 109m, NR)
Yugoslavian comedy centering on four men and their memories of youthful 1950s fascination with the same girl. Gala Videnovic plays the object of their desire. **FF7**

Hey There, It's Yogi Bear (1964, C, 89m, G)
Yogi Bear and Boo Boo star in this animated musical feature about life in Jellystone Park. As spring and picnic basket season approach, the bears try to outsmart Ranger Smith. **FA10**

Hidden, The (1987, C, 96m, R)
A police detective joins forces with an alien cop (in human form) to track a sinister force that possesses people and causes them to go berserk. Michael Nouri and Kyle MacLachlan star in this science fiction/action thriller. **AC8, SF17**

Hidden Fortress, The (1958, B&W, 139m, NR)
Japanese adventure starring Toshiro Mifune as the loyal companion to a spoiled princess making a dangerous journey with precious royal cargo. Directed by Akira Kurosawa. Video version is completely restored print. **CU10, DT57, ST106**

Hide in Plain Sight (1980, C, 98m, PG)
James Caan directed this story of a man (Caan) who frantically searches for his children after they disappear with his ex-wife. With Jill Eikenberry. **MY8**

Hideous Sun Demon, The (1959, B&W, 74m, NR)
Low-budget science fiction yarn about scientist (Robert Clarke) exposed to radiation who turns into the title character in sunlight. Clarke also directed. **SF10**

High and Low (1962, B&W, 142m, NR)
Akira Kurosawa directed this suspenseful study of a businessman (Toshiro Mifune) whose chauffeur's son is mistakenly kidnapped; he agrees to pay the ransom anyway. Deliberately paced, but exceptionally exciting. Available in letterboxed format. **CU19, DT57, MY16, ST106** *Recommended*

High Anxiety (1977, C, 94m, PG)
Mel Brooks spoof of Hitchcock films, about a psychiatrist (Brooks) who finds trouble behind every door when he becomes the head of a sanitarium. With Madeline Kahn, Harvey Korman, and Cloris Leachman. **CO7, DT13**

High Heels (1972, C, 100m, NR)
Jean-Paul Belmondo stars in this French comedy-mystery about a doctor who marries an unattractive woman and falls in love with her sister. Directed by Claude Chabrol. Mia Farrow and Laura Antonelli costar. **ST4**

High Hopes (1988, C, 112m, NR)
British comedy-drama of life in Thatcher's world, with Ruth Sheen and Philip Davis as a working-class couple trying to make ends meet and sense of their zany family. Written and directed by Mike Leigh. **CO2, CO17**

High Noon (1952, B&W, 85m, NR)
Gary Cooper's performance as the honorable sheriff who faces a showdown with outlaws on his wedding day won him an Oscar. With Grace Kelly, Lon Chaney, Jr., Thomas Mitchell, Katy Jurado, Lloyd Bridges, and Lee Van Cleef. Directed by Fred Zinnemann. **CL26, DT120, ST17, ST22, ST82, ST155, WE2, XT2** *Essential*

High Noon, Part II: The Return of Will Kane (1980, C, 100m, NR)
Lee Majors plays a retired marshal who takes the law into his hands when he returns to find a corrupt sheriff in his town. **WE2**

High Plains Drifter (1973, C, 105m, R)
Clint Eastwood directed this spooky, violent western tale about a mysterious character (Eastwood) in a strange frontier town. **ST39, WE5**

High Road to China (1983, C, 106m, PG)
A soldier of fortune agrees to fly a spoiled young woman on a rescue mission to help her father out of China. Tom Selleck and Bess Armstrong star. **AC11, AC14, AC21**

High School Confidential (1958, B&W, 85m, NR)
Camp cult classic which opens with Jerry Lee Lewis singing the title tune (on the back of a flatbed truck) and goes downhill from there. Story has Russ Tamblyn as an undercover agent investigating widespread marijuana use by teens. Also in the cast: Mamie Van Doren, Jackie Coogan, Charlie Chaplin, Jr., and Michael Landon. **CU2, DR25**

High Sierra (1941, B&W, 100m, NR)
Humphrey Bogart plays a gangster running from the police, with the help of his girl friend (Ida Lupino). Written by John Huston; Raoul Walsh directed. **AC22, MY1, ST8** *Essential; Recommended*

High Society (1956, C, 107m, NR)
In this musical remake of *The Philadelphia Story*, Grace Kelly is a wealthy socialite trying to avoid nosy reporters (Frank Sinatra, Celeste Holm) and her ex-husband (Bing Crosby) on the eve of her wedding. Louis Armstrong appears as himself. **MU1, MU14, ST25, ST82, ST138, XT20** *Recommended*

High Spirits (1988, C, 99m, PG-13)
Peter O'Toole plays an impoverished nobleman who claims his castle is haunted, to attract American tourists Steven Guttenberg and Beverly D'Angelo for a paying visit. Daryl Hannah costars as a live ghost in this comedy. **CO11, ST117**

High Tide (1987, C, 120m, PG-13)
Australian drama of a woman (Judy Davis) whose aimless life on the road with musical groups is changed when she's reunited with the daughter she abandoned many years ago. Gillian Armstrong directed. **DR9, DR10, FF5** *Recommended*

High Voltage (1929, B&W, 57m, NR)
A bus is stranded in a mountain snowstorm and its passengers seek help from a lineman, who is in reality a fugitive from justice. William Boyd, Owen Moore, and Carole (billed as "Carol") Lombard star. **ST92**

Higher and Higher (1943, B&W, 90m, NR)
Frank Sinatra made his starring debut in this musical about a down-on-his-luck gentleman who conspires with his servants to raise money. **ST138**

Highlander (1986, C, 111m, R)
Adventure tale of an ancient Scottish warrior who pursues his arch-rival to contemporary Manhattan. Christopher Lambert stars, with Sean Connery. Music by Queen. **SF4, ST21, XT9**

Highpoint (1980, C, 88m, PG)
An innocent man gets involved in a murder after he begins working for a wealthy family in this comedy/thriller. Richard Harris, Christopher Plummer, and Beverly D'Angelo star. **MY9**

Hillbillys in a Haunted House (1967, C, 88m, NR)
A group of country singers get stranded at a haunted house during a storm in this comic horror story. Lon Chaney, Jr. and Basil Rathbone star. **ST17**

Hills Have Eyes, The (1977, C, 89m, R)
Horror film about family whose care breaks down in the desert and are attacked by crazed "family" of mutants. Wes Craven directed this cult film. **CU4, HO14**

Hills of Utah, The (1951, B&W, 70m, NR)
Gene Autry uncovers the truth about his father's death when he visits his hometown. **ST3**

Himatsuri (1984, C, 120m, NR)
Japanese drama of a man who renounces modern ways for Shinto way of life, winds up killing his family and himself. **FF4**

Hindenburg, The (1975, C, 125m, PG)
Drama centering on the disastrous crash in 1937 of the famed German dirigible,

starring George C. Scott, Anne Bancroft, William Atherton, Charles Durning, and Burgess Meredith. Directed by Robert Wise. **AC16, AC23, DT117**

Hired Hand, The (1971, C, 93m, PG)
Peter Fonda directed this western drama set in 1880s New Mexico. He plays a cowhand who returns to work for the woman he abandoned years earlier. Warren Oates costars. **ST115, WE15**

Hiroshima, Mon Amour (1960, B&W, 88m, NR)
Groundbreaking drama about an affair between French woman and Japanese man, with echoes of atomic bomb catastrophe lurking in the background. French-language film directed by Alain Resnais. **FF1** *Essential*

His Double Life (1933, B&W, 67m, NR)
When a famous but retiring artist is thought dead, he happily accepts oblivion to marry a spinster. Roland Young and Lillian Gish star. **ST54**

His Girl Friday (1940, B&W, 92m, NR)
Cary Grant is a newspaper editor whose star reporter, also his ex-wife (Rosalind Russell), is planning to remarry. Ralph Bellamy costars in this breakneck comedy based on the play *The Front Page*. Written by Ben Hecht and Charles Lederer; Howard Hawks directed. **CL10, DT43, ST57** *Essential; Highly Recommended*

His Kind of Woman (1951, B&W, 120m, NR)
Robert Mitchum plays a fall guy for a criminal (Raymond Burr) who wants to re-enter the country from Mexico. With Jane Russell and Vincent Price. **MY1, ST107, ST124**

History of the World—Part I (1981, C, 92m, R)
Mel Brooks' zany revisionist view of human history, starting with prehistoric times. Brooks stars, with Gregory Hines, Dom DeLuise, Madeline Kahn, Harvey Korman, Sid Caesar, and John Hurt as Jesus Christ. **CO6, DT13, HF16**

Hit and Run (1982, C, 93m, NR)
A cabdriver's involvement with a mysterious woman leads to murder. **MY7**

Hit List (1989, C, 87m, R)
Jan-Michael Vincent and Rip Torn star in this action drama of an innocent man whose best friend and son are victimized by a Mob hit man. **ST150**

Hit the Deck (1955, C, 112m, NR)
MGM musical of fun-loving sailors on shore leave, starring Jane Powell, Tony Martin, Debbie Reynolds, Ann Miller, and Vic Damone. Final musical number is presented in letterboxed format. **CU19, MU1**

Hit the Ice (1943, B&W, 82m, NR)
Abbott and Costello are newspaper photographers who get involved with a gangster and his minions at the winter resort of Sun Valley. **ST1**

Hitler (1962, B&W, 107m, NR)
Film portrait of the Nazi dictator, starring Richard Basehart. **DR4, HF12**

Hitler—Dead or Alive (1943, B&W, 70m, NR)
Low-budget wartime thriller about con men trying to assassinate Hitler. Ward Bond stars, with Bobby Watson as Der Fuhrer. **HF12**

Hitler: The Last Ten Days (1973, C, 108m, PG)
Alec Guinness stars in this recreation of the dying days of the Third Reich. **HF12, ST60**

Hobbit, The (1978, C, 76m, NR)
Based on the J.R.R. Tolkien fantasy novel, this animated feature deals with a magical hobbit named Bilbo Baggins. **FA8, FA10, SF13**

Hobson's Choice (1954, B&W, 107m, NR)
A bootshop owner (Charles Laughton) in 1890s Britain decides whom his daughters shall marry, despite their objections. Directed by David Lean. **CO17, DT59**

Hobson's Choice (1983, C, 100m, NR)
TV movie remake of the classic comedy about a shopowner's attempts to control his daughters' lives. Richard Thomas, Sharon Gless, Jack Warden, and Lillian Gish star. **ST54**

Holcroft Covenant, The (1985, C, 112m, R)
A former henchman for Hitler leaves his son (Michael Caine) a fortune intended to

make amends for Nazi atrocities. Thriller based on the bestseller by Robert Ludlum. **MY6, ST15, WR18**

Hold That Ghost (1941, B&W, 86m, NR)
Abbott and Costello are bumbling gas station attendants who inherit a gangster's mysterious mansion. **ST1**

Hole in the Head (1959, C, 120m, NR)
Drama of relationship between a Miami ne'er-do-well (Frank Sinatra) and his adoring son (Eddie Hodges). With Edward G. Robinson, Eleanor Parker, and Thelma Ritter. Directed by Frank Capra; features the Oscar-winning song, "High Hopes." **DT16, ST130, ST138**

Holiday (1937, B&W, 93m, NR)
Bright comedy about a nonconformist (Cary Grant) who becomes engaged to the daughter of a high society family, then falls for her sister (Katharine Hepburn). Directed by George Cukor. **CL10, DT24, ST57, ST66** *Essential; Recommended*

Holiday Inn (1942, B&W, 101m, NR)
Bing Crosby breaks with show-biz partner and rival Fred Astaire to run a Connecticut inn which only opens on holidays. This film introduced the Irving Berlin songs "White Christmas" and "Easter Parade." **MU4, MU6, ST2, ST25**

Hollywood Boulevard (1976, C, 83m, R)
Determinedly low-budget, intentionally sleazy comedy about a young girl trying to "make it" in movies, with dozens of inside gags, especially about filmmaking for producer Roger Corman. Paul Bartel stars; Joe Dante and Allan Arkush directed. **CO8, CU5, CU14, DT4, DT5, DT25**

Hollywood or Bust (1956, C, 95m, NR)
Jerry Lewis plays a zealous movie fan who wins a car in a raffle and travels to Hollywood with a gambler (Dean Martin) to meet his idol, Anita Ekberg. Martin and Lewis's last film. **CO8, FA6, ST91, XT18**

Hollywood Shuffle (1987, C, 82m, R)
Comic saga of a young black actor (Robert Townsend) and his attempts to make an impression in Hollywood. Spoofs various genres of black exploitation filmmaking and racial stereotypes on the screen. Townsend directed and co-wrote. **CO8**

Hollywood Vice Squad (1986, C, 100m, R)
Episodic action thriller set on the mean streets of Hollywood, starring Ronny Cox, Carrie Fisher, Frank Gorshin, and Leon Isaac Kennedy. **AC9**

Holocaust (1978, C, 450m, NR)
Meryl Streep, Fritz Weaver, and Michael Moriarty star in this gripping account of the Nazis' efforts to exterminate all European Jews, and the effects on one family. Originally made for TV. **ST145**

Holy Innocents (1984, C, 108m, NR)
Spanish drama of rural peasants in revolt against wealthy landowners. Alfredo Landa and Francisco Rabal star. **FF7**

Hombre (1967, C, 111m, NR)
A white man (Paul Newman) raised by Indians is the victim of prejudice in frontier Arizona. With Fredric March, Richard Boone, Martin Balsam, and Diane Cilento. Based on a story by Elmore Leonard; directed by Martin Ritt. **DT87, ST111, WE7, WR16**

Home and the World, The (1984, C, 130m, NR)
From Indian director Satyajit Ray, a drama about a woman caught up in the political turmoil that swept her country in the first decade of the 20th century. **DT84**

Home for the Holidays (1972, C, 74m, NR)
An elderly man, threatened by a killer, is protected by his four daughters. Eleanor Parker, Sally Field, Jessica Walter, Julie Harris, Jill Haworth, and Walter Brennan star. Originally made for TV. **ST40**

Home From the Hill (1960, C, 150m, NR)
Melodrama of Texas patriarch (Robert Mitchum) and his two competing sons (George Peppard, George Hamilton). With Eleanor Parker. Directed by Vincente Minnelli. **DR8, DT71, ST107**

Home in Oklahoma (1947, B&W, 54m, NR)
Roy Rogers plays a newspaper editor, Dale Evans a reporter; they're investigating a shifty rancher. **ST132**

Home Is Where the Heart Is *see* Square Dance

Home Movies (1979, C, 90m, PG)
An egotistical film director (Kirk Douglas) gives the star treatment to a nerd,

who then decides to pursue his brother's girlfriend. Comedy about show-biz life directed by Brian DePalma. **CO8, DT29, ST34**

Home of the Brave (1949, B&W, 85m, NR)
A black G.I. is abused by his fellow soldiers during World War II in this classic drama about the effects of racism. James Edwards stars, with Jeff Corey and Lloyd Bridges. **AC1, CL8** *Essential*

Home Sweet Home (1914, B&W, 62m, NR)
D.W. Griffith directed this silent drama inspired by the work of poet and composer John Howard Payne. Dorothy and Lillian Gish star. **DT42, XT8**

Home To Stay (1978, C, 74m, NR)
A young girl runs away from home with her elderly grandfather (Henry Fonda) to avoid her family sending him to a nursing home. Originally made for TV. **ST44**

Homeboy (1989, C, 112m, R)
Boxing saga set in Miami, starring Mickey Rourke as the determined young fighter. With Christopher Walken and Ruben Blades. **DR22, MU12, ST134**

Homer and Eddie (1990, C, 99m, R)
Jim Belushi and Whoopi Goldberg are an unlikely road couple: he's a mentally retarded dishwasher, and she's a homicidal cancer patient. **CO13, XT18**

Honey, I Shrunk the Kids (1989, C, 86m, PG)
A nerdy scientist accidentally trains his miniaturization invention on his own children. Special effects comedy stars Rick Moranis and Matt Frewer. The video version includes a Roger Rabbit cartoon, "Tummy Trouble." **CO5, CO11, CO14**

Honey Pot, The (1967, C, 131m, NR)
Writer-director Joseph L. Mankiewicz updates Ben Jonson's *Volpone*, the story of a wealthy rogue who pretends to be dying to see which of his women will try hardest to curry favor with him. Rex Harrison stars, with Susan Hayward, Cliff Robertson, Capucine, Edie Adams, and Maggie Smith. **DT68**

Honeymoon (1985, C, 98m, R)
A French woman visiting New York marries a man in order to stay in the America, only to find that he's a psychotic killer. Nathalie Baye and John Shea star. **HO9**

Honeymoon Killers, The (1969. B&W, 103m, R)
Cult melodrama, based on fact, about a nurse and her lover posing as brother and sister to lure lonely, rich women to their deaths. Shirley Stoler and Tony LoBianco star. Leonard Kastle directed, his only credit behind the camera. **CU15, DR6, DR16** *Recommended*

Honeysuckle Rose (1980, C, 119m, PG)
Willie Nelson plays a country singer who romances one of his back-up singers, much to his wife's dismay. With Amy Irving, Dyan Cannon, and Slim Pickens. Willie sings "On the Road Again" and many of his hits. **DR12**

Honky Tonk Freeway (1981, C, 107m, R)
Comic free-for-all of the effect on a small Florida town wrought by a highway overpass. The ensemble cast includes William Devane, Beverly D'Angelo, Hume Cronyn, Jessica Tandy, Beau Bridges, and Geraldine Page. Directed by John Schlesinger. **CO2, DT94**

Honkytonk Man (1982, C, 122m, PG)
Clint Eastwood stars in this drama set in the Depression about a broken-down country singer who won't get off the road. Eastwood's son Kyle plays his son on screen. **DR12, ST39, XT8**

Honor Among Thieves (1968, C, 115m, R)
Charles Bronson and Alain Delon star in this action drama of French mercenaries in Marseilles with a big heist in their plans. Also known as *Farewell, Friend*. **ST12**

Hooper (1978, C, 100m, PG)
Burt Reynolds portrays an aging Hollywood stuntman who is challenged by a young maverick to perform a dangerous stunt. Sally Field and Jan-Michael Vincent costar. **CO8, ST40, ST128**

Hoosiers (1986, C, 114m, PG)
Drama about a middle-aged man (Gene Hackman) who accepts a job coaching basketball in smalltown Indiana in the 1950s. He meets opposition from the townspeople for his methods, until the school begins winning. Barbara Hershey and Dennis Hopper costar in this drama based on a true story. **DR22, DR26, ST61, ST71** *Recommended*

Hope and Glory (1987, C, 113m, PG-13)
A young boy suddenly becomes the man of the house when his father goes off to war. John Boorman wrote, produced, and directed this nostalgic, comic view of Britain during World War II. Sebastian Rice-Edwards and Sarah Miles star. **CO5, CO6, CO17, DT11** *Highly Recommended*

Hopscotch (1980, C, 104m, R)
A CIA man who's been phased out of The Company decides to get revenge on his boss by publishing his memoirs. Walter Matthau stars in this comedy, with Glenda Jackson, Sam Waterston, and Ned Beatty. **CO10, ST104**

Horror Express (1972, C, 88m, NR)
A frozen monster thaws out and comes to life on train traveling through Asia, while two anthropologists (Peter Cushing, Christopher Lee) lock horns. **HO8, ST27, ST89, XT19**

Horror Hotel (1960, B&W, 76m, NR)
The spirit of a witch burned at the stake in the 17th century lives at a Massachusetts inn. Several young people who stay there become human sacrifices to the Devil. Christopher Lee stars. **ST89**

Horror of Dracula (1958, C, 82m, NR)
This British film from the famed Hammer studios features Christopher Lee as the cursed count. Peter Cushing costars as Professor Van Helsing. **HF7, HO1, HO5, HO26, ST27, ST89**

Horror of Frankenstein (1970, C, 95m, R)
A self-destructive doctor does away with his father, best friend, and wife while creating a monster. This British version of the classic horror tale is strictly tongue-in-cheek. **HF10, HO26**

Horse Feathers (1932, B&W, 67m, NR)
The Marx Brothers matriculate at Huxley College, and campus life will never be the same again. Thelma Todd costars. Highlights: the speakeasy "password" scene and the football game. **CO18, ST101** *Recommended*

Horse in the Gray Flannel Suit, The (1968, C, 113m, G)
An advertising executive (Dean Jones) designs a campaign to take advantage of his daughter's love for horses. Diane Baker costars in this Disney comedy. **FA1**

Horse Soldiers, The (1959, C, 119m, NR)
Set during the Civil War, this western drama stars John Wayne as a soldier who leads his cavalry troops into Confederate territory. Directed by John Ford. William Holden costars. **DT36, ST68, ST156, WE4, WE6**

Horse's Mouth, The (1958, C, 93m, NR)
Aleç Guinness plays a iconoclastic British painter who doesn't need a canvas to work on. Guinness also adapted the Joyce Cary novel. **CO17, ST60**

Hospital, The (1971, C, 103m, PG)
This offbeat comedy casts George C. Scott as a disillusioned doctor who gets involved with a nutty woman (Diana Rigg) and her father amid the sloppy workings of an inner-city hospital. **CO12**

Hostage Tower, The (1980, C, 105m, NR)
Thriller about a psycho who takes over the Eiffel Tower, holding the U.S. President's mother hostage. Written by Alistair MacLean. Peter Fonda and Billy Dee Williams star, with Keir Dullea, Douglas Fairbanks, Jr., and Rachel Roberts. **MY16, ST159**

Hot Lead and Cold Feet (1978, C, 90m, G)
Disney western features a ranching patriarch and his two sons, a gunfighter and his timid twin, all played by Jim Dale. **FA1**

Hot Rock, The (1972, C, 105m, PG)
A group of thieves blunder their way through a jewel heist. Robert Redford and George Segal star. Based on Donald Westlake's novel. **AC9, CO10, MY18, ST126**

Hot Shot (1986, C, 94m, PG)
Rich American boy runs off to Brazil to meet his idol, soccer superstar Pele (playing himself). Jim Youngs stars in this family drama. **DR22, FA7**

Hot Spell (1958, B&W, 86m, NR)
Anthony Quinn stars as an unfaithful husband whose breakup with his nagging wife (Shirley Booth) has a strong impact on their recently jilted daughter (Shirley MacLaine). **ST96**

Hotel Colonial (1987, C, 104m, R)
International intrigue, involving an Italian man's journey to Colombia to investigate the death of his brother. John Savage

stars, with Rachel Ward and Robert Duvall. **ST38**

Hotel New Hampshire, The (1984, C, 110m, R)
This film version of John Irving's bestselling novel deals with an unusual family's sexual and social adventures. Rob Lowe, Nastassja Kinski, Jodie Foster, and Beau Bridges head the cast. **CO5, DR19, ST47**

Hotel Reserve (1944, B&W, 79m, NR)
Eric Ambler thriller set in a French resort during World War II, revolving around the identity of a mysterious stranger. James Mason stars, with Lucille Mannheim, Herbert Lom, and Patricia Medina. **MY6, MY15, ST102**

Hotel Terminus (1988, C/B&W, 267m, NR)
Oscar-winnning documentary from director Marcel Ophuls which explores the trial in Lyons, France, of Nazi torture specialist Klaus Barbie. **CU16, DT75**

Hound of the Baskervilles, The (1938, B&W, 80m, NR)
A wealthy British family is cursed by a violent hound until Sherlock Holmes (Basil Rathbone) solves the mystery. The first of the series starring Rathbone and Nigel Bruce. **HF14**

Hound of the Baskervilles, The (1959, C, 84m, NR)
Peter Cushing portrays Sherlock Holmes in this remake of the Conan Doyle novel. Produced by Hammer Films; costarring Christopher Lee. **HF14, ST27, ST89**

Hound of the Baskervilles, The (1977, C, 84m, PG)
Sherlock Holmes spoof starring Peter Cook as the great detective, Dudley Moore as Watson (and Holmes' mother), plus Denholm Elliott, Joan Greenwood, Spike Milligan, and Roy Kinnear. Directed by Paul Morrissey. **DT72, HF14, ST109**

Hour of the Star (1985, C, 96m, NR)
A 19-year-old girl from the impoverished northern region of Brazil holds fast to her dream of some day breaking out of her dreary surroundings. **FF6**

House (1986, C, 93m, R)
A novelist (William Katt), plagued by the break-up of his marriage and the disappearance of his son, moves to a house where his late aunt hung herself. **HO3, HO19**

House by the River, The (1950, B&W, 88m, NR)
Melodrama of a dishonest man who commits a crime and gets his wife and brother involved. Louis Hayward, Jane Wyatt, and Lee Bowman star. Directed by Fritz Lang. **DT58**

House Calls (1978, C, 98m, PG)
A widowed doctor (Walter Matthau), who enjoys the single life, meets an opinionated divorcee (Glenda Jackson), who wants a commitment. Art Carney costars in this romantic comedy. **CO1, ST104**

House of Fear (1945, B&W, 69m, NR)
Sherlock Holmes (Basil Rathbone) and Dr. Watson (Nigel Bruce) investigate a murder at Drearcliff, a club whose members are being killed off one at a time. **HF14**

House of Games (1987, C, 102m, R)
A psychologist (Lindsay Crouse) whose patient is a compulsive gambler seeks out the con men who have set him up. Fascinated by their techniques, she allows herself get used by one (Joe Mantegna), then seeks revenge. Written and directed by David Mamet. **DR15, MY9** *Recommended*

House of the Long Shadows (1983, C, 96m, PG)
Four notable horror film stars— Vincent Price, Peter Cushing, John Carradine, and Christopher Lee—have small roles in this tale of a mystery writer (Desi Arnaz, Jr.) spending the night with his girlfriend at mysterious mansion. **HO19, ST27, ST89, ST124**

House of Usher *see* The Fall of the House of Usher

House of Wax (1953, C, 88m, PG)
A vengeful sculptor (Vincent Price), disfigured by a fire, rebuilds his gallery by using human corpses as wax statues. With Frank Lovejoy and Charles Buchinski (Charles Bronson). Remake of *Mystery of the Wax Museum*. **CU18, HO1, HO19, ST12, ST124**

House on Carroll Street, The (1988, C, 111m, PG-13)
Thriller set in 1950s New York, with a photo researcher uncovering a plot to smuggle Nazis into the country. Kelly McGillis, Jeff Daniels, and Mandy Patinkin star. **MY3, MY6**

House on Haunted Hill (1958, B&W, 75m, NR)
Vincent Price plays a wealthy eccentric who offers a group of people $50,000 each if they'll spend the night in a mansion with a history of murder. **HO3, HO19, ST124**

House Party (1990, C, 100m, R)
Comedy centering around a black youth's attempts to make it to the hippest party of the week. Christopher Reid and Christopher Martin (the rap group Kid 'n Play) star, with Robin Harris. **CO4** *Recommended*

House That Dripped Blood, The (1971, C, 101m, NR)
Christopher Lee, Peter Cushing, and Denholm Elliot star in this four-part horror story about a new owner of a mysterious looking mansion who has doubts about living there. **HO23, ST27, ST89**

House 2: The Second Story (1987, C, 88m, PG-13)
Sequel in name only to *House*, with another young man discovering evil that lurks behind the walls of a creepy piece of real estate. **HO3**

House Where Evil Dwells, The (1982, C, 88m, R)
An American family moves into a house in Japan, ignoring warnings that the house is dominated by the ghosts of a 19th-century love affair that ended in tragedy. **HO3**

Houseboat (1958, C, 110m, NR)
A Washington, D.C., widower (Cary Grant) with three children hires a housekeeper (Sophia Loren), and romance blossoms. **ST57, ST93, XT12**

Housekeeper, The (1986, C, 96m, R)
An illiterate woman with severely repressed anxieties takes a job as a maid to a well-to-do family—with murderous results. Rita Tushingham stars. Also known as *Judgment in Stone*. **MY13**

Housekeeping (1987, C, 117m, PG)
Two orphaned sisters are taken in by their loony aunt in this drama set in Montana in the 1940s. Christine Lahti stars, with Sara Walker and Andrea Burchill. Bill Forsyth directed; based on a novel by Marilynne Robinson. **DR9, DR10, DR19, DT38** *Recommended*

How I Got Into College (1989, C, 89m, PG-13)
A high school senior (Corey Parker) determines his choice of colleges by where a certain young lady (Lara Flynn Boyle) is going. **CO18**

How I Won the War (1967, C, 109m, PG)
A man recalls his career in World War II with hilariously exagerrated details. Michael Crawford stars, with John Lennon, Michael Hordern, and Roy Kinnear in this dark comedy from director Richard Lester. **CO6, CO12, CO17, CO21, DT62, MU12** *Recommended*

How the West Was Won (1963, C, 165m, G)
Spencer Tracy narrates this monumental drama about the men and the women who explored and settled the great American West. John Wayne, Henry Fonda, and James Stewart star, with Gregory Peck as Abraham Lincoln. John Ford directed one of the four segments. **DT36, HF17, ST44, ST119, ST143, ST151, ST156, WE1, WE6, XT19**

How To Beat the High Cost of Living (1980, C, 105m, PG)
Susan Saint James, Jane Curtin, and Jessica Lange play three fed-up housewives who plan a robbery at a local shopping mall. **CO13, MY18, ST86**

How To Get Ahead in Advertising (1989, C, 95m, R)
British satire of the ad game, with Richard E. Grant a rising executive who's troubled by a strange growth on his neck that takes on a life of its own. With Rachel Ward. Written and directed by Bruce Robinson. **CO2, CO17**

How To Marry a Millionaire (1953, C, 95m, NR)
Marilyn Monroe, Betty Grable, and Lauren Bacall are the man-hungry young women in pursuit of rich husbands in this comedy. With William Powell, Rory Calhoun, and David Wayne. **ST108, ST122**

How To Murder Your Wife (1965, C, 118m, NR)
Jack Lemmon stars in a comedy about a cartoonist who marries a lovely woman in a weak moment and learns she's a shrew. His solution to his problems are described in the title. With Virna Lisi and Terry-Thomas. **CO10, ST90**

How To Succeed in Business Without Really Trying (1967, C, 121m, NR)
Title says it all, in this Broadway musical starring Robert Morse as the aspiring window washer making good in Rudy Vallee's conglomerate. Michele Lee costars. **MU2**

Howard the Duck (1986, C, 111m, PG)
A duck from another planet comes to Earth and saves the planet from alien invaders. Spoofy special effects comedy stars Lea Thompson. **CO9, CO20**

Howards of Virginia, The (1940, B&W, 140m, NR)
Cary Grant plays a colonial during the Revolutionary War, caught between his father-in-law's loyalist views and his own principles. **ST57**

Howie From Maui *See* HBO Comedy Club

Howling, The (1981, C, 90m, R)
Gory tale of a news reporter sent to a California retreat after she experiences a sexual trauma, only to realize that everyone there is a werewolf. Joe Dante directed; memorable transformation scenes, plenty of in-jokes about other horror movies. Dee Wallace stars, with Patrick Macnee, Dennis Dugan, Kevin McCarthy, John Carradine, Slim Pickens, and (very briefly) Roger Corman. Written by John Sayles. **DT25, DT93, HO4, HO17** *Recommended*

Howling II (1985, C, 98m, R)
After the death of his sister, a law officer discovers that she may have been the victim of a werewolf. Christopher Lee stars in this name-only sequel. Full title: *Howling II: Your Sister Is a Werewolf.* **HO4, ST89**

Howling III: The Marsupials (1987, C, 94m, R)
Australia is the setting for this horror tale about a scientist's investigation into a new breed of werewolf. Barry Otto stars. **HO4**

Howling IV, The (1988, C, 92m, R)
Fourth installment in werewolf series has lovely writer on a woodsy retreat, with predictable results. **HO4**

Huckleberry Finn (1975, C, 78m, NR)
TV movie version of Mark Twain's classic, starring Ron Howard, with Antonio Fargas, Jack Elam, and Merle Haggard. **DT48, FA3, MU12, WR27**

Hud (1963, B&W, 112m, NR)
In contemporary Texas, an arrogant cattleman plays by his own set of rules—and gets away with it. Paul Newman and Oscar winners Patricia Neal and Melvyn Douglas star. Based on Larry McMurtry's novel, *Horseman, Pass By;* directed by Martin Ritt. **DT87, ST111, WE12, XT3, XT4** *Recommended*

Human Comedy, The (1943, B&W, 118m, NR)
William Saroyan's affectionate portrait of small-town life in World War II America. Mickey Rooney stars, with Frank Morgan, Jackie "Butch" Jenkins, James Craig, and Marsha Hunt. **DR19, DR26, ST133**

Human Condition, The
Part I (1958, B&W, 200m, NR)
Part II (1959, B&W, 180m, NR)
Part III (1961, B&W, 190m, NR)
Epic Japanese tale of a pacifist's wartime experiences. In Part I, Kaji (Tatsuya Nakadai) is sent to Manchuria to supervise mine workers; he is betrayed by his enemies and is eventually served with a draft notice. Part II (originally titled *Road to Eternity*) finds Kaji at the front, where he distinguishes himself in battle. In Part III (original title: *A Soldier's Prayer*), Kaji is thrown into despair during the final days of the war, as he comes to understand the true madness of the conflict. Directed by and co-written by Masaki Kobayashi. **FF4**

Human Desire (1954, B&W, 90m, NR)
Drama of weak-willed man involved with a married woman, who'd like to be rid of her husband. Glenn Ford, Gloria Grahame, and Broderick Crawford star. Fritz Lang directed this remake of Jean Renoir's *La Bête Humaine.* **CU18, DT58, FF8**

Human Gorilla, The (1948, B&W, 62m, NR)
Low-budget thriller of a reporter who tracks a judge under suspicion of illegal activity to an asylum. Richard Carlson and Lucille Bremer star. Directed by Oscar (Budd) Boetticher. Original title: *Behind Locked Doors*. **DT10, MY1**

Human Monster, The (1939, B&W, 73m, NR)
Bela Lugosi plays the evil owner of a home for blind men. He persuades them to buy more life insurance, then plots to kill them off. **HO9, ST95**

Human Vapor, The (1964, B&W, 79m, NR)
Japanese science fiction drama of an experiment which transforms a man into a gaseous, deadly monster. **FF5, SF18**

Humanoids From the Deep (1980, C, 80m, R)
A seaside village is menaced by mutated sea monsters who rape women to produce their offspring. Doug McClure, Vic Morrow, and Ann Turkel star. Trashy fun. **HO16, HO25** *Recommended*

Hunchback of Notre Dame, The (1923, B&W, 93m, NR)
Lon Chaney, Sr. portrays the Parisian hunchback in this first film version of the Victor Hugo novel. **ST16**

Hunchback of Notre Dame, The (1939, B&W, 115m, NR)
Charles Laughton plays the handicapped bell-ringer, who is attracted to a beautiful Gypsy girl (Maureen O'Hara) in this version of Victor Hugo's classic. Cedric Hardwicke costars. **CL1** *Recommended*

Hunger, The (1983, C, 97m, R)
A 2000-year old vampire (Catherine Deneuve) searches for fresh blood in a new lover to replace her old one (David Bowie), who is aging rapidly. Susan Sarandon costars. **HO5, MU12, ST29**

Hunt for Red October, The (1990, C, 137m, PG)
A Soviet super-submarine sails toward the United States—is it defecting or about to attack America? This adaptation of Tom Clancy's thriller stars Sean Connery and Alec Baldwin, with Scott Glenn, Sam Neill, James Earl Jones, Joss Ackland, and Courtney B. Vance. Directed by John McTiernan. **MY6, ST21, ST76** *Recommended*

Hunter, The (1980, C, 97m, PG)
Steve McQueen stars as contemporary bounty hunter Pappy Thorson in this action thriller set in Chicago. With Eli Wallach, Kathryn Harrold, and LeVar Burton. **AC8, ST97, XT11**

Hunter's Blood (1987, C, 102m, R)
Five city boys hunting in the country run afoul of some nasty poachers. Sam Bottoms, Kim Delaney, and Clu Gulager star in this survival adventure. **AC24**

Hurricane, The (1937, B&W, 102m, NR)
John Ford directed this tale of a South Seas island and its inhabitants being tormented by a vindictive governor. Climactic storm scenes will blow you away. Dorothy Lamour, Jon Hall, and Mary Astor star; John Ford directed. **AC13, AC23, DT36**

Hurricane (1979, C, 119m, PG)
Remake of disaster story set on an otherwise idyllic South Pacific isle. Jason Robards and Mia Farrow star, with Max von Sydow and Trevor Howard. **AC23, ST129**

Hush . . . Hush, Sweet Charlotte (1965, B&W, 133m, NR)
Bette Davis plays a victimized Southern woman who cannot live down a scandal from her past. Olivia de Havilland and Joseph Cotten costar in this camp cult favorite. **CU2, ST28**

Hustle (1975, C, 120m, R)
Burt Reynolds stars as a detective who gets involved with a call girl (Catherine Deneuve) while investigating a suicide. With Paul Winfield. Directed by Robert Aldrich. **AC9, MY2, ST29, ST128, ST162** *Recommended*

Hustler, The (1961, B&W, 135m, NR)
Paul Newman plays Fast Eddie Felson, a jaded drifter with a talent for shooting pool who challenges the champ, Minnesota Fats (Jackie Gleason). George C. Scott and Piper Laurie costar in this superb drama from writer-director Robert Rossen. Based on a novel by Walter Tevis. **DR22, ST111** *Essential; Highly Recommended*

I Am a Camera (1955, B&W, 98m, NR)
The John van Druten play of Sally Bowles, a young American living in pre-World War II Berlin, performing in a decadent nightclub. Julie Harris stars, with Laurence Harvey and Shelley Winters. Musical remake: *Cabaret*. **DR20, ST164**

I Am a Fugitive From a Chain Gang (1932, B&W, 93m, NR)
Dramatic story of an innocent man (Paul Muni) who is sentenced to prison, victimized by the system. **CL8** *Essential*

I Am the Cheese (1983, C, 95m, PG)
Drama of a young boy who witnesses his parent's deaths, and the fantasies he imagines while under a doctor's care. **FA7**

I Am the Law (1938, B&W, 83m, NR)
Edward G. Robinson plays a law professor hired to clean up a corrupt city government. With Otto Kruger and Wendy Barrie. **ST130**

I Confess (1953, B&W, 95m, NR)
Montgomery Clift portrays a priest who hears a confession of murder and becomes the prime suspect due to his vows of silence. Directed by Alfred Hitchcock. **DT46, MY7**

I Could Go On Singing (1963, C, 99m, NR)
In her final film, Judy Garland plays an American singer on tour in London battling personal problems. Dirk Bogarde costars. **DR12, ST51**

I Dream Too Much (1935, B&W, 95m, NR)
Henry Fonda plays an American composer having marital problems with his lovely opera star wife (Lily Pons). **ST44**

I Hate Your Guts *see* Shame (1961)

I Love You (1981, C, 104, R)
Brazilian drama of a man with nothing left to lose, who finds love. Sonia Braga stars. **FF6, ST9**

I Love You, Alice B. Toklas (1968, C, 93m, R)
Peter Sellers plays a successful Los Angeles lawyer who becomes involved with a lovely flower child (Leigh-Taylor Young) in this comedy co-written by Paul Mazursky. **CO2, ST137**

I Love You to Death (1990, C, 96m, R)
Dark comedy, based on true story, of woman trying unsuccessfully to have her unfaithful husband murdered. Kevin Kline and Tracey Ullman star, with Joan Plowright, River Phoenix, William Hurt, and Keanu Reeves. Directed by Lawrence Kasdan. **CO10, CO12, ST75, ST84**

I Married a Monster From Outer Space (1958, B&W, 78m, NR)
Newlywed can't figure out her husband's strange behavior. Tom Tryon and Gloria Talbot star in this classic of 1950s science fiction. **SF1, SF9** *Recommended*

I Married a Witch (1942, B&W, 77m, NR)
Fantasy comedy about a pesky sorceress (Veronica Lake) determined to make mischief on the descendants of the Puritan (Fredric March) who had her burned at the stake 300 years ago. **SF2**

I Married an Angel (1942, B&W, 84m, NR)
Nelson Eddy and Jeanette MacDonald's swan song as a screen team, the light-hearted tale of a playboy and the heavenly lady who tames him. **CL15**

I Never Sang for My Father (1970, C, 93m, PG)
A middle-aged man (Gene Hackman) takes the responsibility of caring for his elderly, stubborn father (Melvyn Douglas) after his mother dies. With Estelle Parsons; based on a play by Robert Anderson. **DR8, DR11, DR20, ST61**

I Ought To Be in Pictures (1982, C, 107m, PG)
A young New Yorker (Dinah Manoff) travels to Los Angeles to make it in the movies, but her real ambition is to find her father (Walter Matthau). Based on the Neil Simon play. **CO5, ST104, WR23**

I Remember Mama (1948, B&W, 134m, NR)
George Stevens directed this heartwarming film of an immigrant family from Norway adjusting to life in San Francisco. Irene Dunne and Barbara Bel Geddes star. **DT101**

I Sent a Letter to My Love (1981, C, 96m, PG)
A woman and her invalid brother unknowingly begin a romance in a newspaper personals column. Simone Signoret

and Jean Rochefort star in this French drama. **FF1**

I Shot Jesse James (1949, B&W, 81m, NR)
The true tale of Bob Ford, the man who killed the West's most famous desperado (Reed Hadley). Director Sam Fuller's first film. **DT40, HF16**

I Stand Condemned (1935, B&W, 75m, NR)
An officer gets framed by his superior as a spy in a fit of jealousy over a woman. Laurence Olivier stars in one of his early films. **ST116**

I, the Jury (1982, C, 111m, R)
Hard-boiled detective Mike Hammer is played by Armand Assante in this Mickey Spillane thriller. **WR24**

I Wake Up Screaming (1941, B&W, 82m, NR)
An actress' agent (Victor Mature) is the prime suspect in her murder, and he turns to her sister (Betty Grable) for help in clearing his name. With Laird Creagar and Carole Landis. **MY1, MY7**

I Walked With a Zombie (1943, B&W, 69m, NR)
Classic horror tale of nurse coming to Haiti to treat victim of coma-like state, discovering voodoo rituals. Directed by Jacques Tourneur; produced by Val Lewton. **CU4, DT105, HO1, HO6, HO27** *Recommended*

I Wanna Hold Your Hand (1978, C, 104m, PG)
Charming comedy about a group of teenagers who use every trick they can think of to get tickets to the Beatles' debut on *The Ed Sullivan Show* in 1964. Robert Zemeckis directed a lively cast, including Nancy Allen, Bobby DiCicco, Mark McClure, Wendy Jo Sperber, Eddie Deezen, and, as Sullivan, Will Jordan. **CO6** *Recommended*

I Want To Live! (1958, B&W, 122m, NR)
This classic prison drama deals with the story of Barbara Graham, who was framed for murder and sent to the gas chamber. Susan Hayward won an Academy Award for her performance, directed by Robert Wise. **DR18, DT117, XT3**

I Will Fight No More Forever (1975, C, 100m, NR)
Historical account of Chief Joseph, who led his tribe on a 1600 mile trek to Canada to avoid a U. S. Cavalry battle. James Whitmore stars. Originally made for TV. **WE7**

I Will, I Will . . . For Now (1976, C, 110m, R)
Diane Keaton and Elliott Gould play a couple who are bored with their ten-year marriage. They try every means, including therapy and a sex clinic to rekindle the spark. **ST79**

Ice Palace (1960, C, 143m, NR)
Edna Ferber saga set in Alaska, about two friends (Richard Burton, Robert Ryan) turned rivals. With Carolyn Jones, Martha Hyer, Jim Backus, and Shirley Knight. **ST13**

Ice Pirates, The (1984, C, 93, PG)
Science fiction comedy about band of lovable cutthroats out to hijack a drought-stricken galaxy's water supply. Robert Urich, Mary Crosby, and Anjelica Huston star. **SF21**

Ice Station Zebra (1968, C, 148m, G)
Cold War drama under the icecap of the North Pole, starring Rock Hudson as a submarine commander. With Ernest Borgnine, Patrick McGoohan, Jim Brown, and Tony Bill. **MY6, ST73**

Idaho (1943, B&W, 70m, NR)
Roy Rogers and Smiley Burnette clear a judge who's been framed for murder. **ST132**

Identity Crisis (1989, C, 90m, R)
The sudden death of a French fashion designer results in his reincarnation in the body of a hip black street dude. Mario van Peebles stars in this comedy directed by his father, Melvin. **CO20**

Idiot's Delight (1939, B&W, 105m, NR)
Clark Gable, as a song and dance man and Norma Shearer, as his former love, are stranded in a hotel in the Italian Alps at the outset of World War II. Comedy-drama features Gable performing "Puttin' on the Ritz." **MU17, ST49**

Idolmaker, The (1980, C, 119m, PG)
This fictionalized biography of music producer Bob Marcucci shows how he

pushed rock singers Frankie Avalon and Fabian to the top of the charts in the early days of rock 'n' roll. Ray Sharkey stars. Taylor Hackford directed. **DR12, MU4, MU9**

if . . . (1969, C/B&W, 111m, R)
Rebellious boys at a British boarding school finally resort to violence in this drama with darkly comic overtones. Malcolm McDowell stars. Lindsay Anderson directed. **DR9, DR25** *Essential; Recommended*

Ikiru (1952, B&W, 143m, NR)
Japanese drama of a bureaucrat who finds that he has terminal cancer and searches for a sense of purpose in his life. Akira Kurosawa directed. Takashi Shimura stars. **DT57** *Essential; Recommended*

I'll Cry Tomorrow (1956, B&W, 120m, NR)
Susan Hayward plays singer-actress Lillian Roth, whose battles with the bottle were the stuff of show-biz legend. **CL2, CL5**

Ill Met by Moonlight (1957, B&W, 93m, NR)
World War II drama, set in Nazi-occupied Crete, about British commandos kidnapping a German general. Michael Powell directed. Also known as *Night Ambush.* **DT81**

I'm All Right, Jack (1960, B&W, 104m, NR)
British comedy of a factory owner's elaborately crooked schemes being upset by the arrival of his strait-laced nephew. Ian Carmichael and Peter Sellers star. **CO17, ST137**

I'm Dancing as Fast as I Can (1982, C, 106m, PG)
TV producer gets hooked on pills and tries to quit cold turkey, with nearly disastrous results. Jill Clayburgh stars in this true story. **DR10**

I'm Gonna Git You Sucka (1989, C, 89m, R)
Spoof of blaxploitation films, starring Ivory Keenen Wayans (who wrote and directed), with Bernie Casey, Antonio Fargas, Jim Brown, and Isaac Hayes. **CO7, MU12** *Recommended*

Imagine: John Lennon (1988, C, 103m, R)
Documentary tribute to the late musician, singer, and activist, with rare footage from his Beatle days and subsequent years of marriage to Yoko Ono. **MU11**

Imitation of Life (1959, C, 124m, NR)
Glossy tear jerker deals with a white actress, her black housekeeper, and the conflicts they share with their teenage daughters. Lana Turner and Sandra Dee star. Douglas Sirk directed. **CL6, DR2, DT98, ST153**

Immediate Family (1989, C, 95m, PG-13)
Childless, middle-class couple decide to adopt a baby conceived by a young woman and her boyfriend. Glenn Close, James Woods, Mary Stuart Masterson, and Kevin Dillon star. **DR8, ST20, ST165**

Immortal Bachelor, The (1979, C, 95m, NR)
In this Italian comedy, a woman juror (Claudia Cardinale) is skeptical of a female defendant's story—she killed her unfaithful husband—because the man sounds so attractive. With Monica Vitti and Giancarlo Giannini. **FF2**

Immortal Sergeant, The (1943, B&W, 91m, NR)
Henry Fonda plays an inexperienced corporal who has to take command of the troops after their sergeant dies. **ST44**

Importance of Being Earnest, The (1952, C, 95m, NR)
Oscar Wilde's comedy of manners set in Victorian England stars Michael Redgrave and Margaret Rutherford. **CL1**

Impulse (1990, C, 108m, R)
Theresa Russell plays an undercover cop who unwittingly becomes involved with a killer. With Jeff Fahey and George Dzundza. Directed by Sondra Locke. **MY3**

In a Lonely Place (1950, B&W, 93m, NR)
Humphrey Bogart is a frustrated screenwriter in this moody drama from director Nicholas Ray. Gloria Grahame costars. **DT83, MY1, ST8**

In a Shallow Grave (1988, C, 91m, R)
Low-key drama of a scarred war veteran's passion for the girl he left behind but couldn't forget. Michael Biehn and Pat-

rick Dempsey star in this adaptation of the James Purdy novel. **DR1**

In Cold Blood (1967, B&W, 134m, NR)
Drama based on Truman Capote's famed "non-fiction novel" about the senseless murder of a Kansas family by two drifters. Scott Wilson and Robert Blake star. Richard Brooks wrote and directed. **DR6, DR16** *Recommended*

In Country (1989, C, 120m, NR)
Drama of teenager trying to come to grips with the father she never knew—killed almost twenty years before in Vietnam. Emily Lloyd stars, with Bruce Willis, Joan Allen, and Kevin Anderson. Based on the novel by Bobbie Ann Mason; final scene shot at Washington, D.C.'s Vietnam Veterans Memorial. **DR7, DR8, DR19, ST161, XT12**

In Harm's Way (1965, B&W, 165m, NR)
All-star cast in World War II yarn of Navy heroics in the South Pacific, with John Wayne, Kirk Douglas, Patricia Neal, Brandon de Wilde, Jill Haworth, Burgess Meredith, Tom Tryon, Franchot Tone, Patrick Neal, George Kennedy, Slim Pickens, and Henry Fonda. Directed by Otto Preminger. **AC1, DT82, ST34, ST44, ST156**

In Name Only (1939, B&W, 94m, NR)
Cary Grant plays a married man trying to escape a loveless marriage for his beautiful mistress (Carole Lombard). **CL6, ST57, ST92**

In Old Amarillo (1951, B&W, 68m, NR)
During a drought, a courageous cowboy (Roy Rogers) organizes local ranchers. **ST132**

In Old Caliente (1939, B&W, 54m, NR)
A cowpoke (Roy Rogers) is framed for theft by an evil half-breed. With Gabby Hayes. **ST132**

In Old California (1942, B&W, 88m, NR)
A young Boston pharmacist (John Wayne) goes West during the California gold rush. **ST156**

In Old Santa Fe (1934, B&W, 60m, NR)
Gene Autry helps veteran plainsman Ken Maynard recover his horse from bandits. **ST3**

In Search of the Castaways (1962, C, 80m, NR)
An expedition looks for a missing sea captain, and along the way encounters many hardships. Hayley Mills, Maurice Chevalier, and George Sanders star in this Disney adventure based on a Jules Verne story. **FA1, WR28**

In the Good Old Summertime (1948, C, 102m, NR)
Judy Garland and Van Johnson star in this musical remake of *The Shop Around The Corner*, about two coworkers who unknowingly become pen pals. **MU1, MU14, ST51**

In the Heat of the Night (1967, C, 109m, NR)
Oscar winner Rod Steiger plays a small-town Southern sheriff who unwillingly receives help from a black police detective (Sidney Poitier) in a murder case. With Warren Oates and Lee Grant. Directed by Norman Jewison. Winner of four other Oscars, including Best Picture. **DT51, MY10, ST115, ST121, XT1, XT2***Essential*

In the Mood (1987, C, 100m, PG-13)
Comedy based on the true story of Sonny Wisecarver, a 1940s teenager who ran away to marry an older woman and became known as The Woo-Woo Kid. **CO6**

In the Shadow of Kilimanjaro (1986, C, 97m, R)
During a severe drought in the African bush country, herds of baboons begin attacking humans. **HO16**

In the Spirit (1990, C, 93m, R)
Comedy of a Californian (Elaine May) who moves to New York with her husband (Peter Falk) and is befriended by a ditsy mystic (Marlo Thomas). With Jeannie Berlin (May's daughter, who also co-wrote the screenplay) and Melanie Griffith. **CO2, CO12, DT70, ST58, XT8**

In This Our Life (1942, B&W, 97m, NR)
Bette Davis plays the meddling sister to Olivia de Havilland in this melodrama directed by John Huston. With George Brent, Dennis Morgan, and Charles Coburn. **CL5, DT50, ST28**

In Which We Serve (1942, B&W, 115m, NR)
World War II drama of men on board a British battleship recalling the events that

shaped their lives. Written by Noel Coward, who also stars and co-directed with David Lean. With John Mills, Celia Johnson, and Richard Attenborough. **AC1, DT59**

Incident, The (1967, B&W, 107m, NR)
Two punks terrorize a New York subway car in this urban drama. Tony Musante and Martin Sheen star, with Beau Bridges, Thelma Ritter, Ed McMahon, Jack Gilford, and Gary Merrill. **DR15, XT19**

Incredible Invasion: *see* Sinister Invasion

Incredible Journey, The (1963, C, 80m, NR)
Two dogs and a cat make a 250-mile journey across Canada to be reunited with their human owners in this Disney adventure. **FA1, FA5**

Incredible Mr. Limpet, The (1964, C, 102m, NR)
Family fantasy of a mild-mannered man (Don Knotts) who imagines himself a dolphin who helps the U.S. Navy during World War II. **FA8**

Incredible Sarah, The (1976, C, 105m, PG)
Glenda Jackson plays famed stage and silent screen actress Sarah Bernhardt. Daniel Massey costars. **DR4, DR12**

Incredible Shrinking Man, The (1957, B&W, 81m, NR)
A radioactive mist has a terrifying effect on an ordinary man, who's soon battling a spider five times his size. Classic 1950s science fiction with cult following, directed by Jack Arnold. **CU4, FA8, SF1** *Essential; Recommended*

Incredible Shrinking Woman, The (1981, C, 88m, PG)
This take-off on *The Incredible Shrinking Man* stars Lily Tomlin as a housewife who begins to shrink after exposure to household products. With Charles Grodin and Ned Beatty. **CO11, SF21, ST59, ST149**

Incredibly Strange Creatures Who Stopped Living and Became Mixed-up Zombies, The (1963, C, 82m, NR)
Cult horror story of sideshow proprietor who disfigures patrons and puts them on display in his show. Moody cinematography, atrocious acting and dialogue. **CU4**

Independence Day (1983, C, 110m, R)
Small-town woman with big ambitions yearns to break free, but is held back in part by a romance with a local mechanic. Kathleen Quinlan and David Keith star. **DR1, DR10, DR26**

Indestructible Man, The (1956, B&W, 70m, NR)
A thief returns from the dead to get revenge on his cohorts who betrayed him during a robbery. Lon Chaney, Jr. stars. **ST17**

Indiana Jones and the Last Crusade (1989, C, 127m, PG)
Third Indy adventure unites him with his father for derring-do against the Nazis. Harrison Ford and Sean Connery star, with John Rhys-Davies, Denholm Elliott, Alison Doody, and River Phoenix as the young Indiana. Steven Spielberg directed. Available in a letterboxed edition. **AC21, CU19, DT99, ST21, ST46**

Indiana Jones and the Temple of Doom (1984, C, 118m, PG)
This prequel to *Raiders of the Lost Ark* follows the 1930s archeologist as he tries to save a group of children from a murderous cult. Harrison Ford and Kate Capshaw star. Directed by Steven Spielberg. Available in a letterboxed edition. **AC21, CU19, DT99, ST46**

Indiscreet (1958, C, 100m, NR)
Cary Grant is a playboy who romances a famous actress (Ingrid Bergman) and realizes he may be falling seriously in love. Directed by Stanley Donen. **DT30, ST7, ST57**

Indiscretion of an American Wife (1953, B&W, 87m, NR)
Jennifer Jones and Montgomery Clift play adulterous lovers in this drama from director Vittorio De Sica. Also known as *Terminal Station*. **DT26**

Informer, The (1935, B&W, 91m, NR)
Victor McLaglen won an Oscar for his portrayal of a drunk who turns on a friend to collect reward money during the Irish Rebellion. Oscar-winning direction by John Ford. **DT36, XT2, XT6**

Inherit the Wind (1960, B&W, 127m, NR)
Spencer Tracy, Fredric March, and Gene Kelly star in this drama of the Scopes Monkey Trial of 1925, in which a school-

teacher was indicted for teaching Darwin's theory of evolution. Based on the play by Jerome Lawrence and Robert E. Lee; directed by Stanley Kramer. **DR17, DR20, DT55, ST81, ST151**

Inheritance, The (1976, C, 105m, R)
A dying patriarch plans to disinherit his entire family, save his lovely daughter-in-law, with whom he's having an affair. Italian drama starring Anthony Quinn and Dominique Sanda. **FF2**

Inheritors, The (1984, C, 89m, NR)
German drama of an impressionable youth caught up in a neo-Nazi movement. Directed by Walter Bannert. **FF3**

Initiation of Sarah (1978, C, 96m, NR)
When she pledges a sorority, a young girl with telepathic powers falls under the spell of a witch. **HO7**

In-Laws, The (1979, C, 103m, PG)
A quiet, unassuming dentist (Alan Arkin) gets involved in the bizarre schemes of his daughter's father-in-law (Peter Falk), a man claiming to be a CIA agent. Zany comedy written by Andrew Bergman. **CO3, CO10** *Recommended*

Inn of the Sixth Happiness, The (1958, C, 158m, NR)
A missionary (Ingrid Bergman) leads children through enemy territory in pre-World War II China. Robert Donat co-stars. **ST7**

Innerspace (1987, C, 120m, PG)
Dennis Quaid plays a cocky Navy test pilot who is miniaturized for an experiment but is accidentally injected into the body of a timid grocery store clerk (Martin Short). Joe Dante directed. Available in a letterboxed edition. **CO9, CO11, CO14, CU19, DT25, SF3, SF21**

Innocent Man, An (1989, C, 113m, R)
Tom Selleck stars in this thriller as a man set up by two crooked cops, sent off to prison, plotting his revenge. With F. Murray Abraham. **DR18, MY7**

L'Innocente (1979, C, 115m, R)
A faithless Sicilian husband finds that his lovely wife has her own lovers, too. Giancarlo Giannini and Laura Antonelli star. Director Luchino Visconti's last film. **DT108**

Inserts (1976, C, 99m, R)
Richard Dreyfuss plays a 1930s Hollywood director who has turned to making pornographic movies. With Jessica Harper, Veronica Cartwright, and Bob Hoskins. **DR13, ST36, ST72**

Inside Man, The (1984, C, 90m, NR)
Spy drama, made in Sweden, with agents vying for submarine-detecting device. Dennis Hopper stars. **ST71**

Inside Moves (1980, C, 113m, PG)
A suicide survivor (John Savage) who was left cripped gets involved with a group of handicapped men at a local bar. Through these friends and his love for basketball, he regains his self esteem. **DR22**

Insignificance (1985, C, 105m, R)
"Historical" drama about chance encounters between a scientist, a senator, a lovely movie star, and her baseball player husband—resembling Albert Einstein, Joseph McCarthy, Marilyn Monroe, and Joe DiMaggio. Michael Emil, Tony Curtis, Theresa Russell, and Gary Busey star. Nicolas Roeg directed. **DT88**

Inspector General, The (1949, C, 102m, NR)
Musical comedy featuring Danny Kaye as a man who impersonates a bureaucrat in an Eastern European village. **ST78**

Instant Justice (1986, C, 101m, R)
A marine swears vengeance on the drug smugglers who killed his sister. Michael Pare and Tawny Kitaen star. **AC19, AC25**

Interiors (1978, C, 93m, PG)
Woody Allen wrote and directed this drama of a guilt-ridden family trying to come to terms with each other. Geraldine Page, Diane Keaton, E.G. Marshall, Maureen Stapleton, and Mary Beth Hurt star. **DR8, DT1, ST79**

Intermezzo (1936, B&W, 88m, NR)
Swedish-language drama of a a young pianist (Ingrid Bergman) and her affair with a married violinist (Gosta Ekman). Remade two years later in the U.S. **FF7, FF8, ST7**

Intermezzo (1939, B&W, 70m, NR)
Remake of Ingrid Bergman's breakthrough Swedish film about a married violinist (Leslie Howard) who falls in love

with his musical protege (Bergman). **CL4, FF8, ST7**

Internal Affairs (1990, C, 117m, R)
Drama of two L.A. cops, one a corrupt womanizer (Richard Gere), the other a newly married internal investigator (Andy Garcia) on his trail. With Nancy Travis and Laurie Metcalf. Directed by Mike Figgis. **DR16, ST52, MY9, XT10** *Recommended*

International House (1933, B&W, 70m, NR)
W.C. Fields stars with George Burns & Gracie Allen in this comedy set in a hotel in China, where a scientist has invented television and assorted people come from all over the world to buy the rights. **ST41**

International Velvet (1978, C, 127m, PG)
This sequel to *National Velvet* follows a grown Velvet Brown as she primes her niece to take her place as a champion rider. Tatum O'Neal, Nanette Newman, and Christopher Plummer star. **FA5**

Into the Fire (1987, C, 83m, R)
A weird couple at a remote estate involve a young musician and his girlfriend in a complex murder plot. Susan Anspach and Art Hindle star, with Lee Montgomery and Olivia d'Abo. Also known as *Legend of Wolf Lodge*. **MY9**

Into the Night (1985, C, 115m, R)
An insomniac finds himself involved with a beautiful girl, who is being chased by killers. Michelle Pfeiffer and Jeff Goldblum star in this comic thriller, with cameos by many film directors and pop music stars, including Paul Mazursky, Jonathan Demme, David Cronenberg, Don Siegel, David Bowie, and Carl Perkins. **AC14, CU17, DT28, DT23, DT97, MU12, ST56, ST120**

Intolerance (1916, B&W, 123m, NR)
Four stories about man's inhumanity to man, stretching from ancient times to modern day, are interwoven in this silent classic directed by D.W. Griffith. Lillian Gish, Robert Harron, Mae Marsh, Norma Talmadge, and Bessie Love star, with Howard Gaye as Jesus Christ and Erich Von Stroheim in a small role. **CL12, CL14, DT42, DT109, HF16, ST54** *Essential; Highly Recommended*

Intruder, The *see* Shame (1961)

Invaders From Mars (1953, C, 78m, NR)
Small-town boy sees invasion of aliens who brainwash adults, but he can't get anyone to believe him. Classic 1950s science fiction drama, starring Helena Carter, Arthur Franz, and Jimmy Hunt. **SF1, SF9**

Invaders From Mars (1986, C, 100m, PG)
Karen Black, Hunter Carson, and Laraine Newman star in this remake of the 1953 science fiction thriller. Tobe Hooper directed. **CO13, CU18, DT47, SF9**

Invasion of the Bee Girls (1973, C, 85m, R)
Cult science fiction film about sinister alien force that turns women in a small town into sexually ravenous creatures. **CU4**

Invasion of the Body Snatchers (1956, B&W, 80m, NR)
Pods from outer space begin duplicating humans in zombie-like form. Classic science fiction with political overtones for the 1950s, starring Kevin McCarthy, Dana Wynter, King Donovan, and Carolyn Jones, with Sam Peckinpah in a small role. Directed by Don Siegel. **CU4, DT77, DT97, SF1, SF9** *Essential; Highly Recommended*

Invasion of the Body Snatchers (1978, C, 115m, PG)
Remake of the sci-fi classic, updated to 1970s San Francisco, with pointed commentary on self-help trends. Donald Sutherland and Brooke Adams star, with Jeff Goldblum, Veronica Cartwright, and Leonard Nimoy. Directed by Philip Kaufman. **CU4, CU18, DT52, SF9, ST56, XT13** *Highly Recommended*

Invasion U.S.A. (1985, C, 107m, R)
Chuck Norris does his very best to thwart a Russian-backed invasion of America. **AC20, ST114**

Investigation (1979, C, 116m, R)
French thriller set in a vilage where a businessman murders his wife to marry his pregnant mistress. Victor Lanoux, Jean Carmet, and Valerie Mairesse star. **FF1**

Invisible Ghost, The (1941, B&W, 64m, NR)
A man commits murder after his domineering wife hypnotizes him. Bela Lugosi stars. **ST95**

Invisible Man, The (1933, B&W, 71m, NR)
Claude Rains' debut, as he stars in the H. G. Wells story of the mad scientist who makes himself invisible and causes great problems in a small British town. Directed by James Whale. **DT115, HO1, HO20, WR29, XT21** *Recommended*

Invisible Ray, The (1936, B&W, 81m, NR)
Boris Karloff plays a man whose exposure to radiation during an experiment slowly destroys his mind. Bela Lugosi costars. **HO21, ST77, ST95**

Invitation to the Dance (1957, C, 93m, NR)
Gene Kelly directed and stars in this trio of stories told in dance. **MU1, MU3, ST81**

Ipcress File, The (1965, C, 108m, NR)
Michael Caine stars in the first of his three films as Harry Palmer, a British crook who becomes a spy. Based on the character created by Len Deighton. **MY6, ST15**

Iphigenia (1978, C, 127m, NR)
Irene Papas stars in this screen version of the classic Greek tragedy *Iphigenia in Aulis*. **FF7**

Irezumi (1983, C, 88m, R)
Japanese drama of sensual obsession, featuring a woman who has her back elaborately tattooed by her lover. Directed by Yoichi Takabayashi. Also known as *Spirit of Tattoo*. **FF4**

Irma La Douce (1963, C, 142m, NR)
A Paris policeman (Jack Lemmon) falls for a prostitute (Shirley MacLaine), and tries hard to keep her for himself. Comedy directed by Billy Wilder. **DT116, ST90, ST96**

Iron Eagle (1986, C, 117m, PG-13)
When an Air Force officer is taken hostage by terrorists in Northern Africa, his teenaged son and another officer commandeer two jets and attempt a daring rescue mission. Jason Gedrick and Louis Gossett, Jr. star. **AC11**

Iron Eagle II (1988, C, 105m, PG)
More aerial action with Louis Gossett, Jr.. teaming up with the Soviets to wipe out a Middle East nuclear missile installation. Rock soundtrack features Alice Cooper's version of "I Got a Line on You." **AC11**

Iron Triangle, The (1988, C, 94m, R)
Vietnam war drama, told from Vietcong point of view, of American officer's capture and treatment by the enemy. Beau Bridges stars, with Haing S. Ngor. **AC4**

Ironweed (1987, C, 143m, R)
Jack Nicholson and Meryl Streep star as alcoholic outcasts weathering the storm of the Great Depression. Based on the novel by William Kennedy. With Tom Waits. **DR19, MU12, ST112, ST145**

Irreconcilable Differences (1984, C, 117m, PG)
A young girl sues her selfish, materialistic parents for divorce in this modern comedy-drama. Ryan O'Neal, Shelley Long, and Drew Barrymore star. **CO5, DR8**

Isadora (1969, C, 153m, PG)
Vanessa Redgrave plays Isadora Duncan, who was as famous for her free-spirited lifestyle as she was for her influence on modern dance. With Jason Robards and James Fox. Directed by Karel Reisz. Video version restores some footage cut after original theatrical release. **CU10, DR4, ST127, ST129** *Recommended*

Ishtar (1987, C, 107m, PG)
Warren Beatty and Dustin Hoffman play two untalented singer-songwriters who can only get a gig in a war-torn North African kingdom. With Charles Grodin and Isabelle Adjani. Written and directed by Elaine May. **CO3, DT70, ST5, ST59, ST67**

Island, The (1962, B&W, 96m, NR)
Japanese drama, with no dialogue, about family's struggle to survive on a rocky island. Directed by Kaneto Shindo. **FF4**

Island, The (1980, C, 114m, R)
Harrowing drama of modern-day pirates kidnapping an unsuspecting tourist and his son in the Caribbean. Michael Caine and David Warner star. **ST15**

Island at the Top of the World (1974, C, 93m, G)
An arctic expedition uncovers a Viking civilization thought to be extinct. Adventure from the Disney studios. **FA1**

Island Monster (1953, B&W, 87m, NR)
A group of cut-throat drug smugglers elude the law. Boris Karloff stars. **ST77**

Island of Dr. Moreau, The (1977, C, 104m, PG)
Burt Lancaster plays a mad doctor who creates "humanimals" in his island laboratory. Based on an H. G. Wells story. Michael York and Barbara Carrera co-star. **HO20, ST85, WR29**

Island of the Blue Dolphins (1964, C, 93m, NR)
Family adventure set in the 19th century, about a young Indian girl abandoned on a desert island and befriended by a pack of wild dogs. Celia Kaye stars. **FA4**

Islands in the Stream (1977, C, 105m, PG)
Drama based on Ernest Hemingway novel about an artist living in the Caribbean and his relationships with his three sons. George C. Scott stars, with David Hemmings, Claire Bloom, Susan Tyrrell, and Gilbert Roland. **DR8, DR19, WR10**

Isle of the Dead (1945, B&W, 72m, NR)
Boris Karloff stars in this tale about a group of mysterious people stranded on a quarantined Greek Island. Produced by Val Lewton. **HO6, HO27, ST77**

It (1927, B&W, 72m, NR)
Clara Bow plays the "it" girl, a gold-digger who has designs on her boss, in this silent comedy. Gary Cooper has a small role. **CL11, ST22** *Essential*

It Came From Beneath the Sea (1955, B&W, 80m, NR)
Science fiction monster story of massive octopus wreaking havoc in San Francisco. Kenneth Tobey and Faith Domergue star. Special effects by Ray Harryhausen. **SF10**

It Came From Hollywood (1982, C, 80m, PG)
Comedy stars, including Gilda Radner, Dan Aykroyd, and Cheech & Chong, introduce scenes from some of Hollywood's worst science fiction and horror films. **CO13, ST18**

It Came From Outer Space (1953, B&W, 81m, NR)
Classic 1950s science fiction from director Jack Arnold, about an alien spaceship crashing in the desert and its passengers assuming human identities. Richard Carlson and Barbara Rush star. **SF1, SF9** *Recommended*

It Happened at the World's Fair (1963, C, 105m, NR)
Elvis Presley plays a pilot who finds romance during the Seattle World's Fair. **ST123**

It Happened One Night (1934, B&W, 105m, NR)
Clark Gable is a newspaper reporter who meets an heiress (Claudette Colbert); she's running away from her father who is against her marriage. This classic comedy was an Academy Award winner for Best Actor, Best Actress, Best Picture, and Best Director (Frank Capra). **CL10, DT16, ST49, XT1, XT2, XT3, XT6, XT18** *Essential; Highly Recommended*

It Happened One Summer *see* State Fair (1945)

It Lives Again (1978, C, 91m, R)
Sequel to *It's Alive,* featuring more mayhem, this time by three demonic infants. Frederic Forrest and Kathleen Lloyd star. Directed by Larry Cohen. **DT20, HO13**

It Should Happen to You (1954, B&W, 81m, NR)
Judy Holliday plays an unemployed actress who uses her savings to buy New York City billboards to publicize her name. This comedy marked Jack Lemmon's film debut. Directed by George Cukor. **DT24, ST69, ST90, XT9**

It Takes Two (1988, C, 79m, PG-13)
Comedy about a young couple about to be married, only he's getting cold feet. His solution—buy the sportscar of his dreams and ride off for a fling. George Newbern and Leslie Hope star. **CO1**

Italian Straw Hat (1927, B&W, 72m, NR)
Rene Clair directed this silent French comedy of a misunderstanding in which newlyweds must find a replacement for a hat eaten by a horse. **FFA**

It's a Gift (1934, B&W, 73m, NR)
W.C. Fields plays a grocer bedeviled by insomnia, clumsy blind men, and an indifferent family. A classic comedy, perhaps Fields' funniest. **CL10, CU5, ST41** *Essential; Highly Recommended*

It's a Mad Mad Mad Mad World (1963, C, 154m, NR)
Comedy featuring a truly all-star cast of comic performers, with police detective Spencer Tracy watching a frantic group of people search for stolen bank money. Jonathan Winters, Sid Caesar, Dick Shawn, Phil Silvers, Ethel Merman, and Mickey Rooney are among the treasure hunters; watch for guest appearances by dozens of comic personalities. Directed by Stanley Kramer. **CO9, CU17, DT55, FA6, ST133, ST151, XT18**

It's a Wonderful Life (1946, B&W, 129m, NR)
George Bailey (Jimmy Stewart) wishes he had never been born, and an angel shows him what life in his hometown would have been like without him. With Donna Reed and Lionel Barrymore. Frank Capra directed. **CL6, DT16, FA13, ST143** *Essential*

It's Alive! (1974, C, 91m, PG)
Newborn baby turns into rampaging demon in this cult horror film. Directed by Larry Cohen. Sequel: *It Lives Again.* **DT20, HO13**

It's Always Fair Weather (1955, C, 105m, NR)
Gene Kelly, Dan Dailey, and Michael Kidd are three wartime buddies who meet ten years later, only to find that they have nothing in common. Musical written by Betty Comden and Adolph Green, directed by Kelly and Stanley Donen. **MU1, DT30, ST81**

It's an Adventure, Charlie Brown (1983, C, 50m, NR)
The whole Peanuts gang joins in for these six vignettes about a boy named Charlie Brown. **FA10**

It's Good To Be Alive (1974, C, 100m, NR)
Paul Winfield plays all-star Dodger catcher Roy Campanella, who suffered a paralyzing injury that cut short his career. With Louis Gossett, Jr. and Ruby Dee. Originally made for TV. **DR22, ST162**

It's in the Bag (1945, B&W, 87m, NR)
Rare film outing for comic Fred Allen, as the proprietor of a flea circus in search of a hidden inheritance. His encounter with archrival Jack Benny is a classic bit. **CL10**

It's My Turn (1980, C, 91m, R)
A young New York woman (Jill Clayburgh) tries to have it all as a career woman and a lover. With Michael Douglas and Charles Grodin. **CO1, CO2, ST35, ST59, XT9**

Ivan the Terrible, Part One (1943, B&W, 96m, NR)
Part Two (1946, C, 84m, NR)
Russian director Sergei Eisenstein's historical epic about Czar Ivan IV is packed with mesmerizing imagery and features music by Sergei Prokofiev. Tapes available separately or in one package. **DT33** *Essential; Highly Recommended (both Parts)*

Ivanhoe (1952, C, 106m, NR)
Elizabeth Taylor and Robert Taylor star in this family adventure of knights and their ladies fair, based on the Sir Walter Scott novel. With James Mason and Harold Warrender as Robin Hood. **AC13, FA4, HF15, ST102, ST147**

I've Heard the Mermaids Singing (1987, C, 81m, PG)
Comedy-drama, with cult following, about an aimless young woman who finally finds happiness working at a trendy art gallery. Sheila McCarthy stars. **CO12**

Jabberwocky (1977, C, 100m, PG)
Black comedy set in the Middle Ages, directed by Terry Gilliam, stars Michael Palin, both from the Monty Python troupe. **CO15**

Jack and the Beanstalk (1952, B&W/C, 87m, NR)
Abbott and Costello star in a version of the children's fairy tale. **ST1**

Jack and the Beanstalk (1983, C, 60m, NR)
Dennis Christopher stars as the young boy who trades a cow for magic beans, climbs a beanstalk, and encounters a husband/wife giant team (Jean Stapleton, Elliott Gould) in this classic story from the Faerie Tale Theatre collection. **FA12**

Jack the Ripper (1980, C, 82m, R)
Klaus Kinski plays the notorious lady-killer of Victorian London. **HO9, ST83**

Jackie Chan's Police Force (1987, C, 90m, PG-13)
Martial arts thriller about a cop framed for murder. Jackie Chan stars. **AC9, AC26**

Jackie Mason on Broadway (1988, C, 60m, NR)
Highlights from the veteran comic's one-man Broadway show, *The World According to Me*. **CO16** *Recommended*

Jacknife (1989, C, 102m, R)
A Vietnam veteran (Robert DeNiro) tries to pull his one-time war buddy (Ed Harris) out of postwar trauma. Kathy Baker costars in this topical drama. **DR7, ST30**

Jack's Back (1988, C, 97m, R)
Mystery set in contemporary Los Angeles, where a killer is imitating Jack the Ripper's crimes on their 100th anniversary. James Spader plays a young intern who discovers the killer's identity. Cynthia Gibb is one of the potential victims. **MY3, MY7, MY13** *Recommended*

Jacqueline Susann's Once Is Not Enough
see Once Is Not Enough

Jagged Edge (1985, C, 108m, R)
Glenn Close plays an attorney who gets romantically involved with her client (Jeff Bridges), a newspaper publisher accused of murdering his heiress wife. With Peter Coyote and Robert Loggia. **DR3, DR17, MY3, MY5, ST11, ST20**

Jaguar Lives (1979, C, 91m, PG)
A karate expert is hired to travel all over the world to track down narcotics kingpins. Joe Lewis, Christopher Lee, and Barbara Bach star. **ST89**

Jail Bait (1954, B&W, 70m, NR)
From cult director Ed Wood, Jr. comes the tragic tale of a youth led into a crime and then forced to alter his face through plastic surgery to avoid capture. Timothy Farrell, Lyle Talbot, and Steve Reeves star. **DT118**

Jailhouse Rock (1957, B&W, 96m, NR)
Early Elvis Presley musical about a young man who learns to play the guitar while in jail and becomes a successful

rock star after his release. **ST123** *Recommended*

Jake Speed (1986, C, 104m, PG)
A fictional adventure hero and his trusty companion come to life to rescue a lady in distress. Michael Crawford and Dennis Christopher star as the heroes; John Hurt is the villain. **AC21**

Jamaica Inn (1939, B&W, 98m, NR)
Alfred Hitchcock directed this version of Daphne du Maurier's novel about an orphan girl (Maureen O'Hara) who gets involved with a band of smugglers. Charles Laughton costars. **DT46, MY3, WR5**

Jamaica Inn (1985, C, 200m, NR)
New version of the du Maurier classic of a lovely lass in distress at the hands of her evil uncle. Jane Seymour stars, with Patrick McGoohan, John McEnery, and Billie Whitelaw. Originally made for TV. **MY3, WR5**

James Dean Story, The (1957, B&W, 82m, NR)
Documentary about the legendary movie star, co-directed by Robert Altman. **CU16, DT2**

Jane Doe (1983, C, 103m, NR)
Karen Valentine plays an amnesiac stalked by a killer who wants her dead before she can incriminate him. Originally made for TV. **MY3**

Janis (1975, C, 97m, NR)
Documentary about the short life and career of blues/rock singer Janis Joplin; includes extensive concert footage. **MU11**

January Man, The (1989, C, 122m, R)
Kevin Kline is a suspended New York cop on the trail of a serial killer in this crime drama with comic overtones. With Susan Sarandon, Harvey Keitel, and Rod Steiger. **AC9, ST84**

Jason and the Argonauts (1963, C, 104m, NR)
Jason sets out to find the Golden Fleece in order to regain his rightful place on the throne, and encounters many obstacles along the way. Great special effects highlight this fantasy. **AC18, FA8**

Jaws (1975, C, 124m, PG)
Blockbuster horror film about a great white shark's attacks on swimmers at a

New England beach. Steven Spielberg directed. Richard Dreyfuss, Roy Scheider, and Robert Shaw star. **DT99, HO16, ST36** *Essential; Highly Recommended*

Jaws 2 (1978, C, 117m, PG)
The saga of the great white shark continues, with Roy Scheider and his wife in Florida, where they're bedeviled by further attacks. **HO16**

Jaws 3 (1983, C, 98m, PG)
In the third chapter, personnel at a sea world park in Florida are under siege from a shark enraged that its offspring has been captured. Dennis Quaid, Bess Armstrong, and Louis Gossett, Jr. star. **HO16**

Jaws: The Revenge (1987, C, 87m, PG-13)
Lorraine Gary, who played Roy Scheider's wife in the first and second installments, is back to battle another mammoth shark, this time in the Caribbean. Michael Caine costars. **HO16, ST15**

Jazz on a Summer's Day (1959, C, 85m, NR)
Highlights from the 1955 Newport Jazz Festival, featuring performances by Louis Armstrong, Dinah Washington, Gerry Mulligan, Thelonius Monk, and Milt Jackson. **CU16** *Recommended*

Jazz Singer, The (1927, B&W, 89m, NR)
Al Jolson stars as the son of a cantor who'd rather be singing on the stage instead of in a synagogue. A milestone for its use of sound in musical numbers and some dialogue scenes. **MU4** *Essential*

Jazz Singer, The (1980, C, 115m, PG)
Remake of the classic melodrama stars Neil Diamond as the son of a Jewish cantor (Laurence Olivier); Neil breaks with family tradition to become a rock star. **CU18, MU4, ST116**

Jean de Florette (1986, C, 122m, PG)
French drama, based on Marcel Pagnol's tale, about a scheming landowner who conspires with his dim-witted nephew to deprive their new neighbor of water for his crops. Yves Montand, Daniel Auteil, and Gerard Depardieu are the principals. Directed by Claude Berri. Story concludes in *Manon of the Spring*. **FF1, ST31** *Recommended*

Jennifer (1978, C, 90m, PG)
A shy girl is ostracized when she moves to a new school, and her telekinetic powers allow her to unleash deadly snakes on those who snubbed her. **HO7**

Jeremiah Johnson (1972, C, 107m, PG)
A mountain man (Robert Redford) who has turned his back on civilization goes to war with the Crow Indians who killed his family. Directed by Sydney Pollack. **DT80, ST126**

Jerk, The (1979, C, 94m, R)
Steve Martin stars as the title character, a stupid young man who attempts to adjust to life in the "normal" world. **ST99**

Jerry Lewis Live (1985, C, 77m, NR)
This live concert, filmed in Las Vegas, includes many of Jerry Lewis's zaniest routines. **ST91**

Jesse James (1939, C, 105m, NR)
A biography of the famed outlaw starring Henry Fonda in the title role, with Tyrone Power and Randolph Scott. **HF16, ST44, ST136, WE3**

Jesse James at Bay (1941, B&W, 54m, NR)
Roy Rogers and Gabby Hayes team up in a saga of the notorious outlaw's battles with the railroads. **HF16, ST132**

Jesus Christ, Superstar (1973, C, 103m, G)
Screen version of the successful Broadway rock opera portrays the last seven days in the life of Christ. Ted Neeley (in the title role), Carl Anderson, and Yvonne Elliman star. Directed by Norman Jewison. **DT51, FA9, HF16, MU2, MU9**

Jesus of Nazareth (1977, C, 371m, NR)
The life of Christ, portrayed by Robert Powell, features an all-star supporting cast, including Laurence Olivier, James Mason, and Anne Bancroft. Directed by Franco Zeffirelli; originally made for TV. **CL13, HF16, ST102, ST116**

Jet Benny Show, The (1986, C, 77m, NR)
Science fiction spoof featuring a character who resembles Jack Benny. Steve Norman and Kevin Dees star. **CO7, SF21**

Jewel of the Nile (1985, C, 104m, PG)
Kathleen Turner, Michael Douglas, and Danny DeVito return in this sequel to

Romancing the Stone, set in a North African kingdom. Author Joan Wilder is kidnapped by a mad prince, and soldier of fortune Jack Colter is off to the rescue. **AC14, AC21, ST32, ST35, ST152**

Jezebel (1938, B&W, 103m, NR)
Bette Davis plays a willful Southern belle who defies social customs to make her fiance (Henry Fonda) jealous. Davis and supporting actress Fay Bainter both won Oscars under William Wyler's direction. **CL3, DT119, ST28, ST44, XT3, XT5**

Jigsaw Man, The (1984, C, 91m, PG)
A British agent (Michael Caine) who defected to Russia comes back to Britain for a final mission. Laurence Olivier costars. **MY6, ST15, ST116**

Jimi Hendrix (1973, C, 102m, NR)
This documentary on rock's greatest guitarist features interviews with his friends and musical associates, plus rare concert footage. **MU11** *Recommended*

Jimi Plays Berkeley (1973, C, 55m, NR)
Master musician Jimi Hendrix in concert. **MU10**

Jimmy the Kid (1983, C, 85m, PG)
A stuffy young boy, the child of wealthy parents, is kidnapped by a group of bumblers who teach him how to be a kid. Gary Coleman and Paul LeMat star. **FA7**

Jinxed! (1982, C, 103m, R)
Dark comedy of shady doings in Las Vegas involving a lounge singer (Bette Midler), her obnoxious lover (Rip Torn), and a handsome young blackjack dealer (Ken Wahl). **DT97, ST105, ST150**

Jo Jo Dancer, Your Life Is Calling (1986, C, 97m, R)
Richard Pryor stars in this semi-autobiographical story of a comedian who nearly dies from drug abuse. He reflects on his past, starting with his youth in his grandmother's brothel. Debbie Allen, Art Evans, Barbara Williams, Carmen McRae, and Billy Eckstine costar. Pryor co-wrote and directed. **DR12, DR14, MU12, ST125**

Joan of Arc (1948, C, 100m, NR)
Ingrid Bergman portrays the tragic heroine in this adaptation of the Maxwell Anderson play. **CL2, ST7**

Joan of Paris (1942, B&W, 91m, NR)
During World War II, a brave Frenchwoman (Michele Morgan) helps to smuggle downed Allied fliers back to safety. With Paul Henreid, Thomas Mitchell, and Laird Cregar. **AC1**

Jocks (1987, C, 91m, R)
Teen comedy about a traveling tennis team whose hijinks in Las Vegas overshadow their tennis tournament. Look for Christopher Lee and Richard Roundtree in small roles. **ST89**

Joe Cocker: Mad Dogs and Englishmen (1971, C, 119m, NR)
This documentary features highlights of Joe Cocker's 1970 American tour, with outstanding performances by Cocker and Leon Russell. **MU10**

Joe Kidd (1972, C, 88m, PG)
Clint Eastwood is hired on the wrong side of a land war between Mexican natives and American land owners. Robert Duvall costars. Written by Elmore Leonard. **ST38, ST39, WR16**

Joe Piscopo New Jersey Special (1986, C, 60m, NR)
This TV special shows funny man Piscopo kidding his home state with guest star Danny DeVito. **CO16, ST32**

Joe Piscopo Video, The (1984, C, 60m, NR)
Saturday Night Live alumnus does it all in this one-man show, highlighting many of his famous impressions. **CO16**

Joe Versus the Volcano (1990, C, 102m, PG)
Thinking he has only a few months to live, a mild-mannered young man agrees to become a human sacrifice on a small South Pacific island. Tom Hanks stars in this comedy, with Meg Ryan (in three roles), Lloyd Bridges, Robert Stack, and Dan Hedaya. Written and directed by John Patrick Shanley. **CO1, ST62**

Johnny Be Good (1988, C, 91m, R)
A high school quarterback is the object of a mad scramble among unscrupulous recruiters. Anthony Michael Hall and Robert Downey, Jr. star in this comedy. Rated PG-13 in its theatrical release; video version contains additional footage to earn the "R" rating. **CO4, CO19, CU10**

Johnny Belinda (1948, B&W, 103m, NR)
Jane Wyman's Oscar-winning performance highlights this tale of a deaf-mute
and the doctor (Lew Ayres) who comes
to her aid. **CL6, XT3**

Johnny Dangerously (1984, C, 90m, PG-
13)
Spoof of Prohibition-era gangster movies,
starring Michael Keaton, Joe Piscopo and
Danny DeVito. **CO7, CO10, CO13, ST32,
ST80**

Johnny Got His Gun (1971, C, 111m, PG)
A war veteran whose body has been virtually obliterated recalls his past from his
hospital bed. Antiwar parable stars Timothy Bottoms, with Jason Robards and
Donald Sutherland. Dalton Trumbo
adapted and directed his novel. **DR7,
DR19, ST129**

Johnny Guitar (1954, C, 110m, NR)
Offbeat western with women in the two
leads: Joan Crawford as a tough saloon
owner who learns her wealth can't buy
everything, and Mercedes McCambridge
as her rival. Sterling Hayden costars.
Nicholas Ray directed. **CU17, DT83,
ST24, WE8, WE15** *Recommended*

Johnny Handsome (1989, C, 95m, R)
Betrayed in a robbery, a disfigured criminal gets a shot at a new life in prison when
a surgeon rebuilds his face. Out on pa-
role, he goes looking for the couple that
left him behind. Mickey Rourke stars,
with Ellen Barkin, Elizabeth McGovern,
Lance Henriksen, Morgan Freeman, and
Forest Whitaker. Walter Hill directed on
locations in New Orleans. **DR16, DT45,
ST48, ST134, XT14**

Johnny Tremain (1957, C, 80m, NR)
Based on the Esther Forbes novel, this
Disney film deals with a young boy's in-
volvement in the Revolutionary War. **FA1**

Joke of Destiny, A (1983, C, 105m, PG)
Italian comedy of a government official
locked inside his high-tech limo by a computer. Lina Wertmüller directed. **DT114**

Jolson Sings Again (1949, C, 96m, NR)
This sequel to *The Jolson Story* continues
the success story of American entertainer
Al Jolson. Larry Parks stars; Jolie supplied the vocals. **MU5**

Jolson Story, The (1946, C, 128m, NR)
Larry Parks plays Al Jolson in this bio-
graphical film tracing his rise to stardom.
MU5

Jonathan Winters: On the Ledge (1987, C,
60m, NR)
One of America's premier funnymen stars
in this series of sketches, also featuring
Robin Williams and Milton Berle. **CO16,
ST160**

Joshua Then and Now (1985, C, 127m, R)
James Woods plays a Jewish writer trying
to live down his father's reputation as a
gangster. Comedy-drama, adapted from
Mordecai Richler's novel, costars Alan
Arkin and Gabrielle Lazure. **DR8, ST165**

Jour de Fête (1949, B&W, 70m, NR)
Comedy from French director Jacques
Tati about a postman's bizarre attempts
to mechanize mail delivery. **DT104**

Jour Se Leve, Le (1939, B&W, 85m, NR)
Classic French drama of a factory worker
(Jean Gabin) driven to murder, trying to
sort out his life before he's captured.
Marcel Carné directed. **FF1**

Journey Back to Oz (1974, C, 90m, G)
This animated sequel to *The Wizard of Oz*
features the voices of Liza Minnelli,
Mickey Rooney, Margaret Hamilton (the
witch from the original), and Milton
Berle. **FA10, ST133**

Journey Into Fear (1942, B&W, 69m, NR)
An American armaments smuggler (Orson Welles) flees from Turkey in this
World War II thriller, adapted from an
Eric Ambler novel. Joseph Cotten costars; he and Welles wrote the screenplay. **DT112, MY1, MY6**

Journey of Natty Gann, The (1985, C,
101m, PG)
During the Depression, a young girl travels cross-country to see her father and is
protected along the way by a pet wolf.
John Cusack and Meredith Salenger star
in this Disney family adventure. **FA1,
FA4, XT18, XT19**

Journey Through Fairyland (1989, C, 95m,
NR)
Animated adventure for children about a
brave hero's exciting travels, featuring

many classical music pieces on the soundtrack. **FA10**

Journey to the Center of the Earth (1959, C, 132m, NR)
Jules Verne fantasy tale of 19th-century expedition, packed with perils and wonders. James Mason, Arlene Dahl, Pat Boone, and Diane Baker star. **FA4, SF1, SF3, SF13, ST102, WR28**

Journey to the Center of the Earth (1989, C, 79m, PG)
Remake of the Jules Verne classic of "inner space" travel, starring Nicola Cowper, Ilan Mitchell-Smith, and Paul Carafotes. **FA4, SF3, SF13, WR28**

Journey to the Far Side of the Sun (1969, C, 99m,G)
British science fiction adventure, with space voyagers finding a hidden planet. Roy Thinnes, Lynn Loring, and Herbert Lom star. **SF3, SF19**

Joy House (1964, B&W, 98m, NR)
A playboy (Alain Delon) with a secret past stumbles into a mansion in France run by two American women. Jane Fonda costars. **ST45**

Joy of Sex, The (1984, C, 93m, R)
A high school girl, thinking she has only weeks to live, decides to experience it all before it's too late. Michelle Meyrink and Christopher Lloyd star in this comedy. **CO4**

Juarez (1939, B&W, 132m, NR)
This biographical drama stars Paul Muni as Mexican leader Juarez, with Bette Davis as Carlotta. **CL2, ST28**

Jubal (1956, C, 101m, NR)
A rancher becomes jealous of his best friend, who he thinks is having an affair with his lovely wife. Ernest Borgnine and Glenn Ford star, with Valerie French, Rod Steiger, and Charles Bronson. **ST12**

Jubilee Trail (1954, C, 103m, NR)
Vera Ralston plays a saloon singer turned rancher in this western drama. With Joan Leslie, Forrest Tucker, John Russell, and Pat O'Brien. **WE8**

Judge and the Assassin, The (1975, C, 130m, NR)
French drama of a jurist (Philippe Noiret) who must decide the sanity of a man

(Michael Galabra) on trial. With Isabelle Huppert. Directed by Bertrand Tavernier. **FF1**

Judge Priest (1934, B&W, 80m, NR)
John Ford directed this humorous tale of a controversial judge (Will Rogers) in a small town. **DT36**

Judgment at Nuremberg (1961, B&W, 178m, NR)
Spencer Tracy plays an American judge who presides over the Nuremberg war crimes trials. Outstanding performances by Burt Lancaster, Judy Garland, Montgomery Clift, Marlene Dietrich, and Maximilian Schell, who won an Academy Award as the German defense attorney. Directed by Stanley Kramer. **CL8, DR17, DT55, ST33, ST51, ST85, ST151, XT2**

Judgment in Stone *see* The Housekeeper

Juggernaut (1937, B&W, 64m, NR)
A doctor (Boris Karloff) is hired by a woman to murder her husband. But he doesn't stop with one corpse, as he continues to poison people. **ST77**

Juggernaut (1974, C, 109m, PG)
A madman plants four bombs aboard an ocean liner and demands blackmail money from the shipping company. First-rate adventure, with touches of sly wit, starring Richard Harris, Anthony Hopkins, and Shirley Knight. Directed by Richard Lester. **AC23, DT62** *Highly Recommended*

Jules and Jim (1961, B&W, 104m, NR)
Director François Truffaut's modern classic: two men try to share the same free-spirited woman. Jeanne Moreau, Oskar Werner, and Henri Serre star. **DT106, ST110** *Essential; Highly Recommended*

Julia (1977, C, 118m, PG)
True story of how writer Lillian Hellman got involved with World War II Resistance movement in Europe, thanks to a courageous friend. Jane Fonda and Oscar winner Vanessa Redgrave star; Jason Robards also won an Oscar for playing Dashiell Hammett. Meryl Streep's screen debut, in a small role. Directed by Fred Zinnemann. **DR4, DT120, ST45, ST127, ST129, ST145, WR9, XT4, XT5** *Recommended*

Julia and Julia (1988, C, 98m, R)
Kathleen Turner stars as a woman whose husband is killed on their wedding day; years later, he returns with their six-year-old son. She's unable to sort reality from fantasy, which creates tension with her new lover (Sting). **MU12, ST152**

Juliet of the Spirits (1965, C, 148m, NR)
Director Federico Fellini's dream-movie about the fantasies of an ordinary housewife (Giulietta Masina) who's afraid that her husband is cheating on her. **DT53**

Julius Caesar (1953, B&W, 123m, NR)
The Shakespeare drama of power politics in ancient Rome, with Marlon Brando as Mark Anthony, and James Mason, John Gielgud, Louis Calhern, and Deborah Kerr. Joseph L. Mankiewicz directed. **DT68, ST10, ST102, WR22** *Recommended*

Julius Caesar (1970, C, 117m, G)
Charlton Heston, Jason Robards, Diana Rigg, and Christopher Lee are featured in this adaptation of Shakespeare's play about political intrigue in Rome. **ST89, ST129, WR22**

Jumbo (1962, C, 125m, NR)
Rodgers & Hart songs and Busby Berkeley choreography highlight this circus musical starring Doris Day, Stephen Boyd, Jimmy Durante, and Martha Raye. Also known as *Billy Rose's Jumbo*. **DT8**

Jumpin' Jack Flash (1986, C, 100m, R)
Whoopi Goldberg plays a computer programmer who gets involved in international intrigue when a spy contacts her on her computer screen. With Stephen Collins, John Wood, Carol Kane, Annie Potts, and Jim Belushi. **CO10, CO13**

June Night (1940, B&W, 90m, NR)
Ingrid Bergman stars in this melodrama, made in Sweden before her Hollywood career began, about a woman trying to escape her scandalous past. Also known as *A Night in June*. **FF7, ST7**

Jungle Book, The (1942, C, 109m, NR)
Colorful live action fantasy about a boy raised by wolves in the jungle. Great family entertainment, based on the Kipling book. **FA4**

Jungle Raiders (1985, C, 102m, PG-13)
Adventure story featuring Captain Yankee, a fearless soldier of fortune who's off in search of the Ruby of Gloom. Christopher Connelly and Lee Van Cleef star. **AC21, ST155**

Junior Bonner (1972, C, 103m, PG)
Steve McQueen plays a fading rodeo star who returns to his hometown show, determined to be in the spotlight again. With Robert Preston, Ida Lupino, Joe Don Baker, and Ben Johnson. Sam Peckinpah directed. **DT77, ST97, WE12** *Recommended*

Jupiter's Thigh (1983, C, 90m, NR)
Sequel to French comic thriller *Dear Detective* teams up same stars (Annie Girardot, Philippe Noiret) for a mystery that takes place on their honeymoon. **FF1**

Just a Gigolo (1979, C, 98m, R)
Atmospheric drama of Prussian war veteran (David Bowie) adrift in Berlin. Sydne Rome, Kim Novak, and David Hemmings costar; Marlene Dietrich makes a brief appearance. **MU12, ST33**

Just Around the Corner (1938, B&W, 70m, NR)
Shirley Temple teams with Bill "Bojangles" Robinson for some of their best musical numbers, as Shirley puts an end to the Depression by persuading an elderly tycoon to create more jobs. Bert Lahr and Joan Davis costar. **ST148**

Just Between Friends (1986, C, 110m, PG-13)
When a woman's husband is killed in an accident, she learns a terrible secret about her new best friend. Mary Tyler Moore and Christine Lahti star, with Ted Danson and Sam Waterston. **DR10**

Just Tell Me What You Want (1980, C, 112m, R)
A business executive (Alan King) unknowingly pushes his mistress (Ali MacGraw) into the arms of a younger man (Peter Weller), then does everything in his power to get her back. Slam-bang New York comedy directed by Sidney Lumet. With Myrna Loy and Dina Merrill. **DT65, ST94, XT9**

Justine (1969, C, 116m, NR)
A banker's wife (Anouk Aimee) gets involved with politicians from the Middle

East. Adaptation of the Lawrence Durrell novel also stars Dirk Bogarde, Robert Forster, and Michael York. Directed by George Cukor. **DR19, DT24**

K-9 (1989, C, 102m, PG-13)
James Belushi plays a cop whose new partner is a German shepherd in this action comedy. **CO10, CO13**

Kagemusha (1980, C, 159m, PG)
Epic adventure tale of thief who assumes identity of dead warlord, directed by Japan's premier filmmaker, Akira Kurosawa. Tatsuya Nakadai stars. **DT57** *Recommended*

Kameradschaft (1931, B&W, 89m, NR)
Classic German drama of post-World War I enmity between Germans and French forgotten during mining disaster rescue. Directed by G.W. Pabst. **FF3**

Kamikaze '89 (1982, C, 106m, NR)
Thriller set in futuristic Germany about a detective (Rainer Werner Fassbinder) foiling a bomb plot. **FF3, DT34**

Kanal (1956, B&W, 90m, NR)
From Polish director Andrzej Wajda, a drama of the Polish Resistance fighters taking their last stand against the Nazis during the Warsaw Uprising. **FF7** *Recommended*

Kangaroo (1986, C, 105m, R)
Australian drama, based on D.H. Lawrence's autobiographical novel, of a writer scorned in his native England. He and his German-born wife emigrate to Australia, where they become involved with a band of Fascists. Colin Friels and Judy Davis star. **FF5, WR14**

Kansas (1988, C, 111m, R)
Two aimless young men (Matt Dillon, Andrew McCarthy) pull off an impromptu bank robbery. One hides the money, and his partner comes looking for him. **DR16**

Karate Kid, The (1984, C, 126m, PG)
The new kid in town is the punching bag for neighborhood bullies until a kindly handyman teaches him self-defense. Ralph Macchio and Noriyuki "Pat" Morita star. **DR9, DR22, FA7**

Karate Kid II, The (1986, C, 113m, PG)
Further adventures of the young karate student, now in Japan for martial arts

tournament, and his kindly teacher. **DR9, DR22, FA7**

Karate Kid, Part III, The (1989, C, 111m, PG)
Daniel (Ralph Macchio) won't participate in a karate tournament until a bully gets his goat. Noriyuki "Pat" Morita costars. **DR9, DR22, FA7**

Katherine (1975, C, 100m, NR)
Sissy Spacek plays a young woman who turns from political activist to terrorist. With Art Carney and Henry Winkler. Originally made for TV. **DR7, ST139**

Keeper, The (1984, C, 96m, NR)
The patients at an insane asylum are tortured by their sadistic keeper. Christopher Lee stars in this horror drama. **ST89**

Keeping Track (1986, C, 107m, R)
A newsman and a bank teller become pawns in a game of international intrigue after $5 million falls into their laps. Michael Sarrazin and Margot Kidder star. **MY6**

Kelly's Heroes (1970, C, 145m, PG)
A gang of GIs plan a daring robbery behind enemy lines during World War II. Clint Eastwood stars in this comedy-adventure, with Telly Savalas, Donald Sutherland, Carroll O'Connor, and Harry Dean Stanton. **CO21, ST39, ST141**

Kennel Murder Case, The (1933, B&W, 73m, NR)
William Powell plays Philo Vance, the sophisticated detective, as he investigates a murder in New York City. **MY10, ST122**

Kentuckian, The (1955, C, 104, NR)
Burt Lancaster stars in this western about a man starting life over with his son in 1820s Texas. With Diana Lynn and Walter Matthau. Lancaster directed. **ST85, ST104**

Kermit and Piggy Story, The (1985, C, 57m, NR)
The rags-to-riches show biz saga of The Muppets' Miss Piggy, as told by Cheryl Ladd, Raquel Welch, and Tony Randall. **FA14**

Key, The (1958, B&W, 134m, NR)
In World War II London, a woman whose apartment key has passed from one sea captain to another, in a series of affairs,

finally finds true love with a Canadian officer. Sophia Loren and William Holden star. **ST68, ST93**

Key Largo (1948, B&W, 101m, NR)
A gangster (Edward G. Robinson) holds people captive in a Florida hotel during a hurricane. Humphrey Bogart and Lauren Bacall star, with Claire Trevor, who won an Oscar for Best Supporting Actress. Directed by John Huston. **CL15, DT50, MY1, ST8, ST130, XT5** *Recommended*

Keys of the Kingdom (1944, B&W, 137m, NR)
Drama of a missionary sent to China, adapted from the novel by A.J. Cronin. Gregory Peck stars, with Thomas Mitchell and Vincent Price. **ST119, ST124**

Khartoum (1966, C, 134m, NR)
True story of British Major "Chinese" Gordon (Charlton Heston) and his confrontation in 1833 Africa with a wily Arab spiritual leader (Laurence Olivier). **DR5, ST116**

Kickboxer (1989, C, 92m, R)
Jean Claude Van Damme plays this title role in this martial arts saga. **AC26**

Kid, The/Idle Class, The (1921, B&W, 85m, NR)
In his first feature-length film, Charlie Chaplin plays The Little Tramp, who adopts an orphan (Jackie Coogan). Also included on this tape is the Chaplin short, *The Idle Class.* **DT18** *Essential; Highly Recommended*

Kid From Brooklyn, The (1946, C, 113m, NR)
Danny Kaye comedy about a milkman turned pugilist, with Virginia Mayo, Vera-Ellen, and Eve Arden. **ST78**

Kid Galahad (1962, C, 95m, NR)
Elvis Presley plays a successful boxer who would rather be a mechanic. Charles Bronson has a small role. **ST12, ST123**

Kidnapped (1960, C, 97m, NR)
Disney adaptation of Robert Louis Stevenson's book, about a young heir who looks for his uncle, only to be abducted along the way and sold into slavery. Peter Finch and James MacArthur star, with Peter O'Toole. **FA1, ST117**

Kids Are Alright, The (1979, C, 108m, NR)
Documentary on the British rock group The Who, concentrating on the group's memorable concert performances. **MU11**

Kid's Auto Race/Mabel's Married Life (1914/1915, B&W, 21m, NR)
Charlie Chaplin stars in two of his most famous short films. The first deals with a kiddie-car contest. The second focuses on two married people who flirt in the park. **DT18**

Kill and Kill Again (1981, C, 100m, R)
Sequel to *Kill or Be Killed,* with karate star James Ryan foiling the plans of an evil scientist. **AC26**

Kill, Baby, Kill (1966, C, 90m, NR)
The ghost of a murdered girl returns to her European village to avenge her death. Directed by Mario Bava. Also known as *Curse of the Living Dead.* **HO13**

Kill Me Again (1989, C, 94m, R)
A down-and-out private eye decides to help a woman fake her murder—unaware that she's trying to shake a psychotic boyfriend. Joanne Whalley-Kilmer, Val Kilmer, and Michael Madsen star. **MY2, MY4, MY10**

Kill or Be Killed (1980, C, 90m, PG)
Karate champ James Ryan stars in a drama about an ex-Nazi and his Japanese counterpart from World War II meeting years later in a martial arts tournament. **AC26**

Killer Bait (1949, B&W, 98m, NR)
Film noir of a couple who stumble into ill-gotten money; he wants to return it, but she'll do anything to keep it. Lizabeth Scott, Don DeFore, Dan Duryea, and Arthur Kennedy star. Also known as *Too Late for Tears.* **MY1, MY4**

Killer Bats (1941, B&W, 67m, NR)
A cosmetics manufacturer deprives his partner (Bela Lugosi) of his share of the profits, and the partner plots revenge. Also known as *The Devil Bat.* **ST95**

Killer Elite, The (1975, C, 122m, R)
A tale of two professional assassins (James Caan, Robert Duvall) who end up stalking each other. Sam Peckinpah directed on locations in San Francisco. **AC8, AC19, DT77, MY6, ST38, XT13**

Killer Force (1975, C, 100m, PG)
A diamond mine in South Africa is the scene for skullduggery in this action-adventure story, starring Peter Fonda and Telly Savalas, with Hugh O'Brian, Christopher Lee, and O. J. Simpson. **ST89**

Killer Inside Me, The (1976, C, 99m, R)
Stacy Keach plays a deputy sheriff who is near the breaking point. Based on a novel by Jim Thompson. **MY13, WR26**

Killer Party (1986, C, 92m, R)
A trio of sorority pledges are special guests at an April Fool's party held in an abandoned fraternity house. Horror drama starring Elaine Wilkes, with Paul Bartel. **DT5, HO12**

Killers, The (1964, C, 95m, NR)
Thriller, loosely based on Hemingway short story, about hit men learning about their victim's past. Lee Marvin, Angie Dickinson, John Cassavetes, and Ronald Reagan (in his last film) star. Directed by Don Siegel; originally made for TV but deemed too violent, so it was released to theaters. Cult reputation for Reagan's role as sadistic hoodlum. **CU2, DR19, DT97, ST100, WR10, XT22**

Killing, The (1956, B&W, 83m, NR)
Breakthrough film for director Stanley Kubrick, a classic tale of a gang pulling off a complex robbery at a racetrack. Sterling Hayden stars, with Coleen Gray, Vince Edwards, Elisha Cook, Jr., and Timothy Carey. Screenplay by Kubrick and Jim Thompson. **DT56, MY1, MY18.** *Recommended*

Killing Fields, The (1984, C, 142m, R)
Fact-based drama about *New York Times* reporter escaping Cambodia during Vietnam War and his subsequent reunion with his translator. Sam Waterston and Oscar winner Haing S. Ngor star. **DR6, XT4** *Recommended*

Killing of Angel Street, The (1981, C, 101m, PG)
A political activist and a geologist team up to halt greedy real estate developers who are forcing residents to sell their homes. Australian drama stars Liz Alexander and John Hargreaves. **FF5**

Killing of Sister George, The (1968, C, 138m, R)
A middle-aged British actress loses her job on a popular TV series and is also in danger of losing her young female lover to another woman. Beryl Reid, Susannah York, and Coral Browne star. Robert Aldrich directed this drama. **DR3**

Killings at Outpost Zeta, The (1980, C, 92m, NR)
Science fiction mystery about team of scientists and soldiers investigating murders at a remote planet. **SF17**

Killjoy (1981, C, 100m, NR)
Whodunit about a murdered woman and the many possible suspects. Robert Culp and Kim Basinger star. **MY12**

Kim (1950, C, 113m, NR)
Rudyard Kipling's tale of British soldiers fighting against fierce tribesmen in India, starring Errol Flynn and Dean Stockwell. **AC13, FA4, ST43, ST144**

Kind Hearts and Coronets (1949, B&W, 104m, NR)
The black sheep of a wealthy family decides to kill them off. Alec Guinness plays all eight victims in this comic British mystery. **CL10, CL17, MY15, MY17, ST60** *Essential; Recommended*

Kind of Loving, A (1962, B&W, 112m, NR)
British drama of a young couple wed because of her pregnancy. Alan Bates and June Ritchie star. Directed by John Schlesinger. **DR23, DT94**

Kindred, The (1987, C, 92m, R)
A young man discovers that he has been the guinea pig for an experiment combining his tissue with that of a sea monster. Rod Steiger and Kim Hunter star. **HO13**

King (1978, C, 272m, NR)
TV miniseries on the life of Dr. Martin Luther King, Jr. and his leadership in the civil rights struggle. Paul Winfield stars, with Cicely Tyson, Ossie Davis, Roscoe Lee Browne, and Howard Rollins, Jr. Written and directed by Abby Mann. **DR4, DR7, DR14, ST162**

King and I, The (1956, C, 133m, NR)
Yul Brynner won an Oscar for his performance as the King of Siam in this version of the Rodgers and Hammerstein Broadway musical. Deborah Kerr stars as Anna, the governess hired to teach his many children. **FA9, MU2, MU7, XT2**

King Creole (1958, B&W, 116m, NR)
A nightclub singer (Elvis Presley) with a troubled past gets involved with criminals in New Orleans. With Walter Matthau. **ST104, ST123**

King David (1985, C, 114m, PG-13)
Richard Gere stars as the biblical monarch in this drama costarring Edward Woodward as Saul and Alice Krige as Bathsheba. **ST52**

King in New York, A (1957, B&W, 105m, NR)
Charlie Chaplin comedy about a European monarch who visits America during the McCarthy witch hunts and gets a strong taste of American morality. **DT18**

King Kong (1933, B&W, 100m, NR)
The granddaddy of all oversized animal movies, with the big hairy ape terrorizing Skull Island and then demolishing Manhattan. Robert Armstrong, Bruce Cabot, and Fay Wray star. **CU4, FA8, HO1, HO16, SF2, SF10, SF13, SF16, XT9** *Essential; Highly Recommended*

King Kong (1976, C, 134m, PG)
Jeff Bridges and Jessica Lange star in this remake of the classic story about a gigantic ape who captures a young woman and terrorizes Manhattan. With Charles Grodin. **CU18, HO16, ST11, ST59, ST86, XT9**

King Lear (1971, B&W, 137m, PG)
Shakespeare's tragedy of a lonely monarch, starring Paul Scofield, Irene Worth, and Jack MacGowran. Directed by Peter Brook. **WR22**

King Lear (1987, C, 91m, PG)
The title is Shakespeare, but the director is French iconoclast Jean-Luc Godard, who "updates" the tale in his own way. Peter Sellars, Burgess Meredith, and Molly Ringwald head the cast, with appearances by Woody Allen and Norman Mailer. **DT1, DT41, WR22**

King of Comedy (1983, C, 109m, PG)
A stand-up comic kidnaps a popular talk-show host in hopes of getting a shot at the big time. Dark comedy about success and fame, starring Robert DeNiro and Jerry Lewis, with Sandra Bernhard. Directed by Martin Scorsese. **CO2, CO12, CU5, DT95, ST30, ST91, XT9** *Recommended*

King of Hearts (1966, C, 102m, NR)
Midnight movie classic, a fantasy about a World War I soldier separated from his division and coming upon a town occupied only by inmates escaped from an asylum. Alan Bates and Genevieve Bujold star. Available in a letterboxed edition. **CU1, CU5, CU19**

King of Jazz, The (1930, C, 93m, NR)
This revue features a cartoon sequence by Walter Lantz, plus Bing Crosby and the Rhythm Boys, and a performance of Gershwin's "Rhapsody in Blue." **MU15,ST25**

King of Kings (1927, B&W/C, 115m, NR)
Cecil B. DeMille's silent spectacular on the life of Christ (H.B. Warner). The Resurrection is presented in 2-color Technicolor. **CL12, CL13, DT27, HF16**

King of Kings (1961, C, 168m, NR)
Nicholas Ray directed this epic drama centering on the life of Christ. Jeffrey Hunter stars, with Robert Ryan, Rip Torn, and Hurd Hatfield. **CL13, DT83, HF16**

King of the Cowboys (1943, B&W, 67m, NR)
Roy Rogers fights contemporary saboteurs who are plotting to destroy a defense installation. With Smiley Burnette. **ST132**

King of the Grizzlies (1970, C, 93m, G)
In this Disney film, an Indian youth befriends a bear cub, only to grow up to face the same animal as a full-grown grizzly. **FA1**

King of the Gypsies (1978, C, 112m, R)
Eric Roberts stars in the title role as a young man destined to rule his wandering modern clan. With Judd Hirsch, Susan Sarandon, Sterling Hayden, Shelley Winters, Annette O'Toole, and Brooke Shields. **DR8, ST164**

King of the Kongo, The (1929, B&W, 213m, NR)
Silent serial starring Boris Karloff in a tale of ivory thieves in Africa. **ST77**

King of the Mountain (1981, C, 90m, PG)
A mechanic and his pals spend their spare time racing on Los Angeles' winding Mulholland Drive. Harry Hamlin stars, with Joseph Bottoms, Deborah Van Valken-

burgh, and Dennis Hopper as the one-time King of the Mountain. **ST71**

King Rat (1965, B&W, 133m, NR)
In a Japanese POW camp during World War II, an American hustler inspires envy and grudging admiration from his fellow captives. George Segal stars, with Tom Courtenay and James Fox. **AC7** *Recommended*

King Solomon's Mines (1937, B&W, 80m, NR)
First screen version of classic tale of African exploration, starring Paul Robeson, Cedric Hardwicke, and Roland Young. **AC12, AC13, AC21**

King Solomon's Mines (1950, C, 103m, NR)
Second and most popular version of the H. Rider Haggard tale of African adventure, starring Stewart Granger and Deborah Kerr. **AC12, AC13, AC21, FA4**

King Solomon's Mines (1985, C, 101m, PG-13)
Richard Chamberlain stars as the classic British adventurer, Allan Quartermain, as he plunges into deepest, darkest Africa in search of a fabled treasure. **AC12, AC21**

Kings of the Road (1976, B&W, 176m, NR)
Rambling drama from director Wim Wenders about two drifters making their way through the contemporary German landscape. **DT113, XT18**

King's Row (1942, B&W, 127m, NR)
Drama of small town life in the years prior to World War I. Ronald Reagan and Robert Cummings star. **CL6, DR26** *Essential*

Kinjite: Forbidden Subjects (1988, C, 97m, R)
A Los Angeles cop (Charles Bronson) with a grudge against Orientals must change his tune when he must track down the kidnapped daughter of a visiting Japanese businessman. **ST12**

Kismet (1955, C, 113m, NR)
Howard Keel and Ann Blyth star in this colorful musical based on the Broadway show about the Arabian Nights. Directed by Vincente Minnelli. **DT71, MU1, MU2, MU8**

Kiss, The (1988, C, 101m, R)
Horror tale of a young girl (Meredith Salenger) and her spooky aunt (Joanna Pacula), who is determined to infect her niece with the family curse. **HO14**

Kiss and Kill *see* Against All Odds (1969)

Kiss Me Goodbye (1982, C, 101m, PG)
Sally Field plays a young New York socialite visited by the ghost of her dead husband (James Caan) just as she's about to marry another man (Jeff Bridges). Loosely based on *Doña Flor and Her Two Husbands*. **FF8, ST11, ST40**

Kiss Me Kate (1953, C, 109m, NR)
Cole Porter's musical version of *The Taming of the Shrew* stars Howard Keel, Kathryn Grayson, and Ann Miller. Watch for Bob Fosse. **DT39, MU1, MU2, MU14, WR22**

Kiss of the Spider Woman (1985, C, 119m, R)
Oscar winner William Hurt stars with Raul Julia and Sonia Braga in this drama of cellmates, one a political prisoner, the other a homosexual with his film fantasies. Directed by Hector Babenco. **DR18, FF6, ST9, ST75, XT2**

Kiss Tomorrow Goodbye (1950, B&W, 102m, NR)
James Cagney plays the most ruthless of all criminals in one of his last tough-guy roles. **ST14**

Kissin' Cousins (1964, C, 96m, NR)
Elvis Presley in a dual role: a military officer and his down-home relative. The army man is trying to persuade the hick to sell his farm as a site for a missile base. **ST123**

Kitchen Toto, The (1987, C, 96m, PG-13)
Drama set in Kenya in the 1950s, as that country was breaking away from British rule. A young black boy working in the house of the British chief of police watches the violent events of revolution unfold. Edwin Mahinda, Bob Peck, and Phyllis Logan star. Directed by Harry Hook. **DR5, DR9, DR14**

Kitty and the Bagman (1982, C, 95m, R)
Australian comedy-drama about true-life couple in Roaring Twenties, a crooked cop (John Stanton) and his lover (Liddy

Clark), the Underworld Queen of Sydney. **FF5**

Kitty Foyle (1940, B&W, 107m, NR)
Ginger Rogers won an Academy Award for her performance as a working-class girl who falls in love with her boss. **CL5, CL6, ST131, XT3**

Klute (1971, C, 114m, R)
Oscar winner Jane Fonda stars as a New York call girl who is being threatened by sadistic phone calls. She attracts the attention of Klute (Donald Sutherland), a small-town detective searching for a missing friend. **MY3, MY5, MY10, ST45, XT3** *Recommended*

Knife in the Water (1962, B&W, 94m, NR)
Director Roman Polanski's drama of a couple who pick up a hitchhiker and invite him on a boating holiday. In Polish. **DT79, FF7** *Essential; Recommended*

Knight Without Armor (1937, B&W, 101m, NR)
Robert Donat is the secret agent who helps Russian noblewoman Marlene Dietrich escape vengeful revolutionaries. **ST33**

Knightriders (1981, C, 145m, R)
George Romero wrote and directed this unusual drama about a traveling motorcycle gang who stage medieval fairs in which knights joust on cycles. Ed Harris stars. **DT90**

Knights and Emeralds (1986, C, 94m, PG)
Racial tension develops when a young white musician (Christopher Wild) befriends black musicians in this British drama-musical. **DR23**

Knights of the City (1985, C, 87m, R)
Action drama set on the mean streets of Miami, where a street gang tries to go straight and start a career in the music industry. Leon Isaac Kennedy, Nicholas Campbell, and singer Smokey Robinson star. **AC8**

Knights of the Round Table (1953, C, 115m, NR)
Robert Taylor, Ava Gardner, and Mel Ferrer star in this lavish drama of the King Arthur legend. **AC13**

Knock on Any Door (1949, B&W, 100m, NR)
Humphrey Bogart plays a prominent attorney who defends a young hoodlum accused of killing a cop. Directed by Nicholas Ray. **CL8, DT83, MY1, ST8**

Knockout, The/Dough and Dynamite (1914, B&W, 54m, NR)
Charlie Chaplin stars in both these comedy shorts, featuring some of his most famous routines. *The Knockout* features Chaplin as referee of a big fight. *Dough and Dynamite* is about a strike at a bakery where Chaplin works. **DT18**

Knute Rockne—All American (1940, B&W, 96m, NR)
Pat O'Brien plays the legendary Notre Dame football coach and Ronald Reagan is his star player, George Gipp. **CL2, DR22**

Kojiro (1967, C, 152m, NR)
In a followup to Japanese director Hiroshi Inagaki's *Samurai Trilogy,* Tatsuya Nakadai plays a famed swordsman whose exploits young Kojiro (Kikunosuke Onoe) emulates. **FF4**

Kotch (1971, C, 113m, G)
Walter Matthau plays an elderly man who resists his family's attempts to write him off. Jack Lemmon directed this comedy-drama. **DR11, ST90, ST104**

Koyaanisqatsi (1983, C, 87m, NR)
Impressions of nature and man-made structures blend together in this one-of-a-kind documentary meditation on contemporary life. Directed by Godfrey Reggio; music by Philip Glass. **CU16**

Kramer vs. Kramer (1979, C, 105m, PG)
Drama of a marriage breakup and the father's learning to care for his young son, starring Dustin Hoffman, Meryl Streep, and Justin Henry, with JoBeth Williams and Howard Duff. Written and directed by Robert Benton. Oscar winner for Best Picture, Actor, Supporting Actress, and Director. **DR8, DR17, DT6, ST67, ST145, XT1, XT2, XT5, XT6** *Essential; Recommended*

Kriemhilde's Revenge (1924, B&W, 95m, NR)
This silent film, directed by Fritz Lang, is the sequel to *Siegfried,* based on a popu-

lar legend of German mythology. **DT58, FF3**

Kronos (1957, B&W, 78m, NR)
A metallic monster from outer space crash-lands off the coast of Mexico and begins absorbing all the Earth's energy. Science fiction drama stars Jeff Morrow, Barbara Lawrence, and John Emery. **SF1**

Krull (1983, C, 117m, PG)
Sword & sorcery adventure of young man in search of a lost jewel, starring Ken Marshall and Lysette Antony. Lavish production values. **AC18**

Kwaidan (1964, C, 164m, NR)
A quartet of horror stories from Japan, based on works by Lafcadio Hearn. Imaginative use of color; directed by Masaki Kobayashi. **FF4**

La Bamba (1987, C, 103m, PG-13)
Biography of rock 'n' roll's first Hispanic star, Ritchie Valens, starring Lou Diamond Phillips. With Esai Morales, Elizabeth Pena and Marshall Crenshaw as Buddy Holly and Howard Huntsberry as Jackie Wilson. Los Lobos performs Valens' music on the soundtrack. **MU5** *Recommended*

Labyrinth (1986, C, 101m, PG)
A young girl wishes her brother would be captured by goblins—and when her wish comes true, she sets out to rescue him. Family adventure starring Jennifer Connelly and David Bowie, with Terry Jones. **CO15, FA8, MU12, SF13**

Ladies Club, The (1986, C, 86m, R)
Frustrated with the criminal justice system, a policewoman, a rape victim, and several other angry women set out to get justice their own way. **AC19**

Ladies' Man, The (1961, C, 106m, NR)
Jerry Lewis comedy has him playing a handyman at a girls' school. With Helen Traubel, Kathleen Freeman, and Harry James & His Band. **CO18, ST91**

Lady and the Tramp (1955, C, 75m, G)
Classic Disney animated feature about a pampered cocker spaniel and her romance with a street mutt. **FA2** *Highly Recommended*

Lady Caroline Lamb (1972, C, 118m, PG)
True story of wife of British politician and her open affair with poet Lord Byron. Sarah Miles, Peter Finch, and Richard Chamberlain form the romantic triangle; Laurence Olivier costars. **ST116**

Lady Chatterly's Lover (1955, B&W, 102m, NR)
French-language version of D.H. Lawrence's story of forbidden love, starring Danielle Darrieux. **DR3, WR14**

Lady Chatterly's Lover (1981, C, 105m, R)
Second, and more explicit, version of the D.H. Lawrence tale of passion, starring Sylvia Kristel and Nicholas Clay. **DR3, WR14**

Lady Eve, The (1941, B&W, 94m, NR)
A preoccupied scientist (Henry Fonda) is thoroughly confused and fleeced by a smooth con woman (Barbara Stanwyck) in this classic comedy from writer-director Preston Sturges. With Charles Coburn, William Demarest, and Eugene Pallette. **CL10, DT103, ST44, ST142** *Essential; Highly Recommended*

Lady for a Night (1941, B&W, 87m, NR)
A gambling boat owner tries marriage to a wealthy man but is framed for murder. Joan Blondell and John Wayne star in this drama. **ST156**

Lady From Louisiana (1941, B&W, 82m, NR)
John Wayne plays a crusading lawyer in old New Orleans who falls in love with the daughter of a gambling boss he wants to put behind bars. **ST156**

Lady From Shanghai, The (1948, B&W, 87m, NR)
Orson Welles directed this bizarre thriller about a sailor's infatuation with the lovely wife (Rita Hayworth) of a sleazy lawyer. Famous climax in house of mirrors. Welles costars, with Everett Sloane. **DT112, MY1, ST64** *Recommended*

Lady Ice (1973, C, 93m, PG)
An insurance investigator tracks a gang of jewel thieves in this caper mystery. Donald Sutherland, Jennifer O'Neill, and Robert Duvall star. **MY18, ST38**

Lady in a Cage (1964, B&W, 93m, NR)
Olivia De Havilland stars in a thriller about a woman trapped in her home and terrorized by hoodlums. James Caan co-stars. **MY3**

Lady in Cement (1968, C, 93m, NR)
Frank Sinatra plays a seedy private eye who's investigating the murder of a woman who was given special, hard-to-remove footwear. With Raquel Welch, Dan Blocker, Richard Conte, and Joe E. Lewis. Sequel to *Tony Rome*. **MY10, ST138**

Lady in White (1988, C, 113m, PG-13)
In 1962, a ten-year-old boy, locked in a school coatroom, witnesses a murder which took place ten years before. A ghost story with plenty of scares but very little violence. Lukas Haas stars. **HO2, HO19**

Lady Jane (1985, C, 140m, PG-13)
The true story of the 16th-century teen-aged Queen of England, her dramatic rise to the throne, and her sudden downfall. Helena Bonham Carter and Cary Elwes star in this lavish historical drama. **DR5, DR23**

Lady of Burlesque (1943, B&W, 91m, NR)
Barbara Stanwyck plays detective when a murderer begins eliminating strippers in this comic mystery. **MY17, ST142**

Lady of the Evening (1979, C, 110m, PG)
Italian comedy features Sophia Loren and Marcello Mastroianni as a prostitute and a crook who become partners. **ST93, ST103**

Lady on the Bus (1978, C, 102m, R)
A new bride finds her husband unattractive in bed but learns that she is attracted to nearly every other man in sight. Sexy comedy from Brazil starring Sonia Braga. **FF6, ST9**

Lady Sings the Blues (1972, C, 144m, R)
Diana Ross plays famed singer Billie Holiday, who fought a losing battle with drug addiction. Billy Dee Williams and Richard Pryor costar. **DR14, MU5, ST125, ST159**

Lady Takes a Chance, The (1943, B&W, 86m, NR)
John Wayne is a rodeo star and Jean Arthur is the city girl he tames in this light-hearted western. **ST156, WE12, WE14**

Lady Vanishes, The (1938, B&W, 97m, NR)
Hitchcock mystery set aboard a speeding train with a disappearing lady, lots of suspects, sly comedy. Margaret Lockwood, Michael Redgrave and Dame May Whitty star. **DT46, MY15, XT19** *Highly Recommended*

Lady Vanishes, The (1979, C, 99m, PG)
Remake of Hitchcock's classic thriller, starring Cybill Shepherd, Elliott Gould, and Angela Lansbury. **CU18, XT19**

Lady Windermere's Fan (1925, B&W, 80m, NR)
Silent screen version of the Oscar Wilde play of blackmail, deception, and infidelity among British nobility. Ronald Colman, Irene Rich, and May McAvoy star. Ernst Lubitsch directed. **DT63**

Ladyhawke (1985, C, 121m, PG-13)
A magician's spell has doomed a knight (Rutger Hauer) and his maiden fair (Michelle Pfeiffer) always to be apart—until they meet a young pickpocket (Matthew Broderick). **AC14, AC18, ST120**

Ladykillers, The (1955, C, 90m, NR)
Classic British comedy about a bungling band of crooks and a little, old (but quite resourceful) lady. Alec Guinness and Peter Sellers head the cast. **CL10, CO10, CO17, CU5, MY15, MY17, ST60, ST137** *Recommended*

Lair of the White Worm (1988, C, 93m, R)
Director Ken Russell takes on a story by Bram Stoker, about a sexy female vampire. Amanda Donohoe, Catherine Oxenberg, and Sammi Davis star. **DT92, HO5, HO25**

Land Before Time, The (1988, C, 66m, G)
Animated feature set in prehistoric times, with cute dinosaur and his friends undergoing many adventures. **FA10**

Land of Faraway, The (1988, C, 95m, PG)
Family fantasy of an 11-year-old boy who becomes a knight when he releases a spirit in a bottle. Christian Bale stars, with Timothy Bottoms, Susannah York, and Christopher Lee. **FA8, SF13, ST89**

Land of the Minotaur (1976, C, 88m, PG)
A devil-worshipping cult in Greece kidnaps tourists for their bizarre rituals. Donald Pleasence and Peter Cushing star. **HO11, ST27**

Land That Time Forgot, The (1975, C, 90m, PG)
Science fiction fantasy about Germans and Americans discovering a prehistoric land in Latin America. Doug McClure stars. **SF4**

Land Without Bread (1932, B&W, 28m, NR)
Director Luis Buñuel's searing documentary about Las Hurdes, one of the poorest regions of rural Spain. **CU16, DT15** *Recommended*

Laserblast (1978, C, 82m, PG)
A young boy finds a laser gun left behind by aliens and uses it to get even with his tormentors. Family science fiction drama. **SF13**

Lassie Come Home (1943, C, 88m, NR)
Family classic of a collie who is separated from the family who loves him and embarks on a dramatic journey to return to them. Roddy McDowall, Donald Crisp, Dame Mae Whitty, and Edmund Gwenn star, with a young Elizabeth Taylor in a small role. **FA5, ST147**

Lassiter (1984, C, 110m, R)
A handsome cat burglar is forced to go undercover for Scotland Yard against the Nazis. Tom Selleck stars, with Lauren Hutton, Jane Seymour, and Bob Hoskins. **AC14, ST72**

Last American Hero, The (1973, C, 100m, PG)
Jeff Bridges plays a moonshine runner whose driving skills catapult him to fame on the stock-car racing circuit. With Valerie Perrine, Geraldine Fitzgerald, and Gary Busey. Loosely based on the life of Junior Johnson. **DR22, ST11** *Recommended*

Last Angry Man, The (1959, B&W, 100m, NR)
An elderly doctor who has devoted his life to patients in a Brooklyn slum finds himself the unwilling subject of a TV documentary. Paul Muni stars, with Luther Adler, Betsy Palmer, Godfrey Cambridge, Billy Dee Williams, and Cicely Tyson. **CL8, DR15, ST159**

Last Chase, The (1981, C, 101m, R)
In the future, an oil shortage has virtually doomed auto travel—until one man reassembles his Porsche and leads police on a cross-country chase. Lee Majors stars. **AC10, SF11**

Last Command, The (1928, B&W, 88m, NR)
An expatriate Russian general is reduced to playing out his life as a Hollywood extra. Oscar winner Emil Jannings stars, with Evelyn Brent and William Powell. Josef von Sternberg directed this silent classic. **CL7, CL12, DT100, ST122, XT2** *Recommended*

Last Days of Man on Earth, The (1973, C, 79m, R)
British science fiction, with comic overtones, about an impudent scientist who creates a "new messiah" as the world comes to an end. Jon Finch stars. **SF19, SF21**

Last Detail, The (1973, C, 105m, R)
Jack Nicholson stars in this comedy-drama about a pair of Navy "lifers" transporting a young seaman from Norfolk, Virginia, to a naval prison in New Hampshire. Otis Young and Randy Quaid costar. Written by Robert Towne. **CO21, ST112, XT18** *Recommended*

Last Dragon, The (1985, C, 108, PG-13)
Kung Fu meets Motown in this martial arts adventure with musical numbers. Taimak provides the kicks and Vanity the music. **AC26, MU16**

Last Embrace (1979, C, 101m, R)
A CIA agent's wife is murdered and he believes the killers are after him, too. Roy Scheider and Janet Margolin star in this thriller from director Jonathan Demme. With Charles Napier, Christopher Walken, John Glover, and Sam Levene. **DT28, MY4, MY6** *Recommended*

Last Emperor, The (1987, C, 160m, R)
Winner of 9 Oscars (including Best Picture and Director), this lavish drama tells the incredible story of Pu Yi, the Chinese emperor set adrift in the currents of 20th-century history. John Lone stars, with Peter O'Toole and Joan Chen. Bernardo

Bertolucci directed. A visual treat. **DR4, DT9, ST117, XT1, XT6** *Recommended*

Last Exit to Brooklyn (1990, C, 102m, R)
Screen version of Hubert Selby, Jr.'s cult novel of life in 1952 Brooklyn's lower depths, starring Stephen Lang, Jennifer Jason Leigh, Burt Young, Jerry Orbach, and Ricki Lake. **DR15, DR19**

Last Flight of Noah's Ark, The (1980, C, 97m, G)
Disney adventure about a pilot, a female missionary, two young stowaways, and a pair of Japanese soldiers converting a crippled plane into a boat. Elliott Gould and Genevieve Bujold star. **FA1**

Last Four Days, The (1977, C, 91m, PG)
Drama recounting the final days of Italian dictator Benito Mussolini. Rod Steiger and Henry Fonda star. **ST44**

Last House on the Left (1972, C, 91m, R)
Two teenaged girls are tortured and murdered by a sadistic gang, and one girl's father exacts his own revenge. Cult horror film directed by Wes Craven. A loose remake of *The Virgin Spring*. **FF8, HO12**

Last Hurrah, The (1958, B&W, 121m, NR)
Spencer Tracy stars as a Boston Irish politican in the twilight of his career. Directed by John Ford. **DR21, DT36, ST151**

Last Laugh, The (1924, B&W, 77m, NR)
Classic silent drama from Germany about a doorman at a hotel and his meager existence, starring Emil Jannings. Directed by F. W. Murnau. **FF3, CL12** *Essential; Recommended*

Last Man on Earth, The (1964, B&W, 86m, NR)
Vincent Price plays the sole survivor of a world-wide plague who must fight nightly battles against blood-seeking victims. **ST124**

Last Metro, The (1980, C, 133m, PG)
Director François Truffaut's drama of a theater troupe in occupied Paris. Gerard Depardieu and Catherine Deneuve star. **DT106, ST29, ST31**

Last Movie, The (1971, C, 108m, R)
Offbeat drama about an American film company shooting on location in a poor village in Peru. Director Dennis Hopper

stars, with Peter Fonda, Kris Kristofferson, Julie Adams, Sylvia Miles, Rod Cameron, and Sam Fuller. **DR13, DT40, MU12, ST71**

Last Night at the Alamo (1983, B&W, 80m, NR)
The denizens of a Houston bar that's about to be demolished gather for one last stand in this comedy about urban cowboys. **WE12**

Last of Sheila, The (1973, C, 120m, PG)
A yacht party featuring a mystery game turns into something more serious when the hostess is found murdered. James Coburn, Dyan Cannon, James Mason, and Joan Hackett star. Anthony Perkins and Stephen Sondheim wrote the script. **MY9, MY12, ST102**

Last of the Finest, The (1990, C, 106m, R)
Brian Dennehy plays an overzealous cop suspended for his activities against drug dealers; he and his buddies uncover a political conspiracy involving city officials. **AC8**

Last of the Mohicans, The (1936, B&W, 91m, NR)
Randolph Scott stars in this adaptation of James Fenimore Cooper's adventure of the French and Indian War. **AC13, ST136**

Last of the Pony Riders (1953, B&W, 80m, NR)
Gene Autry saddles up for his last feature film, with sidekick Smiley Burnette. **ST3**

Last of the Red Hot Lovers, The (1972, C, 98m, PG)
Neil Simon comedy about a married man's inept attempts at various romantic affairs. Alan Arkin, Sally Kellerman, and Paula Prentiss star. **WR23**

Last Picture Show, The (1971, B&W, 118m, NR)
Screen version of Larry McMurtry's novel of a small Texas town and its frustrated inhabitants. Timothy Bottoms and Jeff Bridges star, with Cybill Shepherd, Ellen Burstyn, Cloris Leachman, Ben Johnson, Clu Gulager, Randy Quaid, and Sam Bottoms. Leach and Johnson won Oscars. Directed by Peter Bogdanovich. **DR19, DR26, ST11, XT4, XT5** *Recommended*

Last Remake of Beau Geste, The (1977, C, 83m, PG)
Spoof of French Foreign Legion movies, directed by and starring Marty Feldman, with Ann-Margret, Michael York, Peter Ustinov, James Earl Jones, and Trevor Howard. **CO7, ST76**

Last Ride of the Dalton Gang, The (1979, C, 150m, NR)
The story of the Old West's notorious gang of outlaws. Cliff Potts and Randy Quaid star, with Jack Palance and Dale Robertson. Originally made for TV. **WE14**

Last Rites (1988, C, 103m, R)
A mysterious woman, seeking sanctuary in a New York church, draws a young priest into a story of murder and revenge. Tom Berenger and Daphne Zuniga star. **DR16**

Last Starfighter, The (1984, C, 100m, PG)
A video game whiz is recruited into an interplanetary war. Science fiction adventure starring Lance Guest, Robert Preston, and Dan O'Herlihy. **SF8, SF13**

Last Tango in Paris (1973, C, 129m, X)
Controversial drama about a casual affair involving an American whose wife has just committed suicide and a free-spirited young Frenchwoman. Marlon Brando and Maria Schneider star, with Jean-Pierre Léaud. Bernardo Bertolucci directed. **CU6, CU13, DR1, DR3, DT9, ST10, XT16** *Essential; Recommended*

Last Temptation of Christ, The (1988, C, 160m, R)
Director Martin Scorsese's controversial adaptation of the Nikos Kazantzakis novel about Christ's human side. Willem Dafoe stars, with Barbara Hershey, Harvey Keitel, Harry Dean Stanton, John Lurie, and David Bowie. Music by Peter Gabriel. **DR19, DT95, HF16, MU12, ST141** *Recommended*

Last Time I Saw Paris, The (1954, C, 116m, NR)
Elizabeth Taylor and Van Johnson star in this drama, loosely based on an F. Scott Fitzgerald story, about Americans adrift in late 1940s Paris. **ST147, WR7**

Last Tycoon, The (1976, C, 125m, PG)
F. Scott Fitzgerald's final novel, the story of a driven movie executive and the people who support and oppose his power.

Robert DeNiro stars, with Jack Nicholson, Jeanne Moreau, Robert Mitchum, Theresa Russell, Ingrid Boulting, Tony Curtis, John Carradine, Ray Milland, Dana Andrews, and Anjelica Huston. Written by Harold Pinter; directed by Elia Kazan and produced by Sam Spiegel. **CU17, DR13, DR19, DT53, ST30, ST107, ST110, ST112, WR7** *Recommended*

Last Unicorn, The (1982, C, 95m, PG)
Animated story about a mythical beast trying to survive in an unfriendly world. Voices supplied by Alan Arkin, Jeff Bridges, and Mia Farrow. **FA10, ST11**

Last Valley, The (1971, C, 128m, R)
Adventure saga of a troop of 17th-century soldiers who stumble into a valley unchanged since the Thirty Years' War. Michael Caine and Omar Sharif star. Directed by James Clavell. **ST15**

Last Waltz, The (1978, C, 117m, PG)
Concert film of rock group The Band's farewell performance on Thanksgiving Day, 1976, featuring many of their hits, plus performances by Bob Dylan, Neil Young, Eric Clapton, Muddy Waters, Van Morrison, Joni Mitchell, and many more. Directed by Martin Scorsese. **DT95, MU10** *Highly Recommended*

Last War, The (1962, C, 79m, G)
From Japan, a science fiction drama about a future conflict that escalates into nuclear annihilation. **FF4, SF18**

Last Wave, The (1977, C, 106m, PG)
Richard Chamberlain stars in this Australian drama about a lawyer who gets more than he bargained for in defending an aborigine on a murder charge. Directed by Peter Weir. **DT111**

Last Woman on Earth (1961, C, 71m, NR)
Low-budget sci-fi drama from director Roger Corman, about a trio of survivors of an atomic holocaust. Antony Carbone, Edward Wain (Robert Towne), and Betsy Jones-Moreland star. Written by Wain. **DT22, SF12**

Last Year at Marienbad (1962, B&W, 93m, NR)
Cryptic, hypnotic film about a young man's attempts to seduce an attractive but enigmatic woman. Directed by Alain Resnais. **FF1** *Essential*

Late Show, The (1977, C, 94m, R)
Art Carney plays a private eye who gets
help from a kooky woman (Lily Tomlin)
in solving the murder of his ex-partner.
An offbeat, likable mystery from writer-
director Robert Benton. **DT6, MY10,
ST149** *Recommended*

Laughing Policeman, The (1974, C, 111m,
R)
San Francisco police track down a crazed
killer who has shot up a busload of peo-
ple. Walter Matthau, Bruce Dern, and
Louis Gossett, Jr. star. **AC9, ST104, XT13**

Laura (1944, B&W, 88m, NR)
Classic mystery starring Gene Tierney as
supposed victim, Dana Andrews as smit-
ten police detective, and Clifton Webb as
Waldo Lydecker, the key to the crime.
With Vincent Price and Judith Anderson.
Otto Preminger directed. **DT82, MY1,
MY3, MY5, ST124** *Essential; Recom-
mended*

Laurel and Hardy Comedy Classics (9 volumes: each B&W, 70-90m, NR)
Each volume of this series contains several short films by the great comedy duo.
ST87 *Recommended*

Lavender Hill Mob, The (1951, B&W,
82m, NR)
A caper comedy from Britain starring
Alec Guinness as a bank clerk who mas-
terminds a safe-cracking scheme. Watch
for Audrey Hepburn in a brief appearance. **CO10, CO17, MY15, MY17, MY18,
ST60, ST65** *Essential*

Law of Desire (1986, C, 100m, NR)
Comedy from Spanish director Pedro Almodóvar about a homosexual director of
adult movies, his transsexual sister, and
their various liaisons. Carmen Maura and
Eusebio Poncala star. **FF7**

Lawrence of Arabia (1962, C, 222m, G)
Peter O'Toole's stunning star debut as
T.E. Lawrence, the Englishman who led
Arab tribesmen against the Turks in the
1920s. With Omar Sharif, Alec Guinness,
Anthony Quinn, Arthur Kennedy, Stanley Baker, and Jack Hawkins. Directed
by David Lean. Available in a letterbox-
format version which includes footage restored from original cut of the film. **CL2,
CU10, CU19, DT59, ST60, ST117, XT1,
XT6, XT21** *Essential; Highly Recommended*

Lean on Me (1989, C, 104m, PG-13)
Real-life story of New Jersey high school
principal Joe Clark, who brought order to
an inner-city school plagued by crime and
dropouts. Morgan Freeman stars. **DR6,
DR25, ST48**

Learning Tree, The (1969, C, 107m, PG)
Gordon Parks directed this version of his
autobiographical novel about a young
black boy growing up in 1920s Kansas.
DR14

Leave 'Em Laughing (1981, C, 100m, NR)
Mickey Rooney plays a clown who takes
in homeless kids in this true story set in
Chicago. Originally made for TV. **ST133**

Left Hand of God, The (1955, C, 87m,
NR)
A priest is caught in the political turbu-
lence of post-World War II China. Hum-
phrey Bogart, Gene Tierney, and Lee J.
Cobb star. **ST8**

Left-Handed Gun, The (1958, B&W,
102m, NR)
Paul Newman plays Billy the Kid in this
psychological study of the Kid's outlaw
ways. Based on Gore Vidal's TV play.
Directed by Arthur Penn. **DT78, HF1,
ST111, WE3**

Legacy, The (1979, C, 100m, R)
Two Americans are kidnapped and taken
to a British mansion where a secret cult
prepares to deal with them. Katharine
Ross and Sam Elliott star. **HO11**

Legal Eagles (1986, C, 116m, PG)
When a New York attorney is caught in a
compromising situation with his female
client who's suspected of murder, he calls
on a female lawyer for help. Robert Redford, Debra Winger, and Daryl Hannah
star in this comedy-mystery. **MY17,
ST126, ST163, XT9**

Legend (1986, C, 89m, PG)
A young hermit living in a magical forest
sets off to rescue a lovely maiden from
the forces of evil. Tom Cruise stars in this
lavishly produced adventure fantasy. Ridley Scott directed. **AC18, DT96, SF13,
SF14, ST26**

Legend of Frenchie King, The (1971, C,
97m, NR)
Brigitte Bardot stars in a western comedy
about female outlaws in New Mexico.

With Claudia Cardinale. Dubbed in English. **ST4**

Legend of Hell House, The (1973, C, 95m, PG)
Horror tale of researchers spending a week in a haunted house. Roddy McDowall and Pamela Franklin star. Richard Matheson wrote the screenplay. **HO2, HO3**

Legend of Lobo, The (1962, C, 67m, NR)
Family drama about a wild wolf from his days as a pup. Disney production features songs by the Sons of the Pioneers. **FA5**

Legend of Sleepy Hollow, The (1949, C, 49m, G)
Washington Irving's fantasy about Ichabod Crane and the Headless Horseman comes to life in this Disney animated feature. Narrated and sung by Bing Crosby. **FA2, ST25**

Legend of the Lone Ranger, The (1981, C, 98m, PG)
The Masked Man rides again in this bigscreen account of his origins. Klinton Spilsbury stars, with Michael Horse, Jason Robards, and Christopher Lloyd. **ST129, WE2**

Legend of the Lost (1957, C, 109m, NR)
Action in the Sahara, with John Wayne and Rossano Brazzi battling the elements—and each other, over Sophia Loren. **ST93, ST156**

Legend of the Werewolf (1975, C, 87m, R)
A Parisian zoo worker has a hairy problem when the moon is full. Peter Cushing stars as the investigator on his trail. **HO4, ST27**

Lemon Drop Kid, The (1951, B&W, 91m, NR)
Bob Hope is in hock to a gangster and tries to use his prowess at the racetrack to make the payment. **ST70**

Lemon Sisters, The (1990, C, 89m, PG-13)
Diane Keaton stars in this wistful comedy about a family show-biz act. With Kathryn Grody, Elliott Gould, Aidan Quinn, Ruben Blades, and Richard Libertini. **CO8, ST79**

Lenny (1974, B&W, 112m, R)
Dustin Hoffman plays controversial comic Lenny Bruce, whose life was plagued by troubles with the law and drugs. With Valerie Perrine. Bob Fosse directed. **DR4, DT39, ST67**

Lenny Bruce (1967, B&W, 60m, NR)
The only filmed performance of the controversial stand-up comic. **CU16** *Recommended*

Leonor (1975, C, 90m, NR)
Liv Ullmann stars in this strange drama about a woman who makes herself mistress to the Devil. **HO10, ST154**

Leopard Man, The (1943, B&W, 66m, NR)
Horror film about a small desert town terrorized by what it thinks is an escaped animal. Directed by Jacques Tourneur; produced by Val Lewton. **DT105, HO16, HO27**

Lepke (1975, C, 110m, R)
Tony Curtis plays real-life gangster Louis Lepke Buchalter, the head of Murder Inc., in this violent crime saga. **AC22**

Les Girls (1957, C, 114m, NR)
A star of a variety show (Gene Kelly) romances three dancing girls (Taina Elg, Kay Kendall, Mitzi Gaynor). Cole Porter wrote the score; Orry-Kelly won an Oscar for his costumes. George Cukor directed. **DT24, MU1, ST81**

Less Than Zero (1987, C, 98m, R)
A wealthy young crowd in Los Angeles hops from party to party and drug to drug. Adapted from the bestselling novel by Bret Easton Ellis. Andrew McCarthy, Jami Gertz, and Robert Downey, Jr. star. **DR9, DR19**

Lesson in Love, A (1954, B&W, 95m, NR)
From director Ingmar Bergman, the story of a married couple's separate affairs. Gunnar Bjornstrand and Eva Dahlbeck star. **DT7**

Let It Be (1970, C, 80m, G)
Documentary chronicles the Beatles' recording one of their last albums. Some memorable musical moments and insights into why the band broke up. **MU11**

Let It Ride (1989, C, 86m, PG-13)
Racetrack comedy, with Richard Dreyfuss as a compulsive gambler on a roll. With Teri Garr and David Johansen. **CO19, MU12, ST36**

Let There Be Light (1945, B&W, 60m, NR)
Director John Huston's documentary about the psychological effects of World War II combat. **CU16, DT50**

Lethal Weapon (1987, C, 110m, R)
Mel Gibson and Danny Glover are cop partners on the trail of vicious drug smugglers. Gary Busey costars in this urban action thriller. **AC9, ST53, ST55**

Lethal Weapon 2 (1989, C, 113m, R)
More buddy-cop action on the streets of L.A., with Mel Gibson and Danny Glover, with the latter marked for murder by South African government agents. With Joe Pesci. **AC9, ST53, ST55, XT10**

Let's Dance (1950, C, 112m, NR)
Fred Astaire and Betty Hutton star in this musical tale of former dance partners fighting for custody of her young son. **ST2**

Let's Do It Again (1975, C, 112m, PG)
Sequel to *Uptown Saturday Night* has Sidney Poitier and pal Bill Cosby as wacky lodge brothers hoping to cash in on a "hypnotized" boxer (Jimmie Walker). **ST121**

Let's Get Harry (1986, C, 98m, R)
An American businessman (Mark Harmon) is kidnapped by terrorists in South America, and a soldier of fortune leads his buddies on a rescue mission. Robert Duvall heads the expedition; Gary Busey and Glenn Frey follow his orders. **AC20, ST38, MU12**

Let's Get Lost (1989, B&W, 120m, NR)
Documentary portrait of jazz trumpeter and singer Chet Baker, whose turbulent life was marked by drug addiction. Directed by Bruce Weber. **CU16**

Let's Make Love (1960, C, 118m, NR)
Yves Montand plays a millionaire who falls for Marilyn Monroe in this show-biz saga. Bing Crosby, Milton Berle, and Gene Kelly have bit parts. George Cukor directed. **DT24, ST25, ST81, ST108**

Let's Spend the Night Together (1982, C, 94m, PG)
Concert film of the Rolling Stones' 1981 tour. **MU10**

Letter, The (1940, B&W, 95m, NR)
Bette Davis stars in the Somerset Maugham drama of a woman who claims self-defense in a twisted murder case. Directed by William Wyler. **CL5, DT119, ST28**

Letter From an Unknown Woman (1948, B&W, 90m, NR)
Joan Fontaine stars as a woman hopelessly in love with a dashing musician (Louis Jourdan). Directed with great style by Max Ophuls; written by Howard Koch. **CL4, CL6, DT76** *Recommended*

Letter to Brezhnev (1985, C, 95m, NR)
Comedy about two Liverpool working-class girls who meet a pair of lonely Russian sailors, with love unexpectedly blossoming between one couple. Alexandra Pigg and Peter Firth star. **CO17**

Leviathan (1989, C, 98m, R)
Undersea adventure, with something very strange and very large lurking in the depths. Peter Weller stars, with Richard Crenna, Amanda Pays, and Daniel Stern. **AC12**

Liaisons Dangereuses, Les (1959, B&W, 111m, NR)
Updating of the 18th-century tale of sexual intrigue among the French aristocracy, starring Gerard Phillipe as Valmont and Jeanne Moreau as Mme. Merteuil. With Jeanne Valerie and Annette Vadim; directed by Roger Vadim. Music by Thelonius Monk and Art Blakey. *Dangerous Liaisons* and *Valmont* used the same material in its original setting. **FF1, ST110**

Lianna (1983, C, 110m, R)
A married woman finds herself attracted to another woman in this drama from writer-director John Sayles. Linda Griffiths and Jane Hallaren star, with Sayles in a small role. **DR3, DT93**

Libeled Lady (1936, B&W, 98m, NR)
Classic comedy of a ruthless newspaper editor (Spencer Tracy) who uses his fiancee (Jean Harlow) and a reporter (William Powell) to get the lowdown on an heiress (Myrna Loy). **CL10, ST94, ST122, ST151** *Recommended*

Liberation of L. B. Jones, The (1970, C, 102m, R)
A hotly contested divorce case threatens to blow the lid off simmering race rela-

tions in a small Southern town. Lee J. Cobb stars in this drama from director William Wyler. **DR14, DR26, DT119**

Licence To Kill (1989, C, 133m, PG-13) James Bond tracks a drug kingpin in the second series installment to star Timothy Dalton. With Carey Lowell, Talisa Soto, Anthony Zerbe, Robert Davi, and Frank McRae. **HF2**

Lt. Robin Crusoe, USN (1966, C, 110m, G) Navy pilot Dick Van Dyke makes the most of his being stranded on a desert island in a family comedy from the Disney studios. **FA1**

Life and Death of Colonel Blimp, The (1943, C, 115m, NR) Epic drama of British soldier through many campaigns and personal crises, starring Roger Livesey and Deborah Kerr (in four roles). Directed by Michael Powell. Original running time: 163m. **DT81**

Life and Times of Grizzly Adams, The (1976, C, 93m, G) Family adventure about a fur trapper and his unlikely friendship with a bear. Dan Haggerty stars. **FA4**

Life and Times of Judge Roy Bean, The (1972, C, 124m, PG) An offbeat western drama from director John Huston, about the famous hanging judge of Texas. Paul Newman heads the cast, which includes Jacqueline Bisset, Stacy Keach, Victoria Principal, Anthony Perkins, Ava Gardner, and the director himself. **DT50, ST111, WE15**

Life of Emile Zola, The (1937, B&W, 116m, NR) Classic biography of French writer, highlighted by his role in the Dreyfus scandal. Paul Muni stars, with Oscar winner Joseph Schildkraut as Dreyfus. Film won Best Picture Oscar as well. **CL2, XT1, XT4**

Life of Oharu, The (1952, B&W, 146m, NR) From Japan, the story of a woman banished because of her forbidden love for a samurai warrior (Toshiro Mifune). Kenji Mizoguchi directed. **FF4, ST106**

Life With Father (1947, C, 118m, NR) Long-running Broadway comedy about colorful family headed by a strong patriarch, in turn-of-the-century New York City. William Powell, Irene Dunne, and Elizabeth Taylor star. **CO5, DR20, ST122, ST147**

Lifeboat (1944, B&W, 96m, NR) The survivors of a German submarine attack struggle to survive in a small boat. Alfred Hitchcock thriller starring Tallulah Bankhead, Walter Slezak, and William Bendix. **AC24, DT46**

Lifeforce (1985, C, 100m, R) Astronauts return to Earth as blood-sucking vampires in this horror-science fiction film from director Tobe Hooper. **DT47, HO5, SF20**

Lift, The (1985, C, 95m, R) From Holland, a horror film about an elevator that begins attacking its passengers. **HO22**

Light at the Edge of the World (1971, C, 126m, PG) Jules Verne saga of lighthouse keeper (Kirk Douglas) and pirate (Yul Brynner) battling for possession of an island and a lovely woman (Samantha Eggar). **ST34, WR28**

Light in the Forest, The (1958, C, 93m, NR) Disney adventure of a white boy raised by Indians and returned to his original family. James MacArthur, Carol Lynley, and Fess Parker star. **FA1**

Light of Day (1987, C, 107m, PG-13) A factory worker and his single-parent sister spend their evenings performing in a bar band in Cleveland. Michael J. Fox, Joan Jett, and Gena Rowlands star in this drama about a family in crisis. **DR8**

Lighthorsemen, The (1987, C, 111m, PG) Australian adventure tale of a company of horse soldiers and their disastrous World War I campaign against the Turks. Directed by Simon Wincer. **AC2, FF5**

Lightning Over Water (1980, C, 91m, NR) A heartfelt documentary portrait of American film director Nicholas Ray, by his German colleague Wim Wenders. Shot during the final days of Ray's life. **CU16, DT83, DT113**

Lightning: The White Stallion (1986, C, 93m, PG)
A horse trainer has his prize stallion stolen and recovers it with the help of two youngsters. Mickey Rooney stars in this family adventure. **FA1, FA4, ST133**

Lights of Old Santa Fe (1944, B&W, 79m NR)
A rodeo trick rider leaves the big time to help a struggling friend's show. Roy Rogers stars, with Dale Evans and Gabby Hayes. **ST132**

Lightship, The (1985, C, 89m, R)
A trio of crooks lay siege to a lightship in this offbeat thriller starring Robert Duvall and Klaus Maria Brandauer. Directed by Jerzy Skolimowski. **ST38**

Lili (1952, C, 81m, G)
Leslie Caron plays a teenaged orphan who joins a circus and helps a bitter puppeteer (Mel Ferrer) see the good things in life. The theme song, "Hi Lili, Hi Lo," helped the film score to win an Oscar. **MU1**

Lilies of the Field (1963, B&W, 93m, NR)
Sidney Poitier won an Oscar for his performance as a handyman who comes to the aid of a group of German nuns trying to build a chapel in the Arizona desert. **ST121, XT2**

Lilith (1964, B&W, 114m, NR)
Warren Beatty plays a naive young therapist who falls under the spell of one of his patients. With Jean Seberg, Peter Fonda, and Gene Hackman. Directed by Robert Rossen. **DR3, ST5, ST61** *Recommended*

Limelight (1952, B&W, 120m, NR)
Charlie Chaplin's sentimental drama of a washed-up comedian who's given inspiration by a young ballerina (Claire Bloom). Buster Keaton appears as a colleague of Chaplin's in one unforgettable scene. **CL6, CL7, DT18, DT54** *Essential*

Link (1986, C, 103m, R)
A crazed scientist and his lovely assistant are endangered species when his experimental chimps launch a revolt. Terence Stamp and Elisabeth Shue star. **HO16, HO19, HO20**

Lion in Winter, The (1968, C, 134m, PG)
Katharine Hepburn is Eleanor of Aquitaine, Peter O'Toole is Henry II in this drama of familial and political intrigue in medieval England. Hepburn won her third Oscar for her performance. **DR5, ST66, ST117, XT3**

Lion, the Witch, and the Wardrobe, The (1983, C, 95m, NR)
When four children walk through a magic wardrobe closet, they're transported into a magical land and meet an evil witch and a kindly lion. An animated adventure based on C.S. Lewis's *Narnia* tales. **FA10**

Lionheart (1990, C, 105m, PG)
Family adventure tale of a young knight (Eric Stoltz) off to join King Richard for the Crusades. With Gabriel Byrne. **AC16, FA4**

Liquid Sky (1983, C, 112m, R)
Cult science fiction film about aliens who land in New York in the middle of the punk-downtown scene. Anne Carlisle plays a male and female role in this highly original film. **CU4, CU6, SF22, XT9** *Recommended*

List of Adrian Messenger, The (1963, B&W, 98m, NR)
Whodunit set on an Irish estate during hunting season, with guest stars in disguise as the suspects. George C. Scott plays detective; Kirk Doulgas, Frank Sinatra, Tony Curtis, Robert Mitchum, and Burt Lancaster are the guest stars. Directed by John Huston, who also appears in a small role. **DT50, MY12, ST34, ST85, ST107, ST138**

Listen to Me (1989, C, 90m, PG-13)
Drama of college students competing on debate squad, with abortion as the Big Topic. Jami Gertz and Kirk Cameron star, with Roy Scheider. **DR7, DR25**

Lisztomania (1975, C, 105m, R)
A stylized, anything-goes biography of composer Franz Liszt, starring rock singer Roger Daltrey, directed by Ken Russell. Not for viewers with tender sensibilities. **DT92, MU5**

Little Big Man (1970, C, 150m, PG)
The tall tale of Jack Crabbe, a 130-year-old man who claims he was the only white to survive Custer's Last Stand. Dustin Hoffman stars, with Faye Dunaway, Chief Dan George, Richard Mulligan as George Armstrong Custer, and Jeff Corey as Wild Bill Hickok. Arthur Penn di-

rected; based on the novel by Thomas Berger. **DR19, DT78, HF6, HF11, ST37, ST67, WE1, WE7**

Little Boy Lost (1953, B&W, 95m, NR)
A journalist travels to post-World War II France to find his orphaned son. Bing Crosby stars. **ST25**

Little Caesar (1930, B&W, 80m, NR)
Edward G. Robinson plays Rico, the mob boss modeled on Al Capone, in this early gangster classic. **AC22, ST130** *Essential; Highly Recommended*

Little Colonel, The (1935, B&W, 80m, NR)
In the Reconstruction South, a little girl reunites her feuding mother and grandpa. Shirley Temple, Lionel Barrymore, and Bill Robinson star. **ST148**

Little Dorritt (1988, C, 360m, G)
Epic version of the Charles Dickens novel about the trials and tribulations of a young girl and her father. Divided into two films: "Nobody's Fault" (177m) and "Dorritt's Story" (183m). Derek Jacobi and Sarah Pickering star, with Alec Guinness. **DR23, ST60, WR4**

Little Drummer Girl, The (1984, C, 130m, R)
From John LeCarre's novel, the story of a British actress recruited by Israeli intelligence to trap a terrorist. Diane Keaton and Klaus Kinski star. **MY6, ST79, ST83, WR15** *Recommended*

Little Foxes, The (1941, B&W, 116m, NR)
Lillian Hellman drama about the collapse of a Southern family, starring Bette Davis in one of her showcase performances. Herbert Marshall and Teresa Wright co-star. Directed by William Wyler. **DR20, DT119, ST28**

Little Girl Who Lives Down the Lane, The (1976, C, 94m, PG)
Subtle horror mystery about a strange girl whose father has been missing for a long time and a menacing man with a special interest in her. Jodie Foster and Martin Sheen star. **HO13, ST47**

Little Gloria. . . Happy at Last (1982, C, 200m, NR)
True story of bitter custody fight over young Gloria Vanderbilt, with Bette Da-

vis, Angela Lansbury, and Christopher Plummer. Originally made for TV. **ST28**

Little Lord Fauntleroy (1936, B&W, 98m, NR)
Freddie Bartholomew plays the young American who suddenly finds himself a British lord in this adaptation of the classic children's story. C. Aubrey Smith and Mickey Rooney costar. **FA3, ST133**

Little Lord Fauntleroy (1980, C, 100m, NR)
TV movie remake of the children's classic about an American lad in Britain. Ricky Schroder and Alec Guinness star. **FA3, ST60**

Little Mermaid, The (1984, C, 55m, NR)
A Faerie Tale Theatre presentation of the Hans Christian Andersen tale. A lovely sea creature (Pam Dawber) has to choose between her home in the ocean and life on land with a sailor (Treat Williams). **FA12**

Little Mermaid, The (1989, C, 82m, G)
Disney animated feature, based on the Hans Christian Andersen tale, with an Oscar-winning musical score. **FA2** *Recommended*

Little Minister, The (1934, B&W, 110m, NR)
Katharine Hepburn plays a gypsy girl who falls in love with a Scottish minister. **ST66**

Little Miss Broadway (1938, B&W, 70m, NR)
Shirley Temple stars in a musical about a theatrical boarding house. George Murphy and Jimmy Durante are on hand, too. **ST148**

Little Miss Marker (1980, C, 103m, PG)
Comedy set in the 1930s about a little girl left with a bookie as an IOU. Walter Matthau, Julie Andrews, Bob Newhart, and Sara Stimson star. **FA6, ST104**

Little Monsters (1989, C, 103m, PG)
Fantasy-comedy of a young boy discovering a gang of monsters under his bed. Fred Savage stars, with Howie Mandel and Daniel Stern. **CO11, FA8**

Little Murders (1971, C, 110m, PG)
Dark comedy, written by cartoonist Jules Feiffer, about life in a New York City

where random killings are the order of the day. Elliott Gould and Marcia Rodd star, with Vincent Gardenia, Elizabeth Wilson, Donald Sutherland, and Alan Arkin, who directed. **CO2, CO12, CU5**

Little Night Music, A (1978, C, 124m, PG) Stephen Sondheim musical, based on Ingmar Bergman's comedy *Smiles of a Summer Night,* about summertime romance among the rich and beautiful people. Elizabeth Taylor and Diana Rigg star. Musical highlight: "Send in the Clowns." **MU2, MU14, MU17, ST147**

Little Nikita (1988, C, 98m, PG) F.B.I. agent has the tough task of telling an American teen that his parents are Soviet agents. Sidney Poitier and River Phoenix star. **ST121**

Little Prince, The (1974, C, 88m, G) Unusual musical based on children's book about a young boy and his friendship with an aviator. Richard Kiley, Bob Fosse, Gene Wilder, and Steven Warner star. Stanley Donen directed. **DT30, DT39, MU16**

Little Princess, The (1939, B&W#, C, 93m, NR) Shirley Temple stars as a Victorian waif searching for her soldier father. With Cesar Romero and Arthur Treacher. **ST148**

Little Red Riding Hood (1985, C, 60m, NR) This Faerie Tale Theatre presentation features Mary Steenburgen as the unsuspecting girl and Malcolm McDowell as the evil wolf. **FA12**

Little Romance, A (1979, C, 108m, PG) Laurence Olivier plays matchmaker in Paris to a young American girl (Diane Lane) and her new French boyfriend (Thelonius Bernard) **CO4, ST116, XT16**

Little Shop of Horrors, The (1960, B&W, 70m, NR) Low-budget horror comedy (supposedly filmed in 3 days) about a man-eating plant and its nerdy keeper. Joanthan Haze stars; Jack Nicholson has a small part as a pain-loving dental patient. Directed by Roger Corman. **CU4, DT22, HO24, ST112**

Little Shop of Horrors (1986, C, 88m, PG-13) Musical version of the horror comedy about a man-eating plant named Audrey II. Rick Moranis and Steve Martin star. Bill Murray, John Candy, and Jim Belushi make brief appearances. **CO13, CO14, MU8, MU14, MU16, ST99**

Little Thief, The (1989, C, 104m, R) French drama of a rebellious adolescent girl growing up in the stifling 1950s, starring Charlotte Gainsbourg. **FF1**

Little Treasure (1985, C, 95m, R) An American stripper journeys to Mexico to visit her father but winds up searching for treasure with an amiable adventurer. Margot Kidder, Burt Lancaster, and Ted Danson are the stars. **ST85**

Little Vera (1989, C, 110m, NR) Comedy from the Soviet Union, centering on a rebellious, sexy teenager (Natalya Negoda) and her family problems. **FF7**

Little Women (1933, B&W, 115m, NR) Louisa May Alcott's classic novel of a family full of varied sisters, starring Katharine Hepburn and Joan Bennett. Directed by George Cukor. **CL1, DT24, ST66**

Little Women (1949, C, 121m, NR) All-star MGM cast is featured in this version of Louisa May Alcott's book, with June Allyson, Margaret O'Brien, Elizabeth Taylor, and Peter Lawford leading the way. **CL1, ST147**

Littlest Horse Thieves, The (1977, C, 104m, G) Three children attempt to save a herd of abused ponies who work in the mines. Disney drama set in turn-of-the-century England. **FA1**

Littlest Outlaw, The (1955, C, 75m, NR) A Mexican boy, fearful that a horse will be destroyed, runs away with it. Disney family drama. **FA1**

Littlest Rebel, The (1935, B&W, 70m, NR) A little girl saves her father from prison during the Civil War by pleading directly to President Lincoln. Shirley Temple stars, with Bill Robinson and Frank McGlynn as Lincoln. **HF17, ST148**

Live a Little, Love a Little (1968, C, 90m, NR)
Elvis Presley plays a photographer who moonlights at a second job—and manages to fit in a little singin' as well. With Michele Carey and Rudy Vallee. **ST123**

Live and Let Die (1973, C, 121m, PG)
Roger Moore's debut as James Bond has 007 chasing down a madman who's distributing drugs as part of his scheme to take over the world. Yaphet Kotto costars. **HF2**

Lives of a Bengal Lancer, The (1935, B&W, 109m, NR)
Gary Cooper heads the cast of this classic adventure tale about a British regiment on patrol in India. **AC13, FA4, ST22**

Living Daylights, The (1987, C, 130m, PG)
Timothy Dalton takes over the James Bond role in this story of a rogue Soviet general (Jeroen Krabbe) and a crooked international arms dealer (Joe Don Baker). Maryam D'Abo and John Rhys-Davies costar. **HF2**

Living Desert, The (1953, C, 73m, G)
Oscar-winning documentary about flora and fauna in the American desert, from the Disney studios. **FA1**

Living Free (1972, C, 91m, G)
Sequel to *Born Free* features more action with Elsa and her cubs in the African wilderness. Susan Hampshire and Nigel Davenport star. **FA5**

Living on Tokyo Time (1987, C, 83m, NR)
Comedy centering on a marriage of convenience between a Japanese woman visiting San Francisco who barely speaks English, and a Japanese-American who speaks no Japanese. Minako Ohashi and Ken Nakagawa star. **CO1, CO2**

Local Hero (1983, C, 111m, PG)
Charming, original comedy about an American oil company trying to buy a Scottish fishing village as a site for a refinery. Peter Riegert and Burt Lancaster star, with Fulton MacKay, Denis Lawson, Jenny Seagrove, and Peter Capaldi. Written and directed by Bill Forsyth; music by Mark Knopfler. **CO2, CO17, DT38, ST85** *Highly Recommended*

Lock Up (1989, C, 105m, R)
Prison drama of rebel convict (Sylvester Stallone) and sadistic warden (Donald Sutherland). **DR18, ST140**

Lodger, The (1926, B&W, 125m, NR)
Silent thriller from Alfred Hitchcock, his first foray into suspense, about a mysterious man suspected of committing a series of murders in London. Ivor Novello stars. **DT46, MY13**

Logan's Run (1976, C, 120m, PG)
Science fiction adventure about a society of unlimited pleasures but extermination at the age of 30, and one man's attempt to escape that fate. Michael York and Jenny Agutter star. The special effects won an Oscar. **SF8, SF15**

Lola (1961, B&W, 90m, NR)
Comedy-drama from France, about a cabaret entertainer (Anouk Aimee) trying to remain faithful to her lover, who left her seven years ago. Written and directed by Jacques Demy. **FF1**

Lola (1969, C, 88m, PG)
A teenager (Susan George) and a middle-aged writer (Charles Bronson) fall in love. Also known as *Twinky*. **ST12**

Lola Montes (1955, C, 110m, PG-13)
The story of a famed circus performer and her many affairs with European nobility. A classic unappreciated on its initial release. Directed by Max Ophuls. Available in letterboxed format. **CL14, CU19, DT76**

Lolita (1962, B&W, 152m, NR)
Dark comedy about a middle-aged man's obsession with a sexy teenager. James Mason stars, with Sue Lyon, Peter Sellers, and Shelley Winters. Stanely Kubrick directed; Vladimir Nabokov adapted his own novel. **CO12, DR19, DT56, ST102, ST137, ST164** *Recommended*

Lone Wolf McQuade (1983, C, 107m, PG)
Chuck Norris, as a Texas Ranger, and David Carradine, as a drug lord, square off in this modern-day western with plenty of martial arts thrown in. **ST114**

Lonely Are the Brave (1962, B&W, 107m, NR)
In the contemporary West, a rebellious cowboy leads a posse on a wild chase.

Kirk Douglas, Gena Rowlands, and Walter Matthau star. **ST34, ST104, WE12** *Recommended*

Lonely Guy, The (1983, C, 91m, R)
When Steve Martin's girl friend walks out on him, he joins the official ranks of America's lonely guys in this contemporary comedy. Charles Grodin costars. **CO2, ST59, ST99**

Lonely Hearts (1981, C, 95m, R)
A romantic drama from Australia about the unlikely pairing of a piano tuner and an awkwardly shy office worker. Wendy Hughes and Norman Kaye star. **FF5**

Lonely Lady, The (1983, C, 92m, R)
A screenwriter claws (and sleeps) her way to the top of the Hollywood heap. This adaptation of the Harold Robbins novel stars Pia Zadora and virtually defines the word "trash." **CU2**

Lonely Man, The (1957, B&W, 87m, NR)
Western drama of a gunfighter trying to put his killing days behind him and find peace with his son. Jack Palance and Tony Perkins star, with Neville Brand, Claude Akins, and Lee Van Cleef. **ST155, WE2**

Lonely Passion of Judith Hearne, The (1987, C, 116m, R)
Maggie Smith stars in this drama of an Irish spinster's troubles. With Bob Hoskins and Wendy Hiller. Based on Brian Moore's novel. **DR19, DR23, ST72**

Lonelyhearts (1958, B&W, 101m, NR)
A reporter takes on his newspaper's advice to the lovelorn column and begins to take his readers' problems to heart. Montgomery Clift stars in this version of Nathanael West's novel, with Robert Ryan, Myrna Loy, and Maureen Stapleton. **DR19, ST94**

Long, Dark Hall, The (1951, B&W, 96m, NR)
Rex Harrison plays a man accused of murder, but his wife (Lilli Palmer) stands by his claims of innocence. **MY15**

Long Day's Journey Into Night (1962, B&W, 170m, NR)
Eugene O'Neill's famous autobiographical play about a family in turmoil, starring Katharine Hepburn, Ralph Richardson, Jason Robards, and Dean Stockwell. Directed by Sidney Lumet. **DR8, DR20, DT65, ST66, ST129, ST144, WR20** *Highly Recommended*

Long Day's Journey Into Night (1987, C, 169m, NR)
Jack Lemmon stars in this made-for-TV version of the O'Neill classic, with Bethel Leslie, Peter Gallagher, and Kevin Spacey. **DR8, DR20, ST90, WR20**

Long Gone (1987, C, 113m, NR)
Comedy-drama of life in baseball's minor leagues, starring William Petersen and Virginia Madsen. Originally made for cable TV. **DR22**

Long Good Friday, The (1980, C, 114m, R)
A British gangster saga, with Bob Hoskins superb as a London crime boss whose empire suddenly begins to crumble. Helen Mirren costars. **AC22, DR23, ST72, XT15** *Highly Recommended*

Long, Hot Summer, The (1958, C, 117m, NR)
William Faulkner's stories are the basis for this starpowered melodrama of Mississippi life, with Paul Newman, Joanne Woodward, Orson Welles, Lee Remick, Anthony Franciosa, and Angela Lansbury. Directed by Martin Ritt. **DT87, DT112, ST111, ST166, WR6**

Long Hot Summer, The (1985, C, 208m, NR)
TV miniseries remake of the 1958 film, based on Faulkner stories, stars Don Johnson, Cybill Shepherd, Jason Robards, Judith Ivey, Ava Gardner, and Wings Hauser. **ST129, WR6**

Long Riders, The (1980, C, 100m, R)
The story of the James Brothers and their friends and enemies, with four real-life sets of brothers (Carradine, Quaid, Keach, and Guest) starring. Stacy and James Keach plays Frank and Jesse James. Directed by Walter Hill; music by Ry Cooder. **DT45, HF16, WE3, XT8**

Long Voyage Home, The (1940, B&W, 105m, NR)
Drama of Swedish seamen, starring John Wayne, Thomas Mitchell, and Barry Fitzgerald. Adapted from Eugene O'Neill's plays; directed by John Ford. **DT36, ST156, WR20**

Longest Day, The (1962, B&W, 180m, NR) Mammoth recreation of the Normandy Invasion, featuring an all-star, nearly all-male cast, including John Wayne, Henry Fonda, Richard Burton, Robert Mitchum, Sean Connery, and many more. **AC1, ST13, ST27, ST44, ST107, ST156** *Recommended*

Longest Yard, The (1974, C, 123m, R) Prison comedy-drama, with an ex-pro football star (Burt Reynolds) leading the cons in a rousing game against the vicious guards and their tyrannical warden. Eddie Albert is the warden; among the players are Michael Conrad, Ed Lauter, and Richard Kiel. **CO19, DR18, ST128**

Longshot, The (1985, C, 110m, PG) Tim Conway—Harvey Korman comedy set at a racetrack, directed by Paul Bartel. **DT5**

Look Back in Anger (1958, B&W, 99m, NR) Classic contemporary British drama of angry young man (Richard Burton) lashing out at society for all its injustices. With Mary Ure and Claire Bloom. Tony Richardson directed on location in London. Based on the play by John Osborne. **DR20, DR23, ST13, XT15** *Essential; Recommended*

Look Who's Talking (1989, C, 90m, PG-13) Gimmick comedy has single mother giving birth to baby whose wisecracking thoughts are voiced by Bruce Willis. Kirstie Alley and John Travolta costar. **CO5, ST161**

Looker (1981, C, 94m, PG) A plastic surgeon uncovers a corporate plot to reproduce female models by computer image and eliminate the real people. Albert Finney, James Coburn, and Susan Dey star in this science fiction mystery. **SF5, ST42**

Looking for Mr. Goodbar (1977, C, 135m, R) Schoolteacher Diane Keaton prowls singles bars at night, with disastrous consequences. Drama based on a true story. With Tuesday Weld, Richard Kiley, William Atherton, Richard Gere and Tom Berenger. **DR3, DR7, ST52, ST79**

Looking Glass War, The (1970, C, 108m, PG) John LeCarre thriller about a photographer out to get picture of a secret rocket in East Berlin. Christopher Jones, Ralph Richardson, and Anthony Hopkins star. **MY6, WR15**

Looney, Looney, Looney Bugs Bunny Movie, The (1981, C, 79m, G) Bugs and all his pals, from Yosemite Sam to Daffy Duck and Porky Pig, are on hand for this collection of Warner Bros. cartoons. **FA11**

Loophole (1980, C, 105m, NR) Albert Finney stars in a thriller about an unemployed architect who takes part in a bank heist. With Martin Sheen and Susannah York. **MY18, ST42**

Loose Cannons (1990, C, 93m, R) Buddy cop comedy matches weary veteran (Gene Hackman) and nutty younger partner (Dan Aykroyd). With Dom DeLuise, Ronny Cox, Nancy Travis, and Robert Prosky. **CO10, CO13, ST61**

Loose Shoes (1980, C, 74m, PG) Comic collection of coming attractions for movies you'll never see: *Skateboarders From Hell, Welcome to Bacon County, The Yid and the Kid,* etc. The cast of this spoof includes Bill Murray, Howard Hesseman, Ed Lauter, Susan Tyrrell, and Buddy Hackett. **CO7, CO13**

Loot . . . Give Me Money, Honey! (1972, C, 101m, PG) Dark comedy, based on Joe Orton play, about a pair of bank robbers who hide their stash in a coffin. Lee Remick, Richard Attenborough, Roy Holder, and Hywel Bennett star. **CO12, CO17**

Lord Jim (1965, C, 154m, NR) Peter O'Toole stars in Joseph Conrad's tale of a British sailor living with guilt over a single act of cowardice. With James Mason, Curt Jurgens, and Eli Wallach. **DR19, ST102, ST117**

Lord of the Flies (1963, B&W, 90m, NR) After an atomic holocaust, a planeload of young boys escaping the devastation crashes on a jungle island. Adapted from William Golding's bestselling novel. **AC12, AC24, DR9, DR19, SF12**

Lord of the Flies (1990, C, 90m, R)
Second version of the Golding classic changes boys to American military school students, removes references to atomic holocaust. **AC12, AC24, CU18, DR9, DR19**

Lord of the Rings (1978, C, 133m, PG)
The first of the famous J.R.R. Tolkien books about the fantastic characters of Middle Earth to be filmed. An animated feature for the entire family. **FA8, FA10, SF13**

Lords of Flatbush, The (1974, C, 88m, PG)
Comedy about a gang of fun-loving guys living in Brooklyn in the 1950s. Sylvester Stallone, Henry Winkler, and Perry King star, with Susan Blakely. **CO6, ST140**

Losin' It (1983, C, 104m, R)
A trio of teens make their way to Tijuana for a wild weekend. Tom Cruise, Jackie Earle Haley, and John Stockwell star, with Shelley Long. **ST26**

Lost Angels (1989, C, 116m, R)
An institution for the children of wealth with emotional problems is the setting for this drama of life in Los Angeles, starring Adam Horovitz and Donald Sutherland. **DR9, MU12**

Lost Boys, The (1987, C, 97m, R)
Horror story of two teenaged brothers up against a gang of teen vampires in a small town. Kiefer Sutherland, Corey Haim, and Jason Patric star. **HO5, HO13**

Lost Command (1966, C, 130m, NR)
Combat action between French and Algerian forces, starring Anthony Quinn, Alain Delon, George Segal, and Claudia Cardinale. **AC6**

Lost Honor of Katharina Blum, The (1975, C, 97m, R)
A political thriller from Germany about a woman (Margarethe von Trotta) who's persecuted by officials after she spends the night with a suspected terrorist. Directed by Volker Schlöndorff. **FF3**

Lost Horizon (1937, B&W, 132m, G)
Director Frank Capra's classic fable about a group of stranded travelers who stumble onto the kingdom of Shangri-la. Ronald Colman stars, with Jane Wyatt, Thomas Mitchell, Margo, and Sam Jaffe. The video version restores about 15 min-

utes of footage from the film's original release. **CU10, DT16, SF2** *Essential*

Lost in America (1985, C, 91m, R)
Writer-director Albert Brooks stars in this brilliant satire about a middle-class couple who decide to quit their jobs and take to the great American road. With Julie Hagerty and Garry Marshall. **CO2, DT12, XT18** *Highly Recommended*

Lost in the Stars (1974, C, 114m, NR)
The Kurt Weill-Maxwell Anderson musical based on Alan Paton's novel *Cry, the Beloved Country,* about a South African minister's trials and tribulations under apartheid. Brock Peters heads the all-black cast. **DR14, MU13**

Lost Patrol, The (1934, B&W, 74m, NR)
A British army patrol is stranded in the African desert, and Arab tribesmen pick them off one by one. Classic adventure directed by John Ford, starring Victor McLaglen and Boris Karloff. **AC13, DT36, ST77** *Recommended*

Lost Squadron, The (1932, B&W, 79m, NR)
Drama of former World War I aces working as movie stunt pilots. Richard Dix stars, with Mary Astor, Joel McCrea, and Erich Von Stroheim as an egomaniacal director. **CL7, DT109**

Lost Weekend, The (1945, B&W, 101m, NR)
Ray Milland plays an alcoholic who lives only for his next drink in this drama. Oscar winner for Best Picture, Actor, and Director (Billy Wilder). **CL8, DT116, XT1, XT2, XT6** *Essential*

Lost World, The (1925, B&W, 77m, NR)
Classic silent adventure about a modern expedition stumbling onto a prehistoric region. One of the first films to make extensive use of special effects techniques. **AC13, SF4, SF16**

Lots of Luck (1985, C, 88m, NR)
An unlucky family find their fortunes reversed when they win a lottery. Unfortunately, they also lose all claims to privacy. Disney comedy stars Martin Mull, Annette Funicello, and Fred Willard. Originally made for cable TV. **FA1**

Louisiana Story (1948, B&W, 79m, NR)
Classic documentary, directed by Robert
Flaherty, centering on the arrival of an
oil-drilling operation in the Louisiana
bayou. Made on commission from Standard Oil Company. Music by Virgil
Thomson. **CU16** *Essential; Recommended*

Loulou (1980, C, 110m, NR)
French drama of a lout (Gerard Depar-
dieu) who persuades a married woman
(Isabelle Huppert) to leave her husband.
Directed by Maurice Pialat. **FF1, ST31**

Love Among the Ruins (1975, C, 100m,
NR)
An aging actress hires a barrister to defend her in a breach of promise suit. She's
unaware but he still recalls that the two
were long-ago lovers. Katharine Hepburn
and Laurence Olivier star. George Cukor
directed. Originally made for TV. **DT24,
ST66, ST116** *Recommended*

Love and Anarchy (1973, C, 108m, R)
From Italian director Lina Wertmüller, a
drama of an Italian peasant's plan to assassinate Mussolini. Giancarlo Giannini
stars. **DT114**

Love and Bullets (1979, C, 95m, PG)
Charles Bronson plays an F.B.I. agent
assigned to retrieve a mobster's girl friend
from Switzerland; instead, he falls in love
with her. **ST12**

Love and Death (1975, C, 82m, PG)
Woody Allen spoofs foreign movies, Russian literature, Napoleon (James Tolkan),
and more. Diane Keaton and Alfred Lutter costar. **DT1, HF18, ST79**

Love and Money (1982, C, 90m, R)
Bizarre drama of rich businessman (Klaus
Kinski) and the wayward man (Ray Shar-
key) he tries to hire. With Ornella Muti
and King Vidor. Written and directed by
James Toback. **DT107, ST83**

Love at First Bite (1979, C, 96m, PG)
Comic twist on the Dracula story has
George Hamilton as a lovesick vampire,
traveling to New York to meet (and nip
on) the girl of his dreams. **CO7, HF7,
HO5, HO24**

Love at Large (1990, C, 97m, R)
A private eye, hired by a mysterious
woman to tail her lover, winds up following the wrong man, who turns out to be a
bigamist. Tom Berenger stars in this mystery with its share of comic moments.
With Elizabeth Perkins, Anne Archer,
Ted Levine, Annette O'Toole, Kate Capshaw, Ann Magnuson, and Neil Young.
Directed by Alan Rudolph. **CO1, DR1,
DT91, MU12, MY10**

Love Bug, The (1968, C, 108m, G)
Herbie is a Volkswagen with a mind of his
own in this popular Disney comedy that
spun off many sequels. Dean Jones and
Michelle Lee costar. **FA1**

Love Butcher, The (1975, C, 84m, R)
A nerdy gardener, spurned by women,
turns up as an alter ego seducer, his
"twin" brother, to murder them. Horror
film stars Erik Stern. **HO9**

Love Finds Andy Hardy (1938, B&W,
90m, NR)
Mickey Rooney has true romance problems, trying to decide among Judy Garland, Lana Turner, and Ann Rutherford.
ST51, ST133, ST153

Love From a Stranger (1947, B&W, 81m,
NR)
Agatha Christie story of a woman (Sylvia
Sidney) who learns that her husband is a
killer. John Hodiak and John Howard co-
star. **MY3, WR3**

Love Happy (1949, B&W, 91m, NR)
Late Marx Brothers film about putting on
a show. Marilyn Monroe has a small part.
ST101, ST108

Love in the Afternoon (1957, B&W, 130m,
NR)
Romance blossoms between Gary Cooper
and Audrey Hepburn in this comedy set
in Paris. Billy Wilder directed. **DT116,
ST22, ST65**

Love in the City (1953, B&W, 90m, NR)
Six Italian directors demonstrate different aspects of love in Rome. Contributors
include Federico Fellini and Michelangelo
Antonioni. **DT3, DT53, XT17**

Love Is a Many Splendored Thing (1955,
C, 102m, NR)
Glossy romantic drama, with a Eurasian
woman (Jennifer Jones) and American reporter (William Holden) learning the
meaning of the title. Drama set in Hong
Kong during the Korean War. **CL4, ST68**

Love Laughs at Andy Hardy (1946, B&W, 93m, NR)
Andy is home form World War II and back in the romantic soup. Mickey Rooney and Bonita Granville star. **ST133**

Love Me or Leave Me (1955, C, 122M, NR)
Musical drama about real life singer Ruth Etting and her affair with a domineering gangster. Doris Day and James Cagney star. **MU5, ST14**

Love Me Tender (1956, B&W, 89m, NR)
Elvis Presley made his film debut in this Civil War western about family conflicts. **ST123, WE6**

Love on the Run (1979, C, 93m, PG)
The fifth installment in French director François Truffaut's series of films about Antoine Doinel, starring Jean-Pierre Léaud. **DT106**

Love Songs (1986, C, 108m, NR)
A woman is deserted by her husband and is uncertain of her new-found freedom. Drama from France, starring Catherine Deneuve. **ST29**

Love Story (1970, C, 99m, PG)
The contemporary classic about a Harvard student (Ryan O'Neal) and his short-lived marriage to a working-class girl (Ali MacGraw). **DR1, DR2** *Essential*

Love With the Proper Stranger (1963, B&W, 100m, NR)
New York is the setting for this romance between a jazz musician (Steve McQueen) and working girl (Natalie Wood). **DR1, ST97, XT9**

Loved One, The (1965, B&W, 122m, NR)
Very dark comedy, based on Evelyn Waugh's novel about a Britisher (Robert Morse) visiting Los Angeles and getting mixed up in the funeral racket when his uncle (John Gielgud) is fired from his job at a movie studio and commits suicide. Incredible supporting cast includes Jonathan Winters (in two roles), Anjanette Comer, Robert Morley, Liberace, Dana Andrews, Milton Berle, James Coburn, Paul Williams, Tab Hunter, Roddy McDowall, Lionel Stander, and Rod Steiger as Mr. Joyboy. Written by Terry Southern and Christopher Isherwood. Advertised as "The movie with something to offend everyone." **CO8, CO12, CU12, CU17, DR19, XT10**

Lover Come Back (1961, C, 107m, NR)
Rock Hudson-Doris Day comedy about rival advertising executives finding romance. With Tony Randall and Edie Adams. **ST73**

Loverboy (1989, C, 98m, PG-13)
A pizza delivery boy finds that many of his customers—bored women—are interested in more than just his pies. Patrick Dempsey stars in this comedy, with Kate Jackson, Nancy Valen, Barbara Carrera, Kirstie Alley, and Carrie Fisher. Directed by Joan Micklin Silver. **CO1**

Lovers, The (1959, B&W, 90m, NR)
Jeanne Moreau plays a bored wife who finds true love with an overnight guest and runs away with him. Louis Malle directed. **ST110**

Lovers and Liars (1979, C, 96m, R)
Marcello Mastroianni and Goldie Hawn are the frantic lovers in this dark comedy made in Italy. **FF2, ST63, ST103**

Lovers and Other Strangers (1970, C, 106m, PG)
Comedy centering around the wedding of a young couple, with the impending ceremony bringing out the best—and worst—in both families. Michael Brandon, Bonnie Bedelia, Bea Arthur, Richard Castellano, and Gig Young star. Diane Keaton's film debut. **CO5, ST79, XT20**

Loves of a Blonde (1965, B&W, 88m, NR)
Boy meets girl, Czech style, in this poignant drama from director Milos Forman. **DT37, FF7**

Loves of Carmen, The (1948, C, 99m, NR)
The famous opera story of passion and betrayal, told in dramatic terms, starring Rita Hayworth and Glenn Ford. **ST64**

Lovesick (1983, C, 95m, PG)
Psychiatrist falls in love with his own patient and calls on Sigmund Freud for advice. Dudley Moore and Elizabeth McGovern star in this romantic comedy, with John Huston, and Alec Guinness as Freud. **DT50, ST60, ST109**

Loving Couples (1980, C, 97m, PG)
Mate-switching comedy starring Shirley MacLaine, James Coburn, Susan Sarandon, and Stephen Collins. **ST96**

Loving You (1957, C, 101m, NR)
Elvis Presley's second film finds him playing a gas jockey whose singing doesn't go unnoticed by a talent scout (Lizabeth Scott). **ST123**

Lower Depths, The (1957, B&W, 125m, NR)
Japanese version of the famed Maxim Gorky play, directed by Akira Kurosawa. Toshiro Mifune plays a thief whose life is changed by an itinerant priest. **DT57, ST106**

Lucas (1986, C, 100m, PG-13)
A sixteen-year-old boy tries out for the school football team, despite his lack of size, to impress his first love. Corey Haim, Charlie Sheen, and Keri Green star in this family drama. **DR9, FA7**

Lucky Luciano (1974, C, 110m, R)
Drama depicting the final years of the deported crime kingpin, starring Gian-Maria Volonte, Rod Steiger, and Edmond O'Brien. **AC22**

Lucky Partners (1940, B&W, 99m, NR)
Comedy starring Ronald Colman and Ginger Rogers as a pair of sweepstakes winners trying to decide what they'll do with their fortune. **ST131**

Lulu in Berlin (1985, C/B&W, 50m, NR)
Documentary portrait of actress Louise Brooks, featuring a rare interview plus generous clips from *Pandora's Box, Diary of a Lost Girl,* and her other films. Directed by Richard Leacock and Susan Woll. **CU16** *Recommended*

Lumiere (1976, C, 95m, R)
Star Jeanne Moreau also directed this drama about four women and their friendships. **FF1, ST110**

Lunatics and Lovers (1975, C, 93m, PG)
Italian comedy about a man with an imaginary wife. Marcello Mastroianni stars, with Claudia Mori. **ST103**

Lust for a Vampire (1971, C, 95m, R)
An all-girls' boarding school is really a haven for vampires in this sexy horror tale. **HO5, HO25, HO26**

Lust for Life (1956, C, 122m, NR)
Biography of tormented painter Vincent Van Gogh (Kirk Douglas), directed by Vincente Minnelli, with an Oscar-winning performance by Anthony Quinn as Paul Gauguin. Outstanding color photography. **CL2, CL9, DT71, ST34, XT4**

Lust in the Dust (1985, C, 85m, R)
Spoof of westerns has Divine and Lainie Kazan playing saloon singers with different parts of a treasure map tattooed on their posteriors. With Tab Hunter, Geoffrey Lewis, and Woody Strode. Directed by Paul Bartel. **CO7, DT5, WE14**

Lusty Men, The (1952, B&W, 113m, NR)
Susan Hayward, Robert Mitchum, and Arthur Kennedy star in this contemporary western drama about the men who tour the rodeo circuit. Directed by Nicholas Ray. **DT83, ST107, WE12**

Luv (1967, C, 95m, NR)
In this comedy, Jack Lemmon plays a would-be suicide who is "saved" by a pal (Peter Falk) who persuades him to take his wife (Elaine May) off his hands. **DT70, ST90**

M (1931, B&W, 99m, NR)
Classic German thriller about a child molester (Peter Lorre) who's hunted down by criminal gangs. Directed by Fritz Lang. **DT58, FF3, HO1, MY13** *Essential; Highly Recommended*

M*A*S*H (1970, C, 116m, R)
Uproarious military comedy about a trio of fun-loving surgeons and their operating procedures during the Korean War. Donald Sutherland, Elliott Gould, and Tom Skerritt star, with Robert Duvall, Sally Kellerman, Rene Auberjonois, Gary Burghoff, Michael Murphy, and Fred Williamson. Robert Altman directed; Ring Lardner, Jr. won an Oscar for his screenplay adaptation of the Richard Hooker novel. **AC3, CO6, CO12, CO21, DT2, ST38** *Essential; Highly Recommended*

MUSE Concert: No Nukes, The (1980, C, 103m, NR)
Concert film, shot at benefit rally opposing nuclear power, includes performances by Bruce Springsteen, James Taylor, Carly Simon, Jackson Browne, and Crosby, Stills & Nash. Also known as *No Nukes*. **MU10**

Macabre Serenade (1969, C, 89m, NR)
Boris Karloff stars in this horror film, one of his last, about a wicked toymaker whose creations are deadly weapons. **ST77**

Macao (1952, B&W, 80m, NR)
Robert Mitchum and Jane Russell star in an adventure yarn set in the exotic title port. Josef von Sternberg directed. **DT100, ST107**

Macaroni (1985, C, 104m, PG)
Marcello Mastroianni and Jack Lemmon are the stars of this comedy about an American returning to the Italian village where he served in World War II. **CO3, FF2, ST90, ST103**

MacArthur (1977, C, 130m, PG)
Gregory Peck plays the fabled general who led the U.S. to victories in World War II but clashed with President Truman over how to wage the Korean War. **DR4, ST119**

MacArthur's Children (1984, C, 120m, PG)
Japanese drama of the effects of the American postwar occupation on a village, especially its youngsters. Directed by Masahiro Shinoda. **FF4**

Macbeth (1948, B&W, 111m, NR)
Orson Welles directed and stars in Shakespeare's play of a suspicious Scottish lord and his scheming wife. **DT112, WR22**

Macbeth (1971, C, 140m, R)
Director Roman Polanski's version of the Shakespeare play of political intrigue in Scotland. Jon Finch and Francesca Annis star. **DT79, WR22**

McCabe and Mrs. Miller (1971, C, 121m, R)
Warren Beatty is a gambler, Julie Christie a frontier madam in this richly textured western set in the Pacific Northwest. With Rene Auberjonois, Keith Carradine, Bert Remsen, Shelley Duvall, Michael Murphy, and Hugh Millais. Directed by Robert Altman; songs by Leonard Cohen. **DT2, ST5, WE8, WE10, WE11, WE15** *Highly Recommended*

Macho Callahan (1970, C, 99m, R)
David Janssen plays a prison escapee in a Civil War western about revenge. **WE5, WE6**

Mack, The (1973, C, 110m, R)
An Oakland pimp just released from prison finds that his old territory has been taken over. Urban action starring Max Julien, Richard Pryor, and Roger E. Mosley. **AC8, ST125**

Mackenna's Gold (1969, C, 128m, PG)
Western saga of the search for a lost canyon filled with gold, starring Gregory Peck, Omar Sharif, Telly Savalas, and Edward G. Robinson. **ST119, ST130, WE1**

Mackintosh Man, The (1973, C, 105m, PG)
Espionage thriller about the elimination of a double agent, starring Paul Newman and James Mason, directed by John Huston. **DT50, MY6, ST102, ST111**

McQ (1974, C, 116m, PG)
John Wayne takes to the streets of Seattle as a veteran cop out to avenge the murder of his partner. **ST156**

McVicar (1980, C, 111m, R)
True-life story of England's most dangerous criminal and his escape from prison. Roger Daltrey stars. **MU12**

Mad Dog Morgan (1976, C, 102m, R)
Fact-based story of a 19th-century outlaw who terrorized the Australian countryside and outwitted the law, starring Dennis Hopper. **FF5, ST71, WE3**

Mad Max (1979, C, 93m, R)
In the near future, a gang of cyclists rule the outback roads of Australia, and only a fearless cop (Mel Gibson) can stop them. George Miller directed this nonstop action adventure. Followed by two sequels. **AC10, AC25, CU7, FF5, ST53** *Highly Recommended*

Mad Max Beyond Thunderdome (1985, C, 106m, PG-13)
In the third Mad Max adventure, Mel Gibson squares off against Tina Turner and her mangy minions in a desert battle to the death. **AC10, AC24, AC25, FF5, MU12, ST53**

Mad Miss Manton, The (1938, B&W, 80m, NR)
A mystery comedy, with socialite Barbara Stanwyck and her society pals involved. Henry Fonda costars. **MY17, ST44, ST142**

Mad Monster Party? (1967, C, 94m, NR)
Animated children's feature, with Frankenstein announcing his retirement at a
gathering of famous monsters. Features
the voice of Boris Karloff. **FA10, ST77**

Madame Bovary (1949, B&W, 115m, NR)
The Flaubert story of a woman's sacrifice
for her husband, lushly told by director
Vincente Minnelli. Jennifer Jones and
James Mason star. **CL1, CL5, DT71,
ST102**

Madame Rosa (1977, C, 105m, NR)
Oscar-winning French drama of a madam
(Simone Signoret) who shelters the chil-
dren of prostitutes. **FF1, XT7**

Madame Sin (1971, C, 73m, NR)
Bette Davis stars as an evil foreign agent
out to make trouble for the U.S. Navy.
With Robert Wagner. Originally made for
TV. **ST28**

Madame Sousatzka (1988, C, 121m, PG-
13)
Shirley MacLaine plays an eccentric Rus-
sian piano teacher in this drama, with
Navin Chowdhry, Twiggy, and Peggy
Ashcroft. Directed by John Schlesinger.
DT94, ST96

Madame X (1966, C, 100m, NR)
The classic soap story about a woman
accused of murder, defended by a man
who has no idea she is really his mother.
Lana Turner stars. **CL5, CL6, DR2, ST153**

Made for Each Other (1939, B&W, 93m,
NR)
Young marrieds James Stewart and Carole Lombard have their ups and downs,
mainly the latter, in this classic melodrama. **CL6, ST92, ST143**

Made in Heaven (1987, C, 103m, PG)
Two souls meet in heaven and begin a
romance that is interrupted when one of
them is sent down to Earth. Timothy
Hutton and Kelly McGillis star in this
romantic drama from director Alan Rudolph. Debra Winger has a small role.
DR1, DT91, ST163

Mademoiselle Striptease (1957, B&W,
99m, NR)
Brigitte Bardot stars in this caper comedy
about the theft of a rare art book. Also
known as *Please! Mr. Balzac.* **ST4**

Madigan (1968, C, 101m, NR)
A police detective (Richard Widmark)
and his commissioner boss (Henry
Fonda) disagree on how to keep the peace
in New York. Directed by Don Siegel.
AC9, DT97, ST44, XT9 *Recommended*

Madigan's Millions (1967, C, 86m, NR)
Comedy about an incompetent U.S. Trea-
sury agent sent to Italy to recover stolen
funds belonging to a late gangster. Dustin
Hoffman stars. Made before *The Graduate* but released only after its success.
ST67

Madman (1979, C, 92m, PG)
A Russian Jew survives years of forced
confinement in an asylum and swears revenge. Sigourney Weaver, Michael Beck,
and F. Murray Abraham star. **ST157**

Maedchen in Uniform (1931, B&W, 90m,
NR)
German drama, once considered daring,
takes place in an oppressive girls' school,
where one student and her teacher form a
lesbian relationship. Dorothea Wieck and
Hertha Thiele star. Leontine Sagan directed. **FF3**

Magic (1978, C, 106m, R)
A high-strung ventriloquist lets his
dummy take over his life. Anthony Hopkins and Ann-Margret star. **HO8, HO19**

Magic Christian, The (1970, C, 93m, PG)
Far-out Terry Southern comedy about the
world's wealthiest man testing to see just
what people will do for money. Peter
Sellers and Ringo Starr head the cast,
which also includes Graham Chapman,
John Cleese, Richard Attenborough, Ro-
man Polanski, Yul Brynner (in drag), and
Christopher Lee as Dracula. **CO12,
CO15, CO17, DT79, HF7, MU12, ST89,
ST137**

Magic Flute, The (1974, C, 134m, G)
Change of pace from director Ingmar
Bergman: a screen version of Mozart's
classic opera. **DT7**

Magic of Lassie, The (1978, C, 100m, G)
Remake of *Lassie Come Home,* with the
popular collie the object of a custody
battle. James Stewart stars—and even
sings, too. With Mickey Rooney. **FA5,
ST133, ST143**

Magic Sword, The (1962, C, 80m, NR)
Adventure film about a young knight's quest to rescue a princess from an evil sorcerer. Basil Rathbone stars. **AC18**

Magical Mystery Tour (1967, C, 60m, NR)
The Beatles' legendary "home movie," originally made for TV, is a loosely connected series of skits incorporating songs from their album of the same name. A midnight movie favorite. **CU1, MU9**

Magician, The (1959, B&W, 102m, NR)
A magician (Max von Sydow) has more than simple tricks up his sleeve in this somber drama from director Ingmar Bergman. **DT7**

Magnificent Ambersons, The (1942, B&W, 88m, NR)
Orson Welles' second film as a director (he narrates but does not appear on screen) is a rich portrait of a turn-of-the-century Midwest family resisting the modern era. Tim Holt, Joseph Cotten, and Agnes Moorehead star. **CL14, DT112**
Essential; Recommended

Magnificent Matador, The (1955, C, 94m, NR)
An aging bullfighter grooms his young protege for a future in the bull ring. Anothy Quinn stars. Directed by Budd Boetticher. **DT10**

Magnificent Obsession (1954, C, 108m, NR)
A playboy carelessly blinds a woman in an auto accident and decides to become a surgeon to restore her sight. Rock Hudson and Jane Wyman star in this tearjerker from director Douglas Sirk. **CL6, DT98, ST73**

Magnificent Seven, The (1960, C, 126m, NR)
Seven cowboys assemble to help a Mexican village besieged by bandits. Yul Brynner heads the cast of future stars, including Steve McQueen, Charles Bronson, Robert Vaughn, and James Coburn. A remake of the Japanese classic, *The Seven Samurai*. **CU17, CU18, FF8, ST12, ST97, WE1** *Recommended*

Magnifique, Le (1976, C, 84m, NR)
A novelist falls in love with a young student, who admires one of his super hero creations. Jean-Paul Belmondo and Jacqueline Bissett star in this French comedy. **ST6**

Magnum Force (1973, C, 124m, R)
The second Dirty Harry adventure, with Clint Eastwood hunting down a band of rogue San Francisco cops trying to dispense justice their own way. **AC9, ST39, XT13**

Mahler (1974, C, 115m, PG)
Director Ken Russell's dramatic portrait of the great composer: his torments, his relationship with his lovely wife, and his triumphs. Robert Powell stars. **DT92, MU5**

Mahogany (1975, C, 109m, PG)
Diana Ross plays a fashion designer with love life problems in this soap opera co-starring Billy Dee Williams and Anthony Perkins. **DR14, ST159**

Main Event, The (1979, C, 112m, PG)
Barbra Streisand comedy has her playing a business executive who decides to manage a luckless prizefighter (Ryan O'Neal). Patti D'Arbanville costars. **ST146**

Major Dundee (1965, C, 124m, NR)
Civil War western about a ragged band of Confederate soldiers at war with the Apaches and French troops. Charlton Heston and Richard Harris star, with Jim Hutton, James Coburn, Warren Oates, Ben Johnson, and Slim Pickens. Sam Peckinpah directed. **DT77, ST115, WE6**

Major League (1989, C, 107m, R)
The new owner of the Cleveland Indians baseball team wants to move the franchise to Miami, so she assembles a ragtag collection to ensure that attendance figures will justify the move. The plan backfires when the misfits are inspired by a flaky pitcher (Charlie Sheen) and veteran catcher (Tom Berenger). With Corbin Bernsen and Margaret Whitton. David S. Ward wrote and directed this comedy. **CO19**

Make Mine Mink (1960, B&W, 80m, NR)
Terry-Thomas heads a gang of fur thieves in this British comedy. Original running time: 100m. **CO17**

Making Contact (1985, C, 80m, PG)
After his father's death, a nine-year-old boy finds he has new powers which he

uses to thwart demons from another dimension. **SF13**

Making Love (1982, C, 113m, R)
A married doctor discovers his true sexual identity when he is attracted to one of his male patients. Michael Ontkean, Harry Hamlin, and Kate Jackson star. **DR3**

Making Mr. Right (1987, C, 100m, PG-13)
Comedy about a hip public relations expert (Ann Magnuson) hired to "sell" a mandroid astronaut to the public. John Malkovich plays the mandroid and his scientist creator. Directed by Susan Seidelman. **CO2, ST98** *Recommended*

Making of a Legend—Gone With the Wind (1989, C/B&W, 120m, NR)
Behind the scenes with the most popular film of all time, including rare outtakes and screen tests. Written by David Thomson. Originally made for cable TV. **CU16**

Makioka Sisters, The (1983, C, 140m, NR)
Japanese drama set in 1938 Osaka, where heiresses to a shipping business watch their family fortune slowly dissolve. Directed by Kon Ichikawa. **FF4**

Malcolm (1986, C, 96, PG-13)
A kooky inventor teams up with a larcenous couple to pull off a heist in this Australian comedy. Colin Friells, John Hargreaves, and Lindy Davies star. Directed by Nadia Tass; written by her husband, David Parker. **CO12, FF5, MY18**

Malice in Wonderland (1985, C, 100m, NR)
Elizabeth Taylor and Jane Alexander play Louella Parsons and Hedda Hopper, the feuding gossip columnists of 1930s and 1940s Hollywood. Originally made for TV. **ST147**

Malicious (1973, C, 97m, R)
Laura Antonelli plays a lusty housekeeper who's the love object of both a father and his teenaged son in this Italian comedy. **FF2**

Malone (1987, C, 92m, R)
An ex-C.I.A. agent blows into a small town Western town, discovers it's dominated by a rich racist and his hate organization. Burt Reynolds and Cliff Robertson star. **ST128**

Malta Story, The (1953, B&W, 98m, NR)
World War II action with British air forces, starring Alec Guinness and Jack Hawkins. **AC1, ST60**

Maltese Falcon, The (1941, B&W, 100m, NR)
Classic Dashiell Hammett detective story of Sam Spade (Humphrey Bogart) and "the stuff that dreams are made of"—the statue of a black bird. With Sydney Greenstreet, Mary Astor, Peter Lorre, and Elisha Cook, Jr. Written and directed by John Huston. **DT50, MY1, ST8, WR9** *Essential; Highly Recommended*

Mame (1974, C, 131m, PG)
Broadway musical version of the *Auntie Mame* tale of a grande dame taking in her impressionable nephew. Lucille Ball and Robert Preston star. **MU2, MU14**

Man Alone, A (1955, C, 96m, NR)
Ray Milland plays a fugitive from a lynch mob hiding under the protection of a sheriff's daughter. Milland also directed this western. With Raymond Burr and Lee Van Cleef. **ST155, WE3**

Man and a Woman, A (1966, C, 102m, NR)
Romantic drama about a widow and widower finding that love is even better the second time around. Anouk Aimee and Jean-Louis Trintignant star. Oscar winner for Best Foreign Language Film. **FF1, XT7**

Man and a Woman: Twenty Years Later, A (1986, C, 112m, PG)
Sequel to the popular romantic drama, with the same stars (Anouk Aimee and Jean-Louis Trintignant) continuing their love affair. **FF1**

Man Betrayed, A *see* Wheel of Fortune

Man Called Flintstone, A (1966, C, 87m, NR)
Feature-length adventures of Fred, Barney, and all the Stone Age cartoon gang, in a spoof of spy movies. **FA10**

Man Called Horse, A (1970, C, 114m, PG)
Richard Harris stars as an English aristocrat captured by Indians and initiated into their tribal ways. Followed by two sequels: *Return of . . and Triumphs of . . .* **WE7**

Man Called Peter, A (1955, C, 119m, NR)
The true story of Peter Marshall, a Scotsman who became a Presbyterian minister and eventually chaplain of the U.S. Senate. Richard Todd and Jean Peters star. **DR4**

Man Facing Southeast (1986, C, 105m, R)
From Argentina, a science fiction drama about a man who mysteriously appears in a mental hospital, claiming to be an alien. **FF6, SF19**

Man for all Seasons, A (1966, C, 120m, NR)
Paul Scofield plays Thomas More, the cleric who defied Henry VIII at the risk of execution. Robert Shaw, Wendy Hiller, Vanessa Redgrave, and Orson Welles costar in this Oscar winner for Best Picture, Actor, and Director (Fred Zinnemann). **DR5, DT112, DT120, ST127, XT1, XT2, XT6**

Man for all Seasons, A (1988, C, 168m, NR)
Charlton Heston heads the cast of this adaptation of Robert Bolt's life of Thomas More. Vanessa Redgrave and John Gielgud costar. Originally made for cable TV. **DR5, ST127**

Man Friday (1976, C, 109m, R)
The Robinson Crusoe story, with a contemporary race relations angle emphasized. Peter O'Toole and Richard Roundtree star. **AC24, ST117**

Man From Cheyenne (1942, B&W, 54m, NR)
A government agent (Roy Rogers) investigates a rustling ring run by a lovely lady. Gabby Hayes costars. **ST132**

Man From Colorado, The (1949, C, 99m, NR)
William Holden stars in a western drama of a cowboy forced to deal with an old Civil War comrade (Glenn Ford) who has become a judge dispensing a brutal form of frontier justice. **ST68**

Man From Laramie, The (1955, C, 104m, NR)
Western revenge drama, with James Stewart out to bring in the men who murdered his brother. Anthony Mann directed. **DT69, ST143, WE5**

Man From Music Mountain, The (1938, B&W, 54m, NR)
Gene Autry and partner Smiley Burnette foil the plans of a swindler. **ST3**

Man From Snowy River, The (1982, C, 104m, PG)
Australian adventure about a pack of wild horses and the young cowboy who would capture them. Tom Burlinson and Sigrid Thornton star, with Kirk Douglas as twin brothers in this family film. Sequel: *Return to Snowy River, Part II*. **AC12, FF5, ST34**

Man From the Alamo, The (1953, C, 79m, NR)
Glenn Ford plays a Texan who escapes from the carnage at the Alamo to warn others but is accused of desertion. Directed by Budd Boetticher. **DT10**

Man in a Cocked Hat *see* Carlton Browne of the F.O.

Man in the Grey Flannel Suit, The (1956, C, 153m, NR)
Gregory Peck stars as the quintessential 1950s Madison Avenue executive. With Jennifer Jones, Fredric March, Marisa Pavan, Lee J. Cobb, and Keenan Wynn. **DR24, ST119**

Man in the Iron Mask, The (1939, B&W, 110m, NR)
Adventure tale of twin brothers, one ascending to royalty, the other becoming a musketeer. Louis Hayward, Joan Bennett, and Warren William star. James Whale directed. **FA4, DT115**

Man in the White Suit, The (1952, B&W, 84m, NR)
Classic British comedy about an inventor (Alec Guinness) who comes up with a miracle fabric and is hounded by the clothing establishment. **CO17, ST60**

Man Like Eva, A (1983, C, 92m, NR)
A young woman impersonates film director Rainer Werner Fassbinder in this drama from Germany. **DT34, FF3**

Man of Flowers (1984, C, 91m, R)
Australian drama about a wealthy bachelor who pays an artist's model to take off her clothes for him. Norman Kaye stars; Werner Herzog plays Kaye's father in flashback scenes. Directed by Paul Cox. **FF5, DT44**

Man of Iron (1980, C, 140m, PG)
Sequel to *Man of Marble*, this Polish drama follows a documentary filmmaker and her romance with the son of a worker-hero whose story she filmed. Andrzej Wajda directed. **FF7** *Essential*

Man of La Mancha (1972, C, 130m, G)
Musical version of the classic novel *Don Quixote*, about a knight in search of his dream. Peter O'Toole and Sophia Loren head the cast. **MU2, MU17, ST93, ST117**

Man of Marble (1977, C, 160m, NR)
Epic Polish drama of a woman filmmaker shooting a documentary about the leader of a workers' uprising. Directed by Andrzej Wajda. **FF7** *Essential*

Man of the Forest (1933, B&W, 62m, NR)
Randolph Scott western has him framed for murder by Noah Beery, Sr. Based on a Zane Grey novel. **ST136**

Man of the Frontier (1936, B&W, 60m, NR)
Early Gene Autry western, featuring the debut of his mighty horse, Champion. Also titled *Red River Valley*. **ST3**

Man on the Eiffel Tower (1949, C, 97m, NR)
Georges Simenon's creation Inspector Maigret is after a murderer in this mystery directed by Burgess Meredith. Charles Laughton and Franchot Tone star. **MY16, XT16**

Man They Could Not Hang, The (1939, B&W, 72m, NR)
A mad scientist is executed for his crimes but brought back to life for revenge on the judge and jury that convicted him. Boris Karloff stars. **HO20, ST77**

Man Who Came to Dinner, The (1941, C, 112m, NR)
The classic play, by George S. Kaufman & Moss Hart, of an obnoxious guest taking up permanent residence in an ordinary household. Monty Woolley stars, with Bette Davis, Ann Sheridan, Billie Burke, and Jimmy Durante. **DR20, ST28**

Man Who Could Work Miracles, The (1937, B&W, 82m, NR)
A shy bank clerk suddenly discovers he has the power to do anything he wants. Family fantasy film, based on an H.G.

Wells story, stars Roland Young and Ralph Richardson. **SF13, WR29**

Man Who Fell to Earth, The (1976, C, 140m, R)
Science fiction drama about an alien (David Bowie) who comes to Earth in search of water for his parched planet but is unable to return home. Brilliantly directed by Nicolas Roeg. With Candy Clark, Rip Torn, and Buck Henry. **CU4, DT88, MU12, SF9, ST150** *Highly Recommended*

Man Who Haunted Himself, The (1970, C, 94m, PG)
Low-key horror film set in London about a man who begins seeing a double of himself after he's injured in a car crash. Roger Moore stars. **HO15**

Man Who Knew Too Much, The (1934, B&W, 75m, NR)
Hitchcock thriller about a couple who accidentally learn intelligence information, and their daughter is kidnapped by spies. Leslie Banks, Edna Best, and Peter Lorre star. **DT46, MY6, MY7**

Man Who Knew Too Much, The (1956, C, 120m, PG)
Hitchcock remade his own film, with the setting now North Africa. James Stewart plays the title character; Doris Day is his wife. **CU18, DT46, MY6, MY7, ST143**

Man Who Loved Cat Dancing, The (1973, C, 114m, PG)
Burt Reynolds and Sarah Miles are trail companions in this western about two people on separate quests. **ST128, WE8**

Man Who Loved Women, The (1977, C, 119m, R)
A man who simply loves all kinds of women tries to come to grips with his obsession by writing his life story. French comedy-drama directed by François Truffaut. American remake released in 1983. **DT106, FF8**

Man Who Loved Women, The (1983, C, 110m, R)
Burt Reynolds stars in a remake of the French comedy about a man with insatiable romantic tendencies. Julie Andrews plays his analyst; Kim Basinger, Marilu Henner, and Cynthia Sikes are the objects of his affections. Directed by Blake Edwards. **DT32, FF8, ST128**

Man Who Shot Liberty Valance, The (1962, C, 122m, NR)
A peace-loving lawyer confronts a violent outlaw. James Stewart, John Wayne, and Lee Marvin star in this western classic, directed by John Ford. With Vera Miles, Woody Strode, and Lee Van Cleef. **DT36, ST100, ST143, ST155, ST156, WE11** *Essential; Recommended*

Man Who Would Be King, The (1975, C, 129m, PG)
Sean Connery and Michael Caine star in the Rudyard Kipling story of two adventurers held captive by a mountain tribe who think one of them is a god. John Huston directed. With Christopher Plummer as Kipling. **AC12, DT50, ST15, ST21** *Recommended*

Man With Bogart's Face, The (1980, C, 106m, PG)
Would-be detective has plastic surgery to resemble Bogart, goes on to solve comic caper. Robert Sacchi stars, with Michelle Phillips, Olivia Hussey, George Raft (in his last film), and Mike Mazurki. **MY17**

Man With One Red Shoe, The (1985, C, 92m, PG)
An innocent man is mistaken for a spy and is caught in a comic crossfire of international agents. Tom Hanks and Jim Belushi star. Remake of French film, *The Tall Blonde Man With One Black Shoe.* **CO10, CO13, FF8, ST62**

Man With the Golden Arm, The (1955, B&W, 119m, NR)
Classic drama of a drug addict (Frank Sinatra) and his desperate attempts to control his problem. With Kim Novak, Darren McGavin, Robert Arnold Stang, Arnold Strauss, and Eleanor Parker. Directed by Otto Preminger; based on Nelson Algren's novel. **CL8, DR19, DT82, ST138** *Essential; Recommended*

Man With the Golden Gun, The (1974, C, 125m, PG)
James Bond (Roger Moore) takes on a vicious international assassin (Christopher Lee). Britt Ekland and Maud Adams costar. **HF2, ST89**

Man With Two Brains, The (1983, C, 90m, R)
Comic tale of a mad scientist (Steve Martin) who marries a lovely but cold woman (Kathleen Turner); his real love is another

woman's brain, which he keeps in his laboratory. **CO7, SF21, ST99, ST152**

Man Without a Star (1955, C, 89m, NR)
Kirk Douglas is the gunslinger who helps a farm woman (Jeanne Crain) in distress. Directed by King Vidor. **DT107, ST34, WE2**

Manchurian Candidate, The (1962, B&W, 126m, PG)
Intelligent, stylish political thriller about a war hero (Laurence Harvey) programmed by communists to be an assassin. Frank Sinatra, Angela Lansbury, and Janet Leigh costar. Adapted by George Axelrod from Richard Condon's novel. Directed by John Frankenheimer. **CU9, DR19, DR21, MY2, MY6, ST138** *Essential; Highly Recommended*

Mandela (1987, C, 135m, NR)
Danny Glover plays South Africa's Nelson Mandela, the heroic leader who has struggled against apartheid. With Alfre Woodard as his wife, Winnie. Originally made for cable TV. **DR4, DR7, DR14, ST55**

Mandingo (1975, C, 127m, R)
Melodrama of antebellum plantation life, with James Mason, Susan George, Perry King, and Ken Norton. **ST102**

Mango Tree, The (1977, C, 93m, NR)
Drama set in Australia around the time of World War I about a young man's coming of age in a small town. Michael Pate and Geraldine Fitzgerald star. **FF5**

Manhattan (1979, B&W, 95m, R)
Woody Allen's comedy about the endless possibilities of love—and heartbreak—in the Big Apple. Diane Keaton, Mariel Hemingway, and Meryl Streep costar as the women in Woody's life. Available in letterboxed format. **CO1, CO2, CU19, DT1, ST79, ST145, XT9** *Essential; Recommended*

Manhattan Merry-Go-Round (1938, B&W, 80m, NR)
A gangster takes control of a record company—but the story is just an excuse to present musical numbers by the likes of Gene Autry, Cab Calloway, Louis Prima, and (believe it or not) Joe DiMaggio. **ST3**

Manhattan Project, The (1986, C, 117m, PG-13)
A teenager creates a unique science project with stolen plutonium. Drama starring Christopher Collet, John Lithgow, and Jill Eikenberry. **DR9**

Manhunter (1986, C, 119m, R)
An F.B.I. agent comes out of retirement to catch a vicious serial killer by imagining how the psycho must plan his crimes. Superb suspense drama, based on Thomas Harris' novel *Red Dragon*. William Petersen stars, with Kim Greist, Brian Cox, Joan Allen, and Dennis Farina. **MY2, MY9, MY13** *Recommended*

Maniac (1980, C, 88m, R)
Extremely graphic horror film about a homicidal killer with a talent for mutilation. Joe Spinell stars. **CU7, HO18**

Manon of the Spring (1987, C, 116m, PG)
Concluding chapter of Marcel Pagnol story, begun with *Jean de Florette*: daughter of wronged French landowner seeks revenge on the neighbors responsible. Emmanuelle Beart, Yves Montand, and Daniel Auteil star. Directed by Claude Berri. **FF1** *Recommended*

Manos, The Hands of Fate (1966, C, 90m, NR)
A couple on an idyllic vacation find themsleves captives of cultists. Ultra low-budget, ultra-bad horror film shot in Texas. **CU11**

Man's Favorite Sport? (1964, C, 120m, NR)
Phony fishing expert (Rock Hudson) is forced to enter an angling competition in this comedy from director Howard Hawks. Paula Prentiss costars. **CO19, DT43, ST73**

Manxman, The (1929, B&W, 90m, NR)
Hitchcock's last silent film, a drama about two best friends, a lawyer and fisherman, who love the same woman. **DT46**

Marat/Sade (1967, C, 115m, NR)
Harrowing version of the stage hit about the Marquis de Sade directing his fellow lunatic asylum inmates in a play about the French Revolution and the murder of Jean-Paul Marat. Patrick Magee is a magnetic de Sade, Glenda Jackson is Charlotte Corday. Full title: *The Persecution and Assassination of Jean-Paul Marat by the Inmates of the Asylum of Charenton Under the Direction of the Marquis de Sade*. **DR5, DR20, DR23** *Recommended*

Marathon Man (1976, C, 125m, R)
Thriller about an innocent New Yorker caught up in international intrigue set in motion by the murder of his secret agent brother. Dustin Hoffman, Laurence Olivier, and Roy Scheider star. Directed by John Schlesinger. **DT94, MY7, ST67, ST116, XT9**

March or Die (1977, C, 104m, PG)
Old-fashioned adventure tale of the French Foreign Legion, starring Gene Hackman, Terence Stamp, Max von Sydow, and Catherine Deneuve. **AC12, ST29, ST61**

Maria's Lovers (1984, C, 100m, R)
Drama set in small Pennsylvania town, to which a World War II veteran returns, with problems for his new bride. John Savage, Nastassia Kinski, Robert Mitchum, and Keith Carradine star. **DR26, ST107**

Marie (1985, C, 113m, PG-13)
The true story of a woman who blew the whistle on corruption in the highest levels of Tennessee state government. Sissy Spacek and Jeff Daniels star, with Morgan Freeman. **DR6, DR10, ST48, ST139**

Marie Antoinette (1938, B&W, 149m, NR)
Norma Shearer plays the haughty French monarch in this lavish costume epic. With Tyrone Power, John Barrymore, and Robert Morley. **CL2**

Marius (1931, B&W, 125m, NR)
French comedy-drama of life in the Provence region, written by Marcel Pagnol. Pierre Fresnay plays the title character, a man torn between his love for Fanny (Orane Demazis) and life at sea. The first of a trilogy, followed by *Fanny* and *Cesar*. **FF1**

Marjoe (1972, C, 88m, PG)
Documentary portrait of pseudo-evangelist Marjoe Gortner. **CU16**

Marjorie Morningstar (1958, C, 123m, NR)
Natalie Wood plays a naive young girl with great ambitions; Gene Kelly is her summer lover. **ST81**

Mark of the Hawk, The (1957, C, 83m, NR)
Sidney Poitier drama set in contemporary Africa, centering on the debate over the means of achieving racial equality. With Eartha Kitt, Juano Hernandez, and John McIntire. **DR14, ST121**

Mark of the Vampire (1935, B&W, 61m, NR)
Bela Lugosi and his *Dracula* director, Tod Browning, are reunited for more blood-sucking thrills. Lionel Barrymore co-stars. **DT14, HO5, ST95**

Marked Woman (1937, B&W, 99m, NR)
Crusading district attorney (Humphrey Bogart) persuades four women to testify against their gangster boss. Bette Davis costars. **ST8, ST28**

Marlene (1986, C/B&W, 96m, NR)
Actor Maximilian Schell's documentary about fabled performer Marlene Dietrich, filmed with her very reluctant cooperation. **CU16, ST33** *Recommended*

Marnie (1964, C, 129m, NR)
A compulsive thief is caught by her boss, who has fallen in love with her. She agrees to marry him to avoid prosecution. Hitchcock thriller starring Tippi Hedren and Sean Connery. **DT46, MY5, ST21**

Marooned (1969, C, 134m, PG)
A group of astronauts is trapped in space, unable to return to Earth, in this science fiction thriller. Gregory Peck, Richard Crenna, and Gene Hackman costar. Special effects won an Oscar. **SF3, SF15, ST61, ST119**

Marriage of Maria Braun, The (1978, C, 120m, R)
In postwar Germany, a war widow builds a financial empire. Acclaimed drama from director Rainer Werner Fassbinder. Hanna Schygulla stars. **DT34** *Essential; Recommended*

Married to the Mob (1988, C, 103m, PG)
Wacky crime comedy set in New York and Miami Beach, with a Mafia hit man's widow pursued by her late husband's boss (and killer), *his* jealous wife, and a bumbling F.B.I. agent. Michelle Pfeiffer stars, with Dean Stockwell, Mercedes Ruehl, Matthew Modine, Alec Baldwin, and Sister Carol. Witty direction by Jon-

athan Demme. **CO10, DT28, ST120, ST144, XT9** *Recommended*

Married Woman, A (1965, B&W, 94m, NR)
Director Jean-Luc Godard's study of a marriage in crisis, with a bored wife taking on a lover. **DT41**

Marseillaise, La (1938, B&W, 130m, NR)
From director Jean Renoir, a drama about the turbulent times of the French Revolution. **DT86**

Martin (1978, C, 95m, R)
A teenaged vampire struggles with his terrible secret in this cult horror film from director George Romero. **CU4, DT90, HO5** *Recommended*

Marty (1955, B&W, 91m, NR)
Oscar-winning story of an ordinary guy, a Bronx butcher, who unexpectedly finds love. Star Ernest Borgnine, director Daniel Mann, and writer Paddy Chayevsky all won Oscars. **CL4, XT1, XT2, XT6** *Essential*

Marvin and Tige (1983, C, 104m, PG)
Drama of unusual friendship between young runaway black boy (Gibran Brown) and middle-aged loner (John Cassavetes). With Billy Dee Williams. **DR14, DR15, ST159**

Mary of Scotland (1936, B&W, 123m, NR)
Katharine Hepburn plays the doomed 16th-century queen. With Fredric March. John Ford directed. **CL3, DT36, ST66**

Mary Poppins (1964, C, 139m, G)
Classic Disney musical about a nanny with magical powers. Oscar winner Julie Andrews (in her movie debut) and Dick Van Dyke star in this combination of live action and animation. **FA1, FA9, MU7, MU8, XT3, XT21**

Masculine-Feminine (1966, B&W, 103m, NR)
A love affair between a journalist and a would-be rock star is the springboard for director Jean-Luc Godard's exploration of mid-1960s Paris. Jean-Pierre Léaud stars. **DT41, XT16**

Mask (1985, C, 120m, PG-13)
True story about a mother's patient love for her teenaged son, whose face is disfigured by an incurable disease. Cher and

Eric Stoltz star in this heart-wrenching drama. **DR2, DR6, DR8, DR9, ST19**

Masks of Death, The (1980, C, 80m, NR)
Peter Cushing plays Sherlock Holmes in this mystery about three unidentified corpses found in London's North End. **HF14, ST27**

Masque of the Red Death, The (1964, C, 86m, NR)
Vincent Price stars as evil Prince Prospero, the madman who throws a massive ball in his castle while a plague sweeps the land. Roger Corman directed this adaptation of two Edgar Allan Poe stories: the title tale and "Hop-Frog." **DT22, HO1, ST124, WR21**

Masque of the Red Death (1989, C, 83m, R)
Second telling of the Poe tale, produced by Roger Corman, starring Patrick Macnee, Clark Hoak, Jeff Osterhage, and Tracy Reiner. **WR21**

Masquerade (1988, C, 91m, R)
A shy young heiress meets a handsome stranger shortly after her mother's mysterious death. Is her stepfather using the man to romance her out of her money? Meg Tilly, Rob Lowe, and John Glover star in this thriller. **MY3, MY5**

Mass Appeal (1984, C, 100m, PG)
Conflict between an eager young priest and a veteran pastor forms the basis of this comedy starring Jack Lemmon and Zeljko Ivanek. **ST90**

Massacre at Fort Holman (1974, C, 92m, NR)
A Civil War western involving the bloody battle for a heavily fortified position. James Coburn and Telly Savalas lead the opposing armies. **WE6**

Massacre in Rome (1973, C, 103m, PG)
During World War II, a Vatican priest pleas for the lives of 330 villagers condemned by Hitler's orders. Richard Burton and Marcello Mastroianni star. **FF2, ST13, ST103**

Master of the House (1925, B&W, 81m, NR)
Silent comedy from Danish director Carl Dreyer, with a woman deserting her abusive husband, returning when he has learned his lesson at the hands of an old nurse. **DT31**

Master of the World (1961, C, 104m, NR)
Vincent Price wants to rule the world from his zeppelin in this science fiction adventure. With Charles Bronson. Based on several Jules Verne stories. **ST12, ST124, WR28**

Masters of the Universe (1987, C, 106m, PG)
A science fiction adventure tale based on the popular children's toys. Dolph Lundgren stars. **AC17, FA8, SF13**

Matewan (1987, C, 130m, PG-13)
Drama based on events surrounding a bitter and bloody coal miner's strike in 1920 West Virginia. Chris Cooper and James Earl Jones star. Written and directed by John Sayles, who also plays a small role. **DR5, DT93, ST76** *Recommended*

Matilda (1978, C, 103m, G)
Family comedy about a boxing kangaroo, starring Elliott Gould, Robert Mitchum, and Lionel Stander. **CO19, FA6, ST107**

Matter of Time, A (1976, C, 99m, PG)
Liza Minnelli and Ingrid Bergman star in this drama about a chambermaid taught lessons in life by a daft noblewoman. Director Vincente Minnelli's last film. **DT71, ST7**

Maurice (1987, C, 100m, NR)
Drama based on E. M. Forster's novel about a young Englishman's gradual awakening to his homosexual nature. Produced by Ismail Merchant; directed by James Ivory. **DR3, DR19**

Mausoleum (1983, C, 96m, R)
A housewife is possessed by a demon from the 17th century in this horror film starring Marjoe Gortner. **HO8**

Maverick Queen, The (1956, C, 92m, NR)
Barbara Stanwyck plays a lady outlaw who falls for a lawman in this western drama. **ST142, WE8**

Max Dugan Returns (1983, C, 98m, PG)
From Neil Simon, a comedy about a schoolteacher whose ex-con father turns up one day with gifts to charm her and her teenaged son. Marsha Mason, Jason Robards, and Matthew Broderick star. **CO5, ST129, WR23**

Max Headroom (1986, C, 60m, NR)
Comic adventure about a computer-created character and his alter ego, a TV news reporter. The original episode of the TV series. Matt Frewer and Amanda Pays star. **CO2, CO11** *Recommended*

Maxie (1985, C, 90m, PG)
Glenn Close stars in this fantasy-comedy about a contemporary San Francisco woman possessed by the spirit of a Roaring Twenties flapper. Mandy Patinkin co-stars, with Ruth Gordon. **CO20, ST20**

Maximum Overdrive (1986, C, 97m, R)
Horror tale directed by Stephen King, based on one of his stories, about the passing of a comet and its effects on all the machinery at a truck stop in the South. Emilio Estevez stars. **HO22, WR12**

Mayerling (1936, B&W, 89m, NR)
Classic story of doomed love, with Charles Boyer as Crown Prince Rudolph of Austria, Danielle Darrieux as the commoner who wins his heart. **CL4, DR3**

Maytime (1937, B&W, 132m, NR)
Nelson Eddy and Jeanette MacDonald team for this love story about a married opera star and poor singer; John Barrymore plays the jealous husband. **CL15**

Me and Him (1989, C, 93m, R)
Offbeat comedy of a man and his talking penis. Griffin Dunne and the voice of Mark-Linn Baker star. Directed by Doris Dorrie. **CO12**

Mean Frank and Crazy Tony (1975, C, 85m, R)
Lee Van Cleef and Tony LoBianco play a mob boss and a street punk who break out of prison together in this crime thriller from Italy. **AC22, FF2, ST155**

Mean Machine, The (1973, C, 89m, R)
Chris Mitchum plays a man with a mission—he's out to get even with the Mob. **AC19**

Mean Streets (1973, C, 112m, R)
In New York's Little Italy, a young hood tries to rise within the organization while keeping his crazy cousin out of trouble. Brilliant portrait of modern urban life, directed by Martin Scorsese, starring Harvey Keitel and Robert DeNiro, with Richard Romanus, David Proval, and Amy Robinson. **DR15, DR16, DT95, ST30, XT9** *Essential; Highly Recommended*

Meatballs (1979, C, 92m, PG)
Bill Murray stars as an amiable camp counselor in this comedy. **CO13**

Mechanic, The (1972, C, 100m, R)
Hit man Charles Bronson passes on his knowledge to understudy Jan-Michael Vincent. **ST12**

Medium Cool (1969, C, 110m, R)
Intense, original drama set in Chicago, during the 1968 Democratic National Convention. An apolitical TV reporter Robert Forster) is galvanized by the turmoil in the city. With Verna Bloom and Peter Bonerz. Haskell Wexler directed. **DR7, DR15, XT11** *Essential; Highly Recommended*

Medusa Touch, The (1978, C, 110m, R)
Richard Burton stars in a psychological thriller about a man who can will people to their deaths. Lee Remick plays his psychiatrist. **HO7, ST13**

Meet John Doe (1941, B&W, 132m, NR)
A sleazy politician hires a naive ex-baseball player to persuade the public that they never had it so good. Gary Cooper and Barbara Stanwyck star in this comedy directed by Frank Capra. **DT16, ST22, ST142** *Essential*

Meet Me in St. Louis (1944, C, 113m, NR)
Musical glimpse into the life of a family visiting the 1903 World's Fair. Judy Garland and Margaret O'Brien, who won a special Academy Award, star. Vincente Minnelli directed. Available in special edition with improved color, plus one song not used in the film and previews of coming attractions. **DT71, FA9, MU1, MU6, ST51** *Essential; Recommended*

Meeting at Midnight (1944, B&W, 67m, NR)
Charlie Chan mystery, set in London, starring Sidney Toler. Also known as *Black Magic*. **HF4**

Melo (1986, C, 110m, NR)
French drama, adapted from stage play, of a romantic triangle set in the world of classical music. Alain Resnais directed a cast headed by Sabine Azema, Pierre Arditi, and Fanny Ardant. **FF1**

Melodie en Sous-Sol (1963, B&W, 118m, NR)
Caper film, French style, as veteran crook (Jean Gabin) and young hothead (Alain Delon) set to take on a Riviera casino. Also known as *Any Number Can Win*. **FF1**

Melody Ranch (1940, B&W, 80m, NR)
Unusual Gene Autry western, mainly because of his costars: Jimmy Durante and Ann Miller. Otherwise, it's business as usual for the singing cowboy. **ST3**

Melvin and Howard (1980, C, 95m, R)
Comedy based on the true story of Melvin Dummar, the gas station owner who claimed to be an heir to billionaire Howard Hughes. Paul LeMat, Jason Robards, and Oscar winner Mary Steenburgen star in this satirical look at fame and fortune from director Jonathan Demme. **CO2, DT28, ST129, XT5** *Highly Recommended*

Member of the Wedding, The (1952, B&W, 91m, NR)
Poignant story of 12-year-old Frankie, a young girl confused by her brother's upcoming marriage. Julie Harris stars, with Ethel Waters and Brandon de Wilde. Fred Zinnemann directed this adaption of Carson McCullers' play. **DR9, DR20, DT120**

Memories of Me (1988, C, 103m, PG-13)
A surgeon suffers a heart attack and while recovering decides to seek a reconciliation with his estranged father, who works as a professional extra in Hollywood. Billy Crystal and Alan King star in this drama, with JoBeth Williams. **CO13, DR8**

Memories of Underdevelopment (1968, B&W, 104m, NR)
Cuban-produced drama of an alienated intellectual who harbors doubts about his country's post-revolutionary society. Directed by Tomás Gutiérrez Alea. **FF6**

Men (1986, C, 99m, R)
From Germany, a comedy about a business executive who becomes buddies with his wife's lover, an artist. Directed by Doris Dorrie. **FF3**

Men, The (1950, B&W, 85m, NR)
Marlon Brando made his film debut in this drama about handicapped World War II veterans trying to adjust to their disabilities. Teresa Wright and Jack Webb costar.

Directed by Fred Zinnemann. **CL8, DT120, ST10, XT21** *Recommended*

Men Don't Leave (1990, C, 113m, PG-13)
A mother with two sons is suddenly widowed and must adjust to life without a mate. Jessica Lange stars in this comedy-drama, with Chris O'Donnell, Charlie Korsmo, Arliss Howard, and Joan Cusack. Remake of French film, *La Vie Continue*. **DR8, DR10, FF8, ST86**

Men in War (1957, B&W, 104m, NR)
Korean War drama starring Robert Ryan, Aldo Ray, and Vic Morrow. Directed by Anthony Mann. **AC3, DT69**

Men of Bronze (1977, B&W/C, 59m, NR)
Documentary of courageous black regiments who fought in World War I. Directed by William Miles. **CU16, DR14** *Recommended*

Men Who Tread on the Tiger's Tail, The (1945, B&W, 58m, NR)
Early film from Japanese director Akira Kurosawa, based on a historical incident: a medieval general flees with his retinue, disguised as priests, from his rival brother. Also known as *They Who Step on the Tiger's Tail*. **DT57**

Mephisto (1981, C, 135m, NR)
Oscar-winning Hungarian drama of a vain actor throwing in with the Nazis during the Occupation, paying a terrible price. Klaus Maria Brandauer stars. **FF7, XT7**

Mephisto Waltz, The (1971, C, 108m, R)
A journalist falls in with a satanic cult after meeting a renowned concert pianist. Alan Alda stars in this horror film, with Jacqueline Bisset, Curt Jurgens, and Barbara Parkins. **HO10, HO11**

Merry Christmas, Mr. Lawrence (1983, C, 122m, R)
Prisoner-of-war drama, with British captives Tom Conti and David Bowie locked in struggle against two Japanese officers (Ryuichi Sakamoto and Takeshi). In English and Japanese; directed by Nagisa Oshima. **AC7, FF4, MU12**

Merry Widow, The (1934, B&W, 88m, NR)
Operetta, starring Jeanette MacDonald and Maurice Chevalier, of a rich widow's courtship in Paris. Directed by Ernst Lubitsch. Original running time: 99m. **DT63**

Messenger of Death (1988, C, 92m, R)
Charles Bronson plays an investigative reporter looking into a mass murder which may be linked to a splinter sect of Mormons. **ST12**

Metalstorm—The Destruction of Jared-Syn (1983, C, 84m, PG)
A peacekeeping ranger is assigned to destroy the evil Jared-Syn, who holds the planet of Lemuria under his tyrranical reign. Adventure fantasy with plenty of swordplay and special effects. **AC18**

Meteor (1979, C, 103m, PG)
A runaway meteor threatens destruction of the earth in this all-star disaster adventure. Sean Connery, Natalie Wood, and Henry Fonda head the cast. **AC23, SF7, ST21, ST44**

Metropolis (1926, B&W, 120m, NR)
Director Fritz Lang's legendary science fiction drama takes place in an underground city, whose workers are enslaved by a cruel dictatorship. Re-released in 1984 in an 87-minute version with some color tinting and a rock music score composed by Giorgio Moroder. Both editions available on home video. **CL12, DT58, FF3, SF2, SF5, SF14, SF16** *Essential (first edition); Highly Recommended* (both editions)

Miami Blues (1990, C, 99m, R)
A middle-aged police detective and a blithe psychopath play a cat-and-mouse game on the streets of Miami. Fred Ward and Alec Baldwin star, with Jennifer Jason Leigh, Charles Napier, and Nora Dunn. Adapted from the Charles Willeford novel by director George Armitage; co-produced by Jonathan Demme. **AC9, MY9** *Recommended*

Micki and Maude (1984, C, 117m, PG-13)
Dudley Moore stars as a man whose wife and mistress both announce they're pregnant—and they have the same doctor. Frantic comedy from director Blake Edwards costars Ann Reinking and Amy Irving. **CO1, DT32, ST109**

Microwave Massacre (1983, C, 75m, NR)
Comedian Jackie Vernon stars in this horror comedy about man and his mysterious oven. **HO24**

Midnight *see* Call It Murder

Midnight Cowboy (1969, C, 113m, R)
Naive young man comes to New York and falls in with a hustling vagrant. Jon Voight and Dustin Hoffman star in this drama which won Oscars for Best Picture and Director (John Schlesinger). **DR15, DT94, ST67, XT1, XT6, XT9** *Essential; Recommended*

Midnight Crossing (1987, C, 96m, R)
Intrigue, double cross, and murder aboard a charter boat on a voyage from the Florida Keys to recover a stolen fortune. Daniel J. Travanti and Faye Dunaway star. **ST37**

Midnight Express (1978, C, 121m, R)
Billy Hayes, an American visiting Turkey, is caught at the airport trying to smuggle drugs out of the country and is thrown into a barbaric prison. Brad Davis, Randy Quaid, and John Hurt star in this true story. **DR6, DR18**

Midnight Girl, The (1925, B&W, 84m, NR)
Silent drama starring Lila Lee as a Russian immigrant in New York and Bela Lugosi as a sophisticated suitor. **ST95**

Midnight Lace (1960, C, 108m, NR)
Thriller set in London with a wife (Doris Day) the victim of anonymous threats that may be coming from her husband (Rex Harrison). With John Gavin, Myrna Loy, and Roddy McDowall. **MY3, ST94, XT15**

Midnight Run (1988, C, 125m, R)
A bounty hunter (Robert DeNiro) accompanies a former Mob accountant (Charles Grodin) on a cross-country journey, with the F.B.I., Mafia hit men, and a rival bountry hunter all in pursuit. Action comedy also features Yaphet Kotto, Dennis Farina, and John Ashton. **CO9, ST30, ST59, XT18**

Midsummer Night's Dream, A (1935, B&W, 132m, NR)
Shakespeare's classic comedy, with an all-star cast, including Mickey Rooney, James Cagney, Dick Powell, and Olivia de Havilland. **ST14, ST133, WR22**

Midsummer Night's Sex Comedy, A (1982, C, 88m, PG)
Sex and romance at a country estate in this Woody Allen comedy set at the turn of the century. The lovers include Mia

Farrow, Jose Ferrer, Julie Hagerty, Mary Steenburgen, and Tony Roberts. **CO1, DT1**

Midway (1976, C, 132m, G)
Drama centering on the key naval battle of World War II, using many clips from previous war films and documentary footage. Charlton Heston heads the cast, which also includes Henry Fonda, Robert Mitchum, and Toshiro Mifune. **AC1, ST44, ST106, ST107**

Mighty Quinn, The (1989, C, 98m, R)
Mystery on a Caribbean island, with murdered white businessman, black police chief, and his boyhood friend (and prime suspect) the main ingredients. Denzel Washington and Robert Townsend star, with James Fox, Mimi Rogers, and M. Emmet Walsh. **MY16**

Mike's Murder (1984, C, 97m, R)
After her boyfriend is murdered, a young woman decides to investigate and finds that he has been involved with drug dealers. Debra Winger and Paul Winfield star. **MY11, ST162, ST163**

Mikey and Nicky (1976, C, 119m, R)
Drama about the friendship of two hoods, one of whom may be setting up his buddy for a rubout. Peter Falk and John Cassavetes star. Elaine May wrote and directed. **DR16, DT70**

Milagro Beanfield War, The (1988, C, 118m, R)
Comedy-drama set in a small New Mexico town, whose citizens are up in arms over water rights and a new recreation development. Robert Redford directed. The cast is headed by Chick Vennera, with Sonia Braga, John Heard, Ruben Blades, Melanie Griffith, Daniel Stern, Freddy Fender, and Christopher Walken. Based on John Nichols' novel. **CO2, DR19, DR26, MU12, ST9, ST58, ST126**

Mildred Pierce (1945, B&W, 109m, NR)
Joan Crawford's classic role (an Oscar winner, too), as a woman whose success in business can't disguise her problems with headstrong daughter Ann Blyth. Based on the James M. Cain novel. **CL5, CL6, MY1, ST24, WR1, XT3** *Essential*

Miles From Home (1988, C, 108m, R)
When a bank forecloses on their family farm, a pair of brothers burn the house and flee the law. Soon, they're regarded as folk heroes. Richard Gere and Kevin Anderson star, with John Malkovich. **DR7, DR16, ST52, ST98**

Milky Way, The (1970, C, 105m, NR)
Director Luis Buñuel's meditations on the history of Christianity. A funny, irreverent film from the master of surrealistic movie art. Paul Frankeur and Laurent Terzieff star, with Bernard Verley as Jesus Christ. **DT15, HF16**

Millennium (1989, C, 108m, PG-13)
Time travel science fiction drama, with Kris Kristofferson as an airplane crash investigator, Cheryl Ladd as a commando from 1000 years in the future. **MU12, SF4**

Millhouse: A White Comedy (1971, B&W, 93m, NR)
A scathing documentary about Richard Nixon, using extensive and by now famous clips from his checkered career. Directed by Emile de Antonio. **CU16** *Recommended*

Million, Le (1931, B&W, 85m, NR)
Rene Clair directed this French comedy of a lucky lottery ticket which sets off a frantic search. **FF1**

Million Dollar Duck, The (1971, C, 92m, G)
Disney comedy about a duck which, after exposure to radiation, lays eggs with gold yolks. Dean Jones and Sandy Duncan play the lucky owners. **FA1**

Million Dollar Mermaid (1952, C, 115m, NR)
Esther Williams plays Annette Kellerman, Olympic swimming champion and silent movie star, in this MGM musical. Production numbers staged by Busby Berkeley. With Victor Mature. **DT8, MU1**

Mind Snatchers, The (1972, C, 94m, PG)
An American soldier in Germany is admitted to a mental hospital, where he discovers that a mad doctor is conducting thought-control experiments on his patients. Christopher Walken stars. **HO20**

Mines of Kilimanjaro, The (1987, C, 88m, PG-13)
A soldier of fortune swears revenge on the Nazis who murdered his professor. Their trail leads to Africa, where he en-

counters many unexpected adventures. Christopher Connelly stars. **AC21**

Miracle Down Under (1986, C, 107m, NR)
Loose adaptation of Dickens' *Christmas Carol*, set in frontier Australia, as a small boy warms a miser's heart. Dee Wallace Stone, John Waters, and Charles Tingwell star. **FA13, FF5, WR4**

Miracle Mile (1989, C, 87m, R)
Thriller about a musician who learns from a ringing pay phone that nuclear war is about to start—and he can't convince anyone of the truth. Anthony Edwards stars, with Mare Winningham and John Agar. **MY6**

Miracle of Morgan's Creek, The (1944, B&W, 99m, NR)
Wacky comedy about a girl who attends an all-night party with wartime soldiers on leave, gets pregnant, but isn't sure who's the father. Betty Hutton, Eddie Bracken, and William Demarest star, with Bobby Watson as Adolf Hitler. Preston Sturges wrote and directed. **DT103, HF12**

Miracle of the Bells, The (1948, B&W, 120m, NR)
When a famous movie star is buried in her hometown, it sets off an unexplained chain of miracles. Frank Sinatra stars as a priest in this drama. **ST138**

Miracle of the White Stallions, The (1963, C, 117m, NR)
True adventure of the evacuation of prized horses from Vienna during World War II. Family fare from the Disney studios. **FA1, FA5**

Miracle on 34th Street (1947, C, 96m, NR)
Classic holiday story of a department store Santa proving to a little girl (and the world) that Mr. Claus (and the spirit he embodies) lives. Oscar winner Edmund Gwenn and Natalie Wood star. **FA13, XT4**

Miracle Worker, The (1962, B&W, 107m, NR)
Oscar winners Patty Duke and Anne Bancroft play Helen Keller and her teacher Anne Sullivan in this vivid recreation of their relationship. Directed by Arthur Penn, from the play by William Gibson. **DR4, DR20, DT78, XT3, XT5**

Mirage (1965, B&W, 109m, NR)
Gregory Peck plays an amnesia victim in this New York-based thriller, with Diane Baker, Walter Matthau, and Kevin McCarthy. **MY7, ST104, ST119, XT9**

Mirror Crack'd, The (1980, C, 105m, PG)
Agatha Christie whodunit, with Angela Lansbury as Miss Marple. Elizabeth Taylor, Rock Hudson, Kim Novak, and Tony Curtis are among the suspects. **ST73, ST147, WR3**

Misadventures of Merlin Jones, The (1964, C, 88m, NR)
A college whiz kid shows off his powers of mind-reading and hypnotism in this Disney comedy starring Tommy Kirk. **FA1**

Misfits, The (1961, B&W, 124m, NR)
Clark Gable and Marilyn Monroe star in a drama (the last film for both) about horse trappers in modern Nevada. With Montgomery Clift, Eli Wallach, and Thelma Ritter. Written by Arthur Miller; John Huston directed. **DT50, ST49, ST108, WE8, WE12, XT22**

Mishima (1985, C/B&W, 120m, R)
The turbulent life of Japan's controversial novelist and self-styled samurai, Yukio Mishima, is told in this stylized film from American director Paul Schrader. Award-winning cinematography, production design, and musical score. **FF4** *Recommended*

Miss Annie Rooney (1942, B&W, 84m, NR)
Shirley Temple gets her first screen kiss (from Dickie Moore) in this tale of a poor girl in love with a boy from a wealthy family. **ST148**

Miss Firecracker (1989, C, 102m, PG)
Zany comedy set in Yazoo City, Mississippi, about a local beauty contest and its eccentric entrants. Holly Hunter stars, with Mary Steenburgen, Alfre Woodard, Tim Robbins, and Scott Glenn. Beth Henley adapted her play, *The Miss Firecracker Contest*. **CO12, DR20, ST74**

Miss Grant Takes Richmond (1947, B&W, 87m, NR)
Lucille Ball plays a secretary who does a little amateur sleuthing in this comic mystery with William Holden. **ST68**

Miss Mary (1986, C, 100m, R)
A drama set in Argentina about a British governess (Julie Christie) and her strange relationship to her family of employers. **FF6**

Miss Sadie Thompson (1953, C, 91m, NR)
Musical remake of Somerset Maugham's *Rain,* with Rita Hayworth as the South Seas lady of the night who seduces a respectable minister. **MU14, ST64**

Missing (1982, C, 122m, R)
Fact-based drama about an American in a Latin American country who's abducted by state police, with his wife and father desperate to find his whereabouts. Jack Lemmon and Sissy Spacek star. Costa-Gavras directed. **DR6, ST90, ST139** *Recommended*

Missing in Action (1984, C, 112m, R)
Chuck Norris stars as a former P.O.W. who returns to Vietnam to free more Americans being held captive. **AC4, ST114**

Missing in Action 2: The Beginning (1985, C, 96m, R)
In this sequel to *Missing in Action,* the story of Chuck Norris' captivity in Vietnam and his escape are told. **AC7, ST114**

Mission, The (1986, C, 126m, PG)
The true story of missionaries in 17th-century South America clashing with slave traders. Robert DeNiro and Jeremy Irons star, with Aidan Quinn and Roy McAnally. Oscar-winning cinematography by Chris Menges; directed by Roland Joffe. **DR5, ST30**

Missionary, The (1982, C, 90m, R)
Comedy about a cleric just back from Africa who is assigned to run a home for women of weak virtue. Michael Palin and Maggie Smith star. **CO15**

Mississippi Burning (1988, C, 125m, R)
The 1964 murder of three civil rights workers is the jumping-off point for this melodrama about the subsequent F.B.I. investigation. Gene Hackman and Willem Dafoe star, with Frances McDormand and Brad Dourif. **DR6, DR7, ST61**

Missouri Breaks, The (1975, C, 126m, PG)
Bounty hunter Marlon Brando squares off against reformed outlaw Jack Nicholson in a leisurely western drama. With Harry

Dean Stanton, Randy Quaid, and Kathleen Lloyd. Written by Tom McGuane; directed by Arthur Penn. **DT78, ST10, ST112, ST141, WE3, WE15**

Mrs. Miniver (1942, B&W, 134m, NR)
Classic story of the effects of World War II on a middle-class British family. Winner of seven Oscars, including Best Picture, Director (William Wyler), Actress (Greer Garson), and Supporting Actress (Teresa Wright). Walter Pidgeon costars. **CL8, DT119, XT1, XT3, XT5, XT6** *Essential*

Mrs. Soffel (1984, C, 113m, PG-13)
Prison warden's wife falls in love with a convict and helps him and his brother escape. True-life romantic drama set in turn-of-the-century Pittsburgh, starring Diane Keaton, Mel Gibson, and Matthew Modine. Directed by Gillian Armstrong. **DR1, DR16, ST53, ST79** *Recommended*

Mrs. Wiggs of the Cabbage Patch (1934, B&W, 80m, NR)
A poor woman raising five children on her own finds time to play matchmaker to a spinster. Pauline Lord stars, with ZaSu Pitts and W. C. Fields as the matched couple. **ST41**

Mr. and Mrs. North (1941, B&W, 67m, NR)
Screen version of popular radio show, with fun-loving couple solving murder mystery. Gracie Allen stars. **MY17**

Mr. and Mrs. Smith (1941, B&W, 95m, NR)
Alfred Hitchcock takes a break from thrillers to make a comedy about a couple who find that their marriage was never legal. Robert Montgomery and Carole Lombard star. **DT46, ST92**

Mr. Arkadin (1955, B&W, 99m, NR)
Twisted tale of mystery millionaire, directed by and starring Orson Welles. **DR24, DT112**

Mr. Blandings Builds His Dream House (1948, B&W, 94m, NR)
New York couple decide to buy their dream home in the Connecticut countryside; the fun begins when they decide to fix it up "a little." Cary Grant, Myrna Loy, and Melvyn Douglas star in this classic comedy. **CL10, ST57, ST94** *Recommended*

Mr. Deeds Goes to Town (1936, B&W, 115m, NR)
Director Frank Capra won an Oscar for this comedy about an ordinary guy who inherits a fortune and decides to give it all away. Gary Cooper and Jean Arthur star, with George Bancroft and Lionel Stander. **CL8, DT116, ST22, XT6** *Essential*

Mr. Halpern and Mr. Johnson (1983, C, 57m, NR)
Modest drama of two men meeting after the funeral of one's wife, the second revealing a longtime secret friendship with the woman. Originally made for cable TV. Laurence Olivier and Jackie Gleason star. **ST116**

Mr. Hobbs Takes a Vacation (1962, C, 116m, NR)
Family comedy about a father who's put through the wringer on a summer vacation. James Stewart and Maureen O'Hara star. **ST143**

Mr. Hulot's Holiday (1953, B&W, 86m, NR)
The first film about M. Hulot, the comic Frenchman with a knack for getting into the strangest situations. Director Jacques Tati also plays the lead role. **DT104** *Essential; Recommended*

Mr. Klein (1977, C, 122m, PG)
In Nazi-occupied France, an art dealer exploiting Jews finds himself confused with another man who's a Jew and under scrutiny from the Germans. Alain Delon and Jeanne Moreau star. Joseph Losey directed. **FF1, ST110**

Mr. Lucky (1943, B&W, 100m, NR)
Cary Grant stars as the dashing owner of a gambling ship who is out to bilk Laraine Day, but she charms him into respectability. **ST57**

Mr. Majestyk (1974, C, 103m, PG)
A Colorado melon grower (Charles Bronson) won't knuckle under to the Mob, which decides to have him eliminated. Adapted by Elmore Leonard from his own novel. **ST12, WR16**

Mr. Mom (1983, C, 92m, PG)
When an executive loses his job and his wife goes to work, their roles are reversed and their lives turned upside-down. Comedy starring Michael Keaton, Teri Garr,

and Martin Mull. Written by John Hughes. **CO2, CO5, CO20, DT49, ST80**

Mr. North (1988, C, 90m, PG)
Gentle comic fable, set in 1920s Newport, Rhode Island, about an extraordinary young man who charms society with his very "electric" personality. Anthony Edwards stars, with Robert Mitchum, Harry Dean Stanton, Anjelica Huston, and Lauren Bacall. Based on a novel by Thornton Wilder. **CO6, ST107, ST141**

Mr. Peabody and the Mermaid (1948, B&W, 89m, NR)
Comedy of a mild-mannered man (William Powell) and his encounter with a finned lady (Ann Blyth). **ST122**

Mister Roberts (1955, C, 123m, NR)
Classic comedy-drama about World War II shipboard battle between high-strung captain (James Cagney) and determined first mate (Henry Fonda). With Oscar winner Jack Lemmon (as Ensign Pulver) and William Powell (in his last film). Co-directed by John Ford. **CL10, DT36, ST14, ST44, ST90, ST122, XT4, XT22** *Recommended*

Mr. Skeffington (1944, B&W, 140m, NR)
Bette Davis and Claude Rains star as a New York society couple whose loveless marriage warms with the passing years. The video version restores 13 minutes of footage from the film's original release. **CL4, CL5, CU10, ST28**

Mr. Smith Goes to Washington (1939, B&W, 129m, NR)
James Stewart plays an idealistic young Congressman in conflict with the Old Guard in the Nation's Capital. With Jean Arthur, Thomas Mitchell, and Claude Rains. Frank Capra directed. **DT16, ST143, XT12** *Essential*

Mr. Winkle Goes to War (1944, B&W, 80m, NR)
Comedy-drama of a mild-mannered man (Edward G. Robinson) who's accidentally drafted and winds up becoming a war hero. **ST130**

Mr. Wong, Detective (1939, B&W, 69m, NR)
Boris Karloff plays an Oriental detective in this low-budget mystery. **ST77**

Mr. Wong in Chinatown (1939, B&W, 70m, NR)
Boris Karloff's third appearance as the wily Oriental detective has him on the trail of the murderer of a Chinese princess. **ST77**

Misunderstood (1984, C, 92m, PG)
Gene Hackman stars in this drama about a family torn apart when the wife dies and the son (Henry Thomas) retreats into a world of his own. With Rip Torn and Susan Anspach. **DR8, ST61, ST150**

Mixed Blood (1985, C, 98m, R)
A comedy-drama about a gang of Brazilian toughs trying to muscle in on New York's drug trade, thwarted by romance between their leader and the daughter of a rival boss. Directed by Paul Morissey. **DT72**

Moby Dick (1956, C, 116m, NR)
Screen version of Herman Melville's classic tale of Captain Ahab (Gregory Peck) and his obsession with the white whale. Directed by John Huston. Orson Welles has one memorable scene as a priest. **CL1, DT50, DT112, ST119**

Modern Problems (1981, C, 91m, PG)
Chevy Chase stars in this comedy about an air traffic controller who discovers he has telekinetic powers. **CO11, CO13**

Modern Romance (1981, C, 93m, R)
A film editor (Albert Brooks) drives his girlfriend crazy with his obsessive behavior about their relationship. With Kathryn Harrold. Brooks co-wrote and directed. **CO1, DT12**

Modern Times (1936, B&W, 89m, G)
Charlie Chaplin's sublime comedy of contemporary man bedeviled by machines. Paulette Goddard costars in this silent, which features music composed by Chaplin. **CL11, DT18** *Essential; Highly Recommended*

Moderns, The (1988, C, 126m, R)
Drama set in 1926 Paris, amid the art and literary world of expatriate Americans, including Ernest Hemingway (Kevin Connor) and Gertrude Stein. Keith Carradine plays an art forger, Wallace Shawn a columnist, John Lone a wealthy art collector, Linda Fiorentino his wife and Carradine's former lover. With Geraldine

Chaplin and Genevieve Bujold. Alan Rudolph directed. **DR5, DT91, WR10**

Mogambo (1953, C, 115m, NR)
Remake of classic adventure story *Red Dust*, with Clark Gable once again the plantation foreman caught between advances of Ava Gardner and Grace Kelly. John Ford directed on location in Africa. **AC12, AC14, CU18, DT36, ST49, ST82**

Mohawk (1956, C, 79m, NR)
An Indian war is prevented by a white man (Scott Brady) and a lovely Indian (Rita Gam). **WE7**

Molly Maguires, The (1970, C, 123m, PG)
In 19th-century Pennsylvania, striking coal miners are betrayed by a union-busting spy. Sean Connery, Richard Harris, and Samantha Eggar star in this historical drama. Directed by Martin Ritt. **DR5, DT87, ST21**

Mommie Dearest (1981, C, 129m, PG)
Movie star and (according to her daughter) monster mom Joan Crawford is portrayed by Faye Dunaway. Has cult following for its campy portrayal of Crawford's obsessions. **CU2, DR12, ST37**

Mon Oncle *see* My Uncle

Mon Oncle d'Amerique (1980, C, 123m, PG)
From French director Alain Resnais, a comedy about modern life, focusing on the work habits of three individuals. Gerard Depardieu stars. **FF1, ST31**

Mona Lisa (1986, C, 104m, R)
In London, a hood just out of jail agrees to return to work for his old boss, chauffeuring (and spying on) a black prostitute who's suspected of pocketing her earnings. Bob Hoskins, Michael Caine, and Cathy Tyson star. **DR16, DR23, ST15, ST72, XT15** *Recommended*

Mondo Trasho (1969, B&W, 95m, NR)
Director John Waters presents a self-described "gutter film" about one day in the life of a hit-and-run driver, played by the inimitable Divine. A cult favorite. **CU12, DT110**

Money Pit, The (1986, C, 91m, PG)
A young married couple (Tom Hanks, Shelley Long) discover that the house of their dreams needs more than a "little"

fixing up. Maureen Stapleton and Alexander Gudonov costar. **ST62**

Monkey Business (1952, C, 97m, NR)
Cary Grant plays a scientist looking for a youth serum in this zany comedy from director Howard Hawks. Ginger Rogers and Marilyn Monroe costar. **DT43, ST57, ST108, ST131**

Monkey Shines (1988, C, 115m, R)
A quadriplegic is helped by a trained monkey, who performs daily tasks for him. Trouble develops when the animal, injected with human brain cells, begins acting strangely. Directed by George Romero. **HO16, DT90**

Monkeys, Go Home! (1967, C, 101m, G)
American inherits an olive farm in France and trains a group of monkeys to pick his harvest. Disney comedy starring Dean Jones and Maurice Chevalier (in his last film). **FA1**

Monkey's Uncle, The (1965, C, 87m, NR)
Sequel to Disney comedy *The Misadventures of Merlin Jones* has college brain Tommy Kirk inventing a flying machine. **FA1**

Monsieur Verdoux (1947, B&W, 123m, NR)
Charlie Chaplin's dark comedy about a man who marries, then murders, a string of women for their money. Martha Raye costars. **DT18** *Recommended*

Monster Club, The (1980, C, 97m, PG)
Vincent Price plays a vampire who narrates three tales of terror, all revolving around a Transylvanian disco. **HO23, ST124**

Monster in the Closet (1986, C, 87m, PG)
A comic tribute to 1950s sci-fi/horror films, about a gang of monsters which hide in closets and kill people. Donald Grant stars, with Claude Akins, Henry Gibson, Howard Duff, Paul Dooley, and John Carradine. **SF21**

Monster Squad, The (1987, C, 82m, PG-13)
A gang of plucky kids meet up with every monster imaginable, from Frankenstein and Dracula to the Wolf Man and the Mummy, in this horror comedy. **HF7, HF10, HO24**

Monte Walsh (1970, C, 99m, PG)
Oldtime cowboys Lee Marvin and Jack Palance won't face the fact that the frontier is closing down. With Jeanne Moreau. **ST100, ST110, WE11**

Montenegro (1981, C, 98m, R)
A bored housewife discovers a new way to approach life when she begins an affair with a Yugoslavian worker. Susan Anspach stars. Dusan Makavejev directed. **FF7**

Monterey Pop (1969, C, 72m, NR)
Concert film of ground-breaking 1967 California pop festival, featuring Jimi Hendrix, Janis Joplin, Otis Redding, The Who, Ravi Shankar, Simon & Garfunkel, The Mamas and the Papas, and more. **MU10** *Highly Recommended*

Monty Python and the Holy Grail (1974, C, 90m, PG)
The boys from TV's most wickedly funny program take on the King Arthur legends. **CO7, CO15**

Monty Python's Flying Circus (17 volumes: all C, 60m, NR)
Each tape in this series contains two half-hour programs from the deliriously silly TV program starring John Cleese, Eric Idle, Graham Chapman, Michael Palin, and Terry Jones, with animated sequences by Terry Gilliam. **CO15** *Highly Recommended*

Monty Python's Life of Brian (1979, C, 90m, R)
Britain's bad boys of humor tell their own version of the Messiah story in this irreverent spoof of religious epics. **CO7, CO15**

Monty Python's The Meaning of Life (1983, C, 107m, R)
More madness from the Python troupe, as they attempt to answer some of life's great questions in this series of bawdy and naughty sketches. **CO15**

Moon in the Gutter, The (1983, C, 126m, R)
Gerard Depardieu and Nastassja Kinski star in this stylized thriller about a man in search of the thug who brutalized his sister. **FF1, ST31**

Moon Is Blue, The (1953, B&W, 95m, NR)
A young woman's virginity is at stake in this comedy, considered daring in its day.

William Holden, David Niven, and Maggie McNamara star. Otto Preminger directed. **DT82, ST68**

Moon Over Parador (1988, C, 93m, PG-13)
An American movie actor, on location in a Latin American country, is forced to impersonate the land's dictator after the despot suffers a fatal heart attack. This comedy, directed by Paul Mazursky, stars Richard Dreyfuss, with Sonia Braga, Raul Julia, Jonathan Winters, and the director (as the dictator's mother). Watch for appearances by Sammy Davis, Jr., Charo, and Dick Cavett. **CO2, CO8, CO20, ST9, ST36**

Moon Pilot (1962, C, 98m, G)
Just before he blasts off, an astronaut meets a lovely alien. Disney comedy starring Tom Tryon, Brian Keith, and Dany Saval. **FA1**

Moon-Spinners, The (1964, C, 118m, NR)
Hayley Mills stars in a Disney mystery about an innocent tourist in Crete becoming involved with a smuggling operation. **FA1**

Moonlighting (1982, C, 97m, PG)
Jeremy Irons plays the foreman of a gang of Polish workmen in London on a temporary construction job. He tries to keep news of political turmoil back home from his co-workers. Directed by Jerzy Skolimowski. Dialogue in English and Polish. **FF7**

Moonlighting (1985, C, 97m, NR)
A classy fashion model and a hip investigator team up to run a detective agency. Cybill Shepherd and Bruce Willis star in this mystery-comedy, originally the pilot for a TV series. **CO10, MY10, ST161** *Recommended*

Moonraker (1979, C, 126m, PG)
James Bond blasts into outer space to take on a madman and his steel-toothed henchman. Roger Moore, Michael Lonsdale, and Richard Kiel star. **HF2**

Moonrise (1948, B&W, 90m, NR)
Melodrama of son of executed killer who's tormented by the memory. In self-defense, he commits a murder and hides out in the swamps. Dane Clark stars. **MY1**

Moon's Our Home, The (1936, B&W, 76m, NR)
Margaret Sullavan and Henry Fonda star in this romantic comedy about the up-and-down relationship between a movie star and a New York writer. **ST44**

Moonstruck (1987, C, 102m, PG)
A young Italian-American widow, set to marry a second time, falls in love with her fiance's younger brother in this romantic comedy set in Brooklyn. Cher and Olympia Dukakis won Oscars for their performances as the widow and her mother. With Nicolas Cage, Vincent Gardenia, and Danny Aiello. Directed by Norman Jewison; written by John Patrick Shanley. **CO1, DT51, ST19, XT3, XT5** *Recommended*

More Ripping Yarns *see* Ripping Yarns (series)

More the Merrier, The (1943, B&W, 104m, NR)
The housing shortage in Washington during World War II is the basis for this clever romantic comedy starring Joel McCrea and Jean Arthur, with Oscar-winning support from Charles Coburn. Directed by George Stevens. **CL10, DT101, XT4** *Recommended*

Morgan: A Suitable Case for Treatment (1966, B&W, 97m, NR)
Madcap British comedy about a loony artist (David Warner) who's obsessed with apes and his ex-wife (Vanessa Redgrave). **CO17, CU5, ST127** *Recommended*

Morgan Stewart's Coming Home (1987, C, 92m, PG-13)
Hip prep school student (Jon Cryer) shows his uptight parents (Lynn Redgrave, Nicholas Coster) how to loosen up in this comedy. **CO5**

Morituri (1965, B&W, 123m, NR)
Marlon Brando plays a German who helps British forces capture a cargo ship in World War II. Yul Brynner costars, with Trevor Howard, Janet Margolin, and Wally Cox. Also known as *Saboteur: Code Name Morituri*. **ST10**

Morning After, The (1986, C, 103m, R)
Jane Fonda stars in this mystery about an alcoholic actress who wakes up one morning next to a corpse—and can't remember what happened the night before.

Jeff Bridges costars, with Raul Julia. Sidney Lumet directed. **DT65, MY3, MY5, ST11, ST45**

Morning Glory (1933, B&W, 74m, NR)
Katharine Hepburn won the first of her four Oscars for her role as an aspiring young actress in this drama. Adolphe Menjou and Douglas Fairbanks, Jr. costar. **CL5, ST66, XT3**

Morocco (1930, B&W, 92m, NR)
Marlene Dietrich's first American film has her succumbing to the charms of legionnaire Gary Cooper. Directed by Josef von Sternberg. **DT100, ST22, ST33**

Moscow Does Not Believe in Tears (1980, C, 152m, R)
Oscar-winning drama from the Soviet Union about a trio of women who emigrate to the capital city in the 1950s to seek their fortunes. **FF7, XT7**

Moscow on the Hudson (1984, C, 115m, R)
A Soviet saxophonist defects—in the middle of Bloomingdale's—in this comedy-drama starring Robin Williams. Paul Mazursky directed. **CO20, DR15, ST160, XT9**

Moses (1975, C, 141m, PG)
Burt Lancaster stars as the Biblical prophet in this condensed version of a 6-hour TV miniseries. **CL13, ST85**

Mosquito Coast, The (1986, C, 119m, PG)
An eccentric inventor (Harrison Ford) moves his family from New England to the jungles of Central America to escape the evil influences of "civilization." River Phoenix and Helen Mirren costar. Peter Weir directed; based on Paul Theroux's novel. **DR8, DR19, DT111, ST46**

Most Dangerous Game, The (1932, B&W, 78m, NR)
Classic adventure saga, based on famous short story about a man and woman pursued for sport by a mad big game hunter. Joel McCrea and Fay Wray star. **AC24**

Motel Hell (1980, C, 102m, R)
Horror film, played for laughs, about a brother and sister whose motel swallows up tourists and recycles them into a popular brand of sausage. Rory Calhoun stars. **HO24**

Mother (1952, B&W, 98m, NR)
Japanese drama of fatherless working class family living in postwar Tokyo. Directed by Mikio Naruse. **FF4**

Mother, Jugs & Speed (1976, C, 95m, R)
Darkly comic adventures of city ambulance drivers, starring Bill Cosby, Raquel Welch, and Harvey Keitel, with Larry Hagman. **CO2**

Mother's Day (1980, C, 98m, NR)
A trio of women out for a hike are brutalized by two backwoods brothers, but the women have the final say in this gruesome horror story. **CU7, HO18**

Mothra (1962, C, 100m, NR)
Japanese monster movie about gigantic flying creature whose destructive ways can be checked only by two tiny twin sisters. **FF4, SF18**

Motown 25: Yesterday, Today, Forever (1983, C, 130m, NR)
Celebration of the black pop music label that recorded such great performers as Stevie Wonder, Marvin Gaye, The Supremes, The Four Tops, The Temptations, and The Jackson 5. Originally shown on TV. **MU10** *Recommended*

Moulin Rouge (1952, C, 123m, NR)
The life of deformed French artist Toulouse-Lautrec, filmed in dazzling color by director John Huston. Jose Ferrer stars, with Zsa Zsa Gabor and Christopher Lee. **CL2, CL9, DT50, ST89**

Mountain Family Robinson (1979, C, 100m, G)
Family drama of clan learning to survive in rugged mountain terrain, starring Robert F. Logan, Susan Damante-Shaw, and Heather Rattray. **FA4**

Mountains of the Moon (1990, C, 135m, R)
The true story of 19th-century British explorers Richard Burton and John Hanning Speke and their search for the source of the Nile River. Patrick Bergin plays Burton, Iain Glen is Speke, with Fiona Shaw (as Isabel Burton) and Richard E. Grant. **AC12, DR4** *Recommended*

Mouse That Roared, The (1959, C, 83m, NR)
Peter Sellers plays three roles in this British comedy about a tiny, mythical kingdom declaring war on America so they

can be eligible for generous foreign aid. **CO17, ST137**

Movers and Shakers (1985, C, 79m, PG)
Hollywood screenwriter tries to sell script called "Love in Sex" in this satire of the contemporary movie scene. Walter Matthau and Charles Grodin star; guest appearances by Steve Martin and Gilda Radner. **CO8, CO13, ST59, ST99, ST104**

Movie Movie (1978, C/B&W, 107m, PG)
Spoof of l930s movies contains two films, one a boxing drama called *Dynamite Hands*, the other a big-budget musical called *Bathing Beauties of 1933*. George C. Scott heads the cast. Stanley Donen directed. **CO7, DT30**

Moving (1988, C, 89m, R)
Richard Pryor stars in this comedy about a man whose job transfer from New Jersey to Idaho is one disaster after another. With Dave Thomas. **CO14, ST125**

Ms. Don Juan (1973, C, 87m, R)
Brigitte Bardot plays a temptress whose conquests include her cousin, a priest. With Maurice Ronet, Robert Hossein, and Jane Birkin. Directed by Roger Vadim. **ST4**

Ms. 45 (1981, C, 84m, R)
In New York City, a mute seamstress is raped twice and goes on a killing spree in revenge. Zoe Tamerlis stars in this action film with a cult following. **AC19, CU7, MY3**

Multiple Maniacs (1971, B&W, 90m, NR)
Cult favorite, described by its creator, director John Waters, as a "celluloid atrocity." Divine stars as the proprietor of a "Cavalcade of Perversions," a carnival at which customers are robbed and beaten. **CU12, DT110**

Mummy, The (1932, B&W, 72m, NR)
Boris Karloff plays the Egyptian wrapped in bandages in the classic horror film. Directed by Karl Freund. **HO1, ST77** *Recommended*

Mummy, The (1959, C, 88m, NR)
British remake of the horror fable of the cursed Egyptian's tomb, starring Christopher Lee and Peter Cushing. **HO26, ST27, ST89**

Muppet Moments (1985, C, 56m, NR)
A collection of musical numbers and comedy skits from the popular TV series. Guest stars include Lena Horne, Liza Minnelli, Pearl Bailey, and Zero Mostel. **FA14**

Muppet Movie, The (1979, C, 94m, G)
The Muppets' feature film debut, in a comedy loaded with human stars as well: Orson Welles, Mel Brooks, Steve Martin, and Richard Pryor head the list. **DT13, DT112, FA14, ST99, ST125**

Muppet Revue, The (1985, C, 56m, NR)
More sketches and songs from the hit TV series, with guest stars Harry Belafonte, Linda Ronstadt, and Rita Moreno. **FA14**

Muppet Treasures (1985, C, 56m, NR)
Kermit, Miss Piggy, and friends welcome human stars Loretta Lynn, Ethel Merman, Peter Sellers, and Paul Simon in this collection of funny moments from the TV series. **FA14, ST137**

Muppets Take Manhattan, The (1984, C, 94m, G)
Broadway-bound frog, pig, and friends take the Great White Way by storm. Liza Minnelli, Joan Rivers, Brooke Shields, Elliott Gould, Art Carney, and Dabney Coleman lend support. **FA14, XT9**

Murder (1930, B&W, 108m, NR)
Herbert Marshall stars in this Hitchcock thriller about a jury member who has second thoughts about a condemned woman. **DT46**

Murder at the Baskervilles *see* The Silver Blaze

Murder at the Vanities (1934, B&W, 89m, NR)
Combination mystery and musical, with detective Victor McLaglen investigating backstage killing. Duke Ellington and his band are among the performers. **MU16, MY12**

Murder by Death (1976, C, 94m, PG)
Mystery comedy featuring an all-star collection of detectives (Charlie Chan, Sam Spade, Miss Marple) attempting to solve a whodunit in the mansion of Truman Capote. Peter Sellers, Peter Falk, and Alec Guinness head the cast. Written by Neil Simon. **CO7, CO10, HF4, MY17, ST60, ST137, WR23**

Murder by Decree (1979, C, 121m, PG)
Sherlock and Dr. Watson track Jack the
Ripper. Christopher Plummer and James
Mason star. **HF14, ST102**

Murder by Natural Causes (1979, C,
100m, NR)
The unfaithful wife of a mentalist tries to
scare her husband to death, with unexpected results. Katharine Ross and Hal
Holbrook star. Written by William Levinson and Richard Link. Originally made
for TV. **MY14**

Murder by Television (1935, B&W, 60m,
NR)
Low-budget mystery about the murder of
a professor working on early TV technol-
ogy. Bela Lugosi plays his assistant, the
prime suspect. **ST95**

Murder Is Announced, A (1984, C, 153m,
NR)
Joan Hickson stars as Miss Marple, Agatha Christie's intrepid sleuth, in this whodunit involving a murder that is advertised ahead of schedule in the classified
ads of a newspaper. Originally made for
British TV. **MY12, WR3**

Murder My Sweet (1944, B&W, 95m, NR)
Dick Powell plays Raymond Chandler's
famous detective Philip Marlowe in this
version of *Farewell, My Lovely*. Filmed
under the original title in 1975. **MY1,
WR2**

Murder on the Orient Express (1974, C,
127m, PG)
Agatha Christie's master sleuth Hercule
Poirot solves the killing of a rich American aboard the famous luxury train. Albert Finney plays Poirot; among the suspects are Oscar winner Ingrid Bergman,
Lauren Bacall, Sean Connery, and Vanessa Redgrave. Sidney Lumet directed.
**DT65, MY12, ST7, ST21, ST42, ST127,
WR3, XT5, XT19**

Murder Over New York (1940, B&W, 64m,
NR)
Ace detective Charlie Chan (Sidney Toler) attends a police convention and
comes up against saboteurs who are crip-
pling the Allied air effort. **HF4**

Murder Story (1989, C, 90m, NR)
A aspiring young novelist copies the tech-
nique of his idol by piecing random newspaper clippings to form a mystery story.

Christopher Lee stars in this thriller,
made in Holland. **ST89**

Murders in the Rue Morgue (1971, C, 87m,
PG)
Horror story, based on Edgar Allan Poe
tale, of Parisian murders by a most mysterious assailant. Jason Robards and Herbert Lom star. **ST129, WR21**

Murmur of the Heart (1971, C, 118m, NR)
French comedy from director Louis
Malle about an unlikely subject: the intimate relationship that develops between
a 14year-old boy and his mother. **FF1**

Murphy's Law (1986, C, 100m, R)
Charles Bronson plays a police detective
framed for murder by an ex-con (Carrie
Snodgress). **ST12**

Murphy's Romance (1986, C, 107m, PG-
13)
A newly divorced mother moves to a
small Arizona town hoping for a new life,
and she falls in love with the town drug-
gist. Sally Field and James Garner star.
Directed by Martin Ritt. **CO1, DR26,
DT87, ST40**

Murphy's War (1971, C, 108m, PG)
Peter O'Toole stars in this drama of a
British seaman who survives a Nazi at-
tack and swears revenge. **ST117**

Music Box (1989, C, 123m, R)
In contemporary Chicago, an elderly man
is accused of participating in World War
II atrocities, and his attorney daughter
agrees to defend him. Jessica Lange and
Armin Mueller-Stahl star, with Frederic
Forrest, Donald Moffat, and Lukas Haas.
Directed by Costa-Gavras. **DR7, DR8,
DR17, ST86, XT11**

Music Box, The/Helpmates (1932, B&W,
50m, NR)
Two classic Laurel and Hardy shorts; the
first, about an inept piano-moving team,
won them their only Oscar. **ST87**

Music Man, The (1962, C, 151m, G)
A con man charms the people of River
City, Iowa, in this all-American musical
starring Robert Preston and Shirley
Jones, with Buddy Hackett and Ronny
Howard. Songs includes "Till There Was
You" and "76 Trombones." **DT48, FA9,
MU2, MU6** *Recommended*

Mussolini and I (1985, C, 126m, PG-13)
Focus in this historical drama is on the dictator's son-in-law, Count Galazzo (Anthony Hopkins). Bob Hoskins plays Il Duce, with Susan Sarandon as his daughter. Originally made for cable TV, where it was shown at 192m. Also known as *Mussolini: The Decline and Fall of Il Duce*. **DR4, ST72**

Mutant (1984, C, 100m, R)
A chemical plant's deadly toxic waste finds its way into the town's water supply, turning everyone into a horrible monster. Wings Hauser, Bo Hopkins, and Jennifer Warren star. **HO21**

Mutilator, The (1985, C, 90m, R)
Five teens at a remote beach house are stalked by a mad killer out for revenge in this horror film. **HO12**

Mutiny on the Bounty, The (1935, B&W, 132m, NR)
The great sea adventure of Captain Bligh (Charles Laughton) and his rebellious first mate Fletcher Christian (Clark Gable). Oscar winner for Best Picture. **AC12, AC13, AC16, CL3, ST49, XT1** *Essential; Recommended*

Mutiny on the Bounty (1962, C, 177m, NR)
Remake of the true-life sea story, with Marlon Brando as Christian and Trevor Howard as Captain Bligh. **AC12, AC16, ST10**

My Beautiful Laundrette (1985, C, 93m, R)
A young Pakistani emigré living in London borrows money from a wealthy uncle to open his own business. He also begins a secret affair with a white British youth. Perceptive comedy-drama, originally made for British TV, stars Saeed Jaffrey, Roshan Seth, Daniel Day-Lewis, and Gordon Warnecke. Directed by Stephen Frears; written by Hanif Kureishi. **DR3, DR7, DR23, XT15** *Recommended*

My Bodyguard (1980, C, 96m, PG)
When bullies harass a small high school student, he hires a very large friend to protect him. Comedy-drama starring Chris Makepeace, Adam Baldwin, and Matt Dillon, with Martin Mull and Ruth Gordon. **CO4, CO18**

My Brilliant Career (1979, C, 101m, G)
In turn-of-the-century Australia, a young woman finds her headstrong ways are getting her into loads of trouble. Judy Davis stars in this superb drama from director Gillian Armstrong. **FF5** *Recommended*

My Darling Clementine (1946, B&W, 97m, NR)
Henry Fonda is Wyatt Earp, Victor Mature is Doc Holliday in this classic telling of the gunfight at the O. K. Corral, directed by John Ford. With Linda Darnell and Walter Brennan. **DT36, HF9, HF13, ST44, WE5, WE8** *Essential; Highly Recommended*

My Dear Secretary (1948, B&W, 94m, NR)
Romantic comedy set in the literary world: Laraine Day plays a bestselling author and Kirk Douglas is a struggling writer. With Keenan Wynn. **ST34**

My Demon Lover (1987, C, 90m, PG-13)
Romantic comedy about a guy who has a problem around girls: whenever he gets turned on, he's transformed into a hideous beast. Scott Valentine and Michelle Little star. **CO11**

My Dinner With Andre (1981, C, 110m, NR)
A New York playwright (Wallace Shawn) and director (Andre Gregory) share a meal and talk about their separate life experiences. A cult comedy, with the performers more or less playing themselves and improvising their dialogue. **CO12, CU5**

My Fair Lady (1964, C, 107m, G)
Hit Broadway musical about a Cockney flower girl learning her manners from stuffy professor. Audrey Hepburn, Rex Harrison, and a great Lerner and Loewe score share the spotlight. Oscar winner for Best Picture, Actor, and Director (George Cukor). **DT24, FA9, MU2, MU7, MU17, ST65, XT1, XT2, XT6**

My Favorite Brunette (1947, B&W, 87m, NR)
Bob Hope comedy about a photographer involved with mobsters, costarring Dorothy Lamour, Peter Lorre, and Lon Chaney, Jr. **ST17, ST70**

My Favorite Wife (1940, B&W, 88m, NR)
A woman thought dead returns from a desert island to find her husband has remarried. Irene Dunne, Cary Grant, and Randolph Scott star in this comedy. **CL10, ST57, ST136**

My Favorite Year (1982, C, 92m, PG)
A young writer for a popular 1950s TV program is assigned to keep watch over a tipsy Hollywood star who's to appear live on the show. Nostalgic comedy starring Peter O'Toole, Mark-Linn Baker, and Joseph Bologna. **CO6, CO8, ST117** *Recommended*

My First Wife (1984, C, 95m, NR)
Intense drama from Australian director Paul Cox of a man trying to cope when his wife leaves him after ten years of marriage. **FF5**

My Left Foot (1989, C, 100m, R)
The life of irish painter and writer Christy Brown, whose affliction afforded only his foot as a means of painting or typing. Oscar winners Daniel Day-Lewis and Brenda Fricker (as Christy's mother) star, with Roy McAnally and Fiona Shaw. **DR4, DR23, XT2, XT5** *Recommended*

My Life as a Dog (1987, C, 101m, NR)
Swedish boy becomes too much for his ill mother to handle, so he's sent to live with relatives in a village. Gentle comedy about pains and pleasures of growing up in the late 1950s, written and directed by Lass Halstrom. (Available in both subtitled and dubbed versions.) **CO4, FF7**

My Life to Live (1962, B&W, 85m, NR)
Director Jean-Luc Godard's portrait of a Parisian prostitute (Anna Karina) is the subject of this groundbreaking experimental film. **DT41**

My Little Chickadee (1940, B&W, 83m, NR)
Mae West and W.C. Fields team up to tame the Old West in this classic spoof. **CL10, ST41, ST158, WE14**

My Little Girl (1986, C, 113m, R)
Drama of a naive girl from a wealthy family who takes a job in an inner city children's detention center. Mary Stuart Masterson stars, with James Earl Jones and Geraldine Page. **DR9, ST76**

My Little Pony: The Movie (1986, C, 90m, G)
Animated feature film starring the beautiful Little Ponies, who befriend humans and fight against evil in the world. **FA10**

My Man Godfrey (1936, B&W, 95m, NR)
Classic comedy of Depression era, with wealthy man turning hobo and becoming butler to a Park Avenue family of eccentrics. William Powell and Carole Lombard star, with Gail Patrick, Eugene Pallette, and Alice Brady. **CL10, CO20, ST92, ST122** *Essential*

My Name Is Nobody (1974, C, 115m, PG)
In this spaghetti western, Henry Fonda plays an aging gunfighter who's idolized by a young cowpoke (Terence Hill). **ST44, WE13**

My New Partner (1985, C, 104m, R)
A French comedy about a veteran cop (Philippe Noiret) training his young partner in the fine art of selective law enforcement. **FF1**

My Night at Maud's (1970, B&W, 105m, PG)
An upright, uptight Catholic intellectual is fascinated by an attractive woman. Jean-Louis Trintignant stars in this French comedy from director Eric Rohmer. **DT89** *Essential*

My Old Man (1979, C, 104m, NR)
Ernest Hemingway's story of a racetrack trainer and his loving daughter stars Warren Oates and Kristy McNichol. Originally made for TV. **ST115, WR10**

My Pal Trigger (1946, B&W, 79m, NR)
Roy Rogers and his faithful horse ride the range in search of adventure. **ST132**

My Pet Monster (1986, C, 60m, NR)
A boy under a mysterious spell turns into a monster every time he gets hungry in this family adventure. **FA4**

My Science Project (1985, C, 94m, PG)
A group of high school students cook up something in their lab that could destroy the whole school. A comedy with plenty of special effects action. John Stockwell stars, with Danielle Von Zerneck and Dennis Hopper. **CO11, CO18, ST71**

My Side of the Mountain (1969, C, 100m, G)
Family drama of a 13-year-old Toronto lad who runs away from home to live in a forest for a year. Teddy Eccles stars, with Theodore Bikel. **FA4, FA7**

My Stepmother Is an Alien (1988, C, 108m, PG-13)
A widowed scientist is romanced by a sexy blonde—who is in reality an alien assigned to enlist his help in saving her imperiled planet. Dan Aykroyd and Kim Basinger star. **CO11, CO13**

My Uncle (1958, C, 116m, NR)
Jacques Tati's Oscar-winning film about the misadventures of M. Hulot (Tati), whose simple life is in contrast to his sister and brother-in-law's gadget-filled home. Also known as *Mon Oncle*. **DT104, XT7**

Myra Breckenridge (1970, C, 94m, R)
Cult movie about decadent Hollywood scene, based on Gore Vidal's novel. Raquel Welch stars, with Mae West, Rex Reed, and John Huston. **CU1, CU2, DR19, DT50, ST158**

Mysterians, The (1959, C, 85m, NR)
Japanese science fiction drama about highly evolved aliens trying to take over our planet. **FF4, SF18**

Mysteries (1984, C, 93m, NR)
French drama starring Rutger Hauer as a rich man obsessed with a young woman he meets in a seaside town. With Sylvia Kristel, David Rappaport, and Rita Tushingham. **FF1**

Mysterious Island (1961, C, 101m, NR)
Jules Verne's tale of prison escapees landing on an island inhabited by gigantic animals. Michael Craig, Joan Greenwood, and Michael Callan star. Special effects by Ray Harryhausen. **FA3, FA4, SF10, WR28**

Mysterious Mr. Wong (1935, B&W, 56m, NR)
Oriental sleuth (Bela Lugosi) uncovers a deadly mystery in Chinatown involving the 13 Coins of Confucious. **ST95**

Mystery of Kasper Hauser, The *see* Every Man for Himself and God Against All

Mystery of the *Mary Celeste*, The: The Phantom Ship, (1937, B&W, 63m, NR)
Mystery story, based on fact, about a ship found in mid-ocean with no one aboard. Bela Lugosi stars. **ST95**

Mystery of the Wax Museum, The (1933, C, 77m, NR)
Classic horror film about a mad doctor (Lionel Atwill) dipping his victims in wax and putting them on display. One of the early films shot in Technicolor. Fay Wray costars. **HO1**

Mystery Train (1989, C, 110m, R)
Off-center comedy from director Jim Jarmusch contains three stories set in Memphis, all related in some way to Elvis Presley (title is one of his great early recordings). Music stars playing "straight" roles in the cast include Screamin' Jay Hawkins, Rufus Thomas, Sy Richardson, Joe Strummer, and Tom Waits. **CO2, CO12, MU12**

Mystic Pizza (1988, C, 101m, R)
In a seaside Connecticut town, three young women who work at a pizza restaurant try to figure what to do with the rest of their lives. Julia Roberts, Annabeth Gish, and Lili Taylor star, with Vincent Philip D'Onofrio, Conchata Farrell, Adam Storke, and William R. Moses. **DR10, DR26**

Nadine (1987, C, 83m, PG)
Austin, Texas, 1954: Vernon and Nadine are about to get divorced, but first there's this matter of some risqué photos, a dead photographer, and a sleazy gangster. Comedy from writer-director Robert Benton, starring Jeff Bridges, Kim Basinger, and Rip Torn. **CO6, DT6, ST11, ST150** *Recommended*

Naked and the Dead, The (1958, C, 131m, NR)
From Norman Mailer's first novel, a drama of men at war—often with each other—in the South Pacific. Aldo Ray and Cliff Robertson star. **AC1, DR19**

Naked Civil Servant, The (1980, C, 80m, NR)
John Hurt portrays Quentin Crisp, a British advocate of rights for homosexuals in the 1930s and 1940s, in this drama. **DR4**

Naked Face, The (1985, C, 103m, R)
A psychiatrist, accused of murdering his own patient, turns detective to find the real killer. Roger Moore, Rod Steiger, and Elliott Gould star. **MY11**

Naked Gun, The (1988, C, 85m, R)
Spoof of cop movies, with Leslie Nielsen a poker-faced detective investigating a plot to assassinate Queen Elizabeth at a California Angels baseball game. With O.J. Simpson, Priscilla Presley, George Kennedy, Ricardo Montalban, and Reggie Jackson. **CO7, CO10** *Recommended*

Naked in the Sun (1957, C, 79m, NR)
Seminole Indians battle slave traders in this western tale, based on a true story. **WE7**

Naked Jungle, The (1954, C, 95m, NR)
Charlton Heston is a South American plantation owner whose property and life are threatened by a mammoth army of ravenous red ants. **AC12, AC24**

Naked Kiss, The (1964, B&W, 93m, NR)
Writer-director Sam Fuller's devastating look at small-town hypocrisy, with an ex-prostitute starting a new life, only to be caught up in a first-class scandal when she murders her fiance. Constance Towers stars, with Anthony Eisley, Virginia Grey, and Michael Dante. **DR26, DT40** *Recommended*

Naked Night, The *see* Sawdust and Tinsel

Naked Prey, The (1966, C, 94m, NR)
Cornel Wilde directed and stars in this adventure story of a Britisher pursued by murderous African tribesmen. **AC12, AC24** *Recommended*

Naked Spur, The (1953, C, 91m, NR)
Bounty hunter James Stewart and fugitive Robert Ryan play a cat-and-mouse game in this classic western. Directed by Anthony Mann. **DT69, ST143**

Naked Truth, The (1957, B&W, 92m, NR)
British comedy about an assortment of people united in their desire to do away with the sleazy editor of a pornographic magazine. Terry-Thomas and Peter Sellers star. Also known as *Your Past Is Showing*. **ST137**

Name of the Rose, The (1986, C, 130m, R)
Sean Connery stars as a monk in 14th-century Italy who solves a bizarre series of murders in a monastery. Based on Umberto Eco's bestselling novel. With F. Murray Abraham and Christian Slater. **DR19, MY11, ST21**

Nanook of the North (1922, B&W, 69m, NR)
Pioneering documentary, directed by Robert Flaherty, about the daily lives of an Eskimo family. **CU16** *Essential; Recommended*

Napoleon (1927, B&W/C, 235m, G)
Grand, epic telling of the life of France's great emperor, played as an adult by Albert Dieudonne. This silent film, directed by Abel Gance, features tinted scenes and a Polyvision, three-screen sequence that was far ahead of its time. **CL1, CL12, FF1, HF18** *Essential; Highly Recommended*

Napoleon (1955, C, 115m, NR)
Orson Welles and Erich Von Stroheim head the cast of this French-made drama about the famed emperor's life. Raymond Pellegrin stars in the title role. **DT109, DT112, HF18**

Napoleon and Samantha (1972, C, 92m, G)
A pair of young children runs off with a pet lion in this Disney drama. Johnny Whitaker, Jodie Foster, and Michael Douglas star. **FA1, ST35, ST47**

Narrow Margin, The (1952, B&W, 70m, NR)
Film noir featuring a cop and gangster's widow on a train dodging hit men. Charles McGraw and Marie Windsor star. **MY1, XT19**

Nashville (1975, C, 159m, R)
Multi-character study of the music scene in Nashville and its connections to a political candidate. Henry Gibson, Karen Black, Ronee Blakley, Keith Carradine, Lily Tomlin, Michael Murphy, and Ned Beatty star, with Gwen Welles, Christina Raines, and Jeff Goldblum. Robert Altman directed. **DR12, DT2, MU6, ST56, ST149** *Essential*

Nasty Habits (1977, C, 96m, PG)
Dark comedy about political machinations inside a convent that mirror the Watergate affair. Glenda Jackson, Geral-

dine Page, Melina Mercouri, and Sandy Dennis star, with Rip Torn, Edith Evans, Jerry Stiller, and Eli Wallach. **CO12, ST150**

Nate and Hayes (1983, C, 100m, PG)
Swashbuckling story of a pirate pair who roam the Caribbean in search of treasure and lovely women. Tommy Lee Jones and Michael O'Keefe star, with Jenny Seagrove. Written by John Hughes. **AC15, DT49**

National Lampoon's Animal House (1978, C, 109m, R)
The groundbreaking comedy about life in the Delta House, the fraternity where disorder always reigns. John Belushi stars, with Tim Matheson, Peter Riegert, Thomas Hulce, and Bruce McGill. **CO4, CO13, CO18** *Recommended*

National Lampoon's Christmas Vacation (1989, C, 97m, PG-13)
Third outing (following the two *Vacation* films) of the comic misadventures of the Griswold clan, headed by Chevy Chase and Beverly D'Angelo, as they entertain for the holidays. With Randy Quaid and Diane Ladd. **CO5, CO13, FA13**

National Lampoon's Class Reunion (1982, C, 84m, R)
A psycho killer stalks a high school reunion party in this comedy written by John Hughes. Gerrit Graham stars. **CO18, DT49**

National Lampoon's European Vacation (1985, C, 94m, PG-13)
The wacky family from *National Lampoon's Vacation* invades the continent for more misadventures in tourism. Chevy Chase, Beverly D'Angelo, and Eric Idle star. Written by John Hughes. **CO5, CO13, CO15, DT49, XT18**

National Lampoon's Vacation (1983, C, 98m, R)
Chevy Chase and family take off for the summer and travel every back road in America on their way to mythical Wally World. Beverly D'Angelo costars, with Christie Brinkley, John Candy, Eddie Bracken, Imogene Coca, Randy Quaid, and Eugene Levy. Written by John Hughes; directed by Harold Ramis. **CO5, CO13, CO14, DT49, XT18**

National Velvet (1944, C, 124m, G)
Classic story of a girl and the horse she must ride in the Grand National—even if it means disguising herself as a boy. Elizabeth Taylor and Mickey Rooney star, with Oscar winner Anne Revere. **FA5, ST133, ST147, XT5**

Native Son (1986, C, 112m, PG)
In 1940, a young black chauffeur accidentally murders the daughter of his employer and becomes the center of a highly publicized trial. Adapted from Richard Wright's novel. Victor Love stars, with Elizabeth McGovern, Oprah Winfrey, and Matt Dillon. **DR14, DR19**

Natural, The (1984, C, 134m, PG)
Robert Redford is baseball star Roy Hobbs, the man with a mysterious past. Glenn Close, Robert Duvall, Barbara Hershey, and Kim Basinger costar. Adapted from the novel by Bernard Malamud. Directed by Barry Levinson; music by Randy Newman. **DR2, DR19, DR22, ST20, ST38, ST126**

Naughty Marietta (1935, B&W, 106m, NR)
Nelson Eddy and Jeanette MacDonald debuted together in this operetta about a runaway princess and dashing Indian scout. Songs include "Ah, Sweet Mystery of Life." **CL15**

Naughty Nineties, The (1945, B&W, 76m, NR)
Abbott and Costello play a couple of riverboat gamblers in this comedy which includes their unforgettable "Who's on First?" routine. **ST1**

Nazarin (1961, B&W, 92m, NR)
From director Luis Buñuel, the story of a Mexican priest and his unsuccessful attempts to bring the word of God to the peasants. **DT15**

Near Dark (1987, C, 94m, R)
A teenaged boy in Oklahoma (Adrian Pasdar) is kidnapped by a family of vampires who roam the roads of the Midwest by night. With Jenny Wright, Lance Henriksen, Bill Paxton, and Jenette Goldstein. Atmospheric horror story with modern twists, directed by Kathryn Bigelow. Music by Tangerine Dream. **HO5, XT18** *Recommended*

Neighbors (1981, C, 94m, R)
Placid suburban man is bedeviled by rude and lewd new next-door neighbors—but is he imagining it all? John Belushi and Dan Aykroyd star in this offbeat comedy, based on Thomas Berger's novel. **CO12, CO13, DR19**

Nelson Mandela 70th Birthday Tribute (1988, C, 120m, NR)
Highlights from a benefit concert held at London's Wembley Stadium to honor the then-jailed South African activist. Among the performers: George Michael, The Eurythmics, Al Green, Tracy Chapman, Peter Gabriel, Whitney Houston, Stevie Wonder, Dire Straits, and Eric Clapton. **MU10**

Neptune's Daughter (1949, C, 93m, NR)
Esther Williams plays a bathing suit designer in this aquatic MGM musical costaring Red Skelton, Betty Garrett, and Mel Blanc. **MU1**

Nest, The (1988, C, 88m, R)
A scientific experiment gone wrong results in a breed of giant cockroaches. Robert Lansing, Lisa Langlois, and a lot of bugs star. **HO16**

Network (1976, C, 121m, R)
An aggressive programmer (Faye Dunaway) at a major TV network clashes with a veteran producer (William Holden) and an unstable anchorman (Peter Finch, in his last film). With Beatrice Straight, Robert Duvall, and Ned Beatty. Directed by Sidney Lumet; Paddy Chayevsky's script brilliantly anticipates many ills of current TV journalism. Finch, Dunaway, and Straight won Oscars. **DR12, DT65, ST37, ST38, ST68, XT2, XT3, XT5, XT22** *Essential; Highly Recommended*

Nevada Smith (1966, C, 135m, NR)
Steve McQueen is an obsessed cowboy out to avenge the murders of his parents. **ST97, WE3, WE5**

Never a Dull Moment (1968, C, 100m, G)
A TV star accidentally becomes involved with gangsters. Disney comedy starring Dick Van Dyke and Edward G. Robinson. **FA1, ST130**

Never Cry Wolf (1983, C, 105m, PG)
Based on a true story, this family adventure drama follows naturalist Farley Mowat as he braves Arctic conditions to

study wolves up close. Charles Martin Smith stars. **AC12, AC24, FA4** *Recommended*

Never Give a Sucker an Even Break (1941, B&W, 71m, NR)
W. C. Fields' last feature film appearance is a zany free-for-all of vintage Fields bits. Margaret Dumont costars. **ST41**

Never Let Go (1963, B&W, 90m, NR)
Rare dramatic outing for Peter Sellers, as he plays a gangster involved with car thefts. **ST137**

Never Love a Stranger (1958, B&W, 91m, NR)
A young hood finds himself caught between his boyhood friends on the right side of the law and his colleagues in the Mob. John Drew Barrymore stars; Steve McQueen has a small supporting role. **ST97**

Never on Sunday (1960, B&W, 91m, NR)
An American visiting Greece tries to "educate" a carefree prostitute, who turns the tables on him. Melina Mercouri and husband Jules Dassin star; Dassin directed. **CO1**

Never Say Never Again (1983, C, 134m, PG)
Sean Connery's return as an older but no less crafty James Bond is a remake of *Thunderball*. Klaus Maria Brandauer is the villain, Kim Basinger and Barbara Carrera are the ladies. **HF2, ST21**

Never So Few (1959, C, 124m, NR)
Frank Sinatra leads a guerrilla band against the Japanese in World War II Burma. Steve McQueen and Charles Bronson head the supporting cast. **AC1, ST12, ST97, ST138**

Never Steal Anything Small (1959, C, 94m, NR)
James Cagney plays a union boss in this offbeat musical comedy-drama. **ST14**

NeverEnding Story, The (1984, C, 92m, PG)
A young boy imagines that the fantasy story he is reading comes true—and he becomes part of a fabulous adventure. **FA8, FF3, SF13**

New Adventures of Pippi Longstocking, The (1988, C, 100m, G)
The children's book heroine embarks on more adventures with her friends Tommy and Annika. Tami Erin stars, with Eileen Brennan, Dennis Dugan, and Dick Van Patten. See also: *Pippi Longstocking* series. **FA4**

New Kids, The (1984, C, 90m, R)
A brother and sister off to live with their uncle suddenly find themselves confronted by a neighborhood gang. Shannon Presby, Lori Loughlin, and Eric Stoltz star in this drama. **DR9**

New Leaf, A (1971, C, 102m, PG)
Elaine May directed and stars in this comedy about a frumpy scientist who's wooed strictly for her money by an unscrupulous playboy (Walter Matthau). **CO12, DT70, ST104**

New Life, A (1988, C, 104m, PG-13)
The comic mishaps of a New York couple who divorce and encounter the world of singles and "dating." Alan Alda and Ann-Margret star, with Hal Linden, Veronica Hamel, and John Shea. Alda wrote and directed. **CO1, CO2**

New Moon (1940, B&W, 105m, NR)
Jeanette MacDonald-Nelson Eddy musical set in Louisiana. Songs include "Softly as in a Morning Sunrise" and "Stout-Hearted Men." **CL15**

New York, New York (1977, C, 163m, R)
Drama set at the end of the Big Band era, centering on the stormy romance between a hot-tempered musician (Robert DeNiro) and a rising singer (Liza Minnelli). Martin Scorsese directed. The video version contains the "Happy Endings" production number, which did not appear in the original release of the film. Also available in a letterboxed edition. **CU10, CU19, DR12, DT95, MU4, MU6, ST30**

New York Stories (1989, C, 123m, PG)
A trio of tales set in contemporary Manhattan. In "Life Lessons," directed by Martin Scorsese, a temperamental artist (Nick Nolte) tries to prevent his protegé-lover (Rosanna Arquette) from leaving him. Francis Ford Coppola's "Life Without Zoe" focuses on the adventures of a girl who lives in a luxurious hotel while her parents are away tending to their separate careers. "Oedipus Wrecks" features director-star Woody Allen as a Jewish attorney whose dominating mother (Mae Questel) ruins his relationship with a Gentile woman (Mia Farrow). **CO2, DR1, DR9, DR15, DT1, DT21, DT95, ST113, XT9** *Recommended*

Newsfront (1978, C, 110m, PG)
Behind-the-scenes drama of the people who made newsreels in Australia during the 1940s and 1950s. **FF5** *Recommended*

Next of Kin (1989, C, 108m, R)
Patrick Swayze plays a Chicago cop whose hometown clan from Kentucky helps him get revenge on the gangsters who killed his brother. **AC19**

Next Year, If All Goes Well (1981, C, 95m, R)
French comedy of a couple (Isabelle Adjani, Thierry Lhermitte) who can't decide if they're really in love, even after conceiving a child. **FF1**

Niagara (1953, C, 89m, NR)
Marilyn Monroe stars in this thriller about a woman planning to murder her new husband on their honeymoon. Joseph Cotten costars. **MY4, ST108**

Nice Dreams (1981, C, 89m, R)
Cheech and Chong, those spaced-out L.A. hipsters, use their ice cream truck as a front for selling marijuana. With Stacy Keach and Timothy Leary. **ST18**

Nicholas and Alexandra (1971, C, 183m, PG)
Epic tale of the final days of Czar Nicholas of Russia and his wife, with court intrigue aplenty. Michael Jayston and Janet Suzman star; Laurence Olivier heads the supporting cast. **DR5, ST116**

Night Ambush *see* Ill Met by Moonlight

Night and Day (1946, C, 128m, NR)
Cary Grant plays composer Cole Porter in this dramatic biography, with Eve Arden and Alexis Smith. Many Porter tunes on the soundtrack. **MU5, ST57**

Night and Fog (1955, B&W, 34m, NR)
Classic documentary about the horrors of the Nazi death camps, directed by Alain Resnais. **CU16** *Essential; Recommended*

Night at the Opera, A (1935, B&W, 92m, NR)
The Marx Bros. journey to America, demolish a production of *Il Travatore*. Margaret Dumont takes a dim view of it all. Stateroom scene an all-time crowd pleaser. Kitty Carlisle and Allan Jones offer a few songs. **ST101** *Essential; Recommended*

Night Before, The (1988, C, 90m, PG-13)
Comedy of errors, set during a teenaged boy's prom night, starring Keanu Reeves, and Lori Loughlin, with Trinidad Silva. Songs by George Clinton, who appears in a nightclub scene. **CO4**

Night Call Nurses (1972, C, 85m, R)
Sexy comedy about wild goings-on at a hospital. Produced by Roger Corman; directed by Jonathan Kaplan. **CU14**

Night Crossing (1981, C, 106m, PG)
True-life drama about two families escaping from East Berlin in a hot-air balloon. John Hurt, Jane Alexander, and Glynnis O'Connor star in this Disney production. **FA1**

Night Flight From Moscow (1973, C, 113m, PG)
A Russian diplomat attempts to defect to the West. Spy thriller starring Yul Brynner, Henry Fonda, and Dirk Bogarde. **ST44**

Night Force (1986, C, 82m, R)
A strike force composed of young recruits engages terrorist during a rescue mission in the jungles of Southeast Asia. Linda Blair is in command. **AC20**

Night Gallery (1969, C, 98m, NR)
Trio of creepy stories, narrated by Rod Serling, each originating with a separate painting. Roddy McDowall, Ossie Davis, and Joan Crawford are among the stars. Steven Spielberg directed the segment with Crawford. Originally made for TV. **DT99, HO23, ST24**

Night Has Eyes, The (1942, B&W, 75m, NR)
British mystery involving a schoolteacher (Joyce Howard) and a friend who turn up missing on the moors. James Mason co-stars. Also known as *Terror House*. **MY5, ST102**

Night in Casablanca, A (1946, B&W, 85m, NR)
The Marx Brothers turn a Moroccan hotel upside-down in search of Nazi spies. **ST101**

Night in June, A *see* June Night

Night in the Life of Jimmy Reardon, A (1988, C, 90m, R)
The comic misadventures of a sexually precocious young man, set in 1962 suburban Chicago. River Phoenix stars, with Ann Magnuson, Meredith Salenger, and Ione Skye. **CO4**

Night Is My Future (1947, B&W, 87m, NR)
Early film from director Ingmar Bergman about a blind veteran who is taken in by a caring housekeeper. Mai Zetterling stars. **DT7**

'night, Mother (1986, C, 97m, PG-13)
A drama about a woman's determination to end her life and her mother's attempts to talk her out of suicide. Sissy Spacek and Anne Bancroft star in this screen version of Marsha Norman's play. **DR8, DR20, ST139**

Night Moves (1975, C, 95m, R)
Detective, hired to find runaway rich girl, uncovers bizarre mystery plot in the Florida Keys. Clever thriller, starring Gene Hackman, with Jennifer Warren, Susan Clark, Melanie Griffith, and James Woods. Directed by Arthur Penn; written by Alan Sharp. **DT78, MY2, MY10, ST58, ST61, ST165** *Highly Recommended*

Night of the Bloody Apes (1968, C, 81m, NR)
Mexican mishmash of horror and wrestling movie. A mad doctor transplants the heart of an ape into his son, who promptly goes bananas. Cult favorite of "bad" movie conoisseurs. **CU11**

Night of the Comet (1984, C, 95m, PG-13)
The passing of a strange comet over the skies of Los Angeles leaves two air-head sisters as survivors to battle zombie victims. Tongue-in-cheek science fiction, starring Catherine Mary Stewart and Kelli Maroney. **SF12, SF21, XT10** *Recommended*

Night of the Creeps (1986, C, 89m, NR)
An alien organism is released through a human carrier, creating monsters and havoc. **HO21**

Night of the Generals, The (1967, C, 148m, NR)
Someone is murdering the generals of the Third Reich in this mystery/war drama. Peter O'Toole, Omar Sharif, and Tom Courtenay star. **ST117**

Night of the Ghouls *see* Revenge of the Dead

Night of the Hunter (1955, B&W, 93m, NR)
Moody thriller about two children fleeing from murderous preacher. Robert Mitchum, Lillian Gish, and Shelley Winters star. The only film directed by actor Charles Laughton; written by James Agee. A cult favorite. **CU15, MY1, ST54, ST107, ST164** *Recommended*

Night of the Iguana, The (1964, B&W, 93m, NR)
Tennessee Williams drama about a minister in Mexico and his worldly temptations. Richard Burton stars, with Ava Gardner, Deborah Kerr, and Sue Lyon as his temptations. John Huston directed. **DT50, ST13, WR30**

Night of the Living Dead (1969, B&W, 96m, NR)
Low-budget horror classic about ghouls returning from the grave to feed on the living. George Romero directed this midnight movie staple. **CU1, CU4, CU7, HO6, HO18, DT90** *Essential; Highly Recommended*

Night of the Shooting Stars, The (1982, C, 106m, R)
During the final days of World War II, the residents of an Italian village try to survive the Nazi retreat. Directed by Paolo and Vittorio Taviani. **FF2** *Recommended*

Night Porter, The (1974, C, 115m, R)
A former concentration camp official and the prisoner he once abused meet years after the war and resume a bizarre sexual relationship. Dirk Bogarde and Charlotte Rampling star in this drama. **CU6**

Night Shift (1982, C, 106m, R)
A nerd and a fast-talking hustler who work nights together at the New York City morgue decide to go into the call girl business. Sweet comedy starring Henry Winkler, Michael Keaton, and Shelley Long. Directed by Ron Howard. **CO1, CO2, DT48, ST80** *Recommended*

Night Stage to Galveston (1952, B&W, 61m, NR)
Gene Autry and pal Pat Buttram are working to uncover corruption in the ranks of the Texas Rangers. Clayton Moore (TV's Lone Ranger) costars. **ST3**

Night They Raided Minsky's, The (1968, C, 99m, PG)
Comedy set in burlesque era in New York, with Quaker girl (Britt Ekland) meeting baggy-pants comic (Jason Robards). Narrated by Rudy Vallee. **CO6, ST129**

Night Tide (1961, B&W, 84m, NR)
Atmospheric thriller about a lonely sailor (Dennis Hopper) obsessed with a sideshow mermaid (Linda Lawson) who may be the real thing. Shot in Venice, California; directed by Curtis Harrington. **CU4, ST71**

Night Time in Nevada (1948, C, 67m, NR)
A western town is caught in the grip of a pair of cattle thievin', embezzlin' varmints, and it's Roy Rogers to the rescue. With Andy Devine and Bob Nolan. **ST132**

Night to Remember, A (1942, B&W, 91m, NR)
Comic mystery about a suspense novelist (Brian Aherne) and his wife (Loretta Young) solving a real murder case. **MY11, MY17**

Night to Remember, A (1958, B&W, 123m, NR)
Dramatic recreation of the infamous sinking of the *Titanic*. Kenneth More and David McCallum head the cast of this disaster adventure. **AC23, CL3, DR5**

Night Visitor, The (1970, C, 106m, PG)
Liv Ullmann and Max von Sydow star in this suspense drama about a man who escapes from a mental institution, intent on revenge. English-language film, shot in Denmark and Sweden. **HO9, ST154**

Night Watch (1973, C, 105m, R)
A wealthy widow claims she witnessed a murder, but police can find no evidence a crime has been committed. Elizabeth

Taylor and Laurence Harvey star in this thriller. **MY3, ST147**

Nightbreaker (1989, C, 99m, NR)
During the 1950s, the U.S. government deliberately exposes thousands of soldiers to an atomic bomb test to determine the effects of radiation. Emilio Estevez and Martin Sheen (son and father in real life) star, with Lea Thompson. Originally made for cable TV. **DR7, XT8**

Nightbreed (1990, C, 99m, R)
Clive Barker wrote and directed this grisly horror tale of a man determined to join a gang of monsters hiding beneath a small-town cemetery. Craig Sheffer stars, with David Cronenberg, Anne Bobby, and Charles Haid. **DT23, HO8, HO18**

Nightcomers, The (1972, C, 96m, R)
Prequel of sorts to Henry James' ghost tale *Turn of the Screw* tries to imagine how the children of that story came to be haunted. Marlon Brando and Stephanie Beacham star. **ST10, WR11**

Nighthawks (1981, C, 99m, R)
Two New York police detectives (Sylvester Stallone and Billy Dee Williams) comb Manhattan for a cold-blooded terrorist (Rutger Hauer). **AC9, ST140, ST159, XT9**

Nightingale, The (1985, C, 60m, NR)
Mick Jagger stars in this Faerie Tale Theatre presentation of the story of a powerful emperor and a magical bird. Barbara Hershey and James Edward Olmos co-star. **FA12, MU12**

Nightmare on Elm Street (series)
Nightmare on Elm Street (1984, C, 92m, R)
Nightmare 2: Freddy's Revenge (1986, C, 87m, R)
Nightmare 3: Dream Warriors (1987, C, 97m, R)
Nightmare 4: The Dream Master (1988, C, 93m, R)
Nightmare 5: The Dream Child (1989, C, 89m, R)
Quintet of horror tales about teenagers with horrible dreams featuring the same demented, scarred killer. Robert Englund stars as the evil Freddy Krueger in all five films. **HO12, HO18**

Nightmare Weekend (1985, C, 88m, R)
Three college coeds answer an ad for an experimental weekend in the country,

only to find themselves captives of a professor's crazed assistant. **HO20**

Nightmares (1983, C, (99m, R)
Four-story horror film, starring Emilio Estevez, Christina Raines, and William Sanderson. **HO23**

Nights of Cabiria (1957, B&W, 110m, NR)
A prostitute in Rome dreams of a better life for herself in this Oscar-winning drama from director Federico Fellini. Giulietta Masina (his real-life wife) stars. **DT53, XT7**

Nightwing (1979, C, 105m, PG)
Horror drama, set in Arizona, about killer vampire bats. David Warner, Kathryn Harrold, and Strother Martin star. **HO16**

Nijinsky (1980, C, 125m, R)
True-life drama of relationship between famed Russian dancer Nijinsky and impressario Sergei Diaghliev. George de la Pena and Alan Bates star, with Leslie Browne, Alan Badel, and Jeremy Irons. **DR3, DR4, DR12**

Nikki, Wild Dog of the North (1961, C, 74m, NR)
Disney adventure about a Canadian wolf-dog and his master. **FA1, FA5**

9 1/2 Weeks (1986, C, 117m, R)
Drama of an intense love affair between two modern New Yorkers, with overtones of sadism and masochism. Mickey Rourke and Kim Basinger star. **CU6, DR3, ST134**

9 to 5 (1980, C 110m, PG)
Comedy about three long-suffering secretaries (Jane Fonda, Lily Tomlin, and Dolly Parton) who take out their frustrations on their loutish boss (Dabney Coleman). **CO3, MU12, ST45, ST149**

1918 (1984, C, 94m, NR)
Matthew Broderick stars in this drama about a small Texas town devastated by the famous influenza epidemic. Written by Horton Foote. Prequel: *On Valentine's Day*. **DR5, DR26**

1984 (1984, C, 117m, R)
Screen version of the George Orwell novel about life under a future dictatorship. John Hurt and Richard Burton (in his last film) star. **DR19, SF11, ST13**

1941 (1979, C, 118m, PG)
Panic erupts in Southern California when residents believe a Japanese attack is imminent. Steven Spielberg directed this comedy with a huge cast that includes John Belushi, Ned Beatty, Treat Williams, Nancy Allen, Dan Aykroyd, Toshiro Mifune, Robert Stack, Warren Oates, Christopher Lee, John Candy, and Slim Pickens. **CO6, CO13, CO14, DT99, ST89, ST106, ST115**

1900 (1977, C, 255m, R)
From Italian director Bernardo Bertolucci, the epic story of two friends, one a landowner, the other a peasant, and how they're affected by the rise of fascism. Robert DeNiro, Gerard Depardieu, Burt Lancaster, and Dominique Sanda star. **DT9, FF2, ST30, ST31, ST85** *Recommended*

92 in the Shade (1975, C, 93m, R)
Bizarre goings-on in the Florida Keys in this comedy about rival fishing guides and their wacky women. Peter Fonda, Warren Oates, Margot Kidder, and Elizabeth Ashley star, with William Hickey, Burgess Meredith, and Joe Spinell. Director Tom McGuane adapted his own novel. **CO12, DR19, ST115** *Recommended*

Ninotchka (1939, B&W, 110m, NR)
Greta Garbo is the Russian agent who falls for suave Melvyn Douglas in one of Garbo's rare comic outings. With Bela Lugosi, Sig Ruman, and Ina Claire. Directed by Ernst Lubitsch; co-written by Billy Wilder. **CL10, DT63, ST50, ST95** *Essential; Highly Recommended*

No Deposit, No Return (1976, C, 112m, G)
Two clever kids stage their kidnapping, just to get some attention. David Niven and Darren McGavin star as villains in this Disney comedy. **FA1**

No Holds Barred (1989, C, 91m, PG-13)
Wrestling star Hulk Hogan makes his motion picture debut in this light-hearted look at the world of professional rassling. **CO19**

No Man of Her Own (1932, B&W, 85m, NR)
Clark Gable and Carole Lombard costar in this drama of a no-good guy and the woman who sets him straight. **ST49, ST92**

No Mercy (1986, C, 108m, R)
A Chicago cop (Richard Gere) travels to New Orleans to nab the gangster who killed his partner. Kim Basinger and Jeroen Krabbe costar. **AC19, MY5, ST52, XT14**

No Nukes *see* MUSE Concert: No Nukes, The

No Retreat, No Surrender (1985, C, 85m, PG)
A karate student squares off against a Russian bully. **AC26**

No Surrender (1985, C, 100m, R)
Comedy-drama set in a Liverpool nightclub, where a prankster has booked two senior citizen lodges—one Catholic, the other Protestant—plus a group of retarded patients from a hospital. Michael Angelis, Roy McAnally, and Joanne Whalley star, with Elvis Costello. Written by Alan Bleasdale. **CO17, DR11, DR23, MU12** *Recommended*

No Way Out (1987, C, 116m, R)
A naval aide to the Secretary of Defense finds himself incriminated in the death of the Secretary's mistress. Kevin Costner, Gene Hackman, and Sean Young star in this political thriller filmed on location in Washington, D.C. With Will Patton, Howard Duff, George Dzundza, and Fred Dalton Thompson. **DR21, MY2, MY5, MY6, ST23, ST61, XT12** *Recommended*

No Way To Treat a Lady (1968, C, 108m, NR)
An actor with a mother fixation dons disguises to commit his crimes against women. Rod Steiger, George Segal, and Lee Remick star. **MY3, MY13**

Nobody's Fault *see* Little Dorritt

Nomads (1986, C, 95m, R)
A scientist discovers a secret cult of ghosts living in modern-day Los Angeles. Horror thriller stars Pierce Brosnan, Lesley-Anne Down, and Adam Ant. **HO11, MU12**

Nomads of the North (1920, B&W, 109m, NR)
In the wilderness of northern Canada, a lovely young woman is forced into marriage with a villain to absolve her father's debts. Silent melodrama starring Lon Chaney, Sr. **ST16**

None but the Lonely Heart (1944, B&W, 113m, NR)
Rare drama for Cary Grant as a Cockney trying to do right by his dying mother (Oscar winner Ethel Barrymore). Grant's only Oscar nomination. **ST57, XT5**

Norma Rae (1979, C, 113m, PG)
Sally Field won an Oscar for her portrayal of a Southern working woman who helps organize a union against enormous pressures. With Beau Bridges and Ron Liebman. Directed by Martin Ritt. **DR10, DT87, ST40, XT3**

Norman Loves Rose (1982, C, 98m, R)
Australian comedy of a teenager (Tony Owen) in love with his sister-in-law (Carol Kane), who becomes pregnant. **FF5**

Norte, El (1984, C, 141m, R)
Heartrending story of a brother and sister fleeing their Latin American country because of political persecution and heading for the United States, where they encounter a different set of problems. Directed by Gregory Nava; produced by Anna Thomas. **DR7** *Recommended*

North Avenue Irregulars, The (1979, C, 99m, G)
A young priest and some of his female parishioners take on local criminals in this Disney comedy. Edward Herrmann, Barbara Harris, and Susan Clark star. **FA1**

North by Northwest (1959, C, 136m, NR)
Hitchcock chase drama, with innocent businessman Cary Grant mistaken for government agent. Many memorable scenes, with exciting climax on Mount Rushmore. Eva Marie Saint and James Mason costar. Written by Ernest Lehman. **DT46, MY7, ST57, ST102, XT18** *Essential; Highly Recommended*

North Dallas Forty (1979, C, 119m, R)
A pro football player finds his love of the game soured by the win-at-all-costs attitudes of his team's coaches and management. A devastating (and often funny) portrait of modern professional sports, starring Nick Nolte and Mac Davis, with Dayle Haddon, Charles Durning, G.D. Spradlin, Bo Svenson, John Matuszak, and Dabney Coleman. **CO19, DR44** *Highly Recommended*

North of the Great Divide (1950, C, 67m, NR)
Roy Rogers stars in this western about a Canadian Mountie and an Indian agent joining forces against a corrupt cannery owner. **ST132, WE10**

North Shore (1987, C, 96m, PG)
Matt Adler and Gregory Harrison star in this drama about surfers living for the big wave on the California coast. **DR22**

North Star (1943, B&W, 105m, NR)
World War II drama set in a Russian village, with noble townspeople resisting the German army. Anne Baxter, Dana Andrews, Walter Huston, and Erich Von Stroheim star. Written by Lillian Hellman; directed by Lewis Milestone. A few years after its release, Cold War politics forced scenes especially sympathetic to the Soviets to be cut; film was retitled *Armored Attack*. **AC1, CU8, DT109**

North to Alaska (1960, C, 122m, NR)
Golddigers on the northern frontier battle the elements and each other. John Wayne, Stewart Granger, and Fabian star. **MU12, ST156, WE10**

Northern Pursuit (1943, B&W, 94m, NR)
Errol Flynn plays a Canadian Mountie tracking a downed Nazi spy pilot. **ST43**

Northwest Passage (1940, C, 125m, NR)
Spencer Tracy stars in this colorful historical drama about Roger's Rangers, a group of scouts in Colonial America. With Robert Young and Walter Brennan. **CL3, ST151**

Nosferatu (1922, B&W, 63m, NR)
Silent film version of the Dracula story, directed by F.W. Murnau, is a classic of mood and atmosphere rather than blood and gore. **HF7, HO1, HO5** *Essential*

Not for Publication (1984, C, 88m, PG)
Comedy about a reporter (Nancy Allen) who moonlights as a campaign worker for a zany mayor and her romance with a photographer (David Naughton). Paul Bartel directed. **DT5**

Nothing in Common (1986, C, 119m, PG)
After a hip advertising executive sees his parents' long-standing marriage fall apart, he finds that his ailing father is now dependent on him. Tom Hanks, Jackie Gleason, and Eva Marie Saint star in this

comedy-drama set in Chicago. **DR8, DR24, ST62, XT11** *Recommended*

Nothing Sacred (1937, C, 75m, NR)
Smooth-talking reporter gets fictional scoop on a Vermont girl supposedly dying of radium poisoning and turns her into a national celebrity. Fredric March and Carole Lombard star in this comedy written by Ben Hecht. **CL10, ST92**

Notorious (1946, B&W, 101m, NR)
Hitchcock's classic mix of suspense and passion, with American agent Cary Grant forcing Ingrid Bergman to spy on Nazi Claude Rains. **CL4, DT46, MY3, MY5, MY6, ST7, ST57** *Essential; Highly Recommended*

Now and Forever (1983, C, 93m, R)
An Australian couple's happiness is shattered when he's falsely accused of rape and sent to prison. Cheryl Ladd stars. **FF5**

Now, Voyager (1942, B&W, 117m, NR)
Classic Bette Davis tearjerker about a spinster's romance. Paul Henreid and Claude Rains costar. **CL4, CL5, ST28**

Now You See Him, Now You Don't (1972, C, 88m, G)
College student Kurt Russell invents a spray that makes him invisible and is pursued by crooks who want the formula. Disney comedy also stars Cesar Romero and Jim Backus. **FA1**

Nowhere to Hide (1987, C, 100m, R)
Amy Madigan is a Marine whose husband, also a member of the Corps, is murdered by assassins. She uses her training to protect herself and her small son. **AC25**

Nuit de Varennes, La (1982, C, 133m, R)
This historical drama has Casanova and Thomas Paine sharing a coach during the violent days of the French Revolution. Marcello Mastroianni, Harvey Keitel, and Hanna Schygulla star. Directed by Ettore Scola. **FF2, ST103**

Number One With a Bullet (1987, C, 101m, R)
Billy Dee Williams and Robert Carradine star as police detectives tracking a drug lord. With Valerie Bertinelli and Peter Graves. **ST159**

Number 17 (1932, B&W, 83m, NR)
Light-hearted Hitchcock thriller about a hobo who gets mixed up with gang of jewel thieves. **DT46, MY15**

Nuns on the Run (1990, C, 90m, PG-13)
British comedy of two small-time hoods on the lam, disguising themselves and hiding out in a convent. Eric Idle and Robbie Coltrane star. **CO15, CO17, CO20**

Nun's Story, The (1959, C, 149m, NR)
Audrey Hepburn stars as a young sister who serves as a missionary in Africa and later decides to leave her order. With Peter Finch, Edith Evans, and Peggy Ashcroft. Fred Zinnemann directed. **DR10, DT120, ST65**

Nuts (1987, C, 116m, R)
A prostitute on trial for murdering a customer must battle her own lawyer and the legal system which wants to declare her insane. Barbra Streisand and Richard Dreyfuss star in this adaptation of Tom Topor's play. With Maureen Stapleton, Karl Malden, Eli Wallach, Robert Webber, James Whitmore, and Leslie Nielsen. Directed by Martin Ritt. **DR10, DR17, DR20, DT87, ST36, ST146**

Nutty Professor, The (1963, C, 107m, NR)
Comic variation on the Dr. Jekyll and Mr. Hyde story, with Jerry Lewis as the supremely nerdy scientist and his alter ego, suave crooner Buddy Love. Stella Stevens costars. **CL14, CO18, ST91**

O. C. and Stiggs (1987, C, 109m, R)
Comedy about two teenagers determined one summer to wreak havoc on their neighborhood. Dan Jenkins and Neill Barry star, with Paul Dooley, Dennis Hopper, and Jon Cryer. Robert Altman directed. **DT2, ST71**

O Lucky Man! (1973, C, 173m, R)
Epic adventures of a plucky young Britisher (Malcolm McDowell) who becomes top coffee salesman, suffers humiliating failure, only to land on his feet again. Unique musical interludes featuring composer Alan Price. With Ralph Richardson, Rachel Roberts, Arthur Lowe, and Helen Mirren. Directed by Lindsay Anderson, who also has a small role. **DR23** *Recommended*

Oblong Box, The (1969, C, 91m, PG)
Vincent Price and Christopher Lee star in
this horror story of two brothers, one a
respectable British aristocrat, the other
his disfigured, reclusive brother. Based
on an Edgar Allan Poe tale. **HO14, ST89,
ST124, WR21**

Obsession (1976, C, 98m, PG)
Years after his wife and daughter are kid-
napped and disappear, a New Orleans
businessman meets a young woman with
an uncanny resemblance to his wife. Cliff
Robertson, Genevieve Bujold, and John
Lithgow star in this thriller from director
Brian DePalma. **DT29, MY5, XT14**

Ocean's Eleven (1960, C, 127m, NR)
Frank Sinatra heads a gang of thieves
with plans to rob five Las Vegas casinos
at one time. Dean Martin, Sammy Davis,
Jr., Peter Lawford, and Angie Dickinson
costar in this comic caper. **MY18, ST138**

Octagon, The (1980, C, 103m, R)
Chuck Norris plays a bodyguard whose
client is in danger from an army of Ninja
assassins. With Lee Van Cleef. **ST114,
ST155**

Octopussy (1983, C, 130m, PG)
James Bond (Roger Moore) travels to India to tangle with a deadly female assassin (Maud Adams) and her cult. **HF2**

Odd Angry Shot, The (1979, C, 90m, R)
A group of Australian soldiers try to cope
with combat life during the Vietnam War.
John Hargreaves and Bryan Brown star.
FF5

Odd Couple, The (1968, C, 105m, G)
Classic Neil Simon comedy about two
newly divorced men (Walter Matthau and
Jack Lemmon) sharing a New York apartment despite their totally incompatible
lifestyles. **CO3, ST90, ST104, WR23, XT9**

Odd Man Out (1947, B&W, 113m, NR)
James Mason plays a wounded Irish gunman on the lam, with no one to shelter
him, in this classic thriller. Directed by
Carol Reed. **MY15, ST102** *Recommended*

Odd Obsession (1959, C, 96m, NR)
In this Japanese drama, an elderly man
persuades his wife to take up with a
younger man, with disastrous consequences. **FF4**

Odessa File, The (1974, C, 128m, PG)
Frederick Forsyth thriller about a German reporter tracking ex-Nazis in 1963
Berlin. Jon Voight and Maximillian Schell
star. **MY6, WR8**

Of Human Bondage (1934, B&W, 83m,
NR)
Classic Somerset Maugham story of a
crippled man's infatuation with a scornful
waitress, starring Bette Davis and Leslie
Howard. **DR19, ST28**

Of Mice and Men (1939, B&W, 107m, NR)
Drama, based on John Steinbeck novel,
about two itinerant workers, clever
George (Burgess Meredith) and dim-witted Lenny (Lon Chaney, Jr.), and the
tragic event that leads to their separation.
DR19, ST17, WR25

Of Unknown Origin (1983, C, 88m, R)
Horror story of a New York businessman
doing battle in his home with a gigantic
rodent. Peter Weller stars. **HO16**

Off Limits (1953, B&W, 89m, NR)
Service comedy, with Bob Hope and
Mickey Rooney trying to put one (or two)
over on the brass. **CO21, ST70, ST133**

Off Limits (1988, C, 110m, R)
A pair of American police detectives
track down a killer in 1968 Saigon. Willem
Dafoe and Gregory Hines star, with
Amanda Pays, Fred Ward, and Scott
Glenn. **AC9, MY16**

Officer and a Gentleman, An (1982, C,
126m, R)
Romance blossoms between a headstrong
naval pilot-in-training and a girl who
works at a local factory. Richard Gere
and Debra Winger star, with Oscar winner Louis Gossett, Jr., David Keith, Robert Loggia, Lisa Blount, and Lisa Eil-
bacher. **DR1, ST52, ST163, XT4**

Official Story, The (1985, C, 110, R)
Oscar-winning film from Argentina about
a woman who discovers that the parents
of her adopted daughter may be among
the "missing" persons executed by the
secret police. Norma Aleandro stars.
FF6, XT7

Offspring, The (1986, C, 99m, R)
A quartet of horror tales, narrated by an
old man (Vincent Price) who lives in a
mysterious small town. **HO23, ST124**

Oh! Calcutta! (1972, C, 105m, NR)
Long-running Broadway musical, actually a series of sketches about sexuality, in which the actors wear no clothes. **MU2**

Oh, God! (1977, C, 104m, PG)
A supermarket manager strikes up a friendship with the earthly presence of the Supreme Being. John Denver and George Burns star in this family comedy. **FA6, MU12**

Oh, God! Book II (1980, C, 94m, PG)
George Burns returns as the Man Upstairs. This time, he's using a little girl to get out the word that reports of his demise have been greatly exaggerated. **FA6**

Oh, God! You Devil (1984, C, 96m, PG)
The third in the series finds George Burns playing both title roles in the story of a singer who sells his soul to you-know-who for fame and fortune. Ted Wass co-stars. **FA6**

Oh! Heavenly Dog (1980, C, 104m, PG)
A private eye (Chevy Chase) is reincarnated in the body of a lovable dog (Benji) in this family comedy. **CO13, FA5**

Oklahoma! (1955, C, 145m, G)
Classic Rodgers and Hammerstein musical about settlers in the Sooner State, starring Gordon MacRae, Shirley Jones, and Rod Steiger. Songs include "Oh, What a Beautiful Mornin' " and "People Will Say We're in Love." Directed by Fred Zinnemann. **DT120, FA9, MU2, MU6**

Oklahoma Kid, The (1939, B&W, 85m, NR)
Unusual casting in this western featuring Humphrey Bogart and James Cagney as the villain and lawman in a revenge struggle. **ST8, ST14, WE15**

Old Barn Dance, The (1938, B&W, 58m, NR)
Singing cowboy Gene Autry exposes some evil businessmen in this modern-day western. Roy Rogers is in the supporting cast under the name Dick Weston. **ST3, ST132**

Old Boyfriends (1979, C, 103m, R)
Drama about a woman who looks up her former lovers to try to understand herself better. Talia Shire stars; John Belushi,

Richard Jordan, and Keith Carradine play the title roles. **CO13, DR10**

Old Corral, The (1936, B&W, 56m, NR)
Contemporary cowboy Gene Autry battles gangsters on the range. The Sons of the Pioneers (featuring Roy Rogers) harmonize. With Lon Chaney, Jr. **ST3, ST17, ST132**

Old Gringo (1989, C, 100m, R)
Historical drama, set during the Mexican Revolution, about an American schoolteacher's fascination with two men: an aging American journalist and a handsome Mexican soldier. Jane Fonda, Gregory Peck, and Jimmy Smits star in this adaptation of Carlos Fuentes' novel. **DR1, DR5, DR19, ST45, ST119**

Old Ironsides (1926, B&W, 111m, NR)
A trio of sailors ship out in search of adventure in this silent adventure classic, starring Wallace Beery, Boris Karloff, and Charles Farrell. **CL12, ST77**

Old Maid, The (1939, B&W, 95m, NR)
Bette Davis and Miriam Hopkins play cousins at war over Davis's illegitimate daughter in this classic soap opera. **CL5, ST28**

Old Yeller (1958, C, 84m, G)
A Texas pioneer family in the 1860s adopts a lovable stray dog in this Disney western drama. Fess Parker, Dorothy McGuire, and Tommy Kirk star. **FA1, FA5**

Oldest Living Graduate, The (1982, C, 75m, NR)
Henry Fonda plays an alumnus of a Texas school who is in conflict with his son. Videotape of a stage performance, originally shown on public TV. **ST44**

Oldest Profession, The (1967, C, 97m, NR)
A comic look at prostitution through the ages, from the viewpoint of six directors, including Jean-Luc Godard. Among the stars: Jeanne Moreau, Elsa Martinelli, Raquel Welch, Anna Karina, and Jean-Pierre Léaud. **DT41, ST110**

Oliver! (1968, C, 153m, G)
Musical version of the Dickens story about an orphan's adventures in London won six Oscars, including Best Picture and Director (Carol Reed). Ron Moody, Oliver Reed, and Mark Lester star. Songs

include ."As Long as He Needs Me."
FA9, MU2, MU7, WR4, XT1, XT6

Oliver and Company (1988, C, 72m, G)
Disney animated feature, loosely based
on Dickens' *Oliver Twist*, with a kitten
adopted by a streetwise pack of dogs in
New York City. Among the character
voices: Billy Joel, Bette Midler, Richard
"Cheech" Marin, and Dom Deluise. **FA2,
ST18, ST105, WR4**

Oliver Twist (1922, B&W, 77m, NR)
Silent version of the Charles Dickens tale
of orphans and thieves, starring Jackie
Coogan and Lon Chaney, Sr. **FA3, ST16,
WR4**

Oliver Twist (1933, B&W, 70m, NR)
The Dickens classic of an orphan caught
up in a world of thieves, starring Dickie
Moore. **FA3, WR4**

Oliver Twist (1948, B&W, 116m, NR)
Director David Lean's version of the
Dickens classic, starring Alec Guinness,
Robert Newton, and Anthony Newley.
Video resotres footage censored for U.S.
release. **CU8, CU10, DT59, FA3, ST60,
WR4**

Olvidados, Los (1950, B&W, 88m, NR)
Drama about the street boys of Mexico
City is one of the most powerful films on
the subject of rebellious youth. Luis Buñuel directed. **DT15** *Essential; Highly Recommended*

Olympia (1938, B&W, 215m, NR)
Legendary documentary of the 1936
Olympic Games, directed by Leni Riefen-
stahl. Available on two tapes: Part I, *The
Festival of the People,* runs 119m; Part II,
The Festival of Beauty, runs 96m. **CU16**
Essential; Highly Recommended

Omen, The (1976, C, 111m, R)
The American ambassador to England
finds out that his step-child is actually the
"anti-christ" incarnate. Horror drama
starring Gregory Peck, Lee Remick, and
David Warner. First in a trilogy that continues with *Damien—Omen II* and *The
Final Conflict.* **HO10, HO13, ST119**

On a Clear Day You Can See Forever (1970,
C, 129m, PG)
Musical fairy tale about a woman whose
psychiatrist discovers she has lived a previous life. Barbra Streisand and Yves

Montand star; Jack Nicholson has a small
role. Directed by Vincente Minnelli.
DT71, MU8, ST112, ST146

On Any Sunday (1971, C, 91m, G)
Documentary on the thrills and spills of
motorcycle racing, featuring Steve Mc-
Queen. **CU16, ST97**

On Dangerous Ground (1952, B&W, 82m,
NR)
A burned-out New York cop is assigned
to a small-town case that involves a teen-
aged killer. Robert Ryan and Ida Lupino
star in this film noir directed by Nicholas
Ray. Music by Bernard Herrmann. **DT83,
MY1**

On Golden Pond (1981, C, 109m, PG)
Katharine Hepburn won her fourth Oscar, Henry Fonda his first (and in his last
film) in this sentimental drama about an
elderly couple and their clashes with their
headstrong daughter (Jane Fonda). **DR11,
ST44, ST45, ST66, XT2, XT3, XT8, XT22**

On Her Majesty's Secret Service (1969, C,
140m, PG)
James Bond not only takes on archenemy
Ernst Stavro Blofeld, but he also decides
to marry a contessa. George Lazenby (in
his only 007 film) stars, with Telly Savalas
and Diana Rigg. **HF2**

On the Beach (1959, B&W, 133m, NR)
After the superpowers destroy one another with atomic weapons, a group of
survivors in Australia await the deadly
radiation clouds. Classic 1950s science
fiction, starring Gregory Peck, Ava Gardner, and Fred Astaire. Directed by Stanley Kramer.**DT55, SF1, SF12, ST2, ST119**

On the Edge (1985, C, 92m, PG)
Bruce Dern plays a middle-aged runner
training for a grueling race that could turn
his life around. **DR22**

On the Nickel (1980, C, 96m, R)
Drama about street persons in Los Ange-
les, starring Ralph Waite and Donald
Moffat, directed by Waite. **DR15**

On the Right Track (1981, C, 98m, PG)
Gary Coleman stars in this family comedy
about a shoeshine boy who lives in a train
station locker. **FA6**

On the Town (1949, C, 98m, NR)
Musical about three sailors (Gene Kelly, Frank Sinatra, Jules Munshin) on shore leave in New York City trying to see all they can in 24 hours. Directed by Gene Kelly and Stanley Donen. **DT30, MU1, MU6, ST81, ST138, XT9** *Essential; Recommended*

On the Waterfront (1954, B&W, 108m, NR)
Drama of life on the New Jersey docks, with Marlon Brando the former prizefighter caught between his fellow workers and his brother, who works for a crooked union boss. With Eva Marie Saint, Rod Steiger, Karl Malden, and Lee J. Cobb. Written by Budd Schulberg, directed by Elia Kazan, produced by Sam Spiegel. Oscar winner for Best Picture, Actor, Supporting Actress, and Director. **CL8, DT53, ST10, XT1, XT2, XT5, XT6** *Essential; Highly Recommended*

On the Yard (1979, C, 102m, R)
Prison drama about young convict making the big mistake of taking on the top con in the joint. John Heard and Thomas Waites star. **DR16**

On Top of Old Smoky (1953, B&W, 59m, NR)
Gene Autry is in hot water when he's mistaken for an outlaw. Smiley Burnette adds comic relief. **ST3**

On Valentine's Day (1986, C, 106m, PG)
A young woman from a small southern town shocks her family by marrying a man with few prospects. Matthew Broderick and Hallie Foote star. Horton Foote wrote this drama about his parents' marriage; sequel to *1918*. **DR5**

Once Is Not Enough (1975, C, 121m, R)
Soap opera deluxe from writer Jacqueline Susann, about young woman's affairs and her ongoing fascination with her father. Deborah Raffin and Kirk Douglas star, with Brenda Vacarro, Alexis Smith, Melina Mercouri, and George Hamilton. Also known as *Jacqueline Susann's Once Is Not Enough*. **ST34**

Once Upon a Honeymoon (1942, B&W, 117m, NR)
Ginger Rogers marries a man she does not know is a Nazi officer; Cary Grant comes to the rescue. Walter Slezak costars in this comedy. **ST57, ST131**

Once Upon a Time in America (1984, C, 225m, R)
Rich, powerful, gangster epic about two Jewish buddies who grow up in New York and turn rivals as adults. Robert DeNiro and James Woods star, with Elizabeth McGovern, Joe Pesci, Burt Young, Tuesday Weld, Treat Williams, Larry Rapp, William Forsythe, and James Hayden. Sergio Leone directed. (Also available in a 143-minute version) **AC22, DT61, ST30, ST165** *Highly Recommended (long version)*

Once Upon a Time in the West (1968, C, 166m, PG)
The ultimate spaghetti western—maybe the ultimate western, with Henry Fonda (as a villain) pitted against Jason Robards and a vengeful Charles Bronson. Claudia Cardinale costars, with Jack Elam, Woody Strode, and Lionel Stander. Photographed on location in scenic Monument Valley, familiar to fans of John Ford's classic westerns.Lovely musical score by Ennio Morricone. Directed by Sergio Leone. **CL14, DT61, ST12, ST44, ST129, WE1, WE5, WE8** *Essential; Highly Recommended*

One and Only Genuine Original Family Band, The (1968, C, 117m, G)
Disney comedy about a musical family from the Dakota Territories who lend their talents to the 1888 Presidential campaign. Walter Brennan stars; Goldie Hawn made her debut in a small role. **FA1, ST63**

One Body Too Many (1944, B&W, 75m, NR)
Jack Haley plays a salesman forced to solve a crime when he's mistaken for a detective. Comedy-mystery costars Bela Lugosi. **ST95**

One Crazy Summer (1987, C, 94m, PG)
Life on Nantucket Island during the tourist season is the basis for this freewheeling comedy, starring John Cusack, Demi Moore, and Joe Flaherty. **CO14**

One Deadly Summer (1983, C, 133m, R)
Isabele Adjani stars in this French thriller about a young girl whose eccentric manner disguises an intricate revenge plan. Also known as *L'Ete Meurtrier*. **MY16**

One-Eyed Jacks (1961, C, 141m, NR)
Marlon Brando stars in this western tale (which he directed) about an outlaw left for dead by his partner. Karl Malden co-stars as the object of Brando's vengeance. **CU15, ST10, WE5, WE15** *Highly Recommended*

One-Eyed Swordsman, The (1963, C, 95m, NR)
Japanese samurai action drama starring Tetsuro Tanba.**FF4**

One Flew Over the Cuckoo's Nest (1975, C, 129m, R)
A misfit decides to get himself committed to a mental hospital for "a little rest." But he doesn't anticipate clashing with a strong head nurse. Adaptation of the Ken Kesey novel won Oscars for Best Picture, Actor (Jack Nicholson), Actress (Louise Fletcher), and Director (Milos Forman). With Brad Dourif, Christopher Lloyd, Danny DeVito, Scatman Crothers, Will Sampson, and Vincent Schiavelli.**DR19, DT37, ST32, ST112, XT1, XT2, XT3, XT6** *Essential; Highly Recommended*

One From the Heart (1982, C, 100m, R)
From director Francis Ford Coppola, a stylized musical drama about a couple in Las Vegas who split up and find other momentary partners. Teri Garr, Frederic Forrest, Raul Julia, and Nastassja Kinski star, with Harry Dean Stanton. Songs by Tom Waits, sung by Waits and Crystal Gayle. **DT21, MU16, ST141**

100 Rifles (1960, C, 110m, PG)
A deputy sheriff pursues a gun thief into Mexico, where the lawman falls in love with a lovely revolutionary. Burt Reynolds, Jim Brown, and Raquel Welch star. **ST128, WE7, WE9**

One Magic Christmas (1985, C, 88m, G)
A modern Christmas fable about a harried mother (Mary Steenburgen) who learns the true meaning of the season from a special angel (Harry Dean Stanton). **FA13, ST141**

One Man Force (1989, C, 89m, R)
Title says it all, with this cop action drama starring John Matuszak, with Ronny Cox and Charles Napier. **AC25**

One Million B.C. (1940, B&W, 80m, NR)
Life in prehistoric times, with cavemen battling dinosaurs. Victor Mature and Lon Chaney, Jr. star. **ST17**

One Minute to Zero (1952, B&W, 105m, NR)
Korean War drama starring Robert Mitchum, with Ann Blyth, William Talman, and Richard Egan. **AC3, ST107**

One of Our Aircraft Is Missing (1941, B&W, 106m, NR)
Drama about British pilots who crash during war mission over Holland and try to make their way home. Michael Powell directed. **AC1, DT81**

One on One (1977, C, 98m, R)
A heavily recruited high school basketball player finds he's just another player on the team at a big university. Robby Benson is the struggling jock; Annette O'Toole is his academic tutor. **DR22**

One-Trick Pony (1980, C, 98m, R)
A rock star tries to juggle the demands of his marriage and his changing audience. Paul Simon, Blair Brown, and Rip Torn star, with musical performers Lou Reed, the B-52's, The Lovin Spoonful, and Sam & Dave. **DR12, MU9, ST150**

One, Two, Three (1961, B&W, 108m, NR)
James Cagney plays a fast-talking American Coca-Cola executive caught up in some hilarious Cold War complications in Berlin. With Arlene Francis, Horst Bucholz, and Pamela Tiffin. Billy Wilder directed. **CL10, CO2, DT116, ST14** *Highly Recommended*

One Woman or Two (1985, C, 97m, PG-13)
A comedy about a French scientist (Gerard Depardieu) and his relationship with the American woman (Sigourney Weaver) who finances his work. **ST31, ST157**

Onion Field, The (1979, C, 122m, R)
True story, based on Joseph Wambaugh book, about a Los Angeles policeman whose partner is murdered by two punks and how he deals with the consequences. John Savage, James Woods, Franklyn Seales, and Ted Danson star. **DR6, DR16, ST165** *Recommended*

Only Angels Have Wings (1939, B&W, 121m, NR)
Superbly realized buddy adventure of mail pilots working the dangeorus routes through the Andes. Cary Grant stars, with Jean Arthur and Rita Hayworth as the women in his life, Richard Barthelmess, Thomas Mitchell, and Noah Beery, Jr. as his fellow fliers. Howard Hawks directed. **AC11, AC13, DT43, ST57, ST64** *Essential; Highly Recommended*

Only the French Can *see* French Cancan

Only the Valiant (1951, B&W, 105m, NR)
Western drama of courageous army man (Gregory Peck) battling Indians. Lon Chaney, Jr. costars. **ST17, ST119**

Only When I Laugh (1981, C, 120m, R)
Change of pace for Neil Simon in this drama about an actress who's a recovering alcoholic and her relationship with her teenaged daughter. Marsha Mason and Kristy McNichol star, with Joan Hackett and James Coco. **DR8, WR23**

Open City (1946, B&W, 105m, NR)
Influential Italian drama about the tense days of Rome's occupation during World War II. Directed by Roberto Rossellini. **FF2, XT17** *Essential*

Operation C.I.A. (1965, B&W, 90m, NR)
Saigon-based thriller with Burt Reynolds as an American agent trying to prevent an assassination. **ST128**

Operation Petticoat (1959, C, 124m, NR)
Cary Grant and Tony Curtis star in this service comedy set aboard a submarine. Directed by Blake Edwards. **CO21, DT32, ST57**

Operation Thunderbolt (1977, C, 125m, PG)
Drama about the Entebbe hijack rescue by Israeli commandoes on July 4, 1976. This film was officially approved by the Israeli government. Klaus Kinski stars. **ST83**

Opportunity Knocks (1990, C, 105m, PG-13)
Dana Carvey plays a con artist in this comedy, with Robert Loggia, Todd Graff, and Julia Campbell. **CO10**

Opposing Force (1986, C, 99m, R)
During a war games maneuver on a remote Pacific island, two officers discover that a third is waging war for real. Tom Skerritt and Lisa Eichorn star. **AC20, AC24**

Orca (1977, C, 92m, PG)
A giant whale goes on a rampage when bounty hunters murder his mate. Horror/disaster story starring Richard Harris and Charlotte Rampling. **HO16**

Ordeal by Innocence (1984, C, 87m, PG-13)
Agatha Christie tale of injustice in a small English town and the amateur sleuth who rights the wrong. Donald Sutherland, Faye Dunaway, and Christopher Plummer star. **ST37, WR3**

Ordet (1955, B&W, 125m, NR)
Danish director Carl Dreyer's classic story of feuding families who must resolve their religious differences when a love affair between one son and daughter of each clan is revealed. **DT31**

Ordinary People (1980, C, 123m, R)
A family is torn apart over the death of its oldest son in this drama. Donald Sutherland, Mary Tyler Moore, and Timothy Hutton (in his debut) star. Robert Redford directed. The film, Redford, and Hutton each won Oscars. **DR2, DR8, DR9, ST126, XT1, XT4, XT6** *Essential; Recommended*

Organization, The (1971, C, 107m, PG)
Sidney Poitier returns for his third stint as Detective Virgil Tibbs in this drama about a dope-smuggling operation. **ST121**

Orphans (1987, C, 120m, R)
Three-character drama about a gangster kidnapped by two loony brothers living in a ramshackle house in New Jersey. Albert Finney, Matthew Modine, and Kevin Anderson star. Lyle Kessler adapted his own stage play; directed by Alan Pakula. **DR20, ST42**

Orphans of the Storm (1922, B&W, 125m, NR)
Silent drama from director D.W. Griffith set amid the turbulence of French Revolution, involving sisters unfairly separated. Lillian and Dorothy Gish star. **DT42, ST54, XT8**

Oscar, The (1966, C, 119m, NR)
Behind-the-scenes soap opera centering on the annual Hollywood Academy Awards show. Eleanor Parker, Stephen Boyd, Elke Sommer, and Ernest Borgnine star. **DR12**

Osterman Weekend, The (1983, C, 102m, R)
A talk show host is persuaded that several of his best friends are Soviet agents. Convoluted thriller, based on the Robert Ludlum novel, stars John Hurt, Rutger Hauer, and Burt Lancaster, with Craig T. Nelson, Dennis Hopper, and Helen Shaver. Director Sam Peckinpah's final film. **DT77, MY6, ST71, ST85, WR18**

Other, The (1972, C, 100m, PG)
Thriller, based on Thomas Tryon's novel, about young twin boys, one good, one evil. Uta Hagen, Diana Muldaur, and Chris and Martin Udvarnoky star. **HO15**

Other Side of Midnight, The (1977, C, 165m, R)
Epic soap opera, from the Sidney Sheldon bestseller, about a woman's ruthless climb to the top of the show business world. Marie-France Pisier, Susan Sarandon, and John Beck star. **DR2**

Our Daily Bread (1934, B&W, 74m, NR)
During the Depression, a couple living on a dilapidated farm invite homeless people to work their land and form a commune of sorts. Classic drama of hard-times 1930s, directed by King Vidor. **CL8, DT107**

Our Hospitality (1923, B&W, 75m, NR)
Buster Keaton's first feature-length comedy is about feuding Southern families. Highlight is incredible stunt rescue at a waterfall. With Natalie Talmadge (Buster's wife), Joseph Keaton (his father), and Buster Keaton, Jr. **CL11, DT54, XT8**

Our Little Girl (1935, C, 65m, NR)
Shirley Temple plays a girl who tries to bring her feuding parents (Rosemary Ames, Joel McCrea) together. **ST148**

Our Relations (1936, B&W, 74m, NR)
Laurel and Hardy comedy in which the boys play two sets of twins, one set happy-go-lucky sailors, the others peaceable married men. **ST87**

Our Town (1940, B&W, 90m, NR)
Thronton Wilder's classic play about life in a small New England town stars William Holden, Martha Scott, and Thomas Mitchell. **DR20, DR26, ST68**

Out of Africa (1985, C, 161m, PG)
Meryl Streep plays writer Isak Dinesen, who journeyed from her native Denmark to live on a plantation in Africa and write about her experiences there. Robert Redford and Klaus Maria Brandauer costar. Sydney Pollack directed this drama, which won 7 Academy Awards, including Best Picture and Director. **DR4, DT80, ST126, ST145, XT1, XT6** *Recommended*

Out of Bounds (1986, C, 93m, R)
A young man visting Los Angeles from Iowa is mistaken for a drug courier in this thriller starring Anthony Michael Hall. **MY7**

Out of Control (1985, C, 78m, R)
A group of high school students are trapped on a desert island and forced to battle a ruthless gang of smugglers for survival. Martin Hewitt stars. **AC24**

Out of the Blue (1980, C, 94m, R)
A teenager tries to deal with the problems of her parents, an ex-con and a drug addict, but finally loses control of her life, too. Linda Manz stars, with Dennis Hopper (who directed) and Sharon Farrell. **DR8, ST71**

Out of the Past (1947, B&W, 97m, NR)
Classic film noir about an ex-con up to his neck in trouble from his former boss and a no-good woman. Robert Mitchum, Kirk Douglas, and Jane Greer are the points in the deadly triangle. Jacques Tourneur directed. Remade as *Against All Odds* (1984).**DT105, MY1, MY5, ST34, ST107** *Essential; Highly Recommended*

Out of Towners, The (1970, C, 97m, PG)
Jack Lemmon and Sandy Dennis play a couple of Ohio tourists who encounter every nightmare situation possible on a trip to New York City. Written by Neil Simon. **ST90, WR23, XT9**

Outland (1981, C, 111m, R)
Sean Connery is an outer space lawman in this futuristic thriller about drug smuggling at a space station. Peter Boyle costars. **SF17, ST21**

Outlaw, The (1943, B&W, 103m, NR)
Cult western, initially banned in some cities, about Billy the Kid (Jack Buetel) and Doc Holliday (Walter Huston), was controversial for its allegedly steamy scenes with Jane Russell (in her film debut). Directed by Howard Hawks and Howard Hughes. **CU8, DT43, HF1, HF13, WE3, WE15, XT21**

Outlaw Josey Wales, The (1976, C, 137m, PG)
Clint Eastwood western saga of a man consumed with hatred for the Union soldiers who killed his family. With Chief Dan George, Sondra Locke, and John Vernon; Eastwood directed. **ST39, WE3, WE5, WE6** *Recommended*

Outrageous! (1977, C, 100m, R)
A lonely young woman and a female impersonator strike up a friendship in this cult comedy starring Craig Russell and Hollis McLaren. **CO12, CU1**

Outrageous Fortune (1987, C, 100m, R)
Bette Midler and Shelley Long play two women who track down the man that two-timed them. Wild chase comedy costars Peter Coyote and George Carlin. **CO2, ST105, XT18**

Outside the Law (1921, B&W, 77m, NR)
Lon Chaney, Sr. and director Tod Browning's first collaboration is this silent melodrama with Chaney playing two roles: Black Mike, the slimy hoodlum, and Ah Wing, the faithful Chinese retainer to the story's heroine. **DT14, ST16**

Outsiders, The (1983, C, 91m, PG)
Three teenaged brothers try to get through life without parents in this drama adapted from S.E. Hinton's novel. C. Thomas Howell, Ralph Macchio, Patrick Swayze, and Matt Dillon star, with Rob Lowe, Emilio Estevez, Diane Lane, and Tom Cruise. Francis Ford Coppola directed. **CU17, DR9, DR19, DT21, ST26**

Over the Edge (1979, C, 95m, R)
In a suburban community, a group of bored, restless teens clash with parents and law enforcement officials. Provocative, disturbing drama starring Michael Kramer and Matt Dillon. Written by Tim Hunter and Charlie Haas; directed by Jonathan Kaplan. **DR7, DR9** *Recommended*

Over the Top (1986, C, 94m, PG)
Sylvester Stallone is a trucker involved in a custody battle and the national arm-wrestling championships. **DR22, ST140**

Overboard (1987, C, 112m, PG)
Goldie Hawn plays a snob who suffers amnesia when she falls off her yacht, and Kurt Russell is the carpenter who claims her for his wife (and mother to his frenetic kids) in this comedy. **CO5, ST63**

Overcoat, The (1960, B&W, 78m, NR)
Soviet drama based on Nikolai Gogol's classic story of a common clerk who buys a new coat and finds his life transformed. **FF7**

Owl and the Pussycat, The (1970, C, 95m, R)
Barbra Streisand and George Segal star in this romantic comedy about a sassy New York prostitute and a fussy, would-be writer. Written by Buck Henry. **CO1, ST146** *Recommended*

Ox-Bow Incident, The (1943, B&W, 75m, NR)
Western tale of injustice, about the lynching of a trio of cowboys who turn out to be innocent. Henry Fonda stars, with Dana Andrews and Anthony Quinn. **ST44, WE5** *Essential; Recommended*

Oxford Blues (1984, C, 98m, PG-13)
An American rower enrolls at Oxford to compete with the best that Britain has to offer. Rob Lowe, Ally Sheedy, and Amanda Pays star. **DR22**

P.O.W. The Escape (1986, C, 90m, R)
David Carrdine plays a hard-bitten officer determined to lead a group of American prisoners out of Vietnam. **AC7**

Pack, The (1977, C, 99m, R)
Wild dogs attack two families in this horror tale starring Joe Don Baker and R.G. Armstrong. **HO16**

Pack Up Your Troubles (1932, B&W, 68m, NR)
Laurel and Hardy enlist in the army to fight in World War I. The Germans almost die laughing. **ST87**

Package, The (1989, C, 108m, R)
Thriller starring Gene Hackman as an army officer transporting a criminal (Tommy Lee Jones), whose escape begins

to unravel a complex political conspiracy. With Joanna Cassidy, John Heard, and Dennis Franz. **MY6, ST61**

Padre Padrone (1977, C, 114m, NR)
Based on a true story, this Italian drama portrays the bitter childhood of a peasant boy who grows up to be a renowned scholar. Directed by Paolo and Vittorio Taviani. **FF2**

Pain in the A—, A (1974, C, 90m, PG)
A hit man and a would-be suicide wind up sharing the same hotel room in this dark comedy from France. American remake: *Buddy, Buddy*. **FF1, FF8**

Paint Your Wagon (1969, C, 166m, G)
Lavish musical about the gold rush in California, starring Clint Eastwood, Lee Marvin, and Jean Seberg. **MU6, MU17, ST39, ST100**

Painted Desert, The (1931, B&W, 75m, NR)
Western drama about two feuding families. Clark Gable's talking pictures debut; he plays a baddie. **ST49**

Paisan (1946, B&W, 90m, NR)
Classic drama of Italian life during World War II, directed by Roberto Rossellini and cowritten by Federico Fellini. **FF2**

Pajama Game, The (1957, C, 101m, NR)
Doris Day and John Raitt square off in this Broadway musical about labor troubles, directed by Stanley Donen and George Abbott. With Carol Haney; choreography by Bob Fosse. **DT30, DT39, MU2**

Pal Joey (1957, C, 111m, NR)
Broadway musical about a colorful hustler (Frank Sinatra) who builds a nightclub in San Francisco, then tries to decide between two lovely women (Rita Hayworth, Kim Novak). Rodgers & Hart songs include "The Lady Is a Tramp," "Bewitched," and "My Funny Valentine." Outstanding use of color. **CL9, MU2, ST64, ST138**

Pale Rider (1985, C, 113m, R)
Clint Eastwood stars in this western story of a mysterious lone gunfighter who comes to the aid of persecuted prospectors. With Carrie Snodgress, John Russell, Michael Moriarty, and Christopher Penn. Eastwood directed. **ST39, WE2**

Paleface, The (1948, C, 91m, NR)
Bob Hope is the world's biggest dude, Jane Russell is his straight-shooting sidekick in this western comedy. **ST70, WE14**

Palm Beach Story, The (1942, B&W, 90m, NR)
Classic comedy about a wife deciding to divorce her inventor husband because her tastes are too rich for them. Claudette Colbert, Joel McCrea, and Rudy Vallee star. Preston Sturges wrote and directed. Among the highlights: Colbert's encounter with Quail & Ale Club on her train ride to Florida. **CL10, DT103, XT19** *Highly Recommended*

Pancho Villa (1972, C, 92m, PG)
Telly Savalas plays the legendary Mexican bandit/revolutionary in this western adventure. **WE9**

Pandora's Box (1928, B&W, 110m, NR)
Classic silent drama of Lulu, the bewitching woman who casts an irresistible spell on all men. Louise Brooks gives a dynamic, sexy performance. Directed by G. W. Pabst. **CL12, CU6, FF3** *Essential; Highly Recommended*

Paper Chase, The (1973, C, 111m, PG)
Portrait of a first-year Harvard Law School student (Timothy Bottoms) and his affair with the daughter of his most feared professor (John Houseman, in an Oscar-winning performance). **DR25, XT4**

Paper Lion (1968, C, 107m, G)
Writer George Plimpton (Alan Alda) goes on assignment with pro football's Detroit Lions, training with the team and quarterbacking in one exhibition game. Alex Karras, then a star lineman, steals the film; also in the cast: Lauren Hutton, Sugar Ray Robinson, and (in a small part) Roy Scheider. **CO19**

Paper Moon (1973, B&W, 102m, PG)
Depression-era comedy about a con man (Ryan O'Neal) and his daughter (Oscar winner Tatum O'Neal) traveling through Middle America with a bible selling routine. **CO6, XT5, XT8**

Paper Tiger (1976, C, 99m, PG)
David Niven plays the cowardly tutor to a Japanese diplomat's son who musters all his courage when he and the boy are kidnapped. Toshiro Mifune costars in this family drama. **ST106**

Paperhouse (1989, C, 92m, PG-13)
British drama of a young girl (Charlotte Burke) whose bout with a fever allows her imagination to run riot. Directed by Bernard Rose. **DR9, DR23**

Papillon (1973, C, 151m, PG)
True story of Henri Charrière, played by Steve McQueen, and his dramatic escape from Devil's Island prison. Dustin Hoffman costars. **AC24, DR18, ST67, ST97**

Paradine Case, The (1948, B&W, 116m, NR)
Alfred Hitchcock courtroom drama, starring Gregory Peck and Valli, with Ann Todd, Charles Laughton, and Ethel Barrymore. **DR17, DT46, ST119**

Paradise Alley (1978, C, 109m, PG)
Sylvester Stallone stars in this comedy of three New York brothers and their dreams for fame and fortune, with one going for a career as a pro wrestler. With Armand Assante. Stallone directed. **ST140**

Paradise, Hawaiian Style (1966, C, 91m, NR)
Elvis Presley returns to the islands after his success with *Blue Hawaii* for some more ukulele strumming and romancing with the local ladies. **ST123**

Parallax View, The (1974, C, 102m, R)
Reporter Warren Beatty uncovers a complex political conspiracy in this very contemporary thriller. With Paula Prentiss, Hume Cronyn, and Jim Davis. Directed by Alan J. Pakula; photographed by Gordon Willis. **CU9, DR21, MY6, MY11, ST5** *Recommended*

Pardon Mon Affaire (1977, C, 105m, PG)
A happily married man is nevertheless fascinated by a gorgeous model he spots in a parking garage. French comedy was remade in the U.S. as *The Woman in Red*. **FF1, FF8**

Pardon Us (1931, B&W, 55m, NR)
Laurel and Hardy are shipped off to prison for making homemade brew during the height of Prohibition. **ST87**

Parent Trap, The (1961, C, 127m, NR)
Hayley Mills plays twin sisters who are separated when their parents divorce and meet years later at a summer camp. Disney comedy costars Brian Keith and Maureen O'Hara. **FA1**

Parenthood (1989, C, 124m, PG-13)
Interlocking stories of a large family, with several generations of problems. Comedy-drama, directed by Ron Howard, stars Steve Martin, with Mary Steenburgen, Dianne Wiest, Jason Robards, Rick Moranis, Thomas Hulce, Martha Plimpton, and Keanu Reeves. **CO5, CO14, DT48, ST99, ST129**

Parents (1989, C, 83m, R)
Dark comedy set in the 1950s, featuring a seemingly normal couple whose young son begins to suspect that their dinners are composed of human meat. Randy Quaid and Mary Beth Hurt star. **CO5, CO6, CO12**

Paris Blues (1961, B&W, 98m, NR)
Quartet of Americans in Paris—two jazz musicians, two female tourists—are the focus of this drama. Paul Newman, Sidney Poitier, Joanne Woodward, and Diahann Carroll star; Louis Armstrong makes an appearance. Directed by Martin Ritt. **DT87, ST111, ST121, ST166, XT16**

Paris Does Strange Things *see* Elena and Her Men

Paris Express, The (1953, C, 83m, NR)
A shy bookkeeper uncovers embezzling by his boss and follows him to Paris, where he's accused of the thief's murder. Claude Rains stars. **MY7**

Paris Holiday (1958, C, 100m, NR)
Bob Hope plays an American in Paris looking to purchase a screenplay, involved in misunderstandings and mixups. With Fernandel, Anita Ekberg, and writer-director Preston Sturges in a rare acting role. **DT103, ST70**

Paris, Texas (1984, C, 150m, R)
Drama of two brothers reunited years after one deserted his son and wife. Harry Dean Stanton, Nastassja Kinski, and Dean Stockwell star. Written by Sam Shepard; directed by Wim Wenders. Music by Ry Cooder. **DR8, DT113, ST141, ST144, XT18**

Paris When It Sizzles (1964, C, 110m, NR)
An American screenwriter and his secretary are in Paris trying to work on a script in this comedy starring William Holden

and Audrey Hepburn. Marlene Dietrich is among the stars who appear in cameos. **ST33, ST65, ST68**

Party, The (1968, C, 99m, NR)
Slapstick comedy set at a large Hollywood party, starring Peter Sellers and Claudine Longet. Directed by Blake Edwards. **DT32, ST137**

Party Line (1988, C, 91m, R)
A brother and sister, unhinged by their mother's suicide and father's abuse, turn killers, using special telephone party lines to lure their victims. Leif Garrett and Greta Blackburn star. **MY14**

Pascali's Island (1988, C, 106m, PG-13)
British period drama set on a Mediterranean outpost, where a Turkish intelligence officer is frustrated in both his professional and love life. Ben Kingsley stars, with Helen Mirren and Charles Dance. **DR23**

Passage to India, A (1984, C, 163m, PG)
From director David Lean comes this screen version of the E.M. Forster novel about an impressionable Englishwoman's tragic experiences in India. Judy Davis, Victor Bannerjee, Alec Guinness, and Oscar winner Peggy Ashcroft star. **DR19, DT50, ST60, XT5**

Passage to Marseilles (1944, B&W, 110m, NR)
Escape drama set on infamous Devil's Island, starring Humphrey Bogart, Claude Rains, Sydney Greenstreet, and Peter Lorre. **DR18, ST8**

Passante, La (1983, C, 106m, NR)
Romy Schneider plays a dual role in this French drama; she's a German refugee and the wife of a world leader. Story of political intrigue also features Michel Piccoli and Maria Schell. **FF1**

Passenger, The (1975, C, 119m, PG)
A journalist in North Africa assumes the identity of a man he finds dead in a hotel room. Jack Nicholson stars in this drama from director Michelangelo Antonioni. **DT3, ST112**

Passion (1919, B&W, 135m, NR)
Silent version of *Madame du Barry*, starring Pola Negri and Emil Jannings and directed by Ernst Lubitsch. **CL12, DT63, FF3**

Passion (1954, C, 84m, NR)
Western drama of revenge set in California, starring Cornel Wilde, Yvonne De Carlo, and Lon Chaney, Jr. **ST17**

Passion of Beatrice, The *see* Beatrice

Passion of Joan of Arc, The (1928, B&W, 114m, NR)
Director Carl Dreyer's austere, gripping recreation of the young martyr's trial and execution. A silent film classic. Maria Falconetti gives a mesmerizing performance. **CL12, DT31, FF1** *Essential; Recommended*

Passion of Love (1982, C, 117m, NR)
Italian drama set in 1862, concerning the cousin of a military commander falling in love with a dashing captain. Valeria D'Obici and Bernard Giraudeau star, with Laura Antonelli and Jean-Louis Trintignant. Directed by Ettore Scola. **FF2**

Pat and Mike (1952, B&W, 96m, NR)
Spencer Tracy—Katharine Hepburn comedy of a hustling sports promoter and his latest find, a superb female athlete. Directed by George Cukor; written by Garson Kanin and Ruth Gordon. With Charles Bronson (billed as Charles Buchinski). **CL10, CL15, CO19, DT24, ST12, ST66, ST151** *Recommended*

Pat Garrett and Billy the Kid (1973, C, 122m, R)
The tragic tale of the famous outlaw and his sheriff friend who gunned him down. James Coburn and Kris Kristofferson star, with Richard Bright, Harry Dean Stanton, Slim Pickens, Katy Jurado, Jason Robards, Richard Jaeckel, R.G. Armstrong, Rita Coolidge, and L.Q. Jones. Directed by Sam Peckinpah, with music by Bob Dylan; both have small roles. This is the version that restores the director's original footage; also available at 106m. **CU10, DT77, HF1, MU12, ST129, ST141, WE3, WE15** *Recommended (long version)*

Patch of Blue, A (1965, B&W, 105m, NR)
Heartfelt tale of a young blind woman who falls in love with a black man. Elizabeth Hartman and Sidney Poitier star, with Oscar winner Shelley Winters. **DR3, ST121, ST164, XT5**

Paternity (1981, C, 94m, PG)
The manager of New York's Madison Square Garden decides to look for the perfect woman to father his first child. Burt Reynolds stars in this comedy, with Beverly D'Angelo, Elizabeth Ashley, and Lauren Hutton. **ST128**

Paths of Glory (1957, B&W, 86m, NR)
World War I drama about a French general who orders his men on a suicide mission, then has three survivors courtmartialed and executed. Powerful antiwar statement from director Stanley Kubrick. Kirk Douglas stars. Co-written by Jim Thompson. **AC2, DT56, ST34** *Essential; Highly Recommended*

Patrick (1978, C, 96m, PG)
A young murderer in a coma uses his telekinetic powers to further destroy those around him. Horror drama from Australia, directed by Richard Franklin. **FF5, HO7**

Patsy, The (1964, C, 101m, NR)
Nerdy bellhop agrees to impersonate a dead comedian so that the star's hangerson can keep the money rolling in. Jerry Lewis stars. **ST91**

Patti Rocks (1988, C, 86m, R)
Foul-mouthed guy takes his buddy for a long car ride to visit his pregnant girlfriend, to talk her into an abortion. Comedy-drama stars Chris Mulkey, John Jenkins, and Karen Landry. **CO2**

Patton (1970, C, 169m, PG)
George C. Scott won an Oscar (which he refused to accept) for his performance as the legendary U.S. Army general with a controversial record in Europe during World War II. The film and its director, Franklin Schaffner, also won Academy Awards. With Karl Malden as Omar Bradley. **AC1, DR4, XT1, XT2, XT6** *Essential; Recommended*

Patty Hearst (1988, C, 100m, R)
True story of publishing heiress kidnapped by political radicals and brainwashed into joining them in a crime spree. Natasha Richardson and William Forsythe star. Paul Schrader directed. **DR6, DR16**

Pauline at the Beach (1983, C, 94m, R)
From French director Eric Rohmer, a comedy about a teenaged girl's experiences during a summer of growing up at a resort. **DT89**

Pawnbroker, The (1965, B&W, 116m, NR)
Rod Steiger stars as a Jewish survivor of the Nazi death camps who runs a pawn shop in Harlem, fighting against his horrible memories. With Jaime Sanchez, Geraldine Fitzgerald, and Brock Peters. Sidney Lumet directed. **DR15, DT65, XT9**

Payday (1973, C, 103m, R)
A country singer pushes himself—and everyone around him—to the brink with his rowdy, uninhibited ways. Rip Torn is the magnetic star of this cult favorite. **DR12, ST150** *Recommended*

Peanut Butter Solution, The (1985, C, 96m, PG)
Family comedy of an 11-year-old boy with a very vivid imagination finds himself in a strange house with more adventures than he ever dreamed of. **FA6, FA7**

Pearl of Death (1944, B&W, 69m, NR)
Sherlock Holmes adventure starring Basil Rathbone and Nigel Bruce. They're out to find a killer who calls himself The Creeper. **HF14**

Pee-wee's Big Adventure (1985, C, 92m, PG)
Pee-wee Herman discovers that his favorite bicycle has been stolen, and he embarks on a cross-country mission to recover it. Silly fun for kids of all ages. **CO11, CO12, CU5, FA6** *Recommended*

Peeping Tom (1960, C, 109m, R)
Legendary cult film, censored and banned in its original release, about a murderous cinematographer (Carl Boehm) who films his crimes. With Anna Massey and Moira Shearer. Michael Powell directed; he also plays the father of the killer in flashback scenes. **CU8, DT81**

Peggy Sue Got Married (1986, C, 103m, PG-13)
At her 20th anniversary high school reunion, a woman passes out and wakes up to find herself in high school again. Will she marry the same no-good guy? Kathleen Turner and Nicolas Cage star in this comedy from director Francis Ford Coppola. **CO6, CO20, DT21, ST152**

Pelle the Conqueror (1988, C, 138m, PG-13)
Oscar-winning drama from Denmark, starring Max von Sydow as an impoverished Swedish widower who moves to Denmark to begin a new life with his son. **FF7, XT7**

Pendulum (1969, C, 106m, PG)
Police detective is framed for murder and must clear himself. George Peppard and Jean Seberg star. **MY7**

Penn and Teller Get Killed (1989, C, 89m, R)
Magicians Penn Jillette & Teller star in this offbeat mystery as themselves, the targets of a mad killer. Directed by Arthur Penn. **DT78, MY17**

Pennies From Heaven (1981, C, 107m, R)
One-of-a-kind musical about a Depression-era sheet music salesman who sings his way through his various troubles. Based on a British TV miniseries created by Dennis Potter. Filled with lavish production numbers, brilliantly photographed by Gordon Willis. Steve Martin stars, with Bernadette Peters, Jessica Harper, and Christopher Walken. **MU3, MU16, ST99** *Recommended*

Penny Serenade (1941, B&W, 125m, NR)
Cary Grant and Irene Dunne star in this tearjerker about a couple who decide to adopt a baby. **CL6, DT101, ST57**

People That Time Forgot, The (1977, C, 90m, PG)
Sequel to *The Land That Time Forgot*, with more adventures in ancient world populated by fierce dinosaurs. Doug McClure stars. **SF4**

Pepe LePew's Skunk Tales (1960, C, 56m, NR)
A collection of Warner Bros. cartoons featuring that misunderstood and amorous skunk. Includes the Oscar-winning cartoon, *For Scent-imental Reasons*. **FA11**

Perfect! (1985, C, 120m, R)
Reporter John Travolta is supposed to do an exposé on fitness clubs as a place to pick up dates; he finds himself falling for aerobics instructor Jamie Lee Curtis. With Laraine Newman and Marilu Henner. **CO2, CO13**

Perfect Furlough, The (1958, B&W, 93m, NR)
Romantic comedy of a young soldier (Tony Curtis) wooing a military psychiatrist (Janet Leigh). Directed by Blake Edwards. **DT32**

Performance (1970, C, 105m, R)
A London gangster on the lam hides out in the home of a reclusive rock star, and their lives begin to intertwine. James Fox and Mick Jagger star in this cult drama, directed by Nicolas Roeg and Donald Cammell. **CU1, CU3, DR16, DT88, MY2** *Recommended*

Permanent Record (1988, C, 91m, PG-13)
A teenager who seems to have it all—good grades, popularity, girl friends—commits suicide, leaving his friends to wonder why. Alan Boyce stars, with Keanu Reeves and Richard Bradford. **DR9**

Persecution and Assassination of Jean-Paul Marat as Performed by the Inmates of the Asylum of Charenton Under the Direction of the Marquis de Sade, The *see* Marat/Sade

Persona (1966, B&W, 81m, NR)
Hypnotic drama from director Ingmar Bergman about the relationship between an actress and a nurse. Liv Ullmann and Bibi Andersson star. **DT7, ST154** *Essential; Recommended*

Personal Best (1982, C, 124m, R)
A pair of women runners, competing for a place on the Olympic team, become lovers. Mariel Hemingway, Patrice Donnelly, and Scott Glenn star. Written and directed by Robert Towne. **DR3, DR10, DR22**

Personal Services (1987, C, 104m, R)
Julie Walters stars as a London working-class girl who stumbles into running a brothel and soon becomes very successful at it. Saucy comedy was directed by Terry Jones of the Monty Python troupe. **CO15, CO17**

Pet Sematary (1989, C, 102m, R)
Stephen King horror tale of an ancient burial ground with powers that can bring dead animals back to life. Dale Midkiff and Fred Gwynne star. King adapted his novel and has a small role as a minister. **HO16, WR12**

Pete Kelly's Blues (1955, C, 95m, NR)
Drama revolving around the jazz scene of the 1920s, starring Jack Webb as a trumpet player and featuring real-life music stars Peggy Lee and Ella Fitzgerald. With Janet Leigh and Lee Marvin. Webb directed. **DR12, ST100**

Pete 'n' Tillie (1972, C, 100m, PG)
Walter Matthau and Carol Burnett star in this romantic comedy-drama about a couple who meet and marry late in life. Co-starring Geraldine Page, Barry Nelson, and Rene Auberjonois. Based on Peter DeVries' novella, *Witch's Milk*. **CO1, DR1**

Peter Pan (1953, C, 76m, G)
Disney feature-length cartoon about the young boy who never grows up, and the trio of children he takes to his magical kingdom. **FA2** *Recommended*

Pete's Dragon (1977, C, 105m, G)
An orphan is befriended by a large and very friendly dragon in this Disney musical. Helen Reddy, Jim Dale, Mickey Rooney, and Shelley Winters star. **FA1, ST133, ST164**

Petrified Forest, The (1936, B&W, 83m, NR)
Escaped convict Humphrey Bogart holds waitress Bette Davis and drifter Leslie Howard hostage in this classic melodrama. Based on the play by Robert Sherwood. **DR20, ST8, ST28**

Petulia (1968, C, 105m, PG)
Drama set in 1967 San Francisco about a divorced surgeon (George C. Scott) and his affair with a restless newlywed (Julie Christie). Powerful portrait of late-1960s America is brilliantly told through multiple flashbacks. With Richard Chamberlain, Arthur Hill, Shirley Knight, Joseph Cotten, Pippa Scott, Kathleen Widdoes, and musical appearances by The Grateful Dead and Big Brother & the Holding Company. Written by Lawrence B. Marcus and directed by Richard Lester; photographed by Nicolas Roeg. **CL14, DR1, DR7, DR15, DT62, XT13** *Essential; Highly Recommended*

Phantom Creeps, The (1939, B&W, 75m, NR)
Condensed version of serial adventure about the evil Dr. Zorka (Bela Lugosi) and his robot and mechanical spider. **ST95**

Phantom Empire (1935, B&W, 245m, NR)
A 12-chapter western serial starring Gene Autry, as he battles the "Thunder Riders" from an underworld kingdom beneath his ranch. Also available in an 80-minute version titled *Radio Ranch*. **ST3**

Phantom of Liberty, The (1974, C, 104m, R)
Director Luis Buñuel presents a series of surrealistic sketches, loosely connected, all designed to satirize contemporary society's claims to freedom. Jean-Claude Brialy, Monica Vitti, and Michel Piccoli star. **DT15**

Phantom of the Opera, The (1925, B&W, 79m, NR)
Lon Chaney, Sr. silent version of the horror classic can't be beat for chills; unmasking scene still an all-time movie highlight. **HO1, HO9, ST16** *Highly Recommended*

Phantom of the Opera (1943, C, 92m, NR)
Second version of horror classic adds brilliant color photography and set design (both Oscar winners). Claude Rains, Susanna Foster, and Nelson Eddy star. **CL9, CU18, HO9**

Phantom of the Opera, The (1989, C, 90m, R)
Robert Englund stars as the masked man of the opera house in this version set in 19th-century London. With Jill Schoelen. **HO9**

Phantom of the Paradise (1974, C, 92m, PG)
Rock 'n' roll version of *Phantom of the Opera,* with a little Faust thrown in. Paul Williams, William Finley, Jessica Harper, and Gerrit Graham star; Brian DePalma directed. **DT29, MU4, MU9, MU14**

Phantom Ship *see* The Mystery of the *Mary Celeste*

Phantom Tollbooth, The (1969, C, 90m, G)
Live action and animation blend in this version of the classic children's book about a boy's adventures in a land of numbers and letters. Animation directed by Chuck Jones. Also known as *The Adventures of Milo in the Phantom Tollbooth*. **FA8**

Phar Lap (1984, C, 107m, PG)
In 1932, Phar Lap became a national hero, a pug ugly horse from New Zealand that won 37 races in Australia. Tom Burlinson stars in this horse lover's drama. **DR22, FA5**

Phase IV (1974, C, 86m, PG)
Science fiction/horror story of three scientists at remote outpost beset by mutant ants. Clever photography and special effects. Directed by Saul Bass. **SF20** *Recommended*

Philadelphia Experiment, The (1984, C, 102m, PG)
Two American sailors fall through a time warp in 1943 and wind up in 1984. After one disappears, the other discovers he's part of a secret government experiment. Michael Pare, Nancy Allen, and Bobby Di Cicco star. **SF4**

Philadelphia Story, The (1940, B&W, 112m, NR)
Witty story of spoiled society girl (Katharine Hepburn) who dumps one husband (Cary Grant), tries to marry another man, falls in love with a third (Oscar winner James Stewart). Directed by George Cukor. **CL4, CL10, DT24, ST57, ST66, ST143, XT2, XT20** *Essential; Highly Recommended*

Philby, Burgess and MacLean: Spy Scandal of the Century (1986, C, 83m, NR)
Dramatization of Britain's major spy scandal, involving three college chums recruited by the Russians and working undetected for thirty years. Anthony Bates, Derek Jacobi, and Michael Culver star. **MY6, MY8, MY15**

Phobia (1980, C, 91m, R)
John Huston directed this mystery about a doctor whose patients, all victims of various phobias, are being murdered one by one. **DT50**

Phone Call From a Stranger (1952, B&W, 96m, NR)
The survivor of a plane crash decides to visit the families of some of the victims. Gary Merrill and Bette Davis star, with Shelley Winters and Michael Rennie. **ST28, ST164**

Physical Evidence (1988, C, 99m, R)
Burt Reynolds is a suspended cop framed for murder whose only hope for acquittal is a snotty public defender (Theresa Russell). **MY7, ST128**

Pick-up Artist, The (1987, C, 81m, R)
A young New York schoolteacher spends his spare time roaming the streets of the city, hitting on women. He meets his match when an attractive young woman accepts his offer for casual sex, then spurns him. Robert Downey, Jr. and Molly Ringwald star, with Dennis Hopper and Harvey Keitel. **ST71, XT9**

Picnic (1955, C, 115m, NR)
The William Inge play of a drifter who shakes things up in a small Kansas town. William Holden stars, with Rosalind Russell, Kim Novak, Betty Field, Cliff Robertson, and Arthur O'Connell. Directed by Joshua Logan. Available in letterboxed format. **CU19, DR20, DR26, ST68**

Picnic at Hanging Rock (1975, C, 110m, PG)
Atmospheric drama set in turn-of-the-century Australia: a girls' school outing to the Outback turns tragic when three students and their teacher disappear. Rachel Roberts stars. Peter Weir directed; based on a true story. **DT111**

Picture of Dorian Gray, The (1945, B&W, 111m, NR)
Oscar Wilde story of a man who never ages, despite a wild and carefree life. Hurd Hatfield, Angela Lansbury, and George Sanders star. Several short sequences in color. **CL1, HO1, HO26**

Piece of the Action, A (1977, C, 135m, PG)
Con men Sidney Poitier and Bill Cosby are roped into helping a social worker and her young charges in this comedy. With James Earl Jones. **ST76, ST121**

Pied Piper of Hamelin, The (1985, C, 60m, NR)
Eric Idle plays both the title role and poet Robert Browning in this Faerie Tale Theatre version of Browning's classic. **CO15, FA12**

Pierrot le Fou (1965, C, 90m, NR)
Episodic adventures of a couple on the lam, from French director Jean-Luc Godard. Screenplay was allegedly improvised as the film was shot. Jean-Paul Belmondo and Anna Karina star, with director Sam Fuller appearing as himself. **DT40, DT41, ST6, XT18** *Recommended*

Pillow Talk (1959, C, 105m, NR)
Doris Day and Rock Hudson share a party line, can't stand each other on the phone, but fall in love when they meet. Fluffy romantic comedy costarring Tony Randall and Thelma Ritter. **CO1, ST73** *Essential*

Pin (1988, C, 103m, R)
Horror tale of a young boy's fascination with his physician father's anatomical dummy, which comes to life for him. **HO16**

Pink Cadillac (1989, C, 122m, PG-13)
Clint Eastwood action comedy of a bounty hunter and the fugitive wife of a white supremacist. With Bernadette Peters. Eastwood directed. **CO10, ST39**

Pink Flamingos (1972, C, 95m, NR)
Director John Waters' look at the cheap and disgusting lives of certain denizens of Baltimore, Maryland. Divine stars in this midnight movie classic. **CU1, CU12, DT110**

Pink Floyd: The Wall (1982, C, 99m, R)
Gloomy rock musical, based on album by British rock group, about the decay of modern society. Bob Geldof and Bob Hoskins star. **MU9, MU16, ST72**

Pink Panther, The (1964, C, 113m, NR)
The comedy that gave the madcap Inspector Clouseau (Peter Sellers) to the world. The theft of a rare jewel (the title reference) is the object of his investigation. With David Niven, Capucine, and Robert Wagner. Blake Edwards directed. **DT32, ST137**

Pink Panther Strikes Again, The (1976, C, 103m, PG)
The fifth in the series about the inept Inspector Clouseau (Peter Sellers) has his ex-boss gone loony and attempting to (dare we say it?) rule the world. Herbert Lom costars. Directed by Blake Edwards. **DT32, ST137**

Pinocchio (1940, C, 87m, G)
Disney animated feature about a marionette who wants to become a boy and must learn some hard lessons about telling the truth. One of the great cartoon features of all time. **FA2** *Essential; Highly Recommended*

Pinocchio (1984, C, 60m, NR)
Paul Reubens (better known as Pee-wee Herman) stars as the marionette who wants to be a boy in this Faerie Tale Theatre presentation. **FA12**

Pippi Longstocking (series)
Pippi Longstocking (1974, C, 99m, G)
Pippi in the South Seas (1974, C, 99m, G)
Pippi Goes on Board (1975, C, 84m, G)
Pippi on the Run (1978, C, 99m, G)
The adventures of a daring little Swedish girl who inherits her spunk from her sea captain father. See also: *The New Adventures of Pippi Longstocking*. **FA4**

Piranha (1978, C, 92m, R)
Horror-movie spoof about a resort lake invaded by tiny but deadly fish. Joe Dante directed. **CU4, DT25, HO16, HO24**

Pirate, The (1948, C, 102m, NR)
Judy Garland believes that Gene Kelly is a famous pirate in this colorful MGM musical directed by Vincente Minnelli. **CL9, DT71, MU1, ST51, ST81**

Pirate Warrior (1964, C, 86m, NR)
Low-budget movie about fierce buccaneers, starring Ricardo Montalban and Vincent Price. **AC15, ST124**

Pirates (1986, C, 117m, PG-13)
A colorful adventure tale starring Walter Matthau as a one-legged rascal seeking revenge on the crew that set him adrift. Directed by Roman Polanski. **AC15, DT79, ST104**

Pirates of Penzance, The (1983, C, 112m, G)
Film version of the classic Gilbert & Sullivan operetta, starring Kevin Kline, Linda Ronstadt, Angela Lansbury, Rex Smith, and George Ross. **FA9, ST84**

Pit and the Pendulum, The (1961, C, 80m, NR)
Vincent Price stars in this adaptation of the Edgar Allan Poe story of an evil torturer. Directed by Roger Corman. **DT22, ST124, WR21**

Pixote (1981, C, 127m, NR)
Powerful drama set on the streets of Rio de Janeiro about a homeless boy's daily struggle for survival. Directed by Hector Babenco. **FF6** *Highly Recommended*

Place in the Sun, A (1951, B&W, 122m, NR)
Montgomery Clift is an ambitious man trapped in a dead-end affair with a factory worker (Shelley Winters) and really in love with a society girl (Elizabeth Taylor). Adapted from Theodore Dreiser's *An American Tragedy*. Directed by Oscar winner George Stevens. **CL4, CL6, CL8, DR19, DT101, ST147, ST164, XT6** *Essential; Recommended*

Places in the Heart (1984, C, 113m, PG)
Heartfelt drama of a farm woman in Texas during the 1930s and her valiant attempts to bring in the harvest after her husband dies. Oscar winner Sally Field stars, with Danny Glover, Lindsay Crouse, Ed Harris, Amy Madigan, and John Malkovich. Written and directed by Robert Benton. **DR2, DR5, DR8, DT6, ST40, ST55, ST98, XT3**

Plainsman, The (1936, B&W, 113m, NR)
With this lavish western, director Cecil B. DeMille manages to pack Annie Oakley (Jean Arthur), Wild Bill Hickok (Gary Cooper), Buffalo Bill (James Ellison), and George Armstrong Custer (John Miljan) into one story. **DT27, HF3, HF6, HF11, HF20, ST22, WE1, WE8**

Plan 9 From Outer Space (1959, B&W, 79m, NR)
Notoriously awful film (and, therefore, a cult classic) from director Ed Wood, Jr. about aliens raising the dead. Bela Lugosi's last film. **CU11, DT118, ST95**

Planes, Trains, and Automobiles (1987, C, 93m, R)
Comedy about the agonies of holiday travel, starring Steve Martin and John Candy as unwilling companions trying to get from New York to Chicago for Thanksgiving. Directed by John Hughes. **CO2, CO3, CO14, DT49, ST99, XT18, XT19**

Planet of the Apes (1968, C, 112m, PG)
Science fiction adventure about astronauts landing on a planet inhabited by a race of intelligent apes—which hold humans captive as beasts. Charlton Heston stars. First film in long-running series; see **SF23** for a complete list of titles. **FA8, SF8, SF12, SF13, SF23**

Platoon (1986, C, 120m, R)
A young recruit is pitched into the horrors of combat in Vietnam. Charlie Sheen, Willem Dafoe, and Tom Berenger star. Oscar winner for Best Picture and Director (Oliver Stone, who also scripted). **AC4, DT102, XT1, XT6** *Recommended*

Play It Again, Sam (1972, C, 87m, PG)
Woody Allen stars in this adaptation of his play about a lovelorn New Yorker with a Humphrey Bogart hang-up. With Diane Keaton and Tony Roberts. Directed by Herbert Ross. **CO1, DT1, ST79**

Play Misty for Me (1971, C, 102m, R)
Clint Eastwood plays a disc jockey whose one-night stand with a fan (Jessica Walter) turns into a nightmare when the woman relentlessly pursues him. With Jessica Walter, Donna Mills, and Don Siegel. Eastwood's first film as a director. **DT97, MY13, ST39** *Recommended*

Playing for Time (1980, C, 150m, NR)
Drama set in a Nazi concentration camp, where certain prisoners played in an orchestra while others met their deaths. Originally made for TV; Emmys to stars Vanessa Redgrave and Jane Alexander, plus writer Arthur Miller. **DR5, ST127**

Playtime (1967, C, 108m, NR)
Jacques Tati directed and stars in this comedy about M. Hulot, the perpetually befuddled Parisian who is trying to keep an important appointment. **DT104**

Plaza Suite (1971, C, 115m PG)
Trio of Neil Simon playlets about goings-on at famous hotel in New York City. Walter Matthau stars in all three episodes; Maureen Stapleton, Lee Grant, and Barbara Harris costar. **ST104, WR23**

Please! Mr. Balzac *see* Mademoiselle Striptease

Plenty (1985, C, 119m, R)
Meryl Streep plays a British woman whose teenaged act of heroism during World War II makes the rest of her life seem dull and unrewarding. With Charles Dance, Tracey Ullman, John Gielgud, and Sting. Adaptation of David Hare's play. **DR10, DR20, MU12, ST145**

Plot Against Harry, The (1969, B&W, 80m, NR)
Comedy of Jewish gangster (Martin Priest) just released from prison, trying to adjust to life with his zany family. Directed by Michael Roemer. **CO5, CO10**

Ploughman's Lunch, The (1983, C, 100m, R)
Dark view of British society and journalism in particular, focusing on the conduct of a reporter (Jonathan Pryce) and colleagues during the Falklands war. **DR23**

Plumber, The (1980, C, 76m, NR)
An overbearing plumber destroys a young couple's bathroom in this comic thriller from Australian director Peter Weir. **DT111, HO24, MY3, MY16**

Pocketful of Miracles (1961, C, 136m, NR)
Bette Davis is Apple Annie, a street-corner vendor of the Depression who's turned into a real lady by a producer (Glenn Ford). Directed by Frank Capra. **DT16, ST28**

Pocketful of Rye, A (1984, C, 102m, NR)
Miss Marple, the indefatigable sleuth created by Agatha Christie, comes to the help of a protege in this whodunit. Joan Hickson stars; originally made for British TV. **MY12, WR3**

Point Blank (1967, C, 92m, NR)
Stylized, violent thriller about a man with a mission: to recover money his partner stole during a heist at abandoned Alcatraz Prison. Lee Marvin stars, with John Vernon, Keenan Wynn, Lloyd Bochner, and Angie Dickinson. Directed with great flair by John Boorman on locations in San Francisco and Los Angeles. **AC8, AC19, AC25, CU7, DR16, DT11, ST100, XT10, XT13** *Highly Recommended*

Poker Alice (1987, C, 109m, NR)
Elizabeth Taylor plays a New Orleans gambler who makes her mark in a frontier saloon. George Hamilton and Tom Skerritt costar in this western originally made for cable TV. **ST147, WE8**

Pollyanna (1960, C, 134m, NR)
An orphan comes to live with her aunt in a small town in New England and her good spirits soon affect everyone around her. Disney classic, starring Hayley Mills, Jane Wyman, and Karl Malden. **FA1**

Poltergeist (1982, C, 115m, PG)
Suburban family is haunted by ghosts through their TV set, with youngest daughter kidnapped into another dimension. Craig T. Nelson and JoBeth Williams star. Tobe Hooper directed and Steven Spielberg produced. **DT47, HO2, HO3, HO19**

Poltergeist II (1986, C, 91m, PG-13)
Same family, different house, same problems, as Craig T. Nelson, JoBeth Williams and children undergo more hauntings. **HO2, HO3**

Poltergeist III (1988, C, 97m, PG-13)
Heather O'Rourke, the young star of the first two chapters, is still in contact with otherworldly demons, while living with her aunt and uncle (Nancy Allen, Tom Skerritt) in a high-rise apartment. **HO2**

Polyester (1981, C, 86m, R)
Suburban Baltimore housewife Francine Fishpaw is romanced by drive-in movie theater owner Todd Tomorrow in this comedy from cult director John Waters. Divine and Tab Hunter star. **CU12, DT110**

Pony Express (1953, C, 101m, NR)
Drama about the founding of the famous mail route that helped to open the West. Buffalo Bill (Charlton Heston) and Wild Bill Hickok (Forrest Tucker) are among the historical figures portrayed. **HF3, HF11**

Poor Little Rich Girl (1936, B&W, 72m, NR)
Shirley Temple is a runaway who teams up with a vaudeville couple in this show-business musical. Alice Faye and Jack Haley costar. **ST148**

Pope John Paul II (1984, C, 147m, NR)
Biography of the first Polish pontiff, portrayed by Albert Finney. Originally made for TV. **DR4, ST42**

Pope of Greenwich Village, The (1984, C, 120m, R)
A pair of smalltime New York hoods (Mickey Rourke and Eric Roberts) decide to challenge the neighborhood crime boss. With Daryl Hannah. **DR15, ST134**

Popeye (1980, C, 114m, PG)
Live action musical of the famous cartoon and comic strip sailor with a taste for spinach. Robin Williams stars, with

Shelley Duvall as Olive Oyl, Paul Dooley as Wimpy. Directed by Robert Altman; songs by Harry Nilsson. **DT2, FA9, ST160**

Pork Chop Hill (1959, B&W, 97m, NR)
Korean War action centering on battle for a strategic position. Gregory Peck, Harry Guardino, and Rip Torn star. **AC3, ST119, ST150**

Porky Pig and Daffy Duck Cartoon Festival (1981, C, 57m, NR)
A collection of Warner Bros. cartoons from the 1940s starring that st-st-stuttering pig and his foolish fowl of a friend. **FA11**

Porky's (series)
Porky's (1981, C, 94m, R)
Porky's II: The Next Day (1983, C, 100m, R)
Porky's Revenge (1985, C, 95m, R)
These comedies depict the zany and raunchy misadventures of a gang of teenagers at a Florida high school in the 1950s. **CO4, CO18**

Port of Call (1948, B&W, 99m, NR)
In a Swedish port town, a young outcast and a seaman strike up a friendship. Directed by Ingmar Bergman. **DT7**

Portrait of Jennie (1948, B&W/C, 86m, NR)
Classic love story of starving artist (Joseph Cotten) and the ethereal object of his desire (Jennifer Jones). With Ethel Barrymore and Lillian Gish. Poroduced by David O. Selznick. Final scene in color. **CL4, ST54**

Poseidon Adventure, The (1972, C, 117m, PG)
When a cruise ship is capsized by a tidal wave, a group of passengers engage in desperate battle for escape and survival. Gene Hackman stars, with Ernest Borgnine, Red Buttons, Stella Stevens, and Shelley Winters. **AC23, ST61, ST164**

Positive I.D. (1987, C, 96m, R)
A housewife victimized by a rapist learns that he's being released from jail. Written and directed by Andy Anderson. **MY3**

Posse (1975, C, 94m, PG)
Kirk Douglas stars in this western as a politically ambitious marshall who has his hands full when he captures a wily and

popular outlaw (Bruce Dern). With Bo Hopkins and James Stacy. **ST34, WE3**

Possessed (1931, B&W, 72m, NR)
Joan Crawford stars in a melodrama of a woman's sacrifice for the man she loves. With Clark Gable. **CL5, ST24, ST49**

Postman Always Rings Twice, The (1946, B&W, 113m, NR)
First screen version of the James M. Cain story of adultery and murder, with Lana Turner (in all-white outfits) and John Garfield the amorous killers. **DR3, MY1, MY5, ST153, WR1** *Essential; Recommended*

Postman Always Rings Twice, The (1981, C, 123m, R)
Jack Nicholson and Jessica Lange are the lovers in this version of James M. Cain's classic tale of adultery and murder. **CU18, DR3, MY5, ST86, ST112, WR1**

Pot o' Gold (1941, B&W, 86m, NR)
James Stewart and Paulette Goddard star in this musical about a boy who wrangles a spot on his uncle's radio show. **ST143**

Potemkin (1925, B&W, 65m, NR)
Classic film based on real-life sailors' mutiny and subsequent massacre of citizens in 1905 Russia. Brilliant editing and imagery give this silent film, directed by Sergei Eisenstein, real emotional power. Also known as *Battleship Potemkin*. **CL12, CU9, DT33** *Essential; Highly Recommended*

Power (1928, B&W, 60m, NR)
Early talkie about a pair of rival dam workers and their love affairs. William Boyd, Alan Hale, Carole Lombard, and Joan Bennett star. **ST92**

Power (1986, C, 111m, R)
A Washington political consultant finds himself representing a mysterious client with some nasty secrets. Richard Gere, Gene Hackman, and Julie Christie star, with Denzel Washington, Kate Capshaw, E.G. Marshall, and Beatrice Straight. Sidney Lumet directed. **DR21, DT65, ST52, ST61, XT12**

Power Play (1978, C, 102m, PG)
A group of military officers plot a coup in a country ruled by a dictatorship and secret police. Peter O'Toole and David Hemmings star. **ST117**

Powwow Highway (1989, C, 90m, R)
Road comedy-drama focusing on two Native Americans driving a beat-up Buick from Montana to Santa Fe, one on a spiritual quest, the other to get his sister out of jail. Gary Farmer and A Martinez star. Good use of rock music on soundtrack. **DR7, XT18**

Prairie Moon (1938, B&W, 58m, NR)
Gene Autry is saddled with three young children after their father dies in this light-hearted western. **ST3**

Prancer (1989, C, 103m, G)
A little girl nurses a sick reindeer back to health, believing that it's one of Santa's helpers. Sam Elliott, Rebecca Harrell, and Cloris Leachman star. **FA13**

Pray for Death (1985, C, 93m, R)
Sho Kosugi stars in this action drama about a former Ninja who reverts to his training when he and his family are threatened by mobsters. **AC26**

Prayer for the Dying, A (1987, C, 107m, R)
A gunman for the Irish Republican Army decides to escape the country. But before he can, he has to carry out a hit for a ruthless mobster. Mickey Rourke, Alan Bates, and Bob Hoskins star. **DR16, DR23, ST72, ST134**

Predator (1987, C, 107m, R)
Arnold Schwarzenegger and his jungle combat buddies are being picked off one by one by an alien creature. Directed by John McTiernan. **AC24, AC25, ST135**

Premature Burial, The (1962, C, 81m, NR)
Ray Milland plays a medical student with an obsession that he'll be buried alive. Roger Corman directed this loose adaptation of Edgar Allan Poe's story. **DT22, WR21**

Premonition (1971, C, 83m, PG)
Drama about three drug-using college students who all experience the same forebodings of death. Directed by Alan Rudolph. **DT91**

Presenting Lily Mars (1943, B&W, 104m, NR)
Early Judy Garland musical about a young singer trying to make it big on Broadway. **ST51**

President's Analyst, The (1967, C, 104m, NR)
James Coburn stars as the title character, a man who knows so many intimate details about the Chief Executive that every spy in the world is after him. Satirical comedy costars Godfrey Cambridge and William Daniels. **CO2, XT12**

President's Plane Is Missing, The (1971, C, 100m, NR)
Thriller, adapted from Robert Serling bestseller, about an attempted overthrow of the U.S. government. Buddy Ebsen, Arthur Kennedy, and Peter Graves star, with Rip Torn, Raymond Massey, and Mercedes McCambridge. Originally made for TV. **MY6, ST150**

Presidio, The (1988, C, 97m, R)
A San Francisco police detective (Mark Harmon) and an army officer (Sean Connery) clash over the investigation of a murder on the latter's base. With Meg Ryan. **AC9, ST21, XT13**

Pretty Baby (1978, C, 110m, R)
In New Orleans around the time of World War I, a strange photographer asks permission of a madam to take pictures of her prostitutes. Based on the true story of E.J. Bellocq. Keith Carradine, Brooke Shields, and Susan Sarandon star. Louis Malle directed; photographed by Sven Nykvist. **DR3, DR5, XT14**

Pretty in Pink (1986, C, 96m, PG-13)
A girl from the wrong side of the tracks and a guy from a wealthy family fall in love and defy their respective crowds at the high school prom. Molly Ringwald and Andrew McCarthy star, with Harry Dean Stanton. John Hughes produced. **DR9, DT49, ST141**

Pretty Woman (1990, C, 117m, R)
A Los Angeles prostitute agrees to pose as an escort to a high-powered takeover specialist, and they fall in love. This Cinderella story stars Julia Roberts and Richard Gere, with Laura San Giacomo, Hector Elizondo, and Ralph Bellamy. Directed by Garry Marshall. **CO1, CO20, ST52, XT10**

Prick up Your Ears (1987, C, 111m, R)
The life of British playwright Joe Orton, who authored several hit comedies before he was murdered by his homosexual lover. Gary Oldman and Alfred Molina

star, with Vanessa Redgrave. **DR3, DR4, DR23, ST127**

Pride and Prejudice (1940, B&W, 118m, NR)
Jane Austen's classic comedy of manners features Greer Garson and Laurence Olivier as romantic sparring partners in 19th-century England. **CL1, ST116**

Pride and the Passion, The (1957, C, 132m, NR)
War drama set in 19th-century Spain, focusing on the capture of a mammoth cannon. Cary Grant, Frank Sinatra, and Sophia Loren star. Directed by Stanley Kramer. **DT55, ST57, ST93, ST138**

Pride of St. Louis, The (1952, B&W, 93m, NR)
The life and wacky times of St. Louis Cardinals pitching great Dizzy Dean, played by Dan Dailey. **CL2, DR22**

Pride of the Yankees, The (1942, B&W, 119m, NR)
Gary Cooper plays New York Yankees star Lou Gehrig, whose brilliant career was cut short by a mysterious disease. **CL2, DR22, ST22**

Prime Cut (1972, C, 91m, R)
Rival mobsters Gene Hackman and Lee Marvin duke it out over the Kansas City meat packing business. Sissy Spacek's film debut. **AC22, ST61, ST100, ST139** *Recommended*

Prime of Miss Jean Brodie, The 1969, C, 116m, PG)
Maggie Smith's Oscar-winning performance highlights this drama of an unconventional teacher in a girls' school. With Robert Stephens and Pamela Franklin. **DR25, XT3**

Primrose Path, The (1940, B&W, 93m, NR)
Ginger Rogers stars in this drama about a girl from the wrong side of town in love with a young man (Joel McCrea) with ambitions. **ST131**

Prince and the Pauper, The (1937, B&W, 120m, NR)
Screen version of Mark Twain's story of royal son and commoner who trade places. Errol Flynn stars, with real-life twins Billy and Bobby Mauch. **FA3, ST43, WR27**

Prince and the Pauper, The (1978, C, 113m, PG)
Remake of the Twain tale of prince and his subject. Mark Lester, Oliver Reed, Raquel Welch, George C. Scott, and Charlton Heston star. Also known as *Crossed Swords*. **FA3, WR27**

Prince and the Showgirl, The (1957, C, 117m, NR)
Unique pairing of Laurence Olivier and Marilyn Monroe in this comedy: title says it all. Olivier directed. **ST108, ST116**

Prince of Darkness (1988, C, 102m, R)
A group of students and scientists discover an ancient cannister in a church, and the contents reap terrifying results. Horror drama from director John Carpenter. **DT17**

Prince of Pennsylvania, The (1988, C, 90m, R)
Family troubles in a working class suburb of Pittsburgh, with teen genius son (Keanu Reeves) hatching a plot to kidnap his father (Fred Ward). With Bonnie Bedelia and Amy Madigan. **DR8**

Prince of the City (1981, C, 167m, R)
True-life drama of New York City cop persuaded by special investigators to go undercover and expose corruption in the force. Treat Williams stars, with Jerry Orbach, Lindsay Crouse, and Richard Foronjy. Sidney Lumet directed. **DR6, DR16, DT65, XT9** *Recommended*

Princess and the Pea, The (1985, C, 60m, NR)
Liza Minnelli, Tom Conti, and Pat McCormick star in this Faerie Tale Theatre presentation of the children's classic. **FA12**

Princess and the Pirate, The (1944, C, 94m, NR)
Pirate comedy with Bob Hope ducking bucaneers Victor McLaglen and Walter Brennan. Virginia Mayo costars. **ST70**

Princess Bride, The (1987, C, 98m, PG)
A fairy tale story for both grownups and kids, with a lovely princess (Robin Wright) tricked by an evil prince (Chris Sarandon) into believing that her lover (Cary Elwes) is dead. The supporting cast includes Mandy Patinkin, Wallace Shawn, Andre the Giant, and Billy Crystal. Directed by Rob Reiner; adapted by William

Goldman from his novel. **AC14, AC15, CO13, DT85**

Princess Tam-Tam (1935, B&W, 77m, NR)
Josephine Baker stars in this French comedy of an African girl educated by a Frenchman and passed off as Indian royalty. **FF1**

Princess Who Never Laughed, The (1984, C, 60m, NR)
A Faerie Tale Theatre presentaiton of the Brothers Grimm classic, starring Howie Mandel, Ellen Barkin, and Howard Hesseman. **FA12**

Principal, The (1987, C, 90m, R)
At an inner-city school, a new principal finds that discipline is his most important subject. Jim Belushi and Louis Gossett, Jr. star in the action drama. **CO13, DR25**

Prisoner, The (1955, B&W, 91m, NR)
Alec Guinness stars in this British drama, set in an Eastern Bloc country, about a cardinal interrogated by a brutal official (Jack Hawkins). **CL8, ST60**

Prisoner of Second Avenue, The (1975, C, 105m, PG)
Neil Simon comedy-drama about an unemployed executive in Manhattan who can't cope with his troubles. Jack Lemmon and Anne Bancroft star. **ST90, WR23**

Prisoner of Zenda, The (1937, B&W, 101m, NR)
First-rate version of the classic adventure tale of commoner filling in for regal relative, gaining revenge. Ronald Colman, Douglas Fairbanks, Jr., and Madeleine Carroll star. **AC13, FA4** *Recommended*

Prisoner of Zenda, The (1952, C, 101m, NR)
The classic swashbuckler about a commoner mistaken for a king. Stewart Granger crosses swords with everyone in sight. With Deborah Kerr and James Mason. **AC13, ST102**

Prisoner of Zenda, The (1979, C, 108m, PG)
Comic version of the classic swashbuckler, with Peter Sellers in the lead. **ST137**

Private Benjamin (1980, C, 100m, R)
A pampered young Jewish woman, widowed on her wedding night, enlists in the army and learns a few lessons in life. Goldie Hawn and Eileen Brennan star in this comedy, with Armand Assante, Harry Dean Stanton, and Albert Brooks. **CO2, CO21, DT12, ST63, ST141**

Private Files of J. Edgar Hoover, The (1977, C, 112m, PG)
Melodramatic recreation of the life of famed F.B.I. chief, starring Broderick Crawford as the man with the goods on everyone in Washington. With Dan Dailey, Jose Ferrer, Rip Torn, Raymond St. Jacques as Martin Luther King, and Michael Parks as Bobby Kennedy. Directed by Larry Cohen. **CU2, DR4, DT20, ST150**

Private Function, A (1985, C, 93m, R)
During the late 1940s, when meat rationing was still in force in Britain, an illegal pig becomes the focus of deception and double-dealing. This comedy stars Michael Palin and Maggie Smith. **CO6, CO15, CO17**

Private Hell 36 (1954, B&W, 81m, NR)
A pair of cops decide to keep some stolen money, then have second thoughts. Ida Lupino stars (she also co-wrote and produced), with Steve Cochran and Howard Duff. Directed by Don Siegel. **DT97, MY1**

Private Life of Henry VIII, The (1933, B&W, 97m, NR)
Oscar winner Charles Laughton stars as the much-married King of England, with Elsa Lanchester as one of his unfortunate brides. **CL2, XT2**

Private Life of Sherlock Holmes, The (1970, C, 125m, PG)
As the title implies, not your everyday Holmes mystery. Robert Stephens, Colin Blakely, and Christopher Lee star in this film from writer-director Billy Wilder with a strong cult following. **DT116, HF14, ST89**

Private Lives of Elizabeth and Essex, The (1939, C, 106m, NR)
Historical drama of the political—and personal—relationship of Queen Elizabeth I (Bette Davis) and the dashing Earl of Essex (Errol Flynn). With Vincent Price. **CL2, CL3, CL21, ST28, ST43, ST124**

Privates on Parade (1982, C, 100m, PG-13)
Comedy about a special theatrical unit performing for British troops in the Pacific during World War II, starring John Cleese. **CO6, CO15, CO21**

Prize Fighter, The (1979, C, 99m, PG)
Family comedy about a lame-brained boxer and his mouthy manager, starring Don Knotts and Tim Conway. **FA6**

Prizzi's Honor (1985, C, 130m, R)
A pair of professional killers meet at a wedding and fall in love, even though one has been assigned to "hit" the other. Jack Nicholson and Kathleen Turner star in this darkly comic tale, based on Richard Condon's novel. Oscar winner Anjelica Huston heads the supporting cast. John Huston directed. **DR16, DT50, ST112, ST152, XT5, XT20**

Producers, The (1968, C, 88m, PG)
Mel Brooks' debut as a writer-director is a daring comedy about an unscrupulous Broadway producer's attempts to intentionally make a flop and walk away with his investors' money. Zero Mostel and Gene Wilder star, with Dick Shawn, Kenneth Mars, and Lee Meredith. **CO8, DT13** *Essential; Recommended*

Professionals, The (1966, C, 117m, NR)
In this western drama, a wealthy man hires four soldiers of fortune to recapture his wife, who has been kidnapped by a Mexican bandit. Burt Lancaster, Lee Marvin, Robert Ryan, and Woody Strode star, with Jack Palance, Claudia Cardinale, and Ralph Bellamy. **ST85, ST100, WE9** *Recommended*

Project X (1987, C, 107m, PG)
An Air Force enlisted man is assigned to a project involving chimpanzees and soon discovers the deadly secret behind the experiments. Matthew Broderick stars, with Helen Hunt. **DR2, DR7**

Promised Land (1988, C, 101m, R)
Story of three small-town high school friends whose lives after graduation diverge and then converge, disastrously. Kiefer Sutherland, Jason Gedrick, and Tracy Pollan star, with Meg Ryan. **DR7, DR26**

Promoter, The (1952, B&W, 88m, NR)
Alec Guinness plays a brash young opportunist in this British comedy, costarring Glynis Johns. Written by Eric Ambler. **ST60**

Proof of the Man (1984, C, 100m, NR)
An American found murdered in Tokyo is the key to a mystery with international implications. Toshiro Mifune, George Kennedy, and Broderick Crawford star. **ST106**

Prophecy (1979, C, 95m, PG)
A doctor and his pregnant wife investigate mercury poisoning in Maine streams and come face to face with a mutant monster. Talia Shire, Robert Foxworth, and Armand Assante star in this science fiction/horror tale. **SF10**

Protector, The (1985, C, 94m, R)
Martial arts star Jackie Chan plays a New York City cop who's after a drug kingpin. **AC26**

Protocol (1984, C, 95m, PG)
Goldie Hawn stars in this comedy about a know-nothing who's given a do-nothing job in the State Department—and winds up involved in serious foreign relations matters. With Chris Sarandon, Richard Romanus, and Andre Gregory. **ST63, XT12**

Proud Rebel, The (1958, C, 103m, NR)
Alan Ladd plays a proud man seeking help for his mute son (David Ladd, the star's real-life son). Olivia de Havilland costars, with Dean Jagger, John Carradine, and (Harry) Dean Stanton. **ST141, XT8**

Providence (1977, C, 104m, R)
From French director Alain Resnais, an English-language film about an aging writer (John Gielgud), his attempts to finish his last novel, and his relationships with his family. Ellen Burstyn and David Warner costar. **DR8, FF1** *Recommended*

Psych-Out (1968, C, 82m, NR)
In late-1960s San Francisco, a young deaf runaway tries to locate her brother and falls in with a local rock band. Susan Strasberg, Bruce Dern, Jack Nicholson, and Dean Stockwell star in this relic from the psychedelic era. **ST112, ST144, XT13**

Psycho (1960, B&W, 109m, R)
Hitchcock's most memorable shocker, about a woman thief, a shabby motel, a shy clerk, and a murderous mother. Anthony Perkins and Janet Leigh star, with John Gavin, Vera Miles, and Martin Balsam. **DT46, HO1, HO9** *Essential; Highly Recommended*

Psycho II (1983, C, 113m, R)
Norman Bates is out of prison for his fiendish crimes, but he just can't stay away from the Bates Motel. Anthony Perkins and Meg Tilly star. Richard Franklin directed. **HO9**

Psycho III (1986, C, 93m, R)
The third entry in the saga of Norman Bates has director-star Anthony Perkins playing the horror for laughs. **HO9**

Psycho Sisters (1972, C, 76m, PG)
A woman whose husband has just died goes to live with her sister, recently released from an insane asylum. Horror drama starring Susan Strasberg and Faith Domergue. **HO14**

Psychomania (1971, C, 95m, R)
A British motorcycle gang returns from the dead after making a special deal in this adult horror film. George Sanders stars. **HO6**

Psychos in Love (1985, C, 88m, NR)
Horror comedy about a romance between a pair of demented killers. **HO24**

Puberty Blues (1981, C, 86m, R)
Two young girls experience the joys and pains of adolescence while they hang out with the surfing crowd in Sydney, Australia. Directed by Bruce Beresford. **FF5**

Public Enemy, The (1931, B&W, 84m, NR)
James Cagney rose to stardom as a tough-talking gangster who packs a mean wallop, especially with a grapefruit in his hand. With Jean Harlow, Eddie Woods, Joan Blondell, and Mae Clark. **AC22, ST14** *Essential; Highly Recommended*

Pudd'nhead Wilson (1984, C, 90m, NR)
Mark Twain's detective tale of mismatched twins and a murder, starring Ken Howard. Originally made for public TV. **WR27**

Puff the Magic Dragon (1985, C, 45m, NR)
Based on the children's song, this animated feature is about a lonely boy and his gigantic fire-breathing friend. **FA10**

Pulp (1972, C, 95m, PG)
Darkly comic tale of a retired Hollywood actor (Mickey Rooney) hiring a hack writer (Michael Caine) to pen his memoirs. With Lizabeth Scott and Lionel Stander. **CO12, ST15, ST133** *Recommended*

Pumping Iron (1976, C, 85m, PG)
Documentary about the world of weightlifters and professional bodybuilders, featuring Arnold Schwarzenegger and Lou Ferrigno. **CU16, ST135**

Pumping Iron II: The Women (1985, C, 107m, NR)
Sequel to *Pumping Iron* concentrates on the female bodybuilders. Bev Francis is the star. **CU16**

Pumpkinhead (1988, C, 87m, R)
Horror story of a vengeance-seeking father who summons a legendary demon to deal with his son's murderers but cannot control it once the killing begins. **HO14**

Punch Line (1988, C, 123m, R)
Tom Hanks and Sally Field play stand-up comics; he's the cynical veteran of the club scene, she's a housewife trying to break into the biz. With John Goodman, Mark Rydell, and Paul Mazursky. Jerry Belson directed this drama. **DR12, ST40, ST62**

Puppet Master (1989, C, 90m, R)
Horror tale of a group of psychics gathered at a remote hotel, terrorized by the fiendish creations of a mad inventor. Paul LeMat stars, with Irene Miracle, Matt Roe, and William Hickey. **HO16**

Purlie Victorious (1963, C, 97m, NR)
Musical fable about a black preacher standing up to a wicked plantation owner. Written by and starring Ossie Davis, with Ruby Dee, Sorrell Booke, and Godfrey Cambridge. **DR14, MU2**

Purple Heart, The (1944, B&W, 99m, NR)
World War II drama of U.S. fliers shot down during bombing raids on Tokyo, starring Dana Andrews, Farley Granger, Sam Levene, and Richard Conte. **AC1**

Purple Hearts (1984, C, 115m, R)
A Navy medic and a nurse fall in love against the backdrop of the war in Vietnam. Cheryl Ladd and Ken Wahl star. **AC4**

Purple Rain (1984, C, 113m, R)
The movie debut of rock star Prince, as he plays a character named The Kid, a rocker battling rival musicians, his own band members, and family problems. With Apollonia Kotero, Morris Day, and Clarence Williams III. **DR12, MU9**

Purple Rose of Cairo, The (1985, C, 84m, PG)
During the Depression, a waitress trapped in a loveless marriage imagines her favorite movie star has come off the screen to romance her. Mia Farrow and Jeff Daniels star in this comedy written and directed by Woody Allen. **CO8, DT1**

Pursued (1947, B&W, 101m, NR)
Robert Mitchum is a cowboy out to find his father's killers. **ST107, WE5**

Pursuit of D.B. Cooper, The (1981, C, 100m, PG)
The tale of the legendary airline bandit who parachuted from the sky with thousands in ransom. Treat Williams and Robert Duvall star. **DR6, ST38**

Pursuit of the Graf Spee (1957, C, 106m, NR)
Michael Powell directed this World War II drama about the British attempts to sink a German battleship. John Gregson, Anthony Quayle, and Christopher Lee star. **AC1, DT81, ST89**

Pursuit to Algiers (1945, B&W, 65m, NR)
Sherlock Holmes mystery, starring Basil Rathbone and Nigel Bruce, has the famous detective and his companion accompanying an heir to a foreign throne on a voyage. Not based on any Arthur Conan Doyle story. **HF14**

Puss 'n' Boots (1984, C, 60m, NR)
Ben Vereen and Gregory Hines star in this Faerie Tale Theatre presentation of the beloved children's story. **FA12**

Putney Swope (1969, C/B&W, 88m, R)
Satirical comedy about a black man taking over a prestigious New York advertising agency and renaming it Truth and Soul, Inc. Arnold Johnson stars; Mel Brooks has a small part. Directed by Robert Downey. **CO2, CO12, DT13**

Pygmalion (1938, B&W, 95m, NR)
The George Bernard Shaw play about a professor's gamble that he can turn a Cockney flower girl into a lady of culture. Leslie Howard and Wendy Hiller star in this comedy that was the basis for *My Fair Lady*. **CL1**

Q & A (1990, C, 132m, R)
Nick Nolte plays a racist New York cop, Timothy Hutton the assistant district attorney investigating him. With Armand Assante and Jenny Lumet. Written and directed by Sidney Lumet. **DR15, DR16, DT65, ST113, XT9** *Recommended*

Q Planes *see* Clouds Over Europe

Q: The Winged Serpent (1982, C, 93m, R)
Horror comedy about a monster from Mexican legend terrorizing Manhattan, nesting on top of the Chrysler Building. Michael Moriarty, Richard Roundtree, and David Carradine star. Larry Cohen directed. **DT20, HO16, XT9**

Quackbusters (1989, C, 76m, G)
Feature-length cartoon, spoofing *Ghostbusters*, starring Daffy Duck as a spook-hunting detective. **FA10**

Quackser Fortune Has a Cousin in the Bronx (1970, C, 90m, R)
Gene Wilder plays an amiable Irishman who collects horse manure from the streets of Dublin and sells it to gardeners. Margot Kidder is an American student who falls in love with him. **CO1**

Quadrophenia (1979, C, 115m, R)
Musical drama about a young Briton in the early 1960s with four separate personalities, based on the rock album by The Who. Superb marriage of music and imagery directed by Franc Roddam. Phil Daniels stars, with Sting in a small role. **MU9** *Recommended*

Quality Street (1937, B&W, 84m, NR)
A woman pretends to be her own niece in order to woo a flame she hasn't seen in ten years. Katharine Hepburn and Franchot Tone star in this comedy directed by George Stevens. **DT101, ST66**

Quartet (1949, B&W, 120m, NR)
W. Somerset Maugham introduces four of his short stories, each with its own cast. Among the players: Mai Zetterling, Ian Fleming, and Dirk Bogarde. Sequels: *Trio* and *Encore*. **DR19**

Quatermass Conclusion, The (1980, C, 107m, NR)
British science fiction adventure about a professor who is the key to stopping a deadly ray from destroying the planet. John Mills stars. Originally made for TV. **SF19**

Que Viva Mexico! (1932, B&W, 85m, NR)
Russian director Sergei Eisenstein's legendary, unfinished documentary about life in Mexico. **DT33**

Queen Christina (1933, B&W, 97m, NR)
One of Greta Garbo's signature roles: the 17th-century Swedish monarch who gave up her throne for love. With John Gilbert. Directed by Rouben Mamoulian. **CL3, CL4, ST50** *Essential; Recommended*

Queen Kelly (1929, B&W, 95m, NR)
Director Erich Von Stroheim's bizarre tale of a young girl's odyssey from a convent school to a brothel. Gloria Swanson stars in this reconstruction of a long-lost and never-finished classic silent drama. **CL12, DT109**

Queen of Hearts (1989, C, 112m, PG)
Charming comedy-drama of an Italian immigrant family living in postwar London, as seen through the eyes of its young son (Ian Hawkes). Joseph Long and Anita Zagaria star. Directed by Jon Amiel. **CO4, CO5, CO17** *Recommended*

Querelle (1982, C, 120m, R)
Director Rainer Werner Fassbinder's last film, about a sailor's discovery of his homosexual nature. Brad Davis and Jeanne Moreau star. **DT34, ST110**

Quest, The (1986, C, 93m, PG)
A young boy learns of an ancient myth in the Australian outback and confronts the source in this adventure. Henry Thomas stars. **FA4, FF5**

Quest for Fire (1981, C, 97m, R)
A drama of life in prehistoric times, filmed on several continents, with special languages and body movements designed for the film. Everett McGill, Ron Perlman,

and Rae Dawn Chong star. Directed by French filmmaker Jean-Jacques Annaud. **AC12, AC24, FF1**

Question of Silence, A (1983, C, 92m, R)
Dutch film about three women on trial for murdering the same man, venting their hostility over a male-dominated society. **FF7**

Quick and the Dead, The (1987, C, 93m, NR)
Louis L'Amour western of a homesteading family falling under the protection of a mysterious stranger. Sam Elliott, Kate Capshaw, and Tom Conti star. Originally made for cable TV. **WR13**

Quiet Cool (1986, C, 80m, R)
A New York cop brings his special brand of street smarts to a small California town being overrun by a gang of pot growers. James Remar and Nick Cassavetes star. **AC9**

Quiet Earth, The (1985, C, 91m, R)
Only three people are left on Earth after a top-secret project goes haywire. Science fiction drama from New Zealand. **SF12**

Quiet Man, The (1952, C, 129m, NR)
American prizefighter returns to his native Ireland and courts local lass in this rollicking comedy from Oscar-winning director John Ford. John Wayne and Maureen O'Hara star, with Victor McLaglen and Barry Fitzgerald. Gorgeous, Oscar-winning color cinematography. **CL9, DT36, ST156, XT6** *Essential; Recommended*

Quiet One, The (1948, B&W, 67m, NR)
Low-budget drama, set in New York, of a black youth trying to stay out of trouble. Donald Thompson stars. **DR14**

Quiller Memorandum, The (1966, C, 105m, NR)
An American agent in Britain hunts down ex-Nazis in this spy thriller starring George Segal, Alec Guinness, and Max von Sydow. Written by Harold Pinter. **MY6, ST60**

Quintet (1979, C, 118m, R)
Science fiction drama about a frozen city of the future and its few inhabitants who play a bizarre game for survival. Paul Newman stars, with Bibi Andersson, Fer-

nando Rey, and Nina Van Pallandt. Robert Altman directed. **DT2, SF8, ST111**

R.P.M. (1970, C, 97m, R)
Drama of campus insurrection, starring Anthony Quinn as a lusty professor, with Ann-Margret, Gary Lockwood, and Paul Winfield as students. Directed by Stanley Kramer. **DR25, DT55, ST162**

Rabbit Test (1978, C, 86m, R)
Billy Crystal stars in a comedy about the world's first pregnant man. Joan Rivers directed. **CO13**

Rabid (1977, C, 90m, R)
From horror director David Cronenberg, the story of a woman who develops a thirst for human blood after she's had plastic surgery. Not for the squeamish. Marilyn Chambers stars. **DT23, HO18**

Race With the Devil (1975, C, 88m, PG)
Two couples on vacation tangle with some devil worshippers in this action thriller that features lots of motorcycle and car chases. Peter Fonda and Warren Oates star. **AC10, HO11, ST115**

Rachel and the Stranger (1948, B&W, 93m, NR)
A romantic triangle, western-style, featuring Loretta Young, William Holden, and Robert Mitchum. **ST68, ST107, WE8**

Rachel Papers, The (1989, C, 92m, R)
Comedy-drama about young man who keeps files on prospective romances in his computer. Dexter Fletcher, Ione Skye, and James Spader star. Based on a novel by Martin Amis. **DR1**

Rachel, Rachel (1968, C, 101m, R)
Joanne Woodward stars in this drama about a lonely schoolteacher looking for love in her mid-thirties. With Estelle Parsons and James Olson; Paul Newman directed. **DR10, ST111, ST166**

Rachel River (1987, C, 90m, PG-13)
Low-key drama of a Minnesota woman who lives in the title small town, eking out a living as a radio journalist. Pamela Reed stars, with Craig T. Nelson, James Olson, and Zeljko Ivanek. **DR10, DR26**

Racing With the Moon (1984, C, 108m, PG)
Nostalgic drama set in small California coastal town in the early 1940s about the romance between a poor boy and a servant's daughter he mistakenly thinks is wealthy. Sean Penn, Elizabeth McGovern, and Nicolas Cage star. **DR1, DR26**

Racket, The (1951, B&W, 88m, NR)
Film noir of a cop (Robert Mitchum) and gangster (Robert Ryan) squaring off. **MY1, ST107**

Racketeer (1929, B&W, 68m, NR)
A gangster tries to go straight for the love of a young woman. Robert Armstrong and Carole Lombard star. **ST92**

Rad (1986, C, 95m, PG)
Family drama centering on the world of BMX bike racing. Bill Allen is the kid with the hot wheels; Talia Shire, Ray Walston, and Jack Weston are the adults on the sidelines. **AC10, DR22, FA7**

Radio Days (1986, C, 85m, PG)
Woody Allen directed this affectionate portrait of New York in the early 1940s, when everyone listened to the nightly radio programs of adventure, romance, and mystery. Mia Farrow heads the large cast; Diane Keaton has a small role as a band singer. **CO5, CO6, CO8, DT1, ST79, XT9** *Highly Recommended*

Radio Ranch *see* Phantom Empire

Rafferty and the Gold Dust Twins (1975, C, 92m, PG)
A nerdy driving instructor is forced by a pair of kooky women to drive them from Los Angeles to New Orleans. Alan Arkin, Sally Kellerman, and Mackenzie Phillips star, with Harry Dean Stanton. **ST141, XT18**

Rage at Dawn (1955, C, 87m, NR)
Randolph Scott and his saddle buddies hunt down an outlaw gang. **ST136**

Rage of Angels (1983, C, 192m, NR)
Sidney Sheldon soaper about a lovely lawyer (Jaclyn Smith) torn between two lovers: a married politician (Ken Howard) and a mob lawyer (Armand Assante). Originally made for TV. **DR2**

Raggedy Man (1981, C, 94m, PG)
Sissy Spacek stars as a widow in a small Texas town during the 1940s who has a romance with a sailor (Eric Roberts) on leave. Sam Shepard costars. **DR10, DR26, ST139**

Raggedy Rawney, The (1988, C, 102m, NR)
Drama of an AWOL British soldier (Bob Hoskins) hiding out with Gypsies. Hoskins also directed. **ST72**

Raging Bull (1980, B&W/C, 129m, R)
Robert DeNiro won an Oscar for his portrayal of New York boxer Jake LaMotta, as brutal outside the ring as in it. With Cathy Moriarty, Joe Pesci, Nicholas Colasanto, and Theresa Saldana. Martin Scorsese directed; photographed by Michael Chapman and edited by Oscar winner Thelma Schoonmaker. **DR4, DR22, DT95, ST30, XT2, XT9** *Essential; Highly Recommended*

Ragtime (1981, C, 156m, PG)
Epic panorama of turn-of-the-century America, adapted from E.L. Doctorow bestseller. James Cagney, Mary Steenburgen, Howard E. Rollins, Jr., Elizabeth McGovern, and Mandy Patinkin head the cast. Milos Forman directed. **DR5, DT37, ST14**

Raid on Entebbe (1977, C, 150m, NR)
Drama about the July 4, 1976 rescue by Israeli commandos of hostages held in Uganda by terrorists. Charles Bronson and Peter Finch star. Originally made for TV. **DR6, ST12**

Raid on Rommel (1971, C, 99m, PG)
Richard Burton stars as the wily German commander in this World War II drama. **ST13**

Raiders of the Lost Ark (1981, C, 115m, PG)
Steven Spielberg's modern tribute to the old-fashioned movie serials, with Harrison Ford as the bullwhip-toting professor, Karen Allen as his companion, and plenty of hair-raising escapes and breath-taking chases. Available in a letterboxed format. **AC14, AC21, CU19, DT99, ST46** *Recommended*

Railroaded (1947, B&W, 71m, NR)
Gangster John Ireland makes life miserable for Sheila Ryan in this thriller. Directed by Anthony Mann. **DT69**

The Railrodder *see* Buster Keaton Rides Again/The Railrodder

Railway Children, The (1972, C, 102m, G)
From Britain, a family adventure about a trio of plucky children determined to clear their father of false charges of espionage. Dinah Sheridan and Bernard Cribbins star. **FA4**

Rain (1932, B&W, 93m, NR)
Joan Crawford and Walter Huston square off in this version of W. Somerset Maugham's tale of a lady of ill repute and a reform-minded preacher. **ST24**

Rain Man (1988, C, 140m, R)
Cross-country odyssey of two brothers (Dustin Hoffman, Tom Cruise), one a hustler, the other a long-institutionalized autistic savant. Oscar winner for Best Picture, Actor (Hoffman), and Director (Barry Levinson). **DR8, ST26, ST67, XT1, XT2, XT6, XT18** *Recommended*

Rain People, The (1969, C, 102m, R)
A housewife deserts her family and takes to the road for an odyssey of self-discovery. Francis Ford Coppola directed this drama starring Shirley Knight, James Caan, and Robert Duvall. **DR10, DT21, ST38, XT18**

Rainbow, The (1989, C, 112m, R)
D.H. Lawrence's story of young love awakening, focusing on a female character who later appeared in *Women in Love*. Sammi Davis stars, with, Paul McGann, Amanda Donohoe, Glenda Jackson, and David Hemmings. Co-written and directed by Ken Russell. **DR1, DR19, DR23, DT92, WR14**

Rainmaker, The (1956, C, 121m, NR)
Katharine Hepburn stars as a spinster living in a parched Southwest town who's wooed by a smooth-talking con man. (Burt Lancaster). **ST66, ST85**

Raintree County (1957, C, 168m, NR)
Elizabeth Taylor is the selfish Southern belle, Montgomery Clift the schoolteacher she ruins in this historical drama of the Confederacy. With Eva Marie Saint and Lee Marvin. **CL3, ST100, ST147**

Raise the Titanic! (1980, C, 112m, PG)
Big-budget version of bestselling novel about the salvage job of a lifetime, starring Jason Robards, with Richard Jordan, David Selby, and Alec Guinness. **ST60, ST129**

Raisin in the Sun, A (1961, B&W, 128m, NR)
Drama of black family life in Chicago, adapted from Lorraine Hansberry's play. Sidney Poitier, Claudia McNeil, Ruby Dee, and Louis Gossett, Jr. star. **DR8, DR14, DR20, ST121**

Raising Arizona (1987, C, 94m, PG-13)
A childless couple decide to kidnap one of a set of quintuplets in this frantic action comedy starring Nicolas Cage and Holly Hunter. **CO5, CO9, CO10, ST74**

Rambo: First Blood Part II (1985, C, 95m, R)
Sylvester Stallone is the Special Forces maverick with a mission: to free Americans still held captive in Vietnam. **AC4, AC25, ST140**

Rambo III (1988, C, 101m, R)
In this installment, John Rambo travels to Afghanistan to rescue his old commander from the Soviet invaders. Sylvester Stallone and Richard Crenna star. **AC25, ST140**

Ramparts of Clay (1971, C, 87m, PG)
French-produced drama, set in Tunisia, concerning a woman's involvement in a strike by villagers. Directed by Jean-Louis Bertucelli. **FF1**

Ramrod (1947, B&W, 94m, NR)
Western tale of a ranch owner (Veronica Lake) involved in a land dispute with her father (Charlie Ruggles). With Joel McCrea, Arleen Whelan, Don DeFore, and Preston Foster. **WE8**

Ran (1985, C, 161m, R)
A Japanese version of Shakespeare's King Lear, with samurai warriors, Oscar-winning costumes, and some of the greatest battle scenes ever filmed. Tatsuya Nakadai stars. Directed by Akira Kurosawa. **DT57, WR22** *Highly Recommended*

Rancho Notorious (1952, C, 89m, NR)
Cowboy Arthur Kennedy, seeking revenge for a murder, winds up at a strange hideout for outlaws run by Marlene Dietrich. Directed by Fritz Lang. **DT58, ST33, WE5, WE8, WE15**

Random Harvest (1942, B&W, 127m, NR)
Romantic drama of a wartime amnesia victim (Ronald Colman) and the woman (Greer Garson) whose love leads him to recovery. **CL4**

Ranger and the Lady, The (1938, B&W, 54m, NR)
Roy Rogers finds romance in the Old West. Gabby Hayes costars—not as the love interest! **ST132**

Rape and Marriage: The Rideout Case (1980, C, 96m, NR)
True story of the landmark court case in which a woman charged her estranged husband with rape. Mickey Rourke and Linda Hamilton star, with Rip Torn. Originally made for TV. **ST134, ST150**

Rape of Love (1977, C, 117m, NR)
French drama of a nurse who's sexually assaulted and then undergoes a worse ordeal in the criminal justice system. Nathalie Neil stars. **FF1**

Rapunzel (1983, C, 60m, NR)
The fairy tale of the girl with long flowing locks, presented by Faerie Tale Theatre. Shelley Duvall, Jeff Bridges, and Gena Rowlands star. **FA12, ST11**

Rare Breed, The (1966, C, 108m, NR)
James Stewart stars in this western drama; Maureen O'Hara can't decide between him and Brian Keith. **ST143**

Rashomon (1951, B&W, 88m, NR)
Classic Japanese drama of a criminal act in a forest and the various versions the story takes in the retelling. Toshiro Mifune stars. Akira Kurosawa directed. Winner of an Oscar for Best Foreign Language Film. **DT57, ST106, XT7** *Essential; Recommended*

Raven, The (1935, B&W, 62m, NR)
Boris Karloff and Bela Lugosi star in the bizarre tale of a mad doctor, who's obsessed with Edgar Allan Poe, and one of his victims. Not based on the Poe poem. **HO1, ST77, ST95**

Raven, The (1963, C, 86m, NR)
A trio of magicians square off in this horror comedy, starring Vincent Price, Peter Lorre, and Boris Karloff. With Jack Nicholson. Roger Corman directed. Very loosely based on Poe's famous poem. **DT22, ST77, ST112, ST124, WR21**

Ravishing Idiot (1965, B&W, 110m, NR)
Comedy about an inept crook who's out to steal some important NATO documents. Anthony Perkins and Brigitte Bardot star. **ST4**

Raw Deal (1986, C, 97m, R)
Arnold Schwarzenegger plays a special F.B.I. agent assigned to clean up Mob activity in Chiago as only he can. **AC25, ST135**

Razorback (1984, C, 95m, R)
A wild hog terrorizes the Australian outback. Gregory Harrison stars. **FF5, HO16**

Razor's Edge, The (1946, B&W, 146m, NR)
Tyrone Power stars in this version of the Somerset Maugham story of a man's disillusionment after his experiences in World War I. With Oscar winner Anne Baxter, Gene Tierney, and Clifton Webb. **DR19, XT5**

Razor's Edge, The (1984, C, 129m, PG-13)
Bill Murray plays it straight in this second screen version of the Somerset Maugham story of a man looking for inner peace. With Theresa Russell, Catherine Hicks, James Keach, and Denholm Elliott. **CO13, DR19**

Real Bruce Lee, The (1980, C, 108m, R)
Highlights of martial arts star Bruce Lee in action from four of his early films. **ST88**

Real Genius (1985, C, 108m, PG)
Comedy about a group of college whiz kids getting revenge on their professor for using their research for a death-dealing government project. Val Kilmer and William Atherton star. **CO2, CO4, CO18** *Recommended*

Real Life (1979, C, 99m, PG)
Pushy documentary filmmaker (Albert Brooks) invades home of typical family to make a movie about them. Brooks also directed this comedy, costarring Charles Grodin. **CO8, DT12, ST59** *Recommended*

Real Men (1987, C, 86m, R)
Jim Belushi and John Ritter star in this action comedy about a CIA agent and a civilian caught up in a dangerous game of international intrigue. **CO13**

Really Weird Tales (1986, C, 85m, NR)
Spoof of *Twilight Zone*-style TV shows, with three episodes starring John Candy, Martin Short, and Catherine O'Hara. **CO14, SF21**

Re-Animator (1985, C, 86m, NR)
Extremely gory horror film with cult following about a young doctor's experiments reviving the dead. Jeffrey Combs and Barbara Crampton star. (Also available in an R-rated version with some of the violence trimmed.) **CU4, CU7, HO18, HO20**

Reap the Wild Wind (1942, C, 124m, NR)
Adventure tale of 19th-century salvagers working off the Georgia coast, starring John Wayne, Ray Milland, and Paulette Goddard. Directed by Cecil B. DeMille. Oscar-winning special effects. **AC12, AC13, DT27, SF15, ST156**

Rear Window (1954, C, 112m, PG)
Classic Hitchcock thriller about a photographer spying on his neighbor, who may have murdered his wife. James Stewart and Grace Kelly star, with Thelma Ritter, Wendell Corey, and Raymond Burr. **DT46, MY11, ST82, ST143** *Essential; Highly Recommended*

Rebecca (1940, B&W, 130m, NR)
Daphne du Maurier story, directed by Alfred Hitchcock, about a young woman's marriage to a widower whose former wife dominates everything around them. Laurence Olivier and Joan Fontaine star, with Judith Anderson and George Sanders. Winner of the Best Picture Oscar. **DT46, ST116, WR5, XT1** *Essential*

Rebecca of Sunnybrook Farm (1938, B&W, 80m, NR)
Shirley Temple stars in this musical about a young radio star. Randolph Scott and Gloria Stuart add some romance. **ST136, ST148**

Rebel (1973, C, 80m, PG)
Sylvester Stallone plays a student radical in this drama made several years before his success with *Rocky*. **ST140**

Rebel (1986, C, 93m, R)
Matt Dillon is an American G.I. deserter adrift in World War II Australia. Bryan Brown costars in this drama. **FF5**

Rebel Rousers (1967, C, 78m, NR)
Low-budget melodrama about motor-cycle gangs, famous mainly for pre- stardom pairing of Jack Nicholson and Bruce Dern. With (Harry) Dean Stanton. **ST112, ST141**

Rebel Without a Cause (1955, C, 111m, NR)
Vintage l950s drama of misunderstood teens, with James Dean, Natalie Wood, and Sal Mineo a trio of outcasts. With Jim Backus, Corey Allen, Nick Adams, and Dennis Hopper. Directed by Nicholas Ray. **CL8, DR9, DT83, ST71** *Essential; Highly Recommended*

Reckless (1983, C, 93m, R)
Straight-arrow student Daryl Hannah falls for moody rebel Aidan Quinn. Stylish high school romance, directed by James Foley. **DR9**

Red Badge of Courage, The (1951, B&W, 70m, NR)
The classic Civil War story, adapted from Stephen Crane's novel, about a young soldier's initiation into the horrors of combat. Audie Murphy stars, with Bill Mauldin, John Dierkes, and Royal Dano. John Huston directed. **AC5, CL1, DT50**

Red Beard (1965. B&W, 185m, NR)
Toshiro Mifune stars as a crusty doctor who tries to impart his knowledge to a young, more kindly intern. Epic drama from director Akira Kurosawa. **DT57, ST106**

Red Dawn (1984, C, 114m, PG-13)
When Soviet-backed troops invade a small town in the American Southwest, a band of teenagers takes to the hills and wages a guerrilla war. Patrick Swayze and C. Thomas Howell star, with Powers Boothe, Ben Johnson, and Harry Dean Stanton. **AC20, ST141**

Red Desert (1964, C, 116m, NR)
Director Michelangelo Antonioni's drama of a woman alienated from modern urban life, on the brink of a breakdown. Monica Vitti and Richard Harris star. Outstanding photography by Carlo DiPalma. **DT3**

Red Dust (1932, B&W, 83m, NR)
Romantic triangle on a rubber plantation: Clark Gable has to pick between lusty Jean Harlow and demure Mary Astor. Classic romantic adventure, remade as

Mogambo. **AC13, AC14, ST49** *Highly Recommended*

Red Headed Stranger, The (1987, C, 108m, NR)
Willie Nelson stars in this western story based on his classic album about a preacher who swears revenge on an unfaithful wife. With Katharine Ross and Morgan Fairchild. **MU12, WE2, WE5**

Red Heat (1988, C, 106m, R)
Soviet cop and his Chicago counterpart team to catch a Russian drug dealer on the lam in the Windy City. Arnold Schwarzenegger and Jim Belushi star. Walter Hill directed. **AC9, CO13, DT45, ST135, XT11**

Red House (1947, B&W, 100m, NR)
Melodrama of simple farmer (Edward G. Robinson) and his fear of a certain house and its mysterious occupants. With Lon McAllister, Judith Anderson, Rory Calhoun, and Julie London. **ST130**

Red Lion (1969, C, 115m, NR)
Toshiro Mifune stars in an action drama about a soldier confronting the corrupt officials in his home town. **FF4, ST106**

Red Pony, The (1949, B&W, 89m, NR)
Drama of young boy's love for his horse and the escape it offers him from family problems. Adapted from the John Steinbeck novel. Robert Mitchum, Myrna Loy, and Peter Miles star. **DR19, FA5, ST94, ST107, WR25**

Red Pony, The (1973, C, 101m, NR)
Latest version of the Steinbeck story, starring Henry Fonda, Maureen O'Hara, Ben Johnson, and Clint Howard. Originally made for TV. **DR19, FA5, ST44, WR25**

Red River (1948, B&W, 133m, NR)
This classic cattle-drive story features John Wayne and Montgomery Clift as a feuding father and son. Directed by Howard Hawks. This video version includes footage restored from original release. **CU10, DT43, ST156, WE1** *Essential; Recommended*

Red River Valley *see* Man of the Frontier

Red Scorpion (1989, C, 102m, R)
Body builder Dolph Lundgren plays a Russian special services officer assigned

to kill the rebel leader of an African free-dom movement. **AC20, AC25**

Red Shoes, The (1948, C, 133m, NR)
Ballerina must choose between her de-voted lover and a hard-driving impressa-rio who knows "what's best" for her career. Director Michael Powell's film won Oscars for photography and art di-rection. Moira Shearer, Anton Walbrook, and Marius Goring star in this cult favor-ite. **CL6, CL7, CL9, DT81, MU3**

Red Sonja (1985, C, 89m, PG-13)
Arnold Schwarzenegger and Brigitte Niel-sen team up as warriors in a land of sacred talismans and magic. **AC18, ST135**

Red Sun (1972, C, 112m, R)
An international cast is featured in this western about a gunslinger and a samurai joining forces. Charles Bronson, Toshiro Mifune, and Ursula Andress star. **ST12, ST106**

Red Tent, The (1971, C, 121m, G)
Based on a true story, this adventure saga dramatizes an ill-fated 1928 expedition to the frozen Arctic led by General Nobile (Peter Finch). Sean Connery costars. **AC12, AC24, ST21**

Reds (1981, C, 195m, PG)
Epic story of John Reed, American jour-nalist and adventurer who chronicled the Mexican and Russian Revolutions. Star Warren Beatty won an Oscar for his di-rection; Diane Keaton, Jack Nicholson, Gene Hackman, and Oscar winner Mau-reen Stapleton head the supporting cast. Narrative is interspersed with interviews with "witnesses," contemporaries of Reed who offer their impressions of him. **DR4, ST5, ST61, ST79, ST112, XT5, XT6** *Recommended*

Reefer Madness (1936, B&W, 67m, NR)
Cheaply made melodrama warning audi-ence of the dangers of marijuana "addic-tion." A cult favorite at midnight show-ings in the 1960s. **CU1, CU11**

Reflections in a Golden Eye (1967, C, 108m, NR)
The dark side of life on a Southern mili-tary base, adpated from Carson Mc-Cullers' novel. Marlon Brando and Eliza-beth Taylor star, with Brian Keith, Julie Harris, and Robert Forster. John Huston directed. **DR3, DR19, DT50, ST10, ST147**

Reflections of Murder (1974, C, 100m, NR)
Remake of French thriller *Diabolique,* about a neglected wife and scorned mis-tress conspiring to murder a school-teacher. Tuesday Weld, Joan Hackett, and Sam Waterston star. Written by Wil-liam Levinson and Richard Link; origi-nally made for TV. **FF8, MY14**

Rehearsal for Murder (1982, C, 100m, NR)
Backstage mystery: star of new Broad-way show is killed on opening night. Rob-ert Preston and Lynn Redgrave star, with Patrick Macnee, Jeff Goldblum, and Wil-liam Daniels. Written by William Levin-son and Richard Link; originally made for TV. **MY12, ST56**

Reivers, The (1969, C, 107m, PG)
Comedy set in turn-of-the-century Mis-sissippi about a young boy's friendship with his family's ne'er-do-well chauffeur. Steve McQueen stars in this adaptation of the William Faulkner novel. **DR19, ST97, WR6**

Relentless (1989, C, 92m, R)
Judd Nelson stars in this thriller about a psychotic known as the Sunset Killer. With Leo Rossi and Robert Loggia. **MY13**

Rendez-vous (1985, C, 83m, R)
French drama of stage actress (Juliette Binoche) involved with a man (Lambert Wilson) who performs in a live sex act. With Jean-Louis Trintignant. Directed by André Techine; available in letterboxed format. **CU6, CU19, FF1**

Renegade Ranger (1938, B&W, 60m, NR)
Rita Hayworth plays a lady outlaw in this western, one of her early screen appear-ances. George O'Brien stars, with Tim Holt. **ST64, WE8**

Renegades (1989, C, 106m, R)
A cop on the trail of stolen diamonds joins forces with a Native American after the same man, who stole a spear sacred to his tribe. Kiefer Sutherland and Lou Dia-mond Phillips star. **AC9**

Rent-a-Cop (1988, C, 95m, R)
Burt Reynolds is the title character, Liza Minnelli the prostitute he's protecting from a serial killer. **ST128**

Repentance (1987, C, 151m, NR)
Soviet parable, an indictment of Stalin's repression, concerns a corpse in a cemetery in a village in Georgia. **FF7**

Repo Man (1984, C, 93m, R)
Offbeat comedy, with sci-fi undertones, about a punked-out kid falling in with a band of car repossessors in Los Angeles and learning the "repo" way of life. Emilio Estevez stars, with Harry Dean Stanton, Vonetta McGee, Sy Richardson, and Tracey Walter. **CO2, CO12, CU5, ST141, XT10** *Recommended*

Repos du Guerrier, Le (1962, C, 100m, NR)
Brigitte Bardot stars in this French drama about a woman involved with a suicidal lover. Directed by Roger Vadim. Also known as *Warrior's Rest*. **ST4**

Repulsion (1965, B&W, 105m, NR)
An unstable young woman, left alone in her sister's apartment, descends into madness. Catherine Deneuve stars in this disturbing psychological study from director Roman Polanski. **DT79, ST29** *Recommended*

Rescue, The (1988, C, 98m, PG)
A band of teens whose U.S. Navy fathers are being held captive in North Korea launch a mission to bring them home. Kevin Dillon, Marc Price, and Christina Howard star. **AC20**

Resurrection (1980, C, 102m, PG)
Ellen Burstyn plays a woman who recovers from an auto accident to learn that she has been endowed with powers of healing. A drama of faith and courage costarring Sam Shepard. **DR2**

Retreat, Hell! (1952, B&W, 95m, NR)
Korean War drama about U.S. withdrawal from the Changjin Reservoir, starring Frank Lovejoy, Richard Carlson, and Russ Tamblyn. **AC3**

Return Engagement (1978, C, 76m, NR)
A lonely professor (Elizabeth Taylor) falls in love with one of her students (Joseph Bottoms). **ST147**

Return From Witch Mountain (1978, C, 93m, G)
Bette Davis and Christopher Lee play kidnappers in this family adventure from the Disney studios. Sequel to *Escape From Witch Mountain*. **FA1, ST28, ST89**

Return of a Man Called Horse, The (1976, C, 129m, PG)
In this sequel to *A Man Called Horse*, Richard Harris again stars as the aristocrat who learns the ways of the Sioux Indians. **WE8**

Return of Captain Invincible, The (1983, C, 90m, PG)
A superhero who has turned into a broken-down drunk is persuaded to don his costume once again to save the world. Bizarre comedy, with musical numbers, stars Alan Arkin and Christopher Lee. **ST89**

Return of Chandu, The (1934, B&W, 206m, NR)
Serial starring Bela Lugosi as a mysterious magician who uses his powers to rescue a maiden from a cat-worshipping cult. **ST95**

Return of Frank James, The (1940, C, 92m, NR)
Henry Fonda plays the outlaw Jesse James's brother, looking to avenge his brother's murder. With Gene Tierney. Fritz Lang directed. **DT58, ST44, WE5**

Return of Martin Guerre, The (1982, C, 111m, PG-13)
French peasant disappears; years later a man (Gerard Depardieu) turns up, claiming to be the missing man. Nathalie Baye costars in this mystery based on a true story. **FF1, ST31**

Return of the Bad Men (1948, B&W, 90m, NR)
Randolph Scott has his hands full with outlaws including Billy the Kid (Dean White), The Sundance Kid, and The Dalton Gang. **HF1, ST136**

Return of the Dragon (1973, C, 91m, R)
Bruce Lee and Chuck Norris match kicks in this action drama about a Chinese in Rome protecting his family from mobsters. **ST88, ST114**

Return of the Fly (1959, B&W, 80m, NR)
Sequel to *The Fly* has son following in his father's footsteps to duplicate dangerous experiment, with dire results. Vincent Price stars. **HO20, ST124**

Return of the Jedi (1983, C, 133m, PG)
The third in the *Star Wars* trilogy finds
Luke Skywalker, Han Solo, and Princess
Leia teaming with the Ewoks to do battle
with Darth Vader and his minions. Harrison Ford, Mark Hamill, and Carrie Fisher
star, with Billy Dee Williams and James
Earl Jones as the voice of Darth Vader.
**FA8, SF11, SF13, SF23, ST46, ST76,
ST159**

Return of the Living Dead, The (1985, C,
91m, R)
Horror spoof, with plenty of gore, about
zombies terrorizing group of people
trapped in a mortuary. Clu Gulager and
James Karen star. **HO6, HO18, HO24**
Recommended

Return of the Pink Panther, The (1975, C,
113m, G)
The fourth installment in the comedy series about the bumbling Inspector Clouseau (Peter Sellers), as he matches what
few wits he has with a master thief (Christopher Plummer). Directed by Blake Edwards. **DT32, ST137**

Return of the Secaucus 7 (1980, C, 100m,
NR)
A reunion of 1960s pals who once got
arrested in New Jersey on their way to a
protest rally is the framework for this
entertaining, insightful comedy-drama.
John Sayles wrote, directed, and plays a
small role. **DR7, DT93** *Recommended*

Return of the Seven (1966, C, 96m, NR)
Sequel to *The Magnificent Seven* has Yul
Brynner rounding up a new collection of
cowboys (including Warren Oates, Robert
Fuller, and Jordan Christopher) to fight
more Mexican bandits. **ST115**

Return of the Soldier, The (1981, C, 101m,
NR)
Alan Bates stars as a World War I veteran
trying to put the pieces of his life back
together. Glenda Jackson, Julie Christie,
and Ann-Margret are the women who offer to help him. **DR5**

Return of the Vampire, The (1943, B&W,
69m, NR)
Bela Lugosi plays a Rumanian vampire
who's dead and buried in London—until
German bombs disturb his grave. Then
he's back to work, with the help of a
werewolf assistant. **HO5, ST95**

Return to Macon County (1975, C, 90m,
PG)
Action and supense down in Dixie, with
two young hotheads ready for hot rod
thrills. Don Johnson and Nick Nolte (in
his film debut) star. **AC10, ST113**

Return to Oz (1985, C, 109m, PG)
Dorothy, the brave heroine of the Oz
tales, goes back to the magic kingdom for
a new set of adventures. Fairuza Balk
stars, with Nicol Williamson, Jean Marsh,
and Piper Laurie. Imaginative special effects. **FA4, SF13**

Return to Snowy River, Part II (1988, C,
97m, PG)
Sequel to *The Man From Snowy River*,
with same young stars (Tom Burlinson,
Sigrid Thornton), same great wild horse
action and lovely Australian scenery.
AC12, FF5

Reuben, Reuben (1983, C, 101m, R)
Tom Conti stars in this wry comedy about
a lecherous poet who finds true, if temporary, love with a young woman (Kelly
McGillis). Adapted from the Peter DeVries novel by Julius Epstein. **CO1, DR19**
Recommended

Reunion in France (1942, B&W, 104m,
NR)
Drama starring John Wayne and Joan
Crawford, as they try to escape Nazi-occupied France. **ST24, ST156**

Revenge (1971, C, 78m, NR)
A vengeful mother (Shelley Winters) imprisons her daughter's rapist in a cage in
her home. Originally made for TV. **ST164**

Revenge (1990, C, 124m, R)
Kevin Costner plays an ex-Navy pilot
who falls in love with the young wife
(Madeline Stowe) of an old buddy (Anthony Quinn). The buddy's henchman
take violent action, and our hero comes
back for retribution. **AC19, ST23**

Revenge of the Dead (1960, B&W, 69m,
NR)
A "bad" horror movie classic, directed
by the legendary Ed Wood, Jr. Narrated
by the psychic Criswell—from a coffin.
And that's just for starters. Also known
as *Night of the Ghouls*. **CU11, DT118**

Revenge of the Nerds (1984, C, 90m, R)
Social outcasts at a university get revenge on the snooty fraternity that runs the school. Robert Carradine stars. **CO4, CO18**

Revenge of the Pink Panther, The (1978, C, 99m, PG)
Peter Sellers' final film as Inspector Clouseau has him in Hong Kong investigating his own murder. With Dyan Cannon, Herbert Lom, and Robert Webber. Directed by Blake Edwards. **DT32, ST137**

Revenge of the Zombies (1943, B&W, 61m, NR)
Low-budget horror film about a mad doctor (John Carradine), his zombie wife, and Nazis lurking in the background. **HO6**

Revolt of Job, The (1983, C, 97m, NR)
In Hungary, a Jewish couple adopt a Gentile boy in the shadow of the Holocaust. **FF7**

Revolution (1985, C, 123m, PG)
A lavishly produced drama about the American colonists' fight for independence from the British. Al Pacino, Nastassja Kinski, and Donald Sutherland star. **AC6, DR5, ST118**

Rhinestone (1984, C, 111m, PG)
Sylvester Stallone and Dolly Parton star in this comedy about a country singer's bet that she can turn a New York cabbie into a singing sensation. **CO8, ST140**

Rich and Famous (1981, C, 117m, R)
Jacqueline Bissett and Candice Bergen play friends/rivals over a 20-year period in this modern soap opera. Directed by George Cukor. **DR10, DT24**

Rich and Strange (1932, B&W, 92m, NR)
Early Hitchcock drama, produced in Great Britain, concerning a couple whose boredom is alleviated by a sudden inheritance. Henry Kendall and Joan Barry star. **DT46**

Rich Kids (1979, C, 101m, PG)
Two teenagers from wealthy New York families find comfort in their friendship as their parents' marriages break up. Trini Alvarado, Jeremy Levy, and John Lithgow star in this comedy-drama. **CO4**

Richard Pryor (concert films)
Live and Smokin' (1971, C, 47m, NR)
Live in Concert (1979, C, 78m, R)
Live on the Sunset Strip (1982, C, 82m, R)
Here and Now (1983, C, 83m, R)
Pryor's no-holds-barred monologues on race, sex, and life's crazy moments. **ST125**

Richard III (1956, C, 155m, NR)
Laurence Olivier directed and stars in this version of Shakespeare's tragedy of the misshapen British monarch and his political problems. This full-length version contains newly restored footage. **CU10, ST116, WR22**

Richard's Things (1980, C, 104m, R)
Liv Ullmann plays a widow who is seduced by her late husband's girl friend. English-language film shot in Great Britain. **ST154**

Ride in the Whirlwind (1966, C, 82m, NR)
A case of mistaken identity has three cowboys fleeing from the law in this cult western. Jack Nicholson and Harry Dean Stanton star. Monte Hellman directed. **ST112, ST141, WE15**

Ride, Ranger, Ride (1936, B&W, 56m, NR)
Gene Autry joins the cavalry and prevents an Indian war. **ST3**

Ride the High Country (1962, C, 94m, NR)
Two aging gunfighters agree to bring a shipment of gold from a mountain camp; one plans to persuade his buddy to steal it. Sam Peckinpah directed this elegiac western starring Joel McCrea and Randolph Scott (in his last movie), with Mariette Hartley, R.G. Armstrong, and Warren Oates. **DT77, ST136, WE11, XT22**
Essential; Highly Recommended

Rider on the Rain (1970, C, 115m, PG)
A woman is attacked by a mysterious stranger, whom she manages to kill—but there's another man following her, too. Charles Bronson stars in this thriller made in France. **FF1, MY3, ST12**

Riders of Death Valley (1941, B&W, 195m, NR)
Western serial about a trio of peacemakers patrolling a crime-riddled mining area. Buck Jones, Dick Foran, and Leo Carillo

star; Lon Chaney, Jr. heads the supporting cast. **ST17**

Riders of the Storm (1986, C, 92m, R)
A pair of loony Vietnam veterans (Dennis Hopper, Michael J. Pollard) run a pirate TV station from their vintage aircraft in this satirical comedy. **ST71**

Riders of the Whistling Pines (1949, B&W, 70m, NR)
Gene Autry rescues a girl about to be swindled out of her land. Jason Robards, Sr. and Clayton Moore (TV's Lone Ranger) costar. **ST3**

Ridin' Down the Canyon (1942, B&W, 62m, NR)
Roy Rogers thwarts a band of horse rustlers who are gumming up the war effort. With Gabby Hayes. **ST132**

Ridin' on a Rainbow (1941, B&W, 79m, NR)
In this western, Gene Autry spends almost as much time singing on a showboat as he does riding the range to nab some outlaws. **ST3**

Rififi (1954, B&W, 115m, NR)
Four French jewel thieves decide to pull off the ultimate caper, but there is immediate mistrust and suspicion in the gang. Directed by Jules Dassin. **FF1, MY16, MY18**

Right of Way (1983, C, 106m, NR)
Bette Davis and James Stewart play an elderly couple who decide to end their lives rather than suffer the indignities of age and illness. Originally made for cable TV. **DR11, ST28, ST143**

Right Stuff, The (1983, C, 193m, PG)
Epic saga of the first Americans in space, adapted from the Tom Wolfe bestseller. Sam Shepard stars as Colonel Chuck Yeager; the large cast also includes Dennis Quaid, Scott Glenn, Ed Harris, Levon Helm, Barbara Hershey, Fred Ward, Pamela Reed, and Jeff Goldblum. Photographed by Caleb Deschanel; directed by Philip Kaufman. **AC11, DR6, DT52, MU12, ST56** *Recommended*

Rikisha-Man (1958, B&W, 105m, NR)
From Japanese director Hiroshi Inagaki, a drama of urban life starring Toshiro Mifune. **ST106**

Rikky and Pete (1988, C, 107m, R)
Australian comedy about brother and sister misfits and their adventures in an isolated mining town. Directed by Nadia Tass; written and photographed by her husband, David Parker, who also designed Pete's wacky inventions. **FF5**

Ring of Bright Water (1969, C, 107m, G)
Family adventure about a man's friendship with his pet sea otter. Bill Travers and Virignia McKenna star. **FA4**

The Rink/The Immigrant (1917, B&W, 79m, NR)
Two Charlie Chaplin shorts. In the first, he plays a waiter in a wacky restaurant; in the second, he's a friendly immigrant who meets a young mother and her child on a boat to America. **DT18**

Rio Bravo (1959, C, 141m, NR)
A cult favorite of westerns fans, starring John Wayne, Dean Martin, and Rick Nelson as a trio trying to uphold the law in a small town. Directed by Howard Hawks. **CL14, CU13, DT43, MU12, WE15, ST156**

Rio Grande (1950, B&W, 105m, NR)
Life in a cavalry outpost in the days after the Civil War. John Wayne stars, with Maureen O'Hara, Ben Johnson, Harry Carey, Jr., and Victor McLaglen. John Ford directed. **DT36, ST156, WE4**

Rio Lobo (1970, C, 114m, G)
For Civil War veteran John Wayne, the war isn't over until he's dealt out his own brand of justice. Director Howard Hawks' last film. **DT43, ST156**

Riot in Cell Block 11 (1954, B&W, 80m, NR)
Classic prison drama of convicts taking over, using the press to convey their demands. Neville Brand stars. Don Siegel directed. **DR18, DT97** *Recommended*

Rip Van Winkle (1985, C, 48m, NR)
The classic tale of the world's greatest sleeper, presented by Faerie Tale Theatre. Harry Dean Stanton stars. Francis Ford Coppola directed. **DT21, FA12, ST141**

Ripping Yarns (series) (1979, C, 90m each, NR)
Three volumes (*Ripping Yarns, More Ripping Yarns*, and *Even More Yarns*) of parodies of schoolboy adventure tales, cre-

ated by Monty Python's Michael Palin and Terry Jones. **CO15**

Risky Business (1983, C, 99m, R)
Suburban Chicago high school student, left alone by traveling parents, becomes involved with call girl and her nasty pimp. Tom Cruise and Rebecca DeMornay star in this comedy with real bite. Written and directed by Paul Brickman; music by Tangerine Dream. **CO4, ST26, XT11** *Highly Recommended*

Rita, Sue and Bob Too (1986, C, 95m, R)
Raunchy British comedy about two teen babysitters involved in a *menage à trois* with the husband of the couple they work for. Siobahn Finneran, Michelle Holmes, and George Costigan star. **CO4, CO17**

Ritz, The (1976, C, 91m, R)
Farce about a man on the run hiding out in gay baths. Jack Weston, Rita Moreno, and Jerry Stiller star. Richard Lester directed. **DT62**

River, The (1951, C, 99m, NR)
Drama, adapted from a Rumer Godden novel, of English children growing up in India. Directed by Jean Renoir, with superb Technicolor cinematography by Claude Renoir. Patricia Walters, Nora Swinburne, and Adrienne Cori star. **CL9, DT86**

River, The (1984, C, 120m, PG-13)
A contemporary farm couple fight to save their land from developers, led by the woman's ex-boyfriend. Sissy Spacek, Mel Gibson, and Scott Glenn star. **DR7, ST53, ST139**

River Niger, The (1976, C, 105m, R)
The intertwined lives of a black family living in Harlem are dramatized in this film version of the award-winning play. James Earl Jones, Cicely Tyson, Glynn Turman, and Louis Gossett, Jr. star. **DR8, DR14, DR20, ST76**

River of No Return (1954, C, 91m, NR)
Western drama has Robert Mitchum caring for abandoned Marilyn Monroe in Indian-infested wilderness. With Tommy Rettig and Rory Calhoun. Directed by Otto Preminger. **DT82, ST107, ST108, WE8**

River's Edge (1987, C, 99m, R)
True-life drama about a group of alienated high school kids, one of whom murders his girl friend, none of whom will report the crime. Crispin Glover, Keanu Reeves, Ione Skye Leitch, and Dennis Hopper star. Directed by Tim Hunter. **DR9** *Recommended*

Road Games (1981, C, 100m, PG)
A trucker and a lovely hitch-hiker join forces to solve murders occurring on lonesome highways in the Australian outback. Stacy Keach and Jamie Lee Curtis star. **MY16**

Road House (1989, C, 114m, R)
Patrick Swayze plays a bouncer in the title location; Ben Gazzara is the town baddie. With Kelly Lynch and Sam Elliott. **AC25**

Road Runner vs. Wile E. Coyote: The Classic Chase (1985, C, 54m, NR)
A collection of superb cartoons, directed by Chuck Jones, about that lovable roadrunner and his inept adversary. **FA11** *Recommended*

Road to Bali (1952, C, 90m, NR)
Bing Crosby and Bob Hope hit the highway for the Far East, with Dorothy Lamour along for laughs and songs. **CL15, ST25, ST70**

Road to Eternity *see* Human Condition, Part II, The

Road to Rio (1947, B&W, 100m, NR)
Bob Hope and Bing Crosby are out to rescue Dorothy Lamour from her evil aunt (Gale Sondergaard). The Andrews Sisters show up for one number. **CL15, ST25, ST70**

Road to Salina (1971, C, 96m, R)
Drifter returns home to mother, proceeds to begin an affair with young girl who may be his sister. Offbeat thriller starring Robert Walker, Jr., Mimsy Farmer, and Rita Hayworth. **MY14, ST64**

Road to Utopia (1945, B&W, 90m, NR)
Bob Hope and Bing Crosby travel to Alaska in search of gold and Dorothy Lamour, not necessarily in that order. Robert Benchley offers color commentary. **CL15, ST25, ST70**

Road to Yesterday, The (1925, B&W, 136m, NR)
Cecil B. DeMille offers two romantic triangle stories, one present-day, the other from the 17th century, in this silent drama. **DT27**

Road Warrior, The (1982, C, 95m, R)
The second Mad Max adventure takes place in a post-apocalypse world where fuel is the most valuable commodity. Mel Gibson stars. The final chase sequence is a classic. Directed by George Miller. **AC10, AC24, AC25, FF5, ST53** *Highly Recommended*

Roadie (1980, C, 105m, PG)
A Texas beer truck driver aspires to meet his rock 'n' idol, Alice Cooper, in this zany comedy from director Alan Rudolph. Meat Loaf stars, with Kaki Hunter and Art Carney. Appearances by music stars Debby Harry & Blondie, Roy Orbison, Asleep at the Wheel, and Hank Williams, Jr. **CO8, DT91, MU9** *Recommended*

Roaring Twenties, The (1939, B&W, 104m, NR)
James Cagney and Humphrey Bogart trade punches and bullets in this classic saga of Prohibition and the gangsters who profited from it. **AC22, ST8, ST14** *Recommended*

Robbery (1967, C, 114m, NR)
Dramatic account of famous Great Train Robbery in 1963 Britain, starring Stanley Baker and Joanna Pettet. **MY8, MY15, MY18**

Robe, The (1953, C, 135m, NR)
Epic religious drama about the Roman centurion who carried out the execution of Christ. Richard Burton and Victor Mature star. **CL13, ST13**

Robert et Robert (1978, C, 105m, NR)
French comedy of friendship struck up by traffic cop and taxi driver while waiting for their respective computer dates. Charles Denner and Jacques Villeret star. Directed by Claude Lelouch. **FF1**

Robert Klein: Child of the 60s, Man of the 80s (1984, C, 60m, NR)
Comic monologues from the comedian who waxes nostalgic about those golden days of protest. **CO16**

Robert Klein on Broadway (1986, C, 60m, NR)
More comic observations about modern life from the stand-up comic. **CO16**

Roberta (1935, B&W, 105m, NR)
Fred Astaire and Ginger Rogers sparkle in this musical which features "Smoke Gets in Your Eyes" and "I Won't Dance." Irene Dunne and Randolph Scott costar. **CL15, ST2, ST131, ST136**

Robin and Marian (1976, C, 112m, PG)
The Robin Hood-Maid Marian story, continued: an aging Robin and Little John return from the Crusades to find that Marian has joined a convent. Sean Connery and Audrey Hepburn star, with Nicol Williamson and Robert Shaw. Richard Lester directed this bittersweet romance. **AC14, AC15, DR1, DT62, HF15, ST21, ST65** *Highly Recommended*

Robin and the Seven Hoods (1964, B&W, 103m, NR)
Gangster spoof starring Frank Sinatra and his Rat Pack pals (Dean Martin, Sammy Davis, Jr., et al.), plus Bing Crosby. Frank sings "My Kind of Town." Look fast for Edward G. Robinson. **ST25, ST130, ST138**

Robin Hood (1973, C, 83m, G)
Disney animated version of the classic tale, with animals playing the parts. **FA2, HF15**

Robin Hood and the Sorcerer (1983, C, 115m, NR)
Michael Praed stars as the legendary bandit of Sherwood Forest; here, his opponent is not the Sheriff of Nottingham, but a wicked magician. **AC18, HF15**

Robin Hood of Texas (1947, B&W, 71m, NR)
Gene Autry is accused of bank robbery and must clear his name to avoid the law. **ST3**

Robin Williams Live! (1986, C, 65m, NR)
From the famed stage of New York's Metropolitan Opera House comes this fast-paced, free-wheeling comic monologue from one of the funniest men alive. **CO16, ST160** *Highly Recommended*

Robinhood of the Pecos (1941, B&W, 56m, NR)
Roy Rogers plays a Confederate veteran battling Northern politicians. **ST132**

Robocop (1987, C, 96m, R)
In the Detroit of the future, a critically wounded policeman is transformed into an impervious robot, who goes after the crooks who assaulted him. Peter Weller and Kurtwood Smith star, with Nancy Allen, Ronny Cox, and Miguel Ferrer. **AC9, AC25**

Robot Monster (1953, B&W, 63m, NR)
Cult ''bad'' movie about an alien (actually, a gorilla with a diving helmet) terrorizing the last remaining family on Earth. **CU11**

Rocco and His Brothers (1960, B&W, 170m, NR)
Episodic account of the trials and tribulations of a poor family living in contemporary Milan. Luchino Visconti directed; the cast is headed by Alain Delon, Renato Salvatori, and Annie Girardot. Video version restores footage to film's original length. **CU10, DT108**

Rock Music With the Muppets (1985, C, 54m, NR)
The Muppets get down with Alice Cooper, Debbie Harry, Paul Simon, Linda Ronstadt, and Helen Reddy. **FA14**

Rock 'n' Roll High School (1979, C, 93m, PG)
Riff Randell, a student at Vince Lombardi High, would rather listen to punk group The Ramones than attend classes. This spoof of teen exploitation movies, directed by Allan Arkush, has become a midnight movie staple. P.J. Soles, Paul Bartel, Mary Woronov, Dey Young, Vincent Van Patten, and Clint Howard star. **CO7, CO18, CU1, DT4, DT5, MU9**

Rock, Pretty Baby (1956, B&W, 89m, NR)
High school rock band competes in a talent contest in this early rock musical. Sal Mineo, John Saxon, Rod McKuen, and Fay Wray star. **MU9**

Rock, Rock, Rock (1956, B&W, 83m, NR)
Tuesday Weld tries to raise money to buy a prom dress, but the story's a flimsy excuse to showcase a long list of rock and pop performers. Chuck Berry, Frankie Lymon and the Teeenagers, and La Vern Baker headline. **MU9**

Rocket Gibraltar (1988, C, 100m, PG)
Family drama centering on the 77th birthday celebration of a patriarch (Burt Lancaster). **DR8, ST85**

Rocket Ship X-M (1950, B&W, 77m, NR)
A spaceship is struck by a meteor and forced to land on Mars, where astronauts find a planet ravaged by nuclear war and inhabited by mutant monsters. One of the first postwar sci-fi films. Lloyd Bridges and Hugh O'Brian star. **SF1, SF3**

Rocky (series)
Rocky (1976, C, 119m, PG)
Rocky II (1981, C, 119m, PG)
Rocky III (1982, C, 99m, PG)
Rocky IV (1985, C, 91m, PG)
Sylvester Stallone plays Rocky Balboa, the prizefighter who rises from obscurity to the heavyweight championship in these four dramas. Talia Shire and Carl Weathers costar. First installment won Best Picture and Director (John G. Avildsen) Oscars. **DR22, ST140, XT1, XT6** *(Rocky only for last two lists)Essential (Rocky only)*

Rocky Horror Picture Show, The (1975, C, 95m, R)
Midnight movie favorite, a rock musical spoof of mad scientist movies. Tim Curry stars, with Susan Sarandon and Barry Bostnick. **CO7, CO12, CU1, CU5, MU9, MU16**

Rodan (1957, C, 70m, NR)
Fire-breathing creature threatens to incinerate Tokyo. **FF4, SF18**

Roe vs. Wade (1989, C, 100m, NR)
Holly Hunter and Amy Madigan star in this drama about the famous court case that legalized abortion. Originally made for TV. **DR6, DR10, ST74** *Recommended*

Roger and Me (1989, C, 90m, NR)
Documentary from filmmaker Michael Moore about the effect on his hometown of Flint, Michigan of a General Motors plant closing. Title refers to his efforts to reach GM chairman Roger Smith. **CU16**

Roger Corman: Hollywood's Wild Angel (1978, C, 58m, NR)
Documentary about the producer/director/talent maven who gave career starts to many great directors and made scores

of low-budget classics. Includes appearances by Corman alumni Martin Scorsese, Jonathan Demme, Allan Arkush, and Joe Dante. **CU16, DT22** *Recommended*

Rollerball (1975, C, 128m, R)
In the near-future, a corporate dictatorship puts on brutal "games" for the masses, and one contestant decides to defy the system. James Caan and John Houseman star. Directed by Norman Jewison. **DT51, SF11**

Rollercoaster (1977, C, 119m, PG)
Madman threatens to destroy popular amusement park ride. George Segal, Timothy Bottoms, and Henry Fonda star. **ST44**

Rolling Thunder (1977, C, 9m,R)
A Vietnam veteran swears revenge on the thugs who killed his family and mutilated him. William Devane and Tommy Lee Jones star in this violent action drama. **AC19**

Rolling Vengeance (1987, C, 92m, R)
Young trucker uses his monster rig to gain revenge on the slimeballs who killed his family and brutalized his girlfriend. Don Michael Paul and Ned Beatty star. **AC10, AC19**

Rollover (1981, C, 118m, R)
When a multimillionaire is murdered, his widow and a financial troubleshooter sort out the financial conspiracy that caused his death. Jane Fonda and Kris Kristofferson star. **DR24, MU12, ST45**

Roman Holiday (1953, B&W, 119m, NR)
Audrey Hepburn won an Oscar for her first starring role, as a princess on the run from stuffy royal life, in love with an American reporter (Gregory Peck). Directed by William Wyler. **DT119, ST65, ST119, XT3, XT17, XT21**

Roman Scandals (1933, B&W, 92m, NR)
Eddie Cantor dreams he's back in ancient Rome in this musical romp. Choreography by Busby Berkeley. **DT8**

Roman Spring of Mrs. Stone, The (1961, C, 104m, NR)
A middle-aged American actress in Rome falls in love with a young Don Juan in this adaptation of a Tennessee Williams short novel. Vivien Leigh and Warren Beatty star. **DR1, ST5, WR30, XT17**

Romance and Riches *see* Amazing Adventure

Romance on the Range (1942, B&W, 54m, NR)
Roy Rogers captures a gang of fur thieves as well as the heart of a lovely lady.**ST132**

Romancing the Stone (1984, C, 105m, PG)
A romance writer finds herself living out one of her stories when her sister is kidnapped in South America. Kathleen Turner and Michael Douglas star in this rousing romantic adventure. With Danny Devito and Zack Norman. Directed by Robert Zemeckis. **AC14, AC21, ST32, ST35, ST152** *Recommended*

Romantic Comedy (1983, C, 102m, PG)
Dudley Moore and Mary Steenburgen are a playwright team with a good professional relationship—but he's looking to get personal. **CO8, ST109**

Romantic Englishwoman, The (1975, C, 115m, R)
Romantic triangle involving a British novelist, his restless wife, and a German houseguest. Michael Caine, Glenda Jackson, and Helmut Berger star. Joseph Losey directed. **DR1, DR23, ST15** *Recommended*

Romeo and Juliet (1936, B&W, 126m, NR)
Classic Hollywood production of the Shakespeare tragedy, with Norma Shearer and Leslie Howard starring. **DR3, WR22**

Romeo and Juliet (1968, C, 138m, PG)
Director Franco Zeffirelli's version of Shakespeare's classic love story, with Leonard Whiting and Olivia Hussey the doomed young lovers. **DR3, WR22**

Romero (1989, C, 105m, PG-13)
Raul Julia plays El Salvador archbishop Oscar Romero, whose outspoken stand against repression earned him a martyr's death. **DR4, DR7**

Ronde, La (1950, B&W, 97m, NR)
Director Max Ophuls spins a romantic web about the interlocking lives and loves of a group of people in Vienna. **DT76, FF1** *Recommended*

Roof, The (1956, B&W, 98m, NR)
Italian drama from director Vittorio De Sica about a couple in postwar Rome looking for a home. **DT26, XT17**

Rooftops (1989, C, 98m, R)
Drama of contemporary gangs in New York living on the tops of buildings. Jason Gedrick stars. Directed by Robert Wise. **DT117, XT9**

Room, The (1987, C, 48m, NR)
A woman and her husband are threatened by the arrival of a strange couple who have been given their room. Linda Hunt stars, with Annie Lennox, Julian Sands, and Donald Pleasence. Written by Harold Pinter; directed by Robert Altman. **DT2, MU12**

Room Service (1938, B&W, 78m, NR)
The Marx Brothers play a trio of penniless producers trying to stay one step ahead of their creditors and their hotel management, which wants them evicted. **ST101**

Room With a View, A (1985, C, 115m, NR)
In the early 1900s, a young Englishwoman visits Florence, and despite her chaperone's best efforts, falls in love with a dashing Englishman. This adaptation of the E.M. Forster novel stars Helena Bonham Carter, Maggie Smith, Julian Sands, Denholm Elliott, and Daniel Day Lewis. **DR19**

Rooster Cogburn (1975, C, 107m, PG)
John Wayne recreates his Oscar-winning role from *True Grit* in this western romp with Katharine Hepburn. **WE2, ST66, ST156**

Rootin' Tootin' Rhythm (1938, B&W, 55m, NR)
Gene Autry and Smiley Burnette settle a range war before things get out of hand. **ST3**

Rope (1948, C, 80m, PG)
Hitchcock drama of two murderers who brazenly throw a party in the room where they've hidden the corpse. James Stewart plays the guest who unravels the crime. Farley Granger and John Dall costar. **DT46, MY9, MY11, ST143**

Rosalie Goes Shopping (1989, C, 96m, PG)
The star (Marianne Sagebrecht) and director (Percy Adlon) of *Bagdad Cafe* and *Sugarbaby* reunite for this comedy of a housewife who lives to shop. **CO2**

Rose, The (1979, C, 134m, R)
Bette Midler plays a rock singer whose hard-living lifestyle is about to catch up with her. With Alan Bates, Frederic Forrest, and Harry Dean Stanton. **DR12, MU4, MU9, ST105, ST141**

Rose Marie (1936, B&W, 110m, NR)
An opera singer (Jeanette MacDonald) searches for her brother (James Stewart) who is also being pursued by a Mountie (Nelson Eddy). The singer and the Mountie fall in love and sing "Indian Love Call." **CL15, MU1, ST143**

Roseanne Barr *see* HBO Comedy Club

Rosemary's Baby (1968, C, 136m, R)
The wife of a New York actor suspects that her pregnancy may not be normal. Mia Farrow, John Cassavetes, and Oscar winner Ruth Gordon star in this modern horror classic from director Roman Polanski. With Ralph Bellamy, Maurice Evans, and, in a small part, Charles Grodin. **DT79, HO10, HO11, HO19, ST59, XT5, XT9** *Highly Recommended*

Rough Cut (1980, C, 112m, R)
A jewel thief and a female agent from Scotland Yard fall in love in this caper comedy. Burt Reynolds and Lesley-Anne Downe star. Directed by Don Siegel. **CO10, DT97, ST128**

Rough Riders' Roundup (1939, B&W, 58m, NR)
Early Roy Rogers western, with plenty of action and some singing as well. Raymond Hatton plays Roy's sidekick. **ST132**

Round Midnight (1986, C, 132m, R)
In the 1950s, an American jazz musician moves to Paris, hoping to find and peace and respect. Based loosely on the lives of jazz greats Bud Powell and Lester Young, this drama stars saxophonist Dexter Gordon. Martin Scorsese has a small role. Directed by Bertrand Tavernier. **DR12, DT95, XT16** *Recommended*

Round-up Time in Texas (1937, B&W, 58m, NR)
One of Gene Autry's early films, featuring sidekick Smiley Burnette and the usual singing and light gunplay. **ST3**

Roustabout (1964, C, 110m, NR)
Elvis Presley musical has The King going to work in a carnival run by Barbara Stanwyck. **ST123, ST142**

Rowlf's Rhapsodies With the Muppets (1985, C, 56m, NR)
Bloopers from the popular TV show, with guests stars Steve Martin, Peter Sellers, Marisa Berenson, and George Burns. **FA14, ST99, ST137**

Roxanne (1987, C, 107m, PG)
In this modern remake of *Cyrano de Bergerac*, Steve Martin plays a small-town fire chief with two problems: a large nose and unrequited love for visiting astronomer Daryl Hannah. With Shelley Duvall and Rick Rossovich. **CO1, ST99** *Recommended*

Royal Wedding (1951, C, 93m, NR)
A brother and sister dance team (Fred Astaire, Jane Powell) perform in London during the wedding festivities of Princess Elizabeth and Prince Phillip. Directed by Stanley Donen. **DT30, MU1, ST2**

Ruby Gentry (1952, B&W, 82m, NR)
Jennifer Jones plays a Southern temptress who marries an older man to spite her real love (Charlton Heston) in this melodrama. Directed by King Vidor. **CL5, DT107**

Rude Awakening (1989, C, 100m, R)
Cheech Marin and Eric Roberts play a couple of refugees form the 1960s who are, like, stuck out of time in the greedy 1980s. With Julie Hagerty and Robert Carradine. **CO20, ST18**

Rude Boy (1980, C, 123m, NR)
Documentary-style drama of an English lad working as a roadie for rock band The Clash. Plenty of concert footage in this midnight movie favorite. **CU1, DR12**

Ruggles of Red Gap (1935, B&W, 92m, NR)
A butler finds that he has been won in poker game by a rude rancher in this comedy western. Charles Laughton stars. **WE14**

Rules of the Game (1939, B&W, 105m, NR)
Director Jean Renoir's classic study of the subtle relationship of the aristocratic class and their servants during a weekend in the country. Marcel Dalio, Nora Gregor, and Renoir star. **DT86** *Essential*

Ruling Class, The (1972, C, 154m, PG)
Zany British comedy about a wacky heir to British lordship (Peter O'Toole) who's convinced that he's Jesus Christ. Irreverent, to say the least, with a cult following. **CO17, CU5, ST117**

Rumblefish (1983, B&W, 94m, R)
Matt Dillon stars as a restless teen, coping with his alcoholic father (Dennis Hopper), idolizing his older brother (Mickey Rourke). Moody, stylized drama from director Francis Ford Coppola, based on a novel by S.E. Hinton. **DR9, DR19, DT21, ST71, ST134**

Rumpelstiltskin (1985, C, 60m, NR)
A Faerie Tale Theatre presentation of the classic story of a dwarf who forces a young maiden to spin gold out of straw. Shelley Duvall and Herve Villechaize star. **FA12**

Run of the Arrow (1957, C, 86m, NR)
A Confederate veteran decides to throw in with the Sioux Indians after the Civil War. Rod Steiger and Charles Bronson star. Samuel Fuller directed. **DT40, ST12, WE6, WE7**

Run Silent, Run Deep (1958, B&W, 93m, NR)
Submarine action during World War II, starring Clark Gable and Burt Lancaster as clashing officers. Directed by Robert Wise. **AC1, DT117, ST49, ST85**

Runaway (1985, C, 99m, PG-13)
Futuristic cops-and-robbers story about a mad inventor unleashing deadly robots on an unsuspecting policeman. Tom Selleck and Gene Simmons star. **MU12, SF6, SF17**

Runaway Barge, The (1975, C, 78m, NR)
A trio of hard-living guys try to eke out a living as riverboat men in modern society. Bo Hopkins, Tim Matheson, and Nick Nolte star. Originally made for TV. **ST113**

Runaway Train (1985, C, 112m, R)
Two escaped convicts (Jon Voight and
Eric Roberts) are trapped aboard a speeding train whose engineer has died of a
heart attack. Shot on location in the Alaskan wilderness. With Rebecca De-
Mornay. **AC24, XT19**

Runner Stumbles, The (1979, C, 99m, PG)
A middle-aged priest is attracted to a
young nun, who winds up murdered.
Dick Van Dyke and Kathleen Quinlan
star. **DR3, DT55**

Running Brave (1983, C, 106, PG)
True story of Billy Mills, the native Amer-
ican who ran for a Gold Medal in the 1964
Olympics. Robby Benson stars. **DR22**

Running Man (1987, C, 101m, R)
Arnold Schwarzenegger plays a cop of
the future who's sentenced by the dictatorship to be a contestant on a deadly
quiz show—a test of skill only the strong-
est survive. **SF11, ST135**

Running on Empty (1988, C, 16m, PG)
A teenager with ambitions to become a
music student is torn by loyalty to his
fugitive parents, former antiwar activists
still purused by the F.B.I. River Phoenix
stars, with Christine Lahti, Judd Hirsch,
and Martha Plimpton. Directed by Sidney
Lumet. **DR7, DR8, DT65**

Running Out of Luck (1986, C, 88m, R)
Mick Jagger stars in this musical adven-
ture, based on songs from his album,
She's the Boss. Shot in South America,
it's about a rock star abandoned and left
for dead. With Dennis Hopper, Jerry
Hall, and Rae Dawn Chong. Directed by
Julien Temple. **MU9, ST71**

Running Scared (1986, C, 106m, R)
Chicago cops Billy Crystal and Gregory
Hines are ready to retire to Florida—but
they'd like to nab just one more scumbag
in this action comedy. **AC9, CO3, CO9,
CO13, XT11**

Running Wild (1927, B&W, 68m, NR)
Silent comedy starring W.C. Fields as his
usual put-upon family man. **CL11, ST41**

**Russians Are Coming! The Russians Are
Coming!, The** (1966, C, 120m, NR)
When a Russian submarine runs aground
off the New England coast, the locals are
thrown into total panic. Satirical comedy

about the Cold War stars Alan Arkin,
Brian Keith, Carl Reiner, and Jonathan
Winters. Directed by Norman Jewison.
CO2, DT51

Rust Never Sleeps (1979, C, 103m, NR)
Concert film featuring rocker Neil Young
and his band, Crazy Horse. Songs include
"Down by the River" and "My, My,
Hey, Hey." **MU10**

Rustler's Rhapsody (1985, C, 88m, PG)
Tom Berenger stars as Rex O'Herlihan,
the last of the singing cowboys in this
comedy. With Andy Griffith and Marilu
Henner. **CO7, WE14**

Ruthless Four, The (1968, C, 96m, NR)
Western drama about four partners in a
gold mine, starring Van Heflin, Gilbert
Roland, Klaus Kinski, and George Hilton. **ST83**

Ruthless People (1986, C, 93m, R)
A desperate couple kidnap a wealthy businessman's wife just as he's about to
bump her off so that he can run off with
his mistress, who is two-timing him.
Frantic comedy starring Bette Midler and
Danny DeVito, with Judge Reinhold, Helen Slater, Anita Morris, and Bill Pullman. **CO10, ST32, ST105**

Rutles, The *see* All You Need Is Cash

Ryan's Daughter (1970, C, 176m, R)
In Northern Ireland, a young woman
trapped in a loveless marriage to a middle-aged schoolteacher embarks on a
scandalous affair with a British soldier.
Sarah Miles, Robert Mitchum, and Christopher Jones star, with Oscar winner
John Mills and Trevor Howard. Directed
by David Lean; photographed by Fred A.
Young. **DR3, DT59, ST107, XT4**

S.O.B. (1981, C, 121m, R)
Broad lampoon of modern Hollywood,
with frantic director trying to talk his
actress wife into doing a nude scene to
rescue his latest bomb. Blake Edwards
wrote and directed; the cast includes Julie
Andrews, William Holden (in his last
film), Robert Preston, Richard Mulligan,
Shelley Winters, and Robert Vaughn.
CO8, DT32, ST68, ST164, XT22 *Highly
Recommended*

S.O.S. Coastguard (1937, B&W, 195m, NR)
Serial adventure about a Coast Guard commander who must stop a mad scientist (Bela Lugosi) from delivering a disintegrating gas to enemies of America. **ST95**

Sabotage (1936, B&W, 76m, NR)
Early Alfred Hitchcock thriller has a woman suspecting that her husband is secretly a mad bomber terrorizing London. Sylvia Sidney and Oscar Homolka star. **DT46, MY6, MY15**

Saboteur (1942, B&W, 108m, NR)
Robert Cummings plays the typical Alfred Hitchcock hero: the man accused of a crime he didn't commit, in this case, sabotage in the munitions industry. Classic finale atop the Statue of Liberty. **DT46, MY6, MY7, XT9, XT18**

Saboteur: Code Name Morituri *see* Morituri

Sabrina (1954, B&W, 113m, NR)
Audrey Hepburn is a chauffeur's daughter romanced by two brothers, played by Humphrey Bogart and William Holden. Sparkling comedy directed by Billy Wilder. **CL4, DT116, ST8, ST65, ST68** *Recommended*

Sacco and Vanzetti (1971, C, 120m, PG)
The story of the infamous trial of two Italian anarchists in the 1920s, with the worldwide protests that arose over their conviction and execution. Gian Maria Volonte stars. **FF2**

Sacketts, The (1979, C, 200m, NR)
Western drama, adapted from two novels by Louis L'Amour, about a trio of brothers (Sam Elliott, Tom Selleck, Jeff Osterhage) making their fortunes on the post-Civil War frontier. Originally made for TV. **WR13**

Sacrifice, The (1986, C, 145m, NR)
Soviet director Andrei Tarkovsky's final film, produced in Sweden, deals with nuclear annihilation and the choices it forces on an aging intellectual. Erland Josephson stars. **FF7**

Sadie Thompson (1928, B&W, 97m, NR)
Silent version of W. Somerset Maugham's story, "Rain," with Gloria Swanson as the woman of ill repute, Lionel Barrymore as the upright minister. Written,

directed, and costarring Raoul Walsh. **CL12**

Safari 3000 (1982, C, 91m, PG)
Action in the wilds of Africa, as an ex-stuntman tries to win an international car race. David Carradine stars, with Stockard Channing and Christopher Lee. **AC10, ST89**

Safety Last *see* Harold Lloyd

Saga of Death Valley (1939, B&W, 56m, NR)
Roy Rogers battles an outlaw with a hidden identity. With Gabby Hayes and Don "Red" Barry. **ST132**

Saga of the Vagabonds, The (1959, C, 115m, NR)
Japanese adventure drama of a band of bandits distributing money to overtaxed peasants. Toshiro Mifune stars. **ST106**

Saginaw Trail (1953, B&W, 56m, NR)
Gene Autry and old pal Smiley Burnette are reunited for this tuneful western. **ST3**

Sahara (1943, B&W, 97m, NR)
During World War II, an Allied battalion is stranded in the desert without supplies or hope of reinforcements. Humphrey Bogart and Dan Duryea star. **ST8**

The Saint (series)
The Saint in New York (1938, B&W, 71m, NR)
The Saint in London (1939, B&W, 72m, NR)
The Saint Strikes Back (1939, B&W, 67m, NR)
The Saint Takes Over (1940, B&W, 69m, NR)
The Saint's Vacation (1941, B&W, 60m, NR)
Series of detective films based on the debonair sleuth created by Leslie Charters. Louis Hayward plays the lead in *New York,* Hugh Sinclair in *Vacation;* George Sanders stars in the other films. Note: *The Saint Strikes Back* is packaged with a second feature, *Criminal Court;* see separate entry. **HF21**

St. Elmo's Fire (1985, C, 107m, R)
Melodramatic look at a group of friends fresh out of Georgetown University, trying to get on with their lives. Andrew McCarthy, Ally Sheedy, Rob Lowe, Demi Moore, Judd Nelson, Emilio Es-

tevez, and Mare Winningham star. **DR7, XT12**

St. Ives (1976, C, 94m, PG)
A writer (Charles Bronson) becomes a pawn in a millionaire's international conspiracy plot. With John Houseman and Jacqueline Bisset. **ST12**

Saint Joan (1957, B&W, 110m, NR)
The life of the French martyr (Jean Seberg), adapted from the George Bernard Shaw play. With John Gielgud, Richard Widmark, and Anton Walbrook. Written by Graham Greene; directed by Otto Preminger. **DR4, DR20, DT82**

St. Valentine's Day Massacre (1967, C, 100m, NR)
Jason Robards portrays Al Capone in this recreation of the events leading up to the famous gangster massacre. With George Segal. Roger Corman directed. **AC22, DT22, ST129**

Sakharov (1984, C, 118m, NR)
Drama about the Soviet scientist and dissident who was imprisoned for many years for defying authorities. Jason Robards and Glenda Jackson star. Originally made for cable TV. **DR6, ST129**

Salaam Bombay! (1988, C, 114m, NR)
Drama of a 10-year-old orphan living by his wits on the streets of Bombay. Directed by Mira Nair **FF7**

Salamander, The (1981, C, 101m, NR)
Political intrigue in Italy, as a band of neo-Fascists plot a coup. Franco Nero stars, with Anthony Quinn, Martin Balsam, Christopher Lee, and Claudia Cardinale. Based on Morris West's novel. **ST89, MY6**

Salem's Lot (1979, C, 112m, PG)
A sinister antiques dealer (James Mason) is the protector of a vampire who takes over a small New England village. It is up to a writer (David Soul) and a teenager (Lance Kerwin) to stop him. Based on the Stephen King novel; directed by Tobe Hooper. A shorter version of the movie made originally for TV, with violent scenes added. **CU10, DT47, HO5, ST102, WR12**

Salesman (1969, B&W, 88m, NR)
Influential documentary, shot in cinema verite style, about a group of bible sales-

men. Directed by Albert and David Maysles. **CU16** *Essential; Recommended*

Sally of the Sawdust (1925, B&W, 91m, NR)
Silent comedy starring W. C. Fields as a con man with a soft heart for a young girl who is an outcast of polite society. Directed by D.W. Griffith. **DT42, ST41**

Salome (1953, C, 103m, NR)
Biblical drama with Rita Hayworth as the title dancer, Stewart Granger as John the Baptist. With Charles Laughton and Judith Anderson. **CL13, ST64**

Salome's Last Dance (1988, C, 90m, R)
Outrageous depiction of imagined night in the life of notorious playwright Oscar Wilde, as a theatrical troupe performs the title play in a brothel before its author. Directed by Ken Russell. Glenda Jackson stars, with Nicholas Grace as Wilde. **DT92**

Salt of the Earth (1953, B&W, 94m, NR)
Cult drama of New Mexico miners' strike, made when the director and major stars were blacklisted in Hollywood during the Red Scare. Will Geer stars. Herbert Biberman directed. **CU9**

Salute to Chuck Jones, A (1985, C, 57m, NR)
The Oscar-winning creator of Wile E. Coyote, the Road Runner, and Pepe Le Pew is showcased in eight cartoons, including the classics *For Scentimental Reasons, One Froggy Evening,* and *What's Opera, Doc?* **FA11** *Highly Recommended*

Salute to Friz Freleng, A (1985, C, 57m, NR)
The veteran animator, winner of six Academy Awards, is represented here by eight of his major Warner Bros. cartoons, including *Birds Anonymous, Speedy Gonzales,* and *Knighty Knight Bugs.* **FA11**

Salute to Mel Blanc, A (1985, C, 58m, NR)
Mel, the man of more than 400 voices, is at his most vocal in the eight cartoons in this compilation, including *Robin Hood Daffy, Bad Ol' Putty Tat,* and *The Rabbit of Seville.* **FA11** *Recommended*

Salvador (1985, C, 123m, R)
American journalist and his wacked-out buddy travel to El Salvador in search of a

story and cheap thrills; they get both as they witness the horrors of civil war raging there. Powerful performance by James Woods; James Belushi and John Savage costar. Written and directed by Oliver Stone. **CO13, DR7, DT102, ST165** *Recommended*

Salvation (1986, C, 80m, R)
Offbeat, timely comedy about a lustful preacher (Stephen McHattie) whose financial empire is threatened by blackmailers. Directed by Beth B. **CO12**

Sammy and Rosie Get Laid (1987, C, 100m, NR)
Drama set in contemporary London about a Pakistani whose son and daughter-in-law are caught up in political and sexual escapades. Shashi Kapoor, Frances Barber, Claire Bloom, and Ayub Khan Din star. Written by Hanif Kureishi; directed by Stephen Frears. **DR23, XT15**

Sam's Song *see* The Swap

Samson and Delilah (1949, C, 128m, NR)
Cecil B. DeMille's Biblical spectacular about the strongman and his downfall at the hands of a temptress. Victor Mature and Hedy Lamarr star, with George Sanders, Angela Lansbury, and Henry Wilcoxon. Spectacular finale. **CL13, DT27**

Samurai *see* The Seven Samurai

Samurai Saga (1959, C, 112m, NR)
Swordplay and a romantic triangle are the ingredients of this Japanese action drama, starring Toshiro Mifune and Yoko Tsukasa. Hiroshi Inagaki directed. **FF4, ST106**

Samurai Trilogy, The
Samurai I (1955, C, 92m, NR)
Samurai II (1955, C, 102m, NR)
Samurai III (1956, C, 102m, NR)
Epic adventure story of Musashi Miyamoto, a warrior who must come to grips with defeat before he can taste true victory. Toshiro Mifune stars. Hiroshi Inagaki directed. **FF4, ST106**

San Francisco (1936, B&W, 116m, NR)
Clark Gable, Spencer Tracy, and Jeanette MacDonald star in this lavish portrait of early 20th-century San Francisco. Highlight is recreation of the infamous earthquake of 1906. **AC13, AC23, CL3, ST49, ST151**

Sand Pebbles, The (1966, C, 179m, NR)
Steve McQueen is an American sailor assigned to a U.S. gunboat anchored in the Yangtze River during the 1926 Chinese Revolution. Candice Bergen, Richard Crenna, and Richard Attenborough costar in this epic adventure, directed by Robert Wise. **AC6, DT117, ST97** *Recommended*

Sandpiper, The (1965, C, 116m, NR)
A free-spirited artist (Elizabeth Taylor) and married minister (Richard Burton) have an affair. Theme song "The Shadow of Your Smile" won an Oscar. With Eva Marie Saint and Charles Bronson. Directed by Vincente Minnelli. **CL15, DT71, ST12, ST13, ST147**

Sands of Iwo Jima, The (1949, B&W, 110m, NR)
John Wayne earned an Oscar nomination for his portrayal of a tough Marine sergeant whose men are responsible for the recapturing of a strategic island during World War II. **AC1, ST156**

Sanjuro (1962, B&W, 96m, NR)
Sequel to *Yojimbo* follows further adventures of scruffy samurai sword-for-hire (Toshiro Mifune). Akira Kurosawa directed. **DT57, ST106**

Sanshiro Sugata (1943, B&W, 82m, NR)
Debut of Japanese director Akira Kurosawa, with the story of a youth trained in the art of judo matched against a jujitsu master. **DT57**

Sansho the Bailiff (1954, B&W, 132m, NR)
Classic drama of Japanese family broken up by a feudal lord and how the son and daughter struggle for survival in a slave labor camp. Directed by Kenji Mizoguchi. **FF4**

Santa Claus, The Movie (1985, C, 112m, PG)
This comedy about St. Nick has an evil toymaker out to steal away his business. David Huddleston plays the title role; John Lithgow and Dudley Moore costar. **FA13, ST109**

Santa Fe Trail (1940, B&W, 110m, NR)
Civil War Western dramatizing the pursuit of fanatic John Brown, played by

Raymond Massey. Errol Flynn and Olivia de Havilland star, with Ronald Reagan as George Armstrong Custer and Charles Middleton as Abraham Lincoln. **HF6, HF18, ST43, WE6**

Saps at Sea (1940, B&W, 57m, NR)
Laurel and Hardy comedy, with Ollie trying to relax on a boat trip, Stanley making his life miserable. **ST87**

Saturday Night Fever (1977, C, 119m, R)
A working class Brooklyn youth (John Travolta) becomes the dancing king at the local disco on Saturday nights. With Karen Lynn Gorney, Barry Miller, and Donna Pescow. Also available in a PG-rated version. **DR15, MU3, XT9***Essential*

Saturn 3 (1980, C, 88m, R)
Two research scientists (Farrah Fawcett, Kirk Douglas) create a Garden of Eden on their outpost. Their ideal life is threatened when a strange man (Harvey Keitel) and his killer robot arrive. Directed by Stanley Donen. **DT30, SF3, SF6, ST34**

Satyricon (1970, C, 129m, R)
Director Federico Fellini's lavish look at the decadence of ancient Rome, starring Martin Potter and Hiram Keller as a pair of pleasure-seeking young men. Also known as *Fellini Satyricon.* Available in a letterboxed edition. **CU19, DT53**

Savage Sam (1963, C, 103m, NR)
In this sequel to *Old Yeller,* two brothers are kidnapped by Indians and their father sets out to rescue them. Brian Keith and Tommy Kirk star. **FA1**

Savage Streets (1984, C, 93m, R)
A nice high school girl turns vigilante to avenge the rape of her sister. Linda Blair stars. **AC8**

Savannah Smiles (1982, C, 107m, PG)
A little runaway hooks up with two criminals and through her love she reforms them. Mark Miller and Donovan Scott star. **FA7**

Save the Tiger (1973, C, 101m, R)
Oscar-winning performance by Jack Lemmon highlights this drama of a dress manufacturer disillusioned with his life, longing for the sweet pleasures of his youth. With Jack Gilford. **DR24, ST90, XT2**

Sawdust and Tinsel (1953, B&W, 92m, NR)
A romantic triangle, set in a traveling circus, is the basis for director Ingmar Bergman's observations on life and love. Also known as *The Naked Night.* **DT7**

Say Amen, Somebody (1983, C, 100m, G)
Documentary celebrating gospel music and its two guiding lights, Rev. Thomas Dorsey and Willie Mae Ford Smith. **CU16** *Recommended*

Say Anything (1989, C, 100m, PG-13)
Romantic comedy-drama of an energetic high school senior (John Cusack) who woos the class valedictorian (Ione Skye), despite the misgivings of her father (John Mahoney). Written and directed by Cameron Crowe.**CO1, CO4** *Recommended*

Sayonara (1957, C, 147m, NR)
Romance blossoms between an Air Force pilot and a Japanese entertainer in this version of James Michener's novel. Marlon Brando and Miiko Taka star, with Oscar winners Red Buttons and Miyoshi Umeki. **ST10, XT4, XT5**

Scalpel (1976, C, 96m, R)
A plastic surgeon, desperate for a family inheritance, transforms a young woman into the image of his late daughter. Robert Lansing stars. **MY14**

Scalphunters, The (1968, C, 102m, NR)
Comic western about a rascal (Burt Lancaster) and his educated slave (Ossie Davis). With Telly Savalas and Shelley Winters. Directed by Sydney Pollack. **DT80, ST85, ST164, WE14**

Scandal (1989, C, 105m, R)
True-life story of the John Profumo—Christine Keeler affair which rocked 1963 Britain and helped bring down that country's Conservative government. John Hurt, Joanne Whalley-Kilmer, Bridget Fonda, and Ian McKellen star. Also available in an unrated version; running time: 115m. **CU10, DR6, DR21, DR23** *Recommended*

Scandalous (1983, C, 93m, PG)
Comic thriller starring Robert Hays as a nosy reporter up to his ears in spies and skullduggery. Pamela Stephenson and John Gielgud costar. **MY17**

Scanners (1981, C, 102m, R)
A small group of people have the ability to read minds; one uses his power for evil and kills innocent people by making their heads explode. A good scanner tracks the evil one to stop him. Cult horror film directed by David Cronenberg. **CU4, CU7, DT23, HO7**

Scaramouche (1952, C, 110m, NR)
Swashbuckler classic, with Stewart Granger as the 18th-century swordsman memorably dueling with villainous Mel Ferrer. With Eleanor Parker and Janet Leigh. **AC13, FA4**

Scarecrow (1973, C, 115m, R)
Gene Hackman and Al Pacino play a pair of drifters in this episodic comedy-drama with Dorothy Tristan, Eileen Brennan, and Ann Wedgeworth. **ST61, ST118, XT18**

Scared to Death (1947, C, 65m, NR)
All those who accuse a woman (Joyce Compton) of murder wind up dead. Bela Lugosi stars. **ST95**

Scarface (1932, B&W, 90m, NR)
Paul Muni stars as a gangster whose career is loosely based on Al Capone. With Boris Karloff, George Raft, and Ann Dvorak. Ben Hecht wrote and Howard Hawks directed this classic. **AC22, DT43, ST77** *Essential; Highly Recommended*

Scarface (1983, C, 170m, R)
Remake and updating of classic gangster drama, with Al Pacino a Cuban immigrant rising to the top of the Miami drug trade. With Michelle Pfeiffer, Steven Bauer, Mary Elizabeth Mastrantonio, F. Murray Abraham, and Robert Loggia. Exceptionally violent film directed by Brian De-Palma. **AC22, CU7, CU18, DT29, ST118, ST120**

Scarlet and the Black, The (1983, C, 155m, NR)
During World War II, a Vatican official (Gregory Peck) tries to protect POWs from a sadistic Nazi commandant (Christopher Plummer). Originally made for TV. **ST119**

Scarlet Claw, The (1944, B&W, 74m, NR)
Sherlock Holmes mystery set in Canada, involving the gruesome murder of a noblewoman. Basil Rathbone and Nigel Bruce star. **HF14**

Scarlet Letter, The (1980, C, 90m, NR)
German director Wim Wenders' version of the classic Hawthorne tale of sin and redemption. **DT113**

Scarlet Pimpernel, The (1934, B&W, 96m, NR)
A British aristocrat becomes the savior of French royalty during the French Revolution. Leslie Howard and Merle Oberon star. **AC13, FA4**

Scarlet Street (1945, B&W, 103m, NR)
A meek, middle-aged man is seduced into a life of crime by a shady lady and her no-good boyfriend. Edward G. Robinson, Joan Bennett, and Dan Duryea star. Fritz Lang directed this classic thriller. **DT58, MY1, MY4, ST130** *Recommended*

Scars of Dracula (1970, C, 94m, R)
A man and woman must fight the legendary Dracula (Christopher Lee) while searching for the man's missing brother. **HF7, HO5, HO26, ST89**

Scene of the Crime (1986, C, 90m, NR)
An escaped convict kidnaps a young boy and forces the child's mother to help him hide from the police. Catherine Deneuve stars in this French-made thriller. **ST29**

Scenes From a Marriage (1973, C, 168m, NR)
Director Ingmar Bergman's portrait of a marriage in crisis, starring Liv Ullmann and Erland Josephson. Originally made for Swedish TV and edited into a theatrical film by the director. **DT7, ST154**

Scenes From the Class Struggle in Beverly Hills (1989, C, 102m, R)
Comedy from cult director Paul Bartel concerning the sexual appetites of the filthy rich and their servants in a Southern California community. Jacqueline Bisset, Ray Sharkey, Robert Beltran, and Mary Woronov star, with Ed Begley, Jr., Wallace Shawn, Paul Mazursky, and Bartel. **DT5**

Schizoid (1980, C, 91m, R)
A psychiatrist's female patients are being killed. The killer tells an advice columnist of the murders and threatens her. Klaus Kinski and Marianne Hill star. **HO9, ST83**

School Daze (1988, C, 120m, R)
One-of-a-kind film, set in an all-black college, combines comedy and drama with

musical numbers to cover variety of subjects, mainly racial identity. Spike Lee wrote and directed and stars as a young fraternity pledge. Uneven, but rewarding for its best segments. **CO2, CO18, DR14, DT60** *Recommended*

Scott of the Antarctic (1948, C, 110m, NR)
An account of the fateful Robert Scott expedition to the South Pole. John Mills stars, with Derek Bond and Christopher Lee. **CL3, ST89**

Scream and Scream Again (1970, C, 95m, PG)
A mad scientist attempts to create a master race of unemotional beings. Vincent Price, Christopher Lee, and Peter Cushing star. **HO20, HO26, ST27, ST89, ST124**

Scream of Fear (1961, B&W, 81m, NR)
A wheelchair-bound young woman (Susan Strasberg) visits her father's Riviera villa, only to be told he's away. When she catches glimpses of his corpse, she begins to suspect her stepmother (Ann Todd) of foul play. British thriller costars Christopher Lee. **MY3, MY15, ST89**

Screamers (1980, C, 89m, R)
A group of convicts escapes to an island that's inhabited by a mad scientist who has created sub-human creatures. Barbara Bach and Joseph Cotten star. **HO20**

Scrooge (1970, C, 118m, G)
A musical adaptation of *A Christmas Carol*. Albert Finney stars, with Alec Guinness, Edith Evans, and Kenneth More. **FA13, MU14, ST42, ST60, WR4**

Scrooged (1988, C, 101m, PG-13)
Contemporary version of Dickens' *Christmas Carol*, with Bill Murray a callous TV executive brought to his senses by a series of wacky angels. With Carol Kane, John Forsythe, Karen Allen, John Glover, Bobcat Goldthwaite, David Johansen, Robert Mitchum, and Alfre Woodard. **CO2, CO13, FA13, MU12, ST107, WR4**

Scruffy (1985, C, 72m, NR)
An orphaned puppy searches for a home and is befriended by a stray. **FA10**

Sea Chase, The (1955, C, 117m, NR)
John Wayne plays a German captain whose World War II ship contains strange cargo and a passenger list that includes

Lana Turner, Tab Hunter, James Arness, and Claude Akins. **AC1, ST153, ST156**

Sea Devils (1953, C, 91m, NR)
British spy yarn set in the Napoleonic era, starring Yvonne DeCarlo and a young Rock Hudson. **ST73**

Sea Gypsies, The (1978, C, 101m, G)
A man, his daughters, a journalist, and a runaway go on a sailing expedition and learn survival techniques when they are shipwrecked. **FA4**

Sea Hawk, The (1940, B&W, 110m, NR)
A buccaneer is given approval by Queen Elizabeth I to wreak havoc on the Spanish fleet and their cities in the New World. Errol Flynn and Flora Robson star. Directed by Michael Curtiz. Home video version contains restored footage of scenes intended to boost British wartime morale. **AC13, CU10, ST43**

Sea of Love (1989, C, 112m, R)
A broken-down cop falls for a woman who may be the serial killer he's seeking. Al Pacino and Ellen Barkin star, with John Goodman. Written by Richard Price. **MY4, MY5, ST118**

Sea Wolves, The (1980, C, 120m, PG)
Two British intelligence officers recruit a retired fighting unit for a top secret mission against the Nazis. Roger Moore, Gregory Peck, and David Niven star. **AC1, ST119**

Seance on a Wet Afternoon (1964, B&W, 115m, NR)
Suspense drama about a shady medium and her husband bilking a couple. Kim Stanley, Richard Attenborough, and Patrick Magee star. **DR23, MY15**

Searchers, The (1956, C, 119m, NR)
John Wayne spends years tracking down the Indians who kidnapped his niece (Natalie Wood). With Jeffrey Hunter, Vera Miles, Ward Bond, and Lana Wood. John Ford directed this cult favorite, more appreciated in the years since its initial release. **CU13, CL14, DT36, ST156, WE5, WE7, WE15, XT8** *Essential; Recommended*

Season of the Witch (1972, C, 89m, R)
A housewife develops an interest in witchcraft and joins a coven. Directed by George Romero. **DT90, HO11**

Second Chorus (1940, B&W, 83m, NR)
Fred Astaire and Burgess Meredith compete for Paulette Goddard in this musical featuring Artie Shaw and his Orchestra. **ST2**

Second Sight (1989, C, 85m, PG)
Comedy of a wacky crime-fighting team: a straight-arrow private eye (John Laroquette) and a zany psychic (Bronson Pinchot). **CO10, CO11**

Secret Agent, The (1936, B&W, 86m, NR)
Madeleine Carroll and John Gielgud are spies posing as man and wife to track down an enemy agent in Switzerland. Directed by Alfred Hitchcock. **DT46, MY6, MY15**

Secret Beyond the Door (1948, B&W, 98m, NR)
Joan Bennett stars in this thriller as a woman who suspects that her husband is a killer. With Michael Redgrave; Fritz Lang directed. **DT58, MY3**

Secret Ceremony (1968, C, 109m, R)
A woman who grieves over her dead daughter forms a strange relationship with a girl whose mother is dead. Elizabeth Taylor and Mia Farrow star in this offbeat drama, with Robert Mitchum. Directed by Joseph Losey. **MY14, ST107, ST147**

Secret Diary of Sigmund Freud, The (1984, C, 129m, PG)
Comedy about the early days of the world's first therapist, starring Bud Cort, Carol Kane, Klaus Kinski, and Carroll Baker. **ST83**

Secret Honor (1984, C, 90m, NR)
Philip Baker Hall stars in this one-man show as Richard Nixon in all his paranoid glory. Directed by Robert Altman; originally made for cable TV. **DT2**

Secret Life of an American Wife, The (1968, C, 92m, NR)
Comedy of a neglected wife who poses as a prostitute. Anne Jackson, Walter Matthau, and Patrick O'Neal star. **ST104**

Secret Life of Walter Mitty, The (1947, C, 105m, NR)
A timid man (Danny Kaye) escapes his dull job and nagging mother through elaborate fantasies. Boris Karloff costars in this adaptation of the James Thurber story. **ST77, ST78**

Secret of My Success, The (1987, C, 110m, PG-13)
An ambitious young man from Iowa climbs the corporate ladder in a New York firm run by his uncle, whose wife has romantic designs on her nephew. Michael J. Fox stars in this comedy, with Richard Jordan, Margaret Whitton, and Helen Slater. **CO2, CO20**

Secret of NIMH, The (1982, C, 83m, G)
Animated adventure about a widowed mouse who seeks help in keeping her home and comes across a secret society of rats. Featuring the voices of Elizabeth Hartman, Derek Jacobi, and Peter Strauss. **FA10**

Secret Policeman's Other Ball, The (1982, C, 91m, R)
Concert film, derived from two London benefits for Amnesty International. Featured are members of the Monty Python troupe doing some of their best routines, plus musical performances by Eric Clapton, Pete Townshend, Jeff Beck, and other British rock stars. **CO15** *Recommended*

Secret Policeman's Private Parts, The (1984, C, 77m, R)
Concert footage from an Amnesty International benefit show starring members of Monty Python, plus Peter Cook and singers Phil Collins, Pete Townshend, and Donovan. **CO15**

Secret War of Harry Frigg, The (1968, C, 110m, NR)
Paul Newman stars as an Army hustler in this World War II comedy about a plot to free five kidnapped U.S. generals. **CO21, ST111**

Secrets of Life (1956, C, 75m, NR)
This Disney documentary, part of the True-Life Adventure series, looks at natural wonders and sea, plant, and insect life. **FA1**

Secrets of Women (1952, B&W, 114m, PG-13)
Three wives at a summer house compare notes on their relationships with their husbands in this comedy-drama from director Ingmar Bergman. **DT7**

Sedcued and Abandoned (1964, B&W, 118m, NR)
Italian comedy about a quirk in the law which allows a man who has seduced and abandoned a young girl to avoid prosecution if he marries her. Saro Urzi and Stefania Sandrelli star. **FF2**

Seduction of Joe Tynan, The (1979, C, 107m, PG)
United States Senator tries his best to resist temptations of political corruption, is less successful at resisting an affair. Alan Alda stars, with Meryl Streep, Barbara Harris, Rip Torn, and Melvyn Douglas. **DR21, ST145, ST150, XT12**

Seduction of Mimi, The (1974, C, 82m, R)
Italian comedy of a working class man (Giancarlo Giannini) and his problems, especially with women. Lina Wertmuller directed. Remade in the U.S. as *Which Way Is Up?* **DT114, FF8**

See No Evil (1971, C, 89m, PG)
A blind woman is stalked by a mad killer, who has already murdered her entire family at a secluded farm. Mia Farrow stars. **MY3**

See No Evil, Hear No Evil (1989, C, 103m, R)
Richard Pryor (as a blind man) and Gene Wilder (as a deaf man) team up in this comedy of mistaken identity: they're accused of a murder and must find the real culprit. **CO3, CO10, ST125**

See You in the Morning (1989, C, 119m, PG-13)
Drama of a second marriage and how the husband's ties to his first wife and set of children complicate his life. Jeff Bridges stars, with Alice Krige and Farrah Fawcett. Written and directed by Alan J. Pakula. **DR8, ST11**

Seems Like Old Times (1980, C, 121m, PG)
Neil Simon comedy about a well-meaning lawyer (Goldie Hawn) whose first husband (Chevy Chase) keeps popping up in her life, much to the annoyance of Husband #2 (Charles Grodin). **CO13, ST59, ST63, WR23**

Seize the Day (1986, C, 93m, NR)
Screen version of Saul Bellow's novel about a loser (Robin Williams) desperately trying to stay out of debt and in his

father's good graces. With Joseph Wiseman, Jerry Stiller, and Glenne Headly. **DR19, ST160** *Recommended*

Seizure (1974, C, 93m, R)
Horror tale of a novelist plagued by a trio of evildoers who put him and his family through hellish tortures—although they may exist only in his imagination. Jonathan Frid stars, with Martine Beswick, Troy Donahue, Herve Villechaize, and Mary Woronov. Written and directed by Oliver Stone. **DT102, HO14**

Semi-Tough (1977, C, 108m, R)
Comedy poking fun at professional sports and self-help groups, among other modern institutions, starring Burt Reynolds, Jill Clayburgh, and Kris Kristofferson. **CO2, CO19, MU12, ST128**

Senator Was Indiscreet, The (1947, B&W, 81m, NR)
The revelations in a lawmaker's diary are the cause for much scandal in this satiric comedy starring William Powell and Ella Raines. Playwright George S. Kaufman directed, his only stint behind the camera. **CL10, CU15, ST122**

Send Me No Flowers (1964, C, 100m, NR)
Rock Hudson-Doris Day comedy of a man who thinks he's dying, assigns his pal (Tony Randall) to find his wife a new husband. Directed by Norman Jewison. **DT51, ST73**

Sense of Loss, A (1972, C, 135m, NR)
Documentary detailing the terrible toll that the Catholic-Protestant conflict in Northern Ireland takes on citizens. Directed by Marcel Ophuls. **CU16, DT75**

Senso (1954, C, 90m, NR)
An aristocratic woman takes a young, poor man for her lover, with tragic consequences. Classic story of infidelity and obsession, directed by Luchino Visconti. Also known as *The Wanton Contessa*. **DT108**

Separate Peace, A (1972, C, 104m, PG)
Screen version of John Knowles' popular novel about friendship between two prep school students during the 1940s. Parker Stevenson and William Roerick star. **DR9, DR19, DR25**

Separate Tables (1958, B&W, 99m, NR)
All-star drama set at English resort, with intertwining stories of guests. Burt Lancaster, Rita Hayworth, David Niven, Deborah Kerr, and Wendy Hiller are the featured players; Niven and Hiller won Oscars. Based on Terence Rattigan's plays. **DR20, ST64, ST85, XT2, XT5**

Separate Tables (1983, C, 108m, PG)
Made-for-cable-TV version of the Terence Rattigan dramas of life at a seaside resort. Alan Bates, Julie Christie, and Claire Bloom star. Directed by John Schlesinger. **DR20, DR23, DT94**

September (1987, C, 82m, PG)
Woody Allen directed this somber drama about a faded movie actress, her daughter, and their tangled lives. Elaine Stritch and Mia Farrow star, with Denholm Elliott, Dianne Wiest, Sam Waterston, and Jack Warden. **DR8, DT1**

Sgt. Pepper's Lonely Hearts Club Band (1978, C, 111m, PG)
Peter Frampton and the Bee Gees create a fantasy world from the songs on the Beatles album of the same name. With Steve Martin. **MU8, MU16, ST99**

Sergeant Ryker (1968, C, 85m, NR)
Lee Marvin plays a soldier on trial for treason during the Korean War. With Bradford Dillman and Vera Miles. **AC3, DR17, ST100**

Sergeant York (1941, B&W, 134m, NR)
Gary Cooper won an Oscar for his portrayal of World War I hero Alvin York.With Walter Brennan and Joan Leslie. Howard Hawks directed. **AC2, CL2, DT43, ST22, XT2**

Serial (1980, C, 86m, R)
Comedy about an affluent California suburb which embraces each new trend as it comes along. Martin Mull and Tuesday Weld star, with Sally Kellerman, Tom Smothers, Bill Macy, and Christopher Lee. **CO2, ST89**

Serpent and the Rainbow, The (1988, C, 98m, R)
An American scientist travels to Haiti to invesitgate voodoo drugs and rituals that turn humans into zombies. Bill Pullman, Cathy Tyson, and Paul Winfield star. Directed by Wes Craven. **HO6, ST162**

Serpent's Egg, The (1978, C, 120m, R)
Director Ingmar Bergman's grim drama of Jews in pre-World War II Germany and the humiliation they suffer in order to survive. David Carradine and Liv Ullmann star. **DT7, ST154**

Serpico (1973, C, 129m, R)
True story of undercover New York cop who blew the whistle on corruption in the department and was nearly murdered for his honesty. Al Pacino stars, with John Randolph, Jack Kehoe, Tony Roberts, M. Emmet Walsh, and F. Murray Abraham. Sidney Lumet directed. **DR6, DR16, DT65, ST118, XT9**

Servant, The (1963, B&W, 115m, NR)
From writer Harold Pinter and director Joseph Losey, the contemporary tale of a manservant (Dirk Bogarde) turning the tables on his decadent master (James Fox). Sarah Miles and Wendy Craig co-star. **DR23** *Essential*

Sesame Street Presents Follow That Bird *see* Follow That Bird

Set-Up, The (1949, B&W, 72m, NR)
Gritty drama of a faded boxer asked to take a fall for gamblers but defying them at the last minute. Robert Ryan stars. Robert Wise directed. **DR22, DT117, MY1** *Essential; Recommended*

Seven Beauties (1976, C, 115m, R)
From Italian director Lina Wertmüller, the tragicomic story of a man who will do anything to survive in a prisoner-of-war camp during World War II. Giancarlo Giannini stars. **DT114** *Essential*

Seven Brides For Seven Brothers (1954, C, 103m, G)
When Howard Keel weds Jane Powell, his six brothers decide to follow suit by kidnapping six townsgirls. Rousing musical western based on Stephen Vincent Benet's "Sobbin' Women." Directed by Stanley Donen; outstanding choreography by Michael Kidd. **DT30, MU1, MU3, MU6, XT20**

Seven Days in May (1964, B&W, 118m, NR)
U.S. President is threatened when one of his high-ranking generals plots a coup. Burt Lancaster and Kirk Douglas star, with Fredric March, Ava Gardner, and Edmond O'Brien. Written by Rod Ser-

ling; directed by John Frankenheimer. First-rate political thriller. **DR21, ST34, ST85** *Recommended*

7 Faces of Dr. Lao, The (1964, C, 101m, NR)
A traveling circus weaves magic and stories to show the inhabitants of a western town the truly important things in life. Tony Randall stars. Directed by George Pal. **FA8, SF13**

Seven Little Foys, The (1955, C, 95m, NR)
When Eddie Foy's wife dies, he is left alone to take care of his seven children. He adds them to his vaudeville act and they become stars. Bob Hope stars, with a special appearance by James Cagney as George M. Cohan. **CL7, MU5, ST14, ST70**

Seven Miles From Alcatraz (1942, B&W, 62m, NR)
Two escaped cons run into a band of Nazi spies and must make a fateful decision. James Craig and Frank Jenks star. **DR18**

Seven Percent Solution, The (1976, C, 113m, PG)
Sherlock Holmes tale, with the famous detective traveling to Vienna for treatment by a certain Dr. Freud for a drug habit. Sounds spoofy, but it's played straight, with a superb cast including Nicol Williamson, Robert Duvall (as Watson), Alan Arkin, Vanessa Redgrave, and Laurence Olivier. **HF14, ST38, ST116, ST127** *Recommended*

Seven Samurai, The (1954, B&W, 200m, NR)
A diverse collection of swordsmen come to the aid of villagers who are being ravaged by bandits. Akira Kurosawa directed. Takashi Shimura and Toshiro Mifune star. Oscar winner for Best Foreign Language Film under the title *Samurai*. Also available in a 141m version. U.S. remake: *The Magnificent Seven*. Arguably the greatest action film of all time. **AC13, DT57, FF8, ST106, XT7** *Essential; Highly Recommended*

Seven Sinners (1940, B&W, 87m, NR)
Marlene Dietrich is a South Seas chanteuse, John Wayne her smitten protector in this melodrama. **ST33, ST156**

Seven-Ups, The (1973, C, 103m, PG)
Roy Scheider heads a special police task force against mobsters that is brutally efficient. Follow-up to *The French Connection*. **AC9**

Seven Year Itch, The (1955, C, 105m, NR)
A married man, with his wife and kids out of town for the summer, gets ideas about a beautiful blonde who has rented the apartment above his. Marilyn Monroe and Tom Ewell star. Directed by Billy Wilder. **DT116, ST108**

1776 (1972, C, 141m, G)
John Adams, Benjamin Franklin, and the rest of the first American Congress sing and dance their way to independence. William Daniels and Howard Da Silva recreate their Broadway roles. **FA9, MU2, MU16**

Seventh Seal, The (1956, B&W, 96m, NR)
Classic allegory from director Ingmar Bergman of medieval knight (Max von Sydow) and his search for truth and beauty. With Bibi Andersson. **DT7** *Essential; Recommended*

Seventh Veil, the (1945, B&W, 95m, NR)
A young woman (Ann Todd) is victimized by a neurotic cousin (James Mason) until a hypnotist (Herbert Lom) helps her out. **ST102**

7th Voyage of Sinbad, The (1958, C, 87m, G)
Sinbad must accomplish several tasks to save a princess who has been miniaturized by an evil magician. Kerwin Matthews and Kathryn Grant are the leads, but the real star is Ray Harryhausen and his special effects. **AC18, FA8, SF13** *Highly Recommended*

sex, lies, and videotape (1989, C, 100m, R)
Four character drama: a young couple whose marriage is on the rocks, a visiting buddy of the husband, and the wife's sister, who's having an affair with her brother-in-law. James Spader, Andie McDowell, Peter Gallagher, and Laura San Giacomo star. Written and directed by Steven Soderbergh. **DR1, DR10** *Recommended*

Sex Shop, Le (1973, C, 92m, R)
The owner of a book shop finds his business multiplying when he begins selling pornographic material. A light, naughty

comedy from France, directed by Claude Berri. **FF1**

Sex With a Smile (1976, C, 100m, R)
Five episodes in this Italian comedy demonstrate how funny good, clean sex can be. Marty Feldman stars. **FF2**

Sextette (1978, C, 91m, R)
Mae West's last film, based on her play, about a woman's eventful honeymoon—her ex-husbands keep making appearances. A movie with "camp" written all over it. **CU2, ST158**

Shack Out on 101 (1955, B&W, 80m, NR)
Mind-blowing thriller set in a hash house on California's coastal highway, about espionage and thwarted romance. Lee Marvin is the cook named Slob who's really a Russian spy, Terry Moore is the lusted-after waitress, Frank Lovejoy is the professor working on a top-secret project. A camp classic. **CU2, MY1, ST100** *Recommended*

Shadow Box, The (1980, C, 100m, NR)
Dramatic story of a trio of terminally ill patients at a rural California hospice, adapted by Michael Cristofer from his play. Paul Newman directed. Joanne Woodward, Christopher Plummer, and James Broderick star. Originally made for TV. **DR7, DR20, ST111, ST166** *Recommended*

Shadow of a Doubt (1943, B&W, 108m, NR)
Hitchcock thriller set in a small town, where a young girl (Teresa Wright) suspects her kindly uncle (Joseph Cotten) of murder. Screenplay co-written by Thorton Wilder **DR26, DT46, MY14** *Essential; Recommended*

Shadow of the Thin Man (1941, B&W, 97m, NR)
Fourth Thin Man mystery, with sleuthing couple Nick and Nora Charles at the racetrack, betting on losers but picking the right murder suspect. William Powell and Myrna Loy star. **CL15, HF5, MY17, ST94, ST122, WR9**

Shadows (1922, B&W, 85m, NR)
A woman, who believes her nasty first husband is dead, remarries and starts a family. Soon after, she starts receiving blackmail threats from her first husband.

Lon Chaney, Sr. stars in this silent drama. **ST16**

Shadows (1960, B&W, 87m, NR)
Director John Cassavetes' groundbreaking independent film about an interracial romance, starring Hugh Hurd, Lelia Goldoni, and Rupert Crosse. **DR3, DR14**

Shadows of Forgotten Ancestors (1964, B&W, 99m, NR)
Drama set in rural Russia of the early 20th century, about the trials and tribulations of a peasant (Ivan Mikolaychuk). **FF7**

Shag (1989, C, 98m, PG)
Four girls travel to Myrtle Beach, South Carolina, in 1963 for a last fling before one gets married. Phoebe Cates, Bridget Fonda, Annabeth Gish, and Page Hannah star in this comedy. **CO6**

Shaggy D.A., The (1976, C, 91m, G)
In this sequel to *The Shaggy Dog*, a lawyer (Dean Jones) who's just been elected District Attorney turns into a sheepdog when an ancient spell is read. Suzanne Pleshette and Tim Conway costar. **FA1**

Shaggy Dog, The (1959, B&W, 104m, G)
A young boy whose father hates dogs discovers his older brother turns into a sheepdog when an ancient spell is read. Fred MacMurray and Tommy Kirk star in this classic Disney comedy. **FA1**

Shaka Zulu (1985, C, 300m, NR)
The true story of Shaka, a tribal leader who united the Zulu nation against the British in Africa during the 1900s. Trevor Howard and Chistopher Lee star. Originally made for TV. **ST89**

Shakedown (1988, C, 90m, R)
A crusading lawyer (Peter Weller) and an undercover cop (Sam Elliott) team to clean up the New York Police Department of corruption. With Patricia Charbonneau. Plenty of wild chases. **AC9**

Shalako (1968, C, 113m, NR)
Western drama about a hunting party of Europeans in New Mexico being attacked by Apaches. Sean Connery and Brigitte Bardot star. **ST4, ST21**

Shall We Dance (1937, B&W, 116m, NR)
A Russian ballet dancer (Fred Astaire) and an American musical performer (Gin-

ger Rogers) marry as a publicity stunt and end up falling in love. **CL15, ST2, ST131** *Recommended*

Shame (1961, B&W, 80m, NR)
Low-budget melodrama from director Roger Corman about a bigot (William Shatner) traveling the South, stirring up racial hatred. Also known as *The Intruder* or *I Hate Your Guts*. **DR7, DT22**

Shame (1988, C, 95m, R)
Australian drama set in a small town which holds a terrible secret: a gang of young men have been attacking women without fear of interference from the community or its law officers. A female barrister, stranded in the town, tries to persuade one of the victims to press charges. **DR26, FF5**

Shampoo (1975, C, 112m, R)
A Beverly Hills hairdresser tries to satisfy his customers in the shop and after hours. Warren Beatty stars, with Julie Christie, Goldie Hawn, and Oscar winner Lee Grant in this satiric comedy, set around the 1968 Presidential election. Written by Beatty and Robert Towne; directed by Hal Ashby. **CO1, CO2, ST5, ST63, XT5, XT10** *Essential; Recommended*

Shamus (1973, C, 106m, R)
Burt Reynolds plays a private eye with some offbeat detection methods in this mystery. Dyan Cannon costars. **MY10, ST128**

Shane (1953, C, 118m, NR)
Alan Ladd plays the lone gunman squared off against evil Jack Palance in this classic western. With Van Heflin, Jean Arthur (in her last film), and Brandon de Wilde. Directed by George Stevens. **DT101, WE2, XT22** *Essential; Recommended*

Shanghai Gesture, The (1941, B&W, 106m, NR)
Josef von Sternberg directed this murky tale of a man who discovers his daughter working in an Oriental den of iniquity. Walter Huston, Gene Tierney, and Victor Mature star. **DT100**

Shanghai Surprise (1986, C, 97m, PG13)
Pop star Madonna plays a missionary in 1930s China. Sean Penn plays a soldier of fortune who helps her out of a tight spot. **AC21, MU12**

Sharad of Atlantis see Undersea Kingdom

Shark! (1969, C, 92m, PG)
Burt Reynolds stars in this underwater adventure of treasure divers encountering toothy creatures of the deep. Directed by Samuel Fuller. **DT40, ST128**

Sharkey's Machine (1981, C, 119m, R)
An Atlanta cop's vendetta against a mobster gets personal when he becomes romantically involved with one of the crime boss's working girls. Burt Reynolds and Rachel Ward star, with Vittorio Gassman, Brian Keith, Bernie Casey, and Charles Durning. **AC9, ST128**

She (1985, C, 90m, NR)
A warrior woman must stop an expedition that is searching for the Flame of Eternal Life. Based on a novel by H. Rider Haggard. Sandahl Bergman stars. **AC18**

She-Devil (1989, C, 99m, PG-13)
Zany, contemporary comedy of a dumpy housewife (Roseanne Barr) seeking vengenace on her faithless husband (Ed Begley, Jr.) and his lover (Meryl Streep), a lovely author. With Linda Hunt and Sylvia Miles. Based on Fay Weldon's novel; directed by Susan Seidelman. **CO2, DR10, ST145**

She Done Him Wrong (1933, B&W, 66m, NR)
Mae West is Diamond Lil; she invites Cary Grant to come up sometime and see her. **ST57, ST158**

She Wore a Yellow Ribbon (1949, C, 103m, NR)
John Wayne is a retiring cavalry officer with one more Indian battle to fight. With Joanne Dru, John Agar, Ben Johnson, and Ward Bond. Directed by John Ford. **AC5, DT36, ST156, WE4** *Essential; Recommended*

Sherman's March (1986, C, 155m, NR)
Unique film, a documentary record of a filmmaker (Ross McElwee) doing research on Civil War general, winding up recording his impressions of women in the contemporary South. Quite rewarding and very funny. **CU16, XT18** *Recommended*

She's Having a Baby (1988, C, 106m, PG-13)
Comedy-drama from writer-director John Hughes, about the second thoughts of a young husband and father-to-be. Kevin Bacon and Elizabeth McGovern star. **CO1, DT49**

Sheena (1984, C, 117m, PG)
A white orphan raised by an African tribe has the ability to communicate with animals. Tanya Roberts stars in this adventure tale. **AC17**

Shenandoah (1965, C, 105m, NR)
A Virginia farmer tries to stay neutral during the Civil War, but his family soon drags him into the fray. James Stewart stars. **AC5, ST143, WE6**

Sherlock Holmes and the Secret Weapon (1942, B&W, 68m, NR)
Basil Rathbone and Nigel Bruce star in this contemporary Holmes case set during World War II, involving the disappearance of an inventor and his important discovery. With Lionel Atwill as Professor Moriarty. **HF14**

Sherlock Holmes and the Spider Woman *see* Spider Woman

Sherlock Holmes and the Voice of Terror (1942, B&W, 65m, NR)
More Holmes detection updated, with the detective battling Nazis who make their terrorist demands over the airwaves. Basil Rathbone and Nigel Bruce star. **HF14**

Sherlock Holmes Faces Death (1943, B&W, 68m, NR)
Basil Rathbone and Nigel Bruce are back for more deducing, this time to solve what appears to be a ritual murder. **HF14**

Sherlock Holmes in Washington (1943, B&W, 71m, NR)
Further adventures of the great detective in the World War II era, this time chasing spies in the Nation's Capital. Basil Rathbone and Nigel Bruce star. **HF14, XT12**

She's Gotta Have It (1986, B&W, 84m, R)
Sexy comedy from director Spike Lee (who also stars as hip messenger boy Mars Blackmon) about a free-spirited woman (Tracy Camila-Johns) with three lovers and no qualms about keeping all of them. **CO1, CO2, CU6, DR14, DT60** *Recommended*

She's in the Army Now (1981, C, 100m, NR)
Comedy of female recruits in today's Army, starring Kathleen Quinlan, Jamie Lee Curtis, and Melanie Griffith. **CO21, ST58**

She's Out of Control (1989, C, 95m, PG)
An overprotective father (Tony Danza) is driven to distraction when his teenaged daughter (Ami Dolenz) begins showing a healthy interest in boys. **CO5**

Shinbone Alley (1971, C, 85m, G)
Animated adventures of an independent alley cat and a poet cockroach who strike up an unusual friendship. Featuring the voices of Eddie Bracken, Carol Channing, and John Carradine. **FA10**

Shine On Harvest Moon (1938, B&W, 60m, NR)
Roy Rogers preserves the peace in the Old West against a gang of desperadoes. **ST132**

Shining, The (1980, C, 142m, R)
Writer agrees to stay at a deserted hotel for the winter with his wife and son, but the solitude (and other forces) prove too much for him. Jack Nicholson stars in this version of Stephen King's novel, directed by Stanley Kubrick. With Shelley Duvall, Scatman Crothers, and Danny Lloyd. **DT56, HO2, HO3, ST112, WR12**

Ship of Fools (1965, B&W, 149m, NR)
Drama set aboard an ocean liner in the dark days just before World War II, with international assortment of characters. Based on Katherine Anne Porter's bestseller. Lee Marvin, Vivien Leigh, Oskar Werner, Simone Signoret, George Segal, Elizabeth Ashley, and Michael Dunne star. Directed by Stanley Kramer. **DR5, DR19, DT55, ST100**

Shirley Valentine (1989, C, 108m, R)
Pauline Collins recreates her comic stage role as a bored working-class British housewife who runs off to Greece for a change of scenery. With Tom Conti. **CO1, CO17, DR10, DR20**

Shoah (1986, C, 570m, NR)
Monumental documentary about the effects of the Holocaust on its survivors

and the townspeople who lived near the death camps. Relies almost exclusively on interview material, with almost no footage of the atrocities themselves. Directed by Claude Lanzmann. **CU16** *Recommended*

Shock, The (1923, B&W, 96m, NR)
A mobster sends a hired gun to a small town to kill a rival banker. The gunman falls in love with a sweet young girl and decides to reform. Lon Chaney, Sr. stars in this silent drama. **ST16**

Shock (1946, B&W, 70m, NR)
Vincent Price and his gang plan to kill a girl who witnessed one of their crimes. **ST124**

Shock to the System, A (1990, C, 87m, R)
Michael Caine stars in this black comedy as a man who's passed up for a promotion, triggering a vendetta against all his enemies. With Elizabeth McGovern, Peter Riegert, Swoosie Kurtz, and Will Patton. **CO12, ST15**

Shock Waves (1977, C, 86m, PG)
A Nazi scientist creates androids to man the Fuehrer's submarines. Peter Cushing stars. **ST27**

Shocker (1989, C, 110m, R)
An executed killer (Mitch Pileggi) is revived through TV waves to continue his nastiness in this horror film. **HO9**

Shoes of the Fisherman, The (1968, C, 152m, G)
A drama about the election of the first Russian Pope and its effect on world peace. Anthony Quinn and Laurence Olivier star, with Vittorio De Sica. **DT26, ST116**

Shogun Assassin (1981, C, 90m, R)
A swordsman travels the Japanese countryside, wheeling his son in a baby carriage, taking on all comers in this extremely violent action saga. Video version of this cult favorite is dubbed in English. **CU7, FF4**

Shoot Loud, Louder. . .I Don't Understand (1966, C, 100m, NR)
Crazy-quilt comedy from Italy about an antiques dealer (Marcello Mastroianni) and his loony adventures with a lovely woman (Raquel Welch) and some bumbling gunmen. **ST103**

Shoot the Living, Pray for the Dead (1973, C, 90m, NR)
Klaus Kinski stars in a western drama about a killer who promises his guide a share in stolen gold. **ST83**

Shoot the Moon (1982, C, 123m, R)
A husband's infidelity leads to the painful breakup of his marriage, with a devastating effect on his three daughters. Albert Finney and Diane Keaton star, with Peter Weller and Karen Allen. Written by Bo Goldman; Alan Parker directed. **DR8, ST42, ST79**

Shoot the Piano Player (1962, B&W, 85m, NR)
A Parisian musician is torn between his musical ambitions and his relationships with gangsters. Moving drama from director François Truffaut, starring Charles Aznavour. Available in letterboxed format. **CU19, DT106, XT16** *Essential; Recommended*

Shoot to Kill (1988, C, 110m, R)
An F.B.I. agent (Sidney Poitier) and mountain guide (Tom Berenger) team to track a fugitive killer who has kidnapped the guide's girlfriend (Kirstie Alley). **AC12, ST121**

Shooting, The (1967, C, 82m, NR)
Cult western starring Jack Nicholson and Warren Oates in a convoluted tale of revenge. Monte Hellman directed. **ST112, ST141, WE15**

Shooting Party, The (1984, C, 108m, NR)
Weekend in the British countryside in 1913, with various personalities, class conflicts, romantic entanglements. James Mason, Dorothy Tutin, Edward Fox, and John Gielgud star. **DR23, ST102**

Shootist, The (1976, C, 99m, PG)
In his last film, John Wayne plays a once-famous gunfighter who finds that he has cancer. With Lauren Bacall, James Stewart, Ron Howard, Richard Boone, and Hugh O'Brian. Directed by Don Siegel. costar. **DT48, DT97, WE2, WE11, ST143, ST156, XT22**

Shop Around the Corner, The (1940, B&W, 97m, NR)
Romantic comedy of two shopworkers (James Stewart, Margaret Sullavan) who become unwitting lovers through corre-

spondence. Directed by Ernst Lubitsch. **CL4, DT63, ST143** *Essential*

Shop on Main Street, The (1965, B&W, 128m, NR)
Oscar-winning drama from Czechoslovakia about the relationship between an elderly Jewish woman and the man who takes over her business during World War II. Directed by Jan Kadar. **FF7, XT7**

Short Circuit (1986, C, 98m, PG)
A robot escapes from its military keepers and is taken in by a lovely young animal lover. Gentle comedy with special effects humor, starring Ally Sheedy, Steve Guttenberg, and Austin Pendleton. **CO11, FA6**

Short Circuit 2 (1988, C, 110m, PG)
More adventures of Johnny 5, the playful robot. Fisher Stevens, Michael McKean, and Cynthia Gibb are the human costars. **CO11, FA6**

Short Eyes (1977, C, 104m, R)
Prison drama of a child molester's fate at the hands of fellow cons. Rewarding drama, but not for the faint of heart. Bruce Davison, José Perez, and Miguel Piñero star; based on Piñero's play. **DR18** *Recommended*

Short Films of D.W. Griffith, The: Volume 1 (1911-12, B&W, 59m, NR)
Three early short films directed by D.W. Griffith. *The Battle* is a Civil War tale about a boy who shows signs of cowardice, then becomes a hero; Charles West and Blanche Sweet star. *The Female of the Species (A Psychological Tragedy)* is a tale of three women who become friends after facing a series of hardships; Mary Pickford stars. *The New York Hat* is about small town hypocrisy and the damage of gossip; Mary Pickford stars. **DT42**

Short Fuse (1987, C, 91m, R)
A Washington, D.C. journalist (Art Garfunkel) investigates a murder in the funky "go-go" clubs of the Nation's Capital. Plenty of music from Chuck Brown & the Soul Searchers, Trouble Funk, and other groups. Released theatrically as *Good to Go*. **AC8, MU12, XT12**

Short Time (1990, C, 97m, PG-13)
Darkly comic story of a police detective who mistaknely thinks he has a terminal

illness, tries to get killed in the line of duty so his family can collect a big insurance check. Dabney Coleman stars, with Matt Frewer and Teri Garr. **CO10, CO12**

Shot in the Dark, A (1964, C, 101m, NR)
Second (and arguably funniest) Pink Panther adventure has Inspector Clouseau trying to prove that a lovely young woman is innocent of murder. Peter Sellers is in top form, as is Elke Sommer; Herbert Lom, George Sanders, and Bert Kwouk are all hilarious. Directed by Blake Edwards. **DT32, ST137** *Essential; Highly Recommended*

Shout, The (1979, C, 87m, R)
A man who believes he can kill people by shouting terrorizes a young couple. Alan Bates, John Hurt, and Susannah York star in this strange drama directed by Jerzy Skolimowski. **HO7**

Shout at the Devil (1976, C, 119m, PG)
Action drama, set in pre-World War I Africa, about a poacher recruiting an Englishman in a plot to blow up a German ship. Lee Marvin and Roger Moore star. **ST100**

Show Boat (1936, B&W, 113m, NR)
The Jerome Kern-Oscar Hammerstein musical of life on the old Mississippi, starring Irene Dunne, Allan Jones, Paul Robeson, and Helen Morgan. Directed by James Whale. **DT115, MU2, MU4, MU6**

Show Boat (1951, C, 107m, NR)
Second screen version of musical about the naive daughter (Kathryn Grayson) of the owners of a show boat falling in love with a gambler (Howard Keel). With Ava Gardner, Joe E. Brown, Marge & Gower Champion, and William Warfield. **MU1, MU2, MU4, MU6**

Show People (1928, B&W, 81m, NR)
Silent comedy set in Hollywood, with Marion Davies as an actress who lets success go to their head. Watch for cameos by Charlie Chaplin, Douglas Fairbanks, and other Movie Town notables of the period. Directed by King Vidor. Carl Davis composed a musical score for the video version. **CL7, CL11, DT18, DT107** *Essential; Recommended*

Showdown at Boot Hill (1958, B&W, 76m, NR)
Charles Bronson is a bounty hunter out to collect his money in this western drama. **ST12**

Shriek in the Night, A (1933, B&W, 66m, NR)
Suspense drama starring Ginger Rogers and Lyle Talbot as reporters out to trap a killer. **ST131**

Shy People (1988, C, 188m, R)
A New York journalist (Jill Clayburgh) travels with her daughter to the Louisiana bayou to meet a cousin (Barbara Hershey) as a subject for a story. **DR8, DR10**

Sicilian, The (1987, C, 146m, NR)
True story of Salvatore Giuliano, the Sicilian bandit who defied the wealthy landowners and gave the peasants a hero to look up to. This is the European cut with footage unseen in the American release. The 115m American version is also available. Christopher Lambert stars. Directed by Michael Cimino. **AC16, CU10, DR5**

Sid and Nancy (1986, C, 111m, R)
The heartbreaking story of English punk rocker Sid Vicious and Nancy Spungen, his American lover and partner in drug addiction. An instant midnight movie classic with stunning performances by Gary Oldman and Chloe Webb. **CU1, DR6, DR12** *Recommended*

Side Out (1990, C, 100m, PG-13)
The beach volleyball scene in Southern California is the backdrop for this drama. C. Thomas Howell and Peter Horton star. **DR22**

Sidewalk Stories (1989, B&W, 97m, R)
Silent comedy about a homeless street artist. Written, produced, directed by, and starring Charles Lane. **CO2**

Sidney Sheldon's Bloodline (1979, C, 116m, R)
Audrey Hepburn stars in this sudsy thriller about a woman who inherits a cosmetics company and is immediately plunged into danger and mystery. With Ben Gazzara, James Mason, Michelle Phillips, Omar Sharif, and Romy Schneider. Also known as *Bloodline*. **MY3, ST65, ST102**

Siege of Firebase Gloria, The (1989, C, 95m, R)
Vietnam War drama centering on combat action at the time of the 1968 Tet Offensive. Wings Hauser and Lee Ermey star. **AC4**

Siegfried (1924, B&W, 100m, NR)
Fritz Lang directed this silent classic, based on the Teutonic legends. **DT58, FF3**

Siesta (1987, C, 97m, R)
Convoluted tale of female stunt pilot (Ellen Barkin) and her fragmented personal affairs. With Gabriel Byrne, Jodie Foster, Martin Sheen, Grace Jones, Julian Sands, and Isabella Rossellini. Music by Marcus Miller, performed by Miles Davis. **DR10, MU12, ST47**

Sign o' the Times (1987, C, 85m, PG-13)
Concert film of controversial rock star Prince also features Sheila E. and Sheena Easton. **MU10**

Signal 7 (1983, C, 92m, NR)
Low-key drama about cabdrivers in San Francisco. Director Rob Nilsson encouraged his actors to improvise their dialogue. **DR15, XT13**

Signs of Life (1989, C, 91m, PG-13)
Drama set in a seaside Maine village, where a boat builder is going out of business. Arthur Kennedy stars, with Kevin J. O'Connor, Vincent Philip D'Onofrio, and Michael Lewis. **DR26**

Silent Movie (1976, C, 86m, PG)
Mel Brooks' tribute to the early days of film comedy: a movie with no dialogue, only music and sound effects. Mel's co-stars are Marty Feldman, Dom DeLuise, Sid Caesar; watch for guest cameos from Paul Newman, Anne Bancroft, and Burt Reynolds. **CO7, CO12, DT13, ST111, ST128**

Silent Night, Deadly Night (1984, C, 79m, R)
A man becomes a homicidal maniac when forced to wear a Santa suit. **HO9**

Silent Partner, The (1978, C, 103m, R)
Thriller about a bank clerk who's tipped off in advance to a robbery and neatly transfers the "stolen" money into his own account. Then the robber comes after him, and things get very nasty. Elliott

Gould and Christopher Plummer star. **MY9** *Recommended*

Silent Rage (1982, C, 105m, R)
Chuck Norris battles a killer who has been rendered virtually indestructible by a scientific experiment. **ST114**

Silent Running (1972, C, 90m, G)
By the 21st century pollution has killed off all the vegetation on Earth. On a specially designed spacecraft, the only botanical specimens left are carefully tended in hopes that one day they can be replanted on Earth. Bruce Dern stars in this science fiction drama directed by Douglas Trumbull. **SF3**

Silent Scream (1984, C, 60m, NR)
A former commandant of a concentration camp collects a variety of animals, including humans. Peter Cushing stars. **ST27**

Silk Stockings (1957, C, 117m, NR)
A cold Russian emissary (Cyd Charisse) visiting Paris warms up to the attentions of a playboy (Fred Astaire). Rouben Mamoulian directed this musical remake of *Ninotchka*. **CU18, MU1, MU14, ST2**

Silkwood (1983, C, 131m, R)
Meryl Streep plays Karen Silkwood, the factory worker who tried to expose safety practices in her nuclear plant and died in a mysterious car accident. With Kurt Russell and Cher. Written by Nora Ephron and Alice Arlen; Mike Nichols directed. **DR6, DT74, ST19, ST145** *Recommended*

Silver Bears (1978, C, 113m, PG)
Comedy-drama of shady dealings in the international silver market, starring Michael Caine and Cybill Shepherd, with Louis Jourdan and Martin Balsam. Based on Paul Erdman's novel. **CO2, DR24, ST15**

Silver Blaze, The (1937, B&W, 60m, NR)
Arthur Wontner stars as Sherlock Holmes in this mystery about a missing racehorse. Also titled *Murder at the Baskervilles*. **HF14**

Silver Bullet (1985, C, 95m, R)
A deranged killer is terrorizing a small town and only a crippled boy (Corey Haim) and his irresponsible uncle (Gary Busey) realize the killer is really a werewolf. Based on a Stephen King novella. Directed by Dan Attias. **HO4, WR12**

Silver Chalice, The (1954, C, 144m, NR)
Drama of ancient Greece, about a sculptor who fashions cup for The Last Supper. Paul Newman's film debut; Virginia Mayo, Pier Angeli, and Jack Palance star. **CL13, ST111**

Silver Spurs (1943, B&W, 54m, NR)
A ranch foreman (Roy Rogers) rides to stop a villainous landgrabber (John Carradine).**ST132**

Silver Streak (1976, C, 113m, PG)
Comic thriller, set aboard a speeding train, with innocent editor (Gene Wilder) becoming involved with murder plot and lovely passenger (Jill Clayburgh). With Richard Pryor and Patrick McGoohan. **CO3, CO10, ST125, XT19**

Silverado (1985, C, 132m, PG-13)
A trio of cowboys ride out to protect the persecuted settlers of a prairie town. Kevin Kline, Scott Glenn, and Danny Glover star. The supporting cast includes Brian Dennehy, Linda Hunt, Rosanna Arquette, Jeff Goldblum, and John Cleese. Written and directed by Lawrence Kasdan. **CO15, ST23, ST55, ST56, ST84, WE1**

Simon (1980, C, 97m, PG)
A group of scientists brainwash a man into believing he is an alien. Alan Arkin and Madeline Kahn star in this comedy written and directed by Marshall Brickman. **SF21**

Simon & Garfunkel: The Concert in Central Park (1982, C, 87m, NR)
Paul Simon and Art Garfunkel sing together for the first time in eleven years. **MU10**

Simon of the Desert (1965, B&W, 45m, NR)
Director Luis Buñuel's sly comedy about a real-life holy man who supposedly spent many years perched on top of a pillar. Claudio Brook and Silvia Pinal star. **DT15** *Recommended*

Simple Story, A (1978, C, 110m, NR)
Romy Schneider is a woman at the crossroads of her life in this French drama. **FF1**

Sin of Harold Diddlebock, The (1947, B&W, 90m, NR)
Harold Lloyd stars in his last sound comedy, about a timid bookkeeper and his first brush with alcohol. Directed by Preston Sturges. **DT103**

Sinbad and the Eye of the Tiger (1977, C, 113m, G)
Sinbad goes on another adventure with a beautiful princess and an evil witch. Special effects by Ray Harryhausen. Patrick Wayne and Jane Seymour star. **FA8**

Since You Went Away (1944, B&W, 172m, NR)
Epic, heart-wrenching story of homefront America during World War II, produced by David O. Selznick. Claudette Colbert, Jennifer Jones, Joseph Cotten, and Shirley Temple star, with Robert Walker, Monty Wooley, Agnes Moorehead, and Hattie McDaniel. **CL5, CL6, ST148**

Sincerely, Charlotte (1986, C, 92m, NR)
A singer is a suspect in her boyfriend's murder and flees from the police with the help of an old lover. Isabelle Huppert stars in this French thriller; her sister Caroline directed. **FF1, MY16**

Sincerely Yours (1955, C, 115m, NR)
Liberace stars as a pianist whose music is an inspiration to all around him. Written by Irving Wallace. As bad as it sounds—but revered by fans of campy movies. **CU2**

Sing (1989, C, 97m, PG-13)
A Brooklyn high school musical competition between seniors and underclassman forms the basis for this drama. Lorraine Braco, Peter Dobson, Louise Lasser, and Patti LaBelle star. **DR12, DR25**

Singe en Hiver, Un (1962, B&W, 105m, NR)
An aging alcoholic gets a new lease on life when a young stranger enters his world. Jean Gabin and Jean-Paul Belmondo star in this French drama. **ST6**

Singin' in the Rain (1952, C, 102m, G)
Grand musical comedy set at the time when sound pictures came to Hollywood. Gene Kelly, Debbie Reynolds, and Donald O'Connor star, with Jean Hagen and Cyd Charisse. Directed by Kelly and Stanley Donen. Many musical highlights, including Kelly's title tune dance, O'Con-nor's "Make 'Em Laugh." **DT30, FA9, MU1, MU4, ST81** *Essential; Highly Recommended*

Sinister Invasion (1970, C, 95m, NR)
A crazed scientist (Boris Karloff) creates a death ray. Also known as *Incredible Invasion.* **ST77**

Sinister Urge, The (1961, B&W, 75m, NR)
A pair of cops set out to break up a porno movies ring in this low-budget, brain-dead drama from director Ed Wood, Jr. **DT118**

Sink the Bismarck! (1960, B&W, 97m, NR)
Action in the North Atlantic, as British forces try to destroy a seemingly impregnable German battleship. Kenneth More and Dana Wynter star. **AC1**

Sioux City Sue (1946, B&W, 69m, NR)
Gene Autry is in Hollywood to try his hand at show business, but there are rustlers even in the Hills of Beverly. **ST3**

Sirocco (1951, B&W, 98m, NR)
Humphrey Bogart plays a gunrunner during the 1920s. Lee J. Cobb and Zero Mostel costar in this thriller. **ST8**

Sister Kenny (1946, B&W, 116m, NR)
True-life story of courageous nurse and her fight against polio. Rosalind Russell stars. **CL2**

Sisters (1973, C, 93m, R)
Horror film about Siamese twins surgically separated at birth, one growing up to become a homicidal maniac (Margot Kidder). With Jennifer Salt and William Finney. Brian DePalma directed; music by Bernard Herrmann. **DT29, HO15** *Recommended*

Six Weeks (1982, C, 107m, PG)
Tearjerker about a politician's friendship with a little girl dying of cancer and her mother. Dudley Moore, Mary Tyler Moore, and Katherine Healy star. **DR2, ST109**

Sixteen Candles (1984, C, 93m, PG)
A girl's 16th birthday is nearly ruined by her family's distractions over her older sister's wedding and her inability to get the attention of a special boy. Molly Ringwald stars. John Hughes wrote and directed. **CO4, DT49, XT20**

Ski Patrol (1990, C, 91m, PG)
Comedy focusing on the antics of young ski enthusiasts who are fighting a greedy developer (Martin Mull) and his plans to take over their resort. With Roger Rose, Corby Timbrook, T.K. Carter, and Ray Walston. **CO19**

Skin Deep (1989, C, 101m, R)
The comic dilemmas of a compulsive ladies' man (John Ritter) in contemporary Los Angeles. Written and directed by Blake Edwards. **CO1, DT32**

Skin Game, The (1931, B&W, 87m, NR)
Early Hitchcock film about a family resorting to blackmail to thwart a neighbor's plans. Edmund Gwenn stars. **DT46**

Skin Game, The (1971, C, 102m, PG)
Amiable, witty comedy about a pair of con men—one black, the other white—traveling through the Civil War South. James Garner and Louis Gossett, Jr. star. **CO6, WE6, WE15** *Recommended*

Sky Is Gray, The (1980, C, 46m, G)
Drama of black child in rural South and his first encounters with racial injustices, based on a story by Ernest Gaines. Olivia Cole, James Bond III, and Cleavon Little star. Originally made for TV. **DR14**

Sky's the Limit, The (1943, B&W, 89m, NR)
A photographer (Joan Leslie) wants to meet a heroic pilot (Fred Astaire). Complications arise when she does meet him, but doesn't recognize him, as he is out of uniform. With Robert Benchley. Astaire sings "One For My Baby." **ST2**

Slamdance (1987, C, 100m, R)
A Los Angeles cartoonist is wrongly accused of murder, takes to the streets to prove his innocence. Tom Hulce stars, with Mary Elizabeth Mastrantonio, Virginia Madsen, and Harry Dean Stanton. Directed by Wayne Wang. **MY7, ST141, XT10**

Slap Shot (1977, C, 122m, R)
Broad, profane comedy about minor-league hockey team and its aging player-coach. Paul Newman stars, with Michael Ontkean, Lindsay Crouse, Jennifer Warren, Melinda Dillon, and Strother Martin. Directed by George Roy Hill. **CO19, ST111**

Slapstick of Another Kind (1984, C, 82m, PG)
Jerry Lewis comedy, based on Kurt Vonnegut, Jr. novel about deformed twins who are really aliens with the solutions to the world's problems. Madeline Kahn co-stars, with Marty Feldman, Samuel Fuller, and Jim Backus. **DT40, ST91**

Slaughter (1972, C, 92m, R)
Jim Brown plays an ex-Green Beret out to avenge his parents' deaths at the hands of organized crime. With Stella Stevens and Rip Torn. **AC19, ST150**

Slaughter in San Francisco (1981, C, 87m, R)
Chuck Norris, in an early role, plays a killer who is being sought by the police. Originally filmed in 1973. **ST114**

Slaughterhouse (1987, C, 87m, R)
An old man with a retarded son doesn't want to sell his slaughterhouse. Soon after the offer is made, people begin to die. **HO24**

Slaughterhouse Five (1971, C, 104, R)
Screen version of the cult novel by Kurt Vonnegut, Jr.: a man becomes unstuck in time and exists where the past, present, and future occur in random order. His most vivid memory of the past is the firebombing of Dresden during World War II, which he and other American POWs survived. Michael Sacks, Valerie Perrine, and Ron Leibman star. **DR19, SF4**

Slave of Love, A (1978, C, 94m, NR)
Russian drama, set during the Revolution, of a love affair between a silent film actress and her cameraman. **FF7**

Slaves of New York (1989, C, 121m, R)
Tama Janowitz' collection of stories about the contemporary art scene in New York was adapted by the writer, concentrating on Eleanor (Bernadette Peters), a hat designer with a heartless painter (Adam Coleman Howard) for a lover. Also in the cast: Chris Sarandon, Mary Beth Hurt, and Mercedes Ruehl. Directed by James Ivory; produced by Ismail Merchant. **DR15, DR19, XT9**

Sleepaway Camp (1983, C, 90m, R)
A psychotic killer is brutally murdering the campers of Camp Arawat. **HO12**

Sleeper (1973, C, 90m, PG)
Woody Allen comedy about a man who is cryogenically frozen and revived two hundred years later to a vastly changed world. Diane Keaton costars. **CO7, DT1, SF4, SF21, ST79**

Sleeping Beauty (1959, C, 75m, G)
An evil witch places a curse on a princess, and it is up to her true love to save her. A classic of Disney animation. **FA2**

Sleeping Beauty (1985, C, 60m, NR)
From the Faerie Tale Theatre series, the tale about a princess who is cursed and her true love who can free her. Christopher Reeve, Bernadette Peters, and Beverly D'Angelo star. **FA12**

Sleeping Dogs (1977, C, 107m, R)
From New Zealand, a political drama of a workers' strike and one man caught between both sides. Sam Neill stars, with Warren Oates. **ST115**

Sleuth (1972, C, 138m, PG)
A vindictive mystery novelist lures his wife's lover into a deadly cat-and-mouse game at a deserted country house. Laurence Olivier and Michael Caine star. Joseph L. Mankiewicz directed; Anthony Shaffer adapted his play. **DR20, DT68, MY9, MY15, ST15, ST116**

Slightly Pregnant Man, A (1973, C, 92m, NR)
Marcello Mastroianni plays a man suffering from morning sickness in this comedy costarring Catherine Deneuve. **ST29, ST103**

Slightly Scarlet (1956, C, 99m, NR)
Thriller about political corruption involving a mayor's secretary and a gangster's secret affair. John Payne, Arlene Dahl, and Rhonda Fleming star. Based on a James M. Cain novel. **MY1, WR1**

Slipstream (1989, C, 92m, PG-13)
Science fiction cop drama of a lawman up against a bounty hunter and his prisoner. Mark Hamill, Ben Kingsley, and F. Murray Abraham star. **SF17**

Slithis (1979, C, 86m, PG)
Radiation leaks into the ocean and causes marine life to mutate, creating a horrifying monster. **HO21**

Slugger's Wife, The (1985, C, 105m, PG-13)
Portrait of a modern romance between a baseball star and a pop singer, whose separate careers threaten to ruin their new marriage. Michael O'Keefe and Rebecca DeMornay star, with Randy Quaid and Martin Ritt. Written by Neil Simon. **DR1, DT87, WR23**

Slumber Party '57 (1980, C, 90m, R)
A group of sorority sisters gather to reveal how each lost her virginity. Debra Winger stars. **ST163**

Slumber Party Massacre (1982, C, 78m, R)
Teenaged girls are menaced by a killer with a power drill. Written by Rita Mae Brown; directed by Amy Jones. **HO9**

Small Change (1976, C, 104m, PG)
Director François Truffaut's loving tribute to children is a loosely connected series of episodes in the lives of youngsters in a French village. **DT106** *Recommended*

Small Town Girl (1953, C, 93m, NR)
MGM musical about title character (Jane Powell) falling for a playboy (Farley Granger). With Ann Miller, Bobby Van, and Nat King Cole. Choreography by Busby Berkeley. **DT8, MU1**

Smile (1975, C, 113m, PG)
Satiric look at a small-town beauty pageant, written by Jerry Belson. Bruce Dern stars, with Barbara Feldon, Michael Kidd, Geoffrey Lewis, Annette O'Toole, and Melanie Griffith. Directed by Michael Ritchie. **CO2, CO8, ST58** *Recommended*

Smiles of a Summer Night (1955, B&W, 108m, NR)
A weekend at a Swedish country estate is the setting for Ingmar Bergman's peerless romantic comedy. **DT7** *Essential; Recommended*

Smith! (1969, C, 101m, G)
In this Disney western, a farmer stands up for the rights of an Indian accused of murder. Glenn Ford stars, with Warren Oates. **FA1, ST115, WE7**

Smithereens (1982, C, 90m, R)
Zany story about a New York hustler whose ambition is to manage a punk rock band. Susan Berman, Brad Rinn, and

Richard Hell star. Susan Seidelman directed. **DR15, XT9**

Smokey and the Bandit (1977, C, 96m, PG)
Burt Reynolds' most popular good ol' boy comedy, about a bootlegger who delights in outwitting a numbskull sheriff (Jackie Gleason). Sally Field costars. **CO9, ST40, ST128**

Smokey and the Bandit II (1980, C, 104m, PG)
Follow-up to first *Smokey* film has Burt Reynolds and Sally Field transporting a pregnant elephant across the South, with sheriff Jackie Gleason in pursuit. **CO9, ST40, ST128**

Smokey and the Bandit 3 (1983, C, 98m, PG)
Third go-round for the action comedy series, with Jerry Reed now the good ol' boy foil for sheriff Jackie Gleason. **CO9**

Smooth Talk (1985, C, 92m, PG13)
A flirtatious adolescent (Laura Dern) meets a slick older man (Treat Williams). With Levon Helm and Mary Kay Place. Based on a short story by Joyce Carol Oates. Originally made for public TV. **DR9, MU12**

Smorgasbord *see* Cracking Up

Snake People, The (1968, C, 90m, NR)
A policeman investigates a series of murders on an island inhabited by a sect of voodoo snake worshipers. Boris Karloff stars. **ST77**

Snoopy Come Home (1972, C, 80m, G)
Snoopy runs away from home and the entire Peanuts gang searches for him in this animated feature. **FA10**

Snow Queen, The (1983, C, 60m, NR)
From the Faerie Tale Theatre series, the story of a queen who teaches a young boy about love and friendship and saves him from a cold curse. Lee Remick, Lance Kerwin, and Melissa Gilbert star. **FA12**

Snow White and the Seven Dwarfs (1983, C, 60m, NR)
Brothers Grimm tale about a beautiful princess helped by seven dwarfs and a handsome prince after her jealous stepmother tries to kill her. Elizabeth McGovern, Vanessa Redgrave, Vincent Price,

and Rex Smith star in this Faerie Tale Theatre production. **FA12, ST124, ST127**

Snowball Express (1972, C, 92m, G)
An accountant (Dean Jones) inherits a hotel in Colorado and tries to turn it into a ski resort. Harry Morgan and Keenan Wynn costar in this Disney comedy. **FA1**

Snows of Kilimanjaro, The (1952, C, 117m, NR)
Hemingway tale of a writer in Africa assessing his life as he lies dying. Gregory Peck stars, with Susan Hayward and Ava Gardner. **ST119, WR10**

So Dear to My Heart (1948, C, 82m, NR)
A young boy tames a wild black sheep in hopes of winning a blue ribbon at the state fair. This Disney film incorporates some animation with live-action sequences. Burl Ives and Bobby Driscoll star. **FA1**

Sodom and Gomorrah (1963, C, 154m, NR)
Biblical spectacle of the twin cities of evil and their destruction. Stewart Granger stars, with Pier Angeli, Stanley Baker, and Anouk Aimee. Directed by Robert Aldrich. **CL13**

Soft Skin, The (1964, B&W, 120m, NR)
A married French businessman finds himself drawn into an affair with a stewardess in this drama from director François Truffaut. Françoise Dorleac stars. **DT106**

Soldier, The (1982, C, 90m, R)
A special agent is dispatched to the Middle East when Soviets hijack a truck packed with deadly plutonium. Ken Wahl and Klaus Kinski star. James Glickenhaus directed. **AC25, ST83**

Soldier Blue (1970, C, 112m, R)
Violent and controversial western focusing on the brutal massacre of an entire Indian village by U.S. cavalry soldiers. Candice Bergen and Peter Strauss star. **WE4, WE7**

Soldier in the Rain (1963, B&W, 88m, NR)
A conniving master sergeant (Jackie Gleason) takes advantage of the G.I. (Steve McQueen) who worships him. Comedy-drama costars Tuesday Weld and Tony Bill. **CO21, ST97**

Soldier of Fortune (1955, C, 96m, NR)
Clark Gable stars in the title role, as he's off to Hong Kong to bring back the kidnapped husband of a lovely woman. With Susan Hayward, Gene Barry, and Michael Rennie. **AC21, ST49**

Soldier of Orange (1979, C, 165m, R)
Epic story of six Dutch university students who enlist when the Nazis invade their homeland. Rutger Hauer and Jeroen Krabbe star. Directed by Paul Verhoeven. **AC1**

Soldiers of Fortune (1970, C, 97m, PG)
Action in war-torn Turkey of the 1920s, with Charles Bronson and Tony Curtis as mercenaries. Original title: *You Can't Win 'Em All.* **AC6, AC21, ST12**

Soldier's Prayer, A *see* Human Condition, Part III, The

Soldier's Story, A (1985, C, 102m, PG)
On a segregated Army base during World War II, an unpopular black officer is murdered, and another black officer is called in to investigate. Howard E. Rollins, Adolph Caesar, and Denzel Washington star in this version of Charles Fuller's play. Directed by Norman Jewison. **DR14, DR20, DT51**

Sole Survivor (1984, C, 85m, R)
The only survivor of a plane crash is haunted by the victims of that disaster. **HO2**

Solid Gold Cadillac, The (1956, B&W/C, 99m, NR)
Comedy set in the world of big business, with Judy Holliday as a heroic stockholder taking on the greedy board of a big corporation. With Paul Douglas, Fred Clark, and John Williams; narrated by George Burns. Last scene in color. **ST69**

Solomon and Sheba (1959, C, 120m, NR)
Biblical spectacle starring Yul Bryunner and Gina Lollobrigida in the title roles. With George Sanders. Directed by King Vidor. **CL13, DT107**

Some Came Running (1958, C, 136m, NR)
James Jones story set in a small town in Indiana, with characters whose lives are going nowhere fast. Frank Sinatra, Shirley MacLaine, and Dean Martin star, with Arthur Kennedy and Martha Hyer. Directed by Vincente Minnelli. **DR26, DT71, ST96, ST138**

Some Kind of Hero (1982, C, 97m, R)
Comedy-drama about a Vietnam veteran who gets a few surprises when he comes home after six years' captivity as a POW. Richard Pryor stars. **ST125**

Some Kind of Wonderful (1987, C, 93m, PG-13)
Teen triangle of guy who loves rich girl, is counseled by his best friend, a girl who loves him. Eric Stoltz, Lea Thompson, and Mary Stuart Masterson star. Produced by John Hughes. **CO4, DT49**

Some Like It Hot (1959, B&W, 119m, NR)
Hilarious comedy about a pair of musicians, on the lam from Al Capone, dressing up like women to join an all-girl jazz band. Jack Lemmon, Tony Curtis, and Marilyn Monroe star, with Joe E. Brown, George Raft, and Pat O'Brien. Written by Billy Wilder and I.A.L. Diamond; directed by Wilder. **CL10, CO10, DT116, ST90, ST108** *Essential; Highly Recommended*

Somebody Up There Likes Me (1956, B&W, 113m, NR)
Bio of boxer Rocky Graziano, who worked his way from the New York slums and a criminal youth to become middleweight champion. Paul Newman stars, with Pier Angeli, Everett Sloane, Sal Mineo, and Robert Loggia. Watch for Steve McQueen in a small role. **DR4, DR22, ST97, ST111**

Someone Behind the Door (1971, C, 95m, PG)
A psychiatrist (Anthony Perkins) discovers that his amnesia patient (Charles Bronson) is a killer and sets him up to kill the psychiatrist's unfaithful wife. **ST12**

Someone To Love (1987, C, 111m, R)
Filmmaker Henry Jaglom invites friends to a Valentine's Day party and records their responses to his questions about romance. Among the guests: Orson Welles, Sally Kellerman, Michael Emil, and Andrea Marcovici. **CO1, DT112**

Someone To Watch Over Me (1987, C, 106m, R)
Cop from Queens, New York, is assigned to protect Manhattan socialite threatened by murder suspect, and romance devel-

ops. Tom Berenger, Mimi Rogers, and Lorraine Braco star. Ridley Scott directed. **DR3, DR15, DT96, MY3, MY5, XT9**

Something for Everyone (1970, C, 112m, R)
Cult comedy about manipulative young man who sexually takes over the house of a poor noblewoman. Michael York and Angela Lansbury star. Harold Prince directed. **CU5, CU6**

Something of Value (1957, B&W, 113m, NR)
Drama set in Kenya during vicious Mau Mau uprising. Rock Hudson, Sidney Poitier, and Wendy Hiller star. **DR14, ST73, ST121**

Something To Sing About (1937, C, 82m, NR)
A bandleader goes Hollywood. James Cagney and William Frawley star. Original running time: 93m. **ST14**

Something Wicked This Way Comes (1983, C, 94m, PG)
The mysterious Mr. Dark and his Pandemonium Circus promise to make everyone's wishes come true—for a very high price. It's up to two small boys and an elderly man to stop him. Jason Robards and Jonathan Pryce star in this version of Ray Bradbury's story. **FA8, HO19, SF13, ST129**

Something Wild (1986, C, 116m, R)
Comedy-drama about an investment analyst "kidnapped" by a free-spirited woman. Jeff Daniels, Melanie Griffith, and Ray Liotta star, with Margaret Colin, Tracey Walter, and, in cameo roles, directors John Waters and John Sayles. Jonathan Demme directed this one-of-a-kind movie. Outstanding use of rock music, including several versions of "Wild Thing." **CO2, CO12, CU1, DT28, DT93, DT110, ST58, XT18** *Highly Recommended*

Sometimes a Great Notion (1971, C, 114m, PG)
Drama of logging family in the Pacific Northwest, adapted from Ken Kesey's novel, starring Paul Newman (who also directed), Henry Fonda, Lee Remick, Michael Sarrazin, and Richard Jaeckel. **DR8, DR19, ST44, ST111**

Somewhere in Time (1980, C, 103m, PG)
Time-travel romance about a man so enthralled by a dead woman's portrait that he wills himself into the past and into her life. Christopher Reeve and Jane Seymour star. **DR1, SF4**

Somewhere Tomorrow (1983, C, 87m, NR)
Teeanged girl bumps her head and believes she's seeing the ghost of a boy killed in a plane crash. Family drama stars Sarah Jessica Parker. **FA7**

Son of Dracula (1943, B&W, 78m, NR)
Classic horror tale with misleading title; it's about the count himself. He's traveling through the American South. Lon Chaney, Jr. stars, with Louise Albritton and Robert Paige. Directed by Robert Siodmak. **HF7, HO1, HO5, ST17**

Son of Flubber (1963, B&W, 100m, G)
Sequel to *The Absent Minded Professor,* with more inventions and trouble. Fred MacMurray and Keenan Wynn star. **FA1**

Son of Frankenstein (1939, B&W, 99m, NR)
The offspring of the famed scientist ressurects his father's creation, with the usual catastrophic results. Basil Rathbone stars, with Boris Karloff as The Monster and Bela Lugosi as Ygor. **HF10, HO1, HO20, ST77, ST95**

Son of Paleface (1952, C, 95m, NR)
Follow-up to *Paleface* finds Bob Hope reunited with Jane Russell. Roy Rogers joins in the fun in this western comedy. **ST70, ST132, WE14**

Son of Sinbad (1955, C, 88m, NR)
Sinbad's son carries on his father's legacy of adventure and romance. Vincent Price costars. **ST124**

Song of Arizona (1946, B&W, 67m, NR)
An outlaw entrusts his son with stolen money, and his gang set out after the boy. Only Roy Rogers can save the day. **ST132**

Song of Bernadette (1943, B&W, 156m, NR)
Jennifer Jones won an Oscar for her portrayal of the young French girl who saw a vision in Lourdes and was ostracized by her village, only to be vindicated years later by sainthood. With William Eythe, Charles Bickford, and Vincent Price. **CL13, DR4, ST124, XT3**

Song of Nevada (1944, B&W, 75m, NR)
Roy Rogers and friends come to the aid
of a girl who's being terrorized by outlaws. Dale Evans and Bob Nolan & the
Sons of the Pioneers costar. **ST132**

Song of Norway (1970, C, 142m, G)
The life of Norwegian composer Edvard
Grieg, starring Florence Henderson, Tor-
alv Maurstad, and Edward G. Robinson.
MU5, ST130

Song of Texas (1953, B&W, 54m, NR)
Roy Rogers helps an alcoholic cowboy
sober up and regain his pride. Bob Nolan
& the Sons of the Pioneers vocalize.
ST132

Song of the Thin Man (1947, B&W, 86m,
NR)
Sixth (and last) *Thin Man* film has Nick
and Nora Charles aboard a gambling ship
when a murder is committed. William
Powell and Myrna Loy star, with Dean
Stockwell (as Nick, Jr.), Keenan Wynn,
and Gloria Grahame. **CL15, HF5, MY17,
ST94, ST122, ST144, WR9** *Recommended*

Song Remains the Same, The (1976, C,
136m, NR)
Led Zeppelin's "home movie" mixes
concert footage with fantasy sequences.
MU11

Song to Remember, A (1945, C, 113m,
NR)
Cornel Wilde plays Frederic Chopin in
this biography costarring Paul Muni and
Merle Oberon (as George Sand). **MU5**

Songwriter (1984, C, 94m, R)
Two country singers plot to "sting" a
greedy promoter in this amiable comedy
starring Willie Nelson and Kris Kristofferson. With Lesley Anne Warren and
Rip Torn. Plenty of fine music from both
leads. Directed by Alan Rudolph. **CO8,
DT91, ST150** *Recommended*

Sons (1989, C, 88m, NR)
A trio of young men take their elderly and
ailing father to France to look up the old
man's wartime flame. William Forsythe,
D.B. Sweeney, and Robert Miranda star,
with Samuel Fuller and Stephane Audran.
DR8, DT40

Sons of Katie Elder, The (1965, C, 112m,
NR)
Four brothers set out to avenge their
mother's death in this spirited western
starring John Wayne and Dean Martin,
with Martha Hyer, Michael Anderson,
Jr., George Kennedy, and Dennis Hopper. **ST71, ST156, WE5**

Sons of the Desert (1933, B&W, 69m, NR)
Classic Laurel and Hardy comedy, with
the boys off to a convention for their
lodge, then concocting a coverup story
for their wives. **CL10, ST87** *Essential;
Highly Recommended*

Sophia Loren: Her Own Story (1980, C,
150m, NR)
The international star plays herself (and
her mother) in this biographical drama,
costarring John Gavin as Cary Grant, Rip
Torn as Carlo Ponti, and Edmund Purdom
as Vittorio De Sica. Originally made for
TV. **ST93**

Sophie's Choice (1982, C, 150m, R)
Intense drama, highlighted by Meryl
Streep's Oscar-winning performance as a
concentration camp survivor living in
postwar Brooklyn. Kevin Kline and Peter
MacNicol play the two men in her life.
Adapted from William Styron's novel; di-
rected by Alan J. Pakula. **DR1, DR2,
DR19, ST84, ST145, XT3, XT9**

Sophie's Place *see* Crooks and Coronets

Sorority House Massacre (1986, C, 74m,
R)
A madman preys on the snobby sisters of
Theta Omega Theta, but his focus is on
the newest pledge, an orphan who suffers
from nightmares. **HO12**

Sorrow and the Pity, The (1970, B&W,
260m, PG)
Epic documentary portrait of France during the German Occupation and the after-
shocks still felt today. Marcel Ophuls directed. **CU16, DT75** *Essential; Highly
Recommended*

Sorrowful Jones (1949, B&W, 88m, NR)
Oft-filmed Damon Runyon story of Little
Miss Marker, the orphan left with a racetrack hustler. Bob Hope stars, with Lucille Ball and William Demarest. **ST70**

Sorry, Wrong Number (1948, B&W, 89m, NR)
Barbara Stanwyck stars in this classic thriller about a woman who overhears her own murder being plotted but can't get anyone to believe her. Burt Lancaster costars. **MY1, MY3, ST85, ST142** *Essential; Recommended*

Sotto, Sotto (1984, C, 105m, NR)
Italian comedy from director Lina Wertmüller of a woman (Veronica Lario) who falls in love with a longtime woman friend (Luisa de Santis). When her husband finds out, he goes berserk. **DT114**

Soul Man (1986, C, 101m, PG-13)
Prospective law school student ups his chances for admission to Harvard when he poses as a black. C. Thomas Howell stars, with Rae Dawn Chong and James Earl Jones. **CO2, CO18, CO20, ST76**

Soul to Soul (1971, C, 95m, NR)
A gathering of soul, jazz, and gospel stars to celebrate the 14th anniversary of Ghanian independence. Performers include Wilson Pickett, Roberta Flack, and Ike & Tina Turner. **MU10**

Sound of Music, The (1965, C, 174m, G)
A novice becomes the governess for the von Trapp children and teaches them and their widowed father the value of love. This film adaptation of the hit Broadway musical won five Academy Awards, including Best Picture and Director (Robert Wise). Julie Andrews and Christopher Plummer star. **DT117, FA9, MU2, MU5, MU7, XT1, XT6**

Sounder (1972, C, 105m, G)
Drama of a black family's struggle in the rural South to survive hardships and injustice, starring Paul Winfield, Cicely Tyson, and Kevin Hooks. Directed by Martin Ritt. **DR14, DT87, ST162**

South of Santa Fe (1942, B&W, 54m, NR)
Roy Rogers falls in love with a young woman who owns a gold mine. **ST132**

South of the Border (1939, B&W, 71m, NR)
Gene Autry and Smiley Burnette head off to Mexico for adventure and a few tunes, too. Duncan Renaldo (TV's Cisco Kid) costars. **ST3**

South Pacific (1958, C, 171m, NR)
Rodgers and Hammerstein's Broadway smash about Navy nurses on the Pacific Islands during World War II. Mitzi Gaynor and Rossano Brazzi star, with John Kerr, Ray Walston, and Juanita Hall. **FA9, MU2**

Southern Comfort (1981, C, 105m, R)
Survival adventure of a Louisiana National Guard troop on weekend maneuvers, lost in the swamps, harassed by vengeful Cajuns. Powers Boothe and Keith Carradine star, with Fred Ward and Peter Coyote. Walter Hill directed; music by Ry Cooder. **AC24, DT45** *Highly Recommended*

Southerner, The (1945, B&W, 91m, NR)
Jean Renoir directed this drama of an American farm family struggling against all odds to make a living. Zachary Scott, Betty Field, and Beulah Bondi star. **DT86**

Southward Ho! (1939, B&W, 54m, NR)
Roy Rogers plays a cowpoke with an itchin' for the warmer climes. **ST132**

Soylent Green (1973, C, 97m, PG)
In the year 2022, a policeman (Charlton Heston) investigates the death of an executive whose company makes soylent green, the only foodstuff left on earth. Edward G. Robinson (in his last film) costars. **SF8, ST130**

Space Rage (1986, C, 78m, R)
A gang of convicts on a penitentiary planet stage a revolt. Skilled weapons specialists are called in to quell the disturbance. Richard Farnsworth and Michael Pare star. **SF17**

Space Raiders (1983, C, 82m, PG)
A young boy and a band of mercenaries battle an evil intergalactic dictator. Vince Edwards stars. **SF13**

Spaceballs (1987, C, 96m, PG13)
Mel Brooks parody of *Star Wars* and other science fiction films. An evil dictator plots to still the atmosphere of a neighboring planet. Brooks stars in two roles, with Daphne Zuniga, Bill Pullman, John Candy, and Rick Moranis. **CO7, CO14, DT13, SF21**

SpaceCamp (1986, C, 107m, PG)
At an astronaut training school, a group of young students and their instructor are

accidentally launched into space. Kate Capshaw and Lea Thompson star. **SF3**

Spaced Invaders (1990, C, 100m, PG)
Five aliens, mistaking an Earth radio station broadcast of "War of the Worlds" as an invitation, invade a small town in the Midwest. Family sci-fi comedy stars Douglas Barr and Royal Dano. **FA8, SF13**

Spacehunter: Adventures in the Forbidden Zone (1983, C, 90m, PG)
Science fiction adventure, starring Peter Strauss and Molly Ringwald, who rescue three beautiful women from the vicious half man/half machine, Overdog (Michael Ironside). **SF3, SF13**

Sparkle (1976, C, 100m, PG)
Three friends form a singing trio in this fictional story based on the early career of The Supremes. Irene Cara and Philip Michael Thomas star. **DR12, DR14, MU4**

Sparrows (1926, B&W, 75m, NR)
Silent melodrama starring Mary Pickford as the protector of a group of orphans. **CL12**

Spartacus (1960, C, 185m, NR)
Epic tale of the Roman gladiator who led a slave revolt and paid a dear price. Kirk Douglas stars, with Jean Simmons, Laurence Olivier, Peter Ustinov (an Oscar winner), Tony Curtis, and Woody Strode. Stanley Kubrick directed. **DR5, DT56, ST34, ST116, XT4**

Special Bulletin (1983, C, 105m, NR)
Riveting drama, presented like a real TV news story with two studio anchors doing running commentary, about radicals engaged in dangerous protest against nuclear weapons. Ed Flanders, Kathryn Walker, Roxanne Hart, and Christopher Allport star. Originally made for TV. **DR7**
Recommended

Special Day, A (1977, C, 106m, NR)
Sophia Loren and Marcello Mastroianni star in this bittersweet story; a housewife and a homosexual have a chance encounter on a day when virtually everyone else in Rome is attending a parade celebrating Hitler's visit. **FF2, ST93, ST103**

Special Effects (1985, C, 106m, R)
A desperate movie producer intends to use footage from a real murder in his latest production, but the dead actress's husband is out for revenge. Zoe Tamerlis and Eric Bogosian star. Larry Cohen directed. **DT20**

Speckled Band, The (1931, B&W, 90m, NR)
Raymond Massey plays Sherlock Holmes, as the famed sleuth helps a girl whose sister has been murdered. Angela Baddely costars. **HF14**

Speed Zone (1989, C, 95m, PG)
In the grand tradition of the *Cannnonball Run* action comedies, here's more cross-country racing with an all-star cast. John Candy, Eugene Levy, Joe Flaherty, Tim Matheson, and Peter Boyle star, with cameo appearances from Brooke Shields (as herself), The Smothers Brothers, Carl Lewis, Michael Spinks, and Lee Van Cleef. **CO9, CO14, ST155**

Speedway (1968, C, 94m, NR)
Elvis Presley plays a singing race car driver who tries to romance his tax auditor (Nancy Sinatra). **ST123**

Spellbound (1945, B&W, 111m, NR)
A psychiatrist (Ingrid Bergman) and her patient (Gregory Peck) fall in love in this classic Hitchcock blend of suspense and romance. With Leo G. Carroll. Salvador Dali contributed sketches for several dream sequences. **DT46, MY5, ST7, ST119**

Spetters (1980, C, 115m, R)
From Holland, a contemporary drama of aimless youth, with Rutger Hauer as a motorcycle racing champion. Paul Verhoeven directed. **FF7**

Spider Baby (1964, B&W, 80m, NR)
Lon Chaney, Jr. stars as the chauffeur for a family of cannibals in this horror tale. Lon warbles the title tune, too. **ST17**

Spider Woman (1944, B&W, 62m, NR)
Sherlock Holmes (Basil Rathbone) and Dr. Watson (Nigel Bruce) take on a wily adversary, a woman (Gale Sondergaard) whose gang poisons wealthy businessmen and disguises the crimes as suicides. Also known as *Sherlock Holmes and the Spider Woman*. **HF14**

Spiders (1919, B&W/C, 137m, NR)
Silent film from German director Fritz Lang about a criminal organization. Color tinted. **DT58**

Spies (1928, B&W, 90m, NR)
A silent film classic from German director Fritz Lang, about a government agent on the trail of a master spy and his gang. **DT58, FF3**

Spies Like Us (1985, C, 103m, PG)
Chevy Chase and Dan Aykroyd star as two bumblers sent by the State Department on a diversionary mission. Features many cameo appearances from such directors as Coista-Gavras, Joel Coen, Martin Brest, and Terry Gilliam, as well as a special guest shot by Bob Hope. **CO13, CO15, CU17, ST70**

Spike of Bensonhurst (1988, C, 101m, R)
Comic tale of a Brooklyn Romeo whose exploits with two young ladies land him in trouble with the local Mob boss. Sasha Mitchell and Ernest Borgnine star, with Sylvia Miles, Maria Pitillo and Talisa Soto. Directed by Paul Morissey. **DT72**

Spinout (1966, C, 90m, NR)
Elvis Presley at the racetrack, singing and shifting gears (and women). Shelley Fabares and Diane McBain costar. **ST123**

Spiral Staircase, The (1946, B&W, 83m, NR)
Dorothy McGuire plays a mute servant who is sure there's a killer hiding in her house but can't get anyone to believe her. Directed by Robert Siodmak. **MY3**

Spirit of Tattoo *see* Irezumi

Spirit of St. Louis, The (1957, C, 138m, NR)
James Stewart plays Charles A. Lindbergh in this drama which focuses on his historic transatlantic solo flight. Billy Wilder directed. **AC11, CL2, DT116, ST143**

Spirit of the Beehive, The (1973, C, 95m, NR)
Spanish drama of a little girl (Ann Torrent) fascinated by the Frankestein monster after she sees the original Boris Karloff film. **FF7, HF10**

Spitfire (1934, B&W, 88m, NR)
Early Katharine Hepburn film has her playing a naive girl in love with a married man (Robert Young). **ST66**

Splash (1984, C, 109m, PG)
A mermaid falls for a young boy, contrives to meet him (on land) when they're a bit older and really ready for love. Daryl Hannah, Tom Hanks, John Candy, and Eugene Levy star. Directed by Ron Howard on location in New York City. **CO1, CO14, CO20, DT48, ST62, XT9** *Recommended*

Splendor in the Grass (1961, C, 124m, NR)
Tragic tale, set in a small town in the 1920s Midwest, about a thwarted love affair that shatters the life of a young girl. Natalie Wood and Warren Beatty (his film debut) star, with Pat Hingle, Sandy Dennis, Phyllis Diller, and Barbara Loden. Elia Kazan directed. **DR1, DR9, DR26, DT53, ST5, XT21**

Split Decisions (1988, C, 95m, R)
Gene Hackman plays an ex-boxer with two sons in the fight game: one has been ordered by the Mob to throw a big fight, while the other wants to go to college and try out for the Olympics. **DR22, ST61**

Split Image (1982, C, 111m, R)
When an impressionable college athlete joins a commune-like cult, his parents have him kidnapped by a ruthless deprogrammer. Michael O'Keefe, Karen Allen, Brian Dennehy, James Woods, Peter Fonda, and Elizabeth Ashley star. **DR8, ST165**

Split Second (1953, B&W, 85m, NR)
An escaped convict (Stephen McNally) holds a group of people hostage in a Nevada town—aware that it's a nuclear bomb test site. With Alexis Smith, Jan Sterling, and Keith Andes. Directed by Dick Powell. **MY1**

Spoilers, The (1942, B&W, 87m, NR)
Action on the Yukon frontier, with prospectors John Wayne and Randolph Scott tussling over dancehall girl Marlene Dietrich. **ST33, ST136, ST156, WE10**

Spontaneous Combustion (1989, C, 97m, R)
Horror tale of a man whose parents were subjected to a radiation experiment in the 1950s; he has grown up with extraordinary powers (see title). Directed by Tobe Hooper. **DT47, SF5**

Spooks Run Wild (1941, B&W, 69m, NR)
The East Side Kids spend the night in a haunted mansion and run into Bela Lugosi. **ST95**

Springtime in the Rockies (1942, C, 91m, NR)
Colorful musical about a Broadway couple's marital and professional ups and downs. Betty Grable and John Payne star, with Carmen Miranda, Cesar Romero, Jackie Gleason, and Harry James and His Band. **MU4**

Springtime in the Sierras (1947, B&W, 75m, NR)
Roy Rogers western: he's battling villainous big-game poachers. Andy Devine provides the laughs. **ST132**

Spy in Black, The (1939, B&W, 82m, NR)
Espionage drama set in World War I Scotland, starring Conrad Veidt as a devious German. Directed by Michael Powell. **DT81, MY6, MY15**

Spy Who Came in From the Cold, The (1965, B&W, 112m, NR)
John LeCarre's story of a Cold Warrior trapped betwen duty and his consicence, starring Richard Burton, with Claire Bloom and Oskar Werner. Directed by Martin Ritt. **DT87, MY6, ST13, WR15** *Recommended*

Spy Who Loved Me, The (1977, C, 125m, PG)
James Bond (Roger Moore) and a sexy Russian agent (Barbara Bach) must join forces to stop a mad mastermind (Curt Jurgens) from destroying the world. Spectacular stunts, especially in the opening sequence. **HF2** *Recommended*

Square Dance (1987, C, 118m, PG-13)
A teenager leaves her granddaddy's Texas farm and strikes out for Ft. Worth and a reunion with her estranged mother. Winona Ryder, Jane Alexander, Rob Lowe, and Jason Robards star. Also known as *Home Is Where The Heart Is*. **DR9, ST129**

Squeeze, The (1987, C, 101m, R)
A con man and a debt collector team to solve a murder case involving the New York State Lottery. Michael Keaton and Rae Dawn Chong star in this comic mystery. **ST80**

Squirm (1976, C, 92m, PG)
During a storm, a high voltage tower falls to the ground and turns the worms into voracious eating machines who devour everything in their path, including humans. **HO16**

Squizzy Taylor (1982, C, 89m, NR)
True saga of an Australian gangster who rose to fame in 1920s Melbourne. David Atkins stars. **FF5**

Stacking (1987, C, 109m, PG)
Coming-of-age drama set in the rural West of the 1950s, starring Megan Follows, Christine Lahti, and Frederic Forrest. **DR9**

Stage Door (1937, B&W, 92m, NR)
A New York boardinghouse is the scene for this comedy-drama about young women with show-biz ambitions. Katharine Hepburn, Ginger Rogers, Lucille Ball, and Eve Arden star. **CL7, ST66, ST131** *Recommended*

Stage Door Canteen (1943, B&W, 132m, NR)
Fictional story of a romance between a G.I. and a hostess at the famous Stage Door Canteen is really an excuse to showcase a variety of stars, including Katharine Hepburn, Harpo Marx, Benny Goodman, Count Basie, and many more. **MU15, ST66**

Stage Fright (1950, B&W, 110m, NR)
An actress's husband is dead, and suspicion falls on a young drama student. Alfred Hitchcock thriller starring Jane Wyman and Marlene Dietrich. **DT46, ST33**

Stage Struck (1936, B&W, 86m, NR)
Busby Berkeley musical starring Dick Powell and Joan Blondell in a story about life behind the scenes of a big show. **DT8**

Stage Struck (1958, C, 95m, NR)
Remake of *Morning Glory*, with Susan Strasberg playing Katharine Hepburn's role of the impressionable young actress. With Henry Fonda. Sidney Lumet directed. **CU18, DT65, ST44**

Stagecoach (1939, B&W, 96m, NR)
The legendary western, starring John Wayne as the Ringo Kid, the outlaw who comes to the aid of a stagecoach in peril. Claire Trevor, Oscar winner Thomas Mitchell, Andy Devine, and John Carradine costar. Directed by John Ford. **DT36, ST156, WE3, XT4** *Essential; Recommended*

Stakeout (1987, C, 115m, R)
Crime comedy-thriller about two cops assigned to watch a waitress whose escaped con boyfriend may show up, with one cop falling in love with her. Richard Dreyfuss, Emilio Estevez, Madeleine Stowe, and Aidan Quinn star. **CO10, ST36** *Recommended*

Stalag 17 (1953, B&W, 120m, NR)
William Holden won an Academy Award for his portrayal of a cynical sergeant in a World War II POW camp. Outstanding supporting cast includes Don Taylor, Otto Preminger, Robert Strauss, Harvey Lembeck, and Peter Graves. Billy Wilder directed. **AC7, DT82, DT116, ST68, XT2** *Essential; Highly Recommended*

Stalking Moon, The (1969, C, 109m, G)
In the Old West, a woman who has been a captive of the Apaches escapes with her half-breed son and seeks protection from an Army scout. Eva Marie Saint and Gregory Peck star. **ST119, WE8**

Stand and Deliver (1988, C, 103m, PG)
True-life drama of a Los Angeles high school math teacher who inspired his underprivileged kids to study hard and perform beyond expectations on standardized tests. Edward James Olmos stars, with Lou Diamond Phillips, Andy Garcia, and Rosana de Soto. **DR6, DR15**

Stand by Me (1986, C, 87m, R)
Comedy-drama of four smalltown pals (Wil Wheaton, River Phoenix, Corey Feldman, Jerry O'Connell) who strike out on an adventure to find a missing boy. Narrated by Richard Dreyfuss. Based on a story by Stephen King; directed by Rob Reiner. **DR9, DT85, ST36, WR12**

Stand Easy *see* Down Among the Z-Men

Stand-In (1937, B&W, 91m, NR)
Comedy poking fun at Hollywood, with Leslie Howard as a lawyer investigating Colossal Pictures, Joan Blondell as a perky stand-in, and Humphrey Bogart as a producer. **CO8, ST8**

Stand Up and Cheer (1934, B&W, 69m, NR)
Shirley Temple does her part to chase away the Depression blues in this musical comedy starring Warner Baxter, Madge Evans, and James Dunn. **ST148**

Stanley and Iris (1990, C, 102m, PG-13)
Romantic drama involving an illiterate cook (Robert DeNiro) and the factory worker (Jane Fonda) who teaches him to read. With Swoosie Kurtz and Martha Plimpton. Directed by Martin Ritt. **DR1, DT87, ST30, ST45**

Stanley and Livingstone (1939, B&W, 101m, NR)
Historical drama of British explorer (Spencer Tracy) searching for famed missionary (Cedric Hardwicke) in the heart of uncharted Africa. With Richard Greene, Nancy Kelly, and Walter Brennan. **CL3, ST151**

Star Chamber, The (1983, C, 109m, R)
Young judge learns of secret tribunal that dispenses its own justice to criminals who beat the legal system. Michael Douglas, Hal Holbrook, and Yaphet Kotto star in this drama. **DR16, ST35**

Star Crystal (1985, C, 93m, R)
A group of scientist astronauts unknowingly pick up a new lifeform which begins to stalk them. **SF20**

Star 80 (1983, C, 117m, R)
True story of model Dorothy Stratten and her murder by her manager-boyfriend. Mariel Hemingway and Eric Roberts star, with Cliff Robertson and Roger Rees. Bob Fosse directed. **DR6, DR13, DT39**

Star Is Born, A (1937, C, 111m, NR)
Classic tale of Hollywood marriage between fading star (Fredric March) and rising one (Janet Gaynor). Co-written by Dorothy Parker; directed by William Wellman. **CL7, DR13**

Star Is Born, A (1954, C, 170m, G)
Judy Garland and James Mason star in this musical remake of the 1937 classic. Many outstanding numbers, including "The Man That Got Away." Directed by George Cukor. This version contains recently restored footage. A 154m version is also available. **CL7, DR13, DT24, MU4, MU14, ST51, ST102** *Essential; Highly Recommended*

Star Is Born, A (1976, C, 140m, R)
A rock 'n' roll remake of the familiar story. Kris Kristofferson plays a rock idol who marries Barbra Streisand, a promising singer, with tragic results. **CU18, MU4, MU9, ST146**

Star of Midnight (1935, B&W, 90m, NR)
Light-hearted mystery starring William Powell as a lawyer accused of murder, forced to prove his innocence. Ginger Rogers costars. **MY7, MY17, ST122, ST131**

Star Trek: The Motion Picture (1979, C, 143m, G)
The *Enterprise* crew is brought back together to battle a strange force field before it can reach Earth. William Shatner and Leonard Nimoy star. Directed by Robert Wise. Video version adds 12 minutes of new footage. **CU10, DT117, FA8, SF3, SF13, SF23**

Star Trek II: The Wrath of Khan (1982, C, 113m, PG)
Khan, a character introduced in the TV series, escapes from exile, looking to destroy Kirk and the rest of the universe. William Shatner and Ricardo Montalban star. **FA8, SF3, SF13, SF23**

Star Trek III: The Search for Spock (1984, C, 105m, PG)
Kirk and his crew head out to find Spock (who "died" at the end of *Star Trek II*) so they can restore him with the essence held in Dr. McCoy's body. Meanwhile, the Klingons decide to get revenge against Kirk by capturing his son. William Shatner and DeForest Kelly star. **FA8, SF3, SF13, SF23**

Star Trek IV: The Voyage Home (1986, C, 119m, PG)
A strange probe, which drains all energy, heads to Earth in search of whales, which are now extinct. Kirk and his crew decide to travel back to 1986 to retrieve a pair of whales, in order to save the Earth of their century. William Shatner and Leonard Nimoy star. **FA8, SF3, SF4, SF13, SF23**

Star Trek V: The Final Frontier (1989, C, 106m, PG)
A Vulcan (Lawrence Luckinbill) forces the *Enterprise* to journey to a distant planet in this installment of the sci-fi series. **FA8, SF3, SF13, SF23**

Star Wars (1977, C, 121m, PG)
Science fiction adventure about a young man (Mark Hamill) who helps rescue a rebel princess (Carrie Fisher) from the clutches of the Empire and goes on to become a general in the rebel forces. An Oscar winner for special effects. With Harrison Ford, Alec Guinness, Peter Cushing, and, as the voice of Darth Vader, James Earl Jones. Directed by George Lucas. Two sequels: *The Empire Strikes Back* and *Return of the Jedi*. **DT64, FA8, SF11, SF13, SF15, SF16, SF23, ST27, ST46, ST60, ST76***Essential; Recommended*

Starchaser: The Legend of Orin (1985, C, 107m, PG)
An animated tale about a young boy who leads a rebellion against an evil dictator. **FA10, SF13**

Stardust Memories (1980, B&W, 91m, PG)
Woody Allen comedy with very dark overtones, about a filmmaker who's frustrated with the demands of his fans, colleagues, and family. Echoes of *8 1/2* and other Fellini movies abound. Charlotte Rampling, Jessica Harper, Marie-Christine Barrault, Tony Roberts, and Daniel Stern head the very large supporting cast. **CO8, DT1** *Recommended*

Starman (1984, C, 115m, PG)
An alien crashlands in Wisconsin and retreats to a farm, where he transforms himself to look like a young widow's late husband. Karen Allen and Jeff Bridges star. John Carpenter directed. **DR1, DT17, SF9, ST11**

Stars and Bars (1988, C, 94m, R)
British satire of contemporary art scene and American eccentrics, with English gallery representative trying to track down a valuable painting purchased by a nouveau riche American. Daniel Day-Lewis and Harry Dean Stanton head the cast. **CO2, CO17, ST141**

Starstruck (1982, C, 95m, PG)
An Australian musical comedy about a waitress with ambitions to be a famous singer. Directed by Gillian Armstrong. **FF5, MU4, MU9**

Start the Revolution Without Me (1970, C, 98m, PG)
Wild comedy set during the French Revolution involving two mismatched sets of twins (Gene Wilder and Donald Sutherland). Orson Welles narrates. **CO5, DT112** *Recommended*

Starting Over (1979, C, 106m, R)
A newly divorced man falls in love with a vulnerable single woman, although he has

trouble shaking his obnoxious ex-wife. Burt Reynolds, Jill Clayburgh, and Candice Bergen star in this romantic comedy. Alan J. Pakula directed. **CO1, ST128** *Recommended*

State Fair (1945, C, 100m, NR)
Musical version of drama filmed in 1933, about a family's adventures at title event. Songs by Rodgers and Hammerstein. Jeanne Crain, Dana Andrews, Dick Haymes, and Vivian Blaine star. Also known as *It Happened One Summer.* **FA9, MU6**

State Fair (1962, C, 118m, NR)
The second musical about an Iowa family's experiences at the title event. Pat Boone stars, with Bobby Darin, Pamela Tiffin, Ann-Margret, and Alice Faye. **FA9, MU6**

State of Siege (1973, C, 120m, NR)
Based on a true story, this French-language political thriller concerns the kidnapping of an American diplomat (Yves Montand) in Latin America by guerrillas opposed to U.S. support of the country's secret police. Costa-Gavras directed. **FF1**

State of the Union (1948, B&W, 124m, NR)
Katharine Hepburn-Spencer Tracy comedy about a Presidential candidate and his fiercely independent wife. Directed by Frank Capra. With Angela Lansbury and Van Johnson. **CL15, DT16, ST66, ST151**

State of Things, The (1982, B&W, 120m, NR)
A moody drama about a film crew on location in Portugal remaking the low-budget cult film, *The Day the World Ended.* Pointed behind-the-scenes look at today's filmmakers and their pretensions, directed by Wim Wenders, shot in English. Patrick Bachau stars, with Sam Fuller, Allen Goorwitz, Paul Getty III, and, in a small role, Roger Corman. **DR13, DT22, DT113**

Stay As You Are (1978, C, 95m, NR)
Middle-aged man romances a teenager, who may be his illegitimate daughter. Marcello Mastroianni and Nastassja Kinski star. **ST103**

Stay Away, Joe (1968, C, 102m, NR)
Elvis Presley plays a Native American in this musical drama, with Burgess Mere-

dith, Joan Blondell, and L.Q. Jones. **ST123**

Stay Hungry (1976, C, 103m, R)
A good ol' boy of the New South is torn between a career in real estate and his affection for a loony group of bodybuilders. Jeff Bridges, Sally Field, and Arnold Schwarzenegger star in this offbeat comedy. Directed by Bob Rafelson.**CO2, ST11, ST40, ST135** *Recommended*

Staying Alive (1983, C, 96m, PG)
This sequel to *Saturday Night Fever* has John Travolta trying to make it as a Broadway dancer. Directed by Sylvester Stallone. **DR12, MU4, ST140**

Staying Together (1989, C, 91m, R)
Three brothers in a small South Carolina town try to keep their family business from being sold off. Sean Astin, Tim Quill, and Dermot Mulroney star, with Stockard Channing, Melinda Dillon, and Levon Helm. **DR8, DR26, MU12**

Stealing Heaven (1989, C, 108m, R)
The Abelard & Heloise story, a forbidden affair between a teacher and his lovely young pupil, with Derek Van Lint and Kim Thomson. An unrated version is also available: running time is 115m. **CU10, DR3**

Stealing Home (1988, C, 98m, PG-13)
A former big-league pitcher recalls his youth when he hears of his babysitter's suicide. Mark Harmon stars, with Jodie Foster, Harold Ramis, and Blair Brown. **CO14, ST47**

Steamboat Bill, Jr. (1928, B&W, 71m, NR)
Buster Keaton plays a young man who has to prove himself to his father, a riverboat captain, in this silent classic. Finale, with cyclone destroying a town, is a highlight. **CL11, DT54** *Essential; Recommended*

Steaming (1985, C, 95m, R)
The setting is a London steam bath for women, and the conversation is frank and revealing. Vanessa Redgrave, Sarah Miles, and Diana Dors star. Director Joseph Losey's last film. **DR23, ST127**

Steel Helmet, The (1951, B&W, 84m, NR)
An American sergeant (Gene Evans) survives a massacre in North Korea and joins up with some other soldiers who have

been cut off from their unit. Samuel Fuller directed. **AC3, DT40**

Steel Magnolias (1989, C, 118m, PG)
The intertwined lives of a group of women in a small Southern town are examined in this comedy-drama. Sally Field, Shirley MacLaine, Dolly Parton, Daryl Hannah, Olympia Dukakis, and Julia Roberts star, with Tom Skerritt and Sam Shepard. Based on the play by Robert Harling. **CO2, DR2, DR10, DR20, DR26, MU12, ST40, ST96**

Steele Justice (1987, C, 95m, R)
A Vietnam vet (Martin Kove) seeks revenge against a druglord who was a Vietcong general and the killer of the vet's best friend. Ronny Cox costars. **AC19**

Steelyard Blues (1973, C, 93m, PG)
Episodic comedy about a group of anti-Establishment types and their pranks, starring Jane Fonda, Donald Sutherland, and Peter Boyle. **CO2, ST45**

Stella (1990, C, 114m, PG-13)
Updated version of *Stella Dallas*, the story of a woman who sacrifices for her illegitimate daughter. Bette Midler stars, with Trini Alvarado, John Goodman, Stephen Collins, and Marsha Mason. **CU18, DR2, DR10, ST105**

Stella Dallas (1937, B&W, 106m, NR)
Barbara Stanwyck stars in the classic soap opera of a woman who gives up everything for her daughter's happiness. Directed by King Vidor. **CL5, CL6, DT107, ST142** *Essential*

Step Lively (1944, B&W, 88m, NR)
Musical remake of *Room Service*, starring George Murphy as a wheeler-dealer producer. With Frank Sinatra, Adolphe Menjou, and Gloria DeHaven. **ST138**

Stepfather, The (1987, C, 89m, R)
A teenaged girl suspects her mother's new husband isn't entirely on the level, and she's right—he's a serial killer who sheds families and identities every few years. Terry O'Quinn and Jill Schoelen star, with Shelley Hack. **MY13, MY14** *Recommended*

Stepfather II (1989, C, 86m, R)
Terry O'Quinn returns as the not-so-dear ol' dad, as he assumes a new identity and picks up with his murderous ways. With

Meg Foster and Caroline Williams. **MY13, MY14**

Steppenwolf (1974, C, 105m, R)
Moody drama of a suicidal writer and his involvement with a mysterious woman, based on Herman Hesse's cult novel. Max von Sydow, Dominique Sanda, and Pierre Clementi star. **DR19**

Sterile Cuckoo, The (1969, C, 107m, PG)
Story of young college boy's first romance, with a girl in desperate need of real affection. Liza Minnelli's film debut; Wendell Burton costars. Directed by Alan J. Pakula; adapted from John Nichols' novel. **DR1, DR19**

Steve Martin Live! (1986, C, 60m, NR)
Footage from a 1979 concert, plus some of his classic bits, including "King Tut" and his Oscar-nominated short film, *The Absent-Minded Waiter*. **CO16, ST99**

Steven Wright Live (1985, C, 53m, NR)
The poker-faced comedian in concert. **CO16**

Stevie (1978, C, 102m, PG)
Glenda Jackson plays eccentric, reclusive British poet Stevie Smith in this unusual film biography. Mona Washbourne costars as Smith's addled aunt. **DR4, DR23**

Stick (1985, C, 109m, R)
Burt Reynolds is an ex-con who gets mixed up in the Miami drug-dealing scene to avenge a friend's death. With Candice Bergen, George Segal, Charles Durning, and Dar Robinson. Based on Elmore Leonard's novel. **AC9, ST128, WR16**

Still of the Night (1982, C, 94m, PG)
Thriller borrowing heavily from Hitchcock has psychiatrist (Roy Scheider) and the girl friend of his murdered patient (Meryl Streep) falling in love. Robert Benton wrote and directed. **DT6, MY5, ST145**

Still Smokin' (1983, C, 91m, R)
Two-part Cheech and Chong comedy has them running wild at an Amsterdam film festival, plus extended concert footage. **ST18**

Sting, The (1973, C, 129m, PG)
Oscar-winning comedy about two Prohibition-era sharpies out to fleece a nasty gambler. Paul Newman and Robert Red-

ford star; Robert Shaw and the music of Scott Joplin offer fine support. Directed by Oscar winner George Roy Hill. **CO6, ST111, ST126, XT1, XT6**

Stir Crazy (1980, C, 111m, R)
A pair of inept bank robbers (Richard Pryor, Gene Wilder) make the most of their stay behind bars by joining the prison rodeo. Sidney Poitier directed. **CO3, CO10, ST121, ST125**

Stolen Kisses (1968, C, 90m, NR)
The third in the Antoine Doinel series of films from star Jean-Pierre Léaud and director François Truffaut finds our hero getting his first taste of real romance. **DT106**

Stolen Life, A (1946, B&W, 107m, NR)
Bette Davis stars in this psychological drama as twin sisters; one takes over with her sister's husband (Glenn Ford). **ST28**

Stone Boy, The (1984, C, 93m, PG)
Montana family is torn apart when one son accidentally shoots and kills his brother. Robert Duvall, Jason Presson, and Glenn Close star, with Wilford Brimley and Frederic Forrest. **DR8, ST20, ST38** Recommended

Stone Killer, The (1973, C, 95m, R)
A dedicated cop (Charles Bronson) works to solve a string of murders linked to organized crime. **ST12**

Stop Making Sense (1984, C, 99m, NR)
This Talking Heads concert film captures the essence of the band, thanks to director Jonathan Demme and his brilliant crew. Three songs added for video version. **CU10, DT28, MU10** Highly Recommended

Storm Boy (1976, C, 90m, NR)
From Australia, a family drama about a young boy learning about life from an elderly aborigine. **FF5**

Storm Over Asia (1928, B&W, 102m, NR)
Silent Soviet historical drama of a Mongolian fur trader leading a fight against occupying British troops in Central Asia. Directed by V.I. Pudovkin. Also known as The Heir to Genghis Khan. **FF7**

Stormy Monday (1988, C, 93m, R)
Moody thriller set in English town of Newcastle, where an American developer

(Tommy Lee Jones) puts the squeeze on a club owner (Sting). With Melanie Griffith and Sean Bean. Written and directed by Mike Figgis, who also composed the music. **DR23, MU12, MY2, MY15, ST58** Recommended

Stormy Weather (1943, B&W, 77m, NR)
A musical that showcases many of the top black entertainers of the 1940s. Lena Horne, Bill Robinson, Fats Waller, Cab Calloway, and The Nicholas Brothers star. **MU3, MU4, MU13** Recommended

Story of Adele H,, The (1975, C, 97m, PG)
True tale of the daughter of French novelist Victor Hugo and her obsession with a young soldier. François Truffaut directed Isabelle Adjani in the title role. **DT106**

Story of Ruth, The (1960, C, 132m, NR)
Biblical tale of faithful daughter-in-law of Naomi, starring Elana Eden, Stuart Whitman, and Tom Tryon. **CL13**

Story of Vernon and Irene Castle, The (1939, B&W, 93m, NR)
Fred Astaire and Ginger Rogers play the real-life husband and wife dance team in this musical biography. **CL15, MU4, MU5, ST2, ST131**

Story of Women (1988, C, 130m, NR)
Intense drama starring Isabelle Huppert as an abortionist in wartime France, being ostracized by a hypocritical community. Directed by Claude Chabrol. **FF1**

Stowaway (1936, B&W, 86m, NR)
A cute little stowaway on a cruise ship helps a young couple find romance. Shirley Temple, Alice Faye, and Robert Young star. **ST148**

Strada, La (1954, B&W, 115m, NR)
Oscar-winning drama from Federico Fellini about a traveling circus and three diverse characters: a lonely waif (Guilietta Masina), a strong man (Anthony Quinn), and an acrobat (Richard Basehart). **DT53, XT7** Essential

Straight Shootin' (1917, B&W, 53m, NR)
Silent western, one of director John Ford's first films, stars Hoot Gibson and Harry Carey, Sr. **DT36**

Straight Time (1978, C, 114m, R)
Ex-con tries to go straight, but is drawn inevitably into old bad habits. Dustin Hoffman stars, with Theresa Russell, Gary Busey, Harry Dean Stanton, and M. Emmet Walsh in this underrated drama. **DR16, ST67, ST141** *Recommended*

Straight to Hell (1987, C, 86m, R)
The last word in western spoofs, with a hip cast that includes Dennis Hopper and rock stars Elvis Costello, Dick Rude, Grace Jones, and Joe Strummer. Directed by Alex Cox. **MU12, ST71, WE14**

Strait-Jacket (1964, B&W, 89m, NR)
Instant camp classic stars Joan Crawford as a just-released convict who served twenty years for ax-murdering her husband and his girl friend in front of her baby daughter. After she moves in with her grown daughter, a series of similar murders occur. **CU2, HO19, ST24**

Strange Brew (1983, C, 91m, PG)
Rick Moranis and Dave Thomas expand their McKenzie Brothers bit from *SCTV* into a feature-length comedy about those Canadian stooges and their search for the perfect beer. **CO14**

Strange Cargo (1940, B&W, 105m, NR)
Allegory of prisoners escaping from Devil's Island in a boat carrying a Christlike character. Joan Crawford and Clark Gable star, with Ian Hunter and Peter Lorre. **ST24, ST49**

Strange Interlude (1988, C, 190m, NR)
Eugene O'Neill drama of a neurotic woman who manipulates the men in her life. Glenda Jackson stars, with Jose Ferrer, David Dukes, and Ken Howard. Originally made for public TV. **DR20, WR20**

Strange Invaders (1983, C, 94m, PG)
Paul LeMat and Nancy Allen star in this gentle spoof of 50s sci-fi movies. An alien force is ready to return home after being on Earth for 25 years, and they want to take the pre-teen daughter of an alien-human union with them. **SF9, SF21**

Strange Love of Martha Ivers, The (1946, B&W, 117m, NR)
Barbara Stanwyck plays a woman with a past that haunts her in this classic film noir, costarring Van Heflin and Kirk Douglas. **MY1, ST34, ST142**

Stranger, The (1946, B&W, 95m, NR)
Ex-Nazi (Orson Welles) lives a second life in New England town until he's tracked down by a relentless pursuer. Welles directed this thriller, with Loretta Young and Edward G. Robinson. **DT112, MY1, MY6, ST130** *Recommended*

Stranger and the Gunfighter, The (1976, C, 107m, PG)
A martial arts spaghetti western. Lee Van Cleef teams with Lo Lieh to track down a killer. **ST155, WE13**

Stranger Is Watching, A (1982, C, 92m, R)
A New York newscaster (Kate Mulgrew) and her daughter are abducted by a madman (Rip Torn). **MY3, ST150, XT9**

Stranger on the Third Floor, The (1940, B&W, 64m, NR)
A reporter's testimony helps convict an innocent man, but the journalist has second thoughts and decides to find the real killer. Peter Lorre stars. **MY7**

Stranger Than Paradise (1984, B&W, 90m, R)
Poker-faced comedy from director Jim Jarmusch about two New York goofs and a 16-year-old Hungarian girl. They sit around in New York apartments, they walk around in the snow in Cleveland, they drive to Florida. John Lurie, Richard Edson, and Eszter Balint star. **CO12, CU1, MU12**

Strangers *see* Voyage to Italy

Strangers Kiss (1984, C, 94m, R)
Drama about the making of a low-budget film whose director tries to encourage a behind-the-scenes romance between his stars to pump up their love scenes on camera. Peter Coyote, Blaine Novak, and Victoria Tennant star, with Richard Romanus. **DR13**

Strangers on a Train (1951, B&W, 101m, NR)
Alfred Hitchcock classic about a psychotic (Robert Walker) trying to talk a tennis pro (Farley Granger) into a murder swap, then carrying out his end of the bargain. Lots of chills, even on repeated viewings; Walker is superb. **DT46, MY9, MY13, XT19** *Essential; Highly Recommended*

Strangers: The Story of a Mother and Daughter (1979, C, 100m, NR)
Bette Davis won an Emmy for her role as a widow whose daughter (Gena Rowlands) comes to visit after twenty years of separation. Originally made for TV. **DR8, ST28**

Strangers When We Meet (1960, B&W, 117m, NR)
Glossy romantic drama of an affair between a married man and woman, starring Kirk Douglas, Kim Novak, Ernie Kovacs, Barbara Rush, and Walter Matthau. **DR1, ST34, ST104**

Strategic Air Command (1955, C, 114m, NR)
James Stewart is a baseball player who puts away his mitt when he's called into the Air Force. Anthony Mann directed. **DT69, ST143**

Straw Dogs (1971, C, 113m, R)
An American academic visiting in rural England is harassed by local toughs and finally fights back in a violent confrontation. Dustin Hoffman stars, with Susan George and David Warner. Sam Peckinpah directed. **DT77, ST67** *Essential; Recommended*

Strawberry Blonde, The (1941, B&W, 100m, NR)
A dentist (James Cagney) is infatuated with a golddigger (Rita Hayworth) but marries a woman (Olivia de Havilland) who really loves him. **ST14, ST64**

Stray Dog (1949, B&W, 122m, NR)
In Tokyo, a police detective's gun is stolen and he has trouble persuading anyone that he's a cop. Toshiro Mifune stars. Akira Kurosawa directed. **DT57, ST106**

Streamers (1983, C, 118m, R)
Intense drama set in an Army barracks at the start of the Vietnam War, starring Matthew Modine, Michael Wright, and Mitchell Lichtenstein. Directed by Robert Altman; screenplay by David Rabe, from his own play. **DR7, DR20, DT2**

Street of Shame (1956, B&W, 96m, NR)
Japanese drama from director Kenji Mizoguchi (his last completed film), about prostitutes in a Tokyo brothel called Dreamland. Machiko Kyo stars. **FF4**

Street Scene (1931, B&W, 80m, NR)
Drama of life in the New York tenements, starring Sylvia Sidney and William Collier, Jr. Directed by King Vidor. **CL8, DT107**

Street Smart (1987, C, 97m, R)
Hotshot reporter, on a tight deadline, concocts story about black pimp; the details happen to match a real pimp who's on trial for murder. Christopher Reeve and Morgan Freeman star in this story of contemporary ethics and life in the media spotlight. With Kathy Baker and Andre Gregory. **DR7, ST48**

Streetcar Named Desire, A (1951, B&W, 122m, NR)
Classic version of Tennessee Williams play of brutal Stanley Kowalski (Marlon Brando), his tough wife Stella (Kim Hunter), and her fragile sister Blanche DuBois (Vivien Leigh). Both actresses and Karl Malden won Oscars. Elia Kazan directed. **DR20, DT53, ST10, WR30, XT3, XT4, XT5** *Essential; Highly Recommended*

Streets of Fire (1984, C, 93m, PG)
A rock singer is kidnapped by the leader of a biker gang, and her ex-boyfriend, a soldier of fortune, sets out to rescue her. Diane Lane, Willem Dafoe, and Michael Pare star in this self-proclaimed "rock 'n' roll fable" with music by Ry Cooder, The Blasters, and others. With Rick Moranis and Amy Madigan. Directed by Walter Hill. **AC8, AC25, CO14, DT45**

Streets of Gold (1986, C, 94m, R)
Russian boxing coach defects to America, finds two fighters to train for international competition against you-know-who. Klaus Maria Brandauer stars. **DR22**

Streetwise (1984, C, 92m, NR)
Documentary portrait of homeless children in Seattle is a searing look at discarded youth. Directed by Martin Bell. **CU16** *Recommended*

Strike (1924, B&W, 70m, NR)
Director Sergei Eisenstein's dramatic account of a 1912 workers' clash with government police. Silent classic of political filmmaking. **CU9, DT33**

Strike Up the Band (1940, B&W, 120m, NR)
A high school band schemes to compete in a radio contest. Mickey Rooney and Judy Garland star. Busby Berkeley directed. **CL15, DT8, MU1, MU4, ST51, ST133**

Stripes (1981, C, 105m, R)
Old-fashioned service comedy with brand-new cast of comedians, featuring Bill Murray, Harold Ramis, and John Candy as the lovable losers, Warren Oates as their perplexed sergeant. **CO13, CO14, CO21, ST115**

Stripper, The (1963, B&W, 95m, NR)
Drama of a no-win love affair between an aging stripper (Joanne Woodward) and a teenager (Richard Beymer). Based on a play by William Inge. **ST166**

Stroker Ace (1983, C, 96m, PG)
Burt Reynolds vehicle has him once again playing the good ol' boy of the car racing circuit. Loni Anderson, Ned Beatty, and Jim Nabors costar. **CO19, ST128**

Stromboli (1950, B&W, 81m, NR)
Ingrid Bergman stars in this drama of a woman and her loveless marriage to an Italian fisherman. Directed by Roberto Rossellini, then her husband. **FF2, ST7**

Strong Man, The (1926, B&W, 78m, NR)
Silent comedy featuring Harry Langdon as a World War I soldier who returns to the U.S. to claim the love of a woman who wrote to him during the war. Directed by Frank Capra. **CL11, DT16**

Studs Lonigan (1960, B&W, 95m, NR)
Drama of aimless Chicago youth in 1920s and his inevitable fate. Based on James T. Farrell's novel, starring Christopher Knight, Frank Gorshin, and (in a small, early role) Jack Nicholson. **DR15, DR19, ST112**

Study in Scarlet, A (1933, B&W, 70m, NR)
Sherlock Holmes mystery which has nothing to do with the story which introduced the famed detective. Reginald Owen stars. **HF14**

Study in Terror, A (1965, C, 94m, NR)
Sherlock Holmes (John Neville) takes on Jack the Ripper in this British-made mystery. Donald Houston costars as Dr. Watson. **HF14**

Stuff, The (1985, C, 93m, R)
A popular new dessert is killing people. A spoof of 1950's sci-fi/horror films. Michael Moriarty and Garrett Morris star. Larry Cohen directed. **CO13, DT20, HO24**

Stunt Man, The (1980, C, 129m, R)
Comedy-drama about filmmaker who offers a fugitive the most dangerous job in movies after the film's stunt man is killed in an accident. Peter O'Toole, Steve Railsback, and Barbara Hershey star in this dazzling look at the way movies create the illusion of reality. **DR13, ST117** *Recommended*

Stunts (1977, C, 89m, PG)
When a stunt man is killed during filming, his brother suspects foul play and decides to investigate on his own. Robert Forster stars. **DR13, MY11**

Suburbia (1984, C, 96m, R)
No-holds-barred drama of society's cast-offs, kids living in deserted tract houses, stealing for food, drinking, and getting high. Directed by Penelope Spheeris. **CU12, DR9** *Recommended*

Subway to the Stars (1987, C, 103m, R)
Brazilian drama of a musician (Guilherme Fontes) in search of his missing girlfriend on the streets of Rio de Janeiro. Directed by Carlos Diegues. **FF6**

Succubus *see* The Devil's Nightmare

Sudden Impact (1983, C, 117m, R)
Dirty Harry is on the trail of a woman who is, one by one, killing the people responsible for the gang rape she and her sister suffered. Clint Eastwood and Sondra Locke star. **AC9, ST39**

Suddenly (1954, B&W, 77m, NR)
Thriller about a gang of thugs planning to assassinate the President as he passes through a small town. Frank Sinatra stars. **DR16, MY1, ST138**

Suddenly, Last Summer (1959, B&W, 114m, NR)
Tennessee Williams drama of a young girl's breakdown and her aunt's manipulative attempts to cure her. Elizabeth Taylor, Katharine Hepburn, and Montgom-

ery Clift star. Written by Gore Vidal; directed by Joseph L. Mankiewicz. **DT68, ST66, ST147, WR30**

Sugar Cane Alley (1984, C, 107m, NR) French drama set in 1930s Martinique, centering on the hopes and dreams of a 10-year-old boy (Garry Cadenat). Directed by Euzhan Palcy. **FF1**

Sugarbaby (1985, C, 87m, R) An odd-couple comedy from Germany about a romance between a plump mortuary attendant and a wimpy subway conductor. Marianne Sagebrecht stars. Percy Adlon directed.**FF3**

Sugarland Express, The (1974, C, 109m, PG) Comedy-drama, based on a true story, about a fugitive couple, their baby, and a hostage state trooper pursued across Texas by a small army of law enforcement agents. Goldie Hawn, William Atherton, and Michael Sacks star, with Ben Johnson. Directed by Steven Spielberg. **DR6, DT99, ST63, XT18** *Recommended*

Suicide Run *see* Too Late the Hero

Sullivan's Travels (1941, B&W, 91m, NR) Writer-director Preston Sturges's satire about a Hollywood director (Joel McCrea) who sets out to make a "serious" film by bumming around the country. Veronica Lake, William Demarest, and Eric Blore head the supporting cast. **CL10, CO20, DT103, XT18** *Essential; Highly Recommended*

Summer (1986, C, 98m, R) From French director Eric Rohmer, a comedy about a Parisian secretary's attempts to escape the city during August. **DT89**

Summer Camp Nightmare (1987, C, 87m, PG-13) At a summer camp run by a strict counselor, the kids stage a revolt and imprison all the adults. **HO12**

Summer City (1976, C, 83m, NR) A quartet of teens are out for a good-times weekend at a seaside resort but run into trouble with resentful locals. Mel Gibson stars in this Australian drama. **FF5, ST53**

Summer Interlude (1951, B&W, 90m, NR) Early Ingmar Bergman drama about a woman sorting out the details of her relationship with a now-dead lover. Also known as *Illicit Interlude*. **DT7**

Summer Lovers (1982, C, 98m, R) A young man and two attractive women enjoy a summer fling on a Greek island in this sexy movie with a cult following. Peter Gallagher, Daryl Hannah, and Valerie Quennessen star. **CU6**

Summer Magic (1963, C, 100m, NR) Disney comedy-drama about a Maine widow raising her family on a meager income. Dorothy McGuire and Hayley Mills star. **FA1**

Summer Night (1987, C, 94m, R) A rich businesswoman (Mariangelo Melato) holds a terrorist captive on an island in this comedy from Italian director Lina Wertmüller. Full title: *Summer Night, With Greek Profile, Almond Eyes and Scent of Basil.* **DT114**

Summer Place, A (1959, C, 130m, NR) Quintessential 1950s romantic drama, set on the coast of Maine, focusing on older couple (Richard Egan & Dorothy McGuire) and younger (Sandra Dee & Troy Donahue). **DR1**

Summer Rental (1985, C, 87m, PG) John Candy stars in this comedy about an air traffic controller's disastrous summer at the beach. With Rip Torn and Richard Crenna. **CO14, ST150**

Summer School (1987, C, 98m, PG-13) A laid-back physical education teacher is roped into teaching a summer course in history to a class of misfits. Mark Harmon stars with Kirstie Alley in this comedy. **CO18**

Summer Solstice (1981, C, 75m, NR) An aging couple (Henry Fonda and Myrna Loy) return to the beach where they first met 50 years ago. With Lindsay Crouse and Stephen Collins. Originally made for TV. **DR11, ST44, ST94**

Summer Stock (1950, C, 109m, NR) Gene Kelly and his troupe invade Judy Garland's farm in order to rehearse their Broadway show. When the female star of the show leaves, Judy fills in. Gene dances with newspapers and Judy sings "Get Happy." **MU4, ST51, ST81**

Summer Wishes, Winter Dreams (1973, C, 93m, PG)
Joanne Woodward plays a New York woman whose emotional distance from everyone around her frustrates her. With Martin Balsam and Sylvia Sidney. **DR10, ST166**

Summertime (1958, C, 98m, NR)
Tearjerker about a spinster (Katharine Hepburn) from Ohio visiting Venice, falling in love with a married man (Rossano Brazzi). David Lean directed. **CL4, CL6, DT59, ST66**

Sunburn (1979, C, 94m, PG)
An insurance investigator (Charles Grodin) is joined by a lovely blonde (Farrah Fawcett) in Mexico to investigate a murder/suicide. With Art Carney, Joan Collins, and William Daniels. **MY10, ST59**

Sunday, Bloody Sunday (1971, C, 110m, R)
Romantic triangle drama, with middle-aged man and young woman competing for the same man. British drama stars Peter Finch, Glenda Jackson, and Murray Head. Screenplay by Penelope Gilliatt; directed by John Schlesinger.**DR3, DR23, DT94**

Sunday in the Country, A (1984, C, 94m, G)
An aging painter invites his loved ones to spend a day at his rural estate. Bertrand Tavernier directed this French drama. **FF1**

Sundays and Cybelle (1962, B&W, 110m, NR)
A war veteran suffering from shell shock finds comfort in the friendship of a young girl. Oscar winner for Best Foreign-Language film. **FF1, XT7**

Sundowners, The (1960, C, 113m, NR)
Drama of Australian sheep herding family, starring Robert Mitchum, Deborah Kerr, and Peter Ustinov. Directed by Fred Zinnemann. **DT120, ST107**

Sunrise at Campobello (1960, C, 143m, NR)
Ralph Bellamy's famed portrait of Franklin D. Roosevelt, adapted from the Dore Schary stage hit. Greer Garson plays Eleanor; Hume Cronyn and Jean Hagen costar. **DR4**

Sunset (1988, C, 105m, PG-13)
In 1920s Hollywood, former Western lawman Wyatt Earp and cowboy movie star Tom Mix team to solve a murder mystery. James Garner and Bruce Willis star. Blake Edwards directed this nostalgic comedy, with plenty of detail about Hollywood in the Jazz Age. **CO6, CO8, DT32, MY17, ST161**

Sunset Boulevard (1950, B&W, 110m, NR)
Legendary look at the seamy underside of Hollywood, with reclusive former star (Gloria Swanson) taking in young screenwriter (William Holden). With Erich von Stroheim, Nancy Olson, Jack Webb, and Buster Keaton and Cecil B. DeMille in bit parts. Billy Wilder directed. **CL7, DR13, DT27, DT54, DT109, DT116, MY1, ST68** *Essential; Highly Recommended*

Sunset in the West (1950, B&W, 67m, NR)
A deputy sheriff (Roy Rogers) battles gunrunners. **ST132**

Sunset on the Desert (1942, B&W, 53m, NR)
Roy Rogers action, with a man returning to his hometown to help his late father's partner out of a jam. **ST132**

Sunset Serenade (1942, B&W, 58m, NR)
Roy Rogers and Gabby Hayes step in the way of some dastardly villains intent on murder and thievery. Bob Nolan & the Sons of the Pioneers add some harmonizing. **ST132**

Sunshine Boys, The (1975, C, 111m, PG)
A pair of ex-vaudeville partners, not on speaking terms, are persuaded to reteam for a TV special. Neil Simon comedy stars Walter Matthau and Oscar winner George Burns. **CO3, CO8, ST104, WR23, XT4**

Superdad (1974, C, 96m, G)
A father (Bob Crane) challenges his daughter's fiance (Kurt Russell) to various competitions to test his worthiness in this Disney comedy. **FA1**

Supergirl (1984, C, 114m, PG)
Supergirl, cousin to Superman, is sent to Earth to recover the Omegahedron, a source of unlimited power, which has fallen into the hands of an evil witch.

Helen Slater stars, with Faye Dunaway and Peter O'Toole. **AC17, FA4, ST37, ST117**

Superman (1978, C, 143m, PG)
The history of Superman, from Krypton to Metropolis. The special effects won an Academy Award. Christopher Reeve stars, with Margot Kidder, Gene Hackman, Ned Beatty, and Marlon Brando. **AC17, FA4, SF15, ST10, ST61** *Essential*

Superman II (1980, C, 127m, PG)
Three villains from Krypton come to Earth with plans to rule the world. Christopher Reeve, Margot Kidder, Gene Hackman, and Terence Stamp star. Directed by Richard Lester. **AC17, DT62, FA4, ST61**

Superman III (1983, C, 123m, PG)
A master villain cons a computer genius into splitting Superman's personalities, one good, one bad. Christopher Reeve, Richard Pryor, and Robert Vaughn star. Richard Lester directed. **AC17, DT62, FA4, ST125**

Superman IV: The Quest for Peace (1987, C, 90m, PG)
Lex Luthor creates a monster to battle Superman, who has just rid the world of nuclear weapons. Christopher Reeve and Gene Hackman star. **AC17, FA4, ST61**

Supernaturals, The (1986, C, 85m, R)
A troop of new recruits on manuevers end up fighting for their lives when a ghost army of Confederate soldiers come to life seeking revenge. Maxwell Caulfield, LeVar Burton, and Nichelle Nichols star. **HO2**

Support Your Local Sheriff! (1969, C, 93m, PG)
Amiable western comedy, with James Garner as a peaceable lawman who has to bring in the bad guys without benefit of a six-shooter. **WE14**

Sure Thing, The (1985, C, 94m, PG-13)
Road comedy about two mismatched college students finding romance as they hitchhike cross-country. John Cusack and Daphne Zuniga star. Directed by Rob Reiner. **CO1, DT85, XT18** *Recommended*

Surrender (1987, C, 95m, PG)
A much-divorced novelist and a struggling artist find romance. Michael Caine, Sally Field, and Steve Guttenberg star in this comedy. **CO1, ST15, ST40**

Survivors, The (1983, C, 102m, R)
Two unemployed men are fingered by the same hit man and flee for their lives to a survivalist commune. Comedy starring Walter Matthau and Robin Williams. **CO3, ST104, ST160**

Susana (1951, B&W, 87m, NR)
Director Luis Buñuel's study of a vagrant girl's alluring hold over a respectable Spanish family. Rosita Quintera stars, with Fernando Soler. **DT15**

Susanna Pass (1949, C, 67m, NR)
Roy Rogers and Dale Evans team up with Cuban star Estelita Rodriguez for western action and plenty of songs. **ST132**

Susannah of the Mounties (1939, B&W, 79m, NR)
Shirley Temple goes West in this sentimental tale of a Mountie (Randolph Scott) who adopts a girl orphaned in an Indian raid. **ST136, ST148**

Suspect (1987, C, 101m, R)
Drama set in Washington, D.C., about a public defender (Cher) whose client is accused of murder and a juror (Dennis Quaid) on the case who uncovers evidence that he decides to share with her. **DR17, ST19, XT12**

Suspicion (1941, B&W, 99m, NR)
Shy young woman is pursued by charming playboy and marries him, then immediately begins to suspect he's targeted her for murder. Classic Alfred Hitchcock suspense starring Oscar winner Joan Fontaine and Cary Grant. **DT46, MY3, MY5, ST57, XT3**

Suspicion (1987, C, 87m, NR)
Remake of the Alfred Hitchcock thriller about a woman who suspects her playboy husband of wanting to murder her, starring Jane Curtin and Anthony Andrews. Originally made for cable TV. **CO13, CU18, MY3, MY5**

Suspiria (1977, C, 92m, R)
Horror tale with cult following, about an American girl who learns that her European dance school is really a coven for witches. Jessica Harper stars. Also available in an unrated version; running time: 97m. **CU4, CU10, HO12**

Svengali (1983, C, 100m, NR)
The classic tale of a young woman's rise to fame and her manipulative benefactor, updated to star Jodie Foster as a rock singer and Peter O'Toole in the title role. Originally made for TV. **ST47, ST117**

Swamp Diamonds (1955, C, 73m, NR)
Four female convicts escape, go looking for treasure amid the muck. Michael Connors, Marie Windsor, and Beverly Garland star. Also known as *Swamp Women*. Directed by Roger Corman. **DT22**

Swamp Thing (1982, C, 91m, PG)
A research scientist who discovers a potion to end world hunger is covered with the substance and becomes a human vegetable. Adrienne Barbeau and Louis Jourdan star. Directed by Wes Craven. **HO16**

Swamp Women *see* Swamp Diamonds

Swann in Love (1984, C, 110m, R)
A French aristocrat finds himself drawn to a woman of less than impeccable breeding in this adaptation of Marcel Proust's classic novel. Jeremy Irons and Ornella Muti star. Directed by Volker Schlöndorff. **DR19, FF1**

Swap, The (1969, C, 90m, R)
Drama about a film editor's search for the killers of his brother, starring Robert DeNiro in an early screen appearance. Originally released in different form as *Sam's Song;* this version adds several new characters. **ST30**

Swarm, The (1978, C, 116m, PG)
Deadly killer bees attack an all-star cast which includes Michael Caine, Katharine Ross, Henry Fonda, and Richard Chamberlain. **HO16, SF7, ST15, ST44**

Swedenhielms (1935, B&W, 88m, NR)
Ingrid Bergman stars in this drama, made in Sweden before her emergence as a star in Hollywood. She's the girlfriend of a young man whose impoverished family is counting on their patriarch to win the Nobel Prize. **FF7, ST7**

Sweet Bird of Youth (1962, C, 120m, NR)
Tennessee Williams drama of fading star and her fling with youthful lover. Geraldine Page and Paul Newman star, with Rip Torn and Oscar winner Ed Begley. **ST111, ST150, WR30, XT4**

Sweet Charity (1969, C, 133m, G)
A dancehall hostess wants a traditional wedding and marriage, but keeps falling in love with ne'er-do-wells who only want her money. The directorial debut of Bob Fosse. Shirley MacLaine stars, with Chita Rivera and Sammy Davis, Jr. **DT39, MU2, MU3, MU14, ST96**

Sweet Dreams (1985, C, 115m, PG13)
Jessica Lange portrays legendary country singer Patsy Cline. With Ed Harris and Ann Wedgeworth. Cline's voice was used on the soundtrack recordings. **DR2, DR4, DR12, MU5, ST86**

Sweet Hearts Dance (1988, C, 101m, R)
A small Vermont town is the setting for this romantic comedy about a couple (Don Johnson, Susan Sarandon) whose shaky marriage isn't helped by his best buddy (Jeff Daniels). **CO1**

Sweet Liberty (1986, C, 107m, PG)
The author of a bestselling book on the American Revolution is appalled when a movie crew arrives in his hometown and begins filming a very loose adaptation of his work. Alan Alda stars, with Michael Caine, Michelle Pfeiffer, Bob Hoskins, and Lillian Gish. Alda also wrote and directed. **CO8, ST15, ST54, ST72, ST120**

Sweet Movie (1975, C, 97m, NR)
Unique film from director Dusan Makavejev about sexuality. Two stories parallel: in one, the winner of a Miss Virginity contest marries a crass Texan; in the second, a female ship's captain and a Soviet sailor have a murderous sexual encounter. Recommended only for the very adventurous. **CU6**

Sweet Sixteen (1981, C, 90m, R)
As beautiful and promiscuous Melissa approaches her sixteenth birthday, her boyfriends start to die. Susan Strasberg and Bo Hopkins star. **HO7**

Sweet Smell of Success (1957, B&W, 96m, NR)
A ruthless New York gossip columnist (Burt Lancaster) uses his power to destroy anyone who doesn't curry favor with him. Tony Curtis costars as a sycophantic press agent. With Martin Milner and Susan Harrison. Superb screenplay by Ernest Lehman and Clifford Odets. **CL7, MY1, ST85** *Essential; Highly Recommended*

Sweet Sweetback's Badasssss Song (1971, C, 97m, R)
A black man kills two racist cops and flees for his life. Written and directed by Melvin Van Peebles, who also stars. **AC8, DR14**

Sweethearts (1938, C, 115m, NR)
Colorful show-biz saga of a Broadway couple (Nelson Eddy, Jeanette MacDonald) whose partnership is threatened when Hollywood beckons. **CL7, CL15**

Sweetie (1989, C, 90m, NR)
Australian story of two sisters (Karen Colston, Genevieve Lemon) and their bizarre relationship. Directed by Jane Campion. **FF5**

Swept Away (1975, C, 116m, R)
An Italian comedy-drama about a shipwrecked odd couple—a snooty rich woman and a lusty sailor. Giancarlo Giannini and Mariangelo Meltao star; Lina Wertmüller directed. **DT114**

Swimmer, The (1968, C, 94m, PG)
Burt Lancaster stars in this drama about a suburbanite who swims through his neighbors' pools on his way home, recalling past experiences along the way. Based on a John Cheever story. **ST85**

Swimming to Cambodia (1987, C, 100m, NR)
Actor/monologist Spalding Gray recounts his experiences on location in Thailand for *The Killing Fields* in this mesmerizing one-man show. Directed by Jonathan Demme. **CO12, DT28** *Recommended*

Swindle, The *see* Bidone, Il

Swing High, Swing Low (1937, B&W, 95m, NR)
Fred MacMurray is a trumpet player whose career hits every note on the scale. Carole Lombard costars. **CL7, ST92**

Swing Shift (1984, C, 100m, PG)
Goldie Hawn goes to work in a factory when her husband goes to fight in World War II. Christine Lahti, Kurt Russell, and Ed Harris star in this nostalgic drama from director Jonathan Demme. **DR3, DR5, DR10, DT28, ST63**

Swing Time (1936, B&W, 103m, NR)
A gambler falls in love with a dance teacher, even though he is engaged to another woman. Fred Astaire and Ginger Rogers star. George Stevens directed this classic musical. **CL15, DT101, MU4, ST2, ST131** *Essential; Highly Recommended*

Swiss Family Robinson (1960, C, 128m, G)
A shipwrecked family learn to survive on a deserted island. John Mills and Dorothy McGuire star in Disney's version of the family adventure classic. **FA1**

Swiss Miss (1938, B&W, 72m, NR)
Laurel and Hardy comedy, set in the Alps, with Ollie a love-smitten yodeler. **ST87**

Switchblade Sisters (1975, C, 91m, R)
Urban action drama centering on the exploits of a female street gang. Robbie Lee, Joanne Nail, and Kitty Bruce star. **AC8**

Switching Channels (1988, C, 108m, PG)
Romantic comedy triangle composed of a TV news producer (Burt Reynolds), his star reporter and ex-wife (Kathleen Turner), and her fiance (Christopher Reeve). A loose remake of *The Front Page* and *His Girl Friday*. **CO1, CU18, ST128, ST152**

Sword and the Rose, The (1953, C, 93m, NR)
Mary Tudor works her charms on a knight, incurs the wrath of a duke, and is noticed by Henry the VIII. Disney version of *When Knighthood Was in Flower*, starring Glynis Johns and Richard Todd. **FA1**

Sword in the Stone, The (1963, C, 75m, G)
Disney animated feature about a young boy who is destined to be king of England and is helped by the wizard Merlin. **FA2**

Sword of Doom (1967, B&W, 120m, NR)
Tatsuya Nakadai stars in this adventure film as a samurai whose lust for action alienates even his own family. Toshiro Mifune appears in a small supporting role. **ST106**

Sword of Sherwood Forest (1961, C, 80m, NR)
Richard Greene stars as Robin Hood in this costume adventure, with Peter Cushing. **AC15, HF15, ST27**

Sword of the Valiant (1982, C, 101m, PG)
In order to become a knight, Gawain (Miles O'Keeffe) must battle the Green Knight (Sean Connery) and solve a riddle. Trevor Howard and Peter Cushing costar. **FA4, ST21, ST27**

Sybil (1976, C, 132m, NR)
Famous case of woman with multiple personalities and the therapist who helped cure her. Sally Field stars, with Joanne Woodward. Originally made for TV with a running time of 198m. **DR6, ST40, ST166**

Sylvester (1984, C, 104m, PG)
Young woman trains her favorite show horse for competition. Melissa Gilbert stars. **DR22, FA5**

Sylvia and the Phantom (1945, B&W, 97m, NR)
French comedy of a teenaged girl's infatuation with the painting of a long-dead nobleman. Odette Joyeux stars, with Jacques Tati. **DT104**

Sylvia Scarlett (1935, B&W, 94m, NR)
Katharine Hepburn and Cary Grant star in this offbeat story of a traveling troupe of players; she's disguised as a boy and he doesn't suspect a thing—for a while. Directed by George Cukor; underappreciated until recent rediscovery. **CL14, DT24, ST57, ST66** *Highly Recommended*

Sympathy for the Devil (1970, C, 92m, NR)
French director Jean-Luc Godard alternates political rhetoric with shots of the Rolling Stones recording the title song. **CU9, DT41**

THX 1138 (1971, C, 88m, PG)
In the future, computers keep the humans drugged so they cannot think and feel for themselves. One man (Robert Duvall) and his roommate (Maggie McOmie) decide to stop taking the drugs and begin to feel human emotions. Director George Lucas's debut feature. **DT64, SF11, ST38**

T-Men (1947, B&W, 96m, NR)
Undercover government agents try to expose a counterfeit ring. Suspenseful drama from director Anthony Mann, starring Dennis O'Keefe. **DT69, MY1**

T.N.T. Jackson (1974, C, 73m, R)
A female karate expert (Jeanne Bell) searches for her missing brother. **AC26**

Tai-Pan (1986, C, 127m, R)
Historical drama about the founding of modern Hong Kong, based on James Clavell's epic novel. Bryan Brown and Joan Chen star. **DR5**

Take a Hard Ride (1975, C, 103m, PG)
Jim Brown, Lee Van Cleef, and Fred Williamson head the cast of this western drama about a cowboy carrying a payroll shipment across the Mexico border. **ST155, WE9**

Take Me Out to the Ball Game (1949, C, 93m, NR)
Busby Berkeley musical about a woman (Esther Williams) who takes over a winning baseball team. Gene Kelly and Frank Sinatra are her star players, who sing and dance better than they hit and field. **DT8, MU6, ST81, ST138**

Take the Money and Run (1969, C, 85m, PG)
Woody Allen's tale of an inept bank robber spoofs documentaries, crime movies, love stories—you name it. Janet Margolin costars. **CO7, CO10, DT1**

Taking of Pelham One Two Three, The (1974, C, 104m, PG)
A gang of hijackers hold the passengers of a New York subway car hostage. Walter Matthau is the cop on the case, Robert Shaw the lead baddie. **AC9, ST104, XT9, XT19**

Tale of the Frog Prince, The (1985, C, 60m, NR)
A spoiled princess is forced to look after a talented frog who turns out to be a cursed prince. Robin Williams and Teri Garr star in this presentation from Faerie Tale Theatre. **FA12, ST160**

Tale of Two Cities, A (1935, B&W, 121m, NR)
Charles Dickens' classic story of the French Revolution and one man's sacrifice for another on the guillotine. Ronald Colman, Elizabeth Allan, and Edna May Oliver star. **CL3, WR4** *Recommended*

Tales From The Crypt (1972, C, 92m, PG)
Five criminally minded people are trapped in the catacombs with a mind-

reading monk. He shows each of them the consequences if they carry out the crimes they are plotting. Joan Collins and Peter Cushing star. **HO23, HO26, ST27**

Tales From the Crypt (1989, C, 81m, NR) Three-part horror film from directors Walter Hill, Robert Zemeckis, and Richard Donner, based on the old E.C. Comics stories. **DT45, HO23**

Tales From the Darkside: The Movie (1990, C, 93m, R) Anthology horror film based on stories by Stephen King, Arthur Conan Doyle, and Michael McDowell. Among the stars: Deborah Harry, Christian Slater, David Johansen, William Hickey, James Remar, and Rae Dawn Chong. **HO23, MU12, WR12**

Tales of Ordinary Madness (1983, C, 107m, NR) Drama of hard-drinking poet who meets unusual assortment of women in his travels. Ben Gazzara, Ornella Muti, and Susan Tyrell star. Based on stories by Charles Bukowski. **CU6**

Tales of Terror (1962, C, 90m, NR) Three stories based on Edgar Allen Poe; "The Black Cat," "Morella," and "The Case of M. Valdemar." Vincent Price and Peter Lorre star. Directed by Roger Corman. **DT22, HO23, ST124, WR21**

Talk of the Town, The (1942, B&W, 118m, NR) Classic comedy with Cary Grant a fugitive hiding out in boardinghouse run by Jean Arthur, debating fellow boarder Ronald Colman on the justice system. Directed by George Stevens. **CL10, DT101, ST57**

Talk Radio (1988, C, 110m, R) Eric Bogosian plays a smart-mouthed radio talk show host whose personal life matches the turmoil he creates on the air. Oliver Stone directed; based on Bogosian's play and true incidents in the life of Alan Berg, a host who was assassinated by white supremacists. **DR6, DR7, DR12, DR20, DT102**

Tall Blonde Man With One Black Shoe, The (1972, C, 90m, PG) French spy spoof starring Pierre Richard as a man caught in the middle of a battle between espionage agents. U.S. remake: *The Man With One Red Shoe*. **FF1, FF8**

Tall Men, The (1955, C, 122m, NR) After the Civil War, two Rebs sign on a cattle drive from Texas to Montana. Clark Gable and Robert Ryan star, with Jane Russell. **ST49**

Tamarind Seed, The (1974, C, 123m, PG) Blake Edwards directed this story of romance and espionage, starring Omar Sharif and Julie Andrews. He's a Russian agent trying to recruit her at a Caribbean resort, but love intervenes. **DT32, MY5, MY6**

Taming of the Shrew, The (1967, C, 126m, NR) Elizabeth Taylor-Richard Burton version of Shakespeare's classic comedy of a headstrong woman and her equallly stubborn suitor. Franco Zeffirelli directed. **CL15, ST13, ST147, WR22***Recommended*

Tampopo (1987, C, 114m, NR) Japanese comedy centering on a widow's attempts to open her own noodle restaurant, with a gruff truck driver coming to her rescue. Numerous subplots and sight gags revolve around the subject of food. Directed by Juzo Itami. **FF4** *Recommended*

Tango and Cash (1989, C, 89m, R) Sylvester Stallone and Kurt Russell play rival L.A. cops who team up to bring down an illegal drug organization. With Teri Hatcher, Jack Palance, and Brion James. **AC9, ST140**

Tank (1984, C, 113m, PG) A teenager is arrested on trumped-up charges by a bigoted sheriff and his father decides to use a surplus tank to free him. James Garner, C. Thomas Howell, G.D. Spradlin, and Shirley Jones star. **DR8**

Tanner '88 (1988, C, 120m, NR) Witty look at contemporary politics, with fictional Presidential candidate slogging through primaries, dealing with ever-present media. Michael Murphy and Pamela Reed star. Written by Garry Trudeau; directed by Robert Altman. Condensed version of a series originally made for cable TV. **CO2, DT2** *Recommended*

Tap (1989, C, 110m, PG-13)
Just out of jail, an ex-dancer is torn between continuing his life of crime and returning to his love of the stage. Gregory Hines stars, with Sammy Davis, Jr. and a host of exponents of old-time tap dancing. **DR12, MU3**

Tapeheads (1988, C, 93m, R)
Comedy about a pair of clumsy but with-it guys (Tim Robbins, John Cusack) trying to make it big in the rock music video biz. With Mary Crosby, Doug McClure, Connie Stevens, and real-life rockers Sam Moore and Junior Walker as a singing duo called The Swanky Modes. **CO8, MU9** *Recommended*

Taps (1981, C, 118m, R)
Timothy Hutton and George C. Scott star in this drama about a rebellious military school student and his commanding officer. With Tom Cruise and Sean Penn. **DR9, DR25, ST26**

Target (1985, C, 117m, R)
When a businessman's wife is kidnapped on a trip to Paris, he's forced to admit to his son his association with the CIA. Gene Hackman and Matt Dillon star in this thriller directed by Arthur Penn. **DT78, MY6, ST61, XT16**

Targets (1968, C, 90m, PG)
Twin stories, which eventually intersect, about an aging horror film star (Boris Karloff) about to retire and a mad sniper. With Tim O'Kelly, Nancy Hsueh, and Peter Bogdanvich, who made his directing debut. Uncredited executive producer: Roger Corman; scenes from his Karloff film, *The Terror*, are used. **CU14, DR13, MY13, ST77**

Tarzan and the Green Goddess (1938, B&W, 72m, NR)
Feature film version of serial *The New Adventures of Tarzan*, starring Herman Brix (aka Bruce Bennett). **HF22**

Tarzan and the Trappers (1958, B&W, 74m, NR)
Gordon Scott plays the Lord of the Apes in this collection of three pilots for an unsold TV series. **FA4, HF22**

Tarzan of the Apes (1918, B&W, 130m, NR)
Elmo Lincoln stars as the screen's first Tarzan. This one's a silent film, so don't listen for that famous yell. **HF22**

Tarzan, the Ape Man (1932, B&W, 98m, G)
Johnny Weissmuller's debut as the jungle hero. Maureen O'Sullivan costars. **FA4, HF22** *Essential*

Tarzan, the Ape Man (1981, C, 112m, R)
An adult version of the famous story, with Miles O'Keeffe as the swingin' jungle man and Bo Derek as a frequently unclad Jane. With Richard Harris. Directed by John Derek. Cult following more for its sheer ineptness than sexiness. **CU11, HF22**

Tarzan the Fearless (1933, B&W, 85m, NR)
Buster Crabbe puts on the loincloth for this feature version of a Tarzan serial. **FA4, HF22**

Tarzaan's Revenge (1938, B&W, 70m, NR)
Olympic athletes Glenn Morris and Eleanor Holm play Tarzan and Jane in this installment of the long-running adventure series. **FA4, HF22**

Taxi Driver (1976, C, 113m, R)
Riveting drama of a paranoid New York cab driver getting involved with a 12-year-old prostitute, whom he tries to "save" from the evils of the streets. Robert DeNiro stars, with Cybill Shepherd, Jodie Foster, Albert Brooks, and Harvey Keitel. Written by Paul Shrader; directed by Martin Scorsese. Violent finale nearly got the film an "X" rating. **CU7, DR15, DT12, DT95, MY2, ST30, ST47, XT9** *Essential; Highly Recommended*

Taxing Woman, A (1988, C, 127m, NR)
Japanese comedy of a female tax collector who has to battle the prejudices of her male colleagues and the deceit of taxpayers. Directed by Juzo Itami. **FF4**

Teachers (1984, C, 106m, R)
Life at a big-city high school, where the students don't care and most of the teachers are just collecting a paycheck. Nick Nolte stars, with JoBeth Williams, Ralph Macchio, and Richard Mulligan. **DR25, ST113**

Teacher's Pet (1958, B&W, 120m, NR)
The editor of a newspaper (Clark Gable) enrolls in a night school class in journalism to make time with the teacher (Doris Day). With Gig Young. **CO18, ST49**

Teahouse of the August Moon (1956, C, 123m, NR)
Service comedy set in postwar Okinawa, with occupying Americans clashing with Japanese. Marlon Brando and Glenn Ford star, with Machiko Kyo and Eddie Albert. **CO21, ST10**

Teddy Ruxpin: Teddy Outsmarts M.A.V.O. (1987, C, 75m, NR)
Animated adventure of Teddy and his friends pursued by the villainous members of M.A.V.O., who want a special crystal Teddy is carrying. **FA10**

Teen Wolf (1985, C, 91m, PG)
A teenager (Michael J. Fox) discovers he is descended from a family of werewolves and becomes popular at school when his classmates find out. **CO4, CO11, HO4**

Teenage Mutant Ninja Turltes (1990, C, 93m, PG)
The popular superheroes—Raphael, Michelangelo, Donatello, and Leonardo—debut in their first live-action feature. **AC17, FA4**

Telefon (1977, C, 102m, PG)
Charles Bronson plays a Russian agent teaming up with the CIA to prevent an unhinged Soviet spy from unleashing a lethal army of hypnotized bombers. With Lee Remick. Don Siegel directed. **DT97, MY6, ST12**

Tell Them Willy Boy Is Here (1969, C, 96m, G)
Robert Blake plays an Indian who kills a man in self-defense and is pursued by a large posse to his death. Based on a true story. Robert Redford stars as the sheriff out to get his man. **ST126, WE3, WE7, WE11**

10 (1979, C, 122m, R)
Comedy about middle-aged man who can't decide between marriage to his charming but predictable girlfriend and a wild fling with woman of his dreams. Dudley Moore, Julie Andrews, and Bo Derek star, with Brian Dennehy, Robert Webber, and Dee Wallace. Blake Ed-

wards directed. **CO1, DT32, ST109** *Essential*

Ten Commandments, The (1923, B&W, 146m, NR)
Cecil B. DeMille's silent classic, combining a modern tale of sin and redemption with the the the story of Moses and the famous tablets. Theodore Roberts, Richard Dix, and Rod La Rocque star. **CL12, CL13, DT27** *Essential*

Ten Commandments, The (1956, C, 220m, G)
Biblical epic about the life of Moses, from birth to his leading the Jews out of Egypt. All-star cast includes Charlton Heston as Moses, Yul Brynner as Ramses, plus Anne Baxter, Debra Paget, Edward G. Robinson, Vincent Price, and John Derek. Directed by Cecil B. DeMille; his last film. **CL9, CL13, DT27, ST124, ST130** *Essential; Highly Recommended*

Ten Days That Shook the World/October (1927, B&W, 104m, NR)
From director Sergei Eisenstein, a documentary of the events surrounding the 1917 Russian Revolution. **CU9, CU16, DT33**

Ten From Your Show of Shows (1973, B&W, 92m, NR)
Classic bits from the legendary TV show of the early 1950s, starring Sid Caesar, Imogene Coca, Carl Reiner, and Howard Morris. Sketch comedy at its absolute best. **CO16** *Highly Recommended*

Ten Little Indians (1975, C, 98m, PG)
Latest version of Agatha Christie's classic whodunit, with setting switched to a hotel in Iranian desert. Oliver Reed, Elke Sommer, and Herbert Lom head the list of victims/suspects. **MY12, WR3**

10 Rillington Place (1971, C, 111m, PG)
True story of the infamous John Christie murders in Britain, and how the real killer's testimony helped send the wrong man to the gallows. Richard Attenborough and John Hurt star. **DR6, DR16, MY7, MY8, MY15**

Ten to Midnight (1983, C, 100m, R)
Charles Bronson stars as a police detective tracking a psycho killer who has made the big mistake of harassing Bronson's daughter. **MY13, ST12**

Ten Wanted Men (1955, C, 80m, NR)
Randolph Scott western, with Richard
Boone as a rival rancher who resorts to
intimidation to get his way. **ST136**

Ten Who Dared (1960, C, 92m, NR)
Disney adventure, based on the exploits
of Major John Wesley Powell (Brian
Keith), who explored the uncharted Col-
orado River in 1869. With Ben Johnson,
R.G. Armstrong, and L.Q. Jones. **FA1**

Tenant, The (1976, C, 125m, R)
Disturbed man moves into the Parisian
apartment of a suicide victim, begins to
assume her identity. Director Roman Polanski stars in this psychological drama,
with Isabelle Adjani, Shelley Winters,
and Melvyn Douglas. **DT79, ST164** *Recommended*

Tender Mercies (1983, C, 93m, PG)
A down-and-out country singer finds redemption in the love of a farm widow and
her son. Oscar winner Robert Duvall
stars, with Tess Harper, Ellen Barkin,
and Betty Buckley as the women in his
life. **DR1, DR2, DR12, ST38, XT2**

Tentacles (1977, C, 90m, PG)
A giant octopus terrorizes a seaside com-
munity. John Huston, Henry Fonda, Bo
Hopkins, and Shelley Winters star. **DT50,
ST44, ST164**

**Tenth Anniversay Young Comedians Spe-
cial** *see* HBO Comedy Club

Tenth Victim, The (1965, B&W, 92m, NR)
In a future society, killing humans is le-
gal, with organized hunting. A science
fiction spoof from Italy, starring Marcello
Mastroianni and Ursula Andress. **FF2,
SF21, ST103**

Tequila Sunrise (1988, C, 116m, R)
Romantic triangle involving an ex-drug
dealer, a narcotics cop (who is also the
ex-dealer's best friend), and the lovely
owner of a posh Italian restaurant. Mel
Gibson, Kurt Russell, and Michelle Pfeiffer star. Written and directed by Robert
Towne. With Raul Julia and, in a small
part, Budd Boetticher.**DR1, DT10, MY2,
ST53, ST120** *Recommended*

Teresa Venerdi (1941, B&W, 90m, NR)
Italian director Vittorio De Sica stars in
this comedy of a doctor at an orphanage

who's involved with three women. Anna
Magnani costars. **DT26**

Terminal Choice (1985, C, 97m, R)
A series of mysterious deaths at a computerized hospital is the basis for this
horror film. Joe Spano stars. **HO20**

Terminal Man, The (1973, C, 104m, PG)
A mini-computer is created to help control a person's psychopathic tendencies.
When the computer is implanted in the
brain of a test subject, it fails and turns
him homicidal. George Segal stars. **SF4**

Terminal Station *see* Indiscretion of an
American Wife, The

Terminator, The (1984, C, 108m, R)
A cyborg assassin from the year 2029 is
sent to 1984 to kill the woman who will
give birth to his opposition's leader. Arnold Schwarzenegger, Michael Biehn,
and Linda Hamilton star, with Paul Winfield. Written and directed by James Cameron. **AC25, ST135, ST162** *Recommended*

Terms of Endearment (1983, C, 132m, PG)
Shirley MacLaine and Debra Winger play
a mother and daughter whose relationship
virtually defines the phrase "love-hate"
in this Oscar-winning drama. With Jeff
Daniels, John Lithgow, and Danny De-
Vito. MacLaine and Jack Nicholson,
writer-director James L. Brooks also won
Oscars. **DR2, DR8, ST32, ST96, ST112,
ST163, XT1, XT3, XT4, XT6** *Highly Recommended*

Terra Trema, La (1947, B&W, 160m, NR)
Documentary-style look at the lives of
Sicilian fisherman from director Luchino
Visconti. One of the key films of the
Italian neorealist movement. **DT108** *Es-
sential*

Terror, The (1963, C, 81m, NR)
A soldier in Napoleon's army (Jack Nicholson) follows a mysterious woman (Sandra Knight) to a castle owned by a sinister
man (Boris Karloff). Directed by Roger
Corman; footage from this film appears in
Targets. **DT22, ST77, ST112**

Terror at Red Wolf Inn (1972, C, 90m,
NR)
A student on vacation stays at an inn run
by two very nice old people who have a
retarded grandson. When several guests

disappear, she discovers that the proprietors are cannibals. **HO24**

Terror by Night (1946, B&W, 60m, NR)
Sherlock Holmes mystery starring Basil Rathbone and Nigel Bruce, set aboard a train, concerning a famous jewel and murders. **HF14**

Terror House *see* Night Has Eyes, The

Terror in the Wax Museum (1973, C, 93m, PG)
A girl inherits a wax museum where a grisly murder took place. When she moves into the apartment above the museum, she is terrorized by the wax figures of famous criminals. Ray Milland and Elsa Lanchester star. **HO26**

Terror of Mechagodzilla (1978, C, 79m, NR)
Aliens who want to invade Japan create a robot Godzilla monster to battle the real Godzilla, now the protector of Japan. **FF4, SF18**

Terror of Tiny Town, The (1938, B&W, 63m, NR)
A one-of-a-kind western drama, with an all-midget cast! This one has to be seen to be believed. **CU11, WE15**

Terror Squad (1987, C, 92m, NR)
Smalltown sheriff (Chuck Connors) leads an ad-hoc army against a band of terrorists who have taken over a nuclear plant. **AC20**

Terror Train (1980, C, 97m, R)
A fraternity party aboard a train is plagued by a mad killer. Jamie Lee Curtis, Hart Bochner, Ben Johnson, and David Copperfield star. **HO12, XT19**

Terrorists, The (1975, C, 97m, PG)
Sean Connery plays a hostage negotiator in this thriller about an airline hijacking. **ST21**

Terrorvision (1986, C, 85m, R)
An alien emerges from a family's television set and wreaks havoc. **SF20**

Terry Fox Story, The (1983, C, 97m, NR)
True, heartfelt tale of a young Canadian runner who loses a leg to cancer and undertakes a cross-country run to raise funds to research his disease. Real-life amputee Eric Fryer stars, with Robert

Duvall. Originally made for cable TV. **DR6, ST38**

Tess (1979, C, 170m, PG)
Literate adaptation of the Thomas Hardy novel of a young girl (Mastassia Kinski) twice wronged in love. Roman Polanski directed. **DR19, DT79** *Recommended*

Testament (1983, C, 89m, PG)
Jane Alexander tries to hold her family together after a nuclear attack, as they wait for the radiation approaching their small town. With William Devane, Rebecca DeMornay, and, in a small role, Kevin Costner.**DR7, DR10, DR26, SF12, ST23**

Testament of Dr. Mabuse, The (1933, B&W, 120m, NR)
A criminal kingpin controls his operations even while he's locked up in an insane asylum. Classic crime drama, with touches of the supernatural, from German director Fritz Lang. **DT58, FF3, SF2**

Tex (1982, C, 103m, PG)
Well-meaning but mischievous teenager (Matt Dillon) is raised by his older brother after their mother dies and father deserts them. Based on S.E. Hinton's novel. **DR9**

Texas (1941, B&W, 93m, NR)
William Holden and Glenn Ford play saddle pals competing for the same woman (Claire Trevor) in this western drama. **ST68**

Texas Chainsaw Massacre, The (1974, C, 83m, R)
A group of teenagers stumble onto a family of cannibals. Cult horror directed by Tobe Hooper. **CU1, CU4, CU7, HO12, DT47**

Texas Chainsaw Massacre II, The (1986, C, 95m, NR)
An ex-lawman (Dennis Hopper) swears revenge on the cannibal family who use human meat in their prize-winning chili. This sequel to *The Texas Chainsaw Massacre* was also directed by Tobe Hooper. **DT47, ST71**

Texas Lady (1955, C, 86m, NR)
Claudette Colbert stars in this low-key western about a newspaper editor battling injustice on the frontier. **WE8**

Texas Legionnaires (1943, B&W, 54m, NR)
Roy Rogers battles Axis spies in this western with a contemporary setting. **ST132**

Thank God, It's Friday (1978, C, 90m, PG)
Musical comedy centering on characters who hang out at a disco, starring Donna Summer and The Commodores, and featuring early screen appearances by Debra Winger and Jeff Goldblum. **ST56, ST163**

Thank Your Lucky Stars (1943, B&W, 127m, NR)
Eddie Cantor puts on a show to support the war effort and has many of Warner Bros.' dramatic stars doing musical and comedy sketches. Highlights include Bette Davis singing "They're Either Too Young or Too Old." Other appearances include Humphrey Bogart, Errol Flynn, and Olivia de Havilland. **MU15, ST8, ST28, ST43**

That Championship Season (1982, C, 110m, R)
A high school basketball team reunites years later with their coach in this drama based on Jason Miller's play. Robert Mitchum stars, with Bruce Dern, Stacy Keach, Martin Sheen, and Paul Sorvino. Directed by Miller. **DR20, DR22, ST107**

That Cold Day in the Park (1969, C, 113m, R)
Suspense drama about a spinster who takes in a young man and holds him prisoner. Sandy Dennis and Michael Burns star. Directed by Robert Altman. **DT2**

That Darn Cat (1965, C, 116m, G)
A pet cat leads the FBI to a gang of kidnappers. Hayley Mills and Dean Jones star in this Disney comedy. **FA1**

That Hamilton Woman (1941, B&W, 128m, NR)
Classic love story, based on historical events, of affair between Lord Nelson and Lady Hamilton. Laurence Olivier and Vivien Leigh star. Directed by Alexander Korda. **CL3, CL5, ST116**

That Obscure Object of Desire (1977, C, 103m, R)
A wealthy man with unconventional sexual ideas falls in love with a maid who accommodatingly teases him. Fernando Rey stars; Carole Bouquet and Angela Molina play the maid. Last film from director Luis Buñuel. **DT15**

That Sinking Feeling (1979, C, 92m, PG)
Comedy set in Glasgow, Scotland about a group of bored youths who turn to stealing sinks to pass the time. Directed by Bill Forsyth. **CO17, DT38**

That Touch of Mink (1962, C, 99m, NR)
Doris Day-Cary Grant romantic fluff about a playboy pursuing a determined woman of virtue. With John Astin. **CO1, ST57**

That Uncertain Feeling (1941, B&W, 84m, NR)
Romantic comedy from director Ernst Lubitsch about a married couple (Merle Oberon, Melvyn Douglas) and their zany musician friend (Burgess Meredith). **DT63**

That Was Rock (1984, B&W, 92m, NR)
A compilation of rock and R&B performances from two films, *The TAMI Show* (1964) and *The TNT Show* (1966). Performers include Chuck Berry, James Brown, The Supremes, The Rolling Stones, and many more. Also known as *Born to Rock*. **MU10**

That Was Then, This Is Now (1985, C, 102m, R)
Drama about relationship between stepbrothers, one of whom is jealous of his brother's new girl friend. Emilio Estevez stars; he also wrote the screenplay, based on an S.E. Hinton novel. With Craig Sheffer, Kim Delaney, and, in a small role, Morgan Freeman. **DR9, ST48**

That'll Be the Day (1974, C, 90m, PG)
A British working class youth in the 1950s decides to become a rock star. David Essex stars, with Ringo Starr and Keith Moon. **MU4, MU9**

That's Dancing (1985, C/B&W, 105m, G)
A compilation of 50 years of dance numbers from MGM musicals, including a Ray Bolger/Scarecrow dance number that was cut from the final version of *The Wizard of Oz*. Fred Astaire, John Travolta, Gene Kelly, Liza Minnelli, and Sammy Davis, Jr. host. **MU1, MU3, MU15, ST2, ST81**

That's Entertainment (1974, C, 132m, G)
To mark its 50th anniversary, MGM produced this compilation of scenes from 100 of their musicals. Among the stars featured: Fred Astaire, Gene Kelly, Bing Crosby, Clark Gable, Judy Garland, and Frank Sinatra. **MU1, MU15, ST2, ST25, ST49, ST51, ST81, ST138** *Recommended*

That's Entertainment, Part II (1976, C, 126m, G)
A sequel to *That's Entertainment,* this time including scenes from non-musical films (featuring Katharine Hepburn & Spencer Tracy, plus the Marx Bros.) as well as more classic MGM numbers. **MU1, MU15, ST2, ST25, ST49, ST51, ST66, ST81, ST101, ST138, ST151**

That's Life! (1986, C, 102m, R)
Jack Lemmon and Julie Andrews play a middle-aged couple preoccupied with their individual problems, less considerate of each other and their children. Drama from director Blake Edwards. Members of Lemmon's, Andrews', and Edwards' families play small roles. **DR8, DT32, ST90, XT8**

Theatre of Blood (1973, C, 104m, R)
A Shakespearean actor begins to kill off all his critics with methods from various Shakespeare plays. Vincent Price at his campy best. With Diana Rigg, Coral Browne, and Robert Morley. **CU4, HO24, HO26, ST124**

Theatre of Death (1967, C, 90m, NR)
The deaths on a Grand Guignol stage are no longer fake. Christopher Lee stars. **ST89**

Thelonius Monk: Straight, No Chaser (1988, C/B&W, 90m, PG-13)
Documentary portrait of pioneering jazz painist. Directed by Charlotte Zwerin; material from the 1960s shot by Christian Blackwood. **CU16**

Them! (1954, B&W, 93m, NR)
Classic 1950s science fiction thriller about giant ants, mutated by radiation. James Whitmore and James Arness star. **CU4, SF1, SF10, SF16** *Recommended*

There Was a Crooked Man (1970, C, 123m, R)
Darkly comic tale, set in the Old West, of convict (Kirk Douglas) who breaks out of prison and is pursued by greedy warden

(Henry Fonda) to a cache of stolen money. With John Randolph, Hume Cronyn, and Warren Oates. Written by Robert Benton and David Newman; directed by Joseph L. Mankiewicz. **DR18, DT68, ST34, ST44, ST115, WE3, WE14, WE15** *Recommended*

There's a Girl in My Soup (1970, C, 95m, R)
Middle-aged businessman falls for flower child in this comedy starring Peter Sellers and Goldie Hawn. **ST63, ST137**

There's No Business Like Show Business (1954, C, 117m, NR)
A husband and wife vaudeville team return to the stage with their three children now in the act. Ethel Merman, Dan Dailey, Donald O'Connor, and Marilyn Monroe star. **MU4, ST108**

Thérèse (1987, C, 96m, NR)
True-life drama from French director Alain Cavalier about Thérèse Martin, a young nun whose devotion and patient suffering resulted in sainthood. **FF1**

These Three (1936, B&W, 92m NR)
Two teachers and a doctor have their professional and personal reputations ruined by the malicious stories of a spoiled little girl. Miriam Hopkins, Merle Oberon, Joel McCrea, and Bonita Granville star. Based on Lillian Hellman's play, *The Children's Hour;* directed by William Wyler. **DR20, DT119**

They All Laughed (1981, C, 115m, PG)
Amiable comedy about three New York private eyes and their various love lives. Ben Gazzara, John Ritter, and Blaine Novak are the gumshoes. With Audrey Hepburn, Dorothy Stratten, Collen Camp, and Patti Hansen. Directed by Peter Bogdanovich. **CO10, ST65, XT9** *Recommended*

They Call Me MISTER Tibbs! (1970, C, 108m, PG)
Sidney Poitier plays his *In the Heat of the Night* character, Virgil Tibbs, in this crime drama set in San Francisco. With Barbara McNair and Martin Landau. **AC9, ST121**

They Call Me Trinity (1971, C, 109m, PG)
In this western spoof, Terence Hill and Bud Spencer play cowboys who agree to

protect settlers from a band of Mexican marauders. **WE13, WE14**

They Came From Within (1975, C, 87m, R)
David Cronenberg directed this horrific tale of parasites who take over the residents of a high-rise apartment building. **DT23**

They Came to Cordura (1959, B&W, 123m, NR)
Gary Cooper stars in this western set in 1916 Mexico, about an officer accused of cowardice and determined to regain his pride. With Rita Hayworth, Van Heflin, and Tab Hunter. **ST22, ST64, WE9**

They Died With Their Boots On (1941, B&W, 138m, NR)
The story of George Armstrong Custer and his infamous Last Stand, with Errol Flynn as the notorious general. Olivia de Havilland costars, with Charles Middleton as Abraham Lincoln. **HF6, HF18, ST43, WE4**

They Drive by Night (1940, B&W, 93m, NR)
A pair of brothers battle the crooked bosses running the trucking industry. Humphrey Bogart, George Raft, and Ann Sheridan star. **CL8, ST8**

They Got Me Covered (1943, B&W, 95m, NR)
Wartime spy comedy set in Washington, D.C., starring Bob Hope, Dorothy Lamour, and Otto Preminger. **DT82, ST70**

They Knew What They Wanted (1940, B&W, 96m, NR)
Romance by correspondence, as an Italian grape grower (Charles Laughton) falls in love with a lonely waitress (Carole Lombard). Garson Kanin directed. **ST92**

They Live (1988, C, 95m, R)
Aliens are taking over Earth, cleverly disguised and only detected through specially-made sunglasses. Roddy Piper stars. John Carpenter directed this low-budget science fiction drama. **DT17, SF9**

They Live by Night (1949, B&W, 95m, NR)
Depression-era tale of young lovers turned outlaws, starring Farley Granger and Cathy O'Donnell. Cult favorite, directed by Nicholas Ray. **DT83, MY1, XT18** *Essential*

They Made Me a Criminal (1939, B&W, 92m, NR)
John Garfield stars in this thriller about a man on the run from the law for a crime he didn't commit. Claude Rains, May Robson, and the Dead End Kids costar. Directed by Busby Berkeley, in a rare non-musical outing. **DT8, MY7**

They Might Be Giants (1971, C, 98m, PG)
Gentle comedy of a man who believes he's Sherlock Holmes and his female shrink, named Dr. Watson. George C. Scott and Joanne Woodward star. **ST166**

They Saved Hitler's Brain (1963, B&W, 74m, NR)
Classic "bad" movie about Nazi cult controlled by Der Fuehrer's still-living head. **CU11**

They Shoot Horses, Don't They? (1969, C, 121m, PG)
Grim drama centering on Depression marathon dance contest. Jane Fonda stars, with Michael Sarrazin, Susannah York, Red Buttons, Bruce Dern, Bonnie Bedelia, and Oscar winner Gig Young. Adapted from Horace McCoy's cult novel; directed by Sydney Pollack. **DR19, DT80, ST45, XT4** *Recommended*

They Went That-A-Way and That-A-Way (1978, C, 95m, PG)
Two amateur comedians, whose specialty is doing Laurel and Hardy impersonations, escape from prison. Tim Conway and Chuck McCann star. **FA6**

They Were Expendable (1945, B&W, 135m, NR)
American PT boats in the Pacific engage Japanese cruisers in battle. John Wayne and Robert Montgomery star. Directed by John Ford. **AC1, DT36, ST156**

They Who Step on the Tiger's Tail *see* Men Who Tread on the Tiger's Tail, The

They Won't Believe Me (1947, B&W, 79m, NR)
On trial for murder, a man tries to explain the twisted circumstances which brought him to his fate. Robert Young plays the philandering man on the witness stand; Susan Hayward, Jane Greer, and Rita

Johnson costar. **DR17, MY1, MY7** *Recommended*

They're Playing With Fire (1984, C, 96m, R)
A sexy teacher and her naive student lover plot a murder in this thriller starring Eric Brown and Sybil Danning. **MY5**

Thief (1981, C, 123m, R)
Drama about the world of a professional thief, starring James Caan and Tuesday Weld, with Robert Prosky and Willie Nelson. Directed by Michael Mann; music by Tangerine Dream. **AC8, DR16, MU12**

Thief of Bagdad, The (1924, B&W, 132m, NR)
Silent film version of the Arabian Nights tale of a professional thief who saves the Princess of Bagdad from an evil Mongol prince. Douglas Fairbanks stars. **AC13, CL12** *Essential*

Thief of Bagdad, The (1940, C, 106m, NR)
Colorful fantasy from the Arabian Nights. with a plucky native boy and a prince dueling a wicked sorcerer. Oscar winner for photography and special effects. Sabu, John Justin, and Conrad Veidt star. Co-directed by Michael Powell. **AC13, CL9, DT81, FA4, FA8** *Essential*

Thief of Hearts (1984, C, 100m, NR)
A burglar's haul includes a married woman's diary, which contains her secret sexual fantasies. The thief conspires to meet the woman and a romance soon develops. Steven Bauer and Barbara Williams star. Some additional scenes were added for the home video version. **CU6, CU10, MY5**

Thief Who Came to Dinner, The (1973, C, 105m, PG)
Computer programmer turns to life of crime as a jewel thief in this comedy starring Ryan O'Neal, with Jacqueline Bisset, Warren Oates, Jill Clayburgh, and Ned Beatty. **CO10, ST115**

Thin Blue Line, The (1988, C, 106m, NR)
Mesmerizing documentary study of a 1976 Dallas, Texas, murder case, for which the wrong man (Randall Dale Adams) was convicted and nearly executed. This film helped to reopen the case and eventually set Adams free. Directed by Erol Morris; music by Philip Glass. **CU16, DT73, MY8** *Highly Recommended*

Thin Man, The (1935, B&W, 90m, NR)
First in the series of films about high society detectives Nick and Nora Charles, created by Dashiell Hammett. William Powell and Myrna Loy mix martinis and murder in a uniquely sophisticated kind of mystery. (For other series titles, see HF5.) **CL10, CL15, HF5, MY17, ST94, ST122, WR9** *Essential; Highly Recommended*

Thin Man Goes Home, The (1944, B&W, 100m, NR)
Fourth in the Nick and Nora Charles series has the high society duo returning to Nick's hometown with baby Nick, Jr. and solving a murder case. William Powell and Myrna Loy star. **CL15, HF5, MY17, ST94, ST122, WR9**

Thing, The (1982, C, 108m, R)
A group of researchers in the Antartic are terrorized by an alien creature who can transform itself into any living organism. Kirk Russell stars in this explicitly gory remake of the 1951 classic. John Carpenter directed. **CU18, DT17, HO17, SF9, SF20**

Thing (From Another World), The (1951, B&W, 86m, NR)
A U.S. outpost at the North Pole finds a crashed spaceship and manage to save its pilot. The alien is made of vegetable matter, feeds on blood, and intends to destroy the humans. Kenneth Tobey stars, with James Arness as the alien. **CU4, SF1, SF9** *Essential; Recommended*

Things Are Tough All Over (1982, C, 92m, R)
Cheech and Chong comedy, with the boys driving around around in a car with $5 million hidden in it. C&C also play two Arab brothers. **ST18**

Things Change (1988, C, 105m, PG)
Comic yarn of an elderly shoemaker (Dom Ameche) persuaded to serve a short jail term for a crime boss he resembles. He and his "guard," a Mob flunky (Joe Mategna), take off for one last fling in Lake Tahoe. David Mamet directed; he and Shel Silverstein wrote the screenplay. **CO10, CO20** *Recommended*

Things To Come (1936, B&W, 91m, NR)
H.G. Wells wrote this science fiction drama about a war which nearly destroys the world and how the survivors try to

construct a utopian society. Raymond Massey, Ralph Richardson, and Cedric Hardwicke star. **SF2, SF12, SF14, WR29**

Think Big (1990, C, 86m, PG-13)
Action comedy featuring a pair of dim-witted, muscular truckers (Peter & David Paul, real-life brothers) hauling toxic waste and a teen stowaway across the country. With Ari Meyers, Martin Mull, David Carradine, and Richard Kiel. **CO9, XT8, XT18**

Third Man, The (1949, B&W, 100m, NR)
Classic Graham Greene thriller set in postwar Vienna, with good guy writer (Joseph Cotten) finding out his old friend Harry Lime (Orson Welles) is working for the bad guys. With Trevor Howard and Valli. Carol Reed directed. **MY6, DT112** *Essential; Highly Recommended*

Third Man on the Mountain (1959, C, 105m, NR)
A young man (James MacArthur) learns about life while attempting to climb the Matterhorn. Drama from the Disney studios. **FA1**

13 Ghosts (1960, B&W, 88m, NR)
A family inherits a haunted house and must solve several mysterious deaths in order to free the spirits. **HO2, HO3, HO19**

13 Rue Madeleine (1946, B&W, 95m, NR)
An Allied agent tries to locate a German missile site in World War II France. James Cagney stars. **AC1, ST14**

Thirteenth Guest, The (1932, B&W, 69m, NR)
A dinner party is held thirteen years after same company saw their host drop dead—and leave his estate to a mystery guest. Ginger Rogers and Lyle Talbot star. **MY12, ST131**

30 Is a Dangerous Age, Cynthia (1968, C, 98m, NR)
Dudley Moore plays a young man whose approaching 30th birthday is driving him loony with anxiety. Moore also co-wrote the screenplay and composed the music. **ST109**

39 Steps, The (1935, B&W, 87m, NR)
One of Alfred Hitchcock's best: innocent man Robert Donat becomes enmeshed in elaborate mystery involving spies and saboteurs. Madeleine Carroll is the woman he's handcuffed to. Many classic moments, including finale with "Mr. Memory." **DT46, MY6, MY7, MY15, XT18** *Essential; Highly Recommended*

39 Steps, The (1978, C, 102m, PG)
Remake of the Alfred Hitchcock classic, starring Robert Powell, David Warner, and Karen Dotrice. **CU18, MY6, MY7, XT18**

Thirty Seconds Over Tokyo (1944, B&W, 138m, NR)
Drama of America's first air raid on Japan during World War II. Van Johnson, Robert Walker, and Spencer Tracy star, with Robert Mitchum in a small role. **AC1, ST107, ST151**

This Gun for Hire (1942, B&W, 80m, NR)
Alan Ladd's first starring role, as the ruthless gunman of Graham Greene's novel, with Veronica Lake a lovely distraction. **MY1**

This Happy Feeling (1958, C, 92m, NR)
Debbie Reynolds plays a woman smitten by a vain actor (Curt Jurgens) and courted by an earnest young man (John Saxon). Comedy from director Blake Edwards. **DT32**

This Is Elvis (1981, C/B&W, 144m, PG)
A biography of The King combining documentary footage with recreated scenes from his life. Video version adds nearly 45 minutes of footage to theatrical release. **CU10, MU5, MU11** *Recommended*

This Is Korea/December 7th (1951/1943, C/B&W, 85m, NR)
John Ford directed these two propaganda documentaries for the Navy. *This Is Korea* praises the U.S. military effort in that conflict. *December 7th* recreates the bombing of Pearl Harbor and won an Academy Award for Best Documentary. **AC1, AC3, CU16, DT36**

This Is Spinal Tap (1984, C, 82m, R)
A British heavy metal group that's beginning to show some signs of rust tours America. Christopher Guest, Michael McKean, and Harry Shearer star in this hilarious parody of rock documentaries. Directed by Rob Reiner, who also plays the pretentious director making a film about the band. Cameos appearances by Paul Shaffer, Billy Crystal, many others. **CO7, CO13, DT85, MU11** *Recommended*

This Island Earth (1954, C, 86m, NR)
Inhabitants from Metaluna come to Earth hoping our scientists can help them find a new energy source before their home is destroyed. Jeff Morrow and Rex Reason star. **SF1, SF3, SF9**

This Land Is Mine (1943, B&W, 103m, NR)
Charles Laughton stars as a French schoolteacher who rises to acts of heroism under Nazi Occupation. Directed by Jean Renoir. **DT86**

This Man Must Die (1970, C, 115m, PG)
A man's son is killed by a hit-and-run driver and he becomes obsessed with exacting his own justice. French thriller from director Claude Chabrol. **FF1**

This Property Is Condemned (1966, C, 109m, NR)
Adaptation of the Tennessee Williams play about a young woman (Natalie Wood) falling for a drifter (Robert Redford) who is staying at her mother's boarding house. With Charles Bronson, Kate Reid, Mary Badham, and Robert Blake. Sydney Pollack directed. **DT80, ST12, ST126, WR30**

This Sporting Life (1963, B&W, 129m, NR)
Powerful, no-holds-barred drama of British rugby player (Richard Harris) whose star rises and falls quickly. With Rachel Roberts. Directed by Lindsay Anderson. **DR22, DR23** *Essential; Recommended*

Thomas Crown Affair, The (1968, C, 102m, R)
A bored millionaire playboy (Steve McQueen) plots the perfect bank robbery. An insurance investigator (Faye Dunaway) is on the case, but she falls in love with her quarry. Directed by Norman Jewison. **DT51, MY5, MY18, ST37, ST97**

Thorn Birds, The (1983, C, 450m, NR)
TV miniseries about the lives and loves of a handsome priest (Richard Chamberlain). With Rachel Ward and Barbara Stanwyck. **DR1, ST142**

Those Calloways (1965, C, 130m, NR)
An eccentric New England family wants to build a bird sanctuary on some land near a lake and must battle some shady developers who want the land as a hunt-ing resort. Brian Keith and Vera Miles star in this Disney film. **FA1**

Those Lips, Those Eyes (1980, C, 107m, R)
A young man working behind the scenes at a summer theater in Cleveland during the 1950s learns about show biz and love from two of the company's performers. Thomas Hulce, Frank Langella, and Glynnis O'Connor star. **CO6, CO8**

Those Magnificent Men in Their Flying Machines (1965, C, 123m, NR)
The early days of aviation races are the subject for this knockabout comedy starring Stuart Whitman, Sarah Miles, and James Fox. **CO6, CO9**

Thousand Clowns, A (1965, B&W, 118m, NR)
A carefree nonconformist and sometime TV writer has his life turned upside down when social workers try to wrest his nephew from his custody. Jason Robards stars, with Barbara Harris, William Daniels, Barry Gordon, and Oscar winner Martin Balsam. Shot on location in New York City. **CO5, ST129, XT4, XT9** *Recommended*

Thousands Cheer (1943, C, 126m, NR)
A commander's daughter (Kathryn Grayson) falls in love with a private (Gene Kelly) and they decide to put on an all-star show for the troops. Mickey Rooney and Judy Garland costar, with appearances by many MGM musical stars. **MU15, ST51, ST81, ST133**

Thrashin' (1986, C, 90m, PG-13)
Drama about competitive downhill skateboarding, with Josh Brolin as the young contender for the championship. **DR22**

Threads (1984, C, 110m, NR)
The devastating aftermath of a nuclear attack and its effects on the lives of working class people in Sheffield, England, are dramatized in this British equivalent of *The Day After*. **SF12, SF19**

Three Ages, The (1923, B&W, 59m, NR)
Buster Keaton comedy spoofing historical epics (and especially D. W. Griffith's *Intolerance*), with segments taking place in prehistoric days, ancient Rome, and modern times. **CL11, DT54**

Three Amigos (1986, C, 105m, PG)
A trio of out-of-work movie actors in 1920s Hollywood are summoned to a Mexican village, which mistakenly thinks they are real cowboys, for a rescue mission. Steve Martin, Chevy Chase, and Martin Short star. **CO3, CO13, CO14, ST99**

Three Brothers (1980, C, 113m, PG)
Italian brothers return to their village for their mother's funeral, sparking many memories. Philippe Noiret stars. Directed by Francesco Rosi. **FF2**

Three Caballeros, The (1945, C, 70m, NR)
Disney trip to Latin America mixes animation and live action, with Donald Duck hosting. **FA2** *Recommended*

Three Days of the Condor (1975, C, 117m, R)
A CIA researcher in New York survives an assassination attack which decimates his entire office, goes on the lam with almost no help from Washington. Robert Redford and Faye Dunaway star, with Max von Sydow, Cliff Robertson, and John Houseman. Sydney Pollack directed. **DT80, MY6, MY7, ST37, ST126**

Three Faces West (1940, B&W, 79m, NR)
Unusual John Wayne vehicle has The Duke leading a group of Austrian refugees to Oregon during World War II. **ST156, WE12**

Three Fugitives (1989, C, 96m, PG-13)
Nick Nolte plays an ex-con who's kidnapped by a loony bank robber (Martin Short) in this chase comedy. With Sarah Rowland Doroff and James Earl Jones. **CO10, CO14, ST76, ST113, XT18**

3 Godfathers (1948, C, 105m, NR)
Western drama of three outlaws (John Wayne, Pedro Armendariz, Harry Carey, Jr.) who find an infant abandoned in the desert. With Ward Bond, Mae Marsh, Jane Darwell, and Ben Johnson. Directed by John Ford. **DT36, ST156, WE3**

Three Little Pigs, The (1985, C, 60m, NR)
From the Faerie Tale Theatre series, a look at three pigs who each build their own home and the wolf who wants to have them for dinner. Billy Crystal, Jeff Goldblum, Valerie Perrine, and Stephen Furst star. **CO13, FA12, ST56**

Three Little Words (1950, C, 102m, NR)
Film biography of songwriters Bert Kalmar and Harry Ruby. Fred Astaire, Red Skelton, Vera-Ellen, and Arlene Dahl star. **MU1, MU5, ST2**

Three Lives of Thomasina, The (1964, C, 98m, NR)
A mysterious woman brings Thomasina, a cat owned by a veternarian's daughter, back from the dead. Patrick McGoohan stars in this Disney fantasy. **FA1**

Three Men and a Baby (1987, C, 95m, PG)
Tom Selleck, Ted Danson, and Steve Guttenberg star as three bachelor roommates with a baby on their hands. American remake of *Three Men and a Cradle*. **CO2, FF8**

Three Men and a Cradle (1985, C, 100m, PG-13)
French comedy about a trio of bachelors who find themselves caring for an infant whom one of them has fathered. U.S. remake: *Three Men and a Baby*. **FF1, FF8**

Three Musketeers, The (1948, C, 125m, NR)
The Dumas tale of a farm boy (Gene Kelly) who wants to be a musketeer and gets caught up in court intrigues. Lana Turner, June Allyson, Van Heflin, and Vincent Price costar. **AC13, ST81, ST124, ST153**

Three Musketeers, The (1974, C, 107m, PG)
Swashbuckling adventure, romance, and splastick are brilliantly mixed in this adaptation of the Dumas tale. Oliver Reed, Richard Chamberlain, Frank Finlay, and Michael York star, with Faye Dunaway, Christopher Lee, Raquel Welch, Charlton Heston, Geraldine Chaplin, and Roy Kinnear. Directed by Richard Lester; followed by sequel, *The Four Musketeers*. **AC15, DT62, ST37, ST89** *Highly Recommended*

Three Sovereigns for Sarah (1985, C, 180m, NR)
Saga of Salem witch trials, starring Vanessa Redgrave, Phyllis Thaxter, and Kim Hunter. Originally made for public TV. **DR5, ST127**

Three Strange Loves (1949, B&W, 84m, NR)
Early drama from director Ingmar Bergman examines the lives of a trio of ballerinas. **DT7**

3:10 to Yuma (1957, B&W, 92m, NR)
A farmer tries to hold an outlaw captive until a prison train arrives. Western suspense starring Glenn Ford and Van Heflin. Based on a novel by Elmore Leonard. **WE15, WR16**

Threepenny Opera, The (1931, B&W, 112m, NR)
Film version of the famous Kurt Weill-Bertolt Brecht musical play about a gangster and his cronies. Rudolph Forster and Lotte Lenya star. **FF3**

Threshold (1981, C, 97m, PG)
Drama of the first articial heart transplant stars Donald Sutherland, with John Marley, Mare Winningham, and Jeff Goldblum. **ST56**

Thrill of It All, The (1963, C, 108m, NR)
Domestic comedy with Doris Day a housewife who suddenly becomes a TV commercials star, much to the dismay of her husband (James Garner). Directed by Norman Jewison. **DT51**

Throne of Blood (1957, B&W, 105m, NR)
Japanese version of *Macbeth,* starring Toshiro Mifune as the ambitious nobleman. Stunning direction by Akira Kurosawa. **DT57, ST106, WR22** *Highly Recommended*

Through a Glass Darkly (1962, B&W, 91m, NR)
Ingmar Bergman's study of a woman recently released from a mental hospital and her relationships with her husband, father, and brother. Harriet Andersson stars in this Oscar-winning film. **DT7, XT7**

Throw Momma From the Train (1987, C, 90m, PG-13)
Comedy teaming Billy Crystal as a writing teacher with a grudge against his wife and Danny DeVito as his student with a monster for a mother (Anne Ramsey). DeVito hits on a "murder swap" scheme after seeing Hitchcock's *Strangers on a Train.* **CO3, CO10, CO13, ST32**

Thumbelina (1983, C, 60m, NR)
From the Faerie Tale Theatre series, a tale about a beautiful and kind princess who is only the size of a human thumb. Carrie Fisher, William Katt, and Burgess Meredith star. **FA12**

Thunder Bay (1953, C, 102m, NR)
Louisiana shrimp fisherman and oil drillers battle over Gulf waters. James Stewart stars. Anthony Mann directed. **DT69, ST143**

Thunder in the City (1937, B&W, 86m, NR)
Edward G. Robinson plays a brash American promoter who takes London by storm with a newly discovered mineral. **ST130**

Thunder Road (1958, B&W, 92m, NR)
Hot-rodding action with a family of moonshiners (Robert and Jim Mitchum, playing brothers; in real life they're father and son) outrunning the feds and gangsters. The elder Mitchum sings the title tune. **AC10, ST107, XT8**

Thunderball (1965, C, 129m, PG)
James Bond (Sean Connery) battles a villain who wants to destroy Miami in this underwater adventure. With Claudine Auger and Adolfo Celi; plenty of underwater action. **AC12, HF2, ST21**

Thunderbolt and Lightfoot (1974, C, 115m, R)
A professional thief (Clint Eastwood) takes on an apprentice (Jeff Bridges) and, together with the thief's old partners, set out to recover money from a previous heist. With George Kennedy and Geoffrey Lewis. Directed by Michael Cimino. **AC9, MY18, ST11, ST39**

Ticket to Heaven (1981, C, 107m, PG)
Canadian drama of young man lulled into joining a cult and his subsequent deprogramming experience. Nick Mancuso, Saul Rubinek, and R.H. Thomson star. **DR9**

Tickle Me (1965, C, 90m, NR)
A rodeo star (Elvis Presley) gets a job at an all-girl dude ranch, goes on a gold hunt, and finds love. **ST123**

Tiger Bay (1959, B&W, 105m, NR)
Hayley Mills stars as a child who witnesses a murder and is kidnapped by the

killer (Horst Bucholz) in this classic British thriller. **FA7, MY15**

Tiger Town (1983, C, 95m, NR)
Young boy idolizes Detroit Tiger ballplayer, tries to help him through a slump. Justin Henry and Roy Scheider star. Originally made for cable TV. **DR22, FA7**

Tiger Walks, A (1964, C, 91m, NR)
Disney drama of a girl who tries to protect a runaway tiger from small-town politicians and bigots. Pamela Franklin stars, with Brian Keith, Vera Miles, Sabu, and Kevin Corcoran. **DR26, FA1**

Tight Little Island *see* Whisky Galore

Tightrope (1984, C, 114m, R)
A New Orleans cop (Clint Eastwood) is searching for a sex murderer and uncovers some nasty truths about himself. With Genevieve Bujold and Alison Eastwood (Clint's real-life daughter). **AC9, ST39, XT8, XT14**

Till the Clouds Roll By (1946, C, 137m, NR)
Robert Walker plays songwriter Jerome Kern in this biography that's really a series of musical numbers. Songs performed by a variety of MGM's stable of stars, including Frank Sinatra and Judy Garland. **MU1, MU5, ST51, ST138**

Till the End of Time (1946, B&W, 105m, NR)
A trio of World War II veterans find heartbreak and frustration back in the States. Guy Madison, Robert Mitchum, and Bill Williams star, with Dorothy McGuire. **CL8, ST107**

Tillie's Punctured Romance (1914, B&W, 73m, NR)
First feature-length comedy, starring Charlie Chaplin as a swindler, Marie Dressler as his victim. Mabel Normand costars. Mack Sennet directed this silent film. **DT18**

Tim (1979, C, 108m, PG)
Australian drama of the friendship between a slightly retarded man (Mel Gibson) and an older woman (Piper Laurie). Based on a novel by Colleen McCullough. **FF5, ST53**

Time After Time (1979, C, 112m, PG)
H. G. Wells (Malcolm McDowell) invents a time machine that Jack the Ripper (David Warner) uses in order to escape from the police. Wells follows him to modern-day San Francisco where, with the help of a bank teller (Mary Steenburgen), he tries to stop the Ripper from launching another killing spree. Adapted from elements in several H. G. Wells stories. **AC14, SF4, WR29** *Recommended*

Time Bandits (1981, C, 110m, PG)
Six dwarfs and a British schoolboy in possession of a time map travel through history in an effort to escape the map's evil owner. Written by Terry Gilliam and Michael Palin; directed by Gilliam. With Sean Connery as Agamemnon, John Cleese, Michael Palin as Robin Hood, Shelley Duvall, Ralph Richardson, David Warner, and Ian Holm as Napoleon. **CO15, FA8, HF15, HF19, SF4, ST21** *Recommended*

Time for Dying, A (1971, C, 87m, PG)
Audie Murphy stars in his last film, a western drama from director Budd Boetticher. **DT10**

Time Machine, The (1960, C, 103m, G)
An inventor (Rod Taylor) constructs a time machine and, after stopping at various intervals, ends up in the year 802701. Based on a story by H. G. Wells. George Pal produced and directed this Oscar winner for special effects. **FA8, SF4, SF13, SF15, WR29**

Time of Destiny, A (1988, C, 118m, PG-13)
Old-fashioned melodrama of revenge, with William Hurt as a World War II soldier pursuing fellow G.I. Timothy Hutton, whom Hurt blames for his father's death. Written by Gregory Nava and Anna Thomas; Thomas produced and Nava directed. **ST75**

Time of Indifference (1964, B&W, 84m, NR)
Social drama of a poor Italian family's struggles during the 1920s. Rod Steiger, Shelley Winters, Claudia Cardinale, and Paulette Goddard star. **FF2, ST164**

Time of Their Lives, The (1946, B&W, 82m, NR)
Abbott and Costello comedy, with Lou and Marjorie Reynolds as ghosts from the

18th century who are haunting a home inhabited by Bud and his pals. **ST1**

Time of Your Life, The (1948, B&W, 109m, NR)
William Saroyan's play about the diverse characters who hang out at a waterfront saloon. James Cagney stars. **ST14**

Time Stands Still (1981, C/B&W, 99m, NR)
Drama set in Hungary in the early 1960s about a group of bored, rebellious, and angry young men who idolize American pop culture heroes like Elvis Presley. **FF7**

Time to Love and a Time to Die, A (1958, C, 132m, NR)
Drama about German soldier who must return to battle after brief romance. John Gavin stars; Klaus Kinski has a small role. Directed by Douglas Sirk. **DT98, ST83**

Time Warp *see* The Day Time Ended

Timerider (1983, C, 93m, PG)
A motocross rider is caught in a government experiment and gets sent back in time to 1877. Fred Ward stars. **SF4**

Times of Harvey Milk, The (1984, C, 87m, NR)
Documentary about San Francisco's first gay public official and his assassination. Oscar winner directed by Robert Epstein. **CU16** *Recommended*

Times Square (1980, C, 111m, R)
Two runaways in New York get a helping hand from a deejay (Tim Curry) who makes them stars. **DR15, MU9, XT9**

Tin Drum, The (1979, C, 142m, R)
Adapted from Günter Grass's bestselling novel, this German drama traces a boy's bizarre adventures during the years of the Third Reich. Oscar winner for Best Foreign Language Film. David Bennent stars. Directed by Volker Schlöndorff. **DR19, FF3, XT7** *Essential; Recommended*

Tin Men (1987, C, 110m, R)
Comic feud between two Baltimore aluminum-siding salesmen in the early 1960s, starring Richard Dreyfuss and Danny DeVito. With Barbara Hershey, Bruno Kirby, John Mahoney, Jackie Gayle, and Michael Tucker. Written and directed by Barry Levinson. **CO3, CO6, ST32, ST36**

Tin Star, The (1957, B&W, 93m, NR)
A tenderfoot sheriff calls on a veteran bounty hunter for help. Anthony Perkins and Henry Fonda star, with Betsy Palmer, Neville Brand, and Lee Van Cleef. Anthony Mann directed. **DT69, ST44, ST155, WE2**

Tingler, The (1959, B&W/C, 82m, NR)
Horror tale of a scientist (Vincent Price) who discovers a growth on people's spines that can be cured only by screaming. One sequence in color. **ST124**

To Be or Not To Be (1942, B&W, 99m, NR)
Bold comedy, considering when it was released, about a troupe of Polish actors defying Nazis with elaborate plan to protect a downed flier. Jack Benny and Carole Lombard (in her last film) star, with Robert Stack and Tom Dugan playing Hitler. Ernst Lubitsch directed. **CL10, CL14, CU5, DT63, HF12, ST92, XT22** *Highly Recommended*

To Be or Not To Be (1983, C, 107m, PG)
Remake of the Lubitsch classic, with Mel Brooks and Anne Bancroft in the Benny and Lombard roles. With Tim Matheson, Jose Ferrer, and Roy Goldman as Hitler. **CU18, DT13, HF12**

To Catch a Thief (1955, C, 103m, NR)
Colorful Alfred Hitchcock thriller, set on the French Riviera, about a suave cat burglar (Cary Grant) and the woman he intends to victimize (Grace Kelly). **DT46, MY5, ST57, ST82**

To Have and Have Not (1944, B&W, 100m, NR)
First teaming of Humphrey Bogart and Lauren Bacall in this loose adaptation of the Hemingway story about the French Resistance. Directed by Howard Hawks; co-written by William Faulkner. **CL15, DR19, DT43, MY4, ST8, WR10**

To Hell and Back (1955, C, 106m, NR)
Audie Murphy, America's most decorated World War II veteran, plays himself in this film based on his autobiography. **AC1, CL2**

To Kill a Mockingbird (1962, B&W, 129m, NR)
Small-town Southern lawyer (Gregory Peck, an Oscar winner) defends an innocent black man accused of rape. Each night, he tries to explain the case to his young children. With Brock Peters, Mary Badham, Philip Alford, and Robert Duvall. Written by Horton Foote. **DR17, DR26, ST38, ST119, XT2** *Recommended*

To Live and Die in L.A. (1985, C, 116m, R)
A counterfeiter kills a Secret Service agent and the agent's partner does everything he can to get revenge. William L. Petersen, John Pankow, and Willem Dafoe star, with Debra Feuer, Darlanne Fluegel and Dean Stockwell. Directed by William Friedkin on location in Los Angeles. **AC9, MY2, ST144, XT10** *Recommended*

To Paris With Love (1955, C, 78m, NR)
Alec Guinness stars in this British comedy of a father taking his son to France for a liberal education. **ST60**

To Sir, With Love (1967, C, 105m, NR)
Sidney Poitier plays a new teacher in London's East End who earns the respect of his rowdy class and teaches them how to get along in the world. Pop singers Lulu and Michael Des Barres play two of his students. **DR25, MU12, ST121**

To the Devil a Daughter (1976, C, 95m, R)
A satanist (Christopher Lee) and his followers pursue a young woman (Natassia Kinski) to force her to mate with the Devil. Her only hope for escape is an occult expert (Richard Widmark). **HO10, HO26, ST89**

To the Last Man (1933, B&W, 74m, NR)
A family feud in Kentucky spills over to the frontier West. Randolph Scott stars in this drama; Shirley Temple has a small role. **ST136, ST148**

To the Shores of Tripoli (1942, C, 86m, NR)
Marine action in World War II, with John Payne the soft, rich kid learning the ropes. With Randolph Scott and Maureen O'Hara. **AC1, ST136**

Toast of New York, The (1937, B&W, 109m, NR)
Colorful tale of turn-of-the-century businessman Jim Fiske, played by Edward Arnold, with Cary Grant as his partner. Frances Farmer costars. **ST57**

Tobruk (1967, C, 110m, NR)
World War II drama, as Allies battle Rommel in the African desert. Rock Hudson stars, with George Peppard and Nigel Green. **AC1, ST73**

Toby Tyler (1960, C, 96m, NR)
At the turn of the century, a young boy runs away from home and joins the circus. Kevin Corcoran stars in this Disney drama. **FA1**

Tokyo-Ga (1983, C, 92m, NR)
German director Wim Wenders' documentary impressions of Japan, which he had only known through the films of Yasujiro Ozu. **CU16, DT113**

Tokyo Joe (1949, B&W, 88m, NR)
Humphrey Bogart plays a World War II veteran in search of his ex-wife and her child in postwar Japan. Sessue Hayakawa costars as a villainous Secret Service agent. **ST8**

Tokyo Olympiad (1966, C, 170m, NR)
Superb documentary of the 1964 Olympic Games, directed by Kon Ichikawa. This is the full-length version in a letterboxed format. **CU16, CU19** *Essential; Recommended*

Tokyo Story (1953, B&W, 134m, NR)
Drama from infleuntial Japanese director Yasujiro Ozu of an elderly couple visiting their children in Tokyo. **FF4** *Essential*

Tom Brown's School Days (1940, B&W, 86m, NR)
A look into life at a boys' school during the Victorian era. Cedric Hardwicke and Freddie Bartholomew star. **FA2**

Tom, Dick and Harry (1941, B&W, 86m, NR)
Ginger Rogers comedy has her choosing from a trio of men: George Murphy, Alan Marshal, and Burgess Meredith. **ST131**

Tom Horn (1980, C, 98m, R)
Steve McQueen plays the legendary Wyoming outlaw and bounty hunter who was

framed by men who hired him. **ST97, WE3, WE11**

Tom Jones (1963, C, 129m, NR)
Oscar-winning comedy about a young British rake lusting his way through the 18th century countryside. Albert Finney stars, with Hugh Griffith, Edith Evans, Susannah York, Joyce Redmond, Diane Cilento, Peter Bull, and David Warner in fine support. Based on the Henry Fielding novel; directed by Tony Richardson. **CL1, CO17, ST42, XT1, XT6** *Essential; Recommended*

Tom Sawyer (1973, C, 104m, G)
Musical version of Mark Twain's classic story, with Johnnie Whitaker, Celeste Holm, Warren Oates, and Jodie Foster. **FA3, ST47, ST115, WR27**

tom thumb (1958, C, 98m, NR)
Children's musical fantasy of a tiny lad (Russ Tamblyn) who's taken in by a kindly couple, then exploited by a pair of crooks (Terry-Thomas, Peter Sellers). Special effects won an Oscar. **FA8, SF15, ST137**

Tomb of Ligeia (1965, C, 81m, NR)
The Edgar Allan Poe tale about a man's dead wife who comes back to haunt him when he remarries. Vincent Price stars. Roger Corman directed. **DT22, ST124, WR21**

Tommy (1975, C, 111m, PG)
Film adaptation of The Who's rock opera about a deaf, dumb, and blind boy's adventures. Roger Daltrey, Oliver Reed, and Ann-Margret star, with special appearances by Elton John, Tina Turner, Eric Clapton, Keith Moon, and Jack Nicholson. Directed by Ken Russell. **DT92, MU8, MU9, ST112**

Tomorrow (1972, C, 103m, PG)
Adaptation of William Faulkner story of farmer who takes in abandoned pregnant woman and learns to love her. Robert Duvall stars. Written by Horton Foote. **DR19, ST38, WR6**

Toni (1934, B&W, 90m, NR)
Early film from director Jean Renoir is a realistic drama set in a French village involving love, jealousy, and murder. **DT86**

Tonight and Every Night (1945, C, 92m, NR)
As their contribution to the war effort, the London's Music Box Revue never misses a performance, not even for an air raid or personal tragedy. Rita Hayworth stars in this musical. **MU4, ST64**

Tonight for Sure (1961, B&W, 66m, NR)
Two men recall their various sexual experiences in this "nudie" film directed by a young Francis Ford Coppola. **DT21**

Tonio Kroger (1965, B&W, 92m, NR)
German drama about a young writer's loves and struggles to find his identity as a man and an artist. Based on a novel by Thomas Mann. **FF3**

Tony Rome (1967, C, 110m, NR)
Frank Sinatra plays a private investigator who's hired by a rich man to look into his daughter's less-than-perfect lifestyle. With Jill St. John, Richard Conte, Sue Lyon, and Gena Rowlands. **MY10, ST138**

Too Late for Tears *see* Killer Bait

Too Late the Hero (1970, C, 133m, PG)
Two soldiers are sent on a suicide mission in the South Pacific during World War II. Michael Caine, Cliff Robertson, and Henry Fonda star. Directed by Robert Aldrich. Also known as *Suicide Run.* **AC1, ST15, ST44**

Tootsie (1983, C, 116m, PG)
Desperate for a job, an actor dresses up in drag and lands a part on a soap opera, where he becomes an overnight sensation. Dustin Hoffman stars in this smashing modern comedy, with Oscar winner Jessica Lange, Bill Murray, Teri Garr, Charles Durning, George Gaynes, and, in a small role, Geena Davis. Directed by Sydney Pollack, who also plays Hoffman's agent. **CO2, CO8, CO13, DT80, ST67, ST86, XT5** *Highly Recommended*

Top Gun (1986, C, 109m, PG)
A hotshot student pilot enrolls in a Naval flying school, where he must compete with other pilots as skilled as he is. Tom Cruise, Kelly McGillis, and Val Kilmer star. **AC11, ST26**

Top Hat (1935, B&W, 99m, NR)
Fred Astaire falls for divorcee Ginger Rogers. who hates most men, particularly him. Then she dances with him . . . With

Edward Everett Horton, Eric Blore, and, in a small role, Lucille Ball. **CL15, ST2, ST131** *Essential; Highly Recommended*

Top Secret! (1984, C, 90m, PG)
An American rock singer touring East Germany ends up helping the French Resistance battle some neo-Nazis. A spy spoof by the makers of *Airplane!* Val Kilmer stars, with Omar Sharif and Peter Cushing. **CO7, ST27**

Topaz (1969, C, 126m, PG)
Alfred Hitchcock Cold War thriller, with American and French spies hunting down a deadly double agent. John Forsythe stars. **DT46, MY6**

Topaze (1933, B&W, 79m, NR)
John Barrymore stars in this version of Marcel Pagnol's story of an honest but naive teacher duped by an aristocrat. With Myrna Loy and Albert Conti. **ST94**

Topkapi (1964, C, 120m, NR)
Elaborate heist story featuring an odd assortment of crooks assembled to steal a jeweled sword from a Turkish museum. Melina Mercouri and Maximilian Schell star, with Oscar winner Peter Ustinov as the gang's designated bumbler. **MY18, XT4** *Recommended*

Topper (1937, B&W, 97m, NR)
A put-upon businessman is haunted by two delightful ghosts in this comedy classic. Roland Young stars, with Cary Grant and Constance Bennett the playful spirits. **SF2, ST57**

Tora! Tora! Tora! (1970, C, 143m, G)
Dramatic recreation of the events that led up to the attack on Pearl Harbor, as seen from both the American and Japanese points of view. Oscar-winning special effects. Martin Balsam, Jason Robards, and E. G. Marshall star. **AC1, ST129**

Torch Song (1953, C, 90m, NR)
Joan Crawford vehicle has her playing a tough Broadway star who falls for a blind pianist (Michael Wilding). **ST24**

Torch Song Trilogy (1988, C, 120m, R)
Harvey Fierstein stars in this adaptation of his play about a gay man whose mother (Anne Bancroft) won't accept his lifestyle. With Matthew Broderick and Brian Kerwin. **DR3, DR20**

Torment (1985, C, 85m, R)
A mid-mannered man on the surface, he's a killer with a hair-trigger temper beneath. Taylor Gilbert stars in this suspense movie about a man who has even his wife and daughter intimidated by his bizarre behavior. **MY14**

Torn Curtain (1966, C, 128m, NR)
Alfred Hitchcock thriller about an American scientist pretending to be a defector in Berlin. Paul Newman and Julie Andrews star. **DT46, MY6, ST111**

Tornado (1983, C, 90m, NR)
American soldiers fighting in Vietnam are pushed to the limit by a sadistic sergeant. **AC4**

Torpedo Alley (1953, B&W, 84m, NR)
Drama of submarine action during the Korean War, starring Dorothy Malone, Mark Stevens, and Bill Williams. **AC3**

Torture Chamber of Dr. Sadism, The (1967, C, 90m, NR)
A mysterious man (Christopher Lee) lures a couple to his castle and takes his revenge by torturing them. Based on Edgar Allan Poe's "The Pit and the Pendulum." **ST89, WR21**

Torture Garden (1968, C, 93m, NR)
A carnival sideshow mystic offers customers a look into their futures. Jack Palance and Peter Cushing star. **HO23, ST27**

Touch and Go (1980, C, 92m, R)
A group of respectable ladies resort to burglary to save their local kindergarten. Wendy Hughes stars in this comedy from Australia. **FF5**

Touch and Go (1986, C, 101m, R)
Michael Keaton plays a hockey star whose self-centered attitude is challenged when he falls in love with the mother of a troubled boy who tried to rob him. Maria Conchita Alonso costars. **ST80**

Touch of Class, A (1973, C, 105m, PG)
Married man is determined to have a carefree affair, even if it nearly kills him. Romantic comedy starring George Segal and Oscar winner Glenda Jackson. **CO1, XT3**

Touch of Evil (1958, B&W, 108m, NR)
Stylized thriller from Orson Welles, with the director playing a crooked border cop

at odds with a Mexican police detective (Charlton Heston) over a car bombing. With Janet Leigh, Akim Tamiroff, Marlene Dietrich, Dennis Weaver, and Mercedes McCambridge. Video version restores 15 minutes cut from original release. **CL14, CU10, DT112, MY1, ST33** *Essential; Highly Recommended*

Tough Enough (1983, C, 106m, R)
An aspiring country singer (Dennis Quaid) turns to amateur boxing in Tough Man competitions. With Carlene Watkins, Stan Shaw, Pam Grier, and Warren Oates. **DR22, ST115**

Tough Guys (1986, C, 103m, PG)
Two train robbers, released after 30 years in prison, try to adjust to life in the 1980s in this comedy pairing Burt Lancaster and Kirk Douglas. **CO3, CO10, CO20, DR11, ST34, ST85**

Tougher Than Leather (1988, C, 92m, R)
Urban action drama of murder and revenge, featuring the rap music group Run-DMC in dramatic roles, with some musical interludes. **AC8**

Tower of London (1962, B&W, 79m, NR)
Political skullduggery with Richard III (Vincent Price) out to eliminate his enemies. Remake of 1939 film, in which Basil Rathbone played Richard and Price had a supporting role. Directed by Roger Corman. **DT22, ST124**

Towering Inferno, The (1974, C, 165m, PG)
An all-star disaster film about a fire that engulfs the world's largest skyscraper. Steve McQueen and Paul Newman star, with William Holden, Faye Dunaway, Fred Astaire, Richard Chamberlain, Susan Blakely, Jennifer Jones, and O. J. Simpson. **AC23, ST2, ST37, ST68, ST97, ST111** *Essential*

Town Like Alice, A (1980, C, 301m, NR)
Epic drama, based on Nevil Shute novel, of couple meeting in a World War II POW camp and reunited later to face a different set of hardships in the Australian outback. Bryan Brown and Helen Morse star. Originally a TV miniseries. **DR5, FF5**

Toxic Avenger (1985, C, 100m, R)
A harassed nerd falls into a vat of nuclear waste and becomes a mutated superhero. A gory spoof of horror films. **HO21, HO24**

Toy, The (1982, C, 99m, PG)
Rich man's son who has everything insists on "owning" a man he sees in a toy store, and Dad obliges. Richard Pryor and Jackie Gleason star. **CO5, ST125**

Toy Soldiers (1984, C, 91m, R)
Two mercenaries (Cleavon Little and Jason Miller) rescue a group of students from a Central American country in the midst of a revolution. **AC20**

Track 29 (1988, C, 90m, R)
Bizarre drama from director Nicolas Roeg, starring Theresa Russell as a woman trapped in a loveless marriage, obsessed with the child she had to give up for adoption when she was raped as a teenager. With Gary Oldman, Christopher Lloyd, and Sandra Bernhard. Written by Dennis Potter. **DT88**

Tracks (1977, C, 90m, R)
Dennis Hopper stars as a Vietnam veteran whose cross-country train ride with the body of a fallen comrade proves to be too much for his fragile state of mind. With Taryn Power, Dean Stockwell, Zack Norman, and Michael Emil. **ST71, ST144, XT19**

Trading Places (1983, C, 118m, R)
A pair of wealthy brothers make a bet and force a black street hustler and white stockbroker to switch positions. Eddie Murphy, Dan Aykroyd, Ralph Bellamy, and Don Ameche star in this comedy from director John Landis. **CO3, CO13, CO20** *Recommended*

Trail of Robin Hood (1950, B&W, 67m, NR)
Roy Rogers hooks up with a collection of famous western stars to aid cowboy actor Jack Holt in delivering Christmas trees to orphans. Rex Allen heads the supporting cast. **ST132**

Trail of the Pink Panther (1982, C, 87m, PG)
The very *last* Pink Panther movie, made after the death of Peter Sellers, has a reporter doing a story on Inspector Clouseau—an excuse to show footage from previous films. David Niven, Herbert

Lom, and Burt Kwouk costar. Directed by Blake Edwards. **DT32, ST137**

Train, The (1965, B&W, 113m, NR)
French Resistance fighters rush to waylay a Nazi train loaded with art treasures. Burt Lancaster and Jeanne Moreau star. **AC1, ST85, ST110, XT19**

Train Robbers, The (1973, C, 92m, PG)
John Wayne and buddies try to help out a lovely widow (Ann-Margret) in this western drama. **ST156**

Tramp, The/A Woman (1915, B&W, 57m, NR)
Two early shorts from Charlie Chaplin. The first is considered to be his first short masterpiece. In the second, he does a hilarious bit in drag. **DT18** *Recommended*

Trancers (1985, C, 85m, PG13)
In the year 2247 an evil cult leader wants to rule the world. His plan is to travel back to 1985 to alter the future to his advantage. It's up to Jack Deth (Tim Thomerson) to follow and destroy him. With Helen Hunt. **SF17**

Transatlantic Tunnel (1935, B&W, 70m, NR)
The trials and tribulations of building a tunnel under the Atlantic Ocean. Spectacularly convincing sets. **SF14**

Transformers: The Movie (1986, C, 86m, PG)
A feature-length film starring the television/toy superheroes battling an evil planet (voice provided by Orson Welles). **DT112, FA10, SF13**

Transmutations (1985, C, 100m, R)
A doctor (Denholm Elliott) creates a drug that mutates its users. Originally titled *Underworld*. **HO21**

Transylvania 6-5000 (1985, C, 93m, PG)
Horror movie spoof, with Jeff Goldblum and Ed Begley, Jr. as reporters snooping around a mad doctor's laboratory in modern-day Transylvania. With Joseph Bologna, Carol Kane, Geena Davis, John Byner, and Petar Buntic as the Frankenstein Monster. **CO7, HF10, ST56**

Transylvania Twist (1990, C, 82m, PG-13)
Horror comedy with Robert Vaughan as Byron Orlock, a vampire, and comic Steve Altman as his sidekick. With Teri

Copley and Boris Karloff (in clips from some of his old films). Executive producer: Roger Corman. **HO24, ST77**

Trapeze (1956, C, 105m, NR)
Romantic triangle among circus performers, starring Burt Lancaster, Gina Lollabrigida, and Tony Curtis. **CL7, ST85**

Trash (1970, C, 110m, NR)
From director Paul Morrissey and producer Andy Warhol, the story of Joe (Joe Dallessandro) and Holly (Holly Woodlawn) and their Lower East Side adventures in the world of drug addiction and trash-can rummaging. **CU12, DT72**

Traveling North (1988, C, 97m, PG-13)
Australian drama of a May-September romance between a retiree (Leo McKern) and a younger woman (Julia Blake). **FF5**

Treasure Island (1934, B&W, 102m, NR)
Adaptation of Robert Louis Stevenson's story about a young boy who travels with pirates in search of treasure. Wallace Beery and Jackie Cooper star. **AC13, FA3**

Treasure Island (1950, C, 96m, G)
Disney version of the Robert Louis Stevenson tale about a young boy's adventures with pirates. Bobby Driscoll and Robert Newton star. **FA1**

Treasure of Pancho Villa, The (1955, C, 96m, NR)
Western action south of the border, with Glenn Ford, Shelley Winters, and Gilbert Rowland. **ST164, WE9**

Treasure of the Four Crowns (1983, C, 97m, PG)
A soldier of fortune is hired to recover an ancient treasure, the source of mystical powers. Tony Anthony stars. **AC21**

Treasure of the Sierra Madre, The (1948, B&W, 125m, NR)
Three men in search of gold in Mexico form an uneasy partnership. Humphrey Bogart, Walter Huston (an Oscar winner), and Tim Holt star in this classic version of B. Traven's novel. Written and directed by Oscar winner John Huston, who also appears in a small role. **AC12, AC13, AC24, DT50, ST8, XT4, XT6, XT8** *Essential; Highly Recommended*

Tree Grows in Brooklyn, A (1945, B&W, 128m, NR)
Warm drama of a young girl's coming of age in turn-of-the-century New York. Dorothy McGuire and Peggy Ann Garner star, with Oscar winner James Dunn. Directed by Elia Kazan. **DT53, XT4** *Essential; Recommended*

Tremors (1990, C, 96m, PG-13)
Tongue-in-cheek sci-fi monster movie about large worms wreaking havoc in a desert town. Kevin Bacon and Fred Ward star, with Finn Carter, Michael Gross, and Reba McIntire. **HO16, HO21, HO24, MU12**

Trial, The (1963, B&W, 118m, NR)
The Franz Kafka story of a man accused of a crime he doesn't know by people he can never see, directed by Orson Welles. Anthony Perkins stars, with Welles, Jeanne Moreau, and Romy Schneider. **DR19, DT112, ST110**

Tribute (1980, C, 121m, PG)
Drama of a man dying with cancer who tries for reunion with his long-estranged son. Jack Lemmon and Robby Benson star. **DR8, ST90**

Trigger, Jr. (1950, C, 68m, NR)
Roy Rogers and his famous horse help to teach a young boy not to be afraid of animals—with the help of Trigger's son. Dale Evans costars. **ST132**

Trilogy of Terror (1975, C, 78m, NR)
Karen Black plays four different characters in three suspenseful tales. The best story is the third, in which a tiny warrior doll comes to life and tries to kill her. **HO23**

Trinity Is STILL My Name! (1972, C, 117m, PG)
Sequel to *My Name Is Trinity* features more western spoofing by Terence Hill and Bud Spencer. **WE13, WE14**

Trio (1950, B&W, 91m, NR)
Sequel to *Quartet* offers three more W. Somerset Maugham stories, starring Harold French, James Hayter, Michael Rennie, and Jean Simmons. **DR19**

Trip, The (1967, C, 85m, NR)
A TV director decides to experiment with LSD, and the results are both beautiful and horrifying. Peter Fonda, Bruce Dern, and Susan Strasberg star, with Dennis Hopper. Roger Corman directed and Jack Nicholson wrote the screenplay. **CU3, DT22, ST71**

Trip to Bountiful, The (1985, C, 105m, PG)
Geraldine Page won an Oscar for her performance as a lonely widow who returns to her small Texas hometown to find that it's completely deserted. Written by Horton Foote. With John Heard, Carlin Glynn, and Rebecca DeMornay. **DR11, XT3**

Triumph of Sherlock Holmes, The (1935, B&W, 75m, NR)
Arthur Wontner stars as the legendary detective in this screen version of Arthur Conan Doyle's "Valley of Fear" tale. **HF14**

Triumph of the Spirit (1989, C, 120m, R)
Grim, fact-based drama of a Greek boxing champ consigned to Nazi death camp, forced to fight for his captors. Willem Dafoe stars, with Edward James Olmos and Robert Loggia. **DR5**

Triumph of the Will (1935, B&W, 110m, PG-13)
Infamous documentary, filmed at Hitler's behest, dramatizes the Nazi appeal to German people at 1934 Nuremberg rally. Directed by Leni Riefenstahl. Chilling content, but a stunning historical document nonetheless. **CU16** *Essential; Recommended*

Triumphs of a Man Called Horse (1983, C, 86m, PG)
The third installment in the *Man Called Horse* trilogy has Richard Harris and his half-breed Indian son battling for Indian rights. **WE7**

Trojan Women, The (1972, C, 105m, PG)
Classic Greek tragedy of the effects of war on the women of Troy, starring Katharine Hepburn, Irene Papas, Genevieve Bujold, and Vanessa Redgrave. **DR20, ST66, ST127**

Troll (1986, C, 86m, PG13)
An evil troll possesses the body of a little girl and sets out to transform her apartment building into a troll kingdom. Shelley Hack, Michael Moriarty, and Sonny Bono star. **HO16**

Tron (1982, C, 96m, PG)
The designer of a vast computer system is pulled into the computer and forced into a videogame competition with the computerized beings who want to overthrow the program that controls their lives. Jeff Bridges and Bruce Boxleitner star. Groundbreaking use of computer animation. **FA1, SF11, SF13, SF16, ST11**

Troop Beverly Hills (1989, C, 105m, PG)
A spoiled Southern California woman finds herself the leader of a Girl Scout troop in this comedy. Shelley Long stars, with Craig T. Nelson. **CO20**

Trouble In Mind (1985, C, 111m, R)
Kris Kristofferson plays an ex-cop just released from prison who gets caught up with a naive girl and her hustler boyfriend. Alan Rudolph directed. With Keith Carradine, Lori Singer, Genevieve Bujold, and Divine. **DR1, DT91, MU12** *Recommended*

Trouble With Angels, The (1966, C, 112m, NR)
Two students at a convent school create havoc with the Mother Superior. Hayley Mills, June Harding, and Rosalind Russell star in this Disney comedy. **CO18, FA1**

Trouble With Girls, The (1969, C, 104m, G)
Elvis Presley musical set in the 1920s, has El in charge of a Chautauqua company, a traveling medicine and educational show. With Marilyn Mason, Sheree North, Vincent Price, and John Carradine. **ST123, ST124**

Trouble With Harry, The (1955, C, 99m, PG)
The good folks of a New England village aren't sure just what to do with a dead body found in the woods. John Forsythe and Shirley MacLaine (her debut) star in this darkly comic mystery from Alfred Hitchcock. **CL14, CO10, CO12, DT46, MY17, ST96, XT21**

True Believer (1989, C, 103m, R)
A lawyer who was an anti-war radical in the 1960s now defends drug dealers. He gets a chance for redemption when he defends a convict on a jail murder charge. The lawyer soon realizes his client has been framed as part of a large-scale political conspiracy. James Woods stars, with Robert Downey, Jr. and Kurtwood Smith. **MY2, MY11, ST165**

True Confessions (1981, C, 108m, R)
A pair of brothers, one a priest (Robert DeNiro), the other a police detective (Robert Duvall), become enmeshed in a murder case in 1940s Los Angeles. Written by John Gregory Dunne and Joan Didion, based on Dunne's novel. **DR16, MY2, MY14, ST30, ST38, XT10** *Recommended*

True Grit (1969, C, 128m, G)
John Wayne won his only Oscar for his portrayal of Rooster Cogburn, the one-eyed sheriff on the trail of a gang of desperadoes. Glen Campbell and Kim Darby costar, with Robert Duvall and Dennis Hopper. **MU12, ST38, ST71, ST156, WE2, XT2**

True Heart Susie (1919, B&W, 93m, NR)
A plain farm girl raises the money to send her true love to college, where he repays her by falling in love with a beautiful and cruel city woman. Lillian Gish stars in this silent drama directed by D. W. Griffith. **DT42, ST54**

True Love (1989, C, 101m, R)
Comedy set before, during, and after an Italian wedding in the Bronx. Ron Eldard and Annabella Sciorra star. Directed by Nancy Savoca. **CO1, CO5, XT20**

True West (1986, C, 110m, NR)
Sam Shepard's powerful drama about two brothers, one a petty thief, the other a respectable screenwriter, starring John Malkovich and Gary Sinise. Originally shown on public TV. **DR8, DR20, ST98** *Recommended*

Truite, La (1982, C, 105m, R)
French country girl (Isabelle Huppert) becomes emeshed in the shady world of high finance in this contemporary drama from director Joseph Losey. **FF1**

Try and Get Me (1951, B&W, 85m, NR)
A hard-luck World War II veteran falls into a life of crime; he and his partner accidentally kill a kidnap victim. Frank Lovejoy and Lloyd Bridges star. Also known as *The Sound of Fury*. **MY1**

Tuck Everlasting (1980, C, 110m, NR)
An adaptation of Natalie Babbitt's novel about a magical family who never age or die. **FA8**

Tucker: The Man and His Dream (1988, C, 111m, PG)
The true story of Preston Tucker, the automobile creator who challenged Detroit's Big Three carmakers with his revolutionary designs. Jeff Bridges stars, with Martin Landau, Joan Allen, Frederic Forrest, Mako, Dean Stockwell (as Howard Hughes), Christian Slater, and Lloyd Bridges. Directed by Francis Ford Coppola. **DR4, DR24, DT21, ST11, ST144, XT8** *Recommended*

Tunes of Glory (1960, C, 106m, NR)
British army drama about the conflict between crusty officer and his replacement. Alec Guinness and John Mills star, with Susannah York. **ST60**

Turk 182 (1984, C, 96m, PG-13)
A New York fireman is injured on the job but can't collect compensation, so his younger brother, a graffiti artist, decides to use his talent to dramatize the predicament. Timothy Hutton and Robert Urich star in this drama. **DR15, XT9**

Turkish Delight (1974, C, 96m, NR)
Dutch drama starring Rutger Hauer as an artist with a very free and easy lifestyle. Directed by Paul Verhoeven. **FF7**

Turn of the Screw (1974, C, 120m, NR)
A governess (Lynn Redgrave) tries to save her two charges from the ghosts of their former governess and her lover. Based on a story by Henry James. **DR19, HO2, HO19, HO26, WR11**

Turner and Hooch (1989, C, 100m, PG)
Comedy of friendship between a cop and his slobbering but resourceful dog. Tom Hanks stars, with Mare Winningham and Craig T. Nelson. **CO10, ST62**

Turning Point, The (1977, C, 119m, PG)
Shirley MacLaine and Anne Bancroft play former dance colleagues whose lives have gone in opposite directions. With Tom Skerritt, Leslie Browne, and Mikhail Baryshnikov. **DR10, DR12, ST96** *Essential*

Turtle Diary (1986, C, 96m, PG)
Unusual love story of two lonely souls in London who unite in a common cause: to kidnap a pair of giant sea turtles from a zoo and return them to their home in the sea. Glenda Jackson and Ben Kingsley star, with Richard Johnson, Michael Gambon, and Eleanor Bron. Original screenplay by Harold Pinter. **DR1, DR23** *Recommended*

Twelve Angry Men (1957, B&W, 96m, NR)
Classic courtroom drama of lone juror holding out for acquittal of murder suspect. Henry Fonda stars; Lee J. Cobb, Jack Warden, Jack Klugman, and E. G. Marshall are among the other deliberators. Directed by Sidney Lumet. **CL8, DR17, DT65, ST44** *Essential; Recommended*

Twelve Chairs, The (1970, C, 94m, G)
Mel Brooks comedy based on Russian story about the race to find one of a set of dining room chairs with a fortune hidden in the seat. Ron Moody, Dom DeLuise, and Frank Langella star, with Brooks hilarious as an idiot servant. **CO6, DT13**

Twelve O'Clock High (1949, B&W, 132m, NR)
American bomber pilots stationed in Great Britain get a new commander (Gregory Peck), who nearly cracks under the responsibility. With Gary Merrill and Oscar winner Dean Jagger. **AC1, AC11, ST119, XT4**

Twentieth Century (1934, B&W, 91m, NR)
Slam-bang comedy, set aboard the title train, involving a Broadway producer (John Barrymore) and the girl he makes a star (Carole Lombard). Both stars are outstanding under Howard Hawks' direction. **CL7, CL10, DT43, ST92, XT19** *Essential; Highly Recommended*

25 X 5: The Continuing Adventures of the Rolling Stones (1990, C, 130m, NR)
Career retrospective of self-proclaimed world's great rock 'n' roll band, with plenty of performance clips and interviews with all the current members of the group. **MU11** *Recommended*

20,000 Leagues Under the Sea (1954, C, 118m, G)
The Jules Verne tale about Captain Nemo (James Mason), a 19th-century inventor

who builds a nuclear-powered submarine which he uses to sink warships. Kirk Douglas, Paul Lukas, and Peter Lorre costar. The special effects in this Disney film won an Academy Award. **FA1, FA3, SF3, SF13, SF15, ST34, ST102, WR28** *Recommended*

Twice Dead (1988, C, 85m, R)
Haunted house story, with spirit of a dead movie star helping a family fend off a gang of punkers. Tom Breznahan and Jill Whitlow star. **HO3**

Twice in a Lifetime (1985, C, 117m, R)
A long-time marriage crumbles when the husband meets an attractive barmaid, leaving his wife confused and one of his grown daughters embittered. Gene Hackman, Ellen Burstyn, Ann-Margret, Amy Madigan, and Ally Sheedy star. **DR8, ST61**

Twice Told Tales (1963, C, 119m, NR)
Three suspense stories based on works by Nathaniel Hawthorne; "Dr. Heidegger's Experiment," "Rapaccini's Daughter," and "The House of the Seven Gables." Vincent Price stars. **HO23, ST124**

Twilight Zone: The Movie (1983, C, 102m, PG)
Four tales of terror patterned after the famous TV show. Dan Aykroyd and Albert Brooks star in a witty prologue; among the segment stars are Vic Morrow (in his last film), Scatman Crothers, Kathleen Quinlan, Jeremy Licht, and John Lithgow. Individual segments directed by John Landis, Steven Spielberg, Joe Dante, and George Miller. **CO13, DT12, DT25, DT99, HO23**

Twilight's Last Gleaming (1977, C, 146m, R)
Renegade American general seizes nuclear warhead facility, threatens to start World War III if his demands aren't met. Burt Lancaster, Paul Winfield, Richard Widmark, and Melvyn Douglas star. Directed by Robert Aldrich. **DR7, ST85, ST162**

Twinky *see* Lola

Twins (1988, C, 107m, PG)
Comedy of long-lost brothers reunited, one a gentle giant (Arnold Schwarzenegger), the other a pint-sized hustler (Danny DeVito). **CO3, CO5, ST32, ST135**

Twins of Evil (1972, C, 85m, R)
One of a set of beautiful twins (Mary and Madeleine Collinson) is a vampire. Peter Cushing costars. **HO15, ST27**

Twister (1989, C, 94m, PG-13)
Comic story set in Kansas about an odd family featuring a loony patriarch (Harry Dean Stanton) and his son and daughter (Crispin Glover, Suzy Amis). They're entertaining various relatives and friends during a storm. Adapted from Mary Robison's novel, *Oh!* **CO5, DR19, ST141**

Two Daughters (1961, B&W, 114m, NR)
From India, a drama in two parts: in "The Postmaster," a young servant girl learns obedience to her employer; in "The Conclusion," a new bride flees an arranged marriage but later returns. Directed by Satyajit Ray. **DT84**

Two English Girls (1972, C, 130m, NR)
French director François Truffaut's study of a romantic triangle involving a Frenchman and two very different British sisters. Jean-Pierre Léaud, Kika Markham, and Stacey Tendeter star. Based on a novel by Henri Roche, also the source author of Truffaut's *Jules and Jim*. Video version includes footage restored by the director in 1984. **CU10, DT106** *Recommended*

Two-Faced Woman (1941, B&W, 94m, NR)
Greta Garbo's last film, a comedy of mistaken identity, with Melvyn Douglas and Constance Bennett. Directed by George Cukor. **DT24, ST50**

Two for the Road (1967, C, 112m, NR)
Literate comedy-drama of romance, marriage, and breakup of an attractive couple (Albert Finney, Audrey Hepburn). Written by Frederic Raphael; directed by Stanley Donen. **DR1, DT30, ST42, ST65, XT18** *Recommended*

Two Girls and a Sailor (1944, B&W, 124m, NR)
MGM musical features romantic title triangle (June Allyson, Gloria DeHaven, and Van Johnson). With Jimmy Durante, Jose Iturbi, Lena Horne, and Harry James. **MU1**

200 Motels (1971, C, 98m, R)
Frank Zappa and the Mothers of Invention satirize suburban America. Ringo

Starr, disguised as Zappa, narrates. **CU1, CU3, MU9**

Two Moon Junction (1988, C, 104m, R)
Steamy trash, with engaged modern Southern belle attracted to an often shirtless carnival worker, causing tongues in her small town to wag. Sherilyn Fenn and Richard Tyson star, with Louise Fletcher, Burl Ives, and Kristy Mc-Nichol. **CU6, DR3, DR26**

Two Mules for Sister Sara (1970, C, 105m, PG)
A prostitute disguised as a nun is befriended by an unsuspecting cowboy. Western action stars Clint Eastwood and Shirley MacLaine. Directed by Don Siegel. **DT97, ST39, ST96, WE8**

Two Rode Together (1961, C, 109m, NR)
James Stewart and Richard Widmark ride off on a rescue mission in this western directed by John Ford. **DT36, ST143**

2001: A Space Odyssey (1968, C, 139m, G)
Stanley Kubrick's masterpiece about the search for the aliens that have been helping humans develop throughout time. The special effects won an Oscar. Keir Dullea and a computer named HAL 9000 star. **CU3, CU4, DT56, SF3, SF6, SF15, SF16** *Essential; Recommended*

2010: The Year We Make Contact (1984, C, 114m, PG)
An American and Soviet space crew journey towards Jupiter in hopes of unraveling the mystery that began in *2001: A Space Odyssey*. Roy Scheider stars. **SF3**

Two Way Stretch (1960, B&W, 87m, NR)
Classic British comedy starring Peter Sellers as a convict who leads his cellmates on a robbery expedition outside the prison. **CO17, ST137**

Two Women (1961, B&W, 99m, NR)
Sophia Loren won an Oscar for her performance as a woman who is brutally attacked, along with her daughter, by soldiers during World War II. With Jean-Paul Belmondo. Directed by Vittorio De Sica. **DT26, ST6, ST93, XT3**

Tycoon (1947, C, 128m, NR)
John Wayne stars in this drama about railroad builders. With Laraine Day, Cedric Hardwicke, and Judith Anderson. **ST156**

UFOria (1986, C, 100m, PG)
Offbeat comedy about a grocery store clerk who is sure that aliens have contacted her. Cindy Williams stars, with Harry Dean Stanton, Fred Ward, and Harry Carey, Jr. Made in 1980. **CO12, ST141**

UHF (1989, C, 96m, PG13)
Al Yankovic stars as a wacky cable TV programmer in this spoof of TV and movies. With Victoria Jackson and Kevin Mc-Carthy. **CO8**

U2: Live at Red Rocks "Under A Blood Red Sky" (1983, C, 55m, NR)
This Irish band in concert at a natural outdoor amphitheatre in Colorado. **MU10**

U2: Rattle and Hum (1988, B&W/C, 90m, PG-13)
Documentary focusing on the popular Irish rock band and their travels in America. One concert segment in color; the rest of the film was shot in B&W. **MU11**

Ugetsu (1953, B&W, 96m, NR)
From Japan, a classic drama of two peasants seeking their fortunes—one as a businessman in the city, the other as a samurai—and bringing disaster upon their families. Directed by Kenji Mizoguchi. **FF4** *Essential; Recommended*

Ugly American, The (1963, C, 120m, NR)
American diplomat in Southeast Asia is caught in political turmoil created by communist elements; he spearheads disastrous official reaction to those events. Marlon Brando stars in this adaptation of the Eugene Burdick's novel. **DR7, ST10**

Ultimate Solution of Grace Quigley, The *see* Grace Quigley

Ulysses (1955, C, 104m, NR)
The classic Greek myth of the warrior who is destined to travel for seven years after the Trojan War before he can return home. Kirk Douglas stars. **AC18, ST34**

Ulzana's Raid (1972, C, 103m, R)
The U.S. Cavalry and a band of Indian marauders battle it out in this violent western tale. Burt Lancaster stars. Directed by Robert Aldrich. **ST85, WE4, WE7, WE15**

Umberto D (1952, B&W, 89m, NR)
Italian director Vittorio De Sica's acclaimed study of a retired bureaucrat (Carlo Battisti) and his struggle to maintain his dignity. **DT26** *Essential*

Umbrellas of Cherbourg, The (1964, C, 91m, NR)
Musical drama (all the dialogue is sung) about two sisters and their umbrella shop in a French seaside resort. Catherine Deneuve stars. **FF1, MU16, ST29**

Unbearable Lightness of Being, The (1988, C, 172m, R)
Adaptation of Milan Kundera's novel of romance and betrayal set against the backdrop of the Czech reforms of 1968 and the Russian invasion of Prague. Daniel Day-Lewis, Lena Olin, and Juliette Binoche star. Directed by Philip Kaufman. **CU6, DR1, DR7, DR19, DT52**

Uncanny, The (1977, C, 85m, NR)
Peter Cushing plays an author who believes that household cats are responsible for a series of unsolved murders. **ST27**

Uncle Buck (1989, C, 100m, PG)
John Candy comedy, as he plays an irrepressible relative who provides an unlikely role model for his little relatives. Directed by John Hughes. **CO5, CO14, DT49**

Uncommon Valor (1983, C, 105m, R)
A retired colonel recruits some Vietnam vets to help him find his MIA son in Laos. Gene Hackman stars, with Robert Stack, Patrick Swayze, and Fred Ward. **AC4, AC20, ST61**

Undefeated, The (1969, C, 119m, G)
Western drama set in the aftermath of the Civil War, starring John Wayne and Rock Hudson as opposing colonels who must find a way to live in peace. **ST73, ST156, WE6**

Under California Skies (1948, B&W, 71m, NR)
When the famous stallion Trigger is kidnapped, Roy Rogers swings into action. With Andy Devine and Bob Nolan & the Sons of the Pioneers. **ST132**

Under Capricorn (1949, C, 117m, NR)
Ingrid Berman plays the weak wife of Australian pioneer Joseph Cotten in this rare costume drama from Alfred Hitchcock. **DT46, ST7**

Under Fire (1983, C, 128m, R)
A trio of American journalists covering the downfall of the dictator Somoza in Nicaragua get personally involved in a story. Powerful drama starring Nick Nolte, Gene Hackman, and Joanna Cassidy. Written by Ron Shelton. **DR7, DR21, ST61, ST113** *Recommended*

Under Milk Wood (1973, C, 90m, PG)
Drama, based on Dylan Thomas play, about the lives of people in a mythical Welsh town. Elizabeth Taylor, Richard Burton, and Peter O'Toole star. **CL15, ST13, ST117, ST147**

Under Nevada Skies (1944, B&W, 68m, NR)
Roy Rogers leads a band of friendly Indians against a gang of claim jumpers. **ST132**

Under the Gun (1989, C, 89m, R)
Cop (Sam Jones) and lovely lawyer (Vanessa Williams) form a team to avenge the death of his brother. With John Russell. **AC9**

Under the Rainbow (1981, C, 98m, PG)
Farce set in a hotel during the making of *The Wizard of Oz,* involving that film's midget actors, spies, and secret agents. Chevy Chase, Carrie Fisher, Eve Arden, and Billy Barty star. **CO8, CO13**

Under the Roofs of Paris (1930, B&W, 92m, NR)
This early sound film from France employs song and mime to tell the comic tale of a romantic triangle. Directed by René Clair. **FF1**

Under the Volcano (1984, C, 112m, R)
Somber drama, set in 1930s Mexico, of alcoholic British diplomat's final days. Albert Finney, Jacqueline Bisset, and Anthony Andrews star in this adaptation of the famed Malcolm Lowry novel. Directed by John Huston. **DR19, DT50, ST42**

Under Western Stars (1945, B&W, 83m, NR)
Roy Rogers stars in this tuneful western with his faithful steed Trigger and Smiley Burnette. **ST132**

Undersea Kingdom (1936, B&W, 223m, NR)
A serial about adventurers finding the lost kingdom of Atlantis. With Lon Chaney, Jr. Also known as *Sharad of Atlantis*. **ST17**

Underworld *see* Transmutations

Underworld, U.S.A. (1961, B&W, 99m, NR)
Young man (Cliff Robertson) swears revenge on the Mob after his father is murdered. Samuel Fuller directed. **AC19, DT40**

Unfaithfully Yours (1948, B&W, 105m, NR)
An orchestra conductor, convinced that his lovely young wife is cheating on him with a musician, plots to do away with both of them. Classic comedy starring Rex Harrison, Linda Darnell, and Kurt Krueger. Written and directed by Preston Sturges. **CL10, DT103**

Unfaithfully Yours (1984, C, 96m, PG)
Remake of the Preston Sturges classic, with Dudley Moore, Nastassja Kinski, and Armand Assante. **CU18, ST109**

Unforgiven, The (1960, C, 125m, NR)
Feuding in frontier Texas between two families and an Indian tribe, which claims a young woman (Audrey Hepburn) as one of theirs. Burt Lancaster stars, with Audie Murphy, Lillian Gish, and Charles Bickford. John Huston directed. **DT50, ST54, ST65, ST85, WE1, WE7, WE8**

Unholy, The (1988, C, 100m, R)
A priest in New Orleans investigates the murders of two fellow clerics—and comes up with a surprising revelation about himself. Horror story stars Ben Cross, Hal Holbrook, Trevor Howard, and Ned Beatty. **HO10**

Unidentified Flying Oddball (1979, C, 92m, G)
A Disney version of *A Conneticut Yankee In King Arthur's Court*. A man gets sent back to medieval times. Dennis Dugan and Jim Dale star. **FA1**

Union City (1980, C, 87m, PG)
Debby Harry plays a housewife in this thriller about paranoia and murder. **MU12, MY2**

Union Station (1950, B&W, 80m, NR)
A madman (Lyle Bettger) kidnaps a blind woman (Allene Roberts) and a police detective (William Holden) heads the manhunt. **ST68**

Unmarried Woman, An (1978, C, 124m, R)
Middle-class Manhattan wife and mother picks up the pieces after her husband leaves her for another woman. Jill Clayburgh stars, with Michael Murphy and Alan Bates. Written and directed by Paul Mazursky, who plays a small role. **DR10, XT9**

Unsinkable Molly Brown, The (1964, C, 128m, NR)
Debbie Reynolds plays a poor miner's daughter who becomes a millionairess and a heroine of the *Titanic* disaster in this musical. Based on a true story. Harve Presnell costars. **MU1, MU6**

Unsuitable Job for a Woman, An (1981, C, 94m, NR)
British private eye story with a twist: the gumshoe's a woman (Pippa Guard) who's investigating the suicide of her boss. Based on a novel by P.D. James. **MY10, MY15**

Until September (1984, C, 95m, R)
Love story set in Paris involving an American woman (Karen Allen) and a married French banker (Thierry L'Hermitte). **DR1**

Untouchables, The (1987, C, 119m, R)
In Prohibition-era Chicago, Al Capone rules over all—until a determined government agent named Elliot Ness arrives in town. Kevin Costner, Robert DeNiro, and Oscar winner Sean Connery star in this gangster saga. With Charles Martin Smith, Andy Garcia, and Billy Drago as Frank Nitti. Written by David Mamet; Brian DePalma directed. **AC22, DT29, ST21, ST23, ST30, XT4**

Up in Arms (1944, C, 106m, NR)
A hypchondriac (Danny Kaye, in his film debut) wreaks havoc on the Army. Constance Dowling and Dinah Shore costar. **CO21, ST78**

Up in Smoke (1980, C, 87m, R)
The movie debut of Cheech and Chong, those lovably stoned L.A. hipsters. **CU3, ST18**

Up the Creek (1958, B&W, 83m, NR)
British service comedy set aboard a mothballed ship, with the emphasis on slapstick humor. David Tomlinson, Wilfrid Hyde-White, and Peter Sellers star. **CO21, ST137**

Up the Sandbox (1972, C, 97m, R)
Comedy-drama of a young New York wife and mother whose overactive imagination results in some bizarre fantasies. Barbra Streisand stars. **DR10, ST146**

Uptown Saturday Night (1974, C, 104m, PG)
Comedy starring Sidney Poitier and Bill Cosby as a couple of screw-ups who are after a valuable lottery ticket. With Harry Belafonte and Richard Pryor. Poitier directed. **ST121, ST125**

Urban Cowboy (1980, C, 135m, R)
Set in contemporary Houston, this drama centers on the life and loves of a young hard-hat who hangs around the mammoth honky-tonk bar, Gilley's. John Travolta and Debra Winger star, with Scott Glenn. **DR15, ST163, WE12**

Urge to Kill (1984, C, 96m, NR)
A convicted killer is released from a mental insitution and has problems readjusting to the outside world. Karl Malden stars, with Holly Hunter, Alex MacArthur, and Paul Sorvino. **ST74**

Used Cars (1980, C, 111m, R)
Wild comedy with cult following about twin car dealer brothers (both played by Jack Warden), one honest, the other totally unscrupulous. Kurt Russell stars in this contemporary slapstick classic, with Gerrit Graham, Frank McRae, Deborah Harmon, David L. Lander, and Michael McKean. Written by Bob Gale and Robert Zemeckis; directed by Zemeckis. **CO12, CU5** *Recommended*

Utopia *see* Atoll K

Vagabond (1985, C, 105, R)
Moody, stylized story of a young woman (Sandrine Bonnaire) and her aimless wandering through the French countryside. Agnes Varda directed. **DR10, FF1** *Recommended*

Valley Girl (1983, C, 95m, R)
Romance blossoms between a San Fernando Valley mall rat and a punked-out dude from Los Angeles. Deborah Foreman and Nicolas Cage star. Martha Coolidge directed. **CO2, CO4** *Recommended*

Valley of Fire (1951, B&W, 63m, NR)
Gene Autry plays matchmaker for a lonely gang of prospectors. **ST3**

Valmont (1989, C, 137m, R)
Director Milos Forman's version of the *Les Liaisons Dangereuses* story of love and intrigue in 18th-century France, filmed before under its original title and as *Dangerous Liaisons*. Colin Firth and Annette Benning star as the schemers, with Meg Tilly, Fairuza Balk, Sian Phillips, Jeffrey Jones, and Henry Thomas. **DR1, DR5, DT37**

Vamp (1986, C, 94m, R)
Four college frat boys decide to hire a hooker for their party. They get more than they paid for when they hire a vampire. Grace Jones plays the prostitute with a taste for blood. **HO5, HO24, MU12**

Vampire Lovers (1971, C, 88m, R)
An erotic thriller from Britain's Hammer Studios about lesbian vampires. Peter Cushing stars. **HO5, HO25, ST27**

Vampire's Kiss (1989, C, 103m, R)
Delirious tale of modern Manhattan vampire (Nicolas Cage), who's a literary agent and womanizer. With Jennifer Beals. **HO5**

Vampyr (1932, B&W, 60m, NR)
Danish director Carl Dreyer's classic horror tale, full of rich imagery and atmosphere. **DT31, HO5**

Vanishing American, The (1925, B&W, 148m, NR)
Classic silent western about the mistreatment of Indians, based on a novel by Zane Grey. **WE7**

Vanishing Point (1971, C, 98m, PG)
A man is hired to drive a car from Denver to San Francisco. He decides to see if he can make the trip in 15 hours without stopping for anything, especially the police. Barry Newman and Cleavon Little star. **AC10**

Vanishing Prairie, The (1954, C, 75m, G)
This Disney documentary, part of the True-Life Adventure series, won an Acad-

emy Award for its look at animal life on the Great Plains. **FA1**

Vanity Fair (1932, B&W, 73m, NR)
Myrna Loy stars in an updated version of the William Thackeray novel about a young social climber. **CL1, ST94**

Variety (1925, B&W, 79m, NR)
Classic silent German drama about a love triangle in a circus mirroring the decadence of 1920s Germany. Emil Janings stars. **CL12, FF3**

Variety Lights (1952, B&W, 86m, NR)
First feature by Federico Fellini (co-directed with Alberto Lattuada) is a drama about a touring company of actors. Giulietta Masina stars. **DT35**

Velvet Touch, The (1948, B&W, 97m, NR)
Rosalind Russell plays a stage actress who turns detective to solve a murder. With Leo Genn, Claire Trevor, and Sydney Greenstreet. **MY11**

Vengeance Valley (1951, C, 83m, NR)
Western drama about feuding brothers and their women, starring Burt Lancaster and Robert Walker. **ST85**

Venom (1982, C, 98m, R)
A black mamba, the world's deadliest snake, is loose in a London home whose residents are being held hostage by kidnappers. Klaus Kinski, Oliver Reed, and Nicol Williamson star. **HO16, ST83**

Vera Cruz (1954, C, 94m, NR)
In 1860s Mexico, two American cowboys become involved in revolutionary politics. Gary Cooper and Burt Lancaster star. Directed by Robert Aldrich. **ST22, ST85, WE9**

Verdict, The (1982, C, 128m, R)
A broken-down defense lawyer tries to rise to the occasion when he's involved in a complicated malpractice case against a skilled and well-funded legal team. Paul Newman stars, with James Mason, Charlotte Rampling, Jack Warden, and Lindsay Crouse. Sidney Lumet directed. **DR17, DT65, ST102, ST111***Recommended*

Vernon, Florida (1981, C, 60m, NR)
Documentary by Erol Morris depicts the lives of folk in a small town in Florida which seems to contain a high proportion of eccentrics. **CU16, DR26, DT73** *Recommended*

Vertigo (1958, C, 128m, PG)
Classic Alfred Hitchcock film, regarded by a growing cult as his best, about one man's obsession with a woman he thinks has died in a tragic fall. James Stewart and Kim Novak star. Shot on location in San Francisco. Music by Bernard Herrmann. **CL14, CU13, DT46, MY5, ST143, XT13** *Essential; Highly Recommended*

Very Curious Girl, A (1969, C, 105m, R)
From France, a comedy about a peasant girl who enjoys making love with the men in her village so much she decides to charge for her services. **FF1**

Very Edge, The (1963, B&W, 82m, NR)
British thriller about a pregnant woman (Anne Heywood) harassed by a sex criminal (Jeremy Brett). **MY3**

Very Private Affair, A (1962, C, 95m, NR)
Marcello Mastroianni and Brigitte Bardot star in this romantic drama in which a theater director gives shelter to a high-strung movie star. Directed by Louis Malle. **ST4, ST103**

Vibes (1988, C, 99m, PG)
Jeff Goldblum and Cyndi Lauper plays a pair of psychics in this adventure comedy about a treasure hunt in Peru. Peter Falk costars. **CO2, CO3, MU12, ST56**

Vice Squad (1982, C, 97m, R)
A man is mutilating prostitutes in Los Angeles, and a hooker helps a cop solve the case. Wings Hauser and Season Hubley star, with Wings Hauser as the memorable villain. **AC9, XT10**

Vice Versa (1988, C, 97m, PG0
A department store executive and his young son find their minds switched through the spell of a magic totem. Judge Reinhold and Fred Savage star. **CO5, CO20**

Victor/Victoria (1982, C, 133m, PG)
Farce of misunderstanding and sexual confusion, as a Paris nightclub singer (Julie Andrews) pretends to be a man impersonating a woman, much to the consternation of an American gangster (James Garner). With Robert Preston, Lesley Anne Warren, and Alex Karas. Blake Edwards directed. **CO1, DT32**

Victory (1981, C, 110m, PG)
Allied personnel in a German POW camp challenge a Third Reich soccer team to a game. Michael Caine, Sylvester Stallone, and Pele star. Directed by John Huston. **DR22, DT50, ST15, ST140**

Videodrome (1983, C, 88m, R)
James Woods plays a cable TV programmer who stumbles onto a show that seduces and then ultimately controls its audience. Debbie Harry plays a kinky woman looking for the ultimate sexual thrill. Directed by David Cronenberg. **DT23, HO11, HO22, MU12, ST165**

Vie Continue, La (1982, C, 93m, NR)
French drama of a woman (Annie Girardot) who must pick up the pieces of her life when her husband suddenly dies. American remake: *Men Don't Leave*. **FF1, FF8**

Vietnam: In the Year of the Pig (1968, B&W, 115m, NR)
Director Emile De Antonio's documentary of the controversial war paints a bleak portrait of American policy and conduct. **CU16**

View to a Kill, A (1985, C, 131m, PG)
In this last James Bond film starring Roger Moore, 007 is up against a pair of villains (Christopher Walken, Grace Jones) who intend to create a devastating earthquake in Silicon Valley. **HF2, MU12, XT13**

Vigilante (1982, C, 90m, R)
An ex-cop joins a gang of vigilantes to avenge the brutal assault of his wife and child. Robert Forster and Fred Williamson star. **AC19**

Vikings, The (1958, C, 114m, NR)
Kirk Douglas and Tony Curtis terrorize the countryside as a pair of nasty Norsemen. With Janet Leigh and Ernest Borgnine costar; narrated by Orson Welles. **AC13, DT112, ST34**

Villa Rides (1968, C, 125m, PG)
Yul Brynner stars as the Mexican bandit and reolutionary, Pancho Villa. Robert Mitchum and Charles Bronson lead the supporting cast. **ST12, ST107, WE9**

Village of the Damned (1960, B&W, 78m, NR)
A strange mist covers an English village and everyone is rendered unconcious until the mist clears. Later, twelve woman discover they are pregnant and give birth to look-alike children with telepathic powers. George Sanders stars. **HO13, HO26, SF9, SF19**

Vilage of the Giants (1965, C, 80m, NR)
H.G. Wells story, updated with teenaged protagonists growing to mammoth size. Tommy Kirk, Johnny Crawford, Beau Bridges, and Ronny Howard star. **DT48, WR29**

Vincent, Francois, Paul, and the Others (1974, C, 113m, NR)
French drama centering on the friendship of three middle-aged men (Yves Montand, Michel Piccoli, Serge Reggiani). Directed by Claude Sautet. **FF1**

Violent Years, The (1956, B&W, 60m, NR)
The king of no-budget trash, Ed Wood, Jr., strikes again with this drama of spoiled debutantes turning to robbery and rape. **DT118**

Violets Are Blue (1986, C, 88m, PG-13)
A successful photographer returns to her hometown and picks up with an old high school flame who's now married. Sissy Spacek and Kevin Kline star, with Bonnie Bedelia. **DR1, ST84, ST139**

Virgin and the Gypsy, The (1970, C, 92m, R)
D.H. Lawrence story of the daughter of a strict priest and her sexual awakening. Joanna Shimkus and Franco Nero star. **DR1, DR19, WR14**

Virgin Queen, The (1955, C, 92m, NR)
Bette Davis plays Queen Elizabeth I in this historical drama about her relationship with Sir Walter Raleigh. Richard Todd and Joan Collins costar. **CL3, ST28**

Virgin Spring, The (1959, B&W, 88m, NR)
Oscar-winning drama from director Ingmar Bergman: a woodsman seeks revenge on the men who raped and murdered his daughter. U.S. horror remake: *Last House on the Left*. **DT7, FF8, XT7**

Virginian, The (1929, B&W, 90m, NR)
Gary Cooper stars in one of his first westerns, based on the classic Owen Wister novel. **ST22**

Viridiana (1961, B&W, 90m, NR)
Controversial drama, banned for years in its native Spain, about a nun (Silvia Pinal) who is constantly thwarted in her attempts to do good in a world full of sinners. Luis Buñuel directed. **CU8, DT15**
Essential; Highly Recommended

Virus (1980, C, 155m, PG)
A deadly manmade virus is accidentally unleashed, sparking a worldwide epidemic. The survivors (858 men and 8 women) must then try to restore civilization. Made in Japan, with a partly American cast that includes Chuck Connors, Glenn Ford, Olivia Hussey, and George Kennedy. **SF12, SF18**

Vision Quest (1984, C, 107m, R)
High school wrestler (Matthew Modine) embarks on ambitious training program for upcoming match, is distracted by the new female boarder (Linda Fiorentino) in his house. **DR9, DR22**

Vital Signs (1990, C, 103m, R)
Drama of first-year medical students, staring Adrian Pasdar, Diane Lane, Jimmy Smits, and Norma Aleandro. **DR25**

Vitelloni, I (1953, B&W, 104m, NR)
Comedy-drama from director Federico Fellini about five boys on the verge of adulthood. **DT53**

Viva Las Vegas (1964, C, 86m, NR)
Ann-Margret thinks Elvis Presley spends too much time with his sports car and sets out to win him over. **ST123**

Viva Zapata! (1952, B&W, 113m, NR)
Marlon Brando plays the legendary Mexican bandit who rose to political power. Oscar winner Anthony Quinn costars. Screenplay by John Steinbeck; directed by Elia Kazan. **DT53, ST10, WE9, XT4**

Vivacious Lady (1938, B&W, 90m, NR)
A professor (James Stewart) marries a fun-loving nightclub singer (Ginger Rogers), which takes his conservative family and his fiancee by surprise. Directed by George Stevens. **DT101, ST131, ST143**

Volpone (1939, B&W, 80m, NR)
French-language version of Ben Jonson's play of a man (Harry Baur) who pretends to be dying to play off his heirs against one another. Directed by Maurice Tourneur. **DR20, DT105, FF1**

Volunteers (1985, C, 107m, R)
An Ivy League student with gambling debts joins the Peace Corps to escape his creditors and winds up paired with a gung-ho boob. Tom Hanks and John Candy star. **CO3, CO14, ST62**

Von Ryan's Express (1965, C, 117m, NR)
World War II drama starring Frank Sinatra as a POW who commandeers a train in a bold escape plan. **AC7, ST138**

Voulez-Vous Danser Avec Moi? (1959, C, 90m, NR)
Brigitte Bardot stars in this comedy/mystery about a woman trying to clear her dance instructor husband of a murder charge. **ST4**

Voyage of the Damned (1976, C, 134m, PG)
Shipload of Jewish refugees fleeing Germany is denied permission to dock and forced to return to Germany. Drama, based on fact, stars Faye Dunaway, Max von Sydow, Oskar Werner, James Mason, and Orson Welles. **DR5, DT112, ST37, ST102**

Voyage Round My Father (1989, C, 85m, NR)
Laurence Olivier stars in this British drama of an elderly man whose longtime blindness hasn't dampened his spirit. With Alan Bates. Written by John Mortimer, based on experiences with his own father. **DR8, DR23, ST116**

Voyage to Italy (1953, B&W, 75m, NR)
A married couple (Ingrid Bergman, George Sanders) travel to Italy in an attempt to patch up their differences. Directed by Roberto Rossellini, then Bergman's husband. Also known as *Strangers*. Original running time: 97m. **ST7**

Voyage to the Bottom of the Sea (1961, C, 105m, NR)
An atomic powered submarine is on its maiden voyage beneath the Antarctic, when it is discovered that the polar cap is melting. Only the sub can save the Earth

from destruction. Directed by Irwin Allen. Walter Pidgeon and Peter Lorre star. **SF3**

W (1984, C, 90m, NR)
Drama of people trying to survive in a post-holocaust world. **SF8**

W. C. Fields Comedy Bag (1930/1932/1933, B&W, 56m, NR)
Three classic Fields shorts: *The Gold Specialist, The Dentist,* and *The Fatal Glass of Beer.* **ST41**

W. C. Fields Festival (1930, B&W, 56m, NR)
Further evidence of W. C. Fields' comic genius, in this collection of his early short films. **ST41**

WR—Mysteries of the Organism (1971, C, 84m, NR)
Yugoslavian director Dusan Makavejev's exploration of the sexual theories of Wilhelm Reich, paralleling a dramatic story of a liberated woman and her Soviet lover. **FF7**

Wackiest Ship in the Army, The (1960, C, 99m, NR)
The Army recruits Jack Lemmon for a top secret mission. On a schooner disguised as a Japanese fishing boat, he and first mate Ricky Nelson must rescue a spy. **CO21, MU12, ST90**

Wages of Fear, The (1952, B&W, 105m, NR)
French thriller about a quartet of desperate men who volunteer to drive two trucks loaded with explosives over dangerous mountain roads. Yves Montand stars. Directed by Henri-Georges Clouzot. **AC13, FF1, MY16** *Essential; Highly Recommended*

Wagner (1983, C, 300m, NR)
The life and times of the famed composer, Richard Wagner. Richard Burton and Vanessa Redgrave star, with Ralph Richardson, Laurence Olivier, and John Gielgud. **MU5, ST13, ST116, ST127**

Wagonmaster (1950, B&W, 86m, NR)
Two cowboys join a group of pioneer Mormons and help them on their way to the promised land. Ben Johnson, Ward Bond, and Harry Carey, Jr. star. Directed by John Ford. **DT36**

Wait Until Dark (1967, C, 108m, NR)
A blind woman unknowingly possesses a doll stuffed with smuggled drugs, and a trio of nasty thugs harass her to get it back. Audrey Hepburn stars, with Alan Arkin, Richard Crenna, and Jack Weston. **MY3, ST65** *Recommended*

Wake of the Red Witch (1948, B&W, 106m, NR)
Adventure in the East Indies, starring John Wayne, Gail Russell, Luther Alder, and Gig Young. **ST156**

Walk, Don't Run (1966, C, 114m, NR)
In his last film, Cary Grant plays matchmaker to Samantha Eggar and Jim Hutton as the three share cramped quarters during the Tokyo Olympics. Remake of *The More the Merrier.* **CU18, ST57, XT22**

Walk in the Spring Rain, A (1970, C, 100m, PG)
Ingrid Bergman and Anthony Quinn star in this romantic drama of a married woman's unexpected love affair. **DR1, ST7**

Walk in the Sun, A (1945, B&W, 117m, NR)
Combat drama about an American infantry unit who are attacking a German stronghold in Italy. Dana Andrews stars. **AC1**

Walk Into Hell (1957, C, 91m, NR)
Adventure tale of an oil mining engineer and his lovely companion stranded in the New Guinea jungle. Chips Rafferty stars in this Australian film. **FF5**

Walk on the Wild Side (1962, B&W, 114m, NR)
A bordello in 1930s New Orleans is the setting for this drama of a drifter seeking his lost love. Laurence Harvey stars, with Barbara Stanwyck as the madam, and Capucine and Jane Fonda among her girls. **ST44, ST142**

Walking Tall (1973, C, 126m, R)
Joe Don Baker plays real life Tennessee sheriff Buford Pusser, who took on local corruption with a baseball bat. Directed by Phil Karlson. **AC9, AC25**

Walking Tall Part 2 (1975, C, 109m, PG)
Walking Tall: The Final Chapter (1977, C, 113m, R)

Bo Svenson takes over the role of Tennessee sheriff Buford Pusser in these two sequels to *Walking Tall*. **AC9, AC25**

Wall Street (1987, C, 124m, R)
Greed and manipulation in the stock market are the subjects of this topical drama, starring Oscar winner Michael Douglas and Charlie Sheen. With Daryl Hannah, Martin Sheen, James Spader, and Sean Young. Written and directed by Oliver Stone. **DR7, DR24, DT102, ST35, XT2, XT8, XT9**

Waltz of the Toreadors (1962, C, 105m, NR)
Peter Sellers stars as a retired military officer with an eye for the ladies in this British comedy classic. With Margaret Leighton. **CO17, ST137**

Wanderers, The (1979, C, 113m, R)
Life on the Bronx streets, 1963, with four tough guys who name their mini-gang after the Dion song. Comedy-drama stars Ken Wahl, Karen Allen, and Linda Manz. Philip Kaufman directed and adapted Richard Price's novel. **DR15, DT52** *Recommended*

Wannsee Conference, The (1984, C, 87m, NR)
German drama, based on actual meeting in January 1942, in which Nazi officials discussed plans for the Final Solution. **FF3** *Recommended*

Wanted: Dead or Alive (1986, C, 104m, R)
Rutger Hauer plays a high-tech bounty hunter who must stop an international terrorist, played by Gene Simmons. **AC25, MU12**

Wanton Contessa, The *see* Senso

War and Peace (1956, C, 208m, NR)
Leo Tolstoy's epic story of Russian society during the struggle against Napoleon, starring Henry Fonda, Audrey Hepburn, and Mel Ferrer, with Herbert Lom as Napoleon. Directed by King Vidor. **CL1, CL3, DT107, HF19, ST44, ST65**

War and Peace (1968, C, 373m, NR)
Mammoth, Russian-produced version of the Tolstoy classic, directed by Sergei Bondarchuk, who also is in the supporting cast. Ludmilla Savelyeva and Vyacheslav Tihonov star, with Vladislav Strzhelchik as Napoleon. Winner of Os-

car as Best Foreign Language Film. Video is English-language dubbed version. **CL1, CL3, FF7, HF19, XT7**

War Lover, The (1962, B&W, 105m, NR)
While in the air, a hotshot World War II combat pilot (Steve McQueen) is considered a good luck charm to the rest of the squad. On the ground, he antagonizes everyone, including his co-pilot (Robert Wagner). **AC1, AC11, ST97**

War of the Roses, The (1989, C, 116m, R)
Domestic comedy starring Michael Douglas and Kathleen Turner as longtime couple whose marital breakup involves custody of their dream home. Director Danny DeVito costars as Douglas's attorney. **CO1, CO2, ST32, ST35, ST152**

War of the Wildcats (1943, B&W, 102m, NR)
John Wayne is an oil wildcatter in frontier Oklahoma. With Martha Scott, Albert Dekker, Gabby Hayes, and Dale Evans. **ST156**

War of the Worlds (1953, C, 85m, G)
Martian war machines invade Earth, intent on destroying all humans. Based on the H. G. Wells novel. Produced by George Pal; Academy Award winner for special effects. Gene Barry stars. **FA8, SF1, SF7, SF9, SF13, WR29**

War Party (1989, C, 99m, R)
In a Montana town, a historical re-enactment of an Indian massacre sets off a Blackfoot Indian, who murders a local white man and in turn is pursued by a posse. **WE7, WE12**

War Wagon, The (1967, C, 101m, NR)
John Wayne and Kirk Douglas pull off a gold heist in this light-hearted western. **ST34, ST156, WE14**

Wargames (1983, C, 114m, PG)
Computer whiz (Matthew Broderick) accidentally taps into Pentagon system and precipitates a serious war exercise. With Ally Sheedy, Dabney Coleman, and John Wood. **DR7, SF5**

Warlock (1959, C, 121m, NR)
Henry Fonda is the gunfighter, Anthony Quinn the gambler, and Richard Widmark the sheriff in this western drama that concentrates on character rather than action. **ST44, WE2**

Warlords of the 21st Century (1982, C, 91m, PG)
During an oil shortage after World War III an ex-commando decides to take a stand against an evil dictator. **SF8**

Warm Nights on a Slow Moving Train (1987, C, 90m, R)
Offbeat Australian drama about a schoolteacher (Wendy Hughes) who moonlights as a prostitute on trains to support her brother's morphine addiction. With Colin Friels. **FF5, XT19**

Warriors, The (1955, C, 85m, NR)
A British prince (Errol Flynn) defends a French village from marauders. With Peter Finch. Flynn's last swashbuckling film. **ST43**

Warriors, The (1979, C, 90m, R)
A New York City gang is falsely accused of murder and must fight its way across its rivals' turfs to get to safety. Michael Beck and James Remar star. Walter Hill directed this controversial film which allegedly sparked violence in several theaters. **AC8, CU7, DR15, DT45, XT9** *Essential; Recommended*

Warriors of the Wasteland (1983, C, 87m, R)
In a post-holocaust world three adventurers protect a band of settlers against the Templars, a gang of very nasty people. **SF8**

Warriors of the Wind (1985, C, 95m, PG)
An animated futuristic fantasy. **AC18**

Warrior's Rest *see* Repos du Guerrier, Le

Wasn't That a Time! (1982, C, 78m, PG)
Loving documentary about the 1980 reunion of The Weavers, folk-singing group who were blacklisted during the McCarthy era. Lee Hays, Pete Seeger, Ronnie Gilbert, and Fred Hellerman offer wonderful harmonizing. Also known as *The Weavers: Wasn't That a Time!* **MU4** *Recommended*

Watch on the Rhine (1943, B&W, 114m, NR)
Nazi agents harass a German (Paul Lukas, in an Oscar-winning performance) and his American wife (Bette Davis) who now live in Washington D.C. With Geraldine Fitzgerald. Dashiell Hammett adapted Lillian Hellman's play. **DR20, ST28, WR9, XT2**

Watcher in the Woods, The (1980, C, 84m, PG)
An American family moves into an English country house and the two children see visions of a missing girl. Bette Davis stars in this Disney horror film. **FA1, FA8, HO2, HO3, HO26, SF13, ST28**

Watchers (1988, C, 92m, R)
A government experiment goes haywire and unleashes a monster named Oxcom and a super-intelligent dog on an unsuspecting populace. Corey Haim stars, with Michael Ironside and Barbara Williams. **HO20**

Water (1985, C 95m, PG-13)
Michael Caine stars in this comedy as the governor of a Caribbean island, where discovery of a valuable mineral water turns things upside-down. With Brenda Vacarro, Leonard Rossiter, and Valerie Perrine. **ST15**

Water Babies, The (1978, C, 92m, NR)
This undersea adventure mixes live action and animation. James Mason stars. **FA8, ST102**

Waterhole #3 (1967, C, 95m, NR)
Comic western about a trio of robbers concealing their loot in the title location. James Coburn stars, with Carroll O'Connor, Claude Akins, and Bruce Dern. **WE14**

Waterloo Bridge (1940, B&W, 103m, NR)
Vivien Leigh and Robert Taylor star in the classic romance about a ballet dancer and soldier falling in love during an air raid. **CL4**

Watership Down (1978, C, 90m, PG)
In this animated adventure, a warren of rabbits pursue freedom in the face of threats from humans, cats, dogs, and their own kind. Featuring the voices of John Hurt, Ralph Richardson, and Denholm Elliott. **FA10**

Wavelength (1983, C, 87m, PG)
A rock star (Robert Carradine) stumbles onto a government cover-up of aliens who crashed landed in California. **SF9**

Way Down East (1920, B&W, 107m, NR)
Classic silent melodrama, starring Lillian
Gish, of a woman shunned because of her
illegitimate baby. D.W. Griffith directed;
the finale on the ice floes is breathtaking.
CL12, DT42, ST54 *Essential; Recommended*

Way Out West (1937, B&W, 65m, NR)
Laurel and Hardy star in this delightful
comedy set in the Old West. **ST87, WE14**
Recommended

Way We Were, The (1973, C, 118m, PG)
Romantic drama about a Jewish political
activist and WASP-y writer, following
their lives from college in the 1930s to
Hollywood and the blacklist in the 1950s.
Barbra Streisand and Robert Redford
star, with Bradford Dillman, Patrick
O'Neal, Lois Chiles, and, in a small role,
James Woods. Directed by Sydney Pol-
lack. **DR1, DR13, DT80, ST126, ST146,
ST165** *Essential*

Way West, The (1967, C, 122m, NR)
The screen version of A.B. Guthrie's
classic novel of pioneers in the Old West.
Kirk Douglas, Robert Mitchum, and
Richard Widmark star; Sally Field has a
small role. **ST34, ST40, ST107, WE1**

We All Loved Each Other So Much (1977,
C, 124m, NR)
From Italy, a comic story of friendship
and love, about three pals who all lust for
the same woman over a 30-year span.
Federico Fellini and Marcello Mastroianni
appear in bit parts as themselves. **DT35,
FF2, ST103**

We of the Never Never (1983, C, 132m, G)
Visually rich adventure of first white
woman to explore the Australian outback.
Angela Punch McGregor and Arthur Dig-
nam star. **AC12, FF5**

We Think the World of You (1989, C, 91m,
R)
British comedy of a pair of male lovers
(Alan Bates, Gary Oldman) who are sep-
arated when one goes to prison and the
other has to care for his friend's dog.
CO17

Weavers, The: Wasn't That a Time! *see*
Wasn't That a Time!

Wedding, A (1978, C, 125m, PG)
Comedy about variety of oddball family
members and guests who show up at a
suburban Chicago wedding. Robert Alt-
man directed a diverse cast, including
Carol Burnett, Desi Arnaz, Jr. Pat Mc-
Cormick, Mia Farrow, Viveca Lindfors,
Paul Dooley, Lillian Gish, Lauren Hut-
ton, Howard Duff, and Vittorio Gassman.
CO5, CU17, DT1, ST54, XT20 *Recommended*

Wedding in Blood (1973, C, 98m, PG)
Two lovers make plans to murder their
respective spouses. French thriller from
director Claude Chabrol, starring Stephane Audran. **FF1, MY16**

Wedding in White (1972, C, 106m, NR)
Canadian drama of young girl (Carol
Kane) made pregnant by older man, a
friend of her father's, and the resulting
family crisis. Donald Pleasence costars.
DR8, XT20

Wedding March, The (1928, C, 113m, NR)
Silent classic, parts of which were restored for home video. Erich von Stroheim directed this drama of depravity set
in pre-World War I Vienna. One of the
earliest films shot in color. **CL12, CU10,
DT109, XT20**

Wedding Party, The (1969, B&W, 92m,
NR)
Comedy about preparations for marriage,
starring Jill Clayburgh and Robert De-
Niro, both in their first film. Brian De-
Palma co-directed, with Cynthia Munroe
and Wilford Leach. **DT29, ST30, XT20**

Wee Willie Winkie (1937, B&W, 100m,
NR)
Rudyard Kipling tale of a British regiment
in India and their mascot (Shirley Temple). With Victor McLaglen. John Ford
directed. **DT36, FA4, ST148**

Weeds (1987, C, 115m, R)
Nick Nolte stars in this drama based on
fact, about a ex-con playwright who takes
a troupe of his fellow former prisoners on
the road with his plays. With Rita Taggart, Lane Smith, and William Forsythe.
DR6, DR18, ST113

Weekend at Bernie's (1989, C, 97m, PG-
13)
Comedy of two young men spending the
weekend at their boss's Long Island digs,

arriving to discover he's dead, trying to cover up the fact. Andrew McCarthy and Jonathan Silverman star, with Terry Kiser as the corpse. **CO9**

Weekend of Shadows (1977, C, 94m, NR)
Australian drama of a Polish immigrant accused of murder, chased by an angry mob. **FF5**

Weird Science (1985, C, 94m, PG-13)
A pair of teen nerds create a lovely woman in their basement laboratory in this comedy. Anthony Michael Hall, Ilan Mitchell-Smith, and Kelly LeBrock star. Directed by John Hughes. **CO11, DT49**

Welcome Home (1989, C, 90m, R)
A returning Vietnam veteran, missing in action for many years, finds that his wife has remarried. Kris Kristofferson stars, with JoBeth Williams and Sam Waterston. **DR7, MU12**

Welcome to L.A. (1977, C, 106m, R)
Episodic drama about contemporary Californians and their aimless lives. Keith Carradine, Sally Kellerman, Geraldine Chaplin, Sissy Spacek, and Harvey Keitel star. Alan Rudolph directed. **DT91, ST139, XT10**

We're No Angels (1955, C, 103m, NR)
Three convicts escape from Devil's Island, hide out with a kind and understanding family, and get themselves into mischief. Humphrey Bogart stars in a rare comedy role, with Peter Ustinov and Basil Rathbone. **ST8**

We're No Angels (1989, C, 108m, PG-13)
Loose remake of the Bogart comedy about escaped cons; this time, there are two (Robert DeNiro, Sean Penn), who masquerade as priests in a small town. With Demi Moore and Hoyt Axton. Written by David Mamet. **CO20, CU18, ST30**

Werewolf of Washington, The (1973, C, 90m, PG)
A personal friend of the President (Dean Stockwell) is bitten by a werewolf while in Budapest. When he returns to Washington as a werewolf, he begins to kill off all opponents of the administration. **HO4, ST144**

Werner Herzog Eats His Shoe (1980, C, 20m, NR)
The German director makes good on a bet involving colleague Erol Morris's ability to finish a film. Directed by Les Blank. **DT44**

West Side Story (1961, C, 151m, G)
Broadway hit musical from Leonard Bernstein and Stephen Sondheim is a Romeo & Juliet story set in contemporary New York. Winner of ten Oscars, including Best Picture, Supporting Actor and Actress (George Chakiris, Rita Moreno), and Director (Robert Wise). Wise and choreographer Jerome Robbins directed; Robbins was awarded a special Oscar. Natalie Wood, Russ Tamblyn, and Richard Beymer star. **DT117, FA9, MU2, MU3, MU6, MU7, MU14, XT1, XT4, XT5, XT6, XT9** *Essential; Recommended*

Western Union (1941, C, 94m, NR)
Drama of the Old West and the establishment of telegraph lines between Omaha and Salt Lake City. Randolph Scott stars. Fritz Lang directed. **DT58, ST136**

Westerner, The (1940, B&W, 100m, NR)
Gary Cooper gets involved in land feuds in this western, with Oscar winner Walter Brennan as Judge Roy Bean. Directed by William Wyler. **DT119, ST22, WE2, XT4**

Westfront 1918 (1930, B&W, 90m, NR)
Classic antiwar drama from German director G.W. Pabst, his first sound picture. **FF3**

Westworld (1973, C, 90m, PG)
An amusement park for the rich is populated by robots who look and act human. One day the robots rebel and slaughter all the human tourists—except one, who desperately tries to escape. Yul Brynner and Richard Benjamin star. **SF6**

Wetherby (1985, C, 97m, R)
British drama of stranger at a Yorkshire home committing suicide, leaving his hosts and others to sort it all out. Vanessa Redgrave, Joely Richardson, Judi Dench, and Ian Holm star. Written and directed by David Hare. **DR23, ST127**

Whales of August, The (1987, C, 91m, NR)
Screen legends Lillian Gish and Bette Davis star in this drama of two elderly sisters spending a summer on the coast of Maine. With Vincent Price, Ann Sothern,

and Harry Carey, Jr. **DR8, DR11, ST28, ST54, ST124**

What Ever Happened to Baby Jane? (1962, B&W, 132m, NR)
An unbalanced ex-child star, Baby Jane Hudson (Bette Davis), terrorizes her crippled sister (Joan Crawford), a former movie idol. A camp classic. Directed by Robert Aldrich. **CU2, DR13, HO14, ST24, ST28** *Essential*

What Have I Done to Deserve This! (1985, C, 100m, NR)
Comedy from Spanish director Pedro Almodóvar about a frantic housewife running a wild working-class family. Carmen Maura stars. **FF7**

What Price Glory (1952, C, 110m, NR)
James Cagney, Dan Dailey, and Robert Wagner are fighting in the French trenches during World War I. Directed by John Ford. **AC2, DT36, ST14**

What's New, Pussycat? (1965, C, 108m, NR)
Woman-crazy man consults loony shrink for help, which only makes his problems worse. Zany comedy starring Peter O'Toole and Peter Sellers, with Woody Allen (who wrote the screenplay), Romy Schneider, Capucine, Paula Prentiss, and Ursula Andress. Tom Jones sings the title tune. **CO1, DT1, ST117, ST137** *Recommended*

What's Up, Doc? (1972, C, 94m, G)
Modern screwball comedy, set in San Francisco, with a free spirit (Barbra Streisand), a straight arrow (Ryan O'Neal), his uptight fiancee (Madeline Kahn), and assorted jewel thieves and other characters. Written by Robert Benton and David Newman; directed by Peter Bogdanovich. **ST146, XT13**

What's Up, Tiger Lily? (1966, C, 80m, NR)
Unique comic film co-written and "directed" by Woody Allen, who took a Grade B Japanese spy thriller called *Key of Keys* and dubbed in hilarious English dialogue. Silly fun. **CO7, DT1** *Recommended*

Wheel of Fortune (1941, B&W, 83m, NR)
John Wayne plays a country lawyer out to put a crooked politician behind bars—even though he loves the man's daughter.

With Frances Dee. Also known as *A Man Betrayed*. **ST156**

Wheels of Fire (1985, C, 81m, R)
A look into the future shows Earth as a wasteland and a car gang terrorizing the populace. **AC10**

When Harry Met Sally . . . (1989, C, 95m, R)
Comedy of a couple who get acquainted as college students moving to New York, strike up a friendship over the years, and eventually fall in love. Billy Crystal and Meg Ryan star, with Carrie Fisher and Bruno Kirby. Written by Nora Ephron; directed by Rob Reiner. **CO1, CO13, DT85, XT9**

When the Legends Die (1972, C, 105m, PG)
Richard Widmark and Frederic Forest star as a rodeo cowboy and his young Indian friend in this contemporary Western. **WE7, WE12**

When the North Wind Blows (1974, C, 113m, G)
A trapper in Siberia tries to protect snow tigers. Henry Brandon stars. **FA4**

When the Whales Came (1989, C, 99m, PG)
British drama set on a remote island off the southwest coast, where a local legend involving a beached whale and a curse seems to be coming true. Paul Scofield stars, with Helen Mirren, David Threlfall, David Suchet, and Helen Pearce. **DR23**

When Time Ran Out (1980, C, 144m, PG)
A posh resort on a Polynesian island and its guests are in danger when a long-dormant volcano erupts. This video version has 20 minutes of additional footage not seen in the theatrical release. Paul Newman, William Holden, and Jacqueline Bisset head the cast. **AC23, CU10, ST68, ST111**

When Wolves Cry *see* Christmas Tree, The

When Worlds Collide (1951, C, 81m, G)
A small band of scientists and students who believe the Earth is on a collision course with a star race against time to build a space ark. Special effects won an Oscar; produced by George Pal. **SF1, SF7**

Where Are the Children? (1982, C, 97m, R)
Jill Clayburgh plays a woman under suspicion when children from her second marriage disappear (she was accused of murdering two children from a previous marriage but found innocent). Frederic Forrest costars in this thriller. **MY14**

Where Eagles Dare (1968, C, 158m, PG)
Richard Burton and Clint Eastwood go undercover to rescue a kidnapped general from a Nazi stronghold. **AC1, ST13, ST39**

Where the Buffalo Roam (1980, C, 96m, R)
The life and very hard times of gonzo journalist Hunter S. Thompson, portrayed by Bill Murray. **CO2, CO13**

Where the Green Ants Dream (1984, C, 101m, NR)
An Australian uranium mining company comes into conflict with a local aborigine tribe when drilling begins on sacred tribal grounds. Bruce Spence stars. Werner Herzog directed. **DT44**

Where the Heart Is (1990, C, 94m, R)
Whimsical comedy of a New York wrecking company tycoon (Dabney Coleman) and his live-in children (Uma Thurman, Suzy Amis, David Hewlett). He gives them a condemned (but historically protected) house to live in, to start their own lives. With Joanna Cassidy, Crispin Glover, and Christopher Plummer. Directed by John Boorman. **CO2, CO5, CU5, DT11, XT9** *Recommended*

Where the Hot Wind Blows (1958, B&W, 120m, NR)
Drama, set in an Italian seaport, about a lusty young girl's many liaisions with the men of the village. Gina Lollabrigida, Marcello Mastroianni, Melina Mercouri, and Yves Montand star. **ST103**

Where the Red Fern Grows (1974, C, 90m, NR)
Family drama set in Depression-era Oklahoma, about a farm boy's devotion to two hunting dogs. James Whitmore, Beverly Garland, and Jack Ging star. **FA5**

Where the River Runs Black (1986, C, 96m, PG)
Young white boy reared in the Amazon jungle swears revenge on the hunters who killed his mother. Charles Durning, Alessandro Rabelo, Marcello Rabelo, and Conchata Ferrel star. **DR9, FA7**

Where Time Began (1978, C, 86m, G)
A group of adventurers travel to the center of the Earth and encounter a time warp. Loosely based on Jules Verne's *Journey To The Centre of the Earth*. Kenneth More stars. **SF4, WR28**

Where's Picone? (1984, C, 122m, NR)
Italian comedy about a tailor living on his wits in modern-day Naples. Giancarlo Giannini stars. **FF2**

Where's Poppa? (1970, C, 92m, R)
Comedy, with cult following for its outrageous humor, about a senile woman whose son is trying to scare her to death. Ruth Gordon and George Segal star, with Trish Van Devere and Ron Liebman. Carl Reiner directed. **CO5, CO12, CU5, CU12**

Which Way Is Up? (1977, C, 94m, R)
Richard Pryor plays three roles in this comedy about a farm worker mixed up in politics and woman troubles. Remake of Italian film *The Seduction of Mimi*. **CO26, FF8**

Which Way to the Front? (1970, C, 96m, G)
Jerry Lewis plays a World War II draftee who's declared 4-F but enlists a bunch of similar misfits to fight the Germans. Jan Murray, John Wood, Kaye Ballard, and Sidney Miller as Adolf Hitler. Lewis directed. **CO21, HF12, ST91**

While the City Sleeps (1956, B&W, 100m, NR)
Fritz Lang directed this suspenseful tale of policemen and reporters looking for a serial killer. Dana Andrews, Ida Lupino, and Vincent Price star. **DT58, MY1, ST124** *Recommended*

Whisky Galore (1949, B&W, 82m, NR)
Classic British comedy about the efforts of island folk to recover booze from a sunken World War II ship. Basil Radford and Joan Greenwood star. Alexander Mackendrick directed. Also known as *Tight Little Island*. **CO17**

Whistle Blower, The (1987, C, 99m, PG)
Michael Caine stars in this British thriller as a former intelligence agent with an idealistic son in a sensitive government

job. With Nigel Havers, Edward Fox, and John Gielgud. **MY15, ST15**

Whistle Down the Wind (1961, B&W, 99m, NR)
Three children find a murderer hiding in their barn and think he is Christ. Hayley Mills and Alan Bates star. **FA7**

White Buffalo, The (1977, C, 97m, PG)
Charles Bronson plays Wild Bill Hickok in this drama about the gunslinger's premonitions of death. With Jack Warden, Will Sampson, Kim Novak, Slim Pickens, and John Carradine. **HF11, ST12, WE2**

White Christmas (1954, C, 120m, NR)
Two army buddies team up and become famous as a song and dance act. With the assistance of two singing sisters, they help out their old army commander, whose hotel is in financial trouble. Bing Crosby, Danny Kaye, Vera-Ellen, and Rosemary Clooney star. **MU4, MU6, ST25, ST78**

White Dawn (1974, C, 110m, PG)
Three whalers stranded in the Arctic take advantage of the Eskimos who rescue them. Warren Oates, Timothy Bottoms, and Louis Gossett, Jr. star. Directed by Philip Kaufman. **AC12, AC24, DT52, ST115**

White Heat (1949, B&W, 114m, NR)
James Cagney plays Cody Jarrett, the gangster with a mother fixation, in this crime drama with the explosive "top of the world" ending. With Edmond O'Brien, Virginia Mayo, Steve Cochran, and Margaret Wycherly as "Ma." Directed by Raoul Walsh. **AC22, MY1, ST14** *Essential; Highly Recommended*

White Lightning (1973, C, 101m, PG)
Moonshiner Burt Reynolds gets revenge on the lawman who killed his brother. **AC19, ST128**

White Mama (1980, C, 105m, NR)
A poor widow (Bette Davis) and a streetwise black kid (Ernest Harden) form an alliance for their mutual survival. Originally made for TV. **ST28**

White Mischief (1988, C, 106m, R)
British colony in 1940s Africa is rocked by scandal: the public affair between the young wife of a diplomat and an army officer, and the officer's mysterious murder. Based on real events, this drama stars Greta Scacchi and Charles Dance as the lovers, with Sarah Miles, Joss Ackland, and John Hurt. **DR5, DR23**

White Nights (1985, C, 135m, PG-13)
An airplane carrying a ex-Soviet dancer crashes in Siberia, and the Russians hold the man in detention, using a black Amercian defector as his guardian. Mikhail Baryshnikov and Gregory Hines are the dancers (and they do dance!). With Jerzy Skolimowski, Isabella Rossellini, Helen Mirren, and Geraldine Page. **DR21**

White of the Eye (1988, C, 113m, R)
Thriller set in Arizona, where a woman suspects her loving husband of being a vicious serial killer. Stylish drama, starring Cathy Moriarty and David Keith, directed by Donald Cammell. **MY13, MY14** *Recommended*

White Rose, The (1983, C, 108m, NR)
German drama about a small group of youths who defy Hitler. **FF3**

White Sheik, The (1951, B&W, 88m, NR)
Italian comedy about a couple on their honeymoon in Rome and the wife's adventures with a cartoon hero called The White Sheik. Alberto Sordi stars. Federico Fellini directed. **DT53, XT17**

White Wilderness (1958, C, 73m, G)
This Disney documentary, part of the True-Life Adventure series, goes to the Arctic to examine the animal and plant life there. **FA1**

White Zombie (1932, B&W, 73m, NR)
The owner of a sugar mill in Haiti cuts down on labor costs by creating an army of zombies. Bela Lugosi stars. **HO1, HO6, ST95**

Who Am I This Time? (1982, C, 60m, NR)
Charming comedy about a troupe of amateur actors in a small town and their bold, talented star—who's a painfully shy nerd off-stage. Christopher Walken and Susan Sarandon star. Directed by Jonathan Demme. **CO1, DT28** *Highly Recommended*

Who Done It? (1942, B&W, 77m, NR)
Abbott and Costello comedy has the boys pretending to be detectives when they're really a couple of radio scriptwriters.

With William Bendix and Mary Wickes. **MY17, ST1**

Who Framed Roger Rabbit (1988, C, 103m, PG)
Mind-boggling combination of live action and animation in the story of a flesh-and-blood 1930s private eye (Bob Hoskins) investigating the murder of a movie studio executive, allegedly by one of his cartoon stars. Christopher Lloyd and Joanna Cassidy head the supporting cast, but the real stars are the cartoon characters, including many familiar faces in "cameo" appearances. Directed by Robert Zemeckis; animation supervised by Richard Williams. **CO8, CO10, CO11, FA6** *Highly Recommended*

Who Killed Baby Azaria (1983, C, 96m, NR)
Australian drama based on the famous Lindy Chamberlain case, of a mother accused of murdering her baby girl. A better-known version of the same events is *A Cry in the Dark*. **FF5**

Who Slew Auntie Roo? (1971, C, 89m, R)
Shelley Winters stars in this horror version of the Hansel & Gretel tale. **ST164**

Who'll Stop the Rain? (1978, C, 126m, R)
An American journalist in Vietnam persuades a Marine buddy to smuggle some heroin back to the States, where all hell breaks loose. Powerful thriller, with underlying commentary on effects of the war. Nick Nolte, Tuesday Weld, and Michael Moriarty star, with Anthony Zerbe, Richard Masur, and Ray Sharkey. Based on Robert Stone's novel, *Dog Soldiers*. **DR7, DR19, MY2, ST113** *Highly Recommended*

Wholly Moses (1980, C, 109m, R)
Irreverent comedy about a nerd (Dudley Moore) who thinks God has picked him to lead the Jews to the Promised Land. With Richard Pryor, Laraine Newman, Madeline Kahn, James Coco, Dom DeLuise, and John Houseman. **CO13, ST109, ST125**

Whoopi Goldberg: Fontaine . . . Why Am I Straight? (1989, C, 51m, NR)
Comedienne Whoopi Goldberg assumes the role a street-smart junkie, just "cured" by the Betty Ford Center. **CO16**

Whoopi Goldberg Live (1986, C, 75m, NR)
The stage show that launched Goldberg's film career, as she plays a wide variety of characters in a tour-de-force performance. **CO16**

Whoops Apocalypse (1981, C, 137m, NR)
Britsh satire lampoons world politics and the news media, as the events leading up to World War III are chronicled. John Barron, John Cleese, and Richard Griffiths star. **CO2, CO15, CO17**

Who's Afraid of Virignia Woolf? (1966, B&W, 129m, NR)
Elizabeth Taylor and Richard Burton in their best film, an adaptation of Edward Albee's play about a battlefield of a marriage. With George Segal and Sandy Dennis costar. Adapted by Ernest Lehman; Mike Nichols directed. Taylor and Dennis won Oscars. **CL15, DR8, DR20, DT74, ST13, ST147, XT3, XT5** *Essential; Recommended*

Who's Harry Crumb? (1989, C, 91m, PG-13)
John Candy plays a private eye who resorts to highly unorthodox methods to rescue a kidnap victim. With Jeffrey Jones, Annie Potts, and Barry Corbin. **CO10, CO14**

Who's That Girl (1987, C, 94m, PG)
Madonna plays a kook just released from prison for a crime she didn't commit. She involves an innocent lawyer (Griffin Dunne) in her zany schemes. **MU12**

Whose Life Is It Anyway? (1981, C, 118m, R)
An artist, paralyzed from the neck down in a car accident, insists that he be allowed to end his life, against the wishes of his girlfriend and doctor. Richard Dreyfuss stars in this version of Brian Clark's play, with Christine Lahti and John Cassavetes. **DR7, DR20, ST36**

Why Shoot the Teacher? (1977, C, 101m, PG)
Canadian drama, set during the Depression, about a young schoolteacher's experiences in a small town. Bud Cort and Samantha Eggar star. **DR25, DR26**

Wicked Lady, The (1945, B&W, 104m, NR)
British adventure tale of female outlaw (Margaret Lockwood) and her exploits with a handsome accomplice (James Mason). Remake released in 1983. **ST102**

Wicked Lady, The (1983, C, 98m, R)
Campy version of the old highwaywoman tale, starring Faye Dunaway as the robber. With Alan Bates and John Gielgud. **CU2, ST37**

Wicked Stepmother (1989, C, 92m, PG-13)
Bette Davis's last film, in which she plays a witch who shrinks people. With Barbara Carrera, Colleen Camp, and Lionel Stander. Davis and writer-director Larry Cohen had a falling-out during shooting, and she left the production; her character disappears about halfway through the story. **DT20, ST28**

Wicker Man, The (1973, C, 95m, R)
While investigating the disappearance of a child, a policeman travels to a remote Scottish island and discovers pagan cultists. Edward Woodward, Christopher Lee, and Britt Ekland star in this thriller with its own cult following. **CU4, HO11, ST89**

Wifemistress (1977, C, 110m, R)
A young woman's husband disappears and she discovers evidence that he has been less than faithful to her. Laura Antonelli and Marcello Mastroianni star in this Italian comedy. **FF2, ST103**

Wilby Conspiracy, The (1975, C, 101m, R)
Chase thriller set in Africa, where a black political activist (Sidney Poitier) is on the lam with a reluctant white journalist (Michael Caine). With Nicol Williamson. **ST15, ST121**

Wild Angels, The (1966, C, 93m, NR)
Director Roger Corman's low-budget biker classic, about the baddest set of dudes ever. Peter Fonda stars, with Nancy Sinatra, Bruce Dern, Michael J. Pollard, Diane Ladd, and Gayle Hunnicutt. **AC10, DT22**

Wild Bunch, The (1969, C, 143m, R)
An aging band of outlaws is pursued along the Tex-Mex border by a ragged band of bounty hunters. Director Sam Peckin-pah's masterful and violent tale of the last days of the frontier stars William Holden and Robert Ryan, with Warren Oates, Ben Johnson, Jaime Sanchez, Edmond O'Brien, Albert Dekker, Emilio Fernandez, Bo Hopkins, Strother Martin, and L.Q. Jones. Arguably the greatest western; certainly one of the most controversial. **CU7, DT77, ST68, ST115, WE3, WE9, WE11** *Essential; Highly Recommended*

Wild Country, The (1971, C, 92m, G)
Disney frontier adventure of a family who moves in the 1880s from Pittsburgh to Wyoming. Steve Forrest and Vera Miles star, with Ronny Howard, Jack Elam, and Clint Howard. **DT48, FA1, XT8**

Wild Duck, The (1983, C, 96m, PG)
Updating of Henrik Ibsen play about a couple and their struggle to raise a blind child. Liv Ullmann and Jeremy Irons star. Produced in Australia. **DR20, FF5, ST154**

Wild Geese, The (1978, C, 134m, R)
Action saga of a band of mercenaries who set out to free a captured African leader, starring Richard Burton, Roger Moore, and Richard Harris, with Hardy Kruger and Stewart Granger. **AC20, ST13**

Wild Geese II (1985, C, 124m, R)
A group of mercenaries are hired to break Nazi Rudolph Hess out of Spandau Prison. Scott Glenn, Barbara Carrera, and Laurence Olivier star. **AC20, ST116**

Wild in the Country (1961, C, 114m, NR)
A backwoods boy (Elvis Presley) gets in trouble with the law; under a psychiatrist's care he is encouraged to write. Script by Clifford Odets. **ST123**

Wild in the Streets (1968, C, 97m, PG)
Satiric look at contemporary youth culture has a rock star elected President when the voting age is lowered to 14. Christopher Jones stars, with Shelley Winters, Diane Varsi, Hal Holbrook, and Richard Pryor. **CO2, ST125, ST164**

Wild Life, The (1984, C, 96m, R)
A high school graduate gets his first apartment and taste of freedom in this comedy about partying hearty. Christopher Penn, Eric Stoltz, and Rick Moranis star. **CO14**

Wild One, The (1954, B&W, 79m, NR)
Biker Marlon Brando and his gang (including Lee Marvin) roar into a small California town and terrorize the locals. Fifties scare movie that has since become a camp classic. **CU2, DR26, ST10, ST100***Essential*

Wild Orchid (1990, C, 100m, R)
Steamy story of the sexual awakening of a lovely young lawyer. Mickey Rourke and Carre Otis star, with Jacqueline Bisset. **CU6, DR3, ST134**

Wild Orchids (1929, B&W, 102m, NR)
A married woman falls in love with another man while on a holiday. Greta Garbo, Lewis Stone, and Nils Asther star in this silent soap opera. **ST50**

Wild Party, The (1975, C, 95m, R)
Hollywood drama about fading film star trying to revive his career with major-league wing-ding. James Coco and Raquel Welch star. James Ivory directed. **DR13**

Wild Ride, The (1960, B&W, 63m, NR)
Early Jack Nicholson film has him playing an amoral hotrodder not above murder or stealing his best buddy's girl. **ST112**

Wild Rovers (1971, C, 138m, PG)
William Holden and Ryan O'Neal star as saddle pals in this cult western drama from director Blake Edwards. The video version contains 29 minutes of footage not included in the theatrical release. **CU10, DT32, ST68, WE15**

Wild Strawberries (1957, B&W, 90m, NR)
An elderly professor (Victor Sjöström), on his way to receive an honorary degree, recalls his past, especially his disappointments. One of director Ingmar Bergman's great achievements. **DT7** *Essential; Recommended*

Wild Style (1982, C, 82m, R)
A rappin' musical about a graffitti artist in New York City. Lee Quinones stars. **MU9**

Wildcats (1986, C, 104m, R)
A divorced mother badly in need of a job agrees to coach an inner city high school football team. Goldie Hawn stars in this comedy, with James Keach, Swoosie Kurtz, and Nipsey Russell. **CO19, ST63**

Wilderness Family Part 2, The (1978, C, 105m, G)
The family who left the city behind in *The Adventures of the Wilderness Family* continue their lives in this sequel. Robert Logan stars. **FA4**

Will Penny (1968, C, 109m, NR)
Western with cult following features Charlton Heston as an aging saddlehand befriending a settler (Joan Hackett) and her young son. With Donald Pleasence, Lee Majors, Bruce Dern, Ben Johnson, Anthony Zerbe, and G.D. Spradlin. **WE15** *Recommended*

Willard (1971, C, 95m, PG)
A disturbed man (Bruce Davison) trains his pet rats to attack all his enemies. With Sondra Locke and Ernest Borgnine. **HO16**

Willie Wonka and the Chocolate Factory (1971, C, 100m, G)
A musical adaptation of Roald Dahl's story, "Charlie and the Chocolate Factory." Charlie wins a trip to a chocolate factory owned by a mysterious man. Gene Wilder stars. **FA8, FA9**

Willow (1988, C, 126m, PG)
Lavish fantasy adventure revolving around the efforts of a brave dwarf (Warwick Davis) to protect an infant from the clutches of an evil witch. Val Kilmer, Joanne Whalley, and Jean Marsh costar. Produced by George Lucas; directed by Ron Howard. **AC18, DT48, FA8, SF13**

Winchester '73 (1950, B&W, 92m, NR)
James Stewart stars in this classic western drama of a man in search of his stolen gun. Anthony Mann directed. With Rock Hudson, Shelley Winters, and Will Geer as Wyatt Earp. **DT69, HF9, ST73, ST143, ST164** *Essential*

Wind, The (1928, B&W, 82m, NR)
Lillian Gish gives one of her finest performances in this silent drama of a young innocent and her hard life on the prairie. Excellent direction by Victor Seastrom. Video version features a new musical score by Carl Davis. **CL5, CL12, ST54** *Essential; Recommended*

Wind and the Lion, The (1975, C, 120m, PG)
An American diplomat's wife (Candice Bergen) and her son are kidnapped by a

Moroccan bandit (Sean Connery), and a romance develops. Based on true events. With Brian Keith (as Theodore Roosevelt) and John Huston. Directed by John Milius. **AC12, AC14, AC16, DT50, ST21**

Wind in the Willows, The (1982, C, 47m, G)
An adaptation of Kenneth Grahame's story about the tale of four gentlemen friends, Mr. Badger, Mr. Mole, Mr. Ratty, and Mr. Toad. Originally part of the 1950 Disney animated feature, *Ichabod and Mr. Toad*. **FA2**

Window, The (1949, B&W, 73m, NR)
Thriller focusing on a young boy (Bobby Driscoll) who witnesses a murder in his New York tenement but can't get anyone to believe his story. With Barbara Hale, Arthur Kennedy, Paul Stewart, and Ruth Roman. **MY1**

Windwalker (1980, C, 108m, PG)
An Indian patriarch returns to his tribe to prevent an act of revenge by his long-lost brother. Trevor Howard stars in this offbeat western. **WE7**

Windy City (1984, C, 103m, R)
A reunion of old neighborhood chums in Chicago dramatizes their successes and failures as adults. John Shea, Kate Capshaw, and Josh Mostel star. **DR7, XT11**

Wings (1927, B&W, 139m, NR)
When the U.S. enters World War I, two friends in love with the same girl enlist in the Army Air Corps. This silent classic won the first Academy Award for Best Picture. Clara Bow, Buddy Rogers, and Richard Arlen star, with Gary Cooper. **AC2, AC11, CL12, ST22, XT1** *Essential*

Wings of Desire (1988, B&W/C, 130m, NR)
From German director Wim Wenders, a captivating fantasy-drama focusing on the adventures of a pair of angels in contemporary Berlin. Bruno Ganz stars, with Otto Sander, Solveig Dommartin, and Peter Falk. Wenders and Peter Handke wrote the screenplay. **DT113** *Recommended*

Wings of Eagles, The (1957, C, 110m, NR)
John Wayne stars as Frank "Spig" Wead, real-life aviator turned screenwriter. With Maureen O'Hara, Dan Dailey, and Ward Bond. Directed by John Ford. **AC11, CL7, DT36, ST156**

Wings of the Morning (1937, C, 98m, NR)
Henry Fonda falls in love with a Gypsy while training a racehorse. The first British film shot in Technicolor. **ST44**

Winning (1969, C, 123m, PG)
Paul Newman plays a race car driver who's driven to become the best in this drama costarring Joanne Woodward and Robert Wagner. **DR22, ST111, ST166**

Winning of the West (1953, B&W, 57m, NR)
Gene Autry and Smiley Burnette ride together to help a crusading newspaper publisher in the Old West. **ST3**

Winter Kills (1979, C, 97m, R)
Wild political thriller about the brother of a slain President searching for the killers and uncovering a massive conspiracy. Based on Richard Condon's novel. Jeff Bridges stars, with John Huston, Toshiro Mifune, Anthony Perkins, Belinda Bauer, Richard Boone, Sterling Hayden, Eli Wallach, and, in a brief role, Elizabeth Taylor. **CU9, CU17, DR19, DR21, DT50, MY6, MY14, ST11, ST106, ST147**

Winter Light (1962, B&W, 86m, NR)
A priest in a Swedish village wrestles with problems of faith in this Ingmar Bergman drama. Ingrid Thulin and Gunnar Bjornstrand star. **DT7**

Winter of Our Dreams, The (1981, C, 90m, R)
A married bookstore owner becomes involved with an embittered prostitute. Australian drama starring Bryan Brown and Judy Davis. **FF5**

Winter People (1989, C, 110m, PG-13)
In the 1934 North Carolina backwoods, romance blossoms between an unwed mother (Kelly McGillis) and a visiting widower (Kurt Russell). With Lloyd Bridges. **DR1**

Wired (1989, C, 108m, R)
Stylized bio of comic John Belushi, starring Michael Chiklis, with Ray Sharkey, J.T. Walsh as Bob Woodward, and Patti D'Arbanville as Cathy Smith. **DR4, DR12**

Wisdom (1986, C, 109m, R)
Emilio Estevez wrote, directed, and stars in this drama of a young man and his girl friend who take to robbing banks and redistributing the money to needy farmers. With Demi Moore. **DR16**

Wise Blood (1979, C, 108m, PG)
Bizarre, fascinating drama, populated by various Southern grotesques, including a young man claiming to be a preacher for The Church Without Christ. Brad Dourif, Daniel Shor, Amy Wright, Harry Dean Stanton, and Ned Beatty star. John Huston directed. Based on Flannery O'Connor's novel. **DR19, DT50, ST141** *Recommended*

Wise Guys (1985, C, 92m, R)
A pair of bumbling hit men are assigned to knock each other off in this comedy starring Joe Piscopo and Danny DeVito. Brian DePalma directed. **CO3, CO10, CO13, DT29, ST32**

Wish You Were Here (1987, C, 91m, R)
British comedy-drama about a teenager (Emily Lloyd) growing up in a stuffy small town in the 1950s, defying the locals with her sexy behavior. Written and directed by David Leland. **CO17**

Witchcraft Through the Ages (1921, B&W, 120m, NR)
Notorious silent film, made in Sweden, banned in several countries for its explicit scenes purporting to explore the dark side of human nature. Available in several versions; above running time is for the full-length version. Also known as *Haxan*. **CU8, FF7**

Witches, The (1990, C, 92m, PG)
A little boy stumbles onto a meeting of witches, and when he is transformed into a mouse, he and his grandmother plot revenge. Jasen Fisher, Mai Zetterling, and Anjelica Huston star. Directed by Nicolas Roeg. **DT88, FA8**

Witches' Brew (1980, C, 99m, PG)
Horror spoof, featuring Teri Garr as a professor's wife who uses witchcraft to help her hubby's career. With Lana Turner and Richard Benjamin. **HO24, ST153**

Witches of Eastwick, The (1987, C, 118m, R)
A New England village becomes a battleground when three contemporary witches collide with a mysterious newcomer. Jack Nicholson, Cher, Michelle Pfeiffer, and Susan Sarandon star. George Miller directed this adaptation of John Updike's novel. **DR10, DR19, DR26, ST19, ST112, ST120**

Witchtrap (1989, C, 90m, R)
Paranormal experts are called in to exorcise the spirit of a man whose house has been inherited by his nephew. James W. Quinn and Kathleen Bailey star. **HO3**

Withnail and I (1987, C, 110m, R)
Two unemployed actors in 1969 London decide to take a holiday in the country, with nearly disastrous results. Dark comedy starring Richard E. Grant, Paul McGann, and Richard Griffiths. Written and directed by Bruce Robinson. **CO17**

Without a Clue (1988, C, 107m, PG)
Sherlock Holmes played for laughs, with the famed detective (Michael Caine) a bungler and Dr. Watson (Ben Kingsley) the real brains of the operation. **HF14, MY17, ST15**

Without a Trace (1983, C, 120m, PG)
True story of a woman whose young son disappears in New York City and her frantic efforts to find him. Kate Nelligan and Judd Hirsch star. **MY8, MY14, XT9**

Without Reservations (1946, B&W, 107m, NR)
The author of a successful novel discovers the perfect man to play her hero in the movies. Claudette Colbert and John Wayne star in this romantic comedy, with cameos by several Hollywood stars. **ST156**

Witness (1985, C, 112m, R)
Drama of Amish boy witnessing murder on a visit to Philadelphia and the cop who befriends him and his mother. Harrison Ford, Kelly McGillis, and Lukas Haas star, with Danny Glover and Alexander Gudonov. Peter Weir directed. **DR16, DT111, ST46, ST55**

Witness for the Prosecution (1957, B&W, 114m, NR)
Agatha Christie courtroom drama, with Charles Laughton defending Tyrone

Power on murder charge. Marlene Dietrich costars as Power's wife. Directed by Billy Wilder. **DR17, DT116, ST33, WR3** *Recommended*

Wiz, The (1978, C, 133m, G)
An update of *The Wizard of Oz,* based on the Broadway musical hit. Diana Ross stars, with Richard Pryor, Michael Jackson, Nipsey Russell, Ted Ross, Mabel King, and Lena Horne. Directed by Sidney Lumet. **DT65, FA9, MU2, MU8, ST125**

Wizard, The (1989, C, 99m, PG)
Family drama of young video-game whiz traveling across country with his brother to compete in a big tournament. Fred Savage and Luke Edwards star, with Beau Bridges and Christian Slater. **FA7**

Wizard of Loneliness, The (1988, C, 110m, PG-13)
During World War II, a young boy is sent to live with his kindly but eccentric grandparents in a Vermont village. Lukas Haas stars in this drama, with Lea Thompson. Based on a novel by John Nichols. **DR9, DR26**

Wizaard of Oz, The (1925, B&W, 93m, NR)
Silent version of the L. Frank Baum classic tale, starring Dorothy Dwan, with Oliver Hardy as the Tin Woodsman. **ST87**

Wizard of Oz, The (1939, C/B&W, 101m, G)
A girl from Kansas discovers the power of friendship and love in a strange land over the rainbow. Judy Garland stars, with Ray Bolger, Bert Lahr, Jack Haley, and Margaret Hamilton. Available in a limited edition celebrating the 50th anniversary of the film's release, containing footage not used in the original release. **CU10, FA9, MU8, SF13, ST51** *Essential; Highly Recommended*

Wizard of Oz, The (1982, C, 78m, NR)
An animated adaptation of Frank L. Baum's classic story about a little girl and her dog and their adventures in the land over the rainbow. **FA10**

Wizards (1977, C, 80m, PG)
Animated adventure set in a world of magic. A good wizard rules his kingdom with kindness. His evil brother sets out to conquer the rest of the planet. **SF13**

Wizards of the Lost Kingdom (1985, C, 78m, PG)
Bo Svenson stars in this futuristic fantasy with plenty of swordplay. **AC18**

Wolf at the Door (1987, C, 90m, NR)
French-produced bio of painter Paul Gauguin, focusing on his middle years, when he returned from Tahiti to Paris to make money. Donald Sutherland stars. **FF1**

Wolf Man, The (1941, B&W, 70m, NR)
Lawrence Talbot (Lon Chaney, Jr.) is bitten by a werewolf (Bela Lugosi) and lives to carry on the curse. A horror classic. **HO1, HO4, HO17, ST17, ST95** *Recommended*

Wolfen (1981, C, 115m, R)
A New York detective (Albert Finney) discovers a race of wolf men living in the slums of the South Bronx. With Gregory Hines, Diane Venora, and James Edward Olmos. Spooky, offbeat thriller which effectively uses real locations. Directed by Michael Wadleigh. **HO4, HO16, ST42, XT9** *Recommended*

Woman Called Golda, A (1982, C, 195m, NR)
The life of former Israeli prime minister, Golda Meir. Ingrid Bergman won an Emmy for her portrayal of this courageous leader. Originally made for TV. **DR4, ST7**

Woman in Flames, A (1982, C, 106m, R)
A housewife deserts her husband and falls into a life of prostitution in this contemporary German drama. Gudrun Landgrebe stars. Robert Van Ackeren directed. **FF3**

Woman in Green, The (1945, B&W, 68m, NR)
Sherlock Holmes and Dr. Watson battle the nefarious Professor Moriarty in this tale of a murderer whose trademark is leaving corpses with one thumb missing. Basil Rathbone and Nigel Bruce star. **HF14**

Woman in Red, The (1984, C, 87m, PG-13)
Romantic comedy starring Gene Wilder as happily married man with hang-up on lovely woman he glimpsed one day in a parking garage. Kelly LeBrock costars, with Gilda Radner, Charles Grodin, and

Judith Ivey. Remake of French film, *Pardon Mon Affaire*. **CO1, CO13, FF8, ST59**

Woman in the Dunes (1964, B&W, 123m, NR)
A scientist becomes trapped in a sandpit with a strange woman who lives there. Offbeat drama from Japan, directed by Hiroshi Teshigahara. **FF4**

Woman in the Moon, The (1929, B&W, 146m, NR)
Fritz Lang directed this silent science fiction tale about the first expedition to the moon. **DT58**

Woman Next Door, The (1981, C, 106m, NR)
A married man's new neighbor, also married, is his ex-lover, and they resume their relationship. French drama from François Truffaut, starring Gerard Depardieu and Fanny Ardant. **DT106, ST31**

Woman of Paris, A (1923, B&W, 81m, NR)
This silent drama is about a woman pledged to marry who becomes a wealthy man's mistress through a series of misunderstandings. Edna Purviance, Adolphe Menjou, and Carl Miller star. A rare dramatic outing for director Charlie Chaplin, who has only a bit part as a railway porter. **CL12, DT18**

Woman of the Year (1942, B&W, 112m, NR)
First pairing of Katharine Hepburn and Spencer Tracy has her playing a political commentator, him a sportswriter. Written by Ring Lardner, Jr. and Michael Kanin (Oscar winners); directed by George Stevens. Sheer joy. **CL10, CL15, DT101, ST66, ST151** *Essential; Highly Recommended*

Woman Rebels, A (1936, B&W, 88m, NR)
Katharine Hepburn stars as a crusader for woman's rights in Victorian England. **CL5, ST66**

Woman Times Seven (1967, C, 99m, NR)
Shirley MacLaine plays seven roles in this series of comic sketches costarring Peter Sellers, Rossano Brazzi, Michael Caine, Alan Arkin, and Vittorio Gassman. Directed by Vittorio De Sica. **DT26, ST15, ST96, ST137**

Woman Without Love, A (1951, C, 91m, NR)
Director Luis Buñuel's drama of infidelity, adapted from a Guy de Maupassant story. **DT15**

Woman's Face, A (1941, B&W, 105m, NR)
A woman with a disfigured face has plastic surgery which transforms her life. Joan Crawford and Melvyn Douglas star. Directed by George Cukor. **CL5, DT24, ST24**

Women, The (1939, B&W, 132m, NR)
Witty comedy about a group of female friends and their love lives, adapted from the Clare Boothe play. Rosalind Russell, Joan Crawford, Norma Shearer, Paulette Goddard, and Joan Fontaine head the all-female cast. George Cukor directed. **CL5, CU2, DT24, ST24** *Highly Recommended*

Women in Love (1970, C, 129m, R)
D.H. Lawrence story of two love affairs, starring Alan Bates, Glenda Jackson (an Oscar winner), Oliver Reed, and Jennie Linden. Vigorous direction by Ken Russell. Prequel: *The Rainbow*. **DR1, DR19, DR23, DT92, WR14, XT3** *Recommended*

Women on the Verge of a Nervous Breakdown (1988, C, 88m, NR)
Spanish comedy from director Pedro Almodóvar, featuring an actress (Carmen Maura) who's trying to learn of her lover's infidelity. Zany look at how popular culture infects our lives. **FF7** *Recommended*

Wonder Man (1945, C, 98m, NR)
Danny Kaye plays twins, one a nightclub singer and one a scholar. The singer gets killed and his ghost pushes his brother into solving the murder. With Virginia Mayo. **MU4, ST78**

Wonderful World of the Brothers Grimm, The (1962, C, 129m, NR)
The lives of the famous German storytellers, with dramatizations of many of their best-loved tales. Laurence Harvey and Karl Boehm star in this family fantasy. **FA8**

Wonderland (1989, C, 107m, R)
British drama, set in Liverpool, of relationship between two young gay men, one (Emile Charles) a mama's boy and movie fan, the other (Tony Forsyth) a hard-

nosed punk. Directed by Philip Saville. **DR3, DR23**

Woodstock (1970, C, 184m, R)
Oscar-winning documentary about three days of peace, love, and music in August 1969. Among the musical highlights: The Who, Ritchie Havens, Joe Cocker, Santana, and Jimi Hendrix performing *The Star-Spangled Banner*. An exceptional filmmaking achievement, directed by Michael Wadleigh. Now available in an edition which letterboxes key musical sequences. **CU19, MU10** *Essential; Highly Recommended*

Words and Music (1948, C, 119m, NR)
This biography of songwriters Richard Rodgers and Lorenz Hart is really a showcase for 36 of their best songs. Mickey Rooney and Tom Drake star, with cameo appearances from many MGM musical stars, including Judy Garland, plus Gene Kelly and Vera-Ellen in an eight-minute ballet. **MU1, MU5, ST51, ST81, ST133**

Work/Police (1915/1916. B&W, 81m, NR)
Two early Charlie Chaplin short films. In the first, he's an inept paper hanger; in the second, he's an ex-con with a penchant for trouble. **DT18**

Working Girl (1988, C, 113m, R)
With her female boss laid up by a skiing injury, a bright, ambitious Wall Street secretary takes over a major deal—and falls in love with a handsome colleague. Melanie Griffith, Harrison Ford, and Sigourney Weaver star in this contemporary romantic comedy. With Joan Cusack and Alec Baldwin. Mike Nichols directed. **CO1, CO2, DR10, DT74, ST46, ST58, ST157, XT9** *Recommended*

Working Girls (1987, C, 93m, NR)
Vivid, sometimes comic portrait of everyday lives of several New York prostitutes, directed by Lizzie Borden. **DR10** *Recommended*

World According to Garp, The (1982, C, 136m, R)
Seriocomic adventures of a college professor and his family, adapted from the John Irving bestseller. Robin Williams stars, with Mary Beth Hurt, Glenn Close, John Lithgow, Hume Cronyn, and Jessica Tandy. **DR8, DR19, ST20, ST160**

World Apart, A (1988, C, 112m, PG)
South Africa is the setting for this drama of a young white girl whose mother neglects her to work in the anti-apartheid movement. Barbara Hershey and Jodhi May star. Shawn Slowo's script was based on her own experiences. **DR7, DR8**

World of Apu, The (1959, B&W, 103m, NR)
The concluding film in Indian director Satyajit Ray's classic *Apu* trilogy finds the young hero finally marrying and becoming a father. **DT84** *Essential*

World of Henry Orient, The (1964, C, 106m, NR)
Two New York teenagers with a crush on a concert pianist make his life miserable by following him everywhere. Peter Sellers stars, with Tippy Walker and Merrie Spaeth. **CO4, ST137, XT9**

World of Suzie Wong, the (1960, C, 129m, NR)
An American artist living in Hong Kong falls in love with an Asian prostitute. William Holden and Nancy Kwan star. **ST68**

World's Greatest Athlete, The (1973, C, 93m, G)
A coach (John Amos) visiting Africa discovers a teenaged Tarzan (Jan-Michael Vincent) who's a super athlete, and takes him to America. Tim Conway costars in this Disney comedy. **FA1**

Worth Winning (1989, C, 102m, PG-13)
A Philadelphia TV weatherman bets his buddies that he can successfully propose to three women—all on videotape. Mark Harmon stars in this comedy, with Madeleine Stowe, Lesley Ann Warren, Maria Holvoe, Mark Blum, and Andrea Martin. **CO1, CO14**

Wraith, The (1986, C, 91m, PG13)
A mysterious car begins to terrorize a group of teenagers. Charlie Sheen, Nick Cassavetes, and Randy Quaid star. **AC10**

Written on the Wind (1956, C, 99m, NR)
From director Douglas Sirk, a lush melodrama about an irresponsible playboy (Robert Stack) and his sexually promiscuous sister (Oscar winner Dorothy Malone) and their wasted lives. Rock Hudson and Lauren Bacall costar. **CL6, DT98, ST73, XT5**

Wrong Arm of the Law, The (1962, B&W, 94m, NR)
A trio of robbers find themselves pursued by crooks and cops in this British comic romp starring Peter Sellers. **ST137**

Wrong Box, The (1966, C, 105m, NR)
Zany British comedy, set in Victorian England, featuring skullduggery over immense inheritance. Great cast includes Ralph Richardson, John Mills, Dudley Moore, Peter Cook, Michael Caine, and Peter Sellers. **CO17, ST15, ST109, ST137** *Recommended*

Wrong Is Right (1982, C, 117m, R)
Satirical look at how modern news media shape political events, with Sean Connery hopscotching the world for news. Written for the screen and directed by Richard Brooks. With George Grizzard, Katharine Ross, Robert Conrad, Henry Silva, Dean Stockwell, and Leslie Nielsen. **CO2, ST21, ST144**

Wrong Man, The (1956, B&W, 105m, NR)
Henry Fonda stars in this low-key Hitchcock thriller about a musician falsely accused of robbery, trying to overcome the system to prove he's innocent. Based on a true case. **DT46, MY7, MY8, ST44**

Wrong Move (1975, C, 103m, NR)
German drama of a young writer's odyssey toward self-discovery and experience. Directed by Wim Wenders. Ridgier Vogler, Hanna Schygulla, and Nastassia Kinski star. **DT113**

Wuthering Heights (1939, B&W, 104m, NR)
Laurence Olivier and Merle Oberon star in this version of the Brontë novel. William Wyler directed this classic romantic drama, photographed by Gregg Toland. **CL1, CL4, CL6, DT119, ST116** *Essential; Recommended*

Wuthering Heights (1954, B&W, 90m, NR)
Director Luis Buñuel's version of the Brontë classic, filmed in Mexico, starring Iraseme Dilian and Jorge Mistral. **CL1, DT15**

X: The Man With the X-Ray Eyes (1963, C, 88m, NR)
Ray Milland invents eye drops to give him X-ray vision, which eventually leads to madness. Directed by Roger Corman. **DT22, SF5**

X: The Unheard Music (1985, C, 87m, R)
A documentary of the L.A.-based punk/country band, filmed between 1980 and 1985. **MU11**

X, Y, and Zee (1972, C, 110m, PG)
A woman (Elizabeth Taylor), her husband (Michael Caine), and his mistress (Susannah York) share each other in a triangular relationship. **DR3, ST15, ST147**

Xanadu (1980, C, 88m, PG)
An angel tries to help a roller-boogie boy achieve stardom. Olivia Newton-John stars, with a special appearance by Gene Kelly. **MU8, ST81**

Xtro (1983, C, 82m, R)
A man disappears and three years later returns to his son. It is then revealed that the man is an alien and that he intends to take his son to his home at any cost. **SF20**

Yakuza, The (1975, C, 112m, R)
Robert Mitchum returns to Japan to rescue Brian Keith's daughter from the Yakuza, the Japanese Mafia. Directed by Sydney Pollack; written by Paul Schrader. **AC22, DT80, ST107**

Yankee Doodle Dandy (1942, B&W, 126m, NR)
James Cagney won an Oscar for his irresistible portrayal of songwriter George M. Cohan. With Joan Leslie and Walter Huston. **FA9, MU5, MU6, MU7, ST14, XT2** *Essential; Recommended*

Year of Living Dangerously, The (1982, C, 115m, PG)
Romantic drama, set in turbulent Indonesia during the mid-1960s, about a naive Australian reporter (Mel Gibson) and a British embassy aide (Sigourney Weaver). Linda Hunt won an Oscar for her portrayal of a male photographer. Peter Weir directed. **DR21, DT111, ST53, ST157, XT5**

Year of the Dragon, The (1985, C, 136m, R)
Cynical police captain intrudes on gang warfare in New York's Chinatown. Mickey Rourke, Ariane, and John Lone star. directed by Michael Cimino. **AC9, ST134**

Year of the Jellyfish, The *see* Annee des Meduses, L'

Year of the Quiet Sun, A (1984, C, 107m, PG)
Drama set in postwar Germany about an affair between an American soldier and a Polish war widow. Directed by Krzystoff Zanussi. **FF7**

Yearling, The (1946, C, 129m, NR)
Family living in the Florida swamps during the Depression find an injured fawn and adopt it. Warm adaptation of the Marjorie Kinan Rawlings book, starring Gregory Peck, Jane Wyman, and Claude Jarman, Jr. Oscar winner for lovely color photography. **CL9, FA5, ST119**

Yellow Rose of Texas, The (1944, B&w, 55m, NR)
Roy Rogers goes undercover to catch some outlaws. Dale Evans costars, with vocal support from Bob Nolan & the Sons of the Pioneers. **ST132**

Yellow Submarine (1968, C, 85m, G)
The Beatles star in this surreal, animated tale about a band who set out to save Pepperland from the Blue Meanies. **CU3, MU8, MU9** *Recommended*

Yellowbeard (1983, C, 101m, PG)
Comic pirate movie with a boatload of stars, including Graham Chapman, Cheech & Chong, Marty Feldman, James Mason, Peter Cook, and Eric Idle. Written by Chapman and Cook. **CO15, ST18, ST102**

Yentl (1983, C, 134m, PG)
Barbra Streisand plays a Jewish woman living in 19th-century Eastern Europe who disguises herself as a male to obtain an education. The star, who also directed and co-wrote the script, sings a dozen soliloquy songs. With Mandy Patinkin, Amy Irving, and Steven Hill. **CO20, ST146**

Yesterday, Today and Tomorrow (1964, C, 119m, NR)
Oscar-winning comedy from Italy, a trio of tales about sex and money, starring Sophia Loren and Marcello Mastroianni. Vittorio De Sica directed. **DT26, ST93, ST103, XT7**

Yin and Yang of Mr. Go, The (1971, C, 89m, R)
Espionage drama, set in Hong Kong, with a CIA agent out to retrieve stolen military plans. Jeff Bridges stars, with James Mason, Burgess Meredith, and Broderick Crawford. **ST11, ST102**

Yojimbo (1961, B&W, 110m, NR)
Classic samurai adventure, exaggerated for comic effect, about a lone swordsman (Toshiro Mifune) playing off two feuding families against one another. Akira Kurosawa directed. Loosely remade as *A Fistful of Dollars*. **AC13, DT57, FF8, ST106** *Essential; Recommended*

Yolanda and the Thief (1945, C, 108m, NR)
A con man tries to convince an heiress that he is her guardian angel. Fred Astaire stars in this colorful musical fantasy directed by Vincente Minnelli. **CL9, MU8, DT71, ST2**

You Can't Cheat an Honest Man (1939, B&W, 76m, NR)
W.C. Fields costars with Edgar Bergen and Charlie McCarthy in this comedy set in a circus. **CL10, ST41**

You Can't Take It With You (1938, B&W, 127m, NR)
The George S. Kaufman-Moss Hart play about a zany family, directed for the screen by Frank Capra. James Stewart and Jean Arthur star, with Lionel Barrymore, Edward Arnold, Mischa Auer, and Ann Miller. Oscar winner for Best Picture and Director. **CL10, DR20, DT16, ST143, XT1, XT6**

You Can't Win 'Em All *see* Soldiers of Fortune

You Only Live Once (1937, B&W, 86m, NR)
Henry Fonda and Sylvia Sidney are the couple on the run in this superb crime drama from director Fritz Lang. **DT58, MY1, ST44, XT18** *Essential; Recommended*

You Only Live Twice (1967, C, 116m, PG)
James Bond (Sean Connery) must outsmart Ernst Stavro Blofeld (Donald Pleasence) before the villain can cause the super powers to go to war. **HF2, ST21**

You Were Never Lovelier (1942, B&W, 97m, NR)
A hotel owner (Adolphe Menjou) allows a gambler (Fred Astaire) to work off his debts by trying to tame the man's headstrong daughter (Rita Hayworth). **ST2, ST64**

You'll Find Out (1940, B&W, 97m, NR)
Kay Kyser and His Orchestra spend the night at a haunted house. Boris Karloff, Bela Lugosi, and Peter Lorre costar. **ST77, ST95**

You'll Never Get Rich (1941, B&W, 88m, NR)
A choreographer (Fred Astaire) starts to romance a chorus girl (Rita Hayworth), then he's drafted. He is able to continue the romance when he arranges to put on a show at his base featuring her. **ST2, ST64**

Young and Innocent (1937, B&W, 80m, NR)
A fugitive from justice is aided by a young girl in proving his innocence. Directed by Alfred Hitchcock. **DT46, MY7, MY15**

Young and Willing (1943, B&W, 82m, NR)
Screen version of stage comedy *Out of the Frying Pan*, about the wacky world of show-biz hopefuls, starring William Holden, Eddie Bracken, and Barbara Britton. **CL7, DR20, ST68**

Young at Heart (1954, C, 117m, NR)
Frank Sinatra romances Doris Day in this musical about small-town life. **ST138**

Young Bill Hickok (1940, B&W, 54m, NR)
Roy Rogers plays the legendary Western scout, as Hickok matches wits with a pair of crafty outlaws. **HF11, ST132**

Young Buffalo Bill (1940, B&W, 54m, NR)
The Legend of the Plains is portrayed by Roy Rogers, who helps the U.S. Army put down an Indian uprising. **HF3, ST132**

Young Doctors in Love (1982, C, 95m, R)
Comedy set in a hospital where anything goes, starring Michael McKean, Sean Young, Harry Dean Stanton, Dabney Coleman, Pamela Reed, many others. **ST141**

Young Einstein (1988, C, 90m, PG)
Wacky Australian comedy which purports to tell the story of how Albert Einstein, with the help of rock 'n' roll and Madame Curie, formulated the theory of relativity. Written and directed by Yahoo Serious, who also stars in the title role. **CO12, FF5**

Young Frankenstein (1974, B&W, 105m, PG)
Mel Brooks' parody of the great black-and-white monster movies from the 1930s, with Gene Wilder as the mad doctor, Peter Boyle as his creation, plus Marty Feldman, Teri Garr, Cloris Leachman, and (in a hilarious cameo) Gene Hackman. Brooks' best film. **CO7, DT13, HF10, ST61** *Essential; Highly Recommended*

Young Guns (1988, C, 107m, R)
Western tale of a youthful band of ruffians, led by Billy the Kid, out for revenge when their kindly rancher friend is murdered. Emilio Estevez stars as Billy, with Charlie Sheen, Kiefer Sutherland, Lou Diamond Phillips, Jack Palance, and Terence Stamp. **HF1, WE5, XT8**

Young Lions, The (1958, B&W, 167m, NR)
In this World War II drama, Marlon Brando plays a sensitive Nazi officer who questions the morality of his orders; Montgomery Clift is an American Jewish soldier contending with anti-Semitism within his unit. Dean Martin costars in this adaptation of Irwin Shaw's novel, with Hope Lange, Barbara Rush, Maximilian Schell, and Lee Van Cleef. **AC1, ST10, ST155**

Young Magician, The (1987, C, 99m, NR)
Family comic fantasy of a young boy who has to learn to control his magical powers. **FA6**

Young Man With a Horn (1950, B&W, 112m, NR)
A talented trumpet player who dreams of the big time heads for destruction when he marries a socialite. Kirk Douglas, Lauren Bacall, and Doris Day star. **MU4, ST34**

Young Mr. Lincoln (1939, B&W, 100m, NR)
Henry Fonda plays the future President as a struggling lawyer in this classic directed by John Ford. **CL2, DT36, HF18, ST44** *Essential; Recommended*

Young Philadelphians, The (1959, B&W, 136m, NR)
Soap opera about an ambitious lawyer (Paul Newman) hoping to crack Philadelphia society with a socialite (Barbara Rush). **ST111**

Young Sherlock Holmes (1985, C, 109m, PG-13)
The movie that asks the question, What if Holmes and Watson had really met as prep school students? Nicholas Rowe and Alan Cox star as the future detective and his sidekick in this fanciful detective story. **FA4, HF14**

Young Winston (1972, C, 145m, PG)
The early days of Winston Churchill, from his schooling up to his first election to Parliament. Simon Ward, Anne Bancroft, Robert Shaw, and John Mills star. Richard Attenborough directed. **DR4**

Youngblood (1986, C, 111m, R)
Brash hockey player has a lot to prove to hard-driving coach, especially when he falls in love with the man's daughter. Rob Lowe, stars, with Patrick Swayze, Ed Lauter, and Cynthia Gibb. **DR22**

Your Past Is Showing *see* The Naked Truth

Your Ticket Is No Longer Valid (1979, C, 91m, R)
Melodrama of an impotent businessman (Richard Harris) and the Parisian madam (Jeanne Moreau) who tries to cure his problem. **ST110**

You're a Big Boy Now (1966,C, 96m, NR)
New York youth falls for a hard-hearted actress, against the wishes of his overbearing parents. Sweet, offbeat comedy from director Francis Ford Coppola, starring Peter Kastner, with Tony Bill, Elizabeth Hartman, Rip Torn, and Geraldine Page. **CO4, DT21, ST150, XT9**

Yours, Mine and Ours (1968, C, 111m, G)
Comedy, based on true story of what happens when a widow (Lucille Ball) with eight children marries a widower (Henry Fonda) with ten. **CO5, FA6, ST44**

Z (1969, C, 127m, PG)
Yves Montand stars as a popular politician whose murder by right-wing thugs sets off a major social movement in his country. Oscar winner for Best Foreign Language Picture; directed by Costa-Gavras. **FF1, MY16, XT7** *Essential; Recommended*

Zabriskie Point (1970, C, 112m, R)
Italian director Michelangelo Antonioni's impressions of life in late-1960s America (and particularly Los Angeles) are wrapped around the story of a campus demonstrator on the run after shooting a policeman. Mark Frechette and Daria Halprin star, with Rod Taylor, Paul Fix, and, in a small role, Harrison Ford. Music by Pink Floyd, the Grateful Dead, Patti Page, and others. **CU3, DR7, DT3, ST46, XT10** *Essential; Recommended*

Zardoz (1974, C, 105m, R)
In the year 2293, the Brutals and the Exterminators are constantly at war, spurred on by the "god" Zardoz. Sean Connery stars, with Charlotte Rampling. John Boorman directed. **CU4, DT11, SF8, SF19, ST21**

Zatoichi Meets Yojimbo (1970, C, 90m, NR)
Showdown between the fabled blind swordsman and mercenary in this action drama, starring Toshiro Mifune. **FF4, ST106**

Zelig (1983, C/B&W, 79m, PG)
Woody Allen spoofs newsreels and documentaries with his tale of the fictional Herbert Zelig, the man who knew every celebrity in the 20th century, from Babe Ruth to Adolf Hitler. Marvelous use of actual newsreel footage with Allen's character inserted. With Mia Farrow; Susan Sontag and Saul Bellow are among the "experts" to offer running commentary. **CO7, CO12, DT1, HF12** *Recommended*

Zelly and Me (1988, C, 87m, PG)
Drama set in 1950s Virginia about a young orphan girl's relationship with her nanny. Alexandra Johnes is the little girl, Isabella Rossellini her nanny. With Glynis Johns, Joe Morton, and David Lynch. **DR9, DT66**

Zero for Conduct (1933, B&W, 44m, NR)
Hilarious, surreal comedy about life in a boys' boarding school from French director Jean Vigo. **CO18, FF1** *Essential; Highly Recommended*

Ziegfeld Follies (1945, C, 110m, NR)
A musical revue showcasing such talents as Judy Garland, Fred Astaire, Gene

Kelly, Lena Horne, Esther Williams, and many more. William Powell opens the show as Flo Ziegfeld in heaven. Directed by Vincente Minnelli. **DT71, MU1, MU4, ST2, ST51, ST81, ST122**

Ziegfeld Girl (1941, B&W, 133m, NR)
MGM musical about the ups and downs of a trio of show-biz hopefuls (Judy Garland, Lana Turner, Hedy Lamarr). James Stewart stars. Choreography by Busby Berkeley. **DT8, MU1, ST51, ST143, ST153**

Ziggy Stardust and the Spiders From Mars (1983, C, 91m, PG)
An early David Bowie alter ego, Ziggy Stardust, filmed at a 1973 performance. **MU10**

Zombie (1979, C, 91m, NR)
The island of Matool is the setting for a zombie epidemic. **HO6, HO18**

Zombie High (1987, C, 91m, R)
All the students are well mannered and obedient at this school. A curious transfer student discovers why. Virginia Madsen stars. **HO12**

Zombie Island Massacre (1984, C, 95m, NR)
A group of tourists commit a sacrilege when they witness an ancient voodoo ceremony. They are then hunted and killed by the island inhabitants. Rita Jenrette plays one of the victims. **HO6**

Zorba the Greek (1964, B&W, 146m, NR)
Anthony Quinn plays the title role, a peasant who teaches a visiting Britisher (Alan Bates) a thing or two about living. Lila Kedrova won an Oscar for her performance as a fatally ill prostitute. **XT5**

Zouzou (1934, B&W, 92m, NR)
Josephine Baker stars in this French musical about a Creole laundress who becomes a stage sensation. **FF1**

Zulu (1964, C, 138m, NR)
British soldiers hold off 4,000 Zulu warriors in this true story about the 1879 battle in Natal, South Africa. Michael Caine and Stanley Baker star. **AC6, ST15**

Zulu Dawn (1979, C, 117m, PG)
This follow-up to *Zulu* is actually about the events leading up to battle between the British Forces and the Zulu nation for control of Natal, South Africa. Peter O'Toole and Burt Lancaster star. **AC6, ST85, ST117**

CHECK LIST INDEX

Finney, Albert	ST42	Hughes, John	DT49
Fitzgerald, F. Scott	WR7	Hunter, Holly	ST74
Flaherty, Joe	CO14	Hurt, William	ST75
Flynn, Errol	ST43	Huston, John	DT50
Fonda, Henry	ST44		
Fonda, Jane	ST45	Idle, Eric	CO15
Ford, Harrison	ST46		
Ford, John	DT36	James, Henry	WR11
Forman, Milos	DT37	James, Jesse	HF16
Forsyth, Bill	DT38	Jesus Christ	HF17
Forsyth, Frederick	WR8	Jewison, Norman	DT51
Fosse, Bob	DT39	Jones, James Earl	ST76
Foster, Jodie	ST47	Jones, Terry	CO15
Frankenstein Monster, The	HF10		
Freeman, Morgan	ST48	Karloff, Boris	ST77
Fuller, Samuel	DT40	Kaufman, Philip	DT52
		Kaye, Danny	ST78
Gable, Clark	ST49	Kazan, Elia	DT53
Garbo, Greta	ST50	Keaton, Buster	DT54
Garland, Judy	ST51	Keaton, Diane	ST79
Gere, Richard	ST52	Keaton, Michael	ST80
Gibson, Mel	ST53	Kelly, Gene	ST81
Gilliam, Terry	CO15	Kelly, Grace	ST82
Gish, Lillian	ST54	King, Stephen	WR12
Glover, Danny	ST55	Kinski, Klaus	ST83
Godard, Jean-Luc	DT41	Kline, Kevin	ST84
Goldblum, Jeff	ST56	Kramer, Stanley	DT55
Grant, Cary	ST57	Kubrick, Stanley	DT56
Griffith, D.W.	DT42	Kurosawa, Akira	DT57
Griffith, Melanie	ST58		
Grodin, Charles	ST59	L'Amour, Louis	WR13
Guinness, Alec	ST60	Lancaster, Burt	ST85
		Lang, Fritz	DT58
Hackman, Gene	ST61	Lange, Jessica	ST86
Hammett, Dashiell	WR9	Laurel & Hardy	ST87
Hanks, Tom	ST62	Lawrence, D. H.	WR14
Hawks, Howard	DT43	Lean, David	DT59
Hawn, Goldie	ST63	LeCarre, John	WR15
Hayworth, Rita	ST64	Lee, Bruce	ST88
Hemingway, Ernest	WR10	Lee, Christopher	ST89
Hepburn, Audrey	ST65	Lee, Spike	DT60
Hepburn, Katharine	CL15, ST66	Lemmon, Jack	ST90
Herzog, Werner	DT44	Leonard, Elmore	WR16
Hickok, Wild Bill	HF11	Leone, Sergio	DT61
Hill, Walter	DT45	Lester, Richard	DT62
Hitchcock, Alfred	DT46	Levy, Eugene	CO14
Hitler, Adolf	HF12	Lewis, Jerry	ST91
Hoffman, Dustin	ST67	Lewis, Sinclair	WR17
Holden, William	ST68	Lewton, Val	HO27
Holliday, Doc	HF13	Lincoln, Abraham	HF18
Holliday, Judy	ST69	Lombard, Carole	ST92
Holmes, Sherlock	HF14	Loren, Sophia	ST93
Hood, Robin	HF15	Loy, Myrna	CL15, ST94
Hooper, Tobe	DT47	Lubitsch, Ernst	DT63
Hope, Bob	ST70	Lucas, George	DT64
Hopper, Dennis	ST71	Ludlum, Robert	WR18
Hoskins, Bob	ST72	Lugosi, Bela	ST95
Howard, Ron	DT48	Lumet, Sidney	DT65
Hudson, Rock	ST73	Lynch, David	DT66

MacDonald, Jeanette	CL15	Pollack, Sydney	DT80
MacDonald, Ross	WR19	Powell, Michael	DT81
MacLaine, Shirley	ST96	Powell, William	CL15, ST122
McQueen, Steve	ST97	Preminger, Otto	DT82
Malick, Terrence	DT67	Presley, Elvis	ST123
Malkovich, John	ST98	Price, Vincent	ST124
Mankiewicz, Joseph L.	DT68	Pryor, Richard	ST125
Mann, Anthony	DT69		
Martin, Andrea	CO14	Radner, Gilda	CO13
Martin, Steve	ST99	Ramis, Harold	CO14
Marvin, Lee	ST100	Ray, Nicholas	DT83
Marx Brothers, The	ST101	Ray, Satyajit	DT84
Mason, James	ST102	Redford, Robert	ST126
Mastroianni, Marcello	ST103	Redgrave, Vanessa	ST127
Matthau, Walter	ST104	Reiner, Rob	DT85
May, Elaine	DT70	Renoir, Jean	DT86
Midler, Bette	ST105	Reynolds, Burt	ST128
Mifune, Toshiro	ST106	Ritt, Martin	DT87
Minnelli, Vincente	DT71	Robards, Jason	ST129
Mitchum, Robert	ST107	Robinson, Edward G.	ST130
Monroe, Marilyn	ST108	Roeg, Nicolas	DT88
Monty Python's Flying Circus	CO15	Rogers, Ginger	CL15, ST131
Moore, Dudley	ST109	Rogers, Roy	ST132
Moranis, Rick	CO14	Rohmer, Eric	DT89
Moreau, Jeanne	ST110	Romero, George	DT90
Morissey, Paul	DT72	Rooney, Mickey	CL15, ST133
Morris, Erol	DT73	Rourke, Mickey	ST134
Morris, Garrett	CO13	Rudolph, Alan	DT91
Muppets, The	FA15	Russell, Ken	DT92
Murphy, Eddie	CO13		
Murray, Bill	CO13	Saint, The	HF21
		Sayles, John	DT93
Napoleon (Bonaparte)	HF19	Schlesinger, John	DT94
Newman, Laraine	CO13	Schwarzenegger, Arnold	ST135
Newman, Paul	ST111	Scorsese, Martin	DT95
Nichols, Mike	DT74	Scott, Randolph	ST136
Nicholson, Jack	ST112	Scott, Ridley	DT96
Nolte, Nick	ST113	Sellers, Peter	ST137
Norris, Chuck	ST114	Shakespeare, William	WR22
		Short, Martin	CO14
Oakley, Annie	HF20	Siegel, Don	DT97
Oates, Warren	ST115	Simon, Neil	WR23
O'Hara, Catherine	CO14	Sinatra, Frank	ST138
Olivier, Laurence	ST116	Sirk, Douglas	DT98
O'Neill, Eugene	WR20	Spacek, Sissy	ST139
Ophuls, Marcel	DT75	Spielberg, Steven	DT99
Ophuls, Max	DT76	Spillane, Mickey	WR24
O'Toole, Peter	ST117	Stallone, Sylvester	ST140
		Stanton, Harry Dean	ST141
Pacino, Al	ST118	Stanwyck, Barbara	ST142
Palin, Michael	CO15	Steinbeck, John	WR25
Peck, Gregory	ST119	Sternberg, Josef von	DT100
Peckinpah, Sam	DT77	Stevens, George	DT101
Penn, Arthur	DT78	Stewart, James	ST143
Pfeiffer, Michelle	ST120	Stockwell, Dean	ST144
Piscopo, Joe	CO13	Stone, Oliver	DT102
Poe, Edgar Allan	WR21	Streep, Meryl	ST145
Poitier, Sidney	ST121	Streisand, Barbra	ST146
Polanski, Roman	DT79	Sturges, Preston	DT103

Tarzan	HF22	Wayne, John	ST156
Tati, Jacques	DT104	Weaver, Sigourney	ST157
Taylor, Elizabeth	CL15, ST147	Weir, Peter	DT111
Temple, Shirley	ST148	Welles, Orson	DT112
Thomas, Dave	CO14	Wells, H. G.	WR29
Thompson, Jim	WR26	Wenders, Wim	DT113
Tomlin, Lily	ST149	Wertmüller, Lina	DT114
Torn, Rip	ST150	West, Mae	ST158
Tourneur, Jacques	DT105	Whale, James	DT115
Tracy, Spencer	CL15, ST151	Wilder, Billy	DT116
Truffaut, François	DT106	Williams, Billy Dee	ST159
Turner, Kathleen	ST152	Williams, Robin	ST160
Turner, Lana	ST153	Williams, Tennessee	WR30
Twain, Mark	WR27	Willis, Bruce	ST161
		Winfield, Paul	ST162
Ullmann, Liv	ST154	Winger, Debra	ST163
		Winters, Shelley	ST164
Van Cleef, Lee	ST155	Wise, Robert	DT117
Verne, Jules	WR28	Wood, Ed, Jr.	DT118
Vidor, King	DT107	Woods, James	ST165
Visconti, Luchino	DT108	Woodward, Joanne	ST166
Von Stroheim, Erich	DT109	Wyler, William	DT119
Waters, John	DT110	Zinnemann, Fred	DT120